T0137319

Lecture Notes in Artificial Intelligence 10989

Subseries of Lecture Notes in Computer Science

More information about this series at http://www.springer.com/series/1244

Jinchang Ren · Amir Hussain
Jiangbin Zheng · Cheng-Lin Liu
Bin Luo · Huimin Zhao
Xinbo Zhao (Eds.)

Advances in Brain Inspired Cognitive Systems

9th International Conference, BICS 2018
Xi'an, China, July 7–8, 2018
Proceedings

Editors
Jinchang Ren
University of Strathclyde
Glasgow
UK

Amir Hussain
Edinburgh Napier University
Edinburgh
UK

Jiangbin Zheng
Northwestern Polytechnical University
Xi'an
China

Cheng-Lin Liu
Chinese Academy of Sciences
Beijing
China

Bin Luo
Anhui University
Hefei
China

Huimin Zhao
Guangdong Polytechnic Normal University
Guangzhou
China

Xinbo Zhao
Northwestern Polytechnical University
Xi'an
China

ISSN 0302-9743 ISSN 1611-3349 (electronic)
Lecture Notes in Artificial Intelligence
ISBN 978-3-030-00562-7 ISBN 978-3-030-00563-4 (eBook)
https://doi.org/10.1007/978-3-030-00563-4

Library of Congress Control Number: 2018954488

LNCS Sublibrary: SL7 – Artificial Intelligence

This Springer imprint is published by the registered company Springer Nature Switzerland AG
The registered company address is: Gewerbestrasse 11, 6330 Cham, Switzerland

Preface

Welcome to the proceedings of BICS 2018 – the 9th International Conference on Brain-Inspired Cognitive Systems. BICS has now become a well-established conference series on brain-inspired cognitive systems around the world, with growing popularity and increasing quality. BICS 2018 followed on from BICS 2004 (Stirling, Scotland, UK), BICS 2006 (Lesvos, Greece), BICS 2008 (Sao Luis, Brazil), BICS 2010 (Madrid, Spain), BICS 2012 (Shenyang, China), BICS 2013 (Beijing, China), BICS 2015 (Hefei, China), and BICS 2016 (Beijing, China).

Geographically located at the heart of China, Xi'an is the largest city of Shaanxi Province. It once served as the capital city of ancient China for 13 dynasties spanning over 1,000 years, with a history of 5,000 years. Xi'an witnessed the most glorious history of China, and now ranks as one of the top ten tourist destinations in China with a distinctive culture. Xi'an is the starting point of the Silk Road and home to the Terracotta Army of Emperor Qin Shi Huang, the first Emperor in Chinese history.

This volume of *Lecture Notes in Artificial Intelligence* constitutes the proceedings of BICS 2018. In this context, BICS 2018 aimed to provide a high-level international forum for scientists, engineers, and educators to present the state of the art in brain-inspired cognitive systems research and applications in diverse fields. The conference featured plenary lectures given by world-renowned scholars, regular sessions with broad coverage, and some special sessions and workshops focusing on popular and timely topics.

The conference received nearly 150 submissions from more than 270 authors in over ten countries and regions across four continents. Based on a rigorous review process carried out by the Program Committee members and reviewers, 84 high-quality papers were selected for publication in the conference proceedings. These papers cover many topics of brain-inspired cognitive systems – related research including biologically inspired systems, cognitive neuroscience, models of consciousness, and neural computation.

Many organizations and volunteers made great contributions toward the success of this event. We are grateful for the great support from the School of Software and Microelectronics, Northwestern Polytechnical University and School of Computer Sciences, Guangdong Polytechnic Normal University (also Guangzhou Key Laboratory of Digital Content Processing and Security Technologies). We also thank the University of Strathclyde and the University of Stirling as well as the IEEE Brain Initiatives for co-organizing the Brain Data Bank Competition with BICS. We would also like to sincerely thank all the committee members for their great effort and time in organizing the event. Special thanks go to the Program Committee members and reviewers, whose insightful reviews and timely feedback ensured the high quality of the accepted papers and the smooth flow of the conference. We would also like to thank the publisher, Springer, for their cooperation in publishing the proceedings in the prestigious series of *Lecture Notes in Artificial Intelligence*. Finally, we would like to thank all the speakers, authors, and participants for their support.

July 2018

Jinchang Ren
Amir Hussain
Jiangbin Zheng
Cheng-Lin Liu
Bin Luo
Huimin Zhao
Xinbo Zhao

Organization

General Chairs

Yanning Zhang	Northwestern Polytechnical University, China
Jiangbin Zheng	Northwestern Polytechnical University, China
Amir Hussain	Edinburgh Napier University, UK
Jinchang Ren	University of Strathclyde, UK
Narisa Nan Chu	IEEE Brain Initiatives, USA
Huimin Zhao	Guangdong Polytechnic Normal University, China

Honorary Co-chairs

Derong Liu	University of Illinois, USA
Igor Aleksander	Imperial College London, UK
Tariq Durrani	University of Strathclyde, UK
Tieniu Tan	Chinese Academy of Sciences, China

Program Chairs

Xiaoya Fan	Northwestern Polytechnical University, China
Cheng-Lin Liu	Chinese Academy of Sciences, China
Bin Luo	Anhui University, China

Workshop Chairs

Meijun Sun	Tianjin University, China
Erfu Yang	University of Strathclyde, UK
Zheng Wang	Tianjin University, China

Publication Chairs

Genyun Sun	China University of Petroleum, China
Xinbo Zhao	Northwestern Polytechnical University, China
Jamie Zabalza	University of Strathclyde, UK

Publicity Chairs

Haibo He	University of Rhode Island, USA
Newton Howard	Massachusetts Institute of Technology, USA
El-Sayed El-Alfy	King Fahd University of Petroleum and Minerals, Saudi Arabia
Mohamed Chetouani	Pierre and Marie Curie University, France

Anna Esposito	Second University of Naples, Italy
Giacomo Indiveri	University of Zurich and ETH Zurich, Switzerland
Stefan Wermter	University of Hamburg, Germany
Erik Cambria	Nanyang Technological University, Singapore
Jonathon Wu	University of Windsor, Canada
Genyun Sun	China University of Petroleum, China

Finance Chairs

Sophia Zhao	University of Strathclyde, UK
Qianru Wei	Northwestern Polytechnical University, China

Registrations and Local Arrangements Chairs

Yuying Wang	Northwestern Polytechnical University, China
Chunxia Xiao	Northwestern Polytechnical University, China
Mingchen Feng	University of Strathclyde, UK
Qiaoyuan Liu	University of Strathclyde, UK

Program Committee

Andrew Abel	Stirling University, UK
Peter Andras	Keele University, UK
Xiang Bai	Huazhong University of Science and Technology, China
Vladimir Bajic	KAUST, Thuwal, Saudi Arabia
Yanchao Bi	Beijing Normal University, China
Erik Cambria	Nanyang Technological University, Singapore
Lihong Cao	Communication University of China, China
Chun-I Philip Chen	California State University, USA
Mingming Cheng	Nankai University, China
Dazheng Feng	Xidian University, China
David Yushan Fong	CITS Group, USA
Marcos Faundez	Zanuy Tecnocampus, Barcelona, Spain
Fei Gao	Beihang University, China
Alexander Gelbukh	CIC IPN, Mexico
Hugo Gravato	Marques ETH Zurich, Switzerland
Claudius Gros Goethe	University of Frankfurt, Germany
Junwei Han	Northwestern Polytechnical University, China
Xiangjian He	University of Technology Sydney, Australia
Bingliang Hu	Xi'an Institute of Optics and Precision Mechanics, Chinese Academy of Sciences, China
Xiaolin Hu	Tsinghua University, China
Kaizhu Huang	Xi'an Jiaotong Liverpool University, China
Tiejun Huang	Peking University, China
Amir Hussain	Edinburgh Napier University, UK
Rongrong Ji	Xiamen University, China

Yi Jiang	Institute of Psychology, Chinese Academy of Sciences, China
Jingpeng Li	Stirling University, UK
Yongjie Li	University of Electronic Science and Technology of China, China
Cheng-Lin Liu	Institute of Automation, Chinese Academy of Sciences, China
Huaping Liu	Tsinghua University, China
Weifeng Liu	China University of Petroleum, China
Iman Yi Liao	University of Nottingham Malaysia Campus, Malaysia
Xiaoqiang Lu	Xi'an Institute of Optics and Precision Mechanics, Chinese Academy of Sciences, China
Bin Luo	Anhui University, China
Mufti Mahmud	University of Padova, Italy
Zeeshan Malik	Stirling University, UK
Deyu Meng	Xi'an Jiaotong University, China
Tomas Henrique Maul	University of Nottingham Malaysia Campus, Malaysia
Junaid Qadir National	University of Sciences and Technology, Pakistan
Jinchang Ren	University of Strathclyde, UK
Simone Scardapane	University of Rome, Italy
Bailu Si	Shenyang Institute of Automation, Chinese Academy of Sciences, China
Mingli Song	Zhejiang University, China
Genyun Sun	China University of Petroleum (East China), China
Meijun Sun	Tianjin University, China
Walid Taha	Halmstad University, Sweden
Dacheng Tao	University of Technology Sydney, Australia
Yonghong Tian	Peking University, China
Isabel Trancoso	INESC-ID, Portugal
Stefano Vassanelli	University of Padua, Italy
Liang Wang	Institute of Psychology, Chinese Academy of Sciences, China
Zheng Wang	Tianjin University, China
Zhijiang Wang	Institute of Mental Health, Peking University, China
Qi Wang	Northwestern Polytechnical University, China
Hui Wei	Fudan University, China
Jonathan Wu	University of Windsor, Canada
Qiang Wu	University of Technology Sydney, Australia
Min Xu	University of Technology Sydney, Australia
Erfu Yang	University of Strathclyde, UK
Tianming Yang	Institute of Neuroscience, China
Zhijing Yang	Guangdong University of Technology, China
Jin Zhan	Guangdong Polytechnic Normal University, China
Daoqiang Zhang	Nanjing University of Aeronautics and Astronautics, China
Li Zhang	University of Birmingham, UK
Yanning Zhang	Northwestern Polytechnical University, China

Contents

Neural Computation

Biologically Inspired Systems

Applications

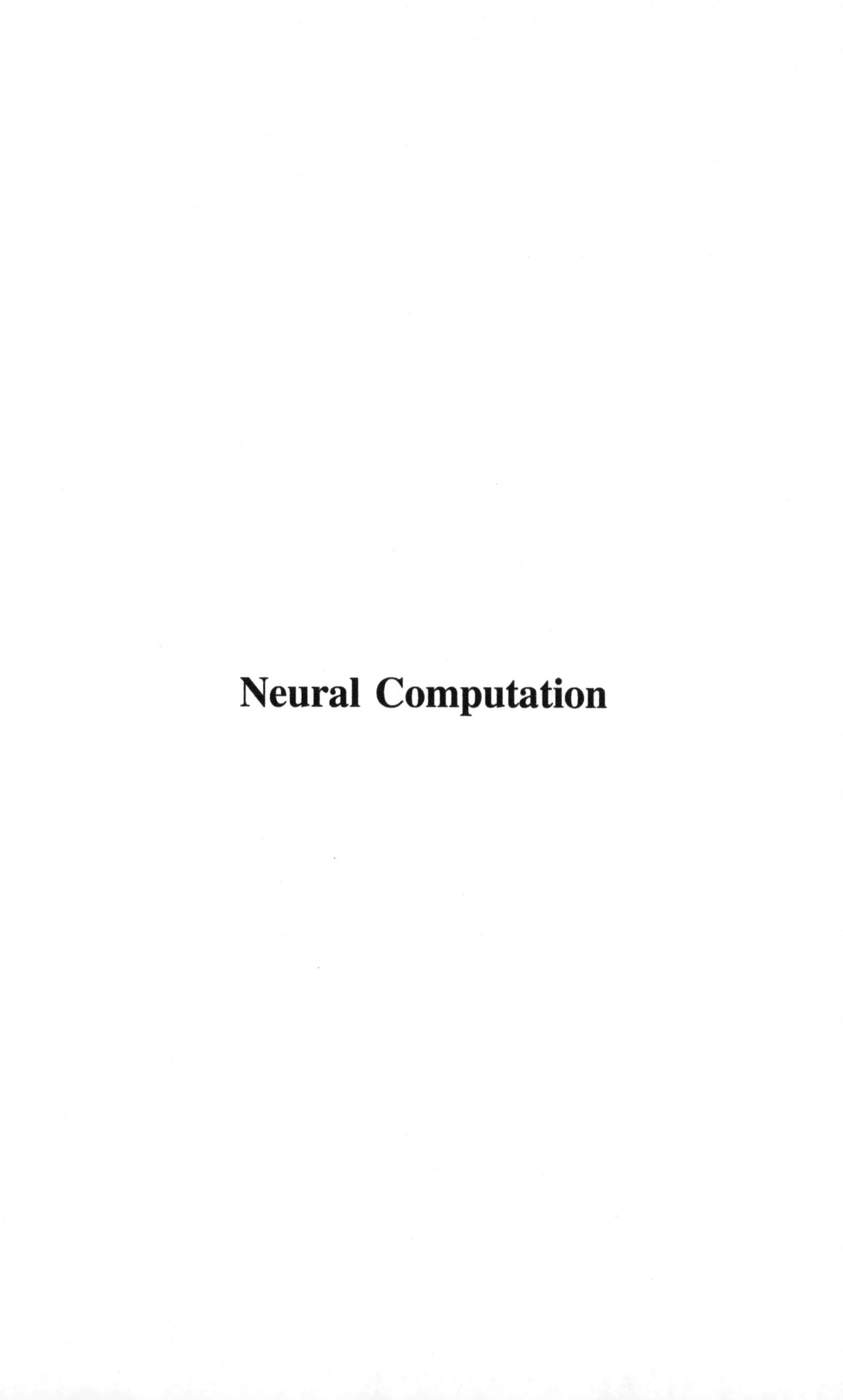

Neural Computation

Style Neutralization Generative Adversarial Classifier

Haochuan Jiang[1], Kaizhu Huang[1(✉)], Rui Zhang[2], and Amir Hussain[3]

[1] Department of EEE, Xi'an Jiaotong - Liverpool University, 111 Ren'ai Rd., Suzhou, Jiangsu, People's Republic of China
kaizhu.huang@xjtlu.edu.cn

[2] Department of MS, Xi'an Jiaotong - Liverpool University, 111 Ren'ai Rd., Suzhou, Jiangsu, People's Republic of China

[3] Division of Computing Science and Maths, University of Stirling, Stirling FK9 4LA, Scotland, UK

Abstract. Breathtaking improvement has been seen with the recently proposed deep Generative Adversarial Network (GAN). Purposes of most existing GAN-based models majorly concentrate on generating realistic and vivid patterns by a pattern generator with the aid of the binary discriminator. However, few study were related to the promotion of classification performance with merits of those generated ones. In this paper, a novel and generalized classification framework called Style Neutralization Generative Adversarial Classifier (SN-GAC), based on the GAN framework, is introduced to enhance the classification accuracy by neutralizing possible inconsistent style information existing in the original data. In the proposed model, the generator of SN-GAC is trained by mapping the original patterns with certain styles (source) to their style-neutralized or standard counterparts (standard-target), capable of generating the targeted style-neutralized one (generated-target). On the other hand, pairs of both standard (source + standard-target) and generated (source + generated-target) patterns are fed into the discriminator, optimized by not only distinguishing between real and fake, but also classifying the input pairs with correct class label assignment. Empirical experiments fully demonstrate the effectiveness of the proposed SN-GAC framework by achieving so-far the highest accuracy on two benchmark classification databases including the face and the Chinese handwriting character, outperforming several relevant state-of-the-art baseline approaches.

1 Introduction

Traditional Generative Adversarial Network (GAN) [5] based approaches aim at generating realistic patterns with the discriminative model by implicitly approximating the high-dimensional real data distribution. Distinctively, in this paper, a novel GAN based classifier named Style Normalization Generative Adversarial Classifier (SR-GAC) is investigated to neutralize diverse style information embedded in the original patterns, promoting classification performance with the aid of the generated samples from the generator.

J. Ren et al. (Eds.): BICS 2018, LNAI 10989, pp. 3–13, 2018.
https://doi.org/10.1007/978-3-030-00563-4_1

Relevant problems were mostly considered previously when data are generated from multiple sources with each one equipped with a specific style information, and different across different groups. It is solved with two major approaches, including the Multi-task Learning [4] (MTL, one classifier is obtained from each group while considering inter-relationship between them), and the field classification [8,10,21] (style-free data is produced by the style normalization transformation, represented by both linear or nonlinear kernelized mapping).

As a generalized framework, the proposed SN-GAC model is capable of obtaining standard patterns by neutralizing style information attached to the original data. Importantly, the generation process (of standard patterns) is designed for and integrated with classifier optimization. It can hence neutralize styles from data and consequently benefit the classification performance in many real applications. Such scenarios can be found in cases including the face recognition task when photos are assigned into several groups while ones from each group are taken with a specific head pose [6], or the handwriting character classification task when they are written by multiple writers according to their own writing habits [15]. Traditional approaches may suffer from degraded performance because of multiple, diverse, and inconsistent style information.

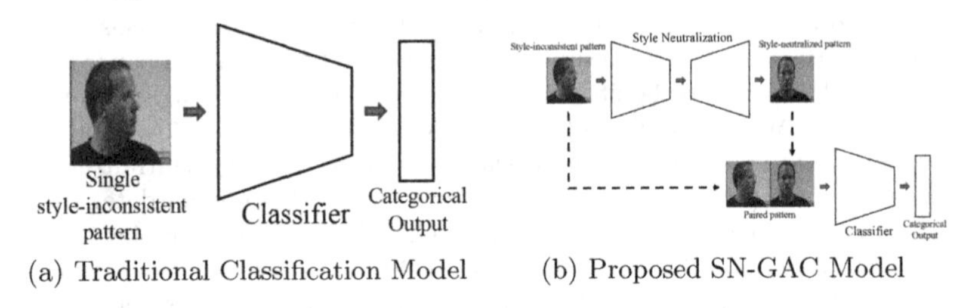

(a) Traditional Classification Model (b) Proposed SN-GAC Model

Fig. 1. Traditional classifier and the proposed SN-GAC model

Specifically, inspired by the recently GAN-based proposed *Pix2Pix* framework introduced in [9], the proposed SN-GAC neutralizes diverse styles from data by learning standard patterns with the final purpose of promoting the classification performance. In more details, the SN-GAC model consists of two independent networks, a *U-Net* [9] based generator (G) and a discriminator with an auxiliary classifier (*D-C* [16]).[1] G is responsible for obtaining high-quality style-neutralized or standard patterns given the input ones with various style information, while *D-C* assigns class labels given the patterns with multiple styles and style-neutralized pattern pairs, as depicted in Fig. 1(b). The proposed classification framework differs significantly from many traditional approaches (Fig. 1(a)) where all the samples are simply fed into the classifier.

[1] The discriminator with auxiliary classifier is termed as *D-C* in this paper since it differs from the D of traditional GAN as in [5]. Moreover, the proposed *D-C* is also different from [16] since the classifier in the SN-GAC model can be directly applied for normal classification after well trained. However, the auxiliary classifier in [16] is only utilized to provide supervising information for better GAN training.

Additionally, in the proposed SN-GAC model, the style-neutralization is fulfilled by the nonlinear G neural network, enabling representation of sufficiently complicated style information. Moreover, as an inherent merit of the GAN approaches, no data distribution assumption is required.

The optimization of the proposed SN-GAC model is a two-stage effort. Initially, G is trained adversarially to generate realistic images, while D-C is optimized with both adversarial and categorical losses. The D-C will be fine-tuned with only the categorical objective to further improve the classification accuracy when G is saturated to produce high-quality style-neutralized patterns. Both the steps are fulfilled with clear purposes, necessary for high-quality style-neutralized examples and accurate classification.

The proposed SN-GAC model is an end-to-end framework capable of improving the recognition accuracy jointly with the adversarial optimization, meanwhile producing realistic samples, saving both time for model learning and storage respectively. It is a generalized framework not only capable of transforming groups of patterns, it can also be applied in a more generalized way for any kind of classification situation for examples with multiple styles.[2]

Major contributions of this paper are listed as follows:

- A novel classification framework named SR-GAC is introduced, which is significantly different from traditional classification models;
- A two-step training strategy is specifically designed for the purpose of generating high-quality style-neutralized patterns as well as achieving high classification accuracy;
- The classification performance is promoted without any extra training effort except the GAN optimization itself.

2 Model Architecture

The SN-GAC model is built on the GAN-based *Pix2Pix* framework [9], while the discriminator is attached with an auxiliary classifier to assign class labels. Several preliminaries will be briefly defined firstly in this section. The detailed model architecture will then be demonstrated, followed by the two-stage training strategy. The SN-GAC model is illustrated in Fig. 2.

2.1 Preliminaries

Definition 1. Source *is noted as data equipped with style information, namely,* x*. It is associated with a class label* y*.*

Definition 2. Standard-Target *is defined as the corresponding pattern equipped with the standard style given the* source x*, denoted as* x_**.*

[2] The proposed SN-GAC model is evaluated only with dataset specifying groups of style patterns in this paper for the simplification purpose.

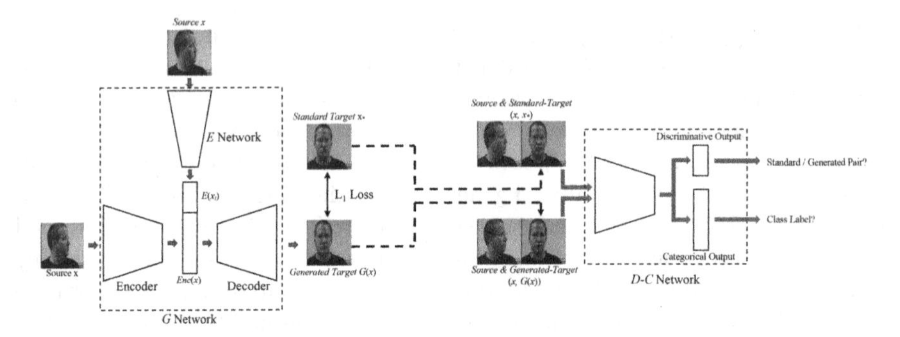

Fig. 2. The SN-GAC architecture: includes a generator (G) and a discriminator with an auxiliary classifier (D-C). G consists an embedder network (E) for style vector inference, a convolutional encoder, and a deconvolutional decoder. It generates a *Generated-Target* (*G(x)*) when given a *Source* (x). *D-C* is a convolutional network, capable to distinguish the input pair coming from the real or from the generated data with the discriminative output; while assigning the class label of the input pair by the categorical output.

Noted that the standard target style needs specified before training. The proposed SN-GAC model builds the neural nonlinear mapping from those multiple and diverse styles to this standard target.

Definition 3. ***Pair of*** **Source** *&* **Standard-Target** *is then denoted as* $\{x, x_*\}$.

Factually, each *target* (x_*) can be corresponded with multiple *sources* (x), originates from over one data generator.

Definition 4. ***Generated-Target*** *is defined as the style-neutralized output of* G *in the proposed SN-GAC model given the* source x. *It is noted as* $G(x)$.

Definition 5. ***Pair of*** **Source** *&* **Generated-Target** *is denoted as* $\{x, G(x)\}$ *to represent the correspondence.*

2.2 U-Net Based Generator

Similar to [9], the G network of the SN-GAC model is based on the *U-Net* [9] with skipping connections. Given that a *source* pattern x is defined in Definition 1, the G network is capable of generating a *Generated-Target* pattern $G(x)$ (as defined in Definition 4) with high quality.

The G network consists of a convolutional encoder network (*Enc*), mapping x to the high-level encoded features (denoted as $Enc(x)$), as well as an upsampling decoder network, transforming high-level encoded features to the targetted style-neutralized counterpart $G(x)$. The deconvolutional operation, seen as the reversed operation of the convolution, is employed as the upsampling function. Moreover, skipping connections from the encoder to the decoder are also applied to align structures and features on the equivalent level. It leads that the input feature of each decoding layer comes not only from the previous decoding layer but also the encoding one at the same level.

The quality of the *Generated-Target* $G(x)$ is well maintained by penalizing the adversarial loss proposed in [5] maximally confusing D. Additionally, the L1 reconstruction error between x_* and $G(x)$, namely, $\mathbb{L}_{l_1} = ||x_* - G(x)||_1$, encouraging to generate sharp and clear image details [9], is also applied.

Moreover, the constant loss introduced in [18] is also engaged as additional restriction to encourage high-quality output patterns. Specifically, it regulates with the L2 difference between encoded spaces of two input patterns. In the proposed SN-GAC model, two constant losses, including $\mathbb{L}_{const_1} = ||Enc(x) - Enc(G(x))||^2$ and $\mathbb{L}_{const_2} = ||Enc(x_*) - Enc(G(x))||^2$, are summed together to form the total constant error, namely, $\mathbb{L}_{const} = \mathbb{L}_{const_1} + \mathbb{L}_{const_2}$.

Instead of explicit random noise fed into G in the traditional GANs, the dropout, severed as the implicit random noise [9], is applied to several layers of both encoder and decoder during training. It is shutdown when performing network inference.

2.3 Embedder Network for Style Representation

An extra embedder network (noted as E) is employed as part of G. It represents the embedded style information of the input source pattern to incorporate with the multi-to-one mapping model. According to [11], patterns in the same style tend to be clustered closer in the deep feature space. In such sense, E can be realized with an extra deep model, fine-tuned from a pre-trained model optimized based on a similar classification task or trained from scratch. It fulfills the function by selecting features from the final layer (inferred logits before the sigmoid or softmax function) as the style vector ($E(x)$). They are then concatenated with the output of the encoder ($Enc(x)$) before fed into the decoder together.

2.4 Discriminator with Auxiliary Classifier

The discriminator with an auxiliary classifier [16] (D-C network) is applied in the proposed SN-GAC model. It is a CNN classifier embedded in the DC-GAN framework. As depicted in Fig. 2, in each training iteration, pattern pair batches consisting of both the *Source* & *Standard-Target* and *Source* & *Generated-Target* are fed into D-C optimized by not only differentiating between both pairs (same with vanilla GAN [5], noted as D training), but also assigning the correct class label (y) of the given pair (C training, as depicted in Fig. 2. The input pair of D (x, x_*) can be considered as an implicit regularization, penalizing over-flexible style transformation between the *Source* (with style) and the style-neutralized targets. Similar ideas are implemented in [8,10,21] with explicit expressions.[3]

[3] Paired input is not evaluated for conventional baselines in Sect. 3 since style-neutralization cannot be achieved with traditional approaches.

2.5 Two-Phase Training Strategy with Multiple Losses

Initial Training for both G and D-C both networks are updated in an iterative fashion. G is trained by minimizing the summation of losses as follows for both sufficiently confusing the D and assigning correct label by C:

$$\mathbb{L}_G = (\mathbb{L}_D - \mathbb{L}_C) + \alpha \cdot \mathbb{L}_{l_1} + \beta \cdot \mathbb{L}_{const} \tag{1}$$

where α and β are hyper-parameters. The adversarial and the categorical losses are given as Eqs. (2) and (3) respectively.

$$\mathbb{L}_D = E_{x,x_*}\left[\log D(x, x_*)\right] + E_x\left[\log(1 - D(x, G(x)))\right] \tag{2}$$

$$\mathbb{L}_C = E_{x,x_*}\left[\log C(x, x_*)\right] + E_x\left[\log C(x, G(x))\right] \tag{3}$$

Meanwhile, the D-C network is optimized not to be fooled by G, meanwhile to assign correct class labels by maximizing the combined loss: $\mathbb{L}_G = (\mathbb{L}_C + \mathbb{L}_D)$.

In each training iteration, G is only accessible to one batch of pairs (*Source & Standard-Target*), while two pair batches including (*Source & Standard-Target*) and (*Source & Generated-Target*) are fed into D-C. As suggested in [13], G will be updated twice while D-C once for balanced training.

Fine-Tuning for C when G is stabilized, it is capable of generating high-quality style-neutralized patterns. The D-C network is then further fine-tuned by fixing the G network while minimizing only the categorical objective $\mathbb{L}_C$.

3 Experiments

Two benchmark data sets including the Point'04 [6] for face recognition, and the CASIA offline database [15] for Chinese handwriting character classification, are used to evaluate the proposed SN-GAC model.

In this section, relevant baselines such as Support Vector Machine (SVM) [3], the Mean Regularized MTL (MR-MTL) model [4], and several field classification approaches including one special case of the Field Bayesian (F-BM) model [21], namely, the Field Nearest Class Mean (F-NCM), the Field Support Vector Classification (F-SVC) model [8] are compared for both sets in this comparison. Moreover, several conventional state-of-the-art techniques not considering style information are also implemented and compared. These models include the Nearest Class Mean (NCM), the Support Vector Classification (SVC) [3] and two specific deep convolutional neural networks, i.e., the Vgg-Face [2] and the Alexnet [14] for the face and handwriting data respectively. Performance of the SVC-based models (including SVC, F-SVC, and MR-MTL) are only reported with the lowest obtained error (for both Linear and RBF Kernel, Ln and RBF for short respectively). The F-SVC model is compared for both style-transferred or not (ST and Non-ST respectively) for the face set.

For each set, some state-of-the-art models are also compared. They are the Style Mixture Model (SMM) [17], the Bilinear Model (BM) [19], and the Fisherface Discriminant Analysis (FDA) [12] for the face set, and the F-BM [21], the Field Modified Quadratic Discriminant Function (F-MQDF) and the Modified Quadratic Discriminant Function (MQDF) for the Chinese handwriting task.

The basic *Pix2Pix* framework can be referred to in [20], while the choice of E depends on different sets. For each set, the *Standard-Target* needs specified, as demonstrated in details in the following sections. The whole model is built on the Google Tensorflow Deep Learning Library (r1.4) [1].

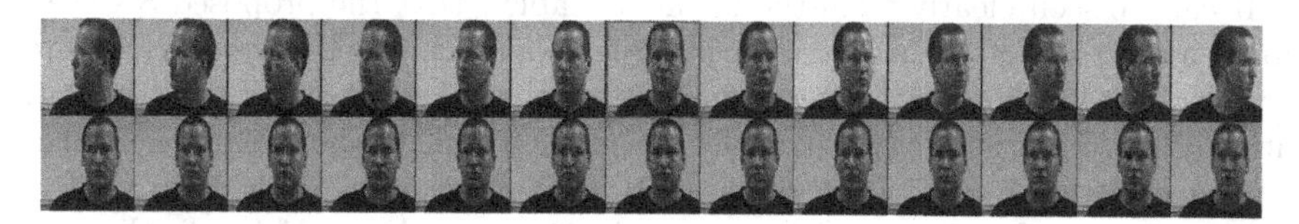

Fig. 3. Examples from the point' 04 database. Each column represents a specific head pose (a style). 1st row: *Source* (x), where the image with a red box is chosen as the *Standard-Target* (x_*); 2nd row: *Generated-Target* ($G(x)$) generated by the generator G.

3.1 Face Classification Across Head Yaw Poses

The experiment involves 15 people in total in the Point' 04 Database [6]. For each one, only the zero pitch pose faces are selected. 13 different yaw angles in the range of [$-90°$,$+90°$] partitioned with $15°$ from each other are chosen, resulting in 195 images. The experiment setting can be referred to in [8], For the proposed SN-GAC model, the images are resized to 256×256 so that they can

Table 1. Error rate on the point' 04 database

Method	Error rate
FDA	30.67%
SMM	26.67%
BM	40.00%
NCM	40.00%
CNN (Vgg-face)	9.33%
F-NCM	21.33%
SVM (RBF)	14.67%
MR-MTL (Ln/RBF)	14.67%
F-SVC (Non-ST, RBF)	12.00%
F-SVC (ST, Ln/RBF)	0.00%
SR-GAC	**0.00%**

be easily incorporated with both the G and the D-C network of the proposed SN-GAC model. It is straightforward to select images with zero yaw angles as style-neutralized *Standard-Targets*.

Images taken of each yaw pose is regarded to be equipped with a consistent style information (as each column in Fig. 3). The classification is conducted based on faces, as examples displayed on the first row in Fig. 3. Images from the first 8 poses (left 8 columns in Fig. 3)) are put into the training set, while the remaining 5 ones are placed into the testing set. For the SN-GAC model, the E network is obtained by fine-tuning the last fully connected and the first convolutional layers from the Vgg-Face model [2].

It can be seen clearly from the result in Table 1 that the proposed SN-GAC model and the F-SVC model with style transfer achieve the zero error rate. However, F-SVC obatin the performance by taking advantage of the test data with a self-training strategy to transfer the trained style to the unseen one. There is no such setting in the proposed SN-GAC framework.

Moreover, by looking into the images in the second row of Fig. 3, the non-linearly mapped generated style-neutralized images by the proposed SN-GAC model can be readily understood by human observers with only insignificant defects. In comparison, in the F-SVC model [8], the obtained standard images may usually be less similar to a real image. In addition, it can only produce style-normalized data by the linear kernel, insufficient to represent multiple, diverse, and complicated style information in real scenarios.

3.2 Chinese Handwriting Classification Across Writers

The offline version of the CASIA dataset [15] is also exploited for evaluation of the proposed SN-GAC model. The original data include 3,755 categories of different Chinese characters. As described in [21], 100 writers (no. 1,101–no. 1,200) are involved in this experiment. For simplicity, only the first 30 characters are chosen in this experiment. Since people are more likely to write texts cursively than isolated characters, the isolated set is chosen as the training set (CASIA-HWDB-1.1), while the cursive text set (CASIA-HWDB-2.1) is used for testing. The total number of samples is 2,995 for the training set and 288 for the testing set. It is noted that each testing sample shares a certain training style. However, there shall be a style difference between isolated characters and their corresponding cursive counterparts. Different from the Point' 04 data, the *Standard-Target* in this evaluation is not coming from the CASIA base. Instead, the standard 'Heiti' font is chosen, as illustrated in the second column of Fig. 4. The Alexnet [14] is introduced with both batch-norm and dropout tricks to form E. It is optimized from scratch without any pre-training strategy.

Pixel values are directly put into the Alexnet after resized to 227×227. Similarly, they are resized to 256×256 for the SN-GAC model. For other baselines, original 256×256 features are compressed to be 512-d with PCA.

As seen in Table 2, the proposed SN-GAC model attains the highest accuracy, along with the self-training F-SVC model. By further examining those incorrectly classified samples as shown in Fig. 4, it can be concluded that most

Table 2. Error rate on the CASIA offline database

Method	Error rate
NCM	5.56%
F-NCM	4.51%
MQDF	5.56%
F-MQDF	4.51%
CNN (Alexnet)	2.78%
SVM (LN/RBF)	3.47%
MR-MTL (RBF)	2.78%
F-SVC (Non-ST, LN)	**2.08%**
SR-GAC	**2.08%**

Fig. 4. Some incorrect classified examples on the CASIA offline database. 1st column: *Source* (x), 2nd column: *Standard-Target* (x_*); 3rd column: *Generated-Target* ($G(x)$); 4th column: class label assigned by *D-C* from the generated sample in the 3rd column.

of the errors come from the confusing and cursive written *Source*. Some of them are even too difficult to be recognized for a human. In this case, the G would generate incorrect or even unclear *Generated-Target* examples. However, even if G does not perform well, the *D-C* may still give reliable class label based on the generated sample.

4 Conclusion and Future Work

A novel classification framework, named Style Neutralized Generative Adversarial Classifier (SN-GAC), based on the emerging Generative Adversarial Network (GAN), is proposed in this paper. It is designed to neutralize diverse and inconsistent style information from the original data by mapping them to patterns with standard style. The style-neutralized features are believed to be better compact and centralized, beneficial to the following classification task [7]. Aiming at promoting the recognition accuracy directly, it trains no extra classification model except the SN-GAC itself. Empirical experiments have demonstrated on two benchmark datasets that the proposed SN-GAC model not only achieves the highest classification performance so-far but taking no advantage of the test data during training with the self-training strategy, while generates high-quality human-understandable style-neutralized patterns. Future work includes the extension of the SN-GAC model to large-category classification (e.g. recognition of 3,755 classes in the whole CASIA dataset [15]), as well as the style transfer scheme to further reduce the classification error due to the style shift difference between training and validation.

Acknowledgements. The work reported here was partially supported by the following: National Natural Science Foundation of China under grant no. 61473236; Natural Science Fund for Colleges and Universities in Jiangsu Province under grant $no.17KJD520010$; Suzhou Science and Technology Program under grant no. SYG201712, SZS201613; Jiangsu University Natural Science Research Programme under grant no. 17KJB-520041; Key Program Special Fund in XJTLU (KSF-A-01)

References

1. Abadi, M., Barham, P., Chen, J., Chen, Z., Davis, A., Dean, J., Devin, M., Ghemawat, S., Irving, G., Isard, M.: TensorFlow: a system for large-scale machine learning. OSDI **16**, 265–283 (2016)
2. Cate, H., Dalvi, F., Hussain, Z.: DeepFace: face generation using deep learning. arXiv preprint arXiv:1701.01876 (2017)
3. Cortes, C., Vapnik, V.: Support-vector networks. Mach. Learn. **20**(3), 273–297 (1995)
4. Evgeniou, T., Pontil, M.: Regularized multi-task learning. In: Proceedings of the Tenth ACM SIGKDD International Conference on Knowledge Discovery and Data Mining, pp. 109–117. ACM (2004)
5. Goodfellow, I., et al.: Generative adversarial nets. In: Advances in neural information processing systems, pp. 2672–2680 (2014)
6. Gourier, N., Hall, D., Crowley, J.L.: Estimating face orientation from robust detection of salient facial structures. In: FG Net Workshop on Visual Observation of Deictic Gestures, vol. 6, p. 7 (2004)
7. Huang, K.Z., Yang, H., King, I., Lyu, M.R.: Machine Learning: Modeling Data Locally and Globally. Springer Science, Heidelberg (2008). https://doi.org/10.1007/978-3-540-79452-3
8. Huang, K., Jiang, H., Zhang, X.Y.: Field support vector machines. IEEE Trans. Emerg. Top. Comput. Intell. **1**(6), 454–463 (2017)
9. Isola, P., Zhu, J.Y., Zhou, T., Efros, A.A.: Image-to-image translation with conditional adversarial networks. arXiv preprint (2017)
10. Jiang, H., Huang, K., Zhang, R.: Field support vector regression. In: Liu, D., Xie, S., Li, Y., Zhao, D., El-Alfy, E.S. (eds.) International Conference on Neural Information Processing. LNCS, pp. 699–708. Springer, Heidelberg (2017). https://doi.org/10.1007/978-3-319-70087-8_72
11. Jiang, Y., Lian, Z., Tang, Y., Xiao, J.: DCFont: an end-to-end deep Chinese font generation system. In: SIGGRAPH Asia 2017 Technical Briefs, p. 22. ACM (2017)
12. Jing, X.Y., Wong, H.S., Zhang, D.: Face recognition based on 2D fisherface approach. Pattern Recognit. **39**(4), 707–710 (2006)
13. Kim, T.: GitHub dcgan-tensorflow (2016). https://github.com/carpedm20/DCGAN-tensorflow
14. Krizhevsky, A., Sutskever, I., Hinton, G.E.: ImageNet classification with deep convolutional neural networks. In: Advances in Neural Information Processing Systems, pp. 1097–1105 (2012)
15. Liu, C.L., Yin, F., Wang, D.H., Wang, Q.F.: CASIA online and offline Chinese handwriting databases. In: 2011 International Conference on Document Analysis and Recognition (ICDAR), pp. 37–41. IEEE (2011)
16. Odena, A., Olah, C., Shlens, J.: Conditional image synthesis with auxiliary classifier GANs. arXiv preprint arXiv:1610.09585 (2016)
17. Sarkar, P., Nagy, G.: Style consistent classification of isogenous patterns. IEEE Trans. Pattern Anal. Mach. Intell. **27**(1), 88–98 (2005)
18. Taigman, Y., Polyak, A., Wolf, L.: Unsupervised cross-domain image generation. arXiv preprint arXiv:1611.02200 (2016)

19. Tenenbaum, J.B., Freeman, W.T.: Separating style and content with bilinear models. Neural Comput. **12**(6), 1247–1283 (2000)
20. Tian, Y.: GitHub zi2zi-tensorflow (2017). https://kaonashi-tyc.github.io/2017/04/06/zi2zi.html
21. Zhang, X.Y., Huang, K., Liu, C.L.: Pattern field classification with style normalized transformation. In: IJCAI Proceedings-International Joint Conference on Artificial Intelligence, vol. 22, p. 1621 (2011)

How Good a Shallow Neural Network Is for Solving Non-linear Decision Making Problems

Hongmei He[1], Zhilong Zhu[2(✉)], Gang Xu[2], and Zhenhuan Zhu[3]

[1] Manufacturing Informatics Centre, SATM, Cranfield University, Cranfield MK43 0AL, UK
h.he@cranfield.ac.uk

[2] School of Electronic Engineering, Anhui Polytechnic University, Wuhu, China
zhuzhilong919@ahpu.edu.cn

[3] Advanced Laser Ltd., 3 Raleigh Street, Stockport SK5 7ER, UK

Abstract. The universe approximate theorem states that a shallow neural network (one hidden layer) can represent any non-linear function. In this paper, we aim at examining how good a shallow neural network is for solving non-linear decision making problems. We proposed a performance driven incremental approach to searching the best shallow neural network for decision making, given a data set. The experimental results on the two benchmark data sets, Breast Cancer in Wisconsin and SMS Spams, demonstrate the correction of universe approximate theorem, and show that the number of hidden neurons, taking about the half of input number, is good enough to represent the function from data. It is shown that the performance driven BP learning is faster than the error-driven BP learning, and that the performance of the SNN obtained by the former is not worse than that of the SNN obtained by the latter. This indicates that when learning a neural network with the BP algorithm, the performance reaches a certain value quickly, but the error may still keep reducing. The performance of the SNNs for the two databases is comparable to or better than that of the optimal linguistic attribute hierarchy, obtained by a genetic algorithm in wrapper or in terms of semantics manually, which is much time-consuming.

Keywords: Shallow neural network
Performance-driven BP learning · Incremental approach
Non-linear decision making · Universe approximate theorem

1 Introduction

An artificial neuron network (ANN) is a computational model, mimicking the structure and functions of biological neural networks. It provides an easy approach to creating the relations between input attributes and the output based on a limit set of data, in stead of an exact mathematic function, which we may

J. Ren et al. (Eds.): BICS 2018, LNAI 10989, pp. 14–24, 2018.
https://doi.org/10.1007/978-3-030-00563-4_2

not be able to create. The ability to learn by examples makes ANNs very flexible and powerful. Although there exists bias to the real relation between inputs and outputs, ANN is still a good approach to solving many non-linear mapping problems.

Deep neural networks (DNNs) have been successfully applied in two main areas: image processing and speech recognition. Especially, deep convolutional nets (ConvNets) have brought about breakthroughs in video [1,2], image processing [3], object detection [4], as well as audio [5] and speech recognition [6]. The properties of compositional hierarchies of images, speech and text promote the capacities of deep neural networks. However, we cannot always see the semantics of higher-level features in many real-world cases as in image and acoustic modelling.

The universal approximation theorem, first with sigmoid activation function proved by Cybenkot in 1989 [7], states that a shallow neural network (with one hidden layer, containing a finite number of neurons) with a non-polynomial activation function can approximate any function, i.e. can in principle learn anything [8,9]. This indicates that we do not always need to use DNNs. A shallow neural network could be enough to solve non-linear approximate problems.

The back-propagation (BP) algorithm is a classic training algorithm of ANNs. Blum and Rivest [10] proved that training a 2-layer, 3 nodes and n inputs neural network with the BP algorithm is NP-Complete. Obviously, the big barrier of blocking the applications of deep neural networks is the computing complexity, although it shows great attractive on solving complex non-linear problems. With the strong capability of GPU, deep learning for 2–20 depth networks is successful (e.g. Google AlphaGo). Also, the success of deep learning in image and acoustic modelling benefits from GPU computing. However, in many cases, we may not need to use GPU, or even we do not have GPU to support the calculation, for example, in an application of embedded intelligence.

Improving learning performance for all ANN applications is necessary. Basically, there are four kinds of approaches to improving the performance of ANNs: (1) improving data, which is important for training an ANN; (2) improving training algorithm, for which many notable algorithms have been developed in addition to the BP algorithm; (3) algorithm tuning, for which, some evolutionary algorithms were developed to optimise the parameters and neural network structures; (4) using ensembles.

Recently, Zhang et al. [11] proposed a dynamic neighborhood learning-based gravitational search algorithm. This approach can improve search performance in convergence and diversity of an evolutionary optimisation. A shallow neural network (SNN) is a feed-forward neural network (FNN) with only one fully connected hidden layer. If we use an evolutionary optimisation to find the best SNN with a specified number of hidden neurons as individuals, then there will be much redundant computing, as SNNs with the same number of hidden neurons but different distribution in the permutation of the individuals in the evolutionary optimisation have the same performance. There was also some research on incremental approach. For example, Bu et al. [12] proposed an incremental back-propagation model for training neural networks by adapting the parameters and the neural structure, and used the Singular Value Decomposition on the weight matrix to reduce some redundant links. The final neural network is not a fully connected FNN. He et al. [13] used the incremental approach based on information gain to select features for SVM spam detector.

In this research, we examine how good a shallow neural network is for solving non-linear decision making problems, and propose a new performance-driven incremental approach to finding the suitable number of hidden neurons in a shallow neural network. This approach overcomes not only the shortages of a population searching in evolutionary algorithm, which is much expensive in computing complexity, but also the shortages in both the randomness and computing complexity of ensembles. We use two case studies on the two benchmark databases, Breast Cancer in Wisconsin [14] and SMS spams [15], from UCI machine learning repository [16] to validate the correction of the universal approximation theorem.

2 Methodology

2.1 A Multi-layer FNN

A multiple layer FNN is a computational graph whose nodes are computing units and whose directed edges transmit numerical information from low layer nodes to upper layer nodes. One neuron represents a linear classifier, the simplest neural network, using an activation function (e.g. sigmoid function in Eq. (2)) to produce the result. A neuron can be described with the following function:

$$v_j = \sum_{i=0}^{k} w_{ij} x_i, \tag{1}$$

$$y = f(v) = \frac{1}{1 + e^{-\alpha(v-b)}}, \tag{2}$$

where, j represents a neuron, to which the outputs of all neurons ($i = 1, ..., k$) in lower layer are input; b is the bias. The sigmoid's output $y \in [0, 1]$. We use $n_1 - n_2 ... - 1$ to denote the structure of a neural network, where n_k is the number of neurons at the kth hidden layer, the last Fig. 1 represents one output neuron, and input neuron number is the number of input attributes by default.

2.2 The Classic BP Algorithm

Neural network learning is to find the optimal weights so that the network function φ approximates the function f representing the given data as closely as possible. Namely, given a training set $(x - 1, t_1), ..., (x_n, t_n)$, it is to minimise the error function of the network, defined as

$$E = \frac{1}{2} \sum_{i=1}^{n} \|o_i - t_i\|^2, \tag{3}$$

where, o_i is the output of the FNN for input sample x_i, t_i is the target output. The basic idea of BP algorithm is to use error back propagation to update weights in a fixed structure of ANN. The process is: (1) initialise the weights of the network randomly, (2) perform feed-forward computation to get the output of the network, and calculate the error between the output of the network and the target value (Eq. (3)), (3) calculate the gradient of the error function for all lower layers, and update the weight in terms of the back-propagated error, and repeat the steps of (2) and (3) until the average error ($\varepsilon = E/n$) is reduced to a specified small value.

Performance Calculation. A true estimation is the result, when the estimated probability $p(y|\boldsymbol{x})$ that the state of a decision variable y with measurement vector $\boldsymbol{x}$ is '+' or '-' is larger than a threshold (e.g. 05). Classic performance measurements include confusion matrices, accuracy (A), and F_1 score, ROC curve, and the area under ROC curve (AUC). Assume P positive samples and N negative samples in the tested data set. The confusion matrices include the four parameters: true positive rate or recall ($\text{TPR} = \text{TP}/P$), true negative rate($\text{TNR} = \text{TN}/N$), false positive rate($\text{FPR} = \text{FP}/N$), and false negative rate ($\text{FNR} = \text{FN}/P$). The accuracy is the ratio of the number of true estimations for both states to the number of testing samples. The F_1 score is the harmonic average of the precision ($\text{TP}/(\text{TP} + \text{FP})$) and recall. A ROC curve is a graphical plot of the true positive rate against the false positive rate at various threshold settings, and the area under the ROC curve has been formalized in [17].

The Updated BP Algorithm. In the general BP algorithm, the stop criteria depends on the average error. The question is how small the average error is sufficient. If the average error is too small, then the number of learning iterations could be large. Usually, a maximum number of iterations is set, in case the average error cannot converge to the specified value. Moreover, the neural network system may produce over fitting problem. To avoid over fitting, usually a small data set is used to validate the performance during the training process. Once the error of the FNN on the validation data is increasing, while the error of the FNN on training data is still decreasing, the training process will be stopped. This increases the complexity of training.

In fact, for a decision making problem, the goal of neural network training is to gain high accuracy. The primary experimental results show that when average error arrives a certain value, the performance for decision making could not be improved further. Therefore, the stop criteria can be set to evaluate the neural network performance, such as Accuracy (A), F1-score (F_1), true positive rate (TPR). Namely, the learning process will be stopped until the performance of the network has not been improved for a certain number (T) of iterations (called convergence tolerance) (Algorithm 1). When the average error is used as the stop criteria p, the line 10 in Algorithm 1 should be $p < best_p$.

Algorithm 1. UpdatedBP(D(X,Y),Net, T)

```
1: Initialise(Net);
2: I = 0, k = 0;
3: p = 0;
4: while (I<MAX_IT) do
5:    Ŷ=feedforward(X);
6:    backpropagation (Y, Ŷ);
7:    Net = updateWeight(Net);
8:    best_p = p;
9:    p = calPerformance(Y, Ŷ);
10:   if (p>best_p) then
11:      k = 0;
12:      best_p=p;
13:   else
14:      k = k+1;
15:      if (k>T) then
16:         break;
17:      end if
18:   end if
19: end while
```

2.3 Incremental Construction of FNN

Recently, David and Greental [18] proposed using a GA to optimise Deep Neural Networks, but they didn't implement it. As we argued in the introduction, the success of deep neural network benefited from the GPU computing. Assume the complexity of deep neural networks is χ, the number of evolutionary generations is $\mathcal{G}$, and the population size $\mathcal{P}$, and assume we have $\mathcal{P}$ processors to parallelises the GA, the complexity of the optimisation process of deep neural network is $O(\mathcal{G}\chi)$ otherwise, it is $O(\mathcal{G}\chi\mathcal{P})$, which may be intolerant. Hence, we propose an incremental approach to finding the best structure of FNN, by starting from one neuron in one hidden layer, increasing a neuron in the hidden layer each step, and then increasing one hidden layer until the performance does not change.

3 Experiments and Evaluation

The test platform is a laptop with Windows 10 and Intel (R) Core (TM)2 Duo CPU T7300 @2 GHZ 2 GB memory. A software tool embedded with the algorithm is implemented in VC++. The FNNs will be evaluated with the accuracy A, F_1 score, TPR and AUC. For each database, five experiments are conducted: (1) Error-driven FNN; (2) A-driven FNN; (3) $F1$-driven FNN; (4) TPR-driven FNN, and (5) a ten folder crossing validation. The convergence tolerance T is set to 200. The best performance will be recorded for each experiment.

First, we apply the incremental approach to changing the structure of FNN on the whole data set, and observe how the performance changes when structure is changed; secondly, examine the training processes of the best structure of neural network, and observe the effect of different termination criteria on the training process and the performance; finally, perform ten folder crossing validation, 10% of data as test set, and the rest 90% of data as training set. Also we compare the performance of the best structural neural networks with ten-folder crossing validation to the performance in literature.

3.1 Case Study on the Database of the Wisconsin Breast Cancer

The Wisconsin Breast Cancer (WBC) database was created by Wolberg [14], containing 699 samples, in which 458 samples are benign, and 241 samples are malignant. There are nine basic attributes $x_0, x_1, ..., x_8$, with integer range [1, 10]. The missing value of an attribute in an instance of the database is replaced with the mean value of the attribute on the corresponding goal class.

Performance of Different Structures of FNN. The experiment is conducted by incrementally changing the structure of the neural network, and the training process of each structure of neural network will be stopped when the minimal average error has not be improved up to 200 epoches. Figure 1(a) shows the performance evolution when the FNN structure changes. Obviously, one hidden neuron can not well represent the function, but the FNN with more than one hidden neurons can well represent the function, although the performances of different structures of FNNs are slightly different. The structure 4-1 of FNN achieves the best performance in all performance measurements of A, F_1, TPR and AUC. The structure 4-3-1 of FNN obtains almost same AUC and TPR as the structure 4-1 of FNN does, but the performance of F_1 and A are slightly lower than that obtained by the structure 4-1 of FNN. Namely, a shallow neural network is enough to represent the function given the data.

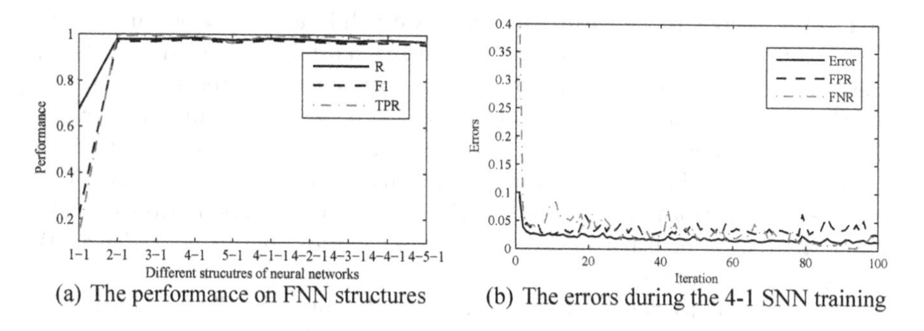

(a) The performance on FNN structures (b) The errors during the 4-1 SNN training

Fig. 1. Performance and training process of the 4-1 SNN.

The Evolution Process During the 4-1 SNN Training. Figure 1(b) shows the error evolution during the training process for the 4-1 FNN. It can be seen that the error (the solid black line in Fig. 1(b) is gradually decreasing during the training process. However, the false negative rate has a large vibration after about 10 iterations, while false positive rate has a decreasing trend although there are many fluctuations. After 20 iterations, the FPR (dashed line) and FNR (dashdotted line) seems having an opposite behaviour. Namely, while FPN is increasing, FNR is decreasing.

Performance of the 4-1 SNN for Different Termination Criteria. For a critical decision making problem, we do not want to make a wrong decision on any positive instances, namely we expect the TPR is 100%. In this section, we observe the end-loop and performances when the criteria of error (ε), A, F_1 and TPR have not be improved for up to 200 iterations, respectively. Table 1 provides the performances of the 4-1 SNN and the iteration index (best iteration) and the training time (best time) after which the observed performance has not been improved. For the four stop criteria, the performances of the 4-1 SNN are almost same, but the end-loops are very different, and error-driven BP learning has the largest end-loop. It means that the performance, arriving a certain value, is not improved further while the average error is still decreasing.

Table 1. Performance parameters of 4-1 FNN for different stop criteria

Criteria	A	F_1	TPR	AUC	$bestIN$	$bestTT$ (ms)
ε	0.9828	0.9757	1	0.9970	527	1015
A	0.9828	0.9755	0.9917	0.9938	154	250
F_1	0.9857	0.9797	1	0.9963	461	750
TPR	0.9814	0.9737	1	0.9960	202	328

Ten-Folder Crossing Validation. Now we validate the performance of the 4-1 SNN for different termination criteria, using ten-folders crossing validation. Table 2 shows the results. Obviously, the performance with ten-folder crossing validation is lower than that in Table 1. This indicates how robust the trained SNN is when it works on unseen data. From Table 2, it can be seen that the performances of A, F_1 and TPR for the termination criteria of ε, A and F_1 are very close. The performance of the 4-1 SNN for the termination criterium TPR is lower than that for other criteria. The average end-loop for error-driven BP learning keeps the largest.

We use (a $\pm$ b) to denote average accuracy (a) and standard deviation (b) for the ten runs of ten folder crossing validation. The average accuracy of (0.955 ± 0.006), obtained by the 4–1 SNN, is slightly lower that of (0.967 ± 0.02), obtained by the optimal linguistic attribute hierarchy (LAH) [17], which was obtained by a GA wrapper. Also an SNN obtains more stable accuracies than the LAH, and the accuracies of the SNN fall in the accuracy range of LAH.

Table 2. Performance parameters of the 4-1 FNN on different stop criteria

Criteria	A	F_1	TPR	End-loop
ε	0.9551	0.9380	0.9643	1372
A	0.9507	0.9249	0.9351	173
F_1	0.9536	0.9349	0.9347	162
TPR	0.9101	0.8475	0.8634	76

3.2 Case Study on the SMSSpamCollection Database

The SMSSpamCollection database [15], has 5574 raw messages, including 747 spams. He et al. [13] extracted 20 features from the database, and the number of features was reduced to 14 by combining some features with similar meanings [19]. We use the 14 attribute database for the experiments.

Performance of Different Structures of FNN. Similar to the experiments on WBC, we apply error-driven BP training on the whole data set. Figure 2(a) shows the performance evolution when the FNN structure changes. It can be seen that the 1-1 FNN can well represent the function from the SMS spams data, and the TPR of the 3-1 FNN is lower than that of the 1-1 FNN. The performances of different structures of FNNs are slightly different. But the performances, A, F_1 and TPR are clearly separated. The F_1 score keep around 0.88, the TPR is waved in [0.8, 0.84], and the accuracy keeps above 0.96. The 6-1 FNN achieves the best performance in F_1 and TPR, but slightly lower performance in A than the 7-1 FNN, and more importantly, the end-loop for training the 6-1 FNN reaches to the preset maximum iteration 20000, while the end-loop for training the 7-1 FNN is only 923. Therefore, the second hidden layer is constructed with the 7 neurons in the first hidden layer. Similar to the WBC experiments, the experimental results show that an SNN is enough to represent the function of the specific data. At the same time, we can conclude that the feature extraction still need to be improved, or additional information is needed for improving the true positive rate of neural networks.

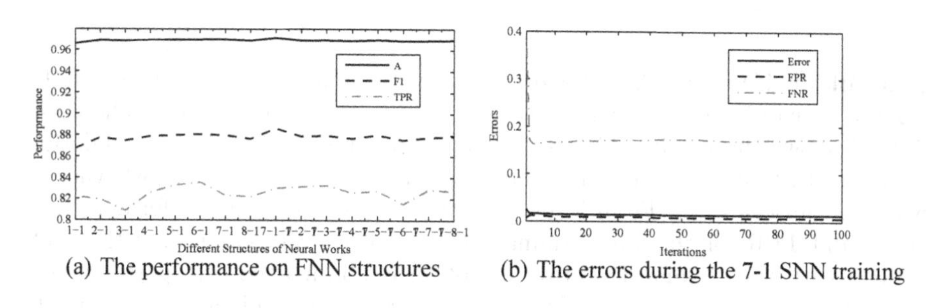

(a) The performance on FNN structures (b) The errors during the 7-1 SNN training

Fig. 2. Performance and training process of the 7-1 SNN.

The Evolution Process During the 7-1 SNN Training. Figure 2(b) shows the error evolution during the training process for the 7-1 SNN. The end-loop of the training process is 923. To clearly show the trend of error evolution, we take the first 100 iterations of the training process for plotting Fig. 2(b). It can be seen that the error (the solid black line) slightly decreases, and the FNR (the red dashed dot line) drops from above 0.35 to 0.15, but the FNR slightly increases at the second iteration. After the second iteration, the average error, FPR and FNR almost do not change.

Performance of the 7-1 SNN for Different Termination Criteria. Similar to the experiments on WBC, we observe the end-loop and performances of SNNs on the SMSSpams data when the criteria of average error (ε), A, F_1 and TPR have not be improved for up to 200 iterations, respectively. Table 3 provides the performances of the trained 7-1 SNN and the iteration index and the training time at the best epoch. It can be seen that the performances in A, F_1 and TPR for the four termination criteria are very close. Especially, for the termination criteria A and F_1, the training stops at the same end-loop. Therefore, the SNNs obtain completely same performances in A, F_1 and TPR. The training process for the termination criterium of average error is the longest, while the termination criterium of TPR produced the shortest training process. The F_1 score and accuracy A do not change after 71 iterations, the TPR is not improved after iteration 3, and the performance A and F_1 are similar at iteration 71 and even at iteration 923. This indicates that the performance of the SNN keeps stable, while the average error continues being slightly reduced.

Table 3. Performance parameters of 7-1 FNN for different termination criteria

Criteria	A	F_1	TPR	AUC	$bestIN$	$bestTT$(ms)
ε	0.9699	0.8798	0.8233	0.9669	923	27406
A	0.9711	0.8851	0.8300	0.9652	71	1906
F_1	0.9711	0.8851	0.8300	0.9652	71	2094
TPR	0.9686	0.8774	0.8380	0.9623	3	109

Ten-Folder Crossing Validation. Now we validate the performance of the 7-1 SNN for different termination criteria, using ten-folders crossing validation. Table 4 shows the results. The performance with ten-folder crossing validation is similar to that in Table 3. This indicates the trained SNN is robust when it works on unseen data. From Table 3, it can be seen that the performances of A, F_1 and TPR for the four termination criteria are very close, even the SNN trained with the termination criterium of TPR obtains the best performance. The performance of the 7-1 SNN with ten-folder crossing validation is much better than that of the linguistic attribute hierarchy in [19], of which, the accuracy on the SMS Spam 0.9458, and the TPR 0.7323. The end-loop for error-driven BP on SMS Spams is much larger than that for performance-driven BP.

Table 4. Performance parameters of the 7-1 FNN for different termination criteria

Criteria	A	F_1	TPR	End-loop
ε	0.9621	0.8615	0.8257	10062
A	0.9627	0.8619	0.8351	97
F_1	0.9645	0.8726	0.8230	53
TPR	0.9670	0.8818	0.8527	54

4 Conclusions

The contribution of the research are summarised as follows: (1) Validating the universe approximate theorem using experiments: a shallow neural network can well represent the function from data, and the number of hidden neurons, taking the half of input number, is good enough. (2) Providing an simple incremental approach to finding the best shallow neural network. This approach overcomes not only the shortages of a population searching in evolutionary algorithm, which is much expensive in computing complexity, but also the shortages in both the randomness and computing complexity of ensembles; (3) Updating the classic BP algorithm with different termination criteria. Performance-driven BP learning could help reduce the training time and avoid over fitting; (4) Having the comparable or better performance of the trained neural network on the two benchmark data bases, compared to the optimal linguist attribute hierarchy. The research results show that a shallow neural network seems matching the property of the human brain: when an individual gets the first impression to a thing, without new information, the individual cannot change the impression. In the future, more relevant research will be surveyed, and partial linked neural network will be investigated.

Acknowledgements. This research is sponsored by the Key project of natural science in universities in Anhui Province (KJ2018A0111).

References

1. Karpathy, A., Toderici, G., Shetty, S., et al.: Large-scale video classification with convolutional neural networks. In: IEEE Conference on Computer Vision and Pattern Recognition (CVPR), Columbus, OH, USA, 23–28 June 2014 (2014). https://doi.org/10.1109/CVPR.2014.223
2. Wang, Z., Ren, J., Zhang, D., et al.: A deep-learning based feature hybrid framework for spatiotemporal saliency detection inside videos. Neurocomputing **287**, 68–83 (2018)

3. Chen, L., Papandreou, G., Kokkinos, I., et al.: DeepLab: semantic image segmentation with deep convolutional nets, atrous convolution, and fully connected CRFs, CoRR, abs/1606.00915. arXiv: 1606.00915 (2016)
4. Ren, S., He, K., Girshick, R.: Faster R-CNN: towards real-time object detection with region proposal networks. J. IEEE Trans. Pattern Anal. Mach. Intell. **39**(6), 1137–1149 (2017)
5. Lee, H., Largman, Y., Pham, P., et al.: Unsupervised feature learning for audio classification using convolutional deep belief networks. In: Proceedings of the 22nd International Conference on Neural Information Processing Systems (NIPS 2009), Vancouver, British Columbia, Canada, 07–10 December 2009, pp. 1096–1104 (2009)
6. Zhang, Y., Pezeshki, M., Brakel, P., et al.: (2017) Towards end-to-end speech recognition with deep convolutional neural networks, CoRR, abs/1701.02720, arXiv: 1701.02720 (2017)
7. Cybenkot, G.: Approximation by superpositions of a sigmoidal function. Math. Control. Signals Syst. **2**, 303–314 (1989)
8. Hornik, K.: Approximation capabilities of multilayer feedforward networks. Neural Netw. **4**(2), 251–257 (1991)
9. Leshno, M., Lin, V., Pinkus, A.: Multilayer feedforward networks with a nonpolynomial activation function can approximate any function. Neural Netw. **6**, 861–867 (1993)
10. Blum, A.L., Rivest, R.L.: Training a 3-node neural network is NP-complete. Neural Netw. **5**, 117–127 (1992)
11. Zhang, A., Sun, G., Ren, J.: A dynamic neighborhood learning-based gravitational search algorithm. IEEE Trans. Cybern. **48**(1), 436–447 (2018)
12. Bu, F., Chen, Z., Zhang, Q.: Incremental updating method for big data feature learning. Comput. Eng. Appl. **3**, 92–101 (2015)
13. He, H., Tiwari, A., Mehnen, J., et al.: incremental information gain analysis of input attribute impact on RBF-kernel SVM spam detection, WCCI 2016, Vancouver, Canada, 24–29 July 2016 (2016)
14. Wolberg, W.H., Mangasarian, O.L.: Multisurface method of pattern separation for medical diagnosis applied to breast cytology. Proc. Natl. Acad. Sci. **87**, 9193–9196 (1990)
15. Almeida, T.A., Hidalgo, J.M.G., Yamakami, A.: Contributions to the study of SMS spam filtering: new collection and results. In: DocEng 2011, Mountain View, California, USA, 19–22 September 2011 (2011)
16. Dua, D., Taniskidou, E.K.: UCI Machine Learning Repository. University of California, School of Information and Computer Science, Irvine, CA (2017). http://archive.ics.uci.edu/ml
17. He, H., Lawry, J.: Linguistic attribute hierarchy and its optimisation for classification problems. Soft Comput. **18**(10), 1967–1984 (2014)
18. David, E., Greental, I.: Genetic algorithms for evolving deep neural networks. In: ACM Genetic and Evolutionary Computation Conference (GECCO), Vancouver, Canada, July 2014, pp. 1451–1452 (2014)
19. He, H., Watson, T., Maple, C., et al.: Semantic attribute deep learning with a hierarchy of linguistic decision trees for spam detection. In: IJCNN2017, Anchorage, Alaska, USA, 14–19 May 2017 (2017)

Predicting Seminal Quality Using Back-Propagation Neural Networks with Optimal Feature Subsets

Jieming Ma[1(✉)], Aiyan Zhen[2], Sheng-Uei Guan[1], Chun Liu[3], and Xin Huang[1]

[1] Department of Computer Science and Software Engineering, Research Institute of Big Data Analytics, Xi'an Jiaotong-Liverpool Univeristy, Suzhou 215123, People's Republic of China
{jieming.ma,steven.guan,xin.huang}@xjtlu.edu.cn

[2] Center of Reproduction and Genetics, Suzhou Municipal Hospital, Suzhou 215002, People's Republic of China

[3] Department of pharmacy, Suzhou Municipal Hospital, Suzhou 215002, People's Republic of China

Abstract. Many studies have shown that there is a decline in seminal quality during the past two decades. Seminal quality may be affected by environmental factors and health status, as well as life habits. Artificial intelligence (AI) technology has been recently applied to recognize this effect. However, conventional AI algorithms are not prepared to cope with the class-imbalanced fertility dataset. To this end, a back-propagation neural network (BPNN) is used to predict the seminal profile of an individual from the dataset. A neural-genetic algorithm (N-GA) is employed to select optimal feature subsets and optimize the parameters of the used neural network. Results indicate that the proposed method outperforms other AI methods on seminal quality prediction in terms of precision and accuracy.

1 Introduction

Seminal quality is a significant factor that reflects male reproductive health. A good number of studies have evaluated possible time trends in sperm concentration or total sperm count in different populations [1–6]. Huang et al. [4] reported a decreasing trend in the seminal quality among young Chinese men from 2001 to 2015. Virtanen et al. [7] reviewed several original studies published since 2000 in various countries and concluded that seminal quality has certainly declined or stabilized to this low level during the past few decades, possibly owing to modern lifestyle factors, including exposure to environmental chemicals.

A good number of factors, such as life habits and health status, can affect the quality of sperms. Semen analysis, the keystone of the male study, is done to evaluate the male fertility potential [8].

In the last two decades, the use of artificial intelligence (AI) technology has also become widely adopted in medical applications [9–11]. In [12], radial

J. Ren et al. (Eds.): BICS 2018, LNAI 10989, pp. 25–33, 2018.
https://doi.org/10.1007/978-3-030-00563-4_3

basis function neural network (RBFNN) is used to study the classification of patients attributes related to seminal quality. Three artificial intelligence techniques, including decision trees (DT), multilayer perceptron (MLP) and support vector machines (SVM), are suggested in [13] to evaluate their performance in the prediction of the seminal quality on fertility dataset. Sahooa and Kumarb [14] proposed more machine learning-based predictive models for seminal quality prediction, such as naive Bayes (kernel) and support vector machine + particle swarm optimization (SVM+PSO), and concluded that these methods can be used to predict a person with or without disease based on environmental and lifestyle parameters (features) rather than undergoing various medical test.

However, the dataset used in a medical domain are usually with a relatively large number of attributes and a very imbalanced class distribution [15,16]. The aforementioned methods are not prepared to cope with imbalanced datasets, which occurs when the class of interest constitutes only a very small minority of the data [17]. To handle this issue, the general approach is to use re-sampling techniques, but there are very few diseases samples.

In this paper, a back-propagation neural network (BPNN) are proposed to predict seminal quality on an imbalanced fertility dataset. A neural-genetic algorithm (N-GA) is used to perform feature subset selection and parameter optimization, which effectively reduces the dimension of attributes and improves the prediction performance of the used BPNN architecture. The experimental results are obtained based on a 10-fold cross validation scheme. Three indicators, including precision, recall, and accuracy, are used in performance evaluation.

The reminder of this paper is organized as follows: Sect. 2 introduces the used fertility dataset. Section 3 presents the proposed seminal quality prediction method. Section 4 focuses on the analysis of experiment results and conclusions are drawn in last section.

2 Fertility Dataset

In this paper, the fertility dataset in [13] is used for predicting seminal quality. Gil et al. [13] undertook a study at the University of Alicante, Spain, which investigates the factors that may affect the seminal quality. Samples of semen were provided by 100 young healthy volunteers between 18 and 36 years old after 3 to 6 days of sexual abstinence, and a semen analysis in accordance with World Health Organization (WHO) guidance was performed.

Table 1 lists the volunteers' life habits and health status. The data values are nominalized according to the following rules:

- Three attributes, including childish diseases, accident or serious trauma, and surgical intervention, are prearranged with binary values (0, 1);
- Two attributes, including high fever in the last year and smoking habit, are prearranged with ternary values (−1, 0, 1);
- Four seasons are expressed by different and equal distance values (1, −0.33, 0.33, 1);

- Numerical attributes, such as age at the time of analysis, number of hours spent sitting per day and frequency of alcohol consumption, obtain a range of more than four independent values and they are normalized to (0, 1).

The data in [13] are divided into two classes: "normal (N)" and "altered (O)". The former is translated as viable and the latter is translated as non-viable.

There are totally 12 samples as "altered" and 88 as "normal", and thus it is an imbalanced dataset where conventional classification algorithms under-perform.

Table 1. Attributes with their descriptions and values range.

No.	Attribute Description	Values range	Normalized
1	Season in which the analysis was performed.	(1) winter, (2) spring, (3) Summer, (4) fall	(−1, −0.33, 0.33, 1)
2	Age at the time of analysis.	18–36	(0, 1)
3	Childish diseases (ie, chicken pox, measles, mumps, polio)	(1) yes, (2) no	(0, 1)
4	Accident or serious trauma	(1) yes, (2) no	(0, 1)
5	Surgical intervention	(1) yes, (2) no	(0, 1)
6	High fevers in the last year	(1) less than three months ago, (2) more than three months ago, (3) no	(−1, 0, 1)
7	Frequency of alcohol consumption	(1) several times a day, (2) every day, (3) several times a week, (4) once a week, (5) hardly ever or never	(0, 1)
8	Smoking habit	(1) never, (2) occasional (3) daily	(−1, 0, 1)
9	Number of hours spent sitting per day	1–16	(0, 1)

3 Seminal Quality Prediction

3.1 Back-Propagation Neural Network

Back-propagation neural network (BPNN) is one of the most widely used neural network models, which are capable of inferring the complex relationships between input and output process variables without a detailed characterization of the mechanisms governing the process.

In this paper, a three-layer BPNN approach is applied for seminal quality prediction. Suppose there are m features, the BPNN obtains l outputs, and its hidden lawyer obtains s neurons.

The mid layer output b_j for the jth unit can be expressed by:

$$b_j = f_1 \left(\sum_{i=1}^{m} w_{ij} x_i - \theta_j \right), \tag{1}$$

where θ_j is the unit threshold of mid layer, and $f_1(\cdot)$ is the transfer function of the mid layer. The usage of a mid layer enables the representation of data that are not linearly separable.

The output layer y_k can be formulated by:

$$y_k = f_2 \left(\sum_{j=1}^{s} w_{ij} b_j - \theta_k \right), \tag{2}$$

where θ_k is the unit threshold of output layer and $f_2(\cdot)$ is the transfer function of output layer. In this paper, the hyperbolic tangent sigmoid (tansig), log-sigmoid (logsig), linear (pureline) transfer functions are used.

Given the network expectation output t_k, the error function is defined as follows:

$$e = \sum_{k=1}^{m} (t_k - y_k)^2. \tag{3}$$

To minimize error function, the weights and threshold values are re-adjusted in network training. Then the predicted results can be obtained by taking the testing set as input.

3.2 Feature Selection and Parameters Optimization

A neural-genetic algorithm (N-GA) is developed for feature subsets selection, initial weight and hidden node size optimization of the BPNN architecture. The chromosome design, fitness function, and genetic operations are described as follows.

(a) Chromosome design

Each individual is coded as a binary vector as shown in Fig. 1. The first P-bit binary number allows 2^P different combinations of the initial weight, the next Q-bit binary number can represent a maximum of 2^Q hidden nodes, and the last R-bit binary number represents a possible feature subset. Value '1' and '0' of the R-bit number indicate the selected and unselected features, respectively. The entire binary vector and its elements are known as chromosome and genes in a GA.

(b) Fitness function

Consider a training dataset $D_t = \{\{x_1, y_1\}, \{x_2, y_2\}, \cdots, \{x_N, y_N\}\}$, where X are d-dimensional input feature vectors and n is the number of instances. After the initialization step, each chromosome is evaluated by the fitness function, which is given by the following equation:

$$F(X) = \frac{1}{\sum_{i=1}^{n} \left(\hat{t}_i - t_i\right)^2}, \tag{4}$$

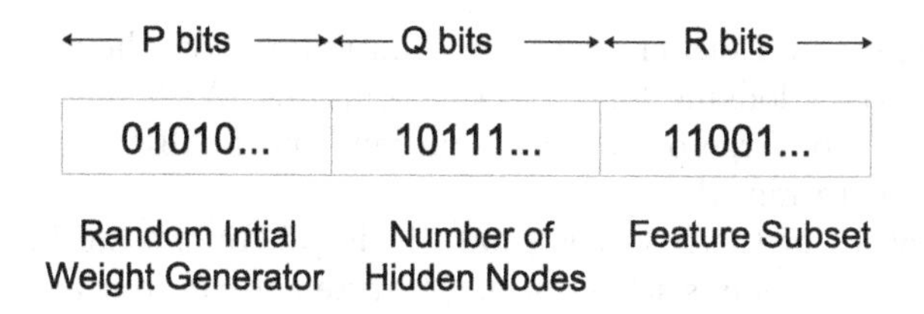

Fig. 1. Chromosome design.

where $F(X)$ is the fitness function in terms of chromosome $\mathbf{X}$; $\hat{t}_i$ is the predicted value for the ith target vector. The chromosomes with higher fitness values will be reproduced more often.

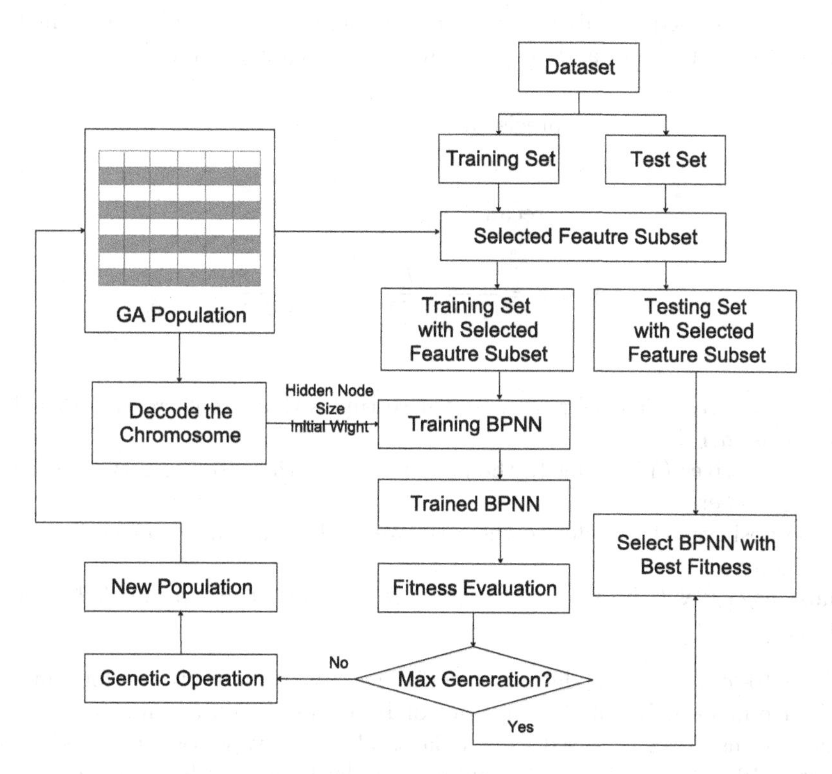

Fig. 2. Structure of the proposed N-GA feature selection and parameters optimization.

(c) Genetic operations

Three operators are iteratively used in the GA. The selection operator determines which individuals may survive [18]. The crossover operator varies the programming of a chromosome or chromosomes from one generation to the next, while the mutation operator arbitrarily alters one or more components of a selected chromosome. Both crossover and mutation allow the search to fan out in diverse directions looking for attractive solutions. With the three operators, the GA tends to converge on optimal solutions and finally the optimal feature subsets can be determined.

The framework of the N-GA is shown in Fig. 2. In this work, the proposed N-GA algorithm not only selects optimal feature subsets, but also supports the simultaneous optimization of connection weights and threshold values for BPNN.

4 Results and Discussions

4.1 Description of Experiments

The fertility dataset [13], which contains 100 instances with nine attributes and two classes, is used in this paper. The used classification performance metrics include precision, recall and accuracy, which are defined as follows:

$$\text{precision} = \frac{TP}{(TP + FP)}; \tag{5}$$

$$\text{recall} = \frac{TP}{(TP + FN)}; \tag{6}$$

$$\text{accuracy} = \frac{(TP + TN)}{(TP + TN + FP + FN)}. \tag{7}$$

where

- true positives (TP) refer to the positive tuples that are correctly labeled by the classifier.
- true negatives (TN) refer to the negative tuples that are correctly labeled by the classifier.
- false positives (FP) refer to the negative tuples that are incorrectly labeled as positive.
- false negatives (FN) refer to the positive tuples that are mislabeled as negative.

The 10-fold cross validation is performed to evaluate the performance of predictive models. In turn, 9 folds out of 10 are used as a training set and the remaining instances are used as test data. The cross-validation process is then repeated 10 times, and the 10 results from the folds are then be averaged to produce the final classification performance metrics.

The performance of proposed N-GA method is compared with four different classification methods, including multilayer perceptron (MLP), support vector machines (SVM), decision trees (DT), and radial basis function neural network (RBFNN). An MLP is a class of feed-forward artificial neural network, which normally consists of input, hidden and output layers. The MLP utilizes a supervised learning to update weights and the thresholds of the MLP. The SVM have been extensively researched and widely applied to applications in various domains. The SVM typically classify data by using a hyperplane, supporting an efficient learning of nonlinear functions by kernel trick. The DT is a classifier in the form of a tree-like graph or model of decisions. The tree can also be represented as rules that are easy to understand. The RBFNN a neural network that uses radial basis functions as activation functions. A linear combination of radial basis functions of the inputs and neuron parameters are used as output.

4.2 Results

In Table 2, a comparison has been carried out among the performance of MLP, SVM and DT, RBFNN and the proposed N-GA technique. The performance metrics of MLP, SVM and DT are given in [13], while prediction results of RBFNN are collected from [12]. The accuracy of these methods are in range between 84% and 86%. The proposed N-GA improving the accuracy by 9.3%-11.9%, achieving an accuracy of 94%. In addition, its precision reaches 100%.

Table 2. Performance comparison of MLP, SVM and DT, RBFNN and the proposed N-GA method.

Parameters	MLP [13]	SVM [13]	DT [13]	RBFNN [12]	N-GA
Precision (%)	89.9	87.4	86.3	84.22	**100**
Recall (%)	94.1	97.7	96.5	**98.75**	93.75
Accuracy (%)	86	86	84	84	**94**

Table 3. Performance comparison of the proposed N-GA by using different transfer functions.

f_1	f_2	Precision (%)	Recall (%)	Accuracy (%)
logsig	purelin	96.25	93.21	91
tansig	purelin	95.35	90.03	87
tansig	tansig	**100**	93.35	**94**
tansig	logsig	0	0	6
logsig	tansig	**100**	**93.75**	**94**
logsig	logsig	0	0	5

It is reported that careful selection of the activation function has a huge impact on the network performance [19]. Therefore, the effects of transfer functions on the performance of the N-GA have also been investigated in Table 3. As mentioned in the previous section, the logsig, tansig and purelin transfer functions have been used for the hidden and output layers. The number of hidden units are set to 50 in this experiment. When the logsig-tansig and tansig-tansig are used as transfer functions for hidden and output layers, the N-GA can obtain an accuracy of 94%. It is observed that low accuracy will be obtained if the tansig-logsig or logsi-logsig functions are adopted in the training phase.

5 Conclusion

We have proposed an N-GA algorithm to automatically select feature subsets. In addition, the N-GA algorithm assists in optimization the connection weights and thresholds in the BPNN. The performance of the proposed method is evaluated in terms of accuracy, precision, and recall. Experimental results have show that the N-GA can effectively improve the accuracy and precision for a fertility dataset with a relatively large number of attributes and a very unbalanced class distribution. A highest accuracy (94%) is obtained when the logsig and tansig transfer functions are applied in the hidden and output layers, respectively. Our future work lies in preprocessing of instances which enables the applied predictive model to detect and measure the intrinsic characteristics of the imbalanced data.

Artificial intelligence technology has grown phenomenally by deep learning. Many recent studies have reported encouraging results for applying deep learning to a variety of applications, such as feature extraction [20,21], object detection [22], and natural language processing [23], etc. Therefore, in future work, we will investigate the feasibility of applying deep learning based approaches to seminal quality prediction.

Acknowledgments. This research is supported by the National Natural Science Foundation of China (Grant No. 61702353), the Natural Science Foundation of Jiangsu Province (Grant No. BK20160355), the Science and Technology Project of Ministry of Housing and Urban-Rural Development (Grant No. 2016-K1-019), the Suzhou Science and Technology Project (SYG201603), and RIBDA research project in XJTLU.

References

1. Lackner, J., Schatzl, G., Waldhör, T., Resch, K., Kratzik, C., Marberger, M.: Constant decline in sperm concentration in infertile males in an urban population: experience over 18 years. Fertil. Steril. **84**, 1657–1661 (2005)
2. Jiang, M., et al.: Semen quality evaluation in a cohort of 28213 adult males from Sichuan area of South-West China. Andrologia **46**, 842–847 (2014)
3. Rao, M., et al.: Evaluation of Semen quality in 1808 university students, from Wuhan, central China. Asian J. Androl. **17**, 111 (2015)
4. Huang, C., et al.: Decline in Semen quality among 30,636 young Chinese men from 2001 to 2015. Fertil. Steril. **107**(2017), 83–88 (2001)
5. Jørgensen, N.: Recent adverse trends in semen quality and testis cancer incidence among finnish men. Int. J. Androl. **34**, e37–e48 (2011)
6. Romero-Otero, J.: Semen quality assessment in fertile men in Madrid during the last 3 decades. Urology **85**, 1333–1338 (2015)
7. Virtanen, H.E., Jørgensen, N., Toppari, J.: Semen quality in the 21st century. Nat. Rev. Urol. **14**, 120 (2017)
8. Kolettis, P.N.: Evaluation of the subfertile man. Am. Fam. Physician **67**, 2165–2172 (2003)
9. Jiang, J., Trundle, P., Ren, J.: Medical image analysis with artificial neural networks. Comput. Med. Imaging Graph. **34**, 617–631 (2010)

10. Ren, J., Wang, D., Jiang, J.: Effective recognition of MCCs in mammograms using an improved neural classifier. Eng. Appl. Artif. Intell. **24**, 638–645 (2011)
11. Ren, J.: ANN vs. SVM: which one performs better in classification of MCCs in mammogram imaging. Knowl.-Based Syst. **26**, 144–153 (2012)
12. Helwan, A., Khashman, A., Olaniyi, E.O., Oyedotun, O.K., Oyedotun, O.A.: Seminal quality evaluation with RBF neural network. Bull. Transilv. Univ. Bras. Math. Inform. Phys. Ser. **9**, 137 (2016)
13. Gil, D., Girela, J.L., De Juan, J., Gomez-Torres, M.J., Johnsson, M.: Predicting seminal quality with artificial intelligence methods. Expert. Syst. Appl. **39**, 12564–12573 (2012)
14. Sahoo, A.J., Kumar, Y.: Seminal quality prediction using data mining methods. Technol. Health Care **22**, 531–545 (2014)
15. Yuan, X., Xie, L., Abouelenien, M.: A regularized ensemble framework of deep learning for cancer detection from multi-class, imbalanced training data. Pattern Recognit. **77**, 160–172 (2018)
16. Zhou, P., Hu, X., Li, P., Wu, X.: Online feature selection for high-dimensional class-imbalanced data. Knowl.-Based Syst. **136**, 187–199 (2017)
17. Galar, M., Fernandez, A., Barrenechea, E., Bustince, H., Herrera, F.: A review on ensembles for the class imbalance problem: bagging-, boosting-, and hybrid-based approaches. IEEE Trans. Syst. Man Cybern. Part C Appl. Rev. **42**, 463–484 (2012)
18. Hertz, A., Kobler, D.: A framework for the description of evolutionary algorithms. Eur. J. Oper. Res. **126**, 1–12 (2000)
19. Trzepiecinski, T., Lemu, H.: Effect of activation function and post synaptic potential on response of artificial neural network to predict frictional resistance of aluminium alloy sheets. In: IOP Conference Series: Materials Science and Engineering, vol. 269. p. 012041. IOP Publishing (2017)
20. Zabalza, J., et al.: Novel segmented stacked autoencoder for effective dimensionality reduction and feature extraction in hyperspectral imaging. Neurocomputing **185**, 1–10 (2016)
21. Wang, Z., Ren, J., Zhang, D., Sun, M., Jiang, J.: A deep-learning based feature hybrid framework for spatiotemporal saliency detection inside videos. Neurocomputing **287**, 68–83 (2018)
22. Han, J., Zhang, D., Hu, X., Guo, L., Ren, J., Wu, F.: Background prior-based salient object detection via deep reconstruction residual. IEEE Trans. Circuits Syst. Video Technol. **25**, 1309–1321 (2015)
23. Mao, Q., Dong, M., Huang, Z., Zhan, Y.: Learning salient features for speech emotion recognition using convolutional neural networks. IEEE Trans. Multimed. **16**, 2203–2213 (2014)

Deep Learning Based Recommendation Algorithm in Online Medical Platform

QingYun Dai, XueBin Hong, Jun Cai(✉), Yan Liu, HuiMin Zhao, JianZhen Luo, ZeYu Lin, and ShiJian Chen

Guangdong Polytechnic Normal University, Guangzhou 510665, China
gzhcaijun@126.com

Abstract. In recent years, with the rapidly development of Internet and pharmaceutical market, online medical platform has become a major place for online medical trading. Recommendation systems have been widely deployed in commercial platform to improve user experience and sales. Motivated by this, we propose two hybrid recommendation algorithms, CB-CF hybrid algorithm and CNN-based CF algorithm, for B2B medical platform to provide accurate recommendations. We also give a brief introduction of two well-known recommendation algorithms, content-based algorithm and model-based CF algorithm. Then we investigate the performance of recommendation algorithms on Apache Spark and Tensorflow with real-world data collected from a china B2B online medical platform. Experimental results show that the hybrid recommendation algorithm performs better than other algorithms.

Keywords: Medical platform · Recommendation system
Collaborative filtering · Deep learning

1 Introduction

Recently, with the rapidly development of Internet and information technology, the volume of online information has grown exponentially. Information overload has become a great challenge faced by Internet. Search engine represented by Google offers a way to solve this problem. However millions of the inquiry results are presented to users by search engines, users' needs cannot be reflected effectively. The accuracy of inquiry results mainly depend on search keywords which are offered by users to represent their information requirements. However, it's a challenge to user for accurately describing their requirements. Recommendation system has been widely adopted in various commercial platforms to provide recommendations to users by considering the diversity of preferences and the relativity of information value, especially unfamiliar items to user. It has been proved that recommendation system is an efficient way to solve the problem of information overload.

With the influencing of ageing populations, the rise of chronic illnesses, and national policy support to medical research, pharmaceutical market in China

J. Ren et al. (Eds.): BICS 2018, LNAI 10989, pp. 34–43, 2018.
https://doi.org/10.1007/978-3-030-00563-4_4

will rapidly grow in next five years. The third-party B2B medical platform has become a major place for medical online trading and low-cast hub of information [1]. Motivated by this, we propose two recommendation algorithms, CB-CF hybrid algorithm and a CNN-based CF algorithm for B2B medical platform to improve user experience and sales of medical platform. For CB-CF hybrid algorithm, the prediction of rating is an weighted sum of two predicted rating calculated by Content-based (CB) algorithm and model-based Collaborative filtering (CF) algorithm respectively. The framework of CNN-based CF algorithm includes two steps: first, the feature matrix of users and items are obtained by decomposing user-item rating matrix according to SVD algorithm; then the two matrices are combined to one as the input data of a CNN (Convolutional Neural Network) model. After the training the CNN model, the prediction of rating score can be obtained. We run our experiments on Apache Spark and Tensorflow. The test dataset is collected from a china online B2B medical platform. Experimental results show that hybrid recommendation model perform better than CB algorithm and model-based CF algorithm.

The rest of paper is organized as follows. Section 2 gives an introduction of related works. Section 3 gives a brief overview of four recommendation algorithms. Section 4 provides the experiment results and Sect. 5 concludes the paper.

2 Related Works

The most important part of recommendation system is recommendation algorithm, which is directly determining the accuracy of recommendation results and the performance of the recommendation system. The mostly used algorithms can be divided into three categories: content based methods, collaborative filtering based methods and hybrid recommendation method.

2.1 Collaborative Filtering Based Recommendation Algorithms

Collaborative filtering (CF) based recommendation algorithms make recommendations according to the opinions of other users who have similar interests or the similarity between items [2]. The CF methods can be divided into two categories: memory-based method and model-based method.

Memory-based methods use users' rating data to calculate the similarity or weight between users or items, recommendations are made by predicting the rating values user haven't rated according to those calculated similarity values [3]. Memory-based CF methods are effective and simple to be implement, so they are widely adopted by commercial systems such as Amazon and Barnes [4,5]. Zhao et al. proposed an user-based CF algorithm to solve the scalability problem of CF and implement the proposed algorithm on Hadoop. Experimental results show that the proposed algorithm can achieve linear speedup by dividing users into groups with a simple method [6]. To improve the scalability of CF algorithms and the quality of recommendations for users, the authors proposed a item-based CF algorithm, which makes recommendations based on relationships between different items. The relationship is identified by analyzing the user-item matrix. Simulation results show that item-based CF algorithm performs much better than user-base CF algorithms [7].

Model-based CF methods have been investigated to overcome shortcoming of memory-based CF methods and achieve better prediction performance. Model-based CF algorithms use rating data to train a model to recognize complex patterns, and then make predication for users. There are many well-known model-based CF algorithms, such as Bayesian belief nets CF algorithms [8], clustering models [9], Markov decision process based CF algorithms [10] and matrix factorization methods [11,12]. Matrix factorization method is the most successful model-based algorithm, which can achieve better accuracy than memory-based method. Guan et al. proposed a series of methods based on matrix factorization to increase the accuracy of recommendation system and reduce computational cost [12].

2.2 Content Based Recommendation Algorithms

Differently from collaborative filtering based methods, content based (CB) recommendation algorithms recommend items based on the portraits of a specific user and items, such as user profiles and attributes of items [13]. Therefore, CB methods can solve the problems of cold start and high sparsity of the data, which are suffered by CF methods. Van den Oord et al. proposed a deep content-based music recommendation system to address cold start problem suffered by CF based recommendation methods, a latent factor model is used for recommendation, and the latent factors from music audio are predicted when they are not be able to obtain from usage data [14].

2.3 Hybrid Recommendation Algorithms

Both CF-based methods and content-based method have their advantages and limitations. Hybrid recommendation systems combine CF with other algorithms to improve recommendation performance [15]. Dong et al. proposed a hybrid CF model with deep structure learning for recommendation system to address the problems of cold start and data sparsity, experimental results show that the proposed hybrid model performs much better than other methods in effectively utilizing side information [16]. Gurbanov et al. proposed a hybrid model by combining CF and sequence mining (SM) to improve prediction accuracy. The proposed system makes prediction on whether a user will take an action of a target type on an item [17]. In recent years, deep learning technology has been widely applied in speech recognition, image process and natural language understanding [18–25]. Several studies show that applying deep learning into recommendation system can improve recommendation performance. A DNN (Deep Neural Network) based recommendation model is proposed by Zhang et al. [26]. The framework of hybrid model includes two Modules: feature representation model and DNN model. When the training of the model is completed, the probability distribution of the rating score can be obtained from the output layer of DNN model.

3 Methods

In this section, we give a brief overview of two well-known recommendation methods, CB method and model-based CF method. Then we propose two hybrid recommendation method, CB-CF hybrid method and CNN-based CF method, for B2B online medical platform to provide precise recommendations.

3.1 Content-Based Recommendation Method

Content-based recommendation algorithm make recommendations by matching up the attributes of user profile with the attributes of items [27]. The user profile, which is generated by analyzing the features of items rated by user in history, reflects user interest. There are three modules in a CB system: content analyzer, profile learner and filtering component.

Content analyzer is responsible for extracting structured information from dataset and generating matrix for representing attributes of items. In this paper, we extract structural information of the type of medicines and map them to a $1 * n$ matrix. Profile learner is responsible for generalizing the data represented user preference and constructing user profile. Filtering component makes recommendations by matching the user profile created by profile learner module to new items. In our model, the matching is realized by calculating the cosine similarity between the attributes of user profile and the attributes of medicines according to Eq. (1). The greater cosine similarity is, the more likely user U is interested in medicine I.

$$cos(U, I) = \frac{\sum_1^n U_i * I_i}{\sqrt{\sum_1^n U_i^2} * \sqrt{\sum_1^n I_i^2}} \tag{1}$$

3.2 Model-Based CF Method

$$R = P * Q \tag{2}$$

Model-based CF algorithms have been investigated to improve prediction performance, which allow the system learn a model from rating data to make intelligent predictions. First step is to generate a $M \times N$ user-item rating matrix, $R \in \mathbb{R}^{M \times N}$; then user-item rating matrix R is presented as the product of two lower dimensional matrix [28], i.e. a $M \times K$ user matrix $P \in \mathbb{R}^{M \times K}$ and a $K \times N$ item matrix $Q \in \mathbb{R}^{K \times N}$, as shown in Eq. (2). Finally, the missing value of R, r_{ui} can be estimated by P and Q according to Eq. (3),

$$\widehat{r}_{ui} = q_i^T * p_u \tag{3}$$

where $\widehat{r}_{ui}$ is the predicted rating of item i rated by user u. The process is described in Algorithm 1.

Algorithm 1. Model-based CF algorithm

Input: R, $r_{ui} = null, r_{ui} \in R$ \\ R is the rating matrix of user-item
Output: r_{ui}
1: generating user matrix P and item matrix Q randomly;
2: updating user matrix P when Q is given;
3: updating item matrix Q when P is given;
4: predicting r_{ui} according to P and Q;
5: return r_{ui};

3.3 CB-CF Hybrid Method

In this paper, we propose a hybrid recommendation method which combines CF and CB algorithms to overcome the problem of cold start and data sparsity, as described in Fig. 1. The predicated rating of item i rated by user u, r_{ui}, is an weighted sum of two predicted rating calculated by CB algorithm and a model-based CF algorithm (LFM) respectively, as shown in Eq. (4),

$$\widehat{r}_{ui} = \alpha r_{ui}^{cb} + \beta r_{ui}^{cf} \tag{4}$$

where r_{ui}^{cb} is the predicted rating value calculated by CB algorithm, r_{ui}^{cf} is the predicted rating value calculated by LFM algorithm, α and β are weighs trained by training data.

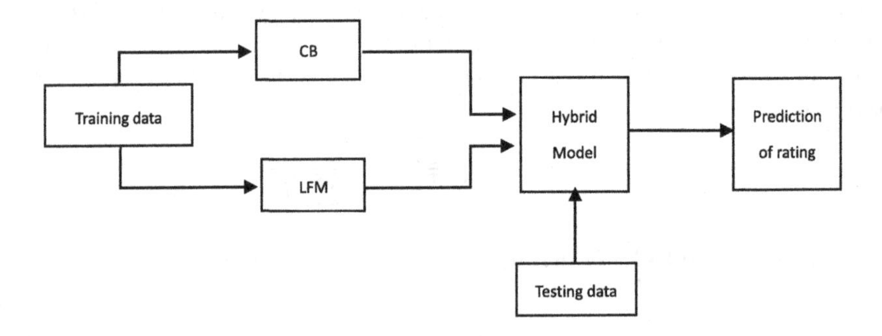

Fig. 1. The architecture of a CB-CF hybrid recommendation system

3.4 CNN-Based CF Method

In this section, we propose a CNN (Convolutional Neural Networks) based recommendation model, as shown in Fig. 2. In our model, users' feature matrix $U \in \mathbb{R}^{m \times k}$ and items' feature matrix $V \in \mathbb{R}^{n \times k}$ can be obtained by decomposing user-item rating matrix $R \in \mathbb{R}^{m \times n}$ according to SVD algorithm, where U_i represents the features of ith user, V_j represents the features of jth item, k is the dimension of the features, R_{ij} is the ith user's rating value on j^{th} item. The two feature vectors are combined to one vector $\boldsymbol{x}^0$ as the input data of CNN model. For each rating R_{ij}, we have

$$\boldsymbol{x}^0 = combine(U_i, V_j) \tag{5}$$

where the function "$combine()$" is used to combine vector U_i and V_j.

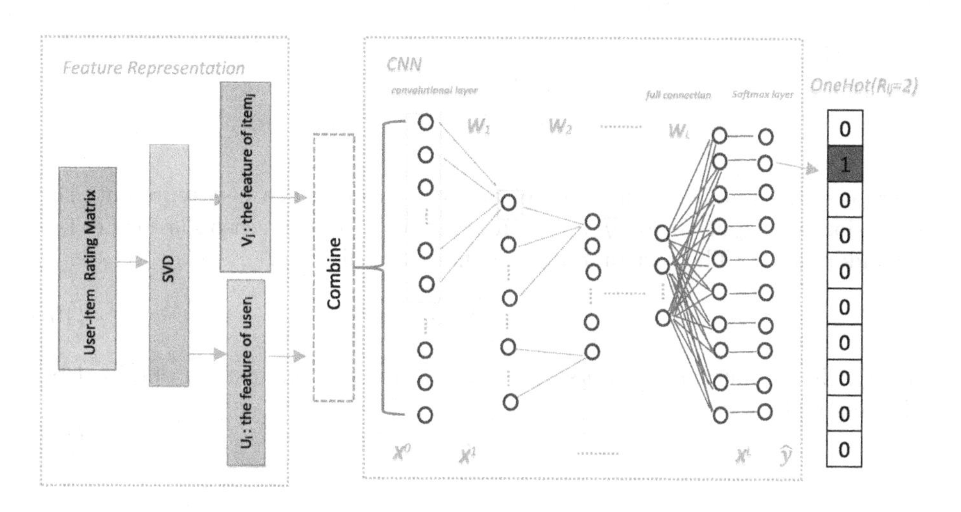

Fig. 2. The frame work of the CNN-based CF model

Our CNN model contains three hidden layer, the first and second hidden are convolutional layer, the last one is full connection layer. Each convolutional layer contains three stage: convolution stage, detector stage and pooling stage. For detector stage of two convolutional layers and full connection layer, we use ReLU function as activation function since it is effective and easy to optimize. When $\boldsymbol{x}^0$ passes through convolution stage and detector stage of first convolutional layer, the output can be obtained by following equation:

$$z_i^1 = ReLU(\sum_m x^0_{(i-1)*s+m} K^1_m + b^1_i) \tag{6}$$

where $\mathbf{K}^1$ is the kernel for first convolutional layer width of m units and is used repeatedly across the entire input, s is the stride of convolution, $\boldsymbol{b}^1$ is the bias vector.

For pooling stage of two convolutional layers, we use max pooling with a pool width of w_p and a stride between pools of s_p. Thus input of second layer (i.e. the output of pooling state) can be obtained by follow equation:

$$x_i^1 = MaxPooling(z^1_{(i-1)*s_p+1}, \ldots, z^1_{(i-1)*s_p+w_p}) \tag{7}$$

where $MaxPooling()$ is the algorithm we chose for pooling stage, w_p is width of the pool, s_p is the stride between pools.

For convenience, we represent the output of lth hidden layer as following:

$$\boldsymbol{x}^l = activation(\boldsymbol{W}_l \boldsymbol{x}^{l-1} + \boldsymbol{b}_l) \tag{8}$$

where $\boldsymbol{W}_l$ is the weight matrix between $(l-1)^{th}$ layer and l^{th} layer, $\boldsymbol{b}_l$ is the bias vector. We choose Softmax layer as the output layer, so the output of Softmax layer can be obtained as follow equation:

$$\widehat{y}_i = \frac{e^{x_i^L}}{\sum_{j=1}^{d} e^{x_j^L}} \tag{9}$$

where d is the number of neurons in Softmax layer, which also represents the dimension of output vector $\widehat{\boldsymbol{y}}$. $\boldsymbol{x}^L$ is the output of full connection layer, i.e. the last hidden layer. The cost function is defined as following:

$$C = -log\widehat{y}_r \tag{10}$$

Finally, the prediction of the $user_i$'s rating score of $item_j$ can be obtained by following equation:

$$\widehat{R}_{ij} = \arg\max_r(\widehat{y}_r). \tag{11}$$

4 Evaluation

4.1 Description of Evaluation

In this section, we investigate the performance of previously mentioned recommendation algorithms, content-based algorithm, model-based CF algorithm and CB-CF hybrid algorithm. We run our experiments on an open-source cluster-computing framework, called Apache Spark. Tensorflow is used to implement our CNN module.

The original dataset contains over 20 GB real-word data collected from a china online B2B medical platform during one year. It contains nearly 20 million order records of 37,100 users for 79,836 items and one billion records of click/watch/browse behavior. The platform is one of the fastest developing medicine B2B trading platforms in China. It provides integrated services for manufacturers, commercial companies and retail terminals through its cargo platform, transfers platform and sharing platform. Over 200,000 retail terminals join the platform, and the monthly turnover exceeds 400 million RMB.

Firstly, the original dataset is divided into twelve million information; then we pre-process these data on Spark to construct a useful dataset for test, including handling missing values, removing duplicates, and extracting feature. Finally, we randomly pick up 80% data from test dataset for training our model and the other 20% data for testing.

We use Mean Absolute Error (MAE) method and Root Mean Squared Error (RMSE) for evaluation purpose, which are widely used in recommendation systems. The expressions are as follows:

$$MAE = \frac{1}{N}\sum_{i,j}|R_{ij} - \widehat{R}_{ij}| \tag{12}$$

$$RMSE = \sqrt{\frac{1}{N}\sum_{i,j}(R_{ij} - \widehat{R}_{ij})^2} \tag{13}$$

where N is the number of testing data samples and $\widehat{R}_{ij}$ refers to the prediction rating value of recommendation algorithm, R_{ij} refers to actual rating value of user. Obviously, the lower of MAE and RMSE values are, the better performance of the algorithm is.

4.2 Evaluation Results

As shown in Figs. 3 and 4, we can see that CB-CF hybrid recommendation algorithm performs much better than content-based algorithm and model-based CF algorithm. This is because hybrid algorithm can overcome the problem of cold start suffered by both CB and CF methods, limited content analysis and over-specialization suffered by CB method, high sparsity of the data suffered by CF methods.

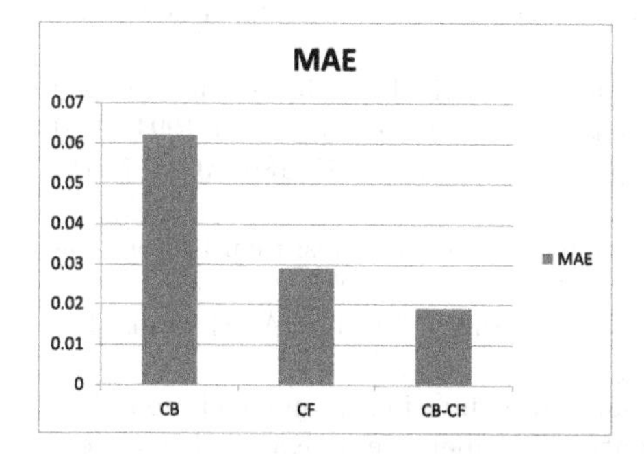

Fig. 3. MAE of different recommendation methods

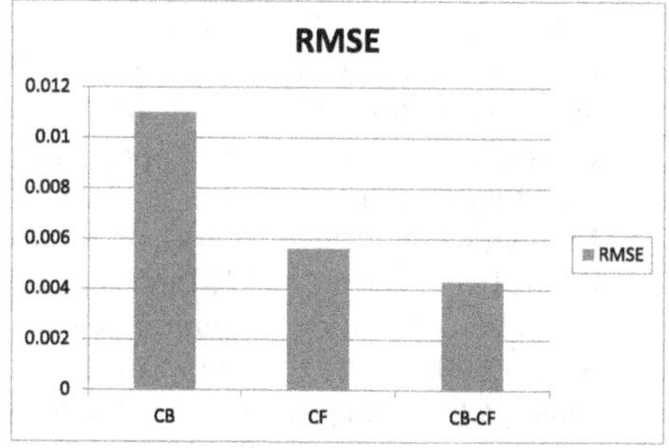

Fig. 4. RMSE of different recommendation methods

5 Conclusion

In this paper, we propose two hybrid algorithms, CB-CF hybrid algorithm and a CNN-based CF algorithm, and give a brief introduction of two well-known recommendation algorithms, content-based algorithm, model-based CF algorithm. Then we investigated the performance of these algorithms on Apache Spark and

Tensorflow. The dataset contains 20 GB real-world data collected from a china online B2B medical platform. The experimental results show that the hybrid algorithm achieves highest predication accuracy. In future work, we will investigate the performance of CNN-based algorithm and further study characteristics of online medical platform and other deep learning models, attempt to design a recommendation model for B2C medical platform to improve user experience and sales.

Acknowledgments. This work was supported by the National Natural Science Foundation of China (Grant No. 61571141, Grant No. 61702120); Guangdong Natural Science Foundation (Grant No. 2014A030313130); The Excellent Young Teachers in Universities in Guangdong (Grant No. YQ2015105); Guangdong Provincial Application-oriented Technical Research and Development Special fund project (Grant No. 2015B010131017, No. 2017B010125003); Science and Technology Program of Guangzhou (Grant No. 201604016108); Guangdong Future Network Engineering Technology Research Center (Grant No. 2016GCZX006); Science and Technology Project of Nan Shan (2017CX004); The Project of Youth Innovation Talent of Universities in Guangdong (No. 2017KQNCX120); Guangdong science and technology development project (2017A090905023).

References

1. Jiang, J., Wang, S.: The legal reform of the third-party medical platform in big data era. Chin. Health Law **22**(5), 22–25 (2014)
2. Jadoon, B., et al.: Collaborative filtering based online recommendation systems: a survey. In: International Conference on Information and Communication Technologies, pp. 125–130 (2017)
3. Resnick, P., Iacovou, N., Suchak, M., Bergstrom, P., Riedl, J.: GroupLens: an open architecture for collaborative filtering of netnews. In: Proceedings of the 1994 ACM Conference on Computer Supported Cooperative Work, pp. 175–186. ACM, North Carolina (1994)
4. Linden, G., Smith, B., York, J.: Amazon.com recommendations: item-to-item collaborative filtering. IEEE Internet Comput. **7**(1), 76–80 (2003)
5. Hofmann, T.: Latent semantic models for collaborative filtering. ACM Trans. Inf. Syst. (TOIS) **22**(1), 89–115 (2004)
6. Zhao, Z.D., Shang, M.S.: User-based collaborative-filtering recommendation algorithms on hadoop. In: 2010 Third International Conference on Knowledge Discovery and Data Mining, pp. 478–481. IEEE, Phuket (2010)
7. Sarwar, B., Karypis, G., Konstan, J., Riedl, J.: Item-based collaborative filtering recommendation algorithms. In: Proceedings of the 10th International Conference on World Wide Web, pp. 285–295. ACM, Hong Kong (2001)
8. Breese, J.S., Heckerman, D., Kadie, C.: Empirical analysis of predictive algorithms for collaborative filtering. In: Proceedings of the 14th Conference on Uncertainty in Artificial Intelligence, pp. 43–52. Morgan Kaufmann Publishers Inc., Madison (1998)
9. Ungar, L.H., Foster, D.P.: Clustering methods for collaborative filtering. In: AAAI Workshop on Recommendation Systems, pp. 114–129 (1998)
10. Shani, G., Heckerman, D., Brafman, R.I.: An MDP-based recommender system. J. Mach. Learn. Res. **6**(1), 1265–1295 (2005)

11. Shahjalal, M.A., Ahmad, Z., Arefin, M.S., Hossain, M.R.T.: A user rating based collaborative filtering approach to predict movie preferences. In: 2017 3rd International Conference on Electrical Information and Communication Technology (EICT), pp. 1–5. IEEE, Khulna (2018)
12. Guan, X., Li, C.T., Guan, Y.: Matrix factorization with rating completion: an enhanced SVD model for collaborative filtering recommender systems. IEEE Access **5**(99), 27668–27678 (2017)
13. Pazzani, M.J., Billsus, D.: Content-based recommendation systems. Adapt. Web **4321**, 325–341 (2007)
14. Oord, A.v.d., Dieleman, S., Schrauwen, B.: Deep content-based music recommendation. In: Proceedings of the 26th International Conference on Neural Information Processing Systems, pp. 2643–2651. Curran Associates Inc., Nevada (2013)
15. Burke, R.: Hybrid recommender systems: survey and experiments. User Model. User-Adapt. Interact. **12**(4), 331–370 (2002)
16. Dong, X., Yu, L., Wu, Z., Sun, Y., Yuan, L., Zhang, F.: A hybrid collaborative filtering model with deep structure for recommender systems. In: Proceedings of the AAAI Conference on Artificial Intelligence, North America, pp. 1309–1315 (2017)
17. Gurbanov, T., Ricci, F.: Action prediction models for recommender systems based on collaborative filtering and sequence mining hybridization. In: Proceedings of the Symposium on Applied Computing, pp. 1655–1661. ACM, Marrakech (2017)
18. Wang, Z., et al.: A deep-learning based feature hybrid framework for spatiotemporal saliency detection inside videos. Neurocomputing **287**, 68–83 (2018)
19. Han, T., et al.: Background prior-based salient object detection via deep reconstruction residual. IEEE Trans. Circuits Syst. Video Technol. **25**(8), 1309–1321 (2015)
20. Zabalza, J., et al.: Novel segmented stacked autoencoder for effective dimensionality reduction and feature extraction in hyperspectral imaging. Neurocomputing **185**, 1–10 (2016)
21. Jiang, J.: Medical image analysis with artificial neural networks. Comput. Med. Imaging Graph. **34**(8), 617–631 (2010)
22. Ren, J.: ANN vs. SVM: which one performs better in classification of MCCs in mammogram imaging. Knowl.-Based Syst. **26**, 144–153 (2012)
23. Noor, S.S.M.: The properties of the cornea based on hyperspectral imaging: optical biomedical engineering perspective. In: Proceedings of International Conference on Systems, Signals and Image Processing (IWSSIP), pp. 1–4. IEEE, Slovakia (2016)
24. Noor, S.S.M.: Hyperspectral image enhancement and mixture deep-learning classification of corneal epithelium injuries. Sensors **17**(11), 2644 (2017)
25. Ren, J.: Effective recognition of MCCs in mammograms using an improved neural classifier. Eng. Appl. Artif. Intell. **24**(4), 638–645 (2011)
26. Zhang, L., Luo, T., Zhang, F., Wu, Y.: A recommendation model based on deep neural network. IEEE Access **6**, 9454–9463 (2018)
27. Lops, P., de Gemmis, M., Semeraro, G.: Content-based recommender systems: state of the art and trends. In: Ricci, F., Rokach, L., Shapira, B., Kantor, P.B. (eds.) Recommender Systems Handbook, pp. 73–105. Springer, Boston, MA (2011). https://doi.org/10.1007/978-0-387-85820-3_3
28. Takacs, G., Pilaszy, I., Nemeth, B., Tikk, D.: Major components of the gravity recommendation system. ACM SIGKDD Explor. Newsl. **9**(2), 80–83 (2007)

The Prediction Model of Saccade Target Based on LSTM-CRF for Chinese Reading

Xiaoming Wang[1,2(✉)], Xinbo Zhao[1], and Meng Xia[1]

[1] Northwestern Polytechnical University, Xi'an, China
wxmgo@163.com
[2] Xi'an International Studies University, Xi'an, China

Abstract. Through introducing the psychology model of reading cognitive, this paper uses the LSTM neural network and the CRF model respectively to simulate the language cognition process and the eye-movement control process in reading, in order to overcome the defect that the traditional CRF prediction model only considers the context information of the label sequence but can not take into account the context information of the text sequence. First, the psychological process of reading cognition is introduced and the prediction model of saccade target based on LSTM-CRF for Chinese reading is proposed. Then, the experimental data, experimental environment, feature templates and parameter settings needed for model training are introduced. Finally, the conclusion is drawn through experimental comparison: (1) The F1 score of prediction model in saccade labeling based on LSTM-CRF is superior to the traditional CRF prediction model; (2) The predictability of the language itself is an important feature of the saccade target prediction model; (3) The best saccade length for Chinese readers is about 2.5 Chinese characters.

Keywords: Eye-tracking · Saccade target prediction
Conditional Random Fields (CRF) · Chinese reading

1 Introduction

The current study of reading eye-movement focuses on the aspect of eye-movements control based on cognitive psychology [2, 4, 6, 8–10, 16–19, 21]. The studies were constructed based on alphabetic writing systems [7], which was not suitable for Chinese reading and needed to be further improved and revised. There are also some language processing studies based on the statistical machine learning model [1, 12]. The studies based on a neural network to realize a classifier [1] or predict the fixation points [12]. However, the built model was relatively simple and didn't integrate with existing research results of landing position effects. The traditional model only considered the context information of the label sequence but can not took into account the context information of the text sequence.

Jiang studied how to apply neural networks to some areas and provided a focused literature survey on neural network developments in computer-aided diagnosis [5]. Ren proposed an improved neural classifier, in which balanced learning with optimized decision making are introduced to enable effective learning from imbalanced samples

J. Ren et al. (Eds.): BICS 2018, LNAI 10989, pp. 44–53, 2018.
https://doi.org/10.1007/978-3-030-00563-4_5

[14]. Ren proposed a new strategy namely balanced learning with optimized decision to enable effective learning from imbalanced samples, which is further employed to evaluate the performance of ANN and SVM in this context [15]. The methods and viewpoints presented in the above article have given us great inspiration. So a new model is needed to simulate the language cognition process and the eye-movement control process in reading respectively. First, the psychological process of reading cognition is introduced and the prediction model of saccade target based on LSTM-CRF for Chinese reading is proposed. Then, the experimental data, experimental environment, feature templates and parameter settings needed for model training are introduced. Finally, the conclusion is drawn through experimental comparison and the next improvement strategy is put forward.

2 The Psychology Model of Reading Saccade

The reader usually supposes that the eye moves smoothly from left to right in the reading process, but in fact, for the limitation of the visual physiological structure, the reader's eye-movement trajectory is made up of a series of fixation and saccade. In order to understand the reading text, the reader needs to obtain the necessary information of the text by continuous saccades. Figure 1 shows the eye-movement trajectory of the adult reader. The number in the circle represents the duration of each fixation (in milliseconds), and the arrow indicates the direction of the saccade.

Fig. 1. Eye-movement trajectory of the adult reader

Since *Javal* first began to study the role of eye-movement in reading in 1879, the eye-movement recording has gradually become an important method for reading research. Eye-movement control is a hot topic in the field of eye-tracking study and contains two sub-problems: the one is what determines ***when*** the reader moves his eyes, and the other is what determines ***where*** the reader moves his eyes [13]. The researchers used computer simulation to integrate a large number of experimental data (mainly from the study of alphabetic writing systems), put forward a variety of eye-movement control models from the perspective of cognitive psychology, and tried to answer the above mentioned two sub-problems [22, 23].

The currently accepted cognitive psychology model for reading processing is the Sequential Attention Shift (SAS) model. The representative models are the Morrison model and the E-Z Reader model. The model emphasizes that vocabulary and lexical processing play a decisive role in the reader's reading process (Reichle et al. 2003), and considers that attention is sequence shifting. Attention resources can only be assigned to one word at a time. If two attention shifts occur within the limited time window, the first eye-movement will be covered by the second eye-movement, that is, a saccade phenomenon. The model considers that reading process contains two independent systems: the language cognitive processing system and the eye-movement control system. The language cognitive processing system includes three stages: early visual processing stage (V), familiarity testing stage (L1) and lexical access stage (L2). The eye-movement control system also includes three stages: an unstable phase of the saccade plan (M1), a stable stage of the saccade plan (M2), and an execution process of the saccade plan (s). The data of each stage has an anterior and posterior correlation. Recurrent Neural Networks (RNN) is the most natural simulation framework for this type of data.

After introducing the psychology model of reading cognition, we next discuss its machine implementation issues.

3 The Prediction Model of Saccade Target Based on LSTM-CRF

As described in the previous section, the psychology model considers that reading process contains two independent systems: the language cognitive processing system and the eye-movement control system, with the cognitive processing in the first place and the saccade in the post. We first consider only the saccade and use Conditional Random Fields to model this process. Conditional Random Fields (CRF) is a conditional probability distribution model for another set of random variable $\boldsymbol{Y}$ with a given input random variable $\boldsymbol{X}$, characterized by the assumption that the output variables constitute Markov Random Fields. In the conditional probability model P(Y|X), $\boldsymbol{Y}$ is the output variable representing the saccade target (fixation) label sequence, and $\boldsymbol{X}$ is the input variable representing the text sequence to be labeled. At this time, the problem of predicting the reading saccade target in this paper is transformed into a sequence labeling problem. In the saccade target prediction task, it is necessary to predict whether the current word is the fixation point (y_i). The result depends not only on the feature value of current word (x), but also on the prediction of whether the last word is the fixation point (y_{i-1}), because the prediction of the last word as a fixation point affects the prediction of the current word, which is exactly in line with the linear-chain CRF model.

However, CRF only takes into account the transfer features and the state features of label sequences, without taking into account the contextual information of text sequence. Long Short-Term Memory Networks (LSTM) is a time-recursive neural network that can process and predict important events of relatively long intervals and delays in time series. Adding LSTM before CRF is equivalent to using a linguistic relationship abstracted by LSTM to train CRF. This makes use of the context of two aspects of text sequence and label sequence, which is more in line with the actual process of reading saccade.

The LSTM-CRF model is divided into three layers: The first layer is the look-up layer, using the pre-trained or random initialized embedding matrix to map each character $\boldsymbol{x_i}$ in the sentence from a one-hot vector to a low-dimensional dense character vector (character embedding). The second layer is bidirectional LSTM neural network, which is used to extract character sequence features automatically. The third layer is the CRF layer, for sentence-level sequence labeling.

If the length of a label sequence y = (y_1,y_2,..., y_n) is equal to the sentence length, the score of the model for the sentence $\boldsymbol{x}$ equal to $\boldsymbol{y}$ is:

$$score(x,y) = \sum_{i=1}^{n+1} A_{y_{i-1},y_i} + \sum_{i=1}^{n} B_{i,y_i} + \Phi(\eta_1, \eta_2, \varepsilon, \Delta, \psi) \tag{1}$$

The score of each location is obtained from two parts, one is determined by the output $\boldsymbol{b}_i$ of LSTM, and the other is determined by the transfer matrix $\boldsymbol{A}$ of CRF. $\boldsymbol{\phi}$ is a penalty function and will be introduced in Sect. 4.3. The learning strategy of the model is to learn so that the conditional probability P(y | x) is maximized, which is:

$$P(y \mid x) = \frac{\exp(score(x,y))}{\sum_{y'} \exp(score(x,y'))} \tag{2}$$

In the prediction process (decoding), the Viterbi algorithm is used to solve the optimal value: $y* = \arg\max_{y'} score(x, y')$.

The structure of the entire model is shown in Fig. 2. We will introduce the parameter settings of the model in the next section.

4 The Experimental Settings

4.1 The Experimental Data and Environment

There is no available Chinese eye-tracking corpus, so we have to spend a lot of energy to build a Chinese eye-tracking corpus as a training set and test set for the model. In building models, we use existing related software [3, 11].

Participants. All the 40 participants were the undergraduate students between 18 and 22 years old with Chinese as their mother tongue, having the corrected or uncorrected visual acuity of 1.0, and none of them had taken the psychology-related courses.

Corpus. The corpus came from the PFR corpus, from which the 55 political essays of the "*People's Daily*" in January 1998 were selected (retrieved from http://www.threedweb.cn/thread-1591-1-1.html). The average length of these paragraphs was 50 Chinese characters (range: 39–62), with an average of 2.5 sentences (range: 1–5). There were 2,382 Chinese characters in total for all these articles.

Apparatus. The eye movements were recorded via an SR Research EyeLink 1000 Plus eye tracker (spatial resolution of 0.01°). Participants were seated 60 cm away from a display with a resolution of 1600 × 900, with approximately three characters facing a viewing angle of 1° (the monitor was 40 × 24 deg of visual angle). The experiment fixed the chin and forehead to minimize head activity and only observed the eye movement record of the right eye. The experiment was controlled by the SR Research Experiment Builder software.

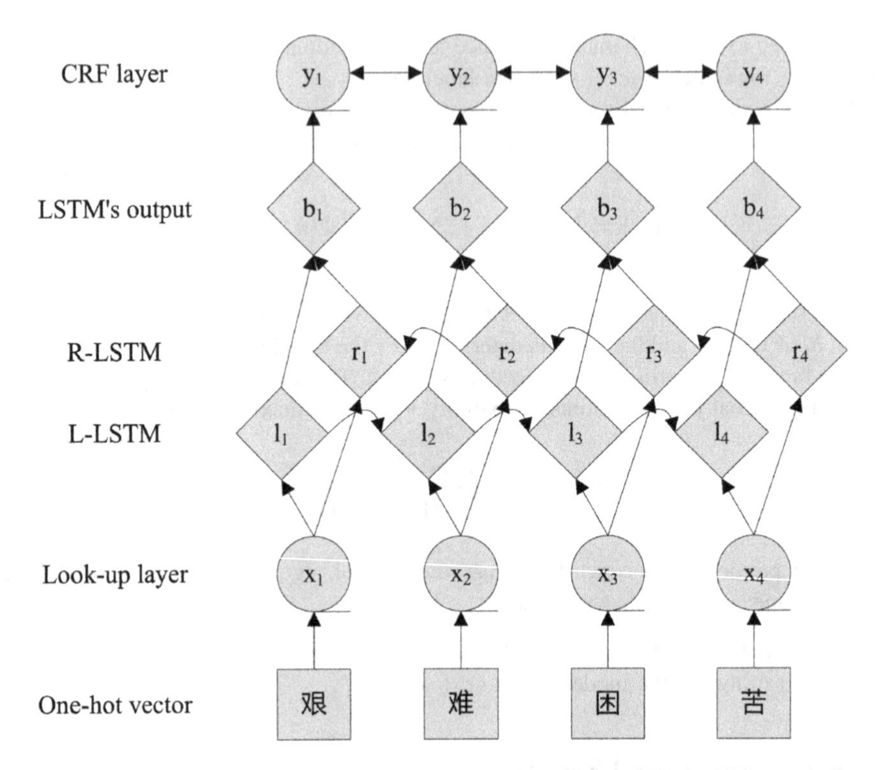

Fig. 2. The prediction model of saccade target based on LSTM-CRF for Chinese reading

Software. The LSTM network was trained using TensorFlow+Keras. CRF training used the CRF++ open source tool under Windows.

4.2 The Feature Templates

There are two types of feature templates: Unigram template and Bigram template, which generate the state feature functions $s_l(y_i, x, i)$ and the transfer feature functions $t_k(y_{i-1}, y_i, x, i)$ respectively. In the above functions, $\boldsymbol{y}$ is the label sequence, $\boldsymbol{x}$ is the observation sequence, and $\boldsymbol{i}$ is the current node location. Each template specifies the token of input data by %x[row, col], in which ***row*** specifies the row offset of the current token, and ***col*** specifies the column offset. The template type is specified by the characters represented by $\boldsymbol{x}$. %U[row, col] is used to describe the template of Unigram feature while %B[row, col] is used to describe the template of Bigram. When traditional CRF is used to model, the templates need to be built from features such as part of speech, word segmentation, and predictability of the character (obtained from the eye-tracking corpus).

When LSTM-CRF is used to model, the LSTM is responsible for processing the state characteristics and context information of the input sequence and the CRF is responsible for processing the transfer characteristics and state characteristics of the label sequence. In this case, only the output sequence ($b_1, b_2, \ldots, b_n$) of the LSTM layer needs to be provided to the CRF layer. The template file is shown in Fig. 3.

艰	b_1	F	的	b_5	F	往	b_9	F	大	b_{13}	S
难	b_2	F	境	b_6	S	成	b_{10}	F	的	b_{14}	F
困	b_3	F	遇	b_7	F	就	b_{11}	S	人	b_{15}	F
苦	b_4	S	往	b_8	S	伟	b_{12}	F	生	b_{16}	F

Fig. 3. Feature templates when using LSTM-CRF to model

As shown in the figure above, when the current token is the character "苦", %x [−2,1] is just the two lines before "苦" and lies in column 1(the column index starts from zero),which is $\boldsymbol{b_2}$. Each row %U[#, #] generates a point (state) function $f(y_i, x)$ of CRF, in which $\boldsymbol{y_i}$ is the label(output) at $\boldsymbol{i}$ time, and $\boldsymbol{x}$ is the context at the $\boldsymbol{t}$ time. Each row of %B[#,#] generates an edge function $f(y_{i-1}, y_i, x)$ of CRF, where $\boldsymbol{y_{i-1}}$ is a label at time $\boldsymbol{i-1}$. This type of template produces L * L * N different characteristics and the generation function is similar to:

```
func1=if(output=F and feature=U02:艰)return 1 else return 0
func2=if(prev_output=F and output=S and feature=B02:苦)
return 1 else return 0
```

Func1 reflects that in the training example, the character is '艰' and the label is F. In this way, each row of the template will generate L * L * N feature functions. After training, the weights of these functions reflect the influence of the label of the previous node on the current node.

4.3 Model Training and Parameter Setting

The performance evaluation adopted *precision*, *recall* and *F1 score* commonly used in the language processing task. For the data test results, there are the following four situations: True Positive (TP), True Negative (TN), False Positive (FP), and False Negative (FN).

The *precision* is for the prediction result. It indicates how many samples in the positive prediction are true positive samples, namely: *precision* = TP/(TP + FP). The *recall* is for the original sample. It indicates how many positive examples in the sample were correctly predicted, namely: *recall* = TP/ (TP + FN).

Generally speaking, the *precision* and *recall* rate demonstrate slightly negative correlation in order to better evaluate the index system. The harmonic average of the two is defined as a comprehensive evaluation index, namely the *F1* score, which is defined as the specific: *F1* = (2 * *precision* * *recall*)/(*precision* * *recall*).

In training the model, we divided the corpus into 3 parts and randomly selected 60% of the data as the training data set, whose F1 score was recorded as $F1_{Training}$, 20%

of the data was randomly selected as the cross-validated data set, whose F1 score was recorded as $F1_{Cross\text{-}validation}$, and the remaining 20% as a test data set, whose F1 score was recorded as $F1_{Test}$.

The output of the model is the probability that a word is labeled as Fixation or Saccade. It is composed of two parts. The first part is determined by the state matrix and the transfer matrix, the second part is a penalty function, which is based on the saccade length to punish the result of the first part. The saccade length mainly includes three parts: the planned saccade length, systematic error and random error. The planned saccade length, systematic error and random error are combined into a penalty function added to the LSTM-CRF model. The systematic error and random error in the reading process are affected by the distance from the take-off position to the best fixation position, so the parameter values of the E-Z Reader model 9 were used for η_1(Intercept: Random error component of the saccade), η_2(Slope: random error component of the saccade), ε(Visual acuity parameters affecting L1) and Δ(Ratio of L1 and L2). The key to adjusting the parameters now is to adjust the value (ψ) of the optimal length of the saccade.

As shown in Fig. 4, since the E-Z Reader model is constructed based on alphabetic writing systems, the optimal length of the saccade plan is not suitable for Chinese reading. In the process of Chinese reading, the F1 score and the cross-validation F1 score was not high when ψ was 3, and the learning curve was underfitting; when ψ was 2, the F1 score was high, but the cross-validation F1 score was not high, which was a typical overfitting; When ψ was 2.5, the learning curve of the model performed best, that is, the reader's planned saccade length is about 2.5 Chinese characters, which is also the bias gaze position distance for Chinese readers.

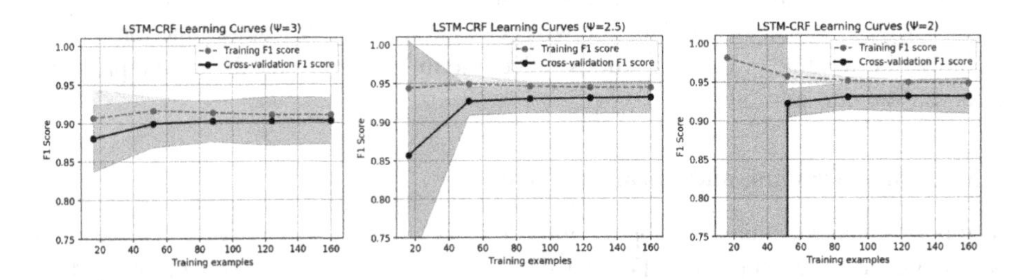

Fig. 4. The learning curve of the LSTM-CRF model

4.4 Experimental Results and Discussion

The simulation experiments were carried out from "CRF Character", "CRF Character + Part of speech", "CRF Character + Word segmentation", "CRF Character + Predictability" and the combination of the previous features, as well as "LSTM + CRF". The results of the simulation experiment are shown in Table 1.

For traditional CRF, the richer the feature template is, the higher the F1 score is, which is obvious. However for a single feature, the "CRF + predictability" pattern is superior to the other two patterns on the F1 score, which shows that the predictability of language plays an important role in reading saccade target selection.

Table 1. Comparison table of F1 score for different models

Model		$F1_{Training}$	$F1_{Cross\text{-}validation}$	$F1_{Test}$
CRF	Character	0.8489	0.8246	0.7932
	+ Part of speech	0.8634	0.8539	0.8443
	+ Word segmentation	0.8558	0.8511	0.8464
	+ Predictability	0.8975	0.8799	0.8623
	+ Part of speech, word segmentation, predictability	0.9039	0.8913	0.8787
LSTM-CRF	Random initialization of character vector	0.9480	0.9378	0.9377

For the LSTM-CRF model, the processing in each layer of this paper is relatively simple, and there is still a space for improvement, such as the initialization method of the character vector embedding, which is only the simplest random initialization here. In the future, it may be considered to segment the sentence and then initialize the character vector to the word vector. It is also possible to try to process low-level features through a RNN or CNN, and then use "combination" to get character-level embedding (using radicals to construct Chinese characters), which is stitched with the randomly initialized character vectors.

5 Conclusion and Future Work

Through introducing the psychology model of reading cognitive processing into the study of reading saccade target prediction, this paper proposes a prediction model of saccade target based on LSTM-CRF for Chinese reading. The conclusion is drawn through experimental comparison: (1) The F1 score of prediction model in saccade labeling based on LSTM-CRF is superior to the traditional CRF model; (2) The predictability of the language itself is an important feature of the prediction model; (3) The best saccade length for Chinese readers is about 2.5 Chinese characters.

Simulation experiments and analysis can be performed from two granularities (characters and words) in the future: CRF are expanded on the E-Z Reader model, SWIFT model, Glenmore model, Chinese word segmentation and vocabulary recognition model [13]. By comparing the fitting degree of the simulation experiment with the actual data, the rationality and applicability of the Sequential Attention Shift Theory and the Guidance by Attentional Gradient Theory in the reading cognitive processing model can be evaluated. Furthermore, the factors influencing landing position effect in Chinese reading process can be analyzed, and whether the granularity of Chinese reading cognitive process is based on characters or words can be figured out. In the aspect of constructing CRF feature template, the existing research results of landing position effect reading should be used for reference, to reduce the feature dependence and formulate effective feature selection strategies in the future. Besides, Wang [20] proposed a deep learning based hybrid spatiotemporal saliency feature extraction framework for saliency detection from video footages, which is a very valuable reference.

Acknowledgments. We would like to thank the associate editor and all of the reviewers for their constructive comments to improve the manuscript. The work is supported by NSF of China (Nos. NCYM0001) and MOE (Ministry of Education in China) Project of Humanities and Social Sciences (Project No. 18YJCZH180).

References

1. Alkhateeb, J.H., Ren, J., Jiang, J., Ipson, S.S., Abed, H.E.: Word-based handwritten Arabic scripts recognition using DCT features and neural network classifier. In: 5th IEEE International Multi-Conference on Systems, Signals and Devices, pp. 517–530. IEEE Press, Amman (2008)
2. Bai, X.J., Yan, G.L., Li, X.: Eye movement control in Chinese reading: a summary over the past 20 years of research. Psychol. Dev. Educ. **31**(1), 85–91 (2015)
3. Cop, U., Dirix, N., Drieghe, D., Duyck, W.: Presenting GECO: an eye-tracking corpus of monolingual and bilingual sentence reading. Behav. Res. Methods **49**(2), 1–14 (2016)
4. Frisson, S., Harvey, D.R., Staub, A.: No prediction error cost in reading: evidence from eye movements. J. Mem. Lang. **95**(4), 200–214 (2017)
5. Jiang, J., Trundle, P., Ren, J.: Medical image analysis with artificial neural networks. Comput. Med. Imaging Graph. **34**(8), 617–631 (2010)
6. Clifton Jr., C., Ferreira, F., Henderson, J.M., Inhoff, A.W., Liversedge, S.P.: Eye movements in reading and information processing: Keith Rayner's 40 year legacy. J. Mem. Lang. **86**(1), 1–19 (2016)
7. Kennedy, A., Pynte, J., Murray, W.S., Paul, S.A.: Frequency and predictability effects in the Dundee Corpus: an eye movement analysis. Q. J. Exp. Psychol. **66**(3), 601–618 (2012)
8. Kuperberg, G.R., Jaeger, T.F.: What do we mean by prediction in language comprehension? Lang. Cognit. Neurosci. **31**(1), 32–59 (2015)
9. Liu, Y., Reichle, E.D.: Eye-movement evidence for object-based attention in Chinese reading. Psychol. Sci. **29**(2), 278–287 (2017)
10. Luke, S.G., Christianson, K.: Limits on lexical prediction during reading. Cogn. Psychol. **88**(6), 22–60 (2016)
11. Luke, S.G., Christianson, K.: The Provo Corpus: a large eye-tracking corpus with predictability norms. Behav. Res. Methods **50**(2), 826–833 (2018)
12. Moch, B.N., Komarudin, K., Susilo, M.S.: Development of eye fixation points prediction model from eye tracking data using neural network. Int. J. Technol. **8**(6), 1082–1091 (2017)
13. Rayner, K., Li, X., Pollatsek, A.: Extending the E-Z Reader model of eye movement control to Chinese readers. Cognit. Sci. **31**(6), 1021–1033 (2007)
14. Ren, J.: ANN vs. SVM: which one performs better in classification of MCCs in mammogram imaging. Knowl. Based Syst. **26**(2), 144–153 (2012)
15. Ren, J., Wang, D., Jiang, J.: Effective recognition of MCCs in mammograms using an improved neural classifier. Eng. Appl. Artif. Intell. **24**(4), 638–645 (2011)
16. Reichle, E.D.: Computational models of reading: a primer. Lang. Linguist. Compass **9**(7), 271–284 (2015)
17. Sheridan, H., Reichle, E.D.: An analysis of the time course of lexical processing during reading. Cognit. Sci. **40**(3), 522–553 (2015)
18. Slattery, T.J., Yates, M.: Word skipping: effects of word length, predictability, spelling and reading skill. Q. J. Exp. Psychol. **71**(8), 1–30 (2017)

19. Su, H., Liu, Z.F., Cao, L.R.: The effects of word frequency and word predictability in preview and their implications for word segmentation in Chinese reading: evidence from eye movements. Acta Psychol. Sin. **48**(6), 625–636 (2016)
20. Wang, Z., Ren, J., Zhang, D., Sun, M., Jiang, J.: A deep-learning based feature hybrid framework for spatiotemporal saliency detection inside videos. Neurocomputing **287**(2), 68–83 (2018)
21. Yu, L., Reichle, E.D.: Chinese versus English: insights on cognition during reading. Trends Cognit. Sci. **21**(10), 721–724 (2017)
22. Reichle, E.D., Pollatsek, A., Fisher, D.L., Rayner, K.: Toward a model of eye movement control in reading. Psychol. Rev. **105**(1), 125–157 (1998)
23. Engbert, R., Longtin, A., Kliegl, R.: A dynamical model of saccade generation in reading based on spatially distributed lexical processing. Vis. Res. **42**(5), 621–636 (2002)

Visual Cognition Inspired Vehicle Re-identification via Correlative Sparse Ranking with Multi-view Deep Features

Dengdi Sun[1,2], Lidan Liu[1], Aihua Zheng[1,2(✉)], Bo Jiang[1,2], and Bin Luo[1,2]

[1] School of Computer Science and Technology, Anhui University, Hefei 230601, China
sundengdi@163.com, liulidan0@163.com
{ahzheng214,jiangbo,luobin}@ahu.edu.cn

[2] Key Lab of Industrial Image Processing and Analysis of Anhui Province, Hefei, China

Abstract. Vehicle re-identification has gradually gained attention and widespread applications. However, most of the existing methods learn the discriminative features for identities by single feature channel only. It is worth noting that visual cognition of human eyes is a multi-channel system. Therefore, integrating the multi-view information is a nature way to boost computer vision tasks in challenging scenarios. In this paper, we propose to mine multi-view deep features via correlative sparse ranking for vehicle re-identification. Specifically, first, we employ ResNet-50 and GoogleNet as two baseline networks to generate the attributes (vehicle color and type) aggregated features. Then we explore the feature correlation via enforcing the correlation term into the multi-view sparse coding framework. The original rankings are obtained by the reconstruction coefficients between probe and gallery. Finally, we utilize a re-ranking technique to further boost the performance. Experimental results on public benchmark VeRi-776 dataset demonstrate that our approach outperforms state-of-art approaches.

Keywords: Vehicle re-identification · Correlative sparse ranking
Multi-view · Deep feature

1 Introduction

With the great progress of computer vision [13,17], vehicle re-identification (Re-ID) has recently drawn much more attention due to its potential applications such as intelligent transportation, urban computing and intelligent monitoring. The aim of the vehicle Re-ID is to identify the same vehicle across non-overlapping cameras, where the license plate of the vehicle is scarcely possible to identify due to motion blur, challenging camera view etc. In addition to person Re-ID, vehicle Re-ID has particular challenges: different identities, especially from the same manufacturer, with similar colors and types possibly.

J. Ren et al. (Eds.): BICS 2018, LNAI 10989, pp. 54–63, 2018.
https://doi.org/10.1007/978-3-030-00563-4_6

Recently, many progresses have been made for vehicle Re-ID. Liu et al. [6] proposed a large surveillance-nature dataset (VehicleID) and explored Coupled Clusters Loss to measure the distance of arbitrary two input vehicle images. Zapletal et al. [15] learnt a linear classifier on color histograms and histograms of oriented gradients by vehicle 3D bounding boxes. Zhang et al. [16] designed a classification-oriented loss and triplet sampling method based on the triplet-wise network. Kanacı et al. [2] proposed to transfer the vehicle model representation for more fine-grained Re-ID tasks via a so-called cross-level vehicle recognition method. Liu et al. [7] proposed a big dataset VeRi-776 for vehicle Re-ID, and extracted the Fusion of Attributes and Color features (FACT). Furthermore, some works tried to integrate the spatio-temporal information into vehicle Re-ID process [8,11,12]. Considering that vehicles have specific attributes such as color and type, Liu [8] designed a progressive searching scheme which employed the appearance attributes of vehicle for a coarse filtering. Li et al. [4] designed a unified vehicle Re-ID framework combing identification, attribute recognition, verification and triplet tasks. However, most of existing methods implement the vehicle Re-ID only from a single feature view. Inspired by the vision system of human eyes which can perceive and decompose the multichannel information, we argue that vehicle can be recognised from multi-view characterizations.

In this paper, we propose to explore the multi-view deep feature correlation for vehicle Re-ID. Specifically, we mine the correlation between two feature space via correlative sparse coding by enforcing the correlation constraint into the multi-view sparse coding framework. It can be regarded as a general framework for multi-view feature fusion for any existing networks. In particular, we employ two attributes aggregated Re-ID networks based on ResNet-50 and GoogleNet as the subnetworks. Furthermore, inspired by the satisfactory performance of the re-ranking techniques in person Re-ID, we further utilize the Expanded Cross Neighborhood (ECN) [10] based re-ranking technique to boost the performance of the proposed method.

2 The Proposed Approach

In this section, first, we shall demonstrate the overall architecture of the proposed method, followed by the implementation details.

2.1 Overview

Given a probe vehicle image, the proposed approach regarding the vehicle Re-ID consists of the following three steps as shown in Fig. 1.

(a) Multi-view deep feature learning: We design two deep learning-based [1] subnetworks, namely ResNet-50 and GoogleNet, to extract the multi-view features by aggregating the attribute information into vehicle ID (ID-Att).
(b) Feature fusion via correlative sparse ranking: We propose to explore the correlation between the multi-view feature spaces via correlative sparse coding,

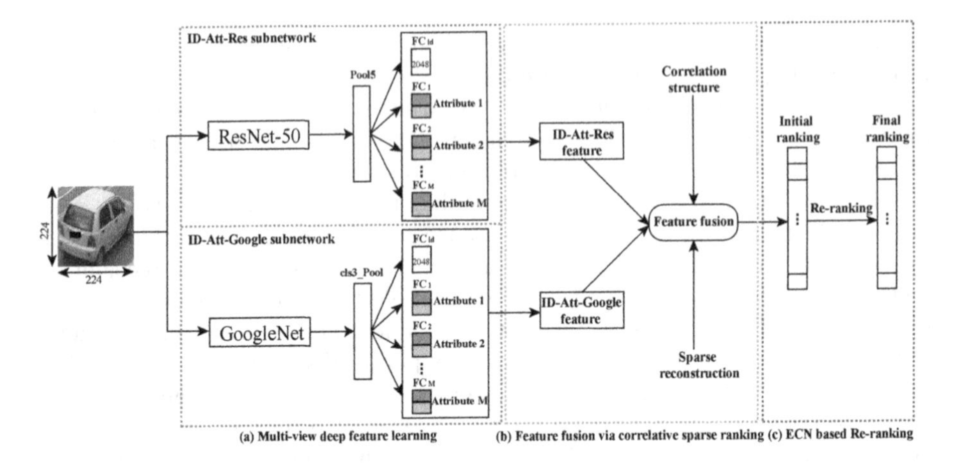

Fig. 1. Overall architecture of the proposed method. (Color figure online)

which enforces the consistency between the sparse coefficients of the multi-view features. The original ranking results are obtained according to the reconstruction coefficients between probe and gallery.

(c) ECN based Re-ranking: The finally ranking results are achieved via Expanded Cross Neighborhood (ECN) [10] based on re-ranking technique.

We shall elaborate the procedure in the following three subsections.

2.2 Multi-view Deep Feature Learning

Inspired by the human visual system, deep learning building hierarchical layers of visual representation to extract the high level features of an image, we design a multi-attribute aggregated deep learning framework to generate the multi-view features for vehicle Re-ID first. As shown in Fig. 1(a), the proposed framework consists of two subnetworks: ResNet-50 and GoogleNet. Specifically, we encode ten color attributes (yellow, orange, green, gray, red, blue, white, golden, brown, black) and nine type attributes (sedan, suv, van, hatchback, mpv, pickup, bus, truck, estate) into the deep framework, since color and type are the most recognizable appearance information.

Without loss of generality, we introduce the ResNet-50 based subnetwork as an example firstly. For the sake of attributes recognition, here we attach $M+1$ fully-connected (FC) layers at the end, including one ID classification and M attributes, where M is the sum of the number of attributes (colors and types). Specifically, for the FC layer for ID classification, the number of output nodes equals to the number of training vehicle identities, C; while each FC layers for one attribute (color or type) link B output nodes corresponding to the B discriminant results. GoogleNet subnetwork is constructed in the same manner.

Furthermore, we append the dropout [3] layers before all FC layers in two subnetworks. The output of each hidden neuron is set to zero with rate $P=0.9$

to avoid overfitting. Finally, for each query image, we extract two 2,048-dim feature vectors X^1 and X^2 from the two dropout layers. For gallery image set H, two feature matrices $\boldsymbol{U^1} = [u_1^1, \cdots, u_N^1]$ and $\boldsymbol{U^2} = [u_1^2, \cdots, u_N^2]$ are generated in the same manner, where u_i^1 and u_i^2 represent the feature vector of the i-th gallery image h_i from two subnetworks respectively.

Loss Computation. Given a probe vehicle image q and a gallery set H with N images of C vehicle identities, $H = \{h_i | i = 1, 2, \ldots, N\}$, Let $D = \{x_i, d_i, l_i\}_{i=1}^N$ be the image-label tuple where d_i and $l_i = \{l_i^1, ..., l_i^M\}$ denote the vehicle identity and the attribute labels of the i-th image x_i respectively, where $M = 10$ (colors) +9 (types), and $l_i^m \in \{0, 1\}$ indicates the binary attribute label.

Take ResNet-50 as the example. As shown in Fig. 1(a), we use the softmax classification loss function to optimise vehicle identity discrimination in vehicle ID classification branch. The output of the last FC layer is $z^{ID} = [z_1^{ID}, z_2^{ID}, ..., z_C^{ID}] \in \mathcal{R}^C$, where z_i^{ID} is the predicted result of the i-th ID. Thus, the prediction probability of each vehicle ID c calculated by softmax is: $p(c) = \frac{exp(z_c^{ID})}{\sum_{i=1}^C exp(z_i^{ID})}$, $c = 1, \cdots, C$. So the total vehicle ID loss is calculated by cross entropy loss function as:

$$L_{ID} = -\sum_{c=1}^{C} f(c) log(p(c)), \tag{1}$$

where $f(c)$ is a $1 \times C$ vector and represents the ground-truth of vehicle ID. Suppose t is the ground-truth of current sample, $f(c) = 1$ when $c = t$, and $f(c) = 0$ for all $c \neq t$.

The output of the FC layer for attribute j is $z_j^{Att} = \left[z_{j_1}^{Att}, \cdots, z_{j_B}^{Att}\right] \in \mathcal{R}^B$, where $B = 2$ denotes the binary discriminant results ("yes" or "no") for attribute j. Therefore, the prediction probability of the j-th attribute label is $p(j_b) = \frac{exp(z_{j_b}^{Att})}{\sum_{j_i=1}^B exp(z_{j_i}^{Att})}$, $j_b = 1, \cdots, B$. Similarly, we can compute the loss function of vehicle attribute j as:

$$L_{Att_j} = -\sum_{j_b=1}^{B} f(j_b) log(p(j_b)), \tag{2}$$

where $f(j_b)$ is $1 \times B$ representing the ground-truth of vehicle attribute.

The final ID-Attribute subnetwork loss is defined as:.

$$L = \beta L_{ID} + \frac{1}{M} \sum_{j=1}^{M} L_{Att_j}, \tag{3}$$

where β is a parameter to balance the contribution of vehicle re-identification loss and attribute loss.

2.3 Feature Fusion via Correlative Sparse Ranking

Above, multi-view deep features of the same vehicle are obtained. In this subsection, based on their closely latent correlations, we formulate the multi-view feature fusion problem via a sparse coding framework due to its robustness to noise, and propose a correlative sparse representation to bridge the multi-view features generated from two subnetworks as shown in Fig. 1(b).

Model Formulation. The main idea of sparse coding is to represent a input vector approximately as weighted linear combination of a small number of basis vectors from the dictionary. These basis vectors thus capture high-level patterns in the input data, while the coefficients consist of the sparse representation of the input data. According to this principle, for each query sample, we calculate sparse representation α^k under the k-th channel, where $X^k \approx \boldsymbol{U}^k \alpha^k$, for $k = 1, \cdots, K$, K is the number of the views and $K = 2$ in this paper. The process above can be converted into a ℓ_1-norm sparsity constraint regularized least squares problem:

$$\min_{\alpha^k} \|X^k - \boldsymbol{U}^k \alpha^k\|_2^2 + \lambda^k \|\alpha^k\|_1, \tag{4}$$

where λ^k controls the trade-off between the ℓ_2-norm reconstruction error and the ℓ_1-norm sparsity constraint of the coefficients under the k-th view.

To explore the correlations of multi-view features, it is natural to punish the diversity between sparse coefficients from arbitrary two corresponding views, that is minimizing the Euclidean distance $\|\alpha^{k_1} - \alpha^{k_2}\|_2^2$ for arbitrary $k_1, k_2 \in 1, \ldots, K$ to find the collaborative representation from multi-views of the same vehicle. Thus, the correlative sparse ranking model can be formulated as:

$$\min_{\alpha^k} \underbrace{\sum_{k=1}^{K} \{\|X^k - \boldsymbol{U}^k \alpha^k\|_2^2 + \lambda_k \|\alpha^k\|_1\}}_{\text{sparse reconstruction item}} + \mu \underbrace{\sum_{k_1 \neq k_2} \|\alpha^{k_1} - \alpha^{k_2}\|_2^2}_{\text{correlation item}}, \quad \text{s.t.} \forall \alpha^k \succeq 0, \tag{5}$$

where μ is the trade-off parameter to balance the sparse reconstruction error and the pairwise correlation constraints. At last, the final sparse representation vector for one query to all gallery images is expressed as: $\alpha = \sum_{k=1}^{K} \alpha^k$.

Model Optimization. Due to the non-negativeness of α^k, Eq. (5) can be written as follows:

$$\min_{\alpha^k} \sum_{k=1}^{K} \{\|X^k - \boldsymbol{U}^k \alpha^k\|_2^2 + \lambda_k \alpha^k \mathbf{1}\} + \mu \sum_{k_1 \neq k_2} \|\alpha^{k_2} - \alpha^{k_2}\|_2^2, \quad \text{s.t.} \forall \alpha^k \succeq 0, \tag{6}$$

where $\mathbf{1}$ denotes the vector with all elements as 1. To solve Eq. (6), we convert it to an unconstrained form as:

$$\min_{\alpha^k} \sum_{k=1}^{K} \{\|X^k - \boldsymbol{U}^k \alpha^k\|_2^2 + \lambda_k \alpha^k \mathbf{1}\} + \mu \sum_{k_1 \neq k_2} \|\alpha^{k_1} - \alpha^{k_2}\|_2^2 + \psi(\alpha), \tag{7}$$

Algorithm 1. Optimization Procedure to Eq. (7)

Input: The feature vector X^k of query image q, the gallery feature matrix $\boldsymbol{U}^k$, $k = 1, \cdots, K$, the parameters λ, μ;
Set $\xi = 2.7 \times 10^5$, $\rho_0 = \rho_1 = 1$, $\varepsilon = 10^{-4}$, $maxIter = 200$, $r = 1$.
Output: α^k
1: **while** not converged **do**
2: Update Ω^k_{r+1} by $\Omega^k_{r+1} = \alpha^k_r + \frac{\rho_{r-1}-1}{\rho_r}(\alpha^k_r - \alpha^k_{r-1})$, where ρ_r is a positive sequence;
3: Update α^k_{r+1} by Eq.(10);
4: Update $\rho_{r+1} = \frac{1+\sqrt{1+4\rho_r^2}}{2}$;
5: Update r by $r = r + 1$;
6: Check the convergence condition: the maximum element change of α^k between two consecutive iterations is less than ε or maximum number of iterations reaches $maxIter$.
7: **return** α^k

where $\psi(\alpha^k_i)$ equals 1 if $\alpha^k_i \geq 0$, and 0 otherwise. α^k_i denotes the representation coefficient of gallery image h_i to the query sample from the k-th subnetwork. In this paper, we utilize the accelerated proximal gradient (APG) approach to optimize efficiently. We denote:

$$\begin{aligned} F &= \min_{\alpha^k} \|X^k - \boldsymbol{U}^k\alpha^k\|_2^2 + \lambda_k \alpha^k \mathbf{1} + \mu \sum_{k_1 \neq k_2} \|\alpha^{k_1} - \alpha^{k_2}\|_2^2, \\ J &= \psi(\alpha). \end{aligned} \tag{8}$$

Obviously, F is a differentiable convex function and J is a nonsmooth convex function. Therefore, according to the APG method, we obtain:

$$\alpha^k_{r+1} = \min_{\alpha^k} \frac{\xi}{2} \|\alpha^k - \Omega^k_{r+1} + \frac{\nabla F(\Omega^k_{r+1})}{\xi}\|_2^2 + J(\alpha^k), \tag{9}$$

where ξ is the Lipschitz constant, r indicates the current iteration, and α^k_{r+1} denotes the sparse representation coefficients of the query image at the $(r+1)$-th iteration based on the k-th subnetworks. $\Omega^k_{r+1} = \alpha^k_r + \frac{\rho_{r-1}-1}{\rho_r}(\alpha^k_r - \alpha^k_{r-1})$, where ρ_r is a positive sequence with $\rho_0 = \rho_1 = 1$. Equation (9) can be solved by:

$$\alpha^k_{r+1} = \max(0, \Omega^k_{r+1} - \frac{\nabla F(\Omega^k_{r+1})}{\xi}). \tag{10}$$

Algorithm 1 summarizes the whole optimization procedure.

After obtaining the collaborative sparse representations α for each query image, we aggregate them as a representation coefficients matrix $\mathbf{A} \in \mathcal{R}^{Q \times N}$. The entry $\alpha_{q,i}$ in $\mathbf{A}$ denotes the representation coefficient of a gallery image h_i to the query image q. Then, the original distance between two vehicle images q and h_i can be calculated by $d(q, h_i) = 1/\alpha_{q,i}$. Therefore, the initial ranking to query sample q is $L(q, H) = \{h^0_1, h^0_2, \cdots, h^0_N\}$, where $d(q, h^0_i) < d(q, h^0_{i+1})$.

2.4 ECN Based Re-ranking

The initial ranking directly compares the distance between the two images, and ignores the correlations among similar images. In order to enhance retrieval performance, here we calculate the distance by averaging the expanded neighbors of probe and gallery image pairs, that is the Expanded Cross Neighborhood (ECN) [10] distance, as shown in Fig. 1(c).

Formally, given the initial ranking $L(q, H) = \{h_1^0, h_2^0, \cdots, h_N^0\}$ for arbitrary query image q, the expanded neighbors of q are defined as the multi-set $N(q, R)$ including two parts: $N(q, l)$ and $N(l, p)$ which represent the top l samples of the query q and the top p neighbors of each of the elements in set $N(q, l)$ respectively:

$$\begin{aligned} N(q,l) &= \{h_i^0 | i = 1, 2, \cdots, l\}; \\ N(l,p) &= \{N(h_1^0, p), \cdots, N(h_l^0, p)\}. \end{aligned} \tag{11}$$

Then we expand the neighbor of each gallery image as a multi-set $N(h_i, R)$ in the same manner, where R is the total number of neighbors in the set $N(h_i, R)$, and $R = l + l \times p$. Finally, the ECN [10] distance of an image pair (q, h_i) is:

$$ECN(q, h_i) = \frac{1}{2R} \sum_{j=1}^{R} [d(qN_j, h_i) + d(h_iN_j, q)], \tag{12}$$

where qN_j is the j-th neighbor in the query expanded neighbor set $N(q, R)$ and h_iN_j is the j-th neighbor in the i-th gallery image expanded neighbor set $N(h_i, R)$. In practise, $l = 4$, $p = 3$.

3 Experiment

3.1 Experiment Settings

Dataset. We evaluate our method on recent public benchmark dataset VeRi-776 dataset [7] for vehicle re-identification. The dataset contains 51035 images of 776 vehicles captured by 20 cameras in real-world traffic surveillance environment. Specifically, there are 37778 images of 576 vehicles for training, 11579 images of 200 vehicles for testing and 1678 for query. Each vehicle is captured by 2-18 cameras along a circular road. Furthermore, each vehicle image is annotated with corresponding attributes e.g. type and color.

Parameters. During the deep feature extraction, we resize all training images into 256×256 pixels and extract randomly 224×224 patches to data augmentation. We train our models using stochastic gradient descent (SGD) with a batch size of 16, momentum of 0.9, and weight decay of $\lambda = 0.0001$. The learning rate is set to 0.1 at the beginning and is changed to 0.01 in the last few epochs. $\beta = 10$ in Eq. (3) and $\lambda_1 = 0.1$, $\lambda_2 = 0.1$ in Eq. (5).

Evaluation Metric. Following the evaluation protocol of re-identification work [8,11], the mean average precision (mAP), Rank-1 and Rank-5 accuracies are utilized to evaluate the performance of re-identification in camera network.

3.2 Evaluation Results

Comparison with Vehicle Re-ID Methods. We evaluate the performance of the proposed method comparing with the state-of-the-art methods on VeRi-776 dataset and report the results in Table 1. Generally speaking, our method outperforms most of existing state-of-the-art methods. Although the mAP of Siamese+Path-LSTM [11] is comparative to ours, it is worth noting that it has utilized additional spatio-temporal path information. Even though, the Rank-1 and Rank-5 accuracies of ours are significantly higher (without any path information). The specifications of the compared methods in Table 1 are described as follows:

Table 1. The mAP, Rank-1 and Rank-5 comparison on VeRi-776 dataset (in %).

Method	mAP	Rank-1	Rank-5
(1) LOMO [5]	9.64	25.33	46.48
(2) BOW-CN [18]	12.20	33.91	53.69
(3) GoogLeNet [14]	17.89	52.32	72.17
(4) FACT [7]	18.49	50.95	73.48
(5) FACT+Plate-SNN+STR [8]	27.70	61.44	78.78
(6) NuFACT [9]	48.47	76.76	**91.42**
(7) Siamese-Visual [11]	29.48	41.12	60.31
(8) Siamese+Path-LSTM [11]	**58.27**	**83.49**	90.04
Ours	**58.21**	**90.52**	**93.38**

(1) **LOMO** [5]. Local Maximal Occurrence Representation (LOMO) is a local feature descriptor coping with illumination variations and viewpoint changes.
(2) **BOW-CN** [18]. Bag-of-Word based hand-crafted features for vehicle Re-ID.
(3) **GoogLeNet** [14]. Pre-trained on ImageNet [3] and then fine-tuned on the CompCars dataset for semantic feature representation of vehicles.
(4) **FACT** [7]. Fused Appearance features including color, texture and shape.
(5) **FACT+Plate-SNN+STR** [8]. **FACT** [7] with additional plate verification and spatio-temporal relations (STR) based on Siamese Neural Network (SNN).
(6) **NuFACT** [9]. The null space based **FACT** [7] to integrate the multi-level appearance features of vehicles and high-level attribute features.
(7) **Siamese-Visual** [11]. Siamese-CNN with only visual information.
(8) **Siamese+Path-LSTM** [11]. Siamese-CNN together with Path LSTM with visual-spatio-temporal path information.

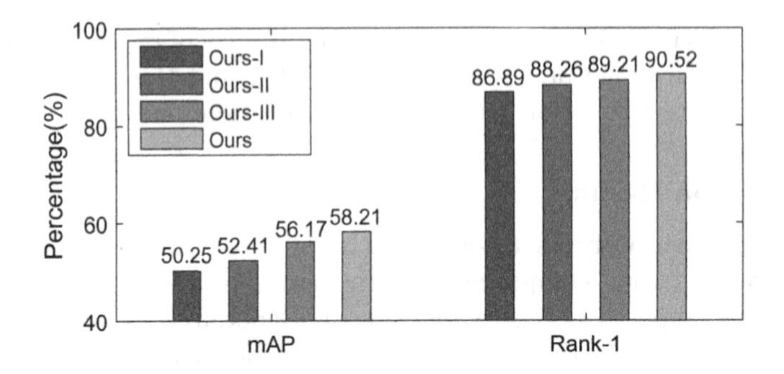

Fig. 2. Component analysis of our method.

Component Analysis. We further evaluate the components of the proposed method with its variants as shown in Fig. 2, where, Ours: the proposed method. Ours-I: only GoogleNet subnetwork without correlative sparse ranking or ECN re-ranking. Ours-II: only ResNet-50 subnetwork without correlative sparse ranking or ECN re-ranking. Ours-III: correlative sparse ranking on two subnetworks but without ECN re-ranking. From Fig. 2 we can see: (1) ResNet-50 subnetwork outperforms the GoogleNet. (2) By correlatively learning on two subnetworks, it can improve the performance of the re-identification. (3) The re-ranking technique can further boost the performance on both mAP and Rank-1.

4 Conclusions

In this paper, inspired by multi-channel visual cognition of human eyes, we discover the correlation between multi-view deep features for vehicle Re-ID. In deep feature extraction, two CNN based attributes aggregated re-identification networks are trained to generate the multi-view deep features. Then we propose the correlative sparse ranking method to jointly learn the coupled sparse coefficients for multi-view features. Furthermore, we re-rank the initial ranking via ECN distance to boost the recognition accuracy. Experimental results on benchmark VeRi-776 demonstrate the promising performance of our method. In the future, we shall further integrate the path and plate information for vehicle Re-ID.

Acknowledgment. This work was partially supported by the National Natural Science Foundation of China (61502006, 61602001 and 61671018), the Key Natural Science Project of Anhui Provincial Education Department (KJ2018A0023) and and Open Project of Anhui University (ADXXBZ201511).

References

1. He, K., Zhang, X., Ren, S., Sun, J.: Deep residual learning for image recognition. In: Proceedings of the IEEE Conference on Computer Vision and Pattern Recognition, pp. 770–778 (2016)

2. Kanaci, A., Zhu, X., Gong, S.: Vehicle re-identification by fine-grained cross-level deep learning. In: Proceedings 5th Activity Monitoring by Multiple Distributed Sensing Workshop, British Machine Vision Conference, London, September 2017
3. Krizhevsky, A., Sutskever, I., Hinton, G.E.: Imagenet classification with deep convolutional neural networks. In: Advances in Neural Information Processing Systems, pp. 1097–1105 (2012)
4. Li, Y., Li, Y., Yan, H., Liu, J.: Deep joint discriminative learning for vehicle re-identification and retrieval. In: IEEE SigPort (2017)
5. Liao, S., Hu, Y., Zhu, X., Li, S.Z.: Person re-identification by local maximal occurrence representation and metric learning. In: Proceedings of the IEEE Conference on Computer Vision and Pattern Recognition, pp. 2197–2206 (2015)
6. Liu, H., Tian, Y., Yang, Y., Pang, L., Huang, T.: Deep relative distance learning: tell the difference between similar vehicles. In: Proceedings of the IEEE Conference on Computer Vision and Pattern Recognition, pp. 2167–2175 (2016)
7. Liu, X., Liu, W., Ma, H., Fu, H.: Large-scale vehicle re-identification in urban surveillance videos. In: 2016 IEEE International Conference on Multimedia and Expo (ICME), pp. 1–6 (2016)
8. Liu, X., Liu, W., Mei, T., Ma, H.: A deep learning-based approach to progressive vehicle re-identification for urban surveillance. In: Leibe, B., Matas, J., Sebe, N., Welling, M. (eds.) ECCV 2016. LNCS, vol. 9906, pp. 869–884. Springer, Cham (2016). https://doi.org/10.1007/978-3-319-46475-6_53
9. Liu, X., Liu, W., Mei, T., Ma, H.: Provid: progressive and multimodal vehicle reidentification for large-scale urban surveillance. IEEE Trans. Multimed. **20**, 645–658 (2018)
10. Sarfraz, M.S., Schumann, A., Eberle, A., Stiefelhagen, R.: A pose-sensitive embedding for person re-identification with expanded cross neighborhood re-ranking. arXiv preprint arXiv:1711.10378 (2017)
11. Shen, Y., Xiao, T., Li, H., Yi, S., Wang, X.: Learning deep neural networks for vehicle re-id with visual-spatio-temporal path proposals. CoRR. vol. abs/1708.03918 (2017)
12. Wang, Z., et al.: Orientation invariant feature embedding and spatial temporal regularization for vehicle re-identification. In: Proceedings of the IEEE Conference on Computer Vision and Pattern Recognition, pp. 379–387 (2017)
13. Yan, Y., et al.: Cognitive fusion of thermal and visible imagery for effective detection and tracking of pedestrians in videos. Cogn. Comput. **10**, 94–104 (2018)
14. Yang, L., Luo, P., Change Loy, C., Tang, X.: A large-scale car dataset for fine-grained categorization and verification. In: Proceedings of the IEEE Conference on Computer Vision and Pattern Recognition, pp. 3973–3981 (2015)
15. Zapletal, D., Herout, A.: Vehicle re-identification for automatic video traffic surveillance. In: Proceedings of the IEEE Conference on Computer Vision and Pattern Recognition Workshops, pp. 25–31 (2016)
16. Zhang, Y., Liu, D., Zha, Z.J.: Improving triplet-wise training of convolutional neural network for vehicle re-identification. In: 2017 IEEE International Conference on Multimedia and Expo (ICME), pp. 1386–1391 (2017)
17. Zhao, C., Li, X., Ren, J., Marshall, S.: Improved sparse representation using adaptive spatial support for effective target detection in hyperspectral imagery. Int. J. Rem. Sens. **34**, 8669–8684 (2013)
18. Zheng, L., Shen, L., Tian, L., Wang, S., Wang, J., Tian, Q.: Scalable person re-identification: a benchmark. In: Proceedings of the IEEE International Conference on Computer Vision, pp. 1116–1124 (2015)

Fully Automatic Synaptic Cleft Detection and Segmentation from EM Images Based on Deep Learning

Bei Hong[1,2], Jing Liu[2,3], Weifu Li[1,2], Chi Xiao[2,3], Qiwei Xie[2,4], and Hua Han[2,3,4](✉)

[1] Faculty of Mathematics and Statistics, Hubei University, Wuhan 430062, China
[2] Institute of Automation, Chinese Academy of Sciences, Beijing 100190, China
{qiwei.xie,hua.han}@ia.ac.cn
[3] University of Chinese Academy of Sciences, Huairou, China
[4] CAS Center for Excellence in Brain Science and Intelligence Technology, Beijing, China

Abstract. The synapse, which is the carrier of neurotransmitter molecules to transmit and store information, is believed to be the key to the reconstruction of the neural circuit. To date, electron microscope (EM) is considered as one of the most important tools for observing and analyzing synaptic structures because they can clearly observe the internal structure of cells. Consequently, many meaningful researches are focused on how to detect and segment the synapses from EM images. In this paper, we propose a novel and effective method to automatically detect and segment the synaptic clefts by using Mask R-CNN. On this base, we utilize the context cues in adjacent sections to eliminate the misleading results. We apply the method to the CREMI challenge and the results demonstrate that our method is effective in segmenting the synaptic clefts of the drosophila. Specifically, we rank first in sample B+ dataset, and the CREMI score is 86.50 which outperforms most of state-of-the-art methods by a large margin.

Keywords: Mask R-CNN · Synaptic cleft · Electron microscopes Segmentation

1 Introduction

It is widely accepted that the synapses are essential to neuronal function for their specified manner by which neuron passes signals to target cell. Analysis

This paper is supported by National Science Foundation of China (No. 61673381, No. 61201050, No. 61701497, No. 11771130), Scientific Instrument Developing Project of Chinese Academy of Sciences (No. YZ201671), Bureau of International Cooperation, CAS (No. 153D31KYSB20170059), and Special Program of Beijing Municipal Science & Technology Commission (No. Z161100000216146).

J. Ren et al. (Eds.): BICS 2018, LNAI 10989, pp. 64–74, 2018.
https://doi.org/10.1007/978-3-030-00563-4_7

of synapse size, morphology, distribution, amount and other information contributes essential information to the understanding of its function and plasticity [10]. Besides, scientists have recently discovered that synaptic abnormalities are associated with autism and alzheimer's disease [9]. Neural circuit seeks to build a graph, neurons with different properties and functions are considered as vertices, while the synapses which are the connection between two neurons as edges. Accordingly, analyzing the three-dimensional (3D) structure of synapses is absolutely an important step in the reconstruction of neural circuits. However, the extracting of brain wiring from large-scale volume is time-consuming and requires considerable manual labor. Hence, fully automatic detection and segmentation of synapses is of vital necessity in cell physiology and neural circuit reconstruction.

High resolution, three-dimensional (3D) representations of cellular ultrastructure are essential in all fields of cell biology. Fortunately, benefiting from the technology of rapid development of electron microscopy (EM), we can look closely into the fine synapse structure with high resolution. As shown in Fig. 1, synapse is composed of presynaptic membrane, postsynaptic membrane and synaptic cleft. Many meaningful synaptic researches were done under the electron microscope images. Typically, Carlos Becker et al. proposed an approach designed to take such contextual cues into account and emulate the human ability to synapses from regions that merely share a similar texture [10]. Kreshuk et al. used a random forest classifier on hand-picked features to detect synapses in EM images [3]. Zhang et al. trained an AdaBoost classifier to optimize detection results in conjunction with context cues, then segmented synaptic clefts using morphological and curve fitting methods [16]. Xiao et al. adopted the Faster R-CNN to detect the synapses in EM images, then Grab Cut was used to segment the synapse [17].

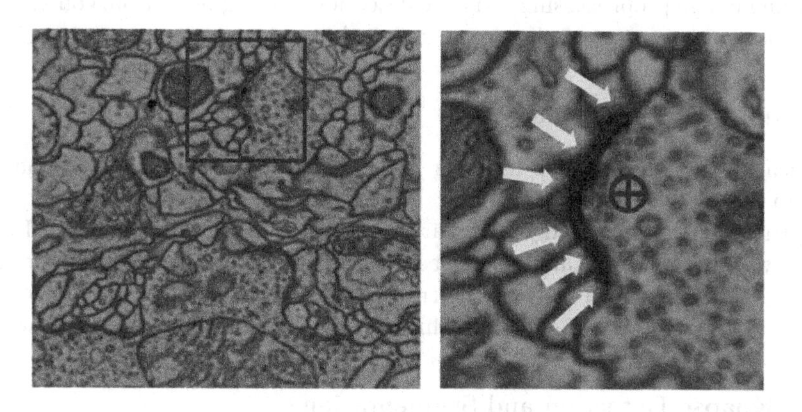

Fig. 1. The structure of the drosophila brain synapse. The red circle, yellow arrow and blue line represent the pre-synaptic, post-synaptic and synaptic cleft respectively (Color figure online)

Despite of the preferable detection and segmentation results for mammal synapses, as for synapses in drosophila brain, the performance of existing methods is not known yet due to the polyadic nature, involving multiple post-synaptic partners for a given pre-synaptic site [4,8]. As we can see from Fig. 1, automatic segmentation of drosophila brain synaptic clefts poses a unique challenge because the membrane and the cleft are hard to distinguish. It is essential to propose a method with stronger characterization ability to detect drosophila's brain synapses. Fortunately, recent years have witnessed the great success of CNNs in the domain of computer vision, and many other fields attempt to apply deep learning to solve some difficult problems, including medical image segmentation and biological structure detection. There are some successful representative work, such as membrane detection in EM images [6], organ segmentation [15], mitochondrial segmentation [12], and etc. Inspired by this, we use the improved Mask R-CNN for synaptic clefts detection and segmentation, which can be trained end to end producing detection and segmentation results in parallel. On this base, we utilize the context cues in the continuous sections and morphological post processing to refine the outputs of network.

The remainder of this study is outlined as follows: Sect. 2 presents a novel and practical method for synapse detection and segmentation from drosophila's brain. Then, the datasets and experimental details are presented in Sect. 3. The experimental results are shown to verify the effectiveness of proposed method in Sect. 4. Finally, in Sect. 5, this study's conclusions are made, and some future research issues are discussed.

2 Methodology

In this section, we present our proposed algorithm that consists of four parts, including image preprocessing, synapse detection and segmentation, context cues correction and post processing for segmentation.

2.1 Image Preprocessing

The learning ability of deep learning has a great deal to do with the quantity of data. The tiny amount of training dataset tends to fit a model without great robustness, so it is critically necessary to expand the limited dataset. In our paper, we enlarge the training dataset by data augmentation, including rotation, flipping, adding noise, and grayscale transformation. After data enrichment, the data size is increased by ten times which is sufficient for training the network.

2.2 Synapse Detection and Segmentation

In recent years, deep learning has become an important technology in the field of neuroscience. Different from hand-crafted features, such as hog feature [5] and sift feature [11], deep learning is actually an effective method to extract features directly through the raw data and therefore the learned features are more robust and accurate than traditional manually designed features. Due to the complexity of background in EM images, it is hard to distinguish synaptic clefts from various subcellular structures. If we segment clefts directly, that is to say, the outputs of network are binary segmentation results which are same size as the inputs of network, other structures are very likely to be considered as synaptic clefts. This way will reduce the accuracy of recognition, so it is necessary to put forward a novel and targeted method based on the situation. Synapse is comprised of axons with vesicles and dendrites appearing bright. Taking the special structure of synapse into account, we can detect the synapses' composition with boxes firstly, then segmentation is performed under every box. In this paper, we adopt the Mask R-CNN network to detect and segment synapses, the architecture of proposed network is illustrated in Fig. 2, and there are three main reasons for consideration:

1. Mask R-CNN is an instance segmentation network [7]. Unlike the traditional segmentation network, Mask R-CNN produces the detection boxes and segmentation results in parallel and almost no additional computation produces. In contrast to the way of segmentation by image processing, such processing not only saves time in reconstructing the synaptic three-dimensional structure, but also reduces the rate of false positives detection for segmentation problems because it is more targeted with less interruption and then contributes to more accurate segmentation.
2. Mask R-CNN is developed based on Faster R-CNN [14]. Compared to Faster R-CNN and some other methods of machine learning, such as adaboost and random forest, it has a deeper feature extraction network which can be trained from raw data to learn features of synapses. In addition, the feature pyramid network (FPN) [13] is used to improve the detection results of small synapses.
3. Mask R-CNN is an end to end model, that is to say, we input raw data to the model of which the outputs are the synapse detection box and the corresponding segmentation mask. It requires less professional knowledge about synapse and promotes efficiency of the reconstruction of the large scale neural circuits under the electron microscope images.

2.3 Context Cues Correction

Due to the diversity of biological tissues, cell internal structure is likely to present similar but different, thus some local ultrastructure that is similar to the synaptic cleft can be detected as synapses inevitably. And our network performs detection and segmentation on 2D images, so it is essential to reduce the false positive detection rate by using the context cues of the continuous section. Considering that the dataset provided from CREMI challenge is stitched and aligned, there is not too much deviation for the locations of synapses in adjacent layers. And synapse is a spatial structure with a size of $\sim$300 nm, so we can find a complete synapse displaying in different sections, while the thickness of a section is only

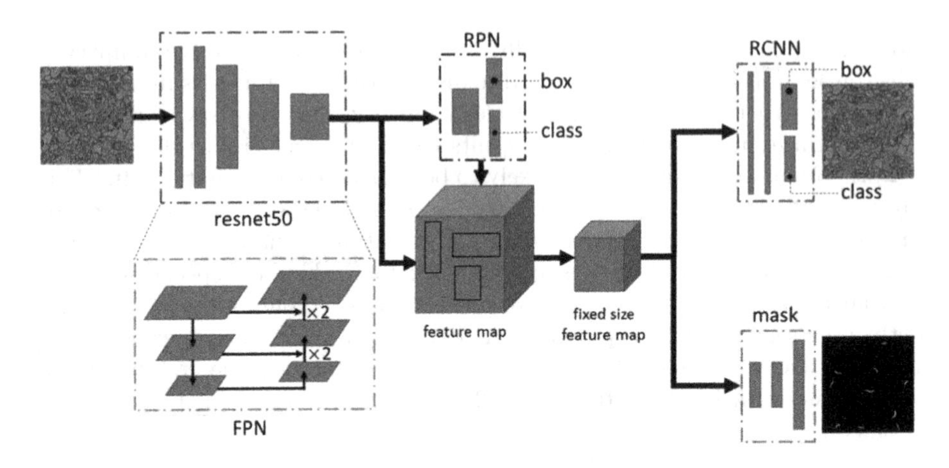

Fig. 2. The architecture of the proposed network. The purple dotted box represents the feature extraction network which uses FPN shown as blue dotted box, the black dotted box includes the two output layers of RPN, the red dotted box generates the synapse detection box and the green dotted box produces the segmentation result based on each detection box. (Color figure online)

40 nm here [16]. For above two reasons, we adopt a new selecting method that combines contextual information in this paper.

We define $L = \{L_1, L_2, \cdots, L_n\}$ as the set of continuous electron microscope sections, that n is the total number of layers,and $L_i \in L$ is ith layer. $T_i = \{T_i^1, T_i^2, \cdots, T_i^{m_i}\}$ represents the detection box set of the ith layer, which the m_i represents the total number of detection boxes of the ith layers, and $T_i^j \in T_i$ is the jth detection box of the ith layer. The main procedure is as follows:

- Denote L_i as the initial layer and set $count = 0$.
- Define the center of the T_i^j as C_{ij}.
- The distance between the T_i^j and the T_k^l is defined as D_{ij}^{kl}, the formula is:

$$D_{ij}^{kl} = \|C_{ij} - C_{kl}\|_2, l = 1, 2 \cdots m_k \tag{1}$$

  that the $k \in \{i-2, i-1, i+1, i+2\}$.
- The closest distance between the T_i^j and the all detection boxes L_k is calculated as:

$$dist_{ij}^k = \arg\min_{m_k} \left\{D_{ij}^{k1}, D_{ij}^{k2}, \cdots, D_{ij}^{km_k}\right\} \tag{2}$$

- if $dist_{ij}^k < \theta$, then the $count = count + 1$, which the θ is set as the distance threshold.

In this article, we consider the information of its adjacent five-layer slices for each slice. The distance threshold θ is set as 100 and we assume that the displacement of the same synapse in adjacent layers will not exceed the threshold. As shown in Fig. 3, if the detection box appears more three times in continuous

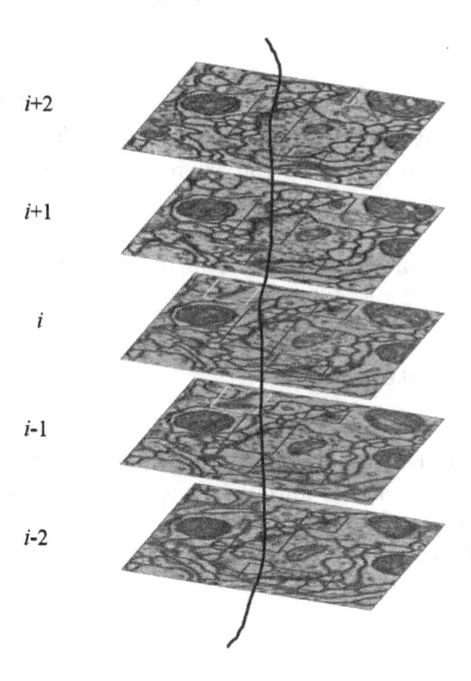

Fig. 3. Correction by context cue. The red box appears five times in continuous five layers, while the yellow box appears two times, so we remove the yellow box and corresponding segmentation result. (Color figure online)

five layers, we believe that the network detects a true synapse and the detection box and the corresponding segmentation result will be kept. In contrast, the detection box and corresponding segmentation result will be removed.

2.4 Post Processing for Segmentation

We have obtained the segmentation results by above network. Although the network can get a relatively well segmentation result, but in this subsection we focus on optimizing the segmentation result by morphological processing in order to obtain a better effect. In this paper, we adopt the image morphological processing method to eliminate some fragmentary areas for each detection box, and then use open operation to eliminate the burrs in synaptic segmentation in order to achieve smoothness.

3 Experimental

In this section, we provide some details related to the experimental dataset and experimental setup.

3.1 Dataset

In this subsection, the experiments are performed on the serial section Transmission Electron Microscopy (ssTEM) datasets that comes from MICCAI Challenge on Circuit Reconstruction from Electron Microscopy Images [2]. MICCAI Challenge provides three datasets taken from different regions of adult fly brain, each consisting of two (5) nm^3 volumes (a training volume and a testing volume), and each volume with a resolution of $4\,nm \times 4\,nm \times 40\,nm$ consists of 125 slices and the size of each slice is 1250×1250.

3.2 Experimental Setup

We implement the Mask R-CNN using the Keras open-source deep learning library [1]. During the training phase, we use the nesterov momentum for better convergence, the learning rate is initially set as 10^{-4} and decreases by a factor 10 when learning stagnates, and the epoch is set to 50. The training and testing tasks are conducted on a server equipped with an Intel i7 CPU of 512 GB main memory and a Tesla K40 GPU.

4 Result

In this section, we conduct several experiments to verify the proposed method. First of all, it's worth mentioning that we evaluate the performance with metrics that defined in CREMI competition. As for the reconstruction of the 3D synapses, we're more concerned about whether the length of the synaptic cleft is correct rather than the classification of the pixel level, which is to say, we count all voxels that are labeled as a synaptic cleft and fall beyond a threshold distance from ground truth labels as false positives (FP), and all voxels in the ground truth that are labeled as synaptic cleft and fall beyond a threshold distance from test labels as false negatives (FN). As is shown in Fig. 4, any detection voxel inside a grown ground truth region is counted as a true positive(TP). In addition, the challenge marks the average distance of any found cleft voxel to the closest ground truth cleft voxel as ADGT, and marks the average distance of any ground truth cleft voxel to the closest found cleft voxel as ADF, then the CREMI score is calculated as:

$$CREMI\ score = \frac{ADGT + ADF}{2} \tag{3}$$

Obviously, the lower score implies the better result for segmentation. We present some detection and segmentation results in Fig. 5. Because the CREMI challenge do not provide the ground truth for test dataset, we can't intuitively show the comparison of our results with the ground truth. In order to measure our approach, we submit the results and the submission is evaluated online, the result is described in Table 1. We evaluate our method in three datasets, which are located in different brain regions, and the morphology of synaptic clefts has

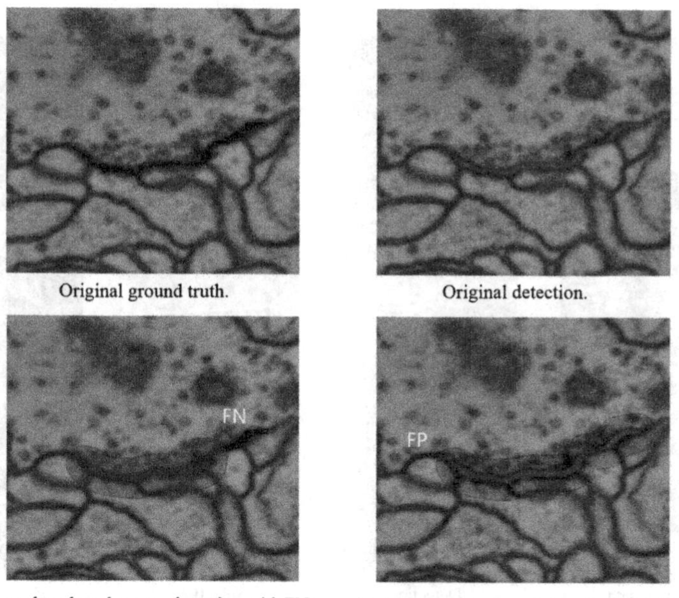

Fig. 4. The metric of the CREMI challenge

great distinction in each dataset. As seen in the Table 1, the CREMI score of the sample B+ ranks first among the 23 submitted models. In sample C+, our method can obtain the comparable result with teams of lower scores. These experiments demonstrate the effectiveness of our approach directly. The result of sample A+ is not good enough, we analyze that it is owing to the synapse is small in sample A+, which makes the detection result of the proposed network not satisfied. Finally we import our segmentation results into software AMIRA for 3D visualization of synaptic clefts, as shown in Fig. 6.

Table 1. Segmentation results on CREMI challenge

Methods	Sample A+	Sample B+	Sample C+	Total score
JRC	60.74	125.41	30.47	72.21
DIVE	65.74	174.72	34.93	88.46
SGD	189.37	129.03	35.90	118.10
IAL	190.85	184.43	37.92	137.73
Our method	148.82	**86.50**	35.02	90.11

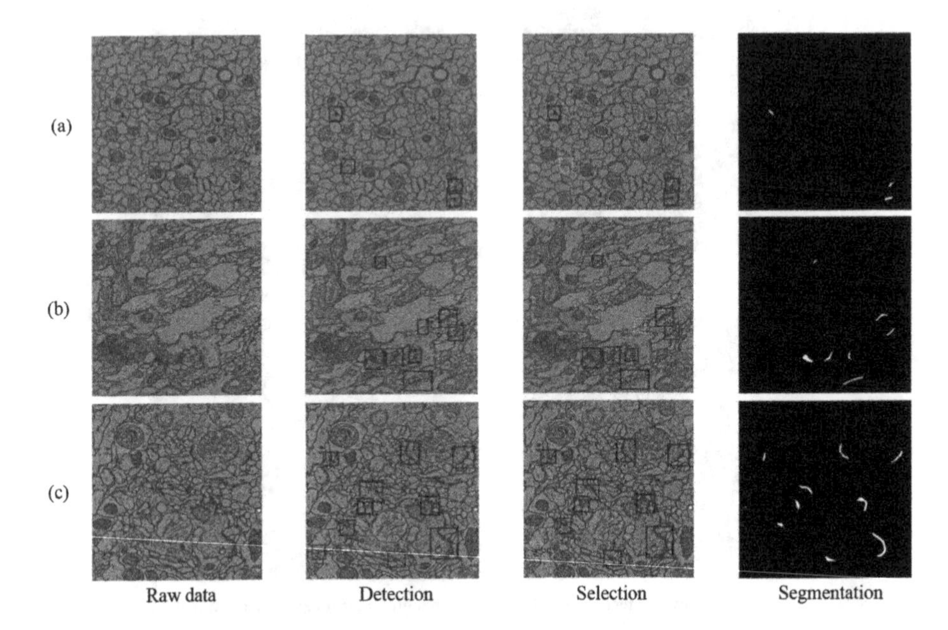

Fig. 5. (a)(b)(c) represent the sample A+, B+, C+ respectively. From left to right: raw data, detection result for network indicated by green rectangles, context cue correction result indicated by red rectangles, and the final segmentation label. (Color figure online)

Fig. 6. 3D visualization of synaptic clefts.

5 Conclusion

Since the reconstruction of synapses is an important step in the building of neural circuits, we present a novel and effective method to detect and segment synapses. Firstly, we adopt the Mask R-CNN to detect and segment synapses, and then combine the context cues to reserve the true detection boxes for a lower false positive rate. Finally, a simple post processing is adopted to optimize the segmentation results. Experimental results demonstrate the effectiveness of the proposed method. Along the line of present research, we plan to improve the classification branch of this network to achieve a better accuracy of detection. In addition, attempting to expand the network to 3D which can get the reconstruction directly is also under our future research.

References

1. Keras: Deep learning library for theano and tensorflow (2015). http://keras.io/
2. Miccai challenge oncircuit reconstruction from electron microscopy images (2016). http://cremi.org/
3. Becker, C., Ali, K., Knott, G., Fua, P.: Learning context cues for synapse segmentation. IEEE Trans. Med. Imag. **32**(10), 1864–1877 (2013)
4. Cardona, A., et al.: An integrated micro- and macroarchitectural analysis of the drosophila brain by computer-assisted serial section electron microscopy, **8**(10), e1000502 (2010)
5. Dalal, N., Triggs, B.: Histograms of oriented gradients for human detection. In: CVPR IEEE Computer Society Conference on 2005, pp. 886–893 (2005)
6. Dan, C.C., Giusti, A., Gambardella, L.M.: Schmidhuber: deep neural networks segment neuronal membranes in electron microscopy images. Adv. Neural Inf. Process. Syst. **25**, 2852–2860 (2012)
7. He, K., Gkioxari, G., Dollár, P., Girshick, R.: Mask R-CNN (2017)
8. Huang, G.B., Scheffer, L.K., Plaza, S.M.: Fully-automatic synapse prediction and validation on a large data set (2016)
9. Kanner, L.: Irrelevant and metaphorical language in early infantile autism. Am. J. Psychiatry **151**(2), 161–164 (1994)
10. Kreshuk, A.: Automated detection and segmentation of synaptic contacts in nearly isotropic serial electron microscopy images. PLoS One **6**(10), e24899 (2011)
11. Kumar, P., Henikoff, S., Ng, P.C.: Predicting the effects of coding non-synonymous variants on protein function using the sift algorithm. Nat. Protoc. **4**(7), 1073–1081 (2009)
12. Li, W., Deng, H., Rao, Q., Xie, Q., Chen, X., Han, H.: An automated pipeline for mitochondrial segmentation on atum-sem stacks. J. Bioinform. Comput. Biol. **15**(3), 1750015 (2017)
13. Lin, T.Y., Dollar, P., Girshick, R., He, K., Hariharan, B., Belongie, S.: Feature pyramid networks for object detection, pp. 936–944 (2016)
14. Ren, S., He, K., Girshick, R., Sun, J.: Faster R-CNN: towards real-time object detection with region proposal networks. In: International Conference on Neural Information Processing Systems, pp. 91–99 (2015)

15. Roth, H.R., Farag, A., Lu, L., Turkbey, E.B., Summers, R.M.: Deep convolutional networks for pancreas segmentation in CT imaging, **9413**(9), 476–484 (2015)
16. Sun, M., Zhang, D., Guo, H., Deng, H., Li, W., Xie, Q.: 3D-reconstruction of synapses based on EM images. In: IEEE International Conference on Mechatronics and Automation, pp. 1959–1964 (2016)
17. Xiao, C., Rao, Q., Chen, X., Han, H.: 3D reconstruction of synapses with deep learning based on EM images. In: SPIE Medical Imaging, p. 101324N (2017)

Deep Background Subtraction of Thermal and Visible Imagery for Pedestrian Detection in Videos

Yijun Yan[1], Huimin Zhao[2,3], Fu-Jen Kao[4], Valentin Masero Vargas[5], Sophia Zhao[1], and Jinchang Ren[1](✉)

[1] Department of Electronic and Electrical Engineering, University of Strathclyde, Glasgow, UK
jinchang.ren@strath.ac.uk
[2] School of Computer Science, Guangdong Polytechnic University, Guangzhou, China
[3] The Guangzhou Key Laboratory of Digital Content Processing and Security Technologies, Guangzhou, China
[4] Institute of Biophotonics, National Yang-Ming University, Taipei, Taiwan ROC
[5] Department of Computer Systems and Telematics Engineering, Universidad de Extremadura, Badajoz, Spain

Abstract. In this paper, we introduce an efficient framework to subtract the background from both visible and thermal imagery for pedestrians' detection in the urban scene. We use a deep neural network (DNN) to train the background subtraction model. For the training of the DNN, we first generate an initial background map and then employ randomly 5% video frames, background map, and manually segmented ground truth. Then we apply a cognition-based post-processing to further smooth the foreground detection result. We evaluate our method against our previous work and 11 recently widely cited method on three challenge video series selected from a publicly available color-thermal benchmark dataset OCTBVS. Promising results have been shown that the proposed DNN-based approach can successfully detect the pedestrians with good shape in most scenes regardless of illuminate changes and occlusion problem.

Keywords: Deep neural network (DNN) · Video salient objects
Pedestrian detection

1 Introduction

Background subtraction is always a crucial step for pedestrian detection. For outdoor surveillance in the urban setting, there are a tremendous amount of available video data. However, most data such as background scenery are redundant, only pedestrians are meaningful information and are necessary to extract. Meanwhile, if the background scenery can be get rid of, both storage and computing resources will be saved. For pedestrian detection, visible camera and thermal imagery are two popularly used sources of image modalities, though not necessarily in a combined solution [5].

J. Ren et al. (Eds.): BICS 2018, LNAI 10989, pp. 75–84, 2018.
https://doi.org/10.1007/978-3-030-00563-4_8

However, either visible image or thermal image has their advantages and disadvantages. The visible image can show detailed color information, but the two biggest challenge for visible images are hard shadow and illumination change. Although many background subtraction methods have been explored in recent years, the performance is still not good enough when facing these challenges. Since the object is detected by its temperature and radiated heat, thermal image can eliminate the influence of color and illumination changes on the objects' appearance [10] in any weather conditions and at both day and night time. However, in some cases e.g. occlusions, the thermal camera may fail to detect the object properly. Moreover, it will detect any objects with surface temperature. Therefore, in this paper, we present a deep pedestrian detection model that fuses the information from both visible and thermal images.

Deep learning technique is a very hot topic recently and has been widely explored in many areas [7, 20, 25]. Fusion strategy is also very popular in many researches (e.g. image retrieval [21, 22], image recognition [4], ROI detection [14, 15, 27], saliency detection [23], etc.) since it can help break the limitation of the single feature. In our work, we first generate the background map for both visible and thermal video sequences. Then, we extract fused features of both visible and thermal image by a DNN to predict the foreground map for pedestrian detection. To prepare the training data patches for DNN, we select 5% video frames and over-segment each video frame, corresponding ground truth and background map into a large number of subsets of the scene. Finally, a cognition-based refinement is applied to smooth the fore-ground map from DNN.

The outline of this paper is as follows: Sect. 2 illustrates the framework of the proposed method. Section 3 describes the detail of our DNN model. Experimental results are presented and discussed in Sect. 4. Finally, some concluding remarks and future work are summarized in Sect. 5.

2 Overview of the Proposed Method

In this paper, we proposed a DNN-based background subtraction model for foreground detection of pedestrians on both visible and thermal video sequences. In the first step, we generate an initial background map for visible and thermal video frames, respectively. Then we over-segment each frame into plenty of regions which overlap with each other. To achieve that, we apply a moving window of size 64 * 64 on each frame (see 'Data preparation' in Fig. 1). Then the train image patches can be obtained in which the information of visible frames, visible background, thermal frames, thermal background and ground truth are included (see 'Training data patches' in Fig. 1). After the deep neural network is trained, we input both visible and thermal frame to the network and get the foreground detection result of pedestrians.

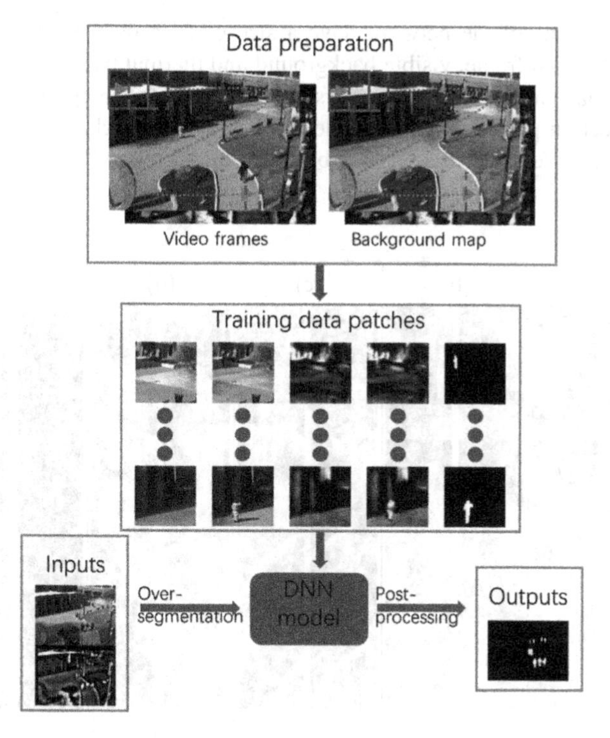

Fig. 1. The framework of our proposed DNN-based background subtraction method.

3 DNN-Based Foreground Detection

We train our proposed DNN with pairs of visible and thermal image patches from video and their background frames. In this section, the data preparation step for network training and network architectures will be explained in detail.

3.1 Data Preparation

To train the DNN, our training data patches consist of the video frame, background map and ground truth. In order to generate background map for visible and thermal image, we compute a median map of N frames randomly selected from the video sequence. Although this pixel-wise temporal median filtering doesn't work very well if there are a lot of moving objects in the scene [1], it works very well in our selected video frames. Because, pedestrians don't move very fast in these frames, and the number of pedestrians is not too much. The other advantage of this method is its simplicity. It doesn't need too much computation cost.

To generate the image patches of visible and thermal video frames, we first random select 5% data samples from the video sequences, which contains various challenging video scenes and their ground truth segmentation. Then we segment each frame into plenty of subsets of a scene with size 64 * 64 and scale the pixel value to [0, 1].

Therefore, our inputs of the network have a size of 64 * 64 * 8 which includes the visible frame, thermal frame, visible background and thermal background. Our outputs of the network have a size of 64 * 64 * 2 since we regard the foreground detection as a binary classification problem. An example of our training patches is shown in Fig. 2. Last but not least, we perform a mean subtraction on each pixel as suggested in many works [8, 12].

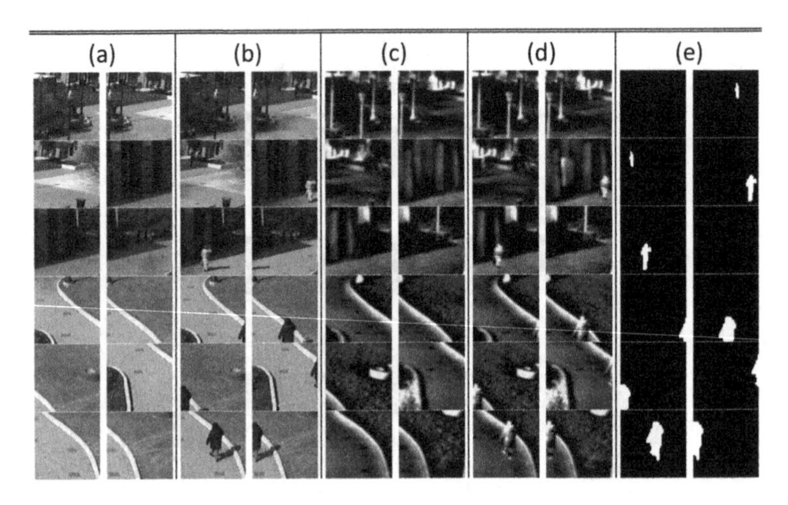

Fig. 2. Visualization of training image patches: (a) visible background patches, (b) visible input patches from visible video sequences, (c) thermal background patches, (d) thermal input patches from thermal video sequences, (e) ground truth patches.

3.2 Network Architecture and Training

The architecture of the proposed deep neural network is shown in Fig. 3. The network contains 4 convolutional layers where several convolution kernels are used to extract different features. For each layer, the size of the kernel is 3 * 3 with a stride of 1 and pad of 1. The number of output of the layer $L \in [1, 2, 3, 4]$ is [48, 246, 512, 2], respectively. The activation function we use is the Rectified Linear Unit (ReLU). It can improve the representation ability of the network model. In addition, the batch normalization (BN) is also applied for first two layers. The advantage of batch normalization layer in DNN is it makes us care less about initialization and can use much higher learning rate. We train our DNN model for 100 epochs with a mini batch size of 20 image patches, and a learning rate of $\alpha = 10^{-3}$. For the loss function, we use the softmax loss, which is defined as follows:

$$Loss = -\frac{1}{N}\sum\nolimits_{i=1}^{N} [y_i \log(\hat{y}_i) + (1 - y_i)\log(1 - \hat{y}_i)] \tag{1}$$

where, N is the number of training image patches, y_i is the ground truth, $\hat{y}_i$ is the predicted foreground result.

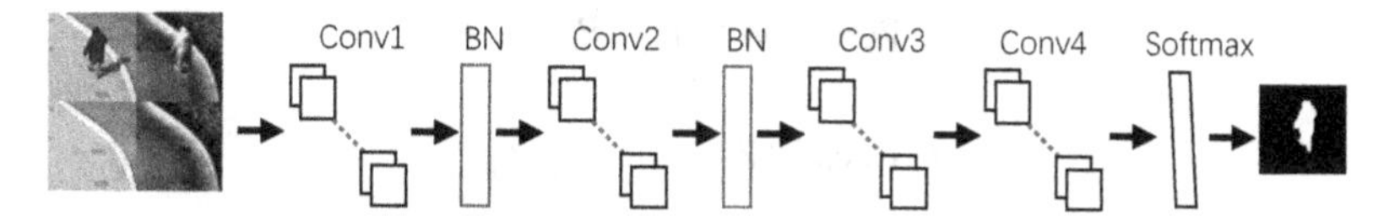

Fig. 3. Architecture of proposed DNN for background subtraction.

3.3 Post Processing

In order to generate the final foreground map and make the result close to human perception, we put a shape constrained morphological refinement to the results from the DNN model. Here, we define a function $D(\cdot)$ that can dilate all the potential objects with a shape based structuring element. The width and height of the rectangle are defined as $2n+1$ and $2n+3\left(n \in Z_0^+\right)$, and we set $n = 0$ because we just want to smooth the edge for each object and connect the small gap between some object pieces. By doing so, the shape of the object will have continuity, which matches human perceptions.

4 Experimental Results

4.1 Dataset Description and Evaluation Criteria

To validate the effectiveness of deep-neural-network-based foreground detection method, we tested our method on three challenging visible and thermal video sequence pairs from a publicly available database '03OSU Color-Thermal Database'. These data are recorded on Ohio State University campus at different times-of-day with different camera gain and level settings. Thermal sequences are captured by Raytheon PalmIR 250D thermal sensor and color sequence are captured by Sony TRV87 Handycam color sensor. All the frames in both sequences have a spatial resolution of 320 * 240 pixels. The number of frames in each video sequence is Sequence-1:2107, Sequence-2:1201, Sequence-3:3399, respectively. Figure 4 shows some examples of the visible and thermal video sequences. It can be seen that video sequences contain several people, some in groups, moving through the scene, and regions of dark shadows and illumination changes in the background.

In our experiment, we do both qualitative and quantitative assessment on some manually segmented silhouettes and we benchmark with our previous work [24] and other 11 methods which have been published in recent years and widely cited i.e. GMG [6], IMBS [3], LOBSTER [16], MultiCue [13], SuBSENSE [17], T2FMRF [26], ViBe [2], FA-SOM [11], PBAS [9], DECOLOR [28] and our previous work [24]. Three commonly used criteria i.e. precision, recall and F-measure, are adopted in our experiments to quantitatively assess the performance of proposed foreground detection method and other benchmarking methods. Three criteria are listed in the following:

- Precision (P) : $P = \frac{T_p}{T_p + F_p}$ (2)

- Recall (R) : $R = \frac{T_p}{T_p + F_n}$ (3)

- F – measure (FM) : $FM = \frac{2 \cdot P \cdot R}{P + R}$ (4)

where T_p, F_p, and F_n respectively refer to the number of correctly detected foreground pixels of the pedestrians, incorrectly detected foreground pixels (false alarms), and incorrectly detected background pixels (or missing pixels from the object). Specifically, these three numbers can be calculated by comparing the binary masks of the detected image and the ground truth. Furthermore, since the database doesn't have ground truth, we obtain a manual segmentation of the pedestrian regions in plenty of frames from selected video sequences.

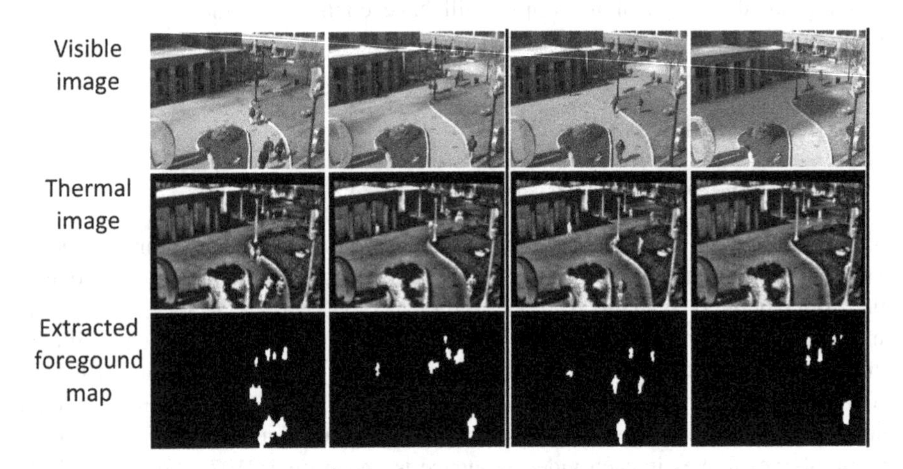

Fig. 4. Visible images, thermal images and results of our foreground detection method.

4.2 Assessment of Foreground Detection Method

To better evaluate the quality of our foreground map and the results from other methods, we do the quantitative comparison in terms of precision, recall and F-measure in Table 1, and qualitative comparison in Fig. 5. Since most benchmarking background subtraction methods are designed for visible images, however, the selected video sequences contain both visible and thermal imagery. Therefore, for a fair comparison, we employed a fusion strategy from our previous work [24] for each method. The final foreground map is integrated by both visible foreground map and thermal foreground map which are generated by those methods on visible and thermal images respectively. In Table 1, it can be seen that our DNN-based method outperforms other mainstream background subtraction approaches on selected three challenge video sequences in terms of precision and F-measure. Although MultiCue [13] yield slightly higher recall (0.2%) than proposed method, its precision is the lowest among all the methods which mean its foreground map contains too much false alarm. For qualitative evaluation, we only show the results of our method and five benchmarking methods. The results of other six methods (i.e. IMBS [3], MultiCue [13], T2FMRF [26], FA-SOM [11], PBAS [9], DECOLOR [28]) are not in this figure, due to the page limit and their relatively low F-measure value. As can be seen in Fig. 5, these methods can detect the pedestrians within close or middle range but not long range from the camera. In addition, affected by light change and weather condition, some details have been lost. For example, some pedestrians' shapes in GMG are fractured (e.g. the pedestrian group in 2nd and 3rd images); some pedestrians that far away from the camera can't be detected in both LOBSTER and SuBSENSE (e.g. the person at up-right in 4th image), and their detection of individual person is melt and stick with each other; most pedestrians' shapes in Vibe are not integrated. Hence, these methods have good quantitative results but their qualitative results don't fit human's cognition. Although the foreground detection of our previous work has been improved a lot, we still can't detect the precise edge of people. However, thanks to the DNN that allow our proposed method can detect the single pedestrian or pedestrian group with more accurate shape even under such a challenge scene with dark shadow and illumination change.

Table 1. Comparison of precision, recall and F-measure values.

Method	Precision	Recall	F-measure
GMG [6]	70.45	70.17	70.31
IMBS [3]	37.03	74.44	49.46
LOBSTER [16]	72.95	72.19	72.57
MultiCue [13]	26.02	88.78	40.25
SuBSENSE [17]	69.31	76.87	72.89
T2FMRF [26]	50.78	29.93	37.66
ViBe [2]	74.06	64.38	68.88
FA-SOM [11]	38.45	82.86	52.53
PBAS [9]	73.02	33.60	46.02
DECOLOR [28]	50.71	91.75	65.32
Previous work [24]	70.16	87.97	78.06
Proposed	**89.22**	**88.54**	**88.88**

In general, our proposed method yields the best performance in terms of quantitative and qualitative performance, but there are still rooms for further improvements. Our current DNN model doesn't contain too many layers which means the feature extraction of the visible and thermal image is not enough. In addition, due to the difference between visible and thermal imagery, each of them should have a typical DNN model. And the final foreground detection can be fused by a statistical fusion strategy.

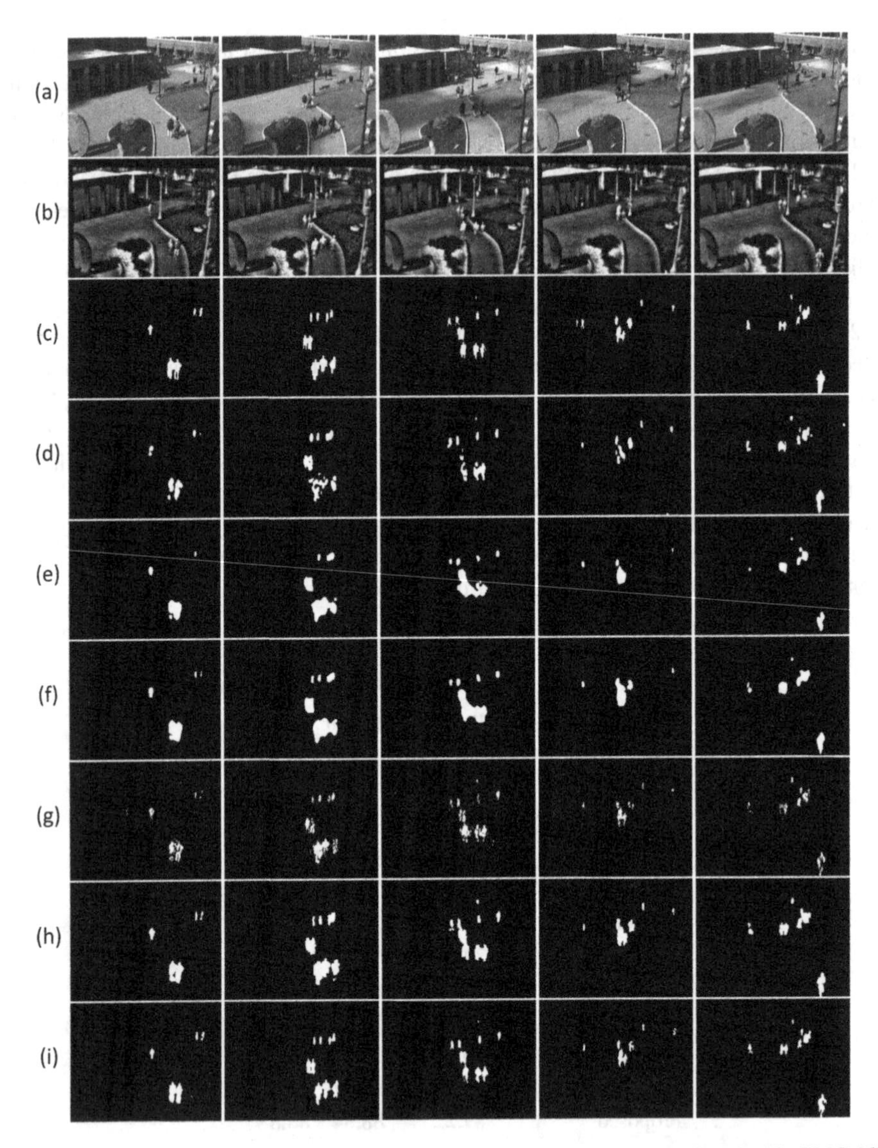

Fig. 5. Visual comparison, (a) RGB images, (b) thermal image, (c) ground truth, (d) GMG [6], (e) LOBSTER [16], (f) SuBSENSE [17], (g) Vibe [2], (h) previous work [24], (i) Proposed method.

5 Conclusion

In this paper, we proposed a background subtraction method using deep neural network for pedestrian detection in visible and thermal imagery. We first generate an initial background map by random median stage and build a lot of ground truth map by manual segmentation. After that, we put all data, initial background map and ground truth to train the DNN model. Finally, a shape constrained morphological refinement is applied to further improve the quality of the foreground detection result. The experimental results show that our approach yields better performance than other classical background modeling approaches in urban scenes. In the future, we would design two typical DNN model for visible and thermal imagery respectively, improve the applicability of our background method approach in different types of scenarios and test our method on more challenge database such as CDnet [19] and BMC [18].

References

1. Babaee, M., Dinh, D.T., Rigoll, G.: A deep convolutional neural network for background subtraction. arXiv preprint arXiv:170201731 (2017)
2. Barnich, O., Van Droogenbroeck, M.: ViBe: a powerful random technique to estimate the background in video sequences. In: IEEE International Conference on Acoustics, Speech and Signal Processing, ICASSP 2009, pp. 945–948. IEEE (2009)
3. Bloisi, D., Iocchi, L.: Independent multimodal background subtraction. In: CompIMAGE, pp. 39–44 (2012)
4. Chai, Y., Ren, J., Zhao, H., Li, Y., Ren, J., Murray, P.: Hierarchical and multi-featured fusion for effective gait recognition under variable scenarios. Pattern Anal. Appl. **19**, 905–917 (2016)
5. Davis, J.W., Keck, M.A.: A two-stage template approach to person detection in thermal imagery. In: Null, pp. 364–369. IEEE (2005)
6. Godbehere, A.B., Matsukawa, A., Goldberg, K.: Visual tracking of human visitors under variable-lighting conditions for a responsive audio art installation. In: American Control Conference (ACC), pp. 4305–4312. IEEE (2012)
7. Han, J., Zhang, D., Hu, X., Guo, L., Ren, J., Wu, F.: Background prior-based salient object detection via deep reconstruction residual. IEEE Trans. Circ. Syst. Video Technol. **25**, 1309–1321 (2015)
8. He, K., Zhang, X., Ren, S., Sun, J.: Deep residual learning for image recognition. In: Proceedings of the IEEE Conference on Computer Vision and Pattern Recognition, pp. 770–778 (2016)
9. Hofmann, M., Tiefenbacher, P., Rigoll, G.: Background segmentation with feedback: the pixel-based adaptive segmenter. In: 2012 IEEE Computer Society Conference on Computer Vision and Pattern Recognition Workshops (CVPRW), pp. 38–43. IEEE (2012)
10. Kim, D.-E., Kwon, D.-S.: Pedestrian detection and tracking in thermal images using shape features. In: 2015 12th International Conference on Ubiquitous Robots and Ambient Intelligence (URAI), pp. 22–25. IEEE (2015)
11. Maddalena, L., Petrosino, A.: A fuzzy spatial coherence-based approach to background/foreground separation for moving object detection. Neural Comput. Appl. **19**, 179–186 (2010)
12. Nguyen, T.P., Pham, C.C., Ha, S.V.-U., Jeon, J.W.: Change detection by training a triplet network for motion feature extraction. IEEE Trans. Circ. Syst. Video Technol. (2018, in press)
13. Noh, S., Jeon, M.: A new framework for background subtraction using multiple cues. In: Lee, K.M., Matsushita, Y., Rehg, J.M., Hu, Z. (eds.) ACCV 2012. LNCS, vol. 7726, pp. 493–506. Springer, Heidelberg (2013). https://doi.org/10.1007/978-3-642-37431-9_38
14. Ren, J., Han, J., Dalla Mura, M.: Special issue on multimodal data fusion for multidimensional signal processing. Multidimension. Syst. Signal Process. **27**, 801–805 (2016)

15. Ren, J., Jiang, J., Wang, D., Ipson, S.: Fusion of intensity and inter-component chromatic difference for effective and robust colour edge detection. IET Image Process. **4**, 294–301 (2010)
16. St-Charles, P.-L., Bilodeau, G.-A.: Improving background subtraction using local binary similarity patterns. In: 2014 IEEE Winter Conference on Applications of Computer Vision (WACV), pp. 509–515. IEEE (2014)
17. St-Charles, P.-L., Bilodeau, G.-A., Bergevin, R.: Flexible background subtraction with self-balanced local sensitivity. In: Proceedings of the IEEE Conference on Computer Vision and Pattern Recognition Workshops, pp. 408–413 (2014)
18. Vacavant, A., Chateau, T., Wilhelm, A., Lequievre, L.: A benchmark dataset for foreground/background extraction. In: ACCV 2012 Workshop: Background Models Challenge (2012)
19. Wang, Y., Jodoin, P.-M., Porikli, F., Konrad, J., Benezeth, Y., Ishwar, P.: CDnet 2014: an expanded change detection benchmark dataset. In: 2014 IEEE Conference on Computer Vision and Pattern Recognition Workshops (CVPRW), pp. 393–400. IEEE (2014)
20. Wang, Z., Ren, J., Zhang, D., Sun, M., Jiang, J.: A deep-learning based feature hybrid framework for spatiotemporal saliency detection inside videos. Neurocomputing **287**, 68–83 (2018)
21. Yan, Y., Ren, J., Li, Y., Windmill, J., Ijomah, W.: Fusion of dominant colour and spatial layout features for effective image retrieval of coloured logos and trademarks. In: 2015 IEEE International Conference on Multimedia Big Data (BigMM), pp. 306–311. IEEE (2015)
22. Yan, Y., Ren, J., Li, Y., Windmill, J.F., Ijomah, W., Chao, K.-M.: Adaptive fusion of color and spatial features for noise-robust retrieval of colored logo and trademark images. Multidimension. Syst. Signal Process. **27**, 945–968 (2016)
23. Yan, Y., et al.: Unsupervised image saliency detection with Gestalt-laws guided optimization and visual attention based refinement. Pattern Recogn. **79**, 65–78 (2018)
24. Yan, Y., et al.: Cognitive fusion of thermal and visible imagery for effective detection and tracking of pedestrians in videos. Cognit. Comput. **10**, 94–104 (2018)
25. Zabalza, J., et al.: Novel segmented stacked autoencoder for effective dimensionality reduction and feature extraction in hyperspectral imaging. Neurocomputing **185**, 1–10 (2016)
26. Zhao, Z., Bouwmans, T., Zhang, X., Fang, Y.: A fuzzy background modeling approach for motion detection in dynamic backgrounds. In: Wang, F.L., Lei, J., Lau, R.W.H., Zhang, J. (eds.) CMSP 2012. CCIS, vol. 346, pp. 177–185. Springer, Heidelberg (2012). https://doi.org/10.1007/978-3-642-35286-7_23
27. Zheng, J., Liu, Y., Ren, J., Zhu, T., Yan, Y., Yang, H.: Fusion of block and keypoints based approaches for effective copy-move image forgery detection. Multidimension. Syst. Signal Process. **27**, 989–1005 (2016)
28. Zhou, X., Yang, C., Yu, W.: Moving object detection by detecting contiguous outliers in the low-rank representation. IEEE Trans. Pattern Anal. Mach. Intell. **35**, 597–610 (2013)

Recent Advances in Deep Learning for Single Image Super-Resolution

Yungang Zhang(✉) and Yu Xiang

Department of Computer Science, Yunnan Normal University,
Kunming 650500, China
{yungang.zhang,yu.xiang}@ynnu.edu.cn

Abstract. Image super-resolution is an important research field in image analysis. The techniques of image super-resolution has been widely used in many computer vision applications. In recent years, the success of deep learning methods in image super-resolution have attracted more and more researchers. This paper gives a brief review of recent deep learning based methods for single image super-resolution (SISR), in terms of network type, network structure, and training methods. The advantages and disadvantages of these methods are analyzed as well.

Keywords: Single image super-resolution · Deep learning
Convolutional neural networks

1 Introduction

Nowadays, the high-definition digital displays are widely used, however the super-resolution techniques are still necessary in many computer vision applications. In many areas such as video surveillance, medical imaging and remote sensing, due to many physical effects, it is common that the quality of images or videos are away from our expectation. Therefore, the users have to enhance resolutions for their original imaging results. Super-resolution (SR) techniques aim to generate a high resolution image from the original obtained low-resolution (LR) image.

The pioneering work of using deep learning in super-resolution can be found in [1], where an end-to-end mapping between the low and high-resolution images is learned, and the mapping is represented as a deep convolutional neural network. Since then, the deep learning based methods have become the mainstream in image and video super-resolution areas. The existing published results show that deep learning is a promising direction in image/video super-resolution.

In this article, a brief review of deep learning based methods in single image super-resolution is given. The rest of the article is organized as follows. Section 2 gives some background concepts in super-resolution. The literature of deep learning techniques for single image super-resolution is reviewed in Sect. 3. Section 4 concludes the article.

Supported by the National Natural Science Foundation of China (No. 61462097) and Yunnan Provincial Education Department Research Grant (No. 2018JS143).

J. Ren et al. (Eds.): BICS 2018, LNAI 10989, pp. 85–95, 2018.
https://doi.org/10.1007/978-3-030-00563-4_9

2 Background

Image Super-resolution (SR) techniques try to construct a high resolution (HR) image from one or more observed low resolution (LR) images [2]. As SR is an ill-posed problem, there may be many solutions exist. From the perspective of input LR images, the SR techniques can be divided into two main categories, namely single image super-resolution (SISR) and multiple image or multi-frame super-resolution. The SISR only uses one input LR image to produce the corresponding HR image, therefore SISR has attracted more focus from researchers as it is more close to the real scenarios in people's daily life. There are two types of SISR techniques:

1. **The learning based methods.** The techniques from machine learning are used in this type of SISR methods to estimate the HR image. The typical methods in this category are: the pixel-based methods [3] and the example-based methods [4]. The techniques such as sparse coding and neighbor embedding are also widely used [5].
2. **The reconstruction based methods.** Which needs prior knowledge to define constraints for the target HR image. The typical techniques used in this category are edge sharpening [6], regularization [7] or deconvolution [8].

In order to alleviate the ill-posed problem of SISR, recent methods try to learn prior information from LR and HR pairs, typical methods are neighbor embedding regression [9], random forest [10] and deep convolutional neural networks [1].

3 Deep Learning for Single Image Super-Resolution

In recent years, deep learning [14], especially convolutional neural networks (CNNs) [11] have become an important tool in computer vision applications. Although CNNs are not perfect [39], the excellent performances of CNNs are reported in various computer vision applications [12,13]. In this section, the recent CNNs-based and relative methods for SISR are briefly reviewed.

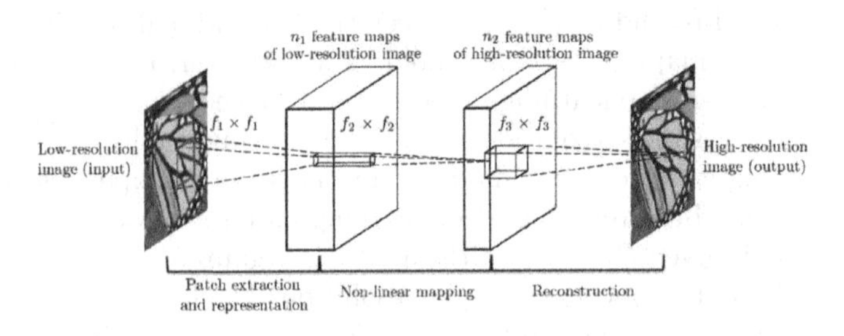

Fig. 1. SRCNN model illustration [15].

3.1 Convolutional Neural Networks for SISR

The first CNNs-based model for SISR is called SRCNN [15], which is illustrated in Fig. 1. The method tries to learn an end-to-end mapping between the input LR image and the corresponding HR image. The bicubic interpolation is used as its pre-processing step, then the image patches are extracted by convolution as feature vectors, which are then non-linearly mapped to find the most appropriate patches to reconstruct the HR image. SRCNN has only convolutional

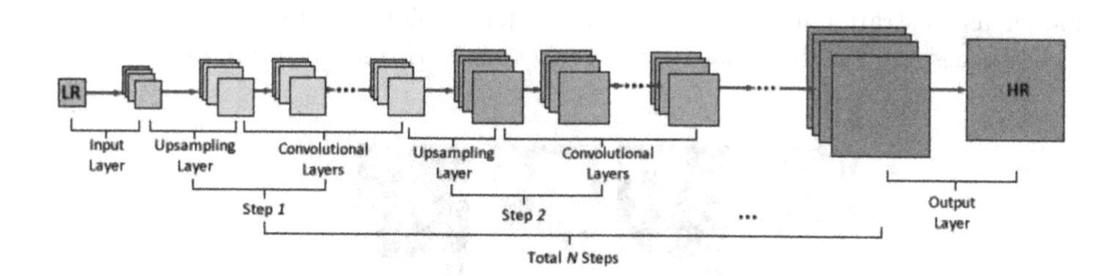

Fig. 2. The GUN model [33].

layers, which has the advantage that the input images can be of any size and the algorithm is not patch-based [16]. SRCNN outperforms many "traditional" models. Although SRCNN is efficient due to a lightweight structure is used, a fast SRCNN (FSRCNN) [17] is proposed to further improve the performance of SRCNN. The FSRCNN replaces pre-processing bicubic interpolation step of SRCNN by a post-processing step in the form of deconvolution. A 40 times improvement on time cost compared to SRCNN was reported by the authors. A deep network cascade (DNC) is introduced in [18], the model upscales an

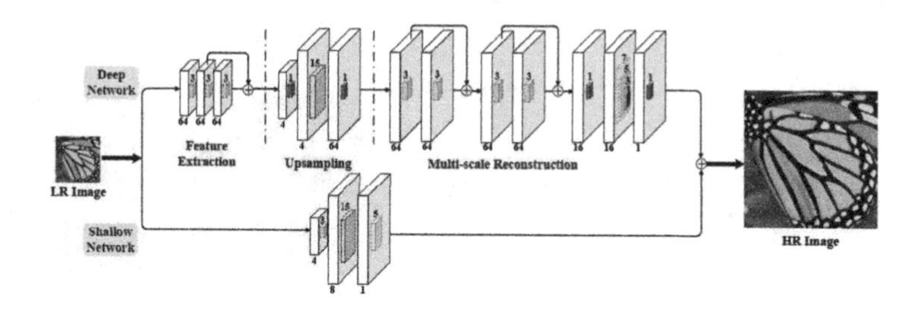

Fig. 3. Network architecture of EEDS [34].

input LR to the HR image layer by layer. The non-local self-similarities are then explored to refine the high-frequency details of the patches. The Gradual Upsampling Network (GUN [33]) gradually magnifies LR to HR. The model (Fig. 2) consists of an input convolution layer, a set of upsampling and convolutional layers, and an output layer. It is believed that the gradual upsampling strategy of adopting very small magnification factor is cost effective in terms of efficiency.

In [34], the authors replace the bicubic upsampling in the first step with feature extraction. Therefore, the LR image can be mapped into a deep feature space. Then a learning based upsampling of the deep features to the desired dimensions is carried out. For the HR reconstruction, context information is derived from the upsampled features, in a multi-scale way that incorporates both short- and long-range contextual information at the same time (Fig. 3).

Inspired by the success of VGG-net in image classification, the VDSR [19] model, as illustrated in Fig. 4, uses a very deep convolution network for SISR [20]. The success of VDSR shows that a deeper network may bring more accurate

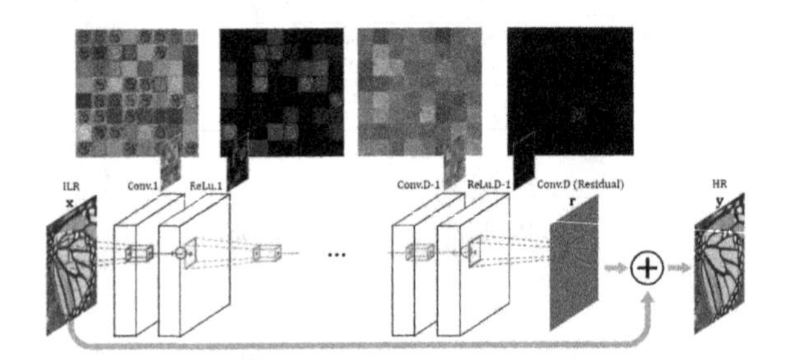

Fig. 4. The VDSR model [19].

outputs. However, deeper networks may introduce two side effects: overfitting and heavy models. Therefore, Kim et al. [21] propose a deeply-recursive convolutional network (DRCN) to apply the same convolutional layer recursively. The core idea of their model is to simultaneously have a very deep network while suppress the number of model parameters. The efficient sub-pixel con-

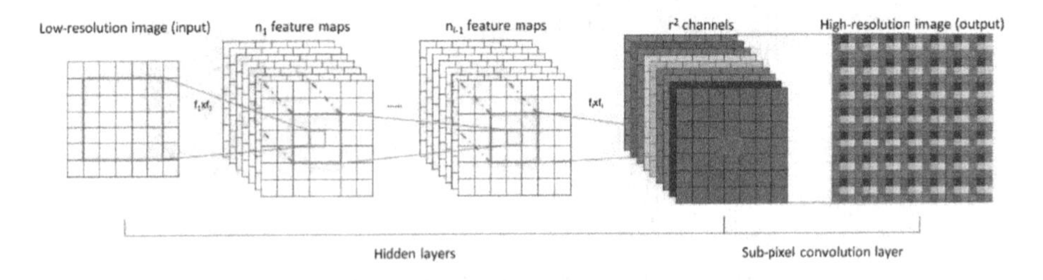

Fig. 5. The ESPCN model [32].

volutional neural network (ESPCN) is proposed in [32] to reduce the space and time complexities in SISR tasks. The model first downsamples the HR images to LR images, then the feature maps are extracted from LR images. Except the last sub-pixel convolution layer, all other layers are characterized by its own upscaling filter for the feature map of the concerned layer. The "sub-pixel convolution layer" then upscales the low resolution image to a super-resolved image. The model is illustrated in Fig. 5. An enhanced deep super-resolution network

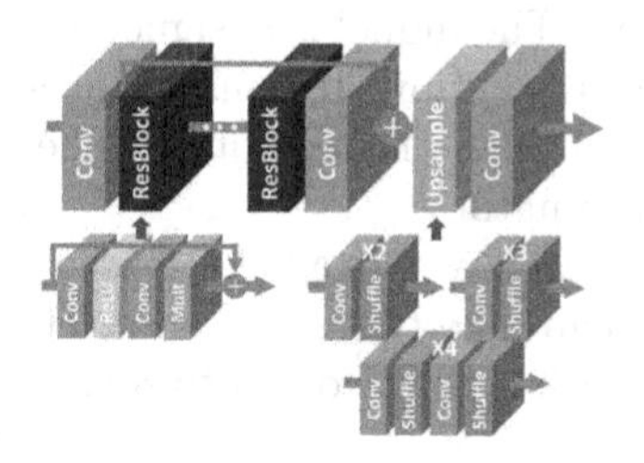

Fig. 6. The EDSR model [40].

(EDSR) is introduced in [40], as illustrated in Fig. 6. The batch normalization layers are removed from the conventional residual networks, and the performance is further improved by expanding the model size. The EDSR achieved the leading performance in CVPR Ntire 2017 challenge.

3.2 Adaptive Models

Besides to use CNN models originally from image classification tasks. Many researchers also try to build models to be more adaptive to the image contents (pixels or structures) for SISR. A Deep Projection CNN (DPN) method is introduced in [25]. DPN uses model adaptation to explore the repetitive structures in LR images. In [26], the pixel recursive super-resolution network is proposed, which comprises a conditioning network and a prior network. The conditioning network transform the LR image to logits to predict the log-likelihood of each HR pixel, and the prior network is a PixelCNN [41]. With this type of structure, the model is able to synthesize realistic details into images while enhancing their resolution. In [27], the authors propose a model named deep joint super resolution (DJSR) in order to adapt deep model for joint similarities.

More recently, Zhang et al. propose a novel adaptive residual network (ARN) [35] for high-quality image restoration. The ARN is a deep residual network, which consists of six cascaded adaptive shortcuts, convolutional layers and PReLUs. Each adaptive shortcut contains two small convolutional layers, followed by PReLU activation layers and one adaptive skip connection. The ARN model can be trained adaptively according to different applications.

3.3 Generative Adversarial Networks Based Models

Generative adversarial networks (GANs) are known for the ability to preserve texture details in images, create solutions that are close to the real image manifold and look perceptually convincing. Therefore, GANs are also can be used for SISR. The first successful application of GAN in SISR can be seen in [43], where the authors propose an adversarial loss and a content loss, a discriminator network is used to differentiate photo-realistic images from SR images created by the generator network.

In [29], the authors propose a Depixelated Super Resolution Convolutional Neural Network (DSRCNN). The model is designed for super-resolving partially pixelated images for super-resolution. It consists of an autoencoder combined with two depixelate layers through deconvolution. The autoencoder is composed of a generator and a discriminator.

GAN is applied in [30] as well, where a GAN-based architecture using densely connected convolutional neural networks (DenseNets) is proposed to super-resolve overhead imagery with a factor of up to 8×.

3.4 Sparsity-Based Models

Some researchers have revealed that combining sparse coding with CNNs can produce better performances than using CNNS only [22,31,37]. A sparse coding based network (SCN) is proposed in [23], with the sparse priors, the model is more compact and accurate compared to SRCNN. Another model called SCRNN-Pr [24] also tries to explore image priors during the training of a deep CNN. Better training time cost and super-resolution performances are reported compared to other state-of-the-art methods.

In [51], a hybrid wavelet convolution network (HWCN) (Fig. 7) is proposed. The LR image is fed into a scattering convolution network (a wavelet tree in nature) to obtain scattering feature maps, sparse codes are then extracted from those maps and used as inputs for a CNN. The model is able to use a tiny dataset to train complex deep networks with better generalization. The authors in

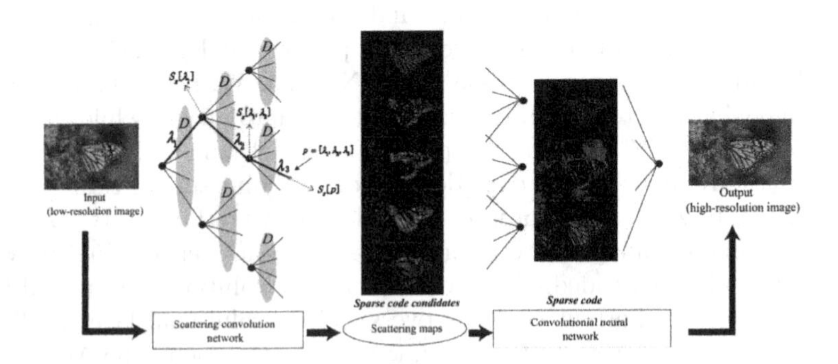

Fig. 7. The HWCN model [51].

[28] propose a very deep Residual Encoder-Decoder Network: RED-Net, which consists of a series of convolutional and deconvolutional layers aim to obtain end-to-end mappings from LR images to HR images. The use of stacked autoencoder

for image restoration can be found in [49], where a non-local stacked autoencoder is proposed. The stacked autoencoder (SAE) is used in [47] and [48] for saliency detection, nevertheless the models can be extended for SISR purpose as well.

3.5 Other Types of Methods

The combining of multiple super-resolution models and ensemble of multiple CNNs are also reported can obtain competitive performance in SISR.

Model Combination. In [42], the authors combines some contemporary state-of-the-art super-resolution methods using conditioned regression models. Their proposed "Regression conditioned" SRCNN has the idea to constructed a single training model to avoid model re-training for different images. The model can be effective for different blur kernels.

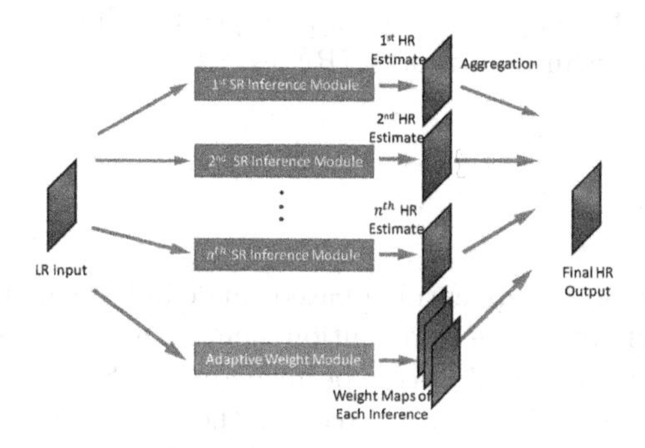

Fig. 8. MSCN [38].

Ensemble of CNNs. The use of multiple CNNs is also a promising direction in this area. In [38], the authors apply a number of SR methods to the LR image independently to get various HR estimates, which are then combined on the basis of adaptive weights to produce the final result. The method is named as MSCN-n, where n is the number of employed inference modules (Fig. 8). Similarly, another multiple CNNs model is proposed in [50], each individual CNN is trained separately with different network structure. A Context-wise Network Fusion (CNF) approach is proposed to integrate the outputs of individual networks by additional convolution layers.

A wavelets guided multiple CNNs method is proposed in [36]. The wavelet decomposition of images are used for multi-scale representations. Then multiple CNNs are trained for approximating the wavelet multi-scale representations, separately. For inference, the trained CNNs regress wavelet multi-scale representations from a low-resolution image, followed by wavelet synthesis that forms a restored high-resolution image. The illustration of the model can be seen in Fig. 9.

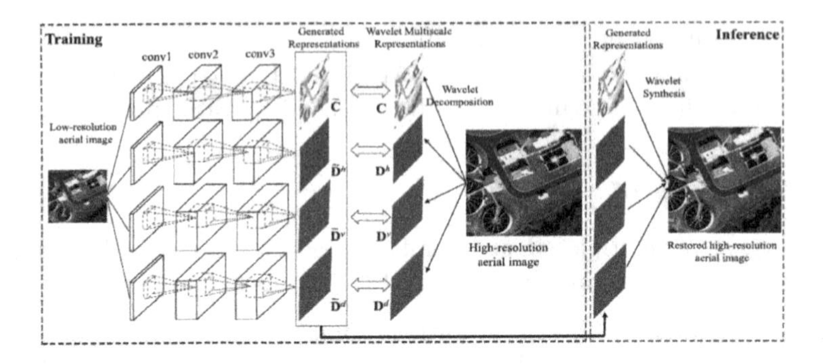

Fig. 9. The wavelet multiscale CNNs model [36].

There are also other types of deep learning methods for SISR, such as deep belief networks [44], the Laplacian Pyramid Super-Resolution Network (LapSRN [45]), and recurrent neural networks (RNNs) [46]. All obtain state-of-the-art performances.

4 Conclusion

In this article, the recent deep learning based single image super-resolution methods are briefly reviewed. The convolution neural networks and relative deep learning models have achieved better performance in SISR than other conventional methods. However, how do we recover the finer texture details when we super-resolve at large upscaling factors is still a question need to be answered. In addition, the models which can be applied in real time scenarios also need further investigations. In our future work, we will pay particular attention to the sparsity-based deep learning models, as sparsity-based models are able to reduce the complexity of the learning processes and extract local information that leads to better performance [48]. Moreover, we believe that the combination of GANs and sparse models is a promising direction in SISR.

References

1. Dong, C., Loy, C.C., He, K., Tang, X.: Learning a deep convolutional network for image super-resolution. In: Fleet, D., Pajdla, T., Schiele, B., Tuytelaars, T. (eds.) ECCV 2014. LNCS, vol. 8692, pp. 184–199. Springer, Cham (2014). https://doi.org/10.1007/978-3-319-10593-2_13
2. Yue, L., et al.: Image super-resolution: the techniques, applications, and future. Sig. Process. **128**, 389–408 (2016)
3. Zhang, K., Gao, X., Tao, D., Li, X.: Single image super-resolution with non-local means and steering kernel regression. IEEE Trans. Image Process. **21**, 4544–4556 (2012)
4. Freeman, W.T., Jones, T.R., Pasztor, E.C.: Example-based super-resolution. IEEE Comput. Graph. Appl. **22**, 56–65 (2002)

5. Gao, X., Zhang, K., Tao, D., Li, X.: Image super-resolution with sparse neighbor embedding. IEEE Trans. Image Process. **21**, 3194–3205 (2012)
6. Dai, S., et al.: Soft edge smoothness prior for alpha channel super resolution. In: Proceedings of CVPR 2007, pp. 1–8. IEEE (2007)
7. Aly, H.A., Dubois, E.: Image up-sampling using total-variation regularization with a new observation model. IEEE Trans. Image Process. **14**, 1647–1659 (2005)
8. Shan, Q., et al.: Fast image/video upsampling. ACM Trans. Graph. **27**, 153:1–153:7 (2008)
9. Timofte, R., De Smet, V., Van Gool, L.: Anchored neighborhood regression for fast example-based super-resolution. In: Proceedings of ICCV 2013, pp. 1920–1927. IEEE (2013)
10. Schulter, S., Leistner, C., Bischof, H.: Fast and accurate image upscaling with super-resolution forests. In: Proceedings of CVPR 2015, pp. 3791–3799. IEEE (2015)
11. Krizhevsky, A., Sutskever, I., Hinton, G.E.: ImageNet classification with deep convolutional neural networks. In: Proceedings of NIPS 2012, vol. 1, pp. 1097–1105. Curran Associates Inc. (2012)
12. Zeiler, M.D., Fergus, R.: Visualizing and understanding convolutional networks. In: Fleet, D., Pajdla, T., Schiele, B., Tuytelaars, T. (eds.) ECCV 2014. LNCS, vol. 8689, pp. 818–833. Springer, Cham (2014). https://doi.org/10.1007/978-3-319-10590-1_53
13. Szegedy, C., et al.: Going deeper with convolutions. In: Proceedings of CVPR 2015, pp. 1–9. IEEE (2015)
14. LeCun, Y., Bengio, Y., Hinton, G.: Deep learning. Nature **521**(7553), 436–444 (2015)
15. Dong, C., et al.: Image super-resolution using deep convolutional networks. IEEE Trans. Pattern Anal. Mach. Intell. **38**, 295–307 (2016)
16. Kappeler, A., et al.: Video super-resolution with convolutional neural networks. IEEE Trans. Comput. Imaging **2**, 109–122 (2016)
17. Dong, C., Loy, C.C., Tang, X.: Accelerating the super-resolution convolutional neural network. In: Leibe, B., Matas, J., Sebe, N., Welling, M. (eds.) ECCV 2016. LNCS, vol. 9906, pp. 391–407. Springer, Cham (2016). https://doi.org/10.1007/978-3-319-46475-6_25
18. Cui, Z., Chang, H., Shan, S., Zhong, B., Chen, X.: Deep network cascade for image super-resolution. In: Fleet, D., Pajdla, T., Schiele, B., Tuytelaars, T. (eds.) ECCV 2014. LNCS, vol. 8693, pp. 49–64. Springer, Cham (2014). https://doi.org/10.1007/978-3-319-10602-1_4
19. J. Kim, J. K. Lee, K. M. Lee: Accurate image super-resolution using very deep convolutional networks. In: Proceedings of CVPR 2016, pp. 1646–1654. IEEE (2016)
20. Simonyan, K., Zisserman, A.: Very deep convolutional networks for large-scale image recognition. CoRR, vol abs/1409.1556. http://arxiv.org/abs/1409.1556. (2014)
21. Kim, J., Kwon Lee, J., Mu Lee, K.: Deeply-recursive convolutional network for image super-resolution. In: Proceedings of CVPR 2016, pp. 1637–1645. IEEE (2016)
22. Gregor, K., Lecun, Y.: Learning fast approximations of sparse coding. In: Proceedings of ICML 2010, pp. 399–406. Omnipress (2010)
23. Liu, D., et al.: Robust single image super-resolution via deep networks with sparse prior. IEEE Trans. Image Process. **25**, 3194–3207 (2016)
24. Liang, Y., et al.: Incorporating image priors with deep convolutional neural networks for image super-resolution. Neurocomputing **194**, 340–347 (2016)

25. Liang, Y., et al.: Single image super resolution - when model adaptation matters. CoRR, vol abs/1703.10889. https://arxiv.org/abs/1703.10889. (2017)
26. Dahl, R., Norouzi, M., Shlens, J.: Pixel recursive super resolution. CoRR, vol abs/1702.00783. http://arxiv.org/abs/1702.00783. (2017)
27. Wang, Z., et al.: Self-tuned deep super resolution. In: Proceedings of CVPR Workshop 2015, pp. 1–8. IEEE (2015)
28. Mao, X., Shen, C., Yang, Y.: Image denoising using very deep fully convolutional encoder-decoder networks with symmetric skip connections. CoRR, vol abs/1603.09056. http://arxiv.org/abs/1603.09056. (2016)
29. Mao, H., et al.: Super resolution of the partial pixelated images with deep convolutional neural network. In: Proceedings of 2016 ACM on Multimedia Conference, pp. 322–326. ACM (2016)
30. Bosch, M., et al.: Super-resolution for overhead imagery using denseNets and adversarial learning. CoRR, vol abs/1711.10312v1. http://arxiv.org/abs/1711.10312v1. (2017)
31. Shi, Y., et al.: Local- and holistic- structure preserving image super resolution via deep joint component learning. CoRR, vol abs/1607.07220. http://arxiv.org/abs/1607.07220. (2016)
32. Shi, W., et al.: Real-time single image and video super-resolution using an efficient sub-pixel convolutional neural network. In: Proceedings of CVPR 2016, pp. 1874–1883. IEEE (2016)
33. Zhao, Y., et al.: Gun: gradual upsampling network for single image superresolution. CoRR, vol abs/1703.0424. http://arxiv.org/abs/1703.0424. (2017)
34. Wang, Y., et al.: End-to-end image super-resolution via deep and shallow convolutional networks. CoRR, vol abs/1607.07680. http://arxiv.org/abs/1607.07680. (2016)
35. Zhang, Y., et al.: Adaptive residual networks for high-quality image restoration. IEEE Trans. Image Process. **27**, 3150–3163 (2018)
36. Wang, T., et al.: Aerial image super resolution via wavelet multiscale convolutional neural networks. IEEE Geosci. Remote. Sens. Lett. **15**, 769–773 (2018)
37. Osendorfer, C., Soyer, H., van der Smagt, P.: Image super-resolution with fast approximate convolutional sparse coding. In: Loo, C.K., Yap, K.S., Wong, K.W., Beng Jin, A.T., Huang, K. (eds.) ICONIP 2014. LNCS, vol. 8836, pp. 250–257. Springer, Cham (2014). https://doi.org/10.1007/978-3-319-12643-2_31
38. Liu, D., et al.: Learning a mixture of deep networks for single image super-resolution. CoRR, vol abs/1701.00823. https://arxiv.org/abs/1701.00823. (2017)
39. Shalev-Shwartz, S., Shamir, O., Shammah, S.: Failures of deep learning. CoRR, vol abs/1703.07950v1. https://arxiv.org/pdf/1703.07950v1.pdf. (2017)
40. Lim, B., et al.: Enhanced deep residual networks for single image super-resolution. In: Proceedings of CVPR Workshop 2017, pp. 1132–1140. IEEE (2017)
41. van den Oord, A., et al.: Conditional image generation with PixelCNN decoders. CoRR, vol abs/1606.05328. http://arxiv.org/abs/1606.05328. (2016)
42. Riegler, G., et al.: Conditioned regression models for non-blind single image super-resolution. In: Proceedings of ICCV 2015, pp. 522–530. IEEE (2015)
43. Ledig, C., et al.: Photo-realistic single image super-resolution using a generative adversarial network. In: Proceedings of CVPR 2017, pp. 105–114. IEEE (2017)
44. Brosch, T., Tam, R.: Efficient training of convolutional deep belief networks in the frequency domain for application to highresolution 2D and 3D images. Neural Comput. **27**, 211–227 (2015)
45. Lai, W., et al.: Deep Laplacian pyramid networks for fast and accurate super-resolution. In: Proceedings of CVPR 2017, pp. 5835–5843. IEEE (2017)

46. Han, W., et al.: Image super-resolution via dual-state recurrent networks. CoRR, vol abs/1805.02704. https://arxiv.org/pdf/1805.02704.pdf (2018)
47. Han, J., et al.: Background prior-based salient object detection via deep reconstruction residual. IEEE Trans. Circuits Syst. Video Technol. **25**, 1309–1321 (2015)
48. Zabalza, J., et al.: Novel segmented stacked autoencoder for effective dimensionality reduction and feature extraction in hyperspectral imaging. Neurocomputing **185**, 1–10 (2016)
49. Wang, R., Tao, D.: Non-local auto-encoder with collaborative stabilization for image restoration. IEEE Trans. Image Process. **25**, 2117–2229 (2016)
50. Ren, H., Elkhamy, M., Lee, J.: Image super resolution based on fusing multiple convolution neural networks. In: Proceedings of CVPR 2017, pp. 1050–1057. IEEE (2017)
51. Gao, X., Xiong, H.: A hybrid wavelet convolution network with sparse-coding for image super-resolution. In: Proceedings of ICIP 2016, pp. 1439–1443. IEEE (2016)

Using GAN to Augment the Synthesizing Images from 3D Models

Yan Ma[1(✉)], Kang Liu[1(✉)], Zhi-bin Guan[1], Xin-Kai Xu[2], Xu Qian[1(✉)], and Hong Bao[2]

[1] School of Mechanical Electronic and Information Engineering, China University of Mining and Technology, Beijing, China
yan.ma@student.cumtb.edu.cn, {kangliu,xuqian}@cumtb.edu.cn
[2] Beijing Union University, Beijing, China

Abstract. Annotation data is the "fuel" of vision cognitive system but hard to obtain. We focus on finding a feasible way to generate high-quality image data. The 3D models can produce rich annotated 2D images, and the generative adversarial nets can create various pictures. We proposed the background augmentation generative adversarial nets to build a bridge between GAN and 3D models for data augmentation. As a result, we use BAGAN and 3D models to generate images which can help deep convolutional classifier improve accuracy score to 93.12% on real data test sets.

Keywords: Self-learning system
Conditional generative adversarial nets · Image synthesizing
Data augmentation · Vision cognitive system

1 Introduction

Is cognitive visual artificial intelligence serving people? In fact, it is served by the human. Supervised learning is the essential engine driving the development of cognitive visual intelligence. As an essential application of supervised learning, computer vision evolved into a "data-hungry" learning algorithm. Data acquisition and annotation spend an enormous amount of time for computer vision researchers and practitioners. Therefore, vision data augmentation is one of the classic issues of deep learning.

Computer vision data augmentation could be divided into two categories: transform-based data augmentation and generation-based data augmentation.

Transform-based data augmentation produces images without changing the basic properties of the images. Krizhevsky [8] applied image reflection to extend data. Szegedy [13] implemented image rescaling to increase the quantity of source data. These methods could build in deep learning algorithms due to little computation and mitigate the overfitting problem of networks. However, these methods cannot avoid the overfitting when the size of annotation data is limited.

J. Ren et al. (Eds.): BICS 2018, LNAI 10989, pp. 96–105, 2018.
https://doi.org/10.1007/978-3-030-00563-4_10

Generation-based data augmentation produces images based on the information of the source data. Krizhevsky [8] derived the images information with the principal component analysis (PCA) and generated images by modifying less information. However, the reality of the generated samples is poor. Goodfellow [5] proposed generative adversarial nets (GAN) to create data by learning the appearance distribution of source data. Nevertheless, the generated images are low-resolution and unordered. Mirza [9] added conditional constraints to solve the unordered problem. Oenda [10] though more complex latent space structure and unique value function product more realistic and high-resolution images.

Both transform-based methods or the generation-based methods are incapable of working under rare hyper-annotation image data such as pose estimation, instance segmentation, and fine-grained classification. Transform-based methods often failed because of small numbers of training data. Generation-based techniques cannot generate complex annotation data.

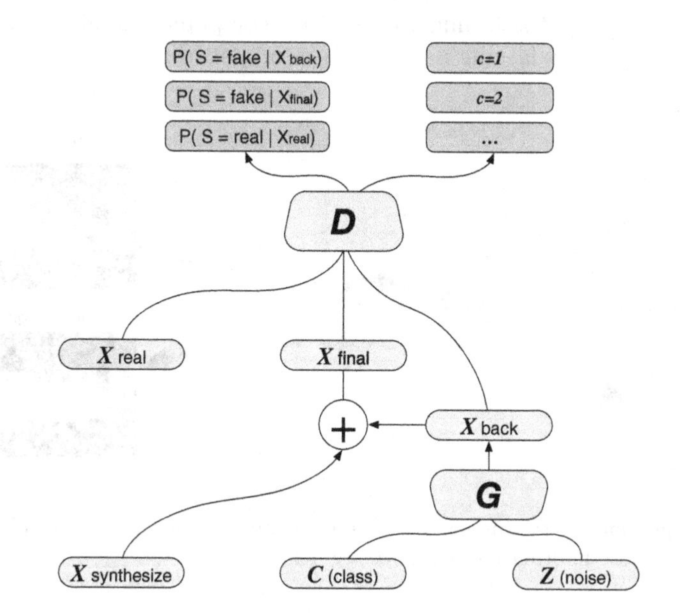

Fig. 1. Background augmentation generative adversarial nets.

Fortunately, the 3D film and 3D game industry provide a large number of sophisticated models and sophisticated tools [4] to synthesize high-quality pictures and videos. The development of virtual reality, augmented reality, game production, and 3D recognition has led to the exploration of a large number of outstanding 3D visual datasets [1] and algorithms [4]. In previous work, we used high-quality 3D models to synthesize the hyper-annotation data[1] and it will be discussed in Sect. 2.

[1] This work described in "Synthetic data from 3D models for real image classification" which had been submitted in "EURASIP Journal on Image and Video Processing."

In this paper, the background augmentation generative adversarial networks (BAGAN) was proposed to generate backgrounds (The network schematic is shown in Fig. 1). The BAGAN augmented the synthesize images from 3D models. Comparing with Cycle-GAN [19] and ACGANs [10], the BAGAN can create solid backgrounds without changing the appearance of the foreground objects. According to classification results, the training data synthesized by the BAGANs achieved 93.12% accuracy.

2 Synthetic Image Data from 3D Models

Synthetic image methods based on GANs intended at learning appearance from source data. There are two major problems of these methods: (1) Modules cannot generate complex annotated data (comment information contains only category information); (2) The generative samples are unrealistic due to the lack of geometric properties. Synthetic images based on computer graphics synthesizing methods are rigorously lacking in appearance properties.

Fig. 2. Our previous work can generate five types annotations: category, subcategory, bounding box, pose information, instance segmentation.

Therefore, in previous work, we proposed a method synthesizing images from 3D models. As the bridge between computer vision and computer graphic, high-quality 3D models possess appearance and geometry information. With the development of 3D animation industry and games, more and more high-quality 3D model warehouses (e.g., ShapeNet database [1]) and agile tools can be useful for data synthesis. We collect 3D models from the ShapeNet database [1] and use kernel density estimation to estimated pose information from ObjectNet3D database [15]. After rendering with blender (open source software[2]), the image was cropped into a valid size and annotated images with pose information, categories, subcategories, instance segmentation (See Fig. 2).

[2] https://www.blender.org/

3 Background Augmentation Generative Adversarial Nets

3.1 Why We Use GAN to Augment Background ?

The effectiveness of synthetic image data should be measured by whether the networks had learned useful features. It is imperative to use GANs powerful appearance learning ability to make the composite images backgrounds more realistic. According to Table 1, we find that background appearance is crucial to recognize the foreground objects.

3.2 Background Loss

Generative adversarial nets (GAN)[5] had two basic models: generator model and discriminator model. The generator G was responsible for generating samples from simple low-dimensional vector z, and the generating samples were denoted as $G(z)$. The discriminator ($D(x)$ or $D(G(z))$) D was subject to distinguish whether the input sample was real x or generated $G(z)$. The expectation of the GAN was that the discriminator cannot distinguish generate samples from the generator. The two-player minimax game is described by Eq. 1.

$$\min_G \max_D \mathcal{L}(D,G) = \mathbb{E}_{x \sim p_{data}(x)}[\log D(x)] + \mathbb{E}_{z \sim p_z(z)}[1 - \log D(G(z))] \quad (1)$$

Conditional generative adversarial nets (CGAN)[9] added conditional constraints y to generate annotated data. The latent space vector z was converted into $z+y$. The two-player minimax game is described by Eq. 2.

$$\min_G \max_D \mathcal{L}(D,G) = \mathbb{E}_{x\ p_{data}(x|y)}[\log D(x)] + \mathbb{E}_{z\ p_z(z)}[\log D(G(z|y))] \quad (2)$$

Auxiliary Classifier Generative Adversarial Nets(ACGANs) [10] constructed more complex architecture to latent space z. Aimed to learn more appearance from the real samples, ACGANs added more constraints for discriminator and separated value function into two parts: similarity Loss $\mathcal{L}_S$ and category Loss $\mathcal{L}_C$ .The two-player minimax game becomes more complex (Eq. 3).

$$\begin{aligned} \mathcal{L}_S &= \mathbb{E}[\log P(S = real|X_{real})] + \mathbb{E}[\log P(S = fake|G(z))] \\ \mathcal{L}_C &= \mathbb{E}[\log P(C = c|X_{real})] + \mathbb{E}[\log P(C = c|G(z))] \end{aligned} \quad (3)$$

where the discriminator maximize $\mathcal{L}_S + \mathcal{L}_C$, the generator maximize$\mathcal{L}_C - \mathcal{L}_S$.

The Background Augmentation Generative Adversarial Nets(BAGANs) assumed that the generator synthesize valid background x_{back} ($x_{back} = G(z)$) for the images x_{syn} which were rendered from 3D models. The discriminator distinguishes both background images x_{back} and synthetic images $x_{final} = x_{back} + x_{syn}$ which combine background and composite images by compositing image's instance semantic segmentation. Based on ACGANs, we redefine the value function of BAGANs into Eq. 4.

$$\begin{aligned}\mathcal{L}_S &= \mathbb{E}[\log P(S = real|X_{real})] \\ &\quad + (1-\lambda)\mathbb{E}[\log P(S = fake|X_{back})] \\ &\quad + \lambda\mathbb{E}[\log P(S = fake|X_{final})] \\ \mathcal{L}_C &= \mathbb{E}[\log P(C = c|X_{real})] + \mathbb{E}[\log P(C = c|X_{final})]\end{aligned} \tag{4}$$

In Eq. 4, We use the final image x_{final} as an important reference for the discriminator correction generator. We consider the trueness of the background image x_{back} to update the discriminator. The responsibility of parameter λ is to adjust the influence of the background and the final image on the network. Because no matter whether a picture contains a foreground object or not, it should be as realistic as possible.

4 Results

We select the cycle generative adversarial networks [19] (Cycle-GAN) as the compared algorithm. Cycle-GAN is the generative model for unaligned image data. In generating process, the synthesizing images from 3D models is a typical unaligned annotation data. The generator backgrounds do not have a corresponding image in the synthesizing images. Figures 3 and 5 show the final results.

As data validation, we regard classification as the verification task, because classification is the essential task in the visual cognitive system. We use the VGG16 [12] networks to train different background images and test on the real image database ObjectNet3D [15].

4.1 Final Images Generated by Cycle-GAN

The generator results of Cycle-GANs is shown in Fig. 3. Through the results, we found Cycle-GANs will change final image's foreground appearance according to

Fig. 3. Cycle-GAN results. Source images are the input of the generator, and conference images are randomly selected by the discriminator to learn appearance from it.

the target real image's foreground object; it would probably change the geometry of final image's foreground. Moreover, the appearance of final results is still unrealistic.

4.2 Final Images Generated by ACGAN

ACGAN is the state-of-the-art GAN algorithms, Fig. 4 shows the samples from the generator of ACGAN. Moreover, we test the generated samples in cifar-10 database, it only achieved 85.23% accuracy. According to Fig. 4, we infer that the foreground geometry of the sample is not sufficient for the image classifier to learn good classification knowledge.

Fig. 4. ACGAN results. Target domain is cifar-10 database.

4.3 Final Images Generated by BAGANs

Compared with different values of λ, good final images should consider the gradient from X_{back} and X_{final}. Because the background image without foreground object should be a realistic image.

Generated samples with different lambda values are shown in Fig. 5.

When $\lambda = 0$, the loss function only considers gradient from X_{back}, the generator can not find the realistic balance of the background image X_{back} and the final image X_{final}.

When $\lambda = 0.25$, the loss function only products the gradient from both X_{back} and X_{final}. Final image has the trend to generate more realistic images, but it

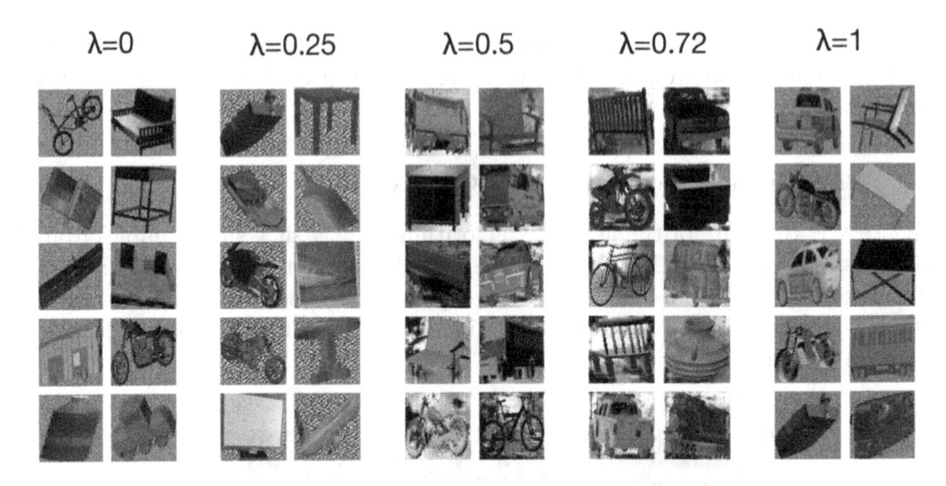

Fig. 5. Samples of BAGAN. This figure shows the different *lambda* BAGANs results. It also shows impact of λ on generative samples.

can not find the realistic balance of the background image X_{back} and the final image X_{final}. When $\lambda = 0.5$, the generator can generate more realistic images.

When $\lambda = 0.72$, the generator can generate the best background in BAGANs.

When $\lambda = 1$, the generator only accepts the gradient from X_{final}. The generator also cannot find the balance between X_{back} and X_{final}.

4.4 Classification Results of Different Training Data

In previous works, we demonstrated different background would have a certain impact on the classification results. Figure 6 shows different backgrounds sample.

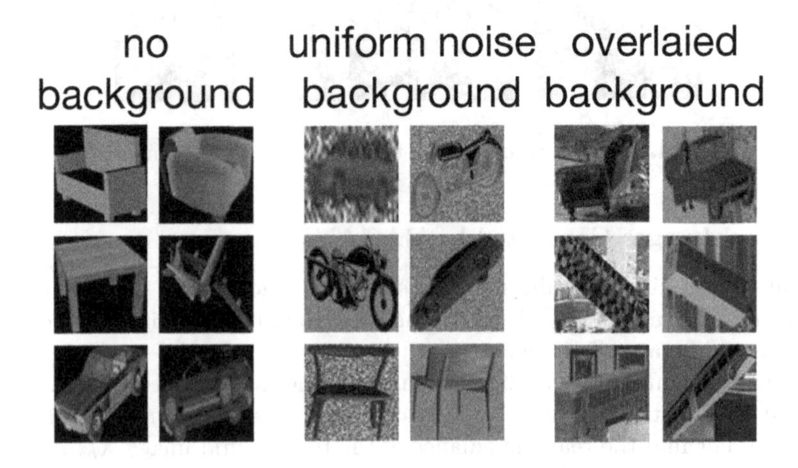

Fig. 6. We use three types of background to increase images appearance information: No background; Uniform noise background; SUN database background [16] (randomly selected image from SUN database as background).

Deep convolutional classifier (VGG-16 Nets)[12] trained on the synthesizing data and tested on the real-images data(ObjectNet3D database [15] and Pascal VOC database [3]). In Table 1, the more complex background appearance in the image has, the higher the accuracy that the classifier can achieve.

Comparing different score of different training data, when $\lambda = 0.73$, the synthesizing images from 3D models will get the best performance which accuracy score is 93.12%, precision is 94.23%, recall score is 97.64%, and f1-score is 95.90%. It is shown in Table 1.

Table 1. The metrics of classifier. This table presents different models test results. Under an adaptive parameters setting, eleven models are trained by Obj3D (ObjectNet 3D database [15], Syn_nobkg (Synthetic data without background), Syn_uniform(Synthetic data with uniform noise background), Syn_SUN (synthetic data with random background from SUN database [16]), Cycle_GANs(adding background though Cycle-GANs) and BAGANs(adding background with different λ values).

Trainingdata	Accuracy	Precision	Recall	F1-score
Objnet_3D	90.29%	92.14%	95.47%	93.78%
No_bkg	87.98%	90.58%	94.23%	92.37%
Uniform_bkg	89.99%	91.80%	95.25%	93.50%
SUN_bkg	92.24%	93.65%	96.19%	94.90%
Cycle_GANs	73.64%	77.52%	82.17%	79.78%
BAGANs ($\lambda = 0$)	88.12%	92.06%	91.67%	91.63%
BAGANs ($\lambda = 0.25$)	90.53%	91.15%	94.77%	93.44%
BAGANs ($\lambda = 0.5$)	91.64%	94.65%	94.58%	94.62%
BAGANs ($\lambda = 0.72$)	93.12%	94.23%	97.64%	95.90%
BAGANs ($\lambda = 1$)	90.42%	91.54%	94.53%	93.01%

5 Discussion

This work is intended to synthesize hyper-vision annotations based on GAN and 3D models. Figure 5 shows the results of BAGANs. The results of BAGANs could help researchers to overcome the overfitting problem due to the shortage of training data. We have demonstrated the final results could help deep convolutional classifier get the better score which accuracy score is 93.12%, precision is 94.23%, recall score is 97.64%, and f1-score is 95.90%. Table 1 shows the useful background can help classifier learning better foreground information and achieve better classification score. The training strategy will help classifier learning appearance from synthesizing images and recognizing foreground from real images. This training strategy was described in previous work.

Content Correction We remake Fig. 5 to make the characters distinct. Again, x_{back} is the background generated by BAGANs $x_{back} = G(z)$. As our methods aimed at improving the realness of an image, the quality of an image is the major consideration of our work, the computational-complexity has low priority in this task. Compared with other generative adversarial nets [2,6,19], our generated samples has a certain metric to compare the quality of generative samples, and the final classification results can evaluate the generative samples. That is more scientific than measuring images by observing the same object with different backgrounds. Furthermore, we reconstruct our paper and show the architecture of the proposed network in Fig. 1.

Strengths and Limitations of the Study. An important strength of the works is that the discriminator can guide generator to generate compelling images through specific lose function. However, our networks use the resized images as input and output, this will loss some appearance information. Furthermore, resizing images will scratch images into a hard-understanding shape. Although Cycle-GAN cannot generate valid images. Its unique learning strategy and value function are worthy of the follow-up research.

6 Conclusion

Our major contributions are: We use GAN and 3D models to synthesize hypervision annotations. Designing BAGAN helps the generative image more realistic. Images generated by BAGANS help deep convolution classifier get 93% accuracy.

In future, we can improve this approach in five ways: (1) Using method proposed by Ren [11] and Zhao [18] to detect and reduce contour, crack and disocclusion artifacts. (2) Wang [14] used attention methods for video saliency detection. We can try to add attention module in order to let networks pay more attention to the quality of the image background. (3) Considering stacked idea (mentioned by Jaime [17]), reconstructing networks architecture may be an effective way to improve the solution of the generated images. (4) Modifying the loss function to merge Cycle-GAN value function. (5) Considering the classification results, we can use the BAGANs generated data to explore saliency image detection [7] with few training data.

References

1. Chang, A.X., et al.: Shapenet: an information-rich 3D model repository. In: Computer Science (2015)
2. Chen, X., Duan, Y., Houthooft, R., Schulman, J., Sutskever, I., Abbeel, P.: Infogan: interpretable representation learning by information maximizing generative adversarial nets. In: Neural Information Processing Systems, pp. 2172–2180 (2016)
3. Everingham, M., Van Gool, L., Williams, C.K.I., Winn, J., Zisserman, A.: The Pascal Visual Object Classes Challenge 2012 (VOC2012) Results. http://www.pascal-network.org/challenges/VOC/voc2012/workshop/index.html
4. Feng, Y., Ren, J., Jiang, J.: Object-based 2D-to-3D video conversion for effective stereoscopic content generation in 3D-tv applications. IEEE Trans. Broadcast. **57**(2), 500–509 (2011)

5. Goodfellow, I.J., et al.: Generative adversarial nets. In: International Conference on Neural Information Processing Systems, pp. 2672–2680 (2014)
6. Gulrajani, I., Ahmed, F., Arjovsky, M., Dumoulin, V., Courville, A.C.: Improved training of wasserstein gans. In: Advances in Neural Information Processing Systems, pp. 5769–5779 (2017)
7. Han, J., Zhang, D., Hu, X., Guo, L., Ren, J., Wu, F.: Background prior-based salient object detection via deep reconstruction residual. IEEE Trans. Circuits Syst. Video Technol. **25**(8), 1309–1321 (2015)
8. Krizhevsky, A., Sutskever, I., Hinton, G.E.: Imagenet classification with deep convolutional neural networks. In: International Conference on Neural Information Processing Systems, pp. 1097–1105 (2012)
9. Mirza, M., Osindero, S.: Conditional generative adversarial nets. In: Computer Science, pp. 2672–2680 (2014)
10. Odena, A., Olah, C., Shlens, J.: Conditional image synthesis with auxiliary classifier gans. In: International conference on machine learning, pp. 2642–2651 (2016)
11. Ren, J., Jiang, J., Wang, D., Ipson, S.S.: Fusion of intensity and inter-component chromatic difference for effective and robust colour edge detection. Image Process. Let **4**(4), 294–301 (2010)
12. Simonyan, K., Zisserman, A.: Very deep convolutional networks for large-scale image recognition. In: International Conference on Learning Representations (2015)
13. Szegedy, C., et al.: Going deeper with convolutions. In: Computer Vision and Pattern Recognition, pp. 1–9 (2015)
14. Wang, Z., et al.: A deep-learning based feature hybrid framework for spatiotemporal saliency detection inside videos. Neurocomputing, 68–83 (2018)
15. Xiang, Y., et al.: Objectnet3D: a large scale database for 3D object recognition. In: European Conference Computer Vision (ECCV) (2016)
16. Xiao, J., Hays, J., Ehinger, K.A., Oliva, A., Torralba, A.: Sun database: large-scale scene recognition from abbey to zoo. In: Computer Vision and Pattern Recognition, pp. 3485–3492 (2010)
17. Zabalza, J.: Corrigendum to novel segmented stacked autoencoder for effective dimensionality reduction and feature extraction in hyperspectral imaging. Neurocomputing **185**(C), 1–10 (2016)
18. Zhao, D., Zheng, J., Ren, J.: Effective removal of artifacts from views synthesized using depth image based rendering. In: The International Conference on Distributed Multimedia Systems, pp. 65–71 (2015)
19. Zhu, J.Y., Park, T., Isola, P., Efros, A.A.: Unpaired image-to-image translation using cycle-consistent adversarial networkss. In: Computer Vision (ICCV) IEEE International Conference on 2017 (2017)

Deep Learning Based Single Image Super-Resolution: A Survey

Viet Khanh Ha[1], Jinchang Ren[1,2(✉)], Xinying Xu[2], Sophia Zhao[1], Gang Xie[3], and Valentin Masero Vargas[4]

[1] Department of Electronic and Electrical Engineering, University of Strathclyde, Glasgow, UK
npurjc@gmail.com
[2] College of Electrical and Power Engineering, Taiyuan University of Technology, Taiyuan, China
[3] College of Electronic Information Engineering, Taiyuan University of Science and Technology, Taiyuan, China
[4] Department of Computer Systems and Telematics Engineering, Universidad de Extremadura, Badajoz, Spain

Abstract. Image super-resolution is a process of obtaining one or more high-resolution image from single or multiple samples of low-resolution images. Due to its wide applications, a number of different techniques have been developed recently, including interpolation-based, reconstruction-based and learning-based. The learning-based methods have recently attracted increasing great attention due to their capability in predicting the high-frequency details lost in low resolution image. This survey mainly provides an overview on most of published work for single image reconstruction using Convolutional Neural Network. Furthermore, common issues in super-resolution algorithms, such as imaging models, improvement factor and assessment criteria are also discussed.

Keywords: Image super resolution · Convolutional neural network
High-resolution image

1 Introduction

Single image super-resolution (SISR) aims to obtain the visually high-resolution (HR) image from one low-resolution (LR) image. It has found practical applications in real-world problems, from remote sensing where restriction of certain bandwidth and pixel size are present, security surveillance imaging where most information regarding particular scene details, and in medical imaging where reducing irradiation is preferred. Since SISR problem usually assumes the observed LR image is to be a non-invertible low-pass filtering, down-sampled and noisy version of HR image, it is a highly ill-posed problem. There are a variety of methods has been developed recently, which can be classified into interpolation-based, reconstruction-based, and example-based methods. Interpolation-based methods typically adopt fixed-function kernels to estimate the unknown pixels in HR image. Although the interpolation-based methods are very simple and effective ways, they are produce overly smooth edges and blurring details.

J. Ren et al. (Eds.): BICS 2018, LNAI 10989, pp. 106–119, 2018.
https://doi.org/10.1007/978-3-030-00563-4_11

Reconstruction-based methods usually introduce certain image priors or constraints between the down-sampling of the reconstructed HR image and the original LR images to tackle the ill-posed problem of image super-resolution. Example-based methods, which recently achieved convincing performance, recovered missing high-frequency based on learning the map between LR patches and its HR counterparts. Example-based methods can be categorized into 5 groups: early research [1–3], sparsity methods [4–6], self-exemplar methods [7, 8], locally linear regression methods [9–15] and deep architectures [16–36], in which the CNN-based methods have drawn considerable attention due to its simple structure and excellent reconstruction quality.

In this paper, we attempt to provide a brief survey of the research on example-based methods, then focus mainly on CNN-based methods in the context of single image super-resolution. The rest of the paper is arranged as follows. Section 2 give brief review of background, followed by early approaches for super-resolution. Section 3 surveys the contemporary CNN-based approaches, mostly on the-state-of-the-art algorithm and the performance comparison among them is given in Sect. 4. Section 5 will discuss further on multi-resolution, among them fusion methods are widely used. Sections 5 and 6 give an overall discussion and a conclusion, respectively.

2 Background

Learning-based algorithm aims to hallucinate missing information of the super-resolved images using relationship between LR and HR images. These algorithms contain training step in which the relationship is learn, then the learned knowledge is then applied to unseen LR images. Although the more training database give more information to apply on unseen data, it is paradox that using larger database does not guarantee better results due to irrelevant examples misleading model to learn more information from noises. Learning-based algorithm for SISR were first introduced in [1–3] in which neighbor embedding [3] was use with idea that low-resolution patches corresponding high-resolution patches share similar local geometries highly influences the subsequent coding-based or dictionary-based methods.

2.1 Sparsity-Based Method

The sparse representation theory each atom unit is a basic unit that can be used to reconstruct larger units. Also, image patches can be well-represent as a sparse linear combination of elements from appropriately chosen over-complete dictionary. By exploiting sparse representation for each patch of low-resolution inputs, the coefficients of this representation can be applied to generate the high-resolution outputs. Let say, if dimensionality of the input image is 64×64 (equal 4096), the dimensionality of dictionary is $N \times 4096$, where N is very large ($N > 4096$, in this case we have over-complete representation).

$$D \times \alpha = X \tag{1}$$

D is basic vector, X is input data and α is unknown. $D >> \dim(X)$ in case for super-resolution, where we want to build dictionary for most scenarios of input. To solve over-complete system, assumption that X is composed of no more than a fix number (k) of bases from *D,* then find the set of k bases that best fit the data point X. The observed low-resolution image Y is blurred and down-sampled version of the high-resolution X:

$$Y = S.H.X \tag{2}$$

Here, H represents a blurring filter and S the down-sampling operation. This is ill-posed problem, since for given low-resolution input, infinitely many high-resolution satisfy the constraint. Yang et al. [4] used joint dictionary training to find α coefficient. Given the sampled training patch pairs P = $\{X^h, Y^l\}$, where $X^h = \{x_1, x_2, \ldots x_n\}$ are the set of sampled high-resolution image patches and $Y^l = \{y_1, y_2, \ldots y_n\}$ are the corresponding low-resolution image patches. Both dictionaries are trained, so sparse representation of high-resolution patch is the same as the sparse representation of the corresponding low-resolution patch. However, limitation appears that two dictionaries are not connected by linear transform also mentioned by authors in this paper. Other works [5, 6] proposed to solve two equations but still have many limitations of extracted features and mapping function, which are not adaptive or optimal for generate HR images.

2.2 Self-exemplar Methods or Internal Database Based Algorithm

Based on the observation that natural image has self-similarity property, which tends to recur many times inside the image, Glasner et al. [7] proposed a scale space pyramid of LR to match LR and HR pairs. Through the training, patches contained in internal data are more relevant than that of external data. Since internal dictionary are constructed only on given limited LR-HR patch pairs, Huang et al. [8] extended search space to both planar perspective and affine transform of patches to achieve lower errors and more accurate prediction. The complexity of computation makes this method not suitable for real time problem.

2.3 Locally Linear Regression Methods

An external database based super resolution methods, use external images to try and find mapping between the high-resolution and low-resolution images. The algorithms use different supervised machine learning techniques such as ridge regression [10], anchored neighborhood regression [10, 12], random forest [13], manifold embedding [15]. The database is categorized separately into clustering using k-mean, random forest dictionary to find linear regression.

3 Deep Architecture Methods

3.1 CNNs-Based Models

The CNNs have been developed rapidly in the last two decades. However, its application to solve SISR problem is first introduced by Dong et al. [16, 17], who described a three-layer CNN for super-resolution as Super-Resolution Convolutional Neural

Network (SRCNN). In this method, CNN has been used to learn the non-linear mapping between the LR and HR images and it significantly outperforms previous non-deep learning methods. The training objective is to find optimal model, given training set $\{x^i, y^i\}_{i=1\ldots N}$. The best mode f then will use to accurately predicts value $\mathbf{Y} = f(\mathbf{X})$, where $\mathbf{X}$ is unobserved examples. The SRCNN [16, 17] consists of following operation, as show in Fig. 1 [16]:

(1) Preprocessing: Upscale LR image to desired HR image using bicubic interpolation.
(2) Feature extraction: Extracts a set of feature map from the upscale LR image.
(3) Non-linear mapping: Maps the feature maps between LR and HR patch.
(4) Reconstruction: Produce the HR image from HR patches.

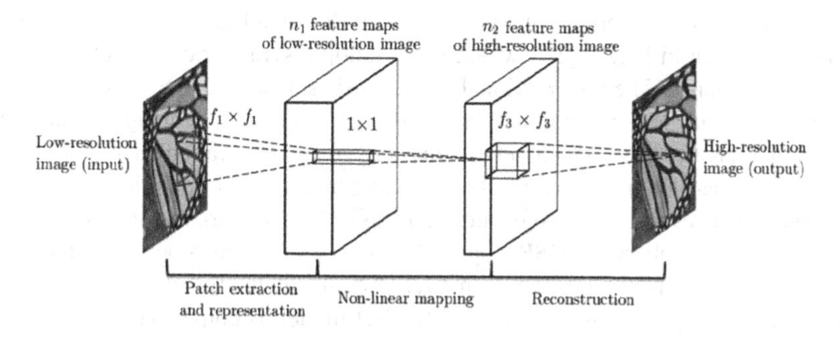

Fig. 1. SRCNN structure [16]

These networks contain only 3 convolutional layers and is improved later with 8 layers [18] impressively outperform conventional non-deep learning methods. However, this model has been mostly restricted to limited training and testing on single scale factor, do not achieve better performance due to the difficulty of deepening networks. This led to observation that whether 'the deeper the better' is or not the case in SR. Inspired of success of very deep networks including Res-Net, Kim et al. [19, 20] proposed two models named Very Deep Convolutional Networks (VDSR) [19] as show in Fig. 2 [19] and Deeply Recursive Convolutional Network [20] (DRCN), both stacking 20 convolutional layers. To speed up training in deep network, the VDSR [19] is trained with very high learning rate (10^{-1} instead of 10^{-4} in SRCNN) in order to accelerate the convergence speed and introduced gradient clipping to control explosion problem. Residual learning is used instead of predict the whole image has several advantages such as fast convergence and better accuracy to compare with SRCNN. In addition, data argumentation allows network adapt well with multiple scale factors (2x, 3x, 4x) without degrading performance. The zero padding also is introduced to avoid the size of feature map reduces quickly through layers of convolution, which appears in deep networks.

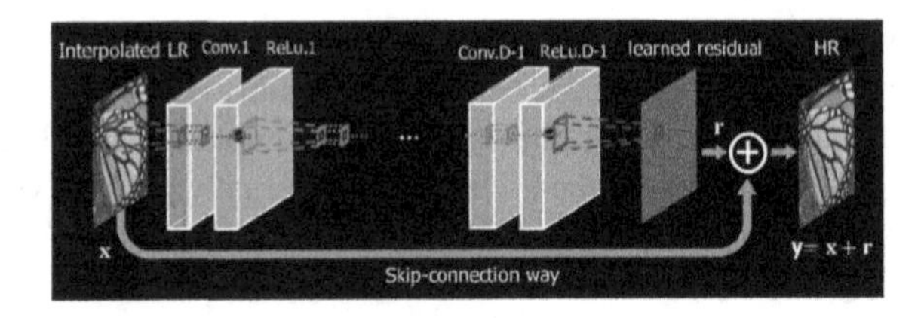

Fig. 2. VDSR model [19] contains 20 convolutional layers, global residual learning represented by skip-connection.

Similar to DRCN [20], Tai et al. [21] proposed Deeply Recursive Residual Network (DRRN), which using both global residual learning and introduces new concept of local residual learning. The global residual learning is used in the identity branch and recursive learning in local residual branch. Mao et al. [22] proposed a 30-layer convolutional auto-encoder network named very deep Residual Encoder-Decoder Network (RED30), as given in Fig. 3 [22], which used multiple symmetric connection to boost training convergence. The convolutional layers work as feature extractor, encode image content, while the de-convolutional layers decode and recover image details. This single model has been testing for several tasks of image restoration such as image de-noising, JPEG de-blocking, non-blind de-blurring and image in-painting [22].

Recent advances in CNN design such as Dense-Net, Network in Network, Residual Network enable numbers of SISR approaches [23, 24, 25] to produce better performances compare to pioneer SRCNN model. Among them, Enhance Deep Residual Networks (EDSR) [26], mostly based on Res-Net model, is convinced to be the-state-of-the-art, as shown in Table 2.

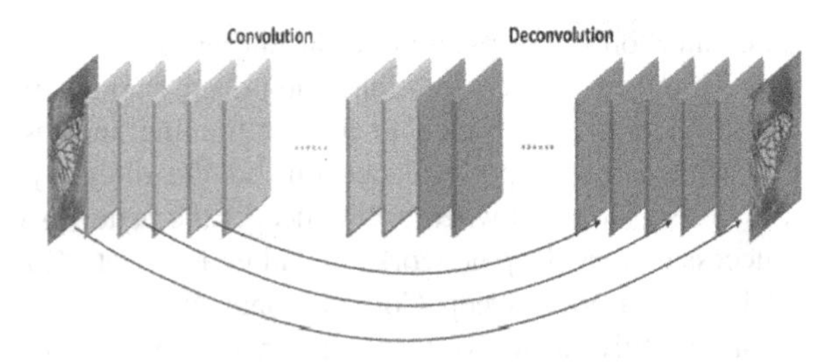

Fig. 3. RED30 structure [22] contain 30 layers. Symmetric skip connection between convolutional and de-convolutional layers

Instead of using interpolation or deconvolution [18] as up-scale method for pre-processing, Lai et al. [27] proposed Laplacian Pyramid Super-Resolution Network (Lap-SRN) to present images as a series of high-pass bands and low-pass bands. This structure enables the residuals (high-pass bands) learn in progressive ways. As shown in Fig. 4 [27], at each step, numbers of convolutional layer learn the residual and one transposed convolutional layer to up-sample feature extraction.

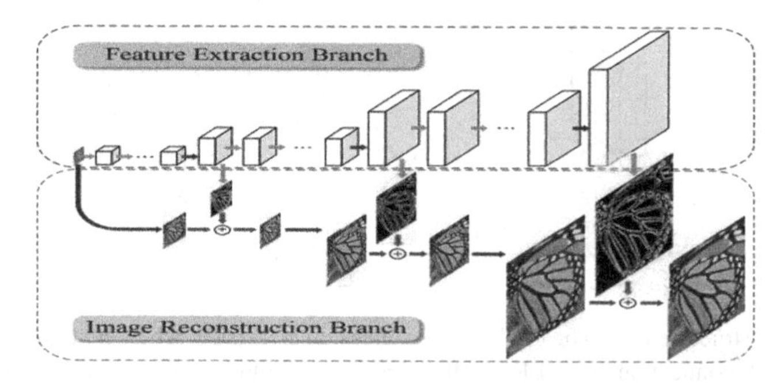

Fig. 4. Lap-SRN structure [27]

One of the drawback with most SISR approaches is that they have been restricted to limit up-scale factors to 2x, 3x, 4x. Otherwise, features available in the LR space have not sufficient to exactly reconstruct the image. To achieve higher scale factor, Wang et al. [28] proposed a fully Progressive Asymmetric Pyramidal Structure to adapt with multiple up-scale factors and up to 8x. Also, a Deep Back Projection Network [29] using mutually connected up- and down-sampling stages has been claimed for reaching such high up-scale factor. To facilitate network training, most CNN-based methods assume that low-resolution image is down-sampled from high-resolution image, they ignored the true degradation in real world application such as noises. Kai Zhang et al. [30] proposed Super-Resolution Multiple Degradation (SRMD) structure with dimensionality stretching strategy scheme to handle blur, noise, and down-sampled image. Shocher et al. [31] inspired by the observation that the natural image has strong internal data repetition, then the information for tiny object is better to be found elsewhere inside the image, other than in any external database of example. Therefore, a 'Zero Shot' SR (ZSSR) is proposed without relying on any prior images example or prior training. It exploits cross-scale internal recurrent of image-specific information, then the test image itself is trained before feed again to resulting trained network.

Although these approaches attempt to higher scale factor and deal with more degradation form of input, they still need to research further to produce persuaded results.

3.2 RNN-CNN-Based Models

On the view of Recurrent Neural Network (RNN), a Dual-State Recurrent Network (DSRN) [32] allows LR path and HR path captions information at different spaces and connected at every step in order to contribute jointly to learning process. At each stage, LR image are sequence inputs of HR image and vice versa, so called dual state, as given in Fig. 5 [32]. Inspired by concept of Long Short Term Memory (LSTM) block in RNN, Tai et al. [33] proposed Memory Network (MemNet), which uses recursive layers follow by memory unit to allow combination short and long-term memory for image reconstruction, as shown in Fig. 6 [33].

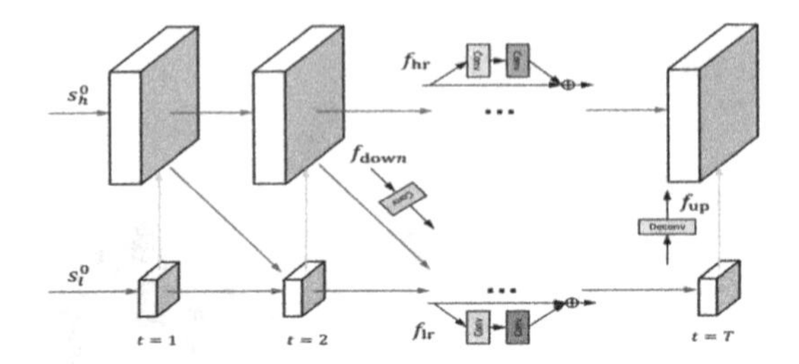

Fig. 5. DSRN structure [32]. The top branch operates on HR space, where bottom branch works on LR space. A connection from LR to HR using de-convolution operation; a delay feedback mechanism to connect previous predicted HR to LR at next stage.

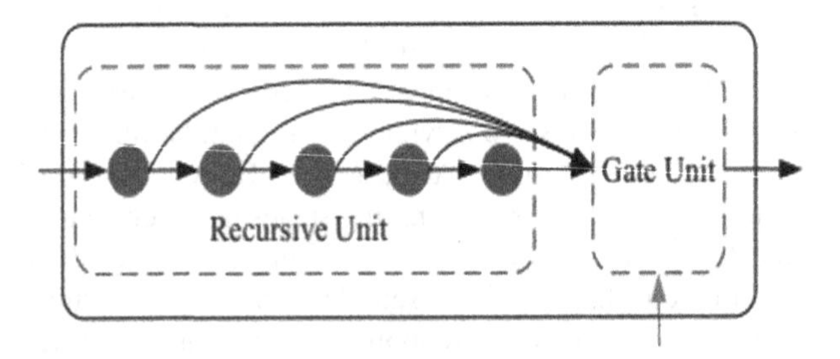

Fig. 6. Memory block in MemNet [33] includes multiple Recursive units and a Gate Unit

3.3 GAN-Based Model

Basically, Generative Adversarial Network (GAN) contains two models, a generative model and a discriminative model. The discriminative model has the task of determining whether a given image looks natural or looks like it has been artificial created. The task of generative model is created images so that the discriminator gets trained to produce a correct output. The interesting point is during the training, the discriminator is aware of the internal represent of data because it has been trained to understand the differences between real image and artificial created.

One major issue in measurement metric is that a performance of algorithm is commonly measured using pixel-wise such as MSE (as in Eq. (4)) in favor of maximizing the peak signal-to-noise ratio (PSNR). This will show poorly visual to human perception even with high PSNR due to the mean of many possible solutions. Ledig et al. [34] proposed Super-Resolution Generative Adversarial Network (SRGAN) in favor of perceptual similarity, has delivered great performance for human perception. The extension GAN model is further used in [35, 36], which improved SRGAN with fusion of pixel-wise loss, perceptual loss, texture matching loss. It is shown in Fig. 7 [34], where the optimization desire to human perception, bring reconstruction image look realistic. One of major advantage of GANs-based SR model is that GANs use a largely unsupervised training process on the real images, so it does not require label or prior condition between LR and HR image.

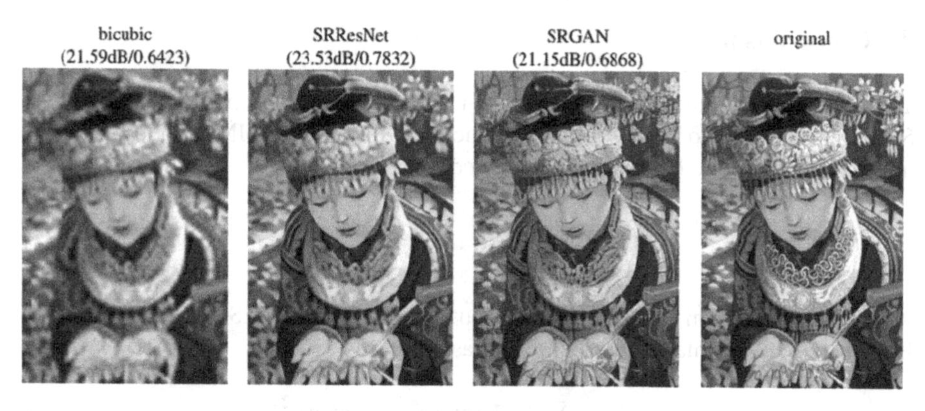

Fig. 7. [34] From left to right, image is reconstructed by bicubic interpolation, deep residual network (SRResNet) measured by MSE, SRGAN optimize more sensitive to human perception, original image. Corresponding PSNR and SSIM are provided on top.

Using MSE-based measurement can have poorly performance even the reconstructed image achieves high PSNR. To support that idea on the side of SRGAN, we also add two of reluctant reconstructed images during implement on SR field. Our model focus on global contextual and get result with low PSNR lower than that of bicubic, as given in Fig. 8. It can be explained that errors on pixel at background deteriorate overall result while the pixel value is not equally important. The bicubic interpolated images has better score, though they are all blur.

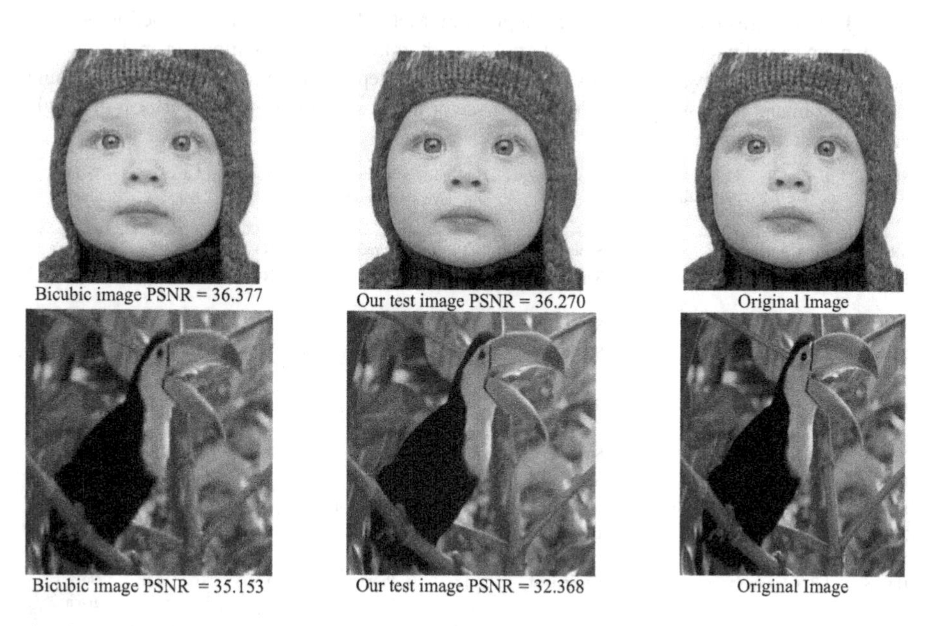

Fig. 8. From left to right, images reconstructed by bicubic interpolation, ours model and original image. PSNR at bottom of each image.

4 Comparison

There are two measures has been mostly used to compare the performance, a Peak Signal-to-Noise Ratio (PSNR) and a Structural SIMlarity (SSIM) index [37]. The higher the PSNR, the better of reconstructed image.

$$\mathrm{PSNR} = 10 * \log_{10}\frac{\mathrm{R}^2}{\mathrm{MSE}} \tag{3}$$

where R is maximum fluctuate in the input image datatype, MSE is Mean Squared Error between two images, has expressed as:

$$\mathrm{MSE} = \frac{\sum_{\mathrm{M,N}}[\mathrm{I}_1(\mathrm{m,n}) - [\mathrm{I}_2(\mathrm{m,n})]^2}{\mathrm{M*N}} \tag{4}$$

Here, M and N are the number of rows and columns in the input images, respectively, and SSIM is quantitative measure used to quantify the similarities of structure between two image.

We compare CNN based SR models including SRCNN [17], FSRCNN [18], VDSR [19], DRCN [20], DRRN [21], RED30 [22], MemNet [33], EDSR [26], LapSRN [27], Zeo Shot [31], Dual State [32], SRGAN [34] on algorithm in Table 1 and performance in Table 2. In Table 2, the benchmark datasets are used including SET5, SET14, B100, URBAN 100 which mostly used for comparison in SR

Table 1. Comparison of CNN based SR algorithm. Methods with direct reconstruction perform one-step up-sampling (with bicubic interpolation of transpose convolution) from LR to HR images, while progressive predict HR images in multiple step. Multiple scale factor mean training and testing image down-scaling with multiple factor at the same process, not perform on single factor separately.

Models	Input	Multiple-scale factor	Type of Network	Number of layers	Reconstruction method	Residual	Loss function	Training time
SRCNN	LR + Interpolation	No	Supervised	3	Direct	No	L2 (MSE)	A week
FSRCNN	LR	Yes	Supervised	8	Direct	No	L2 (MSE)	Few hours
VDSR	LR + Interpolation	Yes	Supervised	20	Direct	Yes	L2 (MSE)	4 h
DRCN	LR + Interpolation	No	Supervised	20	Direct	Yes	L2 (MSE)	6 days
DRRN	LR + Interpolation	Yes	Supervised	52	Direct	Yes	L2 (MSE)	4 days
RED30	LR + Interpolation	Yes	Supervised	30	Direct	Yes	L2 (MSE)	Not given
MemNet	LR + Interpolation	Not given	Supervised	80	Direct	Yes	L2 (MSE)	5 days
EDSR	LR + Interpolation	Yes	Supervised	32	Direct	Yes	L1	8 days
LapSRN	LR	Not given	Supervised	27	Progressive	Yes	Charbonnier	3 days
Zero Shot	LR + Interpolation	Yes	Unsupervised	8	Direct	Yes	L1	days or weeks
Dual Sate	LR + Interpolation	Not given	Supervised	18	Progressive	Yes	L2 (MSE)	Not given
SRGAN	LR through generator network	Yes	Unsupervised + Supervised	54	Direct	Yes	Perceptual loss	Not given

algorithms. Scale factor used include 2x, 3x, 4x, and information that were not provided by the authors is marked by [-]. All quantitative results are duplicated from the original papers.

In Table 2, we observe that EDSR outperformed other algorithms with large margin, reached to the-state-of-the-art model recently. Meanwhile, MemNet, achieved in most case the second best performance on SET5 and SET14. The application of residual learning brings benefits to SR image reconstruction, therefor it has been successfully applied in several network models.

5 Multi-resolution Related Approaches

Image fusion has emerged as a promising research area that aim to combine information from different sources into a single composite for interpretation. It requires the first extraction of the features contained in the various input sources, then characteristics those feature as size, shape, color, contrast, and texture. The fusion is thus enable to detect useful features with higher confidence based on those extracted features. The data fusion has been applied for broad applications in image processing such as in image detection, image registration, image reconstruction. The actual fusion can take place at different types or levels of information representation, from combinations of color and spatial features [38, 39], thermal and visible features [40], spatial and frequency features, spatial and temporal features [41]. When most proposed algorithm processed images in separate colored channel, Yan et al. [38, 39] proposed the fusion of color and spatial features, which is particularly important in retrieval of logo/trademark images. In this method, dominant colors are first extracted via color quantization and k-means clustering, then a component-based spatial descriptor is derived as local features. For detection, Yan et al. [40] proposed the combination of thermal and visible imagery for detection and tracking of pedestrians achieved better distinguishability in human visual perception and less sensitive to these noise effects such as illumination noise and shadows. The fusion of intensity and inter-component chromatic difference has been proposed by Ren et al. [42] for effective and robust color edge detection. Ren et al. also proposed multiresolution decomposition scheme, which decomposes the signal into several components. The 2-D translation is decomposed into two 1-D Fourier transform, which provides improved accuracy in sub-pixel motion estimation [43]. Also, another method [44] based on phase correlation uses linear weighting of the height of the main peak accompany with the difference between two neighboring side peak on the other. This method [44] and gradient-based method [45] effectively deals with noisy image to achieve high accuracy sub-pixel motion estimation. Chai et al. [46] use shape characteristic of a walking object, trajectory-based joint kinematics characteristic motion characteristic of body parts for effective gait recognition.

Last but not least, hyperspectral imagery provides spatial 2-D image in hundreds of different wavelengths, and as the result, gives better capability to see unseen because of its high spectral resolution. However, it requires effective method for dimensionality reduction and feature extraction [47] to reduce level of complexity.

Table 2. Quantitative evaluation of the-state-of-the-art SR algorithm. Average PSNR/SSIM for scale factor 2x, 3, 4x. Red text indicates that the best and blue text indicates the second best performance.

		Set5	Set 14	B100	Urban100
	Scale	PSNR/SSIM	PSNR/SSIM	PSNR/SSIM	PSNR/SSIM
SRCNN	2	36.66/0.9542	32.45/0.9067	-	-
	3	32.75/0.9090	29.30/0.8215	-	-
	4	30.49/0.8628	27.50/0.7513	-	-
FSRCNN	2	37.00/0.9558	32.63/0.9088	-	-
	3	33.16/0.9140	29.43/0.8242	-	-
	4	30.71/0.8657	27.59/0.7535	-	-
VDSR	2	37.53/0.9587	33.03/0.9124	31.90/0.8960	30.76/0.9140
	3	33.66/0.9213	29.77/0.8314	28.82/0.7976	27.14/0.8279
	4	31.35/0.8838	28.01/0.7674	27.29/0.7251	25.18/0.7524
DRCN	2	37.63/0.9588	33.04/0.9118	31.85/0.8942	30.75/0.9133
	3	33.82/0.9226	29.76/0.8311	28.80/0.7963	27.15/0.8276
	4	31.53/0.8854	28.02/0.7670	27.23/0.7233	25.14/0.7510
DRRN	2	37.74/0.9591	33.23/0.9136	-	31.23/0.9188
	3	34.03/0.9244	29.96/0.8349	-	27.53/0.8378
	4	31.68/0.888	28.21/0.7720	-	25.44/0.7638
RED30	2	37.66/0.9599	32.94/0.9144	-	-
	3	33.82/0.9230	29.61/0.8341	-	-
	4	31.51/0.8869	27.86/0.7718	-	-
MemNet	2	37.78/0.9597	33.28/0.9142	-	31.31/0.9195
	3	34.09/0.9248	30.00/0.8350	-	27.56/0.8376
	4	31.74/0.8893	28.26/0.7723	-	25.50/0.7630
LapSRN	2	37.52 / 0.959	33.08 / 0.913	-	30.41 / 0.910
	4	31.54 / 0.885	28.19 / 0.772	-	25.21 / 0.756
	8	26.14 / 0.738	24.44 / 0.623	-	21.81 / 0.581
EDSR	2	38.20 / 0.9606	34.02 / 0.9204	32.37 / 0.9018	33.10 / 0.9363
	3	34.77/0.9290	30.66/0.8481	29.32/0.8104	29.02/0.8685
	4	32.62 / 0.8984	28.94 / 0.7901	27.79 / 0.7437	26.86 / 0.8080
Zero Shot	2	37.37 / 0.9570	33.00 / 0.9108	-	-
	3	33.42/0.9188	29.800.8304	-	-
	4	31.13 / 0.8796	28.01 / 0.7651	-	-
Dual Sate	2	37.66 / 0.959	33.15 / 0.913	-	30.97 / 0.916
	3	33.88/0.922	30.26/0.837	-	27.16/0.828
	4	31.40 / 0.883	28.07 / 0.770	-	25.08 / 0.747
SRGAN	2	-	-	-	-
	3	-	-	-	-
	4	29.40/0.8472	26.02/0.7397	-	-

6 Discussion

One possible contribution to SR field is to propose effective models for image reconstruction. However, it is less likely adding more parameters as solutions since super-resolution aims to recover at pixel-level, which requires much more comparison than in classification. The ways to improve image resolution is how to make the neural networks to learn more about the relationship between LR and HR images. While the regular supervised CNN networks attempt to learn directly the mapping and highly depend on predetermined assumptions, GANs based networks are much more flexible with promising performance due to incorporated unsupervised training. Also, traditional measurements expose several constraints to human perception, and the integrated perceptual assessment produces better results. The fusion of unsupervised/supervised models and multi-resolution can reconstruct image with more accuracy and flexibility, yet it still requires further investigation.

7 Conclusion

This paper contains a survey on recent super-resolution techniques that underlie on learning based methods. Among them, we noticed that convolutional neural network based methods have recently achieved the best performance. There are remain challenges to bring them into real time applications since they are only applied on standard benchmark dataset and require to adapt well with differently structured images.

Although LR image is assumed to be a down-sampled version of the HR image, most CNN-based super resolution models fail to work on large scaling down-sampled factors with the exception of noise. The evaluation metrics also have to consider in different perspective of applications. These will also form the base for our future work.

Acknowledgement. The authors would like to thank the support from the Shanxi Hundred People Plan of China and colleagues from the Image Processing group in Strathclyde University for their valuable suggestions.

References

1. Freeman, W.T., Pasztor, E.C., Carmichael, O.T.: Learning low-level vision. Int. J. Comput. Vis. **40**(1), 25–47 (2000)
2. Freeman, W.T., et al.: Example-based super-resolution. IEEE Comput. Graph. Appl. **22**(2), 56–65 (2002)
3. Chang, H., Yeung, D.Y., Xiong, Y.: Super-resolution through neighbor embedding. In: Proceedings of CVPR, vol. 1, p. I (2004)
4. Zeyde, R., Elad, M., Protter, M.: On single image scale-up using sparse-representations. In: Boissonnat, J.-D., et al. (eds.) Curves and Surfaces 2010. LNCS, vol. 6920, pp. 711–730. Springer, Heidelberg (2012). https://doi.org/10.1007/978-3-642-27413-8_47
5. Dong, W., Zhang, L., Shi, G., Wu, X.: Image deblurring and super-resolution by adaptive sparse domain selection and adaptive regularization. IEEE Trans. Image Process. **20**(7), 1838–1857 (2011)

6. Peleg, T., Elad, M.: A statistical prediction model based on sparse representations for single image super-resolution. IEEE Trans. Image Process. **23**(6), 2569–2582 (2014)
7. Glasner, D., Bagon, S., Irani, M.: Super-resolution from a single image. In: Proceedings of ICCV, pp. 349–356 (2009)
8. Huang, J.B., et al.: Single image super-resolution from transformed self-exemplars. In: Proceedings of CVPR, pp. 5197–5206 (2015)
9. Gu, S., Sang, N., Ma, F.: Fast image super resolution via local regression. In: Proceedings of ICPR, pp. 3128–3131 (2012)
10. Timofte, R., De, V., Van Gool.: Anchored neighborhood regression for fast example-based super-resolution. In: Proceedings of ICCV, pp. 1920–1927 (2013)
11. Yang, C.Y., Yang, M.H.: Fast direct super-resolution by simple functions. In: Proceedings of ICCV, pp. 561–568 (2013)
12. Timofte, R., De Smet, V., Van Gool, L.: A+: adjusted anchored neighborhood regression for fast super-resolution. In: Cremers, D., Reid, I., Saito, H., Yang, M.-H. (eds.) ACCV 2014. LNCS, vol. 9006, pp. 111–126. Springer, Cham (2015). https://doi.org/10.1007/978-3-319-16817-3_8
13. Schulter, S., Leistner, C., Bischof, H.: Fast and accurate image upscaling with super-resolution forests. In: Proceedings of the IEEE Conference on Computer Vision and Pattern Recognition, pp. 3791–3799 (2015)
14. Salvador, J., Perez-Pellitero, E.: Naive Bayes super-resolution forest. In: Proceedings of the IEEE International Conference on Computer Vision, pp. 325–333 (2015)
15. Pérez-Pellitero, E., Salvador, J., Ruiz-Hidalgo, J., Rosenhahn, B.: Psyco: Manifold span reduction for super resolution. In: Proceedings of the IEEE Conference on Computer Vision and Pattern Recognition, pp. 1837–1845 (2016)
16. Dong, C., Loy, C.C., He, K., Tang, X.: Learning a deep convolutional network for image super-resolution. In: Fleet, D., Pajdla, T., Schiele, B., Tuytelaars, T. (eds.) ECCV 2014. LNCS, vol. 8692, pp. 184–199. Springer, Cham (2014). https://doi.org/10.1007/978-3-319-10593-2_13
17. Dong, C., Loy, C.C., He, K., Tang, X.: Image super-resolution using deep convolutional networks. IEEE Trans. Pattern Anal. Mach. Intell. (TPAMI) **38**(2), 295–307 (2016)
18. Dong, C., Loy, C.C., Tang, X.: Accelerating the super-resolution convolutional neural network. In: Leibe, B., Matas, J., Sebe, N., Welling, M. (eds.) ECCV 2016. LNCS, vol. 9906, pp. 391–407. Springer, Cham (2016). https://doi.org/10.1007/978-3-319-46475-6_25
19. Kim, J., et al.: Accurate image super-resolution using very deep convolutional networks. In: Proceedings of CVPR, pp. 1646–1654 (2016)
20. Kim, J., et al.: Deeply-recursive convolutional network for image super-resolution. In: Proceedings of CVPR, pp. 1637–1645 (2016)
21. Tai, Y., Yang, J., Liu, X.: Image super-resolution via deep recursive residual network. In: Proceedings of CVPR, vol. 1, no. 4 (2017)
22. Mao, X.J., Shen, C., Yang, Y.B.: Image restoration using convolutional auto-encoders with symmetric skip connections. arXiv preprint. arXiv preprint arXiv:1606.08921 2 (2016)
23. Yamanaka, J., Kuwashima, S., Kurita, T.: Fast and accurate image super resolution by deep CNN with skip connection and network in network. In: Liu, D., Xie, S., Li, Y., Zhao, D., El-Alfy, E.S. (eds.) ICONIP. LNCS, vol. 10635, pp. 217–225. Springer, Cham (2017). https://doi.org/10.1007/978-3-319-70096-0_23
24. Tong, T., Li, et al.: Image super-resolution using dense skip connections. In: Proceedings of ICCV, pp. 4809–4817 (2017)
25. Zhang, Y., et al.: Residual dense network for image super-resolution. arXiv preprint arXiv: 1802.08797 (2018)
26. Lim, B., et al.: Enhanced deep residual networks for single image super-resolution. In: Proceedings of CVPR, vol. 1, no. 2, p. 3 (2017)

27. Lai, W.S., et al: Deep Laplacian pyramid networks for fast and accurate super-resolution. In: Proceedings of CVPR, pp. 624–632 (2017)
28. Wang, Y., et al: A fully progressive approach to single-image super-resolution. arXiv preprint arXiv:1804.02900 (2017)
29. Haris, M., et al.: Deep back-projection networks for super-resolution. arXiv preprint arXiv: 1803.02735 (2018)
30. Zhang, K., et al.: Learning a single convolutional super-resolution network for multiple degradations. arXiv preprint arXiv:1712.06116 (2017)
31. Shocher, A., et al.: "zero-shot" super-resolution using deep internal learning. arXiv preprint arXiv:1712.06087 (2017)
32. Han, W., et al.: Image super-resolution via dual-state recurrent networks. arXiv preprint arXiv:1805.02704 (2018)
33. Tai, Y., et al: A persistent memory network for image restoration. In: Proceedings of CVPR, pp. 4539–4547 (2017)
34. Ledig, C., et al.: Photo-realistic single image super-resolution using a generative adversarial network. *arXiv preprint* (2016)
35. Sajjadi, M.S., Schölkopf, B., Hirsch, M.: Enhancenet: single image super-resolution through automated texture synthesis. In: Proceedings of ICCV, pp. 4501–4510 (2017)
36. Johnson, J., Alahi, A., Fei-Fei, L.: Perceptual losses for real-time style transfer and super-resolution. In: Leibe, B., Matas, J., Sebe, N., Welling, M. (eds.) ECCV 2016. LNCS, vol. 9906, pp. 694–711. Springer, Cham (2016). https://doi.org/10.1007/978-3-319-46475-6_43
37. Ren, J., Zabalza, J., Marshall, S., Zheng, J.: Effective feature extraction and data reduction in remote sensing using hyperspectral imaging [applications corner]. IEEE Signal Process. Mag. **31**(4), 149–154 (2014)
38. Yan, Y., Ren, J., Li, Y., Windmill, J., Ijomah, W.: Fusion of dominant colour and spatial layout features for effective image retrieval of coloured logos and trademarks. In: Proceedings of IEEE International Conference on Multimedia Big Data, pp. 306–311. IEEE (2015)
39. Yan, Y., Ren, J., Li, Y., et al.: Adaptive fusion of color and spatial features for noise-robust retrieval of colored logo and trademark images. Multidimens. Syst. Signal Process. **27**(4), 945–968 (2016)
40. Yan, Y., et al.: Cognitive fusion of thermal and visible imagery for effective detection and tracking of pedestrians in videos. Cogn. Comput. **10**(1), 94–104 (2018)
41. Wang, Z., Ren, J., Zhang, D., Sun, M., Jiang, J.: A deep-learning based feature hybrid framework for spatiotemporal saliency detection inside videos. Neurocomputing **287**, 68–83 (2018)
42. Ren, J., Jiang, J., Wang, D., Ipson, S.S.: Fusion of intensity and inter-component chromatic difference for effective and robust colour edge detection. IET Image Proc. **4**(4), 294–301 (2010)
43. Ren, J., Vlachos, T., Jiang, J.: Subspace extension to phase correlation approach for fast image registration. In: Proceedings of ICIP, vol. 1, pp. I–481. IEEE (2007)
44. Ren, J., Jiang, J., Vlachos, T.: High-accuracy sub-pixel motion estimation from noisy images in Fourier domain. IEEE Trans. Image Process. **19**(5), 1379–1384 (2010)
45. Ren, J., Vlachos, T., Zhang, Y., Zheng, J., Jiang, J.: Gradient-based subspace phase correlation for fast and effective image alignment. J. Vis. Commun. Image Represent. **25**(7), 1558–1565 (2014)
46. Chai, Y., Ren, J., Zhao, H., Li, Y., Ren, J., Murray, P.: Hierarchical and multi-featured fusion for effective gait recognition under variable scenarios. Pattern Anal. Appl. **19**(4), 905–917 (2016)
47. Zabalza, J., et al.: Novel segmented stacked autoencoder for effective dimensionality reduction and feature extraction in hyperspectral imaging. Neurocomputing **185**, 1–10 (2016)

DAU-GAN: Unsupervised Object Transfiguration via Deep Attention Unit

Zihan Ye[1], Fan Lyu[1], Jinchang Ren[2], Yu Sun[1], Qiming Fu[1], and Fuyuan Hu[1(✉)]

[1] Suzhou University of Science and Technology, Suzhou 215009, China
[2] University of Strathclyde, Glasgow G1 1XW, UK
fuyuanhu@mail.usts.edu.cn

Abstract. Object transfiguration aims to translate objects in image from a kind to another, which is a subtask of image translation. Recently, researchers have proposed many effective approaches for object transfiguration. However, most of them ignore the difference between target objects and background, which would make background deformation, discolor and other problems. We propose a novel attention-based model for unsupervised object transfiguration called Deep Attention Units Generative Adversarial Network (DAU-GAN). We utilize spatial consistencies of objects and background to enable model to preserve background of image. Such an attention-based design enables DAU-GAN to enhance the expression of meaningful features and let the model able to distinguish specific objects and background in images. Experimental results demonstrate that our approach improves the performance of object transfiguration as well as effectively preserves background.

1 Introduction

Object transfiguration, which is one task of image translation, aims to transform a selected kind of object to another one in a given image, for example, translating a horse to a zebra. The task refers to image translation [1–4] and object-related learning [5–9]. Most translation methods are training in supervised setting, where paired training examples are available [1–4]. However, paired examples are difficult and expensive to obtain, people use other ways to get those examples, for example, in the task of de-rain [10], researchers use Photoshop to synthetize training samples. Thus, unsupervised approaches [11] for image translation become popular, such as methods based on Convolutional Neural Network (CNN)[12], which translate images by matching semantically-meaningful features extracted from CNN between two input images, such as VAT [13]. Recently, methods based on GAN are prevalent [14]. Specially, dual structure has achieved impressive results in unsupervised image translation [15,16]. The "dual" means that a translation cycle consist of two mutually reverse directions, like horse → zebra and zebra → horse. In such structures, cycle-consistent

Z. Ye and F. Lyu—The first two authors contributed to this work equally.

J. Ren et al. (Eds.): BICS 2018, LNAI 10989, pp. 120–129, 2018.
https://doi.org/10.1007/978-3-030-00563-4_12

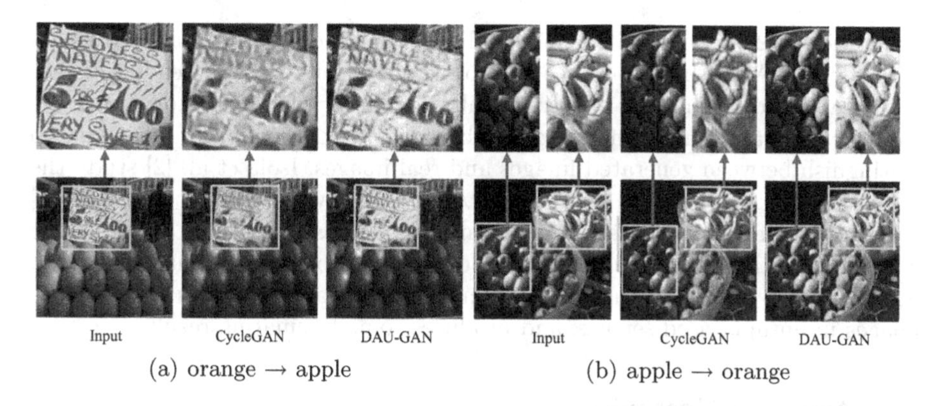

Fig. 1. Yellow rectangles represent regions where be obviously damaged by CycleGAN during translating. For examples, in (a), the words on the billboard are exceedingly blurred; in (b), green apples is purpled and banana redden. (Color figure online)

loss is used as a quantitative measure of changing images after this cycle. They achieve some impressive results.

However, in the task of object transfiguration, most of existing unsupervised approaches fail to distinguish specific objects and background. It would impact background (deformation, discolor and other problems). As shown in Fig. 1, background is considerably impacted. Yellow rectangle where don't include objects is significantly changed. To address this problem, in this paper, we propose an adversarial object transfiguration model by constructing the novel Deep Attention Unit (DAU), which effectively preserves background of translated images. Our approach inspired by the attention mechanism, which tries to select the most important information from a large amount of data, has been applied to many tasks [17,18]. On top of that, the proposed DAU can predict the regions containing the target objects by computing an attention mask. We also construct a background-consistent loss and an attention-consistent loss to train the DAU-GAN. We evaluate our model on two subsets of ImageNet, apple-orange and horse-zebra. The results show that the proposed DAU-GAN is able to preserve images' background during successful translation. For example, as shown in Fig. 1, our approach translates the billboard more clearly than CycleGAN, and successfully preserves other fruits' color. Our main contributions are two-folds: (1) propose a novel framework called DAU-GAN, which can preserve the background of translated image in object transfiguration task; (2) construct a background-consistent loss and an attention-consistent loss to enhance the effectiveness of translation and preserve.

2 Related Work

2.1 Generative Adversarial Network

Recently, researchers has studied GAN vigorously since it was proposed by Goodfellow et al. [19]. GAN were developed to solve many problems, like image generation [4,20], image editing [21], and those have achieved impressive results. The key of GAN's success is that it improve its effectiveness by leading a generator and a discriminator to reciprocally compete. The generator would try to make generated image indistinguishable, and the discriminator would try to distinguish between generated images and real images. Isola et al. [2] study the potential of GAN in image translation. After that, cycle-consistent loss [15,16] was proposed for unsupervised image translation. It assumes that, after a image is translated, the translated image can be translated back to original image, e.g. horse → zebra → horse. It uses the assumption to enhance qualities of translated images in unsupervised setting, and produces some fascinating results.

2.2 Attention Mechanism

The concept of attention originates in human physiology [22].Subsequently, it was introduced in deep learning fields later [17,23]. The essence of attention is a learned weight distribution to make model only care about those interesting parts and to ignore meaningless information. Model consequently gets better effectiveness. Some GANs apply attention mechanism, e.g. DA-GAN [24]. it predicts attention frame and crops those framed parts in image, then encodes those parts. We also integrate attention mechanism into GAN. However, differing with DA-GAN, our approach extracts attention masks from feature maps and then weights corresponding feature maps. In addition, we refer to some structure of residual networks [25,26] to decrease the impact of vanishing gradient.

3 DAU-GAN

3.1 Problem Definition

The goal of object transfiguration is to transform a specific object in a given image to another different type. It can be seen as a domain transforming problem: $G : X \rightarrow Y$, where G is the learning mapping function, X is source domain and Y is target domain. Because our model has a dual structure, we have a reverse translation $F : Y \rightarrow X$.

Our model accepts $\{x, y\} \in \{X, Y\}$ as inputs. For the translation $G : X \rightarrow Y$, it output a image $G(x)$ in domain Y that preserving the background $B(x)$ of x and translating objects in the images. For the translation $F : Y \rightarrow X$, output is $F(y)$ in domain X, with preserving the background $B(y)$ during the translation.

3.2 Proposed Architecture

Our overall architecture is shown in Fig. 2, in which the upper part shows a overall framework for object transfiguration and the lower part shows the details of the generator. Our model has a dual structure, which has been successfully applied to CycleGAN [15], DualGAN [16], and so on. It consists of two generators G and F, and two discriminators D_X and D_Y. To ensure the generated image

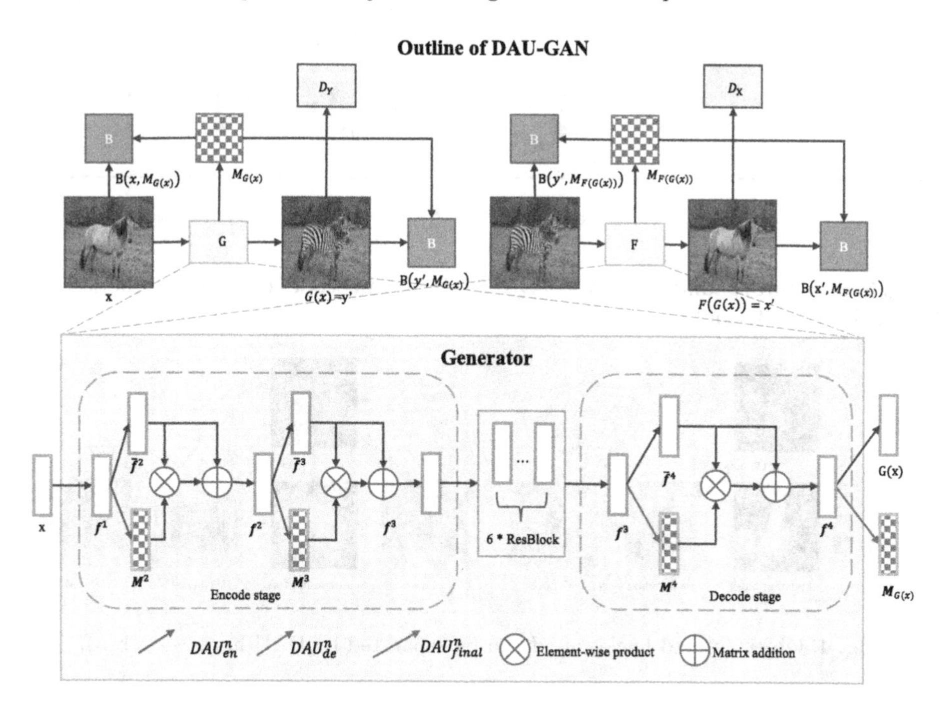

Fig. 2. Architecture of DAU-GAN: the upper part is the outline of our model, and the lower part is the details of generator.

$G(x) = y'$ and $F(y) = x'$ are in the corresponding domains, we employ two discriminators D_X and D_Y to distinguish the real images and synthetic ones. D_X or D_Y takes an image as input and outputs a probability indicating how likely it is a natural image from domain X or Y.

3.3 Deep Attention Unit

we propose a novel Deep Attention Unit (DAU) on the top of dual learning inspired by the dramatic success of attention mechanism in image classification [27], image captioning [28]. The DAU can help model filter out background and objects from an image to preserve background.

In CNN, feature map from each convolutional layer can be divided into many regions. The DAU, which can be attached to any convolutional layer, effectively compute the attention mask for the corresponding feature map. In other word, the DAU can force the model to focus the translation process on the specific objects. The main reason is that the attention mask can separate objects and background, and highlight translated objects.

In this paper, we construct three types of DAU, i.e., DAU_{en}, DAU_{de} and DAU_{final} for encode stage, decode stage and output stage respectively. For DAU_{en} and DAU_{de}, we set the shapes equal to the corresponding feature map, while for DAU_{final}, we shrink the depth to 1 for convenience on visualization.

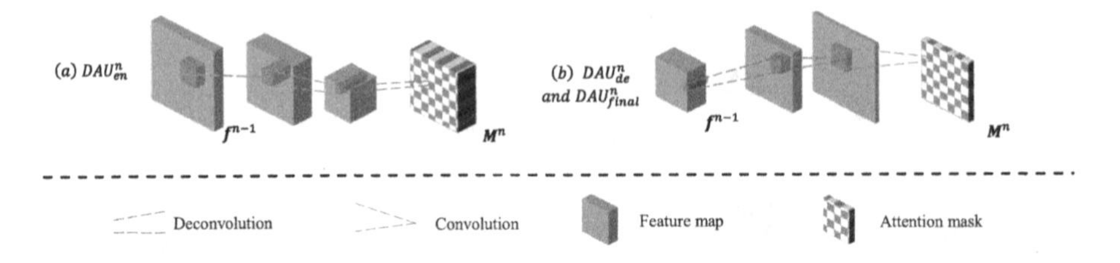

Fig. 3. Structures of different types of DAU. $\mathrm{DAU_{en}}$ for encode stage, $\mathrm{DAU_{de}}$ for decode stage, $\mathrm{DAU_{final}}$ for output stage.

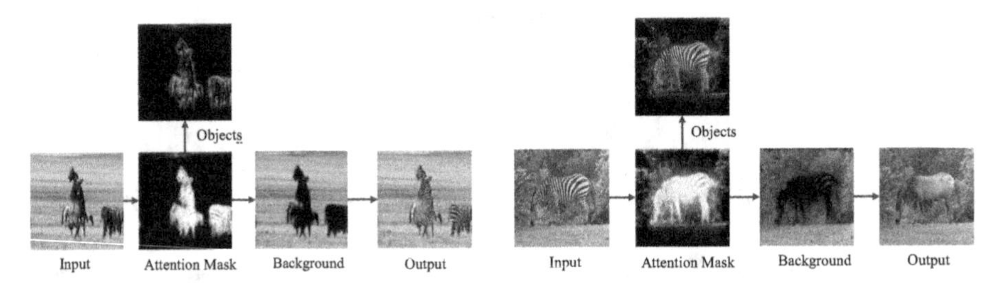

Fig. 4. Object(s) and background can be separated by DAU(horse ↔ zebra).

We regard the feature map from the n-th convolutional layer as $\boldsymbol{f}^n$. As shown in Fig. 3, DAU can extract the mask $\boldsymbol{M}^n$ from $\boldsymbol{f}^{n-1}$, i.e., $\boldsymbol{M}^n = DAU(\boldsymbol{f}^{n-1})$. Specifically, following the dual adversarial learning architecture, we divide the DAU into two main categories for encoder ($\mathrm{DAU_{en}}$) and decoder ($\mathrm{DAU_{de}}$). For the encoder, $\boldsymbol{f}^{n-1}$ first pass through two convolutional layers with the ReLU [29] activation function ($\mathrm{ReLU}(x) = max(0, x)$), and then be sent to one deconvolutional layer with the Sigmoid activation function ($\mathrm{Sigmoid}(x) = \frac{1}{1+e^{-x}}$). The process can be denoted as follows,

$$DAU^n_{en}(x) = Conv^{-1}(Conv(Conv(x))) \tag{1}$$

$$\boldsymbol{M}^n = DAU^n_{en}(\boldsymbol{f}^{n-1}) \tag{2}$$

We define $\bar{\boldsymbol{f}}^n$ as the untreated (n)-th feature map. With the mask $\boldsymbol{M}^n$, we obtain the enhancive feature map by the elements-wise product: $H(\boldsymbol{M}^n, \bar{\boldsymbol{f}}^n)$. In addition, we take a residual architecture [25,26] that we add a shortcut to depress the impact of vanishing gradient. After these operations, the enhancive (n)-th feature map is computed by:

$$\boldsymbol{f}^n = \bar{\boldsymbol{f}}^n + H(\boldsymbol{M}^n, \bar{\boldsymbol{f}}^n). \tag{3}$$

In the decoder, the process is similar except the DAU is inverse. In other word, the feature map first pass through two deconvolutional layers and then go by one convolutional layer. The DAU of the decoder can be represent as follows,

$$DAU^n_{en}(x) = Conv(Conv^{-1}(Conv^{-1}(x))) \tag{4}$$

In the output layer, translated image $y' = G(x)$ and corresponding attention mask $\boldsymbol{M}_{G(x)}$ would simultaneously be exported. As shown in Fig. 4, because the elements of mask represent the probability that objects in the position, we could get $B(x)$ from the equation: $B(x, \boldsymbol{M}_{G(x)}) = H(x, 1 - \boldsymbol{M}_{G(x)})$. We integrate DAU in each layer of generator to enhance meaningful features, even though we use only the last attention mask to compute L_{att} and L_{bg}.

3.4 Attention-Consistent Loss and Background-Consistent Loss

Considering that the position of objects during translating is invariable, we construct an Attention-Consistent Loss to improve the performance of predicting attention mask:

$$L_{att}(x, G, F) = \alpha * \|\boldsymbol{M}_{G(x)} - \boldsymbol{M}_{F(G(x))}\|_1 + \beta * (\boldsymbol{M}_{G(x)} + \boldsymbol{M}_{F(G(x))}) \tag{5}$$

The second term is a regularization, which prevents overfitting.

With attention mask $\boldsymbol{M}$, DAU-GAN can distinguish objects and background. We construct a Background-Consistent Loss to preserve background:

$$L_{bg}(x, G) = \gamma * \|B(x, \boldsymbol{M}_{G(x)}) - B(G(x), \boldsymbol{M}_{G(x)})\|_1 \tag{6}$$

3.5 Full Objective

From GAN, the adversarial losses are

$$L_{GAN}(X, Y, G, D_Y) = log(D_Y(y)) + log(1 - D_Y(y')), \tag{7}$$

$$L_{GAN}(Y, X, F, D_X) = log(D_X(x)) + log(1 - D_Y(x')). \tag{8}$$

In addition, we adopt the structure of dual learning. The key idea of dual learning is to improve the performance of a model by minimizing a cycle-consistent loss. The cycle-consistent loss assumes that for each image x in domain X, model is supposed to be able to translate $y' = G(x)$ to original image. It is formulated as: $F(y') = F(G(x)) \approx x$. Similarly, for each image y in domain Y, the assumption is: $G(x') = G(F(x)) \approx y$. The cycle-consistent loss as follows:

$$L_{cyc}(G, F) = \|F(G(x)) - x\|_1 + \|G(F(y)) - y\|_1. \tag{9}$$

Our full objective is given by:

$$\begin{aligned} L(G, F, D_X, D_Y) = & L_{GAN}(X, Y, G, D_Y) + L_{GAN}(Y, X, F, D_X) \\ & + L_{att}(x, G, F) + L_{att}(y, F, G) \\ & + L_{bg}(x, G) + L_{bg}(y, F) + L_{cyc}(G, F) \end{aligned} \tag{10}$$

Therefore, we solve the optimizing problem:

$$G^*, F^* = arg \min_{G,F} \max_{D_X, D_Y} L(G, F, D_X, D_Y) \tag{11}$$

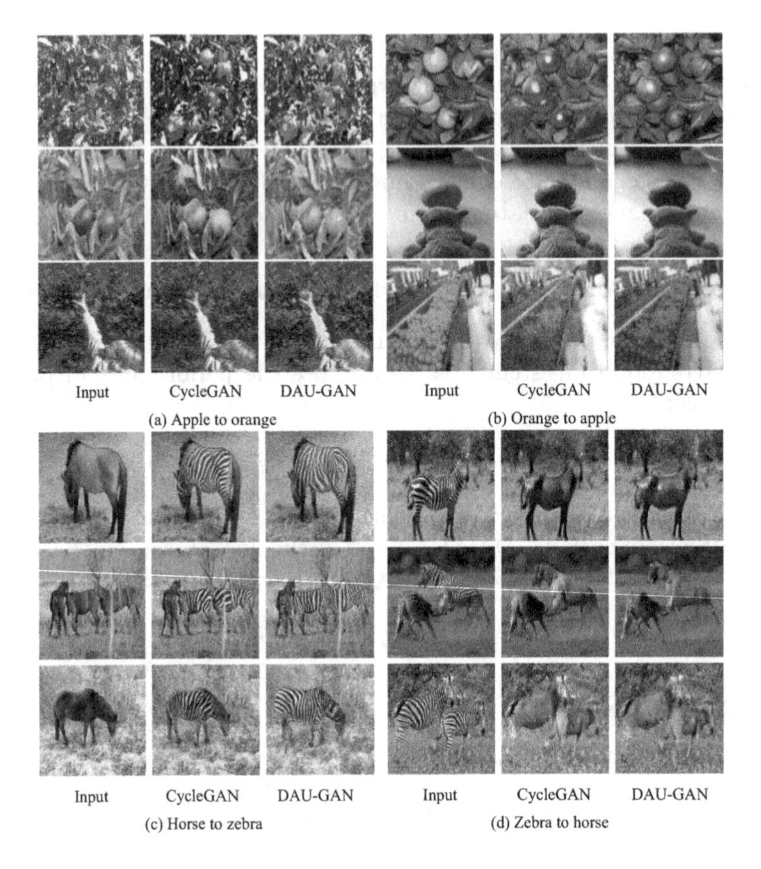

Fig. 5. Experimental results on two subsets of ImageNet.

4 Experiments

4.1 Datasets and Setting

We experiment our model on two subsets (apple-orange and horse-zebra) of ImageNet [30], which is a large-scale labeled image dataset for computer vision. The numbers of images of apple, orange, horse, and zebra respectively are 1,261, 1,267, 1,187 and 1,474.

We run our code on one GeForce GTX 1080 GPU card. More specifically, we adapt the model [1] on generator, in which 6 blocks for 128×128 training images, and 9 blocks for 256×256 or higher resolution training images. And our discriminator is constructed by using 70 * 70 PatchGAN [2]. We respectively set α, β and γ on Eqs. (5) and (6) to 0.000015, 0.000005 and 0.00075. We use the Adam solver with a batch size of 1 and a learning rate of 0.0002.

Fig. 6. Background and objects separated by attention mask(horse $\leftrightarrow$ zebra).

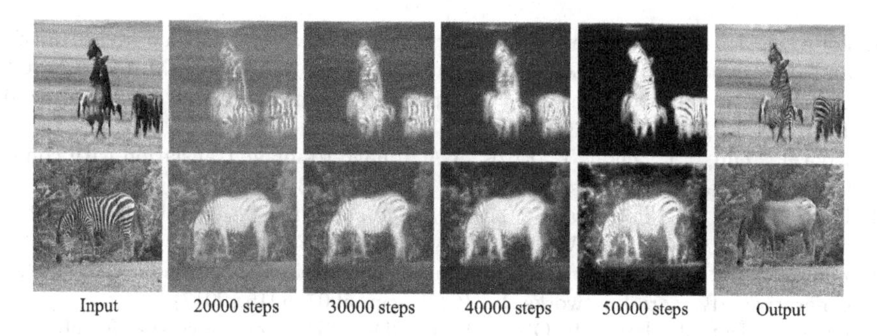

Fig. 7. Attention mask after different training steps(horse $\leftrightarrow$ zebra).

4.2 Performance Comparison

Fig. 5 shows the results of experiment of translation. Obviously, the impact of background in those images translated by CycleGAN are very remarkable. For example, in Fig. 5(a) and (b), leaves discolor from green to gray. However, our approach effectively preserves background besides successfully translating objects that we want to translate. For example, in Fig. 5(c), zebras produced by our approach have more natural streak besides preserving background.

Moreover, we visualize attention mask in Fig. 6 to confirm DAU's effect, where the regions in are black and white represent background and objects. We can see that DAU can correctly predict where objects occurs. Besides, we export attention masks in different training steps in Fig. 7. The results show that high value gradually concentrate where objects is, which verify that DAU do help model learn to distinguish background and objects expected to be translated.

5 Conclusion

In this paper, we propose Deep Attention Unit (DAU) and construct the DAU-GAN for the task of object transfiguration. DAU learns to enhance the most significant information by predicting attention masks, which makes DAU-GAN effectively distinguish specific objects and background during translation process and achieve impressive translation results in two subsets of Imagenet. In the future, we plan to design more robust DAU structures to make model train easier.

Acknowledgments. This work was supported by the Natural Science Foundation of China (Nos. 61472267, 61728205, 61502329, 61672371), Primary Research & Developement Plan of Jiangsu Province (No. BE2017663) and Aeronautical Science Foundation (20151996016).

References

1. Johnson, J., Alahi, A., Fei-Fei, L.: Perceptual losses for real-time style transfer and super-resolution. In: Leibe, B., Matas, J., Sebe, N., Welling, M. (eds.) ECCV 2016. LNCS, vol. 9906, pp. 694–711. Springer, Cham (2016). https://doi.org/10.1007/978-3-319-46475-6_43
2. Isola, P., Zhu, J.Y., Zhou, T., Efros, A.A.: Image-to-image translation with conditional adversarial networks. In: CVPR, pp. 1125–1134 (2017)
3. Ledig, C., et al.: Photo-realistic single image super-resolution using a generative adversarial network. In: CVPR, pp. 4681–4690 (2017)
4. Zhang, H., et al.: Stackgan: Text to photo-realistic image synthesis with stacked generative adversarial networks. In: ICCV, pp. 5907–5915 (2017)
5. Feng, Y., Ren, J., Jiang, J.: Object-based 2D-to-3D video conversion for effective stereoscopic content generation in 3D-TV applications. IEEE Trans. Broadcast **57**(2), 500–509 (2011)
6. Yan, Y., et al.: Cognitive fusion of thermal and visible imagery for effective detection and tracking of pedestrians in videos. Cogn. Comput. **10**(1), 94–104 (2018)
7. Han, J., Zhang, D., Hu, X., Guo, L., Ren, J., Wu, F.: Background prior-based salient object detection via deep reconstruction residual. IEEE Trans. Circuits Syst. Video Technol. **25**(8), 1309–1321 (2015)
8. Ren, J., Jiang, J., Wang, D., Ipson, S.: Fusion of intensity and inter-component chromatic difference for effective and robust colour edge detection. IET Image Process. **4**(4), 294–301 (2010)
9. Han, J., Zhang, D., Cheng, G., Guo, L., Ren, J.: Object detection in optical remote sensing images based on weakly supervised learning and high-level feature learning. IEEE Trans. Geosci. Remote Sens. **53**(6), 3325–3337 (2015)
10. Fu, X., Huang, J., Zeng, D., Huang, Y., Ding, X., Paisley, J.: Removing rain from single images via a deep detail network. In: CVPR, pp. 3855–3863 (2017)
11. Liu, M.Y., Breuel, T., Kautz, J.: Unsupervised image-to-image translation networks. In: NIPS, pp. 700–708 (2017)
12. Krizhevsky, A., Sutskever, I., Hinton, G.E.: Imagenet classification with deep convolutional neural networks. In: NIPS, pp. 1097–1105 (2012)
13. Liao, J., Yao, Y., Yuan, L., Hua, G., Kang, S.B.: Visual attribute transfer through deep image analogy. ACM Trans. Graph. **36**(4), 120 (2017)

14. Choi, Y., Choi, M., Kim, M., Ha, J.W., Kim, S., Choo, J.: Stargan: Unified generative adversarial networks for multi-domain image-to-image translation. arXiv preprint arXiv:1711.09020 (2017)
15. Zhu, J.Y., Park, T., Isola, P., Efros, A.A.: Unpaired image-to-image translation using cycle-consistent adversarial networks. In: CVPR, pp. 2223–2232 (2017)
16. Yi, Z., Zhang, H., Tan, P., Gong, M.: Dualgan: unsupervised dual learning for image-to-image translation. In: CVPR, pp. 2849–2857 (2017)
17. Zhao, B., Feng, J., Wu, X., Yan, S.: A survey on deep learning-based fine-grained object classification and semantic segmentation. Int. J. Autom. Comput. **14**(2), 119–135 (2017)
18. Yan, Y., et al.: Unsupervised image saliency detection with gestalt-laws guided optimization and visual attention based refinement. Pattern Recogn. **79**, 65–78 (2018)
19. Goodfellow, I., et al.: Generative adversarial nets. In: NIPS, pp. 2672–2680 (2014)
20. Radford, A., Metz, L., Chintala, S.: Unsupervised representation learning with deep convolutional generative adversarial networks. arXiv preprint arXiv:1511.06434 (2015)
21. Zhu, J.-Y., Krähenbühl, P., Shechtman, E., Efros, A.A.: Generative visual manipulation on the natural image manifold. In: Leibe, B., Matas, J., Sebe, N., Welling, M. (eds.) ECCV 2016. LNCS, vol. 9909, pp. 597–613. Springer, Cham (2016). https://doi.org/10.1007/978-3-319-46454-1_36
22. Briggs, F., Mangun, G.R., Usrey, W.M.: Attention enhances synaptic efficacy and the signal-to-noise ratio in neural circuits. Nature **499**(7459), 476 (2013)
23. Aboudib, A., Gripon, V., Coppin, G.: A biologically inspired framework for visual information processing and an application on modeling bottom-up visual attention. Cogn. Comput. **8**(6), 1007–1026 (2016)
24. Ma, S., Fu, J., Chen, C.W., Mei, T.: Da-gan: Instance-level image translation by deep attention generative adversarial networks (with supplementary materials). In: CVPR (2018)
25. Wang, F., et al.: Residual attention network for image classification. In: CVPR pp. 3156–3164 (2017)
26. He, K., Zhang, X., Ren, S., Sun, J.: Deep residual learning for image recognition. In: CVPR pp. 770–778 (2016)
27. Fu, J., Zheng, H., Mei, T.: Look closer to see better: Recurrent attention convolutional neural network for fine-grained image recognition. In: CVPR pp. 4438–4446 (2017)
28. Xu, K., et al.: Show, attend and tell: Neural image caption generation with visual attention. In: ICML pp. 2048–2057 (2015)
29. Glorot, X., Bordes, A., Bengio, Y.: Deep sparse rectifier neural networks. In: Proceedings of the Fourteenth International Conference on Artificial Intelligence and Statistics pp. 315–323 (2011)
30. Deng, J., Dong, W., Socher, R., Li, L.J., Li, K., Fei-Fei, L.: Imagenet: a large-scale hierarchical image database. In: CVPR pp. 248–255 (2009)

Gravitational Search Optimized Hyperspectral Image Classification with Multilayer Perceptron

Ping Ma[1,2], Aizhu Zhang[1,2(✉)], Genyun Sun[1,2], Xuming Zhang[1,2], Jun Rong[1,2], Hui Huang[1,2], Yanling Hao[1,2], Xueqian Rong[1,2,3], and Hongzhang Ma[3]

[1] School of Geosciences, China University of Petroleum (East China), Qingdao 266580, China
zhangaizhu789@163.com

[2] Laboratory for Marine Mineral Resources Qingdao National Laboratory for Marine Science and Technology, Qingdao 266071, China

[3] Colledge of Science, China University of Petroleum (East China), Qingdao 266580, China

Abstract. Hyperspectral image classification has been widely used in a variety of applications such as land cover analysis, mining, change detection and disaster evaluation. As one of the most-widely used classifiers, the Multilayer Perception (MLP) has shown impressive classification performance. However, the MLP is very sensitive to the setting of the training parameters such as weights and biases. The traditional parameter training methods, such as, error back propagation algorithm (BP), are easily trapped into local optima and suffer premature convergence. To address these problems, this paper introduces a modified gravitational search algorithm (MGSA) by employing a multi-population strategy to let four sub-populations explore the different areas in search space and a Gaussian mutation operator to mutate the global best individual when swarm stagnate. After that, MGSA is used to optimize the weights and biases of MLP. The experimental results on a public dataset have validated the higher classification accuracy of the proposed method.

Keywords: Hyperspectral remote sensing · Multilayer Perception
Gravitational search algorithm

1 Introduction

In recent years, as a result of advances in optics and photonics, hyperspectral remote sensing has rapidly developed and provided an abundance of data to discriminate between spectrally similar materials [1, 2]. The selection of an appropriate classifier to efficiently model the subtle differences of hyperspectral information plays a critical role in object classification [3, 4]. Classification methods are broadly divided into supervised, unsupervised and semi-supervised methods [5]. Unsupervised classifiers, such as K-Means, construct a pre-defined number of clusters based on a dataset [6]. Supervised classifiers, such as Maximum Likelihood [7], impose a pre-determined classification

J. Ren et al. (Eds.): BICS 2018, LNAI 10989, pp. 130–138, 2018.
https://doi.org/10.1007/978-3-030-00563-4_13

outcome on each input value. Semi-supervised learning models, such as generative models, indirect and low-density separators [8], depend on the model hypothesis. Their classification performances are closely related to the proximity of input data to the assumed distribution.

In order to improve the classification accuracy, many advanced methods have been developed [4], of which multilayer perceptron (MLP) is one of the most popular [9]. Specifically, MLP is trained to classify pixels without prior knowledge of the distribution data. Thus, it has proved to be more robust in processing high-dimensional signals. This property has led to many applications of MLP to hyperspectral image classification. However, MLP has difficulty in determining appropriate training parameters, such as weights and biases [10, 11]. Since these parameters significantly impact on the final classification accuracy, the optimization on their settings inevitably becomes a problematic and a critical issue. Generally, the error back propagation algorithm (BP) [12] is used to adjust weight and biases parameters. However, this method is easy to trap into local optima and experience premature convergence [10].

Recently, swarm intelligence algorithms, due to their superior global optimization and self-organization, have been successfully employed in setting the parameters of neural networks [10]. As a swarm intelligence based optimization approach, the gravitational search algorithm (GSA) [13] has attracted considerable attention. This paper proposes a novel classification method of hyperspectral image classification based on a MLP optimized by a modified GSA algorithm. Specifically, for the purpose of avoiding prematurity due to local minima, a multi-population strategy and Gaussian mutation operator are introduced into the GSA. In this paper, to reduce the dimensionality of hyperspectral image data, an effective feature selection approach, named FODPSO [14], has been utilized to select the most representative features.

The remainder of this paper is organized as follows. In Sect. 2, we review multilayer perceptron and the gravitational search algorithm. The proposed MGSA and MGSA optimized MLP is analyzed in detail in Sect. 3. In Sect. 4, we present experimental settings and discuss the results. Finally, conclusions are drawn in Sect. 5.

2 Related Works

2.1 Multilayer Perceptron

In this paper, we use a three-layer MLP network which includes an input layer, a hidden layer and an output layer, as shown in Fig. 1.

Generally, in MLP, the error back propagation algorithm (BP) [12] is employed as the supervised learning rule. In its learning process, the weights and biases of each layer are tuned based on the reverse propagation errors. However, the BP method easily becomes trapped into local optimum [10]. To address this problem and improve the prediction accuracy, this paper utilizes a modified GSA algorithm to optimize the weights and biases parameters.

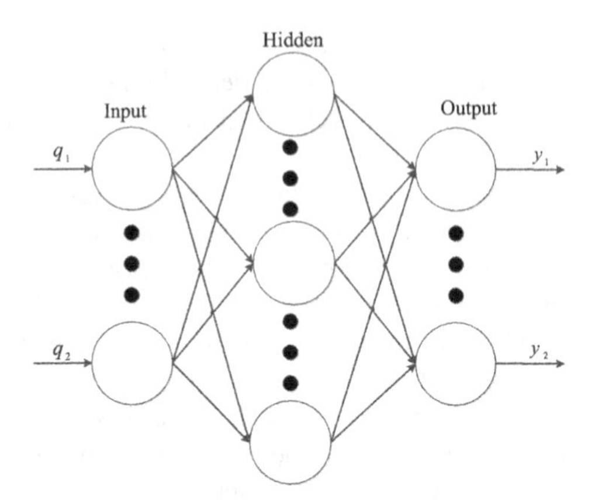

Fig. 1. The structure of MLP network

2.2 Gravitational Search Algorithm

In 2009, Rashedi et al. [13] presented a novel swarm intelligence optimization approach, namely, the gravitational search algorithm (GSA). In GSA, all agents attract each other by the gravitational forces between them. The position of each agent denotes a candidate solution of the problem as defined:

$$\boldsymbol{X}_i = [x_{i1}, \ldots, x_{id}, \ldots, x_{iD}] \quad (i = 1, 2, \ldots, NP) \tag{1}$$

where NP is the population size and x_{id} is the position of the ith agent in the dth dimension.

During the computation intervals, known as epochs, the gravitational force exerted on the agent i from the agent j at a specific time t is as follows:

$$F^t_{id,jd} = G^t \frac{M^t_i \times M^t_j}{\left\|\boldsymbol{X}^t_i, \boldsymbol{X}^t_j\right\|_2 + \varepsilon} \left(x^t_{id} - x^t_{jd}\right) \tag{2}$$

where M^t_j and M^t_i are the mass of agents j and i respectively, $\left\|\boldsymbol{X}^t_i, \boldsymbol{X}^t_j\right\|_2$ is the Euclidian distance between the agents i and j, G^t is the gravitational constant in tth iteration, and ε is a small positive non zero constant.

The mass M^t_i is calculated as follows:

$$mass^t_i = \frac{fit^t_i - worst^t}{best^t - worst^t} \tag{3}$$

$$M^t_i = \frac{mass^t_i}{\sum_{j=1}^{NP} mass^t_j} \tag{4}$$

where fit_i^t is the fitness value of the i-th agent in the iteration t. For the minimum problem, $best^t = \min_{j \in \{1,\ldots,NP\}} fit_j^t$, $worst^t = \max_{j \in \{1,\ldots,NP\}} fit_j^t$.

The gravitational constant G^t is defined as follows:

$$G^t = G_0 \times e^{\left(-\alpha \frac{t}{t_{\max}}\right)} \tag{5}$$

where α is the gravitational constant attenuation factor and $t_{\max}$ is the maximum number of iterations.

In the dth dimension, the total force acting on agent i is defined as:

$$F_{id}^t = \sum_{j \in K_{best}, j \neq i}^{NP} rand_j F_{id,jd}^t \tag{6}$$

where $rand_j$ is a random number in the interval [0,1]. K_{best} is an archive stores K superior agents (with bigger masses and better fitness values) after fitness sorting in each iteration, which size is initialized as NP and linearly decreased with time down to one. Thus, according to the laws of motion, the acceleration of the agent i in the dth dimension in iteration t, a_{id}^t, is calculated by

$$a_{id}^t = F_{id}^t / M_i^t \tag{7}$$

The velocity and position of the agent i are updated according to the following formulae:

$$v_{id}^{t+1} = rand_i \times v_{id}^t + a_{id}^t \tag{8}$$

$$x_{id}^{t+1} = x_{id}^t + v_{id}^{t+1} \tag{9}$$

3 The Proposed Method

3.1 The Modified GSA

The original GSA has the advantages of simple structure and being easy to visualize. However, it readily becomes stuck in local minimum [15]. To improve its performance, this paper introduces a multi-population strategy and a Gaussian mutation operator. Specifically, four simultaneous sub-populations run in parallel over the search space. Meanwhile a counter g, which is initially set to zero, records the number of iterations for which there has been no further improvement in global best value. If g exceeds a defined threshold value mg, then stagnation is deemed to have occurred. At this point, the four sub-populations are re-divided and the global best agent (*gbest*) undergoes mutation as defined by:

$$gbest = gbest \times (1 + \delta \times N(0,1)) \tag{10}$$

where $N(0,1)$ is a random number generated by a Gaussian distribution with zero mean and standard deviation of 1, respectively and δ is a scaling parameter.

In this way, the utilization of multi-population strategy motivates individuals in different sub-populations sufficiently explore the search space, which is helpful to increase the population diversity. The Gaussian mutation operator on the global best individual can effectively avoid the local optima trapping problem. Note the modified GSA is abbreviated as MGSA in this paper.

3.2 MGSA-MLP

In this section, MGSA is utilized to optimize the weights and biases of MLP to achieve a minimum error and improve the classification accuracy of MLP classifier. The specific process of MGSA optimized MLP is shown as follows.

1. Initialization

The initial population with size *NP* is randomly generated to span as much of the search space as possible. The variables of agents represent all the weights and biases of the MLP network.

2. Fitness metric

In the MLP network, a better performance is obtained when the squared error between the actual output value and the expected output value of the network is lower. Hence, the fitness function can be calculated as:

$$f = \sum_{k=1}^{q} \frac{(y(k) - y_m(k))^2}{q} \tag{11}$$

where the variable q is the number of the training samples, $y(k)$ and $y_m(k)$ are the actual output value and the desired output value of MLP network, respectively.

3. MGSA operation

The agents which represent the combination of weights and biases of MLP move to the promising regions under the attraction force of other better performing agents. As such, MLP is configured to iterate towards the optimum parameter settings to realize the higher classification accuracy.

4 Experiment

In this section, the well-known ROSIS-03 Pavia University image dataset [16] is utilized to evaluate the proposed approach. This dataset was collected by the ROSIS optical sensor over an urban area surrounding the University of Pavia, Italy. The data set is of size 610 × 340 × 150 with a spatial resolution of 1.3 m per pixel and a wavelength rang of 0.43–0.86 μm. Figure 2(a) and (b) show the color composite generated by the first three bands of principal component analysis (PCA) [17, 18] and the reference data of the University of Pavia.

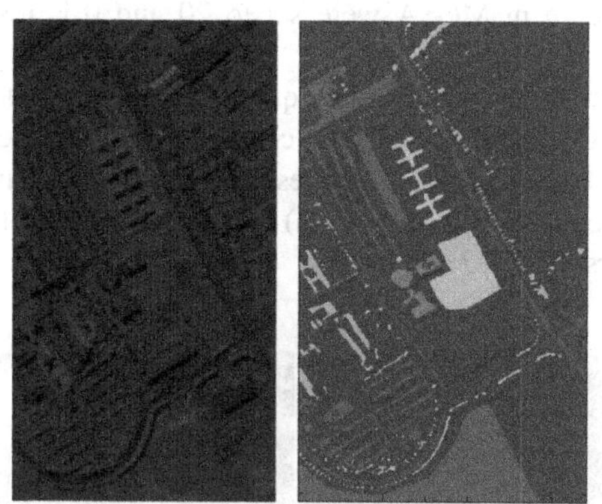

(a) False color composition image. (b) Reference map

Fig. 2. The ROSIS Pavia University data sets.

The data set consists of different classes including: trees, asphalt, bitumen, gravel, metal sheet, shadow, bricks, meadow, and soil. In order to allow a direct comparison between methods, the number of training and test samples were set to be the same as those in the paper [14], which have been used for comparison in many hyperspectral images classification studies. From 3921 training samples, 50% of the samples were chosen for training and the rest for the validation samples. After the feature selection, all 3921 samples are used for training MLP network on the selected bands. The number of training and test samples is given in Table 1.

Table 1. Pavia University: number of training, validation and test samples.

Class		Number of samples		
Number	Name	Training	Validation	Test
1	Asphalt	274	274	6340
2	Meadows	270	270	18146
3	Gravel	196	196	1815
4	Tree	262	262	2912
5	Metal sheet	133	132	1113
6	Bare soil	266	266	4572
7	Bitumen	188	187	981
8	Brick	257	257	3364
9	Shadow	116	115	795

In the experiments, two methods, including the support vector machine (SVM) [14] and BP [10] were selected to compare with the proposed classifier. Note that all methods use the same feature selection approach (FODPSO). The experimental parameter settings of FODPSO and SVM are directly taken from the corresponding literature [14], which is widely considered as an optimal configuration. For the multilayer perceptron, the number of hidden nodes was set to 22. The population size and the scaling parameter δ in MGSA were set to 20 and 0.1, respectively. In BP, the learning rate was set to 0.1.

The classification performances were quantitatively evaluated using two metrics, Overall Accuracy (OA) and the Kappa coefficient (κ). Table 1 shows the results obtained from the experiments. The highest classification accuracy is indicated with bold typeface for each case. Figure 3(a)–(c) illustrated the classification maps obtained by various classifiers (Table 2).

(a) Reference map. (b)Result from SVM. (c) Result from BP. (d) Result from MGSA-MLP.

Fig. 3. Classification maps for the Pavia University image.

As can be seen from the table, the obtained results are coherent for the Pavia University image. The MGSA-MLP classifier yielded significantly higher classification accuracy when compared with other methods. Specifically, the proposed MGSA-MLP method achieved the highest overall classification accuracy, of 88.09% on the Pavia University data set. The results of BP ranked second and obtained the OA of 83.66%. By comparison, SVM achieved the lowest classification accuracy.

As for the classification maps, in general, the proposed MGSA-MLP approach generally performs better than the compared classification methods in terms of visual quality on classification maps. Specially, as can be seen from the rectangle regions in the Fig. 2, some details in Gravel, Bare soil and Bricks areas are misclassified by the compared classifiers, whereas these meaningful detailed structures are accurately classified by the proposed MGSA-MLP.

Table 2. The classification results of three methods.

Classifier	Overall accuracy (OA)	Kappa coefficient (κ)
SVM	78.76%	0.660
BP	83.66%	0.792
MGSA-MLP	88.09%	0.845

5 Conclusion

This paper proposes a modified GSA (MGSA) algorithm to optimize the performance of MLP algorithm for the classification of hyperspectral remote sensing images. In MGSA, the multi-population strategy and mutation operator were adopted for the purpose of avoiding prematurity. Through the optimization of MGSA, an appropriate combination of weights and biases of MLP structure was achieved that resulted in improved classification accuracy. The experimental results verify the improvement resulting from the proposed algorithm. In addition, our future work will comprehensively use the spectral and spatial features to improve the classification accuracy of hyperspectral images.

Acknowledgments. This work was supported by the National Natural Science Foundation of China (41471353), the Shandong Provincial Natural Science Foundation, China (ZR2018BD007, ZR2017MD007), the Fundamental Research Funds for the Central Universities (18CX05030A, 18CX02179A), and the Postdoctoral Application and Research Projects of Qingdao (BY20170204).

References

1. Qiao, T., Ren, J., Wang, Z., et al.: Effective denoising and classification of hyperspectral images using curvelet transform and singular spectrum analysis. IEEE. Trans. Geosci. Remote Sens. **55**(1), 119–133 (2017)
2. Zabalza, J., Ren, J., Zheng, J., et al.: Novel segmented stacked autoencoder for effective dimensionality reduction and feature extraction in hyperspectral imaging. Neurocomputing **185**(C), 1–10 (2016)
3. Qiao, T., Yang, Z., Ren, J., et al.: Joint bilateral filtering and spectral similarity-based sparse representation: a generic framework for effective feature extraction and data classification in hyperspectral imaging. Pattern. Recogn. **77**, 316–328 (2017)
4. Cao, F., Yang, Z., Ren, J., et al.: Sparse representation based augmented multinomial logistic extreme learning machine with weighted composite features for spectral spatial hyperspectral image classification. IEEE. Trans. Geosci. Remote Sens. **99**, 1–17 (2018)
5. Silva, W.D., Habermann, M., Shiguemori, E.H., et al.: Multispectral image classification using multilayer perceptron and principal components analysis. In: Brics Congress on Computational Intelligence and Brazilian Congress on Computational Intelligence, pp. 557–562 (2013)
6. Venkatalakshmi, K., Shalinie, S.M.: Classification of multispectral images using support vector machines based on PSO and K-Means clustering. In: International Conference on Intelligent Sensing and Information Processing, pp. 127–133 (2005)

7. Dempster, A.P.: Maximum likelihood from incomplete data via EM algorithm. J. Roy. Stat. Soc. B **39**(1), 1–38 (2015)
8. Negri, R.G., Sant'Anna, S.J.S., Dutra, L.V.: Semi-supervised remote sensing image classification methods assessment. IEEE. Inter. Geosci. Remote Sens. Symp. **24**(8), 2939–2942 (2011)
9. Tang, J., Deng, C., Huang, G.B.: Extreme learning machine for multilayer perceptron. IEEE. Trans. Neur. Netw. Learn. Syst. **27**(4), 809 (2016)
10. Mirjalili, S., Mirjalili, S.M., Lewis, A.: Let a biogeography-based optimizer train your multi-layer perceptron. Inf. Sci. **269**(8), 188–209 (2014)
11. Mirjalili, S.: How effective is the grey wolf optimizer in training multi-layer perceptrons. Appl. Intell. **43**(1), 150–161 (2015)
12. Xu, J., Yang, Y., Zhang, R.: Graduate enrollment prediction by an error back propagation algorithm based on the multi-experiential particle swarm optimization. In: International Conference on Natural Computation, pp. 1159–1164 (2016)
13. Rashedi, E., Nezamabadi-Pour, H., Saryazdi, S.: GSA: a gravitational search algorithm. Inf. Sci. **179**(13), 2232–2248 (2009)
14. Ghamisi, P., Couceiro, M.S., Benediktsson, J.A.: A novel feature selection approach based on FODPSO and SVM. IEEE Trans. Geosci. Remote Sens. **53**(5), 2935–2947 (2015)
15. Sun, G., Ma, P., Ren, J., et al.: A stability constrained adaptive alpha for gravitational search algorithm. Knowl. Based Syst. **139**, 200–213 (2018)
16. Fang, L., Li, S., Duan, W., et al.: Classification of hyperspectral images by exploiting spectral-spatial information of superpixel via multiple kernels. IEEE Trans. Geosci. Remote Sens. **53**(12), 6663–6674 (2015)
17. Zabalza, J., Ren, J., Ren, J., et al.: Structured covariance principal component analysis for real-time onsite feature extraction and dimensionality reduction in hyperspectral imaging. Appl. Opt. **53**(20), 4440–4449 (2014)
18. Zabalza, J., Ren, J., Yang, M., et al.: Novel folded-PCA for improved feature extraction and data reduction with hyperspectral imaging and SAR in remote sensing. ISPRS J. Photogramm. Remote Sens. **93**(7), 112–122 (2014)

3-D Gabor Convolutional Neural Network for Damage Mapping from Post-earthquake High Resolution Images

Yanling Hao[1,2], Genyun Sun[1,2(✉)], Aizhu Zhang[1,2], Hui Huang[1,2], Jun Rong[1,2], Ping Ma[1,2], and Xueqian Rong[1,2]

[1] School of Geosciences, China University of Petroleum (East China), Qingdao 266580, China
genyunsun@163.com

[2] Laboratory for Marine Mineral Resources, Qingdao National Laboratory for Marine Science and Technology, Qingdao 266071, China

Abstract. Post-earthquake high resolution (HR) remote sensing image classification is crucial for disaster assessment and emergency rescue. 3-D convolutional neural networks (3-D CNNs) exhibit promising performance in remote sensing image classification. However, 3-D CNNs lack the theoretical underpinnings to perform multiresolution approximation for filter learning in view of the scale variance of natural objects. Gabor filtering can effectively extract multiresolution spatial information including edges and textures, which have a potential to reinforce the robustness of learned features in 3-D CNNs against the orientation and scale changes. In this paper, we propose a combined 3-D convolutional neural network and Gabor filters (GNN) method for post-earthquake HR image classification. Instead of choosing a single scale, GNN extends the spatial information to several scales by Gabor filters to take advantage of correlations among multiple scales for damage mapping. The experimental results show that GNN can reflect the multiscale information of complex scenes, obtain good classification results for mapping post-earthquake damage using HR remote sensing images.

Keywords: 3-D convolutional neural networks · Gabor filter
Post-earthquake high resolution images

1 Introduction

Earthquake-induced damage recognition is of vital importance in disaster monitoring, assessment, mitigation and other applications [1]. Earthquake-induced disasters always affect the development of human society and economic progress [1]. In particular, urban areas show typically human-induced stress such as the growing infrastructure and crowded people [2]. These conditions increase the vulnerability of urban areas to natural disasters [3]. Although it is impossible to predict when the disaster strike, it is possible to response to mitigate the loss timely and accurately. For decades, remote sensing techniques have shown the great promise in investigating earthquake-induced damage information due to its prompt availability after disaster and wide coverage.

J. Ren et al. (Eds.): BICS 2018, LNAI 10989, pp. 139–148, 2018.
https://doi.org/10.1007/978-3-030-00563-4_14

More and more attention has been paid to the urban object interpretation with the post-earthquake remote sensing images [2].

In reality, urban environment is very complex which consists of natural and architectural elements (e.g. trees, earth, concrete, metal, stone), thus manifest high spectral variation in remotely sensed data [3]. At the same time, the cities exist in even more complex layouts and patterns after disasters such as landslides [4]. Due to the heterogeneity of urban land covers and the limitation in spatial resolution, problems arise in the inability to define a satisfactory description of urban objects in the earthquake-induced damage affected area [5].

In order to reduce the dilemma, a number of different approaches have been proposed in recent years for automatically feature extraction from remotely sensed images, such as the salient feature [6], midlevel visual elements-oriented feature [7] and so on. However, few of them are suitable for the damage mapping. Deep learning [8], one of the state-of-the-art techniques in the field of computer vision, probably is the best way to extract robust and high-level spatial features. Deep learning can learn non-linear spatial filters automatically and generalize a hierarchy of increasingly complex features [9]. An interesting aspect of deep learning is that instead of requiring prior feature extraction process, it learns relationship between input and output directly from enormous amount of data, showing great flexibility and capability [8]. Convolutional neural networks (CNNs) achieve superior performance on image processing [10].

CNNs are a 2-D model, characterized by local connection, shared weights, and shift-invariance to make it invariant to translation, scaling, skewing and other forms of distortion [11]. This enables CNNs as well as 'improved CNNs' that are combined with other models such as CRF [12], or algorithms such as GSA [13, 14], to be widely utilized in remote sensing image classification [15]. Recently, 2-D CNNs have been extended to 3-D CNNs to extract the spectral and spatial information simultaneously, which can further improve the classification accuracy. 3-D CNNs inherit all the advantages of 2-D CNNs, but also the disadvantages. 3-D CNNs suffer from the fixed receptive fields [9], which lack the theoretical underpinnings to perform multiresolution approximation for filter learning [16]. However, objects in remote sensing images often appear at various observation scales. The fixed receptive fields is unable to characterize the varied objects in images, and leading to incomplete feature representation of the image contents. Consequently, the outputs of 3-D CNNs suffer from speckles.

Fortunately, filter redesigning to enhance the scale-invariant capacity of CNNs has been acknowledged by researchers and some attempts have been made in recent years [17]. Among the existing techniques, Gabor filtering has attracted a lot of attention due to its capability to provide discriminative and informative features [18]. Compared with other filtering approaches, Gabor filtering shows its advantages in spatial information extraction including edges and textures at different scales and orientations [17].

In this paper, we presented a method to combine 3-D convolution neural network and Gabor filter (GNN) for urban object interpretation. First, Gabor filters are designed to filter the multiple channel spatial information by tuning the filters into various spatial and frequency domains. Then, the filter responses are fed into 3-D CNN to take advantage of the correlations among the multiple channel filter responses. GNN exploits the 3-D multi-resolution features within the same layer and the 3-D depth features, which substantially improves the classification results. Comprehensive evaluations and comparisons with the state-of-the-art GNN and support vector machine (SVM) demonstrate that GNN are effective for damage mapping and have substantial practical merit.

The remainder of this article is structured as follows. Section 2 presents the proposed methodology GNN for post-earthquake HR image classification, which consists of multiresolution approximation for Gabor filter learning in terms of the scale variance of natural objects, 3-D CNN-based deep feature learning of urban objects, 3-D GNN based deep feature learning by the fusion of Gabor filtering and 3-D CNN. Experimental results of the proposed method and the comparisons with other segmentation methods are reported in Sect. 3. Finally, some conclusions are drawn in Sect. 4.

2 Methodology

2.1 Framework of the Proposed Method

The framework of the proposed method is shown in Fig. 1. The proposed method GNN used Gabor filtering to extract the spatial features of post-earthquake high resolution image. After that, the extracted features are fed into the 3-D CNN with batch normalization and dropout to extract robust and discriminant features for the subsequent step. At the end of the framework, softmax is employed to produce the final classification map. The proposed framework is elaborated in detail as follows.

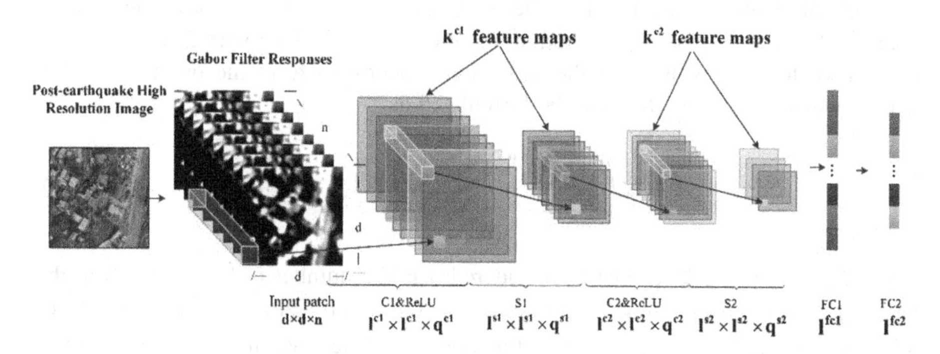

Fig. 1. The framework of the proposed 3-D GNN

2.2 Gabor Filter

The 2-D Gabor function simulates the human visual system. The image is filtered from the spatial domain to the frequency domain. By tuning the filter parameters, the image is analyzed in multiple narrow ranges and directions in frequency domain [19]. The ability of 2-D Gabor filter to clearly describe the local characteristics of both high- and low- frequencies in the imagery has facilitated its good application in high-resolution remote sensing image spatial feature extraction [19]. An even-symmetric linear Gabor filter has the following form:

$$G_{\sigma,\theta}(x,y) = \exp\left\{-\frac{1}{2\sigma^2}\left[(x\cos\theta + y\sin\theta)^2 + (-x\sin\theta + y\cos\theta)^2\right]\right\}$$
$$\cos[\frac{2\pi}{\lambda}(x\cos\theta + y\sin\theta)] \quad (1)$$

where x, y are the coordinates of the pixel p, σ determines the scale (window size), θ specifies the orientation. λ is the frequency space wavelength, and σ/λ defines the half-response spatial frequency bandwidth [20]. The Gabor texture feature image in a specific scale and direction is the magnitude part of the convolution of the Gabor filters and the image P. By tuning to various scales and orientations in frequency space, we can obtain n Gabor filter responses, where $n = \sigma \cdot \theta$, as the spatial feature which gives a detailed and robust delineation of the information.

2.3 3-D Gabor Convolutional Neural Network-Based Feature Extraction

2-D Convolutional Neural Network

The complexity of high-resolution post-earthquake images causes traditional classification methods to fail due to the limited representation power of a few mapping layers. CNN has shown great potential for robust automatic feature extraction in high-resolution images [21]. Usually, the input layer of a CNN imports a raw image, and the output layer produces the classification. Between these two layers are the convolutional layer and sub-sampling layer behaving as feature detector.

The convolutional layer offers filter-like function to generate convoluted feature maps. In the 2-D convolution operation, input data is convolved with 2-D kernels (see Fig. 2a), before going through the activation function to form the output data (i.e., feature maps). This operation can be formulated as

$$v_{lj}^{xy} = f\left(\sum_{m}\sum_{h=0}^{H_{j-1}}\sum_{w=0}^{W_{j-1}} k_{ljm}^{hw} v_{(l-1)m}^{(x+h)(y+h)} + b_{lj}\right) \quad (2)$$

where l indicates the layer that is considered, j is the number of feature maps in this layer, v_{lj}^{xy} stands for the output at position (x, y) on the jth feature map in the lth layer, b is the bias, and $f(\cdot)$ is the activation function, m indexes over the set of feature maps in the $(l-1)$ th layer connected to the current feature map, and finally, k_{ljm}^{hw} is the value at position (h, w) of the kernel connected to the jth feature map, with H_l and W_l being the height and width of the kernel, respectively.

3-D Convolutional Neural Network

In 2-D CNNs, convolutions are applied on the 2-D feature maps to compute features from the spatial dimensions only. To take the advantage of the capability of automatically learning features in deep learning, 3-D CNN uses 3-D kernels for the 3-D convolution operation. The value of a neuron v_{lj}^{xyz} at position (x, y, z) of the jth feature map in the lth layer is given by

$$v_{lj}^{xyz} = f\left(\sum_{m}\sum_{h=0}^{H_{j-1}}\sum_{w=0}^{W_{j-1}}\sum_{r=0}^{R_{j-1}} k_{ljm}^{hwr} v_{(l-1)m}^{(x+h)(y+w)(z+r)} + b_{lj}\right) \tag{3}$$

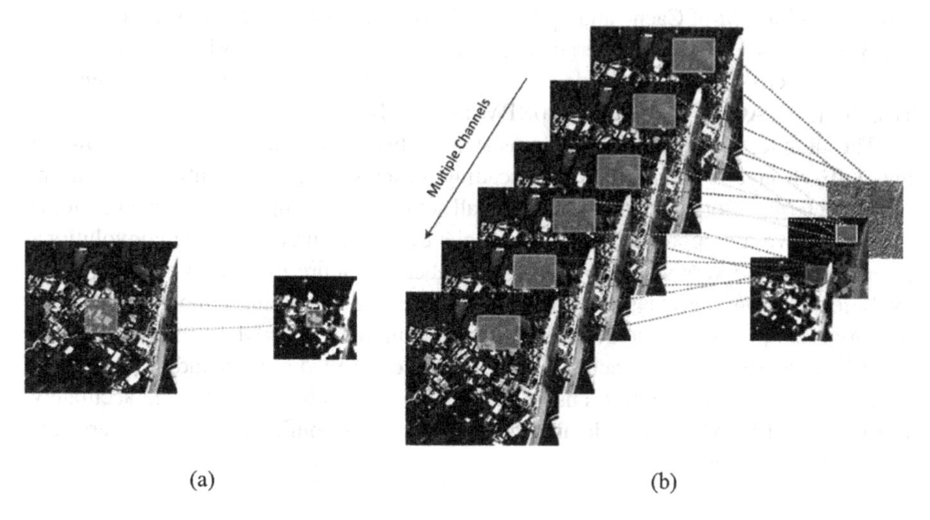

(a) (b)

Fig. 2. (a) 2D convolution operation, as per Formula (2). (b) 3D convolution operation, as per Formula (3).

where Rl is the size of the 3-D kernel along the third dimension, j is the number of kernels in this layer, and k_{ljm}^{hwr} is the $(h, w, r)th$ value of the kernel connected to the mth feature cube in the preceding layer.

3-D Gabor Convolutional Neural Network (GNN)

Gabor filters are widely adopted in the traditional filter design due to their enhanced capability of scale and orientation decomposition of signals, which is unfortunately neglected in most of the prevailing convolutional filters in CNNs [17]. To this end, it is desirable to modulate the learnable convolution filters via traditional hand-crafted Gabor filters into CNNs. Aiming to reduce the number of network parameters and enhance the robustness of learned features to orientation and scale changes, the 3-D CNN are performed on Gabor responses (see Fig. 2b).

In our GNN-based classification model, each feature cube is treated independently. Thus, m is set to 1 in Eq. (2), and the 3-D convolution operation can be (re-)formulated as

$$v_{lj}^{xyz} = f\left(\sum_{h=0}^{H_{j-1}}\sum_{w=0}^{W_{j-1}}\sum_{r=0}^{R_{j-1}} k_{lj}^{hwr} v_{(l-1)}^{(x+h)(y+w)(z+r)} + b_{lj}\right) \tag{4}$$

3 Experiment

3.1 Experimental Configuration

In order to evaluate the performance of our newly presented CNN architecture, we use a hardware environment composed by a 6th Generation Intel Core (TM) i5-6400 K processor with 6 M of Cache and up to 2.70 GHz (4 cores/8 way multitask processing), 8 GB of DDR4 RAM with a serial speed of 2.72 GHz, a GPU NVIDIA GeForce GT 710 with 2 GB GDDR4 of video memory and 10 Gbps of memory frequency, a Toshiba DT01ACA HDD with 7200RPM and 1 TB of capacity.

The architecture of GNN was consisted of two subsequent layers, as shown in Fig. 1. Each layer is composed of cascading structure with convolution and polling stages. In terms of pooling stages, they are all set to be subsampling by a small factor of two to achieve a compromise between efficiency and accuracy. For the convolutional layers, we set the kernel size to five and number of feature maps to 6 and 12 respectively for two convolutional layers considering the size of training samples. Mini-batch strategy is adopted to update trainable parameters in the nets and the size of the training batch is set to 100 samples each. Learning rate is controlled as 0.05 and the number of training epochs is set to 500 to ensure the nets converges both quickly and accurately. The metrics of SVM is set as default in [26]. The GNN configuration parameters have been listed in Table 1.

Table 1. Configuration of the GNN architecture for the T1

GNN proposed topologies								
Images	Convolution layers					Fully Connected Layers		
	Kernals size $k^c \times l^c \times l^c \times q^c$	ReLU	Pooling $l^{mp} \times l^{mp}$	Padding	Dropout	Nneurons l^{fc}	Function	Dropout
T1	6×5×5×3	Yes	2×2×1		Yes (10%)	64	ReLU	Yes (10%)
	12×3×3×1	Yes	2×2×6	1×1×0	Yes (10%)	5	Softmax	No
Common Parameters								
Batch size	Steps (iteration)	Epochs	Learning Rate	Optimizer				
100	5	500	0.05	AdagradOptimizer				

In order to verify the efficacy of the proposed technique, we carried out two groups of experimental validations, including visual assessment and quantitative evaluation. The quantitative evaluation includes the confusion matrixes of two methods. The support vector machine (SVM) [22], an advanced supervised kernel classification approach, was selected to illustrate the efficiency of GNN. The RBF kernel function was selected, and the parameter Gamma in kernel function was set to 0.015 based on the experiment result which achieved the best performance. The ground truths of two test images were manually interpreted in commercial software eCognition [23] by different experienced experts. Figure 3 illustrates the classification results, where

Fig. 3(d) shows the ground truth of T1. Figure 3(a), (b) illustrates the T1 classification result by SVM and GNN respectively.

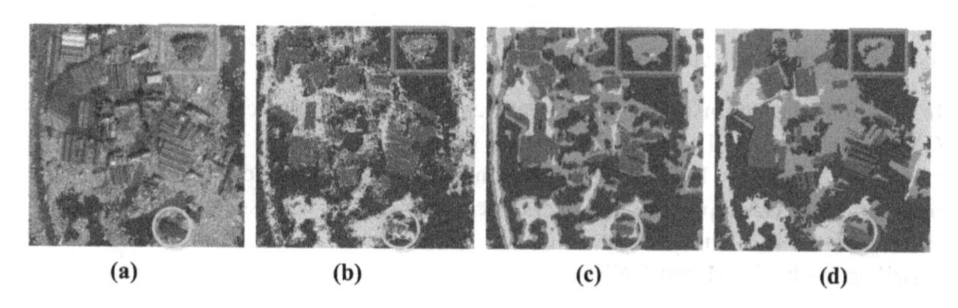

Fig. 3. (a) The post-earthquake HR image, (b)–(c) are the T1 classification results by SVM and GNN, and (d) the ground truths.

3.2 Post-Earthquake High Resolution Image Data

The experiments were conducted on post-earthquake HR images. The image T1 (the spatial resolution is 1 m) were acquired one day after after the devastating Ms 9.0 earthquake and tsunami stricken in Natori, Japan on 11 March 2011 captured by Ikonos Sensor. The earthquake was centered at approximately 38.1 °N and 142.6 °E. The focal depth of this earthquake was 10 km. The earthquake trigger a tsunami of about 10 m in height and then reaches a maximum of 23 m, and devastated a huge area in Japan. The test image covers a variety of damage objects such as collapsed residential sites and flowing ruins. The mapping of the selected damaged areas is challenging.

3.3 Visual Inspection

The visual assessment is to evaluate the classification results by visual judgment in both global and detailed view. According to the classification results, both methods can distinguish different objects to some extent. However, there are still some differences between them. From the Fig. 3, we can find that SVM classification results showed a serious salt-and-pepper appearance throughout the study area Fig. 3(b), whereas the classification maps of GNN were much more homogeneous Fig. 3(c) and in accordance with the ground truth.

Particularly, visually comparing with the ground truths Fig. 3(d), it was easily found that the classification result of SVM suffered a certain misclassifications in some local areas. It is obviously that a part of the grass area was classified into intact buildings [see in the rectangle in Fig. 3(b)]. In specific, SVM identified the intact buildings with homogenous characteristics but failed in detecting these ones with sharp spectral variance [see in the circle in Fig. 3(b)].

GNN located the class accurately. In contrast to the results of SVM, the classification of GNN Fig. 3(c) were more consistent with the ground truth. It is worth noting that compared with SVM classification, the classification by GNN show more realistic object shapes with merit of the combination of different scale information in Gabor responses. Especially the intact buildings areas with varied sizes [see in the rectangle and circle in Fig. 3(c) are detected accurately. The efficient combination of the accurate location from CNN and the abundant boundary information from Gabor filters renders GNN a perfect tool to extract the damaged objects at different scales.

3.4 Quantitative Evaluation

In addition, the confusion matrixes were calculated to evaluate the performance of GNN quantitatively. The numerical values were shown in Table 2. The best obtained results were shown in boldface. PA represents the product accuracy, UA represents the user accuracy, OA represents the overall accuracy, and K represents the Kappa coefficient. Figure 4 is the plotted results of the PA and UA for each classes in the classification by SVM and GNN.

Table 2. The classification accuracy of T1 by CNN and GNN. PA represents product accuracy, UA is user accuracy, OA represents overall accuracy and kappa is the kappa coefficient.

Method test images	/%	SVM				GNN			
		PA	UA	OA	Kappa	PA	UA	OA	Kappa
T1	Intact buildings	41.38	**70.84**	62.64	0.48	**71.42**	57.40	**71.04**	**0.59**
	Forest	56.15	20.90			**58.49**	**55.31**		
	Broken buildings	**83.79**	81.99			81.64	**85.53**		
	Bare land	51.20	67.97			**62.96**	**76.85**		

As shown in Table 2, GNN outperformed SVM with an increase of 8.4% in the OA and an improvement of 0.11 in kappa coefficient.

From the Fig. 4, it can be found that SVM seriously confused the forest into other classes. In contrast, by the effective combination of Gabor filters, GNN can capture the subtle changes between the textures of the geo-objects with similar spectral features, such as the forest and the bare land area. In addition, with the effective of exploitation

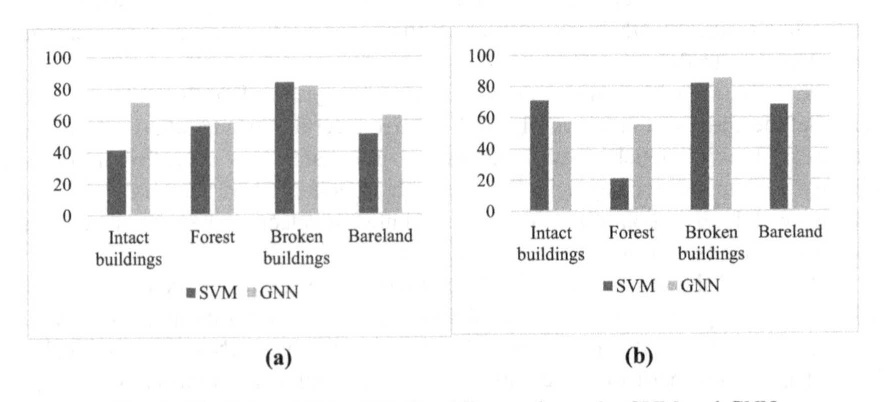

Fig. 4. The PA and UA of T1 for different classes by SVM and GNN

of the multiresolution spatial information of the same class, GNN classification has less salt- pepper noises and spackles than the result of SVM, and also recognize the intact buildings with varied size and characteristics. Therefore, GNN reinforce the robustness of learned features in 3-D CNNs against the orientation and scale changes, and is a robust method in the classification of post-earthquake HR images.

4 Conclusion

Urban object interpretation of post-earthquake HR images has always been a fundamental but challenging issue in the field of damage mapping. More accurate and efficient classification methods for the post-earthquake high resolution images are required. This paper presents a novel GNN approach to combine deep convolution neural network and Gabor filters, and demonstrated its usefulness in urban object interpretation using post-earthquake high resolution images and deep convolutional neural networks. The results showed that the methodology is able to accommodate the rapid damage mapping. The combination of Gabor filtering and 3-D CNN improved the accuracy in the classification significantly in comparison to the conventional SVM algorithm. The quantitative and qualitative evaluations also validated the fact that such scheme renders GNN simple, practical, and appropriate for the post-earthquake HR images classification. Also, we will further investigate the object detection [24] with the GNN with respect to saliency [6] as well as extrapolate our findings to other remote sensing application domains beyond damage mapping.

References

1. Liu, Y., Wu, L.: Geological disaster recognition on optical remote sensing images using deep learning. Proc. Comput. Sci. **91**, 566–575 (2016). https://doi.org/10.1016/j.procs.2016.07.144
2. Gencer, E.A.: Natural disasters, urban vulnerability, and risk management: a theoretical overview. In: Gencer, E.A. (ed.) The Interplay between Urban Development, Vulnerability, and Risk Management: A Case Study of the Istanbul Metropolitan Area, pp. 7–43. Springer, Heidelberg (2013). https://doi.org/10.1007/978-3-642-29470-9_2
3. Geiß, C., Aravena Pelizari, P., Marconcini, M., et al.: Estimation of seismic building structural types using multi-sensor remote sensing and machine learning techniques. ISPRS J. Photogramm. Remote Sens. **104**, 175–188 (2015). https://doi.org/10.1016/j.isprsjprs.2014.07.016
4. Cooner, A., Shao, Y., Campbell, J.: Detection of urban damage using remote sensing and machine learning algorithms: revisiting the 2010 Haiti earthquake. Remote Sens. **8**(10), 868 (2016). https://doi.org/10.3390/rs8100868
5. Béjarpizarro, M., Notti, D., Mateos, R.M., et al.: Mapping vulnerable urban areas affected by slow-moving landslides using sentinel-1 InSAR data. Remote Sens. **9**(9), 876 (2017). https://doi.org/10.3390/rs9090876
6. Yan, Y., Ren, J., Sun, G., et al.: Unsupervised image saliency detection with Gestalt-laws guided optimization and visual attention based refinement. Pattern Recognit. **79**, 65–78 (2018). https://doi.org/10.1016/j.patcog.2018.02.004

7. Cheng, G., Han, J., Guo, L., et al.: Effective and efficient midlevel visual elements-oriented land-use classification using VHR remote sensing images. IEEE Trans. Geosci. Remote Sens. **53**(8), 4238–4249 (2015). https://doi.org/10.1109/TGRS.2015.2393857
8. LeCun, Y., Bengio, Y., Hinton, G.: Deep learning. Nature **521**(7553), 436–444 (2015). https://doi.org/10.1038/nature14539
9. Zhao, W., Du, S.: Learning multiscale and deep representations for classifying remotely sensed imagery. ISPRS J. Photogramm. Remote Sens. **113**, 155–165 (2016). https://doi.org/10.1016/j.isprsjprs.2016.01.004
10. Yu, S., Jia, S., Xu, C.: Convolutional neural networks for hyperspectral image classification. Neurocomputing **219**, 88–98 (2016). https://doi.org/10.1016/j.neucom.2016.09.010
11. Bouvrie, J.: Notes on Convolutional Neural Networks. Neural Nets (2006)
12. Liu, F., Lin, G., Shen, C.: CRF learning with CNN features for image segmentation. Pattern Recogn. **48**(10), 2983–2992 (2015). https://doi.org/10.1016/j.patcog.2015.04.019
13. Sun, G., Ma, P., Ren, J., et al.: A stability constrained adaptive alpha for gravitational search algorithm. Knowl. Based Syst. **139**, 200–213 (2018). https://doi.org/10.1016/j.knosys.2017.10.018
14. Zhang, A., Sun, G., Ren, J., et al.: A dynamic neighborhood learning-based gravitational search algorithm. IEEE Trans. Cybern. **48**(1), 436–447 (2018). https://doi.org/10.1109/TCYB.2016.2641986
15. Sun, G., Hao, Y., Rong, J., et al.: Combined deep learning and multiscale segmentation for rapid high resolution damage mapping. In: IEEE International Conferences (CPSCom, GreenCom, iThings, SmartData), pp. 1101–1105 (2017). https://doi.org/10.1109/ithings-greencom-cpscom-smartdata.2017.238
16. Shi, C., Pun, C.-M.: 3D multi-resolution wavelet convolutional neural networks for hyperspectral image classification. Inf. Sci. **420**, 49–65 (2017). https://doi.org/10.1016/j.ins.2017.08.051
17. Luan, S., Chen, C., Zhang, B., et al.: Gabor convolutional networks. IEEE Trans. Image Process. (2018). https://doi.org/10.1109/tip.2018.2835143
18. Li, J., Wang, T., Zhou, Y., et al.: Using Gabor filter in 3D convolutional neural networks for human action recognition. In: 2017 36th Chinese Control Conference (CCC), 26–28 July 2017, pp. 11139–11144 (2017)
19. Bhagavathy, S., Manjunath, B.S.: Modeling and detection of geospatial objects using texture motifs. IEEE Trans. Geosci. Remote Sens. **44**(12), 3706–3715 (2006). https://doi.org/10.1109/TGRS.2006.881741
20. Yuan, J., Wang, D., Li, R.: Remote sensing image segmentation by combining spectral and texture features. IEEE Trans. Geosci. Remote Sens. **52**(1), 16–24 (2014). https://doi.org/10.1109/TGRS.2012.2234755
21. Gu, J., Wang, Z., Kuen, J., et al.: Recent advances in convolutional neural networks. Pattern Recogn. (2017). https://doi.org/10.1016/j.patcog.2017.10.013
22. Cortes, C., Vapnik, V.: Support-vector networks. Mach. Learn. **20**(3), 273–297 (1995). https://doi.org/10.1007/bf00994018
23. Benz, U.C., Hofmann, P., Willhauck, G., et al.: Multi-resolution, object-oriented fuzzy analysis of remote sensing data for GIS-ready information. ISPRS J. Photogramm. Remote Sens. **58**(3–4), 239–258 (2004). https://doi.org/10.1016/j.isprsjprs.2003.10.002
24. Han, J., Zhang, D., Cheng, G., Guo, L., Ren, J.: Object detection in optical remote sensing images based on weakly supervised learning and high-level feature learning. IEEE Trans. Geosci. Remote Sens. **53**(6), 3325–3337 (2015). https://doi.org/10.1109/TGRS.2014.2374218

Biologically Inspired Systems

A Study of the Role of Attention in Classifying Covert and Overt Motor Activities

Banghua Yang[1], Jinlong Wang[1(✉)], Cuntai Guan[2], Chenxiao Hu[1], and Jianguo Wang[1]

[1] Department of Automation, College of Mechatronics Engineering and Automation, Key Laboratory of Power Station Automation Technology, Shanghai University, No. 149, Yanchang Road, Shanghai 200072, China
genius-wang@foxmail.com

[2] School of Computer Science and Engineering, Nanyang Technological University, 50 Nanyang Avenue, Singapore 639798, Singapore

Abstract. In recent years motor imagery-based brain–computer interface (MI-BCI) is widely used in the rehabilitation of stroke patients and received certain therapeutic effect. The existing imagery mode of brain-computer interface focuses more on the aspect of pure motor imagery and less on the experimental ways of combining other motion and imagination. In this paper, aiming at studying the role of attention in the context of classifying covert and overt motor activities, we design different experiments to explore it in different modes. In our experiments, covert activities are only motor imagery. Overt motor activities are divided into two types—attention to the screen and attention to intended hand. The classification accuracy of six subjects in three modes are compared and analyzed. The average accuracy of overt motor activities with attention to intended hand is the highest, which are respectively 3% and 5% higher than those of covert activities and overt motor activities with attention to screen. At the same time, overt motor activities with attention to intended hand induce more active brain areas according to the spatial pattern of the corresponding EEG data.

Keywords: BCI · WPD-CSP · SVM · Motor imagery
Covert and overt motor activities · Rehabilitation

1 Introduction

A brain-computer interface (BCI) is a communication control system that does not rely on the normal output channels of the peripheral nerves and muscles of the brain. It uses computers or other external electronic devices to communicate directly with the outside world [1–3]. It collects and extracts the features of the human brain by extracting and recognizing the electroencephalogram (EEG) signals and then converts them into some kind of control signals so that people can express their thoughts or manipulate external auxiliary exercise devices directly through the brain without language or action. As a new interdisciplinary subject, BCI technology has attracted the attention of many researchers in the world in recent years [4–6]. BCI technology has shown important

J. Ren et al. (Eds.): BICS 2018, LNAI 10989, pp. 151–160, 2018.
https://doi.org/10.1007/978-3-030-00563-4_15

research value and application prospect in a lot of fields, especially in the rehabilitation of stroke [7–10].

Nowadays, one on one physical therapy by physician and the use of rehabilitation robots are widely used in stroke rehabilitation [11, 12]. However, the rehabilitation robot just drives the movement of patients' limbs mechanically without any voluntary motions. The plasticity theory of the brain tells us that it is usually medically trained to carry out repetitive tasks in patients with specific tasks so that the cortex in the reorganized stores the correct pattern of exercise. A lot of studies have proved that most stroke patients with hemiplegia can be significantly improved or even recovered if they can get timely rehabilitation training. Because the function of remnants of nerve cells gets recovered or enhanced to control corresponding limbs, which fully reflects the existence of neurological function plasticity [13].

BCIs have already shown great potential to induce neural plasticity [14]. Many researchers studied rehabilitation with BCI system [15–17]. They focus more on facilitating paralyzed patients to interact with the environment through external devices controlled by their brain activities [13, 15–17]. In our study, we tried to design three kinds of experiments according to covert and overt motor activities to find how the role of attention matters in brain activity. We collected some EEG data of six subjects and then wavelet packet decomposition-common spatial pattern (WPD-CSP) and support vector machine (SVM) algorithm were used to extract feature and classification respectively.

The experiments and analysis results obtained in this paper provide new training and rehabilitation ideas for the traditional rehabilitation of manipulator, that is, while the robot mechanically drives the affected side for rehabilitation training, the patient also actively carries out the imagination of the affected side with attention to intended hand. It can stimulate the patient's nerves, so that the patient's nervous system directly involved in the training to stimulate the rehabilitation of neurological function, which should have a better rehabilitation effect than the simple mechanical robot arm or covert activities. That is also to say that the patient had better to keep motor imagination with attention to intended hand while the robot drives the movement of patients' limbs mechanically.

2 Experiments

We selected six healthy volunteers (undergraduate students) as experimental subjects, aged 20 to 22 who are all right hand. Volunteers were given the necessary experimental training before the experiment to ensure that they fully understood the experimental procedures and precautions during the experiment. At the same time, volunteers also signed a letter of intent and experimental content to ensure that the rights and interests of volunteers. In addition, part of the labor costs were also given as experimental subsidies to the volunteers participating in the experiment.

During the experiment, the subjects were sitting well in a comfortable armchair in front of a 24 in. screen at a distance of about 1 m. As the Fig. 1 shows, we divide a single trial into three stages–rest, pre-demo and execution. The first stage is rest time when subjects can relax themselves for 2 s. The second stage provides subjects prompt so that they can know how and which side to perform in the third stage. The last stage lasts for 4 s to record corresponding EEG data that the subjects carried out left or right action according to the randomly appeared left or right arrow. The EEG data are recorded during the last stage. The detailed actions include the following three modes:

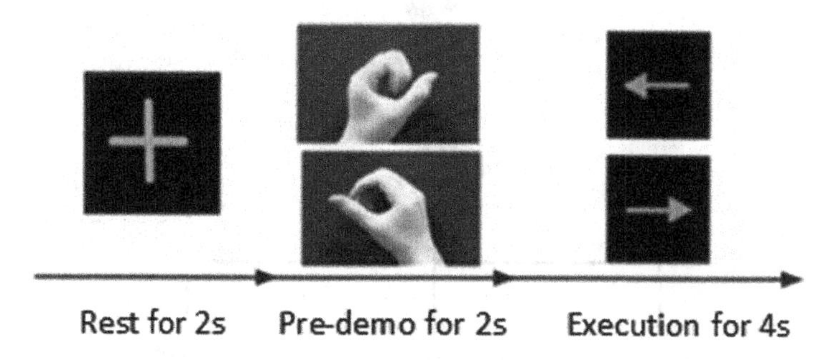

Fig. 1. Process of a single trail.

a. Covert motor activity (Motor Imagery Only, MIO): In the third stage, the subjects start motor imagery of corresponding side of the hand-fist movement when the green arrow shows and always pay attention to their intended hand.
b. Overt motor activity I (Movement Execution Only, MEO, attention to the screen): In the third stage, the subjects only perform hand-fist movement on the corresponding side, and the brain tried not to imagine the hand movement as much as possible. In practice, in order to reduce the imagination of the brain, a calm beautiful sea picture appears in the video of the recording stage. The subjects relax on themselves with their attention focused on the picture instead of their hand movement, and only their hands make a fist movement mechanically.
c. Overt motor activity II (Motor Imagery and Movement Execution, MI&ME, attention to intended hand): In the third stage, the subjects are required to start motor imagery with attention to intended hand and actual movement simultaneously.

In order to ensure that subjects can understand the experimental process to ensure the reliability of experimental data, an extra experiment was arranged before the formal experiment, which was conducted according to the normal experimental standards, so that the subjects can be familiar with the experimental environment and the process.

In the above experimental process, a 32 channels' electrode cap and an amplifier with the sampling rate of 250 Hz were used. And the subjects are required to sit well and the rest of body keeps stationary and quiet except the necessary actions. Every subject was collected EEG data for five groups. Every group contains fifteen sessions. That is, five sessions of EEG data were recorded in three modes respectively. Each session consists of 40 trials. As to every specific subject, the whole experiment lasts about two weeks. Each subject completes five group experiments in two weeks and each group experiment interval is 2–3 days. The whole experimental process is shown in Fig. 2. Three different modes of EEG data are obtained and then are processed including preprocessing, feature extraction and classification.

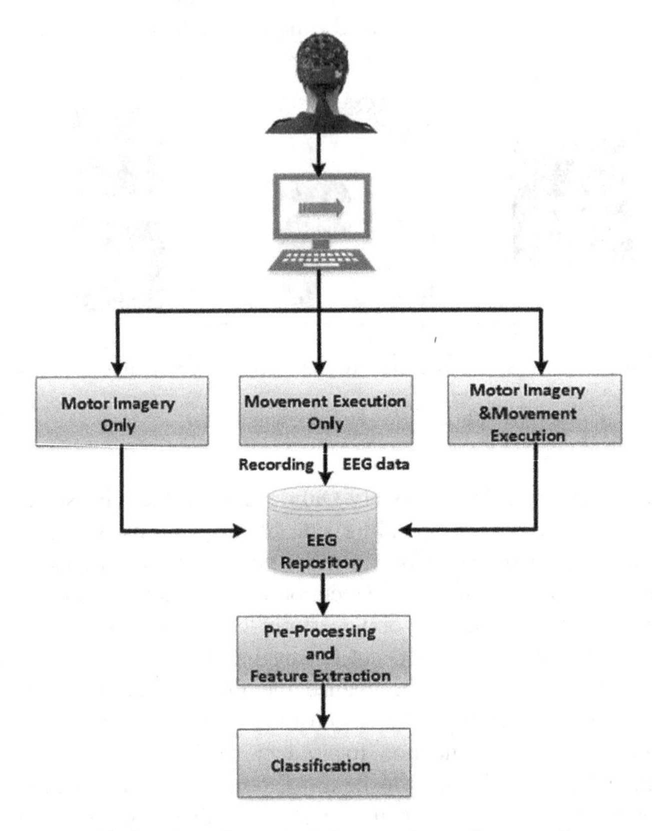

Fig. 2. Flow diagram of the experiment framework.

3 Methodology

3.1 Introduction of CSP

In the current BCI system based on motor imagery, the CSP feature extraction method is widely used as an effective processing method and it essentially finds spatial filters that maximize the variance for one class and simultaneously minimize the variance for the other class. This method decomposes the raw EEG signals into spatial patterns, which are extracted from two classes of single trial EEG. The original EEG signals of each trial are defined as $E_{N\times T}$, N is the number of the channels and T is the number of samples. After the feature extraction of $E_{N\times T}$ by using CSP, a feature vector F = $\{f_1, f_2, \ldots, f_{2m}\}$ is obtained and used as an input for the classifier. The detailed computing process of the CSP can be seen in [18]. But CSP also has some defects. The lack of frequency domain information in the process of its computing process, while mixing some irrelevant frequency signals, seriously affects the effectiveness of eigenvectors.

And only more input can lead to most significant effect [19]. Given these defects of CSP above, we introduce the WPD. It not only reduces the number of EEG signal input and introduces the frequency domain information, which can effectively filter out the frequency components unrelated to the motor imagery. In the case of a small number of inputs, each input is decomposed into 5-dimensional signals by WPD to remedy the defect of CSP algorithm.

3.2 Introduction of Wavelet Packet Decomposition (WPD)

The wavelet packet decomposition (WPD) is an extension of wavelet decomposition. In wavelet analysis, the original signal is decomposed into the approximation parts and the detail parts. The approximation parts are decomposed into another layer of approximation and details again and this process is repeated until the set decomposition level. But in the wavelet packet decomposition, the detail parts are also carried out the same decomposition. The WPD has the characteristics of arbitrary multi-scale and avoids the shortcomings of frequency-fixed in the wavelet decomposition. It provides a great choice for time-frequency analysis and better reflects the nature and characteristics of the signal. The WPD comprises the entire family of the sub band tree. A three level sub band tree is shown in Fig. 3, where S(0, 0) denotes the original signal space, S(j, n) denotes the decomposed subspace, j is the decomposition level, and n is the index of the subspace occurring at the jth level [19].

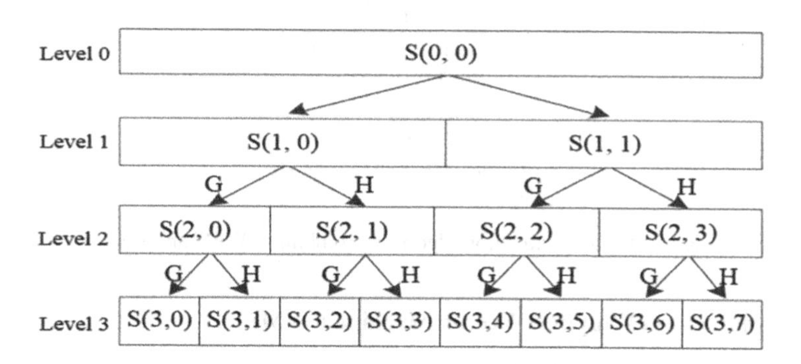

Fig. 3. Process of wavelet packet decomposition.

From the perspective of the energy, the signal energy is decomposed into different time-frequency plane by WPD. The signal energy in the time-frequency window can be reflected by the module value of WPD coefficient. WPD is the promotion of multi-resolution analysis, which can divide the frequency band into levels. Because of the good characteristic in the time-frequency domain, WPD is suitable for the non-stationary EEG signal that has remarkable frequency characteristic and strong randomness [20].

3.3 Feature Extraction Based on WPD-CSP

This paper applies WPD to extract effective frequency range and then obtains feature vector by CSP. The flow chart of this algorithm is shown in Fig. 4. Third-order wavelet packet decomposition is performed for each channel. And then the wavelet coefficients extracted separately for each channel are reconstructed as the input of CSP to extract feature. The detailed steps can be seen in [18].

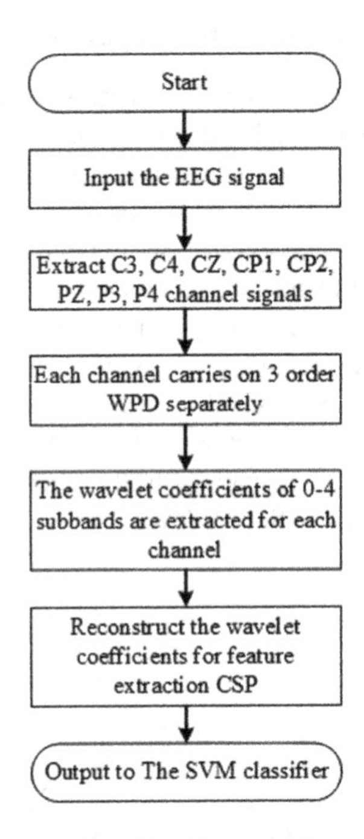

Fig. 4. Feature extraction algorithm combining WPD and CSP.

3.4 Introduction of Support Vector Machine (SVM)

Support vector machine (SVM) is one of the best design criteria proposed by Vapnik et al. for linear classifiers based on years of study of statistical learning theory. For the linear inseparable problem, linearly inseparable samples are transformed into high-dimensional feature space by using nonlinear mapping algorithm. It can solve the practical problems such as small sample, nonlinearity, high dimension and local minimum, which is very suitable for the EEG signals [21].

The central idea of standard SVM is to find the optimal classification hyper-plane, which makes the two classes of training samples separate. The aim of optimization is to maximize the margin between the two bounding planes [22]. Given the above advantages of SVM, this method is used to classify the EEG signals.

4 Data Processing and Results

In this study, the WPD-CSP algorithm was used to train the subject-specific models. First, EEG data segments from 0.5 to 2.5 s after the onset of the maker were used for the analysis, as a range which has been demonstrated to be effective for BCI applications [23].

From the 32 channels' EEG signals, we choose 8 channels (CP1, CP2, C3, C4, CZ, PZ, P3, P4) that are most relevant with the motor area. As to each mode, we carried out the data processing of two types of tasks—left hand and right hand. And then compare the results from the three modes. We use 1000 trials' effective EEG signals to extract data from 0.5 to 2.5 s. Take the above eight channels as input data and each channel was extracted by WPD-CSP. The specific process is as follows: First, we choose the above 8 channels. On the comprehensive consideration of the speed of operation and the resolution of time and frequency, the 'haar' wave is selected as the wavelet base because of the advantages of simple implementation, fast operation speed and small resource consumption. And then the eight channels' signals are respectively performed with three layers WPD. We get eight narrowband signals (S(3,0) $\sim$ S(3,7)) and the corresponding sub-band frequencies are [0, 6.25], [6.26, 12.5], …, [43.75, 50] Hz when the sample frequency of EEG is 250 Hz. As the frequency of motor imagery is always under 30 Hz [24], 5 sub-bands (S(3,0) $\sim$ S(3,4)) are selected to further processing. Each sub-band is reconstructed as a new signal and so 5 new signals are formed. Thus the 40-dimensional array obtained from the eight channels forms the $E_{40 \times T}$.

Then, CSP feature extraction is performed on $E_{40 \times T}$, and a feature vector F of 2 m dimension (m < the half of channels' number) can be obtained. This paper takes m = 3, that is, F is 6-dimensional. Then the obtained 6-dimensional feature vector was sent to the SVM classifier as input data to separate left and right and we got the corresponding classification accuracy.

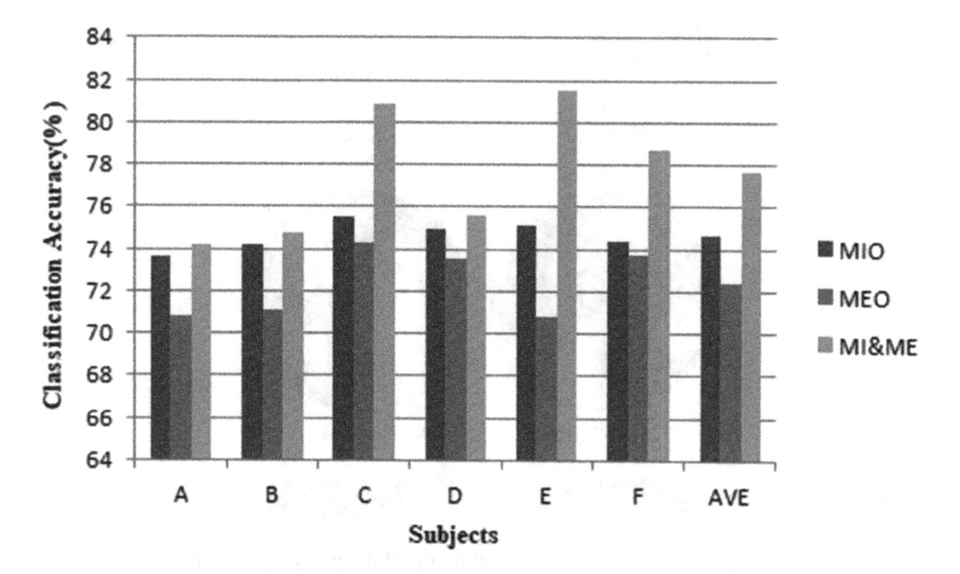

Fig. 5. Corresponding classification accuracy.

Based on the results of EEG analysis of six subjects, the classification accuracy is shown in Fig. 5. It can be concluded that under the experimental conditions of the three different modes, the effect of MI&ME is the best, the second is the MIO, and the effect of MEO is the worst of the three modes. The average accuracy of MI&ME is more than 5% higher than that of MEO, and an average of 3% higher than the accuracy of MIO. The accuracy difference between MI&ME and MEO is statistically significant (p-value is 0.003). On the other hand, spatial pattern energy was drawn with CSP. From the Fig. 6, according to the average spatial pattern of using CSP on our different data respectively, it is clear that some related areas of brain are more active when subjects are in MI&ME mode. The results tell us that, in the rehabilitation of stroke patients, if they focus on the motor imagery of the hand while the external device drives the hand movements, it may activate more brain areas about motor imagery. At the same time, we can get higher classification accuracy.

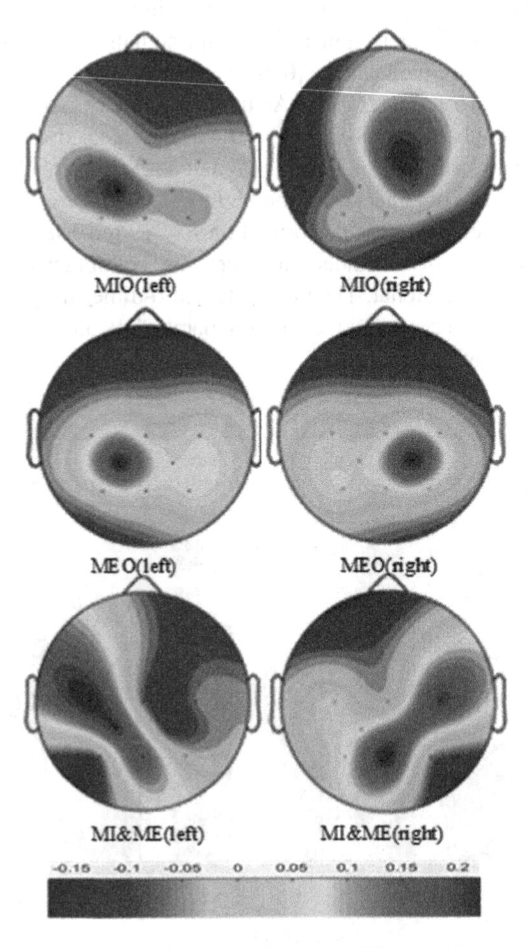

Fig. 6. Spatial pattern of using CSP on our different data respectively.

5 Conclusions and Future Work

In this study, we present three different modes of motor imagery experiments for the existing brain imaging experiments. Some experiments are designed to obtain EEG data under different modes and conduct the corresponding analysis. The experiments conducted in the second section try to find the role of attention in classifying covert and overt motor activities. Actually we do find something different among our designed three experimental modes and these findings may make some contributions to the rehabilitation of stroke patients.

Though Passive movement (i.e., the execution of a movement by an external agency without any voluntary motions) and motor imagery induce similar EEG patterns over the motor cortex [25], from our study, we hypothesize that (1) attention plays an important role in overt and covert motor activities, which may imply that simultaneously overt and covert motor activities may provide better activations in stroke rehabilitation; (2) pure overt movement (like those in robotic rehabilitation) without focusing on the affected limbs may compromised its effect in rehabilitation.

That is, while the robot mechanically drives the affected side for rehabilitation training, the patient should also actively carries out the imagery of the affected limbs. In order to stimulate the patient's nerves, the patient's nervous system should directly involve in the training to motivate the rehabilitation of neurological function. Compared with traditional mechanical arm movement or pure motor imagery, MI&ME should have a better rehabilitation effect.

Upon future work, given that the experiments of this paper are based on healthy people, so we will conduct many experiments on more stroke patients to ensure the reliability of our results. Furthermore, we will use different methods to process the EEG data. Maybe we can apply the deep learning approach to EEG classification problems. We can omit the steps of extracting EEG features and increase the number of trainings and reduce the number of cases when the total data volume is unchanged by using deep learning [26–28]. More samples and new methods will be used to make this study better.

References

1. Birbaumer, N.: Brain–computer-interface research: coming of age. Clin. Neurophysiol. **117**, 479–483 (2006)
2. Wolpaw, J.R., Birbaumer, N., McFarland, D.J., Pfurtscheller, G., Vaughan, T.M.: Brain–computer interfaces for communication and control. Clin. Neurophysiol. **113**, 767–791 (2006)
3. Ahangi, A., Karamnejad, M., Mohammadi, N., Ebrahimpour, R., Bagheri, N.: Multiple classifier system for EEG signal classification with application to brain–computer interfaces. Neural Comput. Appl. **23**(5), 1319–1327 (2002)
4. Hu, S., Tian, Q., Cao, Y., Zhang, J., Kong, W.: Motor imagery classification based on joint regression model and spectral power. Neural Comput. Appl. **21**(7), 1–6 (2012)
5. Ang, K.K., et al.: A large clinical study on the ability of stroke patients to use EEG-based motor imagery brain–computer interface. Clin. EEG Neurosci. **42**, 253–258 (2011)
6. Pfurtscheller, G., Muller-Putz, G.R., Scherer, R., Neuper, C.: Rehabilitation with brain–computer interface systems. Computer **41**, 58–65 (2008)

7. Prasad, G., Herman, P., Coyle, D., McDonough, S., Crosbie, J.: Applying a brain–computer interface to support motor imagery practice in people with stroke for upper limb recovery: a feasibility study. J. Neuroeng. Rehabil. **7**(1), 60 (2010)
8. Butler, A.J., Page, S.J.: Mental practice with motor imagery: evidence for motor recovery and cortical reorganization after stroke. Arch. Phys. Med. Rehabil. **87**, 2–11 (2006)
9. Gu, T., Li, C., Zhan, Q.: Advances in application of rehabilitation robots for upper limb dysfunction in patients with stroke. J. Neurol. Neurorehabilit. **13**(1), 44–50 (2017)
10. Sharma, N., Pomeroy, V.M., Baron, J.C.: Motor imagery: a backdoor to the motor system after stroke? Stroke **37**, 1941–1952 (2006)
11. Vries, S., Mulder, T.: Motor imagery and stroke rehabilitation: a critical discussion. J. Rehabil. Med. **39**, 5–13 (2007)
12. Christa, N., Reinhold, S., Miriam, R., Gert, P.: Imagery of motor actions: differential effects of kinesthetic and visual–motor mode of imagery in single-trial EEG. Cogn. Brain Res. **25**, 668–677 (2005)
13. van Dokkum, L.E., Ward, T., Laffont, I.: Brain computer interfaces for neurorehabilitation – its current status as a rehabilitation strategy post-stroke. Ann. Phys. Rehabilit. Med. **58**, 3–8 (2015)
14. Chaudhary, U., Birbaumer, N., Curado, M.R.: Brain-machine interface (BMI) in paralysis. Ann. Phys. Rehabilit. Med. **58**, 9–13 (2015)
15. Soekadar, S.R., Birbaumer, N., Slutzky, M.W., Cohen, L.G.: Brain–machine interfaces in neurorehabilitation of stroke. Neurobiol. Disease **83**, 172–179 (2015)
16. Ang, K.K., Guan, C.: Brain-computer interface in stroke rehabilitation. J. Comput. Sci. Eng. **7**(2), 139–146 (2013)
17. Zhang, T., Yang, B., Duan, K., Tang, J., Han, X.: Development of hand function rehabilitation system based on motor imagery brain-computer interface. Chin. J. Rehabilit. Theory Pract. **23**(1), 4–9 (2017)
18. Yang, B., Wu, T., Wang, Q., et al.: Motor imagery EEG recognition based on WPD-CSP and KF-SVM in brain–computer interfaces. Appl. Mech. Mater. **556–562**, 2829–2833 (2014)
19. Ang, K.K., Chin, Z.Y., Wang, C., Guan, C.: Filter bank common spatial pattern algorithm on BCI competition IV datasets 2a and 2b. Front. Neurosci. **6**, 1–9 (2012)
20. Yang, B., Li, H., Wang, Q., Zhang, Y.: Subject-based feature extraction by using fisher WPD-CSP in brain–computer interfaces. Comput. Methods Programs Biomed. **129**, 21–28 (2016)
21. Qin, J., Li, Y., Sun, W.: A semisupervised support vector machines algorithm for BCI systems. Comput. Intell. Neurosci. **2007**, 94397 (2007)
22. Ren, J.: ANN vs. SVM: which one performs better in classification of MCCs in mammogram imaging. Knowl. Based Syst. **26**, 144–153 (2012)
23. Tangermann, M., Müller, K.R., Aertsen, A., Birbaumer, N., Braun, C., Brunner, C., et al.: Review of the BCI competition IV. Front. Neurosci. **6**(55), 1–31 (2012)
24. Yuan, L., Yang, B.H., Ma, S.H.W.: Discrimination of movement imagery EEG based on HHT and SVM. Chin. J. Sci. Instrum. **31**(3), 650–654 (2010)
25. Arvaneh, M., Guan, C., Ang, K.K., Ward, T.E., Chua, K.S.G., et al.: Facilitating motor imagery-based brain–computer interface for stroke patients using passive movement. Neural Comput. Appl. **28**, 3259–3272 (2017)
26. Wang, Z., et al.: A deep-learning based feature hybrid framework for spatiotemporal saliency detection inside videos. Neurocomputing **287**, 68–83 (2018)
27. Han, J., et al.: Background prior-based salient object detection via deep reconstruction residual. IEEE Trans. Circ. Syst. Video Technol. **25**(8), 1309–1321 (2015)
28. Zabalza, J., et al.: Novel segmented stacked autoencoder for effective dimensionality reduction and feature extraction in hyperspectral imaging. Neurocomputing **185**, 1–10 (2016)

Attend to Knowledge: Memory-Enhanced Attention Network for Image Captioning

Hui Chen[1], Guiguang Ding[1(✉)], Zijia Lin[2], Yuchen Guo[1], and Jungong Han[3]

[1] School of Software, Tsinghua University, Beijing 100084, China
jichenhui2012@163.com, dinggg@tsinghua.edu.cn,
yuchen.w.guo@gmail.com

[2] Microsoft Research, Beijing 100084, China
zijlin@microsoft.com

[3] School of Computing and Communications, Lancaster University, Lancaster LA1 4YW, UK
jungonghan77@gmail.com

Abstract. Image captioning, which aims to automatically generate sentences for images, has been exploited in many works. The attention-based methods have achieved impressive performance due to its superior ability of adapting the image's feature to the context dynamically. Since the recurrent neural network has difficulties in remembering the information too far in the past, we argue that the attention model may not be adequately supervised by the guidance from the previous information at a distance. In this paper, we propose a memory-enhanced attention model for image captioning, aiming to improve the attention mechanism with previous learned knowledge. Specifically, we store the visual and semantic knowledge which has been exploited in the past into memories, and generate a global visual or semantic feature to improve the attention model. We verify the effectiveness of the proposed model on two prevalent benchmark datasets MS COCO and Flickr30k. The comparison with the state-of-the-art models demonstrates the superiority of the proposed model.

Keywords: Image captioning · Attention mechanism · Memory

1 Introduction

Image captioning aims to enable machines to understand the scene shown in the image and describe it in human language. It has attracted much attention from both academia and industry due to its much value in a wide range of applications, such as childhood education [15], cross-view retrieval [4,13], visual impairment rehabilitation [5], etc.

There are many pioneering works for image captioning [3,17]. The main body of the previous works follows the encoder-decoder framework which has been proven to be effective in dealing with the sequence generation task. Generally,

J. Ren et al. (Eds.): BICS 2018, LNAI 10989, pp. 161–171, 2018.
https://doi.org/10.1007/978-3-030-00563-4_16

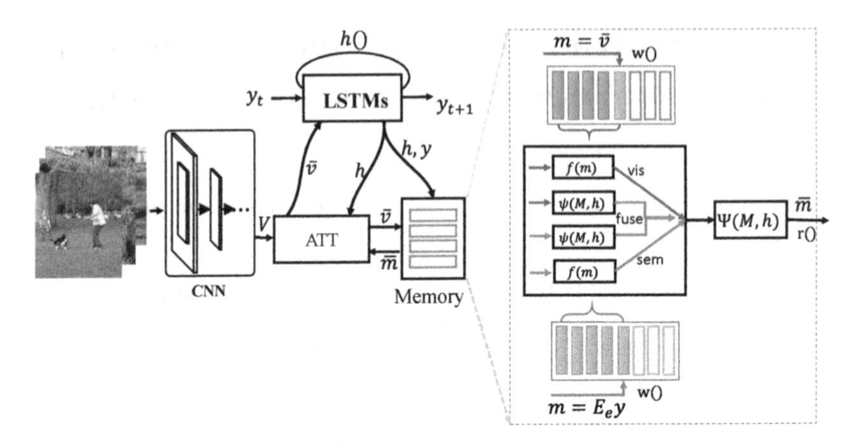

Fig. 1. The framework of the proposed model. For ease of explanation, we leave out the subscript 't' of variables in ATT and Memory module, e.g. h, y, $\bar{v}$, m, $\bar{m}$. M is a matrix consists by m, i.e., $M = [m_0, m_1, ..., m_{t-1}]$. $h()$ means the updating of LSTMs. Three kinds of the memory module are shown in the right red box, where $f(x)$, $w()$, $r()$ refer to the identity function, the write function and the read function, respectively. Details about $\psi()$ are described in Sect. 3. (Color figure online)

a convolutional neural network (CNN) is used as an encoder to extract visual features for a given image, and then a recurrent neural network (RNN) is used to generate sentences conditioned on these visual features by maximizing the likelihood of a sentence. Since it is hard to capture all the informative features of images with only a single context vector [20], attention mechanism is introduced into image captioning [1,2,9,14,19]. The attention mechanism can capacitate the model attend to the most relevant regions for each generated word dynamically, and thus it empowers the model to generate more reasonable sentences (Fig. 1).

In spite of having achieved impressive performance, the attention mechanism still need to be studied further. In the current attention models, the saliency weights greatly rely on the current state of the RNN. However, due to the difficulties of the RNN in capturing the information in the long run, the previous information will vanish gradually along the process. Therefore, the attention procedure is actually guided by the local information (neighboring words) without involving the global information (whole sentence). Although LSTMs [7] are more powerful in memorizing the past information than RNNs due to a more sophisticated memory model, it still struggles to remember words too far in the past [18]. We argue that the global information is helpful to locate the visual concepts, since there likely exists a strong semantic relation between words at a distance and the current word. For example, in sentence "a vase filled with red and green flowers", "vase" is more related to "flowers" than "red" or "green", although it is far from "flowers".

Motivated by this observation, we propose a memory-enhanced attention model targeting at improving the attention mechanism with previous learned knowledge. Our model utilizes the past visual knowledge and semantic knowledge when reasoning where to attend to at the current time step. This help the attention model not only leverage the local information, but also involve both the global spatial information and the temporal information. Our contributions are three folds. (1) We introduce a memory-enhanced attention model to boost the performance of the captioning model. (2) We utilize two types of knowledge, i.e., visual and semantic, by integrating them into our memory-enhanced attention models. (3) We verify the effectiveness of the proposed method by a series of experiments and analyses. The results demonstrate the superiority of the proposed method over the state-of-the-art attention model.

2 Related Work

Many works have been proposed to improve the performance of image captioning models. Encoder-Decoder [3,17] is a prevalent and general framework for image captioning. Motivated by the human being's attention mechanism, attention mechanism is applied to improve the quality of generated captions. The attention-based models can be categorized into visual attention and semantic attention according to what to attend.

Visual Attention. The visual attention model makes the image feature adaptive to the sentence context at hand [2]. Xu *et al.* [19] firstly introduced the visual attention into image captioning, which adopted the soft attention to average the spatial feature with saliency weights and the hard attention to select the most probably attentive region. Chen *et al.* [2] proposed a spatial and channel-wise attention to attend to both salient regions and salient features. Lu *et al.* [14] introduced a visual sentinel allowing attending to regions adaptively. Anderson *et al.* [1] combined both bottom-up attention and top-down attention to generate more informative image features, resulting in better generation.

Semantic Attention. You *et al.* [22] firstly proposed to selectively attend to semantic concepts instead of visual regions. Jia *et al.* [8] used the global semantic correlation between images and captions to guide the decoder to generate better captions. In [2], Chen *et al.* considered the filter kernels of a convolutional layer as a semantic detector, and proposed a channel-wise attention.

3 Attention-Based Network

Before presenting our memory-enhanced attention architecture, we will give a brief introduction about the attention-based network adopted in our work.

The adopted attention-based network follows [1], which is used as the baseline system in this work. Specifically, given an image I, a CNN compresses the image I into a feature map, $V = [v_1, v_2, ..., v_k], v_i \in \mathbb{R}^D$, and a global image feature $\dot{v} \in \mathbb{R}^D$ firstly. Then an RNN generates captions conditioned on the image information extracted by the CNN.

For training, the word y_t in the ground-truth sentence $Y = \{y_0, y_1, ..., y_T\}$ will be fed into the bottom LSTM with the previous hidden states, h_{t-1}^{top} and

h_{t-1}^{btm}, and the global image feature $\dot{v}$. The hidden state of the bottom LSTM, h_t^{btm} updates as follows:

$$h_t^{btm} = \text{LSTM}([h_{t-1}^{top}, \dot{v}, E_e y_t], h_{t-1}^{btm}) \tag{1}$$

where E_e is an embedding dictionary to be learnt, and y_t represents a one-hot vector.

The bottom LSTM can be regarded as a transformation function for the embedding representations of words. Then, the attention module performs a soft attention function over the image's feature map V with the current word's representation h_t^{btm}. We first define a **soft function** denoted by $\psi()$ which takes a matrix $V = [v_1, v_2, ..., v_k], v_i \in \mathbb{R}^D$ and a vector h as inputs, and outputs a vector c:

$$\begin{aligned} c = \psi(V, h) &= \sum_{i=1}^{k} \alpha_i v_i \\ s.t. \quad \alpha &= \text{softmax}(W_a \tanh(W_{av} V + (W_{ah} h)\mathbf{1}^T)) \end{aligned} \tag{2}$$

where W_a, W_{av} and W_{ah} are parameters to be learned.

Then the visual feature $\bar{v}_t$ produced by the attention module at the time step t can be written as follows:

$$\bar{v}_t = \text{att}(V, h_t^{btm}) = \psi(V, h_t^{btm}) \tag{3}$$

where V is the feature map of the image.

Finally, the top LSTM functions as a predictor which will generate a distribution over the whole vocabulary:

$$\begin{aligned} h_t^{top} &= \text{LSTM}([\bar{v}_t, h_t^{btm}], h_{t-1}^{top}) \\ p(y_t | y_{1:t-1}, I) &= \text{softmax}(W_p h_t^{top} + b_p) \end{aligned} \tag{4}$$

where W_p and b_p are parameters to be learned.

4 Memory-Enhanced Attention Network

4.1 Overview

The proposed memory module [6,10,11,16,18] consists of a memory M which stores the knowledge about the image and words that the model has learned. More specifically, the memory is an array of objects indexed by m_t, as in [10,16,18]. In order to utilize the knowledge to improve the attention model, we need to select the most relevant knowledge in the memory. Our memory module can perform two kinds of functions: read and write.

Write. The write function takes in the knowledge you want to memory. Here, we simply store the information into the memory one by one along the process:$m_t = f_t$, where f_t is the knowledge at time step t. We will the representations of f_t in next subsection.

Read. The read function selects the related knowledge for the prediction at the current time step. Since not all knowledge is helpful for the prediction, we need adaptively select the most related information. Here, we let the model learn the selecting strategy by itself. Specifically, we obtain the knowledge feature $\bar{m}_t$ via weighting and summing all knowledge in the memory using soft function in Eq. 2: $\bar{m} = \text{mem}(M, h) = \psi(M, h)$, where $M = \{m_1, m_2, ..., m_k\}$, m_i is the i'th element in the memory and h is the current information, which can be the current hidden state of the decoder.

4.2 Memory Module

In this section, we will describe the construction of the memory module, i.e., what to read and how to read in detail. Our memory module aims to memorize the knowledge which has been exploited by the model. The memory here is flexible and we can fill it with different knowledge. In our work, we explore three kinds of knowledge.

Visual Knowledge. There exists a spatial locality problem in the existing attention models. Here, we propose to use the memory network to solve this issue. We can consider the attention mechanism as a fuzzy function which highlights the region we attend to and makes others blurry. Thus, the feature vector $\bar{v}_t$ produced by the attention model at different time step t contains the global visual information of the image implicitly. Since $\bar{v}_t$ is learned by the model itself, it can be regarded as the visual knowledge about the past impression of the image. Therefore, we store $\bar{v}_t$ in the memory as the visual knowledge. And at any time step t, the attention module reads the global visual information of the image $\bar{m}_t^{vis}$ from the memory by selectively attending to the visual knowledge, which is learned before time step t, using the current information supervised. The write function and read function can be denoted as follows:

$$\begin{aligned} m_{t-1}^{vis} &= \bar{v}_{t-1} \\ \bar{m}_t^{vis} &= \text{mem}(M^{vis}, h_t^{btm}) \end{aligned} \tag{5}$$

where $M^{vis} = \{m_0^{vis}, m_1^{vis}, ..., m_t^{vis}\}$.

Semantic Knowledge. The attention module leverages the hidden state h_t at the time step t to supervise where to attend to. Since the decoder will forget the information too far in the past gradually, the hidden state vector h_t is not adequate to maintain the information that has been known. LSTMs are more powerful in memorizing the past information than vanilla RNNs due to the use of a more sophisticated memory model, but they still have trouble remembering words too far in the past [18]. Thus, current attention models are temporally local because the attention module is not exposed to the information too far in the past. We argue there could be a strong relationship between words at a distance and the current word, and it should be taken into consideration when computing the saliency weights in the attention module. In this paper, we solve the temporal locality problem of attention module by means of the memory module. Specifically, all the information of previously generated words will be kept in a memory storage. And at the time step t, the memory will produce a feature vector $\bar{m}_t^{sem}$ indicating the past semantic knowledge that has been learned by the model. Instead of organizing the memory in an RNN-like way, we let the embedding vector of a word take in one row in the memory and have an attention-like module to adaptively select the semantic knowledge stored in the memory:

$$\begin{aligned} m_t^{sem} &= E_e y_t \\ \bar{m}_t^{sem} &= \text{mem}(M^{sem}, h_t^{btm}) \end{aligned} \tag{6}$$

where E_e is the embedding dictionary to be learned and $M^{sem} = \{m_0^{sem}, m_1^{sem}, ..., m_t^{sem}\}$.

Fusion Knowledge. We also adopt a fusion strategy to combine these two knowledge described above. Instead of directly inputting these two kinds of global features into the attention module, we encourage the model to selectively focus on them with a front-end combination strategy. Specifically, we save the visual knowledge and the semantic knowledge in two memory storages, denoted by M^{vis} and M^{sem} respectively. At time step t, the two memory modules will produce a global visual feature and a global semantic feature about the input image and previously generated words respectively, according to Eqs. 5 and 6, i.e., $\bar{m}_t^{vis}$ and $\bar{m}_t^{sem}$, respectively. Before combining with the attention module, we use the soft function in Eq. 2 and generate a fusion feature:

$$\bar{m}_t^{fuse} = \psi([\bar{m}_t^{vis}, \bar{m}_t^{sem}], h_t^{btm}) \tag{7}$$

where $[.,.]$ means concatenation.

Table 1. Performance of the proposed method on MS COCO dataset.

Dataset	Model	BLEU-1	BLEU-2	BLEU-3	BLEU-4	METEOR	ROUGE-L	CIDEr
MS COCO	top-down	74.1	57.7	43.9	33.6	25.8	54.3	105.7
	top-down+**vis**	75.0	58.2	44.7	34.4	26.4	55.0	108.1
	top-down+**sem**	75.1	58.6	45.0	34.5	26.4	54.9	107.5
	top-down+**vis&sem**	**75.7**	**59.5**	**45.7**	**35.0**	**26.8**	**55.7**	**109.2**

Table 2. Performance comparison of the proposed method with other methods.

Models	Flickr30k							MS COCO						
	B@1	B@2	B@3	B@4	MT	RG	CD	B@1	B@2	B@3	B@4	MT	RG	CD
ATT [22]	64.7	46.0	32.4	23.0	18.9	-	-	70.9	53.7	40.2	30.4	24.3	-	-
Hard-Attention [19]	66.9	43.9	29.6	19.9	18.46	-	-	71.8	50.4	35.7	25.0	23.04	-	-
SCA-CNN [2]	66.2	46.8	32.5	22.3	19.5	44.9	44.7	71.9	54.8	41.1	31.1	25.0	53.1	95.2
Adaptive-attention [14]	67.7	49.4	35.4	25.1	20.4	-	53.1	74.2	58.0	43.9	33.2	26.6	-	108.5
top-down+**vis&sem**	**68.7**	**50.8**	**36.8**	**26.6**	**20.7**	**47.7**	**56.7**	**75.7**	**59.5**	**45.7**	**35.0**	**26.8**	**55.7**	**109.2**

Memory-Enhanced Attention Module. After obtaining the knowledge feature, we plug it into the attention module with the feature map V of the image and the hidden state vector h_t^{btm} of the bottom LSTM:

$$c_t = \mathrm{att}(V, [h_t^{btm}, \bar{m}_t]) \tag{8}$$

where $\bar{m}_t$ is the knowledge representation, which can be either $\bar{m}_t^{vis}$ or $\bar{m}_t^{sem}$ or their combination $\bar{m}_t^{fuse}$ introduced above.

5 Training and Optimization

The captioning model aims to predict the next word given all previously seen words and the input image. Similar to the previous works [2,14,17,19], we encourage the model to directly maximize the cross entropy loss objective during training:

$$\theta^* = \arg\min_{\theta} \sum_{t=1}^{T} \log p(y_t|I, \theta, y_0, y_1, ..., y_{t-1}) \tag{9}$$

where T is the maximum length of sentences and θ denotes the parameter of the proposed network.

6 Experiment

6.1 Dataset

We evaluate the proposed model on two datasets. (1) **Flickr30k** [23] contains 31,783 images, each being attached with 5 captions labeled by human. We follow previous works [2,14], and use 1,000 images for validation, another 1,000 images for test and the remains for training. (2) **MS COCO** [12] consists of 82,783 training images, 40,504 validation images and 40,775 images as the online test set. Following [14], we use 5,000 for validation, 5,000 for test and the remains for training.

Table 3. Evaluation performance of the proposed method on the online MS COCO testing server. † indicates the results of ensemble models.

Models	BLEU-1		BLEU-2		BLEU-3		BLEU-4		METEOR		ROUGE-L		CIDEr	
	c5	c40	c5	c40	c5	c40	c5	c40	c5	c40	c5	c40	c5	c40
ERD [20]	72.0	90.0	55.0	81.2	41.4	70.5	31.3	59.7	25.6	34.7	53.3	68.6	96.5	96.9
MSM† [21]	73.9	91.9	57.5	84.2	43.6	74.0	33.0	63.2	25.6	35.0	54.2	70.0	98.4	100.3
Adaptive attention† [14]	74.6	91.8	58.2	84.2	44.3	74.0	33.5	63.3	26.4	35.9	55.0	70.6	103.7	105.1
SCA-CNN [2]	71.2	89.4	54.2	80.2	40.4	69.1	30.2	57.9	24.4	33.1	52.4	67.4	91.2	92.1
top-down+**vis&sem**	**75.5**	**92.7**	**59.2**	**85.2**	**45.5**	**75.4**	**34.8**	**64.8**	**27.2**	**36.7**	**55.8**	**71.4**	**106.9**	**106.7**

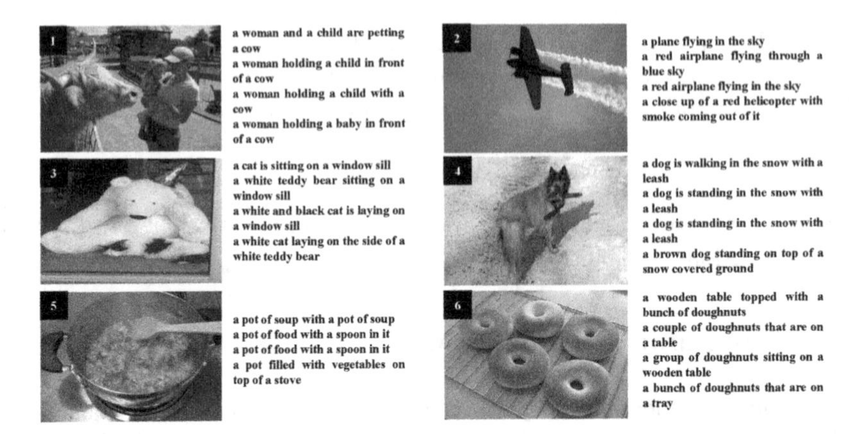

Fig. 2. Examples of four types of models: top-down (black), top-down + **vis** (green), top-down + **sem** (blue) and top-down+**vis&sem** (red). Best viewed in color. (Color figure online)

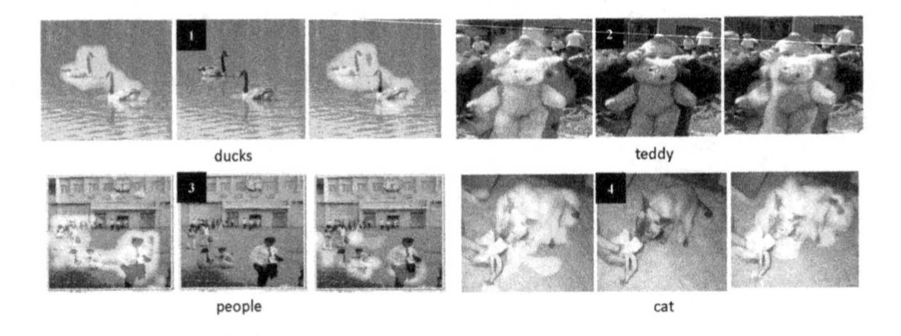

Fig. 3. visualization of the attention maps of objects generated by top-down+**vis&sem** model and the baseline model top-down, listed in the left and right of the given image, respectively.

6.2 Implementation Details

We use the public code[1] to preprocess the captions and end up with 9567 and 7000 words for COCO and Flickr30k respectively. We use ResNet-101 pretrained on ImageNet as the encoder CNN. And we apply spatially average pooling and get the feature map with fixed size of $14 \times 14 \times 2048$. The hidden state size of the decoder LSTM is 512. The embedding dimension of word is fixed to 512. During training, the learning rate is set to 5×10^{-4}. We apply beam search strategy to generate captions with higher probability. By default, we set the beam size as 3, which is common according to the previous works [14]. To compared with other methods, we use the same evaluation metrics, including BLEU (**B@1, B@2, B@3, B@4**), METEOR (**MT**), ROUGE-L (**RG**) and CIDEr (**CD**).

[1] https://github.com/karpathy/neuraltalk.

6.3 Quantitative Analysis

Evaluations of Memory-Enhanced Attention. We compare the the baseline model (top-down) on MS COCO: top-down + **vis**, which only integrates the visual knowledge; top-down + **sem**, which only integrates the semantic knowledge, and top-down + **vis&sem** which integrates both the visual knowledge and the semantic knowledge. The comparison result is listed in Table 1. Compared with the baseline model, our models can achieve better results with improvements of 2.7%, 2.1% and 3.8% in terms of CIDEr on MS COCO dataset. Better performance can be attributed to the introduced global information which is able to assist to highlight the salient regions better. The fusion knowledge-based model (top-down + **vis&sem**) can outperform another two models which integrate only one kind of knowledge in all metrics.

Compared with Others Methods. We further compare our models with several state-of-the-art methods, including ATT [22], Hard-Attention [19], SCA-CNN [2] and Adaptive-Attention [14]. Since here we focus on improving the network structure rather than improving the learning process, for fair comparison, we only compare with those methods without reinforcement learning. We leave using reinforcement learning in our models to the future work. Table 2 shows the performance comparison results. From the comparison, we can conclude that: (1) our proposed memory-enhanced attention model can significantly surpass those captioning models without attention mechanism whose results are listed in the second row in Table 2; (2) our attention model with the fusion knowledge is superior to the current state-of-the-art attention-based models whose results are listed in the third row in Table 2. The results demonstrate that the proposed attention model could capture the global spatial and temporal information and ease the impact of the spatial locality and the temporal locality, which contributes to the performance improvement.

Online Comparison. For online evaluation, we compare our method with other methods on the server of MS COCO[2]. We use the same image feature as [1] to train a new model, and evaluated the performance of the captions for the official test set. The comparison is shown in Table 3. It shows that our single model can obtain a better performance than the state-of-the-art methods.

6.4 Attention Analysis

Figure 3 shows some example generated captions and the attention maps corresponding to specific words in captions. We simply resize the image and the attention weights to the same size (224×224) using bilinear interpolation, and generate a color map for the image. We can see that our model can learn the salient regions for specific words, which is consistent with the human intuition strongly. And we find that the saliency map generated by our model is more smooth than the baseline model, while the salient regions is scatter in the saliency

[2] https://competitions.codalab.org/competitions/3221#results.

map generated by the baseline mode. This demonstrates that the global spatial information introduced to the attention module by the proposed method can improve the quality of the localization of salient regions.

6.5 Quality Analysis

Figure 2 shows some examples of the baseline model and three types of our proposed models. Our best model, i.e. top-down + **vis&sem** can not only learn the objects in the image successfully, but also describe the objects more descriptively than the baseline model: image 1 ("holding"), image 4 ("red helicopter"), image 6 ("on a tray").

7 Conclusion

In this paper, we proposed a memory-enhanced attention network for image captioning. The difficulty of RNN in capturing the information of sequence in the long run makes it hard to expose the attention module adequately to the previous knowledge at a distance. In this paper, we introduce both the global spatial information and the global temporal information to help the attention module. Specifically, we adopt two memory modules, i.e. the visual memory and the semantic memory, to store these two global information. At each time step, the memory modules will generate the fusion information via adaptively selecting the related knowledge to help the attention module localize the salient regions. We carried out a series of experiments and comparisons with the state-of-the-art methods both on MS COCO dataset and Flickr30k. The results demonstrate the effectiveness of the proposed method.

References

1. Anderson, P., et al.: Bottom-up and top-down attention for image captioning and VQA. arXiv preprint arXiv:1707.07998 (2017)
2. Chen, L., Zhang, H., Xiao, J., Nie, L., Shao, J., Chua, T.S.: SCA-CNN: spatial and channel-wise attention in convolutional networks for image captioning. In: CVPR (2017)
3. Chen, M., Ding, G., Zhao, S., Chen, H., Liu, Q., Han, J.: Reference based LSTM for image captioning. In: AAAI (2017)
4. Ding, G., Guo, Y., Zhou, J., Gao, Y.: Large-scale cross-modality search via collective matrix factorization hashing. TIP **25**(11), 5427–5440 (2016)
5. Dodds, A.: Rehabilitating Blind and Visually Impaired People: A Psychological Approach. Springer, Heidelberg (2013). https://doi.org/10.1007/978-1-4899-4461-0
6. Fakoor, R., Mohamed, A.R., Mitchell, M., Kang, S.B., Kohli, P.: Memory-augmented attention modelling for videos. arXiv preprint arXiv:1611.02261 (2016)
7. Hochreiter, S., Schmidhuber, J.: Long short-term memory. Neural Comput. **9**(8), 1735–1780 (1997)
8. Jia, X., Gavves, E., Fernando, B., Tuytelaars, T.: Guiding the long-short term memory model for image caption generation. In: IEEE International Conference on Computer Vision, pp. 2407–2415 (2015)

9. Jin, J., Fu, K., Cui, R., Sha, F., Zhang, C.: Aligning where to see and what to tell: image caption with region-based attention and scene factorization. arXiv preprint arXiv:1506.06272 (2015)
10. Kaiser, L., Nachum, O., Roy, A., Bengio, S.: Learning to remember rare events. In: CVPR (2017)
11. Kumar, A., et al.: Ask me anything: dynamic memory networks for natural language processing. In: International Conference on Machine Learning, pp. 1378–1387 (2016)
12. Lin, T.Y., et al.: Microsoft COCO: common objects in context. In: European Conference on Computer Vision, pp. 740–755 (2014)
13. Lin, Z., Ding, G., Han, J., Wang, J.: Cross-view retrieval via probability-based semantics-preserving hashing. IEEE Trans. Cybern. (2016)
14. Lu, J., Xiong, C., Parikh, D., Socher, R.: Knowing when to look: adaptive attention via a visual sentinel for image captioning (2017)
15. Roopnarine, J., Johnson, J.E.: Approaches to early childhood education. Merrill/Prentice Hall, Upper Saddle River (2013)
16. Sukhbaatar, S., Weston, J., Fergus, R., et al.: End-to-end memory networks. In: Advances in Neural Information Processing Systems, pp. 2440–2448 (2015)
17. Vinyals, O., Toshev, A., Bengio, S., Erhan, D.: Show and tell: a neural image caption generator. In: CVPR, pp. 3156–3164 (2015)
18. Weston, J., Chopra, S., Bordes, A.: Memory networks. arXiv preprint arXiv:1410.3916 (2014)
19. Xu, K., et al.: Show, attend and tell: neural image caption generation with visual attention. In: ICML, pp. 2048–2057 (2015)
20. Yang, Z., Yuan, Y., Wu, Y., Salakhutdinov, R., Cohen, W.W.: Encode, review, and decode: reviewer module for caption generation. In: NIPS (2016)
21. Yao, T., Pan, Y., Li, Y., Qiu, Z., Mei, T.: Boosting image captioning with attributes. arXiv preprint arXiv:1611.01646 (2016)
22. You, Q., Jin, H., Wang, Z., Fang, C., Luo, J.: Image captioning with semantic attention. In: IEEE Conference on Computer Vision and Pattern Recognition, pp. 4651–4659 (2016)
23. Young, P., Lai, A., Hodosh, M., Hockenmaier, J.: From image descriptions to visual denotations: new similarity metrics for semantic inference over event descriptions. Trans. Assoc. Comput. Linguist. **2**, 67–78 (2014)

Direction Guided Cooperative Coevolutionary Differential Evolution Algorithm for Cognitive Modelling of Ray Tracing in Separable High Dimensional Space

Jing Zhao[1(✉)], Jinchang Ren[2], Cailing Wang[3], Ke Li[4], and Yifang Zhao[5]

[1] School of Earth Science and Engineering, Xi'an Shiyou University, Xi'an 710065, China
zhaojing@xsyu.edu.cn
[2] Department of Electronic and Electrical Engineering, University of Strathclyde, Glasgow G1 1XW, UK
[3] School of Computer Science, Xi'an Shiyou University, Xi'an 710065, China
[4] Faculty of Basic Disciplines, Modern College of Northwest University, Xi'an 710130, China
[5] School of Education Science, Shanxi University, Taiyuan 030000, China

Abstract. By simulating how our human brain solves complex and conceptual problems, cognitive systems have been successfully applied in a wide range of applications. In this paper, a cognitive modelling based inversion method, the direction guided differential evolution with cooperative coevolutionary mutation operator (DG-DECCM) algorithm, is proposed to trace the ray path of the seismic waves. The DE algorithm seeks optimal solutions by simulating the natural species evolution processes and makes the individuals become optimal. Classical ray tracing methods were time consuming and inefficiency. The proposed algorithm is suitable for the high and super high dimensional separable model space. It treats the emergent angles of the reflection points as genes of an individual. We introduce a sign function to guide the direction of the mutation and propose two kinds of stopping criteria for effective iteration to speed up the computation. For the complex velocity model, the local optimization methods based on gradient are time consuming to converge or may converge to local minimum but not the optimal value. The proposed global DE algorithm, however, will obtain a global optimum solution more efficiently and has higher convergence rate.

Keywords: Cognitive modelling · Differential evolution · Ray tracing High dimension

1 Introduction

In the geophysics, we study the propagation of the seismic wave to research the subsurface structure of the earth. The ray is the path along which the seismic wave travels through the Earth. It is the high frequency approximate solution of the wave equation. Ray tracing is one of the key steps of tomography, which is used at the

J. Ren et al. (Eds.): BICS 2018, LNAI 10989, pp. 172–183, 2018.
https://doi.org/10.1007/978-3-030-00563-4_17

beginning of the iterative inversion to simulate the forward model. Fast and effective ray tracing algorithm is the key to improve the inversion efficiency. There are lots of ray tracing methods, such as the wave-front method [1], the shortest path method [2], the travel-time epenthesis method [3], and ordinal wave-front construction method [4], etc. The above methods are inefficient in calculating, poor in convergence and low in resolution. The shortest travel time ray tracing method meshed the underground medium and traced all the nodes. The grids cannot be too small, otherwise the tracing speed would be very slow. It however decreases the resolution if the grids are too large. The stepwise iterative method [5] had to assume a ray which would introduce artificial factors. Ray tracing equation describes the trajectory of the seismic energy with the high frequency. Ray tracing [6] will be faster and more accurate by using the ray equation as it has an analytic expression.

This paper focuses on the ray equation method based on pre-stack seismic record. The locations of the shot points and the receivers are known, if the reflection point and the emergence angles are also known, we can define a ray. This paper focuses on the calculation of the emergence angles using inversion method. Researchers have already developed various inversion approaches such as local optimization waveform inversion and global optimization. In local optimization, the minimum of the objective function can be determined by gradient, conjugate gradient, Newton, Gauss-Newton, and quasi-Newton methods. Among these, the gradient-based waveform inversion methods have got some success, but they have the limitation of nonlinearity of the inversion and dependence on the initial model. In fact, Virieux [7] pointed out that some challenges of waveform inversion are related to building exact initial models, defining new minimization criterion and improving multi-parameter inversion capability.

On the other hand, there are many global optimization methods such as evolutionary algorithm (EA) [8], simulated annealing algorithm [9] and the Monte Carlo method [10]. Compared with the gradient-based waveform inversion method, the global optimization methodology is less dependent on the initial values and requires no gradient. However, it needs a large amount of computation. Despite this fact, it is widely used in recent years with the development of high performance computing.

On a different note, cognitive computing can handle human problems. It has the capability in studying, reasoning, and solving specific problems. Cognitive systems can understand the problems adequately and model the thought process as computing models. Their ability of studying abstract features is similar to the study processing of the brain. Hence the cognitive computing can enhance the human intellectual and decision-making capacity.

The EAs are a kind of cognitive computing and they simulate the natural species evolution processes by computers, and make the individual become optimal. However, the conventional EAs often lose their effectiveness when applied to high-dimensional problems. Pan [11] proposed CRsADE method which use individual crossover rate and subcomponent crossover rate to adaptively improve the efficiency of crossover operation. C. Wang proposed DE with cooperative coevolution selection (DE-CCS) [12] and DE with cooperative coevolution mutation (DE-CCM) [13]. These methods divided the high-dimension problem to several subproblems and judged the subproblems by local fitness functions. Chandra [14] proposed coevolutionary multi-task learning used for multi-step chaotic time series prediction. This paper presents a network architecture which is capable of predicting multi-step. Gao [15] proposed a highly efficient DE algorithm (HEDE) which used a new population evolution strategy to decrease the population size. A new multimutation scheme was later proposed to accelerate the convergence [16]. Cui [17] improved particle swarm optimization used for poststack impedance inversion. This method combined the swarm intelligence and probabilistic theory for global optimization. Mahdavip [18] reviewed metaheuristics in large-scale global continues optimization, including large-scale global optimization (LSGO), evolutionary algorithm (EAs), cooperative coevolution (CC). Lots of DEs such as cooperative coevolution (CC) [19], ND-CC [20] and Co-evolutionary multi-task learning were proposed to solve high-dimensional optimization problems. Meanwhile, most existing methods have the problems of "dimensional bottleneck". The optimizing ability of these methods declined sharply with the increasing of the dimensions. To make the fine subsurface medium, we need to divide the medium into small pieces which let the parameters of the model to be huge. To inverse thousands of parameters can result in the existing CCs becoming invalid or making a large number of iterations.

In this paper, we derive a direction guided DE algorithm to estimate angles for ray tracing. The result can used to synthesize pre-stack seismic reflection record. Meanwhile, a sign function is introduced to guide the mutation direction and a stopping criteria are introduced to speed up the computation.

2 Our Proposed Method

The seismic reflection wave method is easy to operate. The geophones are located on the surface which reduce the cost because of no drilling. Compared to the post-stack reflection data, the pre-stack seismic reflection data is not affected by normal move-out (NMO), and have exact layer information, abundant frequency and travel-time information. We can observe the minute stratum features such as the variation of the waveform at the thin interbed series from the pre-stack data. The observation system of the pre-stack common shot-point gather is shown in Fig. 1(a). The source is located at the shot-point and the geophones are located along the survey line at the surface. Forward simulation is one of the key steps in an inversion problem. In this paper, we study the forward modeling which is carried out by ray tracing based on the pre-stack seismic data. Because the ray equation cannot calculate the reflected rays, we divide a complete ray from shot to receiver into two parts as shown in Fig. 1(b), one part is from the shot to the reflection point and the other one is from the receiver to the reflection point. p_x and p_z represent the slowness along x and z axes respectively, which are the components of the reciprocal of the velocity. Two rays take travel time T_s and T_r to proceed from the reflection point with angles θ_s and θ_r. The 2D ray equations are:

$$\begin{gathered}\frac{\partial x(t)}{\partial t} = v^2(X)p_x, \quad \frac{\partial z(t)}{\partial t} = v^2(X)p_z, \quad \frac{\partial p_x}{\partial t} = -\frac{1}{v(X)} \cdot \frac{\partial v(X)}{\partial x}, \\ \frac{\partial p_z}{\partial t} = -\frac{1}{v(X)} \cdot \frac{\partial v(X)}{\partial z}. \end{gathered} \tag{1}$$

where t is the travel time, v is the velocity at a certain space point, $X = (x, z)$ is the coordinate of the ray. The integration variable of the ray equation is time, and the numerical solutions of differential Eq. (1) are the positions and the gradient directions at each sampling time. Hence, the position of the ray is a function of the emergent angle. If the reflection point and the emergent angles θ_s and θ_r are known, the ray equations can be solved by 4 order Runge-Kutta method. We calculate the emergent angles by DG-DECCM method.

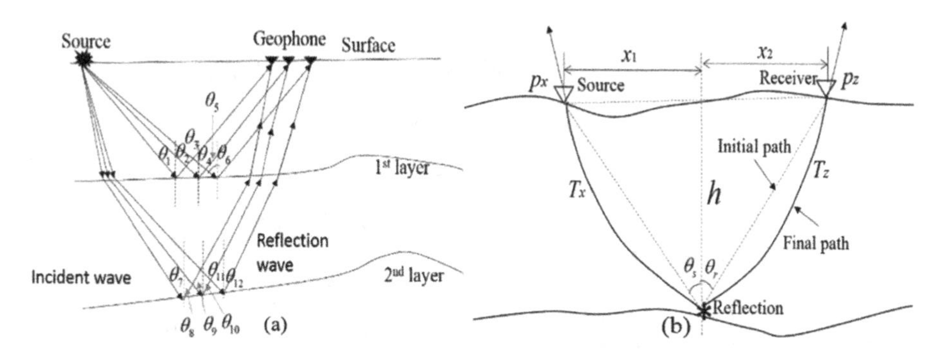

Fig. 1. (a) The observation system of the pre-stack CSP record. (b) Illustration of the initial angles and the final ray

The DE algorithm seeks optimal solutions by simulating the processes in natural species evolution. Cognitive science can be utilized to mimic the evolution process. First, we provide an initial population, and then mutate some individuals of it. We use the algorithm to learn autonomously, to think independently and judge whether the mutation is the optimal direction of evolution. Finally, all the individuals become optimum by iterations. Based on the result, we can find the optimum parameters and make quicker and better decisions. The proposed DE algorithm starts with a population $\boldsymbol{P}$ which has M initial individuals:

$$\boldsymbol{P} = [\boldsymbol{p}_1, \boldsymbol{p}_2, \cdots, \boldsymbol{p}_M]. \tag{2}$$

The kth individual can be expressed as:

$$\boldsymbol{p_k} = [p_{k,1}, p_{k,2}, \cdots, p_{k,N}] = [\theta_1, \theta_2, \theta_3, \theta_4, \theta_5, \theta_6, \cdots, \theta_M], \quad k = 1, \cdots, M. \tag{3}$$

where N is the number of the estimated parameters, $\theta_1, \theta_2, \ldots, \theta_M$ is shown in Fig. 1(a) or Fig. 2(b). For a pre-stack seismic record with $N/2$ data traces, there are N angles to be estimated, so the dimension of the estimated parameters is N. The local fitness function is used to control the mutation direction defined by the error energy between the observed and the calculated data. The local fitness function of the kth individual is defined as:

$$f_{k,j} = \sqrt{\left[x_{k,o}(j) - x_{k,c}(j)\right]^2 + \left[z_{k,o}(j) - z_{k,c}(j)\right]^2}. \tag{4}$$

where $\left[x_{k,o}(j),\ z_{k,o}(j)\right]$ is the end point of the jth observed ray, $\left[x_{k,c}(j),\ z_{k,c}(j)\right]$ is the end point of the jth calculated ray. x and z are the horizontal and vertical axis. Local fitness value is a $M \times N$ matrix, $\mathbf{f} = \begin{bmatrix} f_{1,1} & f_{1,2} & \cdots & f_{1,N} \\ \cdots & & & \\ f_{M,1} & f_{M,2} & \cdots & f_{M,N} \end{bmatrix}$.

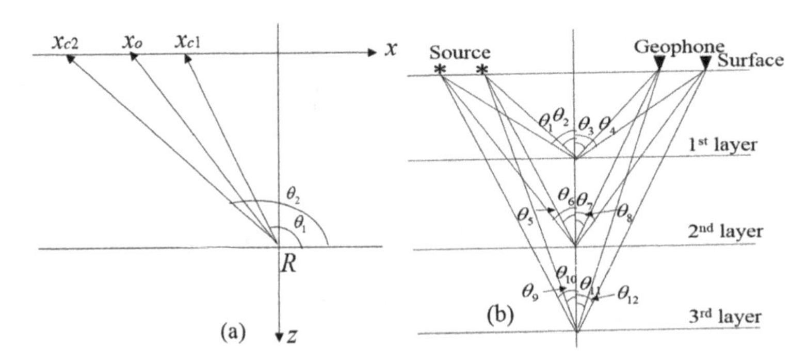

Fig. 2. (a) Illustration of the definition of the sign function. (b) The observation system of the CMP gather

A good mutation strategy can modify the genes (namely, angles) of the individuals effectively, and the optimal solution can be approached after several iterations. A population includes M individuals. M can be any number, if M is too small, we do not always obtain the global optimal parameters; if M is too large, the running time is too long. In the experiments we choose M as 100. If there are N estimated parameters, the number of the genes is N. The M initial individuals of each population are mutated and updated, and finally we will choose an optimum individual as the result.

Picking the variable $p_{r,j}$ corresponding to the minimal value of the sorted local fitness function, and choosing other two variables $p_{r1,j}$ and $p_{r2,j}$ randomly, the mutation strategy of the jth component of the kth individual is derived as:

$$p^m_{k,j} = p_{r,j} + F \cdot \left|p_{r1,j} - p_{r2,j}\right| * S. \tag{5}$$

where F is the control factor whose value is between 0 and 1. S is the sign function defined as:

$$S = \begin{cases} -1, & x_o > x_c \\ 1, & x_o < x_c \end{cases}. \tag{6}$$

where x_o and x_c are the horizontal axis of the observed and calculated end rays individually. The diagram is shown in Fig. 2(a). If the horizontal axis x_{c1} of the end point of the calculated ray is larger than that of the observed ray, the emergency angle θ_1 should be larger. In this case, the optimal variable may be at the right side of the variable $p_{r,j}$, so

S is positive. Otherwise, if x_{c2} is at the left side of x_o, the angle θ_2 should be smaller, so S is negative. The mutated gene disturbs nearby the optimum value.

The table of the DG-DECCM method is summarized as follow:

Algorithm 1. The DG-DECCM Workflow

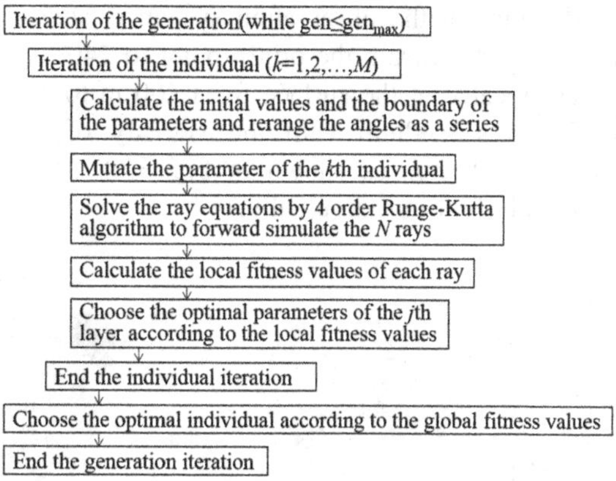

- Iteration of the generation(while gen≤gen$_{max}$)
  - Iteration of the individual (k=1,2,…,M)
    - Calculate the initial values and the boundary of the parameters and rerange the angles as a series
    - Mutate the parameter of the kth individual
    - Solve the ray equations by 4 order Runge-Kutta algorithm to forward simulate the N rays
    - Calculate the local fitness values of each ray
    - Choose the optimal parameters of the jth layer according to the local fitness values
  - End the individual iteration
- Choose the optimal individual according to the global fitness values
- End the generation iteration

where gen$_{max}$ defines a given hard threshold whose value can be 100–500. We set two kinds of iteration stopping criteria. One is hard threshold criteria, where if the iteration times reach the given threshold, then the program exits from the loop. The other one is soft threshold criteria:

$$Ea_j < E_{\min}. \tag{7}$$

where $Ea_j = {}^1\!/_M \sum_{k=1}^{M} f_{k,j}$ is the average error energy and $E_{\min}$ is the given threshold of the minimal precision which is according to the production request. If the above inequality in Eq. 7 is satisfied, then the program is forced to exit from the iteration.

We can see from the flow that there are N separate and independent angles to estimate and N rays to obtain. All the subcomponents are mutated and selected simultaneously and independently under the guidance of the local fitness function, being the new individuals and the original ones crossed randomly. The initial angles are defined according to the geometric relationship shown in Fig. 1(b):

$$\theta_s = \arctan\left(\frac{x_s}{h}\right), \quad \theta_r = \arctan\left(\frac{x_r}{h}\right). \tag{8}$$

where x_s is the distance between the shotpoint and the midpoint, x_r is the distance between the receiver point and the midpoint, and h is the depth of the reflection point. The emergency angle of the ray is defined between the z-axis and the ray, so we should adjust the angles as:

$$\theta_s = \arctan\left(\frac{x_s}{h}\right) + 180, \quad \theta_r = 360 - \theta_s = 180 - \arctan\left(\frac{x_r}{h}\right). \tag{9}$$

3 Experiments and Results

3.1 The Pre-stack Common Midpoint Gather (CMP) Model

We test the proposed method using a CMP data based on the horizontally layered velocity model. The diagram of the observation system is shown in Fig. 2(b). The sources are located at the surface from the origin point to 240 m with the interval of 5 m. The geophones are located at the surface from 260 m to 500 m with the equal interval. There are 5 layers medium with the velocity of 2000 m/s, 2200 m/s, 2400 m/s, 2600 m/s and 2800 m/s as shown in Fig. 3(a). The depths are 200 m, 400 m, 600 m, 800 m, and 1000 m individually.

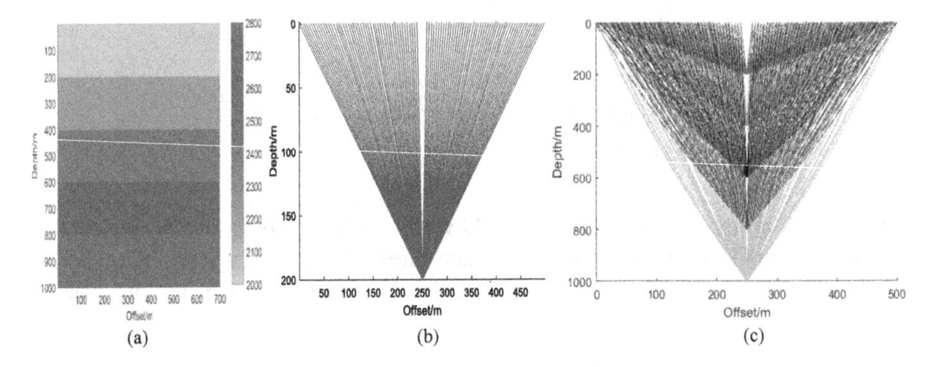

Fig. 3. (a) The velocity of the 5 layers medium. (b) The rays travelling in the first layer medium. (c) The rays in the 5 layers medium

There are 100 initial individuals in the population, and the values of the genes of each individual are generated randomly. In order to optimize the individuals quickly and efficiently, the search space is defined by the lower and upper bounds. The initial angles are calculated according to the geometrical relationship and used to define the upper and lower bounds by superimposing $\pm 30°$ on them. We choose the range of the bounds according to the experience. If the bounds are too narrow, it may not obtain the global optimal solution. DE method uses only the low frequency trends of the initial values but not the initial values themselves, hence it is not dependent on the initial values.

The rays in the first layer are shown in Fig. 3(b). We can see from the figure that the rays in the uniform medium travel in straight lines. The forward simulated rays of the 5 layers are shown in Fig. 3(c). When the rays travel through the interface of the velocity, they will refract into the broken lines. The convergence curve of the error energy is shown in Fig. 4(a) which decreases monotonously. The error energy is defined as the distance of the end of the observed and the calculated rays. There are 49 geophones, so the total rays are $49 \times 2 \times 5 = 490$. After 50 iterations, the error is below 50 m which means the average error energy of each ray is about 0.1 m which is acceptable in field. Figure 4(b) is showing the synthetic single trace-gather based on the calculated rays.

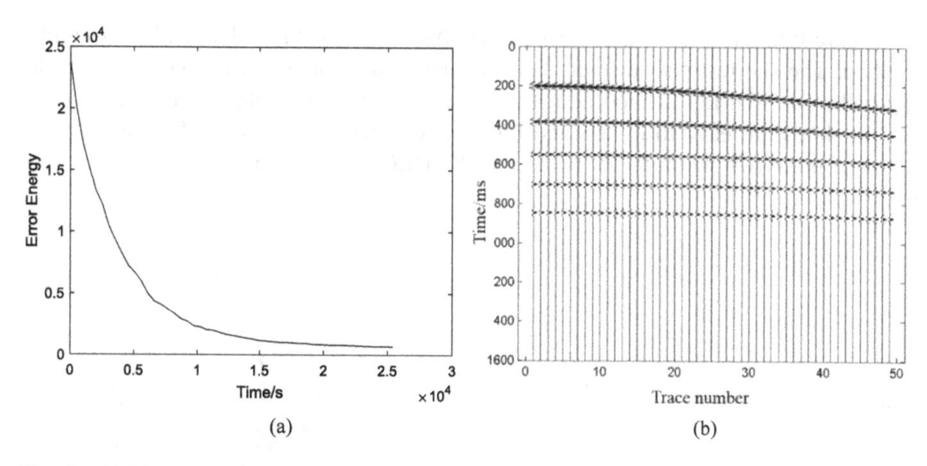

Fig. 4. (a) The convergence curve of the error energy with time. (b) The synthetic CMP record

Figure 5(a) and (b) are the convergence curves of the error energy using a local optimal ray tracing method called adaptive angle-step ray tracing algorithm [21]. We can see from the figure that the error energy oscillates with constant amplitude. This is because the error energy is the quadratic function of the incident angle as shown in Fig. 5(c). To find the optimal incident angle is to search for the "bowl bottom" of the error energy curve. The error energy however cannot converge to the minimum value because the two ends of the dash line in Fig. 5(c) have the equal distances from the minimum value point. This leads to the oscillation of the error energy between the two ends. There are 5 × 49 × 2 = 490 rays, and it takes 6 h to get these rays on a personal computer. In fact, the time spent to trace each ray ranges from 0.1 s to 80 s. Experiment results indicate that the deeper the event is, the more time it takes to trace the rays. This is because the more complex the media structure is, the harder the convergence is. Hence this local optimal method is not suitable for complex subsurface geology.

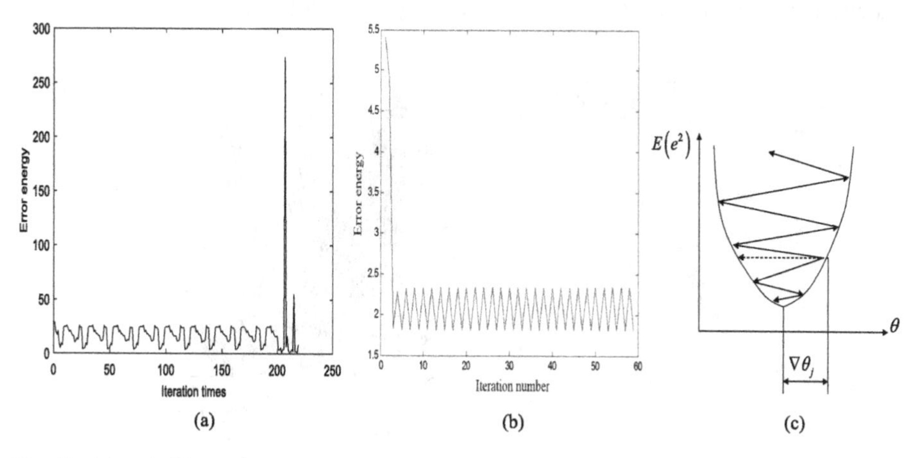

Fig. 5. (a) and (b) are the convergence curves of error energy using a local optimal algorithm called adaptive angle-step ray tracing method. (c) The diagram of the function of the error energy

Figure 6(a) and (b) are the rays obtained by shortest path method and the trial ray method. The shortest path method traverses the whole nodes and retraces the suitable ray path. The trial ray method adjust the initial emergency angle step by step. These two methods are easy to understand but time-consuming and low efficiency. Spend hours of these two methods are twice the DG-DECCM method.

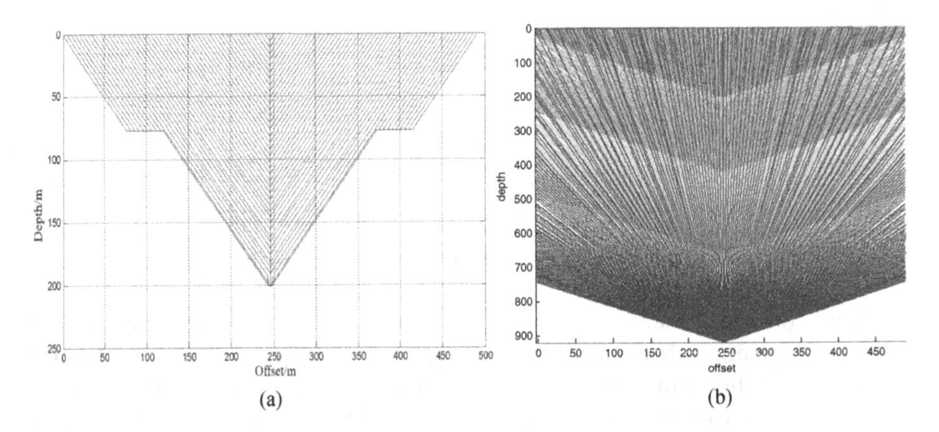

Fig. 6. The rays traced by (a) shortest path method and (b) trial ray method

3.2 The Pre-stack Common Shotpoint (CSP) Gather Model

We test the validity of the proposed method using a CSP model. The velocity model is the same as in Fig. 3(a). The observation system is shown in Fig. 1(a). The depths are 200 m, 400 m, 600 m, 800 m, and 1000 m. The source is located at the origin of the surface. The geophones are located from 20 m to 500 m with the interval of 10 m. Figure 7(a) is the traced rays of the 5 layers and Fig. 7(b) is the rays of the 4th layer. The conclusion is the same as the Sect. 3.1: the rays are straight lines in uniform velocity field and broken lines in horizontally layered velocity field.

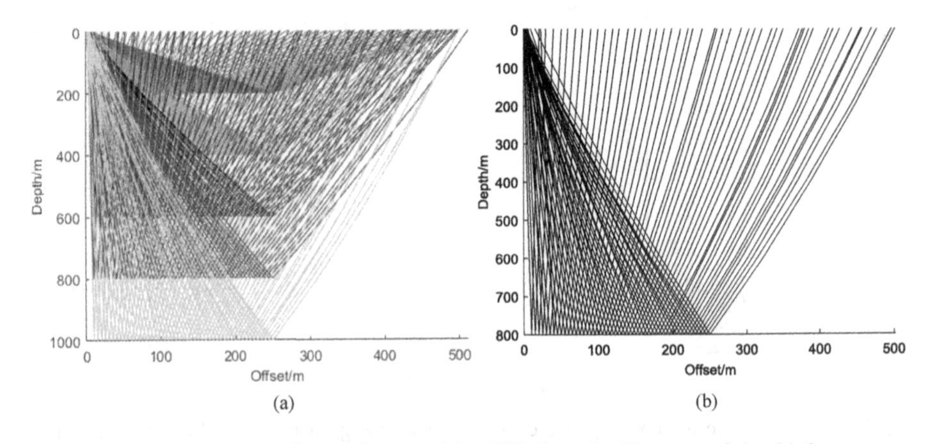

Fig. 7. (a) The rays of the 5 layers of the CSP data. (b) The rays of the 4th layer

3.3 The High Velocity Body Model

We also test the method by a high velocity body model. The velocity model is shown in Fig. 8(a) which is defined by equation v = 2 + 0.4sin(0.25πz)sin(0.5πx) km/s. The velocity varies continuously. The x-axis is from the origin to 2000 m and the depth is from the origin to 4000 m. The reflection point locates at the midpoint (1000, 4000) m. The sources is from the origin to 960 m with the interval of 20 m, and the receivers locate from 1060 m to 2000 m with the equal interval at the surface. Figure 8(b) is the traced rays where the rays bend to the outside of the abnormal high velocity areas.

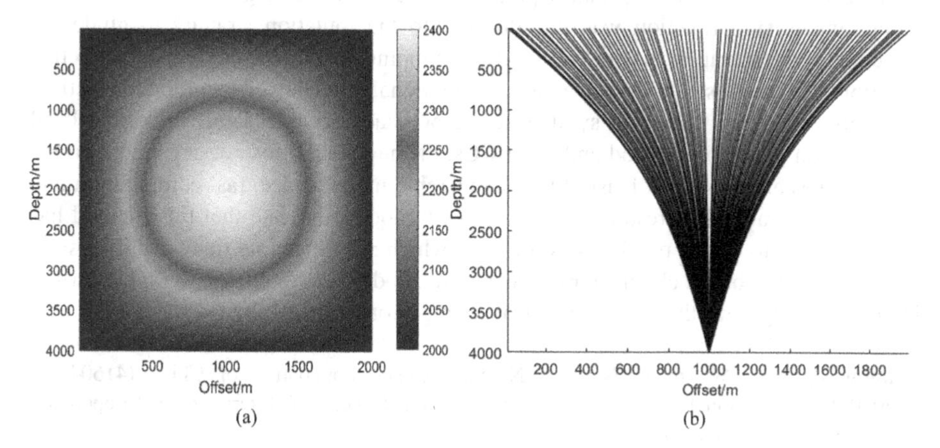

Fig. 8. (a) The high velocity body model. (b) The traced rays of the high velocity body

3.4 The Low Velocity Body Model

The last example is the low velocity body model. The velocity model is shown in Fig. 9(a) which is defined by the equation $v = 2 - 0.4\sin(0.25\pi z)\sin(0.5\pi x)$ km/s.

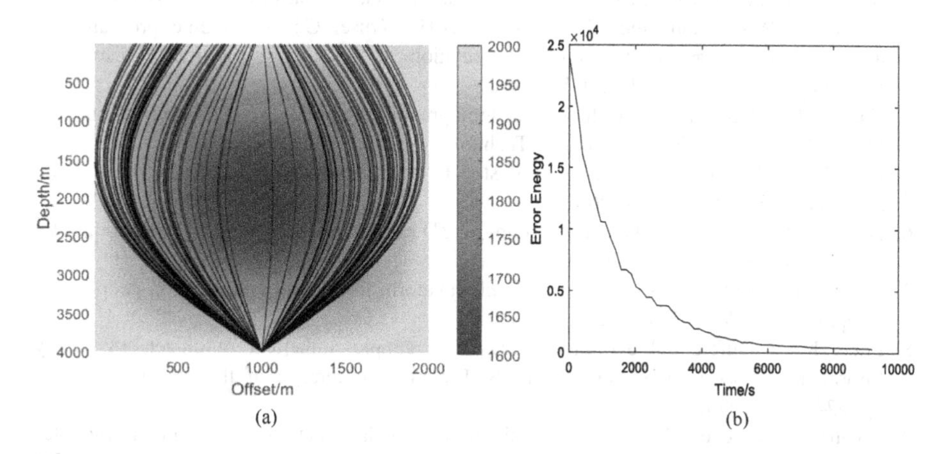

Fig. 9. (a) The velocity of the low velocity body model and the rays of the model. (b) The convergence curve of the error energy

The velocity varies continuously. The reflection point locates at the midpoint (1000, 4000) m. The locations of the sources and the receivers are the same as the Sect. 3.3. The black line is the traced rays where the rays bend to the inside of the abnormal low velocity areas. Figure 9(b) is the convergence curve which is decreased monotonically.

4 Conclusion

In this paper, we proposed a direction guided differential evolution algorithm that is suitable for the high-dimensional separable model space. Being based on cognitive computing, a sign function was introduced into the mutation strategy to guide the direction of the mutation, where two kinds of stopping criteria for flexible and effective iteration were proposed to improve the computational efficiency. The proposed method was applied for ray tracing to synthesize the pre-stack seismic data. Unlike the local optimization inversion method and other CCs, the new method is not dependent on the initial values and has good feasibility for separable model space, fast computation and good convergence. Test results on four velocity models indicate that this method has great potential to derive reliable seismic rays, which may speed up the wave inversion. Compared with other classical ray tracing methods, our approach will be further improved along with the development of high performance computing.

Acknowledgment. We thank National Natural Science Foundation of China (41604113, E070101) and National Nature Science Foundation Project of International Cooperation (41711530128) for their support.

References

1. Huang, J.L., Li, Y., Wu, R.: The wave-front ray tracing method for image reconstruction. Chin. J. Geophys. **35**, 223–232 (1992)
2. Moser, T.J.: Shortest path calculation of seismic ray. Geophysics **56**(1), 59–67 (1991)
3. Schneider, W.A., Ranzinger, K.A., Balch, A.H., Kruse, C.: A dynamic programming approach to first arrival traveltime computation in media with arbitrarily distributed velocities. Geophysics **57**(1), 39–50 (1992)
4. Zhao, L.F.: Study on crosswell seismic tomography combining velocity and attenuation. Ph.D. Thesis, Chengdu University of Technology (2002)
5. Gao, E.G., Xu, G.M.: A new kind of step by step iterative ray-tracing method. Chin. J. Geophys. **39**, 302–308 (1996)
6. Dwornik, M., Pieta, A.: Efficient algorithm for 3D ray tracing in 3D anisotropic medium. In: EAGE Conference, p. 138 (2009)
7. Virieux, J., Operto, S.: An overview of full-waveform inversion in exploration geophysics. Geophysics **74**, WCC1–WCC26 (2009)
8. Price, K.V.: Differential evolution: a fast and simple numerical optimizer. In: Fuzzy Information Processing Society. NAFIPS, Biennial Conference of the North American, pp. 524–527 (1996)
9. Corana, A., Marchesi, M., et al.: Minimizing multimodal functions of continuous variables with the "simulated annealing" algorithm Corrigenda for this article is available here. ACM Trans. Math. Soft. (TOMS) **13**, 262–280 (1987)

10. Press, F.: Earth models obtained by Monte Carlo inversion. J. Geophys. Res. **73**, 5223–5234 (1968)
11. Pan, Z., Wu, J., Gao, Z., Gao, J.: Adaptive differential evolution by adjusting subcomponent crossover rate for high-dimensional waveform inversion. IEEE Geosci. Remote Sens. Lett. **12**, 1327–1331 (2015)
12. Wang, C., Gao, J.: A new differential evolution algorithm with cooperative coevolutionary selection operator for waveform inversion. In: IEEE International Geoscience and Remote Sensing Symposium (IGARSS), pp. 688–690 (2010)
13. Wang, C., Gao, J.: High-dimensional waveform inversion with cooperative coevolutionary differential evolution algorithm. IEEE Geosci. Remote Sens. Lett. **9**, 297–301 (2012)
14. Chandra, R., Ong, Y.S., Goh, C.K.: Co-evolutionary multi-task learning with predictive recurrence for multi-step chaotic time series prediction. Neurocomputing **243**, 21–34 (2017)
15. Gao, Z., Pan, Z., Gao, J.: A new highly efficient differential evolution scheme and its application to waveform inversion. IEEE Geosci. Remote Sens. Soc. **11**, 1702–1706 (2014)
16. Gao, Z., Pan, Z., Gao, J.: Multimutation differential evolution algorithm and its application to seismic inversion. IEEE Trans. Geosci. Remote Sens. **54**(6), 3626 (2016)
17. Cui, X.F., Gao, J.H., Zhang, B., Wang, Z.: Poststack impedance inversion using improved particle swarm optimization. SEG Technical Program Expanded Abstracts, pp. 3809–3813 (2016)
18. Mahdavi, S., Shiri, M.E., Rahnamayan, S.: Metaheuristics in large-scale global continues optimization: a survey. Inf. Sci. **295**, 407–428 (2015)
19. Govindan, R., Kumar, R., Basu, S., Sarkar, A.: Altimeter-derived ocean wave period using genetic algorithm. IEEE Geosci. Remote Sens. Lett. **8**, 354–358 (2011)
20. Gomes, J., Mariano, P., Lyhne, A.: Novelty-driven cooperative coevolution. Evol. Comput. **25**, 275–307 (2017)
21. Zhao, J., Gao, J.H., Wang, D.X., Zhang M.L.: Estimation of quality factor Q from pre-stack CMP records using EPIFVO analysis. In: SEG and 81st Annual Meeting, pp. 1835–1839 (2011)

P300 Brain Waves Instigated Semi Supervised Video Surveillance for Inclusive Security Systems

Anurag Singh and Jeevanandam Jotheeswaran(✉)

Galgotias University, Greater Noida, Uttar Pradesh, India
Anurag.singh485@gmail.com, jeevanandamj@gmail.com

Abstract. Soldier patrolling is a risky task at the cross borders which leads to loss of life. To overcome such risks, many researchers working on reduction of human effort using Cognitive Science through Brain Computer Interface (BCI) application. Human brain is a complex organ of body and researchers aim to build a direct communication of human brain with computer system including the Artificial Intelligence (AI) and Computational Intelligence (CI). In order to achieve such objectives, a proper brain signal capturing mechanism to be used. The appropriate signals are captured using Electroencephalogram (EEG) cap which is used to record electrical activity of brain and classified to filter P300 brain wave which is an Event Related Potential (ERP) to detect abnormal events like crawling under the Line of Control (LoC) or any illegal cross border movements of goods, drugs supply, arms supply and cargos. Brain signal is contaminated with artifacts and noises. Further work is carried on improving the Signal to Noise Ratio (SNR) quality by using appropriate filtration algorithm. The proposed filter is to use sliding Hierarchal Discriminant Classification Algorithm (sHDCA) for P300 signal to detect and classify between the target and non target component based on a multi Rapid Serial Visual Presentation (RSVP) using real time video frames from the region. As a result, it reduces the false alarm and creating the threat signature library from the filtered and classified brain signals for Comprehensive Integrated Border Management System (CIBMS).

Keywords: Brain Computer Interface (BCI)
Fast Independent Component Analysis (Fast ICA)
Comprehensive Integrated Border Management System (CIBMS)
Event Related Potentials (ERP) · Human Computer Interaction (HCI)

1 Introduction

Terrorism or any type of abnormal activity across the borders of any country is the major threat that leads to many losses of lives of soldiers and innocent people. As per [1] in 2016, a total number of 11,072 terrorist attacks occurred worldwide which resulting to 25,621 total death and more than 33,800 people got injured. India is one among the countries which is affected by terrorist activities across its border. As India shares its boundaries about 15,106.7 km (7516 km costal area, 5422 km coastline main land, 2094 km bordering islands) with its neighboring countries like Bangladesh,

J. Ren et al. (Eds.): BICS 2018, LNAI 10989, pp. 184–194, 2018.
https://doi.org/10.1007/978-3-030-00563-4_18

Nepal, China, Myanmar, Bhutan and Pakistan, which is very complex and critical to operate in various climate conditions because of that various soldiers martyr and civilians gets killed in terrorist attacks (Figs. 1 and 2).

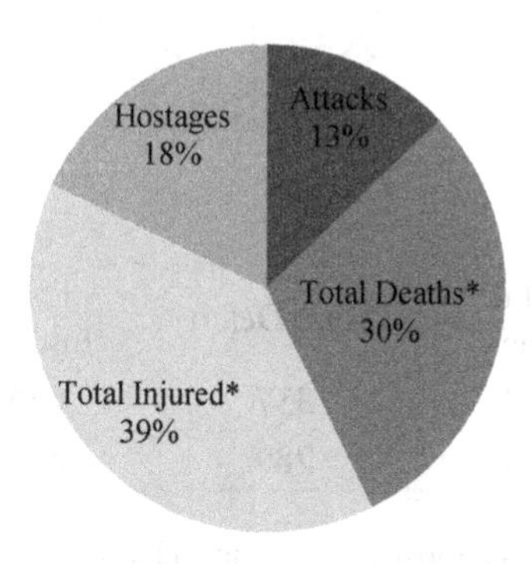

Fig. 1. Bureau of counterterrorism and countering

To protect people, government of India started creating 14000 bunkers and check points at border which will be costing more than Rs. 415 crore but again bunkers to be managed by soldiers and still illegal border surpassing cross border infiltration and terrorist attacks are not stopped due to failure in man operated systems and border management. Governments of various countries started using advance systems and sensors for border surveillance. Indian borders are equipped with various advance surveillance systems for their border areas such as Unmanned Ariel Vehicles (UAVs) commonly known as drones, target identifying binoculars, handheld thermal imagers, Night Vision Devices (NVDs), unattended ground sensors, Satellite Based Augmentation Systems (SBAS) etc.

To avoid such losses of lives and increase in accuracy to identify the potential threats, researchers and engineers developed surveillance systems and incorporating these systems and technologies with Brain Computer Interface (BCI).

BCI is an emerging area of research which makes a human brain to interact with computer systems. It is an unconventional human machine interaction expertise that uses observers brain waves captured by electroencephalogram (EEG) and examines the meanings to interact with the peripheral situation directly. There are various examples of BCI based applications such as in medical area to identify the brain disorder, a wheel chair which was recent developed by researchers that can make a disabled person to operate with the help of brain waves using BCI systems, cyborg is a biomechatronic body parts which works with human action performed using brain waves.

Brain is a tiny organ which typically consumes 20% of power from human body for controlling all body functions, emotions, behaviors that includes receiving and interpreting information from outside world. Different sensory organs are used for receiving information specifically smell, touch, taste and hearing that works according to the arranged patterns of nerve cells. Human brain generates electrical signal which is

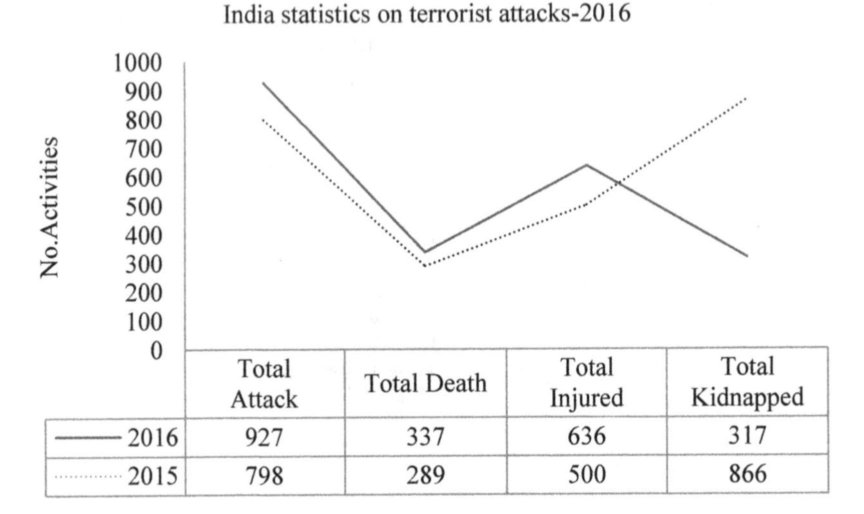

	Total Attack	Total Death	Total Injured	Total Kidnapped
2016	927	337	636	317
2015	798	289	500	866

Fig. 2. Terrorist activities in India in 2015, 2016

obtained from neuron cells particularly are of three types such as sensory neurons, motor neurons and interneuron which transfers these signals at the rate of 250 mph. It is made up of three major parts commonly known as forebrain, midbrain and hindbrain. Forebrain covers the largest part of the brain which performs sensory information, non rational functions for example temperature and reproduction, eating, sleeping, controlling and displaying of signals. Midbrain performs the motor movement contains blinking of eyes, auditory function and visual processing. Hindbrain works outside conscious control, to illustrate flow of blood circulation and breathing.

EEG signals are of five types and all the brain waves works on various brain conditions these waves are named as Delta, Theta, Alpha, Beta and Gamma and captured as discussed in Fig. 3. These signal frequency range from 0.5 Hz to 31 Hz and more.

Normally for cognitive task and alert related activity beta waves are more suitable and efficient whose frequency varies from 12 Hz to 30 Hz. Human brain signals are captured with the help of 10-10 electrode silver/silver-chloride or gold electrodes (T7-Cz-T8-P7-**P3**-PZ-P4-P8-O1-O2). It is internationally accepted that 64 scalp electrodes arranged at distance to place the electrode is 10-20 system. The processing of signals can be done with the help of MATLAB tool.

2 Related Work

BCI is an advanced Human Machine Interaction (HMI) that is extracted by using brain monitoring techniques like EEG, MEG, EcoG and implementing them with various real time applications. Earlier doctors used EEG devices in the field of neuroscience for identifying brain disorder functionalities. Researchers in last two decade started using the brain signal to communicate with computer system for enhancement of BCI.

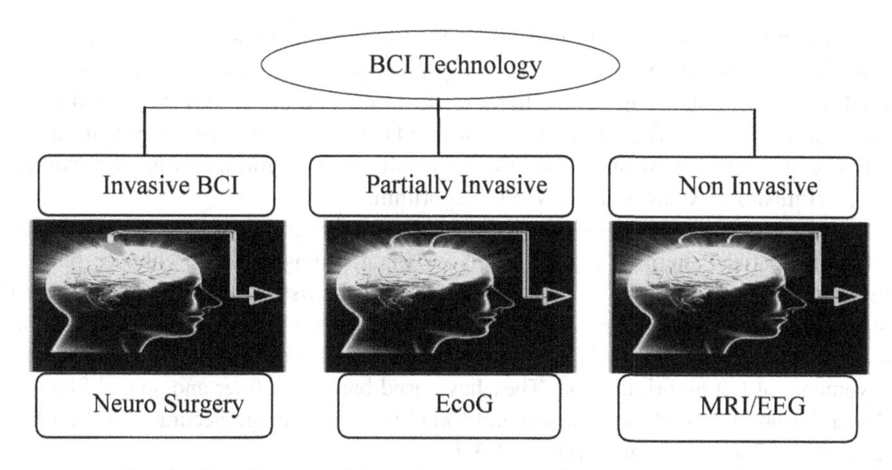

Fig. 3. Classification of Brain Computer Interface (BCI) Technology.

BCI2000 is one of the general purpose software platforms for BCI research. Various researchers using BCI2000 system for data acquisition, stimulus presentations and brain monitoring applications.

Tamara et al. [2] discussed oddball paradigm, which uses repetitive sequence of stimuli and recognition of memory in which low probability target items are mixed with high probability non target items. In the oddball paradigm the target detection task is done by using P300 signals. In the research the users responds to the target stimuli which was occurring on the computer screen in different series and sequences that to be identified. These target detection evokes on the cortical region of the brain. In the research they have found a signal issue in identifying the objects which was later rectified after incorporating effects at the time of hemodynamic brain activity using EEG headset. A set of random objects were presented in front of users and they have to click the left right buttons for identifications of the object such as odd one out.

Farwell et al. [3] in their research proposed the use of P300 signal which is more efficient in beta waves for Spell check and they have used Stepwise Linear Discriminant Analysis (SWLDA) one of the machine learning classification algorithm to detect P300 components. In their research P300 Speller presents 6 rows and 6 columns containing the set of the characters including an item attended by the observer described as the rare set and the others described as the frequent set. The SWLDA algorithm utilized in the research for linear model that relates an arrangement of information features (i.e. filtered brain responses) to output labels (i.e. to identify the P300 signals belongs to brain response or not) utilizing number of multiple regressions and iterative statistical procedures. This system chooses only brain signal features which includes P300 component in brain responses. Alvarado-González et al. [4] used twenty one observers which used P300 brain waves and applied SWLDA algorithm for shape feature vector that results to 93%. P300 signals were used for detection and pattern recognition techniques on its shape. They perform a calibration algorithm to analyze the performance of P300 detection using shape feature vector and classifying the P300 waves using SWLDA and SVM. Accuracy of both the algorithm was calculated by confusion matrix and found SWLDA accuracy was poor compared to SVM. Barachant et al. [5] proposed a classification methods for event related potentials based on an Information geometry framework. In their research they have used P300 based game invader. They have tested with xDawn algorithm commonly used for feature extraction, MDM and SWLDA. As result MDM algorithm suits and worked fine as compare to xDawn and SWLDA algorithm.

Blankertz et al. [6] proposed to remove noises and blurs of EEG recordings using Common Spatial Pattern (CSP) algorithm for signal strength and to enhance blurred EEG signals from brain signal using second order statistics of the signal between electrodes and the solution is obtained by solving a generalized Eigen value problem. In the research method they have focused on binary classification between imagined movements of left and right hand. They have used band pass filter and spatial filter on 14 healthy observers for comparison and found that the average accuracy of the EEG signal with 93.4% with the duration of 3.5 to 2.7 s.

In the research discussed by Marathe et al. [7] a set of five consecutive video frames were showed to participants with the duration of 100 ms and at a frequency of 2 Hz, each video clip was presented with duration of 500 ms. They have used Sliding Hierarchal Discriminant Classification Algorithm (sHDCA) which decreased the classification error by 50% when compared to standard HDCA. In the research they have improved the SNR and enable more accurate single trail analysis which includes both spatial and temporal features of the brain wave to improve the classification. In the proposed system by them they have removed artifacts of EOG and EMG using ICA feature extraction algorithm contaminated in brain signals and later it undergoes sHDCA algorithm for classification and performs 10 fold cross validation to determine the accuracy. As a result the classification error decreased to 75%.

Lin et al. [8] proposed multi rapid serial visual presentation frame work based on EEG-based target detection. In their research they have used two different P300 detection algorithms utilized in triple RSVP framework which flashes three images consecutively with delay of 750 ms for improving target detection accuracy. The target image first shown at the left side of the screen at 0 ms, then it is displayed with the delay of 750 ms on the right side and third image at the bottom with the delay of 1500 ms with the frequency of 4 Hz. The observers have to click left and right button to identify the potential threat from the sequence of images.

Waytowich et al. [9] proposed an unsupervised transfer method known as Spectral Transfer using Information Geometry (STIG). In the research STIG validates in both off line and online real time analyses on RSVP paradigm based on user independent BCI. In the research they have proposed zero calibration data which do not require any dataset for classification, it perform classification on real time using Riemannian Mean classifiers to make predictions observers in combination with spectral meta learning. Wavelet transformation mathematical tool widely used for both feature extraction, classification and preprocessing of EEG signals and discussed about Wavelet transformation is of two types:

- Continuous Wavelet Transformation (CWT)
- Discrete Wavelet Transformation (DWT).

Das et al. [10] discussed about cognitive load which was experienced during critical task and emotional states based on stimulus. The results displayed unsupervised learning method is better than supervised method. For accuracy measurement they have proposed Component based fuzzy c-Mean than that of traditional Fuzzy c-Means (FCM). Amin et al. [11] discussed about various feature extraction techniques such as ICA, wavelet transformation and SVM, KNN for pattern recognition from the recorded EEG brain waves containing cognitive task. In the research they have done comparison between various classifier algorithms and found SVM results to 98.57%, and KNN with 93.3%. They proposed to use feature extraction using the combination of DWT with Fischer Component Analysis (FCA) and Principal Component Analysis (PCA) along with classification algorithm to enhance the result of pattern recognition.

In the related work researchers have discussed about oddball paradigm based on BCI for identifying a target and non target objects from the sequence of images. Types of artifacts, noises, loss of signal strengths and to overcome these problems uses filtration techniques commonly low pass filters, band pass filter, CSP for removal of noise and enhancing the strength of the blur signals are discussed. For extracting features from the brain waves ICA, FastICA, MDM, xDawn, Wavelet transformation etc techniques with their accuracy discussed. For classification, supervised algorithms commonly SVM, SWLDA, sHDCA, KNN based on multiple RSVP paradigm analyzed and compared with accuracy and response time. Some of the researchers discussed about unsupervised algorithms to identify the abnormal activity from the set of videos.

3 Proposed P300 Signal Based BCI System

The system consist of sequence of multi RSVP of video frames captured by operators brain waves assembled with EEG headset storing the raw brain signals after visualizing any event related potential also known as Visual Evoked Potential (VEP) by visual stimulus across border areas. The brain waves captured in the form of beta signals undergoes for signal preprocessing to be fed into low pass filter for filtration of signal with a frequency lower than certain cutoff and thin with higher frequency, Notch filter used for suppressing or cancelling a particular range of frequencies to avoid unwanted interference within a circuit configuration and post filter. After amplification of brain signals, it undergoes for signal acquisition phase for analog to digitization. Under feature extraction phase signals fed into filtration algorithm proposing to use Independent Component Analysis (ICA) algorithm for removing noise from the signals and Fast Independent Component Analysis (FastICA) that is used for extracting the feature vector of P300 EEG signal which later fed into classification algorithm sHDCA for process classification. sHDCA is a supervised learning method which leads to classification, regression and outliers detection. After classification the signal undergoes BCI system and feedback signal acknowledgment by the soldier (Fig. 4).

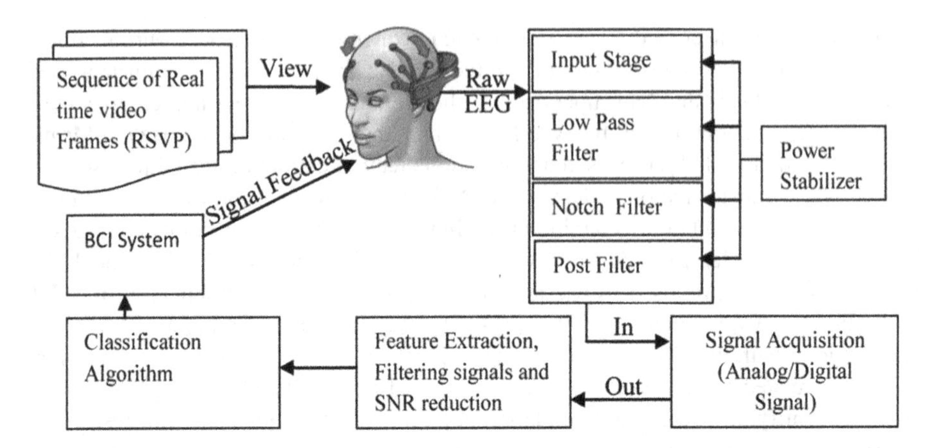

Fig. 4. EEG based BCI for Comprehensive Integrated Border Management System

3.1 Procedure for Visual Stimulation

The system proposed in this research on visualization of all type abnormal activity across border that includes throwing grenade, firing with guns, crawling and jumping over the LoC etc. We will be concatenating the abnormal activity signal generated while capturing the Visual Evoked Potential (VEP) from the border areas with soldiers brain wave that triggers when any event related potential occurs.

3.2 Classification Algorithm/Translational Algorithm

After filtration of EEG signal using ICA algorithm, signals undergoes translation for classification between target and non target and set the output signals that controls the output devices. Translation algorithm used for classification and regression approach. For extracted features single trial P300 signal requires accurate classification. Many researchers have attempted to enhance classification algorithm, by utilizing linear and non liner methods for classification. For classification supervised learning algorithm commonly sHDCA, SVM were used as a classifier.

3.2.1 Principal of sHDCA

sHDCA is a classifier algorithm to extract more information from sequence of events and classifying between target and non target object. Fischer linear Discriminant (FLD) or Logistic Regression (LR) works as a initial classifier in sHDCA. sHDCA classifier using epoch data from 100 ms to 1600 ms post stimulus matching the data using sHDCA. HDCA algorithm performs on two layers. First, to calculate the average data and second by dividing the original EEG data by the time window size. To calculate difference between target and non target classes is:

$$a_k = \left(\frac{1}{N}\right) \sum_n \sum_i w_{ki} bi[(k-1)N + n] \quad (1)$$

Where $bi[(k-1)N+n]$ denotes kth separate time window value for single trial data.

n = EEG activity from data sample
i = Electrode
w = Set of spatial weight
w_{ki} = Weight vector with i electrode and k window

$$N = T \times f_s \quad (2)$$

f_s = Time window
T = Temporal resolution of time window

$$a_{is} = \sum_k d_k a_k \quad (3)$$

a_k = Single after dimension reduction using kth separate window
d_k = Temporal coefficient
a_{is} = Final intersect score

$$z_{min} = (1 - z_k)^N \quad (4)$$

z_{min} = Target missed
z_k = Target
N = No. of ignored video images

$$Accuracy = \left(\frac{|RT - pRT|}{RT} * 100\right) \quad (5)$$

RT = Actuall time
pRT = Predicted reaction time

Algorithm 1: EEG Classification
Input: Source real time EEG signals from operator brain wave
Output: Target and Non target classification

Start
n= EEG signals;
For i = 1 to 20
Compute time window to obtain N;
N= No. of ignored video images;
End for
Compute N to obtain a_k;
While(n>0)
Compute to obtain $a_k = \sum_i w_{ki} bi[(k-1)N + n]$;
Compute to obtain $a_{is} = \sum_k d_k a_k$;
Return a_{is}
Compute to obtain $z_{min} = (1 - z_k)^N$;
Return z_{min}

4 Result and Discussions

The dataset taken from multiple RSVP was presented in front of 8 observers wearing EEG headset and each of the observers asked to press the button when they identify any potential threat in a sequence of images. To classify event related potential, P300 brain waves is generated falls under beta waves and captured using EEG headset asked to wear on each observers head. The signals generated at the time of component analysis undergoes filtration process using low pass filters for thinning process of signals and later the signals under goes to notch filter to remove noise more than 50 Hz. ICA algorithm used for removing artifacts mostly blinking of eyes and eye movements. After the SNR reduction the waves undergoes feature extraction using Fast ICA algorithm to remove blurness from the signals and making it ready for classification process. The removal of artifacts and accuracy of signals reached to 97% after the preprocessing. Each observers brain waves after feature extraction under goes classification of potential threat displayed in Fig. 5 demonstrate the comparison of same data set applied to two different classification algorithms and result was much higher in sHDCA compared to SWLDA algorithm in multiple RSVP representation. In Fig. 5 observers 4 has the same result but for other observers the accuracy was high than that of SWLDA.

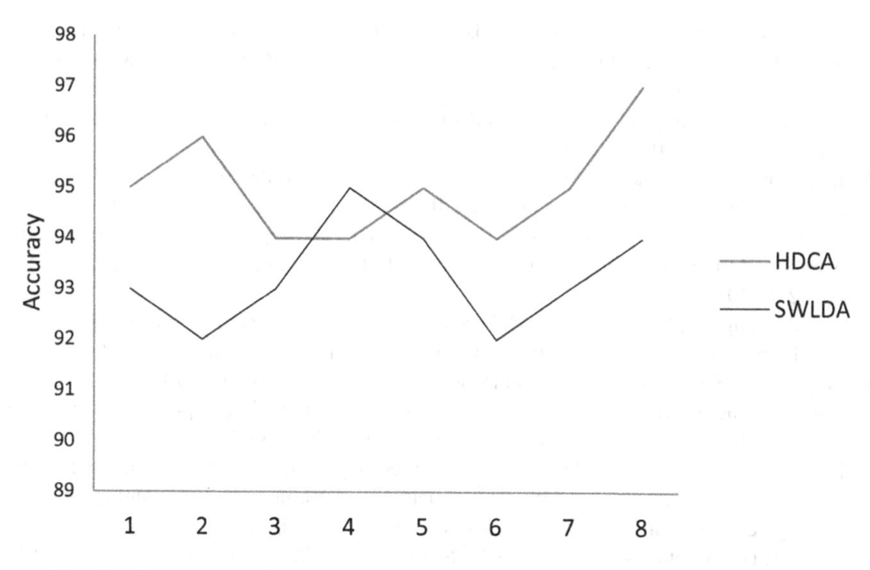

Fig. 5. Graph comparison between HDCA and SWLDA classification algorithm

5 Conclusion and Future Work

According to the proposed system the sequence of video frames undergoes multiple RSVP paradigms for observers testing and various filtration and classification algorithm, we found that the system is compatible with the EEG signal filtration and noise removing process. After filtration EEG signal fed into feature extraction algorithm where FastICA performed independent component analysis of signal and removing blurriness from the EEG signals and making it better for classification between target and non target objects. The sHDCA algorithm proposed for the classification of target from the EEG signal successfully performed classification of target with higher accuracy as compared to SWLDA. Our future work is to capture the brain signals at the time of playing a combat game or mission game and generating the data set for classification and feature extraction from the captured EEG signals.

References

1. www.state.gov: National Consortium for the Study of Terrorism and Responses to Terrorism: Annex of Statistical Information (2016). https://www.state.gov/j/ct/rls/crt/2016/272241.htm. Accessed 25 Jan 2018
2. Tamara, B., Howard, J.: Privacy by design in brain-computer interfaces. University of Washington, UWEE, Technical report number UWEETR-2013-0001 (2013)
3. Farwell, L.A., Donchin, E.: Talking off the top of your head: toward a mental prosthesis utilizing event-related brain potentials. Electroencephalogr. Clin. Neurophysiol. **70**(6), 510–523 (1988)

4. Alvarado-González, M., Garduño, E., Bribiesca, E., Yáñez-Suárez, O., Medina-Bañuelos, V.: P300 detection based on EEG shape features. Comput. Math. Methods Med. **2016**, 14 (2016). Article ID 2029791
5. Barachant, A., Congedo M.: A Plug&Play P300 BCI using information geometry. White paper. arXiv:1409.0107 (2014)
6. Blankertz, B., Tomioka, R., Lemm, S., Kawanabe, M., Muller, K.R.: Optimizing spatial filters for robust EEG single-trial analysis. IEEE Signal Process. Mag. **25**(1), 41–56 (2008)
7. Marathe, A.R., Ries, A.J., McDowell, K.: Sliding HDCA: single-trial EEG classification to overcome and quantify temporal variability. IEEE Trans. Neural Syst. Rehabil. Eng. **22**(2), 201–211 (2014)
8. Lin, Z., Zeng, Y., Gao, H., et al.: Multirapid serial visual presentation framework for EEG-based target detection. BioMed Res. Int. **2017**, 12 (2017). Article ID 2049094
9. Waytowich, N.R., Lawhern, V.J., Bohannon, A.W., Ball, K.R., Lance, B.J.: Spectral transfer learning using information geometry for a user-independent brain-computer interface. Front. Neurosci. **10**, 430 (2016). https://doi.org/10.3389/fnins.2016.00430
10. Das, D., Chatterjee, D., Sinha, A.: Unsupervised approach for measurement of cognitive load using EEG signals. In: 13th IEEE International Conference on BioInformatics and BioEngineering, Chania, pp. 1–6. https://doi.org/10.1109/bibe.2013.6701686 (2013)
11. Amin, H.U., Mumtaz, W., Subhani, A.R., Saad, M.N.M., Malik, A.S.: Classification of EEG signals based on pattern recognition approach. Front. Comput. Neurosci. **11**, 103 (2017). https://doi.org/10.3389/fncom.2017.00103

Motor Imagery EEG Recognition Based on FBCSP and PCA

Banghua Yang[1], Jianzhen Tang[1(✉)], Cuntai Guan[2], and Bo Li[2]

[1] Department of Automation, School of Mechanical Engineering and Automation, Shanghai University, No. 149, Yanchang Road, Shanghai 200072, China
{yangbanghua, tjz31521}@shu.edu.cn
[2] School of Computer Science and Engineering, Nanyang Technological University, 50 Nanyang Avenue, Jurong West 639798, Singapore

Abstract. In motor imagery-based Brain Computer interfaces (BCIs), the classification accuracy of using the Common Spatial Pattern (CSP) algorithm to deal with the electroencephalogram (EEG) is closely related to the frequency range selected. Due to individual differences, the frequency range selected that reaches the best performance is different, which limits the generality and the actual use of the algorithm. To solve this problem, this paper proposes a motor imagery recognition method based on Filter Bank Common Spatial Pattern (FBCSP) and Principal Components Analysis (PCA), which is called FBCSP +PCA. The feasibility of the FBCSP+CSP is preliminary verified using the 2008 BCI competition data and further verified using data collected by our laboratory with wireless dry electrode device. The average classification accuracy of the data collected by our laboratory reaches 75.7% in the absence of individual band selection. That is also to say that the proposed method has good generality and and practical value because it can obtain high performance without the need of giving each individual a specific optimum frequency band.

Keywords: Motor imagery · FBCSP · PCA · Dry electrode

1 Introduction

Currently, a Brain-Computer Interfaces (BCI) system based on motor imagery is slowly approaching public view as a newly emerging rehabilitation method in the field of clinical rehabilitation. It achieves the human-computer interaction between the human brain and the computer by real-time measurement and analysis of the electroencephalogram (EEG) generated when motor imaging [1].

Effective and rapid feature extraction and classification methods are important in the practical application of BCI systems. The feature extraction method of Common Spatial Patterns (CSP) has good performance and is the most widely method used in the BCI system based on motor imagery [2]. However, the CSP method itself lacks frequency domain information, and the classification accuracy is closely related to the frequency range selection of EEG signals [3]. In actual use, because of the individual

J. Ren et al. (Eds.): BICS 2018, LNAI 10989, pp. 195–205, 2018.
https://doi.org/10.1007/978-3-030-00563-4_19

differences of EEG signals, it is necessary to manually adjust a specific frequency range for each individual to obtain a higher correct rate, which limits its generality and practical application.

In order to solve the problem of manually selecting the subject-specific frequency range for the CSP algorithm, several methods have been proposed, including the Common Spatio-Spectral Pattern (CSSP) [4], the Common Sparse Spetral Spatial Pattern (CSSSP) [5], the Sub-band Common Spatial Pattern (SBCSP) and Filter Bank Common Spatial Pattern (FBCSP) [3, 6]. In the method of CSSP and CSSSP, due to the inherent nature of the optimization problem, the solution of filter coefficients is also strongly dependent on the choice of initial parameters. When using SBCSP, a comparative study of using different sub band score fusion techniques and classification algorithms are not available [6]. FBCSP algorithm comprises four stages: frequency filtering, spatial filtering, feature selection and classification. In the first stage, the EEG measurements are band-pass filtered into multiple frequency bands. In the second stage, CSP features are extracted from each of these bands. In the third stage, the Mutual Information (MI)-based feature selection algorithm is used to automatically select discriminative pairs of frequency bands and corresponding CSP features. In the fourth stage, a classification algorithm is used to classify the CSP features. And the FBCSP has been shown to yield superior classification accuracy compared against SBCSP on a publicly available dataset [3].

In this paper, a motor imagery recognition method based on FBCSP and Principal Components Analysis (PCA), which is called FBCSP+PCA, is proposed. The method uses a set of band-pass filters to decompose the EEG signal from 4–40 Hz into a plurality of frequency bands with a specific bandwidth, which enriches the frequency domain information. Meantime, intercepting a specific time period of EEG during imaging task through a time window eliminates the brain waves caused by the state conversion of thinking and visual evoked [7]. The CSP algorithm is used to extract the features of EEG from multiple frequency bands. The extracted multidimensional features are filtered by PCA for feature dimension reduction, which can solve the problem manually selecting a specific frequency caused by individual differences. Finally, the feature after dimension reduction are classified by Support Vector Machine (SVM) and K-NearestNeighbor (KNN). The method has achieved good experimental results, which lays the foundation for the practical application of the algorithm in BCIs.

2 Method

2.1 Introduction of CSP

The CSP technique has become a popular feature extraction approach in EEG-based BCI applications and it essentially finds spatial filters that maximize the variance for one class and simultaneously minimize the variance for the other class [8]. This method decomposes the raw EEG signals into spatial patterns, which are extracted from two classes of single trial EEG. Suppose the EEG signals of each trial are E_{D*N}, where D is the number of channels and N is the number of samples. The detailed computing process of the CSP can be seen in [9]. After the feature extraction by using CSP, a feature vector $F = \{f_1, f_2, \cdots, f_{2m}\}$, where m is the number of feature pairs chosen, is obtained and used as an input for the feature dimension reduction.

2.2 Filter Bank Common Spatial Pattern

In this paper, the FBCSP algorithm comprises four stages: frequency filtering, spatial filtering, feature reduction and classification. In the first stage, the EEG signal is band-pass filtered into multiple frequency bands. In the second stage, CSP features are extracted from each of these bands. In the third stage, the PCA-based feature reduction algorithm is used to automatically get the most effective CSP features. In the fourth stage, the SVM algorithm and KNN algorithm are used to classify the CSP features. The specific description is as follows: (1) two groups of IIR (Infinite Impulse Response) band-pass filter are respectively used to divide EEG signals from 4–40 Hz with bandwidth 4 Hz and 2 Hz, which leads to a group of 9 bands signal and a group of 18 bands signal. According to the bandwidth selection in the reference [3] and that the smaller the bandwidth is, the more sub-bands are decomposed, the more frequency information is provided in principle. So the bandwidth of 4 Hz and 2 Hz are selected to decompose EEG. (2) The each band signal of two groups is respectively as input of the CSP filter to extract 2-dimensional features. The group of signals with a bandwidth of 4 Hz obtains a feature vector $F_1 = \{f_1, f_2, \cdots, f_{18}\}$ and the other group of signals with a bandwidth of 2 Hz obtains a feature vector $F_2 = \{f_1', f_2', \cdots, f_{36}'\}$. (3) The PCA algorithm is used for the feature reduction from two groups of CSP features. (4) The two groups of features after dimensionality reduction are used as input of SVM and KNN algorithm to obtain classification results. The processing of EEG signal is shown in Fig. 1.

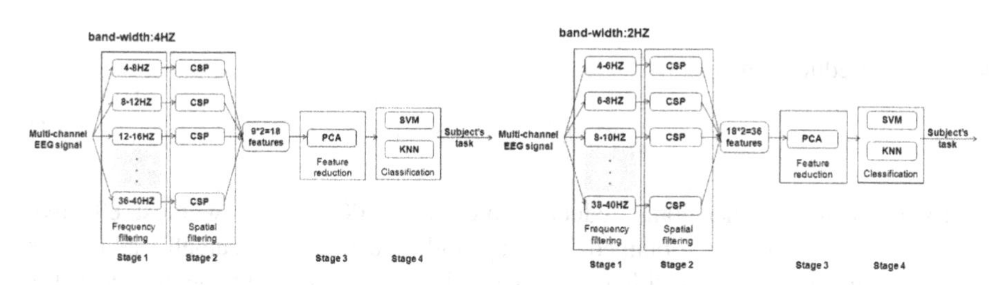

(a)Single-band bandwidth 4HZ decomposition signal (b)Single-band bandwidth 2HZ decomposition signal

Fig. 1. The processing of EEG signal

2.3 PCA Algorithm

PCA is a multivariate statistical method that examines the correlations among multiple variables, which derives a small number of principal components that retain the information of the original variables as much as possible from the original variables. Using PCA to extract features of multidimensional features, we can extract the most relevant signal features of EEG from motor imagery, and remove the noise signals and irrelevant components to improve classification accuracy and speed.

Suppose there is an extracted multidimensional feature matrix f_{n*M} where we can consider n is the total task number of left-handed imaging tasks and right-handed imaging tasks, and M is the dimension of the extracted features. The detailed steps of PCA can be described as follows:

- Step 1: Center features

$$A_{n*M} = f_{n*M} - \bar{f} \tag{1}$$

  where $\bar{f}$ is the matrix formed by the average of each dimension in f_{n*M}.
- Step 2: Calculate the covariance matrix of the centralized matrix

$$B_{M*M} = \frac{A^T A}{n} \tag{2}$$

- Step 3: Calculate the eigenvector matrix U and the eigenvalue matrix $L(l_1, l_2, \cdots l_M)$ of the covariance matrix B, where $l_1, l_2 \cdots l_M$ is the eigenvalue of the B matrix and is expressed as descending order.
- Step 4: Select the eigenvectors corresponding to the first k largest eigenvalues according to the cumulative contribution rate G to form a transformation matrix T_{M*k}.

$$G = \frac{\sum_{i=1}^{k} l_i}{\sum_{i=1}^{M} l_i} \tag{3}$$

- Step 5: Reduce dimension

$$newf_{n*k} = f_{n*M} * T_{M*k} \tag{4}$$

By the feature dimensional reduction process of PCA, the few most effective features are automatically obtained, which avoids the need to manually adjust the optimal frequency range for different individuals and different time segments of the same individual. It improves the generality and practicability of the CSP algorithm.

3 Datasets

3.1 Dataset I

The first dataset used in this study is from "Data sets 1" of BCI Competition 4, which is launched on July 3rd 2008. The EEG data from four subjects (c, d, e, g) of the dataset are selected in this study, because the EEG data from these four subjects include two classes of motor imagery tasks, left hand and right hand. The main purpose of this paper is to distinguish between motor imagery tasks. These EEG signals were recorded from 59 channels. The signals were band-pass filtered between 0.05 and 200 Hz and then sampled at 1000 Hz. More details were described in [10].

3.2 Dataset II

The second dataset was from the authors' laboratory experiments. The experiment used g.Nautilus-8 wireless dry electrode of g.tec to collect EEG data. Sampling frequency is 250 Hz, cycle of each trial is 8 s. Each experimental cycle is divided into the following three links, as shown in Fig. 2:

- Link 1: 0–2 s black screen, subjects are in a relaxed state.
- Link 2: Cross appears on 2–4 s screen "+", subject is ready.
- Link 3: 4–8 s left or right arrow appears on the screen, the subjects carry on left or right hand motor imagery task according to the arrow instructions.

In the experiment, EEG data of eight subjects were collected. The EEG data of each subject contains four groups of left and right hand motor imagery EEG data. Each group of experimental data contains 40 times left-hand motor imagery tasks and 40 times right-hand motor imagery tasks. The electrodes distribution of EEG signals is shown in Fig. 3.

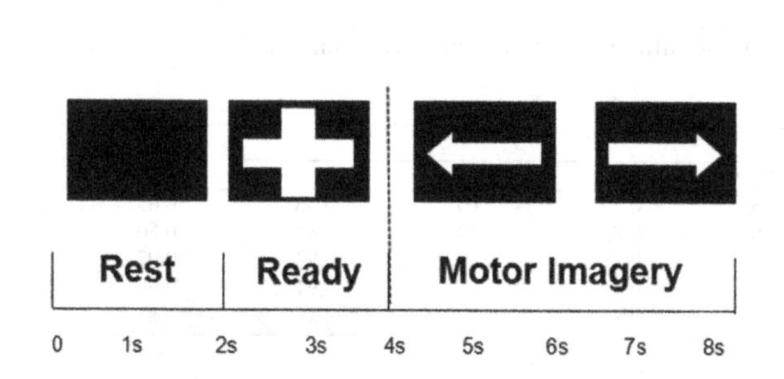

Fig. 2. Experimental flow chart

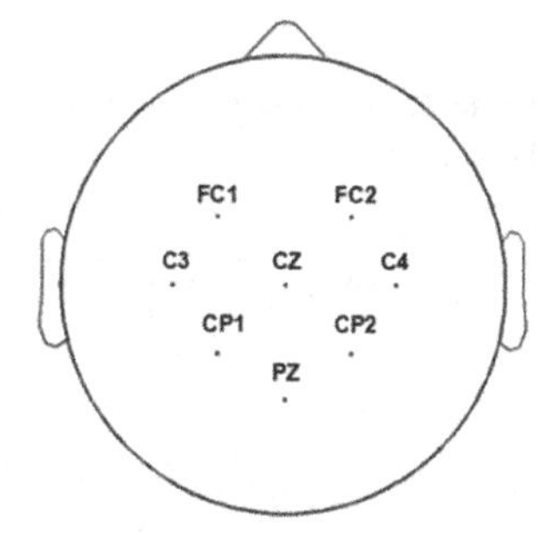

Fig. 3. The electrodes distribu tion

4 Results

4.1 Experimental Results Based on the First Dataset from BCI Competition 4

This paper first verifies the EEG data of four subjects (c, d, e, g) from Data sets 1 provided by the 4th BCI competition in 2008. In the competition data, each participant's data contains 100 left-handed imaging tasks and 100 right-handed imaging tasks, with a sampling frequency of 1000 Hz. Fifty left-handed and fifty-right-handed data were extracted from each set of data for training and the rest were used for testing. The feature extraction method is FBCSP, then PCA is used for feature dimension reduction, the SVM and KNN methods are used to classify the left hand and right hand motor imagery. The detailed theory and Implementation of SVM and KNN can be seen in [11–13]. When the two feature vectors F_1 and F_2 are reduced by the PCA, the final feature dimension k needs to be determined in order to obtain the best classification result. In the experiment, the classification accuracy is closely related to the feature dimension k. And through the prior verification of the experiment, it is learned that when k is greater than or equal to 5, the classification effect is less than that k is small. So $k = 2, 3, 4$ is selected as the feature dimension for the final selection. The classification accuracy of the data set with bandwidths of 2 Hz and 4 Hz at different values of k is shown in Tables 1 and 2 respectively.

Table 1. The classification accuracy of different subjects at 2 Hz bandwidth from the first dataset

K	2		3		4	
Subjects	*SVM*	*KNN*	*SVM*	*KNN*	*SVM*	*KNN*
c	0.72	0.73	0.78	0.75	0.76	0.75
d	0.85	0.83	0.90	0.87	0.90	0.85
e	0.96	0.93	0.97	0.97	0.96	0.95
g	0.87	0.84	0.90	0.89	0.89	0.85
mean	0.85	0.832	0.887	0.87	0.877	0.85

Table 2. The classification accuracy of different subjects at 4 Hz bandwidth from the first dataset

K	2		3		4	
Subjects	*SVM*	*KNN*	*SVM*	*KNN*	*SVM*	*KNN*
c	0.67	0.62	0.70	0.67	0.68	0.63
d	0.83	0.80	0.85	0.84	0.86	0.80
e	0.96	0.94	0.97	0.95	0.93	0.92
g	0.88	0.84	0.92	0.92	0.91	0.90
mean	0.835	0.80	0.86	0.845	0.845	0.812

The Tables 1 and 2 shows that: (1) When the value of k is 3, the feature dimension after dimension reduction is 3 dimensions, the highest average classification accuracy rate can be achieved in both groups of features with bandwidth of 2 Hz and 4 Hz. (2) The accuracy from two groups features with a bandwidth of 2 Hz are all higher on average than that with a bandwidth of 4 Hz. The results can also be interpreted as a data set with a bandwidth of 2 Hz decomposes more frequency bands than a set of signals with a bandwidth of 4 Hz, and the extracted frequency domain information is more abundant.

4.2 Experimental Results Based on the Second Dataset from Laboratory Data

Twenty left hand and twenty right hand motor imagery data from each set of 8 subjects collected in our laboratory were adopted for training and the rest for testing. After the same processing as the above competition data, the average classification accuracy with bandwidths of 2 Hz and 4 Hz under different *k* values are shown in Tables 3 and 4 respectively.

Table 3. The classification accuracy of different subjects at 2 Hz bandwidth from the second dataset

K	*2*		*3*		*4*	
Subjects	*SVM*	*KNN*	*SVM*	*KNN*	*SVM*	*KNN*
A	0.718	0.743	0.75	0.787	0.675	0.731
B	0.731	0.762	0.756	0.781	0.681	0.718
C	0.706	0.718	0.743	0.756	0.637	0.675
D	0.681	0.681	0.731	0.718	0.675	0.669
E	0.718	0.706	0.737	0.743	0.687	0.693
F	0.743	0.75	0.781	0.775	0.706	0.718
G	0.699	0.706	0.75	0.743	0.675	0.687
H	0.713	0.687	0.756	0.756	0.693	0.687
mean	0.714	0.719	0.751	0.757	0.678	0.697

Table 4. The classification accuracy of different subjects at 4 Hz bandwidth from the second dataset

K	*2*		*3*		*4*	
Subjects	*SVM*	*KNN*	*SVM*	*KNN*	*SVM*	*KNN*
A	0.706	0.681	0.693	0.718	0.637	0.625
B	0.669	0.706	0.7	0.725	0.637	0.675
C	0.681	0.675	0.693	0.706	0.643	0.657
D	0.637	0.625	0.681	0.675	0.625	0.613
E	0.681	0.657	0.706	0.7	0.663	0.675
F	0.718	0.7	0.743	0.718	0.687	0.663
G	0.675	0.687	0.706	0.699	0.675	0.657
H	0.663	0.637	0.687	0.7	0.643	0.663
mean	0.678	0.671	0.701	0.705	0.651	0.655

The Tables 3 and 4 shows that: (1) When the value of *k* is 3, the highest average classification accuracy can be achieved in both groups of features with bandwidths of 2 Hz and 4 Hz. After feature dimension reduction, 3 dimensions is the best feature dimension for each subject. (2) A set of signals with a bandwidth of 2 Hz is 4.3% higher on average than that with a bandwidth of 4 Hz, which is more obvious than that obtained with the competition data. It also shows the method has a good performance with the data collected from the authors' laboratory experiments by g.Nautilus-8 wireless dry electrode EEG acquisition equipment.

Figure 4 shows the most significant Spatial Patterns using the frequency range that is autonomously selected in FBCSP+PCA. The results show that the left hemisphere and right hemisphere discriminates the right hand action and left hand action respectively for eight subjects from the authors' laboratory experiments. These results verify the neurophysiological plausibility of the CSP projection matrix computed for these subjects. However, the results for subjects 'D' and 'E' do not show such patterns. This is a plausible reason for the relative inferior test accuracy obtained for subjects 'D' and 'E'.

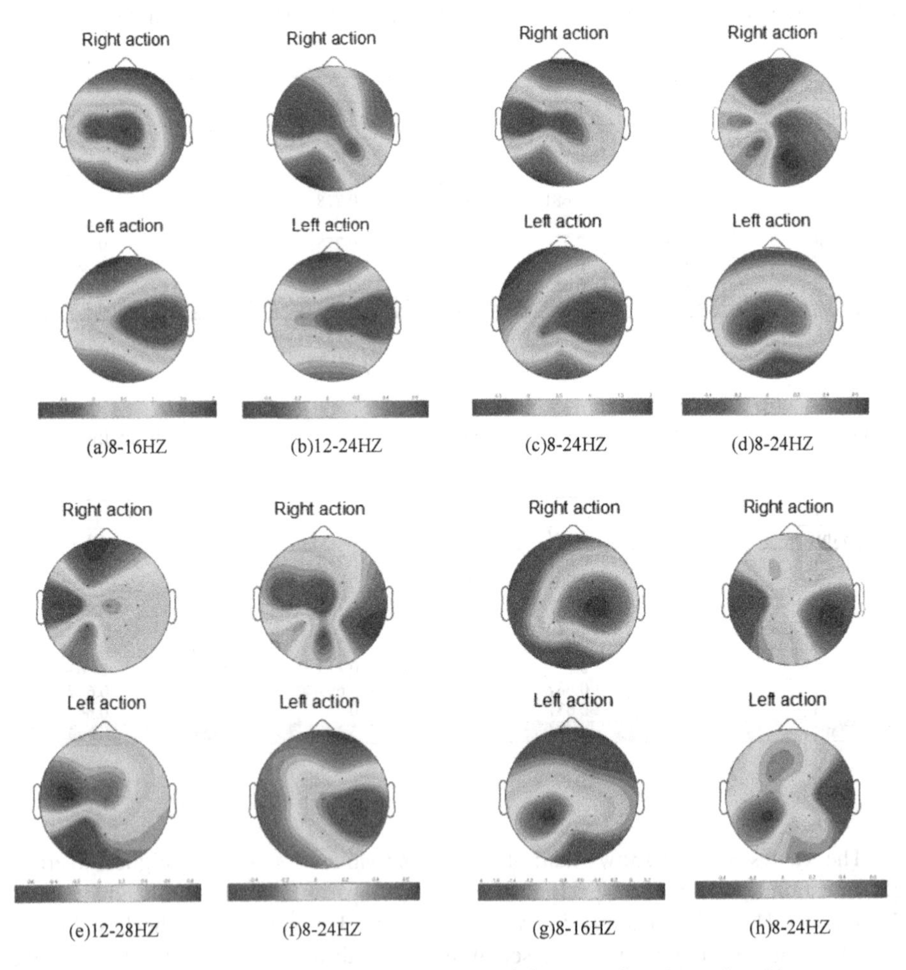

Fig. 4. Spatial patterns of using FBCSP on laboratory data for each subject

4.3 EEG Signal Processing Based on Time Window

The motor imagery time of each trial is four seconds. When subjects perform motor imagery tasks, there are the problems of visual evoked and delay of imaging especially in the beginning and end of 4 s, which would produce more volatility and reduce the signal-to-noise ratio, thus reducing the classification accuracy. To solve this problem, five time windows (0 to 4 s, 0.5 to 4 s, 0 to 3.5 s, 0.5 to 3.5 and 1 to 3 s) are chosen in the experiment.

Table 5 shows the average classification accuracy of different time windows for 8 subjects respectively under the bandwidth is 2 Hz and k takes 3. The result shows that when the time window is set to 0.5 to 4 s and 0 to 3.5 s, the average classification accuracy is higher than 0 to 4 s, and the classification accuracy of the time window (0.5 to 3.5 s) is the highest, which verifies it can eliminate the problems of visual evoked and delay of thinking and improves the classification accuracy by time window setting. When the time window is set to 1 to 3 s, the classification accuracy is down compared with 0.5 to 3.5 s. It shows that it can diminish the effect of EEG signal amplitude fluctuations, however, it also lose part of the useful information related to motor imagery under this time window.

Table 5. When bandwidth is 2 Hz and k takes 3, the average classification accuracy of different time windows for 8 subjects respectively

Time_window / Subject	*0-4s*	*0.5-4s*	*0-3.5s*	*0.5-3.5s*	*1-3s*
A	0.675	0.718	0.706	0.75	0.725
B	0.669	0.693	0.7	0.756	0.731
C	0.657	0.693	0.706	0.743	0.706
D	0.643	0.681	0.693	0.731	0.7
E	0.65	0.675	0.681	0.737	0.718
F	0.687	0.706	0.731	0.781	0.743
G	0.669	0.681	0.699	0.75	0.718
H	0.657	0.687	0.699	0.756	0.725
mean	0.663	0.691	0.702	0.751	0.721

Figure 5 shows the average classification accuracies of the traditional CSP and the method proposed in this paper for 8 subjects from the authors' laboratory experiments respectively. The result shows the average accuracy of the method proposed in this paper is higher than the traditional CSP and reaches 75.7%. It verifies the method FBCSP+PCA can effectively eliminate the individual differences of EEG signals and gets better classification results.

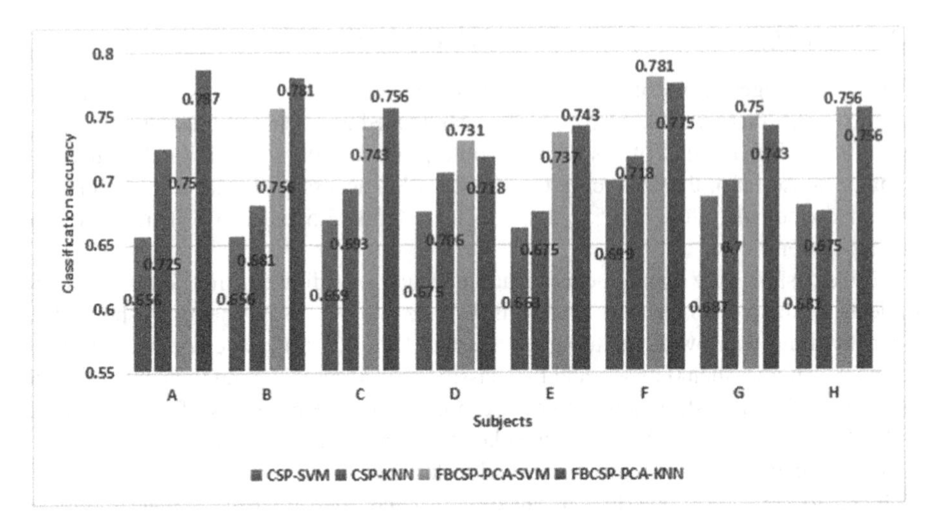

Fig. 5. The average classification accuracy of the traditional CSP and the method proposed in this paper for 8 subjects respectively

5 Discussion

Furthermore, the reason for using PCA as the feature reduction method is the PCA can reduce the correlation of the components in multidimensional features and so it increases the significance of each component. However, there is a drawback of the PCA method. The drawback is it can cause the presence of unexpected observations within the data to be processed by the PCA, which results in an incorrect de-correlation of the different features and so it may lacks part of information of motor imagery when feature reducing. There is a method called Robust PCA (RPCA) based on the Minimum Covariance Determinant (MCD) estimator, which has a good performance on this problem [14, 15]. Using this method to replace the conventional PCA method in FBCSP+PCA may has a better performance in getting the most effective features from different individuals and can improve the practical use of the method proposed in the paper.

6 Conclusion

In this paper, a motor imagery recognition algorithm called FBCSP+PCA is presented. The FBCSP algorithm can enrich the frequency domain information of feature extracted. The PCA algorithm can get the few most effective motor imagery features by feature reduction. The combination of these two algorithm effectively avoid the problem that need to manually adjust the certain frequency range selected caused by individual differences when using traditional CSP algorithm. By verifying two EEG data set from BCI Competition 4 and the authors' laboratory experiments, the method showed a good performance, which lays a foundation for in-depth study of practical application of portable BCI system based on motor imagery.

Acknowledgments. This project is supported by National Natural Science Foundation of China (60975079, 31100709).

References

1. Yang, B., Li, H., Wang, Q., et al.: Subject-based feature extraction by using fisher WPD-CSP in brain-computer interfaces. Comput. Methods Prog. Biomed. **129**(C), 21–28 (2016)
2. Blankertz, B., Kawanabe, M., Hohlefeld, F.U., et al.: Invariant common spatial patterns: alleviating nonstationarities in brain-computer interfacing. In: International Conference on Neural Information Processing Systems, pp. 113–120. Curran Associates Inc. (2007)
3. Kai, K.A., Zheng, Y.C., Zhang, H., et al.: Filter bank common spatial pattern (FBCSP) in brain-computer interface. In: IEEE International Joint Conference on Neural Networks, pp. 2390–2397. IEEE (2008)
4. Lemm, S., Blankertz, B., Curio, G., et al.: Spatio-spectral filters for improving the classification of single trial EEG. IEEE Trans. Biomed. Eng. **52**(9), 1541–1548 (2005)
5. Dornhege, G., Blankertz, B., Krauledat, M., et al.: Combined optimization of spatial and temporal filters for improving brain-computer interfacing. IEEE Trans. Bio-Med. Eng. **53** (11), 2274 (2006)
6. Novi, Q., Guan, C., Dat, T.H., et al.: Sub-band common spatial pattern (SBCSP) for brain-computer interface. In: International IEEE/EMBS Conference on Neural Engineering, pp. 204–207. IEEE (2007)
7. Xu, Y., Haykin, S., Racine, R.J.: Multiple window time-frequency distribution and coherence of EEG using Slepian sequences and hermite functions. IEEE Trans. Biomed. Eng. **46**(7), 861–866 (1999)
8. Wang, Z., Logothetis, N.K., Liang, H.: Extraction of percept-related induced local field potential during spontaneously reversing perception. Neural Netw. **22**(5), 720–727 (2009)
9. Yang, B.H., Wu, T., Wang, Q., et al.: Motor imagery EEG recognition based on WPD-CSP and KF-SVM in brain computer interfaces. Appl. Mech. Mater. **556–562**, 2829–2833 (2014)
10. Blankertz, B., Dornhege, G., Krauledat, M., et al.: The non-invasive Berlin brain-computer interface: fast acquisition of effective performance in untrained subjects. Neuroimage **37**(2), 539 (2007)
11. Nishino, K., Nayar, S.K., Jebara, T.: Clustered blockwise PCA for representing visual data. IEEE Trans. Pattern Anal. Mach. Intell. **27**(10), 1675 (2005)
12. Joachims, T.: Making large-scale SVM learning practical. Technische Universität Dortmund, Sonderforschungsbereich 475: Komplexitätsreduktion in multivariaten Datenstrukturen, pp. 499–526 (1998)
13. Yu, C., Ooi, B.C., Tan, K.L., et al.: Indexing the distance: an efficient method to KNN processing. In: VLDB (2001)
14. Zabalza, J., Clemente, C., Caterina, G.D., et al.: Robust PCA micro-doppler classification using SVM on embedded systems. IEEE Trans. Aerosp. Electron. Syst. **50**(3), 2304–2310 (2014)
15. Zabalza, J., Ren, J., Yang, M., et al.: Novel Folded-PCA for improved feature extraction and data reduction with hyperspectral imaging and SAR in remote sensing. ISPRS J. Photogramm. Remote Sens. **93**(7), 112–122 (2014)

A Hybrid Brain-Computer Interface System Based on Motor Imageries and Eye-Blinking

Jin Liu[1,2], Xiaopei Wu[1,2(✉)], Lei Zhang[1,2], and Bangyan Zhou[1,2]

[1] Key Laboratory of Intelligent Computing and Signal Processing, Ministry of Education, AnHui University, Hefei, China
wxp2001@ahu.edu.cn
[2] School of Computer Science and Technology, Anhui University, Hefei, China

Abstract. This paper focuses on the online implementation of a hybrid brain computer interface (BCI) involving electroculogram (EOG) and electroencephalogram (EEG) of motor imagery (MI). The hybrid BCI system comprises of modules of eye-blinking detection, ICA spatial filter, zero-training classifier and cursor movement controlling. Eye-blinking information contained in EOG signal was achieved for locating EEG segments related to motor imageries. Then, independent component analysis (ICA) was applied to the filtered EEG data to yield the motor-related potentials, whose features were fed into a zero-training classifier. Finally, the classification results regarding the types of moving imagination were transferred into commands to control the cursor moving along a predesigned path shown on the computer screen. Four subjects attended the online BCI tests, the average moving accuracy reached 84.56% for all tests, and the response time was about 4.13 trials/min. The experimental results demonstrate that the hybrid MIBCI system in this study is feasible for the real-time control of peripheral devices.

Keywords: BCI · EEG · Asynchronous control · EOG · ICA

1 Introduction

Brain-Computer interface (BCI) provides a new direct communication method with external devices but does not depend on nerves or muscles [1]. A large number of brain researches have proved that there is a close relationship between mind and cerebral activity [2–4]. Reasonably, we can interpret the intention of people from the activities of brain. As a widely concerned BCI, Motor imagery BCI (MIBCI) enables severely disabled people to communicate with the outside world better [5]. The MIBCI system can be divided into asynchronous and synchronous BCI. The difference lies in that synchronous BCI system relies on cues or fixed mode to motor imagery but asynchronous does not. The users can control the motor imagery autonomously in asynchronous system. Nowadays, most of the researches in BCI concentrate on synchronous system. The main difficulty for asynchrony is to identify the time when the imagery tasks begin to perform, which is about detecting when the user change the mental pattern between the no-task state and task state [6]. Fortunately, the hybrid BCI system is proposed to solve some problems faced by traditional BCI. It can avoid the

J. Ren et al. (Eds.): BICS 2018, LNAI 10989, pp. 206–216, 2018.
https://doi.org/10.1007/978-3-030-00563-4_20

disadvantage of single mode BCI and achieve more effective control function. Some researches have demonstrated that the combination of P300 and steady-state visual evoked potential (SSVEP) can improve the performance of BCI significantly [7, 8]. In this paper we propose a new hybrid MIBCI system, which combines EEG and EOG signals to realize asynchronous control. The EOG signal is accompanied with an obvious process of rising and falling of energy when the subject is blinking, and the feature does not vary from person to person. Therefore, we regard blinking behavior as the command for the start of task status. But by analyzing the EEG signals, we can recognize the mental state of the brain.

The signal processing algorithm is to extract the feature from EEG signal to reflect the state of mind. The spatial filtering method can make good use of the spatial distribution of scalp electrodes and the mutual information of the channels to extract the effective features [9]. In recent years, independent component analysis (ICA), as a typical blind source separation algorithm based on higher order statistical analysis, has received extensive attention in BCI [10]. ICA can make full use of the multi-channel signals by designing a signal transmission model between brain sources and channels without training [11]. The independent signal sources of cerebral nerve activity can be separated by the spatial filter.

The paper is organized as follows: Sect. 2 describes the EEG and EOG data acquisition, the algorithm of signals processing, blinking detection, automatic selection of motor related independent components (MRICs) detection filters, the structure diagram and GUI control mechanism of system. Experiment and results are presented in Sect. 3. Section 4 provides the results analysis and discussions, and the conclusions are summarized in Sect. 5.

2 Methods

2.1 EEG and EOG Data Acquisition

The EEG and EOG data acquisition equipment comes from American NeuroScan company, including 40 channel EEG amplifier, electrode cap, acquisition software and connectors. The position of electrode is strictly in accordance with the standard of the international 10/20 System. The data was recorded from 16 electrodes (VEOU, VEOL, Fp1, Fp2, FC3, FCz, FC4, C3, Cz, C4, CP3, CPz, CP4, O1, Oz, O2) as shown in Fig. 1. In order to avoid interference and operate conveniently, we choose 9 electrodes (VEOU, Fp1, Fp2, C3, Cz, C4, O1, Oz, O2)for analysis. The electrode of VEOU is placed just right above the brow to detect eye movement. The motor imagery begin with the two consecutive blinks of subjects, and the duration of single trial lasts 4 s. The EEG and EOG signals are amplified firstly, then band-pass filtered between 0.1 and 100 Hz, and sampled at 250 Hz.

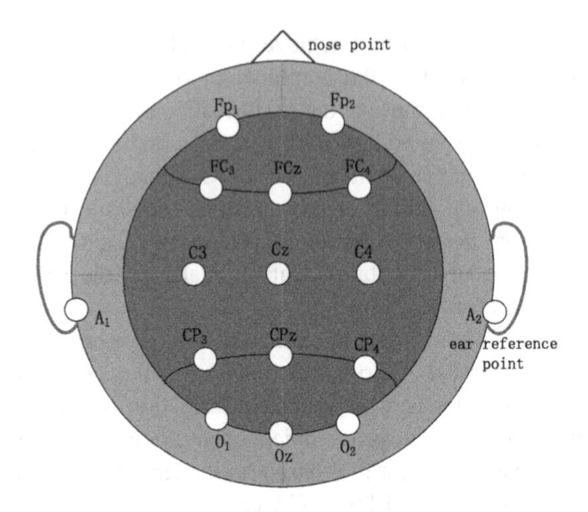

Fig. 1. The positions of placement for 16 EEG electrodes

2.2 ICA Algorithm

ICA algorithm is a typically blind source separation algorithm, it assumes the sources are non-Gaussian distribution, and the separated sources are independent of each other [12]. The basic process as follows:

Step1: The original N-channel EEG signals $x(t) = [x_1(t),\ldots x_N(t)]^{\mathrm{T}}$ are assumed linear and instantaneous mixtures of several independent sources.

$$x(t) = A\ s(t) \tag{1}$$

Step2: Regarding $u(t)$ as the estimation source signals $s(t)$, and W as the separation matrix

$$u(t) = W\,x(t) \tag{2}$$

Step3: The maximum information criterion as the independence measure criterion of each source signal, the separation matrix W processed by iterative learning with natural gradient

$$\Delta \mathbf{W} \infty [I - E[K \cdot \tanh(u)u^T + uu^T]]\mathbf{W} \tag{3}$$

Step 4: The estimated source $u(t)$ was normalized by the variance normalization process, And at the same time the A and W to do the corresponding adjustment, and get the mixed matrix A.

$$u = u/diag(std(u)) \tag{4}$$

$$A = W^{-1} \cdot diag(std(u)) \tag{5}$$

Where $A = [a_1, \ldots, a_N]$ is a mixing matrix, each column vector $a_i(i = 1, 2, \ldots, N)$ as a spatial pattern which reflects the weights of the independent sources $s(i)$ on scalp electrodes. The separation matrix W is the ICA spatial filter that can separate the components of the source signal. I is a unit matrix, K for diagonal matrix, tanh() for the hyperbolic tangent function, diag() is to diagonalization of matrix.

2.3 Blinking Detection

The energy of EOG signals will rise when the subject is blinking, and it falls obviously when the blinking ends. Given the obvious characteristics, we set a high threshold D_H when the EOG energy rises, meanwhile a low threshold D_L is set when energy falls on the analysis of large amounts of blinking data. We detect the number of blinking in a slide window for 4 s. Under the status of detecting blinking, the sliding window is sliding forward on receiving EOG data. The system enters the motor imagery status when the blinking more than two times in succession. Our method is more simple, convenient and low complexity compare to the traditional method of blink detection such as finite difference method. Figure 2 presents the process of blink detection method.

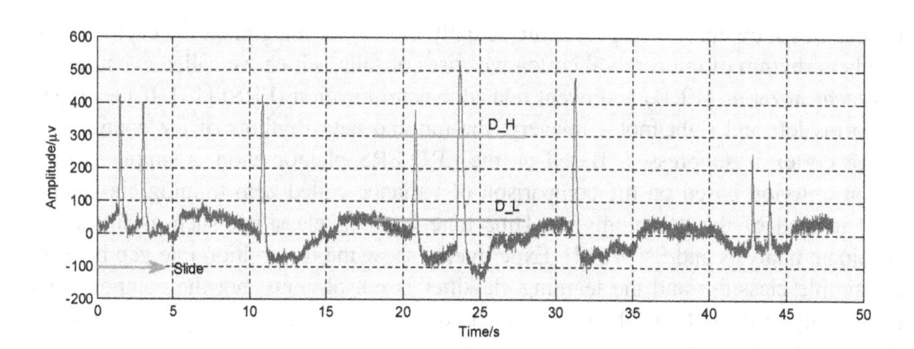

Fig. 2. The schematic diagram of blinking detection

2.4 Automatic Selection Method of MRICs Detection Filter

BCI system based on motor imagery EEG is susceptible to the interference of non-objection noise. It is necessary to extract the correct MRICs, which represent the motor imagination. The selection process of MRICs filters is briefly introduced: we take the 8 channel EEG{Fp1, Fp2, C3, Cz, C4, O1, Oz, O2} as a example. After processing by ICA algorithm, the obtained EEG sources and spatial mixture model of scalp electrodes are $A = [a_1, \ldots a_8]$ and $W = [w_1, \ldots, w_8]$ respectively. a_j represents the j-th estimated source $u_j(t)$ in the projection coefficients of 8 scalp detecting electrodes, its absolute value reflects the attenuation of EEG sources transferred to scalp electrode, approximately in inverse proportion to spatial transmission distance. According to the position of C3, Cz, and C4 electrodes in Fig. 1, the three EEG sources located in the motor cortex should be in C3, Cz, and C4 with the maximum projection coefficients. The processing of specific algorithm is shown in Fig. 3.

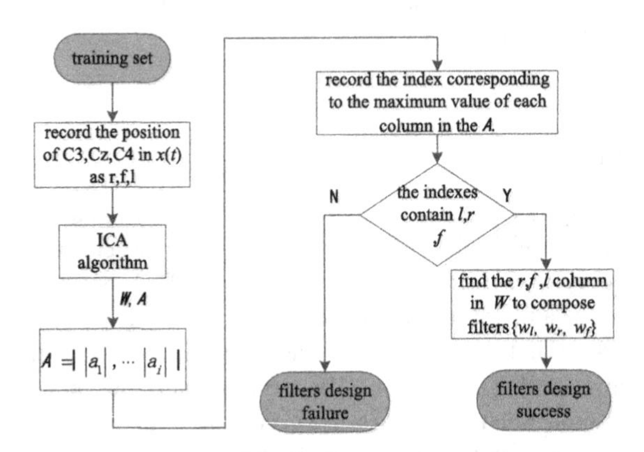

Fig. 3. The design of ICA spatial filter

2.5 Classification

Researches show that when people are actually moving or imagining, the energy of mu and beta rhythm of the cerebral cortex will rises or falls, which we called event related desynchronization (ERD) and event related synchronization (ERS) [13]. If the subject performs left and right motor imagery, the mu and beta rhythms of the contralateral motor cortex is suppressed. Based on the ERD/ERS phenomenon, a simple classification criterion based on the comparison of variance called zero training classifier is used instead of the commonly used machine learning classifier, such as linear discriminant analysis and SVM [14]. Experiments show the recognition rate gap between the simple classifier and the learning classifier is not obvious, but the computational complexity of the latter is obviously increased. Figure 4 describes the process of motor imagery classification.

2.6 The Structure of Hybrid BCI System and GUI Control Mechanism

The diagram of BCI system as shown in Fig. 5, the hardware platform composes of NeuroScan multi-channel EEG acquisition amplifier, SCAN collection server software, and ICA-MIBCI system client. The basic process of hybrid BCI system is as follows: after receiving the EEG signals, the system will collect the EEG training 100 s duration EEG segment to design ICA spatial filter. By the way, we can also read offline filters which designed on the simulation platform in advance. Then the system enters the blink detection status, the user control the start of motor imagery by blinking. When the system detects more than 2 times blinks in the sliding window, the status of the current system will change to motor imagery mode. The subject decide the motor imagery type according to the planned path in GUI represented by green square. After the end of the

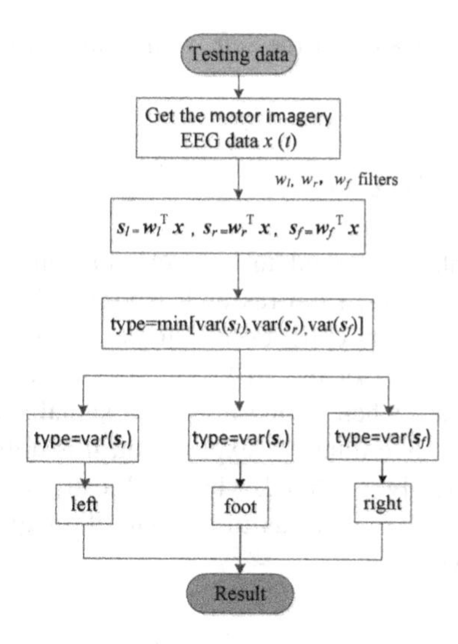

Fig. 4. The flowchart of three type motor imagery classification

4 s motor imagination, the feature is extracted by MRICs detection filters, combined with zero training classifier to get the type of motion imagination, then the result is send to the controlled ball as a command. The ball move a step according to the result. If the ball has not reached the destination, the status change to blink detection, the subjects prepare for the next motor imagination until the ball reach the destination. The blue squares represent the trajectories of the subjects' motor imagery, and the red mark represents the destination in GUI. As for moving commands, The left, right and foot

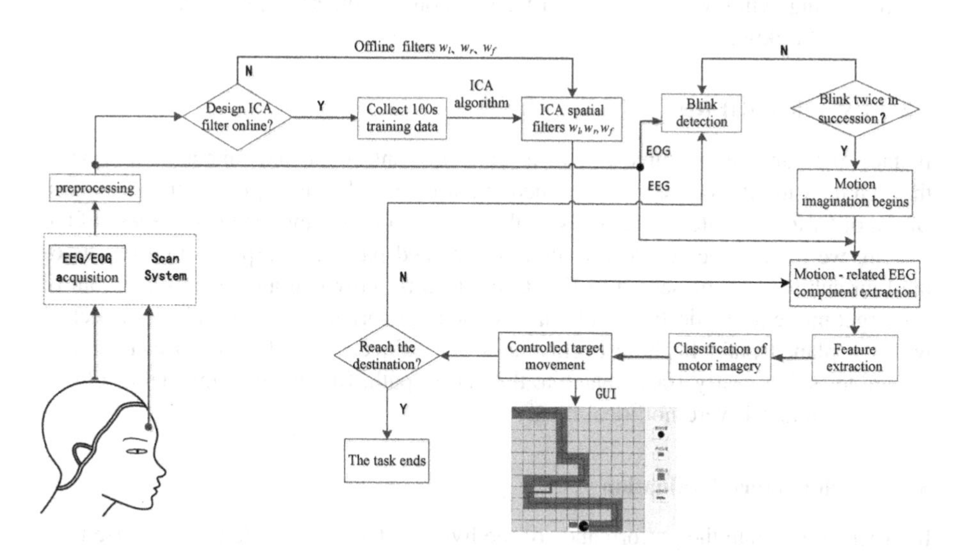

Fig. 5. The flow chart of the hybrid BCI system (Color figure online)

imaginary movements correspond to the left, right and downward movement of the ball.

3 Experiments and Results

All the online experiments performed in a quiet and comfortable laboratory. Four healthy subjects (S1, S2, S3, S4) from research laboratory attended the experiments, They have already had some prior experience of motor imagery before the experiment, and have a good understanding of the BCI system. The subjects are required to sit quietly and smoothly in chair when testing in case of signal abnormality. Each subject performs experimental tests five times. In experiment, it is difficult to ensure that each motor imagery can be correctly identified, which will cause the inconsistency with the planed route. But this does not affect us to evaluate the experiment, and the planed route is only as a reference.

3.1 Description of Different States

- **Motor imagery state:**
  When the system enters the status of motor imagery, the subject determine the type of motor imagery according to the planed path in GUI. Each motor imagery complete at 4 s. the system will remind the subject of the status of the system has switched into blinking detection from motor imagery when motor imagery ends.
- **Blinking detection/resting state:**
  The blinking detection state as a node of the conversion between different states. The number of blinking set in advance as the beginning of motor imagery. At the same time, the subjects can choose to have a rest without continuous blinking, and the sliding window moves forward continuously detects whether there is a continuous blinking.

3.2 Experimental Results

In fact, the subjects are involved in a game to control the movement of the target through their mind. We are more inclined to allow the subjects to plan their own routes. But in order to illustrate the accuracy of the recognition rate and the effectiveness of the system, we require the subjects to along the planed path. The experimental results of the four subjects are presented in Fig. 6, the results show that all subjects can control the target move to the destination though some trajectories are not completely matched with the planed path. In these twenty tests, the subject S1 and S2 even can achieve several tests that nearly 100% match to the planed path. But the experimental results of subject S3 and S4 were not ideal relatively.

3.3 Performance Evaluation

In order to illustrate the performance of the hybrid BCI system, We use response time (*RT*) to represent the ratio of total time to the trials of motor imagery. And the right path

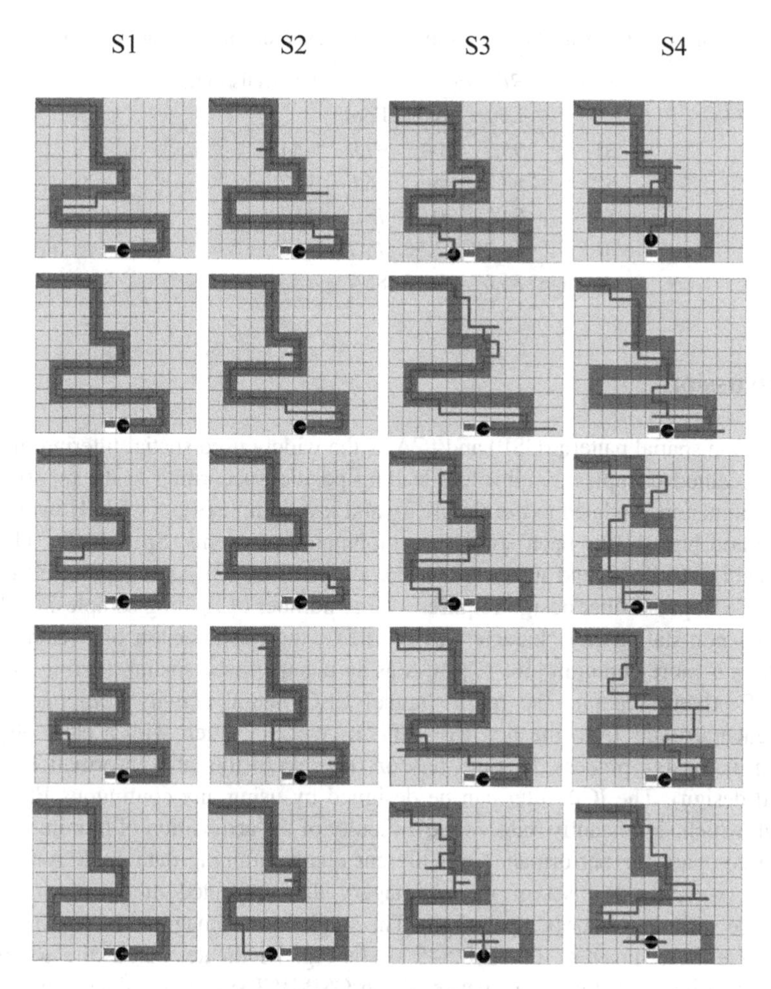

Fig. 6. The experimental results of online motor imagery for four subjects

(*RP*) representing the consistency with the path is to evaluate the effectiveness of BCI asynchronous control system. When the trajectory of the target is not consistent with the planned path, the subject can try his best to finish the game along the planned route or back to former path, we regard this kind of inconsistency as right path. Table 1 is the statistics of all evaluation indicators for experiments. The experimental results show that subjects can basically control the movement of target on their own motor imagery mode. The average *RP* and *RT* of the four subjects were 84.56% and 4.13 trials/min respectively.

$$RP = \frac{right\ path}{total\ path} \quad RT = \frac{total\ time}{total\ trials} \tag{6}$$

Table 1. The evaluation of motor imagery experiments for four subjects

Subjects	*RP* (%)			*RT* (trials/min)
	Left	Right	Foot	
S1	95.2	100	97.9	5.11
S2	87.8	94	95.6	3.67
S3	84.37	70.3	78.37	4.03
S4	64.25	67.56	71.72	3.18
Average	86.42	82.15	85.76	4.13

4 Discussion

The common spatial pattern (CSP) and ICA as the widely used spatial filtering method, the CSP method occupies the absolute leading position according to the reports [15]. This phenomenon is related to the simplicity and low complexity of CSP. However, the CSP method has always been some insurmountable problems. Specifically, (1) It is very sensitive to noise and artifact interference in EEG. (2) As a supervised design method, CSP spatial filter design requires a large number of training samples. (3) Since the strong non-stationarity characterizes the EEG, the phenomenon of over-fitting in CSP filters is more common [16, 17]. ICA as an unsupervised spatial filtering method, it can effectively separate the multi-channel EEG neural activity components and interference artifacts from the original EEG. ICA spatial filter, with a clear physical meaning, its design process does not rely on the data of the label information (unsupervised design). The ICA filter can be designed by using any continuous EEG data segment, which significantly reduces the difficulty of the acquisition of training data. In order to compare the performance of different quality training data on ICA-BCI and CSP-BCI, we choose a set of motor imagery data collected in the laboratory in accordance with the prescribed paradigm. The single motor imagination lasts 10 s, and the effective motor imagery time is 0.5–5 s. The Fig. 7 indicates that as the non-motor imagery data increase, the performance of the CSP-BCI system declines significantly while ICA-BCI is barely affected.

The brain-machine asynchronous control technology is a difficult technical bottleneck in the process of BCI application [18]. Under the mode of asynchronous control, the user can switch between the task status and the idle state at any time. While the synchronous system requires the user to follow the specified paradigm to complete the corresponding motor imagery task. The hybrid MIBCI system combines the EEG and EOG bio-signals reasonably to achieve brain-to-machine control. In this way, the user autonomously determines the beginning of motor imagery by blinking. What's more, the combination of eye-brain-controlled game can play a positive role in relieving eye/brain fatigue. Therefore, The hybrid brain-machine system has great application potential and market value in related fields. Moreover, the system can be used as a training platform which can evaluate training and testing data offline for motor imagery BCI. Undeniably, the system also has some problems. The differences of individual can result in a significant difference in the experimental results. Some subjects have to be trained many times to achieve the desired results. And the system

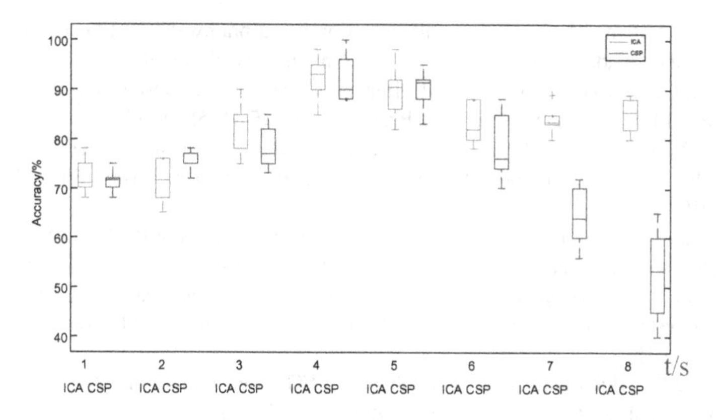

Fig. 7. The performance comparison between ICA-BCI and CSP-BCI on different time periods of training sample

achieves asynchronous control by detecting blinking, Each time after motor imagery, the system will be in the status of the detecting blinking again instead of the continuous motor imagery. Some new signal processing approaches may achieve better results [19, 20].

5 Conclusions

In order to face the challenge of high freedom and real-time control of practical BCI system. This paper presents a hybrid MIBCI system to realize asynchronous control, which can overcome the lack of single-mode BCI system. We provide a new approach to design asynchronous MIBCI system by taking blinking behaviour as the converter of no-task and task state. This method can obviously improve the rate of information transmission due to the independent features selected by system. At the same time, the ICA algorithm is used to extract the features of EEG signals without much training. The experimental results indicate that the hybrid MIBCI is effective in asynchronous control, which provides a novel mode of brain-computer interaction system. But there are still some problems that can not be ignored. The focuses of future work are to improve the asynchronous control function of the system and increase the type of classification.

References

1. Pavitrakar, V.R.: Survey of brain computer interaction. Int. J. Adv. Res. Electr. Electron. Instrum. Eng. **2**(4), 1647–1652 (2013)
2. Fox, M.D., Raichle, M.E.: Spontaneous fluctuations in brain activity observed with functional magnetic resonance imaging. Nat. Rev. Neurosci. **8**(9), 700–711 (2007)
3. Singer, W.: Synchronization of cortical activity and its putative role in information processing and learning. Annu. Rev. Physiol. **55**(1), 349–374 (1993)

4. Marcel, S., Millan, J.D.R.: Person authentication using brainwaves (EEG) and maximum a posteriori model adaptation. IEEE Trans. Pattern Anal. Mach. Intell. **29**(4), 743–752 (2007)
5. Rivet, B., Cecotti, H., Maby, E., et al.: Impact of spatial filters during sensor selection in a visual P300 brain-computer interface. Brain Topogr. **25**(1), 55–63 (2012)
6. Wu, Z., Yao, D., Tang, Y., et al.: Amplitude modulation of steady-state visual evoked potentials by event-related potentials in a working memory task. J. Biol. Phys. **36**(3), 261–271 (2010)
7. Li, Y., Pan, J., Wang, F., Yu, Z.: A hybrid BCI system combining P300 and SSVEP and its application to wheelchair control. IEEE Trans. Biomed. Eng. **60**(11), 3156–3166 (2013)
8. Fan, X.A., Bi, L., Teng, T., et al.: A brain-computer interface-based vehicle destination selection system using P300 and SSVEP signals. IEEE Trans. Intell. Transp. Syst. **16**(1), 274–283 (2015)
9. Wolpaw, J.R., McFarland, D.J.: Multichannel EEG-based brain-computer communication. Electroencephalogr. Clin. Neurophysiol. **90**(6), 444–449 (1994)
10. Khan, O.I., Farooq, F., Akram, F., et al.: Robust extraction of P300 using constrained ICA for BCI applications. Med. Biol. Eng. Comput. **50**(3), 231–241 (2012)
11. Jonmohamadi, Y., Poudel, G., Innes, C., Jones, R.: Source-space ICA for EEG source separation, localization, and time-course reconstruction. Neuroimage **101**, 720–737 (2014)
12. Hyvärinen, A., Oja, E.: Independent component analysis: algorithms and applications. Neural Netw. **13**(4), 411–430 (2000)
13. Ghaheri, H., Ahmadyfard, A.R.: Extracting common spatial patterns from EEG time segments for classifying motor imagery classes in a brain computer interface (BCI). Sci. Iran. **20**(6), 2061–2072 (2013)
14. Zabalza, J., et al.: Robust PCA micro-doppler classification using SVM on embedded systems. IEEE Trans. Aerosp. Electron. Syst. **50**(3), 2304–2310 (2014)
15. Brunner, C., Naeem, M., Leeb, R., Graimann, B., Pfurtscheller, G.: Spatial filtering and selection of optimized components in four class motor imagery EEG data using independent components analysis. Pattern Recogn. Lett. **28**(8), 957–964 (2007)
16. Zhou, B., Wu, X., Lv, Z., et al.: A fully automated trial selection method for optimization of motor imagery based brain-computer interface. PLoS ONE **11**(9), e0162657 (2016)
17. Abdulkader, S.N., Atia, A., Mostafa, M.S.M.: Brain computer interfacing: applications and challenges. Egypt. Inform. J. **16**(2), 213–230 (2015)
18. Fruitet, J., Clerc, M., Papadopoulo, T.: Preliminary study for an offline hybrid BCI using sensorimotor rhythms and beta rebound. Int. J. Bioelectromagn. **13**(2), 70–71 (2011)
19. Zhang, A., et al.: A dynamic neighborhood learning-based gravitational search algorithm. IEEE Trans. Cybern. **48**(1), 436–447 (2018)
20. Qiao, T., et al.: Effective denoising and classification of hyperspectral images using curvelet transform and singular spectrum analysis. IEEE Trans. Geosci. Remote Sens. **55**(1), 119–133 (2017)

Goal-Directed Behavior Control Based on the Mechanism of Neuromodulation

Dongshu Wang[1(✉)], Hui Shan[1], and Lei Liu[2]

[1] School of Electrical Engineering, Zhengzhou University, Zhengzhou 450001, China
wangdongshu@zzu.edu.cn, 1240361158@qq.com

[2] Department of Research, The Peoples Bank of China, Zhengzhou Central Sub-Branch, Zhengzhou 450020, China
luckyliulei@126.com

Abstract. Due to the role of the brain's neuromodulatory system, biological organisms have the capacity of responding to the ever-changing environment rapidly. This work presents that the mechanism of the neuromodulatory systems through a developmental network can provide a control framework for the artificial agent to regulate its behavior. With the dopamine, serotonin, acetylcholine and norepinephrine modulation, the agent can operate autonomously, effectively carry out specific functions, e.g., to pursue a friend and avoid the enemy, and make suitable and instant decision when the environment changes. Goal-directed pursuing behavior in two simulation scenarios demonstrate the effect of the proposed neural modulatory systems, such as attentional effort, reinforcement learning and addressing the unexpected uncertainty.

Keywords: Neuromodulatory system · Developmental network
Unexpected uncertainty · Reinforcement learning

1 Introduction

Vertebrates have sub-cortical structures, called neuromodulatory systems, which can modulate the organisms' fundamental behavior, and are very important for them to survive [1]. When the environment changes, it is the neuromodulatory system that causes the organism to respond to the change quickly and accurately. There exist several neuromodulators which can response to reward [2], threat [3], effort [4] and novelty [5], respectively. Therefore, understanding the basic principle and function of the neuromodulatory system may provide a basis for controlling the autonomous robots.

Although there are many types of neural transmitters, we concentrate on four types here: dopamine (DA), serotonin (5-HT), acetylcholine (Ach) and norepinephrine (NE). Some form of dopamine are related to reward and some forms of serotonin are related to aversion and punishment. Particularly, 5-HT is considered to be related with control of stress, social interactions, and risk-taking

Supported by National Natural Science Funds of China (61603343, 61703372).

J. Ren et al. (Eds.): BICS 2018, LNAI 10989, pp. 217–226, 2018.
https://doi.org/10.1007/978-3-030-00563-4_21

behavior [6], while DA with prediction of rewards, incentive salience or "wanting" [7,8]. Ach and NE systems are considered to be crucial in attention and judging uncertainty [9,10], and Yu and Dayan [5] proposed that Ach is involved in expected uncertainty and NE is involved with unexpected uncertainty. For simplicity, we hypothesize that 5-HT and DA are used to denote the punishment and reward, respectively, while Ach and NE are used to indicate attention and novelty, respectively, as we discussed below.

2 Realization of the Neuromodulatory System

2.1 Structure of the Neuromodulatory System

Figure 1 provides a framework according to the principles of the vertebrate neuromodulatory system, used to design an autonomous system. This ascending neuromodulatory systems encompass serotonergic, cholinergic, noradrenergic, and dopaminergic projections from the brainstem and basal forebrain regions to wide areas of the nervous system, such as the neocortex, prefrontal cortex, the thalamus, and hippocampus, etc. In this work, the neuromodulatory system will be used as a controller for an artificial agent, to simulate the goal-directed driving behavior through the developmental network.

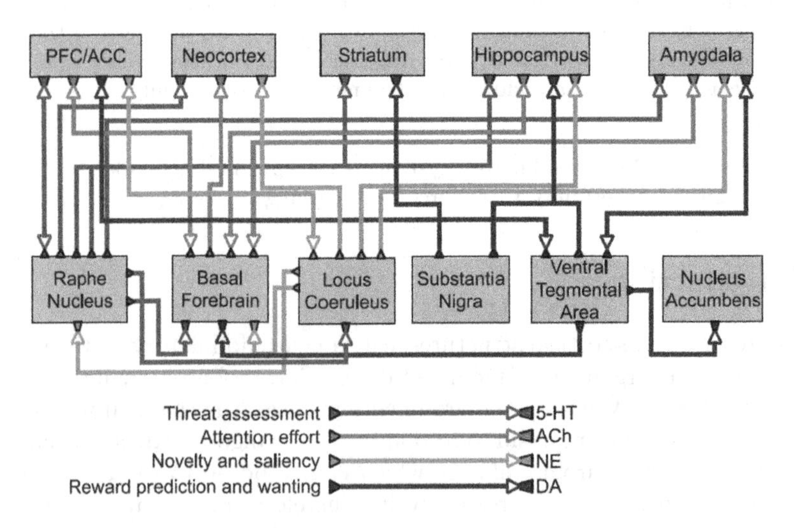

Fig. 1. Architecture of the neuromodulatory systems. The raphe nucleus (RN) is the source of serotonin (5-HT), the basal forebrain (BF) is the source of acetylcholine (ACh), the locus coeruleus (LC) is the source of norepinephrine (NE), and the substantia nigra and ventral tegmental area (VTA) are the sources of dopamine (DA). From Krichmar [1].

2.2 Theory of the Developmental Network

The simplest version of a developmental network has three areas, the sensory area X, the internal area Y, and the motor area Z, with an example in Fig. 2. The internal area Y as a "bridge" to connect its two "banks"— the sensory area X and the motor area Z. In the DN, input areas are X and Z, output areas are X and Z, Y is skull-closed inside the brain, not directly accessible by the external world after the birth. The detailed DN algorithm can be found in [11–13].

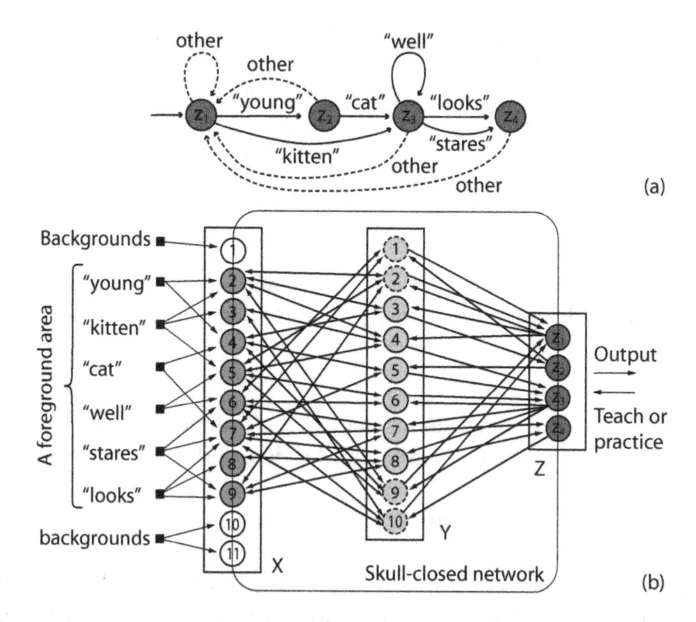

Fig. 2. Relate a "skull-open" Agent Finite Automaton (AFA) with a "skull-closed" DN. (a) An AFA, handcrafted and static, reasons in the symbolic world. (b) A corresponding DN that lives and learns autonomously in the real physical world.

2.3 Architecture of the Motivated DN (MDN)

In the MDN as shown in Fig. 3, the sensory area X can be denoted as $X = (X_u, X_p, X_s)$, where X_u means the unbiased input vector, while X_p and X_s are the pain input vector and sweet input vector, respectively. At any time step, X will produce a response vector based on the state of the external physical world.

Y area is also divided into 3 sub-areas, Y_u, Y_p and Y_s are the unbiased, pain and sweet area, respectively, corresponding to the three sub-areas in X area. If the switch of the X_p and (or) X_s is opened, there is punishment and (or) reward, neurons with the maximal pre-action energy in Y_p and Y_s area will be activated, their weights and ages will be updated.

The released serotonin and dopamine give a nonzero response to certain neurons in Y_p and Y_s areas, respectively, and this nonzero response will affect

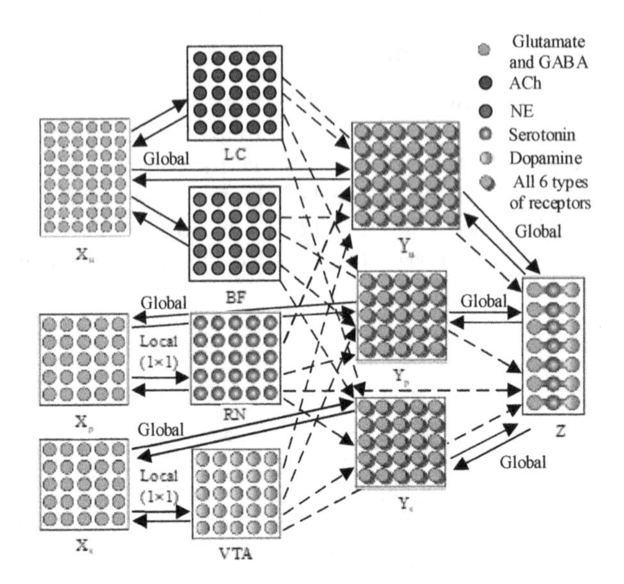

Fig. 3. A motivated DN with Ach/NE, dopamine and serotonin modulatory systems. Y_u, Y_p and Y_s have cholinergic/noradrenergic, serotonergic and dopaminergic receptors, respectively.

the neuron learning rate in Y_u area. Due to the influence of the serotonin and dopamine, the learning rate of Y area can be deduced as [14]:

$$\omega_2(n_j) = \min((1 + \alpha_{RN} + \alpha_{VTA})\frac{1}{n_j}, 1) \tag{1}$$

where α_{RN} and α_{VTA} are constants related with RN and VTA, respectively.

The motor area Z can be represented by a series of neurons $Z = (z_1, z_2, \cdots, z_m)$, where m is the neuron number in Z area. Each z_i has three neurons $z_i = (z_{iu}, z_{ip}, z_{is})$ as shown in Fig. 3, where z_{iu}, z_{ip} and z_{is} $(\mathrm{i}=1, 2, \cdots, m)$ are unbiased, pain and sweet motors, respectively. The composite pre-action energy of a motor neuron can be computed as follows:

$$z_i = z_{iu} + \alpha z_{ip} + \beta z_{is} \tag{2}$$

where α and β are both positives. The j-th motor neuron fires and action is released where

$$j = \arg\max_{1 \le i \le m} \{z_i\} \tag{3}$$

3 Simulation Experiments Setting

3.1 Simulation Design

We will use three artificial robots to test the above algorithm, one is the agent which can think and decide, controlled by the MDN. The other two are its friend and enemy. For simplicity, we define the following entities: a (agent), f (friend), e (enemy), their position scheme is provided in Fig. 4, then we can get the following expressions:

$$\begin{aligned}
\theta_f &= \arctan(a_x - f_x, a_y - f_y) \\
d_f &= \sqrt{(a_x - f_x)^2 + (a_y - f_y)^2} \\
\theta_e &= \arctan(a_x - e_x, a_y - e_y) \\
d_e &= \sqrt{(a_x - e_x)^2 + (a_y - e_y)^2} \\
x_u &= \{\cos\theta_f, \sin\theta_f, \cos\theta_e, \sin\theta_e, \frac{d_f}{d_f + d_e}, \frac{d_e}{d_f + d_e}\}
\end{aligned} \tag{4}$$

where θ_f and θ_e are the angle between the heading of the agent and the direction of the friend and enemy, respectively; d_f and d_e are the distance between the agent and the friend and the enemy, respectively.

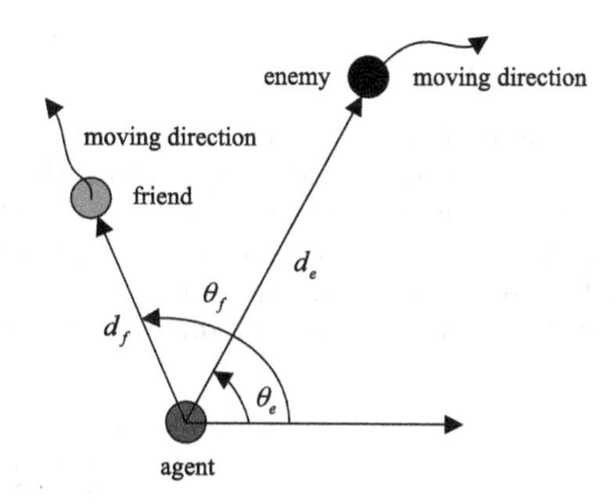

Fig. 4. The setting of the wandering plan which includes the agent, the friend agent and enemy agent. The size of the square space used is 500×500.

The punishment threshold is set to 65, namely, if $d_e > 65$, there is no punishment. If $22 < d_e < 65$, punishment value is set to 3. Otherwise, the punishment value is computed through the threshold divided by the actual distance de. Similarly, the desire threshold is set to 45, if $d_f < 45$, there is no reward. If $45 < d_f < 200$, the reward value is computed through the actual distance d_f divided by the desire threshold. Otherwise, the reward value is set to 2.

3.2 Simulation Setup

In the experiment, we write the training data according to the relative positions between the agent and its friend and enemy. In actual movement, after calculating the move direction of each step, the agent moves according to the most approximate direction among the 37 directions. During the train, we consider three cases, with reward and without punishment ($d_e > 65$, $d_f > 45$), with punishment and reward ($d_e < 65$, $d_f > 45$), with punishment and without reward ($d_e < 65$, $d_f < 45$), while the agent is under the condition of without punishment and reward ($d_e > 65$, $d_f < 45$) or $d_f < 20$, end the train. We design two simulation scenarios to display how the agent to approach the friend and avoid the enemy.

4 Experiment Results and Analysis

In this section, we design two scenarios to illustrate the effect of the neuromodulatory systems, through comparing the performance of the current MDN (proposed in this work) and the original MDN [15]. [15] only considers the effects of serotonin and dopamine on the motor area qualitatively, while the current MDN considers not only the effects of serotonin and dopamine on the motor area (formula 2), but also their effects on the Y_u area (formula 1). Moreover, we further consider the role of ACh/NE in the neural modulatory systems.

4.1 The First Experiment

In this experiment, there are only the agent and its friend. Figure 5 provides the distance between the agent and friend, changing with the experiment step. Figure 5 shows that when there only exist the agent and friend in the environment, the pursuing paths of the agent with the original MDN and current MDN are totally identical. If there is the reward, the agent will move towards the friend under the guidance of the reward. If there is no reward, the agent can still move

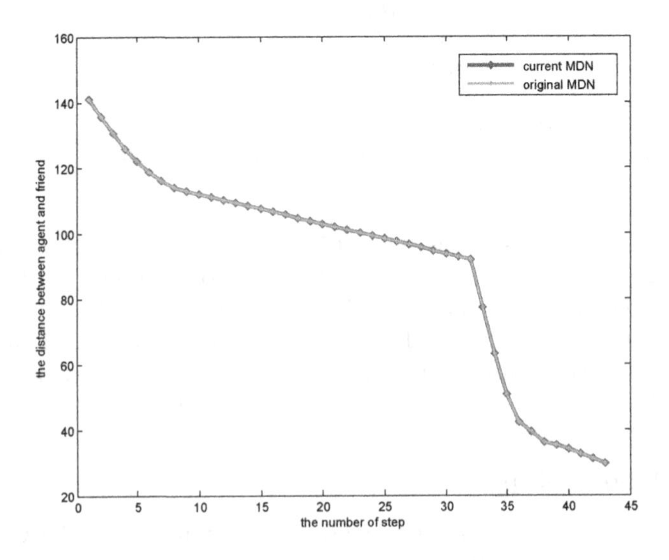

Fig. 5. Distance between the agent and its friend changing with the time step.

and gradually approach the friend, so their pursuing paths are identical, but the times they consumed are different as displayed in Table 1. Figure 5 illustrates that before time step 32, the agent gradually moves towards the friend, but at step 32, the distance between the agent and friend decreases suddenly, resulting from the fact that at step 32, the friend meets the environment boundary and rebounds back towards the agent. The pursuing behavior after step 32 efficiently demonstrates that the agent can rapidly change its moving behavior to pursue the friend as soon as possible, which displays the influence of ACh on the agent behavior. The Ach system makes the agent to attention the friend continuously, and quickly modify the agent's moving behavior to suit the variation of the external environment.

From Table 1, we can see that the average time with the current MDN (8.32 s) is a little bit smaller than that of the original MDN (8.454 s), which means the current MDN is more decisive and more attentive than those of the original MDN.

Table 1. Time consumed in ten operations with the two MDNs (unit: second)

Experiment	1	2	3	4	5	6	7	8	9	10	Average
Original MDN	8.65	8.37	8.41	8.38	8.55	8.52	8.42	8.37	8.42	8.45	8.454
Current MDN	8.16	8.28	8.35	8.44	8.32	7.94	8.51	8.29	8.43	8.48	8.32

4.2 The Second Experiment

In this experiment, in the early 3 s, there are only the agent and friend, with the same initial positions as the first experiment, and the agent pursues the friend without obstacles in the environment. After 3 s, in order to test the agent's response to the novelty (unexpected uncertainty), an enemy is designed to appear suddenly and randomly move, so the agent is required to not only pursue the friend but also to avoid the enemy simultaneously.

From the Fig. 6, we can see that before step 8 (corresponding to the early 3 s), agent is always pursuing the friend, at step 8, the enemy suddenly appears, and the current MDN can response immediately to the sudden change, while the original MDN responses at near step 9. Similarly, in Fig. 7, before step 8, the distance between the agent and the enemy is 0, at step 8, the enemy appears suddenly, so the distance increases to 55.75 instantly, Fig. 7 shows that the current MDN response quickly and the distance increases immediately, while the original MDN responses slowly and after near step 9, the distance begins to increase. These differences demonstrate that the current MDN can response the unexpected uncertainty more rapidly than the original MDN, because the current MDN considers not only the role of NE, but also the effects of serotonin and dopamine on the Y_u area, while the original MDN does not.

Moreover, based on the Figs. 6 and 7, we can see that at step 8, the enemy suddenly appears, the distances between the agent and the friend and enemy

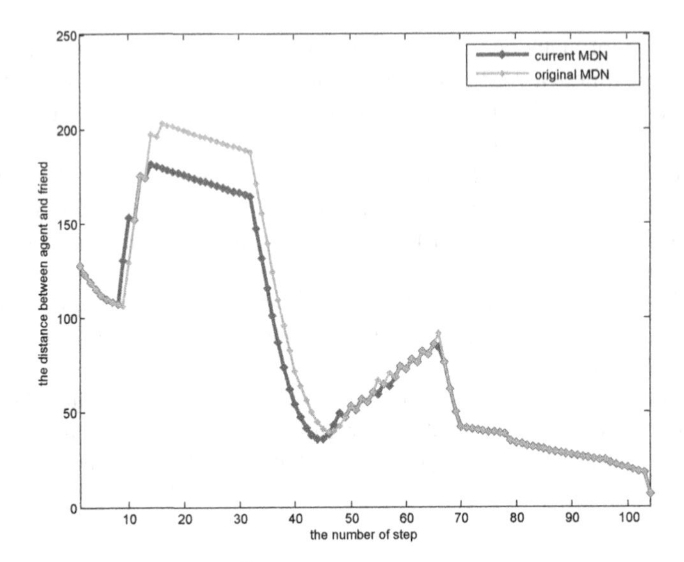

Fig. 6. Distance between the agent and its friend changing with the time step.

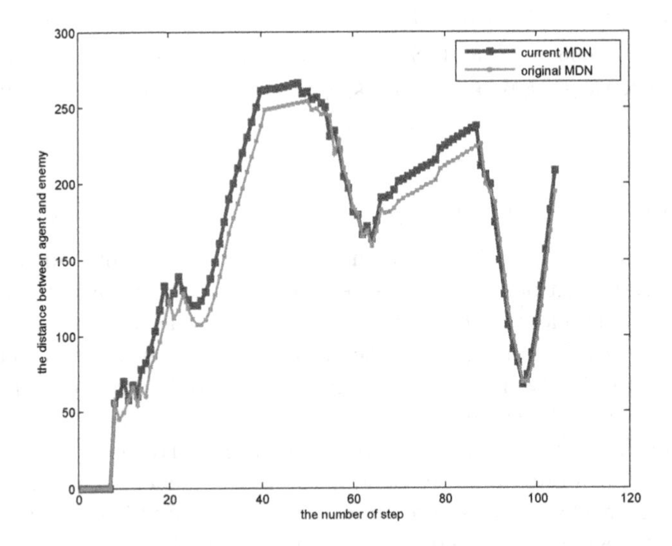

Fig. 7. Distance between the agent and its enemy changing with the time step.

suddenly increases, it resulting from the fact that the initial position of the enemy is located between the agent and the friend, and the agent chooses to avoid the enemy first, resulting in the two increasing distances. During the pursuing, when $8 < \text{step} < 14$, disturbance of the enemy on the agent causes it to move away from the friend, resulting in an increasing distance d_f, In addition, the agent moves away from the enemy, resulting in the increasing d_e. Due to the increasing d_e, the influence of the enemy on the agent becomes weaker, so at step 14, the agent begins to approach the friend gradually (i.e., decreasing d_f). At step 44, the enemy brings the weak influence on the agent again, the d_f increases again. At step 65, the influence of the enemy begins to fade away gradually, the agent approaches the friend slowly until it reaches the friend finally.

Table 2. Time consumed with the two MDNs in the second experiment (unit: second)

Experiment	1	2	3	4	5	6	7	8	9	10	Average
Original MDN	22.09	22.89	21.94	21.91	22.03	22.36	21.86	22.04	21.92	22.03	22.107
Current MDN	21.88	21.79	21.63	21.8	21.73	21.91	21.79	21.87	21.86	21.83	21.809

Similar with the results of Table 1, Table 2 shows that the average time with the current MDN is still a little bit smaller that that of the original MDN, which again proves that the current MDN is more decisive than the original MDN, for the ACh/NE mechanism.

5 Conclusion

Brain's neuromodulatory systems play an important function in regulating decision-making, controlling goal-directed behavior, and responding to environment changes. In this work, we introduce a developmental network to simulate the neural modulatory systems, which are composed of serotonin, dopamine, ACh and NE, to direct an artificial agent's behavior control, i.e., pursuing its friend and avoiding the enemy. Two simulation experiments illustrate that the proposed neural modulatory systems play a key role in regulating attentional effort, addressing the unexpected uncertainty and realizing the reinforcement learning. Next, we will design more complex scenarios, such as the anxious, emotion, etc, to further test the functions of the neuromodulatory systems.

References

1. Krichmar, J.L.: The neuromodulatory system: a framework for survival and adaptive behavior in a challenging world. Adapt. Behav. **16**, 385–399 (2008)
2. Kakade, S., Dayan, P.: Dopamine: generalization and bonuses. Neural Netw. **15**, 549–559 (2002)
3. Cavallaro, S.: Genomic analysis of serotonin receptors in learning and memory. Behav. Brain Res. **195**(1), 2–6 (2008)
4. Dayan, P.: Twenty-five lessons from computational neuromodulation. Neuron **76**, 240–256 (2012)
5. Yu, A.J., Dayan, P.: Uncertainty, neuromodulation, and attention. Neuron **46**, 681–692 (2005)
6. Talanov, M., et al.: Simulation of serotonin mechanisms in NEUCOGAR cognitive architecture. Procedia Comput. Sci. **123**, 473–478 (2018)

7. Takahashi, Y.K., Langdon, A.J., Niv, Y., Schoenbaum, G.: Temporal specificity of reward prediction errors signaled by putative dopamine neurons in rat VTA depends on ventral striatum. Neuron **91**, 182–193 (2016)
8. Lau, B., Monteiro, T., Paton, J.J.: The many worlds hypothesis of dopamine prediction error: implications of a parallel circuit architecture in the basal ganglia. Curr. Opin. Neurobiol. **46**, 241–247 (2017)
9. Okon-Singer, H.: The role of attention bias to threat in anxiety: mechanisms, modulators and open questions. Curr. Opin. Behav. Sci. **19**, 26–30 (2018)
10. Payzan-LeNestour, E., Dunne, S., Bossaerts, P., ODoherty, J.P.: The neural representation of unexpected uncertainty during value-based decision making. Neuron **79**, 191–201 (2013)
11. Wang, D., Chen, J., Liu, L.: How internal neurons represent the short context: an emergent perspective. Prog. Artif. Intell. **6**(1), 67–77 (2017)
12. Wang, D., Wang, J., Liu, L.: Developmental network: an internal emergent object feature learning. Neural Process. Lett. https://doi.org/10.1007/s11063-017-9734-z
13. Wang, D., Shan, H., Tian, Y., Liu, L.: Emergent face orientation recognition with internal neurons of the developmental network. Prog. Artif. Intell. https://doi.org/10.1007/s13748-018-0150-z
14. Wang, D., Duan, Y., Weng, J.: Motivated optimal developmental learning for sequential tasks without using rigid time discounts. IEEE Trans. Neural Netw. Learn. Syst. https://doi.org/10.1109/TNNLS.2017.2762720
15. Daly, J., Brown, J., Weng, J.: Neuromorphic motivated systems. In: Proceedings of International Joint Conference on Neural Networks, San Jose, California, USA, 31 July–5 August 2011, pp. 2917–2924 (2011)

Automated Analysis of Chest Radiographs for Cystic Fibrosis Scoring

Zhaowei Huang[1(✉)], Chen Ding[2], Lei Zhang[2], Min-Zhao Lee[1], Yang Song[1], Hiran Selvadurai[3], Dagan Feng[1], Yanning Zhang[2], and Weidong Cai[1]

[1] Biomedical and Multimedia Information Technology (BMIT) Research Group, School of IT, University of Sydney, Sydney, Australia
zhua7630@uni.sydney.edu.au

[2] Shaanxi Key Lab of Speech and Image Information Processing (SAIIP), School of Computer Science, Northwestern Polytechnical University, Xi'an, China

[3] Children's Hospital at Westmead, Sydney Children's Hospitals Network, Sydney, Australia

Abstract. We present a framework to analyze chest radiographs for cystic fibrosis using machine learning methods. We compare the representational power of deep learning features with traditional texture features. Specifically, we respectively employ VGG-16 based deep learning features, Tamura and Gabor filter based textural features to represent the cystic fibrosis images. We demonstrate that VGG-16 features perform best, with a maximum agreement of 82%. In addition, due to limited dimensionality, Tamura features for unsegmented images achieve no more than 50% agreement; however, after segmentation, the accuracy of Tamura can reach 78%. In combination with using the deep learning features, we also compare back propagation neural network and sparse coding classifiers to the typical SVM classifier with polynomial kernel function. The result shows that neural network and sparse coding classifiers outperform SVM in most cases. Only with insufficient training samples does SVM demonstrate higher accuracy.

Keywords: Cystic fibrosis · Computer-assisted score · Deep learning feature VGG-16

1 Introduction

Cystic fibrosis (CF) is a widespread life-threatening genetic disease, which affects up to 1 in 3000 people born in the highest-risk regions [1]. For example, Cystic Fibrosis Community Care[1] shows that 1 in 25 people in Australia are carrying defective CF genes and nearly 90 babies each year are born with this disease. The disease causes considerable morbidity and mortality, affecting multiple organs and ultimately with an average life expectancy at birth of close to 38 years despite ongoing medical care [2].

[1] www.cysticfibrosis.org.au/nsw/collaborative-research-project.

J. Ren et al. (Eds.): BICS 2018, LNAI 10989, pp. 227–236, 2018.
https://doi.org/10.1007/978-3-030-00563-4_22

Cystic fibrosis causes major disease in the lungs. People with cystic fibrosis generally suffer from difficulty breathing, and frequent episodes of pneumonia. Half of patients with CF will require lung transplants. Clinicians usually assess the severity degree of cystic fibrosis by analyzing radiological images of the diseased lungs. For example, plain chest radiographs (CXRs) are often used to assess cystic fibrosis in children [3]. Shwachman-Kulczycki scoring is usually used in Australia to quantify the degree of abnormality in the lungs [4], with reference to the visible changes associated with the disease as seen on CXRs. In particular, clinicians look for signs of airflow obstruction (expanded shape of the chest cavity), bronchial and vascular thickening (linear markings), nodules and cysts, and gross regional abnormalities in lungs to give the assessment result. In this work, we mainly focus on the Shwachman-Kulczycki scoring system.

Shwachman-Kulczycki scoring classifies CXRs into five categories, which are quantified into a range from 5 to 25 with interval 5, in the order of decreasing severity. Table 1 describes the CXR findings for each score, as initially proposed by Shwachman and Kulczycki. Clinicians assign a Shwachman-Kulczycki score based on their own observations, which is a subjective determination and thus varies between different clinicians. Therefore, the development of an automatic scoring system providing clinicians with an objective measure of the CXR changes is still a challenging problem.

CF is an interstitial lung disease. The visual appearances of CF are mainly in the regional textures in the lungs. A recent study used Tamura, Gabor filter and other textural features to build a fully automated scoring of chest radiographs in cystic fibrosis and obtained 75% and 51% agreement with clinicians [5]. To the best of our knowledge, this is the best computer-assisted score for CF chest radiographs.

Recently, neural networks, represented by Convolutional Neural Network (CNN), have shown excellent learning and classifying abilities. Moreover, some studies applied CNN to medical image processing [6–9]. The deep structure of neural networks enables the extraction of much more complicated features than the traditional textural features.

The purpose of our study is to build a framework for automated scoring with various feature extraction techniques and find more appropriate feature extraction methods and suitable classifiers to improve the accuracy and stability of the system. In contrast to previous methods considering textural features with support vector machine (SVM), this study proposes to employ deep learning methods to build an experimental system with deep learning features and deep learning classifiers for CXRs.

2 Methods

In order to ensure the correctness of the result, the proposed scoring framework consists of three steps, including the preprocessing, feature extraction and classification steps. In this paper, we use pre-existing fined-tune VGG-16 and seven-fold cross-validation to build up whole system (Fig. 1).

Table 1. Shwachman-Kulczycki X-ray scoring [4]

Grading	Points	Findings
Excellent	25	Clear lung fields
Good	20	Minimal accentuation of bronchovascular markings; early emphysema
Mild	15	Mild emphysema with patchy atelectasis; increased bronchovascular markings
Moderate	10	Moderate emphysema; widespread areas of atelectasis with superimposed areas of infection; minimal bronchial ectasia
Severe	5	Extensive changes in pulmonary obstructive phenomena and infection; lobar atelectasis and bronchiectasis

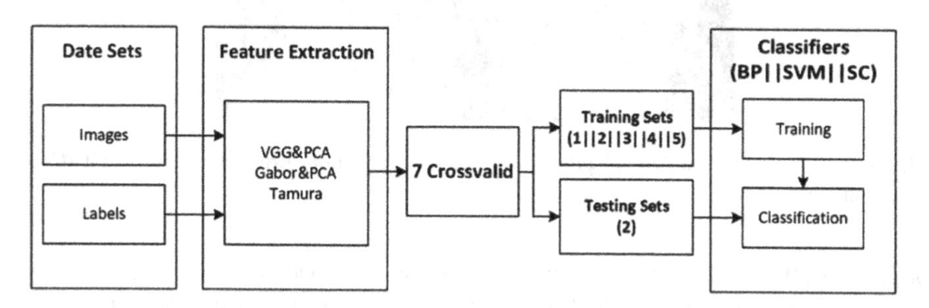

Fig. 1. The proposed scoring framework for cystic fibrosis in lungs

2.1 Acquisition of CXR Data

In this study, all experiment data come from the CXR data of 139 patients with cystic fibrosis, which are identified from an Australian pediatric cystic fibrosis registry and are aged between 2 to 16.

To evaluate the performance of scoring framework quantitatively, we consider the clinicians' reviewed results for all 139 images to be the standard score results. Out of all 139 images, clinical scoring assigned 36 images a score of 10, 56 images with a score of 15 and 47 images with a score of 20.

2.2 Preprocessing

CXR images were taken with different protocols and stored in several different formats. For each image, the preprocessing step includes edge clipping, resampling, and gray scale normalization.

In order to eliminate regions of the image outside the body, and to simplify resampling, we used the difference between the lung field and the background to get the axis-x and axis-y projection and crop out the external regions ("edge clipping"), as shown in Fig. 2. The green lines are the local maximum for left or right, and the red line is the midline.

Original CXR image dimensions ranged from 721×696 to 1131×951 pixels, with gray values between 0–30000. After edge clipping, images still contain the

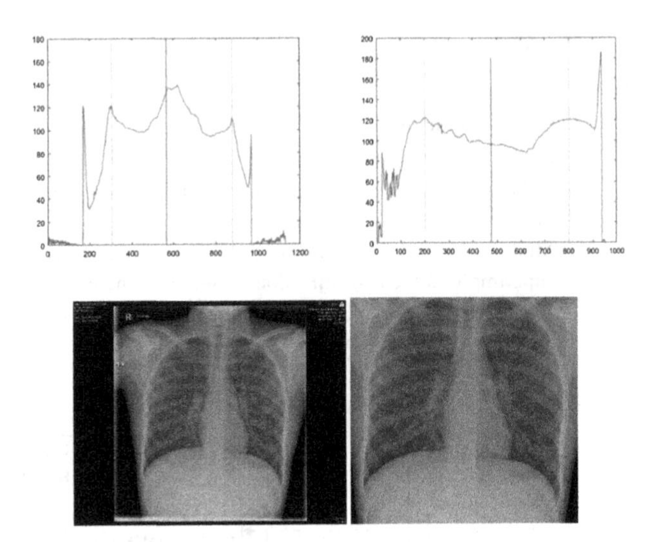

Fig. 2. Edge clipping: horizontal projection, vertical projection, original image, result (Color figure online)

original depth for later experiments. To control the standard input dimension, we resample images to a size of 512 $\times$ 512 pixels, and gray levels scaled to 0–255. To retain discriminating information, we do not apply noise reduction or enhancement. We also perform automated segmentation [5], which we evaluated using overlap as our performance measure. The result was 0.939 in [5] and we achieve 0.899. The sample of segmentation results are listed in Fig. 3.

2.3 Feature Extraction

In the feature extraction step, we investigate the comparison between deep learning features and textural features. Since in the previous study, Tamura achieved the best performance and Gabor achieved fair results [5], we decided to use Tamura and Gabor as the textural features for comparison.

The Tamura features are based on psychophysical studies of the characterizing elements that are perceived in textures by humans: Contrast, Directionality, Coarseness, Linelikeness, Regularity, and Roughness. Among these, the first three are of greater importance. Contrast measures the way in which gray levels vary in the image and to what extent their distribution is biased to black or white. Directionality considers the edge strength and the directional angle. They are computed using pixel-wise derivatives according to Prewitt's edge detector. Coarseness relates to the distances of important spatial variations of grey levels, that is, implicitly, to the size of the primitive elements forming the texture [10–12].

The Gabor filter is a linear filter that can be used for edge detection. It provides orientation selection and is biologically plausible [13]. The Gabor filter is generated by scaling and rotation from a parent wavelet so that it could extract the relevant features

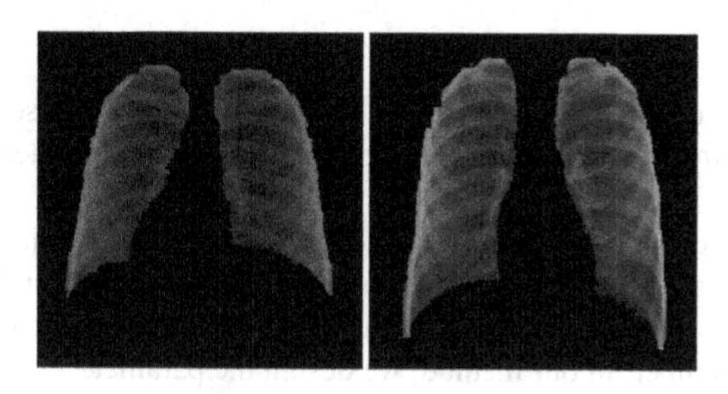

Fig. 3. Segmented results

in different scales and directions in the frequency domain. We set 6 directions and 2 scales over each image, for a total of 12 filters to be used for feature extraction.

In contrast to the hand-crafted texture features mentioned above, deep learning features can be task-driven and learned from extensive training examples. More importantly, deep learning enables the learned feature to capture more flexible and complicated structure in the data, and thus improves the task performance. Witnessing the success of deep learning feature in various computer vision tasks, we turn to leverage deep learning features to represent abnormalities in cystic fibrosis.

Due to the limited data set, we adopt pre-trained deep learning features. Without generality, we choose the VGG-16 based deep learning features. The VGG-16 based deep learning feature set is pre-trained from the ImageNet database with 16 layers of deep convolutional neural network [14, 15]. VGG-16 consists of 13 convolution layers and three fully connected layers. The VGG-16 based deep learning feature vector is the output of the last fully connected layer.

The VGG-16 network is pre-trained using an extensive collection of nature images. However, the cystic fibrosis CXR image is distributed completely differently from the nature images, which makes it difficult to depict cystic fibrosis well with the pre-trained VGG-16 feature. To address this problem, we employ the labeled cystic fibrosis images to fine-tune the pre-trained VGG-16 feature. Specifically, we modify the last fully connected layer to the size of the classification problem in cystic fibrosis. Then, we adjust the network parameters according to the classification error with backpropagation techniques. By doing this, the VGG-16 network can be adapted to fit the distribution of the cystic fibrosis images.

In this paper, we use the output of the 15th layer of the VGG-16 as a feature. This output contains 4096 nodes, so the feature has 4096 dimensions, and Gabor filter's output has 360 dimensions. To improve the computational efficiency and reduce the overfitting problem, we use the classical PCA dimensionality reduction algorithm to reduce the dimensions: the features from VGG-16 are reduced to 140-dimensions, and features from Gabor Filter were reduced to 60-dimensions.

2.4 Classifiers

We choose back propagation based neural network (BP) and Sparse Coding (SC) as classifiers and compare their performance with polynomial-kernel support vector machine (SVM).

BP is a neural network that uses error back propagation for training [16]. BP model is built up by three main element layers: input layer, hidden layer, and output layer. In hidden layer, the tunable parameters are the learning rate, number of iterations, and number of nodes number. In our method, we design the parameters as follows: learning rate: 0.0021; number of nodes in hidden layer: 850, 105 and 50; number of iterations: 10 (due to the initial parameters of the back propagation neural network.

SC [17] is an effective way of exploiting the data structure. In particular, through representing the data onto a given dictionary, SC exploits the underlying correlation among different data samples by depicting the sparsity on the representation. We set the lambda = 0.01 using the cross-validation test.

SVM is a supervised learning method that has been widely used. It uses kernel functions to avoid the increase in computational complexity caused by increased dimension [18]. Due to the limited number of samples, we choose the polynomial kernel function. The values of the training parameters C and gamma are 1.8, determined by grid search and cross-validation test.

2.5 Cross-Validation

In this step, we adopt cross-validation for validating the proposed method. Since the samples number is 139, we randomly choose one sample to copy and then add it to the dataset. The total 140 samples in the dataset can be evenly divided into seven groups. We randomly choose some groups for training and the other group for testing.

3 Experiment and Results

We conducted two experiments to check the classification effect of the deep learning features and deep learning classifiers, deep learning features (VGG-16) compared with textural features (Tamura, Gabor); and deep learning classifiers (BP and SC) compared with machine learning algorithm (SVM), and the difference between using different numbers of training sets.

3.1 Deep Learning Classification Performance Verification

From randomly assigning 140 samples into seven groups of 20, we randomly selected two groups as a test set, and four groups from the remaining five groups as a training set of five different cycles. The results can be seen in Table 2.

From the perspective of features, whether it was in the deep learning classifiers or the SVM classifier, VGG-16's classification results were significantly better than the textural features. In back propagation neural network, VGG-16 achieved a result 6% higher than Gabor and 34% higher than Tamura. In sparse coding, VGG-16 was 3%

Table 2. Comparison of classification performance

Feature	Classifier		
	BP	SC	SVM
VGG-16	0.82 ± 0.06	0.80 ± 0.05	0.79 ± 0.08
Gabor	0.76 ± 0.04	0.77 ± 0.03	0.77 ± 0.05
Tamura	0.48 ± 0.02	0.41 ± 0.04	0.42 ± 0.05

better than Gabor and 39% better than Tamura. in SVM, VGG-16 was 2% better than Gabor and 37% better than Tamura. We also noticed that the variance of the VGG-16 feature is greater than the textural features. It is possible that for deep convolution neural networks such as VGG-16, the number of training samples in this paper is too small and pre-training is limited by the effect of parameter debugging.

From the perspective of classifiers, for both the deep learning features and traditional texture features that were used, the results of all three classifiers were similar. Overall, back propagation neural network classifier was slightly better than the other two classifiers. In VGG-16, BP classifier performed 2.5% better than both sparse coding and SVM; In Tamura, BP classifier was 7% better than sparse coding and 6% better than SVM; in Gabor, BP classifier was 1.3% below than other two classifiers. We also noticed that the variance of the deep learning classifier was less than that of the SVM classifier.

The results of this paper have a significant difference with [5]. First of all, the classification performance of Tamura features is obviously smaller than that of [5], which was 0.75. Second, even if the SVM classifier is used, the Gabor feature classification (0.77) is better than that of [5] (0.51). In this paper, the parameters of all three classifiers were optimized for the feature set after combining the three features, making the SVM core and parameter configuration was more reasonable. We also added an experiment to test the segmented images, with results shown in Table 3. It is obvious that segmentation is an important preprocessing step for Tamura.

VGG-16 and neural network produce 17.1% more agreement than an independent clinician observer (0.70). Even when combining VGG-16 and SVM, the results remain 12.9% better. Comparing with [5] (Tamura and SVM, 0.75), VGG-16 and neural network produced 9.3% improvement; with VGG-16 and SVM, the results were 5.3% better.

3.2 Training Set Size Optimization

From randomly assigning 140 samples into seven groups of 20, we randomly selected two groups as a test set, and between 1 and 5 groups from the remaining five groups as training sets to determine the effect of different training samples on the classifications.

Table 4 shows the relationship between classification performance, and training set size for VGG-16 features with different classifiers. Table 5 shows the relationship between classification performance and training set size for Gabor feature with different classifiers.

Table 3. Comparison for Tamura

Feature	Classifier		
	BP	SC	SVM
Segmented	0.78 ± 0.03	0.79 ± 0.04	0.75 ± 0.02
Unsegmented	0.48 ± 0.02	0.41 ± 0.04	0.42 ± 0.05

Table 4. Training sets size optimization for VGG-16

Training sets	Feature-classifier		
	VGG-BP	VGG-SC	VGG-SVM
20	0.51 ± 0.09	0.51 ± 0.09	0.55 ± 0.05
40	0.63 ± 0.10	0.63 ± 0.07	0.64 ± 0.07
60	0.73 ± 0.11	0.71 ± 0.06	0.71 ± 0.08
80	0.82 ± 0.06	0.80 ± 0.05	0.79 ± 0.08
100	0.48 ± 0.12	0.42 ± 0	0.45 ± 0

Table 5. Training sets size optimization for Gabor

Training sets	Feature-classifier		
	Gabor-BP	Gabor-SC	Gabor-SVM
20	0.51 ± 0.09	0.56 ± 0.12	0.56 ± 0.08
40	0.59 ± 0.11	0.62 ± 0.10	0.60 ± 0.07
60	0.68 ± 0.07	0.69 ± 0.08	0.71 ± 0.03
80	0.76 ± 0.04	0.77 ± 0.03	0.77 ± 0.05
100	0.42 ± 0.04	0.26 ± 0	0.35 ± 0

The result shows that, for both VGG-16 and Gabor features, the classification accuracy of the three classifiers increased with increasing training set size at first, reaching a maximum at a training set size of 80; but decreasing significantly when training set size increased to 100. One possible reason is that the number of experimental samples is small (140), and the characteristic dimension (140) and Gabor feature dimension (60) of VGG-16 are higher, resulting in overfitting.

Table 6 shows the results for Segmented Tamura features. It appears that Tamura achieves a better result than Gabor but is still lower than VGG-16.

Table 6. Training sets size optimization for Segmented Tamura

Training sets	Feature-classifier		
	Tamura-BP	Tamura-SC	Tamura-SVM
20	0.51 ± 0.09	0.49 ± 0.10	0.50 ± 0.08
40	0.62 ± 0.12	0.65 ± 0.09	0.67 ± 0.05
60	0.77 ± 0.07	0.71 ± 0.03	0.71 ± 0.02
80	0.78 ± 0.03	0.79 ± 0.04	0.79 ± 0.02
100	0.50 ± 0.12	0.47 ± 0	0.40 ± 0

4 Conclusion

In this study, we present an automated scoring system for chest radiographs (CXRs) in cystic fibrosis. In order to improve the performance of the computer-aided scoring system, we compare the effectiveness of various features and classifiers. The VGG-16 based neural network is fine-tuned to transfer the knowledge learned from extensive nature images classification to CF severity scoring, and ultimately results in an improved VGG network (modified-VGG) suitable for CF chest radiography. A three-layer back propagation neural network and sparse coding were used for classification. Through 7-fold cross validation training and test sample ratio optimization, a satisfactory score was obtained, and the best classification accuracy rate was up to 0.82. We have demonstrated that the CF chest radiograph scoring based on deep convolution neural network can obtain better accuracy than with normal textural features, with better agreement than independent clinician observer in some cases.

In the future, further experiments can be conducted on the following three aspects. First, the number of samples used in this paper is limited. We can increase the number of experimental samples to carry out more detailed and in-depth study to improve the accuracy and stability of the score. Second, we could go deeper by using ResNet-152, or investigate with mixture deep learning classifiers, and transfer learning methods [19–21]. Last, we can further investigate new finds in other medical applications [22–24].

References

1. Ratjen, F., Döring, G.: Cystic fibrosis. In: Lancet, vol. 361, pp. 681–689 (2003)
2. Yankaskas, J.R., Marshall, B.C., Sufian, B., Simon, R.H., Rodman, D.: Cystic fibrosis adult care: consensus conference report. Chest **125**(1 Suppl), 1S–39S (2004)
3. Cleveland, R.H., Zurakowski, D., Slattery, D.M., Colin, A.A.: Chest radiographs for outcome assessment in cystic fibrosis. Proc. Am. Thorac. Soc. **4**, 302–305 (2007)
4. Shwachman, H., Kulczycki, L.L.: Long-term study of one hundred five patients with cystic fibrosis. AMA J. Dis. Child. **96**, 6–15 (1958)
5. Lee, M.Z., Cai, W., Song, Y., Selvadurai, H., Feng, D.D.: Fully automated scoring of chest radiographs in cystic fibrosis. In: 2013 35th Annual International Conference of the IEEE Engineering in Medicine and Biology Society (EMBC), Osaka, pp. 3965–3968 (2013)
6. Li, Q., Cai, W., Wang, X., Zhou, Y., Feng, D.D., Chen, M.: Medical image classification with convolutional neural network. In: 13th International Conference on Control Automation Robotics & Vision (ICARCV), Singapore, pp. 844–848 (2014)
7. Tajbakhsh, N., Shin, J.Y., Gurudu, S.R., et al.: Convolutional neural networks for medical image analysis: full training or fine tuning? IEEE Trans. Med. Image **35**(5), 1299–1312 (2016)
8. Song, Y., Li, Q., Huang, H., Feng, D., Chen, M., Cai, W.: Low dimensional representation of fisher vectors for microscopy image classification. IEEE Trans. Med. Imaging **36**(8), 1636–1649 (2017)
9. Orlando, J.I., Prokofyeva, E., Fresno, M.D., et al.: Convolutional neural network transfer for automated glaucoma identification. https://doi.org/10.1117/12.2255740 (2017)
10. Tamura, H., Mori, S., Yamawaki, T.: Textural features corresponding to visual perception. In: IEEE Transactions on Systems, Man, and Cybernetics, SMC-8, pp. 460–472 (1978)

11. Niblack, C.W., et al.: The QBIC project: querying images by content using color, texture, and shape. In: Proceedings of SPIE, Storage and Retrieval for Image and Video Databases, vol. 1908, San Jose, pp. 173–187 (1993)
12. Castelli, V., Bergman, L.D.: Image Databases: Search and Retrieval of Digital Imagery. Wiley, New York (2002)
13. Fogel, I., Sagi, D.: Gabor filters as texture discriminator. Biol. Cybern. **61**, 103–113 (1989)
14. Deng, J., Dong, W., Socher, R., Li, L.J., Li, K., Li, F.: ImageNet: a large-scale hierarchical image database. In: IEEE Conference on Computer Vision and Pattern Recognition, Miami, FL, pp. 248–255 (2009)
15. Simonyan, K., Zisserman, A.: Very deep convolutional networks for large-scale image recognition. In: Proceedings of the International Conference on Learning Representations http://arxiv.org/abs/1409.1556 (2014)
16. Ding, C., Xia, Y., Li, Y.: Supervised segmentation of vasculature in retinal images using neural networks. In: International Conference on Orange Technologies, Xian, pp. 49–52 (2014). https://doi.org/10.1109/icot.2014.6954694
17. Schölkopf, B., Platt, J., Hofmann, T.: Sparse representation for signal classification. In: 19th Proceedings of the 2006 Conference on Advances in Neural Information Processing Systems, edn. 1, pp. 609–616. MIT Press (2007)
18. Cortes, C., Vapnik, V.: Support-vector networks. Mach. Learn. **20**, 273–297 (1995)
19. Noor, S.S.M., et al.: Hyperspectral image enhancement and mixture deep-learning classification of corneal epithelium injuries. Sensors **17**(11), 2644 (2017)
20. Ren, J.: ANN vs. SVM: which one performs better in classification of MCCs in mammogram imaging. Knowl. Based Syst. **26**, 144–153 (2012)
21. Wang, X., et al.: ChestX-ray8: hospital-scale chest X-ray database and benchmarks on weakly-supervised classification and localization of common thorax diseases. In: CVPR, pp. 3462–3471 (2017)
22. Zabalza, J., et al.: Novel segmented stacked autoencoder for effective dimensionality reduction and feature extraction in hyperspectral imaging. Neurocomputing **185**, 1–10 (2016)
23. Wang, Z., et al.: A deep-learning based feature hybrid framework for spatiotemporal saliency detection inside videos. Neurocomputing **287**, 68–83 (2018)
24. Noor, S.S.M., et al.: The properties of the cornea based on hyperspectral imaging: optical biomedical engineering perspective. In: Systems, Signals and Image Processing, IWSSIP (2016)

Mismatching Elimination Algorithm in SIFT Based on Function Fitting

Xiaoni Zhong(✉), Yunhong Li, and Jie Ren

Xi'an Polytechnic University, Xi'an 710048, China
1549003771@qq.com

Abstract. In order to solve the problems such as time consuming and mismatching in the experiment of eliminating SIFT mismatch points in RANSAC algorithm, proposed Mismatching Elimination Algorithm in SIFT Based on Function Fitting; Firstly, we use SIFT algorithm to direct the matching of the image and the matching image, using iterative least squares fitting method to construct function model for the key points of matched Image; secondly, fit the function model with the key points of matching image features; Finally, the errors of the two algorithms are calculated, when the error is greater than the set threshold, verify that the point is a mismatch point, and it is eliminated. The experimental results show that using Mismatching Elimination Algorithm in SIFT Based on Function Fitting than RANSAC algorithm in time to save the 2 s on average, the correct matching rate is increased by 11.75%, and more correct matching points can be reserved.

Keywords: Image matching · Function fitting · Iterative least square method Mismatching Elimination

1 Foreword

Image matching is a key technology in image processing, Its task is to find the correspondence between feature points in two or more images in the same scene; The goal is to get similar regions in two images and identify points of the same name by matching them [1, 2]. Image matching has been extended to many industries, and its development has been greatly improved, and has been widely and practically applied in many fields. For example, image stitching and fusion [3–5], target recognition and tracking [6–8], photogrammetric remote sensing [9, 10], image retrieval [11, 12] etc.; In recent years, many image matching algorithms have appeared, especially the scale invariant feature transform (SIFT) algorithm as well as a variety of SIFT improved algorithms, SIFT algorithm, scaling invariant feature transformation algorithm, published by David Lowe [13] in 1999, based on points of interest in some parts of the object, regardless of the size or rotation of the image. Cheng [14] and so on, proposed the image matching method based on improved SIFT algorithm, the research and improvement of images with different resolution and different scales can improve the accuracy and efficiency of image matching; Hou [15] proposed an image matching algorithm based on local features. For each sample point in the image, the local coordinates of the relative feature point were established in turn, and the corresponding

J. Ren et al. (Eds.): BICS 2018, LNAI 10989, pp. 237–247, 2018.
https://doi.org/10.1007/978-3-030-00563-4_23

relationship between the sample point and the feature point was found. In this way, the rotation invariance can be satisfied and the error caused by the main direction estimation can be avoided at the same time; Tian [16] proposes a cylindrical image matching algorithm based on curve fitting, which increases the number of matching points near the edge of cylindrical image after eliminating mismatch, and improves the accuracy of cylindrical image matching. However, no matter what kind of image matching algorithm is adopted, due to some unavoidable external factors such as illumination, imaging angle, geometric deformation, etc., there are always mismatch points in the result of image matching. Therefore, in the image matching technology, in order to obtain the high accuracy matching effect, it is very important to eliminate the mismatch points of the matched image.

At present, there are a lot of researches on the algorithm of eliminating mismatch points. The common method is to use random sampling consistency, (RANSAC) [17], eliminate the mismatched points of the matched image, the model parameters are random used in RANSAC algorithm when eliminating mismatch points. It is mainly composed of random selected sample points, so the calculated model parameters can not reflect the characteristic information of more experimental points, and it is difficult to distinguish the correct matching points and mismatch points. Although some mismatch points can be eliminated, but at the same time, a large number of correct matching points are eliminated, which reduces the matching accuracy [18–20]. In order to solve this problem, this paper proposes Mismatching Elimination Algorithm in SIFT Based on Function Fitting. The function model of the image to be matched is determined by iterative least square method, and then the error between the matching point and the model to be matched is determined to determine whether the point is a mismatched point, and the detected mismatch point is eliminated. Experimental results show that Mismatching Elimination Algorithm in SIFT Based on Function Fitting is more robust than RANSAC algorithm.

2 SIFT Matching

When matching the SIFT, the two images are connected with color lines. In order to make the matching effect more clear and reduce the error caused by the color image, it is necessary to convert the color image into gray image before matching. Firstly, the original color image is transformed into gray image, and then the SIFT algorithm is used to coarse match the two grayscale images; The SIFT feature matching consists of the following two stages.

2.1 SIFT Feature Generation

The feature vectors of scale scaling, rotation and brightness change are extracted from multiple images. The principle of SIFT feature generation is shown in Fig. 1.

The characteristic vector generation process is as follows: First of all, using Gao Si fuzzy (Gao Si smoothing) to construct the scale space, search all the image position on the scale space, Lindeberg and others [21, 22] have proved that Gao Si convolution kernel is the only transformation kernel to realize scale transformation, and is the only

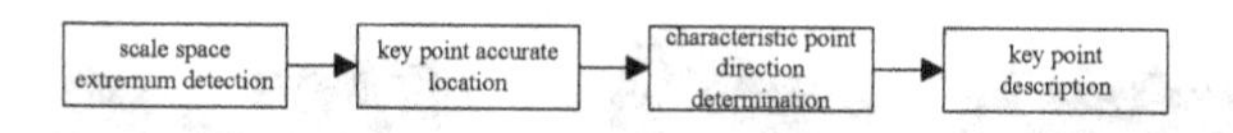

Fig. 1. SIFT feature generation principle diagram

linear kernel. We can obtain the scale and rotate invariant interest point by Gao Si differential function; Then the subpixel interpolation method is used to obtain the continuous spatial extremum (maximum value point) by discrete spatial point interpolation, and the relative interpolation center is obtained, when the offset is greater than the specified value, the interpolation center is offset, the point is deleted, and the current key point is changed, at the same time, the new position needs to be redetermined, and the subpixel interpolation method is used to repeat the interpolation in the new position until the offset is less than the specified value; then, the local features of the image are used to assign the corresponding reference direction to each key point; Using Lowe [23] suggestion, the window size of 4 * 4 in the key point scale space is selected, the gradient information in 8 directions is calculated, and the 128-dimensional feature descriptor is generated.

2.2 Matching of SIFT Feature Vectors

When the SIFT feature vectors of two images are generated, the Euclidean distance of the key point feature vectors is used to determine the similarity of the key points in the two images. Select a key point in the image to be matched, find the nearest two key points in the matching image by traversing, calculate the ratio of the second close distance to the nearest distance, and make a judgment, when the ratio is less than the set threshold value, this pair of key points can be confirmed as a pair of matching points.

Experiment 1: The image material is a close-range image, image size: The first picture of Fig. 2 is 377 pixels * 384 pixels, and is an image to be matched; The second picture of Fig. 2 is 377 pixels * 360 pixels, which is a matching image; The third picture of Fig. 2 is the SIFT direct matching result diagram.

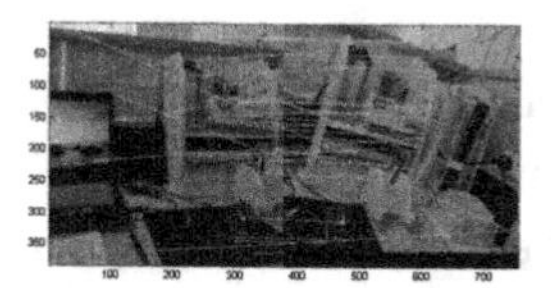

Fig. 2. SIFT matching results

Experiment 2: Image material is medical image, image size: The first picture of Fig. 3 is 640 pixels * 572 pixels, which is the image to be matched; The second picture of Fig. 3 is 762 pixels * 745 pixels, which is a matching image, the rotation is added to the original base, and the rotation angle is 20°; The third picture of Fig. 3 is the SIFT direct matching result diagram.

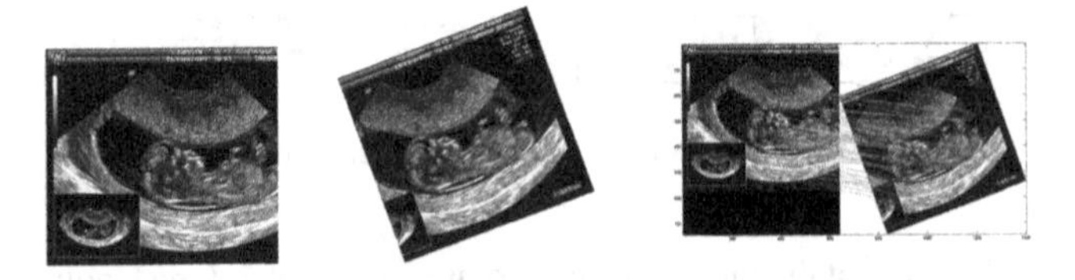

Fig. 3. SIFT matching results

3 Function Fitting Eliminating Mismatch

3.1 Fundamental

The basic principle of function fitting is to select the appropriate function model according to the size and geometric deformation of the original image, and to construct the function model according to the feature key points of the image to be matched after matching (selecting polynomial function model), then the coefficients of the function model are solved by the iterative least square fitting method, and the exact function model of the image to be matched is obtained, the error between the key points of the matching image and the function model of the image to be matched is calculated, and the relationship between the error and the threshold value is compared; When the error of a matching point is greater than the set threshold, the matching point is considered to be a mismatched point, which needs to be eliminated. The error-matching point removal flowchart is shown in Fig. 4.

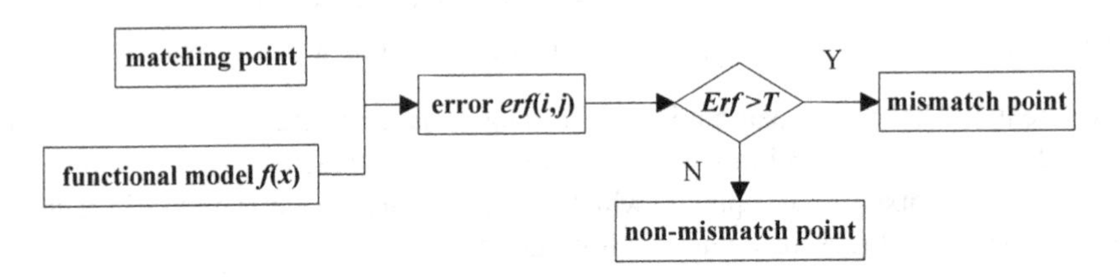

Fig. 4. Flow chart of mismatching point elimination

3.2 Mismatch Elimination

Solving the Coefficients of the Image Model to be Matched

The selected image function model to be matched is cubic polynomial, using iterative least Squares fitting method to solve the coefficients of the function Model, the least square method is called the least mean method, and its basic idea is to match the best function of the data by minimizing the square of the error, and to make all the data to the maximum degree to satisfy the function parameter as far as possible. Set up $f(x)$ as a function that needs to be fitted, x_i for actual data, the minimum model of square sum of deviation between fitting data and actual data is the best function model of the image to be matched. Expressed as follows (1):

$$\min \sum_{i=1}^{n} [f(x_i) - x_i]^2 \tag{1}$$

n is the number of characteristic keys of the image to be matched.

The function model is obtained by least square fitting of all the points to be matched by iterative least squares fitting method, the error between each point to be matched and the function model is calculated, and the two points to be matched with the largest error are eliminated; then, the least square method is used to solve the function model again for the remaining points to be matched, the error is calculated, the two points to be matched with the largest error are eliminated, and the above process is repeated in turn. Until the error between all the points to be matched and the function model is less than the set threshold; A more accurate functional model of the image to be matched can be obtained. The solution of the function model of the image to be matched is as follows:

Select a set of data $r_0(x), r_1(x), r_2(x), r_3(x), \quad 3 < n$, let

$$f(x) = a_0 r_0(x) + a_1 r_1(x) + a_2 r_2(x) + a_3 r_3(x) \tag{2}$$

Of which, a_0, a_1, a_2, a_3 to be determined.

Minimize the sum of distance squared between the feature points (x_i, y_i) to be matched and the curve $y = f(x)$, remember

$$\begin{aligned} J(a_0, a_1, a_2, a_3) &= \sum_{i=1}^{n} [\, f(x_i) - y_i]^2 \\ &= \sum_{i=1}^{n} \left[\sum_{k=0}^{3} a_k r_k(x_i) - y_i \right]^2 \end{aligned} \tag{3}$$

Pair derivative $J(a_0, a_1, a_2, a_3)$, let $\frac{\partial J}{\partial a_k} = 0$, reach

$$\begin{cases} \sum\limits_{i=1}^{n} r_0(x_i) \left[\sum\limits_{k=0}^{3} a_k r_k(x_i) - y_i \right] = 0 \\ \sum\limits_{i=1}^{n} r_1(x_i) \left[\sum\limits_{k=0}^{3} a_k r_k(x_i) - y_i \right] = 0 \\ \sum\limits_{i=1}^{n} r_2(x_i) \left[\sum\limits_{k=0}^{3} a_k r_k(x_i) - y_i \right] = 0 \\ \sum\limits_{i=1}^{n} r_3(x_i) \left[\sum\limits_{k=0}^{3} a_k r_k(x_i) - y_i \right] = 0 \end{cases} \tag{4}$$

To ensure that the coefficient $\{a_0, a_1, a_2, a_3\}$ has a unique solution, $\{r_0(x), r_1(x), r_2(x), r_3(x)\}$ regardless of linearity, desirable $\{r_0(x), r_1(x), r_2(x), r_3(x)\} = \{1, x, x^2, x^3\}$. The coefficients of the function model can be obtained by substituting the matching points in the formula of (4).

To calculate the error between the point to be matched and the function model, the threshold value is 0.002, and the two points to be matched with the largest error are eliminated, the remaining $n-2$ points to be matched are fitted again by least square fitting to solve the function model, and the error between the function model and the obtained function model is calculated; Repeat the above operation until the error between the point to be matched and the function model is less than 0.002. Finally, the function model of the image to be matched is obtained. After many iterations, the final coefficients of the image function model to be matched are expressed as follows (5):

$$\begin{cases} a_0 = \dfrac{n\left(\sum_{i=1}^{n} x_i^2 \sum_{i=1}^{n} x_i^2 y_i + \sum_{i=1}^{n} x_i^3 \sum_{i=1}^{n} x_i^3 y_i\right)}{\sum_{i=1}^{n} x_i y_i \cdot \sum_{i=1}^{n} x_i^2 y_i \cdot \sum_{i=1}^{n} x_i^3 y_i} \\ a_1 = \dfrac{\sum_{i=1}^{n} x_i \left(\sum_{i=1}^{n} x_i^2 \sum_{i=1}^{n} x_i^2 y_i + \sum_{i=1}^{n} x_i^3 \sum_{i=1}^{n} x_i^3 y_i\right)}{n \sum_{i=1}^{n} x_i^2 y_i \cdot \sum_{i=1}^{n} x_i^3 y_i} \\ a_2 = \dfrac{\sum_{i=1}^{n} x_i^2 \left(\sum_{i=1}^{n} x_i \sum_{i=1}^{n} x_i y_i + \sum_{i=1}^{n} x_i^3 \sum_{i=1}^{n} x_i^3 y_i\right)}{n \sum_{i=1}^{n} x_i y_i \cdot \sum_{i=1}^{n} x_i^3 y_i} \\ a_3 = \dfrac{\sum_{i=1}^{n} x_i^3 \left(\sum_{i=1}^{n} x_i \sum_{i=1}^{n} x_i y_i + \sum_{i=1}^{n} x_i^2 \sum_{i=1}^{n} x_i^2 y_i\right)}{n \sum_{i=1}^{n} x_i y_i \cdot \sum_{i=1}^{n} x_i^2 y_i} \end{cases} \quad (5)$$

Rejecting Mismatching Point

Calculate the errors of all matching points and function models, taking the average, the error threshold $T = 0.0032$, to compare the relationship between the error and the threshold value, the hard threshold shrinkage method is used formula (6). The corresponding error of each point is calculated, and the relationship between the error and the set threshold value is judged. When the error of the point is less than the set threshold value, the matching point is determined as the correct matching point and the point is retained; when the error is greater than a set threshold, the matching point is considered to be a mismatch point.

$$erf = \begin{cases} erf(i,j) & |erf(i,j)| \geq T \\ 0 & |erf(i,j)| < T \end{cases} \quad (6)$$

Elimination Curve Fitting Result Chart

Close-range image fitting: According to the functional model of the right image feature points and the left image feature points in SIFT matching picture 2, three order polynomial fitting is applied; The first picture of Fig. 5 is a fitting map after rough matching of SIFT, and the second picture of Fig. 5 is a fitting map after elimination of mismatched points.

Medical image fitting: According to the functional model of the right image feature points and the left image feature points in SIFT matching picture 3, three order polynomial fitting is applied; The first picture of Fig. 6 is a fitting map after SIFT rough

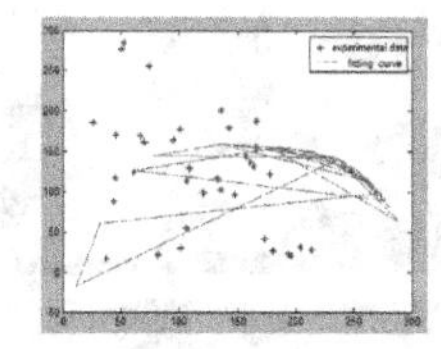 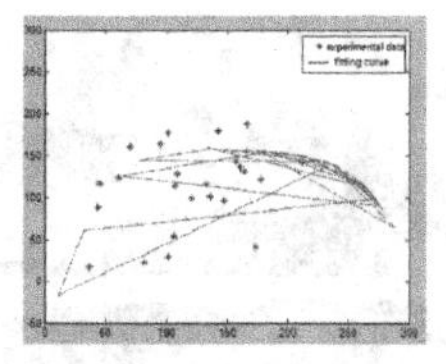

Fig. 5. Eliminate the false matching points before and after the fitting results

matching, and the second picture of Fig. 6 is a fitting map after the elimination of mismatched points.

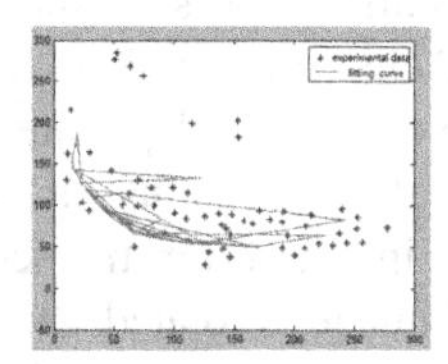 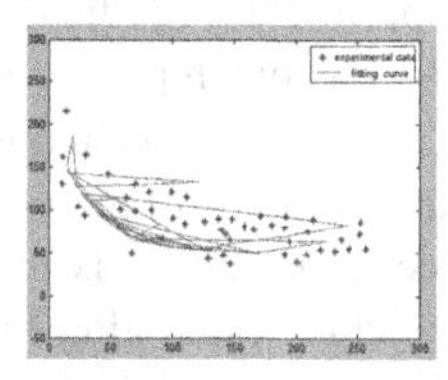

Fig. 6. Eliminate the false matching points before and after the fitting results

Based on the fitting results of close-range image Fig. 5 and medical image Fig. 6, it is concluded that the remote key points have been eliminated, and the matching points in figure are basically gathered around the curve, the results show that the function fitting algorithm can effectively eliminate the mismatch points in the matching process, and the elimination effect is significant and the accuracy is high.

4 Experimental Results and Analysis

In order to verify the validity of the algorithm, the function fitting algorithm is compared with the RANSAC algorithm. The error threshold of the function fitting algorithm is 0.0032. Analysis of the results of experiment 1 close-range images: The first picture of Fig. 7 is the result of eliminating mismatch points by RANSAC algorithm, and the result of function fitting algorithm culling mismatch points is shown in second picture of Fig. 7.

Based on the function fitting algorithm, the mismatch points can be eliminated effectively, and the correct matching points can be retained. Compared with the elimination result of RANSAC algorithm, it can be seen in second picture of Fig. 7 that the function fitting algorithm can be processed, the matching points reserved in books and other parts are more dense, from the experimental results of the third picture of Fig. 7, we can see that a matching point of the left image is on the right side of the pen, while the right image has no corresponding matching point in the same position, and a key point appears in the left position of the pen. In fourth picture of Fig. 7, there is a key point in the left position of the left and right image pen, and two pairs of correct matching points are also found in the nearby position of the pen.

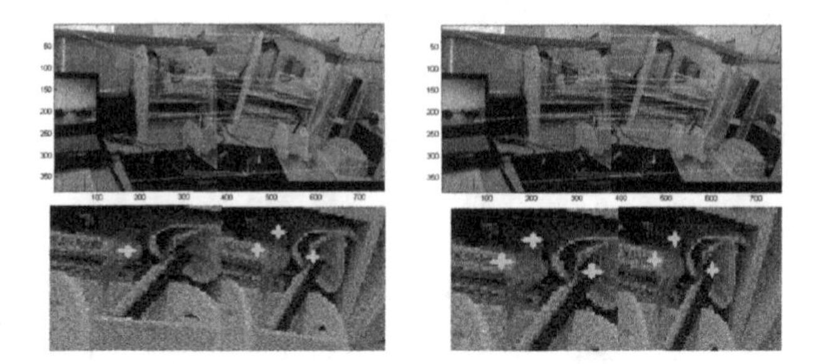

Fig. 7. Experimental processing results 1

Analysis of Experiment 2 Medical Imaging Results: The first picture of Fig. 8 is the result of eliminating mismatch points by RANSAC algorithm, and the result of function fitting algorithm culling mismatch points is shown in second picture of Fig. 8. The experimental images come from medical images, and the matching images are obtained by rotating processing on the basis of the original image. From the second picture of Fig. 8, it can be concluded that after the matching image is rotated, the function fitting algorithm can still carry on the effective experiment to it; It can be seen that the function fitting algorithm has a strong advantage in extracting feature points.

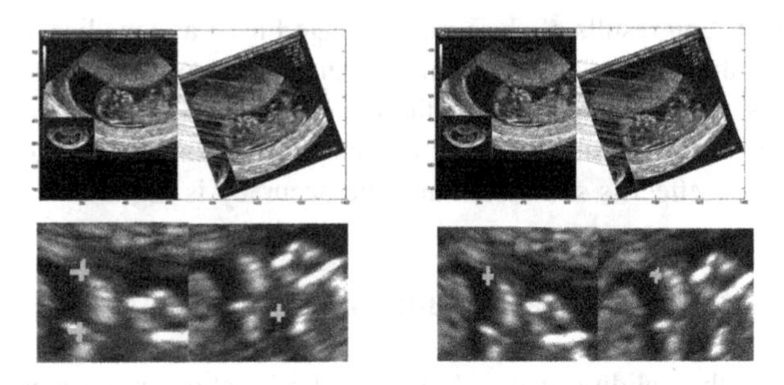

Fig. 8. Experimental processing results 2

The third picture of Fig. 8 is an enlarged map of RANSAC algorithm to eliminate mismatched points, and the fourth picture of Fig. 8 is a magnification map of error-matching points eliminated by function fitting algorithm, By contrast, in third picture of Fig. 8, the left image has a feature point in the black bend, the lower right part and the middle area, and the same position in the right image has no corresponding point, and a feature point appears in the rest of the image. Then the two feature points are mismatched points and the RANSAC algorithm does not eliminate the error points; compared with the fourth picture of Fig. 8, there is no matching point in the black bending and the lower right part of the left image. It can be seen that the function fitting algorithm has eliminated the point and has a pair of correct matching points in the same position of the left and right images.

The function fitting algorithm can accurately eliminate the mismatch points and retain more correct matching points, so the accuracy is greatly improved. The results of the two algorithms are shown in Tables 1 and 2.

Table 1. Comparison of culling results in experiment 1.

Parameter	Matching point logarithm	Correct matching point logarithm	Error matching point logarithm	Correct match Rate/%	Time/s
SIFT	37	28	9	75.68	
RANSAC	18	15	3	83.33	3
Function fitting	25	24	1	96	1

Table 2. Comparison of culling results in experiment 2.

Parameter	Matching point logarithm	Correct matching point logarithm	Error matching point logarithm	Correct match Rate/%	Time/s
SIFT	60	50	10	83.33	
RANSAC	42	38	4	90.48	4
Function fitting	50	49	1	98	2

From SIFT matching, In experiment 1, 9 pairs of mismatch points appeared in 37 key points. After eliminating the mismatch points, the RANSAC algorithm found 15 pairs of 18 pairs of correct matching. Compared with RANSAC algorithm, the function fitting algorithm found 24 pairs of 25 pairs of correct matching; The matching efficiency is increased from 75.68% to 96% compared with SIFT direct matching, Compared with RANSAC algorithm, the matching efficiency is improved by 15.2% in the experiment of rejecting mismatching; Experimental results show that the number of feature points extracted by image matching is 60, and the average time is 4 s, After matching, the number of feature points extracted by RANSAC algorithm is 42, the average time is 2 s, and the number of feature points extracted by function fitting algorithm is 8 more than that of RANSAC algorithm, and 49 pairs of 50 pairs of correct matching are found. Compared with RANSAC, the matching efficiency is improved from 90.48% to 98 s, and the time is increased by 2 s.

5 Conclusion

In order to gain more accurate matching effect, after the direct matching of SIFT algorithm, we use iterative least square method to construct the function model to avoid the model error caused by large error points, the function fitting algorithm is used to eliminate the mismatch points. Compared with the RANSAC algorithm, the function fitting algorithm can not only accurately identify and eliminate the mismatch points, but also not lose the correct matching points, so it can find more key points and more matching points. Moreover, the distribution is dense, the accuracy is greatly improved, and the matching efficiency is increased at the same time. The matching efficiency of the two groups was increased by 15.2% and 8.31% respectively, and the processing time was saved by 2 s on average.

References

1. Liu, X., Lei, Z.: Multi-modal image matching based on local frequency information. EURASIP J. Adv. Signal Process. **3**(1), 1–11 (2013)
2. Ren, G., Peng, D., Gu, Y.: Fast image stitching algorithm based on cylindrical surface mapping. Appl. Res. Comput. **34**(11), 1–8 (2017)
3. Li, G., Chen, Z.: Research status and prospect of visual tracking technology. Appl. Res. Comput. **27**(8), 2814–2821 (2017)
4. Tan, S., Liu, Y., Li, Y.: Kernel correlation filtering target tracking algorithm based on Gauss scale space. Comput. Eng. Appl. **53**(1), 29–33, +141 (2017)
5. Liu, L., Sun, K., Xu, H.: A fast matching algorithm for large scale images based on Hash characteristics. Comput. Eng. Appl. **53**(17), 202–206, +211 (2017)
6. Wang, Q., Wang, B.: Local matching algorithm for image shopping search. Comput. Eng. Appl. **53**(6), 246–251 (2017)
7. Wu, X., He, Y., Yang, L.: Two valued image retrieval based on improved shape context feature. Opt. Precis. Eng. **23**(1), 302–309 (2015)
8. Yong, C., Lei, S.: Improved SIFT image registration algorithm on characteristic statistical distributions and consistency constraint. Opt.-Int. J. Light. Electron Opt. **127**(2), 900–911 (2016)
9. Zhang, J., Zhang, H., Luo, Y.: An improved image registration method based on Harris corner detection. Laser Infrared **47**(2), 230–233 (2017)
10. Chen, Y., Sun, Q., Xu, H.: Remote sensing image matching method based on SURF algorithm and RANSAC algorithm. Comput. Sci. Explor. **6**(9), 822–828 (2012)
11. Yu, B., Guo, L., Zhao, T.: An adaptive hybridz bilateral filtering algorithm for infrared images. Infrared Laser Eng. **41**(11), 3102–3107 (2012)
12. Di, N., Li, G., Wei, Y.: Terminal guidance chart using SIFT image matching technology. Infrared Laser Eng. **40**(8), 1589–1593 (2011)
13. Yan, Y.: Cognitive fusion of thermal and visible imagery for effective detection and tracking of pedestrians in videos. Cogn. Comput. **10**(1), 94–104 (2018)
14. Cheng, D., Li, Y., Yu, R.: Image matching method based on improved SIFT algorithm. Comput. Simul. **28**(7), 285–289 (2011)
15. Hou, X.: The Research of Image Matching Technology Based on Local Feature Detection. Xidian University, Xi'an (2014)
16. Tian, J.: Cylindrical image matching algorithm based on curve fitting. Electron Meas. Technol. **39**(2), 61–63, +68 (2016)
17. Wang, Z.: A deep-learning based feature hybrid framework for spatiotemporal saliency detection inside videos. Neurocomputing **287**, 68–83 (2018)
18. Han, J.: Object detection in optical remote sensing images based on weakly supervised learning and high-level feature learning. IEEE Trans. Geosci. Remote Sens. **53**(6), 3325–3337 (2015)

19. Ren, J.: Real-time modeling of 3-D soccer ball trajectories from multiple fixed cameras. IEEE Trans. Circuits Syst. Video Technol. **18**(3), 350–362 (2008)
20. Zhou, Y.: Hierarchical visual perception and two-dimensional compressive sensing for effective content-based color image retrieval. Cogn. Comput. **8**(5), 877–889 (2016)
21. Yan, Y.: Unsupervised image saliency detection with Gestalt-laws guided optimization and visual attention based refinement. Pattern Recogn. **79**, 65–78 (2018)
22. Yan, Y.: Adaptive fusion of color and spatial features for noise-robust retrieval of colored logo and trademark images. Multidimens. Syst. Signal Process. **27**(4), 945–968 (2016)
23. Chai, Y.: Hierarchical and multi-featured fusion for effective gait recognition under variable scenarios. Pattern Anal. Appl. **19**(4), 905–917 (2016)

Novel Group Variable Selection for Salient Skull Region Selection and Sex Determination

Olasimbo Ayodeji Arigbabu[1], Iman Yi Liao[1(✉)], Nurliza Abdullah[2], and Mohamad Helmee Mohamad Noor[3]

[1] School of Computer Science, University of Nottingham Malaysia Campus, Semenyih, Malaysia
khyx5oaa@exmail.nottingham.edu.my, iman.liao@nottingham.edu.my
[2] Department of Forensic Medicine, Hospital Kuala Lumpur, Kuala Lumpur, Malaysia
azilrun@gmail.com
[3] Radiology Department, Hospital Kuala Lumpur, Kuala Lumpur, Malaysia
emeemd71@gmail.com

Abstract. Sex determination in forensic analysis involves individual examination of different sites of the skull and combination of these sites to understand their impact on the estimation results. Conventionally, forensic experts perform a stepwise combination of several skull region assessment parameters to determine the most important regions with regard to the sex estimation results. This paper introduces a novel group variable selection algorithm: Graph Laplacian Based Group Lasso with split augmented Lagrangian shrinkage algorithm (SALSA) to automatically learn from data by structuring the data into a set of disjointed groups and imposing a number of group sparsity to discover the salient groups which influence the sex determination results. In order to attain this, the skull is partitioned into smaller regions (local regions) using fuzzy c-means (FCM), which are further arranged into clusters as structured groups. Then, we implement the SALSA based group lasso algorithm to impose sparsity on the groups. Our experiments are conducted on 100 skull samples obtained from hospital kuala lumpur (HKL) and the best estimation result obtained is 84.5%.

Keywords: Forensic anthropology · Skull sex estimation
Skull partition · Group variable selection · Clustering

1 Introduction

Forensic anthropologists study sex as a biological characteristic, which is useful for ascertaining the identity of an unknown individual. Some of the skeletal parts of the body that are usually examined for sex determination are pelvis, skull, mandible, and long arm bone [16]. It has been convincingly demonstrated

J. Ren et al. (Eds.): BICS 2018, LNAI 10989, pp. 248–259, 2018.
https://doi.org/10.1007/978-3-030-00563-4_24

in the literature that skull is the second best predictor of sex because of its longer decomposition period when compared to every other skeletal part [18]. Skull sex determination can be achieved using morphological assessment and morphometric analysis [12]. Morphological assessment is concerned with analysis of anatomical regions of the skull using semantic or verbal terms, while Morphometric analysis is based on annotation of anatomical landmarks, and linear or geometric measurement of the distance between the landmarks. Eventually a discriminant function analysis (DFA) model is constructed to determine the sex of the skull. In depth understanding of the factors influencing the determination of sex from human skull, remains one of the focal points of forensic analysis. Whether the choice of approach for sex determination is morphological assessment or morphometric analysis, forensic experts are not only interested in obtaining the final estimation outcome but to understand which parts of the skull contribute toward the eventual estimation results. A commonly utilized approach in conventional forensic examination is to conduct stepwise combination of every possible skull region estimation parameters [7]. However, while this common approach has yielded favorable results, the computation could rapidly become exhaustive as the number of traits increases. Therefore, in this paper we introduce a novel method for discovering the important skull regions directly from data using the idea of graph based group variable selection.

The proposed approach centers around utilizing the shape property of the local regions of the skull to construct graphs with discriminating shape information and then use the graph as a form of regularization to displace less important skull regions. There are some aspects of computer vision focusing on discovering salient parts of objects in images and videos [15,20,23,24]. The remainder of the paper is organized as follows. Section 2 presents the related works on skull sex estimation and region selection. Section 3 describes the proposed method in detail composing of pseudo-anatomical method for skull partitioning into smaller regions and mathematical formulation of group LASSO and the proposed optimized graph based group LASSO, with the implementation details. In Sect. 4, we present the experiments on sex estimation and skull region selection. Finally, we conclude our work in Sect. 5.

2 Related Works

In the literature, some of the prominently assessed anatomical regions of the skull include the nuchal crest, mastoid process, supraorbital margin, glabella, mental eminence, and etc. Walker [19] examined 5 anatomical sites underunivariate and multivariate statistical analysis with linear and quadratic discrimanant analysis. It was discovered that under independent test, the glabella and mastoid process are more sexually dimorphic than other traits with prediction of 70%, with the nuchal crest showing the least dimorphic characteristics (57%). Though the best result was achieved using the 5 traits with a prediction of 90%, a combination of only 3 traits produced a prediction of 88%. Graw et al. [8] investigated how the shape of supraorbital margin can be assessed for sex determination and their result gave indication that this anatomical region can be independently used for sex prediction with an accuracy of 70%. Likewise, Pinto et al. [13] studied this anatomical region based on computer-aided method by using 2D wavelet transform on 3D reconstruction of the scanned supra-orbital impression to study its shape variation. Williams and Rogers [21] studied 21 sexually dimorphic traits for sex determination. Each trait was assessed and ranked according to its inter-observer error and accuracy when predicting male and female samples. The authors discovered that the size of the mastoid and supraorbital ridge, rugosity of the zygomatic extension, size and shape of the nasal aperture, and gonial anglewere ranked higher than the remaining characteristics, with $\leq$10% inter-observer error and accuracy $\geq$80%. Langley et al. [11] recently reported the analysis of the 5 traits of Walker and one additional trait (zygomatic extension) using decision tree model, with the aim eliminating the traits with high possibility of low inter-observer consistency. Conforming with previous standards, the authors adopted the standardized 5 ordinal-scale built by Buikstra and Ubelaker [4], which has been commonly reported in the literature. In order to make prediction, the ratings from these traits were used to construct classification and regression trees (CART). Their study showed that the decision tree which derived the combination of 3 traits (glabella, zygomatic extension, and mastoid process) provided the most accurate result with a prediction rate of 93.5%, whereas the nuchal crest, supraorbital margin, and mental eminence were not chosen by the tree model.

3 Materials and Methods

3.1 Experimental Dataset

We used post-mortem computed tomography (PMCT) scan slices of 100 subjects obtained from Hospital Kuala Lumpur (HKL), which has been compiled between 01-05-2012 and 30-09-2012. Legal consent for the use of the dataset was obtained prior to commencing this research. The data is composed of 54 male and 46 female subjects between the ages of 5 to 85 years, from south east asia. The scanning device is Toshiba CT scanner with scanning settings of 1.0 slice thickness, and 0.8 slice interval. The original data contains the full body of the subjects, which average between 2000 to 4000 slices per-subject. The resolution of the data is $512 \times 512 \times$ No of slices. For the purpose of this work, the slices belonging to the head region have been chosen for each subject. Therefore, the resulting input samples have resolutions between $512 \times 512 \times 261$ and $512 \times 512 \times 400$, depending on size of the skull of each subject.

3.2 Skull Preprocessing

Each skull sample undergo a two stage data preprocessing. In the first stage, the 3D volumetric data from Sect. 3.1 is filtered using 3D noise filtering technique based on 3D discrete cosine transform based penalized least square regression

(DCT-PLS) on equally spaced high dimension data, introduced by Garcia [6]. The second stage of preprocessing involves noisy background object removal by learning an online sequential linear systems with gaussian mixture model (GMM) sample initialization. The details of these approaches have been described in [2].

3.3 Skull Region Partition

The pre-processed skull is partitioned into local geometric regions, which is referred to as pseudo-anatomical regions in this paper due to its similarity to the standard forensic cranial sites in [4]. In order to partition each skull into similar local regions, we first select a model skull, which is used to register every other target skull in the dataset using coherent point drift (CPD). Assuming the model skull has M vertices and a target skull has T vertices, the registration correspondence between the two samples obtained via CPD is represented as C. Thus the indices relation between the samples can be established as $T = M\{C\}$. To geometrically partition the skulls into pseudo-anatomical regions, we consider clustering the model skull into N clusters using fuzzy c-means (FCM) and transferring the labels of the indices of the clustered model skull to every target skull by taking advantage of the established registration correspondence C. Hence, consider clustering model skull M in N clusters $\{M_1, \ldots, M_N\}$, the labels of the indices of the clusters of M can be propagated (transferred) to the target skull using relation $T_N = M_N \cap T$, where T_N is the propagated cluster in the target skull. Example of partitioned skulls are depicted in Fig. 1a. Once the skull has been partitioned into local regions, we extract 3D local shape representations. Some existing techniques for object representation describe the shape, texture and intensity information [22,25,26] but we used mesh local binary pattern (MeshLBP), local depth scale invariant feature transform (LD-SIFT), and spin image which have been used in our previous work [2]. The local features are computed on each vertex point in the local regions, which are then aggregated into compact representation following the illustration in [2], as shown in Fig. 1b.

3.4 Novel Graph Laplacian Based Group Lasso with Split Augmented Lagrangian Shrinkage Algorithm (SALSA)

3.4.1 Graph Based Group LASSO

The proposed algorithm lies under the concept of group variable selection and one of the most well known technique in this domain is the group LASSO. As such, this novel algorithm improves on the formulation of group LASSO and incorporates optimization solver to improve the performance of the algorithm. Fundamentally, the standard group LASSO can be formulated as [5]

$$\min_{w \in \mathbb{R}^p} \left(||y - \sum_{k=1}^{K} X_k w_k||_2^2 + \lambda \sum_{k=1}^{K} \sqrt{p_k} ||w_k||_2 \right) \tag{1}$$

where $\sqrt{p_k}$ is the term that accounts for the size of the group and $||\cdot||$ is the euclidean norm (non-squared). This is with the assumption that our p predictors

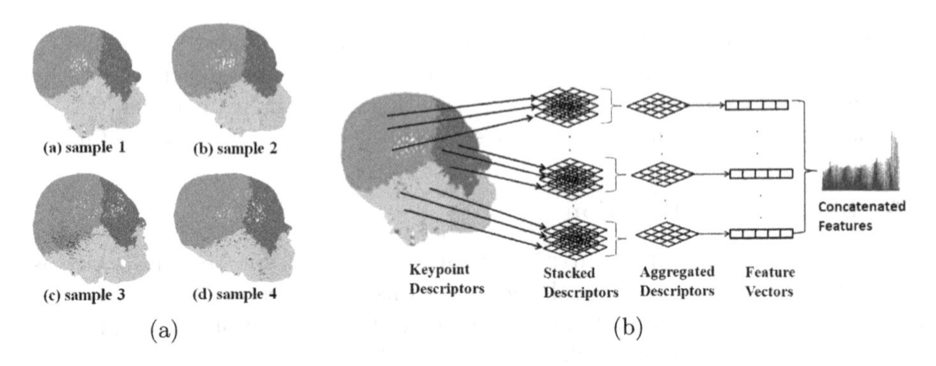

Fig. 1. (a) Illustration of pseudo-anatomical partitioning with FCM after registration using CPD; (b) An example of local shape representation from pseudo-anatomical partitioned skull.

can be divided into K groups, and p_k denotes the number of predictors from group k. Thus, the corresponding data matrix and coefficients for that group will be X_k and w_k respectively. This form of group variable selection is able to work effectively under well structured data setting. In an event where the structure of the input needs to be preserved, the learned coefficients will become unreliable and inefficiently derived. Therefore, we incorporate another term to cater for the structure of the data as a form of graph [9]. The essence of constructing a graph for each region is to represent each region with its own shape property (such that the shape property of each region are different) as opposed to the single general graph for the entire regions on the skull. The new formulation is expressed as:

$$\min_{w \in \mathbb{R}^p} \left(||y - \sum_{k=1}^{K} \varphi(X_k) w_k||_2^2 + \lambda \sum_{k=1}^{K} \sqrt{p_k} ||w_k||_2 \right) \tag{2}$$

where $\varphi(X_k)$ is now the manifold defined on each group data. The graph is an undirected graph $G = (V, E)$ where V are the vertex set and E are the edge set, and the unnormalized graph Laplacian of G is defined as $L = D - W$, where D is a diagonal matrix with diagonal entries $D_{ii} = \sum_{j=1}^{l+u} = W_{ij}$ and W is a symmetric matrix which is sparse with W_{ij} containing the weight value of the edge joining vertices i and j and 0 when there no such edge (see [9]). The eigenvalue decomposition of the manifold embedding can be expressed as [9]:

$$\varphi(X_k) = XA \tag{3}$$

where A consists of the eigenvectors $\mathbf{a}$ of a generalized eigenvalue decomposition problem $XLX^T\mathbf{a} = \lambda X^T DX\mathbf{a}$ [9]. The values of A are different for each region. To make the formation discriminant, we compute:

$$\boldsymbol{D}_k = \left\{ \sum_{k \neq l}^{K} \varphi(X_k) \right\}^{-1} * \varphi(X_k) \tag{4}$$

Thus, the objective is reformulated as:

$$\min_{w \in \mathbb{R}^p} \left(||y - \sum_{k=1}^{K} \boldsymbol{D}_k w_k||_2^2 + \lambda \sum_{k=1}^{K} \sqrt{p_k}||w_k||_2 \right) \tag{5}$$

The main idea behind the proposed approach is to be able to transform the original data into a new space where the shape property between different skull regions is well maximized. Thus, we obtain the shape property of each region through graph construction. Then we make the graph discriminant by dividing a particular graph with the remaining of the graphs formed on the skull. In other words, we map training data into the basis space to obtain their new representations $\varphi(X_k)$ based on the concept of manifold learning (the kNN is used to generate the graph and in particular we used the heat kernel to generate the k nearest neighbor). Then by generating $\varphi(X_k)$, we compute the discriminant induction graph $\mathbf{D}_k$ using Eqs. 4 and 5.

3.4.2 Graph Based Group LASSO with SALSA Optimization

SALSA is an optimizer which has been used for image inverse problem such as restoration and reconstruction. Of recent, its application to general least square minimization was demonstrated in [17]. In this research, SALSA is initially used to solve the inner least square problem of each group (i.e. the least square which target the coefficients (column space) instead of the groups) before applying the euclidean norm to determine the penalization of the groups. Assuming the minimization problem of the inner least square of each group k can be expressed as [17]:

$$\arg\min_{w_k} \frac{1}{2}||y - \mathbf{D}_k w_k||_2^2 + \ ||\lambda \odot w_k||_1 \tag{6}$$

where the $\lambda \odot w_k$ is the element-wise multiplication of the equal size vectors, λ and w_k. When all elements are equal then it simply becomes w_k. However, in the idea of variable splitting, it is commonplace to create a new term which allows for non-uniform regularization. Thus we can express the variable splitting problem as:

$$\arg\min_{w_k, u_k} \frac{1}{2}||y - \mathbf{D}_k w_k||_2^2 + \ ||\lambda \odot u_k||_1 \qquad \text{such that} \ \ u_k - w_k = 0 \tag{7}$$

The problem in Eq. 7 can be expressed in the augmented lagrangian form. We briefly recall that for a constrained optimization problem:

$$\arg\min_{z_k} E(z) \qquad \text{subject to} \ \ \mathbf{D}_k \mathrm{z} - \mathrm{y} = 0 \tag{8}$$

where $\mathrm{b} \in \mathrm{R}^P$ and $\mathbf{D} \in \mathrm{R}^{\mathrm{pxn}}$ meaning that we have p linear equality constraints. The augmented Lagrangian of the problem can be expressed as:

$$L(z, \lambda, \mu) = E(z) + \lambda^T(\mathrm{y} - \mathbf{D}_k z) + \frac{\mu}{2}||\mathbf{D}_k z - \mathrm{y}||_2^2 \tag{9}$$

where $\lambda \in R^P$ is a vector of Lagrange multipliers and $\mu \geq 0$ is penalty parameter. The Augmented Langragian Method simply iterates between minimizing $L(z, \lambda, \mu)$ with respect to z, keeping λ fixed, and updating λ until some convergence criterion is satisfied.

The problem in Eq. 7 can be expressed in the form of Eq. 8 by setting:

$$z_1 = w_k,\ z_2 = u_k,\ z = \begin{bmatrix} z_1 \\ z_2 \end{bmatrix} \tag{10}$$

$$E(z) = \frac{1}{2}||y - \mathbf{D}_k z_1||_2^2 + ||\lambda \odot z_2||_1 \tag{11}$$

Iterative augmented lagragian method (ALM), also known as method of multipliers (MM) [10,14] can be applied as [1]

Algorithm 1. ALM/MM

Initialize $\mu > 0, d_k$

repeat

$$w_k, u_k = \arg\min \frac{1}{2}||y - \mathbf{D}_k z_1||_2^2 + ||\lambda \odot u_k||_1 + \frac{\mu}{2}||u_k - w_k - d_k||_2^2 \tag{12}$$

$$d_k \leftarrow d_k - (u_k - w_k) \tag{13}$$

end when stopping criteria is reached

where d_k is the estimate coefficient which should be initialized prior to iterative process. In this work, d_k is initialized to zero. In order to attain the global minimum, the alternating direction method of multipliers (ADMM) [3] is used to alternate between w_k and u_k, which can be expressed in Algorithm 2.

Algorithm 2. ADMM

Initialize $\mu > 0, d_k$

repeat

$$u_k \leftarrow \arg\min_{u_k} ||\lambda \odot u_k||_1 + \frac{\mu}{2}||u_k - w_k - d_k||_2^2 \tag{14}$$

$$w_k \leftarrow \arg\min_{w_k} \frac{1}{2}||y - \mathbf{D}_k z_1||_2^2 + \frac{\mu}{2}||u_k - w_k - d_k||_2^2 \tag{15}$$

$$d_k \leftarrow d_k - (u_k - w_k) \tag{16}$$

end when stopping criteria is reached

Once the coefficient estimate d_k has been obtained, they are used as the vector for each group and the group sparsity is determined if $\frac{w_k}{||w_k||} = 0$ otherwise the group is not sparse because $\frac{w_k}{||w_k||} < 1$ but not 0. The overall algorithm is illustrated in Algorithm 3.

Algorithm 3. Graph based Group LASSO with SALSA

Input: $X = [X_1, X_2, \ldots, X_k]$
\\ *Make a graph for each group offline*
Construct graph L on each X_k
Compute $\varphi(X_k)$ following Eq. 3
\\ *obtain the discriminant graph*
Compute discriminant graph $\mathbf{D}_k$ using Eq. 4
\\ *run SALSA to solve Group LASSO on constructed graph*
Initialize $w_k = w_0$
for each k **do**
  Apply Eq. 7
  Apply **Algorithm 1** and **Algorithm 2**
  Set $w_k = d_k$
  Compute $\frac{w_k}{||w_k||}$
  $W = [w_1, w_2, \ldots, w_k]$
end for
Output: W

4 Experiment

The aim of the experiments in this section is two-fold: (1) To discover the salient regions of the skull through group regularization. (2) To predict the sex of each skull from the learned regions. To achieve the first aim of this section, it is necessary to determine the group coefficients that are representative of the salient or important skull regions. Hence, we first selected 50 random samples of male and female classes to model the group LASSO algorithm. From the samples, we perform over-representation of the skull, which simply means that the skull is repeatedly partitioned into regions from coarse to fine scale, as shown in Fig. 2.

As such, we consider partitioning the skull into: $\{5, 11, 15, 17, 19, 21\}$ scales forming a total of 88 regions. Then local shape representation is computed and aggregated from each region, and the regional features are concatenated forming 88 regional feature groups. On these regional groups, the group variable selection algorithm is implemented. For a particular value of regularization (we tried $2^{-15}: 2^{10}$) the sparse groups can be obtained following the mathematical derivation in Sect. 3.4.1 for group LASSO, and solution in Sect. 3.4.2 for graph based group LASSO with SALSA optimization. The resulting coefficient from the learned groups are placed in: $\hat{W} = \hat{w}_1, \hat{w}_2, \ldots \hat{w}_k$.

Thus, for every new skull sample x_i, the sparse local regions can simply be discovered by computing the hadamard (element-wise) product as:

$$\hat{w}^* = x_i \odot \hat{W} \tag{17}$$

where $\hat{w}^*$ denotes the sparse index of the new sample. Once the non-sparse regions have been selected, the local features are aggregated and concatenated

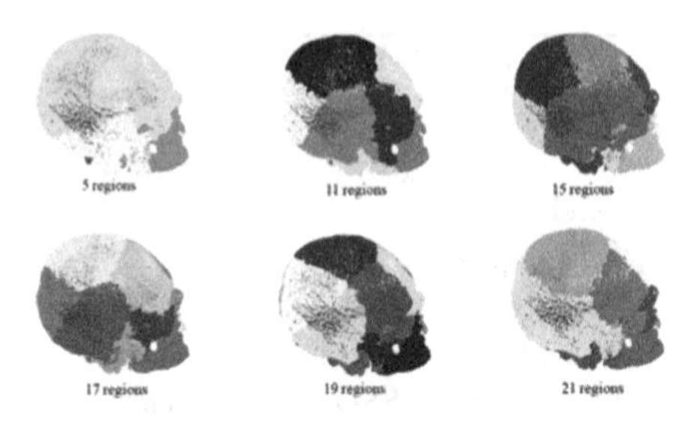

Fig. 2. Illustration of pseudo-anatomical partitioning with FCM

for each sample as described in Sect. 3.3. To achieve the second aim of this section (sex determination), kernel principal component analysis (KPCA) is utilized to reduce the dimension of the features and support vector machine (SVM) with linear kernel is used for classification. The experiments are conducted on 100 HKL samples, where 60 random samples are chosen for training and 40 samples for testing. The results obtained in our experiments are illustrated in Fig. 3b and Table 1.

Table 1. Result of skull region selection based on group variable selection

Local descriptor	Group LASSO	Graph based group LASSO with SALSA
LD-SIFT	79.3	83.8
Spin image	83.75	84.5
MeshLBP	81	83.3

From the experiments, it can be observed that embedding shape property through graph construction preserves the locality of the partitioned regions, which guides the structure the concatenated features from the resulting regions, and in turn improves the sex determination results. To understand this observation, we visually examine the illustration in Fig. 3b. It can be noticed that the discovered regions align toward similar geometrical locality of skull, while it can be noticed that the region are inconsistently selected in Fig. 3a due to the absence of graph. Another observation is that the selected regions indicate that the full skull is not needed for sex identification. Looking at majority of the partitions, it can be noticed that the back area is commonly displaced, showing that sexually dimorphic features are concentrated on the frontal part of the skull. This further confirms the findings in forensic morphological assessment [19] that the nuchal crest (back part) have the least sexually dimorphic information.

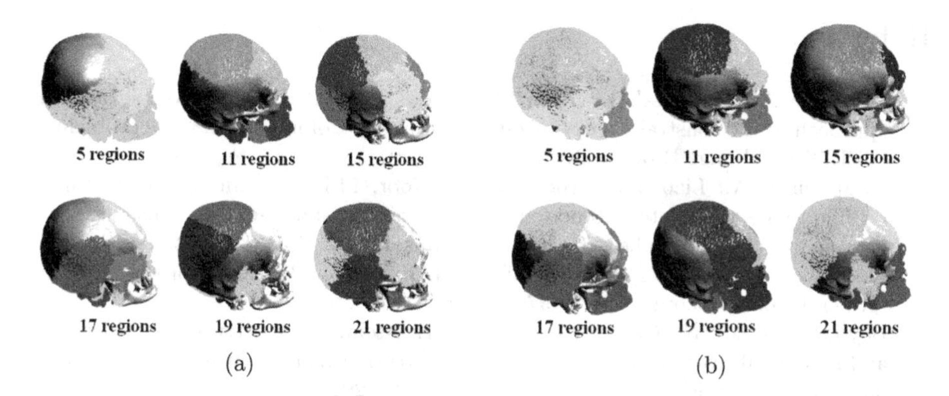

Fig. 3. (a) Illustration of group patch selection from the clustered regions by group LASSO; (b) Illustration of group patch selection from the clustered regions by graph based group LASSO with SALSA optimization.

5 Conclusion

This paper has presented a novel group variable selection algorithm for automatically discovering the salient regions of the skull toward sex determination. This is an improvement on the conventional forensic examinations methods which make use of stepwise combination of estimation parameters to understand the impact of anatomical skull sites on sex estimation performance. The proposed algorithm embed shape property of the skull in the group variable selection objective function, by using the concept of graph construction and group regularization. Then, we consider the problem as an optimization problem that is solved using both augmented Lagrangian and variable splitting in an iterative algorithm which provides a more flexible way of handling the problem. The results attained are intuitive from visual examination and better than standard group LASSO algorithm. In future works, we will examine the performance of other variants of group LASSO to obtain more results which could lead to further analysis.

Acknowledgement. This research is sponsored by the eScienceFund grant 01-02-12-SF0288, Ministry of Science, Technology, and Innovation (MOSTI), Malaysia. The project has received full ethical approval from the Medical Research & Ethics Committee (MREC), Ministry of Health, Malaysia (ref: NMRR-14-1623-18717) and from the University of Nottingham Malaysia Campus (ref: IYL170414). Iman Yi Liao would like to thank the National Institute of Forensic Medicine (NIFM), Hospital Kuala Lumpur, for providing the PMCT data, and is grateful to Dr. Ahmad Hafizam Hasmi (NIFM) and Ms. Khoo Lay See (NIFM) for their assistance in coordinating the data preparation.

References

1. Afonso, M.V., Bioucas-Dias, J.M., Figueiredo, M.A.: An augmented Lagrangian approach to the constrained optimization formulation of imaging inverse problems. IEEE Trans. Image Process. **20**(3), 681–695 (2011)
2. Arigbabu, O.A., Liao, I.Y., Abdullah, N., Noor, M.H.M.: Can computer vision techniques be applied to automated forensic examinations? A study on sex identification from human skulls using head CT scans. In: Lai, S.-H., Lepetit, V., Nishino, K., Sato, Y. (eds.) ACCV 2016. LNCS, vol. 10114, pp. 342–359. Springer, Cham (2017). https://doi.org/10.1007/978-3-319-54190-7_21
3. Boyd, S., Parikh, N., Chu, E., Peleato, B., Eckstein, J.: Distributed optimization and statistical learning via the alternating direction method of multipliers Foundations and Trends®. Mach. Learn. **3**(1), 1–122 (2011)
4. Buikstra, J.E., Ubelaker., D. H.: Standards for data collection from human skeletal remains. In: Proceedings of a Seminar at the Field Museum of Natural History, Arkansas Archaeology Research Series, vol. 44 (1994)
5. Friedman, J., Hastie, T., Tibshirani, R.: A note on the group lasso and a sparse group lasso. arXiv:1001.0736 [math, stat], p. 8 (2010)
6. Garcia, D.: Robust smoothing of gridded data in one and higher dimensions with missing values. Comput. Stat. Data Anal. **54**(4), 1167–1178 (2010)
7. Garvin, H., Klales, A.: A validation study of the Langley et al. (2017) decision tree model for sex estimation. J. Forensic Sci. **63**, 1243–1251 (2017)
8. Graw, M., Czarnetzki, A., Haffner, H.T.: The form of the supraorbital margin as a criterion in identification of sex from the skull: investigations based on modern human skulls. Am. J. Phys. Anthropol. **108**, 91–96 (1999)
9. He, X., Niyogi, P.: Locality preserving projections. In: Neural Information Processing Systems, vol. 16, p. 153 (2004)
10. Hestenes, M.R.: Multiplier and gradient methods. J. Optim. Theory Appl. **4**(5), 303–320 (1969)
11. Langley, N.R., Dudzik, B., Cloutier, A.: A decision tree for nonmetric sex assessment from the skull. J. Forensic Sci. **61**(3), 743–751 (2017)
12. Luo, L., Chang, L., Liu, R., Duan, F.: Morphological investigations of skulls for sex determination based on sparse principal component analysis. In: Sun, Z., Shan, S., Yang, G., Zhou, J., Wang, Y., Yin, Y.L. (eds.) CCBR 2013. LNCS, vol. 8232, pp. 449–456. Springer, Cham (2013). https://doi.org/10.1007/978-3-319-02961-0_56
13. Pinto, S.C.D., Urbanová, P., Cesar, R.M.: Two-dimensional wavelet analysis of supraorbital margins of the human skull for characterizing sexual dimorphism. IEEE Trans. Inf. Forensics Secur. **11**(7), 1542–1548 (2016)
14. Powell, M.J.: A method for non-linear constraints in minimization problems. In: UKAEA (1969)
15. Ren, J., Jiang, J., Wang, D., Ipson, S.S.: Fusion of intensity and inter-component chromatic difference for effective and robust colour edge detection. IET Image Process. **4**, 294–301 (2010)
16. Scheuer, L.: Application of osteology to forensic medicine. Clin. Anat. **15**(4), 297–312 (2002)
17. Selesnick, I.: L1-norm penalized least squares with SALSA. Connexions (2014). http://cnx.org/content/m48933/
18. Spradley, M.K., Jantz, R.L.: Sex estimation in forensic anthropology: skull versus postcranial elements. J. Forensic Sci. **56**(2), 289–296 (2011)

19. Walker, P.L.: Sexing skulls using discriminant function analysis of visually assessed traits. Am. J. Phys. Anthropol. **136**(1), 39–50 (2008)
20. Wang, Z., Ren, J., Zhang, D., Sun, M., Jiang, J.: A deep-learning based feature hybrid framework for spatiotemporal saliency detection inside videos. Neurocomputing **287**, 68–83 (2018)
21. Williams, B.A., Rogers, T.L.: Evaluating the accuracy and precision of cranial morphological traits for sex determination. J. Forensic Sci. **51**(4), 729–735 (2006)
22. Yan, Y., Ren, J., Li, Y., Windmill, J., Ijomah, W.: Fusion of dominant colour and spatial layout features for effective image retrieval of coloured logos and trademarks. In: 2015 IEEE International Conference on Multimedia Big Data (BigMM), pp. 306–311 (2015)
23. Yan, Y., Ren, J., Sun, G., Zhao, H., Han, J., Li, X.: Unsupervised image saliency detection with Gestalt-laws guided optimization and visual attention based refinement. Pattern Recognit. **79**, 65–78 (2018)
24. Yan, Y., Ren, J., Zhao, H., Sun, G., Wang, Z., Zheng, J.: Cognitive fusion of thermal and visible imagery for effective detection and tracking of pedestrians in videos. Cogn. Comput. **10**, 94–104 (2018)
25. Zheng, J., Liu, Y., Ren, J., Zhu, T., Yan, Y., Yang, H.: Fusion of block and keypoints based approaches for effective copy-move image forgery detection. Multidimens. Syst. Signal Process. **27**, 989–1005 (2016)
26. Zhou, Y., Zeng, F.Z., Zhao, H.M., Murray, P., Ren, J.: Hierarchical visual perception and two-dimensional compressive sensing for effective content-based color image retrieval. Cogn. Comput. **8**(5), 877–889 (2016)

AFSnet: Fixation Prediction in Movie Scenes with Auxiliary Facial Saliency

Ziqi Zhou[1], Meijun Sun[1], Jinchang Ren[2], and Zheng Wang[3](✉)

[1] School of Computer Science and Technology, Tianjin University, Tianjin, China
[2] Department of Electronic and Electrical Engineering, University of Strathclyde, Glasgow, UK
[3] School of Software, Tianjin University, Tianjin, China
wzheng@tju.edu.cn

Abstract. While data-driven methods for image saliency detection has become more and more mature, video saliency detection, which has additional inter-frame motion and temporal information, still needs further exploration. Different from images, video data, in addition to rich semantic information, also contains a large number of contextual information and motion features. For different scenes, video saliency also has different tendencies. In the movie scene, the face has the strongest visual stimulus to the viewer. In view of the specific movie scene, we propose an efficient and novel video attention prediction model with auxiliary facial saliency (AFSnet) to predict human eye locations in movie scene. The proposed model takes FCN as the basic structure, and improves the prediction effect by adaptively combining facial saliency hints. We give qualitative and quantitative experiments to prove the validity of the model.

Keywords: Video saliency · Eye fixation detection
Fully convolutional neural networks

1 Introduction

According to biology and neuroscience, human beings selectively filter out useless or uninteresting information when view visual images or videos, focusing only on some local areas of interest. This is the concept of human visual attention mechanism. Features such as the color, contour, and luminance may be the initial impact factor influencing the point of focus. However, if the viewing is task-driven, the dominant factors may be high-level semantic information or motion information. In the field of computer vision, image data, as a data source containing abundant information, has been studied deeply in recent years, such as edge detection [1], image retrieval [2–4], object detection and so on. As a key step in preprocessing image data, saliency detection has been widely studied and studied. The study in this field can be roughly divided into the following categories: salient object detection [5–13] and eye fixation prediction [26–35].

Compared with the traditional manual feature extraction method, in recent years, most of the researches on saliency detection have been focused on deep learning,

J. Ren et al. (Eds.): BICS 2018, LNAI 10989, pp. 260–270, 2018.
https://doi.org/10.1007/978-3-030-00563-4_25

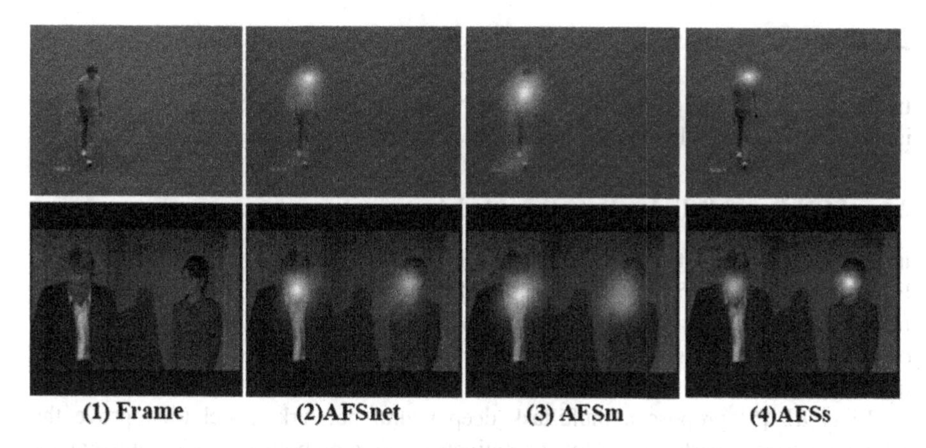

Fig. 1. Detection results from our proposed model AFSnet and two branches AFSm and AFSs.

especially fully convolutional neural networks (FCNs) [5–12, 14]. Lots of research has proved that FCNs is powerful in learning spatial information and high-level semantic information in pixel level tasks. However, most of the deformation and optimization of FCNs are done for image data, and it is obviously not enough to simply focus on the non-linear combination of high-level features extracted from the last convolutional layers for video saliency detection. As a challenging task in the field, video saliency detection not only needs to take into account the semantic information within the frame, but need to learn the sequence content of the time dimension. In particular, in the movie scene, human faces may have the strongest visual stimulus to the viewer. How to balance among multiple salient objects and find the most salient position that is suitable for the current scene is the problem that video saliency detection task needs to solve.

Based on the above discussion, the following aspects should be taken into account in the research of video saliency based on movie scene: (1) extracting intra-frame high-level semantic knowledge, (2) capturing inter-frame temporal information, (3) considering face influences and (4) simultaneously utilizing intra-frame saliency cues, inter-frame temporal information and face saliency cues to get the final saliency result. To resolve these problems, we propose an encoder-decoder framework with a sub facial saliency prediction branch (AFSnet), which effectively utilizes intra- and inter-frame information for precise eye fixation detection by adaptively selecting face saliency results. Some prediction results are shown in Fig. 1.

In general, our main contributions are summarized as follows:

(1) We propose a novel and efficient model AFSnet, which takes the current frame and the pre-saliency map from previous frame as the input, and outputs a spatial-temporal prediction that ensures the time and space consistency.
(2) We utilize the face detection model proposed in [23] and selectively adopt the facial saliency clues to help improve the precision of prediction.
(3) The proposed model achieves new state-of-the-art performance on two large-scale video salient detection datasets, including Hollywood2 [24] and UCF [25].

2 Related Works

In this section, we briefly review existing representative FCNs-based models for saliency detection. We also review video saliency detection.

2.1 FCN-Based Saliency Detection Models

In the past two years, the study of FCN in the field has attracted wide attention. Many FCNs-based models [5, 6, 12] has proposed, some other works [7–10, 14] learn ideas from FCN and take an encoding-decoding model structure to obtain more fine-grained detection results by upsampling and merging the feature maps of different convolutional layers.

Li *et al.* [5] propose a multi-task deep neural network model to improve the saliency detection performance by alternatively training on both semantic segmentation data sets and salient object detection data sets. Lu *et al.* [6] also use the idea of multitasking and adopts the simultaneous training method to enable the semantic segmentation task assisting the training of saliency models. On the basis of [6], they find that the lower the convolution layer is, the stronger the perception of edge information, while the high level convolution has a stronger sense of semantic information, so they suggested two different multi-level way [7, 8] to simultaneously incorporate coarse semantics and fine details. In order to make the edges of test results smoother, they further put forward two new optimization method: global recurrent localization network (RLN) [9] and progressive attention guided recurrent network [10]. Wang *et al.* [14] propose a skip-layer network to capture hierarchical saliency information for eye fixation detection.

2.2 Video Saliency Detection

The data that video saliency detection tasks need to process are continuous frame sequences, which is more challenging. The recently proposed video saliency model are [12, 15–20]. For instance, Wang *et al.* [12] use the encoder-decoder model, take the detection results of the previous frame, and two successive frames as input to extract the saliency results of the current frame. In their early work [16], a spatiotemporal saliency detection approach was proposed which use intra-frame boundary information and inter-frame motion information together to estimate salient regions in videos based on the gradient flow field and energy optimization. In [15], authors build a spatiotemporal saliency model, they utilize the shortest path algorithm on the graph for saliency measurement and to reasonably generate *MS* maps by using super-pixel-level motion, color histograms and global motion histograms as features. Han *et al.* [17] extract two types of bottom-up features and spatiotemporal motion energy to predict temporal visual attention and spatial visual attention based on spatiotemporal gaze density and inter-observer gaze congruency.

Our proposed approach clearly differs from the aforementioned methods. We focus on the four important problems mentioned in the introduction section and develop an efficient deep video saliency detection model with auxiliary face saliency (AFS). The main branch AFSm extracts inter-frame high-level semantic knowledge and captures inter-frame temporal information simultaneously. The sub branch AFSs computes intra-frame facial saliency. The final saliency result is gained by adaptively combining the detection results of AFSm and AFSs.

3 Ground Truth Computation

In this section, we introduce how the corresponding ground truth is obtained for a video frame being observed, which is crucial for our proposed model.

3.1 Dataset Introduction

For model training and performance evaluations, the ground truth fixation maps for raw videos are required. The data set we use has a large number of eye fixations captured by eye tracker, and we calculate the ground truth according to certain existing algorithms. As the method proposed in [17], we compute the ground truth in a similar method using two large datasets: the Hollywood2 [24] and the UCF-sports [25], which contain different sports scenes and complicated movement scenarios.

3.2 Ground Truth Computation

Similar to the method proposed in [17], the spatiotemporal saliency map is obtained through the following process. We map all the eye fixations to the specific location of the corresponding video frame and select the adaptive diffusion coefficient according to the eye pupil size of the subject for a Gaussian processing, finally, we fuse all the eye location Gaussian models and normalized to form the spatial-temporal fixation map.

To be exact, assuming that there are S subjects, for the k-*th* subject, the eye tracker recorded M^k gaze positions. Each gaze position can be denoted as $g_k^i = (x, y, f)$, $i \in [1, M^k]$, $k \in [1, S]$. For g_k^i, the corresponding Gaussian model $G_k^i(g)$ centered around g_k^i can be obtained by:

$$G_k^i(g) = \exp\left\{ -\frac{\left(g - g_k^i\right)^2}{2\left(\delta_x^2 + \delta_y^2 + \delta_f^2\right)} \right\} \tag{1}$$

The final spatial-temporal fixation map ST_{map} can be computed by combining all the Gaussian models by:

$$ST_{map}(g) = \sum_{i=1}^{M^k} \sum_{k=1}^{S} G_k^i(g) \tag{2}$$

Here, g refers to a pixel in the spatial-temporal fixation map ST_{map}, represents the probability to be fixated. The spatial standard deviation (STD) of the smoothing Gaussian kernel δ_x, δ_y is set at one degree of the visual angle point, which corresponds to about 0.01 in image width. The temporal STD δ_f of the Gaussian equals to 150 ms. In order to weaken the central bias, eye data obtained in the first 3 s is discarded.

4 AFSnet: Video Attention Detection Model

4.1 Model Structure

In a movie sequence with context information, human eye fixation will be affected by the context information and change the bottom-up view to a task driven way. For example, with the movie playing, once identifying the protagonist, the eye locations of the subject often follows the leading character, or falls around the leading role even if there are other moving objects. Based on this fact, we propose a video attention detection model AFSnet with auxiliary facial saliency prediction. The main branch AFSm performs the extraction of intra-frame high-level semantic information and the extraction of temporal information inter-frames. The sub branch AFSs captures the significant face saliency locations intra-frame. The final saliency result is obtained by integrating AFSm prediction and AFSs results. The overall architecture is illustrated in Fig. 2.

4.2 The Main Branch: AFSm

To extract spatial information from a movie sequence and to take the human memory mechanism into account to reflect the fact that the prior frame will form a relatively significant object in human brain, we design a FCN-based saliency detection model which named AFSm.

As shown in Fig. 2, AFSm takes the current frame I, saliency map $I - 1$ of previous frame as input, and outputs the spatiotemporal fixation map of frame I. The design is motivated by the fact that context information plays a key role in eye movement of subjects. That is to say when watching movies, fixations from the previous frame will influence the eye fixation in the current frame. Taking the eye fixation result of the previous frame as part of the input of the current frame detection process, it is hoped that the context information will be incorporated into the model training and thus achieve a more comprehensive and accurate eye fixation identification. The model has a clearly structure. The encoder part of the model is based on the VGG16 net by discarding the full connected layer behind, and the decoder part of the model aims to up-sample the feature maps to get the same size as the input.

Specifically, the first convolutional layer of AFSm has an input with four channels, we need to concatenate the pre-saliency $I - 1$ and the current frame I to form the input data. Hence, the first convolutional operation is modified as:

$$f(F_i, P_{i-1}; W_{F_i}, W_{P_{i-1}}, b) = W_{F_i} * F_i + W_{P_{i-1}} * P_{i-1} + b \tag{3}$$

Here, W_{Fi} corresponds to the weight of the input frame F_i, and correspondingly, $W_{Pi\text{-}1}$ corresponds to the weight of the pre-saliency map P_{i-1}, b is the bias term and f represents the activation function ReLU.

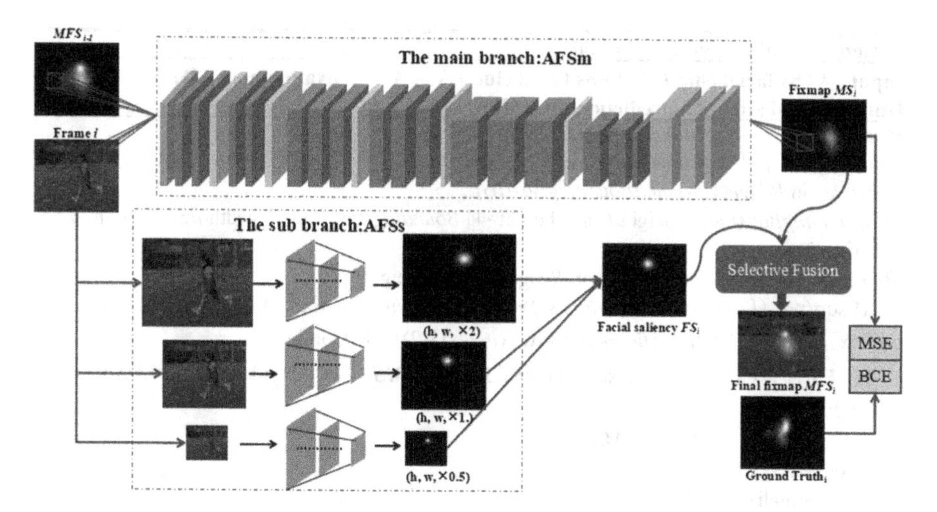

Fig. 2. Flow chart of our proposed model AFSnet. The input of AFSm is a tensor of h × w × 4.

In order to effectively train the model, we utilize binary cross entropy (BCE) and mean squared error (MSE) to calculate the content loss. The loss function is designed as:

$$L_{total}(P,G) = L_{MSE}(P,G) + L_{BCE}(P,G) = \frac{1}{2}\sum_{i=1}^{w}\sum_{j=1}^{h}\left\|G_{i,j} - P_{i,j}\right\|_2^2 + \alpha\sum_{i=1}^{w\times h}\left[G_{i,j}logP_{i,j} + \left(1 - G_{i,j}\right)log\left(1 - P_{i,j}\right)\right] \quad (4)$$

Where α is the super parameter showing the importance of the corresponding loss item.

4.3 The Sub Branch: AFSs

The AFSs model uses the tiny face detection model proposed in [23] to detect facial features. The model is based on Resnet-101, which can capture the different size of face areas according to the different scales of the input image. According to the size of the bounding box, we calculate the positions of the eyes, nose and lips, and get the simulated eye fixation map of facial saliency clue FS_i by randomly generating the noise points, then a Gaussian model is used for smoothing. Since the clue is used for auxiliary detection, the final attention detection result is obtained through adaptively integrate FS_i with MS_i from AFSm. The fusion algorithm is shown in Algorithm 1.

Fusion Algorithm : Saliency Fusion

Input: AFSs facial clue FS_i, AFSs facial clue FS_{i-1}, AFSm fixation map MS_i

Output: Final attention prediction map MFS_i

```
BoundingBox_i= list(getBoundingBoxInfo(i));
BoundingBox_{i-1}= list(getBoundingBoxInfo(i-1));
For index in Range(1, NumOfBoundingBox(i))):
  If BoundingBox_i(index).height/frame.height>4|| BoundingBox_i (index).width/frame.width>4:
      Continue;
  For x in Range(1:frame.width), y in Range(1, frame.height)
    If sqrt(pow(BoundingBox_i (index).x,2)+ pow(BoundingBox_i (index).y,2)) - sqrt(pow(BoundingBox_{i-1} (index).x,2)+ pow(BoundingBox_{i-1} (index).y,2))>10: Continue;
    If (FS_i (x,y)>avg(FS_i)+(max(FS_i)-min(FS_i))/2&& MS_i (x,y) > avg(MS_i)+ (max(MS_i)- min(MS_i))/2:
          MFS_i(x,y)= FS_i(x,y)+ MS_i(x,y);
    Else: MFS_i(x,y)= MS_i(x,y)
MFS_i = normalize(MFS_i);
End
```

5 Experimental Results

5.1 Datasets

To verify the effectiveness of the proposed model, intensive experiments were conducted on two publicly available datasets Hollywood2 [24] and UCF [25] in line with the majority of previous efforts. Using the method described in Sect. 3, we got the ground truth of all the movie clips and divided them into the training set and the testing set. The Hollywood2 dataset contains 823 train videos and 884 test videos. The UCF dataset consists of 92 short videos, we randomly select train set and test set.

5.2 Implementation Details

The element of AFSnet is implemented based on the Caffe [36] toolbox. We initialize the encoder with convolution blocks of the pre-trained VGG16, the decoder has three de-convolution layers with ReLU activation, and parameters of decoder are initialized from Gaussian distribution and iteratively updated by back propagation. The SGD learning procedure is accelerated using a NVIDIA Geforce GTX 1080ti GPU. The learning rates and momentum value are empirically set.

5.3 Metrics for Evaluations

To evaluate the performance effectively, we adopted seven widely used indicators for eye fixation detection, including the ROC, the precision recall (PR), area under the ROC (shuffled-AUC), the linear correlation coefficient (CC) [21], the similarity (SIM), the Earth mover's distance (EMD) [22], and the normalized scanpath saliency (NSS).

5.4 Performance Comparison

To validate the advantages of our proposed model, we compared it with 11 state-of-the-art models including MTDS [5], RFCN [6], GAFL [16], SUN [28], MSS [29], PQFT [30], GBVS [31], FES [32], SP [33], UHF [34], and HSSR [35]. Some specific experimental results are presented in Figs. 3, 4 and Table 1.

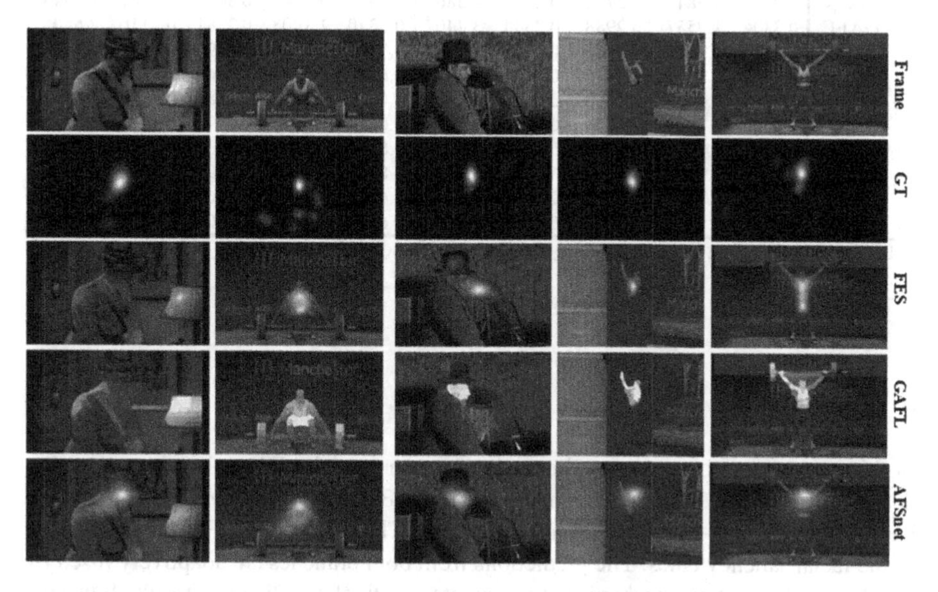

Fig. 3. Visualization of some test results from AFSnet, FES [32] and GAFL [16].

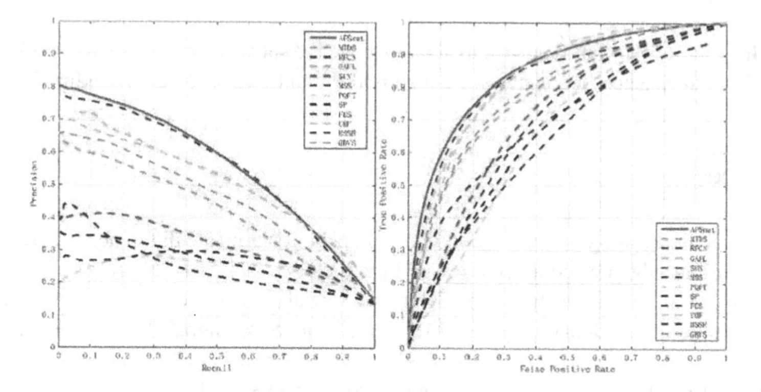

Fig. 4. Precision-Recall and ROC curves of the Hollywood2 dataset. We can clearly see that AFSnet in red line achieves an advanced performance compared with the others. (Color figure online)

Table 1. Model performance comparison for Hollywood2 and UCF

	HOLLYWOOD2					UCF-sports				
	sAUC	**NSS**	**CC**	**SIM**	**EMD↓**	**sAUC**	**NSS**	**CC**	**SIM**	**EMD**
AFSnet	0.9127	1.2825	0.3686	0.3228	3.1484	0.8990	1.2672	0.4748	0.3119	3.0411
MTDS	0.8334	1.2464	0.3561	0.2639	3.0745	0.7791	1.0525	0.3598	0.2733	3.5393
RFCN	0.7567	0.9845	0.2792	0.2297	3.5861	0.6923	-	0.3049	0.2067	3.2845
GAFL	0.8304	1.0557	0.2988	0.2344	3.4407	0.8350	1.1908	0.3881	0.3110	2.6805
SUN	0.6620	0.5071	0.1366	0.1362	4.4743	0.7183	0.7614	0.2290	0.1585	4.4155
MSS	0.6506	0.3606	0.0945	0.1414	4.1072	0.6518	0.4959	0.1749	0.1735	4.0080
PQFT	0.6718	0.4582	0.1066	0.1420	4.4180	0.6599	0.3067	0.1089	0.1514	4.7652
SP	0.6500	0.3083	0.0864	0.1363	4.5863	0.6669	0.5378	0.1979	0.1779	4.3314
FES	0.8291	1.1936	0.3807	0.2819	2.6970	0.8246	1.2875	0.4431	0.3577	2.2495
UHF	0.7907	0.9890	0.2510	0.1700	3.8098	0.8339	1.2867	0.3497	0.1962	3.6832
HSSR	0.7618	0.7275	0.1829	0.1490	4.2837	0.6983	0.6625	0.1962	0.1501	4.4801
GBVS	0.7168	0.9515	0.25587	0.1975	3.5416	0.6839	1.2035	0.3604	0.2295	3.1090

The top three results are shown in red, blue, and brown, respectively.

6 Conclusions

In this study, we propose a novel encoder-decoder model AFSnet for video attention detection in movie scenes. The main branch AFSm extracts intra-frame semantic knowledge and inter-frame temporal information. The sub branch AFSs provides intra-frame facial saliency clues. The predictions from both branches are adaptively fused by the designed selection mechanism to generate the final eye fixation result. Intensive experiments validate the superiority of our proposed model in comparison with 11 recently proposed attention detection models.

Acknowledgment. The authors wish to acknowledge the support for the research work from the National Natural Science Foundation of China under grant Nos. 61572351, and 61772360.

References

1. Ren, J., et al.: Fusion of intensity and inter-component chromatic difference for effective and robust colour edge detection. IET Image Process. **4**(4), 294–301 (2010)
2. Yan, Y., et al.: Adaptive fusion of color and spatial features for noise-robust retrieval of colored logo and trademark images. Multidimension. Syst. Signal Process. **27**(4), 945–968 (2016)
3. Yan, Y., Ren, J., et al.: Fusion of dominant colour and spatial layout features for effective image retrieval of coloured logos and trademarks. In: Multimedia Big Data (2015)
4. Zheng, J., Liu, Y., Ren, J., et al.: Fusion of block and keypoints based approaches for effective copy-move image forgery detection. Multidimension. Syst. Signal Process. **27**(4), 989–1005 (2016)
5. Li, X., Zhao, L., Wei, L., et al.: DeepSaliency: multi-task deep neural network model for salient object detection. IEEE Trans. Image Proc. **25**(8), 3919–3930 (2016)

6. Wang, L., Wang, L., Lu, H., Zhang, P., Ruan, X.: Saliency detection with recurrent fully convolutional networks. In: Leibe, B., Matas, J., Sebe, N., Welling, M. (eds.) ECCV 2016. LNCS, vol. 9908, pp. 825–841. Springer, Cham (2016). https://doi.org/10.1007/978-3-319-46493-0_50
7. Zhang, P., Wang, D., Lu, H., Wang, H., Ruan, X.: Amulet: aggregating multi-level convolutional features for salient object detection. In: IEEE International Conference on Computer Vision (2017)
8. Zhang, P., Wang, D., Lu, H., Wang, H., Yin, B.: Learning uncertain convolutional features for accurate saliency detection. In: IEEE International Conference on Computer Vision (2017)
9. Lu, H., Yang, G., Ruan, X., Borji, A.: Detect globally, refine locally: a novel approach to saliency detection. In: IEEE Computer Vision and Pattern Recognition (2018)
10. Zhang, X., Wang, T., Qi, J., Lu, H., Wang, G.: Progressive attention guided recurrent network for salient object detection. In: IEEE Computer Vision and Pattern Recognition (2018)
11. Lee, G., et al.: ELD-Net: an efficient deep learning architecture for accurate saliency detection. IEEE Transactions on Pattern Analysis and Machine Intelligence, August 2017
12. Wang, W., Shen, J.: Video salient object detection via fully convolutional networks. IEEE Trans. Image Proc. **27**(1), 38–49 (2018)
13. Yan, Y., et al.: Unsupervised image saliency detection with Gestalt-laws guided optimization and visual attention based refinement. Pattern Recogn. **79**, 65–78 (2018)
14. Wang, W., Shen, J.: Deep visual attention prediction. IEEE Trans. Image Proc. **27**(5), 2368–2378 (2018)
15. Liu, Z., Li, J.H., Ye, L.W., et al.: Saliency detection for unconstrained videos using superpixel-level graph and spatiotemporal propagation. IEEE Trans. Circuits Syst. Video Technol. **27**(12), 2527–2542 (2016)
16. Wang, W., Shen, J., et al.: Consistent video saliency using local gradient flow optimization and global refinement. IEEE Trans. Image Proc. **24**(11), 4185–4196 (2015)
17. Han, J., Sun, L., Hu, X., Han, J., Shao, L.: Spatial and temporal visual attention prediction in videos using eye movement data. Neurocomputing **145**(2014), 140–153 (2014)
18. Dehkordi, B., et al.: A learning-based visual saliency prediction model for stereoscopic 3D video (LBVS-3D). Multimed. Tools Appl. **76**(22), 23859–23890 (2017)
19. Wang, Z., et al.: A deep-learning based feature hybrid framework for spatiotemporal saliency detection inside videos. Neurocomputing **287**(2018), 68–83 (2018)
20. Yan, Y., et al.: Cognitive fusion of thermal and visible imagery for effective detection and tracking of pedestrians in videos. Cogn. Comput. **10**(1), 94–104 (2018)
21. Toet, A.: Computational versus psychophysical bottom-up image saliency: a comparative evaluation study. IEEE Trans. Patt. Anal. Mach. Intell. **33**(11), 2131–2148 (2011)
22. Ofir, P., Michael, W.: Fast and robust earth mover's distances. In: IEEE International Conferences on Computer Vision, pp. 460–467 (2009). https://doi.org/10.1109/iccv.2009.5459199
23. Hu, P., Ramanan, D.: Finding tiny faces. In: IEEE Conferences on Computer Vision and Pattern Recognition, pp. 1522–1530, July 2017
24. Mathe, S., et al.: Actions in the eye: dynamic gaze datasets and learnt saliency models for visual recognition. IEEE Trans. Pattern Anal. Mach. Intell. **37**(7), 1408–1424 (2015)
25. Soomro, K., Zamir, A.R.: Action recognition in realistic sports videos. In: Moeslund, T.B., Thomas, G., Hilton, A. (eds.) Computer Vision in Sports. ACVPR, pp. 181–208. Springer, Cham (2014). https://doi.org/10.1007/978-3-319-09396-3_9
26. Han, J., Zhang, D., Wen, S., Guo, L., Liu, T.: Two-stage learning to predict human eye fixations via SDAEs. IEEE Trans. Cybern. **46**(2), 487–498 (2016)

27. Cornia, M., Baraldi, L., Serra, G., Cucchiara, R.: Predicting human eye fixations via an LSTM-based saliency attentive model. arXiv preprint, arXiv:1611.09571 (2017)
28. Zhang, L.Y., Tong, M.H., Marks, T.K.: SUN: a bayesian framework for saliency using natural statistics. J. Vis. **8**, 32 (2008)
29. Achanta, R., Susstrunk, S.: Saliency detection using maximum symmetric surround. IEEE Trans. on Image Processing, vol. 119, no. 9, pp. 2653–2656 (2010)
30. Guo, C., et al.: Spatio-temporal saliency detection using phase spectrum of quaternion Fourier transform. In: Proceedings of the IEEE International Conference on Computer Vision and Pattern Recognition, June 2008
31. Harel, J., Koch, C., Perona, P.: Graph-based visual saliency. In: Proceedings of the Neural Information Processing Systems, pp. 545–552 (2007)
32. Rezazadegan Tavakoli, H., Rahtu, E., Heikkilä, J.: Fast and efficient saliency detection using sparse sampling and kernel density estimation. In: Heyden, A., Kahl, F. (eds.) SCIA 2011. LNCS, vol. 6688, pp. 666–675. Springer, Heidelberg (2011). https://doi.org/10.1007/978-3-642-21227-7_62
33. Li, J., Tian, Y., Huang, T.: Visual saliency with statistical priors. Int. J. Comput. Vis. **107**(3), 239–253 (2014)
34. R. Tavakoli, H., Laaksonen, J.: Bottom-up fixation prediction using unsupervised hierarchical models. In: Chen, C.-S., Lu, J., Ma, K.-K. (eds.) ACCV 2016. LNCS, vol. 10116, pp. 287–302. Springer, Cham (2017). https://doi.org/10.1007/978-3-319-54407-6_19
35. Hou, X., Harel, J., Koch, C.: Image signature: highlighting sparse salient regions. IEEE Trans. Pattern Anal. Mach. Intell. **34**(1), 194–201 (2011)
36. Jia, Y., Shelhamer, E., Donahue, J., et al.: Caffe: convolutional architecture for fast feature embedding. In: Proceedings of ACM Multimedia, pp. 675–678 (2014)

A Visual Attention Model Based on Human Visual Cognition

Na Li[1], Xinbo Zhao[1(✉)], Baoyuan Ma[1], and Xiaochun Zou[2]

[1] School of Computer Science, Northwestern Polytechnical University, Xi'an, China
xbozhao@nwpu.edu.cn
[2] School of Electronics and Information, Northwestern Polytechnical University, Xi'an, China

Abstract. Understanding where humans look in a scene is significant for many applications. Researches on neuroscience and cognitive psychology show that human brain always pays attention on special areas when they observe an image. In this paper, we recorded and analyzed human eye-tracking data, we found that these areas mainly were focus on semantic objects. Inspired by neuroscience, deep learning concept is proposed. Fully Convolutional Neural Networks (FCN) as one of methods of deep learning can solve image objects segmentation at semantic level efficiently. So we bring forth a new visual attention model which uses FCN to stimulate the cognitive processing of human free observing a natural scene and fuses attractive low-level features to predict fixation locations. Experimental results demonstrated our model has apparently advantages in biology.

Keywords: Visual attention model · FCN · Human visual cognition

1 Introduction

Researching human visual attention mechanism is essential to many computer vision tasks. For example, for video compression, those human RoIs (regions of interest) which contain important information of images usually be key points to be handled. Besides, knowing where humans look in a scene is vital for satisfying the user's requirements, such as human computer interaction, advertisement design and so on.

Visual biological cognition researches provide biological basis for human visual attention mechanisms [1, 2]. When the human eyes are observing the surrounding visual information, selected information are imaged on the macula on the retina of the human eye and some region of observer's brain selectively focus on specific areas of imaged information. For example, FMRI (Functional magnetic resonance imaging) studies that human brain's fusiform face area responds selectively to faces [3], and human brain's parahippocampal place area responds selectively to places and buildings [4, 5]. According to these biological cognition researches, we assume that semantic objects areas are more likely to be selected as human attention high-awareness areas, and for verifying our assumption, we recorded and analyzed human eye-tracking data,

J. Ren et al. (Eds.): BICS 2018, LNAI 10989, pp. 271–281, 2018.
https://doi.org/10.1007/978-3-030-00563-4_26

and our experimental evidence shows that semantic object features attract most visual attention.

FCN which is a neural network model proposed by Long [6] in 2015, as one of methods of deep learning can solve image objects segmentation at semantic level efficiently. It is inspired by the organization of the animal visual cortex, whose individual neurons are arranged in such a way that they respond to overlapping regions tiling the visual field. FCN is trained by dense feedforward computation and back-propagation. Besides, FCN can accept arbitrary-sized inputs, which lead FCN to more suitable to be used to extract semantic object features.

Therefore, as Fig. 1 shown, we proposed a new visual attention model, which mainly use FCN to extract semantic object features and combines low-level features to predict human fixations locations based on human visual cognition research.

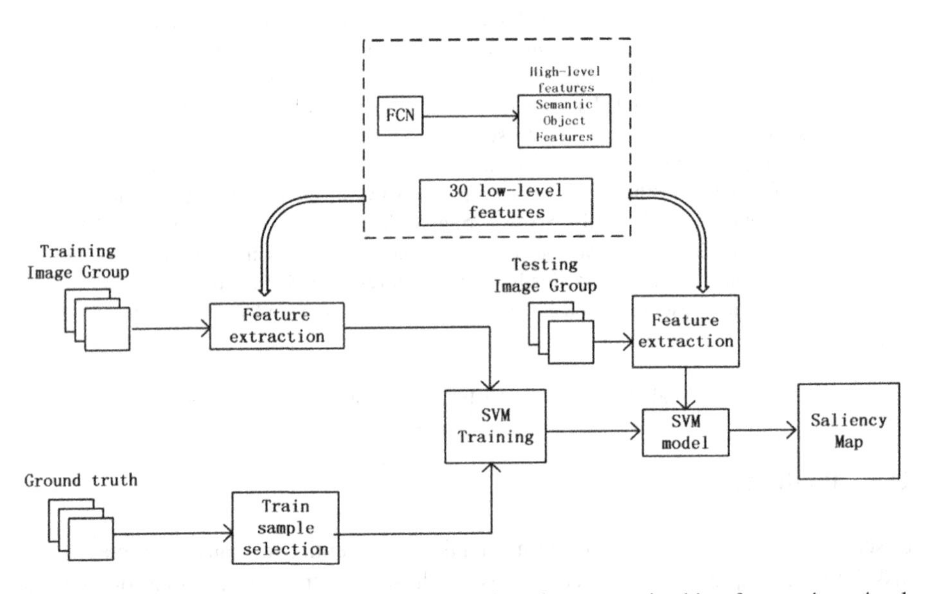

Fig. 1. The algorithm flow chart of this paper. We introduce semantic object features into visual attention model and establish a visual attention model based on human visual cognition. In processing of feature extract, we use FCN to obtain semantic object feature, besides we select typical 30 low-level features. Then we use human real fixation as ground truth, and train those features by SVM model to predict human fixations locations.

In this paper, we make four contributions: Firstly, we established an eye-tracking database contained eye tracking data of 10 viewers on 2000 images, after analyzing we concluded that human always pay attention on semantic objects when they look in a scene under the 'free-viewing'. Secondly, because FCN were inspired by biological processes and have remarkable advantages, so we used a FCN-8s framework [6] to segment semantic objects features of images as human brain's processing of cognition does. Then we selected typical 30 low-level features. Finally, we combined those objects features to train a learning-based visual attention model, which can predict human fixations in a free viewing context.

2 Related Work

Past few years, there were many researches on human eye movements, and many saliency models based on various techniques with compelling performance exist. Some researchers have made some headway on low level attention models. One of the most influential ones is a pure bottom-up attention model proposed by Itti et al. [7], based on the feature integration theory [8]. In this theory, an image is decomposed into low-level attributes such as color, orientation, and intensity. Based on the idea of decorrelation of neural responses, Garcia-Diaz et al. [9] proposed an effective model of saliency known as Adaptive Whitening Saliency (AWS). Zhang et al. [10] put forward SUN (Saliency Using Natural statistics) model in which bottom-up saliency emerges naturally as the self-information of visual features. Similarly, Torralba [11] proposed a Bayesian framework for visual search which is also applicable for saliency detection. Graph Based Visual Saliency (GBVS) [12] is another method based on graphical models.

Though those models do well qualitatively, they discount attraction of object information for human visual mechanisms. Judd et al. [13] and Zhao et al. [14] integrated the low-level features and object features in a learning framework to obtain the superimposed weight of each feature in the process of feature integration. However, the object features used by the model are limited, such as faces, people, and vehicles. Experimental results show that the introduction of object features greatly improves the performance of the model. In general, although some models have used object features as top-down guidance information, but these types of feature are only for a few objects.

There are many researches based on human visual cognition have achieved success. Inspired by Gestalt laws optimization and background connectivity theory, Yan et al. [15] proposed a cognitive framework to combine bottom-up and top-down vision mechanisms for unsupervised saliency detection. Inspired by three cognitive properties of human vision, namely, hierarchical structuring, color perception and embedded compressive sensing, Zhou [16] proposed a new CBIR approach. Chai [17] proposed a hierarchal and multi-featured fusion approach for effective gait recognition.

Inspired by human visual cognition, this paper proposes a visual attention model that combines semantic object features and low-level features. And the experimental results show that the prediction results are more close to human visual attention.

3 Fixations Analysis

For learning common people visual behaviors when they look at a scene, we selected 2000 images called VOC2012-E with semantic segmentation label from Visual Object Classes Challenge 2012 database (VOC2012) [18], which always is used to semantic objects segmentation, and recorded human eye-tracking data when observe those images. The VOC2012-E allows quantitative analysis of fixation points and provides ground truth data for saliency model research. Compared with several objects segmentation datasets that are publicly available, the main motivation of our new dataset is for analyzing eye-tracking.

We used a Tobii TX300 Eye Tracker device to record eye movements, which has very high precision and accuracy and robust eye tracking, besides, it also has compensation for large head movements extends the possibilities for unobtrusive research of oculomotor functions and human behavior.

There are 10 viewers participate in the experiments, and each image was presented for 5 s and followed by a rapid and automatic calibration procedure. During first 1 s viewing, viewers maybe free viewed the images, so we discarded the first 1 s viewing tracking results of each subject.

We counted each image's fixations that fall into semantic objects areas account for total fixations, then calculate the average proportion as Table 1 shown. According to our experiment, the average proportion was more than 83.53%, which shows that the semantic object features attract human attention. Therefore, for improving the accuracy of visual attention model's prediction, we introduced semantic object features into our visual attention model.

Table 1. The ratio of eye movement points dropping into semantic objects areas.

Total eye movement points	Eye movement points dropping into semantic objects areas	Ratio (%)
556395	464766	83.53

As Fig. 2(a) shows, there are 8 sample images of VOC2012-E. We overlapped the eye-tracking data collected from all viewers (Fig. 2(b)). From Fig. 2(c), we can know that semantic object attract most of eye fixation. Besides, to obtain a continuous ground truth of an image from the eye-tracking data of a viewer, we convolved a Gaussian filter across the viewer's fixation locations, similar to the 'landscape map' (Fig. 2(d)).

4 Obtaining Semantic Objects Features

According to the experiments in Sect. 3, we extract semantic objects features for closing to human visual cognition behaviors. FCN has excellent performance [19, 20] in semantic objects segmentation, especially under experiment results of [6], FCN-8s has mean IU 62.2% on VOC2012 database, which has better semantic objects segmentation performance than other model. Therefore, we use trained FCN-8s model, whose network parameters have been trained in image segmentation tasks, to increase the speed of calculation.

Figure 3 shows the structure of FCN-8s model. In the first 5 layers, convolutional layers (Conv1..,5) and pooling layers (Pool1…,5) are connected one by one. Convolution barely change the size of image, but pooling reduces an image in half. In Conv6-7, fully connected layers are converted into convolution. Conv7 is amplified by a

Fig. 2. We collected eye-tracking data on 2000 images from ten viewers. First row is the 8 sample of original images (a) in VOC2012-E. Gaze tracking paths and fixation locations are recorded in second row (b). Third row (c) shows most of eye fixation in the semantic object area. A continuous ground truth (d) is found by convolving a Gaussian over the fixation locations of all subjects.

4× upsampling layer. Then a 1 × 1 convolution layer on top of pool4 to produce additional class predictions at stride 16, and this output is amplified by a 2× upsampling layer. Then fusing these two features with the prediction computed on top of pool3 at stride 8 by adding a 1 × 1 convolution layer. Finally, the segmentation result is the 8x upsampled prediction. There are the samples of semantic objects features we obtaind by FCN-8s (Fig. 4).

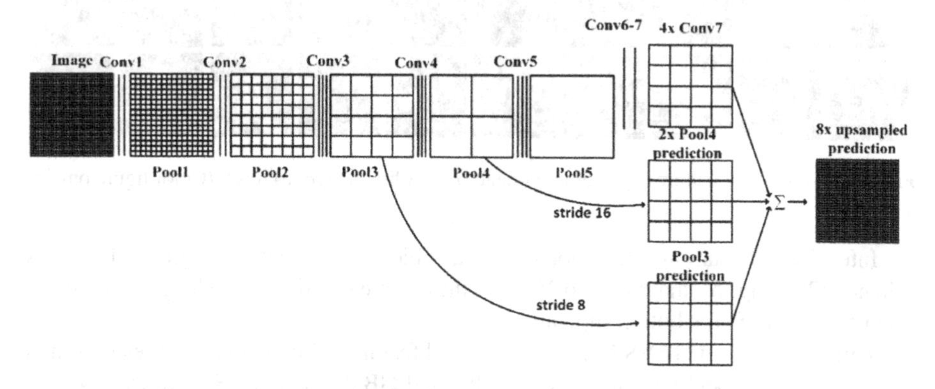

Fig. 3. The structure of FCN-8s model. Layers are shown as grids that reveal relative spatial coarseness.

Fig. 4. The samples of semantic objects features we obtained by FCN-8s. (a) is original images, (b) is the semantic object features obtained by FCN-8s model, (c) is the groundtruth.

5 Features Integration

For human visual attention, except for top-down visual attention controlled by human's cognition, there is also bottom-up visual attention which is a subconscious mechanism that attracts us to conspicuous features [21]. Therefore, we also extract attractive 30 low-level features, such as intensity, colors and orientations and so on. Based on feature integration theory, we process those features in parallel and combined those later [7].

The local energy of the steerable pyramid filters [19], which are used as features in four orientations and three scales (see Fig. 5, first 13 images).

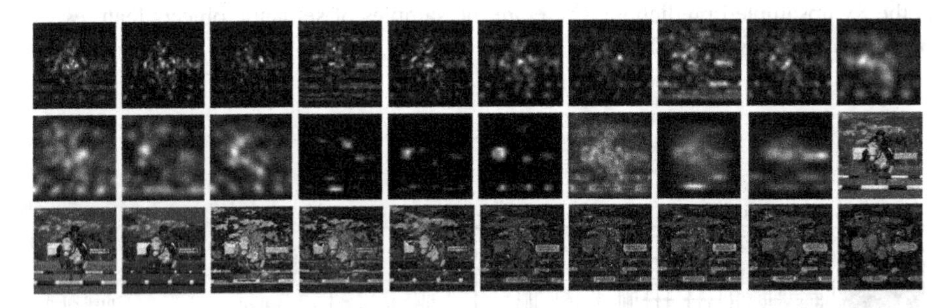

Fig. 5. 30 low-level features of a sample image (Fig. 4 first image (a) row). (Color figure online)

Intensity, orientation and color contrast, which is calculated by Itti and Koch's saliency [22] (Fig. 5, images 14 to 16), and these three channels have long been seen as important features for bottom-up saliency.

Torralba [11] and GBVS [12], and AWS [9] features. We include features used in a simple saliency model described by Torralba and GBVS, and AWS features based on subband pyramids (Fig. 5, images 17 to 19).

Red, green and blue channels. We extract the value of these three channels, and the probabilities of each of these channels are used as features (Fig. 5, images 20 to 25).

Probability of each color, which is as computed from 3D color histograms of the image filtered with a median filter at six different scales (Fig. 5, images 26 to 30).

After the feature extraction process, the features of the top 5% (bottom 30%) points in the ground truth are selected as training samples in each training image. All of the training samples are sent to train a SVM model.

6 Experiments

We validate our visual attention model and compare it with eight well-known techniques which had to deal with similar challenges in natural scene. We used them as the baseline because our method is biologically inspired and they also mimic the visual system, these eight models were AIM [23], AWS [9], Judd [13], ITTI [22], GBVS [12], SUN [10], STB [24], and Torralba [11]. We evaluate these methods in 3 ways: Firstly, we measure performance of each model by Area Under the ROC Curve (AUC). Secondly, we examine the performance of different models on Normalized Scan Path Saliency (NSS). Finally, we compute linear correlation coefficient (CC). We use 10-fold cross-validation to estimate performance of those 9 models.

In Fig. 6, we see that compared with other 8 model, Ours's performance is obviously more close to human visual cognition, in which semantic object features are high

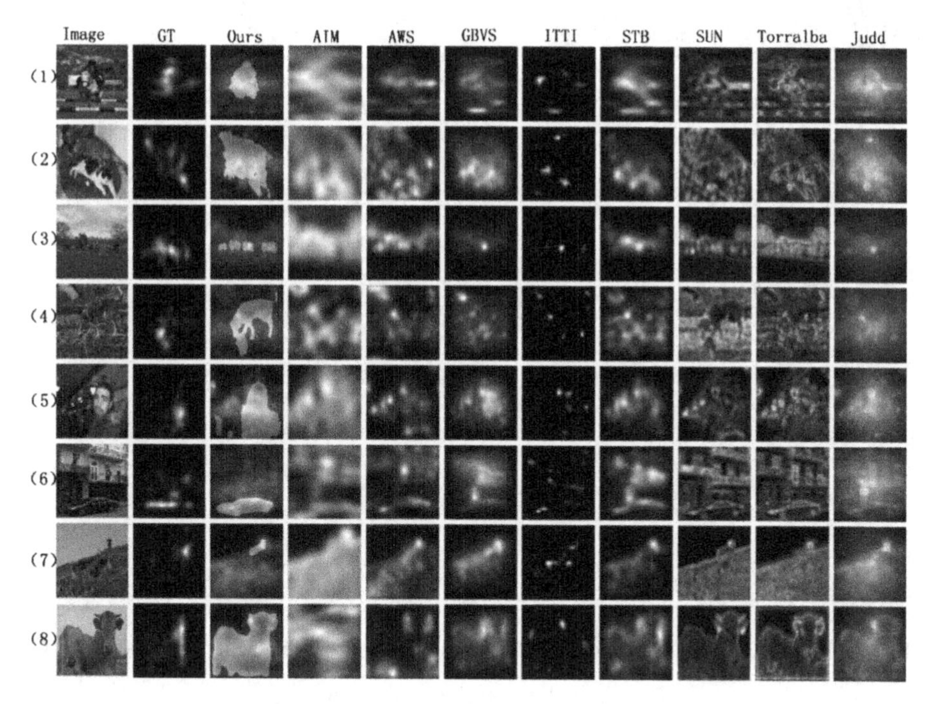

Fig. 6. Some saliency maps produced by 9 different models from the VOC2012-E database along with predictions of several models using ROC. Each example shown by one row. From left to right: original image, ground truth, Ours, AIM, AWS, GBVS, ITTI, STB, SUN, Torralba and Judd.

saliency. In Fig. 7, we see the ROC curves of eight examples in Fig. 6 describing the performance of different saliency models. The size of the salient region plays an important role in the ROC method, since it cannot separate salient regions from backgrounds using a certain threshold, the ROC method treats a saliency map as a binary classifier for ground truth under various thresholds.

As shown in Fig. 7, except for image (1) and image (7), the ROC of Ours in other images were higher than other models under 40% salient region. For image (1), the performance of Ours was close to STB under 20% salient region, and STB outperformed slightly Ours between 20% and 40% salient region, which same as GBVS and Ours in image (7). When the salient region was larger than 60%, the performance of the nine saliency model were roughly similar. However, the salient RoIs which can be used to distinguish from other objects in an image are generally under 40% and even smaller in many cases. As a result, the performance of our method is better than other models when the salient region is small.

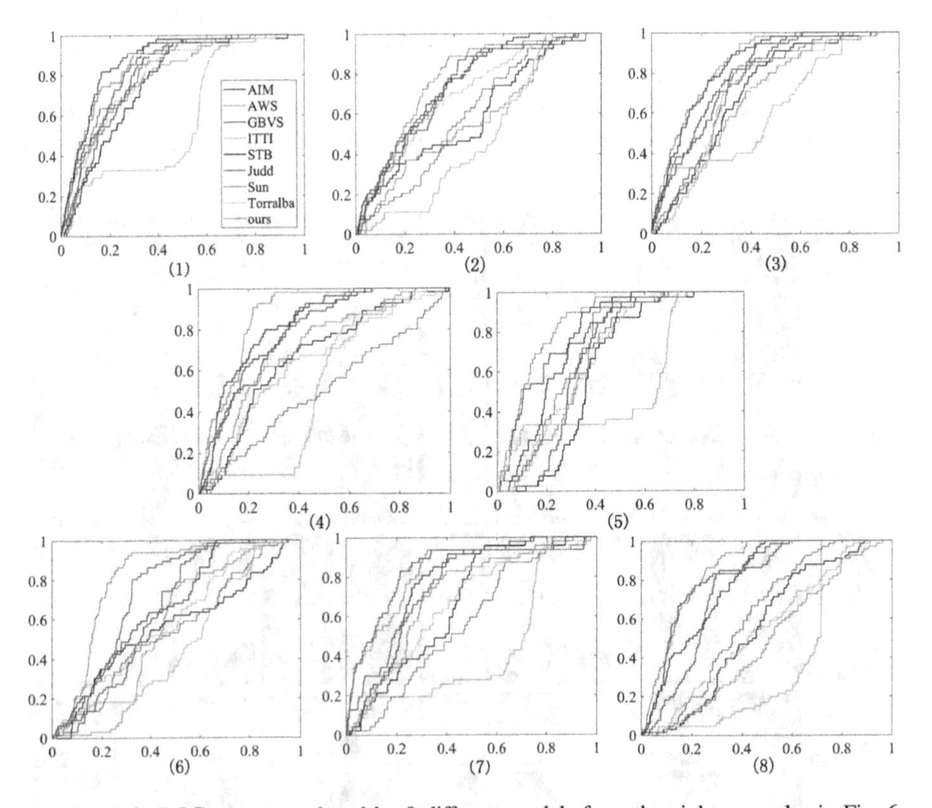

Fig. 7. Eight ROC curves produced by 9 different models from the eight examples in Fig. 6.

As shown in Table 2, all AUC, NSS, and CC measurements evidence that our model outperforms the other models. The AUC of our model is highest (0.823), followed by Judd (0.822) and GBVS (0.810). However, the average is only 0.716. It

Table 2. Performances of nine models in three metrics.

Metrics	Ours	AIM	AWS	GBVS	ITTI	STB	SUN	Torralba	Judd	Average
AUC	0.823	0.664	0.718	0.810	0.531	0.779	0.619	0.679	0.822	0.716
NSS	1.360	0.595	0.892	1.263	0.674	0.399	0.460	0.681	1.242	0.888
CC	0.557	0.241	0.351	0.521	0.145	0.453	0.184	0.275	0.518	0.360

means the results of Ours are more identical with ground truth than other models. Generally speaking, Ours has good performance in this metric.

The NSS of our model is 1.360, which surpasses the average sensitivity 0.472, followed by GBVS with 1.263 and Judd with 1.242. However, STB had the lowest rate (only 0.399), which only approximate a quarter of Ours.

And the larger value of CC (0.557) is also shown in our model, and the indisputable fact is the higher CC is, the higher the correlation between attention model and human real fixation. Thus, Ours is more close to predict human fixation locations, because Ours is inspired by cognitive processing of human free observing a natural scene and fuses semantic object features and attractive low-level features.

7 Conclusion

The present paper has introduced a new visual attention model based on Human Visual Cognition which has apparently advantages in biology. In this work we make the following contributions:

Firstly, we established an eye-tracking database from 10 people across 2000 images, called VOC2012-E, to learn common people visual behaviors record their eye-tracking data when human observe images. According to our experiment, we concluded that the semantic object features attract human attention. Secondly, inspired by human visual cognition, we introduced semantic object features into visual attention model training. We used the excellent deep learning method FCN to obtain objects feature. Then, we selected 30 typical low-level features. Finally, we built a learning-based visual attention model on VOC2012-E database, which is trained by machine learning based on semantic object features and low-level image features. Our model has the ability to automatically learn the relationship between saliency and features. And our model simultaneously considers appearing frequency of features and the pixel location of features, which intuitively have a strong influence on saliency. As a result, our model can determine saliency regions and predict human's fixation more precisely.

In the future, to improve the performance of our model, we can optimize the processing of feature extraction and further research on features integration, meanwhile, improve the speed of computation.

Acknowledgements. We would like to thank the associate editor and all of the reviewers for their constructive comments to improve the manuscript. The work is supported by NSF of China (Nos. NCYM0001 and 61201319).

References

1. Scholkopf, B., Smola, A.: Learning with Kernels. MIT Press, Cambridge (2002)
2. Smola, A.J., Mika, S., Scholkhopf, B., et al.: Regularized principal manifold. J. Mach. Learn. Res. **1**(3), 179–209 (2001)
3. Kanwisher, N., Mcdermott, J., Chun, M.: The fusiform face area: a module in human extrastriate cortex specialized for perception of faces. J. Neurosci. **17**(11), 4302–4311 (1997)
4. Epstein, R., Kanwisher, N.: A cortical representation of the local visual environment. Nature **392**(6676), 598–601 (1998)
5. Epstein, R., Stanley, D., Harris, A., Kanwisher, N.: The parahippocampal place area: perception, encoding, or memory retrieval? Neuron **23**(2000), 115–125 (2000)
6. Long, J., Shelhamer, E., Darrell, T.: Fully convolutional networks for semantic segmentation. In: IEEE Conference on Computer Vision and Pattern Recognition, CVPR 2015, vol. 79, pp. 3431–3440 (2015)
7. Itti, L., Koch, C., Niebur, E.: A model of saliency-based visual attention for rapid scene analysis. IEEE Trans. Pattern Anal. Mach. Intell. IEEE **20**, 1254–1259 (2002)
8. Koch, C., Ullman, S.: Shifts in selective visual attention: towards the underlying neural circuitry. Hum. Neurobiol. **4**(4), 219–227 (1985)
9. Garcia-Diaz, A., Fdez-Vidal, X.R., Pardo, X.M., Dosil, R.: Decorrelation and distinctiveness provide with human-like saliency. In: Blanc-Talon, J., Philips, W., Popescu, D., Scheunders, P. (eds.) ACIVS 2009. LNCS, vol. 5807, pp. 343–354. Springer, Heidelberg (2009). https://doi.org/10.1007/978-3-642-04697-1_32
10. Zhang, L., Tong, M.H., Marks, T.K., Shan, H., Cottrell, G.W.: SUN: a Bayesian framework for saliency using natural statistics. J. Vis. **8**(7), 1–20 (2008)
11. Torralba, A.: Modeling global scene factors in attention. J. Opt. Soc. Am. A **20**(7), 1407–1418 (2003)
12. Schölkopf, B., Platt, J., Hofmann, T.: Graph-Based Visual Saliency, vol. 19, pp. 545–552. MIT Press, Cambridge (2010)
13. Judd, T., Ehinger, K., Durand, F., Torralba, A.: Learning to predict where humans look, vol. 30, pp. 2106–2113 (2009)
14. Zhao, Q., Koch, C.: Learning a saliency map using fixated locations in natural scenes. J. Vis. **11**(3), 74–76 (2011)
15. Yan, Y., Ren, J., Zhao, H., Sun, G., Wang, Z., Zheng, J., et al.: Cognitive fusion of thermal and visible imagery for effective detection and tracking of pedestrians in videos. Cognit. Comput. **9**, 1–11 (2017)
16. Zhou, Y., Zeng, F.Z., Zhao, H.M., Murray, P., Ren, J.: Hierarchical visual perception and two-dimensional compressive sensing for effective content-based color image retrieval. Cognit. Comput. **8**(5), 877–889 (2016)
17. Chai, Y., Ren, J., Zhao, H., Li, Y., Ren, J., Murray, P.: Hierarchical and multi-featured fusion for effective gait recognition under variable scenarios. Pattern Anal. Appl. **19**(4), 905–917 (2016)
18. Everingham, M., Van Gool, L., Williams, C.K.I., Winn, J., Zisserman, A.: The PASCAL Visual Object Classes Challenge 2012 (VOC2012) Results. http://www.pascal-network.org/challenges/VOC/voc2012/workshop/index.html
19. Yu, S., Cheng, Y., Xie, L., et al.: Fully convolutional networks for action recognition. IET Comput. Vision **11**(8), 744–749 (2017)
20. Dai, J., He, K., Li, Y., Ren, S., Sun, J.: Instance-sensitive fully convolutional networks. In: Leibe, B., Matas, J., Sebe, N., Welling, M. (eds.) ECCV 2016. LNCS, vol. 9910, pp. 534–549. Springer, Cham (2016). https://doi.org/10.1007/978-3-319-46466-4_32

21. Koch, C., Ullman, S.: Shifts in selective visual attention: towards the underlying neural circuitry. Hum. Neurobiol. **4**(4), 219–227 (1985)
22. Itti, L., Koch, C.: A saliency-based search mechanism for overt and covert shifts of visual attention. Vis. Res. **40**(12), 1489–1506 (2000)
23. Bruce, N.D.B., Tsotsos, J.K.: Saliency based on information maximization. Adv. Neural. Inf. Process. Syst. **18**(3), 298–308 (2005)
24. Walther, D., Koch, C.: Modeling attention to salient proto-objects. Neural Netw. Off. J. Int. Neural Netw. Soc. **19**(9), 1395–1407 (2006)

An Extended Common Spatial Pattern Framework for EEG-Based Emotion Classification

Jingxia Chen[1,2](✉), Dongmei Jiang[1], and Yanning Zhang[1]

[1] Northwestern Polytechnical University, Xi'an 710072, Shaanxi, People's Republic of China
chenjx_sust@foxmail.com

[2] Shaanxi University of Science and Technology, Xi'an 710021, Shaanxi, People's Republic of China

Abstract. A major challenge for emotion classification using electroencephalography (EEG) is how to effectively extract more discriminative feature and reduce the day-to-day variability in raw EEG data. This study proposed a novel spatial filtering algorithm called Ext-CSP which combined common spatial patterns (CSP) and the regularization term into a unified optimization framework based on Kullback-Leibler (KL) divergence. The experiment was carried out on a five-day Music Emotion EEG dataset of 12 subjects. Four classifiers were applied to make emotion classification. The experiment results demonstrated our unified Ext-CSP algorithm could effectively increase the robustness and generalizability of the extracted EEG features and gain 14% better performance than traditional PCA algorithm, and 1.7% better performance than the stepwise DSA-CSP iteration algorithm on EEG-based emotion classification.

Keywords: CSP · DSA · EEG · Emotion classification

1 Introduction

A brain-computer interface (BCI) provides a direct communication path between the brain and an external device. Nowadays, the BCI system is interacting with an external device not only through decoding of mental states, but also based on some preliminary responses of visual, auditory, sensorimotor, e.g., P300, SSVEP. Emotion classification using noninvasively measured electrical brain activity, namely electroencephalography (EEG), has attracted growing interests in recent years. Most efforts devoted to improving emotion-classification performance by developing novel or refining previous machine-learning schemes. For example, Wang et al. [1] proposed a feature-smoothing method following feature extraction to deal with strong fluctuations and information unrelated to emotion responses. Liu et al. [2] introduced a new feature type of kernel eigen-emotion patterns upon multichannel spectral power. Lin et al. [3] demonstrated the advantages of incorporating multi-modal information to augment low-density EEG data. Feng et al. [4] proposed a novel ensemble margin-based algorithm to constructing higher quality balanced feature for each base classifier. Jiang et al. [5] developed an artificial neural

J. Ren et al. (Eds.): BICS 2018, LNAI 10989, pp. 282–292, 2018.
https://doi.org/10.1007/978-3-030-00563-4_27

network to resolve the medical imaging problem. Ren et al. [6] suggested a new balanced learning strategy with optimized decision making to improve the performance of ANN and SVM on imbalanced samples.

However, the efficiency of machine-learning scheme is not the only factor affecting classification performance, lack of sufficient training data and the inherent EEG variability posed a great challenge in characterizing spatial-spectral EEG dynamics with implicit emotional responses. To address this issue, Lin et al. [7] recently explored to extract differential laterality (DLAT) and differential causality (DCAU) EEG features to improve the accuracy of emotion classification by leveraging a 5-day EEG dataset of 12 subjects and alleviating the inherent inner-day and cross-day EEG variability. The study in [8] used independent component analysis (ICA) to remove artifacts prior to EEG feature extraction effectively and alleviated some but not all of the inter-day variability. Some studies showed that BCI performance can be improved by using data space adaptive (DSA) procedures to minimize the changes among different trials or sessions, such as bias adaptation [9], feature space adaption [10], and covariate shift adaptation [11] which adapted the training data to minimize the mismatch between the training and evaluation sessions. Some studies focused on extracting invariant features by regularizing the common spatial patterns (CSP) algorithm [12, 13] to find a feature subset robust to changes and alleviate the nonstationary effects in BCI applications. Although impressive improvements in BCI efficiency have been achieved, especially for SSVEP-based BCIs, the current affective BCI system are far from being perfect in terms of reliability and generalizability. More efforts are still needed to resolve the inherent inter-day and cross-day variability in EEG.

In this paper, we propose a novel spatial filtering algorithm which extends the CSP algorithm into a unifying optimization framework based on divergence maximization, namely Ext-CSP. Based on the maximum entropy principle, the robust Gauss function is used to model the EEG distribution with zero mean and covariance matrix, and the difference between the two Gauss distributions is usually measured by Kullback Leibler (KL) divergences. Therefore, we firstly use the CSP spatial filter to span a subspace with maximum symmetric KL divergence between the two class EEG distributions. Then the regularization term also measured as KL divergences is added to alleviate the cross-day variability and the accompanied background perturbations on each day. The experiment is carried out on the five-day longitudinal Music Emotion EEG dataset of 12 subjects. We compare the performance of the Ext-CSP algorithm with other two methods, including principal component analysis (PCA) and the stepwise DSA-CSP iteration method. The experiment results show that our proposed Ext-CSP algorithm can effectively increase the robustness and generalizability of the extracted EEG features.

2 Dataset and Data Preprocessing

2.1 EEG Dataset

This study adopts the five-day EEG dataset of 12 subjects collected in [7] for testing the feasibility of using the Ext-CSP algorithm to deal with day-to-day variability. The data collection experiment was carried out by the Human Research Protections Program of University of California, San Diego. Each subject participated in the same music-listening experiments for five days. The study used a 14-channel Emotiv headset (with T7 and T8 excluded) to sample the EEG signals at 128 Hz and in a bandwidth of 0.16 and 43 Hz during music listening. In each experiment, the subjects were instructed to assign one of the target emotions (happiness or sadness) or neutral (no feeling) to each of 24 music excerpts (each lasted around 37 s on average) according to what they had experienced. That is each experiment day resulted in 24 $\times$ 37-s EEG trials labeled by self-reported emotions (happiness, sadness, or neutral). Please refer to [7] for more details regarding the headset setup, experiment settings and the music excerpts.

2.2 Data Preprocessing and Feature Extraction

The EEG signals are firstly processed with a 1-Hz high-pass finite impulse response filter to remove low-frequency drifts. Then we sample the EEG signals at 128 Hz, exclude irrelevant T7 and T8 channels, concatenate all the happy data and sad data of any 4-day out of 5 days for each subject as the training data, and the left 1-day data is as the testing data. The average is removed from each channel of training data and testing data separately. Due to great difference of feature magnitude over different channels will leads instable numerical calculation and poor testing performance, the z-score function is used to normalize the training data, and its normalized parameters Mu and sigma are used to normalize the testing data. Then our proposed Ext-CSP spatial filtering algorism is used to project the normalized training data to the subspace with maximum symmetric KL divergence between the two different class distributions and minimum KL divergence between different day's trials for each subject. The same spatial filtering work is down on the testing data. The dimension of projected subspace and the regularization weight of Ext-CSP can be adjusted to get different filtered result, and the detail is in part B of Sect. 3.

Meanwhile, we also apply the traditional PCA method and stepwise DSA-CSP iteration method to preprocess the raw EEG data and use them as the baselines to make comparation with our Ext-CSP method. Because the DLAT and DCAU features correlate EEG dynamics with emotion states and get better performance in multi-day EEG emotion recognition [14], after the preprocessing, we extract the DLAT and DCAU feature that characterize the differential normalized data in left-right and frontal-posterior electrode pairs respectively which is called DLAT&DCAU feature. As the power spectral density (PSD) feature is more discriminative in EEG emotional classification, we then extract the PSD of the DLAT&DCAU feature on training data and testing data respectively. The short-time Fourier transform with a 1-s nonoverlapping hamming window was then applied to calculate the band powers in five frequency bands, including δ (1–3 Hz), θ (4–7 Hz), α (8–13 Hz), β (14–30 Hz), and γ (31–43 Hz). For 12-dimensional subspace, 12 original EEG channels form six left-right pairs and four frontal-posterior pairs, DLAT&DCAU PSD feature in five frequency bands has a dimension of 50 (30 for DLAT and 20 for DCAU), and the pure PSD feature without DLAT and DCAU in five frequency bands has a dimension of 60. We test on these two types of features to find out which one has better performance.

3 Methods

3.1 Divergence-Based CSP Framework

Like many machine learning algorithms such as independent component analysis [15] or stationary subspace analysis [16], the CSP algorithm can be cast into the framework of information geometry and formulated as divergence optimization problems. The subspace mapped by CSP maximizes the KL divergence between the average distributions. The symmetric KL divergence $\tilde{D}_{kl}$ between two class distributions f(x) and g(x) is defined as [17]:

$$\int f(x)\log\frac{f(x)}{g(x)}dx + \int g(x)\log\frac{g(x)}{f(x)}dx \tag{1}$$

It can be interpreted as distortion measure between two probability distributions and it is always positive and equals zero if and only if $g = f$. In this paper, we compute divergences between zero mean Gaussian distributions. Let Σ_1 and Σ_2 are covariance matrices of two emotion classes of EEG, $W \in R^{D\times d}$ is the top d (sorted by α_i) spatial filters computed by CSP and let $V^T = \tilde{R}P \in R^{d\times D}$ be a matrix that can be decomposed into a whitening projection $P \in R^{D\times D}$ with $(P(\sum_1 + \sum_2)P^T = I)$ and an orthogonal projection $\tilde{R} = I_d R \in R^{d\times D}$ with $I_d \in R^{d\times D}$ being the identity matrix truncated to the first d rows and $R^T R = I \in R^{(D\times D)}$. Then the following relation exists between the spatial filters extracted by CSP and the symmetric KL divergence:

$$\text{span}(W) = \text{span}(V^*) \tag{2}$$

$$V^* = \arg\max_V \tilde{D}_{kl}(V^T\Sigma_1 V \parallel V^T\Sigma_2 V) \tag{3}$$

Here, span(W) means the subspace spanned by the columns of the matrix W. The proof can be referred in appendix of [18]. The CSP filters matrix W project the data to a subspace with maximum discrepancy between the d-dimensional Gaussian distributions $\mathcal{N}(0,\ W^T\ \Sigma_1 W)$ and $\mathcal{N}(0,\ W^T\ \Sigma_2 W)$ measured by symmetric KL divergence. Thus, instead of computing spatial filters with CSP, we obtain an equivalent solution (up to linear transformations within the subspace) when maximizing (3). Note that [19] has provided a proof for the special case of one spatial filter, i.e., for $V \in R^{D\times 1}$. In the following, we present the subspace method for divergence maximization.

3.2 The Proposed Ext-CSP Framework

Previously, we showed that CSP can be formulated in a divergence maximization framework, however, maximizing the band power ratios may not be the only objective for feature extraction. A natural way of regularizing the extracted spatial filters toward stationarity is to combine the objective function of CSP with a divergence term that accounts for the stationarity of the features. We propose to extend CSP by adding the regularization term that minimizes the cross-day non-stationarity and permits utilizing information from other day's trials. Since the optimization process is not affected by changing the way how stationarity is measured, as long it is a divergence, our framework integrates CSP objective function with regularization term and the new objective function can be written as:

$$\mathcal{L}(V) = \underbrace{(1-\lambda)\tilde{D}_{kl}\left(V^T\Sigma_1 V \parallel V^T\Sigma_2 V\right)}_{CSP\,Term} - \underbrace{\lambda\Delta}_{Reg.Term} \tag{4}$$

Where Δ is the regularization term, and λ is a regularization parameter trading off the influence of the CSP objective function and the regularization term. The objective functions can be written as weighted sum of divergences and the goal is to find a projection to a d-dimensional subspace that maximizes this sum. We concatenated recordings of five day's trials of the same class for each subject, and then divided the data into a set of smaller epochs. The non-stationarity of the extracted features is measured as average divergence between the data distribution of each day's trial and the whole 5-day data distribution for each class separately (see [9]). More precisely, we compute the regularization term as:

$$\Delta = \frac{1}{2N}\sum\nolimits_{c=1}^{2}\sum\nolimits_{i=1}^{N} D_{kl}\left(V^T\Sigma_c^i V \parallel V^T\Sigma_c V\right) \tag{5}$$

where N denotes the number of sessions (here is 5, number of days) and Σ_c^i stands for the estimated covariance matrix of class c and session i. We use the KL divergence to capture the changes. Adding the regularization term Δ to (4) reduces the cross-day variability of the extracted training features within each class.

3.3 Optimization Algorithms

We use the subspace approach [18] to solve the optimization of (4). The first step of the method consists of the computation of a whitening matrix $P \in R^{D \times D}$ that projects the data onto the unit sphere, i.e., $P(\Sigma_1 + \Sigma_2)P^T = I$. This whitening transformation is applied to the class covariance matrices Σ_1 and Σ_2 followed by a random rotation with $R_0 \in R^{D \times D}$. The rotation matrix satisfies $R_0^T R_0 = I$, where I is the identity matrix. The optimization process then consists of finding a rotation matrix $R \in R^{D \times D}$ that maximizes the KL divergence in the first d sources. More precisely, we optimize the following objective function:

$$\mathcal{L}_{kl}(R) = \underbrace{\tilde{D}_{kl}\left(I_d R\tilde{\sum}_1 R^T I_d^T \parallel I_d R\tilde{\sum}_2 R^T I_d^T\right)}_{CSP\,Term} - \underbrace{\frac{\lambda}{2N}\sum\nolimits_{c=1}^{2}\sum\nolimits_{i=1}^{N} D_{kl}\left(I_d R\tilde{\sum}_c^i R^T I_d^T \parallel I_d R\tilde{\sum}_c R^T I_d^T\right)}_{Reg.Term} \tag{6}$$

where the whitened covariance matrices $\tilde{\Sigma} = P\Sigma P^T$ and the projected ones as $\bar{\Sigma} = I_d RP\Sigma P^T R^T I_d^T$. So $\tilde{\Sigma}_1$and $\tilde{\Sigma}_2$ denote the whitened covariance matrices of two classes and $I_d \in R^{d \times D}$is the identity matrix truncated to the first d rows. Note that although R is a $D \times D$ rotation matrix, we only evaluate the first d rows of it, i.e., we only evaluate the divergence in a d-dimensional subspace.

The optimization is performed by gradient descend on the manifold of orthogonal matrices. More precisely, we start with an orthogonal matrix R_0 and find an orthogonal update U in the kth step such that $R^{k+1} = UR^k$. This ensures that we stay on the manifold of orthogonal matrices at each step (see [20] and [21] for more details). The gradients $\nabla R\mathcal{L}$ of the algorithm used in this paper are summarized in Table 1.

Since the objective function in (6) is invariant to rotations within the d-dimensional subspace, we rotate the projection matrix V in the last step of the algorithm with a matrix G, so that it maximally separates the two classes and minimally reduces the non-stationarity of different trails along the projection directions. The spatial filters can be rearranged so that they capture the class differences with decreasing strength (α_i sorting). Through adjusting the dimension of projected subspace and the regularization weight λ, we get different spatial filtered results.

Table 1. Gradient of the Ext-CSP using KL divergence.

Item	Gradient $\nabla R\,\mathcal{L}$
CSP term	$(1-\lambda)I_d^T((\bar{\Sigma}_2)^{-1}I_d\tilde{\Sigma}_2 - (\bar{\Sigma}_1)^{-1}\bar{\Sigma}_2 - (\bar{\Sigma}_1)^{-1}I_d\tilde{\Sigma}_1 + (\bar{\Sigma}_1)^{-1}I_d\tilde{\Sigma}_1 - (\bar{\Sigma}_2)^{-1}\bar{\Sigma}_1(\bar{\Sigma}_2)^{-1}I_d\tilde{\Sigma}_2)R$
Reg. term	$-\frac{\lambda}{2N}\sum_{c=1}^{2}\sum_{c=1}^{N}(I_d^T((\bar{\Sigma}_c^i)^{-1}I_d\tilde{\Sigma}_c^i - (\bar{\Sigma}_c)^{-1}\bar{\Sigma}_c^i(\bar{\Sigma}_c)^{-1}I_d\tilde{\Sigma}_1 - (\bar{\Sigma}_c^i)^{-1}I_d\tilde{\Sigma}_c^i + (\bar{\Sigma}_c)^{-1}I_d\tilde{\Sigma}_c)R)$

3.4 Classification

This study firstly tests the relation between the cross-day emotion classification accuracy and the number of training days involved to demonstrate the steady improvement in cross-day classification accuracy. Then it tests the applicability and effectiveness of our proposed Ext-CSP algorithm which could extract the robust and discriminative features from cross-day EEG dataset for binary emotion classification task (happiness versus sadness). The EEG data labeled as neutral by subjects are discarded. Four state-of-the-art classification algorithms including Bagging tree (BT) [22], Linear discriminative analysis (LDA) [23], Bayesian linear discriminative analysis (BLDA) [24] and Support Vector Machine (SVM) [25] are used to distinguish EEG data between happiness and sadness. To report the 5-day emotion classification performance, we employed q-day leave-day-out (LDO) validation method, where q (1–4) indicates the data collected within the number of days are used to train the classification model and the trained model is tested against on an unseen day.

4 Experiments and Results

In experiment of testing the relation between the classification accuracy and the number of training days involved, we separately select the data of one day out of two days, two days out of three days, three days out of four days, four days out of five days as the training data and the rest days' data as the testing data. The results are shown in Tables 2 and 3, which demonstrate the steady improvement in cross-day classification accuracy as the days involved increase.

Table 2. Classification accuracy of pure PSD feature

Training data	BT	SVM	LDA	BLDA
4 days out of 5 days data	0.5836	0.5761	0.6117	0.6118
3 days out of 4 days data	0.5858	0.5694	0.6114	0.6072
2 days out of 3 days data	0.5747	0.5739	0.5917	0.6064
1 day out of 2 days data	0.5605	0.5644	0.5820	0.5935

Table 3. Classification accuracy of Ext-CSP filtered PSD feature

Training data	BT	SVM	LDA	BLDA
4 days out of 5 days data	0.6436	0.6401	0.6817	0.6923
3 days out of 4 days data	0.6158	0.6094	0.6470	0.6416
2 days out of 3 days data	0.5896	0.5863	0.6098	0.6152
1 day out of 2 days data	0.5675	0.5721	0.5937	0.6036

This improvement may account for more EEG features regarding emotions along days. The results also show us for 5-day leave-day-out validation dataset, the classification accuracy of four classifiers on Ext-CSP filtered PSD feature is higher than that on pure PSD feature without Ext-CSP filtering. The accuracy of the optimal BLDA classifier on Ext-CSP filtered PSD feature is 0.6923, which is 8% higher than 0.6118 on pure PSD feature. This indicates the applicability and effectiveness of our proposed Ext-CSP algorithm.

We also compare the performance of our proposed Ext-CSP framework with traditional PCA and the stepwise DSA-CSP iterative algorithm. These three algorithms are all used to preprocess the EEG data before feature extraction and classification. The PCA algorithm transforms the original EEG data into a set of linear independent vectors in each dimension by linear transformation, which is mainly used to extract the primary features of the data. For the stepwise DSA-CSP iterative algorithm, the DSA algorithm [26] was firstly used to preprocess the 5-day EEG data to minimize the inconsistency and non-stationarity between different days for each subject, and then the CSP algorithm [27] is applied to transform the DSA's output result into a subspace to maximize the difference between two classes. The output of each CSP transformation is then taken as the input of next-round DSA-CSP transformation, and so forth the results of different iterations are obtained and their classification accuracy on DLAT&D-CAU&PSD feature is shown in Table 4.

From Table 4, we can see the classification accuracy does not increase with the number of iterations and as a result the DSA-CSP with 1 iteration gets the optimal performance. This may account for DSA and CSP is not optimized synchronously in a unified framework which leads to the DSA transformation for minimizing cross-day

Table 4. Classification accuracy of stepwise DSA-CSP iteration

Classifier	1-Iteration	2-Iteration	3-Iteration	4-Iteration	5-Iteration
BT	0.6306	0.6138	0.6124	0.6053	0.5858
SVM	0.6307	0.6015	0.6043	0.6034	0.6031
LDA	0.6744	0.6428	0.6456	0.6240	0.6310
BLDA	0.6834	0.6618	0.6408	0.6182	0.5970

variability inevitably reduces some discriminative features of two classes. For Ext-CSP algorithm, we apply an extended CSP transformation function [18] to project the raw EEG data into the d-dimensional subspace with maximum symmetric KL divergence between the two class distributions, and through the regularization term to alleviate the cross-day variability. After preprocessing with these three kinds of algorithms, we extract two types of feature including pure PSD feature and DLAT& DACU&PSD feature respectively. Then we make classification on these features with four baseline classifiers. The classification accuracy of PCA, stepwise DSA-CSP 1-iteration and the Ext-CSP algorithms on 5-day different features are shown in Table 5.

Table 5. Classification accuracy of three algorithms on 5-day different features

Algorithm and feature	BT	SVM	LDA	BLDA
PCA + PSD	0.5380	0.5501	0.5510	0.5520
PCA + DLAT&DCAU&PSD	0.5458	0.5694	0.5576	0.5611
DSA-CSP(1-iteration) + PSD	0.6183	0.6152	0.6627	0.6786
DSA-CSP(1-iteration) + DLAT&DCAU&PSD	0.6306	0.6307	0.6744	0.6834
Ext-CSP + PSD	0.6436	0.6401	0.6817	0.6923
Ext-CSP + DLAT&DCAU&PSD	0.6512	0.6438	0.6975	0.7006

The experiment results show that totally the DLAT& DCAU&PSD feature has better performance than PSD feature, the best BLDA classification accuracy on the stepwise DSA-CSP 1-iteration filtered feature is 0.6834, which is 12.2% better than the best performance 0.5611 of PCA algorithm. While the best BLDA classification accuracy on our proposed Ext-CSP filtered feature reaches 0.7006, which is 14% better than that of PCA and 1.7% better than that of stepwise DSA-CSP 1-iteration algorithm.

Table 6. Classification accuracy of Ext-CSP with different λ parameters

Classifier	Ext-CSP preprocessed DLAT&DCAU&PSD feature (d = 10)					
	$\lambda = 0$	$\lambda = 0.1$	$\lambda = 0.3$	$\lambda = 0.5$	$\lambda = 0.7$	$\lambda = 1$
BT	0.6355	**0.6512**	0.6355	0.4625	0.3207	0.2461
SVM	0.6280	**0.6438**	0.6382	0.4132	0.2992	0.2209
LDA	0.6734	**0.6975**	0.6691	0.5064	0.4345	0.2658
BLDA	0.6802	**0.7006**	0.6774	0.5278	0.4611	0.2872

We compute the Ext-CSP spatial filter with $\lambda = \{0, 0.1, 0.3, 0.5, 0.7, 1\}$. Table 6 shows the average classification accuracy of all subjects with increasing regularization parameter λ. One can see that the accuracies of four classifiers are all best when λ is 0.1 and decreases with increasing regularization when $\lambda > 0.3$. The method relies completely on other days' data if the parameter is 1 and corresponds to standard CSP if the parameter is 0.

5 Conclusion

This study proposes an Ext-CSP framework to maximize the discrepancy between two classes, as well as alleviate the cross-day variability in the EEG data for the emotion classification problem based on KL divergence. The experiment results demonstrate that our unified Ext-CSP framework not only extracted more discriminative feature and increased the robustness and generalizability of the extracted EEG features, but also reduced the day-to-day non-stationarity. Sequentially, leveraging the Ext-CSP filtered EEG features from multiple days appeared to improve the emotion classification performance steadily, which was not the case when using the raw EEG features. Meanwhile, the cross-day performance improvement may also better account for the Ext-CSP filtered EEG features regarding emotions along days. In the future, we will explore the deep learning method [28, 29] and attention-based algorithm [30] for spatiotemporal salient feature extraction for EEG-based emotion recognition.

References

1. Wang, X.W., Nie, D., Lu, B.L.: Emotional state classification from EEG data using machine learning approach. Neurocomputing **129**, 94–106 (2014)
2. Liu, Y.H., Wu, C.T., Kao, Y.H., Chen, Y.T.: Single-trial EEG based emotion recognition using kernel Eigen-emotion pattern and adaptive support vector machine. In: 35th Annual International Conference of the IEEE Engineering in Medicine and Biology Society (EMBC), pp. 4306–4309 (2013)
3. Lin, Y.P., Yang, Y.H., Jung, T.P.: Fusion of electroencephalographic dynamics and musical contents for estimating emotional responses in music listening. Front. Neurosci. **8**, 94 (2014)
4. Feng, W., Huang, W., Ren, J.: Class imbalance ensemble learning based on the margin theory. Appl. Sci. **8**(5), 815 (2018)
5. Jiang, J., Trundle, P., Ren, J.: Medical image analysis with artificial neural networks. Comput. Med. Imag. Graph. **34**(8), 617–631 (2010)
6. Ren, J.: ANN vs. SVM: which one performs better in classification of MCCs in mammogram imaging. Knowl.-Based Syst. **26**, 144–153 (2012)
7. Lin, Y.P., Hsu, S.H., Jung, T.P.: Exploring day-to-day variability in the relations between emotion and EEG signals. In: Schmorrow, D.D., Fidopiastis, C.M. (eds.) AC 2015. LNCS, vol. 9183, pp. 461–469. Springer, Cham (2015). https://doi.org/10.1007/978-3-319-20816-9_44
8. Lin, Y.P., Jung, T.P.: Exploring day-to-day variability in EEG-based emotion classification. In: IEEE International Conference on System, Man, and Cybernetics, SMC, pp. 2226–2229 (2014)

9. Samek, W., Kawanabe, M., Vidaurre, C.: Group-wise stationary subspace analysis—A novel method for studying non-stationarities. In: Proceedings of 5th International Brain Computer Interface Conference, pp. 16–20. IOPscience, Bristol (2011)
10. Thomas, K.P.C., Guan, C.T., Lau, V., Prasad, A., Ang, K.K.: Adaptive tracking of discriminative frequency components in EEG for a robust brain computer interface. J. Neural Eng. **8**(3), 1–15 (2011)
11. Sugiyama, M., Krauledat, M., Müller, K.R.: Covariate shift adaptation by importance weighted cross validation. J. Mach. Learn. Res. **8**, 985–1005 (2007)
12. Blankertz, B., Müller, K.R., Krusienski, D.: The BCI competition III: validating alternative approaches to actual BCI problems. IEEE Trans. Neural Syst. Rehabil. Eng. **14**(2), 153–159 (2006)
13. Tangermann, M., Müller, K.R., Aertsen, A.: Review of the BCI competition IV. Front. Neurosci. **6**, 55 (2012)
14. Lin, Y.P., Yang, Y.H., Jung, T.P.: Fusion of electroencephalographic dynamics and musical contents for estimating emotional responses in music listening. Front. Neurosci. **1**, 88–94 (2014)
15. Hyvärinen, A.: Survey on independent component analysis. Neural Comput. Surv. **2**, 94–128 (1999)
16. Kawanabe, M., Samek, W., von Bünau, P., Meinecke, F.C.: An information geometrical view of stationary subspace analysis. In: Honkela, T., Duch, W., Girolami, M., Kaski, S. (eds.) Artificial Neural Networks and Machine Learning—ICANN 2011. LNCS, vol. 6792, pp. 397–404. Springer, Heidelberg (2011). https://doi.org/10.1007/978-3-642-21738-8_51
17. Samek, W., Blythe, D., Müller, K.R., Kawanabe, M.: Robust spatial filtering with beta divergence. In: Proceedings of Advances in Neural Information Processing System, NIPS, vol. 26, pp. 1007–1015 (2013)
18. Samek, W., Kawanabe, M., Müller, K.R.: Divergence-based framework for common spatial patterns algorithms. IEEE Rev. Biomed. Eng. **7**, 50–72 (2014)
19. Wang, H.: Harmonic mean of Kullback-Leibler divergences for optimizing multi-class EEG spatio-temporal filters. Neural Process. Lett. **36**(2), 161–171 (2012)
20. Von Bünau, P.: Stationary subspace analysis—Towards understanding non-stationary data. Ph.D. dissertation. Department Software Engineering Theoretical Computer Science, Technik University at Berlin, Berlin, Germany (2012)
21. Plumbley, M.D.: Geometrical methods for non-negative ICA: manifolds, lie groups and toral subalgebras. Neurocomputing **67**, 161–197 (2005)
22. Chuang, S.W., Ko, L.W., Lin, Y.P., Huang, R.S., Jung, T.P., Lin, C.T.: Co-modulatory spectral changes in independent brain processes are correlated with task performance. Neuroimage **62**, 1469–1477 (2012)
23. Scholkopft, B., Mullert, K.R.: Fisher discriminant analysis with kernels. Neural Netw. Signal Process. **IX**(1), 1 (1999)
24. Hoffmann, U., Vesin, J.M., Ebrahimi, T., Diserens, K.: An efficient P300-based brain–computer interface for disabled subjects. J. Neurosci. Methods **167**, 115–125 (2008)
25. Cortes, C., Vapnik, V.: Support-vector networks. Mach. Learn. **20**, 273–297 (1995)
26. Arvaneh, M., Guan, C., Ang, K.K., Quek, C.: EEG data space adaptation to reduce intersession non-stationarity in brain-computer interface. Neural Comput. **25**, 2146–2171 (2013)
27. Wang, Y.J., Gao, S.K., Gao, X.R.: Common spatial pattern method for channel selection in motor imagery based brain-computer interface. In: Proceedings of the 2005 IEEE Engineering in Medicine and Biology 27th Annual Conference, Shanghai, China, pp. 5392–5395 (2005)

28. Wang, Z., Ren, J., Zhang, D., Sun, M., Jiang, J.: A deep-learning based feature hybrid framework for spatiotemporal saliency detection inside videos. Neurocomputing **287**, 68–83 (2018)
29. Han, J., Zhang, D., Hu, X., Guo, L., Ren, J., Wu, F.: Background prior-based salient object detection via deep reconstruction residual. IEEE Trans. Circuits Syst. Video Technol. **25**(8), 1309–1321 (2015)
30. Yan, Y., Ren, J., Sun, G., Zhao, H., Han, J., Li, X., et al.: Unsupervised image saliency detection with gestalt-laws guided optimization and visual attention based refinement. Pattern Recogn. **79**, 65–78 (2018)

CSA-DE/EDA: A Clonal Selection Algorithm Using Differential Evolution and Estimation of Distribution Algorithm

Zhe Li[1], Yong Xia[1,2](✉), and Hichem Sahli[2,3,4]

[1] Shaanxi Key Lab of Speech and Image Information Processing (SAIIP), School of Computer Science and Engineering, Northwestern Polytechnical University, Xi'an 710072, China
yxia@nwpu.edu.cn

[2] Centre for Multidisciplinary Convergence Computing (CMCC), School of Computer Science and Engineering, Northwestern Polytechnical University, Xi'an 710072, China

[3] Audio Visual Signal Processing (AVSP), Department of Electronics and Informatics (ETRO), Vrije Universiteit Brussel (VUB), VUB-ETRO, Pleinlaan, 2, 1050 Brussels, Belgium

[4] Interuniversity Microelectronics Center, Kapeldreef 75, 3001 Leuven, Belgium

Abstract. The clonal selection algorithm (CSA), which describes the basic features of an immune response to an antigenic stimulus, has drawn a lot of research attention in the bio-inspired computing community, due to its highly-adaptive and easy-to-implement nature. However, despite many successful applications, this optimization technique still suffers from limited ability to explore the solution space. In this paper, we incorporate the differential evolution (DE) and estimation of distribution algorithm (EDA) into CSA, and thus propose a novel bio-inspired computing algorithm called CSA-DE/EDA. In this algorithm, the hypermutaion and receptor editing processes are implemented based on DE and EDA, which provide improved local and global search ability, respectively. We have applied this algorithm to brain image segmentation. Our comparative experimental results suggest that the proposed CSA-DE/EDA algorithm outperforms several bio-inspired computing techniques on the segmentation problem.

Keywords: Bio-inspired computing · Clonal selection algorithm (CSA) Differential evolution (DE) · Estimation of distribution algorithm (EDA) Image segmentation

1 Introduction

Optimization problems are commonly studied in almost every field of engineering for effective and efficient solutions [1]. Despite their wide-spread applications, traditional optimization algorithms, such as the gradient descent [2], pose many constraints on the objective function, including convexity, continuity, derivability and unimodality,

J. Ren et al. (Eds.): BICS 2018, LNAI 10989, pp. 293–302, 2018.
https://doi.org/10.1007/978-3-030-00563-4_28

which, unfortunately, are not always satisfied in most real-life problems [1]. With the explosive growth of computational power, bio-inspired computing techniques, which are capable of imitating the key principles in nature, such as the natural selection and clonal selection, have been applied to several optimization problems. These techniques are highly-adaptive and easy-to-implement, and pose less constraints on the objective function [3].

There are two important categories of bio-inspired computing techniques: evolutionary algorithms and swarm intelligence [4]. As one of the most prevalent evolutionary algorithms, the genetic algorithm (GA) uses heuristics-guided search that simulates the process of natural selection and survival of the fittest, and generates the next population of solutions via performing a combination of genetic operators on the current population, including selection, crossover and mutation, which enable GA to adapt to the changing environments. Although GA has the potential to search the global optimal, it often falls into local optima due to the limited runtime [3].

To improve the performance of GA, many enhancements have been proposed. Among them, the differential evolution (DE) [3] and estimation of distribution algorithm (EDA) [5] are two of the most well-known algorithms. DE generates the trial individuals by perturbing existing individuals with the scaled difference between two randomly selected individuals [6]. It has proven itself in competitions and a variety of real applications by producing more accurate results than several other optimization methods including GA, simulated annealing and evolutionary programming [7]. EDA, also known as the probabilistic model-building genetic algorithm, replaces the crossover and mutation operators with learning and sampling from the solution distribution in generating new offspring [8]. The advantages of EDA include the expressiveness and transparency of the probabilistic model that guides the search process, the absence of multiple parameters to be tuned, compact representation and the ability to avoid premature convergence. EDA has been proven to be better suited to some applications than GAs, while achieving competitive and robust results in the majority of the tackled problems [9].

As a well-known paradigm in swarm intelligence [4], the artificial immune system (AIS) [10] has drawn a lot of research attentions recently. Many AIS algorithms are designed to solve multimodal function optimization problems via mimicking the behavior of living organisms in protecting themselves against antigens. Inspired by the clonal selection principle of acquired immunity that explains how B and T lymphocytes improve their response to antigens over time [11], De Castro and Von Zuben [11] developed the clonal selection algorithm (CSA), which has shown superior performance compared to several other bionic algorithms and traditional optimizing mechanisms in a variety of applications [11, 12]. CSA is designed to simulate the affinity maturation process based on the clonal selection theory, which claims that only those cells that recognize the antigens will be selected to proliferate, and these cells will improve their affinity through an affinity maturation process [13].

Despite its success and prevalence, CSA can be further improved [14]. A good optimization algorithm should use both the local information around the current solutions and the global information about the search space [6]. The former is of great importance for exploitation, and the later can guide the search space for promising areas [6]. In CSA, antibodies are updated mainly via hypermutation and receptor editing, which perform local and global search, respectively. Considering the superior performance of DE and EDA, we suggest using them to perform local and global search in CSA, and thus combining the strength of both evolutionary algorithms and swarm intelligence. Therefore, in this paper we use DE and EDA to perform hypermutation and receptor editing, respectively, and accordingly propose the CSA-DE/EDA algorithm for global optimization problems. Since brain magnetic resonance (MR) image segmentation of gray matter (GM), white matter (WM) and cerebrospinal fluid (CSF) is pivotal for quantitative brain analyses and can popularly be transformed into the optimization problem by some models such as hidden Markov random field (HMRF) [15], the proposed algorithm has been evaluated against state-of-the-art brain image segmentation approaches on clinical brain MR images.

2 CSA-DE/EDA Algorithms

Similar to CSA, the proposed CSA-DE/EDA algorithm analogizes the clonal selection process to solve optimization problems

$$x^* = arg\max_{x \in R^D} f(x). \tag{1}$$

Each admissible solution x is encoded as an antibody $\boldsymbol{Ab}_i^k = \left[Ab_{i,1}^k, Ab_{i,2}^k, \ldots, Ab_{i,D}^k\right] \in R^D$, and the objective function $f(x)$ is defined as the adaptive immune response, namely the affinity, to the corresponding antigen. Solving this optimization problem is equivalent to searching the antibody that has the maximum affinity [11]. To this end, CSA-DE/EDA evolves (at kth generation) a population of antibodies, denoted by $\boldsymbol{Ab}^k = \{\boldsymbol{Ab}_1^k, \boldsymbol{Ab}_2^k, \ldots, \boldsymbol{Ab}_N^k\}$, where N is the population size and k gives the generation index. The population can be randomly initialized and updated on a generation-by-generation basis using five operators, including the selection, clone, DE-based hypermutation, reselection and EDA-based receptor editing [11], until a stopping criterion, such as a predefined maximum number of generations, is met. The diagram of CSA-DE/EDA is shown in Fig. 1.

2.1 Selection and Clone

For the kth generation of antibodies $\boldsymbol{Ab}^k = \{\boldsymbol{Ab}_1^k, \boldsymbol{Ab}_2^k, \ldots, \boldsymbol{Ab}_N^k\}$, the corresponding affinities are evaluated and presented as $\boldsymbol{f}^k = \{f(\boldsymbol{Ab}_1^k), f(\boldsymbol{Ab}_2^k), \ldots, f(\boldsymbol{Ab}_N^k)\}$. We select n highest-affinity antibodies, denoted by $\left\{\boldsymbol{Ab}_{\{1\}}^k, \boldsymbol{Ab}_{\{2\}}^k, \ldots, \boldsymbol{Ab}_{\{n\}}^k\right\}$, and clone each selected antibody n_i times. Then the number of antibodies in the clone set $\boldsymbol{C}^k$ is

$$N_c = \sum_{i=1}^{n} n_i = \alpha * n, \tag{2}$$

where α is the clonal multiplying factor that takes a positive integer and controls the cloning number [11]. In this paper, n_i is the same to all selected antibodies.

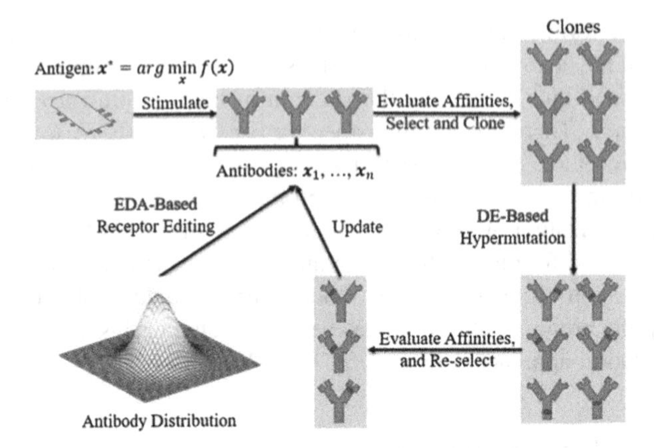

Fig. 1. Diagram of the proposed CSA-DE/EDA algorithm.

2.2 Hypermutation

The DE-based hypermutation is applied to each selected antibody $\boldsymbol{Ab}_i^k$ and its clones in $\boldsymbol{C}^k$ in three steps. First, a temporary antibody is generated as follows

$$\boldsymbol{Z} = \frac{\left(\boldsymbol{Ab}_d^k + \boldsymbol{Ab}_i^k\right)}{2} + F \cdot \left[\left(\boldsymbol{Ab}_d^k - \boldsymbol{Ab}_i^k\right) + \left(\boldsymbol{Ab}_b^k - \boldsymbol{Ab}_c^k\right)\right], \tag{3}$$

where $\boldsymbol{Ab}_d^k$ is randomly selected from $\boldsymbol{C}^k$ such that $f\left(\boldsymbol{Ab}_d^k\right) \leq f\left(\boldsymbol{Ab}_i^k\right)$, $\boldsymbol{Ab}_b^k$ and $\boldsymbol{Ab}_c^k$ are also randomly selected from $\boldsymbol{C}^k$, and F is a user specified scaling factor that controls the scaling of the difference vector. Second, the following crossover is applied to each temporary antibody $\boldsymbol{Z}$ and its parent $\boldsymbol{Ab}_i^k$ to generate a trial antibody $\boldsymbol{Ab}_i^{*k}$

$$Ab_{i,j}^{*k} = \begin{cases} Z_j & \textit{if } (rand < CR) \\ Ab_{i,j}^k, & \textit{otherwise} \end{cases}, j = 1, \cdots\cdots, D \tag{4}$$

where *rand* is a uniform distributed random value within the range $[0,\ 1]$ and CR is the user specified crossover rate. At the combination step, the obtained trial antibody $\boldsymbol{Ab}_i^{*k}$ replaces $\boldsymbol{Ab}_i^k$ in $\boldsymbol{C}^k$ if it has a higher affinity than the original antibody $\boldsymbol{Ab}_i^k$; otherwise, $\boldsymbol{Ab}_i^k$ is kept. After the hypermutation, $\boldsymbol{C}^k$ is termed $\boldsymbol{C}^{*k}$. Since CSA-DE/EDA uses the arithmetic combination rather than randomly changing, it can capture the local information in the current population for more efficient exploitation [3].

2.3 Reselection

For each antibody $\boldsymbol{Ab}_i^k$, there are n_i cloned and hypermutated copies, which form a subset of antibodies. To keep the size of antibody population unchanged, we reselect the best antibody in each subset and thus form a trial population.

2.4 Receptor Editing

Next, the EDA-based receptor editing is applied to the trial population. To explore the global information, we assume that the probabilistic distribution of the elite antibody is Gaussian and each component of the antibody is mutually independent. Thus, we have

$$p(\boldsymbol{Ab}^*) = \prod\nolimits_{d=1}^{D} p\left(Ab_d^*\right) = \prod\nolimits_{d=1}^{D} N\left(Ab_d^*;\, \mu_d,\, \sigma_d\right), \tag{5}$$

where $\boldsymbol{Ab}^* = \left[Ab_1^*, Ab_2^*, \ldots, Ab_D^*\right]$ is the globally optimal antibody, and $N(\cdot;\mu,\sigma)$ is a univariate Gaussian distribution with mean μ and standard deviation σ. To estimate the distribution $p(\boldsymbol{Ab}^*)$, we select m highest-affinity antibodies from the current generation $\boldsymbol{Ab}^k$ using the truncation selection [6] and apply the maximum likelihood estimation [6] to them, which results in the estimated Gaussian parameters $\left\{\mu_d^k,\, \sigma_d^k;\, d = 1, 2, \cdots, D\right\}$. Then, we sample $r * N$ antibodies from the distribution $\prod_{d=1}^{D} N\left(Ab_d^*;\, \mu_d^k,\, \sigma_d^k\right)$ and use them to replace $r * N$ lowest-affinity antibodies in the trial population. Usually, the number of selected antibodies m, denoted by $\boldsymbol{Ab}_{\{M\}}^k$, is set to $N/2$ [6].

2.5 Summary

The major steps of the proposed CSA-DE/EDA algorithm are summarized in Table 1.

Table 1. The CSA-DE/EDA algorithm.

Line	Pseudo code of CSA-DE/EDA
1	**Initialization:** Randomly generate N antibodies $\boldsymbol{Ab}^{\boldsymbol{0}}$ $(k = 0)$
2	**while** the stopping criterion is not met
3	Evaluate the vector $\boldsymbol{f}^{\boldsymbol{k}}$
4	Select $\boldsymbol{Ab}_{\{n\}}^{\boldsymbol{k}}$
5	Select $\boldsymbol{Ab}_{\{M\}}^{\boldsymbol{k}}$
6	Clone $\boldsymbol{Ab}_{\{n\}}^{\boldsymbol{k}} \rightarrow \boldsymbol{C}^{\boldsymbol{k}}$
7	DE-based hypermutation $\boldsymbol{C}^{\boldsymbol{k}} \rightarrow \boldsymbol{C}^{*\boldsymbol{k}}$
8	Reselect from $\boldsymbol{C}^{*\boldsymbol{k}}$ to obtain $\boldsymbol{Ab}^{\boldsymbol{k+1}}$
9	EDA-based receptor editing to replace the $r * N$ lowest affinity antibodies from $\boldsymbol{Ab}^{\boldsymbol{k+1}}$
10	**end**

3 Application to MR Image Segmentation

The proposed CSA-DE/EDA algorithm can be applied to many image segmentation problems, such as the segmentation of brain MR images that aims to delineate the gray matter (GM), white matter (WM) and cerebrospinal fluid (CSF) from the brain.

Let an observed brain MR image be an instance of the image random field $\boldsymbol{Y}$, and the corresponding segmentation result be an instance of the label random field $\boldsymbol{X}$.

According to the HMRF model, this segmentation task can be converted into the following optimization problem.

$$\boldsymbol{X}^* = \arg\max_{\boldsymbol{X}} p(\boldsymbol{X}|\boldsymbol{Y}, \boldsymbol{b}, \boldsymbol{\theta}^*) \tag{6}$$

$$\boldsymbol{\theta}^* = \arg\max_{\boldsymbol{\theta}} p(\boldsymbol{\theta}|\boldsymbol{Y}, \boldsymbol{b}, \boldsymbol{X}^*) \tag{7}$$

where $\boldsymbol{b}$ is the bias field, $\boldsymbol{\theta} = \{\theta_k|k = 1, 2, \cdots, K\}$ the ensemble of model parameters, K the number of classes, and

$$p(\boldsymbol{\theta}|\boldsymbol{Y}, \boldsymbol{b}, \boldsymbol{X}^*) \propto p(\boldsymbol{Y}|\boldsymbol{X}^*, \boldsymbol{b}, \boldsymbol{\theta})p(\boldsymbol{\theta}) = \prod_j \sum_k \left[N(Y_j - b_j|X_j = k;\, \theta_k)p(\theta_k)\right], \tag{8}$$

with $N(x;\, \theta_k)$ a Gaussian distribution with parameter $\theta_k = (u_k, \sigma_k)$. This problem can be solved using a three-step iterative process, which starts from a random initialization and iteratively (1) using the method in [16] to update the bias filed $\boldsymbol{b}$, (2) using the CSA-DE/EDA algorithm to solve the sub-problem given in Eq. (7) and update the model parameters (i.e. $\boldsymbol{\theta}$ being the antibody), and (3) using the iterated conditional mode (ICM) approach [17] to update the segmentation result.

Since the region-based HMRF method [18] is more robust to noise and artifacts than pixel-based HMRF but may offer a too smooth and relatively holistic view of the image to be segmented, we jointly used both region- and pixel-based HMRF methods. We first adopted the super pixel algorithm-TurboPixel [19] to over-segment a brain MR image into small regions $\boldsymbol{R} = \{R_i|i = 1, 2, \ldots, m\}$, where m is the number of regions. Then the region adjacency graph (RAG) can be defined on $\boldsymbol{R}$, where each region R_i corresponds to a node of the graph. The intensity of each node is the average intensity of all pixels in this region. So, we perform region-based segmentation to generate a coarse result. Next, we estimate the ranges of model parameters based on the coarse result and perform pixel-based segmentation to produce the final result. This process is summarized in Algorithm 2.

Algorithm 2: HMRF-CSA/DE/EDA MR segmentation algorithm

Input: observed brain MR image $\boldsymbol{Y}$

Output: optimal voxel class labels $\boldsymbol{X}$ and model parameters $\boldsymbol{\theta}$.

1 **Initialization:** segmentation by k-means, random model parameters and initial bias field $\boldsymbol{b}$

2 **while** the stopping criterion is not met (region-based)

3 Evaluate the vector $\boldsymbol{f^k}$ through Eq. (8)

4 Select $\boldsymbol{Ab^k_{\{n\}}}$

5 Select $\boldsymbol{Ab^k_{\{M\}}}$

6 Clone $\boldsymbol{Ab^k_{\{n\}}} \rightarrow \boldsymbol{C^k}$

7 Hypermutation using DE $\boldsymbol{C^k} \rightarrow \boldsymbol{C^{*k}}$

8 Reselect from $\boldsymbol{C^{*k}}$ to partly replace $\boldsymbol{Ab^k}$

9 EDA-based receptor editing

10: Update class labels in Eq. (6) by ICM

11: Update the bias field using the method in [16]

12: **end**

13 Execute step 2 to 12 again with the ranges of $\boldsymbol{\theta}$ (pixel-based)

4 Experiments and Results

The proposed CSA-DE/EDA algorithm has been applied to the segmentation of clinical brain MR images obtained from the internet brain segmentation repository (IBSR). The segmentation experiment was performed on 18 T1-weighted clinical brain MR images with expert segmentations (IBSR_V2.0) [20]. Each image was first spatially normalized into the Talairach orientation, and then resliced into a dimension of 256 * 256 * 128 voxels with a voxel size of 1.0 * 1.0 * 1.5 mm^3. The parameters used in this algorithm were empirically set as follows: population size $N = 50$, scaling factor $F = 0.9$, crossover rate $CR = 0.1$, clonal multiplying factor $\alpha = 2$, replacement ratio $r = 0.1$ and the maximum iterations is 15, including 5 iterations for region-based segmentation and 10 iterations for pixel-based segmentation. The accuracy of delineating gray matter and white matter was assessed quantitatively by using the Dice similarity coefficient (DSC).

$$D(V_s(k), V_g(k)) = 2 * \frac{|V_s(k) \cap V_g(k)|}{|V_s(k)| + |V_g(k)|} \tag{9}$$

where $V_s(k)$ is the volume of brain tissue class k in the segmentation result, $V_g(k)$ is the corresponding volume in the ground truth, and $|V|$ represents the number of voxels in volume V. DSC takes a value from the range $[0, 1]$, and a higher value represents more accurate brain tissue delineation. The accuracy of segmenting the entire brain volume is measured by the percentage of correctly classified voxels.

Figure 2 shows the 68th coronal slice of the study "IBSR_09", the intermediate segmentation result and final result of the proposed algorithm, and the ground truth brain tissue map. It reveals that the final result after the region- and pixel-based segmentation processes is more similar to the ground truth than the result obtained by using only the region-based segmentation.

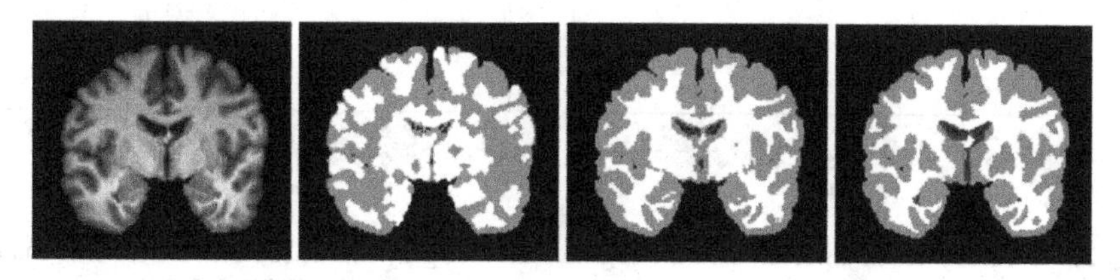

Fig. 2. An example coronal slice from the Brain MRI study "IBSR_09" (left), and the corresponding result of region-based segmentation (middle left), result of region- and pixel-based segmentation (middle right) and ground truth (right).

Next, the proposed algorithm was quantitatively compared to the GMM-based unified registration-segmentation routine in SPM [21], the classic HMRF-EM algorithm of the FSL packages [22], the GA-GMM algorithm of the GAMixute package [23], the D-C algorithm [24] and the HMRF-CSA [25]. The accuracy of these six algorithms in the segmentation of gray matter, white matter and overall brain volume on each image is depicted in Fig. 3, and the average segmentation accuracies of these algorithms are compared in Table 2. As it can be noticed, the proposed HMRF-CSA/DE/EDA algorithm can produce more accurate segmentation of gray matter and overall brain volume than the other five algorithms on the IBSR_V2.0 dataset.

We conducted the ablation experiment with HMRF-CSA/DE/EDA and HMRF-CSA/DE/EDA without region-based part (PHMRF-CSA/DE/EDA). The average accuracy and time cost of the two algorithms on one 3D MR image of IBSR_V2.0 are shown in Table 3 (Intel Core i7-4710HQ CPU, 16 GB memory and Matlab R2015a). It shows that HMRF-CSA/DE/EDA outperforms PHMRF-CSA/DE/EDA, which means that the region-based HMRF can indeed improve the pixel-based HMRF as an auxiliary. However, HMRF-CSA/DE/EDA still has a relatively high computational complexity due to the time-consuming nature of bio-inspired algorithms.

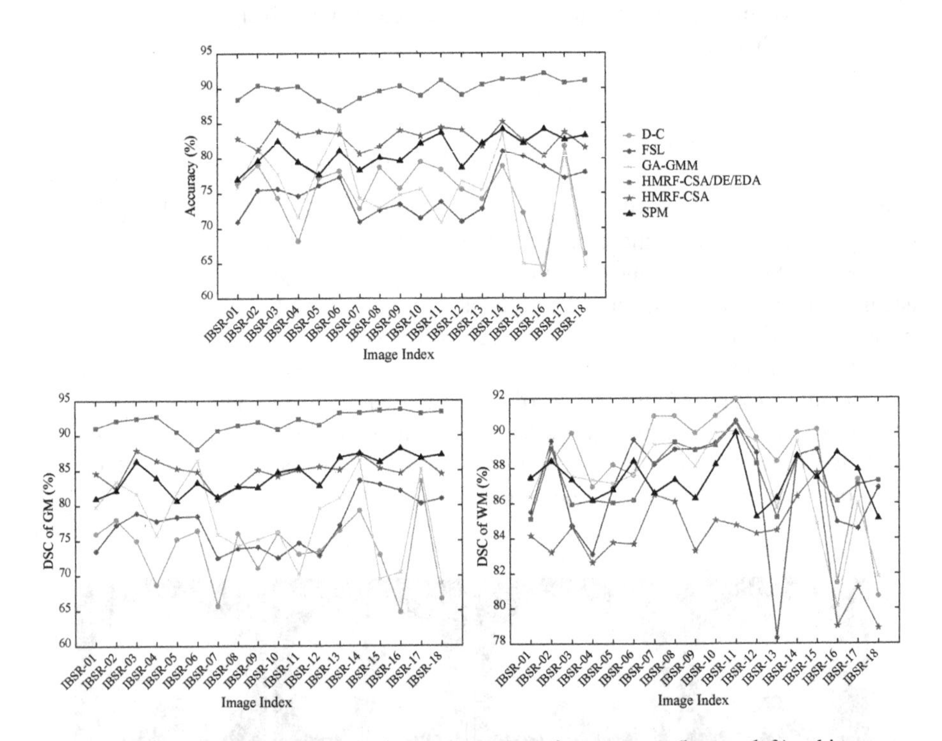

Fig. 3. Accuracy of six algorithms in the segmentation of gray matter (bottom left), white matter (bottom right) and overall brain volume (top) on each image in the IBSR_V2.0 dataset.

Table 2. Average segmentation accuracy of six algorithms on the IBSR_V2.0 dataset.

Accuracy	FSL	D-C	SPM	GA-EM	HMRF-CSA	HMRF-CSA/DE/EDA
Overall	75.06%	75.02%	81.02%	74.97%	82.95%	**89.90%**
GM	77.35%	73.80%	84.42%	77.90%	84.92%	**92.02%**
WM	87.08%	**88.41%**	87.38%	87.23%	83.88%	87.52%

Table 3. Average accuracy and time cost of PHMRF-CSA/DE/EDA and HMRF-CSA/DE/EDA

	Accuracy	GM	WM	Time
HMRF-CSA/DE/EDA	**89.90%**	**92.02%**	**87.52%**	**1510** s
PHMRF-CSA/DE/EDA	85.09%	86.85%	86.66%	2164 s

5 Conclusion

In this paper, we proposed the CSA-DE/EDA algorithm for optimization problems. This algorithm incorporates DE and EDA into the CSA process, and thus generates offspring solutions by jointly using both local and global information from the current generation. Our experimental results indicated that the proposed algorithm outperforms the GA-GMM, HMRF-CSA, D-C algorithms and the brain image segmentation routine in the commonly used SPM and FSL packages for brain MR image segmentation. In future work we will mainly focus on reducing the computation time of the algorithm by using parallel computing techniques and designing adaptive parameters to further improve the robustness of CSA-DE/EDA [26, 27].

References

1. Zhang, A., Sun, G., Ren, J., Li, X., Wang, Z., Jia, X.: A dynamic neighborhood learning-based gravitational search algorithm. IEEE Trans. Cybern. **48**(1), 436–447 (2016)
2. Ji, L., Zhou. T.: On gradient descent algorithm for generalized phase retrieval problem. In: International Conference on Signal Processing, ICSP, pp. 320–325 (2016)
3. Binitha, S., Sathya, S.S.: A survey of bio inspired optimization algorithms. Int. J. Soft Comput. Eng. **2**(2), 137–151 (2012)
4. Timmis, J., Andrews, P., Hart, E.: On artificial immune systems and swarm intelligence. Swarm Intell. **4**(4), 247–273 (2010)
5. Peña, J.M., Robles, V., Larrañaga, P., Herves, V., Rosales, F., Pérez, M.S.: GA-EDA: hybrid evolutionary algorithm using genetic and estimation of distribution algorithms. In: Orchard, B., Yang, C., Ali, M. (eds.) IEA/AIE 2004. LNCS, vol. 3029, pp. 361–371. Springer, Heidelberg (2004). https://doi.org/10.1007/978-3-540-24677-0_38
6. Sun, J., Zhang, Q., Tsang, E.P.K.: DE/EDA: a new evolutionary algorithm for global optimization. Inf. Sci. **169**(3–4), 249–262 (2005)
7. Onwubolu, G.C., Babu, B.V.: New Optimization Techniques in Engineering. Springer, Berlin (2004). https://doi.org/10.1007/978-3-540-39930-8
8. Huda, S., Yearwood, J., Togneri, R.: A constraint-based evolutionary learning approach to the expectation maximization for optimal estimation of the hidden Markov model for speech signal modeling. IEEE Trans. Syst. Man Cybern. Part B Cybern. **39**(1), 182–197 (2009). A Publication of the IEEE Systems Man & Cybernetics Society
9. Armañanzas, R., Inza, I., Santana, R., Saeys, Y., Flores, J.L., Lozano, J.A., et al.: A review of estimation of distribution algorithms in bioinformatics. Biodata Min. **1**(1), 6 (2008)
10. Vidal, J.M., Orozco, A.L.S., Villalba, L.J.G.: Adaptive artificial immune networks for mitigating DoS flooding attacks. Swarm Evolut. Comput. **38**, 94–108 (2018)
11. Castro, L.N.D., Zuben, F.J.V.: Learning and optimization using the clonal selection principle. IEEE Trans. Evol. Comput. **6**(3), 239–251 (2002)

12. Batista, L., Guimaraes, F.G., Ramirez, J.A.: A distributed clonal selection algorithm for optimization in electromagnetics. IEEE Trans. Magn. **45**(3), 1598–1601 (2009)
13. Castro, L.N.D., Zuben, F.J.V.: Clonal selection algorithm with engineering applications. In: GECCO 2002—Workshop Proceedings, pp. 36–37 (2002)
14. Zhang, L., Gong, M., Jiao, L., Yang, J.: Optimal approximation of linear systems by an improved Clonal Selection Algorithm. In: IEEE Congress on Evolutionary Computation, pp. 527–534 (2008)
15. Zhang, Y., Brady, M., Smith, S.: Segmentation of brain MR images through a hidden Markov random field model and the expectation-maximization algorithm. IEEE Trans. Med. Imag. **20**(1), 45–57 (2001)
16. Li, C., Gatenby, C., Wang, L., Gore, J.C.: A robust parametric method for bias field estimation and segmentation of MR images. In: IEEE Conference on Computer Vision and Pattern Recognition, pp. 218–223 (2009)
17. Besag, J.: On the statistical analysis of dirty pictures. J. Roy. Stat. Soc. Ser. B (Methodol.) **48** (3), 259–302 (1986)
18. Zheng, C., Yijun, H., Leiguang, W., Qianqing, Q.: Region-based MRF model with optimized initial regions for image segmentation. In: International Conference on Remote Sensing, Environment and Transportation Engineering, RSETE, pp. 3354–3357 (2011)
19. Levinshtein, A., Stere, A., Kutulakos, K.N., Fleet, D.J., Dickinson, S.J., Siddiqi, K.: TurboPixels: fast superpixels using geometric flows. IEEE Trans. Pattern Anal. Mach. Intell. **31**(12), 2290–2297 (2009)
20. Rohlfing, T.: Image similarity and tissue overlaps as surrogates for image registration accuracy: widely used but unreliable. IEEE Trans. Med. Imag. **31**(2), 153–163 (2012)
21. Flandin, G., Friston, K.J.: Statistical parametric mapping (SPM). Scholarpedia **3**(4), 6232 (2008)
22. FMRIB Software Library, in http://fsl.fmrib.ox.ac.uk/fsl/
23. Tohka, J., Krestyannikov, E., Dinov, I.D., Graham, M.K., Shattuck, D.W., Ruotsalainen, U., et al.: Genetic algorithms for finite mixture model based voxel classification in neuroimaging. IEEE Trans. Med. Imag. **26**(5), 696–711 (2007)
24. Zhang, T., Xia, Y., Feng, D.D.: A deformable cosegmentation algorithm for brain MR images. In: Engineering in Medicine and Biology Society, EMBC, pp. 3215–3218 (2012)
25. Zhang, T., Xia, Y., Feng, D.D.: Hidden Markov random field model based brain MR image segmentation using clonal selection algorithm and Markov chain Monte Carlo method. Biomed. Signal Process. Control **12**(1), 10–18 (2014)
26. Sun, G., Ma, P., Ren, J., Zhang, A., Jia, X.: A stability constrained adaptive alpha for gravitational search algorithm. Knowl. Based Syst. **139**, 200–213 (2018)
27. Wei, F., Wenjiang, H., Jinchang, R.: Class imbalance ensemble learning based on the margin theory. Appl. Sci. **8**(5), 815 (2018)

Early Identification of Alzheimer's Disease Using an Ensemble of 3D Convolutional Neural Networks and Magnetic Resonance Imaging

Yuanyuan Chen[1], Haozhe Jia[1], Zhaowei Huang[2], and Yong Xia[1(✉)]

[1] National Engineering Laboratory for Integrated Aero-Space-Ground-Ocean Big Data Application Technology, School of Computer Science and Engineering, Northwestern Polytechnical University, Xi'an 710072, China
yxia@nwpu.edu.cn

[2] Biomedical and Multimedia Information Technology (BMIT) Research Group, School of IT, University of Sydney, Sydney, NSW 2006, Australia

Abstract. Alzheimer's disease (AD) has become a nonnegligible global health threat and social problem as the world population ages. The ability to identify AD subjects in an early stage will be increasingly important as disease modifying therapies for AD are developed. In this paper, we propose an ensemble of 3D convolutional neural networks (en3DCNN) for automated identification of AD patients from normal controls using structural magnetic resonance imaging (MRI). We first employ the anatomical automatic labeling (AAL) cortical parcellation map to obtain 116 cortical volumes, then use the samples extracted from each cortical volume to train a 3D convolutional neural network (CNN), and finally assemble the predictions made by well-performed 3D CNNs via majority voting to classify each subject. We evaluated our algorithm against six existing algorithms on 764 MRI scans selected from the Alzheimer's Disease Neuroimaging Initiative (ADNI) database. Our results indicate that the proposed en3DCNN algorithm is able to achieve the state-of-the-art performance in early identification of Alzheimer's Disease using structural MRI.

Keywords: Alzheimer's disease · Computer-aided diagnosis
Ensemble learning · 3D convolutional neural network

1 Introduction

Alzheimer's disease (AD) is the most common neurodegenerative disease among elderly people, mainly characterized by cognitive dysfunction and behavior disorder, occupying 50% to 70% of all dementia types. According to the world health bureau, the number of people suffering from AD worldwide is about 47 million in 2015 and is expected to be 141 million in 2050. Today, treatments can only help with relieving the symptoms of this disease, and there are no available treatments that can stop or reverse its progression. Nevertheless, the early diagnosis of AD affords the AD patients awareness of the severity and allows them to take prevention measures, e.g., lifestyle changing and medications [1], which could improve their cognition and enhance their life quality. Thus it is of great importance to accurately diagnose AD at an early stage.

J. Ren et al. (Eds.): BICS 2018, LNAI 10989, pp. 303–311, 2018.
https://doi.org/10.1007/978-3-030-00563-4_29

To support AD diagnosis, several modalities of biomarkers have been investigated to explore the difference of the brains between AD patients and normal controls (NCs). Magnetic resonance imaging (MRI), which is a non-invasive neuroimaging tool, has been employed for developing computer-aided diagnosis [2]. Structural MRI provides good contrast between gray matter and subcortical brain structures and abundant information on the structural integrity of the brain tissue. Hence it has been regularly used to diagnose AD patients and NCs.

Many machine learning methods have been proposed to aid the diagnosis of AD using structural MRI, including region-of-interest (ROI) analysis [3] and whole brain analysis [4]. Specifically, ROI-based measures (e.g., cortical thickness [5], hippocampal volume [3], and gray matter volume [6]) are traditionally adopted to measure regional anatomical volume and to investigate abnormal tissue structures in the brain. Kloppel et al. [7] used the gray matter (GM) voxels as features and trained a support vector machine (SVM) to discriminate the AD subjects from the NC ones. To quantify the hippocampus shape for feature extraction, Gerardin et al. [8] segmented and aligned the hippocampus regions for various subjects and modeled their shape with a series of spherical harmonics. Zhang et al. [9] proposed a landmark-based feature extraction method that does not require nonlinear registration and tissue segmentation for AD diagnosis. Whole brain analysis captures structural changes to quantify brain atrophy, among which voxel-based morphometry (VBM) [10], deformation-based morphometry (DBM) [11] and tensor-based morphometry (TBM) [12] are the typical examples. Specifically, VBM directly measures local tissue density of a brain via voxel-wise analysis, DBM detects morphological differences from non-linear deformation fields that align/warp images to a common anatomical template, and TBM identifies regional structural differences from local Jacobians of deformation fields, respectively.

Recently, deep learning had been successfully applied to medical images analysis with its fast development in the field of natural image classification [13, 14]. It can achieve feature extraction and image classification in an end to end manner and remove the subjectivity and workload that comes with the hand-crafted features [15]. Ortiz et al. [16] applied the deep belief network to the early diagnosis of the Alzheimer's disease using both MRI and PET scans. Suk and Shen [17] used a stacked autoencoder to extract features from MRI, PET, and cerebrospinal fluid (CSF) images, respectively. Suk et al. [18] used a multimodal deep Boltzmann machine (DBM) to extract one feature from each selected patch of the MRI and PET scans and predict AD with an ensemble of SVMs. Liu et al. [19] extracted 83 regions-of-interest (ROI) from the MRI and PET scans and used multimodal fusion to create a set of features to train stacked layers of denoising autoencoders. Vu et al. [20] used sparse autoencoder and convolutional neural network (CNN) to train and test on combined PET-MRI data to diagnose the disease status of a patient. Li et al. [21] proposed a classification method based on the combination of multi-model 3D CNNs to learn the various features from MR brain images. Li et al. [22] present a robust deep learning system to identify different progression stages of AD patients based on MRI and PET scans and utilized the dropout technique to improve classical deep learning by preventing its weight coadaptation.

In this paper, we propose an ensemble of 3D CNNs (en3DCNN) for the differentiation of AD patients from NCs using structural MRI. We first employ the

Anatomical Automatic Labeling (AAL) cortical parcellation map to obtain 116 types of anatomical volumes of the brain. Then, we use the volumes sampled from each cortical type to train a 3D CNN. Finally, we assemble the predictions made by well-performed 3D CNNs via majority voting to classify each MRI case. We evaluated our algorithm on 764 MRI scans selected from the Alzheimer's Disease Neuroimaging Initiative (ADNI) database, and achieved the state-of-the-art performance.

2 Dataset

Data used in this paper were obtained from the ADNI database (adni.loni.usc.edu). The ADNI was launched in 2003 as a public-private partnership, led by Principal Investigator Michael W. Weiner, MD. The primary goal of ADNI is to test whether serial MRI, PET, other biological markers, and clinical and neuropsychological assessment can be combined to measure the progression of MCI and early AD.

The obtained data are raw Digital Imaging and Communications in Medicine (DICOM) structural MRI scans, including 347 patients with Alzheimer's disease and 417 NCs. The demographic information of subjects is shown in Table 1. MRI data acquisition was performed according to the ADNI acquisition protocol [23]. Scanning was performed on different 3 Tesla scanners: General Electric (GE) Healthcare, Philips Medical Systems, and Siemens Medical Solutions based on identical scanning parameters. Anatomical scans were acquired with a 3D MPRAGE sequence (TR = 2 s, TE = 2.63 ms, FOV = 25.6 cm, 256 $\times$ 256 matrix, 160 slices of 1 mm thickness). We preprocessed these data through a pipeline that includes motion correction, non-uniformity (NU) intensity correction, Talairach space conversion, normalization and skull stripping with the software FreeSurfer [24] of Neuroimaging Informatics Technology Initiative (NIFTI) format. Then we aligned these data to an AAL atlas [25] using the statistical parametric mapping (SPM) package [26].

Table 1. Demographics data of patients in our dataset

Diagnosis	Number	Gender (F/M)	Age (mean $\pm$ std)
AD	347	170/152	74.8 $\pm$ 9.1
NC	417	189/200	73.8 $\pm$ 8.2

3 Method

The proposed en3DCNN algorithm consists of four major steps: volume partition, data augmentation, VOI classification, and ensemble decision. The diagram of our proposed algorithm is shown in Fig. 1.

3.1 Volume Partition

The AAL cortical parcellation map [27] is a digital human brain atlas with 116 labeled anatomical volumes, including 54 pairs of symmetrical volumes and 8 asymmetrical

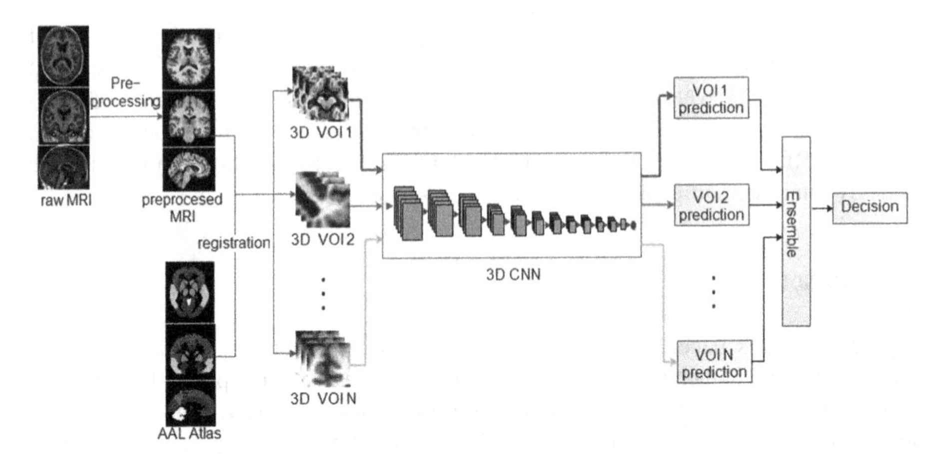

Fig. 1. Diagram of the proposed en3DCNN algorithm.

volumes. For each volume, we calculated a 3D bounding box by its specific voxel value on the AAL atlas. As all 3D brain images were aligned to the AAL atlas in the preprocessing procedure, we employed the obtained 116 bounding boxes to extract 116 anatomical volumes on the 3D brain image of each subject.

For each subject, since the obtained 116 volumes have different size, we resized each volume to a size of $60 \times 60 \times 60$. In order to consider the symmetry of the 54 pairs of symmetrical volumes, we concatenated every two symmetrical volumes together as a volume of interest (VOI) with the size of $60 \times 120 \times 60$. As a result, we obtained 62 VOIs, including 54 VOIs with the size of $60 \times 120 \times 60$ and 8 VOIs with the size of $60 \times 60 \times 60$.

3.2 Data Augmentation

Since the number of the original 3D brain images is limited, we employed data augmentation to enlarge our dataset. For each extracted 3D VOI, we flipped it along three dimensions, respectively. Thus the number of our data was increased by 3 times. Considering the other augmentation techniques may disrupt the original information in images, we didn't employ other augmentation techniques.

3.3 VOI Classification

For each ROI, we designed a 3D CNN to verify whether it can be used to classify AD patients from NCs or not. The architecture of the 3D CNN is shown in Fig. 2. The 3D CNN consists of 7 convolutional layers. The first five convolutional layers have rectified linear unit (ReLU) activation and are followed by max-pooling procedures to perform a down-sampling operation for their outputs. Then, we utilized two convolutional layers to replace fully connected layers by setting its kernel size same to its input size. The input of the 3D CNN are 3D VOIs with size of $60 \times 120 \times 60$ and $60 \times 60 \times 60$. The kernel size of the first five 3D convolutional layers is $3 \times 3 \times 3$, and for all the pooling layers it is $2 \times 2 \times 2$. The kernel size is same as its input size in both Conv6 and Conv7. To make the input and output have consistent size, zero padding is used in convolutional layers. At last, a flattening operation was added to obtain the final class label.

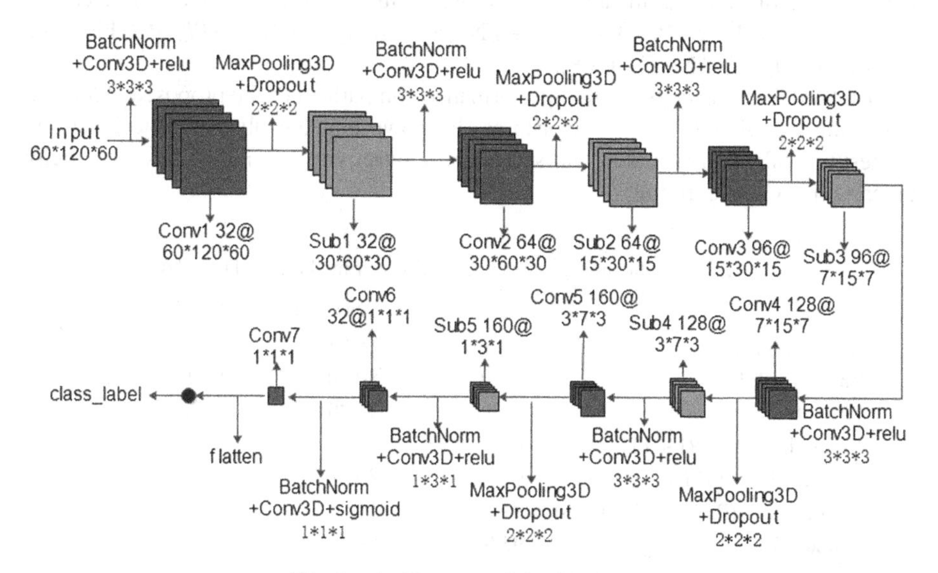

Fig. 2. Architecture of the 3D CNN.

The 3D CNN used for this study was implemented based on Keras and all layers were randomly initialized. We applied batch normalization before each convolutional layer to improve convergence of the network and added a dropout layer with a ratio of 0.5 after each pooling layer to avoid overfitting. The network was optimized by the stochastic gradient descent (SGD) algorithm with the momentum coefficient of 0.9 and the batch size of 16. The learning rate was set to $1e^{-3}$ in the first 20 epochs and was reduced to $1e^{-4}$ for the rest. The training process ended when the network did not significantly improve its performance on the validation set within epochs. We adopted the 5-fold cross validation scheme. The training set was split further into training and validation parts. Each time, all 3D CNN models used the same training, validation and testing parts.

3.4 Ensemble of 3D CNNs

For each VOI, we run the proposed 3D CNN to get an independent prediction result. After obtaining the predictions for all VOIs, we simply employed a majority voting strategy with the threshold of 0.75 to obtain the final decision.

4 Results

We use TP, TN, FP and FN to denote numbers of true positive, true negative, false positive, and false negative classification results for a given set of data items. Then the performance of AD classification is measured with the following metrics: accuracy (ACC) = (TP + TN)/(TP + TN + FP + FN); sensitivity (SEN) = TP/(TP + FN) and specificity (SPE) = TN/(TN + FP).

Table 2 gives the classification performance comparison of the proposed algorithm with other six state-of-the-art algorithms. It shows that our algorithm achieves the highest classification accuracy, the second best sensitivity and the highest specificity among all seven algorithms.

Table 2. Classification performances of seven methods (AD vs. NC)

Methods	Accuracy (%)	Sensitivity (%)	Specificity (%)
Liu et al. [19]	82.59	86.83	/
Zhang et al. [9]	83.10	80.50	85.10
Li et al. [21]	88.31	**91.40**	84.42
Vu et al. [20] (MRI + PET)	90	/	/
Ortiz et al. [16] (PET + MRI)	90	86	94
Li et al. [22] (PET + MRI + CSF)	91.4	/	/
Proposed	**93.9**	89.4	**95.1**

We finally used 10 VOIs with classification accuracy more than the threshold of 0.75 on testing set to assemble for the final prediction. These 10 VOIs are Hippocampus, Fusiform, ParaHippocampal, Amygdala, Calcarine, Postcentral, Caudate, Pallidum, Thalamus and Temporal_Sup.

5 Discussion

5.1 Ensemble Threshold

We discussed five different values of the ensemble threshold. The changing curves of the classification performances with different threshold values are shown in Fig. 3. Figure 3 implies we can obtain the highest accuracy, sensitivity and specificity when setting the threshold to 0.75.

5.2 Computational Complexity

The training time of the proposed en3DCNN is about 35 h (Intel Xeon E5-2678V3, NVIDIA Titan Xp GPU $\times$ 4, 128 GB Memory, 120 GB SSD). The test time of one case in our method is around 12 s. It is worth noting that although the preprocessing time for each scan is a little long (about 20 min), it has a great impact on the

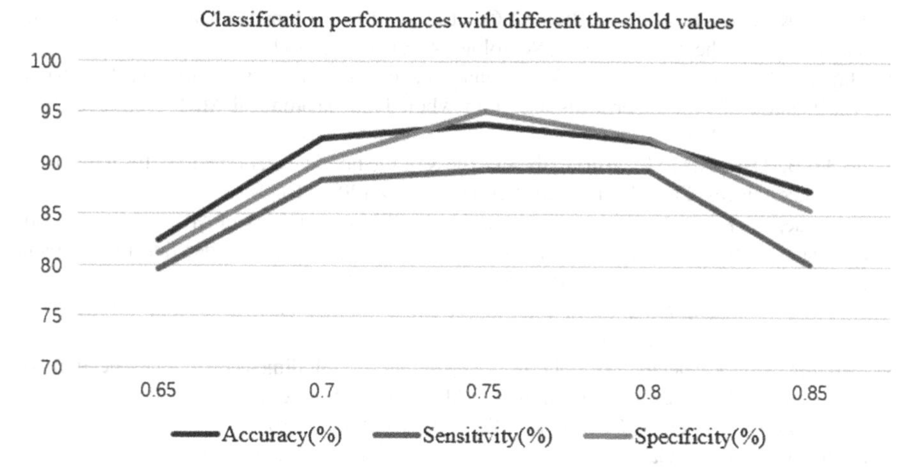

Fig. 3. Classification performances with different threshold values.

classification accuracy of AD. Thus it is necessary to do a preprocessing procedure for the raw data from ADNI dataset.

6 Conclusion

In this study, we propose en3DCNN algorithm for computer-aided diagnosis of AD patients and NCs. We first employ the AAL cortical parcellation map to obtain 62 anatomical VOIs for each 3D brain image, then use each VOI to train a 3D CNN, and finally employ majority voting strategy to assemble the prediction results of 10 VOIs. The evaluation on ANDI dataset indicates that the proposed en3DCNN outperforms the state-of-the-art approaches in differentiating AD cases from NCs.

Acknowledgements. This work was supported by the National Natural Science Foundation of China under Grants 61471297 and 61771397. Data collection and sharing for this project was funded by the Alzheimer's Disease Neuroimaging Initiative (ADNI) (National Institutes of Health Grant U01 AG024904) and DOD ADNI (Department of Defense award number W81XWH-12-2-0012). ADNI data are disseminated by the Laboratory for Neuro Imaging at the University of Southern California.

References

1. Baumgart, M., Snyder, H.M., Carrillo, M.C., et al.: Summary of the evidence on modifiable risk factors for cognitive decline and dementia: a population-based perspective. Alzheimers Dement. **11**(6), 718–726 (2015)
2. Jr, J.C., Albert, M.S., Knopman, D.S., et al.: Introduction to the recommendations from the National Institute on Aging-Alzheimer's Association workgroups on diagnostic guidelines for Alzheimer's disease. Alzheimers Dement. **7**(3), 257–262 (2011)

3. Jack, C.R., Petersen, R.C., O'Brien, P.C., et al.: MR-based hippocampal volumetry in the diagnosis of Alzheimer's disease. Neurology **42**(1), 183–188 (1992)
4. Magnin, B., Mesrob, L., Kinkingnéhun, S., et al.: Support vector machine-based classification of Alzheimer's disease from whole-brain anatomical MRI. Neuroradiology **51**(2), 73–83 (2009)
5. Fischl, B., Dale, A.M.: Measuring the thickness of the human cerebral cortex from magnetic resonance images. Proc. Natl. Acad. Sci. U. S. A. **97**(20), 11050–11055 (2000)
6. Yamasue, H., Kasai, K., Iwanami, A., et al.: Voxel-based analysis of MRI reveals anterior cingulate gray-matter volume reduction in posttraumatic stress disorder due to terrorism. Proc. Natl. Acad. Sci. U. S. A. **100**(15), 9039–9043 (2003)
7. Kloppel, S., Stonnington, C.M., Chu, C., et al.: Automatic classification of MR scans in Alzheimer's disease. Brain **131**(3), 681–689 (2008)
8. Gerardin, E., Chételat, G., Chupin, M., et al.: Multidimensional classification of hippocampal shape features discriminates Alzheimer's disease and mild cognitive impairment from normal aging. Neuroimage **47**(4), 1476–1486 (2009)
9. Zhang, J., Gao, Y., Gao, Y., et al.: Detecting anatomical landmarks for fast Alzheimer's disease diagnosis. IEEE Trans. Med. Imag. **35**(12), 2524–2533 (2016)
10. Ashburner, J., Friston, K.J.: Voxel-based morphometry—The methods. Neuroimage **11**(6), 805–821 (2000)
11. Gaser, C., Nenadic, L., Buchsbaum, B.R., et al.: Deformation-based morphometry and its relation to conventional volumetry of brain lateral ventricles in MRI. Neuroimage **13**(6), 1140–1145 (2001)
12. Hua, X., Leow, A.D., Parikshak, N., et al.: Tensor-based morphometry as a neuroimaging biomarker for Alzheimer's disease: an MRI study of 676 AD, MCI, and normal subjects. Neuroimage **43**(3), 458–469 (2008)
13. Jiang, J., Trundle, P., Ren, J., et al.: Medical image analysis with artificial neural networks. Comput. Med. Imag. Graph. **34**(8), 617–631 (2010)
14. Zabalza, J., Ren, J., Zheng, J., et al.: Novel segmented stacked autoencoder for effective dimensionality reduction and feature extraction in hyperspectral imaging. Neurocomputing **185**, 1–10 (2016)
15. Wang, Z., Ren, J., Zhang, D., et al.: A deep-learning based feature hybrid framework for spatiotemporal saliency detection inside videos. Neurocomputing **287**, 68–83 (2018)
16. Ortiz, A., Munilla, J., Górriz, J.M., et al.: Ensembles of deep learning architectures for the early diagnosis of the Alzheimer's disease. Int. J. Neural Syst. **26**(7), 1650025 (2016)
17. Suk, H.-I., Shen, D.: Deep learning-based feature representation for AD/MCI classification. In: Mori, K., Sakuma, I., Sato, Y., Barillot, C., Navab, N. (eds.) MICCAI 2013. LNCS, vol. 8150, pp. 583–590. Springer, Heidelberg (2013). https://doi.org/10.1007/978-3-642-40763-5_72
18. Suk, H.I., Lee, S.W., Shen, D.: Hierarchical feature representation and multimodal fusion with deep learning for AD/MCI diagnosis. Neuroimage **101**, 569–582 (2014)
19. Liu, S., Liu, S., Cai, W., et al.: Multimodal neuroimaging feature learning for multiclass diagnosis of Alzheimer's disease. IEEE Trans. Biomed. Eng. **62**(4), 1132–1140 (2015)
20. Vu, T.D., Yang, H.J., Nguyen, V.Q., et al.: Multimodal learning using convolution neural network and Sparse Autoencoder. In: IEEE International Conference on Big Data and Smart Computing, BigComp 2017, pp. 309–312 (2017)
21. Li, F., Cheng, D., Liu, M.: Alzheimer's disease classification based on combination of multi-model convolutional networks. In: IEEE International Conference on Imaging Systems and Techniques, IST 2017, pp. 1–5 (2017)
22. Li, F., Tran, L., Thung, K.H., et al.: A robust deep model for improved classification of AD/MCI patients. IEEE J. Biomed. Health Inf. **19**(5), 1610–1616 (2015)

23. Jack, C.R., Bernstein, M.A., Fox, N.C., et al.: The Alzheimer's disease neuroimaging initiative (ADNI): MRI methods. J. Magn. Reson. Imag. **27**(4), 685–691 (2008)
24. Fischl, B.: FreeSurfer. Neuroimage **62**(2), 774–781 (2012)
25. Nielsen, F.A., Hansen, L.K.: Automatic anatomical labeling of Talairach coordinates and generation of volumes of interest via the BrainMap database. Neuroimage **16**, 2–6 (2002)
26. Valerius, K.P., Mai, J.K., Assheuer, J., et al.: Atlas of the human brain. Mamm. Biol. **71**(1), 62 (2003)
27. Tzourio-Mazoyer, N., Landeau, B., Papathanassiou, D., et al.: Automated anatomical labeling of activations in SPM using a macroscopic anatomical parcellation of the MNI MRI single-subject brain. Neuroimage **15**(1), 273–289 (2002)

Image Recognition: Detection, Tracking and Classification

A Novel Semi-supervised Classification Method Based on Class Certainty of Samples

Fei Gao[1], Zhenyu Yue[1(✉)], Qingxu Xiong[1], Jun Wang[1], Erfu Yang[2], and Amir Hussain[3]

[1] Beihang University, Beijing 100191, China
feigao2000@163.com, zhenyu_yue@163.com
[2] University of Strathclyde, Glasgow G1 1XJ, UK
[3] University of Stirling, Stirling FK9 4LA, UK

Abstract. The traditional classification method based on supervised learning classifies remote sensing (RS) images by using sufficient labelled samples. However, the number of labelled samples is limited due to the expensive and time-consuming collection. To effectively utilize the information of unlabelled samples in the learning process, this paper proposes a novel semi-supervised classification method based on class certainty of samples (CCS). First, the class certainty of unlabelled samples obtained based on multi-class SVM is smoothed for robustness. Then, a new semi-supervised linear discriminant analysis (LDA) is presented based on class certainty, which improves the separability of samples in the projection subspace. Finally, the nearest neighbor classifier is adopted to classify the images. The experimental results demonstrate that the proposed method can effectively exploit the information of unlabelled samples and greatly improve the classification effect compared with other state-of-the-art approaches.

Keywords: Remote sensing images · Semi-supervised classification Class certainty · Semi-supervised LDA

1 Introduction

With the rapid development of the remote sensing (RS) technology, the higher-resolution and more informative RS images can be acquired, and are already used in target surveillance, disaster relief, environmental protection and *etc.* [1–3]. The process of RS images interpretation consists of three parts: target detection, image segmentation and image classification [4, 5]. Besides, image classification is the most critical step. However, since the sample labeling for RS image is time-consuming, it's difficult to achieve accurate classification of RS images when the labelled samples are insufficient, which has become one of research hotspots [6, 7].

Generally, the working mechanism of human cognitive system have inspired researchers to improve the classification accuracy of images with insufficient labelled samples. Since most of the information received by the brain is unlabelled, the human cognition is a semi-supervised learning process, where the unlabelled information is utilized based on the priori knowledge. Inspired by this, many semi-supervised learning

J. Ren et al. (Eds.): BICS 2018, LNAI 10989, pp. 315–324, 2018.
https://doi.org/10.1007/978-3-030-00563-4_30

methods have been presented, such as generative mode, semi-supervised SVM [8], graph-based model [9], self-training model and co-learning model [10]. For the semi-supervised algorithms, unlabelled samples are used to enlarge initial labelled samples set and make the classification surface pass through the space with sparse samples. In [11], the transductive support vector machine (TSVM) is developed to search the optimal classification surface based on margin maximization by iteratively assigning the sample positive label or negative one. Persello and Bruzzone present a progressive semi-supervised SVM with diversity (PS3VM-D) to make candidate samples within and closer to the margin band [12]. Then, samples are incrementally selected among the candidates considering the kernel cosine-angular similarity. Based on co-training model, Zhou designed a tri-training algorithm by training three classifiers. Then, reliable unlabelled samples are selected by one classifier and added to the labelled samples set of the other two classifiers in an iterative way [13]. Although the aforementioned algorithms are proved to be effective experimentally, semi-supervised learning methods are not always helpful because of the strict requirements of data distribution, selection method and labeling method for unlabelled samples.

To effectively improve RS images classification performance, this paper proposes a novel semi-supervised classification method by utilizing unlabelled samples based on class certainty of samples (CCS). Different from other semi-supervised algorithms, CCS initially assigns the class certainty to unlabelled samples and integrates it to the scatter matrixes of linear discriminant analysis (LDA). The new scatter matrixes can effectively describe the true characteristic distribution, which makes samples more separable in the projection subspace. Since the class certainty is used to measure the class reliability of samples, the unlabelled samples with high reliability play a more important role than those with low reliability in CCS. To ensure the sufficient class reliability of unlabelled samples in the subsequent semi-supervised process, the class certainty is smoothed through normalization and threshold considering the complicated distribution of samples. As a result, the performance of CCS is greatly improved.

The rest of this paper is organized as follows. Section 2 describes the proposed method in detail. The experiments for the SAR targets classification are provided in Sect. 3 and the conclusions are drawn in Sect. 4.

2 Proposed Method

In this part, we first present the related definition. The training samples $X = [L, U] \in R^{d \times N}$ are divided into two parts according to the label of samples. Let $L = [x_1, x_2, \cdots, x_l] \in R^{d \times l}$ be the feature matrix of labelled samples with label vector $[y_1, y_2, \cdots, y_l]$, $y_i \in \{1, 2 \cdots, k\}$ and $U = [x_{l+1}, x_{l+2}, \cdots, x_{l+u}] \in R^{d \times u}$ be the feature matrix of unlabelled samples. $N = l + u$ denotes the number of training samples and the test set is T. Then, as shown in Fig. 1, the proposed novel semi-supervised method (CCS) consists of four main ingredients.

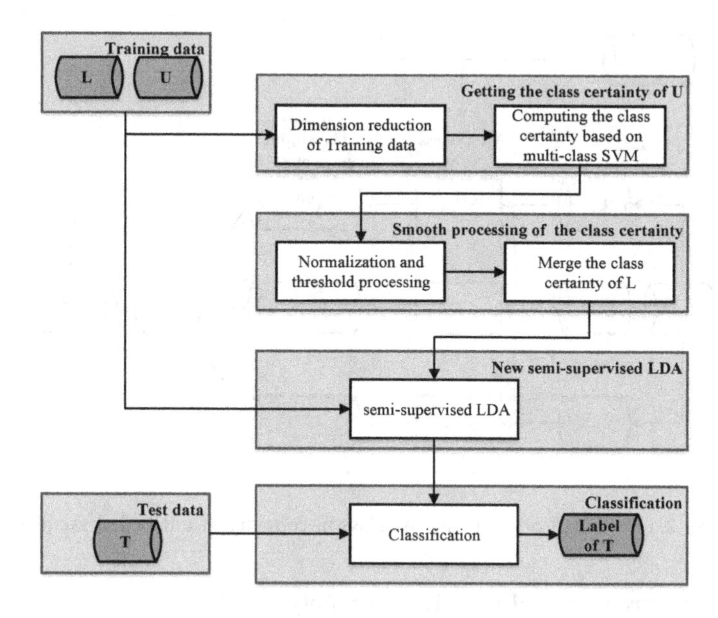

Fig. 1. Flowchart of the proposed method CCS.

2.1 Getting the Class Certainty of Unlabelled Samples

Dimension Reduction of Training Data. In Fig. 1, the inputs of CCS are the original RS training data L and U in high-dimension. To get the class certainty information, the computational complexity and the dimension of training data should be reduced. Thus, based on KLDA algorithm, the projection characteristics L_1 and U_1 are obtained.

Computing the Class Certainty Based on Multi-class SVM. The output of SVM can effectively measure the class certainty of samples. After the dimension reduction, SVM can be trained based on the labelled samples L_1. Because the samples are generally multi-class, we construct multi-class SVM based on the "one-against-one" approach. To express more clearly, an example of obtaining the class m certainty of unlabelled samples is shown in Fig. 2.

In Fig. 2, L_1^m denotes labelled samples of class m with reduced dimension. Let L_1^m and samples of the other classes be positive labels and negative labels, respectively. Then, after training k − 1 binary SVM between L_1^m and other classes of samples, the corresponding output vector is derived by passing U_1 to every binary SVM. For example, $f^{m,m-1} = (w^T\phi(U_1) + b)^T$ denotes the output vector of the SVM trained by L_1^m and L_1^{m-1}. To get the class m certainty f_U^m, the output vectors are added based on the voting method. Similarly, other class certainty f^i, $i = 1, 2, \cdots, k$, $i \neq m$ can be obtained according to the corresponding implementation.

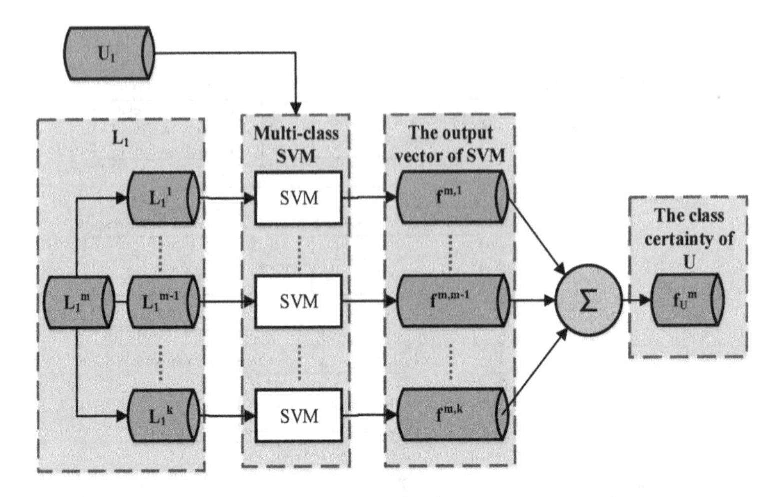

Fig. 2. Flowchart of obtaining the class m certainty of unlabelled samples.

2.2 Smooth Processing of the Class Certainty

Normalization and Threshold Processing. Since the class i certainty $f_U^i(i \in \{1, 2, \cdots, k\})$ contains elements ranged from less than 0 to larger than 1, they should be normalized and threshold processed before utilizing. Accordingly, we utilize the min-max standard method, which can be written as

$$p_U^i = \frac{f_U^i - \min}{\max - \min}, \; i \in \{1, 2, \cdots, k\} \tag{1}$$

where p_U^i represents the class i certainty of U after normalization processing. Then, we choose threshold $t \in [0, 1]$. If the element of p_U^i is less than t, we set it to 0.

$$p_{U,j}^i = \begin{cases} 0, & p_{U,j}^i < t \\ p_{U,j}^i, & others \end{cases}, \; i \in \{1, 2 \cdots, k\}, \; others \, j \in \{1, 2, \cdots, u\} \tag{2}$$

where $p_{U,j}^i$ denotes the j-th element of vector p_U^i. The greater threshold t means higher reliability requirement for the utilized unlabelled samples.

Merge the Class Certainty of Labelled Samples. Assuming that L^i, $i \in \{1, 2, \cdots, k\}$ is the original labelled sample set of class i. It's obvious that the corresponding class i certainty is 1 and the other class certainty is 0. Thus, the class i certainty vector p_L^i of L can be derived as,

$$p_{L,j}^i = \begin{cases} 1, & y_j = i \\ 0, & y_j \neq i \end{cases}, \; i \in \{1, 2, \cdots, k\}, \; j \in \{1, 2, \cdots, l\} \tag{3}$$

where $p^i_{L,j}$ denotes the j-th element of vector p^i_L and y_j denotes the label of x_j, respectively. By combining p^i_L and p^i_U, the class i certainty vector of training data $X = [L, U]$ is obtained:

$$p^i = [p^i_L, p^i_U],\ i \in \{1, 2, \cdots, k\} \tag{4}$$

2.3 New Semi-supervised LDA

In this section, we propose a novel semi-supervised LDA method by integrating class certainty into the scatter matrixes so that the samples are more separable in the projection subspace. At first, we define the within-class mean vector u_i and the total mean vector u,

$$\begin{aligned} u_i &= \frac{\sum_{j=1}^{N} p^i_j x_j}{\sum_{j=1}^{N} p^i_j} = X\left(p^i_j / \sum_{j=1}^{N} p^i_j\right) = X\widetilde{p^i} \\ u &= \frac{\sum_{i=1}^{K}\sum_{j=1}^{N} p^i_j x_j}{\sum_{i=1}^{K}\sum_{j=1}^{N} p^i_j} = X\left(\sum_{i=1}^{K} p^i / \sum_{i=1}^{K}\sum_{j=1}^{N} p^i_j\right) = X\widetilde{p} \end{aligned} \tag{5}$$

where p^i_j is the element of vector p^i.

Next, to obtain the "generalized Rayleigh quotient" of semi-supervised LDA, the new between-class scatter matrix S_b, within-class scatter matrix S_w and total-class scatter matrix matrixes S_t are defined as:

$$\begin{aligned} S_b &= \sum_{i=1}^{K} n_i (u_i - u)(u_i - u)^T \\ &= X[\sum_{i=1}^{K} m_i (\tilde{p}^i - \tilde{p})(\tilde{p}^i - \tilde{p})^T]X^T = X\tilde{S}_b X^T \end{aligned} \tag{6}$$

where $n_i = \sum_{j=1}^{N} p^i_j$.

$$\begin{aligned} S_w &= \sum_{i=1}^{k}\sum_{j=1}^{N} p^i_j (x_j - u_i)(x_j - u_i)^T \\ &= X[\sum_{i=1}^{k}\sum_{j=1}^{N} p^i_j (h_j - \tilde{p}^i)(h_j - \tilde{p}^i)^T]X^T = X\tilde{S}_w X^T \end{aligned} \tag{7}$$

$$S_t = \sum_{i=1}^{k}\sum_{j=1}^{N} p_j^i (x_j - u)(x_j - u)^T$$
$$= X[\sum_{i=1}^{k}\sum_{j=1}^{N} p_j^i (h_j - \tilde{p})(h_j - \tilde{p})^T]X^T = X\tilde{S}_t X^T \quad (8)$$

where $h_j \in R^{N \times 1}$ is expressed as:

$$h_{j,i} = \begin{cases} 1, & i = j \\ 0, & else \end{cases} \quad (9)$$

and $h_{j,i}$ denotes the element of h_j.

Since the new scatter matrixes have been proven to satisfy $S_t = S_b + S_w$, any two scatter matrixes can be utilized to construct the "generalized Rayleigh quotient". Generally, it is expressed in the following criterion,

$$\max_{w} \frac{w^T S_b w}{w^T S_w w} \quad (10)$$

where $w \in R^{d \times (k-1)}$ is the projection matrix. Then, w can be calculated by (11)

$$S_b w = \lambda S_w w \quad (11)$$

The closed-form solution of w related to k − 1 characteristic vectors of $S_w^{-1} S_b$.

2.4 Classification

After the dimension reduction, the test data will be classified. There are several classifiers to be selected, such as SVM, random forest, nearest neighbor classifier (NNC) and so on. We adopts the NNC in this part because the training samples of the same class in the projection subspace are very close, which makes the mean vectors fully represent the characteristic information of every class. The mean vectors $\tilde{u}_i$ after dimension reduction can be expressed as

$$\tilde{u}_i = w^T u_i, \ i \in \{1, 2, \cdots, k\} \quad (12)$$

Then the class of test sample is determined by the nearest $\tilde{u}_i$.

3 Experiment

In this section, the performance of the proposed method is investigated on the Moving and Stationary Target Acquisition and Recognition (MSTAR) database. The discussion of CCS is performed initially to demonstrate the feasibility of CCS-related steps. Subsequently, the effectiveness of the proposed method is verified by comparing CCS with other semi-supervised algorithms. As shown in Fig. 3, we choose BMP2 (sn-c21), T72 (sn-132) and BTR70 (sn-c21) as the training data in the following experiments. Meanwhile, we select BMP2 (sn-c9566), T72 (sn-s7) and BTR70 (sn-c70) as the testing data. Table 1 lists the number of vehicles in the aforementioned dataset.

(a) T72 (b) BMP2 (c) BTR70

Fig. 3. The SAR images of three classes of vehicles.

Table 1. Types and quantities of training data and testing data.

	Training data			Testing data		
Type	T72	BMP2	BTR70	T72	BMP2	BTR70
Model	sn_132	sn_c21	sn_c71	sn_s7	sn_9566	sn_c70
Quantity	232	232	232	191	191	191

3.1 Discussion of CCS

To demonstrate the effectiveness of the semi-supervised LDA method, we compare it with the LDA method which only utilizes the labelled samples. We select 10% of the training data as the labelled samples and the remaining data as the unlabelled samples. As shown in Fig. 4, test-BMP represents a testing sample selected from the BMP vehicles. BMP, BTR, T72 denote the class mean vectors of the three types of vehicles obtained by the LDA method, and u-BMP, u-BTR, u-T72 denote the class mean vectors obtained by the semi-supervised LDA method. The direction of arrow represents the class judgment result of the test-BMP.

In Fig. 4(a), since test-BMP is closest to the mean vector of T72, the classification result is mistaken. Different from LDA, semi-supervised LDA can represent the truer feature distribution of samples by absorbing the characteristic information of unlabelled samples. As presented in Fig. 4(b), the test-BMP is obviously closest to the u-BMP and is correctly classified into BMP.

When obtaining the class certainty of unlabelled samples, we utilize the threshold processing to ensure the sufficient class reliability. Next, we discuss the impact of changing the threshold t on the performance of CCS. With the change of the percentage of labelled samples, the overall accuracy of different threshold is shown in Fig. 5.

When the percentage of labelled samples is small, the performance of CCS with $t = 0.2$ is highest, and the performance with $t = 0$ is the second highest. If the thresholds are relative big, which are set as 0.7 and 1, the classification performance of CCS is not good. The experimental result shows that when labelled samples are insufficient, compared with $t = 0$ which exploits all the class certainty information of unlabelled samples, setting t as a small value helps to improve the classification performance, which ensures the reliability of class certainty used in the semi-supervised LDA.

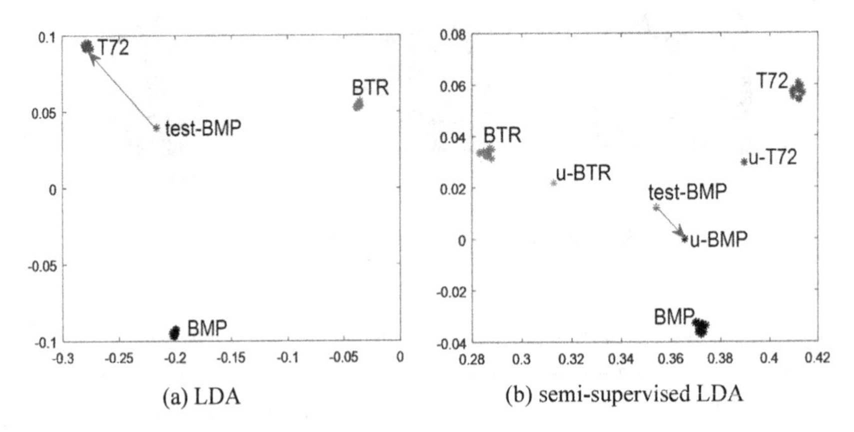

Fig. 4. The effectiveness of the semi-supervised LDA method compared with the LDA method.

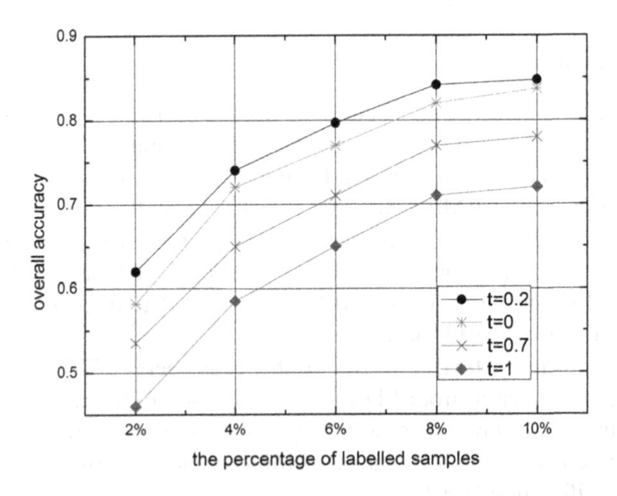

Fig. 5. Classification performance of CCS with different threshold setting.

3.2 Comparison with Other Semi-supervised Algorithms

In this section, we compare the performance of our method with that of the label propagation (LP) [14], progressive semi-supervised SVM with diversity (PS3VM-D) [12], constrained KMeans (C-KMeans) [15] and semi-supervised discriminant analysis

(SDA) [16]. As the percentage of labelled samples changes, the overall accuracy of different methods can be derived, as shown in Fig. 6.

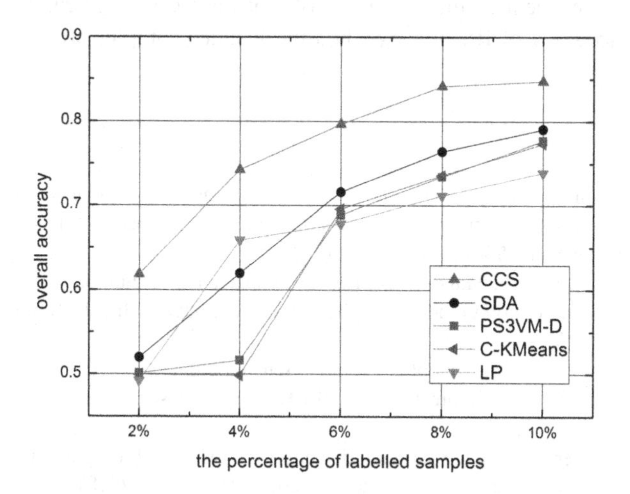

Fig. 6. Classification performance of CCS and the other four semi-supervised algorithms.

Obviously, the classification accuracy of CCS outperforms the other four semi-supervised algorithms by at least 8% when the labelled samples are insufficient. Generally, LP and PS3VM-D assign pseudo labels to unlabelled samples. However, the wrong pseudo labels will cause a bad influence on subsequent classifier training process. In terms of the C-KMeans, it can't make full use the spectrum information by adding constraints, which leads to little performance improvement. As for SDA, it focuses on maintaining the neighborhood relationship between samples, but has a high requirement of data distribution. Compared with the aforementioned four methods, CCS not only utilizes the class information of labelled samples, but also reliably absorbs the characteristic information of unlabelled samples through integrating the class certainty of samples into LDA, which makes the classification performance more stable and accurate.

4 Conclusion

To effectively solve the problem of RS images classification when labelled samples are insufficient, this paper proposes a novel semi-supervised classification method (CCS). There are three major findings:

(a) Based on the dimensional reduction of training samples and multi-class SVM based learning, the class certainty information is obtained and assigned to unlabelled samples for further processing.
(b) The pre-processed class certainty reassigns the weight for the unlabelled samples by normalizing and threshold processing.

(c) By combining class certainty, the proposed LDA can make full use of class information of labelled samples while characterizing reliably unlabelled samples.

From the experiment results, we observe that the CCS significantly improves the classification accuracy of RS images when the labelled samples are insufficient.

References

1. Zabalza, J., Ren, J., Zheng, J., Han, J.: Novel two-dimensional singular spectrum analysis for effective feature extraction and data classification in hyperspectral imaging. IEEE Trans. Geosci. Remote Sens. **53**(8), 4418–4433 (2015)
2. Zhao, C., Li, X., Ren, J., Marshall, S.: Improved sparse representation using adaptive spatial support for effective target detection in hyperspectral imagery. Int. J. Remote Sens. **34**(24), 8669–8684 (2013)
3. Han, J.: Object detection in optical remote sensing images based on weakly supervised learning and high-level feature learning. IEEE Trans. Geosci. Remote Sens. **53**(6), 3325–3337 (2015)
4. Yan, Y.: Unsupervised image saliency detection with Gestalt-laws guided optimization and visual attention based refinement. Pattern Recogn. **79**, 65–78 (2018)
5. Wang, Z.: A deep-learning based feature hybrid framework for spatiotemporal saliency detection inside videos. Neurocomputing **287**, 68–83 (2018)
6. Bian, X., Zhang, T., Zhang, X.: Clustering-based extraction of near border data samples for remote sensing image classification. Cogn. Comput. **5**(1), 19–31 (2013)
7. Cao, F.: Sparse representation-based augmented multinomial logistic extreme learning machine with weighted composite features for spectral-spatial classification of hyperspectral images. IEEE Trans. Geosci. Remote Sens. **99**, 1–17 (2018)
8. Pasolli, E., Melgani, F., Tuia, D., Pacifici, F., Emery, W.J.: SVM active learning approach for image classification using spatial information. IEEE Trans. Geosci. Remote Sens. **52**(4), 2217–2233 (2014)
9. Blum, A., Chawla, S.: Learning from labeled and unlabeled data using graph mincuts. In: Eighteenth International Conference on Machine Learning, pp. 19–26. Morgan Kaufmann Publishers, USA (2001)
10. Blum, A.: Combining labeled and unlabeled data with co-training. In: Proceedings of the Eleventh Annual Conference on Computational Learning Theory, pp. 92–100 (2000)
11. Joachims, T.: Transductive inference for text classification using support vector machines. In: Sixteenth International Conference on Machine Learning, pp. 200–209. Morgan Kaufmann Publishers, Slovenia (1999)
12. Persello, C., Bruzzone, L.: Active and semisupervised learning for the classification of remote sensing images. IEEE Trans. Geosci. Remote Sens. **52**(11), 6937–6956 (2014)
13. Zhi-Hua, Z., Ming, L.: Tri-training: exploiting unlabeled data using three classifiers. IEEE Trans. Knowl. Data Eng. **17**(11), 1529–1541 (2005)
14. Wang, F., Zhang, C.: Label propagation through linear neighborhoods. IEEE Trans. Knowl. Data Eng. **20**(1), 55–67 (2007)
15. Wagstaff, K., Cardie, C., Rogers, S.: Constrained K-means clustering with background knowledge. In: Eighteenth International Conference on Machine Learning, pp. 577–584. Morgan Kaufmann Publishers, USA (2001)
16. Cai, D., He, X., Han, J.: Semi-supervised discriminant analysis. In: 11th International Conference on Computer Vision, pp. 1–7. IEEE, Brazil (2007)

Texture Profiles and Composite Kernel Frame for Hyperspectral Image Classification

Cailing Wang[1(✉)], Hongwei Wang[2], Jinchang Ren[3], Yinyong Zhang[3], Jia Wen[4], and Jing Zhao[1]

[1] School of Computer Science, Xi'an Shiyou University, Xi'an, China
azering@163.com
[2] Engineering University of CAPF, Xi'an, China
[3] Department of Electronic and Electrical Engineering, University of Strathclyde, Glasgow, UK
[4] School of Electronics Engineering, Tianjin Polytechnic University, Tianjin, China

Abstract. It is of great interest in spectral-spatial features classification for High spectral images (HSI) with high spatial resolution. This paper presents a new Spectral-spatial method for improving accuracy of hyperspectral image classification. Specifically, a new texture feature extraction algorithm based on traditional LBP method is proposed directly. Texture profiles is obtained by the proposed method. A composite kernel framework is employed to join spatial and spectral features. The classifiers adopted in this work is the multinomial logistic regression. In order to illustrate the good performance of the proposed framework, the two real hyperspectral image datasets are employed. Our experimental results with real hyperspectral images indicate that the proposed framework can enhance the classification accuracy than some traditional alternatives.

Keywords: Hyperspectral image classification · Spectral-spatial analysis Generalized composite kernel

1 Introduction

Hyperspectral image (HSI) captures reflectance values from Visible to Infrared spectrum which cover the wide spectral range with hundreds of bands for each pixel in the image. This rich spectral information provides possibility to distinguish different materials spectrally. HSI classification plays an important role in hyperspectral image application, such as crop analysis, plant and mineral identification, among others.

In traditional HSI classification systems, classifiers solely consider spectral signatures without considering the correlations between the pixel of interest and its neighboring pixels [1–3]. Numerous classification techniques for HSI have been developed such as K-nearest-neighbor (K-NN) classifier [4], maximum-likelihood estimation (MLE) [5], artificial neural networks [6], and kernel-based techniques [7]. However, it is a very challenging task due to the only tiny distinction among spectral signatures of various types in same families, such as tillage in the corn fields. Meanwhile the spatial

J. Ren et al. (Eds.): BICS 2018, LNAI 10989, pp. 325–333, 2018.
https://doi.org/10.1007/978-3-030-00563-4_31

resolution is increasing during last decades, it is of great interest in exploiting spectral-spatial proposing to improve the accuracy of HSI classification [8–10]. There are two main directions of employing spatial information for HSI classification, the one is extracting spatial features such as statistic features, morphological profiles [11], texture features [12, 13], etc. to join the spectral features as the input of classifier, which is called Feature-level fusion, the other is classifying HSI in spectral and spatial domain separately and fusing the two classification results into a final one with decision-making methods [14], which is called Decision-level fusion.

In this paper, we develop a new Spectral-spatial method which exploits texture profiles and composite kernel framework for HSI classification. Specifically, a new texture feature extraction algorithm based on traditional LBP method is proposed, texture profiles is obtained by the feature extraction method and a composite Kernel Framework is employed to join spatial and spectral features. Finally, we chose multinomial logistic regression as classifier. Our experimental results, conducted with a real hyperspectral scene collected by the Reflective Optics Spectrographic Imaging Instrument (ROSIS) of the Deutschen Zentrum for Luftund Raumfahrt (DLR, the German Aerospace Agency) over the city of Pavia, Italy, indicate that the proposed method can enhance the classification accuracy compare to traditional alternatives.

2 Proposed Approach

2.1 Texture Feature Extraction with Spectral-Spatial LBP

To exploit texture feature, we calculate the similarity in spectrum domain firstly. In this paper, Spectral Angle Cosine (SAC) is employed to quantify differences between reflectance spectrums.

Assume that hyperspectral pixel $X = (x_1, x_2, \ldots, x_L)$, each component x_i is the pixel of band B_i acquired at a particular wavelength λ_i. $\{\lambda_i\}_{l=1}^{L}$ is a set of L wavelengths. Denoted another hyperspectral pixel $Y = (y_1, y_2, \ldots, y_L)$ vector. The SAC is calculated by Eq. (1).

$$SAC = \cos\frac{\sum XY}{\sqrt{\sum X^2 \sum Y^2}} \tag{1}$$

Supposed that the central hyperspectral pixel X and the neighborhood hyperspectral pixels $\{Y_1, Y_2, \cdots, Y_N\}$, N is the number of neighborhood pixels the threshold for binary is chosen by calculating the Mean of SAC, shown in Eq. (2).

$$\delta = \frac{1}{N}\sum_{num=1}^{N} SAC(X, Y_n) \tag{2}$$

Then the proposed LBP is shown in Eq. (3).

$$LBP_{N,R(X)} = \sum_{num=1}^{N} s(SAC(X, Y_n) - \delta)2^{num}$$
$$s(x) = \begin{cases} 1, & (SAC(X, Y_n) - \delta) \geq 0 \\ 0, & (SAC(X, Y_n) - \delta) < 0 \end{cases} \tag{3}$$

2.2 Texture Profiles for Hyperspectral Image

Some texture features may have a high response for a local region size, and a lower response for other sizes. A single size approach appears loses some important information. For this reason, it is often a good idea to use a multi-scale approach based on a range of different local region size. A range of different texture features could be employed.

Given the above-proposed notion of the texture features. It is straightforward to extend the same concepts to multi-scale processing. The texture profiles is defined as a vector where the histogram of local region is stored for every step of increasing region size.

Figure 1 illustrates the implementation of traditional LBP feature extraction and SID_LBP feature extraction. Figure 1a gives the implementation of LBP feature extraction applied to each selected band image. Figure 1b gives the SID-LBP features extraction.

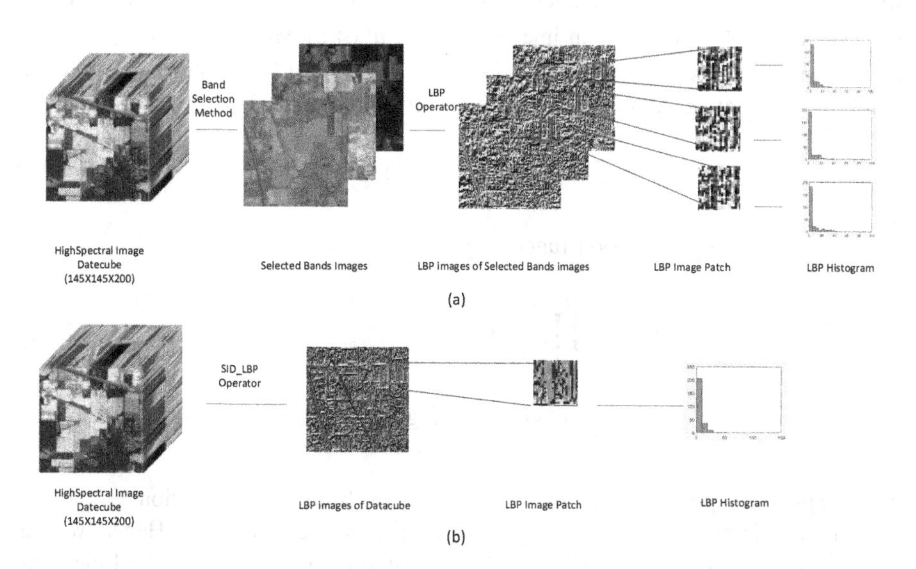

Fig. 1. Comparison on implementation of traditional LBP and SIDLBP feature extraction. (a) Implementation of traditional LBP feature extraction; (b) implementation of SID_LBP feature extraction.

Obviously, the computations will be more time-consuming because of calculating histogram of local region by increasing region size. However, better information should be extracted from the hyperspectral data than LBP used on selected bands. There are some redundancies should be observed for the texture profiles. Therefore, feature extraction should be used as well as data redundancy method.

2.3 Data Redundancy

Data redundancy can be viewed as finding a set of vectors that represents an observation while reducing the texture profiles dimensionality [15]. Extracting meaningful features (or components) from multidimensional data is typically done using the principal component analysis (PCA) [16], aka Empirical orthogonal functions (EOF). Nevertheless, many other data reduction methods are available in the literature [17, 18]. PCA disregards the target data and exploits correlations between the input variables to maximize the variance of the projections. We do PCA here for data redundancy.

2.4 Generalized Composite Kernel Framework

The generalized composite kernel framework is proposed by Li at for spectral-spatial feature classification. Denoted the X_i^W as the spectral information and X_i^S as the spatial information for pixel vector X_i, the GCK method stacks the spectral and spatial kernels as follows:

$$K(x_i, x_j) = [K^{\omega}(x_i^{\omega}, x_j^{\omega}), K^s(x_i^s, x_j^s)] \tag{4}$$

where $x = (x_1, \ldots, x_n) \in R^d$ denotes the HSI make up of d-dimensional feature vectors $y = (y_1, \ldots, y_n) \in R^d$ denotes an image of labels, $h(x_i) := [h_1(x_i), \ldots, h_l(x_i)]^T$ denotes the features of the samples data, $\upsilon = [\upsilon^{(1)T}, \ldots, \upsilon^{(K-1)T}]^T$. The problem is shown as follow by calculating the maximum a posteriori estimate:

$$\hat{\upsilon} = \arg\max_{\upsilon}(\mathrm{l}(\upsilon)) + \log p(\upsilon) \tag{5}$$

where $\mathrm{l}(\upsilon)$ is the log-likelihood function given by

$$\begin{aligned} \mathrm{l}(\upsilon) &= \log \prod_{i=1}^{L} p(y_i | x_i, \upsilon) \\ &= \sum_{i=1}^{L} (h^T(x_i)^{\upsilon(y_i)} - \log(\exp(h^T(x_i)^{\upsilon(k)}))) \end{aligned} \tag{6}$$

And $\log p(\upsilon)$ is a prior over υ which is independent from the observation X.

Let's define pixel spectral features as x_i^w and spatial features as x_i^s. Hence, we can refer to the spectral kernel is $K^w(x_i^w, x_j^w)$, the spatial kernel is $K^s(x_i^s, x_j^s)$ and the composite kernel is define as $K(x_i, x_j)$ and is shown as follow:

$$K(x_i, x_j) = [K^w(x_i^w, x_j^w), K^s(x_i^s, x_j^s)] \tag{7}$$

Hence, $h(x_i)$ can be represented as follow by kernel function:

$$\begin{aligned} h(x_i) &= [1, K^T(x_i, x_1), \ldots, K^T(x_i, x_L)]^T \\ &= [1, (K^w)^T(x_i^w, x_1^w), \ldots, (K^w)^T(x_i^w, x_L^w), (K^s)^T(x_i^s, x_1^s), \ldots, (K^s)^T(x_i^s, x_L^s)]^T \end{aligned} \tag{8}$$

In this paper, we take advantage of the logistic regression via variable splitting and augmented Lagrangian (LORSAL) algorithm with overall complexity $o(L \times (l_1 + l_l) \times K)$. At this point, we recall that L is the number of training samples, K is the number of classes, and l_j is the number of elements in the jth linear/nonlinear feature. LORSAL is able to deal with high-dimensional features and plays a central role in this work. Therefore, in this paper the LORSAL algorithm was adopted to compute the logistic regressions υ.

2.5 Proposed Classification Approach

In the paper, we proposed a new Spectral-spatial method classification. The proposed method consists of spatial texture profiles by SAD_LBP and GC-MLR for classification step. The procedure is as shown in Table 1.

Table 1. The procedure of proposed method

Input: Training set with N samples for each class, initial texture patch size sets W_1 and Window size step: Output: Classification maps and accuracy
1 Calculate the texture feature histograms by SAC_LBP with different window size
2 Calculate spectral channel features
3 Normalize, stack and reduce spatial-spectral features
4 Train a classification model
5 Classify the test set and assess accuracy
6 Return accuracy

3 Experimental Results

In this section, we evaluate the proposed approach using two real hyperspectral datasets. These data sets include different contexts, different spatial resolutions and different bands in order to make possible the assessment of the performance of the proposed approach.

The first data was collected by Airborne Visible/Infrared Image Spectrometer (AVIRIS) over Northwest Indiana test, Indiana, USA, in June 1992. The image presents a classification scenario with the spatial coverage of 145 × 145 pixels covering 16 classes of different crops at 20-m spatial resolution and 220 bands in 0.4 to 2.45 μm region of visible and infrared spectrum. After uncalibrated and noisy bands were removed, 200 bands remained to experiment. The second data set was collected by the Reflective Optics System Imaging Spectrometer sensor covering the city of Pavia, Italy. The data set consists of 115 spectral bands with 610 × 340 pixels covering 9 classes with a spectral range from 0.43 to 0.86 μm and spatial resolution of 1.3 m. After removed 12 noisy channels, the remaining 103 bands were used for the test. All the datasets present the challenging classification scenarios. The class information of three images is detailed in Tables 1 and 2; Fig. 1.

Table 2. The class information of Indian Pine

Order	Class name	Number of samples
1	Alfalfa	54
2	Corn-notill	1034
3	Corn-mintill	834
4	Corn	234
5	Grass-pasture	497
6	Grass-trees	747
7	Grass-pasture-mowed	26
8	Hay-windrowed	489
9	Oats	20
10	Soybean-notill	968
11	Soybean-mintill	2468
12	Soybean-clean	614
13	Wheat	212
14	Woods	1294
15	Building-grass-trees-drives	380
16	Stone-steel-towers	95
	Total	10366

Table 3. The class information of Pavia

Order	Class name	Number of samples
1	Asphalt	6631
2	Meadows	18649
3	Gravel	2099
4	Trees	3064
5	Metalsheets	1345
6	Bare soil	5029
7	Bitumen	1330
8	Bricks	3682
9	shadow	947
	Total	42776

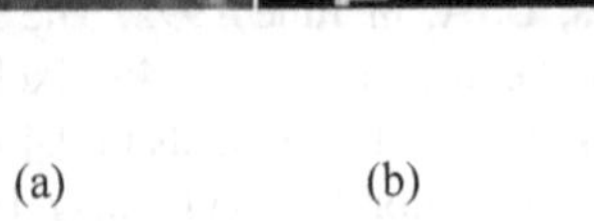

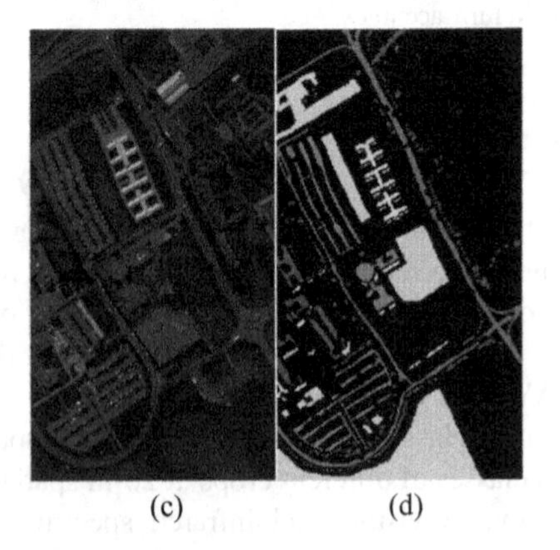

(a) (b) (c) (d)

Fig. 2. (a) The 10th band of Indian Pine image; (b) Indian Pine ground survey; (c) the 10th band of the University of Pavia; (d) The University of Pavia ground survey

For two datasets, we randomly chose a certain number of samples from each class for training and used the rest for testing. There are two methods for training samples selection: one is selecting training samples as ratio of training samples and total samples (Table 3). The other method is same number training samples in different classes. In this experiment, we chose the 5% training samples per class in Indian Pine dataset and 500 training samples per class in the University of Pavia dataset (Fig. 2).

In order to show the performance of our proposed approach, we employ the traditional LBP for texture feature extraction. The bands selection method we chose is PCA and the first three bands are used. We calculated the accuracy with different region size on two datasets to evaluate the impact of region size on classification. The classification accuracy is shown in Tables 4 and 5.

Table 4. The classification accuracy with different region size in Indian Pine dataset with 5% training samples

Region size	Overall accuracy (OA)	Kappa statistic
5	0.7691	0.7358
7	0.8742	0.8561
9	0.9319	0.9221
11	0.9463	0.9388
13	0.9442	0.9363
15	0.9595	0.9537
17	0.9634	0.9583
19	0.9643	0.9643
21	0.9717	0.9677
23	0.9749	0.9719
25	0.9706	0.9706
27	0.9665	0.9618

Table 5. The classification accuracy with different region size in Pavia dataset with 5% training samples

Region size	Overall accuracy (OA)	Kappa statistic
5	0.7699	0.6931
7	0.8442	0.7376
9	0.9243	0.7324
11	0.9299	0.8288
13	0.9354	0.8789
15	0.9433	0.9012
17	0.9554	0.9283
19	0.9667	0.9443
21	0.9517	0.9577
23	0.9455	0.9719
25	0.9436	0.9606
27	0.9399	0.9518

Finally, we designed the experiment with region size started from 5 to 25 by step size is 2. The classification accuracy is shown in Table 6.

Table 6. The classification accuracy with the proposed method in two datasets (with the region size is 17×17)

Dataset name	Overall accuracy (OA)	Kappa statistic
Indian Pine with 5% training samples	0.9891	0.9792
The university of Pavia with 500 training samples per class	0.9929	0.9441

As shown in Tables 4 and 5, firstly, we can conclude that the region size has great influence on classification accuracy. Secondly, we can see that the accuracy tends to be the maximum with 17 × 17 or larger in two datasets. We can suppose that the optimal region size is not easy to find because of image resolution and content. Finally, we can get the information that the proposed spectral-spatial texture extraction by SAC gets higher accuracy than the traditional one.

From the Table 6, we can see that the proposed method offers 21.21% higher accuracy than traditional LBP method when region size is 5 and 1.47% higher than traditional one when region size is 17 × 17 in Indian Pine dataset. Meanwhile, the proposed method offers 22% higher accuracy than traditional LBP method when region size is 5 and 2% higher than traditional one when region size is 17 × 17.

4 Conclusion

In this paper, we have developed a new classification method for HSI. Specifically, we proposed a new texture feature extraction method exploits spatial texture feature from spectrum. We combined the new texture feature with different region size into texture profiles for classification. A composite kernel framework is employed to join spatial and spectral features. We have got good experiment performance in experiment above.

Acknowledgments. This work has been supported by the National Science foundations of China (Grant Nos. 41301382, 61401439, 41604113, 41711530128) and foundation of key lab of spectral imaging, Xi'an Institute of Optics and Precision Mechanics of CAS.

References

1. Richards, J.A.: Remote sensing digital image analysis **10**(2), 343–380 (1995)
2. Bandos, T.V., Bruzzone, L., Camps-Valls, G.: Classification of hyperspectral images with regularized linear discriminant analysis. IEEE Trans. Geosci. Remote Sens. **47**(3), 862–873 (2009)
3. Li, W., Prasad, S., Fowler, J.E., Bruce, L.M.: Locality-preserving dimensionality reduction and classification for hyperspectral image analysis. IEEE Trans. Geosci. Remote Sens. **50**(4), 1185–1198 (2012)
4. Ma, L., Crawford, M.M., Yang, X., Guo, Y.: Local-manifold-learning-based graph construction for semisupervised hyperspectral image classification. IEEE Trans. Geosci. Remote Sens. **53**(5), 2832–2844 (2015)
5. Zenzo, S.D., Degloria, S.D., Bernstein, R., Kolsky, H.G.: Gaussian maximum likelihood and contextual classification algorithms for multicrop classification experiments using thematic mapper and multispectral scanner sensor data. IEEE Trans. Geosci. Remote Sens. **GE-25**(6), 815–824 (1987)
6. Stathakis, D., Vasilakos, A.: Comparison of computational intelligence based classification techniques for remotely sensed optical image classification. IEEE Trans. Geosci. Remote Sens. **44**(8), 2305–2318 (2006)
7. Tuia, D., Camps-Valls, G., Matasci, G., Kanevski, M.: Learning relevant image features with multiple-kernel classification. IEEE Trans. Geosci. Remote Sens. **48**(10), 3780–3791 (2010)

8. Gu, Y., Wang, C., You, D., Zhang, Y., Wang, S., Zhang, Y.: Representative multiple kernel learning for classification in hyperspectral imagery. IEEE Trans. Geosci. Remote Sens. **50** (7), 2852–2865 (2012)
9. Li, J., Marpu, P.R., Plaza, A., Bioucas-Dias, J.M., Benediktsson, J.A.: Generalized composite kernel framework for hyperspectral image classification. IEEE Trans. Geosci. Remote Sens. **51**(9), 4816–4829 (2013)
10. Fang, L., Li, S., Duan, W., Ren, J., Benediktsson, J.A.: Classification of hyperspectral images by exploiting spectral-spatial information of superpixel via multiple kernels. IEEE Trans. Geosci. Remote Sens. **53**(12), 6663–6674 (2015)
11. Fauvel, M., Benediktsson, J.A., Chanussot, J., Sveinsson, J.R.: Spectral and spatial classification of hyperspectral data using SVMs and morphological profiles. IEEE Trans. Geosci. Remote Sens. **46**(11), 3804–3814 (2008)
12. Zhang, L., Zhang, L., Tao, D., Huang, X.: On combining multiple features for hyperspectral remote sensing image classification. IEEE Trans. Geosci. Remote Sens. **50**(3), 879–893 (2012)
13. Qiao, T., Ren, J., Wang, Z., Zabalza, J., Sun, M., Zhao, H., et al.: Effective denoising and classification of hyperspectral images using curvelet transform and singular spectrum analysis. IEEE Trans. Geosci. Remote Sens. **55**(99), 1–15 (2017)
14. Kettig, R.L., Landgrebe, D.A.: Classification of multispectral image data by extraction and classification of homogeneous objects. IEEE Trans. Geosci. Electron. **14**(1), 19–26 (1976)
15. Benediktsson, J.A., Palmason, J.A., Sveinsson, J.R.: Classification of hyperspectral data from urban areas based on extended morphological profiles. IEEE Trans. Geosci. Remote Sens. **43**(3), 480–491 (2005)
16. Zabalza, J., Ren, J., Liu, Z., Marshall, S.: Structured covariance principal component analysis for real-time onsite feature extraction and dimensionality reduction in hyperspectral imaging. Appl. Opt. **53**(20), 4440 (2014)
17. Zabalza, J., Ren, J., Yang, M., Zhang, Y., Wang, J., Marshall, S., et al.: Novel folded-PCA for improved feature extraction and data reduction with hyperspectral imaging and SAR in remote sensing. ISPRS J. Photogramm. Remote Sens. **93**(7), 112–122 (2014)
18. Zabalza, J., Ren, J., Liu, Z., Qing, C., Yang, Z.: Novel segmented stacked autoencoder for effective dimensionality reduction and feature extraction in hyperspectral imaging. Neurocomputing **185**(C), 1–10 (2016)

High-Resolution Image Classification Using the Dynamic Differential Evolutionary Algorithm Optimized Multi-scale Kernel Support Vector Machine Method

Xueqian Rong[1,2], Aizhu Zhang[1,2(✉)], Genyun Sun[1,2], Hui Huang[1,2], and Ping Ma[1,2]

[1] School of Geosciences, China University of Petroleum (East China), Qingdao 266580, China
zhangaizhu789@163.com

[2] Laboratory for Marine Mineral Resources, Qingdao National Laboratory for Marine Science and Technology, Qingdao 266071, China

Abstract. With the fast development of remote sensing techniques, the spatial resolution of remote sensed image are improved significantly. However, the excessive spatial resolution leads to a sharp increase in data volume and spectral information confusion of objects. The multi-scale kernel learning (MSKL) method has shown an excellent advantage in classification of high-resolution satellite image. Nevertheless, the performance of the MSKL is dramatically influenced by the widths and weights of the Radial Basis Function (RBF) kernel, since its multi-scale kernel function is constructed by several RBF kernels. In order to achieve efficient multi-scale classifier, a new dynamic differential evolution (DE) algorithm is introduced in this paper. In addition, the spectral features and spatial fractal texture features of images are synthetically employed to construct the multi-scale kernel. The experimental results show that the multi-scale kernel based on the dynamic DE algorithm is superior to the traditional multi-scale kernel in obtaining a better multi-scale kernel classifier and with higher classification accuracy.

Keywords: High-resolution image · Multi-scale kernel learning
Dynamic differential evolution strategies · Fractal texture

1 Introduction

With the continuous advancement of remote sensing technology, the spatial resolution of the available remote sensing images is also increasing. High-resolution remote sensing images not only enrich the spectral features of the objects, but also make it easy to observe and apply the spatial features of objects such as textures and structures. The complication of the features lead to poor performance of the spectral features based traditional methods, such as the maximum likelihood method, the minimum distance method and K-means method. Therefore, more effective classification technology has become a hotspot in the field of remote sensing [1–3]. Vapnik et al. proposed a Support

J. Ren et al. (Eds.): BICS 2018, LNAI 10989, pp. 334–341, 2018.
https://doi.org/10.1007/978-3-030-00563-4_32

vector machines (SVM) based on the idea of empirical risk minimization principle has attracted much attention [4, 5]. Comparing with other algorithms, such as Bayesian network [6] and deep-learning [7, 8], SVM has the characteristics of high precision, strong generalization ability, and it is suitable for remote sensing image classification with high-dimensional sample features [9].

In recent years, the theory and application have proved that the use of multi-kernel SVM, instead of single-kernel SVM can enhance the interpretability of the decision function, and get better performance than the single-kernel model or a single-kernel machine combination model [10–12]. Actually, the multi-scale kernel learning (MSKL) method is a multi-kernel learning method with higher flexibility and more complete scale selection property, which is usually composed of several radial basis function (RBF) with different widths and different weights. However, the classifier is extremely sensitive to the weights and the widths of the RBF kernel. The traditional algorithm for parameter selection has high computational complexity and it is difficult to obtain optimal parameters. In contrast, the nature-inspired algorithms can be more efficient when solving the multi-parameter optimization problems [13, 14]. Zheng et al. [15] utilized the expectation-maximization (EM) algorithm to train multi-scale support vector regression. Phienthrakul et al. [16] proposed an evolutionary strategy for multi-scale radial basis kernel parameter selection. Feature selection plays an important role in image processing [17]. In this paper, we show that the proposed kernels with the help of a simple improved dynamic differential evolution (DE) algorithm [18] can provide better performance combined with the spectral features and fractal texture features of the image.

The remainder of this paper is organized as follows. The general principle of multi-scale RBF kernels and DE is briefly described in Sect. 2. Section 3 introduces the details of the proposed DE-based MSKL method. In Sect. 4, the comparison experiments are presented. At last, Sect. 5 provides a conclusion for this work.

2 Background

2.1 Multi-scale RBF Kernels

The multi-kernel model is a more flexible kernel-based learning model. MSKL method is a specialization of multi-kernel learning, which involves the fusion of kernels at multiple widths. It has been proved in practice, this method can provide more complete scale selection than other multi-kernel methods, and a good theoretical background by introducing the scale space.

In most of all instances, the foundation of the MSKL method is to find a set of RBF kernel functions with multi-scale representation capabilities. The mathematical formulation of RBF kernel is:

$$k(x, \mathrm{y}) = \exp\left(-\frac{\|x - \mathrm{y}\|^2}{2\sigma^2}\right) \tag{1}$$

where x and y are samples, $k(x, \mathrm{y})$ is dot production function, and σ is width of RBF kernel which affect the performance.

The RBF kernel is the most successful kernel in many problems, and the combination of RBF kernels of different widths has also been proved to meet the mercer condition. For example, multiscale RBF kernel can be defined as:

$$k\left(-\frac{\|x-y\|^2}{2\sigma_1^2}\right),\ldots,k\left(-\frac{\|x-y\|^2}{2\sigma_m^2}\right) \tag{2}$$

where $\sigma_1 < \cdots < \sigma_m$. It can be seen that these classifiers can classify those samples that change drastically when σ are small, and when σ are large, they can be used to classify those samples that change steadily, to obtain better generalization ability.

In this paper, a differential evolution strategy is introduced to select the multi-scale RBF parameters. The combination of this multi-scale RBF kernel function is:

$$k(x,y) = \sum_{i=1}^{n} \alpha_i k(x,y,\sigma_i) \tag{3}$$

$$k(x,y,\sigma_i) = \exp\left(-\sigma_i\|x-y\|^2\right) \tag{4}$$

where α_i are the arbitrary nonnegative weighting constants, there are $2n$ parameters that need to be determined, includes n weight parameters and n width parameters. These parameters affect the performance of the combined kernel and ultimately affect the classification accuracy.

2.2 Differential Evolution Algorithm

DE algorithm is an optimization algorithm based on swarm intelligence theory proposed by Storn et al. [19]. In DE, the population is randomly initialize in the search space $p^0 = \left[x_1^0, x_2^0, \ldots, x_N^0\right]$, N is the population size. Individual $x_i^0 = \left[x_{i,1}^0, x_{i,2}^0, \ldots, x_{i,n}^0\right]$ represents a solution of the problem, n represents the dimension of the optimized problem. Then the mutation operation are first utilized follows Eq. (5).

$$v_i^{t+1} = x_{r_1}^t + F\left(x_{r_2}^t - x_{r_3}^t\right) \tag{5}$$

where $r_1, r_2, r_3 \in \{1, 2, \ldots, N\}$ different from each other and different from i,$x_{r_1}^t$ is the parent base vector, $\left(x_{r_2}^t - x_{r_3}^t\right)$ is called the parental difference vector, F is the scaling factor, t is the current algebra.

Then, individual x_i^t and v_i^{t+1} are crossed to generate experimental u_i^{t+1} by Eq. (6).

$$u_{i,j}^{t+1} = \begin{cases} v_{i,j}^t, & \text{if } rand(j) \le CR \text{ or } j = rnbr(i) \\ x_{i,j}^t, & \text{else} \end{cases} \tag{6}$$

where *rand(j)* is a uniformly distributed random number within [0, 1], $CR \in [0,1]$ is the crossover probability, $rnbr(i)$ is a random number belongs to $\{1, 2, \ldots, n\}$.

Finally, in this algorithm, the position of the individual x_i^t can be updated follows Eq. (7) (for a maximization problem):

$$x_i^{t+1} = \begin{cases} u_i^{t+1}, & \text{if } f\left(u_i^{t+1}\right) > f\left(x_i^t\right) \\ x_i^t, & \text{esle} \end{cases} \tag{7}$$

where *f(g)* is the individual objective function value.

3 Background

In this section, a novel MSKL method is proposed based on a dynamic DE algorithm to obtain the optimal parameters and classification results effectively. The main principle of the proposed method is to extract the spectral information and texture information based on the fractal theory [20], and combine the spectral and texture information to segment the images [21]. The multi-scale kernel classifier is used to classify the segmented objects, in which the kernel parameters are determined by the dynamic DE algorithm. The processing steps mainly include extraction of attribute feature information, image segmentation, and extraction of training samples, parameters selection by DE algorithm, multi-scale kernel based classification, and finally, accuracy assessment, as shown in Fig. 1.

In the dynamic DE algorithm, the population is first divided into three subpopulations, which contains N_1, N_2, and N_3 individuals, respectively. These subpopulations are dynamically adjusted in each iteration. In particular, after each iteration of the DE algorithm, the whole N individual will be ranked by its corresponding objective function value, and then the N_1 individuals with the higher objective function value will be treated as the first-level subpopulation, using the $DE/best/1$ mutation strategy to update:

$$v_i^{t+1} = x_{best}^t + F\left(x_{r_2}^t - x_{r_3}^t\right) \tag{8}$$

These N_1 individuals are used for local search to speed up algorithm convergence. Another N_2 individuals with a general objective function value as a second-level subpopulation, using the $DE/rand\,to\,best/1$ mutation strategy:

$$v_i^{t+1} = x_i^t + F\left(x_{best}^t - x_i^t\right) + F\left(x_{r_1}^t - x_{r_2}^t\right) \tag{9}$$

These N_2 individuals are used to balance the algorithm's local search ability and global search ability. The rest N_3 individuals with lower objective function values are used as the third-level subpopulations, and using $DE/rand/2$ mutation strategy:

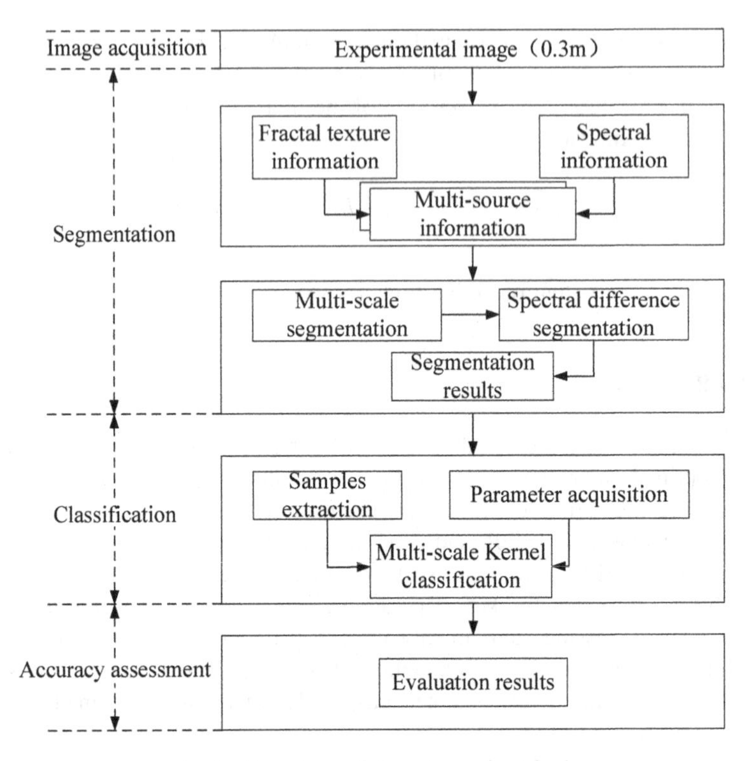

Fig. 1. Flowchart of the proposed method.

$$v_i^{t+1} = x_{r_1}^t + F\left(x_{r_2}^t - x_{r_3}^t\right) + F\left(x_{r_4}^t - x_{r_5}^t\right) \tag{10}$$

These N_3 individuals are used to enhance global search capabilities and jump out of local optima, avoid precocious convergence.

In addition, it should be noted that the objective function value used in this paper is the classification accuracy of the test samples. Moreover, to speed up the convergence of the algorithm, when the experimental individual has a better objective function than the target individual, the experimental variable replaces the target variable and immediately enters the current population to participate in the subsequent evolution.

4 Results and Discussion

In this section, San Diego's high-resolution remote sensing image with 0.3 m resolution acquired at May 3rd, 2010 was taken as the experimental area, as shown in Fig. 2a with a size 600 × 600. As shown in Fig. 2a, this area mainly contains 7 kinds of objects [22]: road (C1), vegetation (C2), water body (C3), house (C4), shadow (C5), bare land (C6), and rocky beach (C7).

In order to illustrate the effectiveness of the proposed algorithm (E1), the obtained results are compared with the classification results based on the spectral information

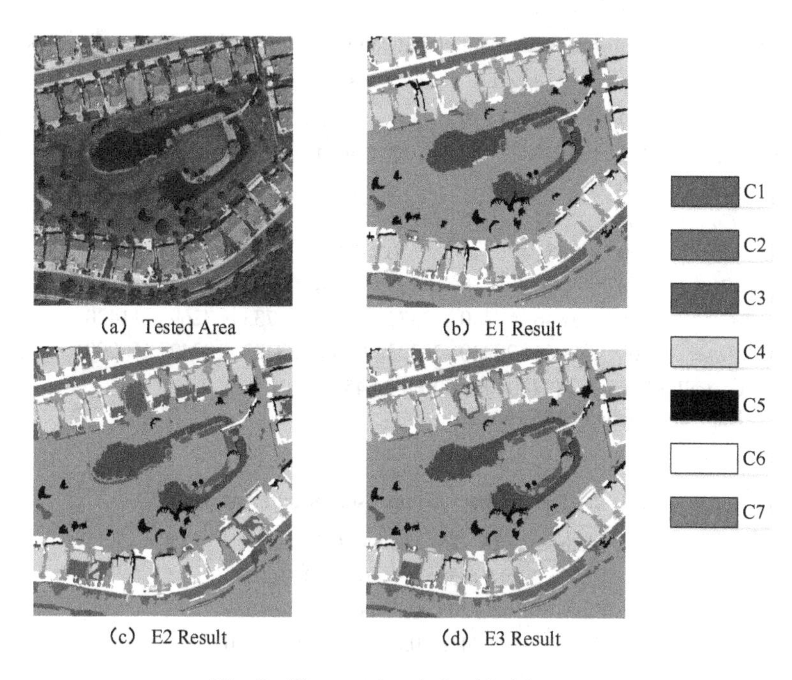

Fig. 2. The tested and classified images.

only (E2) and the classification with parameters obtained by cross-validation (E3). In the experiment, the parameters of the dynamic DE algorithm are: population N = 40, in the early stage of evolution, $N_1 = 20$, $N_2 = 10$, $N_3 = 10$, in the middle stage of evolution, $N_1 = 10$, $N_2 = 20$, $N_3 = 10$, in the last stage of evolution, $N_1 = 10$, $N_2 = 10$, $N_3 = 20$, the widths of RBFs are between 0.0 and 100.0, the maximum number of iterations is 200, the scaling factor F = 0.6, the crossover probability CR = 0.9. The corresponding classification results are presented in Fig. 2(b), (c) and (d). Further, confusion matrix and classification accuracy produced by the proposed method is listed in Table 1 and the comparison of the three classification methods, including the overall classification accuracy (OA) and Kappa coefficient (Kappa) is reported in Table 2.

From the classification and the accuracy evaluation results, we can see that the road, vegetation, house, bare land, and water can be better classified, while shadow and rocky beach are more difficult to distinguish, and there are different degrees of misclassification. Nevertheless, the overall classification results and accuracy are good enough. Compared with the experiments without texture information, the addition of texture information significantly improves the classification accuracy of the house. This is due to the fact that the spectral features of houses in the tested image facing to the sunlight and are easily confused with the spectral features of the rocky beach, while the other side of the house is easily confused with the road. In addition, although the classification results of the cross-validation based method are similar to the dynamic DE algorithm, the proposed method has obvious advantages in the construction efficiency of the classifier.

Table 1. The confusion matrix and classification accuracy of the proposed method.

	C1	*C2*	*C3*	*C4*	*C5*	*C6*	*C7*	*Total*
C1	19669	288	0	311	0	0	0	20268
C2	327	184654	0	713	3924	0	0	189618
C3	0	0	20891	0	1292	0	0	22183
C4	64	587	0	74704	0	2213	2579	80147
C5	0	2671	49	0	7376	0	0	10096
C6	0	0	0	423	174	25477	194	26268
C7	0	846	0	2572	0	733	7269	11420
Total	20060	189046	20940	78723	12766	28423	10042	360000

Overall accuracy = (340040/360000) 94.4556%
Kappa coefficient = 0.9160

Table 2. The accuracy comparison of different method.

Methods	OA (%)	Kappa	CPU time
E1	94.4556	0.9160	2.3827e+03
E2	88.9203	0.8348	2.2764e+03
E3	93.3458	0.8989	3.288673e+03

5 Conclusion

This paper proposes a multi-scale kernel learning (MSKL) method for object-oriented classification of high-resolution images based on the dynamic DE algorithm for determine the multi-scale kernel parameters. The experimental results indicate that the proposed method has high feasibility and can effectively improves the classification accuracy of the high-resolution images. On one hand, the application of multi-scale kernel method can effectively solve the problem of high dimensionality and high data volume of high-resolution image samples. On the other hand, the dynamic DE algorithm improves the efficiency and effectiveness of the selection of multi-scale kernel parameter compared to traditional cross-validation methods.

Moreover, the addition of texture features provides rich spatial features in multi-scale kernel classifiers, which makes effective use of spatial information and enhances the effect of classification. Furthermore, there are the other combination techniques and algorithms that can be used to improve the efficiency of SVM kernels, which will be investigated in the near future.

Acknowledgments. This work was supported by the National Natural Science Foundation of China (41471353), the Natural Science Foundation of Shandong Province (ZR201709180096, ZR201702100118), the Fundamental Research Funds for the Central Universities (18CX05030A, 18CX02179A), and the Postdoctoral Application and Research Projects of Qingdao (BY20170204).

References

1. Yuan, J., Wang, D., Li, R.: Remote sensing image segmentation by combining spectral and texture features. IEEE Trans. Geosci. Remote Sens. **52**(1), 16–24 (2014)
2. Yan, Y., Ren, J., Sun, G., et al.: Unsupervised image saliency detection with Gestalt-laws guided optimization and visual attention based refinement. Pattern Recogn. **79**, 65–78 (2018)
3. Han, J., Zhang, D., Hu, X., et al.: Background prior-based salient object detection via deep reconstruction residual. IEEE Trans. Circuits Syst. Video Technol. **25**(8), 1309–1321 (2015)
4. Vapnik, V.: The Nature of Statistical Learning Theory. Springer, New York (1995)
5. Vapnik, V.: Statistical Learning Theory. Wiley, New York (1998)
6. LeCun, Y., Bengio, Y., Hinton, G.: Deep learning. Nature **521**(7553), 436–444 (2015)
7. Jawad, H., Olivier, P., Ren, J., et al.: Performance of hidden Markov model and dynamic Bayesian network classifiers on handwritten Arabic word recognition. Knowl. Based Syst. **24**(5), 680–688 (2011)
8. Wang, Z., Ren, J., Zhang, D., et al.: A deep-learning based feature hybrid framework for spatiotemporal saliency detection inside videos. Neurocomputing **287**, 68–83 (2018)
9. Ren, J.: ANN vs SVM: which one performs better in classification of MCCs in mammogram imaging. Knowl. Based Syst. **26**, 144–153 (2012)
10. Zheng, D., Wang, J., Zhao, Y.: Non-flat function estimation with a multi-scale support vector regession. Neurocomputing **70**(1–3), 420–429 (2006)
11. Schölkopf, B., Smola, A.: Learning with Kernels: Support Vector Machines, Regularization, Optimization, and Beyond. MIT Press, Cambridge (2001)
12. Yang, Z., Guo, J., Xu, W., Nie, X., Wang, J., Lei, J.: Multi-scale Support Vector Machine for Regression Estimation. In: Wang, J., Yi, Z., Zurada, J.M., Lu, B.-L., Yin, H. (eds.) ISNN 2006. LNCS, vol. 3971, pp. 1030–1037. Springer, Heidelberg (2006). https://doi.org/10.1007/11759966_151
13. Sun, G., Ma, P., Ren, J., et al.: A stability constrained adaptive alpha for gravitational search algorithm. Knowl. Based Syst. **139**, 200–213 (2018)
14. Zhang, A., Sun, G., Ren, J., et al.: A dynamic neighborhood learning-based gravitational search algorithm. IEEE Trans. Cybern. **48**(1), 436–447 (2018)
15. Zheng, D., Wang, J., Zhao, Y.: Training sparse MS-SVR with an expectation–maximization algorithm. Neurocomputing **69**(13–15), 1659–1664 (2006)
16. Phienthrakul, T., Kijsirikul, B.: Evolutionary strategies for multi-scale radial basis function kernels in support vector machines. In: Conference on Genetics and Evaluation Computer, pp. 905–911. ACM, Washington, DC (2005)
17. Han, J., Zhang, D., Cheng, G., et al.: Object detection in optical remote sensing images based on weakly supervised learning and high-level feature learning. IEEE Trans. Geosci. Remote **53**(6), 3325–3337 (2015)
18. Xu, S., Long, W.: Differential evolution algorithm with dynamically adjusting number of subpopulation individuals. J. Comput. Appl. **31**(11), 3101–3103 (2011)
19. Storn, R., Price, K.: Differential evolution-a simple and efficient heuristic for global optimization over continuous spaces. J. Glob. Optim. **11**(4), 341–359 (1997)
20. Peleg, S., Naor, J., Hartley, R.: Multiple resolution texture analysis and classification. IEEE Trans. Pattern. Anal. PAMI **6**(4), 518–523 (2009)
21. Zhang, J., Pan, Y., He, C.: The high spatial resolution remote sensing image classification based on SVM with the multi-source data. In: Symposium on 2005 IEEE International Geoscience and Remote Sensing, pp. 3818–3821 (2005)
22. Cheng, G., Han, J., Guo, L., et al.: Effective and efficient midlevel visual elements-oriented land-use classification using VHR remote sensing images. IEEE Trans. Geosci. Remote Sens. **53**(8), 4238–4249 (2015)

Eigenface Algorithm-Based Facial Expression Recognition in Conversations - An Experimental Study

Zixiang Fei[1], Erfu Yang[1](✉), David Li[2], Stephen Butler[3], Winifred Ijomah[1], and Neil Mackin[4]

[1] Department of Design, Manufacture and Engineering Management, University of Strathclyde, Glasgow G1 1XJ, UK
{zixiang.fei,erfu.yang,w.l.ijomah}@strath.ac.uk
[2] Strathclyde Institute of Pharmacy and Biomedical Sciences, University of Strathclyde, Glasgow G4 0RE, UK
david.li@strath.ac.uk
[3] School of Psychological Sciences and Health, University of Strathclyde, Glasgow G1 1QE, UK
stephen.butler@strath.ac.uk
[4] Capita plc, London SW1H 0XA, UK
Neil.Mackin@capita.co.uk

Abstract. Recognizing facial expressions is important in many fields such as computer-human interface. Though different approaches have been widely used in facial expression recognition systems, there are still many problems in practice to achieve the best implementation outcomes. Most systems are tested via the lab-based facial expressions, which may be unnatural. Particularly many systems have problems when they are used for recognizing the facial expressions being used during conversation. This paper mainly conducts an experimental study on Eigenface algorithm-based facial expression recognition. It primarily aims to investigate the performance of both lab-based facial expressions and facial expressions used during conversation. The experiment also aims to probe the problems arising from the recognition of facial expression in conversations. The study is carried out using both the author's facial expressions as the basis for the lab-based expressions and the facial expressions from one elderly person during conversation. The experiment showed a good result in lab-based facial expressions, but there are some issues observed when using the case of facial expressions obtained in conversation. By analyzing the experimental results, future research focus has been highlighted as the investigation of how to recognize special emotions such as a wry smile and how to deal with the interferences in the lower part of face when speaking.

Keywords: Facial expression recognition · Eigenface algorithm
Facial expressions in conversations

J. Ren et al. (Eds.): BICS 2018, LNAI 10989, pp. 342–351, 2018.
https://doi.org/10.1007/978-3-030-00563-4_33

1 Introduction

Facial expressions play an important role in communicating with other people, expressing feelings, emotions and can be argued to be one of the most salient social signals in the visual world. Recognizing facial expressions is important in many fields such as computer-human interface.

Machine learning has many good applications in the areas such as medical and data processing. Face feature analysis is a hot topic in machine learning and image processing [1, 2]. In this paper, a large amount of images acquired from the facial expressions of the author and one elderly person are used in the training stage, which includes lab-based facial expressions and facial expressions generated during conversations. By training the given images of facial expressions, the system which is originally written by Md. Iftekhar Tanveer will be able to recognize typical emotional facial expressions such as neutral, happy, angry, sad and surprise [3]. In this system, the Eigenface algorithm is adopted since it can reduce the size of the training images and improve efficiency in the training stage.

Nowadays, there are many algorithms for facial expression recognition and researchers continue doing the research in this topic. For example, Fathallah et al. used deep learning for facial expression recognition and Jun et al. used 28 facial feature keypoints in images detection and Gabor wavelet filter for facial expression recognition [4, 5]. However, many existing approaches have weaknesses in dealing with complex backgrounds and head motions. There are also several good survey papers which summarize the advantages and drawbacks for recognizing facial expressions [6–10]. For instance, Fasel et al. discuss issues relating to current facial expression recognition systems [7].

Among the many approaches available, the Eigenface algorithm has proven to be the effective methods for facial expression recognition. Originally proposed by Turk and Pentland [11], this algorithm has been employed by several researchers to deal with other related problems [12–15].

Hok-chun [12] employed the Eigenface algorithm to recognize facial expression in performance animation. In this approach, the process of recognizing facial expression is achieved by matching the input images with the images for a variety of facial expression in a database. Its simplicity allows the system to work in real time.

In a different approach, Suranga et al. employed the Eigenface algorithm to both recognize different facial features and assign descriptive words to each feature [13]. In this approach, after the training stage, the system is able to match the input image with a pattern in the training set which can be described as the best match. The experiment showed that the current system is able to recognize some well-defined features like eyes, but it seemed that it was unable to cover all the features in a face.

In related research, Mohamed et al. used the Eigenface technique to attempt to match the input face images with face images in the database with known identity [14]. The system mainly involved three parts, i.e., Generating Eigenfaces, Face Classification and Face Identification. In addition, Chung-Hsien researched the recognition of facial expression by the Eigenface algorithm where it was focused on speaking effect removal [15].

This paper will mainly present an experimental study employing the Eigenface algorithm-based facial expression recognition approach in the Matlab environment. In addition, the Eigenface algorithm will be particularly studied using conversational facial expressions. This paper aims to probe the problems that arise when attempting to recognize facial expressions during conversations using the Eigenface algorithm.

This paper is organized as follows. Section 1 has a general overview and sets out the outline of the paper. Subsequently, fundamental knowledge on Eigenface algorithm and principal components analysis is introduced in Sect. 2. Section 3 outlines the main processes required for the implementation of the algorithm in a Matlab environment. The experiments and discussions are provided in Sect. 4. Section 5 provides a summary and conclusion.

2 Introduction to Principal Components Analysis and Eigenface Conversion

2.1 Principal Components Analysis

Recognition of facial expressions using the Eigenface algorithm requires several steps. In these steps, the principal components analysis (PCA) is considered to be fundamental for Eigenface algorithm. In Matlab, the following main steps are required:

1. Obtain one set of random data sets
2. Adjust the dataset and minus the dataset with the average value
3. Calculate the Covariance of the adjusted dataset
4. Calculate the eigenvector, and eigenvalue of the covariance
5. Obtain the feature vector by choosing some larger eigenvalue
6. Obtain the final data by multiply the adjusted data with Feature Vector

2.2 Eigenface Conversion

The classic Eigenface algorithm contains the following steps. First, the dataset for both training and testing obtained, employing various facial expressions, is used as input. Next, the adjusted dataset is obtained by the following step: take the average image for facial expressions in the dataset as (1); minus the origin dataset with the average image as (2):

$$\psi = \frac{1}{M}\sum_{i=1}^{M} T_i, \tag{1}$$

$$\phi_i = T_i - \psi. \tag{2}$$

Then, the eigenvector and eigenvalue of the covariance of the matrix of the adjusted image dataset are obtained in (3):

$$u_l = \sum_{k=1}^{M} v_{lk}\phi_k, \quad l = 1\ldots M. \tag{3}$$

Also, the weight of each input image is defined below in (4):

$$\omega_k = u_k^T(T_i - \psi), \quad k = 1\ldots M. \tag{4}$$

After that, only major weights are selected, and the others are ignored. Both training and testing datasets are projected to the face subspace. Finally, they are compared to give the result.

3 Implementation of Eigenface Conversion

The implementation of the Eigenface conversion in Matlab is shown in Fig. 1. Many functions in Matlab are used, allowing the Eigenface conversion to be simplified to some extent. The detailed steps are as follows:

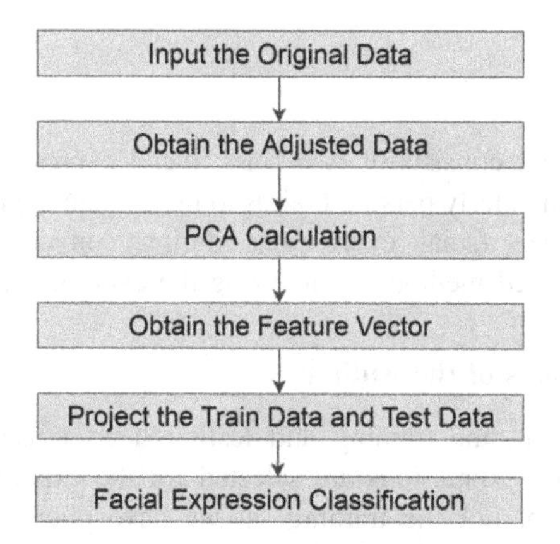

Fig. 1. Flowchart for the eigenface conversion

(1) Data Input

In this step, the dataset of both the training and testing phase for various facial expressions are used as input. Note that the actual facial expression for each image in the training dataset is also known.

(2) Obtain the Adjusted Dataset

Next, the adjusted dataset is obtained as follows: take the average image for facial expressions; minus the origin dataset with the average image.

(3) Obtain the Feature Vector

Then, the PCA calculation is performed to obtain the eigenvector of the covariance. The feature vector is also obtained by choosing some larger eigenvalue. There are 23, 17 and 20 images in the training dataset in the three experiments respectively. 8 largest eigenvalues are chosen in the both three experiments.

(4) Project the Training and Testing Data

In this step, the training image dataset and the testing image dataset are projected to the Facespace. They are obtained by multiplying the adjusted dataset to the feature vector.

(5) Compare and Classify the Facial Expression

In addition, the test images of facial expression are compared with the ones in the training dataset by calculating the Euclidean distance. It is assumed that the testing image has the same facial expression as the training image that has the shortest Euclidean distance. As a result, the facial expression is recognized.

(6) Generate Results

Finally, the results of recognizing facial expression are generated in a file.

4 Experiment

The reported experiment consists of two parts: facial expressions of the author and facial expressions of an elderly person. It aims to investigate the problems that occur in attempting to recognize facial expressions during conversations employing the Eigenface algorithm-based method by analyzing the experimental result.

4.1 Facial Expressions of the Author

For the first experiment, the training and testing dataset used the author's facial expressions. Five facial expressions are selected for the experiment: neutral, happy, sad, angry and surprise. For the training set we have obtained a range of images acquired in different contexts, i.e., in home and in work, with glasses and without glasses, under different background and different lighting conditions. Currently, only some images are used. In the first experiment, 23 images are in the training dataset and 9 images are in the testing dataset. The images used in the testing dataset are shown below in Fig. 2:

In addition, the facial expressions of the images in the training dataset are also included in a text file as the input. Results for the test of recognition of facial expression is shown in Table 1 below. The first column is the number of image in the testing dataset. The second column is the actual facial expression displayed in each image. The third column is the facial expression recognized by the Matlab program. The Matlab program was developed by Tanveer and (which is described in [3]). The fourth column is the comparative results from the actual facial expression and the expression recognized by the Matlab program. As shown in Table 1, all the facial expressions in the 9 testing images are recognized correctly.

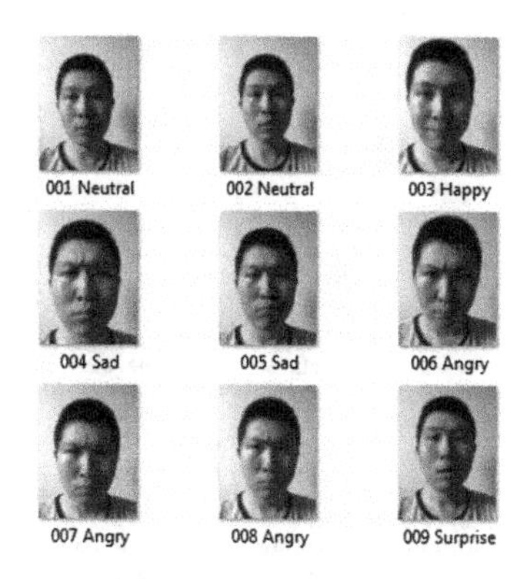

Fig. 2. Testing dataset

Table 1. The experiment result with author's own facial images

Test image number	Actual facial expression	Expression recognized	Test result
1	Neutral	Neutral	Correct
2	Neutral	Neutral	Correct
3	Happy	Happy	Correct
4	Sad	Sad	Correct
5	Sad	Sad	Correct
6	Angry	Angry	Correct
7	Angry	Angry	Correct
8	Angry	Angry	Correct
9	Surprise	Surprise	Correct

In the second experiment the facial expressions employed are either positive emotions (happy, enjoyment, relaxed), negative emotions (unhappy, sad, angry) or emotionally neutral. This experiment investigated how to recognize the author's facial expressions when talking. There are 28 images in the testing dataset and 17 images in the training dataset. The images in the testing dataset are shown in the Fig. 3. The recognition accuracy of facial expression is 85.7%. In particular, images 5, 25, 26, & 28 are inaccurately classified. Naturally occurring emotional life facial expressions show more changes and variation. Moreover, there are changes in the head pose and mouths. Thus, the complexity of the task of recognition complexity is increased.

4.2 Facial Expressions of an Elderly Person

For the experiment employing the facial expressions of an elderly person, screenshots of a video of the interview of one elderly person were used as the training and testing dataset. There are 20 images in the testing dataset and 20 images in the training dataset. The images of the elderly person are not shown in the paper, because of some privacy

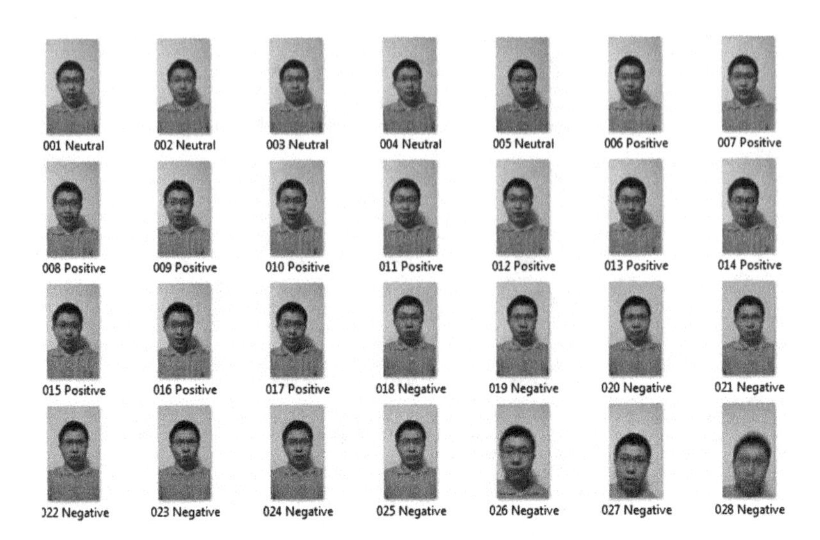

Fig. 3. 2nd testing dataset

reasons. This experiment was designed to test the Eigenface algorithm for facial expression recognition of elderly people in a natural communication situation.

Facial expressions in the images in the training dataset are also included in the text file as the input. Table 2 illustrates the result of recognizing the facial expression of the elderly person. The first column is the number of images in the test dataset. The second column is the actual facial expression displayed within each image. The third column is the facial expression recognized by the Matlab program. The fourth column is the comparative results from the actual facial expression and the expression recognized by the Matlab program. The result of the recognition of facial expression for the selected elderly person is 70.0%, with images 7, 8, 9, 10, 19, 20 were incorrectly classified. Again, we observed that in an accurate real-life situation, natural facial expressions show more changes and variation, including some changes in head pose and mouth shape. Thus difficulty of recognition is greatly increased.

Of particular interest, we observed that a wry smile, which may be considered a negative feeling, is recognized as a happy emotion by the system. As a result, some sad emotions are recognized wrongly in the experiment. The problem mainly results from recognition of the facial expression by calculating the Euclidean distance to the nearest facial expression in the training dataset. The problems that observed in the process of facial expression recognition can be summarized as follows: firstly, that recognition of facial expressions by calculating similarity may result in incorrect recognition for some emotions, such as a wry smile. Secondly, during conversation, the lower parts of the facial features may change in various ways during speech. On the other hand, currently, the facial expression is recognized by finding the most similar image in the training dataset to the image in the testing dataset by calculating the Euclidean distance. As a result, the recognition result may be affected by some factor like appearance of the person. For future improvement, the facial expressions should be recognized using action units, or be classified in detailed categories. Additionally, the issue of changes to

Table 2. The result for facial expression recognition

Test image number	Actual facial expression	Expression recognized	Test result
1	Happy	Happy	Correct
2	Sad	Sad	Correct
3	Sad	Sad	Correct
4	Happy	Happy	Correct
5	Neutral	Neutral	Correct
6	Neutral	Neutral	Correct
7	Sad	Neutral	Wrong
8	Sad	Neutral	Wrong
9	Sad	Neutral	Wrong
10	Sad	Neutral	Wrong
11	Sad	Sad	Correct
12	Sad	Sad	Correct
13	Neutral	Neutral	Correct
14	Neural	Neural	Correct
15	Happy	Happy	Correct
16	Neutral	Neutral	Correct
17	Neutral	Neutral	Correct
18	Neutral	Neutral	Correct
19	Happy	Neutral	Wrong
20	Happy	Neutral	Wrong

lower facial features during speech requires a solution. Thirdly, the performance of facial expression recognition needs to be compared with other algorithms in more detail. Also, dataset consisting of more images should be used. Finally, the influence of the key parameter in the PCA process should be discussed.

For extension of the work in the future, the computer vision techniques could be applied into other machine learning approaches and applications by further research. Relevant research work should be learned. For example, Jawad *et al.* proposed a word-based off-line recognition system using Hidden Markov Models [16]. Jinchang *et al.* proposed an improved neural classifier for early detection of breast cancer [17]. Yanmei *et al.* researched about hierarchical and multi-featured fusion for effective gait recognition [18]. There are some other related tasks including human-computer interaction, unsupervised image saliency detection, handwritten Arabic Scripts Recognition and automatic gait recognition [19–22].

5 Conclusion

This paper described the process of recognizing facial expressions using the Eigenface algorithm, which was conducted using Matlab. First, this paper gave an introduction to the recognition of facial expressions. Next, the fundamental knowledge relating to PCA was provided; then, the Eigenface process in Matlab was detailed. In addition, an experiment on the result of experimental testing of the recognition of both the author's facial expression, and the expressions of one elderly person were reported.

In this approach, although the simplicity of comparing and classifying the facial expressions is an advantage, there are some drawbacks. For instance, this approach relies on a good training set. It cannot recognize facial expressions or facial features that are not included in the training set. In addition, when there are some inferences, the recognition accuracy will be affected. Moreover, problems that occurred in the process of the recognition of some less common facial emotions, those such as a wry smile, or that occur when lower facial features change during speech.

References

1. Machine learning for facial recognition – EFavDB. http://efavdb.com/machine-learning-for-facial-recognition-3/
2. Chen, J., Jenkins, W.K.: Facial recognition with PCA and machine learning methods. In: Midwest Symposium on Circuits and Systems, pp. 973–976 (2017)
3. Eigenface based Facial Expression Classification - File Exchange - MATLAB Central. https://uk.mathworks.com/matlabcentral/fileexchange/33325-eigenface-based-facial-expression-classification?requestedDomain=true
4. Fathallah, A., Abdi, L., Douik, A.: Facial expression recognition via deep learning. In: Proceeding of IEEE/ACS International Conference on Computer Systems and Applications, AICCSA, pp. 745–750 (2018)
5. Ou, J., Bai, X.-B., Pei, Y., Ma, L., Liu, W.: Automatic facial expression recognition using Gabor filter and expression analysis. In: ICCMS 2010–2010 International Conference on Computer Modeling and Simulation, pp. 215–218 (2010)
6. Samal, A., Iyengar, P.A.: Automatic recognition and analysis of human faces and facial expressions: a survey. Pattern Recognit. **25**, 65–77 (1992). https://doi.org/10.1016/0031-3203(92)90007-6
7. Fasel, B., Luettin, J.: Automatic facial expression analysis: a survey. Pattern Recognit. **36**, 259–275 (2003). https://doi.org/10.1016/s0031-3203(02)00052-3
8. Sandbach, G., Zafeiriou, S., Pantic, M., Yin, L.: Static and dynamic 3D facial expression recognition: a comprehensive survey. Image Vis. Comput. **30**, 683–697 (2012). https://doi.org/10.1016/j.imavis.2012.06.005
9. Zeng, Z., Pantic, M., Roisman, G.I., Huang, T.S.: A survey of affect recognition methods: audio, visual, and spontaneous expressions. IEEE Trans. Pattern Anal. Mach. Intell. **31**, 39–58 (2009). https://doi.org/10.1109/tpami.2008.52
10. Sariyanidi, E., Gunes, H., Cavallaro, A.: Automatic analysis of facial affect: a survey of registration, representation, and recognition. IEEE Trans. Pattern Anal. Mach. Intell. **37**, 1113–1133 (2015). https://doi.org/10.1109/tpami.2014.2366127
11. Turk, M., Pentland, A.: Eigenfaces for recognition. J. Cognit. Neurosci. **3**, 71–86 (1991)
12. Lo, H.-C., Churig, R.: Facial expression recognition approach for performance animation. In: Proceedings of 2nd International Workshop on Digital and Computational Video, DCV 2001 (2001)
13. Wijeratne, S., Jayawardena, S., Jayasooriya, S., Lokupathirage, D., Patternot, M., Kodagoda, G.N.: Eigenface based automatic facial feature tagging. In: Proceedings of the 2008 4th International Conference on Information and Automation for Sustainability, ICIAFS 2008 (2008)

14. Toure, M.L., Beiji, Z.: Intelligent sensor for image control point of eigenfaces for face recognition. J. Comput. Sci. **6**, 484–491 (2010). https://doi.org/10.3844/jcssp.2010.484.491
15. Wu, C.-H., Wei, W.-L., Lin, J.-C., Lee, W.-Y.: Speaking effect removal on emotion recognition from facial expressions based on eigenface conversion. IEEE Trans. Multimedia **15**, 1732–1744 (2013). https://doi.org/10.1109/tmm.2013.2272917
16. Alkhateeb, J.H., Ren, J., Jiang, J., Al-Muhtaseb, H.: Offline handwritten Arabic cursive text recognition using Hidden Markov Models and re-ranking. Pattern Recognit. Lett. **32**, 1081–1088 (2011). https://doi.org/10.1016/j.patrec.2011.02.006
17. Ren, J., Wang, D., Jiang, J.: Effective recognition of MCCs in mammograms using an improved neural classifier. Eng. Appl. Artif. Intell. **24**, 638–645 (2011). https://doi.org/10.1016/j.engappai.2011.02.011
18. Chai, Y., Ren, J., Zhao, H., Li, Y., Ren, J., Murray, P.: Hierarchical and multi-featured fusion for effective gait recognition under variable scenarios. Pattern Anal. Appl. **19**, 905–917 (2016). https://doi.org/10.1007/s10044-015-0471-5
19. Ren, J., Vlachos, T., Argyriou, V.: Immersive and perceptual human-computer interaction using computer vision techniques. In: 2010 IEEE Computer Society Conference on Computer Vision and Pattern Recognition - Workshops, CVPRW 2010, pp. 66–72 (2010)
20. Yan, Y., et al.: Unsupervised image saliency detection with Gestalt-laws guided optimization and visual attention based refinement. Pattern Recognit. **79**, 65–78 (2018). https://doi.org/10.1016/j.patcog.2018.02.004
21. Alkhateeb, J.H., Ren, J., Jiang, J., Ipson, S.S., El Abed, H.: Word-based handwritten arabic scripts recognition using DCT features and neural network classifier. In: 2008 5th International Multi-conference on Systems, Signals and Devices, SSD 2008 (2008)
22. Chai, Y., Ren, J., Zhao, R., Jia, J.: Automatic gait recognition using dynamic variance features. In: Proceedings of the 7th International Conference on Automatic Face and Gesture Recognition, FGR 2006, pp. 475–480 (2006)

Unsupervised Hyperspectral Band Selection Based on Maximum Information Entropy and Determinantal Point Process

Zhijing Yang[1(✉)], Weizhao Chen[1], Yijun Yan[2], Faxian Cao[1], and Nian Cai[1]

[1] School of Information Engineering, Guangdong University of Technology, Guangzhou 510006, China
yzhj@gdut.edu.cn

[2] Department of Electronic and Electrical Engineering, University of Strathclyde, Glasgow G1 1XW, UK

Abstract. Band selection is of great important for hyperspectral image processing, which can effectively reduce the data redundancy and computation time. In the case of unknown class labels, it is very difficult to select an effective band subset. In this paper, an unsupervised band selection algorithm is proposed which can preserve the original information of the hyperspectral image and select a low-redundancy band subset. First, a search criterion is designed to effectively search the best band subset with maximum information entropy. It is challenging to select a low-redundancy spectral band subset with maximizing the search criteria since it is a NP-hard problem. To overcome this problem, a double-graph model is proposed to capture the correlations between spectral bands with full use of the spatial information. Then, an improved Determinantal Point Process algorithm is presented as the search method to find the low-redundancy band subset from the double-graph model. Experimental results verify that our algorithm achieves better performance than other state-of-the-art methods.

Keywords: Unsupervised band selection · Maximum information
Graph model · Determinantal Point Process (DPP)

1 Introduction

Hyperspectral data is a three-dimension image with the spatial information and abundant spectral information which makes great development of hyperspectral images in the field of remote sensing [1, 2]. Multidimensional spectral bands can improve the representation of the ground objects. However, not all the bands play an important role in hyperspectral image processing [3]. That is because high dimensional hyperspectral data may cause a lot of problems, such as redundancy of information, noise bands and Hughes phenomenon. Therefore, an effective dimension reduction method is necessary for the hyperspectral data. Traditional dimensionality reduction methods mainly include two types: band selection and feature extraction [5–7]. Compared with feature extraction, band selection can effectively protect the original information as much as possible.

The research of band selection can be mainly divided into two directions: supervised band selection [8, 9] and unsupervised band selection [10–12]. Supervised band

J. Ren et al. (Eds.): BICS 2018, LNAI 10989, pp. 352–361, 2018.
https://doi.org/10.1007/978-3-030-00563-4_34

selection method can select a spectral band subset that have a strong correlation with class labels. However, it's time-consuming to label the hyperspectral images. Therefore, the unsupervised band selection method is more applicable. In this paper, we propose an unsupervised band selection method to select a low-redundancy band subset with maximum amount of information.

The unsupervised band selection process mainly contains two steps: the selection criteria and search strategy. At present, the unsupervised selection methods can be divided into the ranking-based methods [13], clustering-based methods [17], and greedy-algorithms [15]. However, most of the above-mentioned band selection methods only consider the property of the band combination ignoring the latent structure between spectral bands in the high dimensional space [3]. This defect will cause the lack of global considerations. In addition, most band selection methods do not consider the correlation between pairwise bands from the spatial information. Spatial information helps to make the measurement of spectral redundancy more comprehensive. In [3], Yuan et al. proposed a multiple graph to measure similarity between spectral bands by spectral clustering method. However, the spectral clustering has very high computation complexity and high memory requirements. In view of this, this paper proposes a double-graph structure to describe the complex correlation between spectral bands with both pixels information and neighborhood information of pixels.

In addition, selecting a low-redundancy band subset from the graph model with traditional search methods is a challenging work. DPP [16] is a probabilistic model that can select a diverse subset of features. The k-DPP [17], as an improved algorithm of the DPP, can select a low-redundancy band subset with dimension k. The original k-DPP can only be applied to select from single graph model without full use of the spatial information of hyperspectral images. Furthermore, it does not consider the physical properties of each band in the selecting process.

To solve the above problems, a double-graph model DPP is proposed with full use of pixel information and its domain information. To attain a high-performance band subset, a spectral band selection criterion: maximum band subset information [4] is used which means that the selected spectral band subset has a rich amount of information.

2 The Proposed Framework

2.1 Hyperspectral Data Representation

A hyperspectral dataset is represented by $\mathrm{B} = \{\mathrm{b}_1, \mathrm{b}_2, \mathrm{b}_3, \ldots, \mathrm{b}_l\} \in R^{n \times l}$, where n represents the number of pixels in each spectral band and l is the total number of all spectral bands. $\mathrm{b}_i (1 \leq i \leq l)$ indicates the i-th spectral band. Given a pixel point p_x^j, we use $\hat{p}_x^j$ to represent the mean of the neighbourhood of pixel p_x^j. Then, the neighbour information can be rewritten as a new dataset $\hat{\mathrm{B}} = \left\{\hat{\mathrm{b}}_1, \hat{\mathrm{b}}_2, \hat{\mathrm{b}}_3, \ldots, \hat{\mathrm{b}}_l\right\} \in R^{s \times l}$, where s is the total number of $\hat{\mathrm{b}}_i (1 \leq i \leq l)$.

2.2 Double Graph Model

In [3], a multi-graph structure with spectral clustering method is proposed that can effectively represent the relationship between bands. In this section, we construct a double graph model to capture the complex relationships between pairwise spectral bands with statistical property of space. In graph model, each vertex represents a band b_i and each edge corresponds to the correlation between pairwise bands. The correlation of vertices can be described as an adjacency matrix which can be defined by a Gram matrix. The adjacency matrix of bands is defined as follows:

$$L_B = B^T B \tag{1}$$

And the adjacency matrix of neighbour information data can be expressed as follows:

$$L_{\hat{B}} = \hat{B}^T \hat{B} \tag{2}$$

L_B and $L_{\hat{B}}$ are both $l \times l$ positive semidefinite similarity matrices. According to the reference [18], it is clear that

$$\det(L_Y) = \mathrm{Vol}^2\left(\{\mathrm{b}_i\}_{i \in Y}\right) \tag{3}$$

where $\det(\mathrm{L}_Y)$ is equal to the squared k-dimensional volume of the parallelepiped spanned by the $\{\mathrm{b}_i\}_{i \in Y}$ of B corresponding to bands in subset Y, where k is the dimension of subset Y.

2.3 Search Criterion

To select a band subset with rich information, the evaluation criteria of maximum information entropy [4] is used here. The information entropy of the spectral band subset is defined as:

$$\max\ H_k = -\frac{1}{k}\sum\nolimits_{i=1}^{k} \sum\nolimits_{x=1}^{n} P\left(p_x^i\right) \log P\left(p_x^i\right) \tag{4}$$

where p_x^i represents the pixel value of the i-th spectral band and k is the number of band subset. Equation (4) can be used as the evaluation criteria for the performance of each band subset, which is called **MI** for short.

2.4 MI-DPP Band Selection Method

The k-DPP [14] can be expressed as follows:

$$\sum\nolimits_{|Y'|=k} \det(L_{Y'}) = \det(L+I) \sum\nolimits_{|Y'|=k} \mathrm{P}_L(Y') \tag{5}$$

where $\mathrm{P}_L(Y')$ represents the probability of any band subset Y' with dimension k. According to Eq. (5), k-DPP can be expressed as follows:

$$P_L^k(Y) = \frac{\det(\mathrm{L}_Y)}{\sum_{|Y'|=k} \det(L_{Y'})} \tag{6}$$

According to reference [13], we can get

$$P_L^k = \frac{1}{e_k^N}\det(L+I)\mathrm{P}_L = \frac{1}{e_k^N}\sum\nolimits_{|Y|=k} P^{V_Y}(Y')\Pi_{n\in Y}\lambda_n \tag{7}$$

Equation (7) is the mathematical expression of k-DPP which shows that P_L^k is a mixture of the elementary DPPs P^{V_Y}.

With full use of the spatial information, our algorithm can be written as follows:

$$P_{L_B,L_{\hat{B}}}^k(Y) = \frac{1}{e_{B,k}^N}\sum\nolimits_{|Y|=k} uP^{V_Y^B}(Y')\prod\nolimits_{n\in Y}\lambda_n^B + \frac{1}{e_{\hat{B},k}^N}\sum\nolimits_{|Y|=k} \hat{u}P^{V_Y^{\hat{B}}}(Y')\prod\nolimits_{n\in Y}\lambda_n^{\hat{B}} \tag{8}$$

where u and $\hat{u}$ are scalars that balance the weight of two k-DPPs. Equation (8) shows that our algorithm is a mixture of two elementary DPPs $P^{V_Y^B}$ and $P^{V_Y^{\hat{B}}}$, where λ_n^B and $\lambda_n^{\hat{B}}$ are the eigenvalues of the adjacent matrices L_B and $L_{\hat{B}}$ respectively. $e_{B,k}^N = \sum_{|Y|=k}\prod_{n\in Y}\lambda_n^B$ and $e_{\hat{B},k}^N = \sum_{|Y|=k}\prod_{n\in Y}\lambda_n^{\hat{B}}$ are the eigenvalue polynomials of the adjacent matrices L_B and $L_{\hat{B}}$, respectively. $P_{L_B,L_{\hat{B}}}^k(Y)$ is the probability of sampling a band subset Y. Combined with the search criterion MI mentioned in Sect. 2.3, we call the proposed algorithm as MI-DPP. Details of the sampling process of MI-DPP are summarized in Algorithm 1.

Algorithm 1 Sampling Process of MI-DPP

Input:

$\boldsymbol{B}$: a hyperspectral image

$\boldsymbol{k}$: number of selected bands

Output:

Y: index of feature vectors

1) Computing similarity matrix: $L_B = B^T B \;\; L_{\hat{B}} = \hat{B}^T\hat{B}$
2) Characteristic decomposition: $\{\lambda_n^B, \mathbf{v}_n^B\}_{n=1}^l \Leftarrow L_B \;\; \{\lambda_n^{\hat{B}}, \mathbf{v}_n^{\hat{B}}\}_{n=1}^l \Leftarrow L_{\hat{B}}$
3) for $\boldsymbol{n} = \boldsymbol{l}, \ldots, \mathbf{2}, \mathbf{1}$ do
4) select eigenvectors sets V_B and $V_{\hat{B}}$ with cardinality $\mathbf{k}$ with probability $\lambda_n^B \frac{e_{B,k-1}^{n-1}}{e_{B,k}^n}$ and $\lambda_n^{\hat{B}} \frac{e_{\hat{B},k-1}^{n-1}}{e_{\hat{B},k}^n}$
5) end for
6) while $|\mathbf{V}_{\boldsymbol{B}}| > \mathbf{0}$ **and** $|\mathbf{V}_{\hat{\boldsymbol{B}}}| > \mathbf{0}$ do
7) select band $\boldsymbol{i}$ with probability:

$$\boldsymbol{P_r(i)} = u\frac{1}{|V_B|}\sum\nolimits_{\mathbf{v}_n^B\in V}\left(\mathbf{v}_n^{B^T}\boldsymbol{e_i}\right)^2 + \hat{u}\frac{1}{|V_{\hat{B}}|}\sum\nolimits_{\mathbf{v}_n^{\hat{B}}\in V_{\hat{B}}}\left(\mathbf{v}_n^{\hat{B}^T}\boldsymbol{e_i}\right)^2$$

8) If $\boldsymbol{u \sim U[0,1] < P_r(i)}$

$\boldsymbol{Y \leftarrow Y \cup \{i\}}$

9) end if
10) $\boldsymbol{V_B} \leftarrow \boldsymbol{V_{B\perp}}, \boldsymbol{V_{\hat{B}}} \leftarrow \boldsymbol{V_{\hat{B}\perp}}$ an orthonormal basis for the subspace of $\boldsymbol{V_B}$, $\boldsymbol{V_{\hat{B}}}$ orthogonal to $\boldsymbol{e_i}$
11) end while

Output: Y

We repeat Algorithm 1 for α times to obtain α spectral band subsets Y with the dimension k. Then we select the band subset that meets the maximum search criteria H_k from the α spectral band subsets. With the proposed algorithm MI-DPP, the selected band subset will have the advantages of low redundancy and high information.

3 Experimental Result

In this section, we test the performances of the proposed algorithm and compare with several well-known unsupervised selection algorithms, including MIC [18] and Lscore [19].

3.1 Hyperspectral Datasets

AVRIS sensor: Indian Pines dataset

The India Pines dataset was obtained by the Airborne Visible/Infrared Imaging Spectrometer sensor (AVIRIS) in 1992 [20]. The image covers Indian Pines test site in North-western Indiana which has 220 spectral bands covering the spectrum range of 0.2–2.4 μm. And 20 water absorption spectral bands [104–108], [150–163] are removed and remaining 200 spectral bands form the dataset. It has 145 $\times$ 145 spatial pixels, including 16 classes ground truth.

Table 1. The numbers of training and test samples for each category of the Indian Pines image

Class	Training	Test	Samples
1. Alfalfa	4	50	54
2. Corn - notill	142	1292	1434
3. Corn - mintill	83	751	834
4. Corn	23	211	234
5. Grass - pasture	49	448	497
6. Grass - trees	73	674	747
7. Grass - pas - turemowed	3	23	26
8. Hay - windrowed	48	431	489
9. Oats	2	18	20
10. Soybean - notill	97	871	968
11. Soybean - mintill	245	2223	2468
12. Soybean - clean	59	555	614
13. Wheat	20	192	212
14. Woods	127	1167	1294
15. Building - grass-trees	39	341	380
16. Stone - steel-towers	9	86	95
Total	1023	9343	10366

3.2 Experimental Parameter Setup

In this section, we will introduce the parameter settings. The weight scalar u and $\hat{u}$ are set to be $u = \hat{u} = 0.5$. The number of iterations $\alpha = 5$. The number of selected bands increased by 10 and up to 100 bands. We use the SVM algorithm [21] to test the performance of the selected bands. The parameters C and γ of RBF kernel of SVM are in the range of $10^{\{1:4\}}$ and $2^{\{-4:4\}}$, and are determined by five-fold cross validation. In all experiments, 10% of the samples were randomly selected for training, and the rest of the samples were used for testing. In Table 1, we show the numbers of training samples and test samples for Indian Pines dataset. The results of the experiment are evaluated through three widely used indexes: overall accuracy (OA), average accuracy (AA) and kappa coefficient [22].

3.3 Runtime Analysis

As showed in [18], k-DPP has a time complexity of $\mathcal{O}(Nk^3)$. It spends $\mathcal{O}(N^3)$ time to decompose s adjacent kernel matrices of bands. The MI-DPP algorithm takes total time $\mathcal{O}(nN^3 + nNk^3)$ to sample k bands, where n is the number of the similar kernel matrices. The computation time of the algorithm will greatly increase when N and k are large. However, the numbers of N and k are normally small in the selecting progress. We pre-calculate the information entropy for each band and establish lookup tables for Indian Pines dataset. Establishing lookup tables for Indian Pines dataset takes only 0.05 s. All the experiments are carried out on Matlab with Intel CPU E5-1620@3.5 GHz with 32 GB RAM.

In Fig. 1, the computing time of the three algorithms is shown as the number of selected spectral bands increases from 10 to 100. It's obvious that the calculation time of the proposed MI-DPP is the least comparing with the other algorithms when the dimension of band subset is low. As the number of selected spectral bands increases,

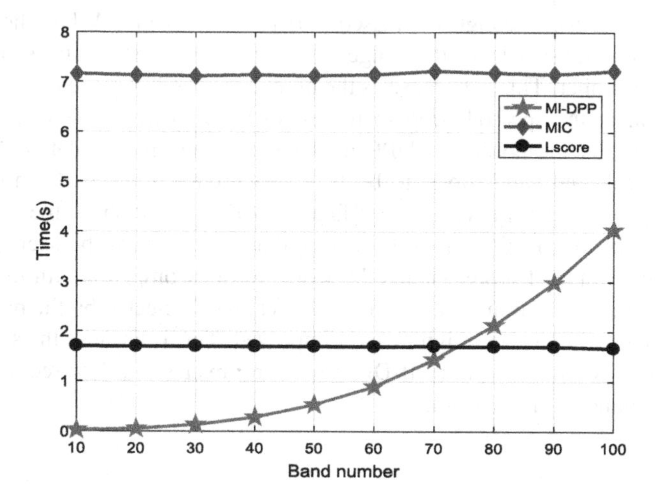

Fig. 1. Runtime of MI-DPP, MIC, Lscore on the Indian Pines

the calculation time of the MIC and Lscore does not change significantly. The calculation time of the algorithm MI-DPP will increase as the dimension of selected band subset increases. In general, the proposed algorithm MI-DPP takes less time than the other band selection algorithms.

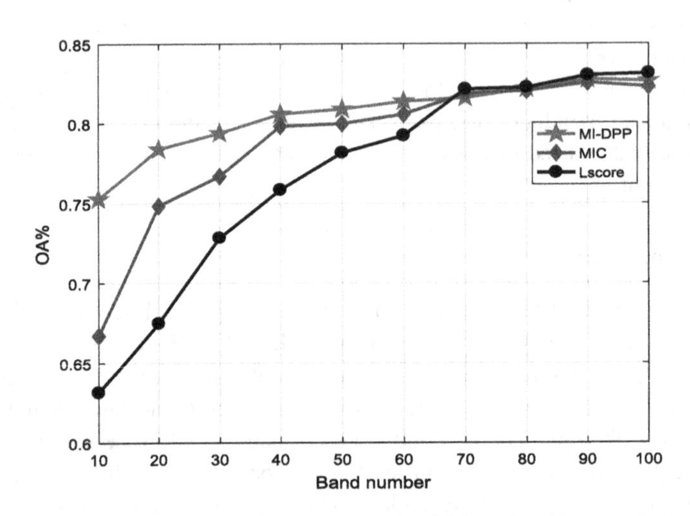

Fig. 2. Classification accuracy of the three band selection algorithms on Indian Pines

3.4 Classification Results

In this subsection, we test the performance of the selected subsets of spectral bands on Indian Pines image. In Fig. 2, we compared the classification accuracy of the band subset selected by different algorithms. When the dimension of band subsets is in the range of 10–70, our proposed band selection method MI-DPP is significantly better than other algorithms. The algorithm Lscore performs the worst. When the dimension of spectral band subsets is in the range of 70–100, the performances of the three algorithms are similar. This is because as the number of bands is increasing, the amount of information in the spectral band increases. In the following, we will analyse the performance of the proposed MI-DPP in the low dimension in detail. We set the dimension of selected band subset to be 10 for each dataset and perform the classification tests. The results are shown in Table 2. In Fig. 3, we show the classification maps of three band selection algorithms on Indian Pines. It can be seen that among these three algorithms, Lscore obtains the worse result. Compared with the other two algorithms, the classification accuracy of the optical band selected by the proposed MI-DPP in all categories has been significantly improved. This is because the spectral band subset selected by the algorithm MI-DPP are more diverse and low-redundant which can provide abundant information.

Table 2. Classification accuracy of the band set on the Indian pines image selected by Lscore, MIC and the proposed MIMN-DPP

Class	Lscore	MIC	Proposed
1. Alfalfa	22.0 ± 19.7	32.6 ± 25.1	**44.6 ± 16.6**
2. Corn - notill	46.7 ± 3.5	55.3 ± 3.8	**60.2 ± 4.8**
3. Corn - mintill	34.2 ± 3.4	32.6 ± 5.8	**55.6 ± 2.5**
4. Corn	10.9 ± 7.5	12.4 ± 6.3	**53.7 ± 7.9**
5. Grass - pasture	78.1 ± 3.9	83.2 ± 4.4	**88.5 ± 2.7**
6. Grass-trees	88.4 ± 3.1	90.8 ± 1.9	**91.8 ± 2.1**
7. Grass - pas - turemowed	26.9 ± 78.9	63.4 ± 21.7	**82.2 ± 10.1**
8. Hay - windrowed	82.1 ± 6.1	95.6 ± 1.9	**95.7 ± 2.5**
9. Oats	11.1 ± 11.7	16.1 ± 13.7	**57.2 ± 27.3**
10. Soybean - notill	55.6 ± 3.6	44.3 ± 6.8	**65.1 ± 6.1**
11. Soybean - mintill	71.5 ± 2.3	75.1 ± 2.7	**79.6 ± 3.1**
12. Soybean - clean	36.4 ± 3.4	52.7 ± 4.7	**66.1 ± 3.1**
13. Wheat	91.3 ± 4.7	90.1 ± 4.9	**94.4 ± 3.1**
14. Woods	92.6 ± 1.3	93.6 ± 0.6	**94.5 ± 1.3**
15. Building - grass-trees	24.0 ± 5.4	37.1 ± 3.5	**47.2 ± 6.5**
16. Stone - steel-towers	81.4 ± 8.7	77.0 ± 16.6	**87.7 ± 8.6**
OA (%)	63.1 ± 0.1	66.7 ± 0.9	**75.2 ± 0.7**
AA (%)	53.3 ± 2.6	59.5 ± 3.2	**72.8 ± 2.4**
Kappa (%)	57.4 ± 0.9	61.5 ± 1.5	**71.5 ± 0.8**

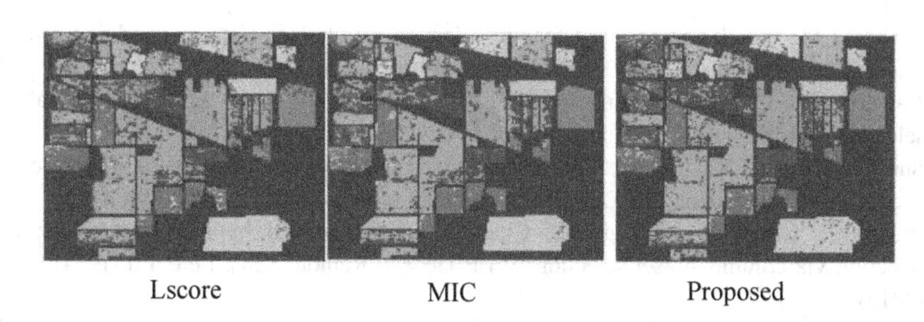

Fig. 3. Classification maps of three band selection algorithms on Indian Pines

4 Conclusion

In this paper, an unsupervised band selection algorithm called MI-DPP is proposed for hyperspectral images. We use the evaluation criterion to evaluate the spectral band performance, aiming to maintain the maximum band information. A double graph model is used to capture the complex relationship between bands. Furthermore, an improved k-DPP is proposed to sample a diversity and low-redundancy band subset from the two-graph structure. The experimental results on Indian Pines image dataset show that the proposed algorithm has a good expression in the task of band selection.

Acknowledgements. This work is supported by the National Nature Science Foundation of China (nos. 61471132 and 61372173), and the Training program for outstanding young teachers in higher education institutions of Guangdong Province (no. YQ2015057).

References

1. Qiao, T., Yang, Z., Ren, J., et al.: Joint bilateral filtering and spectral similarity-based sparse representation: a generic framework for effective feature extraction and data classification in hyperspectral imaging. Pattern Recogn. **77**, 316–328 (2017)
2. Qiao, T., Ren, J., et al.: Effective denoising and classification of hyperspectral images using curvelet transform and singular spectrum analysis. IEEE Trans. Geosci. Remote Sens. **55**(1), 119–133 (2017)
3. Yuan, Y., Zheng, X., Lu, X.: Discovering diverse subset for unsupervised hyperspectral band selection. IEEE Trans. Image Process. **26**(1), 51–64 (2017)
4. Feng, J., Jiao, L., Liu, F., Sun, T., Zhang, X.: Unsupervised feature selection based on maximum information and minimum redundancy for hyperspectral images. Pattern Recogn. **51**, 295–309 (2016)
5. Zabalza, J., Ren, J., Yang, M., et al.: Novel folded-PCA for improved feature extraction and data reduction with hyperspectral imaging and SAR in remote sensing. ISPRS J. Photogram. Remote Sens. **93**, 112–122 (2014)
6. Zabalza, J., et al.: Structured covariance principal component analysis for real-time onsite feature extraction and dimensionality reduction in hyperspectral imaging. Appl. Opt. **53**(20), 4440–4449 (2014)
7. Ren, J., Zabalza, J., Marshall, S., Zheng, J.: Effective feature extraction and data reduction in remote sensing using hyperspectral imaging. IEEE Sig. Process. Mag. **31**(4), 149–154 (2014)
8. Sotoca, J.M., Pla, F.: Supervised feature selection by clustering using conditional mutual information-based distances. Pattern Recogn. **43**(6), 2068–2081 (2010)
9. Yang, H., Du, Q., Su, H., Sheng, Y.: An efficient method for supervised hyperspectral band selection. IEEE Geosci. Remote Sens. Lett. **8**(1), 138–142 (2011)
10. Sui, C., Tian, Y., Xu, Y., Xie, Y.: Unsupervised band selection by integrating the overall accuracy and redundancy. IEEE Geosci. Remote Sens. Lett. **2**(1), 185–189 (2015)
11. Wang, C., Gong, M., Zhang, M., Chan, Y.: Unsupervised hyperspectral image band selection via column subset selection. IEEE Geosci. Remote Sens. Lett. **12**(7), 1411–1415 (2015)
12. Zhang, M., Ma, J., Gong, M.: Unsupervised hyperspectral band selection by fuzzy clustering with particle swarm optimization. IEEE Geosci. Remote Sens. Lett. **4**(5), 773–777 (2017)
13. Chang, C., Wang, S.: Constrained band selection for hyperspectral imagery. IEEE Trans. Geosci. Remote Sens. **44**(6), 1575–1585 (2006)
14. Jia, S., Ji, Z., Qian, Y., Shen, L.: Unsupervised band selection for hyperspectral imagery classification without manual band removal. IEEE J. Sel. Top. Appl. Earth Observ. Remote Sens. **5**(2), 531–543 (2012)
15. Geng, X., Sun, K., Ji, L., Zhao, Y.: A fast volume-gradient-based band selection method for hyperspectral image. IEEE Trans. Geosci. Remote Sens. **52**(11), 7111–7119 (2014)
16. Kulesza, A., Taskar, B.: Determinantal point processes for machine learning. Found. Trends Mach. Learn. **5**(2–3), 123–286 (2012)
17. Kulesza, A., Taskar, B.: k-DPPs: fixed-size determinantal point processes. In: Proceedings of International Conference on Machine Learning, pp. 1193–1200 (2016)

18. Mitra, P., Murthy, C.A., Pal, S.K.: Unsupervised feature selection using feature similarity. IEEE Trans. Pattern Anal. Mach. Intell. **24**(3), 301–312 (2002)
19. He, X., Cai, D., Niyogi, P.: Laplacian score for feature selection. In: NIPS, pp. 507–514 (2006)
20. Green, R.O., et al.: Imaging spectroscopy and the airborne visible/infrared imaging spectrometer (AVIRIS). Remote Sens. Environ. **65**(3), 227–248 (1998)
21. Bazi, Y., Melgani, F.: Toward an optimal SVM classification system for hyper-spectral remote sensing images. IEEE Trans. Geosci. Remote Sens. **44**(11), 3374–3385 (2006)
22. Foody, G.M.: Status of land cover classification accuracy assessment. Remote Sens. Environ. **80**, 185–201 (2002)

Dense Pyramid Network for Semantic Segmentation of High Resolution Aerial Imagery

Xuran Pan[1,2], Lianru Gao[2(✉)], Bing Zhang[2], Fan Yang[1], and Wenzhi Liao[3]

[1] Tianjin Key Laboratory of Electronic Materials and Devices, School of Electronics and Information Engineering, Hebei University of Technology, Tianjin 300401, China
[2] Key Laboratory of Digital Earth Science, Institute of Remote Sensing and Digital Earth, Chinese Academy of Sciences, Beijing 100094, China
gaolr@radi.ac.cn
[3] Department of Telecommunications and Information Processing, IMEC-Ghent University, 9000 Ghent, Belgium

Abstract. In this work, a dense pyramid network is proposed to provide fine classification maps of high resolution aerial images. The network applied densely connected convolutions to take full advantage of features and deepen the network without concerning the disappearance of gradients. Pyramid pooling module is introduced to bring flexible context information to the segmentation task and accomplish the fusion of multi-resolution features. Additionally, in order to preserve more information of multi-sensor data, group convolutions and channel shuffle operation are applied at the beginning of the network. We evaluate the dense pyramid network on the ISPRS Vaihingen 2D semantic labeling dataset, and the results demonstrate that the proposed framework exhibits better performance compared to the state of the art methods.

Keywords: High resolution aerial images · Semantic segmentation
Densely connected convolutions · Pyramid pooling module

1 Introduction

Semantic segmentation of high resolution remote sensing images plays a key role in many applications, like environmental monitoring, agriculture, forestry and urban planning, which makes the real-time and effective labeling of high resolution remote sensing images a significant task. However, the higher spatial resolution not only brings more details of the earth objects, but also challenges the semantic segmentation task due to the large intra-class variance and small inter-class differences.

Over the past decades, different approaches have been proposed for image classification and detection, including methods based on spectral statistical features [1], methods based on machine learning [2–4] and some new approaches like object-oriented classification [5] and sparse representation [6]. These methods achieved satisfactory classification performances, but they typically suffer of major drawbacks

J. Ren et al. (Eds.): BICS 2018, LNAI 10989, pp. 362–369, 2018.
https://doi.org/10.1007/978-3-030-00563-4_35

which were caused by the deficiency of high level features such as spatial contextual information.

Over the last few years, deep learning have been widely applied in each field [7–9]. Indeed, convolutional neural networks (CNNs) achieved outstanding results in semantic segmentation of high resolution imagery. CNNs' deeper structure can learn high level concepts from remote sensing data, which makes it widely applied in high resolution remote sensing image classification. Paisitkriangkrai et al. [10] proposed to use patch-based CNNs to predict probability maps and then combine with the probabilities of random forest (RF) classifier by conditional random field to provide a sooth result. But the patch-based CNNs suffer from limited receptive field and huge RAM cost, and soon be outperformed by pixel-based CNNs. Volpi et al. [11] proposed CNN full patch labeling, which belongs to pixel-based CNNs category, to accomplish high resolution remote sensing imagery classification, and compared it with two patch-based CNNs. The experimental results indicated that pixel-based CNNs outperforms these patch-based models. In [12], Liu et al. fused multi-sensor data by using higher order CRFs, in which color-infrared (CIR) images were processed by fully convolutional network and light detection and ranging (LiDAR) data were trained by a logistic regression. Sherrah et al. [13] proposed a no-downsampling fully convolutional netwrok (FCN) to mitigate information loss caused by pooling operation, and combined the features of CIR images and LiDAR in the decision level. Although this architecture improved the state-of-the-art semantic segmentation accuracy, its limitation of receptive field made it soon be outperformed by the downsampling then upsampling architectures. Audebert et al. [14] applied SegNet [15] to the high resolution aerial imagery classification and proposed dual stream SegNet to accomplish multi-sensor features fusion through residual correction. However, they trained separable networks for CIR images and LiDAR data, and fused the features in the back end of the architecture which often suffers from the multi-fold increase of parameters. Maggiori et al. [16] proposed to combine multi-resolution feature maps by using multi-layer perceptron, and analyzed some recently proposed CNNs deeply. In [17], an hourglass-shape network was proposed for high resolution aerial images classification. Inception module and residual module are introduced to bring flexible receptive fields and feed information from encoder to decoder directly. However, they stacked all data as input to the network, and this resulted in classification ambiguities to some classes without obvious height information.

From the analysis above, the existing methods often suffer from the insufficient exploitation of the spatial and contextual information, and the multi-sensor data fusion is not always appropriate enough. To overcome these problems, we proposed a dense pyramid network (DPN) to obtain fine-grained classification maps of high resolution aerial images. Group convolutions and shuffling operation are applied to each channel of input separately to take full advantage of multi-sensor information; densely connected convolutions are introduced to deepen the network to achieve wider receptive field; pyramid pooling module fuses multi-resolution feature maps at the back end of the network through an effective global contextual prior manner. The rest of the paper is organized as follows. The proposed dense pyramid network architecture is presented in Sect. 2. Experimental settings and results are given in Sect. 3, and conclusions are drawn in Sect. 4.

2 The Proposed Dense Pyramid Network

In this section, we will detail the architecture of the proposed dense pyramid network. The architecture is presented as three parts: the group convolutions and channel shuffling operation for channel-wise feature extraction of multi-sensor data; the densely connected convolutions for high-level semantic feature extraction; and the pyramid pooling module for multi-resolution features fusion. The architecture of the proposed dense pyramid network (DPN) is shown in Fig. 1.

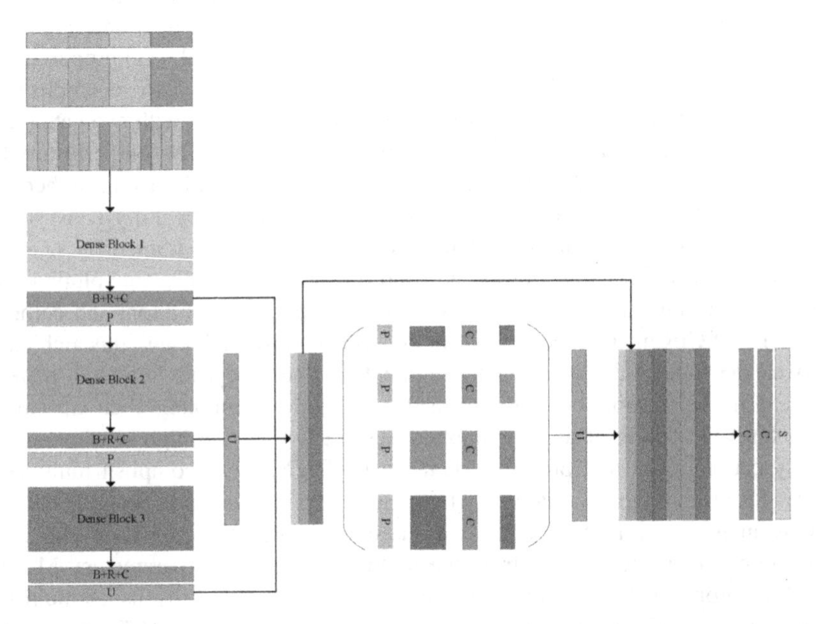

Fig. 1. Architecture of dense pyramid network: B + R + C: Batch normalization + ReLU + Convolutional layer (kernel size: 1 × 1, stride: 1), where P: Pooling layer (kernel size: 2 × 2, stride: 2); U: Upsampling layer; C: Convolutional layer (kernel size: 3 × 3, stride: 1); S: Softmax layer.

2.1 Group Convolutions and Channel Shuffling Operation

Normally, multi-sensor data are stacked together and inputted into the network, and depth-wise convolution combines all channels together at the very first layer. This rough combination can lead to the waste of information, also brings ambiguity to certain ground objects. In this work, we introduce 1 × 1 group convolutions [18] to deal with the multi-sensor data in channel-wise to extract feature maps of each channel separately, so that we can preserve more information of different channels and avoid the channel disorder to some distance. However, when the output channels are only derived from a limited fraction of input channels, the ability of information representation can be reduced. To overcome this bottleneck, the group convolutions are followed by a channel shuffling operation [19] in the proposed network to enhance the representation ability.

2.2 Densely Connected Convolutions

Three densely connected blocks [20] are then applied to mitigate the vanishing gradient problem caused by the network deepening and take full advantage of all features. The structure of dense block is illustrated in Fig. 2, and take 4 layers as an example, each layer is connected to every other layer in a feed-forward fashion. In this work, we applied 16 convolutional layers in each dense block.

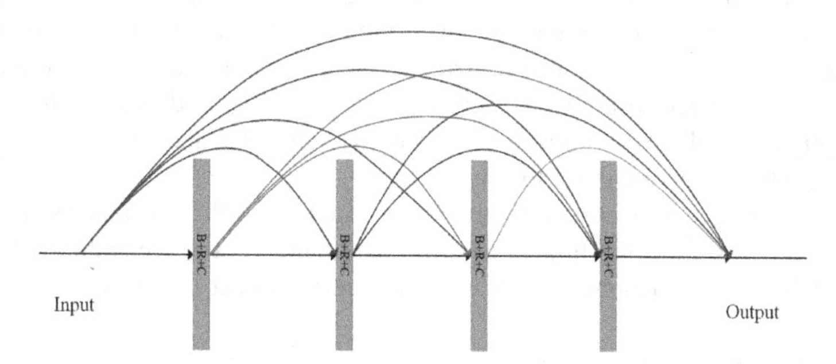

Fig. 2. Architecture of dense block (4 layers). B + R + C: Batch normalization + ReLU + Convolutional layer (kernel size: 3 × 3, stride: 1)

Each dense block is connected by the so called bottleneck layer, which consists of one convolutional layer and one average pooling layer, to reduce dimensions and integrates features of each layer.

2.3 Pyramid Pooling Module

In order to mitigate the trade-off between recognition and localization, multi-resolution feature maps of different layers are first concatenated in varying depth and then combined by the pyramid pooling module [21]. By doing so, multi-resolution features are fused through an effective global contextual prior manner. The pyramid pooling module consists of multi-scale pooling and upsampling layers, as depicted in dotted-line box in the Fig. 1, and different level features are then concatenated to create the final pyramid pooling global feature. Two convolutional layers are followed to reduce dimensions. Finally, a softmax cross entropy layer is used in the training phase of the network.

3 Experiments

3.1 Dataset

The dataset used in the experiment is Vaihingen dataset provided by Commission III of ISPRS [22]. This dataset contains 33 true orthophoto (TOP) tiles which have three channels including near-infrared, red and green. Digital surface models (DSMs) and normalized DSMs (nDSMs) [23] are also provided for each tile. The average size of the

TOP is 2494 $\times$ 2064 pixels. Only 16 of 33 TOP tiles have ground truth maps which are labeled in six classes, namely: impervious surfaces, building, low vegetation, tree, car and clutter. We selected 11 tiles (1, 3, 5, 7, 13, 17, 21, 23, 26, 32, 37) for training and 5 tiles (11, 15, 28, 30, 34) for validation following the practice of [11, 17].

3.2 Experimental Setup

The image tiles are cropped to the size of 256 $\times$ 256 pixels with 50% of overlap. Data augmentation is applied to mitigate the overfitting caused by the limitation of training data. Therefore all data are flipped horizontally and vertically, and then are rotated at 90° intervals. A sparse softmax cross entropy with logits is used as loss function, and Adam optimizer [24–26] is utilized with learning rate 10^{-3} and step down 10 times every 5 epoch. Batch size is set to 3.

In the inference stage, we applied sliding window to clip the images into small patches in order to meet the limitations of video memory. And the sliding window is applied with 75% overlapping size to solve the border effect [14, 17].

3.3 State of the Art Comparison

In this section, the proposed DPN, DPN without group convolutions and shuffling operation version (DPN-noGS) are compared with the state of the art semantic labeling of high resolution aerial image. Among which DPN-noGS fuses the multi-sensor data at the first layer (similar to hourglass-shape network (HSN) [17]) to evaluate whether group convolutions and shuffling operation can achieve better feature extraction of multi-sensor data than rough fusion at the first layer. Table 1 reports the numerical evaluation results of each method, from which we can observe that DPN and DPN-noGS outperform HSN (presented in [17]), SegNet [15] and FCN-8s [27] in most evaluation metrics, and DPN further exceed DPN-noGS which proves group convolutions and shuffling operation can preserve more information from multi-sensor data. It is worth noting that most per class F1 scores of FCN-8s and SegNet are significantly lower than other three methods. The main reason of this phenomenon is that FCN-8s and SegNet suffers from insufficient contextual information, moreover, they utilize VGG16 as its encoder which makes it only suitable for processing 3-channel images, therefore LiDAR data are ignored in the training phase. In comparison to HSN which designed for both CIR images and LiDAR data, DPN achieves higher F1-score in most classes and higher overall accuracy, even DPN-noGS outperforms HSN in most evaluation metrics which indicate the superiority of the dense pyramid design.

The above analysis clearly indicates that DPN can take full advantage of multi-sensor data and have sufficient spatial and contextual information which lead to the significant improvements in segmentation performance.

Figure 3 shows the qualitative results comparison of FCN-8s, HSN (presented in [17]), DPN-noGS and DPN. From row 1 of Fig. 3, it can be seen that bare soil is similar to sparse grass land and some building roof, and it accounts for a low percentage of pixels in the training set, so most networks fail to label this kind of impervious surfaces. Thanks to richer contextual information and appropriate fusion

Table 1. Numerical results for the vaihingen validation set. All evaluation metrics except for OA (overall accuracy) are F1 scores in [%] using the reference with eroded boundaries.

Methods	Imp. surf.	Build	Low veg.	Tree	Car	Aver. F1	OA
FCN-8s [27]	89.13	92.90	77.18	87.66	79.02	85.18	87.09
SegNet [15]	90.00	94.01	78.35	88.21	81.56	86.43	88.02
HSN [17]	91.32	94.66	**79.73**	88.30	83.60	87.52	88.79
DPN-noGS	**91.72**	95.03	79.34	88.30	**83.69**	87.62	88.96
DPN	91.68	**95.36**	79.51	**88.54**	83.53	**87.72**	**89.14**

with LiDAR data, DPN can label this kind of impervious surfaces correctly. Building with cement roof and cement share the similar color and hard to be recognized correctly without the help of LiDAR data, as shown in row 2 of Fig. 3, FCN-8s fails to label this kind of building while other four methods achieve better results, especially the result of DPN have more accurate outlines of buildings. The same effect can be also observed in row 3 of Fig. 3, DPN have sharper outlines of building than that of FCN-8s, SegNet, HSN and DPN-noGS.

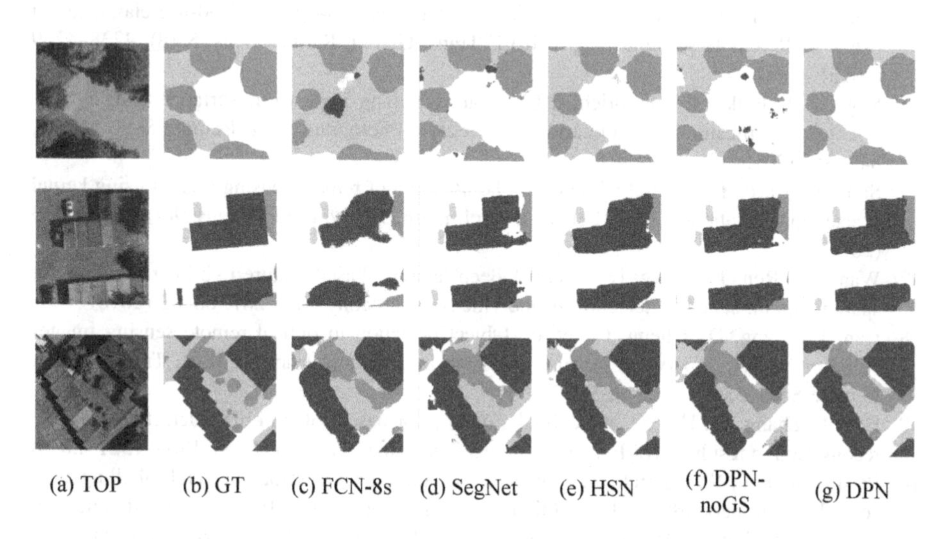

Fig. 3. Comparison of segmentation results using FCN-8s, SegNet, HSN, DPN-noGS and the proposed DPN for the ISPRS Vaihingen dataset.

4 Conclusion

In this paper, a dense pyramid network is proposed to deal with the semantic segmentation of high resolution aerial imagery. The architecture based on densely connected convolutions and pyramid pooling module achieves wider receptive area and different-region-based context aggregation. In particular, group convolutions and shuffling operation are applied at the beginning of the network to preserve more information of multi-sensor data. Experiments on the ISPRS 2D Vaihingen dataset indicate that the proposed DPN is more effective to fuse multi-sensor data and provide a better semantic labeling accuracy.

Acknowledgement. This research was supported by the Strategic Priority Research Program of the Chinese Academy of Sciences under Grant No. XDA19080302, and by the National Natural Science Foundation of China under Grant No. 91638201.

References

1. Sun, J., Yang, J., Zhang, C., et al.: Automatic remotely sensed image classification in a grid environment based on the maximum likelihood method. Math. Comput. Model. **58**(3–4), 573–581 (2013)
2. Yan, Y., Ren, J., Sun, G., et al.: Unsupervised image saliency detection with Gestalt-laws guided optimization and visual attention based refinement. Pattern Recognit. **79**, 65–78 (2018)
3. Ren, J.: ANN vs. SVM: which one performs better in classification of MCCs in mammogram imaging. Knowl. Based Syst. **26**, 144–153 (2012)
4. Cheng, G.: Effective and efficient midlevel visual elements-oriented land-use classification using VHR remote sensing images. IEEE Trans. Geosci. Remote Sens. **53**(8), 4238–4249 (2015)
5. Sugg, Z.P., Finke, T., Goodrich, D.C., et al.: Mapping impervious surfaces using object-oriented classification in a semiarid urban region. Photogram. Eng. Remote Sens. **80**(80), 343–352 (2015)
6. Song, B., Li, P., Li, J., et al.: One-class classification of remote sensing images using kernel sparse representation. IEEE J. Sel. Top. Appl. Earth Observ. Remote Sens. **9**(4), 1613–1623 (2016)
7. Wang, Z., Ren, J., Zhang, D., et al.: A deep learning based feature hybrid framework for spatiotemporal saliency detection inside videos. Neurocomputing **287**, 68–83 (2018)
8. Han, J., Zhang, D., Cheng, G., et al.: Object detection in optical remote sensing images based on weakly supervised learning and high-level feature learning. IEEE Trans. Geosci. Remote Sens. **53**(6), 3325–3337 (2015)
9. Han, J., Zhang, D., Hu, X., et al.: Background prior-based salient object detection via deep reconstruction residual. IEEE Trans. Circuits Syst. Video Technol. **25**(8), 1309–1321 (2015)
10. Paisitkriangkrai, S., Sherrah, J., Janney, P., et al.: Effective semantic pixel labelling with convolutional networks and conditional random fields. In: 2015 IEEE Conference on Computer Vision and Pattern Recognition Workshops (CVPRW), pp. 36–43 (2015)
11. Volpi, M., Tuia, D.: Dense semantic labeling of subdecimeter resolution images with convolutional neural networks. IEEE Trans. Geosci. Remote Sens. **55**, 881–893 (2017)
12. Liu, Y., Piramanayagam, S., Monteiro, S., et al.: Dense semantic labeling of very-high-resolution aerial imagery and LIDAR with fully-convolutional neural networks and higher-order CRFs. In: IEEE Conference on Computer Vision and Pattern Recognition Workshops (CVPRW), pp. 1561–1570 (2017)
13. Sherrah, J.: Fully convolutional networks for dense semantic labelling of high-resolution aerial imagery. arXiv arXiv:1606.02585v1 (2016)
14. Audebert, N., Le Saux, B., Lefèvre, S.: Semantic segmentation of earth observation data using multimodal and multi-scale deep networks. In: Asian Conference on Computer Vision (ACCV), pp. 180–196 (2016)

15. Badrinarayanan, V., Kendall, A., Cipolla, R.: Segnet: a deep convolutional encoder-decoder architecture for image segmentation. IEEE Trans. Pattern Anal. Mach. Intell. **39**, 2481–2495 (2017)
16. Maggiori, E., Tarabalka, Y., Charpiat, G., et al.: High-resolution aerial image labeling with convolutional neural networks. IEEE Trans. Geosci. Remote Sens. **55**, 7092–7103 (2017)
17. Liu, Y., Minh Nguyen, D., Deligiannis, N., et al.: Hourglass-shape network based semantic segmentation for high resolution aerial imagery. Remote Sens. **9**, 522 (2017)
18. Krizhevsky, A., Sutskever, I., Hinton, G.E.: ImageNet classification with deep convolutional neural networks. In: Advances in Neural Information Processing Systems, pp. 1097–1105 (2012)
19. Zhang, X., Zhou, X., Lin, M., et al.: ShuffleNet: an extremely efficient convolutional neural network for mobile devices, arXiv preprint arXiv:1707.01083 (2017)
20. Huang, G., Liu, Z., Weinberger, K.Q.: Densely connected convolutional networks. CoRR, abs/1608.06993 (2016)
21. Zhao, H., Shi, J., Qi, X., et al.: Pyramid scene parsing network. In: IEEE Conference on Computer Vision and Pattern Recognition (2017)
22. ISPRS Vaihingen 2D semantic labeling dataset. http://www2.isprs.org/commissions/comm3/wg4/2d-sem-label-vaihingen.html
23. Gerke, M.: Use of the stair vision library within the ISPRS 2D semantic labeling benchmark (Vaihingen) (2015)
24. Kingma, D., Ba, J.: Adam: a method for stochastic optimization. In: International Conference on Learning Representations (ICLR) (2015)
25. Sun, G., Ma, P., Ren, J., et al.: A stability constrained adaptive alpha for gravitational search algorithm. Knowl. Based Syst. **139**, 200–213 (2018)
26. Zhang, A., Sun, G., Ren, J., et al.: A dynamic neighborhood learning-based gravitational search algorithm. IEEE Trans. Cybern. **48**(1), 436–447 (2018)
27. Long, J., Shelhamer, E., Darrell, T.: Fully convolutional networks for semantic segmentation. In: 2015 IEEE Conference on Computer Vision and Pattern Recognition (CVPR), pp. 3431–3440 (2015)

Gaussian-Staple for Robust Visual Object Real-Time Tracking

Si-Bao Chen(✉), Chuan-Yong Ding, and Bin Luo

Key Laboratory of Intelligent Computing and Signal Processing of Ministry of Education, School of Computer Science and Technology, Anhui University, Hefei 230601, China
sbchen@ahu.edu.cn

Abstract. Correlation Filter-based trackers have achieved excellent performance and run at high frame rates. Recently, Staple, which utilizing a simple combination of a Correlation Filter (using HOG features) and a global color histogram, has achieved excellent performance. It shows strong robustness in challenging situations including motion blur, illumination changes and deformation changes. However, Staple is only a linear combination of two methods. It is not reliable to determine the confidence level only by the peak. In this paper, we propose Gaussian-Staple that utilize a more sensible way of fusion without destroying the response distribution after fusion. Gaussian prior is added to the response of the output, which is used to determine whether to fine tune by local search. Extensive experiments on a commonly used tracking benchmark show that the proposed method significantly improves Staple, and achieves a better performance than other state-of-the-art trackers.

Keywords: Correlation filter · Staple · Gaussian prior
Object tracking

1 Introduction

In the field of computer vision, object real-time tracking is regarded as one of the most challenging tasks and has various applications such as robotics, video surveillance and intelligent vehicles, which is closely related to object detection [5,18], pedestrian analysis and tracking [11,21], scene analysis [14–16] and so on.

In this paper, we consider a single target tracking, where the target is given in the first frame. The tracking methods can be divided into generative and discriminative respectively. Recently, Sum of Template And Pixel-wise LEarners (Staple) [1] have aimed to combine two representations of image patches that have complementary aspects to learn tracking model. The results have better

B. Luo—This work was supported in part by National Natural Science Foundation of China under Grant 61472002, 61572030 and 61671018, and Collegiate Natural Science Fund of Anhui Province under Grant KJ2017A014.

J. Ren et al. (Eds.): BICS 2018, LNAI 10989, pp. 370–381, 2018.
https://doi.org/10.1007/978-3-030-00563-4_36

performances on color changes and deformations. It exploits the inherent structure of the template and histogram to solve two independent ridge-regression problems. Although much success has been demonstrated, through this simple weighting fusion, the drifting still exists in the background color similar, fast deformation and other challenges. To alleviate such risks of drifting, we advocate a new way of fusion that does not damage correlation response. We propose to prevent the drifting by controlling maximum response of the response map to follow the Gaussian distribution, which not only gains the robustness for variations, but also reduces the effect of noisy frames.

In this paper, we propose Gaussian-Staple tracker which uses a new fusion method to combine two representations of image patches that are sensitive to complementary factors. We model the correlation response of fusion to reduce the effect of incorrect location samples and achieve stable tracking. Comparing with other methods that fuse the predictions of multiple models, the proposed Gaussian-Staple significantly improves the final tracking performances.

2 Related Works

Correlation Filter-based trackers has been getting more and more attentions and researches. This is because in CF, all training and detection with densely-sampled examples and high dimensional features are converted by fast Fourier transform (FFT) to the frequency domain. MOSSE [2] was proposed to introduce the correlation filter into the visual tracking field. Henriques [7] proposed a high speed tracker with kernelized correlation filters (KCF) using multi-channel features (HOG) to achieve better performance.

To further improve performance of correlation filter based trackers, a number of methods were proposed. Several trackers take incorporating contextual information into consideration to further improve performance. In addition, color information can be used to distinguish the object from the background. Color histograms have been widely used in early tracking methods [13], and recently they have demonstrated the good performances in benchmarks in Distractor-Aware Tracker [12].

Recently, ensemble methods, which combine the estimates of several methods, have been widely adopted to mitigate inaccurate predictions, since the weaknesses of different trackers are reciprocally compensated. Staple [1] has combined two representations of image patches that are sensitive to complementary factors to learn a model that is inherently robust to both colour changes and deformations. Experiments show that the Staple outperforms competition is far more sophisticated trackers according to multiple benchmarks OTB50 [19], OTB100 [20] and all entries in the popular VOT14 [10]. However, when there exists similarity between the target and background color, there will be drift phenomenon. In this paper, we propose a more sensible way of fusion, without destroying the response distribution after fusion, we model the correlation response to the accurate location of the tracking and solve the model drift problem.

3 Staple

In this section, we briefly review Staple [1] which is closely related to the proposed tracking method. Staple also adopts the tracking-by-detection paradigm, and proposes a score function:

$$f(x) = \gamma_t f_t(x) + \gamma_h f_h(x), \tag{1}$$

where subscript t denotes the template score and h denotes the histogram score. The template score $\phi_x : \tau \rightarrow \mathcal{R}^k$, is a linear function of a k-channel feature image that obtained from x and defined on a finite grid $\tau \subset \mathcal{Z}^2$, where the template α is also a k-channel image,

$$f_t(x; \alpha) = \sum_{z \in \tau} \alpha[z]^{\mathrm{T}} \phi_x[z]. \tag{2}$$

Likewise the histogram score is computed to utilize m-channel feature image $\psi_x : \hbar \rightarrow \mathcal{R}^m$ that obtained from x and defined on a finite grid $\hbar \subset \mathcal{Z}^2$,

$$f_h(x; \beta) = \beta^{\mathrm{T}}(\frac{1}{|\hbar|} \sum_{z \in \hbar} \psi[z]), \tag{3}$$

which is rewritten as:

$$f_h(x; \beta) = \frac{1}{|\hbar|} \sum_{z \in \hbar} \zeta_{(\beta,\psi)}[z], \tag{4}$$

where $\zeta_{\beta,\psi}[z] = \beta^{\mathrm{T}} \psi[z]$. $\theta = (\alpha, \beta)$ denotes parameters of the overall model. The training loss is a weighted linear combination of per-image losses:

$$L(X_T, \theta) = \sum_{t=1}^{T} \omega_t \ell(x_t, p_t, \theta_t). \tag{5}$$

T is the number of images and $\ell(x_t, p_t, \theta_t)$ is the per-image loss function:

$$\ell(x_t, p_t, \theta_t) = c(p, \arg\max_{q \in \vartheta} f(T(x, q); \theta)), \tag{6}$$

where $c(p, q)$ denotes the cost when choosing rectangle p while the correct rectangle is q and T is an image transformation. Therefore, $f(T(x, q); \theta)$ can assign a score to the rectangular window p in image x according to the model parameters θ.

In order to efficiently learn the model, we need to solve two independent ridge regression problems:

$$\beta_t = \arg\min_{\beta} L_t(\beta; X_t) + \frac{1}{2}\lambda_t ||\beta||^2, \tag{7}$$

$$\alpha_t = \arg\min_{\alpha} L_t(\alpha; X_t) + \frac{1}{2}\lambda_t ||\alpha||^2. \tag{8}$$

First learning the template score, the per-image loss is

$$\ell(x, p, \alpha) = ||\sum_{k=1}^{K} \alpha^k \bullet \phi^k - y||^2, \tag{9}$$

where α^k is a channel k of multi-channel image α, ϕ and y are the input and output respectively, and $\bullet$ refers to cross-correlation operation. The FFT of x denoted by $\hat{x}$. From (9) we have:

$$\hat{\alpha}[z] = (\hat{\Phi}[z] + \lambda I)^{-1} \hat{\Psi}[z], \tag{10}$$

for all $z \in \tau$, where $\hat{\Phi}[z]$ is a $K \times K$ matrix with elements $\hat{\Phi}^{ij}[z]$ and $\hat{\Psi}[z]$ is a K-dimensional vector with elements $\hat{\Psi}^i[z]$. For the sake of simplicity,

$$\hat{\alpha}[z] = \frac{1}{(\hat{D}[z] + \lambda)} \cdot \hat{\Psi}[z], \tag{11}$$

where $\hat{D} = \sum_{i=1}^{K} (\hat{\phi}^i) \odot \hat{\phi}^i$. Then the online version update is

$$\begin{cases} \hat{D}_t = (1 - \eta_t) \hat{D}_{t-1} + \eta_t \hat{D}_t \\ \hat{\Psi}_t = (1 - \eta_t) \hat{\Psi}_{t-1} + \eta_t \hat{\Psi}_t. \end{cases} \tag{12}$$

Learning the histogram score, the per-image loss is

$$\ell(x, p, \beta) = \sum_{(q,y) \in W} (\beta^{\mathrm{T}} [\sum_{z \in \hbar} \Upsilon_{(x,q)}] - y)^2, \tag{13}$$

where W denotes a set of pairs (q, y) of rectangular windows q and their corresponding regression target y. From (13) we have

$$\ell(x, p, \beta) = \frac{1}{|\mathcal{O}|} \sum_{z \in \mathcal{O}} (\beta^{\mathrm{T}} \Upsilon(z) - 1)^2 + \frac{1}{|\mathcal{B}|} \sum_{z \in \mathcal{B}} (\beta^{\mathrm{T}} \Upsilon(z) - 1)^2, \tag{14}$$

where $\mathcal{O}$ and $\mathcal{B}$ denote object and background respectively, which is rewritten as

$$\ell(x, p, \beta) = \sum_{j=1}^{M} [\frac{N^j(\mathcal{O})}{|\mathcal{O}|} \cdot (\beta^j - 1)^2 + \frac{N^j(\mathcal{B})}{|\mathcal{B}|} \cdot (\beta^j)^2], \tag{15}$$

$$\beta_t^j = \frac{\rho^j(\mathcal{O})}{\rho^j(\mathcal{O}) + \rho^j(\mathcal{B}) + \lambda}, \tag{16}$$

where j is feature dimension, $j = 1, \ldots, M$, where $\rho^j(A) = N^j(A)/|A|$ is the proportion of pixels in a region for which feature j is non-zero. Then the model parameters are updated

$$\begin{cases} \rho_t(\mathcal{O}) = (1 - \eta_h) \rho_{t-1}(\mathcal{O}) + \eta_h \rho_t(\mathcal{O}) \\ \rho_t(\mathcal{B}) = (1 - \eta_h) \rho_{t-1}(\mathcal{B}) + \eta_h \rho_t(\mathcal{B}), \end{cases} \tag{17}$$

where $\rho_t(A)$ is the vector of $\rho_t^j(A)$ for $j = 1, \ldots, M$.

4 Gaussian-Staple

In this section, we propose a new method to compute the response output, where the response output is constrained by a Gaussian distribution.

$$\hat{y}^t \sim \mathcal{N}(\mu^t, \sigma^{2,t}), \tag{18}$$

where $\hat{y}^t$ is the regression response label for sample x in the tth frame. The score (response of output) of tracker should follow a Gaussian distribution whenever it is template or histogram score in ideal cases. This is not discussed in the existing works. In this section, we propose a new fusion approach that ensures the fusion of score following gaussian distribution,

$$f(x) = f_t(x) \odot f_h(x), \tag{19}$$

where $\odot$ denotes the element-wise product, $f_t(x)$ is template score and $f_h(x)$ is histogram score.

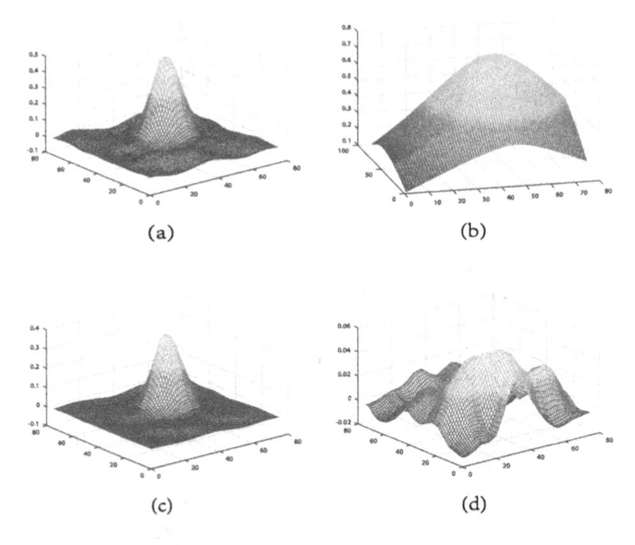

Fig. 1. Illustration that the fusion response are still a near Gaussian distribution on Boy sequences. (a) Response of the template on Boy sequences. (b) Response of the color histogram on Boy sequences. (c) Response of the fusion on Boy sequences. (d) Response of the Staple on Jumping sequence, which is far from one-peak Gaussian distribution. (Color figure online)

As is shown in Fig. 1, the final response map is still basically consistent with the Gaussian distribution. Figure 1(a) is response of the template on Boy sequences. Figure 1(b) is response of the color histogram on Boy sequences. Figure 1(c) is response of the fusion on Boy sequences, the final response map still conforms to the Gaussian distribution. Staple has achieved good performances in many cases. However, when there exists background color similarity and rapid deformation, Staple still exists drifting. Figure 1(d) shows the response of Staple on Jumping sequence. We can see that the Gaussian distribution of the response graph has undergone a severe change and eventually causes the drifting. Through our fusion approach, the final response still satisfies the Gaussian distribution. We propose that the property of Gaussian prior can well prevent drifting.

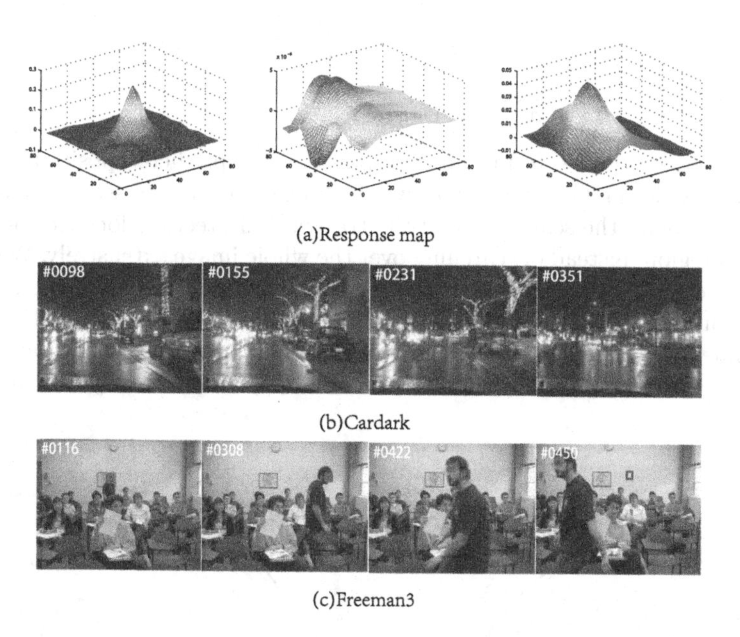

Fig. 2. Illustration of Staple and Gaussian-Staple on Cardark and Freeman3 sequences. The correlation response of Staple on Cardark sequence follows a near-Gaussian distribution as in the left sub-figure of (a) so that both Gaussian-Staple (green rectangular) and Staple (red rectangular) achieve good performances on Cardark sequence as in (b) when correlation response satisfies the Gaussian distribution. However, the correlation response of Staple on Freeman3 sequence fails to follow a near-Gaussian distribution as in the middle sub-figure of (a) while that of the proposed Gaussian-Staple still follows a near-Gaussian distribution as in the right subfigure of (a). Therefore, Staple (red rectangular) is a failed tracker while Gaussian-Staple (green rectangular) is better on Freeman3 sequence as in (c) when the correlation response is sharply changed. (Color figure online)

As Fig. 2(a) shows that the proposed method can ensure response map to follow a near-Gaussian distribution, so that the proposed method achieves better performances on the Freeman3 sequence. The proposed method is that we decide whether the position of prediction is reliable based on the Gaussian prior of correlation response. Only when its response output belongs to a Gaussian distribution, the position of prediction can be considered to be reliable. That is the correlation response should meet the following interval. If correlation response exceeds this threshold, it is an unreliable sample.

$$|\frac{\hat{y}^t - \mu^t}{\sigma^t}| < \xi_g, \tag{20}$$

where set $\xi_g = 1.6$, y is response of the predicted position, μ and σ^2 are the mean and variance of the Gaussian. For simplicity, μ and σ^2 are considered as constant in per-fame. The μ and σ^2 are calculated by all response map of previous frame.

$$\mu = \frac{\sum_{i=1}^{t-1}(\hat{y}^i)}{t-1}, \tag{21}$$

$$\sigma^2 = var(\hat{y}^1, \ldots, \hat{y}^i, \ldots, \hat{y}^{t-1}), \tag{22}$$

where $\hat{y}^i$ denote the ith frames max response of the predicted position.

After restricting Gaussian prior, we then introduce a local search strategy to explicitly expand the search area of the tracker and precisely localize the target in a local region, instead of searching over the whole image extensively. We determine to activate the local search strategy by examining whether the maximal correlation response is out of the confident region of Gaussian distribution. That is the time when there is a drift in our tracking. When we activate the local search strategy, considering the displacement of the target between adjacent frames is

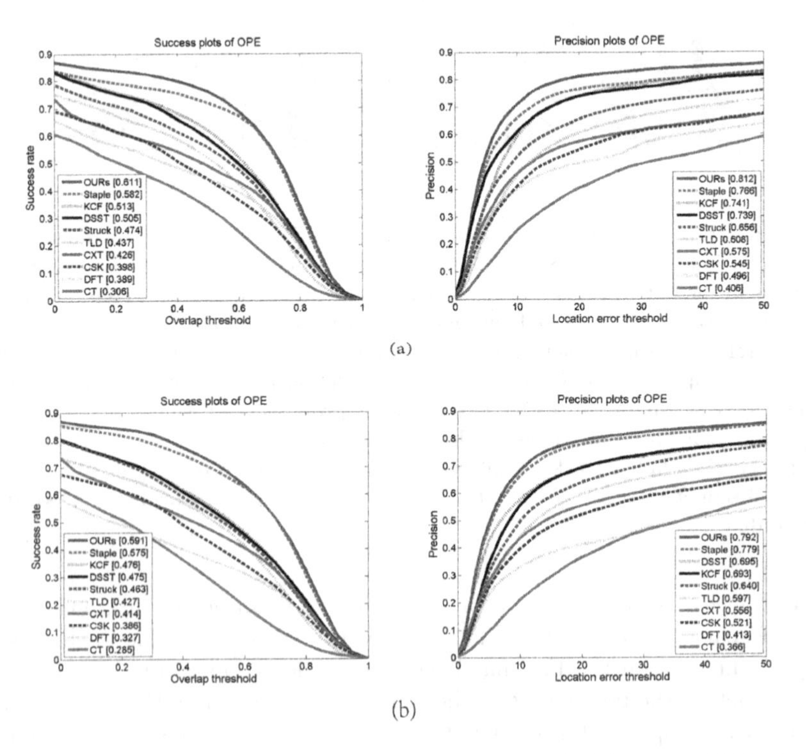

Fig. 3. Success and precision plots on OTB50 benchmark (a) and OTB100 benchmark (b).

very small, we first detect the central region, where the object is supposed to be close to the location in previous frame. We then search a central region from D directions taking the latest location (x_0, y_0) as center. The coordinates of center location for central regions are calculated by

$$p_x = \begin{cases} x_0 + ir\sin(jd) & j \; mod \; 2 = 0 \\ x_0 + ir\sin(jd + \epsilon) & j \; mod \; 2 = 1 \end{cases} \tag{23}$$

$$p_y = \begin{cases} y_0 + ir\sin(jd) & j \; mod \; 2 = 0 \\ y_0 + ir\sin(jd + \epsilon) & j \; mod \; 2 = 1 \end{cases} \tag{24}$$

where R is the radius of the search area, $r = (R/N)$ denotes the distance step, $i \in 1, \ldots, N$, $d = 2\pi/D$ denotes the angle step, $j \in 1, \ldots, N$, $\epsilon = d/2$. In our experiments, we set $N = 5$, $D = 16$. We can get $N \times D$ pathes centered around the last predicted position.

$$P = \{p_1, p_2, \ldots, p_{N\times D}\}. \tag{25}$$

In the local search process, the maximal response of each patch is obtained by

$$r_i = \max(\gamma_t f_t(p_i) \odot \gamma_h f_h(p_i)). \tag{26}$$

Then calculate the response map between the target appears and each patch in central regions

$$\hat{p} = \arg\max_i \{p_1, \ldots, p_i, \ldots, p_{N\times D}\}. \tag{27}$$

The patch with the largest peak value in response map is considered as the correct patch, and its location is used to update the newly predicted position.

5 Experiments

In this section, we compare the proposed Gaussian-Staple tracker with competing methods on OTB50 [19] and OTB100 [20]. The trackers used for comparison include: Staple [1], DSST [3], KCF [7], TLD [9], Struck [6], CXT [4], CSK [8], CT [22] and DFT [17].

Figure 2 shows illustration of Staple and Gaussian-Staple on Cardark and Freeman3 sequences. The correlation response of Staple on Cardark sequence follows a near-Gaussian distribution as in the left sub-figure of Fig. 2(a) so that both Gaussian-Staple (green rectangular) and Staple (red rectangular) achieve good performances on Cardark sequence as in Fig. 2(b) when correlation response satisfies the Gaussian distribution. However, the correlation response of Staple on Freeman3 sequence fails to follow a near-Gaussian distribution as in the middle sub-figure of Fig. 2(a) while that of the proposed Gaussian-Staple still follows a near-Gaussian distribution as in the right subfigure of Fig. 2(a). Therefore, Staple

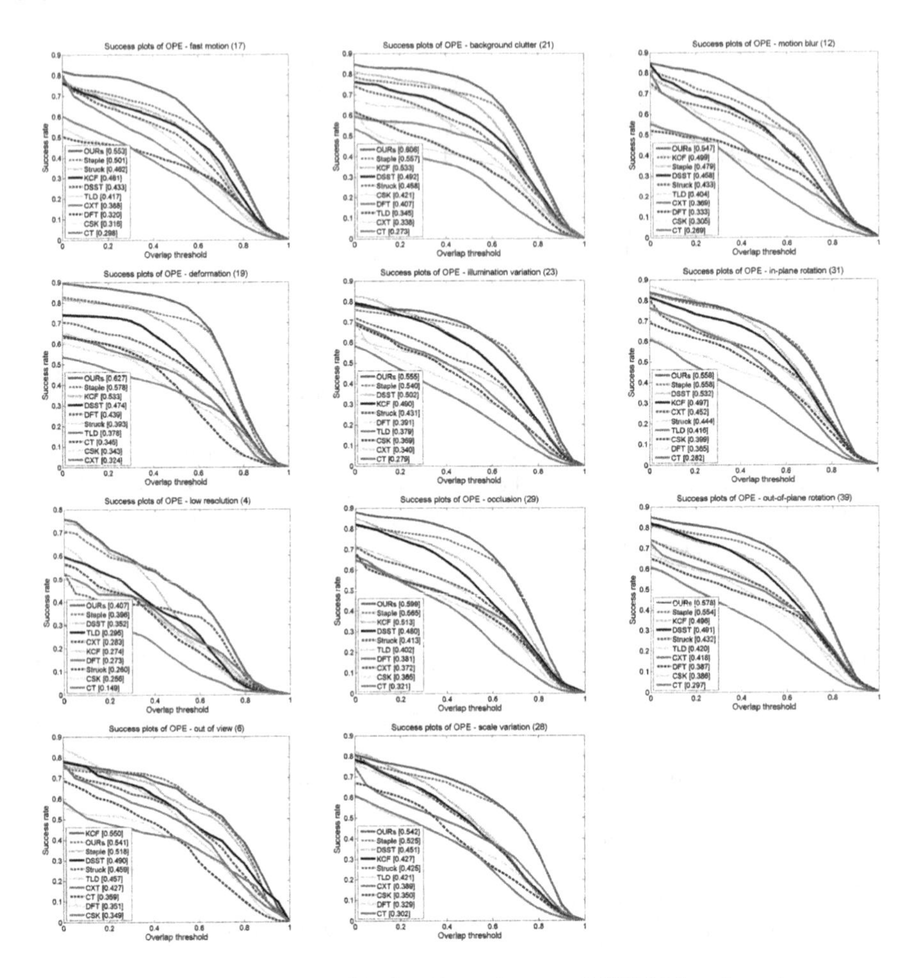

Fig. 4. Success plots for the 11 attributes of OTB50 benchmark.

(red rectangular) is a failed tracker while Gaussian-Staple (green rectangular) is better on Freeman3 sequence as in Fig. 2(c) when the correlation response is sharply changed.

We evaluate the accuracy and robustness to failure of the proposed Gaussian-Staple trackers on OTB50 [19] and OTB100 [20]. The overall success and precision plots generated by the benchmark toolbox are also reported. As shown in Fig. 3, the proposed method reports the best results. The Gaussian-Staple and Staple achieve 61.1% and 58.2% based on the average success rate on OTB50, while other famous trackers, KCF, DSST and Struck achieve 51.3%, 50.5% and 47.4% respectively. In terms of precision, the proposed Gaussian-Staple and Staple, can achieve 81.2% and 76.6% when the threshold is set to 20. Comparing with other trackers, the proposed Gaussian-Staple method has greatly improvement. Comparing with the baseline Staple tracker, both the average precision

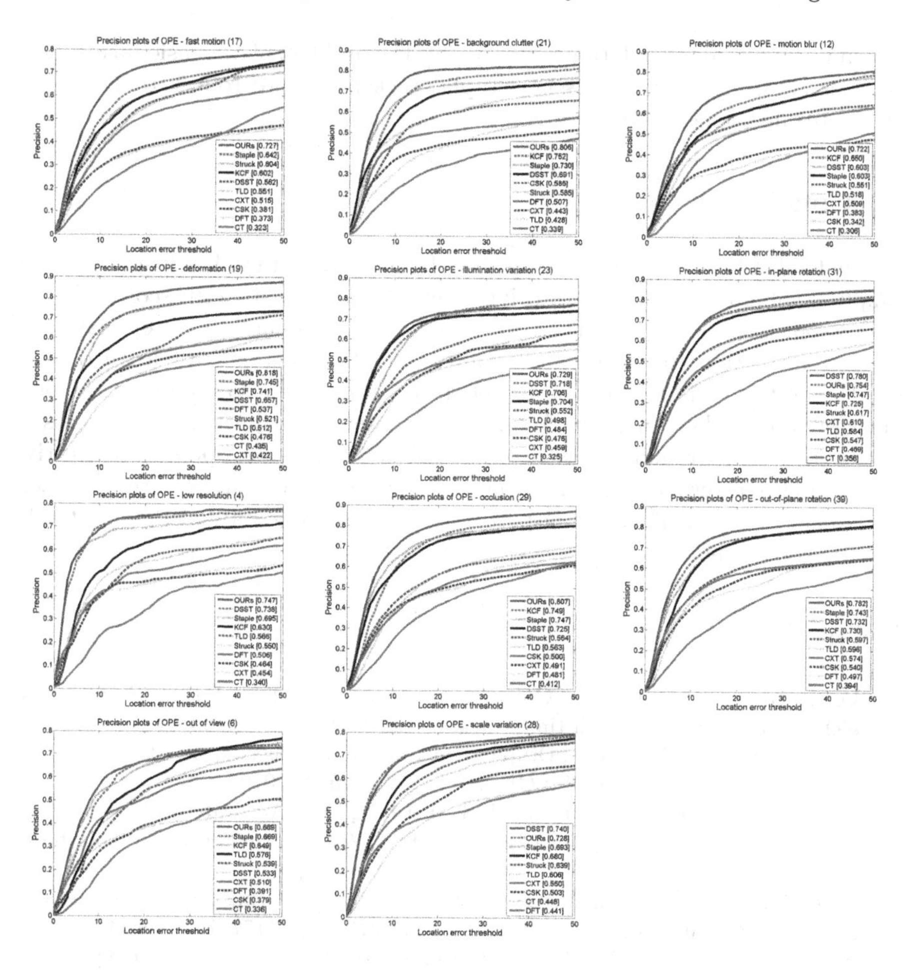

Fig. 5. Precision plots for the 11 attributes of OTB50 benchmark.

rate and success rate of our proposed Gaussian-Staple tracker have a significant improvement. As shown on OTB100 in Fig. 3(b), we have the same results that our performance has improved significantly. These results confirm the effectiveness of our tracker and verify that it performs better than state-of-the-art trackers.

Figures 4 and 5 show the full sets of plots generated by the benchmark toolbox. In Fig. 4, we can see that the proposed Gaussian-Staple achieves significant higher performance in cases of illumination variations, background clutters, scale variations, deformations, motion blur, abrupt motion, occlusions, in-plane rotation, out-of-plane rotation, out-of-view and low resolution, except for out-of-view. Likewise, in Fig. 5, it can be seen that the proposed Gaussian-Staple achieves significant higher performance in most cases except in-plane rotation and scale variations. This could be solved by DSST [3] which learns discriminative scale correlation filter to solve the problem of dimensional changes. All this shows that the Gaussian-Staple tracker is more robust to variations attributes mentioned above.

6 Conclusion

It is not reliable to determine the levels of confidence through a fusion peak by simply combining individual learning templates with histogram scores. Therefore, we proposed a new method to improve the combination of template and histogram fractions to increase the robustness. This method was learned independent of the variations of the target. In addition, we also restricted the output response of the tracker to follow the Gaussian distribution on the basis of our fusion. What is more, based on Gaussian prior, we proposed an effective local search strategy to fine-tune the predicted position. The resulting tracker, Gaussian-Staple, significantly outperforms many complex state-of-the-arts trackers in several benchmarks.

References

1. Bertinetto, L., Valmadre, J., Golodetz, S., Miksik, O., Torr, P.H.S.: Staple: complementary learners for real-time tracking. **38**(2), 1401–1409 (2015)
2. Bolme, D.S., Beveridge, J.R., Draper, B.A., Lui, Y.M.: Visual object tracking using adaptive correlation filters. In: CVPR, pp. 2544–2550 (2010)
3. Danelljan, M., Hager, G., Khan, F.S., Felsberg, M.: Accurate scale estimation for robust visual tracking. In: British Machine Vision Conference, pp. 65.1–65.11 (2014)
4. Dinh, T.B., Vo, N., Medioni, G.: Context tracker: exploring supporters and distracters in unconstrained environments. In: CVPR, pp. 1177–1184 (2011)
5. Han, J., Zhang, D., et al.: Object detection in optical remote sensing images based on weakly supervised learning and high-level feature learning. IEEE TGRS **53**(6), 3325–3337 (2015)
6. Hare, S., Saffari, A., Torr, P.H.S.: Struck: structured output tracking with kernels. In: IEEE ICCV, pp. 263–270 (2012)
7. Henriques, J.F., Caseiro, R., Martins, P., Batista, J.: High-speed tracking with kernelized correlation filters. IEEE T-PAMI **37**(3), 583 (2015)
8. Henriques, J.F., Caseiro, R., Martins, P., Batista, J.: Exploiting the circulant structure of tracking-by-detection with kernels. In: Fitzgibbon, A., Lazebnik, S., Perona, P., Sato, Y., Schmid, C. (eds.) ECCV 2012. LNCS, vol. 7575, pp. 702–715. Springer, Heidelberg (2012). https://doi.org/10.1007/978-3-642-33765-9_50
9. Kalal, Z., Matas, J., Mikolajczyk, K.: P-N learning: bootstrapping binary classifiers by structural constraints. In: CVPR, pp. 49–56 (2010)
10. Kristan, M., Pflugfelder, R., et al.: The visual object tracking VOT2013 challenge results. In: IEEE ICCV Workshops, pp. 98–111 (2013)
11. Liu, Q.: Decontaminate feature for tracking: adaptive tracking via evolutionary feature subset. J. Electron. Imaging **26**(6), 1 (2017)
12. Possegger, H., Mauthner, T., Bischof, H.: In defense of color-based model-free tracking. In: CVPR, pp. 2113–2120 (2015)

13. Pérez, P., Hue, C., Vermaak, J., Gangnet, M.: Color-based probabilistic tracking. In: Heyden, A., Sparr, G., Nielsen, M., Johansen, P. (eds.) ECCV 2002. LNCS, vol. 2350, pp. 661–675. Springer, Heidelberg (2002). https://doi.org/10.1007/3-540-47969-4_44
14. Ren, J., Orwell, J., Jones, G.A., Xu, M.: Tracking the soccer ball using multiple fixed cameras. Comput. Vis. Image Underst. **113**(5), 633–642 (2009)
15. Ren, J., Xu, M., Orwell, J., Jones, G.A.: Real-time modeling of 3-D soccer ball trajectories from multiple fixed cameras. IEEE T-CSVT **18**(3), 350–362 (2008)
16. Ren, J., Xu, M., et al.: Multi-camera video surveillance for real-time analysis and reconstruction of soccer games. Mach. Vis. Appl. **21**(6), 855–863 (2010)
17. Sevilla-Lara, L., Learned-Miller, E.: Distribution fields for tracking. In: IEEE Conference on CVPR, pp. 1910–1917 (2012)
18. Wang, Z., Ren, J., Zhang, D., Sun, M., Jiang, J.: A deep-learning based feature hybrid framework for spatiotemporal saliency detection inside videos. Neurocomputing **287**, 68–83 (2018)
19. Wu, Y., Lim, J., Yang, M.H.: Online object tracking: a benchmark. In: IEEE CVPR, pp. 2411–2418 (2013)
20. Wu, Y., Lim, J., Yang, M.H.: Object tracking benchmark. IEEE T-PAMI **37**(9), 1834–1848 (2015)
21. Yan, Y., Ren, J., et al.: Cognitive fusion of thermal and visible imagery for effective detection and tracking of pedestrians in videos. Cogn. Comput. **10**(1), 94–104 (2018)
22. Zhang, K., Zhang, L., Yang, M.H.: Real-time compressive tracking. In: Fitzgibbon, A., Lazebnik, S., Perona, P., Sato, Y., Schmid, C. (eds.) ECCV 2012. LNCS, vol. 7574, pp. 864–877. Springer, Heidelberg (2012). https://doi.org/10.1007/978-3-642-33712-3_62

Saliency-Weighted Global-Local Fusion for Person Re-identification

Si-Bao Chen(✉), Wei-Ming Song, and Bin Luo

Key Laboratory of Intelligent Computing and Signal Processing of Ministry of Education, School of Computer Science and Technology, Anhui University, Hefei 230601, China
sbchen@ahu.edu.cn

Abstract. Many features have been proposed to improve the accuracy of person re-identification. Due to the illumination and viewpoint changes between different cameras, individual feature is less discriminative to separate different persons. In this paper, we propose a saliency-weighted feature descriptor and global-local fusion optimization for person re-identification. Firstly, the weights on pixels are calculated via saliency detection method, then the computed weights are integrated into local maximal occurrence (LOMO) feature descriptor. Secondly, the saliency weights are used to update the metric learning distance in training so that we can learn a new metric matrix for testing. And then, the whole person image is divided into upper and lower halves. A novel global-local fusion method is proposed to combine local and global regions together in the most appropriate way. After that an optimization algorithm is proposed to learn the weights among upper half, lower half and the whole image. According to those weights, a final fused distance is obtained. Experimental results show that the proposed method outperforms many state-of-the-art person re-identification methods.

Keywords: Person re-identification · Global-local fusion Saliency-weighting

1 Introduction

Person re-identification is focused on identifying the co-occurrence of individuals across a set of disjoint cameras. There have many interests in person re-identification research due to its wide application prospect. Matching pedestrians which across disjoint camera views is the core problem of person re-identification. Specifically, given a probe image, person re-identification aims to match the identical person from gallery images. This is a challenging problem because of viewpoints, poses, illumination, occlusion and many other factors.

B. Luo—This work was supported in part by National Natural Science Foundation of China under Grant 61472002, 61572030 and 61671018, and Collegiate Natural Science Fund of Anhui Province under Grant KJ2017A014.

J. Ren et al. (Eds.): BICS 2018, LNAI 10989, pp. 382–393, 2018.
https://doi.org/10.1007/978-3-030-00563-4_37

Two major problems in person re-identification are feature representation, which is robust against the various changes and metric learning, which gives small values to images of the same person and large values for those of different people. Feature representation plays an important role in person re-identification which is the foundation of person re-identification. Many feature representation methods are proposed. Color features and texture features are widely employed because of their good performance. There are many good features such as Local Binary Patterns (LBP) and Scale-invariant feature transform (SIFT) features. Local Maximal Occurrence (LOMO) [6] analyzes the horizontal occurrence of local features, and maximizes the occurrence to make a stable representation against viewpoint changes.

Another aspect of person re-identification is how to get a robust metric learning. Learning a metric is the key point of metric learning which makes sure the images coming from the same class are closer, while the images coming form different classes are farther apart.

In this paper, we propose a novel weighted feature descriptor via saliency detection to enhance the discrimination of person re-identification. Furthermore, we take some effective measures to combine different regions together. The main contribution of this paper is: (1) A novel saliency-weighted LOMO feature descriptor is proposed via saliency detection to enhance the discrimination of person re-identification. It focus on enhancing the foreground cues on the person image. (2) In order to make the same class distance smaller, we calculate the average weight of the same person images across non-overlapping camera views. Then the weighted images are used to update the metric learning distance in training so that we can learn a new metric matrix $\mathbf{M}$ for testing. (3) We proposed a novel global-local fusion optimization method to calculate weights on different regions. Fusing various regions according to their weights is the key point in this paper. An optimization algorithm is proposed to obtain optimal weights.

2 Related Works

Feature representation and metric learning are the two most important works in person re-identification. Due to the illumination and viewpoint changes between different cameras, individual feature is less discriminative to separate different persons. Fusing multiple features is preferred.

Specially, there are two fundamental methods for multiple feature fusion: early fusion and late fusion. The descriptors of early fusion are focus on feature level or sensor level. However, late fusion pays attention to score or decision levels. In late fusion, Han et al. [5] uses simulated annealing algorithm to learn different distance weights. These methods determine a fixed weight for each classifier.

And there are many robust fusion methods such as [1,7,10,11,13,15]. But they also have some disadvantages. For example, simulated annealing algorithm in [5] is not stable on the accuracy of person re-identification. According to its shortcomings, we design an optimization method to obtain stable fusion weight estimation.

Besides, robust metric learning is necessary to person re-identification. Many robust and discriminative metric learning have been proposed to improve the accuracy of person re-identification. For example, Yang et al. [14] proposed a novel metric learning called Large Scale Similarity Learning (LSSL) which introduces an efficient strategy to learn it by using only similar pairs for person re-identification. Liao et al. [6] proposed an effective metric learning called Cross-view Quadratic Discriminant Analysis (XQDA) which is learned on the derived subspace with LOMO features.

Furthermore, deep features for person re-identification are newly appeared. Fusing deep learnt feature and hand-craft feature together which called Feature Fusion Net (FFN) is proposed in [9]. Visual saliency is considered to be a key attentional mechanism that facilitates learning, and there are many saliency prediction methods such as [12] and [8].

3 Our Approach

3.1 Saliency-Weighted Feature

People can recognize human beings on small salient regions, which means that human saliency is reliable and distinctive for person re-identification. However, when calculating the similarity, these valuable information is often hidden. Inspired by the experimental results on the person re-identification, we propose a novel method to integrate the saliency weights into person images.

In order to highlight the importance of the person in a image, we use saliency detection method to acquire the weight on pixels. The pixel weight value on the person is higher than others. Then we can integrate the weights into the image for enhancing the recognition performance of person re-identification. It is noteworthy that any saliency detection method can be adopted in our framework.

We choose the saliency detection method proposed in [3] in the experiments. It's easy to get the saliency weights on pixel according to the original image. Then the local maximal occurrence (LOMO) descriptor [6] is selected as our original feature descriptor which include color descriptor and texture descriptor. As we all know the saliency is a color characteristic. Due to the speciality of the saliency, we just integrate the weights into color descriptor in the local maximal occurrence. The whole procedure of saliency-weighted feature extraction is shown in Fig. 1. Saliency weights of all pixels from the original image are obtained firstly. Then the weights are integrated into the feature descriptor by pixel-wise multiplication.

3.2 Improved Metric Learning by Saliency-Weighting

After getting the saliency weights, all probe and gallery images have their own weight. In order to make the same class distance smaller and get a high accuracy,

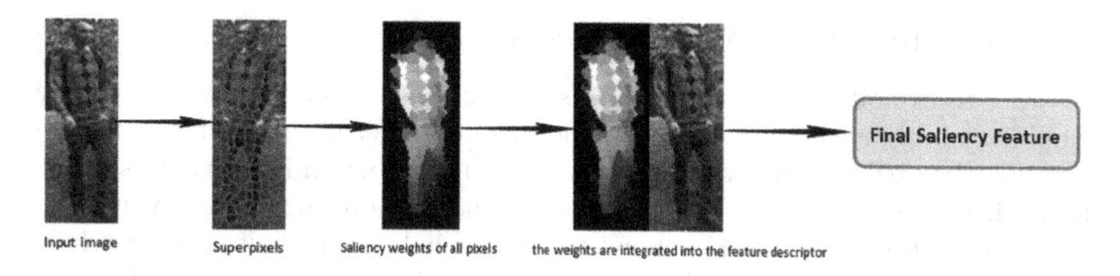

Fig. 1. Illustration of saliency-weighted feature extraction. Saliency weights of all pixels from the original image are obtained firstly. Then the weights are integrated into the feature descriptor by pixel-wise multiplication. (Color figure online)

we calculate the average weight of the same person images across non-overlapping camera views. And then the average weight is used to improve metric learning in training so that we can learn new metric matrix $\mathbf{M}$ for testing. The new metric matrix $\mathbf{M}$ can be used directly in testing stage with original features of pedestrian images. It is no need to multiply saliency weights on pedestrian images first and then calculate the metric distance separately. It can reduce computational time in the testing stage. As we all know that the metric learning distance is gained as the following:

$$d = (\mathbf{x}_i - \mathbf{x}_j)^\top \mathbf{M}(\mathbf{x}_i - \mathbf{x}_j), \tag{1}$$

where $\mathbf{x}_i$ and $\mathbf{x}_j$ are the same person images from non-overlapping camera views. Metric matrix $\mathbf{M}$ is a positive semi-definite matrix. After getting the saliency weights, $\mathbf{x}_i$ and $\mathbf{x}_j$ can be replaced by their weighted version $\tilde{\mathbf{x}_i}$ and $\tilde{\mathbf{x}_j}$, which is weighted as the following,

$$\tilde{\mathbf{x}_i} = w_i \cdot \mathbf{x}_i, \tag{2}$$

where $\cdot$ is element-wise multiplication operator. The formula above can be rewritten in the form of matrix-vector multiplication,

$$\tilde{\mathbf{x}_i} = diag(w_i)\mathbf{x}_i. \tag{3}$$

Similarly, $\tilde{\mathbf{x}_j} = w_j \cdot \mathbf{x}_j$ can be rewritten in the form of matrix-vector multiplication, $\tilde{\mathbf{x}_j} = diag(w_j)\mathbf{x}_j$, where w_i and w_j are the saliency weights of $\mathbf{x}_i$ and $\mathbf{x}_j$. Therefore, we can rewrite (1) as the following,

$$\begin{aligned} d &= (\tilde{\mathbf{x}}_i - \tilde{\mathbf{x}}_j)^\top \mathbf{M}(\tilde{\mathbf{x}}_i - \tilde{\mathbf{x}}_j) \\ &= (\mathbf{x}_i - \mathbf{x}_j)^\top diag(\frac{(w_i + w_j)}{2})\mathbf{M} \times diag(\frac{(w_i + w_j)}{2})(\mathbf{x}_i - \mathbf{x}_j). \end{aligned} \tag{4}$$

We define $\mathbf{W} = diag(\frac{(w_i+w_j)}{2})$ to simplify the formula (4),

$$d = (\mathbf{x}_i - \mathbf{x}_j)^\top \mathbf{WMW}(\mathbf{x}_i - \mathbf{x}_j). \tag{5}$$

Finally the improved metric learning distance (saliency-weighted metric) is obtained as the following:

$$d = (\mathbf{x}_i - \mathbf{x}_j)^\top \tilde{\mathbf{M}}(\mathbf{x}_i - \mathbf{x}_j), \tag{6}$$

where $\tilde{\mathbf{M}}$ is the simplification of $\mathbf{WMW}$.

3.3 Global-Local Fusion of Distances

In order to exploit the complementary strengths of global and local regions, we employ a novel fusion method to combine them together in the most appropriate way. Firstly, we divide the whole person image into upper and lower halves. After that, their saliency weights are calculated. Then an optimization algorithm is proposed to learn the weight among the upper half, lower half and the whole image. According to those weights, a final fused distance is obtained. To compensate the insufficiency of local regions, we also make use of the global region. The global region and local regions are combined as the following:

$$d_{final} = (w_{up} * d_{up}) + (w_{down} * d_{down}) + (w_{global} * d_{global}), \tag{7}$$

where w_{up}, w_{down} and w_{global} are the weights of upper, lower and global region respectively, d_{up}, d_{down} and d_{global} are the metric learning distances of upper, lower and global region respectively.

We can reformulate a weighted distance function as the following:

$$d = \Sigma_{i=1}^{C}(w_i * d_i), \tag{8}$$

where C is the number of all regions include local regions and global region. The w_i and d_i are the weight and distance of the ith region. The whole procedure of global-local fusion optimization is shown in Fig. 2.

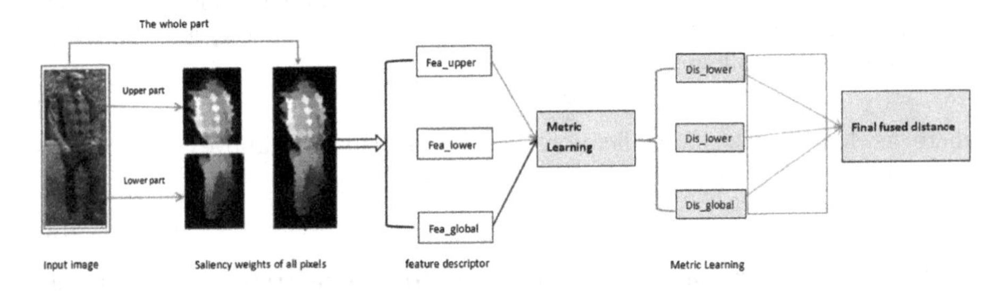

Fig. 2. Illustration of global-local fusion optimization. The whole image is firstly divided into upper and lower halves. Then we get their saliency weights by saliency detection. An optimization algorithm is adopted to learn the global-local weights and the final fused distance is obtained via global-local weights.

We hope to learn a suitable weighted distance function using our optimization function as follow:

$$min\Sigma_{i=1}^{C}(w_i^2 * d_i^+) \qquad s.t. \quad \Sigma_{i=1}^{C}(w_i) = 1, \tag{9}$$

where w_i and d_i^+ is the ith region weight and distance of the same person across a set of disjoint cameras. C is the number of all regions include local regions and global region. We will show the strategy of the above optimization problem in the next subsection.

3.4 Optimization of Global-Local Fusion Weights

The Lagrange function of the constrained optimization problem (9) is as the belowing:

$$L = min(\Sigma_{i=1}^{C}(w_i^2 * d_i^+) - \lambda(\Sigma_{i=1}^{C}(w_i) - 1)), \tag{10}$$

where w_i and d_i^+ are the ith region weight and distance of the same person across a set of disjoint cameras. C is the number of all regions include local regions and global region. We can get the w_i from the optimization function easily. Compute the derivative of L with respective to w_i and let it equal to zero,

$$\frac{\partial L}{\partial w_i} = 2w_i * d_i^+ - \lambda = 0\,. \tag{11}$$

$$\frac{\partial L}{\partial \lambda} = \Sigma_{i=1}^{C}(w_i) - 1 = 0\,. \tag{12}$$

From Eq. (11) we can get:

$$w_i = \lambda / 2d_i^+\,. \tag{13}$$

From Eqs. (12) and (11) we can get:

$$w_i = 1/((\Sigma_{i=1}^{C} 1/d_i^+) * d_i^+)\,. \tag{14}$$

According to those weights, we can calculate the final fused metric learning distance in Eq. (7).

4 Experiments

It is noteworthy note that the saliency weights can be integrated with any color-based feature descriptors. To simplify the experiments, we simply integrate the saliency weights into local maximal occurrence (LOMO) [6] features. After saliency-weighted LOMO features are obtained, we employ principal component analysis (PCA) to reduce the dimensionality and remove noises. Four widely used datasets are selected for experiments, including VIPeR [4], PRID450S, iLIDS-VID and PRID2011 [2].

4.1 Effect of Saliency-Weighting

In this subsection, we investigate the effect of saliency-weighting. Saliency-weighted local maximal occurrence (LOMO) descriptor is invoked as feature representation. We choose Cross-view Quadratic Discriminant Analysis (XQDA) [6] as the metric learning.

Results on VIPeR dataset are listed in Table 1. From the second line in the table, we can see that our saliency-weighted LOMO descriptor improves the rank-1 rates by 10.0%, than the original LOMO descriptor, which shows the effect of the proposed saliency-weighting method.

Table 1. Effects of saliency-weighted LOMO and global-local fusion optimization on recognition accuracy (%) via XQDA as metric on VIPeR dataset.

Method	Rank = 1	Rank = 5	Rank = 10	Rank = 20	Rank = 30
Saliency-weighted + Global-local fusion	**63.4**	**86.5**	**92.5**	**97.0**	**98.2**
Saliency-weighted LOMO	**50.0**	**77.7**	**86.7**	**93.3**	**96.2**
Original LOMO	40.0	68.0	80.5	91.1	95.5

Table 2. Effects of saliency-weighted LOMO and global-local fusion optimization on recognition accuracy (%) via XQDA as metric on PRID450S dataset.

Method	Rank = 1	Rank = 5	Rank = 10	Rank = 20	Rank = 30
Saliency-weighted + Global-local fusion	**80.3**	**94.4**	**97.1**	**98.7**	**99.1**
Saliency-weighted LOMO	**67.3**	**88.3**	**94.1**	**97.7**	**98.8**
Original LOMO	58.7	81.6	88.9	94.1	96.7

Results on PRID450S dataset are shown in Table 2. From the second line of the table, we can see that our saliency-weighted LOMO descriptor improves the rank-1 rates by 8.6%, than the original LOMO descriptor, which shows the effect of the proposed saliency-weighting method.

Table 3 shows the results on the iLIDS-VID dataset. It can be seen that these images have poor image quality and low resolutions, containing large variations of illumination and viewpoint. Experimental result that our saliency-weighted LOMO descriptor improves the rank-1 rates by 29.6%, than the original LOMO descriptor, which is shown in the second line in Table 3. It indicates the effect of the proposed saliency-weighting method.

Table 3. Effects of saliency-weighted LOMO and global-local fusion optimization on recognition accuracy (%) via XQDA as metric on iLIDS-VID dataset.

Method	Rank = 1	Rank = 5	Rank = 10	Rank = 20	Rank = 30
Saliency-weighted + Global-local fusion	**52.2**	**77.6**	**86.3**	**93.7**	**96.5**
Saliency-weighted LOMO	**46.2**	**73.6**	**83.0**	**91.3**	**95.1**
Original LOMO	16.6	39.1	52.4	66.8	75.5

Table 4 is the results on PRID2011 dataset. It can be observed that the accuracy of our Saliency-weighted LOMO improves the rank-1 rates by 6.7% than the original LOMO descriptor, which is shown in the second line in Table 4. It indicates the effect of the proposed saliency-weighting method.

4.2 Effect of Global-Local Fusion Optimization

In this subsection, we investigate the effect of global-local fusion optimization. Firstly, we integrate the saliency weights into the image after we get their saliency

Table 4. Effects of saliency-weighted LOMO and global-local fusion optimization on recognition accuracy (%) via XQDA as metric on PRID2011 dataset.

Method	Rank = 1	Rank = 5	Rank = 10	Rank = 20	Rank = 30
Saliency-weighted + Global-local fusion	**70.9**	**93.5**	**96.2**	**98.2**	**99.2**
Saliency-weighted LOMO	**55.5**	**85.5**	**94.1**	**97.3**	**98.6**
Original LOMO	48.8	77.2	87.6	95.1	95.1

weights from Saliency Detection [3]. After that, we divide the whole image into upper and lower halves. Then we employ the proposed global-local fusion method to combine various region together with an optimization algorithm to learn the weights among upper half, lower half and the whole image. According to those weights, a final fused distance is obtained. XQDA [6] is chosen as the metric learning.

The results on VIPeR dataset are shown in the first line in Table 1. Experimental results show that our saliency-weighted with global-local fusion method improves the rank-1 rates by 26.3%, than the original LOMO descriptor. And experimental results show that our saliency-weighted with global-local fusion method improves the rank-1 rates by 5.8%, than saliency-weighted LOMO method without global-local fusion, which is shown in Table 1.

Results on PRID450S dataset are shown in the first line in Table 2. Experimental results show that our saliency-weighted with global-local fusion method improves the rank-1 rates by 21.6%, than the original LOMO descriptor. Experimental results show that our saliency-weighted global-local fusion method improves the rank-1 rates by 3.7%, than saliency-weighted LOMO method without global-local fusion, which is shown in Table 2.

The results on iLIDS-VID dataset are shown in the first line in Table 3. Experimental results show that our saliency-weighted with global-local fusion method improves the rank-1 rates by 35.6%, than the original LOMO descriptor. And experimental results show that our saliency-weighted global-local fusion method improves the rank-1 rates by 6.0%, than saliency-weighted method without global-local fusion, which is shown in Table 3.

The results on PRID2011 dataset are shown in the first line in Table 4. Experimental results show that our saliency-weighted with global-local fusion method improves the rank-1 rates by 22.1%, than the original LOMO descriptor. Experimental results show that our saliency-weighted global-local fusion method improves the rank-1 rates by 5.2%, than saliency weighted method without global-local fusion, which is shown in Table 4.

We can make a conclusion easily that both saliency-weighted descriptor and global-local fusion optimization in our proposed method can improve the recognition performance of person re-identification.

4.3 Comparison with State-of-the-Arts

In this subsection, we evaluate the proposed saliency-weighted LOMO and global-local fusion optimization method and compare it with state-of-the-art methods. Experimental settings are the same as the above. And we choose XQDA [6] as the metric learning.

First we compare the proposed method with state-of-the-art methods on VIPeR dataset, whose results are listed in Table 5. From the table we can see that our saliency-weighted LOMO and global-local fusion method with XQDA improves the rank-1 rates by 26.3%, than the original LOMO+XQDA. And experimental results show that our saliency-weighted LOMO descriptor and global-local fusion method improve the rank-1 rates by 9.9%, than the second one. Our proposed method has shown good performance in rank-1 identification rates comparing with state-of-the-art methods.

Table 5. Recognition rate on VIPeR dataset

Method	Rank = 1	Rank = 5	Rank = 10	Rank = 20	Rank = 30
The proposed	**63.4**	**86.5**	**92.5**	**97.0**	**98.2**
SCSP	53.5	82.6	91.5	96.6	–
Kernel X-CRC	51.6	80.8	89.4	94.2	97.4
Cheng et al.	47.8	74.7	84.8	91.1	94.3
LSSL	47.8	77.9	87.6	94.2	–
Ding et al.	40.5	60.8	70.4	84.4	90.9
LOMO+XQDA	40.0	68.0	80.5	91.0	95.5
SCNCD	37.8	68.5	81.2	90.4	94.2

Results on PRID450S dataset are shown in Table 6. The proposed method is compared with state-of-the-art methods. In this dataset, we also have a better accuracy than other state-of-the-art methods. Experimental results show that our saliency-weighted LOMO descriptor and global-local fusion method improve the rank-1 rates by 19.8%, than the second one, which is shown in Table 6.

Table 7 shows the results on the iLIDS-VID dataset. The proposed method is compared with state-of-the-art methods. It can be seen that these images have poor image quality and low resolutions, containing large variations of illumination and viewpoint. Experimental result that our saliency-weighted LOMO descriptor and global-local fusion method with XQDA improves the rank-1 rates by 35.6%, than the original LOMO+XQDA. And experimental results show that our saliency-weighted LOMO descriptor and global-local fusion improve the rank-1 rates by 23.8%, than the second one, which is shown in Table 7.

Table 8 is the PRID2011 dataset results. In this dataset, we are also given a better accuracy than other state-of-the-art method. Experimental results show that our saliency-weighted LOMO descriptor and global-local fusion method improves the rank-1 rates of 27.2% than the second one.

Table 6. Recognition rate on PRID450S dataset

Method	Rank = 1	Rank = 5	Rank = 10	Rank = 20	Rank = 30
The proposed	**80.3**	**94.4**	**97.1**	**98.7**	**99.1**
LSSCDL	60.5	–	88.6	93.6	–
Chen et al.	55.4	79.3	87.8	93.9	–
Kernel HPCA	52.8	80.9	89.0	97.2	97.2
X-KPLS	52.8	82.1	90.0	95.4	97.3
Shen et al.	44.4	71.6	82.2	89.8	93.3
Shi et al.	44.9	71.7	77.5	86.7	–
SCNCD	41.6	68.9	79.4	87.8	95.4
EIML	35.0	58.5	68.0	77.0	83.0
KISSME	33.0	59.8	71.0	79.0	84.5

Table 7. Recognition rate on the iLIDS-VID dataset

Method	Rank = 1	Rank = 5	Rank = 10	Rank = 20	Rank = 30
The proposed	**52.2**	**77.6**	**86.3**	**93.7**	**96.5**
FAST3D	28.4	54.7	66.7	78.1	–
LOMO+XQDA	16.6	39.1	52.4	66.8	75.5
ELF	8.1	20.9	31.7	47.1	–
HistLBP	7.9	21.0	30.0	43.9	–
CN color	5.0	17.3	26.2	38.0	–

Table 8. Recognition rate on the PRID2011 dataset

Method	Rank = 1	Rank = 5	Rank = 10	Rank = 20	Rank = 30
The proposed	**70.9**	**93.5**	**96.2**	**98.2**	**99.2**
LFDA	43.7	72.8	81.6	90.8	–
LADF	47.3	75.5	82.6	91.1	–
PRSVM	36.9	60.4	72.4	83.0	–
KISSME	34.3	61.8	72.1	81.0	–
TopRank	31.6	62.2	75.2	89.4	–
LMNN	27.1	53.7	64.9	75.1	–
FAST3D	31.1	60.3	76.4	88.6	–

It can be observed that our model always outperformed all the compared re-id methods on all datasets, which show the effectiveness of the proposed method.

5 Conclusion

Due to the illumination and viewpoint changes between different cameras, individual feature is less discriminative to separate different persons. In this paper, we proposed a saliency-weighted feature LOMO descriptor and global-local fusion optimization method for person re-identification. The saliency weights are integrated into the image after their saliency weights are obtained. After that, the whole image is divided into upper and lower halves. And then a novel fusion method is employed to combine various region together in the most appropriate way. An optimization algorithm is proposed to learn the weights among upper half, lower half and the whole image. Final fused distance is obtained according to those weights. Experiments on four well-known person re-identification datasets show that the proposed method outperforms many state-of-the-art methods significantly.

References

1. Chai, Y., Ren, J., Zhao, H., Li, Y., Ren, J., Murray, P.: Hierarchical and multi-featured fusion for effective gait recognition under variable scenarios. Pattern Anal. Appl. **19**(4), 905–917 (2016)
2. Chen, C.L., Xiang, T., Gong, S.: Multi-camera activity correlation analysis. In: CVPR, pp. 1988–1995 (2009)
3. Frintrop, S., Werner, T., Garcła, G.M.: Traditional saliency reloaded: a good old model in new shape. In: 2015 IEEE CVPR, pp. 82–90 (2015)
4. Gray, D., Brennan, S., Tao, H.: Evaluating appearance models for recognition, reacquisition, and tracking (2007)
5. Han, K., Wan, W., et al.: Distance aggregation for person re-identification using simulated annealing algorithm. In: International Conference on Audio, Language and Image Processing, pp. 399–403 (2016)
6. Liao, S., Hu, Y., et al.: Person re-identification by local maximal occurrence representation and metric learning. In: CVPR, pp. 2197–2206 (2015)
7. Ren, J., Han, J., Mura, M.D.: Special issue on multimodal data fusion for multidimensional signal processing. Multidimens. Syst. Signal Process. **27**(4), 1–5 (2016)
8. Wang, Z., Ren, J., Zhang, D., Sun, M., Jiang, J.: A deep-learning based feature hybrid framework for spatiotemporal saliency detection inside videos. Neurocomputing **287**, 68–83 (2018)
9. Wu, S., Chen, Y.C., et al.: An enhanced deep feature representation for person re-identification. In: Applications of Computer Vision, pp. 1–8 (2016)
10. Yan, Y., Ren, J., Li, Y., Windmill, J., Ijomah, W.: Fusion of dominant colour and spatial layout features for effective image retrieval of coloured logos and trademarks. In: IEEE International Conference on Multimedia Big Data, pp. 306–311 (2015)
11. Yan, Y., Ren, J., Li, Y., Windmill, J.F.C., Ijomah, W., Chao, K.M.: Adaptive fusion of color and spatial features for noise-robust retrieval of colored logo and trademark images. Multidimens. Syst. Signal Process. **27**(4), 1–24 (2016)

12. Yan, Y., et al.: Unsupervised image saliency detection with gestalt-laws guided optimization and visual attention based refinement. Pattern Recognit. **79**, 65–78 (2018)
13. Yan, Y., et al.: Cognitive fusion of thermal and visible imagery for effective detection and tracking of pedestrians in videos. Cogn. Comput. **9**, 1–11 (2017)
14. Yang, Y., Liao, S., et al.: Large scale similarity learning using similar pairs for person verification. In: AAAI, pp. 3655–3661 (2016)
15. Zheng, J., Liu, Y., Ren, J., Zhu, T., Yan, Y., Yang, H.: Fusion of block and keypoints based approaches for effective copy-move image forgery detection. Multidimens. Syst. Signal Process. **27**(4), 989–1005 (2016)

Spectral and Spatial Kernel Extreme Learning Machine for Hyperspectral Image Classification

Zhijing Yang[1(✉)], Faxian Cao[1], Jaime Zabalza[2], Weizhao Chen[1], and Jiangzhong Cao[1]

[1] School of Information Engineering, Guangdong University of Technology, Guangzhou 510006, China
yzhj@gdut.edu.cn

[2] Department of Electronic and Electrical Engineering, University of Strathclyde, Glasgow G1 1XW, UK

Abstract. Kernel extreme learning machine (ELM) has attracted more and more attentions due to its good performance compared with support vector machine (SVM). Since the original Kernel ELM (KELM) is just a spectral classifier, it can't extract the rich spatial information of hyperspectral images (HSIs). This hence refrains the performance of KELM. In view of this, based on the fact that the neighbors of a pixel are more likely to belong to the same class, this paper proposes a spectral and spatial KELM, which exploits the local spatial information to improve the KELM for HSIs classification. Experimental results on two well-known datasets demonstrate the good performance of the proposed spectral and spatial KELM compared with the original KELM and other state-of-the-art methods.

Keywords: Kernel extreme learning machine (KELM)
Hyperspectral images (HSIs) · Spectral and spatial information

1 Introduction

Hyperspectral images (HSIs) have been widely applied in many application, such as environment mapping, geology and crop analysis, which attribute to the fast development of science technology [1]. The rich spectral information makes the HSIs available to be classified for each pixel of different applications [2]. However, supervised HSIs learning is still a changing problem due to the Hughes phenomenon [3] which caused by the large number of spectral bands and limited samples of training pixels. To tackle this problem, some state-of-the-art methods have been proposed for feature extraction, data reduction, and classification for hyperspectral images. Feature extraction and data reduction are relative [11, 25]. Principal component analysis (PCA) and its variations [15–17] have been widely used for feature extraction and data reduction [2, 7], which can successfully remove correlation inherent in the data. Singular spectrum analysis (SSA) [12–14] is another well-known feature extraction method. It can be used to remove the noisy components, and enhance the signal for improving the final classification. Classification is a crucial step for HSIs processing. Many methods have been proposed, such as the multi-kernel (MK) classification [4],

J. Ren et al. (Eds.): BICS 2018, LNAI 10989, pp. 394–401, 2018.
https://doi.org/10.1007/978-3-030-00563-4_38

the sparse multinomial logistic regression [5–7], support vector machine (SVM) [8] and extreme learning machine (ELM) [9, 10]. Among these methods, ELM has acquired many attentions due to its good performance.

ELM has been proven a good method for many applications. It has many good properties, such as straightforward solution, fast implementation, and strong generalization capability [18]. The kernel ELM (KELM) which is an improvement of the traditional ELM, has comparable classification performance compared with SVM and faster speed than SVM [19]. However, there is a drawback in KELM for HSIs classification that it can't explore the rich spatial information of HSIs [20].

In HSIs, there are some large homogenous regions where the neighborhood pixels have the same class materials and similar spectral feature [21]. Therefore, the pixels in such region are more likely belong to the same class [9]. In view of this, this paper proposes a spectral and spatial KELM (SSKELM) for HSIs classification in order to incorporate the spectral and spatial information of HSIs. Details will be discussed in Sect. 3.

The rest of this paper can be summarized as follows. Section 2 introduces the principal of KELM. The proposed SSKELM is presented in Sect. 3. The experimental results and discussion can be found in Sect. 4. Conclusions and remarks are given in Sect. 5.

2 Kernel Extreme Learning Machine

Given N training samples $X \equiv (x_1; x_2; \ldots; x_N) \in R^{N \times d}$ of a HSI and the corresponding labels which are denoted by $Y = (y_1; y_2; \ldots; y_N) \in R^{N \times M}$, where d denotes the spectral bands of a HSI, M is the number of classes in the HSI that need to be classified. ELM is a generalized single layer feedforward neural network [22]. The ELM model with activation function H(x) and L hidden neurons can be expressed by the following equation:

$$\sum\nolimits_{j=1}^{L} \beta_j H\left(w_j^T * x_i + b_j\right) = y_i, \quad i = 1, 2, \ldots, N \tag{1}$$

where β_j is the weight vector from the hidden layer to the output layer, $\beta = [\beta_1, \beta_2, \ldots, \beta_M] \in R^{L \times M}$, w_j and b_j represent the weight vector and bias between the input layer and hidden layer of ELM, respectively, and $H(w_j x_i + b_j)$ denotes the output of the j-th hidden neuron of the input sample x_i. Then the solution of Eq. (1) can be directly obtained by:

$$\beta = H^{\dagger} Y \tag{2}$$

where $\beta = [\beta_1, \beta_2, \ldots, \beta_M] \in R^{L \times M}$, and $H^{\dagger}$ is the Moore-Penrose generalized inverse of matrix H [23]. Hence $H^{\dagger} = H^T(HH^T)^{-1}$ or $H^{\dagger} = (H^T H)^{-1} H^T$ and

$$H = \begin{bmatrix} h(w_1, b_1, x_1) & \cdots & h(w_1, b_1, x_N) \\ \vdots & \ddots & \vdots \\ h(w_L, b_L, x_1) & \cdots & h(w_L, b_L, x_N) \end{bmatrix} \tag{3}$$

A positive value $\frac{I}{C}$ can be added to the diagonal element of $H^T H$ or HH^T [19] in order to improve the generalization and stale ability of the inverse operator. Then the final ELM model can be denoted as:

$$\beta = H\left(H^T H + \frac{I}{C}\right)^{-1} Y \tag{4}$$

The KELM is an improvement of ELM which can be expressed by:

$$\beta_{KELM} = H\left(\frac{I}{C} + K_{KELM}\left(x_i, x_j\right)\right)^{-1} Y^T \tag{5}$$

where $K_{KELM}\left(x_i, x_j\right) = H(x_i)^T * H\left(x_j\right) = \exp\left(-\frac{\|x_i - x_j\|^2}{2*\sigma_{KELM}^2}\right)$ is the Gaussian RBF [19].

3 Spectral and Spatial Kernel Extreme Learning Machine

Given $\mathrm{X}_{\mathrm{KELM}}^* \equiv \left(\mathrm{x}_1^*; \mathrm{x}_2^*; \ldots; \mathrm{x}_\mathrm{N}^*\right) \in \mathrm{R}^{\mathrm{N} \times \mathrm{d}}$ as the N training samples of HSIs, and $\mathrm{Y} = \left(\mathrm{y}_1; \mathrm{y}_2; \ldots; \mathrm{y}_\mathrm{N}\right) \in \mathrm{R}^{\mathrm{N} \times \mathrm{M}}$ as the corresponding labels, we can extract the neighboring/spatial information for KELM. Let p denote the four neighbors of a given pixel. Then given the training pixels, all their corresponding 4 adjacent pixels can be integrated. Let $\mathrm{X}_{\mathrm{SSKELM}}^* \equiv \left(\mathrm{x}_1^*; \mathrm{x}_2^*; \ldots; \mathrm{x}_\mathrm{N}^*; \mathrm{x}_{11}^*; \mathrm{x}_{21}^*; \ldots; \mathrm{x}_{\mathrm{N}1}^*; \ldots; \mathrm{x}_{14}^*; \mathrm{x}_{24}^*; \ldots; \mathrm{x}_{\mathrm{N}4}^*\right) \in \mathrm{R}^{5\mathrm{N} \times \mathrm{d}}$ denote the spectral and spatial information of all the training samples. Then the proposed Spectral and Spatial Kernel Extreme Learning Machine (SSKELM) can be expressed as follows:

$$\beta_{SSKELM} = H_{SSKELM}^*\left(\frac{I_1^*}{C} + K_{SSKELM}\left(x_i^*, x_j^*\right)\right)^{-1} Y^* \tag{6}$$

where $\mathrm{I}_1^* \in \mathrm{R}^{5\mathrm{N} \times 5\mathrm{N}}$ is an unit matrix, and $\mathrm{Y}^* = (\mathrm{Y}, \mathrm{Y}, \ldots, \mathrm{Y}) \in \mathrm{R}^{5\mathrm{N} \times \mathrm{M}}$, and

$$\begin{aligned} H_{SSKELM}^* &= \left[H_{SSKELM}^*\left(x_1^*\right), H_{SSKELM}^*\left(x_2^*\right), \ldots, H_{SSKELM}^*\left(x_{(p+1)N}^*\right)\right] \\ &= \left[\begin{pmatrix} h\left(w_1, b_1, x_1^*\right) & \cdots & h\left(w_1, b_1, x_{(p+1)N}^*\right) \\ \vdots & \ddots & \vdots \\ h\left(w_L, b_L, x_1^*\right) & \cdots & h\left(w_L, b_L, x_{(p+1)N}^*\right) \end{pmatrix}\right]. \end{aligned} \tag{7}$$

$$K_{SSKELM}\left(x_i^*, x_j^*\right) = \exp\left(-\frac{\| x_i^* - x_j^* \|^2}{2 * \sigma_{SSKELM}^2}\right) \tag{8}$$

Then given a whole HSI $\hat{\mathrm{X}} = \left(\hat{\mathrm{x}}_1, \hat{\mathrm{x}}_2, \ldots, \hat{\mathrm{x}}_\mathrm{n}\right) \in \mathrm{R}^{\mathrm{n} \times \mathrm{d}}$, the test process of the proposed SSKELM can be expressed by the following equations:

$$f(\hat{x}_i) = H^*_{SSKELM}(\hat{x}_i)\beta = K^*_{SSKELM}\left(\frac{I^*_1}{C_1} + K_{SSKELM}\left(x^*_i, x^*_j\right)\right)^{-1} Y^* \tag{9}$$

$$K^*_{SSKELM}\left(\hat{x}_i, x^*_j\right) = H^*_{SSKELM}(\hat{x}_i)H^*_{SSKELM}\left(x^*_j\right) = \exp\left(-\frac{\| \hat{x}_i - x^*_j \|^2}{2 * \sigma^2_{SSKELM}}\right) \quad j = 1, \ldots, N \tag{10}$$

4 Experimental Results and Discussion

4.1 Hyperspectral Image Description

(1) Indian Pines Dataset: The Indian Pines dataset was acquired by Airborne Visible Imaging Spectrometer (AVIRIS) sensor in June 1992, in which the size is 145 × 145 pixels with 220 bands between 0.4 to 2.45 visible and infrared spectrum region. The Indian Pines dataset has 16 classes and 10366 samples need to be classified. Also, there are 200 bands after removing 20 water absorption [19].
(2) Pavia University Dataset: This Pavia University dataset was obtained by the Reflective Optics System Imaging Spectrometer (ROSIS) sensor over the area surrounding University of Pavia [19]. Nine reference classes where total 42776 samples in this datasets need to be classified. The Pavia University dataset has 610 × 340 pixels with 103 bands after removing 12 noisy and water absorption bands.

4.2 Experiment Results and Discussions

In this subsection, we will compare the proposed SSKELM with the original KELM and kernel SVM (KSVM) [9]. The penalty parameter and kernel Gaussian radial basis function parameter of KELM, KSVM and the proposed KSVM are set as the same. That is to say we set the penalty parameter $C = [2^1, 2^2, \ldots, 2^{20}]$ and the kernel parameter $\sigma = [2^{-4}, 2^{-3}, \ldots, 2^4]$. Three crossing validation is used to choose the best parameter. All the experiments are conducted in Matlab R2015a and tested on a computer with 2.9 GHz i7 CPU and 32.0 RAM, and are repeated 10 times with the average classification and computation time reported for comparison. It should be noted that the LIBSVM [24] software is used for the implementation of the KSVM. The code of KELM and KSVM can be downloaded at this website: http://www.fst.umac.mo/en/staff/fstycz.html. OA, AA and K mean the overall accuracy, average accuracy and kappa coefficient, respectively [9]. We vary and randomly select the number of the training samples from each class, denoted by Q. That is Q = 5, 10, 15, 20, 25, 30 in our experiments. Only 50% of the samples in each class is selected for training if Q is more than 50% of the total samples in that class.

Tables 1 and 2 show the classification accuracies of KSVM, KELM and SSKELM in Indian Pines dataset and Pavia University, respectively. From Tables 1 and 2, we can see that the proposed SSKELM can greatly improve the classification results of KELM, and also have better classification accuracies than KSVM. In the last line of Tables 1 and 2, we report the computation time of KELM, KSVM and the propose SSKELM. It can be seen that the computation time of SSKELM is slightly more than KELM. Besides, SSKELM has less computation than KSVM in Indian Pines dataset.

Based on above analysis, we can conclude that the proposed SSKELM obtains very good results according to the classification and computation time. Figures 1 and 2 show the classification results map under 30 training samples per class in Tables 1 and 2, respectively.

Table 1. Classification accuracy (%) and standard deviation with different numbers of labeled samples in Indian Pines dataset (best result of each row is marked in bold type).

Training number	Indexes	KSVM	KELM	SSKELM
5	OA	55.98 ± 3.99	57.40 ± 4.47	**69.59 ± 1.99**
	AA	67.04 ± 2.42	70.27 ± 2.30	**79.93 ± 0.91**
	K	50.80 ± 4.35	52.80 ± 4.60	**65.91 ± 2.15**
10	OA	66.34 ± 2.26	67.50 ± 2.15	**75.61 ± 2.44**
	AA	76.58 ± 1.53	78.36 ± 1.53	**85.50 ± 1.20**
	K	62.20 ± 2.39	63.46 ± 2.31	**72.55 ± 2.71**
15	OA	70.45 ± 2.51	70.75 ± 1.63	**79.70 ± 1.36**
	AA	80.03 ± 2.35	81.65 ± 0.59	**88.38 ± 0.71**
	K	66.87 ± 2.76	67.25 ± 1.76	**77.14 ± 1.49**
20	OA	73.68 ± 1.92	73.70 ± 1.91	**81.52 ± 1.29**
	AA	83.51 ± 0.83	84.52 ± 0.74	**89.86 ± 0.67**
	K	70.38 ± 2.12	70.45 ± 2.05	**79.12 ± 1.45**
25	OA	75.57 ± 1.31	76.19 ± 1.22	**83.20 ± 0.96**
	AA	85.06 ± 1.00	85.95 ± 0.89	**90.99 ± 0.64**
	K	72.48 ± 1.43	73.16 ± 1.34	**80.99 ± 1.07**
30	OA	77.24 ± 1.31	76.91 ± 1.26	**84.25 ± 0.83**
	AA	86.29 ± 0.85	86.94 ± 0.90	**91.91 ± 0.64**
	K	74.34 ± 1.44	74.05 ± 1.35	**82.18 ± 0.93**
5	Time (seconds)	3.17	0.25	1.57

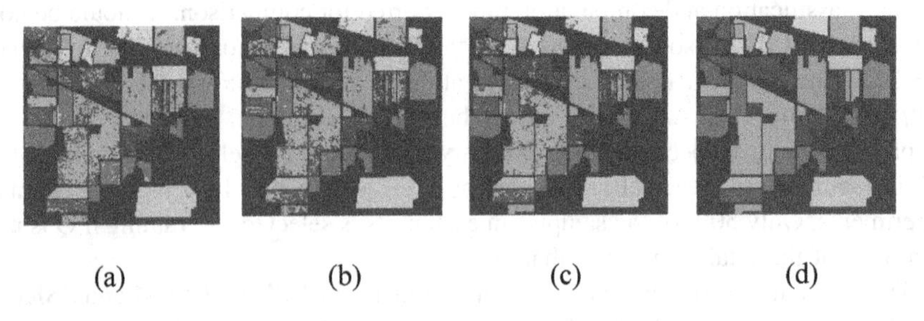

Fig. 1. Results in Indian Pines dataset (with about 30 training samples per class): (a) KSVM (OA = 77.24 ± 1.31); (b) KELM (OA = 76.91 ± 1.26); (c) SSKELM (OA = 84.25 ± 0.83); (d) reference map.

Table 2. Classification accuracy (%) and standard deviation with different numbers of labeled samples in Pavia University dataset (Best result of each row is marked in bold type).

Training number	Indexs	KSVM	KELM	SSKELM
5	OA	61.74 ± 10.75	59.08 ± 6.66	**62.57 ± 8.02**
	AA	73.09 ± 4.94	72.04 ± 3.95	**76.39 ± 3.73**
	K	53.18 ± 10.81	50.25 ± 7.18	**54.61 ± 8.56**
10	OA	71.27 ± 4.43	68.12 ± 2.93	**72.01 ± 3.26**
	AA	79.03 ± 1.94	77.57 ± 2.25	**82.75 ± 1.73**
	K	63.80 ± 4.87	60.23 ± 3.12	**65.26 ± 3.55**
15	OA	74.09 ± 6.45	72.94 ± 6.67	**79.03 ± 5.08**
	AA	81.17 ± 3.10	80.68 ± 2.79	**86.07 ± 2.31**
	K	67.27 ± 7.40	65.93 ± 7.57	**73.52 ± 5.93**
20	OA	75.91 ± 3.67	75.73 ± 2.75	**82.84 ± 1.65**
	AA	82.60 ± 1.12	83.04 ± 1.18	**88.09 ± 0.63**
	K	69.50 ± 4.14	69.32 ± 3.02	**78.04 ± 1.92**
25	OA	80.61 ± 2.37	78.68 ± 3.12	**84.49 ± 0.96**
	AA	85.55 ± 1.22	84.83 ± 1.57	**88.94 ± 0.47**
	K	75.17 ± 2.79	72.91 ± 3.64	**80.05 ± 1.14**
30	OA	81.89 ± 1.33	80.27 ± 2.80	**85.93 ± 1.79**
	AA	86.10 ± 0.82	85.53 ± 1.33	**89.71 ± 0.67**
	K	76.68 ± 1.59	74.74 ± 3.36	**81.84 ± 2.17**
5	Time (seconds)	0.95	0.49	1.90

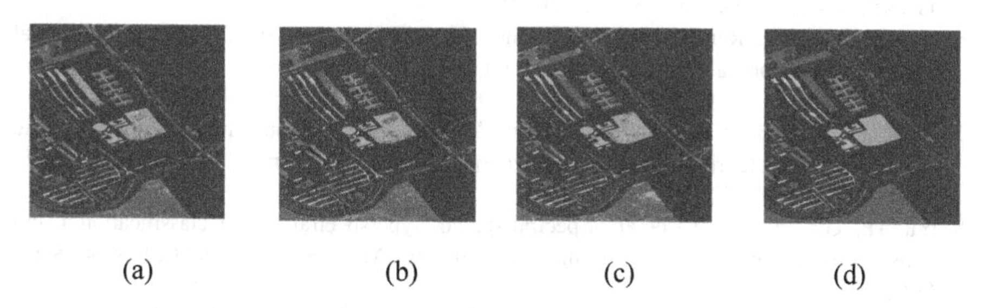

(a) (b) (c) (d)

Fig. 2. Results in the Pavia University dataset (with about 30 training samples per class): (a) KSVM (OA = 81.89 ± 1.33); (b) KELM (OA = 80.27 ± 2.80); (c) SSKELM (OA = 85.93 ± 1.79); (d) reference map.

5 Conclusion

In this paper, a novel spectral and spatial kernel extreme learning machine (SSKELM) method has been proposed for spectral and spatial classification of HSIs. The proposed method considers the fact that the neighborhoods of a given pixel are more likely to belong to the same class. The local spatial information can be extracted by the SSKELM which is very important for the HSIs classifications. Experimental results on

Indian Pines and Pavia University show the better performances of proposed SSKELM than the well-known KELM and KSVM.

For the further work, we will resort to reduce the computation of the proposed SSKELM using sparse representation method [26]. Also, we will further improve the classification accuracies of the proposed SSKELM by extended multi-attribute profiles method [27] and gravitational search algorithms [28, 29].

Acknowledgements. This work is supported by the National Nature Science Foundation of China (nos. 61471132 and 61372173), and the Training program for outstanding young teachers in higher education institutions of Guangdong Province (no. YQ2015057).

References

1. Zhou, Y., Peng, J., Chen, C.L.P.: Dimension reduction using spatial and spectral regularized local discriminant embedding for hyperspectral image classification. IEEE Trans. Geosci. Remote Sens. **53**(2), 1082–1095 (2015)
2. Plaza, A., Benediktsson, J.A., Boardman, J.W., et al.: Recent advances in techniques for hyperspectral image processing. Remote Sens. Environ. **113**(1), S110–S122 (2009)
3. Hughes, G.: On the mean accuracy of statistical pattern recognizers. IEEE Trans. Inf. Theory **14**, 55–63 (1968)
4. Fang, L., Li, S., Duan, W., Ren, J., Benediktsson, J.A.: Classification of hyperspectral images by exploiting spectral-spatial information of superpixel via multiple kernels. IEEE Trans. Geosci. Remote Sens. **53**, 6663–6674 (2015)
5. Li, J., Bioucas-Dias, J.M., Plaza, A.: Spectral-spatial hyperspectral image segmentation using subspace multinomial logistic regression and Markov random fields. IEEE Trans. Geosci. Remote Sens. **50**, 809–823 (2012)
6. Cao, F., Yang, Z., Ren, J., Ling, W.K., Zhao, H., Marshall, S.: Extreme sparse multinomial logistic regression: a fast and robust framework for hyperspectral image classification. Remote Sens. **9**(12), 1255 (2017)
7. Krishnapuram, B., Carin, L., Figueiredo, M.A.T., et al.: Sparse multinomi al logistic regression: fast algorithms and generalization bounds. IEEE Trans. Pattern Anal. Mach. Intell. **27**, 957–968 (2005)
8. Yu, H., Gao, L., Li, J., et al.: Spectral-spatial hyperspectral image classification using subspace-based support vector machines and adaptive Markov random fields. Remote Sens. **8**(4), 355 (2016)
9. Zhou, Y., Peng, J., Chen, C.L.P.: Extreme learning machine with composite kernels for hyperspectral image classification. IEEE J. Sel. Top. Appl. Earth Observ. Remote Sens. **8**, 2351–2360 (2015)
10. Cao, F., Yang, Z., Ren, J., Jiang, M., Ling, W.K.: Linear vs nonlinear extreme learning machine for spectral-spatial classification of hyperspectral image. Sensors **17**, 2603 (2017)
11. Zabalza, J., et al.: Novel segmented stacked autoencoder for effective dimensionality reduction and feature extraction in hyperspectral imaging. Neurocomputing **185**, 1–10 (2016)
12. Qiao, T., Ren, J., et al.: Effective denoising and classification of hyperspectral images using curvelet transform and singular spectrum analysis. IEEE Trans. Geosci. Remote Sens. **55**, 119–133 (2017)

13. Zabalza, J., et al.: Novel two dimensional singular spectrum analysis for effective feature extraction and data classification in hyperspectral imaging. IEEE Trans. Geosci. Remote Sens. **53**, 4418–4433 (2015)
14. Qiao, T., Ren, J., Craigie, C., Zabalza, Z., Maltin, C., Marshall, S.: Singular spectrum analysis for improving hyperspectral imaging based beef eating quality evaluation. Comput. Electron. Agric. **115**, 21–25 (2015)
15. Zabalza, J., Ren, J., Liu, Z., Marshall, S.: Structured covaciance principle component analysis for real-time onsite feature extraction and dimensionality reduction in hyperspectral imaging. Appl. Opt. **53**, 4440–4449 (2014)
16. Zabalza, J., et al.: Novel folded-PCA for improved feature extraction and data reduction with hyperspectral imaging and SAR in remote sensing. ISPRS J. Photogramm. Remote Sens. **93**, 112–122 (2014)
17. Dalla Mura, M., Villa, A., Benediktsson, J.A., et al.: Classification of hyperspectral images by using extended morphological attribute profiles and independent component analysis. IEEE Geosci. Remote Sens. Lett. **8**, 542–546 (2011)
18. Huang, G.B., Zhou, H., Ding, X., et al.: Extreme learning machine for regression and multiclass classification. IEEE Trans. Syst. Man Cybern. Part B (Cybern.) **42**(2), 513–529 (2012)
19. Li, W., Chen, C., Su, H., Du, Q.: Local binary patterns and extreme learning machine for hyperspectral imagery classification. IEEE Trans. Geosci. Remote Sens. **53**(7), 3681–3693 (2015)
20. Chen, C., et al.: Spectral-spatial classification of hyperspectral image based on kernel extreme learning machine. Remote Sens. **6**(6), 5795–5814 (2014)
21. Chen, Y., Nasrabadi, N., Tran, T.: Hyperspectral image classification using dictionary-based sparse representation. IEEE Trans. Geosci. Remote Sens. **49**(10), 3973–3985 (2011)
22. Huang, G., Zhu, Q., Siew, C.: Extreme learning machine: theory and applications. Neurocomputing **70**(1), 489–501 (2006)
23. Banerjee, K.S.: Generalized Inverse of Matrices and Its Applications. Wiley, New York (1971)
24. Chang, C.C., Lin, C.J.: LIBSVM: a library for support vector machines. ACM Trans. Intell. Syst. Technol. **2**(3), 27 (2011)
25. Ren, J., Zabalza, Z., Marshall, S., Zheng, J.: Effective feature extraction and data reduction with hyperspectral imaging in remote sensing. IEEE Signal Process. Mag. **31**(4), 149–154 (2014)
26. Cao, F., Yang, Z., Ren, J., Ling, W., et al.: Sparse representation based augmented multinomial logistic extreme learning machine with weighted composite features for spectral-spatial classification of hyperspectral images. IEEE Trans. Geosci. Remote Sens. **99**, 1–17 (2018)
27. Mura, M.D., Benediktsson, J.A., Waske, B., et al.: Morphological attribute profiles for the analysis of very high resolution images. IEEE Trans. Geosci. Remote Sens. **48**(10), 3747–3762 (2010)
28. Sun, G., Ma, P., Ren, J., Zhang, A., Jia, X.: A stability constrained adaptive alpha for gravitational search algorithm. Knowl. Based Syst. **139**, 200–213 (2018)
29. Zhang, A., Sun, G., Ren, J., Li, X., Wang, Z., et al.: A dynamic neighborhood learning-based gravitational search algorithm. IEEE Trans. Cybern. **48**(1), 436–447 (2018)

Local-Global Extraction Unit for Person Re-identification

Peng Wang[1], Chunmei Qing[1(✉)], Xiangmin Xu[1], Bolun Cai[1], Jianxiu Jin[1], and Jinchang Ren[2]

[1] School of Electronic and Information Engineering, South China University of Technology, Guangzhou, China
winper001@gmail.com, {qchm,xmxu,jxjin}@scut.edu.cn, caibolun@gmail.com

[2] Department of Electronic and Electrical Engineering, University of Strathclyde, Glasgow, UK
jinchang.ren@strath.ac.uk

Abstract. The huge variance of human pose and inaccurate detection significantly increase the difficulty of person re-identification. Existing deep learning methods mostly focus on extraction of global feature and local feature, or combine them to learn a discriminative pedestrian descriptor. However, rare traditional methods have been exploited the association of the local and global features in convolutional neural networks (CNNs), and some important part-wise information is not captured sufficiently when training. In this paper, we propose a novel architecture called **Local-Global Extraction Unit (LGEU)**, which is able to adaptively re-calibrate part-wise information with integrating the channel-wise information. Extensive experiments on Market-1501, CUHK03, and DukeMTMC-reID datasets achieve competitive results with the state-of-the-art methods. On Market-1501, for instance, LGEU achieves 91.8% rank-1 accuracy and especially 88.0% mAP.

Keywords: Person re-identification · Local-Global Extraction Unit Convolutional neural networks

1 Introduction

Person re-identification (ReID), matching two specified person images crossing non-overlapping camera views, has been receiving rapid attention in recent years. However, ReID remains a challenging problem due to following factors: human pose changes, background cluster, and local occlusion [24].

In the gallery, we aim at searching for images containing the same person in a cross-camera mode. To address this problem, two crucial facts must be considered. First, discriminative features are required to represent both the query

C. Qing—This work is supported by the National Natural Science Foundation of China (61401163, 61702192).

J. Ren et al. (Eds.): BICS 2018, LNAI 10989, pp. 402–411, 2018.
https://doi.org/10.1007/978-3-030-00563-4_39

and gallery images. Second, suitable distance metrics are inevitable to determine whether a gallery image contains the same person as the query image. Early ReID methods mainly focus on discriminative feature representation or robust distance measure. With the development of deep learning, CNN-based approaches concentrate on better feature representation for pedestrians, which can be roughly divided into three aspects.

- **Global descriptors** [2,3] pay more attention on global information, such as gender, stature, and body shape. However, they lose the explicit information or crucial details because of pose variations and person detection errors [9, 21,22,30].
- **Local descriptors** [1,20,23] directly divide the whole image into some fixed patches, and roughly feed them into the model. Therefore, they omit the fact that fixed-length strips are sensitive to the pose variance.
- **Global and local representation** [5,24] are combined to form a fusion descriptor, and achieve satisfactory performance. In [29], the global features is extracted for jointly learning local features. Cheng *et al.* [18] simply splits the convolutional maps into several parts, and fuses the local features with the global features. However, these method require more computation and additional storage space.

In this paper, we propose a novel architectural unit called **Local-Global Extraction Unit (LGEU)**, which exploits the selection of part-wise and channel-wise information to optimize global feature discriminative capabilities. LGEU embedded in backbone network replaces the original global pooling layer, which expresses the importance of each part and each channel for pedestrian images. Then, we fuse both part-wise and channel-wise information to get a global descriptor as the final feature. Largely different from existing methods, LGEU is not simply combines local and global information, but regards the local features as complementary information that benefits global features.

2 Local-Global Extraction Unit

During the CNN training for ReID, we expect the convolutional layer to learn integrated information by fusing part-wise and channel-wise information. Inspired by [7], we propose a novel unit called LGEU to address this problem. LGEU can do work on any networks, and we employ the ResNet50 as the backbone network in this paper. As shown in Fig. 1, the proposed architecture actually includes two part: local selection and global fusion.

2.1 Local Selection

Differently from the previous works, the proposed architecture embeds local selection to directly train the network as final descriptor. Local selection pays more attention to part-wise and channel-wise information. In some ways, local

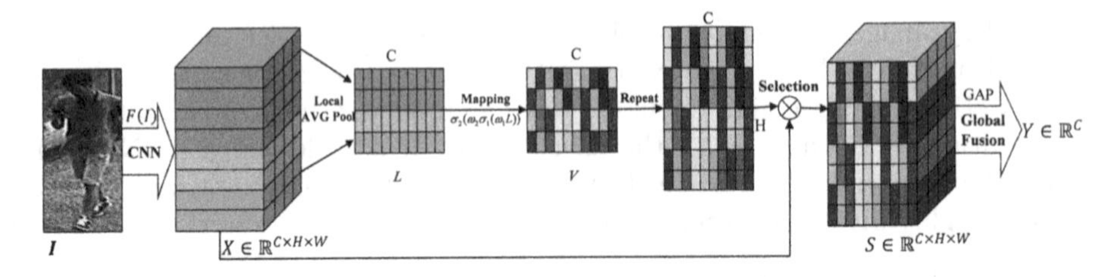

Fig. 1. The architecture of LGEU. We feed the raw image I into the backbone network (ResNet50) $\mathcal{F}$, and define the output $X \in \mathbb{R}^{C\times H\times W}$ of the last convolutional layer as $X = \mathcal{F}(I)$. For the sake of understanding, the LGEU can be shallowly represented as $f : X \rightarrow Y$, where $Y \in \mathbb{R}^{C}$ is integration of part-wise and channel-wise information.

selection works like activation functions [6,7] for feature re-weighting, which would be discussed detailedly in Sect. 2.3.

Along the vertical direction, a pedestrian body can be divided into different parts, such as head, upper clothes, lower clothes, and shoes. As is shown in Fig. 1, we integrate the part-wise feature $L \in \mathbb{R}^{C\times K}$ by local average pooling with $(H/K)\times W$ receptive fields. In this paper, the input feature $X \in \mathbb{R}^{C\times H\times W}$ is divided into $K = 4$ pieces, and each element is calculated by

$$L^{c,k} = \frac{1}{(WH)/K} \sum_{i=(k-1)\Delta+1}^{k\Delta} \sum_{j=1}^{W} X^{c,i,j}, \tag{1}$$

where $\Delta = H/K$.

Then we take these part-wise features L into K branches, separately. Each branch is sequentially composed by weight, ReLU, weight, and Sigmoid function. The non-linear mapping aims to learn the importance feature of each part. We concatenate them to single tensor $V \in \mathbb{R}^{C\times K}$, whose elements can be expressed by

$$V^{c,k} = \sigma_2(\omega_2^k \sigma_1(\omega_1^k L^{c,k})), \tag{2}$$

where σ_1, σ_2 refer to the ReLU function and sigmoid function, respectively. The size of ω_1^k is $R \times C$, and ω_2^k is $C \times R$. Here R is the reduction dimension and set to 16 in the paper.

If we let $K = 1$, it means that the whole pedestrian discriminator is fed into the unit. As pointed in Sect. 2.3, the block is a little similar to SE unit. However, LGEU has many differences in mechanism or results. The results of LGEU on these public datasets would show its powerful ability, which is explained in Sect. 3.3.

Finally, we select the channel-wise information in each part-wise branch. Each element of V along the vertical direction can be repeated by H/K times to have the same height as X. The result of local selection can be written as follow:

$$S^{c,i,j} = X^{c,i,j} \otimes V^{c,\lceil i/\Delta \rceil}, \tag{3}$$

where $\otimes$ denotes point-wise multiplication, and $\lceil\rceil$ means the operation of rounded up.

2.2 Global Fusion

As described above, local selection takes account of both part-wise and channel-wise information to re-weight the input X. Similarly to many CNN-based frameworks, we straightforward embed global average pooling for feature fusion, which can be expressed by

$$Y^c = \frac{1}{WH}\sum_{i=1}^{H}\sum_{j=1}^{W} S^{c,i,j}, \tag{4}$$

where Y^c is the mean value responsing to each feature map. Indeed, the global feature contains more high-level information, such as shape and pose, and it benefits to avoid overfitting on small training sets. Then a Softmax loss function is appended for global feature learning.

2.3 Comparison

In this section, we will discuss the mechanism of LGEU, and compare it with ReLU [6] and SE unit [7].

ReLU. ReLU [6] sparsely selects which element in the feature maps from previous layer can be fed into the next layer. As illustrated in Fig. 2, ReLU, as a special form of LGEU, can be regarded as a point-wise multiplication of an linear mapping and a gate function. LGEU is capable of learning how these patches and channels are selected, while ReLU cannot do so. Moreover, the derivative of ReLU switch function is zero, which causes that the training error cannot be back-propagated though the switch during the training process. LGEU uses Sigmoid as gate function, which is able to optimize the whole selection control as training error can be back-propagated through itself.

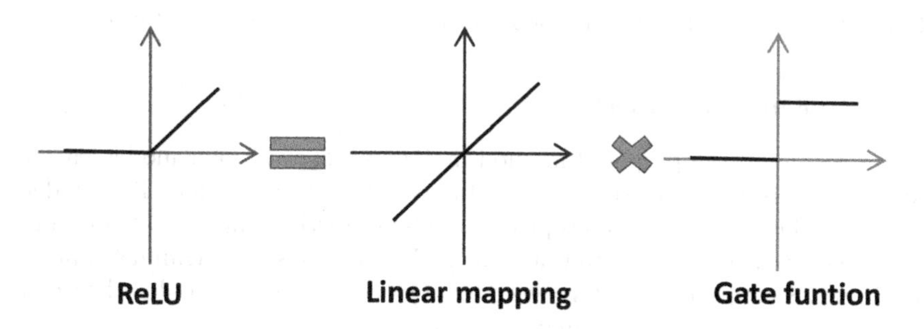

Fig. 2. Mechanism of ReLU. ReLU can be re-defined as a point-wise multiplication of an identity mapping and a switch.

SE Unit. In some ways, LGEU could be compared with SE unit [7] in architecture. However, they have many differences, especially in function. SE unit fuses the global spatial information into channel descriptor, aiming to fully capture channel-wise dependencies. While LGEU not justly consider channel-wise information, but lay more emphasis on part-wise. In addition, SE squeezes the each feature map into a scalar, which is used for re-weighting the channel, but we do not do so. In short, LGEU focus on more information than SE unit when training the network.

3 Experiments

3.1 Datasets and Evaluation Protocol

Datasets. We conduct the proposed method on three widely used datasets: Martket-1501 [8], CUHK03 [4], and DukeMTMC-reID [10,11]. **Market-1501** dataset contains 1501 identities observed by 6 cameras, 19732 gallery images, and 12936 training images. We split the dataset with standard protocol: 751 identities for training and 750 identities for testing. **CUHK03** dataset includes 1467 identities and 13164 images, and offers both hand-labeled and DPM-detected bounding boxes. In this work, we use latter, and employ the new training/testing protocol introduced in [12]. **DukeMTMC-reID** dataset, which contains 1404 identities (702/702 for training and testing), 2228 queries, 17661 gallery images, and 16552 training images, is captured with 8 cameras. The single-query setting is used in all our experiment.

Evaluation Protocol. For the distance measure, we compute the cosine distance between a query and a gallery. Our experiments adopt the cumulative matching characteristic (CMC) and mean average precision (mAP) as performance measure. Moreover, we also employ re-ranking approach [12] to improve ReID accuracy, which combines original distance and Jaccard distance.

3.2 Implementation Details

We implemented the proposed method in *Pytorch* package. For model learning, we use the ResNet50 fine-tuned from ImageNet as our baseline. The model is trained for 60 epochs with SGD optimizer, whose starting learning rate initialized at 0.1 and decayed to 0.01 after 40 epochs. We set the size of training inputs to be 256×128, and set the batchsize to 32. All the images are random horizontal flipped and cropped for data augmentation.

3.3 Performance Evaluation

The Effectiveness of LGEU. As is shown in Fig. 3, the backbone network inserted LGEU achieves a great promotion in all these datasets. Without re-ranking approach in test, mAP on three datasets increases from 69.8%, 41.6%,

57.4% to **74.5% (+4.7%), 47.4% (+5.8%), 62.3% (+4.9%)**, respectively. And rank-1 increases from 86.5%, 46.5%, 73.9% to **90.0% (+3.5%), 50.7% (+4.2%), 77.4% (+3.5%)**, respectively. On the other hand, LGEU is more superior than SE unit [7], which is shown in Table 1. The significant raise indicates that the combination of part-wise and channel-wise information enhances the discriminative ability of the network.

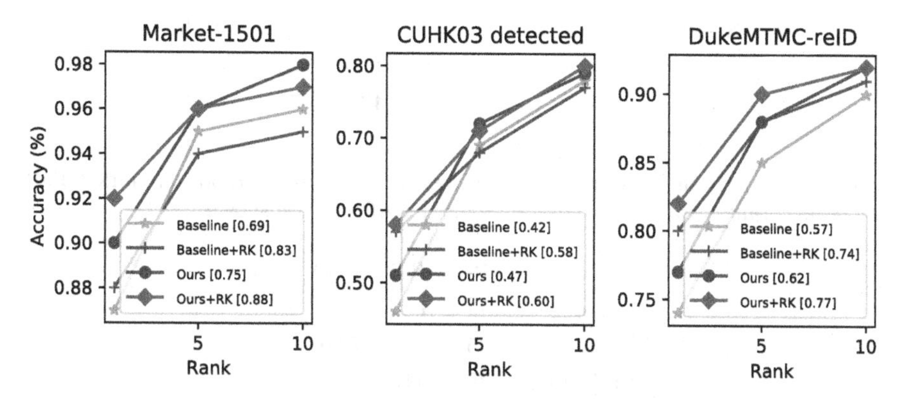

Fig. 3. The comparison of the baseline of and our methods. Note that the score in the parenthesis means the mAP corresponding to each method. RK stands for re-ranking approach.

Comparison with Other Methods. The comparisons of the proposed methods on **Market-1501** in terms of rank-1, rank-5, rank-10 matching rate are given in Table 2. Related methods are roughly divided into three groups: (1) hand-crafted methods, such as [8,13,14]. (2) CNN-based methods with employing global features [15,16]. (3) CNN-based methods with employing local features [19,23,24]. GLAD [24] gets the best rank-1 accuracy (89.9%) and mAP (73.9%), which is surpassing the other methods. However, our result is 0.1% higher than its in rank-1 accuracy, and 0.6% higher in mAP. When using re-ranking, we can obtain 91.8% rank-1 accuracy, and the mAP further surpass GLAD.

For **CUHK03-detected** dataset, we use the training/testing protocol as [12]. The comparison is summarized in Table 3. SVDNet [26] is comparatively higher than other works either rank-1 accuracy or mAP, while we get better result than it. Our method obtains 50.7% accuracy and 47.4% mAP. After using re-ranking, the rank-1 accuracy increases to 57.7% (+10%), and the mAP increases to 60.0% (+12.6%).

We also show our result for **DukeMTMC-reID**. The comparison with related methods is depicted in Table 4. Our method outperforms most the state-of-the-art approaches, but slightly lower the DPFL [1] in rank-1, which takes multi-scale images as input and calculates more complicatedly than ours. However, our method gets the best mAP (62.35%) among the all approaches. When employing the re-ranking, our performance is improved enormously from 77.40% to 81.96% in accuracy, from 62.35% to 77.17% in mAP.

Table 1. Comparison of our method with the baseline and Se-Unit, respectively. The rank-1 accuracy (%) and mAP (%) are shown. All the methods are conducted without re-ranking approach.

Methods	Datasets					
	Market-1501		CUHK03		DukeMTMC	
	Rank-1	mAP	Rank-1	mAP	Rank-1	mAP
Baseline	86.5	69.8	46.5	41.6	73.9	57.4
Se-Unit	89.8	74.3	47.6	43.9	74.1	57.5
Ours	**90.0**	**74.5**	**50.7**	**47.4**	**77.4**	**62.3**

Table 2. Comparison of our method with the state of the art methods on Market-1501. The rank-1, rank-5, rank-10 accuracy (%) and mAP (%) are shown.

Methods	R-1	R-5	R-10	mAP
Bow+kissme [8]	44.4	63.5	72.2	20.8
WARCA [13]	45.2	68.1	76.0	-
KLFDA [14]	46.5	71.1	79.9	-
SOMAnet [15]	73.9	-	-	47.9
SVDNet [16]	82.3	92.3	95.2	62.1
PAN [17]	82.8	-	-	63.4
PAR [19]	81.0	92.0	94.7	63.7
MultiLoss [20]	83.9	-	-	64.4
PartLoss [23]	88.2	-	-	69.3
DPFL [1]	88.9	-	-	73.1
GLAD [24]	89.9	-	-	79.3
Ours	90.0	**96.2**	**97.2**	74.5
Ours+RK	**91.8**	95.7	96.9	**88.0**

Table 3. Comparison with state of the art methods on CUHK03-detected. rank-1 accuracy (%) and mAP (%) are shown.

Methods	R-1	R-5	R-10	mAP
Bow+kissme [8]	6.4	-	-	6.4
LOMO+XQDA [25]	12.8	-	-	11.5
SVDNet [16]	41.5	-	-	37.5
PAN [17]	36.3	-	-	34.0
DPFL [1]	40.7	-	-	37.0
SVDNet+Era [26]	48.7	-	-	43.7
Ours	50.7	71.6	78.9	47.4
Ours+RK	**57.7**	**70.8**	**79.8**	**60.0**

Table 4. The result of DukeMTMC-reID. The rank-1 accuracy (%) and mAP (%) are shown.

Methods	R-1	R-5	R-10	mAP
Bow+kissme [8]	25.13	-	-	12.17
LOMO+XQDA [25]	30.75	-	-	17.04
LSRO [10]	67.68	-	-	47.13
AttIDNet [27]	70.69	-	-	51.88
PAN [17]	71.59	-	-	51.59
ACRN [28]	72.58	-	-	51.98
SVDNet [16]	76.70	-	-	56.80
DPFL [1]	79.20	-	-	60.60
Ours	77.4	88.11	92.10	62.35
Ours+RK	**81.96**	**89.45**	**92.37**	**77.17**

4 Conclusion

To obtain discriminative features, we proposed a novel architecture named Local-Global Extraction Unit (LGEU) to exploit both part-wise and channel-wise information aiming to optimize global feature discriminative ability. LGEU is largely different from tradition methods, which either focus on local and global features, or combination of them. LGEU work more like the mechanism of activation function, such as ReLU, but it can automatically select discriminative information. Moreover, LGEU is a little bit like the SE units, which only focus on channel-wise information. While LGEU pays attention to part-based information too. Abundant experiments with state-of-the-art methods on the challenging datasets demonstrated that our method achieves favorable results in terms of rank-1 accuracy and mAP. In the next work, we would like to combine other mechanism to select crucial information for person re-identification.

Acknowledgment. This work is supported by the National Natural Science Foundation of China (61401163, 61702192).

References

1. Chen, Y., Zhu, X., Gong, S.: Person re-identification by deep learning multi-scale representations. In: Proceedings of the IEEE Conference on Computer Vision and Pattern Recognition, pp. 2590–2600. IEEE, Hawaii (2017)
2. Li, D., Chen, X., Zhang, Z., Huang, K.: Learning deep context-aware features over body and latent parts for person re-identification. In: Proceedings of the IEEE Conference on Computer Vision and Pattern Recognition, pp. 384–393. IEEE, Hawaii (2017)
3. Chen, W., Chen, X., Zhang, J., Huang, K.: A multi-task deep network for person re-identification. In: AAAI, San Francisco, vol. 1, p. 3 (2017)

4. Li, W., Zhao, R., Xiao, T., Wang, X.: DeepReID: deep filter pairing neural network for person re-identification. In: IEEE Conference on Computer Vision and Pattern Recognition, pp. 152–159. IEEE, Hawaii (2014)
5. Su, C., Li, J., Zhang, S., Xing, J., Gao, W., Tian, Q.: Pose-driven deep convolutional model for person re-identification. In: 2017 IEEE International Conference on Computer Vision (ICCV), pp. 3980–3989. IEEE, Venice (2017)
6. Nair, V., Hinton, G.E.: Rectified linear units improve restricted Boltzmann machines. In: Proceedings of the 27th International Conference on machine learning (ICML-2010), Haifa, pp. 807–814 (2010)
7. Hu, J., Shen, L., Sun, G.: Squeeze-and-excitation networks. In: Proceedings of the IEEE International Conference on Computer Vision. IEEE, Venice (2017)
8. Zheng, L., Shen, L., Tian, L., Wang, S., Wang, J., Tian, Q.: Scalable person reidentification: a benchmark. In: Proceedings of the IEEE International Conference on Computer Vision, pp. 1116–1124. IEEE, Santiago (2015)
9. Wang, Z., Ren, J., Zhang, D., Sun, M., Jiang, J.: A deep-learning based feature hybrid framework for spatiotemporal saliency detection inside videos. Neurocomputing **287**, 68–83 (2018)
10. Zheng, Z., Zheng, L., Yang, Y.: Unlabeled samples generated by GAN improve the person re-identification baseline in vitro. In: 2017 IEEE International Conference on Computer Vision (ICCV), pp. 3774–3782. IEEE, Venice (2017)
11. Ristani, E., Solera, F., Zou, R., Cucchiara, R., Tomasi, C.: Performance measures and a data set for multi-target, multi-camera tracking. In: Hua, G., Jégou, H. (eds.) ECCV 2016. LNCS, vol. 9914, pp. 17–35. Springer, Cham (2016). https://doi.org/10.1007/978-3-319-48881-3_2
12. Zhong, Z., Zheng, L., Cao, D., Li, S.: Re-ranking person re-identification with k-reciprocal encoding. In: Computer Vision and Pattern Recognition (CVPR), pp. 3652–3661. IEEE, Hawaii (2017)
13. Jose, C., Fleuret, F.: Scalable metric learning via weighted approximate rank component analysis. In: Leibe, B., Matas, J., Sebe, N., Welling, M. (eds.) ECCV 2016. LNCS, vol. 9909, pp. 875–890. Springer, Cham (2016). https://doi.org/10.1007/978-3-319-46454-1_53
14. Karanam, S., Gou, M., Wu, Z., Rates-Borras, A., Camps, O., Radke, R.J.: A comprehensive evaluation and benchmark for person re-identification: features, metrics, and datasets. arXiv preprint arXiv:1605.09653 (2016)
15. Barbosa, I.B., Cristani, M., Caputo, B., Rognhaugen, A., Theoharis, T.: Looking beyond appearances: synthetic training data for deep CNNs in re-identification. arXiv preprint arXiv:1701.03153, 2017
16. Sun, Y., Zheng, L., Deng, W., Wang, S.: SVDNet for pedestrian retrieval. In: Proceedings of the IEEE Conference on Computer Vision and Pattern Recognition. IEEE, Hawaii (2017)
17. Zheng, Z., Zheng, L., Yang, Y.: Pedestrian alignment network for large-scale person re-identification. In: 2017 IEEE International Conference on Computer Vision (ICCV. IEEE, Venice (2017)
18. Cheng, D., Gong, Y., Zhou, S., Wang, J., Zheng, N.: Person re-identification by multi-channel parts-based CNN with improved triplet loss function. In: Proceedings of the IEEE Conference on Computer Vision and Pattern Recognition, pp. 1335–1344. IEEE, Nevada (2016)
19. Zhao, L., Li, X., Wang, J., Zhuang, Y.: Deeply-learned part-aligned representations for person re-identification. In: 2017 IEEE International Conference on Computer Vision (ICCV). IEEE, Venice (2017)

20. Li, W., Zhu, X., Gong, S.: Person re-identification by deep joint learning of multiloss classification. In: International Joint Conference on Artificial Intelligence (2017)
21. Zaihidee, E.M., Ghazali, K.H., Ren, J., Salleh, M.Z.: A hybrid thermal-visible fusion for outdoor human detection. J. Telecommun. Electron. Comput. Eng. (JTEC) **10**(1–4), 79–83 (2018)
22. Ren, J., Jiang, J., Wang, D., Ipson, S.: Fusion of intensity and inter-component chromatic difference for effective and robust colour edge detection. IET Image Process. **4**(4), 294–301 (2010)
23. Yao, H., Zhang, S., Zhang, Y., Li, J., Tian, Q.: Deep representation learning with part loss for person re-identification. arXiv preprint arXiv:1707.00798 (2017)
24. Wei, L., Zhang, S., Yao, H., Gao, W., Tian, Q.: Glad: global-local-alignment descriptor for pedestrian retrieval. In: Proceedings of the 2017 ACM on Multimedia Conference, pp. 420–428. ACM (2017)
25. Liao, S., Hu, Y., Zhu, X., Li, S.Z.: Person re-identification by local maximal occurrence representation and metric learning. In: Proceedings of the IEEE Conference on Computer Vision and Pattern Recognition, pp. 2197–2206. IEEE, Boston (2015)
26. Zhong, Z., Zheng, L., Kang, G., Li, S., Yang, Y.: Random erasing data augmentation. arXiv preprint arXiv:1708.04896 (2017)
27. Lin, Y., Zheng, L., Zheng, Z., Wu, Y., Yang, Y.: Improving person re-identification by attribute and identity learning. arXiv preprint arXiv:1703.07220 (2017)
28. Schumann, A., Stiefelhagen, R.: Person re-identification by deep learning attribute complementary information. In: Computer Vision and Pattern Recognition Workshops (CVPRW), pp. 1435–1443. IEEE, Hawaii (2017)
29. Zhang, X., et al.: AlignedReID: surpassing human-level performance in person reidentification. arXiv preprint arXiv:1711.08184 (2017)
30. Yan, Y., et al.: Cognitive fusion of thermal and visible imagery for effective detection and tracking of pedestrians in videos. Cogn. Comput. **10**(1), 94–104 (2018)

Robust Image Corner Detection Based on Maximum Point-to-Chord Distance

Yarui He(✉), Yunhong Li, and Weichuan Zhang

Xi'an Polytechnic University, Xi'an 710048, China
heyarui0202@163.com

Abstract. This paper first analysed the state-of-the-art corner detection algorithms and then proposed a novel corner detection approach based on a maximum point-to-chord distance. The proposed corner detector consists of three steps: First, several curves of original image is extracted using Canny edge detector. Second, a method of maximum point-to-chord distance is used in each curve to get the initial corner points. Third, non-maximum suppression and threshold are used to remove corner points with low curvature and get the final result. Different from the CPDA (chord-to-point distance accumulation) corner detector, our proposed detector neither need to accumulate each distance from a moving chord, nor need to computer the accumulation of each point in a curve, therefore achieves better speed while keeping the good average repeatability and accuracy. Compared with the existing methods, the proposed detector attains better performance on average repeatability and localization error under affine transforms, JPEG compression and Gaussian noise.

Keywords: Corner detection · Point-to-chord distance
Non-maximum suppression

1 Introduction

Corner points in images represent critical information in describing object features, which play a crucial and irreplaceable role in computer vision and image processing. Many computer vision tasks rely on the successful detection of corner points, including image matching, object recognition and object tracking, image retrieval, 3-D reconstruction, [1–4] etc. Feature tracking are also a fundamental problem of image processing research. In tracking problem, a set of efficient algorithms [5–10] are proposed for tracking salient objects from images and videos.

However, there still not exists a strict mathematical definition for corners; corners are in the past decades, a substantial number of promising corner detection methods based upon the different corner definitions have been proposed by vision researchers. The existing corner detection methods can be broadly classified into two classes: intensity-based [12–19] and contour-based methods [21–27]. The presence of two categories methods have their strengths and weaknesses, which makes the corner detection become research hotspot in the field of computer vision and image processing.

J. Ren et al. (Eds.): BICS 2018, LNAI 10989, pp. 412–421, 2018.
https://doi.org/10.1007/978-3-030-00563-4_40

This paper is organized as follows. Section 2 gives a systematic review of state-of-the-art corner detection methods. Section 3 presents the new corner detector with detailed flowchart. Section 4 shows the comparison results of the proposed corner detector with other three popular detectors in the respect of repeatability and localization accuracy under affine transforms, JPEG compression and Gaussian noise. Finally, a conclusion is given.

2 Literature Survey

This section presents a review of the existing literature on corner detection methods. In the literature, the terms "point feature", "dominant point", "critical point" and "corner" are taken as equivalent. However, the terms "interest point" and "salient point" include not only "corner", but also junctions and blobs, as well as significant texture variation [11].

2.1 Intensity-Based Methods

The key of the intensity-based corner detection is to extract gray-variation and structural information. Moravec [12] considered corners as points which are not self-similar in an image. Harris and Stephens [13] presented an operation by modifying the Moravec's interest operator, using the first order derivative to approximate the second derivatives. Lowe [14] proposed a scale invariant feature transform (SIFT), which combines a scale invariant region detector and a descriptor based upon on the gradient distribution in the detected region. Bay et al. [15] presented SURF detector that locates the feature points at which the determinant of the Hessian reaches its maximum. Meanwhile, the low complexity is enabled by employing the box filters and the integral images. Leutenegger et al. [16] proposed BRISK detector, a method for key point detection, description and matching. Later, KAZE detector [17] finds local extreme by diffusing filtering, which is used to provide multi scale spaces and preserves natural image boundaries. Ramakrishnan et al. [18] introduced a novel technique to accelerate the Harris corner detectors, which using simple approximations to quickly prune away non-corners. Wang et al. [19] implemented an adaptive Harris corner detection algorithm based on the iterative threshold; the technique was an improvement of the Harris corner detection algorithm.

2.2 Contour-Based Methods

Contour-based methods first obtain image's planar curves by some edge detector (e.g., Canny edge detector [20]) and then analyze the properties of the contours' shape to detect corners. Thereafter, the points of local curvature maxima, line intersects or rapid changes in the edge direction are marked as corners. Kitchen and Rosenfeld [21] developed a corner measure based upon the change of gradient direction along an edge contour multiplied by the local gradient magnitude as follows:

$$C_{KR}(x,y) = \frac{I_{xx}I_y^2 - 2I_{xy}I_xI_y + I_{yy}I_x^2}{I_x^2 + I_y^2}. \quad (1)$$

Later, Mokhtarian and Suomela [22] proposed a curvature scale space (CSS) corner detector. For a given parametric vector equation of a planar curve $\Gamma(u) = \{x(u), y(u)\}$, the curvature is defined as

$$K(u,\sigma) = \frac{\dot{X}(u,\sigma)\ddot{Y}(u,\sigma) - \ddot{X}(u,\sigma)\dot{Y}(u,\sigma)}{\left[\dot{X}(u,\sigma)^2 + \dot{Y}(u,\sigma)^2\right]^{3/2}} \quad (2)$$

Where,

$$\begin{aligned} \dot{X}(u,\sigma) &= x(u) \otimes \dot{g}(u,\sigma) \quad & \ddot{X}(u,\sigma) &= x(u) \otimes \ddot{g}(u,\sigma) \\ \dot{Y}(u,\sigma) &= y(u) \otimes \dot{g}(u,\sigma) \quad & \ddot{Y}(u,\sigma) &= y(u) \otimes \ddot{g}(u,\sigma) \end{aligned} \quad (3)$$

Here, $\otimes$ is the convolution operator, σ is the scale factor, $\dot{g}(u,\sigma)$ and $\ddot{g}(u,\sigma)$ are the first- and second derivatives of Gaussian $g(u,\sigma)$, respectively. To improve corner localization and noise suppression, an enhanced CSS algorithm [23] is proposed by using different scales of the CSS for contours with different length. He and Yung [24] used an adaptive curvature threshold in a dynamic region of support to judge corners. The chord-to-distance accumulation technique [25] is applied to compute curvature and detect corners. Zhang and Shui [26] presented a contour-based corner detector using the angle difference of the principal directions of anisotropic Gaussian directional derivatives (ANDDs) on contours. Lin et al. [27] introduced two novel corner detectors to measure the response of contour points using Manhattan distance and Euclidean distance.

3 Proposed Corner Detector

In this section, we give a new corner detection method using a maximum point-to-chord distance. Like the most contour-based methods, our proposed corner detector first uses Canny to extract image's planar curves. Then the maximum point-to-chord distance algorithm is applied to each curve to estimate an initial corner point. Next, the curvature on each initial corner point is computed. Finally, non-maximum suppression and threshold are used to remove weak corner points with low curvature and the final corner points are detected.

3.1 Planar Curves Extraction

Canny edge detector is one of the most widely used edge detectors in contour-based corner detectors and has also become a standard gauge in edge detection. An edge pixel is defined as if the gradient magnitudes at either side of it are lower than itself. However, the output contours may have small gaps and these gaps may possibly contain corners. These small gaps are formed because of two main reasons. First, the gradient magnitudes around junctions become very small, which results in the exclusion of junctions from the edge map. Although in some branching edges, the gradient magnitudes are not small but the maximal value is not at the gradient direction which will be discarded after the non-maximum suppression. Therefore, filling the small gaps between contours before corner detection is a necessary work to avoid loss of corners.

3.2 The Maximum Point-to-Chord Distance

After we extract the planar curves from the Sect. 3.1, we use a maximum point-to-chord distance method to select the corner point on the image. The detailed algorithm is outlined as follows:

1. Let C be a set of N discrete point P_1 to P_N that compose a curve in sequence $C = \{P_1, P_2, P_3, \ldots, P_N\}$.
2. Connect P_1 and P_N with a line, so we get a chord $L_{1,N}$.
3. The perpendicular distance of all points in the curve C to the chord $L_{1,N}$ is measured, denoted as $D = \{D_{1,L}, D_{2,L}, D_{3,L}, \ldots, D_{N,L}\}$.
4. Find the maximal distance D_{max} in D and the corresponding point P_{max}.
5. If the maximal distance D_{max} is beyond a threshold T_{min}, mark the corresponding point P_{max} as a corner point, and divide the curve C into two curves C_1 and C_2.
6. Repeat the step 1–6 for C_1 and C_2, until the maximal distance D_{max} is below a threshold T_{min} (Fig. 1).

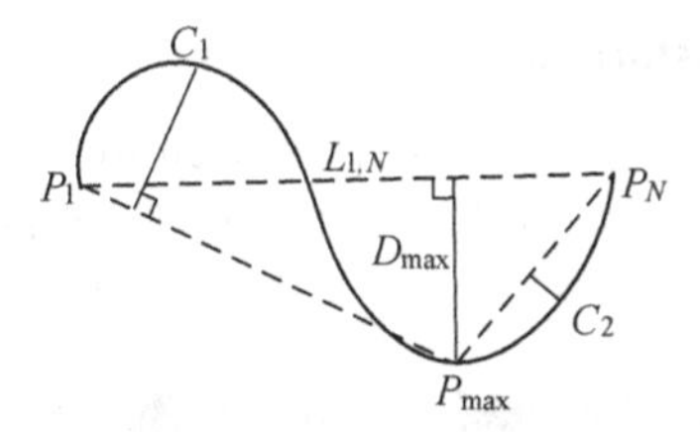

Fig. 1. Diagrammatic sketch of point-to-chord distance calculation

3.3 False Corner Removal

After the maximum point-to-chord distance algorithm that presented in Sect. 3.2, we got a series of initial corner points. Although the threshold T_{min} prevents the weak corner to be selected, there are still some occasions that our algorithm could choose some weak corner as the output corner points. These false corners have a common characteristic that they are located in flat curves, which have low curvature value. Thus, by removing the initial corner with low curvature value, the false corners could be eliminated. After the curvature of each corner point been computed, the non-maximum suppression algorithm and a threshold are used to suppress the corner points with small curvature and too close to other corner points. Figure 2 shows the false corner removal result.

Fig. 2. False corner removal

4 Experimental Results and Performance Evaluation

In this section, we focus on experiments and performance evaluation. The proposed detector is compared with three popular detectors (Harris [13], BRISK [16], He and Yung [24] and CPDA [25]). The average repeatability and localization error is used to evaluation the four detectors including our proposed detector with no manual intervention. The evaluation programmer can be running on any size of database, apply basic transformations like rotation, scaling, shear, image quality compression and Gaussian noise. Each image in the input database is applied these transformations and the average repeatability and localization error are computed for each detector. Finally, the average repeatability and localization error curves are drawn to have a visualized performance comparison of each detector.

4.1 Database and Transformation

As can be seen from Fig. 3, fifteen images collected from standard evaluation dataset [29] are used to evaluate the four detectors including our proposed detector.

Fig. 3. Fifteen standard test images

Each image from the dataset is transformed by the following six types of transformations:

1. Rotations: Rotate from −90° to 90° in 10° increments for each transformation.
2. Uniform Scaling: Scale factors $s_x = s_y$, in 0.1 increments from 0.5 to 2.0.
3. Non-uniform Scaling: Scale factors $s_x = 1$ and s_y in 0.1 increments from 0.5 to 2.0.
4. Shear transforms: Shear factor c in 0.1 increments from −1.0 to 1.0.

$$\begin{bmatrix} x' \\ y' \end{bmatrix} = \begin{bmatrix} 1 & c \\ 0 & 1 \end{bmatrix} \begin{bmatrix} x \\ y \end{bmatrix}$$

5. JPEG quality compression: JPEG quality factor in 5% increments from 5% to 100%.
6. Gaussian noise: zero mean white Gaussian noise at 15 standard deviation in [1, 15] at 1 apart.

4.2 Evaluation Criterion

We employ the performance evaluation metrics that used in [28]. The average repeatability and localization error represent the robustness and consistency of the detectors under different transformations that we introduced in 4.1.

The average repeatability R_{avg} measures the average number of detected corner point in the same position between original images and transformed images. It is defined as

$$R_{avg} = (1/2) \times N_r \times (1/N_o + 1/N_t). \tag{4}$$

Where N_o and N_t denote the number of interest point from original images and transformed images respectively. N_r is the number of repeated interest points between them. Let p_i be one of the corner point detected in the original images, q_j be the corner point detected in the corresponding geometric transformed image.

The localization error L_e is defined as the average distance between the corner points detected in the original images with those detected in the transformed images.

$$L_e = \sqrt{\frac{1}{N_r} \sum_{i=1}^{N_r} (x_{oi} - x_{ti})^2 + (y_{oi} - y_{ti})^2}. \tag{5}$$

Where (x_{oi}, y_{oi}) and (x_{oi}, y_{oi}) are the location of repeated corner i in the original and transformed images respectively.

4.3 Summary of the Proposed Parameter Setting

In this subsection, we summarized the proposed parameter setting. The parameters T_{min} and the non-maximum suppression threshold were decided by experimentation. Figure 4 shows the effect of the point-to-chord distance T_{min} on the proposed corner detector. When it was set small, the average repeatability was relatively high, but its robustness to localization was quite low. However, when it was increased above 6, both the average repeatability and localization error remain stable. Therefore, we have chosen $T_{min} = 6$ as default for the detector. Figure 5 shows the average repeatability did not change much. Thus, we selected the parameter produced the least localization error as default value.

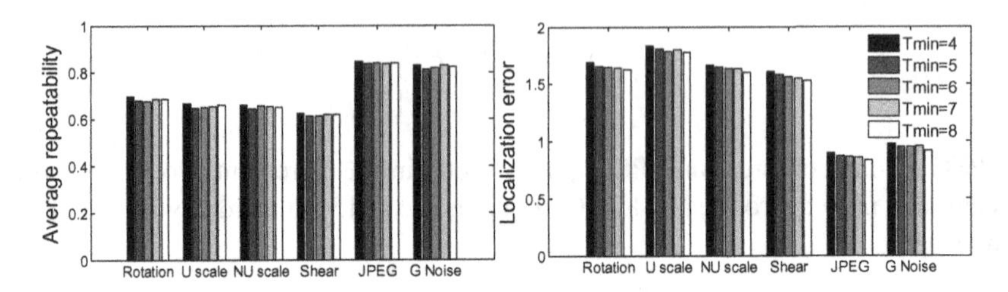

Fig. 4. The effect of threshold $T_{\min}$ on the new corner detector

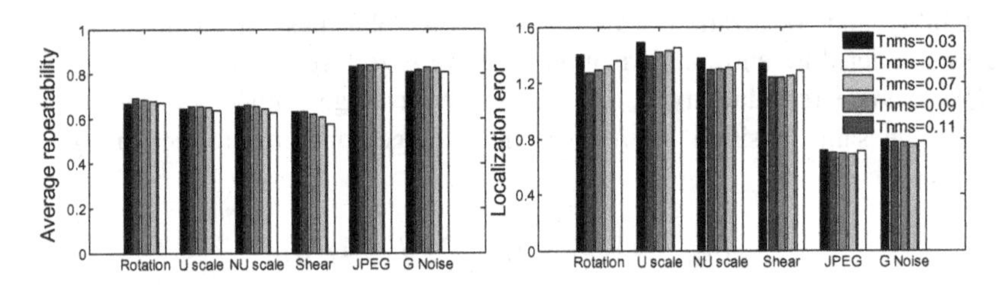

Fig. 5. The effect of threshold T_{nms} on the new corner detector

4.4 Comparative Results

In this section, a comparison of the average repeatability and localization error between the proposed and three other detectors (Harris [13], BRISK [16], He and Yung [24] and CPDA [25]) are presented.

The results of the average repeatability and localization error under six different transforms are shown in Fig. 6. In general, the four corner detectors achieved the highest average repeatability in JPEG quality compression and the worst localization error in shear transformation. The proposed and CPDA corner detectors performed better than other detectors in geometric transformations. In terms of JPEG quality compression and Gaussian noise, the proposed method achieves the highest average repeatability and lowest localization error than other three detectors. The experimental results show that the proposed detector attains better overall performance.

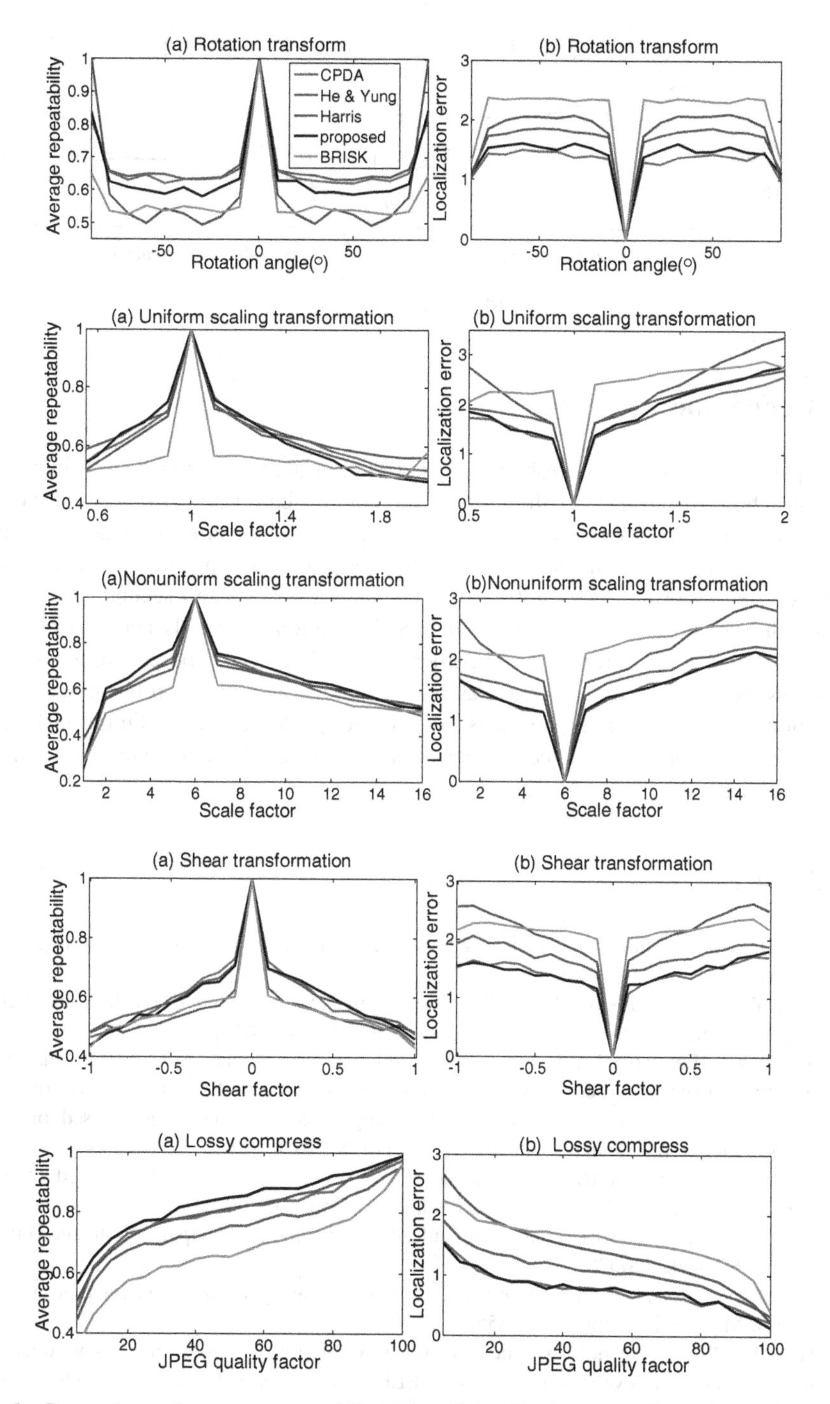

Fig. 6. Comparison of average repeatability (a) and localization error (b) under six different transforms

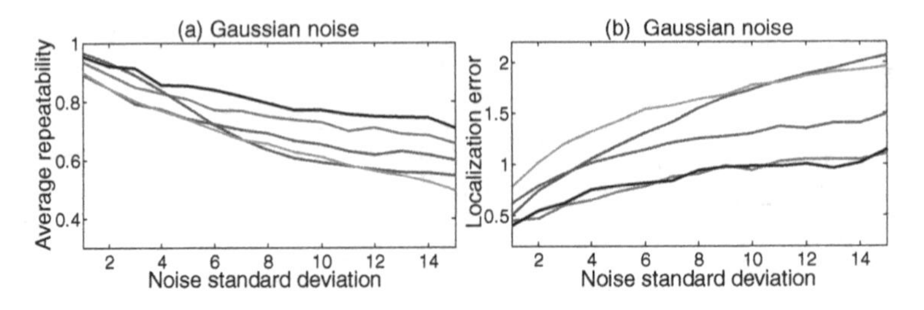

Fig. 6. *(continued)*

5 Conclusion

This paper proposed a new robust corner detection algorithm based on a maximum point-to-chord distance. Like the most of the contour-based corner detectors, the first step is to extract the edge map of original image and extracts edge contours from it. Compared with the existing corner detection algorithms based on curvature calculation, the proposed algorithm does not need to calculate the first- and second- derivatives, avoids the calculation error caused by the local variation effectively and very robust to noise. It can be seen from the experiment result that the proposed corner detector performs better than other three classical detectors in term of robustness. Corner detection algorithm of this paper has good detection performance. Future tasks may continuously improve its detection performance and apply it in many of computer vision research.

References

1. Zhu, J., Wu, S.: Multi-image matching for object recognition. IET Comput. Vis. **12**(3), 350–356 (2018)
2. Yan, Y.: Cognitive fusion of thermal and visible imagery for effective detection and tracking of pedestrians in videos. Cognit. Comput. **10**(1), 94–104 (2018)
3. Zhou, Y.: Hierarchical visual perception and two-dimensional compressive sensing for effective content-based color image retrieval. Cognit. Comput. **8**(5), 877–889 (2016)
4. Bi, Y.X., Wei, S.M.: 3D reconstruction of high-speed moving targets based on HRR measurements. IET Radar Sonar Navig. **11**(5), 778–787 (2017)
5. Ren, J.: Real-time modeling of 3-D soccer ball trajectories from multiple fixed cameras. IEEE Trans. Circuits Syst. Video Technol. **18**(3), 350–362 (2008)
6. Ren, J.: Tracking the soccer ball using multiple fixed cameras. Comput. Vis. Image Underst. **113**(5), 633–642 (2009)
7. Ren, J.: Multi-camera video surveillance for real-time analysis and reconstruction of soccer games. Mach. Vis. Appl. **21**(6), 855–863 (2010)
8. Han, J.: Object detection in optical remote sensing images based on weakly supervised learning and high-level feature learning. IEEE Trans. Geosci. Remote Sens. **53**(6), 3325–3337 (2015)
9. Liu, Q.: Decontaminate feature for tracking: adaptive tracking via evolutionary feature subset. J. Electron. Imaging **26**(6), 025–063 (2017)

10. Wang, Z.: A deep-learning based feature hybrid framework for spatiotemporal saliency detection inside videos. Neuro Comput. **287**, 68–83 (2018)
11. Mikolajczyk, K., Schmid, C.: Indexing based on scale invariant interest points. In: Proceedings of Eighth International Conference on Computer Vision, pp. 525–531 (2001)
12. Moravec, H. P.: Towards automatic visual obstacle avoidance. In: Proceedings of 5th International Joint Conference on Artificial Intelligence, p. 584 (1977)
13. Harris, C., Stephens, M.: A combined corner and edge detector. In: Proceedings of Alvey Vision Conference, University of Manchester, pp. 147–151 (1988)
14. Lowe, D.: Distinctive image features from scale-invariant keypoints. Int. J. Comput. Vis. **2** (60), 91–110 (2004)
15. Bay, H., Ess, A.: Speeded-up robust features (SURF). Comput. Vis. Image Underst. **110**(3), 346–359 (2008)
16. Leutenegger, S., Chli, M., Siegwart, R. Y.: BRISK: binary robust invariant scalable keypoints. In: IEEE International Conference on Computer Vision (ICCV), pp. 6–13 (2011)
17. Alcantarilla, P. F., Bartoli, A., Davison, A. J.: Kaze features. In: Proceedings of European Conference on Pattern Recognition, (ECCV), pp. 214–227 (2012)
18. Ramakrishnan, N., Wu, M.Q., Lam, S.K.: Enhanced low-complexity pruning for corner detection. J. Real-Time Image Proc. **1**(1), 197–213 (2016)
19. Wang, Z. C., Li, R.: Adaptive Harris corner detection algorithm based on iterative threshold. Modern Phys. Lett. B **31**(15) (2017)
20. Canny, J.: A computational approach to edge detection. IEEE Trans. Pattern Anal. Mach. Intell. **8**(6), 679–698 (1986)
21. Kitchen, L., Rosenfeld, A.: Gray-level corner detection. Pattern Recogn. Lett. **1**(2), 95–102 (1982)
22. Mokhtarian, F., Suomela, R.: Robust image corner detection through curvature scale space. IEEE Trans. Pattern Anal. Mach. Intell. **20**(12), 1376–1381 (1998)
23. Mokhtarian, F., Mohanna, F.: Enhancing the curvature scale space corner detector. In: Proceedings of Scandinavian Conference on Image Analysis, pp. 145–152 (2001)
24. He, X.C., Yung, N.H.C.: Corner detector based on global and local curvature properties. Opt. Eng. **47**(5), 1–12 (2008)
25. Awrangjeb, M., Lu, G.: Robust image corner detection based on the chord-to-point distance accumulation technique. IEEE Trans. Multimedia **10**(6), 1059–1072 (2008)
26. Zhang, W.C., Shui, P.L.: Contour-based corner detection via angle difference of principal directions of anisotropic Gaussian directional derivatives. Pattern Recognit. **48**(9), 2785–2797 (2015)
27. Lin, X.Y., Zhu, C., Zhang, Q., et al.: Efficient and robust corner detectors based on second-order difference of contour. IEEE Signal Process. Lett. **24**(9), 1393–1397 (2017)
28. Schmid, C., Mohr, R., Bauckhage, C.: Evaluation of interest point detectors. IJCV **37**(2), 151–172 (2000)
29. The Image Database. http://figment.csee.usf.edu/edge/roc

Fabric Defect Detection Based on Sparse Representation Image Decomposition

Jun-Feng Jing(✉), Hao Ma, and Zhuo-Mei Liu

Xi'an Polytechnic University, 19th of Jinhua South Road, Xi'an, China
jingjunfeng0718@qq.com

Abstract. Due to the distribution of fabric defect shown the sparseness, it is possible to describe the fabric defects feature using sparse representation in particular transform. In this paper, we proposed a novel approach based on sparse representation for detecting patterned fabric defect. In our work, the defective fabric image is expressed by sparse representation model, it is represented as a linear superposition of three components: defect, background and noise. The defective components can be decomposed effectively by using the principle of base pursuit denoising algorithm and block coordination relaxation algorithm. The fabric defect detection is realized by analyzing the defect components. Experimental results demonstrate that the proposed approach is more efficient to detect a variety of fabric defects, in particularly the pattern fabrics.

Keywords: Patterned fabric · Defect detection · Sparse representation
Blind source separation · Morphological component analysis

1 Introduction

Chinese textile industry competition is becoming increasingly as well as the rapid development of science and technology. Effective detection and control of textile surface defects are of the key link to modern textile enterprises, controlling costs and improving product competitiveness. The traditional fabric defect detection methods are mainly done by manual work, which will result in false detection, missed detection and low detection rate, as well as waste a lot of manpower and material resources. Therefore, it is of great significance to develop an efficient, reliable and accurate automatic fabric defect detection algorithm.

Until now, many effective detection algorithms have been proposed for fabric defect detection, which can be broadly classified into three categories: statistical, spectral and model-based [1]. The objective of defect detection based on statistical approaches is to separate the defect area of the inspection image from the background texture. The general algorithms are fractal dimension, gray level co-occurrence matrix, morphological, and cross correlation belong to this category. In an earlier work, the one-dimensional fractal extraction fabric feature is used to realize the detection of defects, and the contrast efficiency greatly improves the efficiency of feature extraction [2]. The statistical histogram and the gray level co-occurrence matrix are used in to extract fabric texture features, and 27 types of defects were detected [3]. The detection success rate was 93.1%. In reference [4], semi-supervised sparse representation-based

J. Ren et al. (Eds.): BICS 2018, LNAI 10989, pp. 422–429, 2018.
https://doi.org/10.1007/978-3-030-00563-4_41

classification for face recognition is proposed, which faces are represented in terms of two dictionaries. Zhao et al. [5] used the improved sparse representation approaches for effective target detection in hyperspectral imagery. To solve the problem of improper random weights, in reference [6], the sparse representation is employed to derive the optimized output weights. Liu et al. [7] proposed a weighted joint sparse representation (WJSR) model to simultaneously encode a set of data samples, which can reduce the influence of outliers.

This paper presents a novel of fabric defect detection that based on sparse representation. We use non decimated wavelets (UWT) to construct defect dictionaries and local discrete cosine transform (LDCT) to construct background dictionaries. The classification of the background and the detection target. The method of sparse representation of defective images based on the distribution of fabric defect shown the sparseness, the blind source separation theory and the morphological composition analysis. Under the sparse representation conditions, the image features are characterized with the simplest sparse structure. The dictionary maximizes the overall structural features of the extracted image. The sparse coefficient uses the few nonzero vectors to cover the details of the image and the edge characteristics. Not only simplifies the process of fabric image processing, while ensuring the diversity of fabric inspection defects and accurate and effective.

The main contributions of the proposed method are:

1. A novel detection algorithm is proposed for fabric defect detection.
2. It enables to efficiently cope with several types of fabrics and defects, such as gray cloth (simple textured) and dyed-fabric (complex textures).
3. At present, the defect detection can be accurate to the level of image. The overall detection success rate of the gray cloth and dyed-fabric in this paper reach 97% and 95%, respectively.

2 Sparse Representation Model of Fabric Defect Image Separation

Assuming that the fabric defect image represents the observation vector y. The defective components and the background components represent two source signal vectors y_1 and y_2. The noise components in the image represented the additive noise vector v. According to Fig. 1, which the linear instantaneous mixing model in the blind source separation [8]. In the Fig. 1, S_n represents the superposition of n source signals. Likewise, n_m, x_m, and y_m represent noise, observed signals and separated signals, respectively. The mathematical model of the fabric defect image is:

$$y = y_1 + y_2 + v \tag{1}$$

The sparseness is an important feature of defective images, so defective images can be sparse represented in a particular transformation. Assuming that there are two dictionaries A_1 and A_2, which can be sparse representation for the defective components and the background components respectively, the model is [9]:

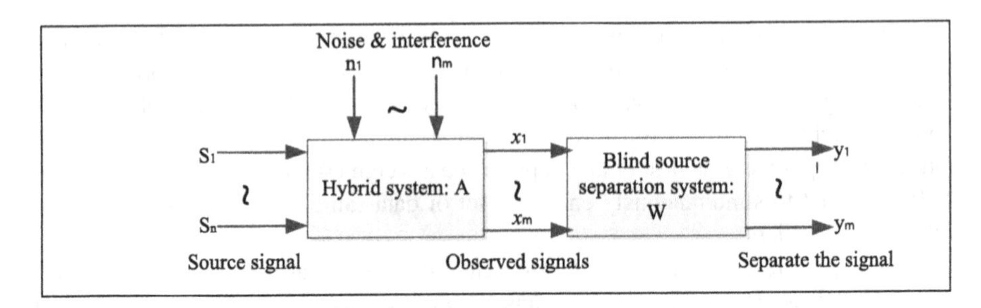

Fig. 1. Linear instantaneous blind source separation model.

$$\min\|x_1\|_0 \quad s.t. \quad y_1 = A_1x_1 \tag{2}$$

$$\min\|x_2\|_0 \quad s.t. \quad y_2 = A_2x_2 \tag{3}$$

The above formulas are sparse representation in the case of ignoring the error term.

Based on the analysis of the defective image, which can be regarded as combination of background component which is composed of a relatively strong texture, a randomly distributed defect component and an additive noise component. It can be seen from the Morphological Component analysis [10] that there are differences between the components of the defect image (i.e. the morphological components), so that the defective image can be separated. The difference in the morphological components of the defective images allows them to be sparsely represented by different dictionaries, and there are only dictionaries corresponding to sparse representations. The model can be transformed into a morphological analysis model:

$$\min\|x_1\|_0 + \|x_2\|_0 \quad s.t. \quad y = A_1x_1 + A_2x_2 \tag{4}$$

The above equation ignores the noise and error information. In order to make the above model beneficial to the calculation, the base pursuit denoising of the approximation algorithm is used to transform the nonconvex problem into convex optimization problem (i.e. replace the l_0 norm with l_1 norm) and use the error and additive noise as constraints item [11, 12]. Equation (4) is transformed into:

$$\min\|x_1\|_1 + \|x_2\|_1 \quad s.t. \quad \|y - A_1x_1 - A_2x_2\|_2^2 \le \delta \tag{5}$$

Here, the parameter δ depends on the noise and the model error of sparse representation.

After the above step-by-step analysis, we can realize that the defective components and the background components of the fabric defect image effectively separated, which is equivalent to the reconstruction of y1 and y2. Figure 2 shows the patterned image separation model of fabric based on sparse representation [13]. The sparse representation model of fabric defect image separation is obtained as follows:

$$\hat{x}_1, \hat{x}_2 = \arg\min_{x1,x2} \|x_1\|_1 + \|x_2\|_1 + \lambda \|y - A_1 x_1 - A_2 x_2\|_2^2 \tag{6}$$

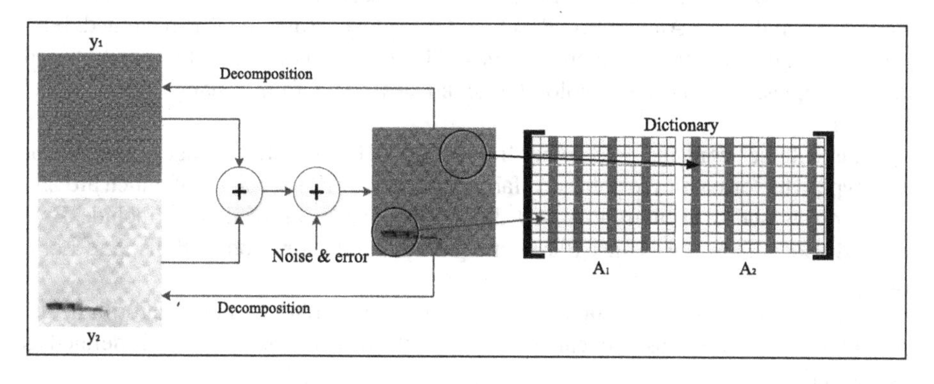

Fig. 2. Image separation model of patterned fabrics based on sparse representation.

Equation (6) is to replace the constrained optimization in [11] with an unconstrained penalized optimization. The parameter λ denotes a weighting coefficient, that is, the weight of the reconstructed error and noise. By finding the right pseudo inverse matrix of A1 and A2, the substitution, $\hat{x}_1 = A_1^{-1} y_1, \hat{x}_2 = A_2^{-1} y_2$ is used, then the model is converted to [14]:

$$\hat{y}_1, \hat{y}_2 = \arg\min_{y1,y2} \left\|A_1^{-1} y_1\right\|_1 + \left\|A_2^{-1} y_2\right\|_1 + \lambda \|y - y_1 - y_2\|_2^2 \tag{7}$$

Because the defect components have random uncertainty, it is possible to use the undecimated wavelet as the defect components dictionary. The texture of the background components is periodic, so the locally discrete cosine transform is used as the background components dictionary. In this case, since the transformed image is analyzed in the direction of the image at different scales, the smooth section and smooth edges can be obtained. So the general variation normalization is used to strengthen the quality of the defective component separation, and restrain edge ringing effect. The model is further converted to [15]:

$$\hat{y}_1, \hat{y}_2 = \arg\min_{y1,y2} \left\|A_1^{-1} y_1\right\|_1 + \left\|A_2^{-1} y_2\right\|_1 + \lambda \|y - y_1 - y_2\|_2^2 + \gamma \mathrm{TV}\{y_1\} \tag{8}$$

Where γ denotes the weighting factor of the total variation penalized optimization. Finally, the block coordinate relaxation algorithm [16] is used to solve the objective function Eq. (8), which makes the defect components and the background components get effective separation and achieve the goal of commendably dividing the defect target.

3 Experimental Results and Discussion

In order to verify the effectiveness of the proposed method, we use the MATLAB R2014a environment for testing. Patterned fabric data set is from the University of Hong Kong Industrial Automation Research Laboratory, providing star-patterned, box-patterned, and dot-patterned fabric images, TILDA database fine lattice and striped fabric samples, and the solid color fabric images come from Guang Dong Esquel Textiles.

This data set contains 100 defect-free images, 100 defective images, and 20 for each type. The format of the patterned fabric image is BMP format, all of which are 256 * 256 pixels and a resolution of 600 dpi image. The types of defects include BrokenEnd, Hole, Thin Bar, Thick Bar, Netting Multiple, Color, Cotton Balls, Sao Loss, etc.

In order to accurately evaluate the performance of our detection algorithm, the detection success rate is used to calculate. Where the detection success rate is defined as follows [17]:

$$Detection\,Success\,Rates = \frac{Number\,of\,Samples\,Correctly\,Detected}{Total\,Number\,of\,samples} \tag{9}$$

Figure 3 contains 8 defective images with 3 types of background texture, and 5 types of defect detection results. To our knowledge, fabric images with smaller texture cycle unit for example gray cloth, can be regarded as patterned fabric. Figure 4 shows the detection results of fine lattice image, gray pattern and net color cloth, which showing 9 defective images with 6 types of background texture, and 9 types of defect detection results. It can be seen from Figs. 3 and 4 that the algorithm proposed in this paper performs well, not only effective for most defects including BrokenEnd, Hole, Thin Bar, Thick Bar, Netting Multiple, Color, Cotton Balls, Sao Loss and so on, but also the location of the fabric defect and the shape of the defect details have been more accurately visualized.

We compared with the proposed method and the other two advanced defect detection algorithms including Gabor filter [18], and Sparse Coding Dictionary Learning (SCDL) [19]. The detection results of the 3 defect detection algorithms are shown in Table 1.

From the comparison of the test results shown in Table 1, the detection algorithm proposed in this paper has more obvious advantages than other detection algorithms. The main reason is that the method of this paper is to separate the image signal according to the difference of the morphological components, and can keep the information of each components well, aiming at the precise positioning and keeping the details. Under the same conditions, the detection rate of SCDL algorithm is higher than Gabor filter algorithm. The defect detection algorithm based on Gabor filter has higher requirement for parameters setting of filter. The method proposed in this paper not only recognizes the noise, but also uses the sparsity of the defect and the morphological difference of the components of the fabric defect to preserve the details and morphological characteristics of the defect, having good robustness and achieving higher detection rates.

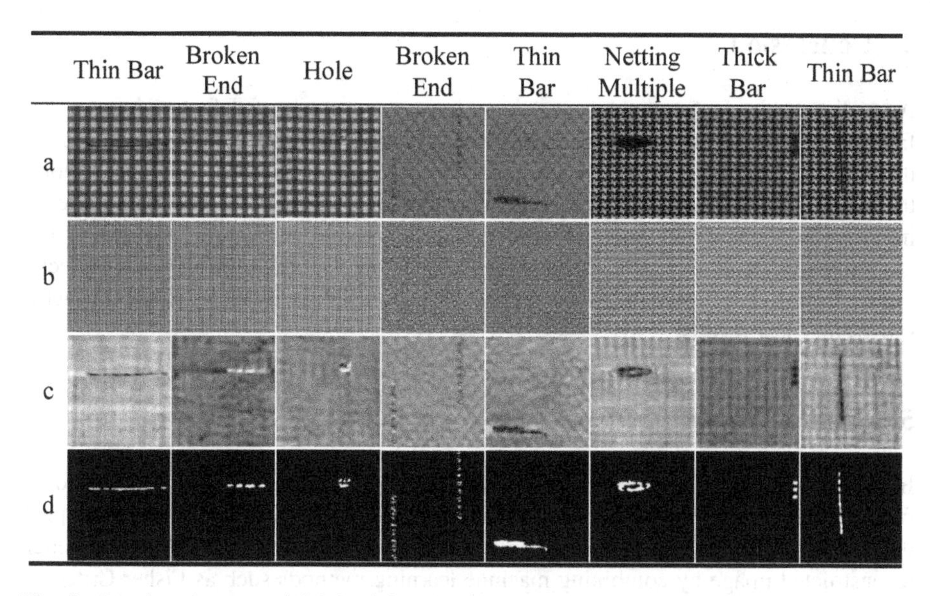

Fig. 3. Results of patterned fabric defect detected with proposed method: (a) original defect image. (b) Background image. (c) Defective components by proposed method. (d) Binary image.

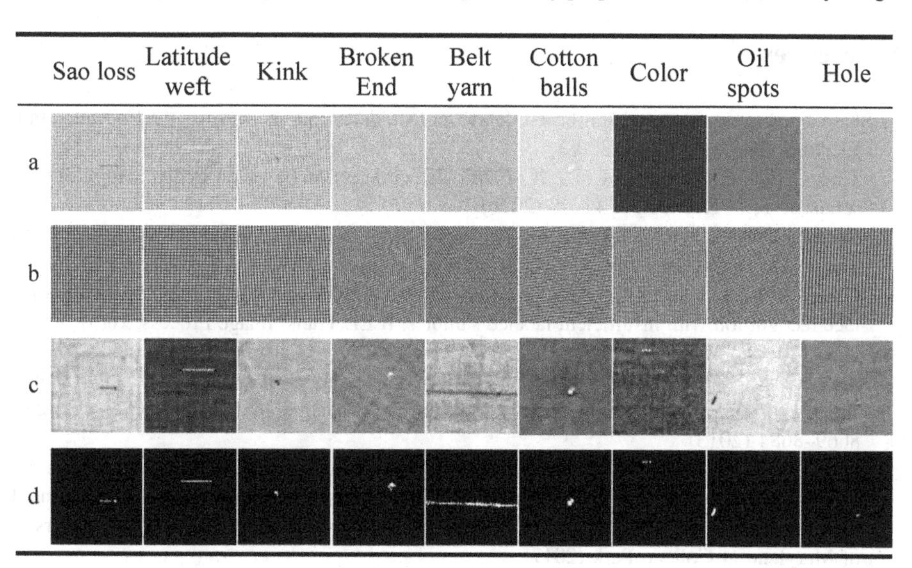

Fig. 4. Results of patterned fabric defect detected with proposed method: (a) original defect image. (B) background image. (c) Defective components by proposed method. (d) Binary image.

Table 1. The comparison of detection rate of the proposed algorithm and others.

Algorithms	Box-patterned	Star-patterned	Dot-patterned	Gray cloth
Proposed method	96%	97%	95%	97%
Gabor filter	93%	92%	90%	94%
SCDL	95%	92%	85%	95%

4 Conclusion

According to the fact that sparseness is an important feature of defective images, the fabric defect based on the sparse representation image decomposition is proposed. In this method, the components are alternately separated based on the difference among the morphological components of the defective images. Our method can preserve information of each components that including the precise positioning, the details and morphological features of the defect. It can also be applied to various types of defects, especially for complex textures texture of the pattern fabric images, which can get a satisfactory test results.

5 Future Work

Based on the results obtained in this paper, some ideas arise that can be followed as future work. One direction involves the speeding up the dictionary generation [20] process to enable real-time defect localization. The second direction is to obtain better reconstructed image by combining machine learning methods such as Fisher Criterion [21].

References

1. Kumar, A.: Computer-vision-based fabric defect detection: a survey. IEEE Trans. Ind. Electron. **55**(1), 348–363 (2008)
2. Tian, C., Bu, H., Wang, J., Chen, X.: Fabric defect detection based on fractal feature of time series. J. Text. Res. **31**(5), 44–48 (2010)
3. Selver, M.A., Avşar, V., Özdemir, H.: Textural fabric defect detection using statistical texture transformations and gradient search. J. Text. Inst. **105**(9), 998–1007 (2014)
4. Gao, Y., Ma, J., Yuille, A.L.: Semi-supervised sparse representation based classification for face recognition with insufficient labeled samples. IEEE Trans. Image Process. **26**(5), 2545–2560 (2017)
5. Zhao, C., Li, X., Ren, J., Marshall, S.: Improved sparse representation using adaptive spatial support for effective target detection in hyperspectral imagery. Int. J. Remote Sens. **34**(24), 8669–8684 (2013)
6. Cao, F., Yang, Z., Ren, J., Ling, W.: Sparse representation based augmented multinomial logistic extreme learning machine with weighted composite features for spectral spatial hyperspectral image classification. In: CVPR, pp. 1–15. eprint arXiv:1709.03792, University of Maryland at College Park (2017)
7. Liu, L., Chen, L., Chen, C., Tang, Y., Chi, M.: Weighted joint sparse representation for removing mixed noise in image. IEEE Trans. Cybern. **1**(99), 1–12 (2017)
8. Bridwell, D.A., Rachakonda, S., Rogers, F.S., Pearlson, G.D., Calhoun, V.D.: Spatiospectral decomposition of multi-subject EEG: evaluating blind source separation algorithms on real and realistic simulated data. Brain Topogr. **31**(1), 1–15 (2018)
9. Georgiev, P., Theis, F., Cichocki, A.: Sparse component analysis and blind source separation of underdetermined mixtures. IEEE Trans. Neural Netw. **16**(4), 992–996 (2005)
10. Starck, J.L., Murtagh, F., Fadili, J.: Sparse Image and Signal Processing: Wavelets, Curvelets, Morphological Diversity. Cambridge University Press, Cambridge (2010)

11. Elad, M.: From exact to approximate solutions. In: Elad, M. (ed.) Sparse and Redundant Representations. Springer, New York (2010). https://doi.org/10.1007/978-1-4419-7011-4_5
12. Sardy, S., Bruce, A.G.: Block coordinate relaxation methods for nonparamatric signal denoising. Proc. SPIE. **3391**, 75–86 (1998)
13. Starck, J.L., Elad, M., Donoho, D.L.: Image decomposition via the combination of sparse representations and a variational approach. IEEE Trans. Image Process. **14**(10), 1570–1582 (2005)
14. Ngan, H.Y.T., Pang, G.K.H., Yung, N.H.C.: Automated fabric defect detection, a review. Image Vis. Comput. **29**(7), 442–458 (2011)
15. Wright, S.J., Nowak, R.D., Figueiredo, M.A.T.: Sparse reconstruction by separable approximation. IEEE Trans. Signal Process. **57**(7), 2479–2493 (2009)
16. Elad, M., Figueiredo, M.A.T., Ma, Y.: On the role of sparse and redundant representations in image processing. Proc. IEEE **98**(6), 972–982 (2010)
17. Yuan, X., Wu, L., Peng, Q.: An improved Otsu method using the weighted object variance for defect detection. Appl. Surf. Sci. **349**, 472–484 (2015)
18. Zhang, Yu., Lu, Zhaoyang, Li, Jing: Fabric defect detection and classification using gabor filters and gaussian mixture model. In: Zha, Hongbin, Taniguchi, Rin-ichiro, Maybank, Stephen (eds.) ACCV 2009. LNCS, vol. 5995, pp. 635–644. Springer, Heidelberg (2010). https://doi.org/10.1007/978-3-642-12304-7_60
19. Liu, S., Li, P., Zhang, L., Zhang, H., Zhang, H., Jing, J.: Defect detection based on sparse coding dictionary learning. J. Xi'an Polytech. Univ. **29**(5), 594–599 (2015)
20. Xie, J., Zhang, L., You, J., Shiu, S.: Effective texture classification by texton encoding induced statistical features. Pattern Recognit. **48**(2), 447–457 (2014)
21. Li, Y., Zhao, W., Pan, J.: Deformable patterned fabric defect detection with Fisher criterion-based deep learning. IEEE Trans. Autom. Sci. Eng. **14**(2), 1256–1264 (2017)

Salient Superpixel Visual Tracking with Coarse-to-Fine Segmentation and Manifold Ranking

Jin Zhan[1,2] and Huimin Zhao[1,2](✉)

[1] School of Computer Science, Guangdong Polytechnic Normal University, Guangzhou, China
{gszhanjin, zhaohuimin}@gpnu.edu.cn

[2] The Guangzhou Key Laboratory of Digital Content Processing and Security Technologies, Guangzhou, China

Abstract. We propose a novel salient superpixel based tracking algorithm using Coarse-to-Fine segmentation on graph model, where target state is estimated by a combination of pixel-level cues and middle-level cues to achieve accurate target appearance model. We exploit temporal optical flow and color distribution characteristics as coarse grained information from pixel-level processing, and propagate to fine-grained superpixels to improve initial target appearance segmentation from bounding box annotations. Our algorithm constructs a graph model with manifold ranking by improved superpixels to estimate the saliency of target foreground and background in subsequent frames. The tracking result is located by calculating the weight of multi-scale box, where the weight depends on the similarity of scores of foreground and background superpixels in the scale box. We compared our algorithm with the existing techniques in OTB100 dataset, and achieved substantially better performance.

Keywords: Visual tracking · Superpixels · Graph model · Manifold ranking

1 Introduction

Robust visual tracking algorithm has been one of the research focuses in computer vision. The challenging task is accuracy of real-time tracking in practical and complicated video scenes. In the representation model of the target, segmentation-based tracking algorithms [3–7] mainly rely on pixel-level information such as color and gradient, or utilize external segmentation algorithms such as Grabcut [4]. Although pixel-level information almost unchanged with video sequence, it is not sufficient to model semantic structure of target. Recently, tracking-by-detection methods [8–11] use target texture or other high-level features, build classifier to distinguish the target and the background. However, they typically depend on bounding boxes for target representations, and often easy to lose the targets details and suffer from drifting problem.

Superpixels are middle-level cues which contain the local structure information of target visual characteristics, and are closer to the basic perception when people understand the image. Many computer vision tasks have used superpixels to represent the interest objects in the image, such as object segmentation [20], object recognition

J. Ren et al. (Eds.): BICS 2018, LNAI 10989, pp. 430–440, 2018.
https://doi.org/10.1007/978-3-030-00563-4_42

[21], human posture estimation [22, 23], and saliency detection [1, 24, 25]. Since a superpixel can be treated as a whole, using superpixels can greatly reduce the computation time of sophisticated image processing, and have flexibility compared with high level and low level features.

In visual tracking problem, Wang et al. [12] proposed superpixel based tracking in 2011, and trained a Bayesian classifier by using Meanshift clustering. Then Yang et al. [13] incorporate particle filtering to find the optimal target by superpixel tracking. However, since both methods achieve accurate tracking results in the process of occlusion and scale change, they are slow to run. The main cost is to cluster the super pixels and the spatio-temporal relations between superpixels are not considered. To overcome the limitation induced from the flat representations, Zhou et al. [14] propose a level set tracking method based on a discriminative speed function, which produces a superpixel driven force for effective level set evolution. Hong et al. [15] and [16] both presented a multi-level appearance modeling which maintains pixel, superpixel and bounding box, and have improved performance in non-rigid object deformation handling and occlusions. Recently, tracking-by-segmentation algorithms that combines Graph model have been proposed [17, 18]. The edges of graph are encoded by the underlying spatial, temporal, and appearance fitness constraints. These superpixel tracking algorithms based on graph model facilitate more accurate online update when a target involves substantial non-rigid or articulated motions.

We propose a novel salient superpixel based tracking algorithm using Coarse-to-Fine segmentation on graph model. Here, coarse-grained denotes temporal optical flow information and color distribution characteristics from pixel-level processing, and are propagated to fine-grained superpixels to improve initial target appearance segmentation from bounding box annotations. Furthermore, we construct a graph model where the improved superpixels are vertices and edges are encoded by k-regular connected similarity of nodes degree. Target saliency is obtained from manifold ranking and is conducive to find target area with maximum response at the scope of target surrounding in subsequent frames.

2 Target Appearance Model by Coarse-to-Fine Segmentation

2.1 Graph Construction Based on Manifold Ranking

Based on the graph-based manifold sorting algorithm [1], we combine the two-dimensional geometric structure and color information of target to further distinguish the foreground superpixels and background superpixels.

Define a graph $G = (V, E)$, where the graph vertices V correspond to superpixels, and divided into two subsets: some vertices are defined for query point; the remaining vertices are ranked according to their relevance with the query points. Given a superpixel set $SP = \{sp_1, \ldots, sp_n\} \subset R^m$, n is the number of superpixels, m is the feature dimension. Let f: $SP \to R^m$ denote a ranking function which assigns a ranking value f_i to each point x_i, and f can be viewed as a vector $f = [f_1, \ldots, f_n]^T$. The edges E are weighted by an affinity matrix $W = [w_{ij}]_{n \times n}$. Given G, the degree matrix is $D = diag\{d_{11}, \ldots, d_{nn}\}$, where $d_i = \sum_j w_{ij}$, where the relationship matrix W is a sparse matrix since the structural relationship of vertices, adjacent vertices and vertices with shared border. The optimal rankings of queries f^* is computed by solving the following optimization problem:

$$f^* = \arg\min_f \frac{1}{2}\left(\sum_{i,j=1}^{n} w_{ij}\left\|\frac{f_i}{\sqrt{d_{ii}}} - \frac{f_j}{\sqrt{d_{jj}}}\right\|^2 + \mu\sum_{i=1}^{n}\|f_i - y_i\|^2\right) \tag{1}$$

where the parameter μ controls the balance of the smoothness constraint and the fitting constraint, $Y = [y_1, \ldots, y_n]^T$ denote an indication vector, in which $y_i = 1$ if sp_i is a query point, and $y_i = 0$ otherwise. Set the derivative of the above function to be zero, the resulted ranking function can be written as:

$$f^* = (D - \alpha w)^{-1} Y,\ \alpha = \frac{1}{1+\mu} \tag{2}$$

The weight of each edge is given by the similarity of the relevance with vertices. Considering that the same color Superpixels should have high relevance than those superpixels with different colors, and adjacent superpixels represents the spatial geometric relevance of target. The superpixels with the same color and the same connected area in spatial will have more consistent ranking fits with the target appearance, and more uniformly highlight the whole target. Therefore, we learn the edges weights by maximizing the scores between superpixels in target foreground with color distance and geometric distance. Let c_i and c_j are CIELab color distance of relevance vertices, p_i and p_j are Euclidean distance of relevance vertices, w_{ij} is computed by the following formula:

$$w_{ij} = e^{-\left(\frac{\|c_i - c_j\|}{\sigma_1^2} + \lambda\frac{\|p_i - p_j\|}{\sigma_2^2}\right)} \tag{3}$$

where λ is coefficient of balance.

2.2 Saliency Detection for Superpixels

By ranking the vertices on the constructed graph, the nonzero relevance value between superpixels can be computed. This relevance value matrix naturally captures spatial relationship information which is an important cue for saliency detection. In tracking problem, target is given in the first frame, and the center of the target is the most important foreground location. We exploit two-stage scheme for saliency detection using ranking with background and center queries [1].

Firstly, four saliency maps are constructed using boundary priors and then be integrated as the final map. Taking top image boundary as an example, the vertices on this side are the queries and other vertices as the unlabeled data. According to the ranking scores of Eq. (3), the saliency of the vertex i on top boundary is calculated.

$$S_t(i) = 1 - \bar{f}^*(i) \tag{4}$$

where $\bar{f}^*(i)$ is the ranking score normalized to [0, 1]. In the same way, the saliency $S_b(i)$, $S_l(i)$, $S_r(i)$ of the vertex i relative to the bottom, left and right boundaries can be calculated by the Eq. (4). Then, the saliency of vertex i is:

$$S_{bg}(i) = S_t(i) \times S_b(i) \times S_l(i) \times S_r(i) \tag{5}$$

Since some background superpixels may not be adequately suppressed, the saliency map is further improved via ranking with foreground queries. Literate [1] then use the adaptive threshold segmentation method for $S_{bg}(i)$, and select the foreground salient superpixels as new query points. The new ranking vector $\bar{f}'^*$ is calculated by Eq. (2) which normalized to [0, 1], and the saliency of vertex i in the first stage is:

$$S(i) = \bar{f}'^*(i) \tag{6}$$

The graph model based salient superpixel detection algorithm can provide sufficient cues to identify the interesting target.

2.3 Target Segmentation by Coarse-Grained and Fine-Grained Cues

The target information includes various contents, such as temporal relation, color distribution and texture information. The temporal relation contains the smooth motion attribute of the target on the time axis and affords coarse-grained cues such as the contour boundary of the target. In addition, the color distribution of target is relatively stable and is almost unchanged in the video sequences, which can combine with middle-level visual cues. Therefore, we expect that the final target appearance foreground is extracted by multiple connected components of superpixels within the initial coarse segmentation.

For the purpose, we adopt a Coarse-to-Fine Segmentation (see Fig. 1), where the outline boundary of target is given by motion flow from successive frames, which are learned with the layer-wise optical flow. Image segmentation with the same color is divided in color feature space, and should be coarser than those superpixels computed by the SLIC algorithm [2]. Given a superpixel set $SP = \{sp_1, \ldots, sp_n\} \subset R^m$, n is the number of superpixels. For a color segment c of image color segment set C, we defined background Boundary Length (BL) of c is the numbers of superpixels on image boundary:

$$BL(c) = \sum_{h=1}^{n} sp_h \cdot \delta_h \tag{7}$$

where δ_h is Indicator vector, when sp_h contains boundary pixels then $\delta_h = 1$, others $\delta_h = 0$. Note that the background Boundary Length (BL) of color segments is computed with different indicator vector. Obviously, a color segment with maximum BL should be the background, whereas the segment with the minimum BL is the foreground. For further divide color segments of target foreground, we incorporate the relative spatial dispersion of color segment to measure foreground connectivity. Assuming that color segment c has N pixels, we can get its center-of-mass coordinates:

$$x_c = \frac{\sum_I \sum_J i \cdot V(i,j)}{\sum_I \sum_J V(i,j)},\ y_c = \frac{\sum_I \sum_J j \cdot V(i,j)}{\sum_I \sum_J V(i,j)} \tag{8}$$

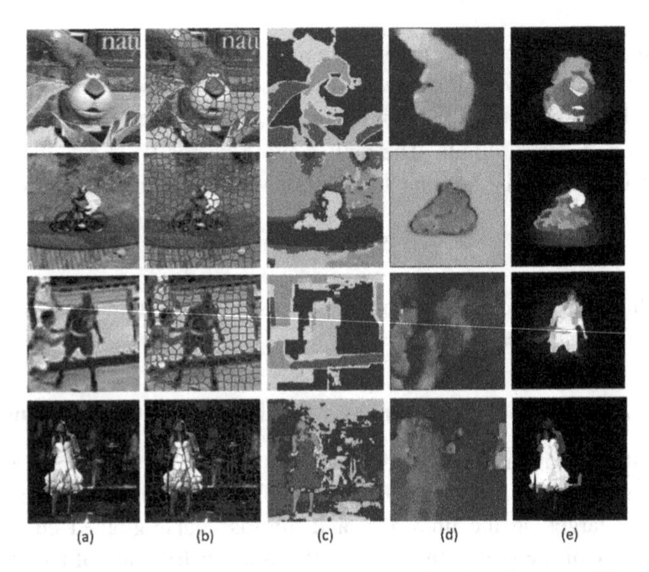

Fig. 1. Illustration of the salient target appearance procedure by Coarse-to-Fine segmentation. (a) Image; (b) Superpixels; (c) Color Segmentation; (d) Optical flow; (e) Saliency map;

Then, we define the spatial dispersion degree of color segment c is the distance between its center-of-mass and target center:

$$SD(c) = \gamma\left(\left\|x_c - I_0^x\right\| + \left\|y_c - I_0^y\right\|\right) \tag{9}$$

where I_0^x, I_0^y are image coordinates of target center, and γ is the normalizing turning parameter. While most color segments are highlighted with the superpixel patches, some background may not be adequately suppressed. To alleviate this problem and improve the results, the motion flow maps are further improved via ranking with foreground queries. A confidence of superpixel k is measured to indicate the probability of belong to the target:

$$H(k) = \gamma \cdot BL_c^k \cdot SD_c^k \cdot FL^k \cdot S(k),\ k = 1,\ldots,n \tag{10}$$

where FL^k is the motion flow maps for superpixe k. The larger score $H(k)$ of each superpixel indicates it is more likely to appear in the target foreground, and vice versa.

3 Tracking by Salient Superpixels Using Confidence Map

When a new frame arrives, we first exact a surrounding region of the target and handle it with optical flow [19], color segmentation and superpixels segmentation [2]. The target surrounding confidence map generated by the pure Coarse-to-Fine approach described in the previous subsection and may be located the target foreground as the best tracking result. To find the target location, we use multi-scale sliding window around the superpixel with the maximum confidence value. The size of multi-scale sliding window is the proportional value of the tracking result on the previous frame. Once the multi-scale sliding windows are given, we formulate a score to evaluate each sliding window. The produce is shown in Fig. 2.

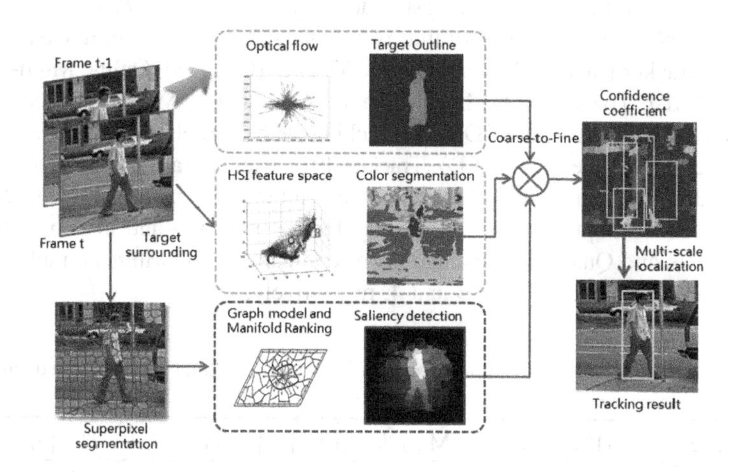

Fig. 2. The procedure of proposed algorithm using superpixel confidence map.

In confidence map, we cut the target foreground and background for superpixel by adaptive threshold segmentation algorithm Otsu [25]. Each sliding window contains different ratio of foreground and background superpixels and can be used to weight the sliding window. Let N_{fg} and N_{bg} denote the number of foreground and background superpixels in sliding window m, respectively. Then, the weight of sliding window m is given by

$$sw_m = \frac{\sum_{i=1}^{N_{fg}} area(sp_i)}{\sum_{j=1}^{N_{bg}} area(sp_j)} \tag{11}$$

where area(.) is the sum of pixels in the superpixel. However, instead of the area of the background superpixel, we employ total pixels of the sliding window for simplified calculation. In addition, the best sliding window should be as close as the tracking result size of the previous frame. So, the modified weight of sliding window m is

$$sw_m = \rho_m \cdot \sum_{i=1}^{N_{fg}} \frac{area(sp_i)}{area(m)} \tag{12}$$

where ρ_m is scaling coefficients which measure the size similar between sliding window m and tracking result of last frame. Then, the sliding window with maximum value of sw is the best tracking location in current frame.

4 Experiments

We evaluate our algorithm in OTB100 dataset [27] and select six typical video sequences as algorithm evaluation test videos: *Boy*, *CarScale*, *Basketball*, *David3*, *Jogging*, *Tiger1*. Our tracking algorithm is compared with six recent trackers, include Superpixel Tracker (SPT) [12], Compressive Tracker (CT) [28], Online Multi-instance Learning (MIL) Tracker [29], Local Sparse Appearance Model and K-selection (LSK) Tracker [30], Structured Output Tracking with Kernels (Struck) Method [11], Tracking-Learning-Detection (TLD) Tracker [9]. The overall performances of six compared algorithms in six video sequences are summarized in Tables 1 and 2, where the optimal and suboptimal trackers are highlighted with red and blue, respectively. Precision plots and Qualitative evaluations of comparative algorithms on all six video sequences are illustrated in Figs. 3 and 4, respectively.

Table 1. Average center location error (lower is better) of trackers on test sequences.

Sequence	SPT[12]	CT[28]	MIL[29]	LSK[30]	Struck[11]	TLD[9]	Ours
Boy	**4.7**	21.9	16.1	180.7	5.8	8.8	**4.0**
CarScale	**12.7**	26.0	68.6	37.7	36.8	99.8	**12.1**
Bassketball	**17.1**	122.1	103.8	146.1	90.4	173.5	**20.1**
David3	22.7	**18.6**	93.5	227.1	67.5	222.5	**5.7**
Jogging	19.4	111.1	88.4	84.9	44.0	**5.6**	**7.4**
Tiger1	**23.6**	35.3	92.3	53.4	64.3	139.7	**23.8**

Heavy Occlusion: Our proposed tracker performed best and second best on two sequences, respectively. In the *Jogging* sequence, the MIL, LSK and Struck trackers drift when heavy occlusion occurs at frame 68. TLD performs best due to its long-time detection scheme and re-locates the target after the target appears at frame 80. In *david3* sequence, the proposed tracker performed best and the CT tracker performed second best. The Struck tracker lost the target at frame 86 when target was completely obscured by the trees.

Fast Motion and Scale Change: The target object also undergoes some occlusions. The proposed tracker and SPT tracker achieved best performance in the entire sequence. This is mainly because our superpixel-based tracking algorithm is integrated

Table 2. Tracking success rate (higher is better) of the comparative trackers on six sequences.

Sequence	SPT[12]	CT[28]	MIL[29]	LSK[30]	Struck[11]	TLD[9]	Ours
Boy	**98.8**	61.9	12.6	41.8	96.0	76.1	**99.6**
CarScale	**75.4**	45.6	45.2	64.7	43.3	40.1	**84.5**
Bassketball	**89.4**	24.8	25.1	2.2	34.6	2.8	**62.6**
David3	23.0	**67.5**	31.8	15.1	56.8	9.5	**97.6**
Jogging	33.2	22.2	21.5	20.2	50.5	**96.4**	**96.7**
Tiger1	**42.4**	24.4	7.5	12.0	12.0	12.5	**56.5**

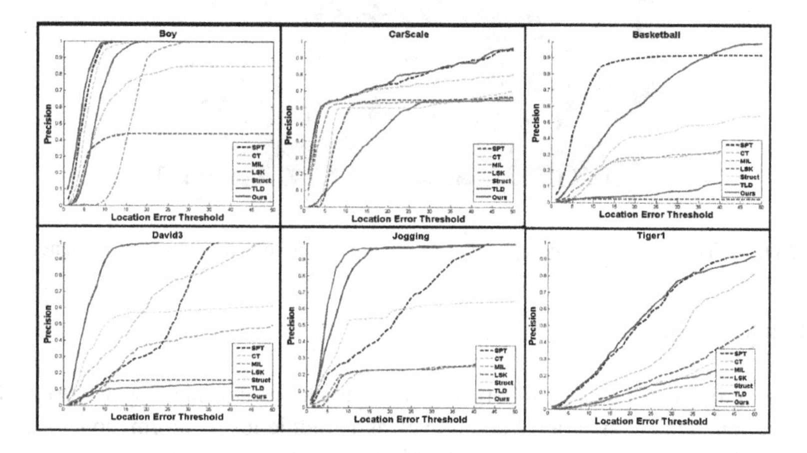

Fig. 3. The precision plots of the compared algorithms.

with dynamic optical flow which can get the structure and motion estimation of the object. In Boy sequence, MIL and CT is able to track the target in some frames but fails when fast motion and motion blue occur. The LSK and MIL tracker fail to track the object in the CarScale sequence with large scale change, so they have small success rate and large center-pixel error.

Pose Variation and Background Clutter: In basketball sequence, SPT tracker performed best and the proposed tracker performed second best. This is mainly because superpixel-based tracking algorithms are effective to follow articulated or deformable objects. LSK, TLD and MIL trackers drifted away when the target has noticeable pose variation at frame 95. In Tiger1 sequence, SPT tracker and the proposed tracker performed best. Struck, TLD and LSK tracker drifted at frame 37 and MIL tracker drifted at frame 89 with the target fast motion and external rotation.

Fig. 4. Tracking results compared with the comparative trackers on six sequences.

5 Conclusion

We have proposed a salient superpixel based tracking algorithm by Coarse-to-Fine segmentation, which integrated pixel-level and middle-level information to achieve accurate target appearance represent model, and improve initial target appearance representation from bounding box annotations. A graph model with manifold ranking is constructed by improved superpixels to estimate the saliency of target foreground in the subsequent frames. The tracking result is located by calculating the weight of multi-scale box, where the weight depends on the similarity of scores of foreground and background superpixels in the scale box. The experimental results show that our algorithm has effective performance and better stability on handling various scenarios, such as occlusion, pose variation, scale change and background clutter.

Acknowledgment. This research is supported by National Natural Science Foundation of China (61772144, 61672008), Innovation Research Project of Education Department of Guangdong Province (Natural Science) (2016KTSCX077), Foreign Science and Technology Cooperation Plan Project of Guangzhou Science Technology and Innovation Commission (201807010059), Guangdong Provincial Application-oriented Technical Research and Development Special Fund Project (2016B010127006), the Natural Science Foundation of Guangdong Province (2016A030311013), and the Scientific and Technological Projects of Guangdong Province (2017A050501039). The corresponding author is Huimin Zhao.

References

1. Yang, C., Zhang, L.: Saliency detection via graph-based manifold ranking. In: IEEE Conference on Computer Vision and Pattern Recognition (CVPR), pp. 3166–3173. IEEE, Portland (2013)
2. Achanta, R.: SLIC superpixels compared to state-of-the-art superpixel methods. IEEE Trans. Pattern Anal. Mach. Intell. **34**(11), 2274–2282 (2012)
3. Belagiannis, V., Schubert, F., Navab, N., Ilic, S.: Segmentation based particle filtering for real-time 2D object tracking. In: Fitzgibbon, A., Lazebnik, S., Perona, P., Sato, Y., Schmid, C. (eds.) ECCV 2012. LNCS, vol. 7575, pp. 842–855. Springer, Heidelberg (2012). https://doi.org/10.1007/978-3-642-33765-9_60
4. Rother, C., Kolmogorov, V.: Grabcut: interactive foreground extraction using iterated graph cuts. In: ACM SIGGRAPH, Los Angeles, vol. 23, pp. 309–314 (2004)
5. Liu, Q.: Decontaminate feature for tracking: adaptive tracking via evolutionary feature subset. J. Electron. Imaging **26**(6), 1 (2017)
6. Son, J., Jung, I.: Tracking-by-segmentation with online gradient boosting decision tree. In: International Conference on Computer Vision (ICCV), pp. 3056–3064. IEEE, Santiago (2015)
7. Ren, X., Malik, J.: Tracking as repeated figure/ground segmentation. In: IEEE Conference on Computer Vision and Pattern Recognition (CVPR), pp. 1–8. IEEE, Hawaii (2007)
8. Yan, Y., Ren, J.: Cognitive fusion of thermal and visible imagery for effective detection and tracking of pedestrians in videos. Cognit. Comput. **10**(1), 94–104 (2018)
9. Kalal, Z., Mikolajczyk, K.: Tracking-learning-detection. IEEE Trans. Pattern Anal. Mach. Intell. **34**, 1409–1422 (2012)
10. Xu, C.: Robust visual tracking via online multiple instance learning with Fisher information. Pattern Recognit. **48**(12), 3917–3926 (2015)
11. Hare, S., Saffari, A., Torr, P.H.S.: Struck: structured output tracking with kernels. In: 13th International Conference on Computer Vision (ICCV), pp. 263–270. IEEE, Barcelona (2011)
12. Wang, S., Lu, H.: Superpixel tracking. In: 13th International Conference on Computer Vision (ICCV), pp. 1323–1330. IEEE, Barcelona (2011)
13. Yang, F.: Robust superpixel tracking. IEEE Trans. Image Process. **23**(4), 1639–1651 (2014)
14. Zhou, X.: Learning a superpixel-driven speed function for level set tracking. IEEE Trans. Cybern. **46**(7), 1498–1510 (2016)
15. Hong, Z., Wang, C., Mei, X., Prokhorov, D., Tao, D.: Tracking using multilevel quantizations. In: Fleet, D., Pajdla, T., Schiele, B., Tuytelaars, T. (eds.) ECCV 2014. LNCS, vol. 8694, pp. 155–171. Springer, Cham (2014). https://doi.org/10.1007/978-3-319-10599-4_11
16. Xiao, J., Stolkin, R., Leonardis, A.: Single target tracking using adaptive clustered decision trees and dynamic multilevel appearance models. In: Computer Vision and Pattern Recognition (CVPR), pp. 4978–4987. IEEE, Boston (2015)
17. Yeo, D., Son, J., Han, B., Han, J.H.: Superpixel-based tracking-by-segmentation using Markov chains. In: Computer Vision and Pattern Recognition (CVPR), pp. 511–520. IEEE, Hawaii (2017)
18. Wang, L., Lu, H., Yang, M.H.: Constrained superpixel tracking. IEEE Trans. Cybern. **48**(3), 1030–1041 (2018)
19. Liu, C.: Beyond pixels: exploring new representations and applications for motion analysis. Doctoral Thesis. Massachusetts Institute of Technology (2009)

20. Lucchi, A., Li, Y., Smith, K., Fua, P.: Structured image segmentation using kernelized features. In: Fitzgibbon, A., Lazebnik, S., Perona, P., Sato, Y., Schmid, C. (eds.) ECCV 2012. LNCS, pp. 400–413. Springer, Heidelberg (2012). https://doi.org/10.1007/978-3-642-33709-3_29
21. Rosenfeld, A., Weinshall, D.: Extracting foreground masks towards object recognition. In: IEEE International Conference on Computer Vision (ICCV), 1371–1378. IEEE (2011)
22. Chai, Y., Ren, J., Zhao, H., et al.: Hierarchical and multi-featured fusion for effective gait recognition under variable scenarios. Pattern Anal. Appl. **19**(4), 905–917 (2016)
23. Ezrinda, M.Z., Kamarul Hawari, G., Ren, J., Mohd Zuki, S.: A hybrid thermal-visible fusion for outdoor human detection. J. Telecommun. Electron. Comput. Eng. (JTEC) **10**(1–4), 79–83 (2018)
24. Yan, Y., et al.: Unsupervised image saliency detection with Gestalt-laws guided optimization and visual attention based refinement. Pattern Recognit. **79**, 65–78 (2018)
25. Wang, Z., et al.: A deep-learning based feature hybrid framework for spatiotemporal saliency detection inside videos. Neurocomputing **287**, 68–83 (2018)
26. Otsu, N.: A threshold selection method from gray-level histograms. IEEE Trans. Syst. Man Cybern. **9**(1), 62–66 (1979)
27. Wu, Y.: Object tracking benchmark. IEEE Trans. Pattern Anal. Mach. Intell. (PAMI) **37**(9), 1834–1848 (2015)
28. Zhang, K., Zhang, L., Yang, M.-H.: Real-time compressive tracking. In: Fitzgibbon, A., Lazebnik, S., Perona, P., Sato, Y., Schmid, C. (eds.) ECCV 2012. LNCS, vol. 7574, pp. 864–877. Springer, Heidelberg (2012). https://doi.org/10.1007/978-3-642-33712-3_62
29. Babenko, B., Yang, M.-H.: Visual tracking with online multiple instance learning. In: Computer Vision and Pattern Recognition (CVPR), pp. 983–990. IEEE, Florida (2009)
30. Liu, B., Huang, J.: Robust tracking using local sparse appearance model and k-selection. In: Computer Vision and Pattern Recognition (CVPR), pp. 1313–1320. IEEE (2011)

A Regenerated Feature Extraction Method for Cross-modal Image Registration

Jian Yang[1], Qi Wang[1,2(✉)], and Xuelong Li[3]

[1] School of Computer Science and Center for OPTical IMagery Analysis and Learning (OPTIMAL), Northwestern Polytechnical University, Xi'an 710072, Shaanxi, People's Republic of China
crabwq@nwpu.edu.cn
[2] Unmanned System Research Institute (USRI), Northwestern Polytechnical University, Xi'an 710072, Shaanxi, People's Republic of China
[3] Xi'an Institute of Optics and Precision Mechanics, Chinese Academy of Science, Xi'an 710119, Shaanxi, People's Republic of China

Abstract. Cross-modal image registration is an intractable problem in computer vision and pattern recognition. Inspired by that human gradually deepen to learn in the cognitive process, we present a novel method to automatically register images with different modes in this paper. Unlike most existing registrations that align images by single type of features or directly using multiple features, we employ the "regenerated" mechanism cooperated with a dynamic routing to adaptively detect features and match for different modal images. The geometry-based maximally stable extremal regions (MSER) are first implemented to fast detect non-overlapping regions as the primitive of feature regeneration, which are used to generate novel control-points using salient image disks (SIDs) operator embedded by a sub-pixel iteration. Then a dynamic routing is proposed to select suitable features and match images. Experimental results on optical and multi-sensor images show that our method has a better accuracy compared to state-of-the-art approaches.

Keywords: Feature regeneration · MSER · SIDs · Image registration Dynamic routing

1 Introduction

Image registration is the process that spatially overlays two or more images containing the same scene captured at different time, from different viewpoints or

---

This work was supported by the National Key R&D Program of China under Grant 2017YFB1002202, National Natural Science Foundation of China under Grant 61773316, Fundamental Research Funds for the Central Universities under Grant 3102017AX010, and the Open Research Fund of Key Laboratory of Spectral Imaging Technology, Chinese Academy of Sciences.

J. Ren et al. (Eds.): BICS 2018, LNAI 10989, pp. 441–451, 2018.
https://doi.org/10.1007/978-3-030-00563-4_43

by different sensors [1]. In most applications, image registration directly determines the accuracy of follow-up processing, e.g., structure from motion (SFM) [2], simultaneous localisation and mapping (SLAM) [4], and stereo matching [3]. Thus, it is necessary to develop a robust and accurate registration method.

Over past few years, extensive methods have been proposed for registration. These methods can be divided into two categories, i.e., area-based and feature-based methods [5]. The former usually use image intensity to estimate the transformation between input images. Differently, the later [6] first detect some salient structures from images and then calculate the transformation by the structures. Because image features are less sensitive to image deformations [7], such type of methods are more robust than area-based ones. Particularly, point feature has higher position accuracy. So, it is widely applied and plenty of methods based on it [8,9] have been proposed. For example, Hsu *et al.* [10] combines speeded up robust features (SURF) with edge feature extraction (EFE) to register rat brain slices, which performs well on the rat brain images with less distortions. Al-khafaji *et al.* [11] explore both spectral and spatial dimensions simultaneously to extract spectral and geometric transformation invariant features and proposed spectral-spatial scale invariant feature transform (SS-SIFT)for spectral-spatial image matching. Seregni *et al.* [12] used SIFT detector to extract liver landmarks trajectories for real-time motion tracking in MRI-Guided radiotherapy and obtained high efficiency with limited loss of accuracy. Although these methods achieve a better result in real scenarios, there also exist some problems, e.g., many more points are extracted, the distributions of features are dense and uneven, which cause a high computing expense and lots of false matches.

To avoid above problems, some methods based on region feature are developed, typically including Harris-Laplace [13], Hessian-Laplace and MSER [14], which can detect more reliable support regions efficiently. Since real images often suffer from badly random noise, different occlusions, various data sources or other complex deformations. For such cases, only using one type of features is difficult to obtain a satisfactory result. So, the methods based on hybrid feature [15] are proposed, which colligate the merits of different features. For example, [16] detected more stable control points centered at a local neighborhood with high-intensity contrast, which can be a fusion of region and points feature. Zhang *et al.* [17] applied the MSER [14] and phase congruency points to align the images with affine deformations. In general, most hybrid features based methods only combine two types of features (e.g., points, regions) by a coarse-to-fine framework. And the features used in the paper are designed for specific types of images. Even if the feature is for the specified image, it is also unsuitable sometimes due to illumination, occlusion and viewpoint changes. Especially, existing features becomes helpless and infeasible for cross-modal matching.

In this paper, a novel cross-modal feature extraction method is proposed. A regenerating and dynamic routing mechanism is designed for feature extraction and matching, i.e., re-extract another feature from one feature and adaptively select one or more suitable features from the feature sequence for different modal images. Figure 1 shows the framework of our method. Affine-invariant region

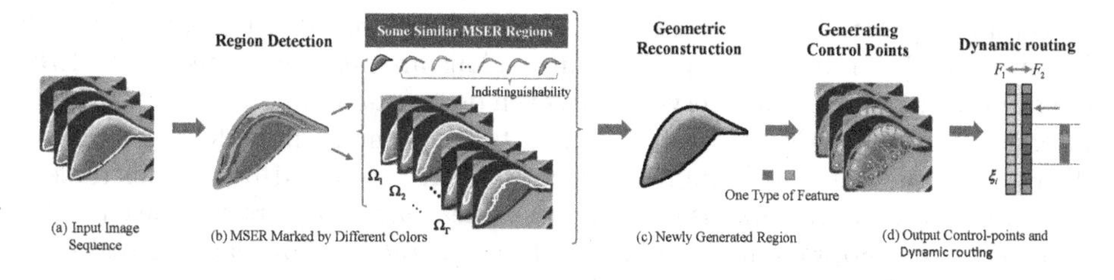

Fig. 1. An overview of the proposed method. In the figure, the overlapping MSER are marked by different colors, and some similar regions with white contours are shown as well. The green circles are the control points with different scales regenerated on the regions. And the feature sequence are matched via dynamic routing. (Color figure online)

feature is used as the primitive of feature regeneration to re-extract points with high position accuracy. MSER regions are first detected, and then a geometry-based rebuilding is used to trim the MSER regions and regenerates some well-identified non-overlapping regions. After that, a multistage isotropic matched filtering (MIMF) [16] is used to accurately localize the control-points of the regions. To match the multi-features, a dynamic routing is presented to adaptively select suitable features for input images. Our main contributions are:

- A feature fusion and regeneration is first proposed for cross-modal image matching, which improves the adaptation of the same method to diverse types of images;
- A dynamic routing mechanism is first introduced to match images, which addresses the problem of feature selection for different types of images and improves the matching efficiency;
- A non-overlapping region detection with point re-extraction over the region is given, which is taken as an example that proves the effectiveness of such feature fusion and regeneration to cross-modal registration.

2 Feature Regeneration

In this section, we first introduce the non-overlapping region detection method, which is taken as the primitive of feature regeneration, and then describe the process of generating control-points on the regions. Finally, we illustrate the dynamic routing and align the given image pairs.

2.1 Non-overlapping Region Detection

Compared to points or lines feature, region feature is more easily identified. While point feature is more stable against image distortions in localization. So, if we re-extract points feature from the region, more robust and precise points with high feature repeatability can be obtained. Since MSER detector [14] performs better in computation efficiency and detection accuracy over other region detectors [13], MSER is selected as the primitive to re-extract points feature. However, as shown in Fig. 1(b), abundant regions are often extracted by MSER operator, some of which are very similar, even one part contains another. If these interlaced regions is directly used to extract points, much more feature redundancies are inevitable and the new generated features would be also unstable. Some regions with small intensity variation or clear boundary are reliable enough to align images. So, we refine the MSERs to regenerate non-overlapping regions, which are free from the interference of these similar regions.

As shown in Fig. 1, different MSER regions are intertwined and also complex. However, when we regard MSER regions as some geometric figures in plane geometry, this position relation can be just described as intersection, deviation or tangent in geometry. Thus, we can employ the geometric positions to refine these overlapping MSERs. Whereas the regions with a smaller or larger area are more unstable (the area of a region is the number of pixels within the region), we restrict the regenerated region within the smallest area Ω_{min} and largest area Ω_{max}. Denote notation $\mathbf{G}$ as the newly generated region set, which is an empty set $\emptyset$ at first. For any two MSERs Ω_i, Ω_j, it is clear that they are either intersecting or disjoint in geometry. If they are disjoint, the two regions have no effect on each other. So, they are directly treated as available regions and are added into the new region set $\mathbf{G}$.

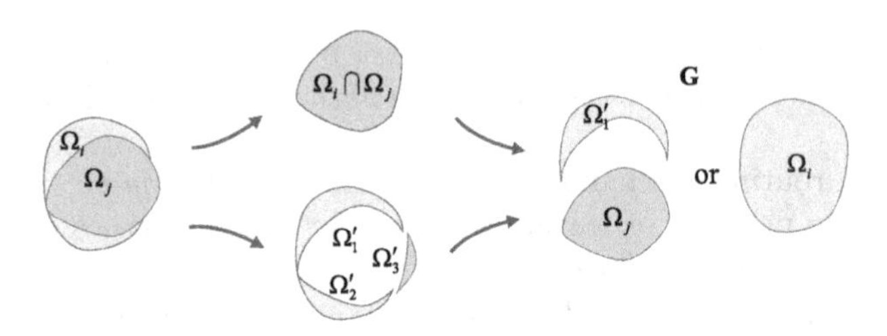

Fig. 2. Schematic diagram for non-overlapping region extraction. Notation Ω_i' denotes the connected component of complementary set.

Obviously, it becomes complex when the regions intersect each other. It is necessary to distinguish the differences between the two regions. If the differences are indeed very small, they can be treated as the same region, which means they can be replaced by either. However, if the differences are large, new regions based on the two original regions is rebuild and the new regions are non-overlapping for less redundancy. Specifically, as shown in Fig. 2, we divide it into two cases according to the region area. First, when one region is larger than the sum of their overlapping part $|\Omega_i \cap \Omega_j|$ and a constant δ, we keep its corresponding complementary set's largest connected component (e.g., Ω_1' in Fig. 2) and also directly add the other region into the set $\mathbf{G}$. Next, when the area of one region is less than $|\Omega_i \cap \Omega_j| + \delta$ but larger than the other region, it shows the two regions almost have no differences. So, only the region with larger area (e.g., Ω_i' in Fig. 2) are kept and added into $\mathbf{G}$. More details are shown in Algorithm 1.

Algorithm 1. Non-overlapping region detection

Input: Initial region set $\Omega = \{\Omega_1, \Omega_2, \cdots, \Omega_\Gamma\}$, parameters $\delta \in R^+$, Ω_{min}, Ω_{max}.
Output: a set of new MSER, named $\mathbf{G}$

1: ***Initialize*** $\mathbf{G} = \Omega_i$, *with* $|\Omega_i| \geq \Omega_{min} \wedge |\Omega_i| \leq \Omega_{max}$.
2: **for** $j = 1$ to Γ **do**
3:     **if** $|\Omega_j| \geq \Omega_{min} \vee |\Omega_j| \leq \Omega_{max}$;
4:       **if** $\mathbf{G} \cap \Omega_j \neq \emptyset$, record Ω_j into $\mathbf{G}$;
5:       **else** find the set Ω_k in $\mathbf{G}$, $\Omega_k \cap \Omega_j \neq \emptyset$;
6:       **end if**
7:       **if** the set Ω_j contains Ω_k
8:           **delete** Ω_k from $\mathbf{G}$ and record Ω_j into $\mathbf{G}$
9:       **else if** $|\Omega_k|$ is less than $|\Omega_j|$;
10:           **if** $|\Omega_j|$ is less than $|\Omega_k \cap \Omega_j| + \delta$;
11:               **delete** Ω_k from $\mathbf{G}$ and record Ω_j into $\mathbf{G}$
12:           **else** record the largest connected components $\Omega_j^{'}$
13:               of Ω_j with $|\Omega_j^{'}| > \Omega_{min}$ into $\mathbf{G}$
14:       **else if** $|\Omega_k| > |\Omega_j \cap \Omega_k| + \delta$
15:           remain the largest connected components $\Omega_k^{'}$
16:           of Ω_k with $|\Omega_k^{'}| > \Omega_{min}$ and record Ω_j into $\mathbf{G}$;
17:     **else continue**;
18:     **end if**
19:     **end if**
20: **end for**
21: **return** $\mathbf{G}$;

2.2 Iteratively Extraction of Regenerated Points

Unlike existing points (e.g. centroid, corners), the control-point SIDs implies the structural properties of the region, which detects local salient feature directly based on image intensity. A SID is a circular fragment with a variable diameter while a homogeneous region is circumscribed into it. In SIDs extraction, the scale of each point is first estimated, which is defined as the maximum of the isotropic local contrast with a homogeneity constraint over a given scale range Λ.

From Fig. 3, the scale range Λ is traversed for estimating the scale, which is a time-consuming process. Besides, a SID is always circumscribed by homogeneous regions, and the detected region is exactly homogeneous, which can be used to fast estimate the scale ρ of SIDs feature. For each detected region Ω, we define the distance ϑ_{ij} from its inner arbitrary point υ_{ij} to its boundary ζ composed of point ζ_i as:

$$\vartheta_{ij} = \min_{\zeta_i \in \zeta} \|\upsilon_{ij} - \zeta_i\|, \tag{1}$$

According to ϑ_{ij}, the scale ρ can be set in a smaller range within the given scale range Λ. To enhance the robustness of scale estimation, we set the scale searching range as $(\alpha \max(\vartheta_{ij} - \epsilon, 1), \alpha \min(\vartheta_{ij} + \epsilon, \Lambda))$, where α is a coefficient and ϵ is a threshold. Ignoring the lower limit, more points are obtained. Moreover, if $\Lambda < \vartheta_{ij} - \epsilon$, the scale upper limit remains unchanged at this time.

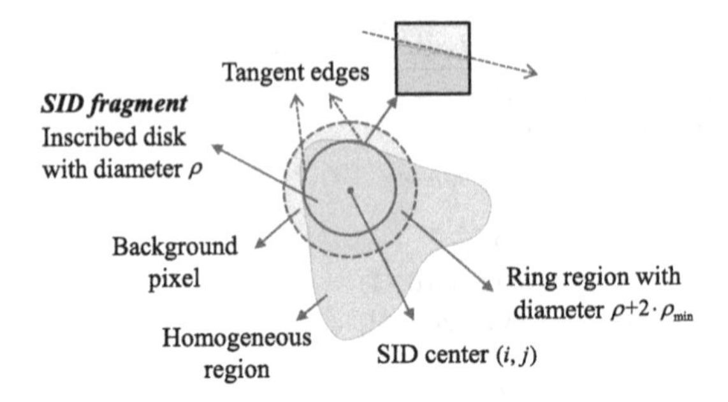

Fig. 3. Schematic diagram of SID feature extraction on a homogeneous region.

After scale estimation, the control point of SIDs is determined via the scale. the SIDs operator directly select the extreme point of MIMF response as the control point in an interest region A. It is not enough accurate. There often exists location offset between local extreme point in discrete space and the real ones. So, we interpolate MIMF response to iteratively select stable and accurate SIDs points. Denote the MIMF response as the scale-space function $\psi(x, y, \rho)$. The migration between the extreme point and the extreme point to be estimated in the local neighborhood is $\mathbf{x} = (x, y, \rho)$, then the second-order Taylor expansion of scale-space function $\psi(x, y, \rho)$ can be written as:

$$\psi(\mathbf{x}) = \psi + \frac{\partial \psi^{\mathrm{T}}}{\partial \mathbf{x}}\mathbf{x} + \frac{1}{2}\mathbf{x}^{\mathrm{T}}\frac{\partial^2 \psi}{\partial \mathbf{x}^2}\mathbf{x}, \tag{2}$$

The location of the extremum $\hat{\mathbf{x}}$ is determined by taking the derivative of Eq. 2 with respect to $\mathbf{x}$, and set the derivatives equation to zero, i.e.,

$$\hat{\mathbf{x}} = -\frac{\partial^2 \psi^{-1}}{\partial \mathbf{x}^2}\frac{\partial \psi}{\partial \mathbf{x}}, \tag{3}$$

Then if we plug the corresponding extreme point into Eq. 2, it would be

$$\psi(\hat{\mathbf{x}}) = \psi + \frac{1}{2}\frac{\partial \psi^{\mathrm{T}}}{\partial \mathbf{x}}\hat{\mathbf{x}}, \tag{4}$$

The migration obtained by Eq. 4, reveals which point is more closer to the extremum point. If the offset is greater than half a pixel in any dimensions, the extremum point lies closer to its neighbor. Continue this process until $\hat{\mathbf{x}}$ in any dimension is less than half a pixel. In fact, this iterative process can be also limited a few steps for a lower computing. Furthermore, $\psi(\hat{\mathbf{x}})$ also embodies the strength of response and consistency. When the extremum response $\psi_(\hat{\mathbf{x}})$ is small, the extremum points are unstable. So, to gain more robust and accurate extremum points, only the points that the responses $|\psi_(\hat{\mathbf{x}})|$ are more than threshold δ_ψ are remained in iterative process. More details can refer to Algorithm 2.

Algorithm 2. Accurate extraction of regenerated points

Input: Candidate control-points set $\mathbf{P}$, parameters $\delta_{\mathbf{x}}$, δ_{ψ}. **Output**: Regenerated points set $\mathbf{P}_{\psi}$

1: ***Initialize*** $\boldsymbol{P}_{\psi} = \emptyset$, $\delta_{\mathbf{x}} = (0.5, 0.5, 0.5)^{\mathrm{T}}$.
2: **for** $i = 1$ to N_{iter} **do**
3: Compute the offset $\hat{\mathbf{x}}$ by Eq. 3, the extreme $\psi(\hat{\mathbf{x}})$;
4: **if** the extreme $\psi(\hat{\mathbf{x}})$ is less than $\mathbf{P}_{\psi}$;
5: **while** $|\hat{\mathbf{x}}| > \delta_{\mathbf{x}}$ **do**
6: Update $\hat{\mathbf{x}}$ with rounding down $\psi(\hat{\mathbf{x}}) + sgn(\hat{\mathbf{x}})\delta_{\mathbf{x}}$
7: Recompute the $\hat{\mathbf{x}}$ and extreme $\psi(\hat{\mathbf{x}})$ by Eq. 3, Eq. 4;
8: **if** $|\psi(\hat{\mathbf{x}})|$ is less than δ_{ψ} **continue**;
9: **end if**;
10: **end while**
11: Record $\hat{\mathbf{x}}$ into $\mathbf{P}_{\psi}$;
12: **end if**;
13: **end for**
14: **return** $\mathbf{P}_{\psi}$;

2.3 Dynamic Routing and Parameters Estimation

Feature extraction and matching are the most curial steps in image registration. By feature regeneration, we generate some new features towards more precise aligning and a feature sequence is obtained. For fast matching the obtained features with least cost, a dynamic routing mechanism is developed to adaptively select a feature subsequence that can align the input images precisely, and this dynamic routing can be synchronized with the feature extraction of each step. Once there is a feature subsequence that can align images precisely, the following features are not extracted anymore. If one feature matching fails, record the former results and restart to extract the following features. When there is no such feature subsequences fulfilling the accuracy, only choose the best one from recorded results as the final result. Specifically, denote the feature to be extracted as an ordered set $F = \{\xi_1, \xi_2, \cdots, \xi_\tau\}$, and matching the feature sequens $\xi_1, \xi_2, \cdots, \xi_\tau$ can be regarded as finding a feature subsequence from F which can precisely estimate the transformation parameters between the input images, that is, search minimum ℓ, $\kappa \in Z^+$,$1 \leq \ell \leq \kappa \leq \tau$, which makes

$$\|\xi_\kappa^{'} - H(\xi_\ell, \xi_{\ell+1}, \cdots, \xi_{\ell+\kappa})\xi_\kappa^{''}\| \leq \varepsilon, \tag{5}$$

where $\xi_i^{'}$, $\xi_i^{''}$ denotes the i-th type of features detected from image I_1, I_2 (e.g., MSER, SIDs), respectively. ε is matching error and H is the homography matrix estimated by the selected feature subsequence $(\xi_\ell^{'}, \xi_\ell^{''}), (\xi_{\ell+1}^{'}, \xi_{\ell+1}^{''}), \cdots, (\xi_\kappa^{'}, \xi_\kappa^{''})$.

Take region-to-point matching as example, to obtain affine invariant features, each region pairs are first normalized into circular region with matrix $A_{ci} = 2V_i\Sigma_i^{\frac{1}{2}}$, $i = 1, 2$, where V, Σ correspond the **SVD** decomposition of the second-order moments matrix of the region. Denote the transformation matrix estimated by the regenerated points pairs as A_f. If both region and point feature are selected, the final homography matrix between input images would be

$H(\xi_c, \xi_f) = A_{c1}^{-1} A_f A_{c2}$. And the matrix H can be also A_f or estimated by matched regions as long as the accuracy meets the requirements. Finally, the images are registered via H.

3 EXPERIMENTAL RESULTS

In this section, we apply our method for cross-modal image alignment, i.e., matching optical images and remote sensing images captured by different sensors. Matching errors and visual quality is analyzed and compared. For optical images, the Oxford dataset is used for testing, which consists of more than 40 images with blurring, compression, occlusions, lighting changes. Besides, three pairs of remote sensing images are also tested. All the experiments are performed on MATLAB with a 4 GHz CPU, 16.0 GB RAM windows system.

Parameter Setting. In the experiments, there are crucial parameters to set, i.e., area constant δ, Λ and the region size. The area constant δ is used for evaluating the similarity of two regions. When the area difference of two regions is very small, they can be regarded as the same region. And we set $\delta = 200$. To estimate the scale of SID feature, Λ is set as in [13] and the coefficient α actually has the same effect with ϵ, which reflects the accuracy of extracted regions. Since MSER is very accurate and is also refined, α is set as 1 and ϵ is set to 10. The region size are set as $\Omega_{min} = 200$, $\Omega_{max} = max(0.15 \times MN, 8000)$, where M, N is image size and iterations N_{iter} is 5 for efficiency. Besides, the matching error ε is set to 1, which means the matching reaches sub-pixel level.

Figure 4 shows the optical image matching result. Clearly, some images are well-aligned only using regions. There's no need to extract SIDs anymore, which shows the necessity of dynamic routing selection. The typical state-of-the-art registration methods, e.g., SIFT [13], ASIFT [18], SIDs [16], are made comparisons. To quantitatively evaluate the performance of different methods, we calculate the root mean square error (RMSE) between the matched features (Fig. 4).

Fig. 4. Results for optical images. L-to-R: input images, the detected and matched regions marked by white or red color, and the aligned images via matched regions.

Table 1 shows the testing results on the six images (Figs. 4 and 5). A matching examples with large deformations are displayed in Fig. 6. From Table 1, our method outperforms others, and the accuracies are less than one pixel, even for the multi-sensor images with complex deformations, which shows that more robust feature is obtained by feature regeneration. Especially, although many more matched points (SIFT 19, ASIFT 40, SIDs 20, Ours **30**) are obtained, the matched points focus on local region and the distributions are more even. This leads to a bad result for the image with local deformation. As shown in Fig. 6, it is clear that our method can align the local details better. In terms of running

Table 1. RMSE results on registration accuracy

Images	SIFT [13]	ASIFT [18]	SIDs [16]	**Ours**
Canton	0.7453	1.4310	0.9094	**0.7386**
Graffiti	0.8203	0.9428	1.1445	**0.5865**
Leuven	0.5761	0.7479	0.8324	**0.6125**
Pairs(a)	0.8634	1.0967	1.1647	**0.7320**
Pairs(b)	1.1715	**0.8081**	1.0432	0.9255
Pairs(c)	1.0448	1.5741	1.0655	**0.8743**

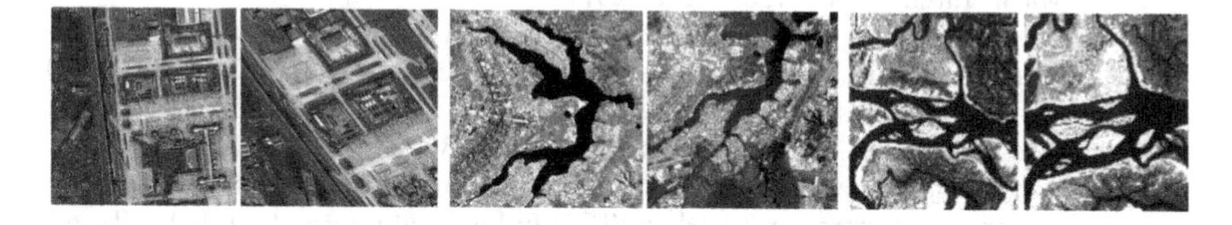

Fig. 5. Multi-modal images taken from google earth, SPOT and Landsat.

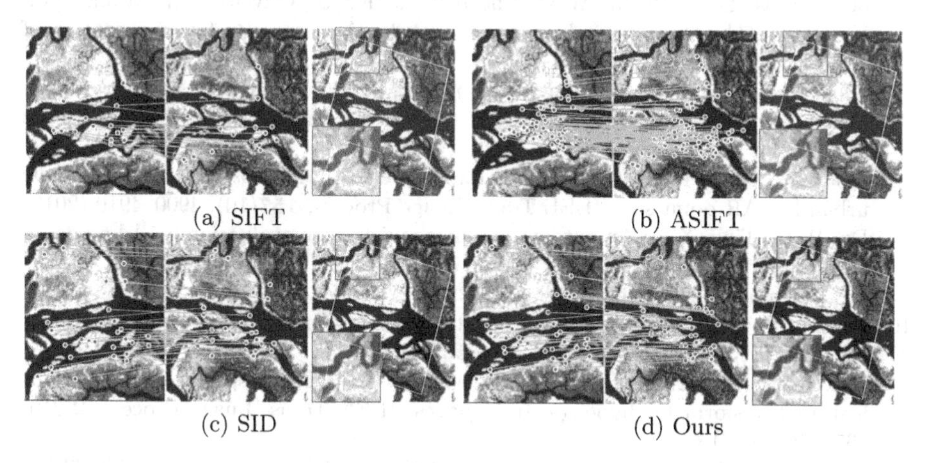

Fig. 6. Registration results for images with complex deformations.

time, our feature extraction takes about 3 s per image. The experiments show that our method performs better than the state-of-art methods.

4 Conclusion

In this paper, a novel feature fusion and regeneration method is proposed for cross-modal image registration. By feature regeneration, more robust and accurate features are generated, which enhances the performance of feature extraction and also forms a multi-feature registration system. Considering the applicability of diverse features to different modal images, a dynamic routing is used to fast select feasible features for specific image. Experiments show that our method can align the different modal images and has better results in both registration accuracy and visual quality.

References

1. Barbara, Z., Jan, F.: Image registration methods: a survey. Image Vis. Comput. **11**(21), 977–1000 (2003)
2. Collins, T., Bartoli, A.: Planar structure-from-motion with affine camera models: closed-form solutions, ambiguities and degeneracy analysis. IEEE Trans. Pattern Anal. Mach. Intell. **39**(6), 1237–1255 (2017)
3. Kim, S., Min, D., Kim, S., Sohn, K.: Feature augmentation for learning confidence measure in stereo matching. IEEE Trans. Image Process. **26**(12), 6019–6033 (2017)
4. Li, J., Kaess, M., Eustice, R., Johnson-Roberson, M.: Pose-graph SLAM using forward-looking sonar. IEEE Robot. Autom. Lett. **3**, 2330–2337 (2018)
5. Gong, M., Zhao, S., Jiao, L., Tian, D., Wang, S.: A novel coarse-to-fine scheme for automatic image registration based on SIFT and mutual information. IEEE Trans. Geosci. Remote Sens. **52**(7), 4328–4338 (2014)
6. dos Santos, D.R., Basso, M.A., Khoshelham, K., de Oliveira, E., Pavan, N.L., Vosselman, G.: Mapping indoor spaces by adaptive coarse-to-fine registration of RGB-D data. IEEE Geosci. Remote Sens. Lett. **13**(2), 262–266 (2016)
7. Guislain, M., Digne, J., Chaine, R., Monnier, G.: Fine scale image registration in large-scale urban LIDAR point sets. Comput. Vis. Image Underst. **157**, 90–102 (2017)
8. Rister, B., Horowitz, M.A., Rubin, D.L.: Fine scale image registration in large-scale urban LIDAR point sets. IEEE Trans. Image Process. **157**(10), 4900–4910 (2017)
9. Du, W.L., Tian, X.L.: An automatic image registration evaluation model on dense feature points by pinhole camera simulation. In: 2017 IEEE International Conference on Image Processing (ICIP), pp. 2259–2263. IEEE, Beijing (2017)
10. Hsu, W.Y., Lee, Y.C.: Rat brain registration using improved speeded up robust features. J. Med. Biol. Eng. **37**(1), 45–52 (2017)
11. Al-khafaji, S.L., Zhou, J., Zia, A., Liew, A.W.C.: Spectral-spatial scale invariant feature transform for hyperspectral images. IEEE Trans. Image Process. **27**(2), 837–850 (2018)
12. Seregni, M., Paganelli, C., Summers, P., Bellomi, M., Baroni, G., Riboldi, M.: A hybrid image registration and matching framework for real-time motion tracking in MRI-guided radiotherapy. IEEE Trans. Biomed. Eng. **65**(1), 131–139 (2018)

13. Mikolajczyk, K., Schmid, C.: Scale & affine invariant interest point detectors. Int. J. Comput. Vis. **60**(1), 63–86 (2004)
14. Matas, J., Chum, O., Urban, M., Pajdla, T.: Robust wide-baseline stereo from maximally stable extremal regions. Image Vis. Comput. **22**(10), 761–767 (2004)
15. Han, J., Pauwels, E.J., De Zeeuw, P.: Visible and infrared image registration in man-made environments employing hybrid visual features. Image Vis. Comput. **34**(1), 42–51 (2013)
16. Palenichka, R.M., Zaremba, M.B.: Automatic extraction of control points for the registration of optical satellite and LiDAR images. IEEE Trans. Geosci. Remote Sens. **7**, 2864–2879 (2010)
17. Zhang, Q., Wang, Y., Wang, L.: Registration of images with affine geometric distortion based on maximally stable extremal regions and phase congruency. Image Vis. Comput. **36**, 23–39 (2015)
18. Morel, J.M., Yu, G.: ASIFT: a new framework for fully affine invariant image comparison. SIAM J. Imaging Sci. **2**(2), 438–469 (2009)

Bottom-Up Saliency Prediction by Simulating End-Stopping with Log-Gabor

Ke Zhang[1(✉)], Xinbo Zhao[2], and Rong Mo[1]

[1] Key Laboratory of Contemporary Design and Integrated Manufacturing Technology of Ministry of Education, Northwestern Polytechnical University, Xi'an 710072, China
ake020675@163.com

[2] School of Computer Science, Northwestern Polytechnical University, Xi'an 710129, China

Abstract. This paper presents a bottom-up saliency model inspired by end-stopping mechanism in primary visual cortex (V1). By modelling an end-stopped cell as multiplication of the outputs from two different orientations tuned selective neurons, corners, line intersections, and line endings, which are called end-stopping features in this paper, are extracted and integrated to indicate saliency cues. The proposed model is constructed as follow: firstly we utilize log-Gabor filters to represent orientation selectivity in V1 neurons; then energy maps of the log-Gabor response from two different orientations are multiplied to extract median features perceived by end-stopped cells; finally the resulting feature maps are combined with color features computed by the traditional center-surround operation to obtain the final saliency map. Results on public eye tracking datasets show the proposed model achieves state-of-the-art performance compared to other models.

Keywords: Bottom-up saliency · End-stopping · Log-Gabor · Visual attention

1 Introduction

Saliency map is usually defined as a topographical image that represent the probability of visual attention on each pixel location in an image. Study of saliency prediction may reveal the attentional mechanisms of biological visual systems, or facilitate high-level vision processing by reducing computational cost in real-time applications such as object detection or recognition [1].

Visual saliency prediction has received extensive attention, and many models have been proposed based on different assumptions. Generally speaking, there are two different visual attention processes that influence saliency: One is top-down and depends on the task at hand and the other is bottom-up, which is driven by the input image. Early models of saliency prediction often focus on bottom-up factors of visual attention, the main idea of which is that several low level features are computed in parallel and then their values are summed in a representation which is called a saliency map [2]. Subsequently many models incorporate top-down factors by including object level features like face, car, and horizontal line, or learn the weights of features from

J. Ren et al. (Eds.): BICS 2018, LNAI 10989, pp. 452–461, 2018.
https://doi.org/10.1007/978-3-030-00563-4_44

eye tracking data [3]. Although deep learning methods have further boosted saliency prediction performance amazingly in recent years [4–6], bottom-up saliency model driven by low-level visual cues remains meaningful and challengeable [7].

End-stopping is referred as the property of a type of visual processing neuron in the visual cortex, which responds more strongly to short stimuli than to long ones. This type of neuron is named end-stopped or hypercomplex neuron, and discovered by David Hubel and Torsten Wiesel [8]. End-stopped neurons, which are ubiquitous in V1, V4 and posterior IT (PIT) of monkeys and respond best to high-curvature contours, have shown a big capacity to identify corners and curves on the edges and borders of objects with high saliency [9]. Though low level vision system has inspired almost all bottom-up saliency models directly or indirectly, end-stopping has not been well studied and utilized in saliency models yet.

We present a biological-inspired model to compute saliency using a bottom-up methodology based upon end-stopping mechanism. Our work is an effort to incorporate end-stopping into a basic framework of saliency by directly modelling end-stopped neurons. In this paper, we utilize the response of the log-Gabor filters instead of Gabor to enhance the production of edge responses. The proposed model has achieved the performance of state-of-the-art saliency models in predicting eye-fixations for two datasets and using three metrics.

The rest of this article is structured as follows: Sect. 2 reviews bottom-up saliency models related to end-stopping; Sect. 3 gives the details of the proposed model; experimental results are discussed in Sect. 4; Finally, Sect. 5 concludes this work and suggests further improvements.

2 Related Work

Generally early human visual pathway inspires bottom-up saliency model in two aspects: 1. visual stimuli are decomposed to color-opponent and intensity channels according to cone and rod cells in retina; 2. widely-used center-surround operators are analogous to receptive fields of neurons in early visual areas (ganglion cells in retina and simple/complex cells in V1). As a classic bottom-up saliency model, [3] simulated the visual pathway to extract image intensity, colors, and orientations features, which are processed and integrated to obtain the final saliency map. Specially, orientation information was obtained by approximating impulse response of the receptive field of simple neurons in V1 with Gabor filters. The model cannot detect targets salient for unimplemented feature types like T junctions or line terminators as end-stopping mechanism is not taken into consideration.

As end-stopped cells could perceive high-curvature contours and corners which indicate possible locations where may exist visual objects that are high salient in a scene, some saliency models based on corner or curvature features were proposed. [10, 11] used a convex hull on Harris corners to obtain coarse saliency region. [12] replaced the orientation feature in [3] with edge and corner features extracted by a linear structure tensor. [13] investigated the relationship between interest point and visual attention, and proposed a mixture saliency strategy by integrating all the interest point algorithms including SIFT, SURF, FAST detectors. [14] proposed a model that utilized corner features to extract possible salient locations in natural images. They pointed that corners are very important for correct border ownership assignment in Gestalt principles that promote proto-object based methods. Some studies also added curvature features to bottom-up visual attention model [15–17].

Different from the above-mentioned models based upon corners or other features, our paper computes saliency by directly modelling end-stopping inspired by [18], which is based on multiplication of the outputs from two different orientations tuned neurons. Our model is similar to [14], but that model uses corners which respond to all four orientations as salient cues, and our model extracts end-stopping features by multiplying the outputs from two different orientations tuned cells as in [18].

3 Our Model

End-stopped cells are recognized as a subtype of simple and complex cells in visual cortex, which are sensitive to visual stimuli in specific orientations and can be used in combination to detect corners, line intersections, and line endings, where multi-directional responses exist [9]. We model end-stopping using a similar method to [18] for its biological plausibility and easiness to implement. In [18], the receptive fields of two orientation-selective neurons which correspond to complex cells were simulated as 2-D Gabor functions at different orientations, then end-stopped cell was generated by combining the amplitudes from the two resulting filtered spectra of the stimuli.

2D Gabor filters have been widely used in saliency models to simulate the receptive fields of simple cells to extract directional features [2, 19–21], but we differ here in the option of log-Gabor filters, which have a Gaussian transfer function when viewed on a log scale and allow arbitrarily large bandwidth filters while maintaining a zero DC component in the even symmetric filter.

The architecture of our approach is illustrated in Fig. 1. In this framework, we first extract edge maps with 2D Log-Gabor filters at 4 different orientations on the luminance channel of the input. Amplitudes of two different orientation responses are then multiplied to simulate an end-stopped cell. Finally all resulting feature maps are integrated with color contrast feature maps from the opponent color channels to construct a final saliency map.

3.1 Image Decomposition

The input image is firstly transformed into Lab color coordinates. Since orientation selectivity is only weakly associated with color selectivity, we model end-stopping on the luminance channel, and the opponent color channels a and b are processed with the same method as [2].

The luminance channel is transformed into a multi-oriented multiresolution representation by a bank of log-Gabor filters defined as:

$$\log Gabor(\rho, \theta, s, o) = exp\left(-\frac{(\rho-\rho_s)^2}{2\sigma_\rho^2}\right) exp\left(-\frac{(\theta-\theta_{so})^2}{2\sigma_\theta^2}\right) \tag{1}$$

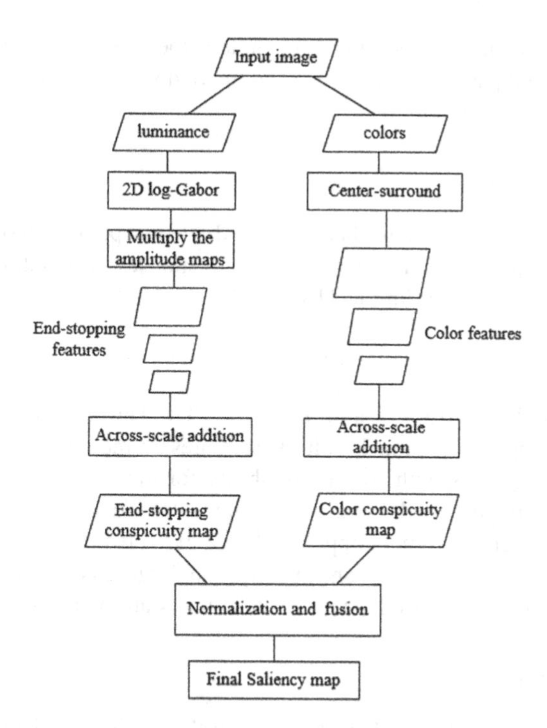

Fig. 1. Architecture of our method

where (ρ, θ) is log-polar coordinates of pixels; (s, o) indicate the scale and orientation of the filter; (ρ_s, θ_{so}) is frequency center of filter and $(\sigma_\rho, \sigma_\theta)$ is the bandwidths in (ρ, θ).

To detect all the irregularities in the preattentive features, a set of filters with different scales and orientations is required. Our choice of the bandwidth in orientation is motivated by [18], which simulates an end-stopped cell from two simple cells differing by 40°. In our experiments, we utilized a log-Gabor bank with s = 5, o = 4. The parameters are chosen such that the log-Gabor bank spans roughly two octaves with some degree of overlap between successive filters. The aim of adjusting these parameters is to vary the scale of regions which respond strongly to orientation, thus they are chosen to compromise between edges with different scales and orientations.

For each scale s and orientation o, a measure of the local energy En_{so} in the input signal, i.e. the amplitude of the response can be obtained to model complex cells by taking the modulus of the complex filter response:

$$En_{so} = \sqrt{(L * f_{so})^2 + (L * h_{so})^2} \tag{2}$$

where L is the luminance channel, f and h denote respectively the even symmetric log-Gabor giving the real part of the response, and the odd symmetric log-Gabor giving the imaginary part of the response.

3.2 Feature Extraction

Once orientation feature maps have been obtained, the receptive field of an end-stopped cell can be modelled as the multiplication of the responses of two different orientation tuned complex neurons according to [18]:

$$E_i = En(o_i) * En(o_{i+1}) \tag{3}$$

where $o \in \{0°, 45°, 90°, 135°\}$, and $i = \{1, 2, 3\}$. Thus for each scale, 3 end-stopping feature maps are obtained with (3) to represent the responses of end-stopped cells. In E_i, only locations with strong possibility for the existence of multiple orientational responses are promoted, therefore saliency cues like corners, line intersections, and line ending detected by end-stopped cells are extracted.

The opponent color channels a and b simply undergo a center-surround operation described in [2], then a total of 12 color feature maps are obtained.

3.3 Saliency Map

Since a total of 15 end-stopping feature maps on the luminance channel and 12 color feature maps on opponent color channels have been obtained, the saliency map can be computed by normalizing and fusing all these feature maps, first within each feature dimension and then over the resulting end-stopping saliency and color saliency maps.

Firstly, each feature map is normalized into [0, 1] to make all maps comparable, and summed up with across-scale addition to obtain the conspicuity maps C:

$$C^f = \bigoplus_i F_i \tag{4}$$

where f $\in \{L, a, b\}$, F_i are feature maps on each channel, the across-scale addition $\oplus$ interpolates each feature map to the finest scale.

Then conspicuity maps can be fused to calculate the estimated saliency map S:

$$S = \sum g(C^f) \tag{5}$$

Where g is a fusion operation. A non-linear weighting function for g that favors maps with few peaks [22] is computed as:

$$W = C^f / \sqrt{m} \tag{6}$$

where m is the number of local maxima above a certain threshold. The purpose of such a weighting is to strengthen outliers which appear only in one feature channel.

At last, S is normalized again and convolved with a Gaussian filter to make it smooth like the ground truth saliency map.

4 Experiments

The common strategy to evaluate the performance of saliency model is to compare the estimated saliency map with the ground truth fixation map generated by human's eye movement data. We have compared our approach with several saliency models with three evaluation measures on two open-access eye movement datasets.

4.1 Metrics

This article used sAUC, CC, and NSS, three of the most popular measures to evaluate model performance [1].

AUC-shuffled (sAUC) is a variant from AUC (Area under the ROC Curve) where human fixations are considered as the positive set and some points from the image are uniformly chosen as the negative set. The saliency map is then treated as a binary classifier to separate the positive samples from negatives. By thresholding over this map and plotting true positive rate vs. false positive rate an ROC curve is achieved and its underneath area is calculated. AUC was the most widely used metrics for saliency method evaluation in the past. However, factors such as border cut and center-bias setting have been shown to have a dramatic influence over AUC. To control for these factors, we adopted the sAUC proposed by [23], which has become a standard evaluation method used in many recent works. Under the sAUC metric, a perfect prediction will give a score of 1.0, while any static saliency map will give a score of approximately 0.5.

NSS (normalized scanpath saliency) is the average saliency value at human fixation positions in the normalized saliency map of a model and measures how well the saliency map correlates with human fixation points during each saccade. The larger the NSS, the more accurate the predicted fixation points are. A value of 1 means that fixation points fall in an area with a predicted density of one standard deviation above the mean. Meanwhile, NSS = 0 indicates that the model performs no better than picking a random position on the map.

The Pearson's Correlation Coefficient, CC, is a statistical method used generally in the sciences for measuring how correlated or dependent two variables are. CC can be used to interpret saliency and fixation maps as random variables to measure the linear relationship between them. High positive CC values occur at locations where both the saliency map and ground truth fixation map have values of similar magnitudes.

4.2 Datasets and Models

Since statistics of different datasets vary, we employed two popular image datasets often used for saliency evaluation:

- Toronto [24]: One of the earliest and most widely used datasets. It contains 120 images mainly indoor and in-city scenes.
- MIT1003 [3]: This dataset contains 1,003 images with fixation and saliency map. The fixation map comes from 15 viewers when free viewing the original image for 3 s recorded by the eye-tracking system.

Our model was compared with four state-of-the-art saliency models (AWS [25], BMS [26], Cor [14], and eDN [27]). AWS, BMS and Cor are three outstanding bottom-up models currently available, and eDN is a deep learning based method. In addition, we also added the end-stopping saliency map, i.e. the saliency map generated by end-stopping features into the comparation to evaluate the contribution of end-stopping features to saliency. Figure 2 shows some examples of output saliency map of each model on Toronto dataset. The end-stopping saliency maps are denoted as "es-saliency", and the final saliency maps of our model are shown in the last column.

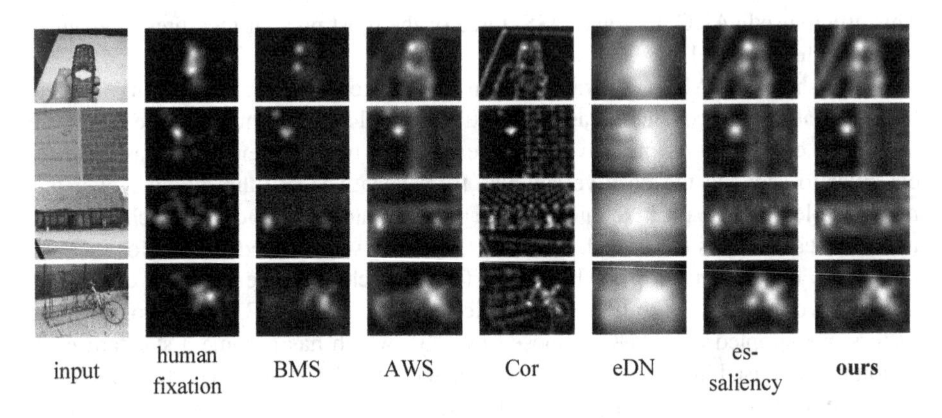

Fig. 2. Examples of output saliency maps on Toronto dataset

4.3 Center Bias

Due to the characteristic of sAUC, higher sAUC means the model is less sensitive to Gaussian blurring in evaluation, therefore sAUC can be used to evaluate the effect of center-bias on model performance. As in many models, we smooth the saliency maps of each method by varying the Gaussian blur standard deviation (STD), and show in Fig. 3 its influence on the average sAUC scores of each method on two datasets.

As shown in Fig. 3, the rank is almost same over two datasets. Specifically, our model performs better than Cor [14] and eDN [27], and worse than BMS [26] and AWS [25] in subtle differences. It's notable that the sAUC curves of end-stopping saliency map and final saliency map of our model are both smoother than all other models, indicating that the proposed model is insensitive to STD and is least affected by center bias among all five models.

4.4 Eye Fixation Prediction

The mean values of all three metrics for each model over two datasets are shown in Tables 1 and 2 respectively. The Overall performance of our model is slightly worse than BMS, better than AWS on Toronto dataset and worse on MIT1003. The differences are all quite small. Surprisingly, our model outperforms eDN [24], which is an early work based on deep learning. While recent deep learning models [4–6] have

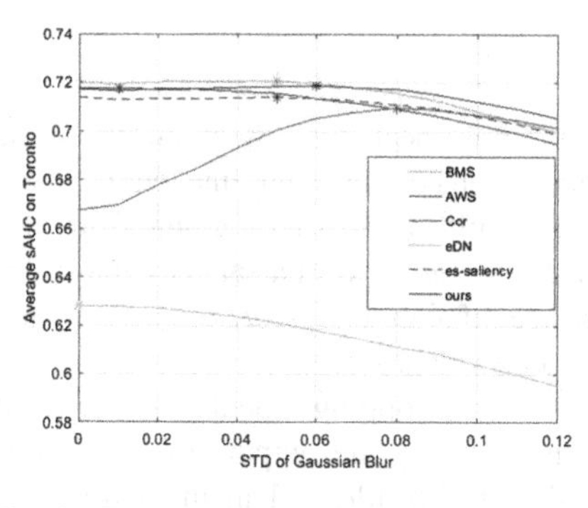

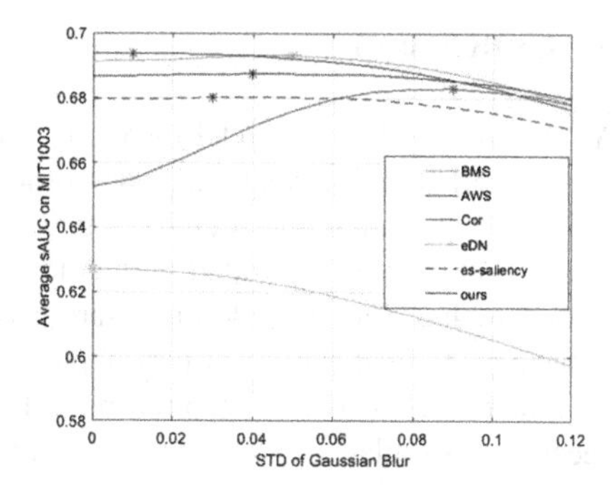

Fig. 3. Average sAUC against the STD of Gaussian Blur. X-axis represents the Gaussian blur standard deviation (STD) in image width and Y-axis represents the average sAUC score on one dataset. "*" is the peak of the curve.

achieved a much higher level, enormous calculation and large scale datasets are required for the training. Compared to Cor, the end-stopping saliency map and final saliency map of our model both show obvious advantages on CC and NSS score, which indicate the output saliency map of our model has a stronger relevance to the ground truth. The reason lies in two parts. First, biologically speaking end-stopped cells can capture many different types of features not just including corners, therefore multiscale end-stopping features used in this paper are much richer than corner features. Second, we combined color contrast features and end-stopping features together into the final saliency map.

Table 1. Results of the performance on Toronto

Model	sAUC	CC	NSS
BMS	0.7209	0.5212	1.4351
AWS	0.7175	0.4321	1.1745
eDN	0.6279	0.4982	1.2214
Cor	0.7097	0.3000	0.8842
es-saliency	0.7104	0.4412	1.1908
Ours	**0.7198**	**0.4487**	**1.2170**

Table 2. Results of the performance on MIT1003

Model	sAUC	CC	NSS
BMS	0.6931	0.3571	1.2287
AWS	0.6938	0.3220	1.1251
eDN	0.6271	0.4096	1.2880
Cor	0.6829	0.2243	0.8371
es-saliency	0.6811	0.2974	1.0186
Ours	**0.6905**	**0.3113**	**1.0629**

5 Conclusion

A bottom-up saliency model inspired by end-stopping mechanism is proposed in this paper. End-stopping features like corners, line intersections, and line endings are extracted by modelling an end-stopped cell as multiplication of the outputs from two complex cells, and integrated with color contrast features to form a saliency map. Our algorithm has shown state-of-the-art performance of fixation prediction and strong robustness to center bias on two popular open-access datasets.

Our model is mainly inspired by [14, 18]. The end-stopping model [18] is chosen because it simulates end-stopping by directly multiplying the outputs from two different orientations tuned complex neurons based on Gabor filters. This method is easy to implementation and biologically plausible, and displays the main characteristics of end-stopping cells. Compared to [14] which is based on corners extracted on edge maps of the intensity and color contrast maps that response to four orientations, our paper simulates end-stopping on the luminance channel and extracts end-stopping features that response to two different orientations, because end-stopping is mainly associated with orientation selectivity on intensity channel rather than color information, and end-stopping can perceive many other features except for corners. Higher NSS and CC values indicate our model outperforms [14] which is bothered by the sparseness of corner features in fixation prediction.

End-stopping features are integrated into final saliency map in a traditional way in this paper, thus the contribution of end-stopping to saliency is preliminarily explored and confirmed. Further research on end-stopping phenomenon or other methods like learning the precise weights of end-stopping features from eye tracking data are required to reveal the real role of end-stopping in bottom-up attention.

Acknowledgments. We acknowledge support by the Chinese National Natural Science Foundation (NSFC 61231016).

References

1. Borji, A., Itti, L.: State-of-the-art in visual attention modeling. IEEE Trans. Pattern Anal. Mach. Intell. **35**(1), 185–207 (2013)
2. Itti, L., Koch, C., Niebur, E.: A model of saliency-based visual attention for rapid scene analysis. IEEE Trans. Pattern Anal. Mach. Intell. **20**(11), 1254–1259 (1998)
3. Judd, T., Ehinger, K., Durand, F., Torralba, A.: Learning to predict where humans look. In: 2009 IEEE 12th International Conference on Computer Vision, pp. 2106–2113. Kyoto, Japan (2009)
4. Wang, Z., Ren, J., Zhang, D., Sun, M., Jiang, J.: A deep-learning based feature hybrid framework for spatiotemporal saliency detection inside videos. Neurocomputing **287**, 68–83 (2018)
5. Pan, J., Sayrol, E., Giro-I-Nieto, X., Mcguinness, K., O'Connor, N.E.: Shallow and deep convolutional networks for saliency prediction. In: IEEE Conference on Computer Vision and Pattern Recognition, pp. 598–606. IEEE, Las Vegas (2016)

6. Huang, X., Shen, C., Boix, X., Zhao, Q.: Salicon: reducing the semantic gap in saliency prediction by adapting deep neural networks. In: IEEE International Conference on Computer Vision, pp. 262–270. IEEE, Santiago (2015)
7. Kummerer, M., Wallis, T.S.A., Gatys, L.A., Bethge, M.: Understanding low- and high-level contributions to fixation prediction. In: IEEE International Conference on Computer Vision, pp. 4799–4808. IEEE, Venice (2017)
8. Hubel, D.H., Wiesel, T.N.: Receptive fields and functional architecture in two nonstriate visual areas (18 and 19) of the cat. J. Neurophysiol. **28**, 229–289 (1965)
9. Ponce, C.R., Hartmann, T.S., Livingstone, M.S.: End-stopping predicts curvature tuning along the ventral stream. J. Neurosci. **37**(3), 648 (2017)
10. Yan, Y., et al.: Unsupervised image saliency detection with gestalt-laws guided optimization and visual attention based refinement. Pattern Recognit. **79**, 65–78 (2018)
11. Xie, Y., Lu, H., Yang, M.H.: Bayesian saliency via low and mid level cues. IEEE Trans. Image Process. **22**(5), 1689–1698 (2013)
12. He, Z., Chen, X., Sun, L.: Saliency mapping enhanced by structure tensor. Comput. Intell. Neurosci. **2015**(4), 1–8 (2015)
13. Zhang, X., Wang, S., Ma, S., Gao, W.: A study on interest point guided visual saliency. In: Picture Coding Symposium, pp. 307–311. IEEE, Cairns (2015)
14. Rueopas, W., Leelhapantu, S., Chalidabhongse, T.H.: A corner-based saliency model. In: International Joint Conference on Computer Science and Software Engineering, pp. 1–6. IEEE, Khon Kaen (2016)
15. Lei, Y., Mei-ling, S., Guo-qin, P., Dan, X.: Object detection based on saliency map. J. Comput. Appl. **30**(S2), 82–85 (2010)
16. Benyosef, G., Benshahar, O.: Curvature-based perceptual singularities and texture saliency with early vision mechanisms. J. Opt. Soc. Am. A Opt. Image Sci. Vis. **25**(8), 1974–1993 (2008)
17. Van, Z.W., Kerzel, D.: The effects of saliency on manual reach trajectories and reach target selection. Vis. Res. **113**(12), 179–187 (2015)
18. Skottun, B.C.: A model for end-stopping in the visual cortex. Vis. Res. **38**(13), 2023 (1998)
19. Hamel, S., Guyader, N., Pellerin, D., Houzet, D.: Contribution of color information in visual saliency model for videos. In: Elmoataz, A., Lezoray, O., Nouboud, F., Mammass, D. (eds.) ICISP. LNCS, vol. 8509, pp. 213–221. Springer, Cherbourg (2014)
20. Chen, D., Jia, T., Wu, C.: Visual saliency detection: from space to frequency. Signal Process. Image Commun. **44**, 57–68 (2016)
21. Chen, Z.H., Liu, Y., Sheng, B., Liang, J.N., Zhang, J., Yuan, Y.B.: Image saliency detection using gabor texture cues. Multimed. Tools Appl. **75**(24), 16943–16958 (2016)
22. Frintrop, S.: Vocus: A Visual Attention System for Object Detection and Goal-Directed Search. Springer-Verlag GmbH, Berlin (2006)
23. Zhang, L., Tong, M.H., Marks, T.K., Shan, H., Cottrell, G.W.: Sun: a bayesian framework for saliency using natural statistics. J. Vis. **8**(7), 32.1–32.20 (2008)
24. Bruce, N.D.B., Tsotsos, J.K.: Saliency based on information maximization. In: Advances in Neural Information Processing Systems 18(NIPS2005), pp. 155–162. MIT Press, Vancouver (2005)
25. Leborn, V., Garca-Daz, A., Fdez-Vidal, X.R., Pardo, X.M.: Dynamic whitening saliency. IEEE Trans. Pattern Anal. Mach. Intell. **39**(5), 893–907 (2016)
26. Zhang, J., Sclaroff, S.: Exploiting surroundedness for saliency detection: a Boolean map approach. IEEE Trans. Pattern Anal. Mach. Intell. **38**(5), 889–902 (2016)
27. Vig, E., Dorr, M., Cox, D.: Large-scale optimization of hierarchical features for saliency prediction in natural images. In: Computer Vision and Pattern Recognition, pp. 2798–2805. IEEE, Columbus (2014)

Learning Collaborative Sparse Correlation Filter for Real-Time Multispectral Object Tracking

Yulong Wang, Chenglong Li(✉), Jin Tang, and Dengdi Sun

School of Computer Science and Technology, Anhui University, Hefei, China
wylemail@qq.com, lcl1314@foxmail.com, tj@ahu.edu.cn, sundengdi@163.com

Abstract. To track objects efficiently and effectively in adverse illumination conditions even in dark environment, this paper presents a novel multispectral approach to deploy the intra- and inter-spectral information in the correlation filter tracking framework. Motivated by brain inspired visual cognitive systems, our approach learns the collaborative sparse correlation filters using color and thermal sources from two aspects. First, it pursues a sparse correlation filter for each spectrum. By inheriting from the advantages of the sparse representation, our filers are robust to noises. Second, it exploits the complementary benefits from two modalities to enhance each other. In particular, we take their interdependence into account for deriving the correlation filters jointly, and formulate it as a $l_{2,1}$-based sparse learning problem. Extensive experiments on large-scale benchmark datasets suggest that our approach performs favorably against the state-of-the-arts in terms of accuracy while achieves in real-time frame rate.

Keywords: Visual tracking · Information fusion
Sparse representation · Correlation filter

1 Introduction

Visual tracking is an active research area in the computer vision community, since it is an essential and significant task in visual surveillance [20], human-computer interaction [18], and self-driving systems [1]. Despite of many breakthroughs recently, the visual tracking mainly relies on traditional RGB sensors and thus tracking target objects in case of cluttered background and low visibility at night and in bad weather is still regarded as a challenging problem.

Vision is one of the most important ways that the human brain perceives the outside world to acquire information, and the eye is the "window" to receive visual information. It is worth noting that visual cognition of human eyes is a multi-channel system. Therefore, integrating the multi-source information is a nature way to boost vision tasks in challenging scenarios [21]. Moreover, at progressively higher levels of sensory processing, information is carried by fewer

J. Ren et al. (Eds.): BICS 2018, LNAI 10989, pp. 462–472, 2018.
https://doi.org/10.1007/978-3-030-00563-4_45

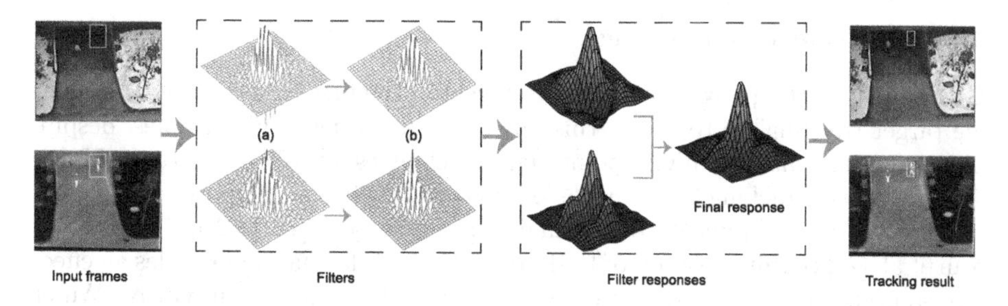

Fig. 1. Pipeline of the proposed approach. (a) and (b) denote the correlation filters optimized by our proposed model without and with collaborative sparse constraint, respectively.

neurons because the system is organized to a near complete a representation with the fewest active neurons. In other terms, the encoding of sensory information gets"sparser" as one moves up into higher levels of sensory processing [7].

Motivated by the above observations, we propose a novel approach that uses collaborative sparse correlation filters to integrate multiple source data, i.e., visible and thermal infrared spectrums, for visual tracking. Our method deploys both the intra- and inter-spectral information in the correlation filter tracking framework. First, instead of using l_2-regularization on the filters [10], we pursue a sparse correlation filter to select most significant parts to enhance the discriminative ability [6,26]. It will make our filters efficient and robust by inheriting from both advantages of the sparse representation and the correlation filter. The effectiveness of using the sparse is demonstrated in Fig. 1. Second, we exploit the complementary benefits from two modalities to enhance each other. In particular, we observe that different spectrums should have similar filters such that they have consistent localization of the target object, as shown in Fig. 1(b). Therefore, we jointly learn the correlation filters of color and thermal spectrums to collaboratively distinguish the target from the background.

We summarize our contributions to multispectral object tracking and related applications as follows. First, we propose a novel approach that carries out efficient and effective fusion of multiple spectral data, and performs favorably against the state-of-the-art multispectral trackers on two benchmark datasets, i.e., GTOT [12] and RGBT210 [16]. Second, we employ a sparse- and collaborative sparse-based regularizations on the joint filter to deploy both intra- and inter-modal complementary benefits from of color and thermal spectrums. Third, extensive analysis and evaluation on large-scale benchmark datasets verify the effectiveness and efficiency of the proposed approach.

2 Related Work

The most relevant methods and techniques are discussed. We review the related work to us from two research streams, i.e., multispectral tracking and correlation filter tracking.

2.1 Multispectral Tracking

Given the bounding box of an unknown target in the first frame, the goal of "single target tracking" is to locate this object in subsequent video frames, despite object motion, changes in viewpoint, lighting changes, or other variations. Multispectral object tracking has drawn a lot of attentions in the computer vision community with the popularity of thermal infrared sensors [12,13,16,17,19,22,23]. Yan et al. [23] cognitive fusion of RGB and thermal information provides an effective solution for effective detection and tracking of pedestrians in videos. Wu et al. [22] and Liu and Sun [17] directly employ the sparse representation to calculate the likelihood score using reconstruction residues or coefficients in Bayesian filtering framework. They ignore modality reliabilities in fusion, which may limit the tracking performance when facing malfunction or occasional perturbation of individual sources. Li et al. [12] and Li et al. [16] introduce modality weights to handle this problem, and propose sparse representation based algorithms to fuse color and thermal information. Different from these methods, we make the best use of intra- and inter-spectrum information in the correlation filter tracking framework to perform efficient and effective multispectral tracking.

2.2 Correlation Filter Tracking

Correlation filters have achieved great breakthroughs in visual tracking due to its accuracy and computational efficiency [2–4,6,9,10,14,15,26]. Bolme et al. [2] first introduce correlation filters into visual tracking, named MOSSE, and achieve hundreds of frames per second, and high tracking accuracy. Recently, many researchers further improve MOSSE from different aspects. For example, Henriques et al. [9,10] extend MOSSE to non-linear one with kernel trick, and incorporate multiple channel features efficiently by summing all channels in kernel space. To handle scale variations, Danelljan et al. [4] learn correlation filters for translation and scale estimation separately by using a scale pyramid representation. Dong et al. [6] propose a sparse correlation filter for combining the robustness of sparse representation and the efficiency of correlation filter. Zhang et al. [26] integrate multiple parts and multiple features into a unified correlation particle filter framework to perform effective object tracking.

3 Proposed Algorithm

In this section, we first present the technical details of the proposed algorithm and then describe the optimization process of the model.

3.1 Formulation

For a typical correlation filter, many negative samples are used to improve the discriminability of the track-by-detector scheme. In this work, denote $\mathbf{x}_k \in \mathbb{R}^{M\times N\times D}$as the feature vector of k-th spectrum, where M, N, and D indicates the width, height, and the number of channels, respectively. We consider all the circular shifts of $\mathbf{x}_k$ along the M and N dimensions as training samples. Each shifted sample $\mathbf{x}^k_{m,n}$, $(m,n) \in \{0,1,\ldots,M-1\} \times \{0,1,\ldots,N-1\}$, has a Gaussian function label $y(m,n)$. Let $\mathbf{X}_k = [\mathbf{x}_{0,0},\ldots,\mathbf{x}_{m,n},\ldots\mathbf{x}_{M-1,N-1}]^{\mathrm{T}}$ denote all training samples of the k-th spectrum. The goal is to find the optimal correlation filters $\mathbf{w}_k$ for K different spectrums,

$$\min_{\mathbf{w}_k} \sum_{k=1}^{K} \frac{1}{2}||\mathbf{X}_k\mathbf{w}_k - \mathbf{y}||_2^2 + \lambda_1||\mathbf{w}_k||_2^2, \tag{1}$$

the last term of Eq. (1) is the regularization of $\mathbf{w}_k$. For each spectrum k, only a few possible locations $\mathbf{x}_k^{m,n}$ should be selected to localize where the target object is at next frame. Ideally, only one possible location corresponds to the target object. Based on this observation, we suggest that the regularization should use the l_1 norm instead of the l_2 norm,

$$\min_{\mathbf{w}_k} \sum_{k=1}^{K} \frac{1}{2}||\mathbf{X}_k\mathbf{w}_k - \mathbf{y}||_2^2 + \lambda_1||\mathbf{w}_k||_1. \tag{2}$$

Among different spectrums, the learned $\mathbf{w}_k$ should select similar circular shifts so that they have similar motion. As a result, the learned $\mathbf{w}_k$ should be similar. In this work, we use the convex $l_{2,1}$ mixed norm to learned their correlation filters jointly to distinguish the target from the background, and the final structure of our model is as follows:

$$\min_{\mathbf{w}_k} \sum_{k=1}^{K} \frac{1}{2}||\mathbf{X}_k\mathbf{w}_k - \mathbf{y}||_2^2 + \lambda_1||\mathbf{w}_k||_1 + \lambda_2||\mathbf{W}||_{2,1}, \tag{3}$$

where $\mathbf{W} = [\mathbf{w}_1, \mathbf{w}_2, \ldots, \mathbf{w}_K] \in \mathbb{R}^{MN \times K}$, and λ_1, λ_2 are regularization parameters. The definition of the $l_{p,q}$ mixed norm is $||\mathbf{W}||_{p,q} = (\sum_i(\sum_j |[\mathbf{W}]_{ij}|^p)^{\frac{q}{p}})^{\frac{1}{q}}$ and $[\mathbf{W}]_{ij}$ denotes the element at the i-th row and j-th column of $\mathbf{W}$.

3.2 Optimization

In this section, We present algorithmic details on how to efficiently solve the optimization problem (3). We first use the linearized ADM with adaptive penalty to avoid some matrix inversions in optimization. Two auxiliary variables $\mathbf{p}_k \in \mathbb{R}^{MN \times 1}$ and $\mathbf{Q} \in \mathbb{R}^{MN \times K}$ are introduced to make Eq. (3) separable:

$$\min_{\mathbf{w}_k} \sum_{k=1}^{K} \frac{1}{2}||\mathbf{X}_k\mathbf{w}_k - \mathbf{y}||_2^2 + \lambda_1||\mathbf{p}_k||_1 + \lambda_2||\mathbf{Q}||_{2,1}, s.t. \mathbf{w}_k = \mathbf{p}_k, \mathbf{W} = \mathbf{Q} \tag{4}$$

We use the fast first-order Alternating Direction Method of Multipliers (ADMM) to efficiently solve the optimization problem (4). By introducing augmented Lagrange multipliers to incorporate the equality constraints into the objective function, we obtain a Lagrangian function that can be optimized through a sequence of simple closed form update operations in (5).

$$\begin{aligned}
&\min_{\mathbf{w}_k,\mathbf{p}_k,\mathbf{Q}} \sum_{k=1}^{K} \frac{1}{2}||\mathbf{X}_k\mathbf{w}_k - \mathbf{y}||_2^2 + \lambda_1||\mathbf{p}_k||_1 + \frac{\mu}{2}||\mathbf{w}_k - \mathbf{p}_k||_F^2 + \langle \mathbf{Y}_{1,k}, \mathbf{w}_k - \mathbf{p}_k \rangle \\
&+ \lambda_2||\mathbf{Q}||_{2,1} + \langle \mathbf{Y}_2, \mathbf{W} - \mathbf{Q} \rangle + \frac{\mu}{2}||\mathbf{W} - \mathbf{Q}||_F^2 \\
&= \sum_{k=1}^{K} \frac{1}{2}||\mathbf{X}_k\mathbf{w}_k - \mathbf{y}||_2^2 + \lambda_1||\mathbf{p}_k||_1 + \frac{\mu}{2}||\mathbf{w}_k - \mathbf{p}_k + \frac{\mathbf{Y}_{1,k}}{\mu}||_2^2 - \frac{1}{2\mu}||\mathbf{Y}_{1,k}||_2^2 \\
&+ \lambda_2||\mathbf{Q}||_{2,1} + \frac{\mu}{2}||\mathbf{W} - \mathbf{Q} + \frac{\mathbf{Y}_2}{\mu}||_F^2 - \frac{1}{2\mu}||\mathbf{Y}_2||_F^2
\end{aligned} \tag{5}$$

Here, $\langle \mathbf{A}, \mathbf{B} \rangle = \mathrm{Tr}(\mathbf{A}^{\mathrm{T}}\mathbf{B})$ denotes the matrix inner product. $\mathbf{Y}_{1,k}$ and $\mathbf{Y}_2$ are Lagrangian multipliers. We then alternatively update one variable by minimizing (5) with fixing other variables. Besides the Lagrangian multipliers, there are three variables, including $\mathbf{W}$, $\mathbf{p}_k$ and $\mathbf{Q}$, to solve. The solutions of the subproblems are as follows:

w-Subproblem: Given fixed $\mathbf{p}_k$ and $\mathbf{Q}$, $\mathbf{w}_k$ is updated by solving the optimization problem (6) with the solution (7)

$$\min_{\mathbf{w}_k} \sum_{k=1}^{K} \frac{1}{2}||\mathbf{X}_k\mathbf{w}_k - \mathbf{y}||^2 + \frac{\mu}{2}||\mathbf{w}_k - \mathbf{p}_k + \frac{\mathbf{Y}_{1,k}}{\mu}||_2^2 + \frac{\mu}{2}||\mathbf{W} - \mathbf{Q} + \frac{\mathbf{Y}_2}{\mu}||_F^2, \tag{6}$$

$$\mathbf{w}_k = (\mathbf{X}_k^{\mathrm{T}}\mathbf{X}_k + 2\mu\mathbf{I})^{-1}(\mathbf{X}_k^{\mathrm{T}}\mathbf{y} + \mu(\mathbf{p}_k + \mathbf{Q}_k) - (\mathbf{Y}_{1,k} + \mathbf{Y}_{2,k})). \tag{7}$$

Here, $\mathbf{w}_k$, $\mathbf{P}_k$ and $\mathbf{Q}_k$ denote the k-th column of $\mathbf{W}$, $\mathbf{P}$, $\mathbf{Q}$, respectively. Note that, all circulant matrices are made diagonal by the Discrete Fourier Transform (DFT), regardless of the generating vector. If $\mathbf{X}_k$ is a circulant matrix, it can be expressed with its base sample $\mathbf{x}_k$ as

$$\mathbf{X}_k = F diag(\hat{\mathbf{x}}_k) F^{\mathrm{H}}, \tag{8}$$

where $\hat{\mathbf{x}}_k$ denotes the DFT of the generating vector, $\hat{\mathbf{x}}_k = \mathcal{F}(\mathbf{x}_k)$, and F is a constant matrix that does not depend on $\mathbf{x}_k$. The constant matrix F is known as the DFT matrix. $\mathbf{X}_k^{\mathrm{H}}$ is the Hermitian transpose, i.e., $\mathbf{X}_k^{\mathrm{H}} = (\mathbf{X}_k^*)^{\mathrm{T}}$, and $\mathbf{X}_k^*$ is the complex-conjugate of $\mathbf{X}_k$. For real numbers, $\mathbf{X}_k^{\mathrm{H}} = \mathbf{X}_k^{\mathrm{T}}$. It (Eq. (7)) can be calculated very efficiently in the Fourier domain by considering the circulant structure property of $\mathbf{X}_k$,

$$\mathbf{w}_k = \mathcal{F}^{-1}[\frac{\hat{\mathbf{x}}_k^* \odot \hat{\mathbf{y}} + \mu(\hat{\mathbf{p}}_k + \hat{\mathbf{Q}}_k) - (\hat{\mathbf{Y}}_{1,k} + \hat{\mathbf{Y}}_{2,k})}{\hat{\mathbf{x}}_k^* \odot \hat{\mathbf{x}}_k + 2\mu}]. \tag{9}$$

Here, $\mathcal{F}^{-1}$ denotes the inverse DFT, while $\odot$ as well as the fraction denote the element-wise product and division, respectively. The $\mathbf{x}_k$ is the base sample of circulant matrix $\mathbf{X}_k$.

Algorithm 1. Optimization Procedure to Eq.(4).

Input: The spectra feature matrix $\mathbf{X}_k(k = 1, 2..., K)$ and Gaussian function label $\mathbf{y}$, the parameters λ_1 and λ_2;
Set $\mathbf{w}_k = \mathbf{p}_k = \mathbf{Y}_{1,k} = 0, \mathbf{W} = \mathbf{Q} = \mathbf{Y}_2 = 0, \mu_0 = 0.1, \mu_{max} = 10^{10}, \rho = 1.2, \epsilon = 10^{-15}, maxIter = 10$ and $t = 0$.
Output: The filter $\mathbf{w}_k$.
while not converged **do**
Update $\mathbf{w}_{k,t+1}$ by Eq.(7);
Update $\mathbf{p}_{k,t+1}$ by Eq.(11);
Update $\mathbf{Q}_{t+1}$ by Eq.(13);
Update Lagrange multipliers as follows:
$\mathbf{Y}_{1,k,t+1} = \mathbf{Y}_{1,k,t} + \mu_t(\mathbf{w}_k - \mathbf{p}_k)$;
$\mathbf{Y}_{2,t+1} = \mathbf{Y}_{2,t} + \mu_t(\mathbf{W} - \mathbf{Q})$;
Update μ_{t+1} by $\mu_{t+1} = \min(\mu_{max}, \rho\mu_t)$;
Update t by $t = t + 1$;
Check the convergence condition, i.e. the maximum element changes of $\mathbf{w}_k, \mathbf{p}_k$ and $\mathbf{Q}$ between two consecutive iterations are less than ϵ or the maximum number of iterations reaches maxIter.
end while

p-Subproblem: Given fixed $\mathbf{w}_k$ and $\mathbf{Q}$, Eq. (5) can be rewritten as

$$\min_{\mathbf{p}_k} \sum_{k=1}^{K} \frac{\mu}{2} ||\mathbf{w}_k - \mathbf{p}_k + \frac{\mathbf{Y}_{1,k}}{\mu}||_2^2 + \lambda_1 ||\mathbf{p}_k||_1. \tag{10}$$

According to (Lin et al. 2009), an efficient closed-form solution of Eq. (10) can be computed by the soft-thresholding (or shrinkage) method:

$$\mathbf{p}_k = S_{\frac{\lambda}{\mu}}(\mathbf{w}_k + \frac{\mathbf{Y}_{1,k}}{\mu}), \tag{11}$$

where the definition of $S_\lambda(a)$ is $S_\lambda(a) = \text{sign}(a)\max(0, |a| - \lambda)$.

Q-Subproblem: Given fixed $\mathbf{W}$, $\mathbf{P}$, Eq. (5) can be rewritten as

$$\begin{aligned} &\min_{\mathbf{Q}} \frac{\mu}{2} ||\mathbf{W} - \mathbf{Q} + \frac{\mathbf{Y}_2}{\mu}||_F^2 + \lambda_2 ||\mathbf{Q}||_{2,1} \\ &= \min_{\mathbf{Q}_1,\dots,\mathbf{Q}_m} \sum_{i=1}^{m} (\frac{\mu}{2} ||\mathbf{W}_i - \mathbf{Q}_i + \frac{\mathbf{Y}_{2,i}}{\mu}||_2^2 + \lambda_2 ||\mathbf{Q}_i||_2). \end{aligned} \tag{12}$$

$\mathbf{W}_i$, $\mathbf{Q}_i$ and $\mathbf{Y}_{2,i}$ denote the i-th row of the matrix $\mathbf{W}$, $\mathbf{Q}$ and $\mathbf{Y}_2$, respectively. For each row of $\mathbf{Q}_i$ in the subproblem (12), an efficient closed-form solution can be computed:

$$\mathbf{Q}_i = max(0, 1 - \frac{\lambda_2}{\mu ||\mathbf{H}_i||_2})\mathbf{H}_i, \tag{13}$$

where $\mathbf{H}_i = \mathbf{W}_i + \frac{1}{\mu}\mathbf{Y}_{2,i}$.

Since each subproblem of Eq. (4) is convex, we can guarantee that the limit point by our algorithm satisfies the Nash equilibrium conditions. And the main steps of the optimization procedure are summarized in Algorithm 1.

3.3 Target Position Estimation

After solving this optimization problem, we obtain the correlation filter $\mathbf{w}_k$ for each type of modality. Given an image patch in the next frame, the feature vector on the k-th modality is denoted by $\mathbf{z}_k$ and of size $M \times N \times D$. We first transform it to the Fourier domain $\hat{\mathbf{z}}_k = \mathcal{F}(\mathbf{z}_k)$, and then the final correlation response map is computed by

$$S = \sum_{k=1}^{K} \mathcal{F}^{-1}(\hat{\mathbf{z}}_\mathbf{k} \odot \hat{\mathbf{w}}_\mathbf{k}). \tag{14}$$

The target location then can be estimated by searching for the position of maximum value of the correlation response map S of size $M \times N$.

3.4 Model Update

In practice, we adopt an incremental strategy, which only uses new samples $\mathbf{x}_k$ in the current frame to update models as shown in (15), where t is the frame index and η is a learning rate parameter.

$$\mathcal{F}(\mathbf{w}_\mathbf{k})^t = (1-\eta)\mathcal{F}(\mathbf{w}_\mathbf{k})^{t-1} + \eta\mathcal{F}(\mathbf{w}_\mathbf{k})^t. \tag{15}$$

4 Experimental Results

4.1 Experimental Setups

Implementation Details: There are two hyperparameters, i.e., λ_1 and λ_2, in Eq. (3). The value of them are estimated by performing a grid search from 0 to 1 with step 0.01. Evaluations show that the best performance is achieved when $\lambda_1 = 0.11$ and $\lambda_2 = 0.14$, and use a kernel width of 0.1 for generating the Gaussian function labels. Their learning rate η in (15) is set to 0.025. To remove the boundary discontinuities, the extracted feature channels are weighted by a cosine window. We implement our tracker in MATLAB on an Intel I7-6700K 4.00 GHz CPU with 32 GB RAM. Furthermore, all the parameter settings are available in the source code to be released for accessible reproducible research.

Datasets: Our algorithm is evaluated on two large datasets: GTOT and RGBT210. GTOT includes 50 aligned RGB-T video pairs with about 12K frames in total, and RGBT210 includes 210 highly-aligned RGB-T video pairs with about 210K frames in total. They are annotated with ground truth bounding boxes and various visual attributes.

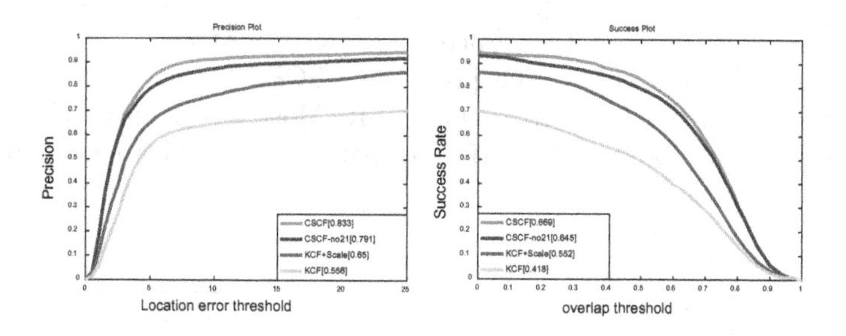

Fig. 2. PR and SR plots on GTOT. The performance of CSCF tracker is improved gradually with the addition of collaborative sparse constraint.

Evaluation Protocol: As a measure of tracking results, we use the success rate (SR) to evaluate the RGB-T tracking performance. SR is the ratio of the number of successful frames whose overlap is larger than a threshold. By changing the threshold, the SR plot can be obtained, and we employ the area under curve of SR plot to define the representative SR.

4.2 Model Analysis

KCF [10] is intended as the baseline in this work, and is achieved by using the released code with default parameter settings. KCF + Scale utilize an adaptive multi-scale strategy to handle scale variations. CSCF-no21 is our model without using the mixed $l_{2,1}$ norm. Scale processing also apply to CSCF-no21 and CSCF, and all trackers use grayscale feature. Figure 2 shows the performance of our model is improved gradually with the addition of l_1 and $l_{2,1}$ norm on the benchmark of GTOT. CSCF-no21 dramatically improves the performance by a SR score of 9.3% compared with KCF + Scale. Our overall model achieves about 4.2%/2.4% improvement with PR and SR metrics in comparison with CSCF-no21, which demonstrates the effectiveness of the proposed mechanism in practical tracking.

4.3 Comparison with State-of-the-Arts

Evaluation on GTOT: We first evaluate our CSCF algorithm with 9 trackers on GTOT, including CSR [12], Struck [8], SCM [27], CN [5], STC [25], KCF [10], L1-PF [22], JSR [17] and TLD [11]. Among all the trackers, our CSCF tracker achieves the best results as shown in Fig. 3(a). Compared with CSR, CSCF achieves about 4.9% improvement with SR on the GTOT dataset. Furthermore, compared with KCF, CSCF achieves much better performance with about 24.7% improvement.

Evaluation on RGBT210: For further demonstrate the effectiveness of the proposed approach, we construct experiments on the public RGBT210 dataset with comparisons to 6 trackers, including DSST [4], MEEM [24] + RGBT, CSR,

KCF + RGBT, L1-PF, JSR. Figure 3(b) shows that our tracker significantly outperform them. In particular, The proposed CSCF obtains 4.2% performance gains in SR, which is much better than CSR. Most importantly, the proposed tracker performs at about 50 FPS (frames per second), which has enabled real-time object tracking.

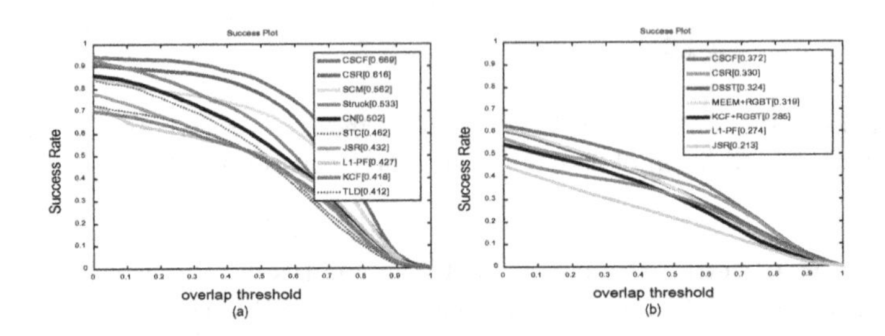

Fig. 3. (a) and (b) denote the evaluation results on GTOT and RGB210 dataset, respectively. The representative score of SR is presented in the legend.

5 Conclusion

In this paper, we propose a novel learning collaborative sparse correlation filters for multispectral object tracking. The proposed tracking algorithm can effectively exploit interdependencies among different spectrums to learn their correlation filters jointly. Experimental results compared with several state-of-the-art methods on two visual tracking benchmark datasets demonstrate the effectiveness and robustness of the proposed algorithm.

Acknowledgment. This work was jointly supported by National Natural Science Foundation of China (61672002, 61702002, 61402002), Natural Science Foundation of Anhui Province (1808085QF187), Natural Science Foundation of Anhui Higher Education Institution of China (KJ2017A017, KJ2018A0023) and Co-Innovation Center for Information Supply & Assurance Technology of Anhui University.

References

1. Bengler, K., Dietmayer, K., Farber, B., Maurer, M.: Three decades of driver assistance systems: review and future perspectives. ITSM **6**(4), 6–22 (2014)
2. Bolme, D.S., Beveridge, J.R., Draper, B.A., Lui, Y.M.: Visual object tracking using adaptive correlation filters. In: Proceedings of the IEEE Conference on CVPR (2010)
3. Danelljan, M., Bhat, G., Khan, F.S., Felsberg, M.: ECO: efficient convolution operators for tracking. In: Proceedings of the IEEE Conference on CVPR (2017)
4. Danelljan, M., Hager, G., Khan, F., Felsberg, M.: Accurate scale estimation for robust visual tracking. In: Proceedings of the BMVC (2014)

5. Danelljan, M., Khan, F.S., Felsberg, M., Weijer, J.V.D.: Adaptive color attributes for real-time visual tracking. In: Proceedings of the IEEE Conference on CVPR, pp. 1090–1097 (2014)
6. Dong, Y., Yang, M., Pei, M.: Visual tracking with sparse correlation filters. In: Proceedings of the IEEE ICIP, pp. 439–443 (2016)
7. Donoho, D.L.: Compressed sensing. IEEE IT **52**(4), 1289–1306 (2006)
8. Hare, S., Saffari, A., Torr, P.H.S.: Struck: structured output tracking with kernels. In: Proceedings of the IEEE ICCV, pp. 263–270 (2011)
9. Henriques, J.F., Caseiro, R., Martins, P., Batista, J.: Exploiting the circulant structure of tracking-by-detection with kernels. In: Fitzgibbon, A., Lazebnik, S., Perona, P., Sato, Y., Schmid, C. (eds.) ECCV 2012. LNCS, vol. 7575, pp. 702–715. Springer, Heidelberg (2012). https://doi.org/10.1007/978-3-642-33765-9_50
10. Henriques, J.F., Rui, C., Martins, P., Batista, J.: High-speed tracking with kernelized correlation filters. IEEE TPAMI **37**(3), 583–596 (2015)
11. Kalal, Z., Mikolajczyk, K., Matas, J.: Tracking-learning-detection. IEEE TPAMI **34**(7), 1409–1422 (2012)
12. Li, C., Cheng, H., Hu, S., Liu, X., Tang, J., Lin, L.: Learning collaborative sparse representation for grayscale-thermal tracking. IEEE TIP **25**(12), 5743–5756 (2016)
13. Li, C., Hu, S., Gao, S., Tang, J.: Real-time grayscale-thermal tracking via Laplacian sparse representation. In: Tian, Q., Sebe, N., Qi, G.-J., Huet, B., Hong, R., Liu, X. (eds.) MMM 2016. LNCS, vol. 9517, pp. 54–65. Springer, Cham (2016). https://doi.org/10.1007/978-3-319-27674-8_6
14. Li, C., Liang, X., Lu, Y., Zhao, N., Tang, J.: RGB-T object tracking: benchmark and baseline. arXiv:1805.08982 (2018)
15. Li, C., Lin, L., Zuo, W., Tang, J., Yang, M.: Visual tracking via dynamic graph learning. arXiv:1710.01444 (2018)
16. Li, C., Zhao, N., Lu, Y., Zhu, C., Tang, J.: Weighted sparse representation regularized graph learning for RGB-T object tracking. In: Proceedings of the ACM MM, pp. 1856–1864 (2017)
17. Liu, H., Sun, F.: Fusion tracking in color and infrared images using joint sparse representation. Inf. Sci. **55**(3), 590–599 (2012)
18. Liu, L., Xing, J., Ai, H., Xiang, R.: Hand posture recognition using finger geometric feature. In: Proceedings of the ICPR, pp. 565–568 (2013)
19. Ren, J., Orwell, J., Jones, G.A., Xu, M.: Tracking the soccer ball using multiple fixed cameras. CVIU **113**(5), 633–642 (2009)
20. Ren, J., Xu, M., Orwell, J., Jones, G.A.: Multi-camera video surveillance for real-time analysis and reconstruction of soccer games. MVA **21**(6), 855–863 (2010)
21. Wang, Z., Ren, J., Zhang, D., Sun, M., Jiang, J.: A deep-learning based feature hybrid framework for spatiotemporal saliency detection inside videos. Neurocomputing **287**, 68–83 (2018)
22. Wu, Y., Blasch, E., Chen, G., Bai, L., Ling, H.: Multiple source data fusion via sparse representation for robust visual tracking. In: Proceedings of the ICIF, pp. 1–8 (2011)
23. Yan, Y., Ren, J., Zhao, H., Sun, G., Wang, Z., Zheng, J., Marshall, S., Soraghan, J.: Cognitive fusion of thermal and visible imagery for effective detection and tracking of pedestrians in videos. Cogn. Comput. **9**, 1–11 (2017)
24. Zhang, J., Ma, S., Sclaroff, S.: MEEM: robust tracking via multiple experts using entropy minimization. In: Fleet, D., Pajdla, T., Schiele, B., Tuytelaars, T. (eds.) ECCV 2014. LNCS, vol. 8694, pp. 188–203. Springer, Cham (2014). https://doi.org/10.1007/978-3-319-10599-4_13

25. Zhang, K., Zhang, L., Liu, Q., Zhang, D., Yang, M.-H.: Fast visual tracking via dense spatio-temporal context learning. In: Fleet, D., Pajdla, T., Schiele, B., Tuytelaars, T. (eds.) ECCV 2014. LNCS, vol. 8693, pp. 127–141. Springer, Cham (2014). https://doi.org/10.1007/978-3-319-10602-1_9
26. Zhang, T., Xu, C., Yang, M.H.: Multi-task correlation particle filter for robust object tracking. In: Proceedings of the IEEE Conference on CVPR, pp. 4819–4827 (2017)
27. Zhong, W., Lu, H., Yang, M.H.: Robust object tracking via sparse collaborative appearance model. IEEE TIP **23**(5), 2356 (2014)

Saliency Detection via Multi-view Synchronized Manifold Ranking

Yuanyuan Guan, Bo Jiang(✉), Yuan Zhang, Aihua Zheng, Dengdi Sun, and Bin Luo

School of Computer Science and Technology, Anhui University, No. 111 Jiulong Road, Hefei, China
jiangbo@ahu.edu.cn

Abstract. Saliency detection is an important problem in computer vision. Recently, graph-based manifold ranking (GMR) has been successfully employed in image saliency detection problem. Traditional GMR involves two main ranking stages, i.e., ranking with background queries and ranking with foreground queries. However, these two ranking stages are conducted separately which obviously ignores the correlation between background and foreground queries. Also, traditional GMR uses a single graph which lacks of considering multi-view features. To overcome these problems, in this paper, we propose a new multi-view synchronized manifold ranking for saliency detection problem. Our method aims to perform background and foreground ranking simultaneously by exploiting multiple kinds of features and thus performs more robustly and discriminatively for saliency detection problem. Experimental results on three benchmark datasets demonstrate the effectiveness of the proposed saliency detection method.

Keywords: Saliency detection · Graph ranking · Multi-scale graph Multi-views

1 Introduction

Image saliency detection aims to locate the important and informative regions in an image. It is an important problem in image or video analysis and has been widely used in many computer vision applications. Most of existing saliency detection methods can be roughly categorized into three classes including bottom-up, top-down, and combination of bottom-up and top-down methods. Top-down models [13,18,20,36] are usually supervised and need some manually labeled object as training data while bottom-up models [1,4,6,16,30,37,39,40] are generally unsupervised. They only exploit low-level visual cues to compute saliency map.

In recent years, graph-based bottom-up saliency detection methods have been widely studied. These methods generally represent an image by using a graph

J. Ren et al. (Eds.): BICS 2018, LNAI 10989, pp. 473–483, 2018.
https://doi.org/10.1007/978-3-030-00563-4_46

whose nodes denote the super-pixels and edges represent the spatial relationship among super-pixels. Then, they use some graph based learning models to compute the optimal saliency for each super-pixel. For example, Harel et al. [19] propose the graph-based visual saliency model. Chang et al. [5] construct a graphical model which combines both objectness and regional saliency together to obtain a better saliency estimation. Yan et al. [39] present a graphical model based hierarchical optimization formulation for saliency detection. Yang et al. [7] rank the super-pixels via graph-based manifold ranking based on foreground or background queries, respectively. Zhu et al. [43] propose a saliency optimization model based on robust background detection. They first introduce background and foreground measurement and then present a general energy optimization framework to combine background and foreground cues together. Li et al. [21] propose to use a regularized random walks ranking model to conduct saliency estimation and computation. Recently, Wang et al. [35] put forward a saliency detection approach by exploiting both local graph structure and background priors. Peng et al. [27] present a hybrid of local feature-based saliency and global feature-based saliency detection model.

As a popular bottom-up method, graph-based manifold ranking (GMR) [7] has been shown effectively in image saliency detection problem. GMR involves two main stages, i.e., ranking with background queries and ranking with foreground queries. However, one limitation is that these two stages are conducted separately, which ignores the correlation between background and foreground cues. Also, traditional GMR uses a single graph which lacks of considering multiple different kinds of features. To overcome these problems, in this paper, we propose a new multi-view synchronized manifold ranking for saliency detection problem. Our method aims to perform background and foreground ranking simultaneously by exploiting multiple kinds of features and thus performs more robustly and discriminatively for saliency detection problem. A simple effective iterative algorithm has been proposed to find the optimal solution for the proposed multi-view model. Experimental results on three benchmark datasets demonstrate the effectiveness and robustness of the proposed multi-view saliency detection method.

2 Multi-view Synchronized Manifold Ranking

In this section, we first present the synchronized manifold ranking (SMR) model [12]. Then, we extend the model to multi-view case and propose our new multi-view Synchronized Manifold Ranking model, followed by an algorithm to solve it.

2.1 Synchronized Manifold Ranking

Given an input image $\mathcal{I}$, we first segment it into n non-overlapping super-pixels $S = \{s_1, \cdots s_q, s_{q+1}, \cdots s_n\}$ by using simple linear iterative clustering (SLIC) approach [2]. Similar to work [7], we first construct a neighbor graph $G = (V, E)$

whose nodes V represent the super-pixels S and edges E denote the relationship between pairs of super-pixels. W_{ij} is edge weight between s_i and s_j. Let $Y = (y^f, y^b) \in \mathbb{R}^{n\times 2}$, where y^f, y^b denote the foreground and background queries, respectively. Then, by considering the correlation between f_i and g_i, Guan et al. [12] propose a synchronized manifold ranking model as,

$$\begin{aligned} &\min_F \frac{1}{2}\sum_{i,j=1}^{n} W_{ij}\|F_i - F_j\|^2 + \mu\sum_{i=1}^{n} d_i\|F_i - \frac{Y_i}{\sqrt{d_i}}\|^2 + \lambda\sum_{i=1}^{n} f_i g_i \\ &s.t. \quad F = (f, g) \end{aligned} \tag{1}$$

where $d_i = \sum_j W_{ij}$, parameter $\mu, \lambda > 0$ are two balance parameters. F_i and F_j denote the i-th and j-th rows of variable matrix F, and variable f, g denote the first and second column of F, respectively. The last term $\sum_{i=1}^{n} f_i g_i$ indicates the correlation between foreground and background measurement f_i and g_i. Using matrix notation, the problem can be rewritten as,

$$\begin{aligned} &\min_F \frac{1}{2}\sum_{i,j=1}^{n} W_{ij}\|F_i - F_j\|^2 + \mu\sum_{i=1}^{n} d_i\|F_i - \frac{Y_i}{\sqrt{d_i}}\|^2 + \lambda f^T g \\ &s.t. \quad F = (f, g) \end{aligned} \tag{2}$$

Note that, the penally term $\lambda f^T g$ guarantees that the correlation between the background probability and the foreground probability is as low as possible. When $\lambda = 0$, our model degenerates to traditional two stage GMR ranking process.

2.2 Multi-view Model

The above ranking model only considers conducting ranking on a single graph. In real application, multiple graphs can usually be obtained by exploring multi-view features (such as HOG, RGB, LBP and so on), respectively, in which each feature corresponds to a graph. For each super-pixel s_i, we extract multi-view visual features as x_i^k, where $k = 1, 2 \ldots K$. Let $X = \{X^1, X^2, \ldots X^K\}$, where $X^k = \{x_1^k, x_2^k \ldots x_n^k\}$ denote the feature collection of the k-th view feature. For each view X^k, we construct graph $G^k(V, E^k)$ whose nodes V represent the super-pixels S and edges E^k denote the relationship between visual features of the k-th view. Let W^k be the corresponding weight matrix of the graph $G^k(V, E^k)$. Then, the k-th view ranking model as follows,

$$\begin{aligned} &\min_F \frac{1}{2}\sum_{i,j=1}^{n} W_{ij}^k\|F_i - F_j\|^2 + \mu\sum_{i=1}^{n} d_i^k\|F_i - \frac{Y_i}{\sqrt{d_i}}\|^2 + \lambda f^T g \\ &s.t. \quad F = (f, g) \end{aligned} \tag{3}$$

By a simple algebra formation, Eq. (3) can be reformulated more compactly as,

$$\min_F Tr(F^T A^k F - \mu F^T Y) + \lambda f^T g \tag{4}$$

where $A^k = (1+\mu)D^k - W^k$ and D^k is diagonal matrix with $D^k_{ii} = \sum_j W^k_{ij}$. $Tr(\cdot)$ denotes the trace operator. Then, by taking the contributions of different views together, we combine all views together using an adaptive non-negative view-weight α_k. That is,

$$\min_F \sum\nolimits_{k=1}^{K} \alpha_k Tr(F^T A^k F) - Tr(\mu F^T Y) + \lambda f^T g \tag{5}$$

$$s.t. \quad \sum\nolimits_{k=1}^{K} \alpha_k = 1,\ \alpha_k \geq 0,\ F = (f, g) \tag{6}$$

2.3 Optimization Algorithm

In this section, we introduce an iterative algorithm to solve this problem. The proposed algorithm iteratively conducts the following two steps until convergence.

(1) Fixing $F = (f, g)$ while optimizing α. First, we fix $F(f, g)$ to optimize α. By using a lagrange multiplier β to ensure the constraint $\Sigma_{k=1}^{K} \alpha_k = 1$, we get the Lagrange function as Eq. (5) ,

$$L(\alpha, \beta) = \sum_{k=1}^{K} \alpha_k Tr(F^T A^k F) - Tr(\mu F^T Y) + \lambda f^T g + \beta(\sum\nolimits_{k=1}^{K} \alpha_k - 1) \tag{7}$$

Note that, the solution of α in Eq. (7) is $\alpha_{k^0} = 1$ and other entries in α equal to 0, which is corresponding to find the minimum J over different views. It means that only one view is selected by this method, which is not desirable. Therefore, following the work in [11], we handle this problem by setting $\alpha_k \leftarrow \alpha_k^r$ with $r > 1$ and solve,

$$L(\alpha, \beta) = \sum_{k=1}^{K} \alpha_k^r Tr(F^T A^k F) - Tr(\mu F^T Y) + \lambda f^T g + \beta(\sum\nolimits_{k=1}^{K} \alpha_k - 1) \tag{8}$$

where $r > 1$. Then, the optimal solution is computed by setting the first derivative of the above function $L(\alpha, \beta)$ w.r.t α and β to be zero, i.e.,

$$\begin{cases} \dfrac{\partial L(\alpha, \beta)}{\partial \alpha_k} = r\alpha_k^{r-1} Tr(F^T A^k F) - \beta = 0, \\ \dfrac{\partial L(\alpha, \beta)}{\partial \beta} = \sum\nolimits_{k=1}^{K} \alpha_k - 1 = 0, \end{cases} \tag{9}$$

Therefore, the update formula for α_k can be obtained as

$$\alpha_k = \frac{\left(\frac{1}{Tr(F^T A^k F)}\right)^{\frac{1}{(r-1)}}}{\sum_{k=1}^{K} \left(\frac{1}{Tr(F^T A^k F)}\right)^{\frac{1}{(r-1)}}} \tag{10}$$

where the parameter r controls α_k.

If $r \to +\infty$, a different α_k will be close to each other, and if $r \to 1$, only $\alpha_k = 1$ corresponding to the minimum J over different views, and $\alpha_k = 0$

otherwise. Therefore, the selection of r should be based on the complementary property of all view features. That is, a large value of r is preferable for the features with rich complementary information and vice versa.

(2) Fixing α while optimizing $F = (f, g)$. Then, the optimal $F^* = (f^*, g^*)$ can be obtained by fixed α. The problem becomes,

$$\min_F \sum_{k=1}^{K} \alpha_k^r Tr(F^T A^k F) - \mu Tr(F^T Y) + \lambda f^T g \qquad s.t.\ \ F = (f, g), \tag{11}$$

which can be rewritten as follows,

$$\min_F Tr(F^T BF) - Tr\mu(F^T Y) + \lambda f^T g \qquad s.t.\ \ F = (f, g), \tag{12}$$

where $B = \sum_{k=1}^{K} \alpha_k^r A^k$. Substituting $F = (f, g)$ and $Y = (y^b, y^f)$ into Eq. (12), we have the following,

$$\min_F Tr\Big[(f,g)^T B(f,g)\Big] - Tr\Big[\mu(f,g)^T(y^b, y^f)\Big] + \lambda f^T g \tag{13}$$

Simplify the above formulation, we can obtain,

$$L = f^T Bf + g^T Bg - \mu(f^T y^b + g^T y^f) + \lambda f^T g \tag{14}$$

Then, the optimal $F^* = (f^*, g^*)$ can be obtained by setting the first derivation w.r.t f, g to zero, respectively, i.e.,

$$\begin{cases} \dfrac{\partial L}{\partial f} = 2Bf^* - \mu y^b + \lambda g^* = 0 \\ \dfrac{\partial L}{\partial g} = 2Bg^* - \mu y^f + \lambda f^* = 0 \end{cases} \tag{15}$$

At last, we obtain the optimal f^* and g^* as follows,

$$\begin{cases} f^* = \mu(\lambda^2 I - 4B^2)^{-1}(\mu y^f - 2By^b) \\ g^* = -\frac{1}{\lambda}(2Bf^* - \mu y^b) \end{cases} \tag{16}$$

3 Saliency Detection

In this section, we summarize our saliency detection method. Overall, it contains three main steps, i.e., multi-view feature extraction, graph construction and the final ranking saliency computation.

3.1 Multi-view Feature Extraction

In this paper, we use two kinds of features to capture different characteristics of each superpixel, i.e., low-level appearance feature and high-level semantic feature. For low-level appearance features are used in this work, we use both color and texture features. For high-level semantic feature, we use deep convolutional neural networks (CNNs) to extract features which have been demonstrated effectively on detection tasks [22,42]. Specifically, we employ the ResNet [14] model, and pre-trained it on the ImageNet [8] dataset to extract the high-level semantic features.

3.2 Graph Construction

We construct a multi-layer graph whose lower layer of the graph represents the more detailed image structures and the higher layer encodes the overall visual information. For each input image, we first build an image pyramid to generate multi-layer representations $\mathcal{I}^m, m = 1 \cdots M$. For each m-th layer, we use SLIC algorithm [2] to segment it into n_m non-overlapping super-pixels $S = \{s_1^m, s_2^m, \cdots s_{n_m}^m\}$. Here, we set the numbers of superpixels to $n_m, m = 1, 2, 3$ to 200, 300, 400 respectively. In the m-th layer, each node s_i^m is not only connected to its neighboring nodes s_j^m but also connected to the 2-hop neighboring nodes s_h^m. In addition, any pair of nodes on the image boundary are also connected. We compute the weight of graph for each view as,

$$W_{ij}^k = e^{-\frac{\|\mathbf{c}_i^k - \mathbf{c}_j^k\|^2}{\sigma^2}} \tag{17}$$

where $\mathbf{c}_i^k, \mathbf{c}_j^k$ denote the feature vectors of the k-th view, and σ is a constant that controls the strength of the weight. For each node pair $s_i^{m_1}$ and $s_j^{m_2}$ on different layers, we connect them if their corresponding overlapping is larger than a threshold δ. For the edge across different layers, we set weight as a constant ν.

3.3 Ranking Saliency Computation

By ranking the nodes on the constructed graph according to the Eq. (1), we can obtain an initial saliency value $f_{N \times N}^*$, where $N = \sum_{m=1}^{3} n_m$. The saliency value of each super -pixel is successively assigned to the corresponding pixels. In order to make the results more consistent, we simply average all saliency value on three layers. The final result Sal can be computed by $Sal_i = \frac{1}{3} \sum_{m=1}^{3} f_{n_m \times n_m}^*$ at pixel level.

Background and Foreground Queries Generation: It is usually observed that salient objects are rarely occur on the boundaries of the image. Thus, the image boundary regions are usually regarded as query regions in traditional ranking saliency detection methods [7]. Therefore, for background queries y^1, we use image boundary super-pixels as background queries and obtain the optimal background ranking result f^* using the standard GMR model [7]. For foreground queries y^2, we select the super-pixels as the foreground queries that have high ranking values f^* (higher than mean value) of the first stage of GMR (Here, we can use any kind of existing good method as a prior to select foreground queries).

Saliency Detection: Based on constructed multi-scale graph model, and the background queries y^1 and foreground queries y^2 obtained above, we then obtain the optimal ranking result $F^* = (f^*, g^*)$ using the proposed multi-view optimized ranking model. We use the optimal f^* as the final saliency result.

4 Experiments

For the performance evaluation, we evaluate the proposed model on three public datasets including ASD [30], SED [3] and SOD [25].

Parameter Setting: We set the number of superpixels $n_1 = 200, n_2 = 300, n_3 = 400$ in multiple layers. The parameter μ, δ, λ are set to 0.008, 0.6 and 0.01 in all the experiments. Besides, the edge weight ν between different layers are set to 0.01.

Evaluation Metrics: We evaluate all methods by using the metric of precision, recall and F-measure. These evaluation metrics are commonly used in many related works [6,7,28,30]. We compare our algorithm with some other methods: SR [37], SUN [41], SER [32], SEG [29], SWD [9], FES [31], SIM [26], SF [28], SS [15], LMLC [38], COV [10], MC [17], PCA [24], HS [39], MR [7], MS [33],DSR [23], RBD [43], RR [21], and MST [34]. We use source codes with default parameters provided by the authors for all methods.

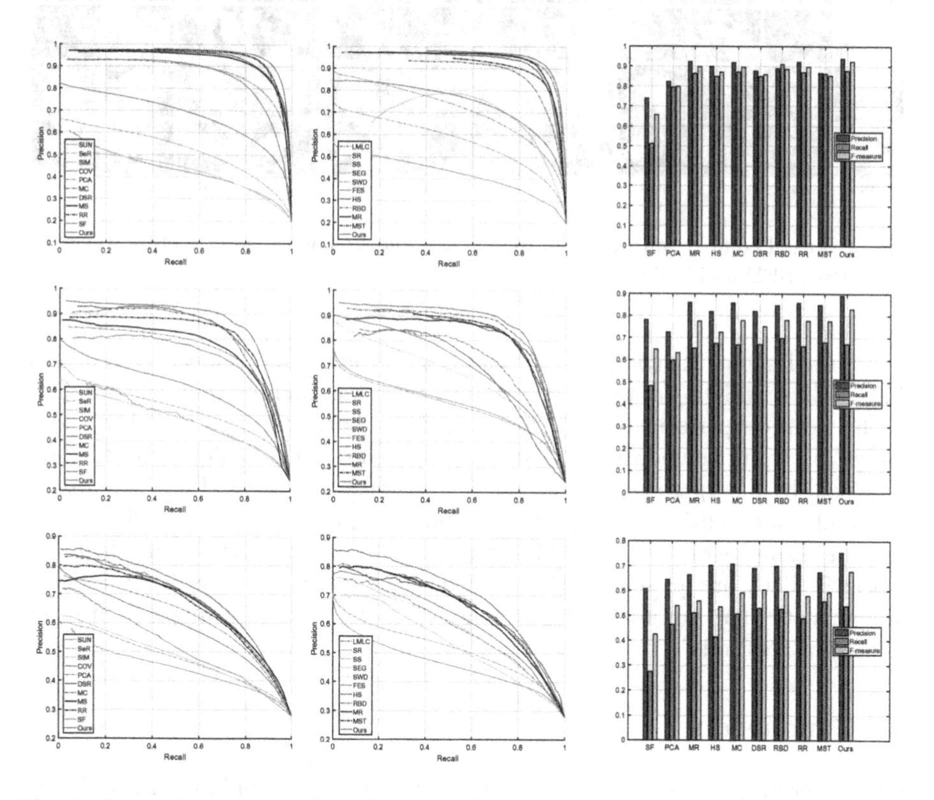

Fig. 1. Comparison results of precision-recall curves and F-measure for different methods on three different datasets. From top to down: ASD, SED, SOD.

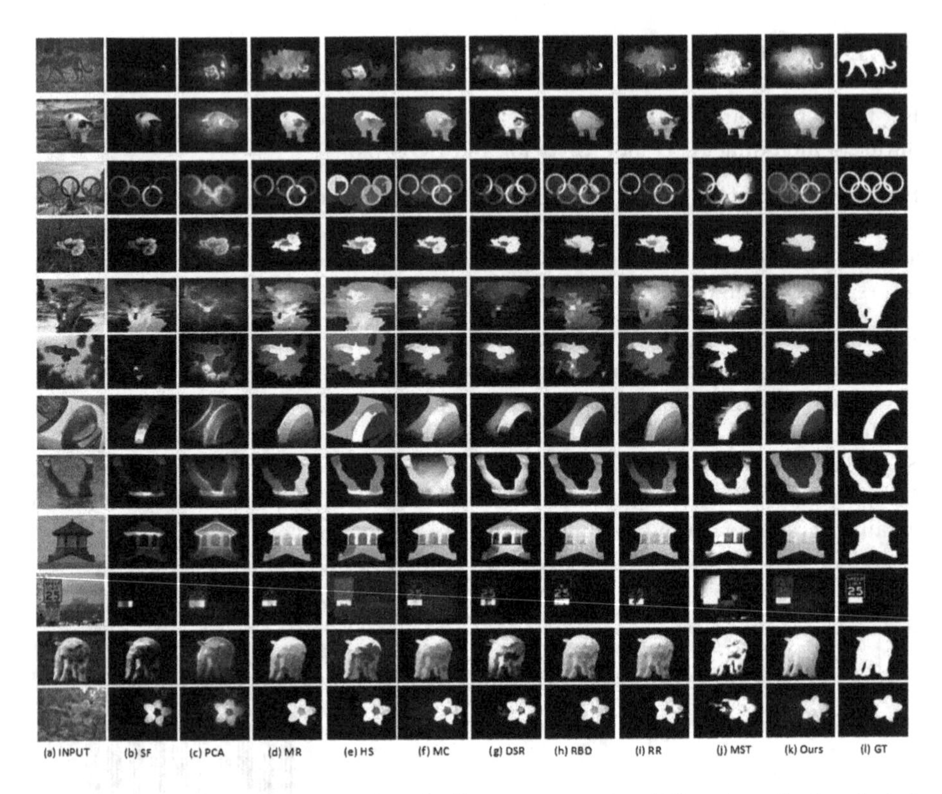

Fig. 2. Visual comparison examples of saliency maps using different methods selected from ASD, SED and SOD datasets.

Figure 1 shows the comparison results of PR-curves and F-measure values on ASD, SED and SOD datasets, respectively. Here, we can note that, the proposed method can outperform than other methods on both PR-curve and F-measure values. All results demonstrate that the proposed ranking model is effective and beneficial by incorporating the correlation between background and foreground cues and using multi-scale graph model and multiple features. Some visual comparison examples of the proposed method and the top 9 methods are displayed in Fig. 2. They are all selected from ASD, SED and SOD datasets. Intuitively, we can note that our method can generate clearer saliency maps than other competing methods.

5 Conclusion

This paper proposes a novel multi-view synchronized manifold ranking for image saliency detection problem. The main aspect of the proposed method is to conduct background and foreground ranking by exploiting multiple kinds of features simultaneously and thus performs more robustly and discriminatively for salient object detection. An new iterative updating algorithm has been derived to solve the proposed ranking model. Experimental results show the effectiveness and benefits of the proposed method.

Acknowledgments. This work was supported by the National Nature Science Foundation of China (61602001, 61502006, 61402002); Natural Science Foundation of Anhui Higher Education Institutions of China (KJ2016A020, KJ2018A0023), Natural science foundation of Anhui Province (1508085QF127).

References

1. Achanta, R., Estrada, F., Wils, P., Süsstrunk, S.: Salient region detection and segmentation. In: Gasteratos, A., Vincze, M., Tsotsos, J.K. (eds.) ICVS 2008. LNCS, vol. 5008, pp. 66–75. Springer, Heidelberg (2008). https://doi.org/10.1007/978-3-540-79547-6_7
2. Achanta, R., Shaji, A., Smith, K., Lucchi, A., Fua, P., Ssstrunk, S.: Slic superpixels. EPFL 149300 (2010)
3. Alpert, S., Galun, M., Basri, R., Brandt, A.: Image segmentation by probabilistic bottom-up aggregation and cue integration. In: CVPR, pp. 1–8 (2007)
4. Borji, A., Cheng, M.M., Jiang, H., Li, J.: Salient object detection: a benchmark. IEEE Trans. Image Process. **24**(12), 5706–5722 (2015)
5. Chang, K.Y., Liu, T.L., Chen, H.T., Lai, S.H.: Fusing generic objectness and visual saliency for salient object detection. In: ICCV, pp. 914–921 (2011)
6. Cheng, M.M., Zhang, G.X., Mitra, N.J., Huang, X., Hu, S.M.: Global contrast based salient region detection. In: CVPR, pp. 409–416 (2011)
7. Chuan, Y., Lihe, Z., Huchuan, L., Xiang, R., Ming-Hsuan, Y.: Saliency detection via graph-based manifold ranking. In: CVPR, pp. 3166–3173 (2013)
8. Deng, J., Dong, W., Socher, R., Li, L.J., Li, K., Fei-Fei, L.: Imagenet: a large-scale hierarchical image database. In: 2009 IEEE Conference on Computer Vision and Pattern Recognition, pp. 248–255 (2009)
9. Duan, L., Wu, C., Miao, J., Qing, L., Fu, Y.: Visual saliency detection by spatially weighted dissimilarity. In: CVPR, pp. 473–480 (2011)
10. Erdem, E., Erdem, A.: Visual saliency estimation by nonlinearly integrating features using region covariances. J. Vis. **13**(4), 11 (2013)
11. Feng, Y., Xiao, J., Zhuang, Y., Liu, X.: Adaptive unsupervised multi-view feature selection for visual concept recognition. In: Lee, K.M., Matsushita, Y., Rehg, J.M., Hu, Z. (eds.) ACCV 2012. LNCS, vol. 7724, pp. 343–357. Springer, Heidelberg (2013). https://doi.org/10.1007/978-3-642-37331-2_26
12. Guan, Y., Jiang, B., Xiao, Y., Tang, J., Luo, B.: A new graph ranking model for image saliency detection problem. In: IEEE International Conference on Software Engineering Research, Management and Applications, pp. 151–156 (2017)
13. Han, J., Zhang, D., Cheng, G., Guo, L., Ren, J.: Object detection in optical remote sensing images based on weakly supervised learning and high-level feature learning. IEEE Trans. Geosci. Remote. Sens. **53**(6), 3325–3337 (2015)
14. He, K., Zhang, X., Ren, S., Sun, J.: Deep residual learning for image recognition. In: 2016 IEEE Conference on Computer Vision and Pattern Recognition (CVPR), pp. 770–778 (2016)
15. Hou, X., Harel, J., Koch, C.: Image signature: highlighting sparse salient regions. IEEE TPAMI **34**(1), 194–201 (2012)

16. Itti, L., Koch, C., Niebur, E.: A model of saliency-based visual attention for rapid scene analysis. IEEE TPAMI **20**, 1254–1259 (1998)
17. Jiang, B., Zhang, L., Lu, H., Yang, C., Yang, M.H.: Saliency detection via absorbing Markov chain. In: ICCV, pp. 1665–1672 (2013)
18. Jimei, Y., Ming-Hsuan, Y.: Top-down visual saliency via joint CRF and dictionary learning. In: CVPR, pp. 2296–2303 (2012)
19. Jonathan, H., Christof, K., Pietro, P.: Graph-based visual saliency. In: NIPS, pp. 545–552 (2006)
20. Kanan, C., Tong, M.H., Zhang, L., Cottrell, G.W.: Sun: top-down saliency using natural statistics. Vis. Cogn. **17**(6–7), 979–1003 (2009)
21. Li, C., Yuan, Y., Cai, W., Xia, Y., Feng, D.D.: Robust saliency detection via regularized random walks ranking. In: CVPR, pp. 2710–2717 (2015)
22. Li, G., Yu, Y.: Visual saliency based on multiscale deep features. In: 2015 IEEE Conference on Computer Vision and Pattern Recognition (CVPR), pp. 5455–5463 (2015)
23. Li, X., Lu, H., Zhang, L., Ruan, X., Yang, M.H.: Saliency detection via dense and sparse reconstruction. In: ICCV, pp. 2976–2983 (2013)
24. Margolin, R., Tal, A., Zelnik-Manor, L.: What makes a patch distinct? In: CVPR, pp. 1139–1146 (2013)
25. Movahedi, V., Elder, J.H.: Design and perceptual validation of performance measures for salient object segmentation. In: CVPRW, pp. 49–56 (2010)
26. Murray, N., Vanrell, M., Otazu, X., Parraga, C.A.: Saliency estimation using a non-parametric low-level vision model. In: CVPR, pp. 433–440 (2011)
27. Peng, Q., Cheung, Y.M., You, X., Tang, Y.Y.: A hybrid of local and global saliencies for detecting image salient region and appearance. IEEE Trans. Syst. Man Cybern. Syst. **PP**(99), 1–12 (2017)
28. Perazzi, F., ähenb ühl, P.K., Pritch, Y., Hornung, A.: Saliency filters: contrast based filtering for salient region detection. In: CVPR, pp. 733–740 (2012)
29. Rahtu, E., Kannala, J., Salo, M., Heikkilä, J.: Segmenting salient objects from images and videos. In: Daniilidis, K., Maragos, P., Paragios, N. (eds.) ECCV 2010. LNCS, vol. 6315, pp. 366–379. Springer, Heidelberg (2010). https://doi.org/10.1007/978-3-642-15555-0_27
30. Ravi, A., Sheila, H., Francisco, E., Sabine, S.: Frequency-tuned salient region detection. In: CVPR, pp. 1597–1604 (2009)
31. Rezazadegan Tavakoli, H., Rahtu, E., Heikkilä, J.: Fast and efficient saliency detection using sparse sampling and kernel density estimation. In: SCIA, pp. 666–675 (2011)
32. Seo, H.J., Milanfar, P.: Static and space-time visual saliency detection by self-resemblance. J. Vis. **9**(12), 15 (2009)
33. Tong, N., Lu, H., Zhang, L., Ruan, X.: Saliency detection with multi-scale superpixels. IEEE Signal Process. Lett. **21**(9), 1035–1039 (2014)
34. Tu, W.C., He, S., Yang, Q., Chien, S.Y.: Real-time salient object detection with a minimum spanning tree. In: CVPR, pp. 2334–2342 (2016)
35. Wang, Q., Zheng, W., Piramuthu, R.: Grab: visual saliency via novel graph model and background priors. In: CVPR, pp. 535–543 (2016)
36. Wang, Z., Ren, J., Zhang, D., Sun, M., Jiang, J.: A deep-learning based feature hybrid framework for spatiotemporal saliency detection inside videos. Neurocomputing **287**, 68–83 (2018)
37. Xiaodi, H., Liqing, Z.: Saliency detection: a spectral residual approach. In: CVPR, pp. 1–8 (2007)

38. Xie, Y., Lu, H., Yang, M.H.: Bayesian saliency via low and mid level cues. IEEE TIP **22**(5), 1689–1698 (2013)
39. Yan, Q., Xu, L., Shi, J., Jia, J.: Hierarchical saliency detection. In: CVPR, pp. 1155–1162 (2013)
40. Yan, Y., et al.: Unsupervised image saliency detection with Gestalt-laws guided optimization and visual attention based refinement. Pattern Recogn. **79**, 65–78 (2018)
41. Zhang, L., Tong, M.H., Marks, T.K., Shan, H., Cottrell, G.W.: Sun: a Bayesian framework for saliency using natural statistics. J. Vis. **8**(7), 32.1–32.20 (2008)
42. Zhao, R., Ouyang, W., Li, H., Wang, X.: Saliency detection by multi-context deep learning. In: 2015 IEEE Conference on Computer Vision and Pattern Recognition (CVPR), pp. 1265–1274 (2015)
43. Zhu, W., Liang, S., Wei, Y., Sun, J.: Saliency optimization from robust background detection. In: CVPR, pp. 2814–2821 (2014)

Robust Visual Tracking via Sparse Feature Selection and Weight Dictionary Update

Penggen Zheng[1,2], Jin Zhan[1,2], Huimin Zhao[1,2(✉)], and Hefeng Wu[3]

[1] School of Computer Science, Guangdong Polytechnic Normal University, Guangzhou, China
penggengg@gmail.com,
{gszhanjin, zhaohuimin}@gpnu.edu.cn

[2] Guangzhou Key Laboratory of Digital Content Processing and Security Technologies, Guangzhou, China

[3] School of Information Science and Technology, Guangdong University of Foreign Studies, Guangzhou, China
wuhefeng@gmail.com

Abstract. Sparse representation-based visual tracking methods do not adapt well to changes in the target and backgrounds, and the sparseness of samples does not guarantee optimality. In this paper, we propose a robust visual tracking algorithm using sparse multi-feature selection and adaptive dictionary update based on weight dictionaries. We exploit the color features and texture features of the learning samples to obtain different discriminative dictionaries based on the label consistent K-SVD algorithm, and use the position information of those samples to assign weights to the dictionaries' base vectors, forming the weight dictionaries. For robust visual tracking, we adopt a novel feature selection strategy that combines the weights of dictionaries' base vectors and reconstruction errors to select the best sample. In addition, we introduce adaptive noise energy thresholds and establish a dictionary updating mechanism based on noise energy analysis, which effectively reduces the error accumulation caused by dictionary updating and enhances the adaptability to target and background changes. Comparison experiments show that the proposed algorithm performs favorably against several state-of-the-art methods.

Keywords: Visual tracking · Similarity weights · Sparse representation Adaptive update · Multi-feature selection

1 Introduction

Visual tracking is an important problem of computer vision. In the past few years, we have witnessed rapid advancements in visual tracking, but it is still a challenging task due to complex situations, such as occlusions, target deformation, rotation, scale changes and cluttered background. Most of existing methods can be roughly divided into generative methods [1–4] and discriminative methods [5–9]. The generative methods describe the appearance characteristics of the target and search for candidate targets by minimizing the reconstruction error. Based on classifiers, the discriminative methods mainly find the decision boundaries of the target and the background.

J. Ren et al. (Eds.): BICS 2018, LNAI 10989, pp. 484–494, 2018.
https://doi.org/10.1007/978-3-030-00563-4_47

In recent years, there have been many target tracking algorithms based on sparse representation [1–3], correlation filters (CF) [10–13] and deep learning [14–17], where deep learning and correlation filters are research hotspots now. The main advantage of deep learning-based tracking methods lies in their powerful characterization of depth features. SO-DLT [16] and MDnet [17] use non-task video datasets for pre-training, and then adjust the tracking model to make the model adapt to the current tracking task. However, these methods are computationally intensive and depend strongly on pre-trained samples. CF-based tracking methods show strong computational efficiency and tracking robustness. Heriques et al. [10] proposed an efficient tracking method based on HOG features using cyclic transform and kernel transform. Danelljan et al. [11, 12] later used multi-scale models to solve the problem of target scale change. The correlation filters have a great advantage in tracking efficiency. However, the tracking effect is easily affected by the boundary effect, and the target background information cannot be fully utilized.

Sparse representation-based tracking methods [1–3] select the target location by comparing the reconstruction errors of the features. Because of insensitivity to the target noise, this kind of method has a strong tracking robustness when target deformation occurs. Based on the Label Consistent K-SVD (LC-KSVD) method [18], the work [19] used the positive and negative samples together to train a discriminative sparse dictionary, making the model have stronger discriminative performance during the tracking process. However, fixed discriminative dictionary ignores the variations cues between foreground and background. Also, it used single-feature which lacks of considering color distribution of target.

The main innovations of our method are as follows:

- **Sparse Multi-feature Selection.** According to the center distance from the learning sample to the target, we assign Gaussian weights to the basis vectors of different feature dictionaries. We use the multi-feature weight of the samples to measure the similarity between the samples and the target to obtain candidate samples, and then to select the best sample by synthesizing the multiple features reconstruction error of them. The complementary effect between the various features improves the stability of the tracking.
- **Adaptive Weight Dictionary Update.** We analyze the changes of the average noise energy during tracking. In order to select the best update time for the dictionary, we use the quantile threshold of all previous average noise energies to determine the anomalous changes in the tracking scene.

2 Proposed Approach

The overall framework of our approach is shown in Fig. 1. It can be divided into two parts in general. (1) *Update-related.* In frame t, we set a threshold for the noise energy of the tracking results based on all previous tracking results, combined with the target noise and samples average noise to determine whether the update conditions are satisfied. The updated dictionary is learned from the positive and negative samples of frame t and the positive sample of frame 1, and used for the tracking detection of the next frame. (2) *Selection-related.* In frame $t + 1$, we perform sparse coding on samples obtained from Gaussian sampling using the latest weight dictionary, and then compare sample similarity weights and reconstruction errors to select the best sample.

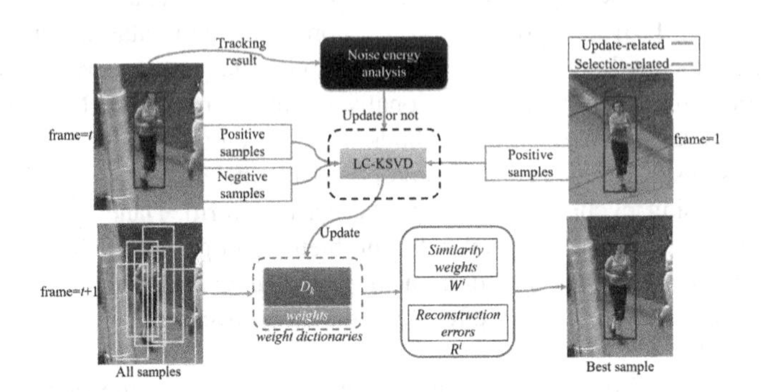

Fig. 1. The tracking flowchart of the proposed approach.

2.1 Weight Dictionary Model

Discriminative Dictionary Composition. In this paper, we use three types of templates (the target template *T*, the background template *B* and the noise template *I*) to collectively represent the target appearance. In the process of template sampling in first frame, all pixels in the range of radius r_0 are sampled to obtain the positive samples. And then dense sampling is performed in the range of radius between r_1 and r_2 to obtain negative samples. If the dimension of a sample feature is *m*, then the target templates and the background templates define as:

$$T = \{F_i | d(i) \leq r_0\}^{m \times p},\ B = \{F_i | r_1 < d(i) \leq r_2\}^{m \times q}, \tag{1}$$

where F_i represents the sample *i*, *d*(*i*) is the center distance from sample F_i to the target, *i* is the label of the samples, *p* and *q* are the number of positive samples and negative samples. The three radiuses in Eq. (1) satisfy the relationship: $0 < r_0 \leq r_1 < r_2$.
The sparse discriminative dictionary *D* learned from all samples consists of three parts: $D = [D^T, D^B, D^I]$, then D^T, D^B and D^I respectively corresponding to template *T*, *B* and *I*. In the tracking process, the sparse representation formula for the feature *y* is:

$$y \approx D\gamma = [D^T, D^B, D^I] \begin{bmatrix} z \\ v \\ e \end{bmatrix}, \tag{2}$$

where *D* is a discriminative dictionary, *z* is target coefficients, *v* is background coefficients, *e* is noise coefficient, and γ is sparse coding.

Weight Dictionary Learning. In this paper, the LC-KSVD [18] method is used to unify dictionary learning and classification labeling. The solution to Eq. (2) can be transformed into solving four local dictionaries respectively. The solution process is expressed as follows:

$$\underset{D,A,\gamma}{arg\ min}\|Y - D\gamma\|_2^2 + \beta\|G - A\gamma\|_2^2 + \lambda\|\gamma\|_1. \tag{3}$$

Matrix G is the discriminative sparse coding of the initial template classification, so that γ approximates the sparse coding of the initial label, and the transfer matrix A makes γ in the sparse feature space has stronger discriminant ability of samples category. β is a range control coefficient that is consistent with the regular term contribution in Formula (3). According to the samples category of the target template T, the background template B and the noise template I, matrix G is defined as follows:

$$G = \begin{bmatrix} g_1 & 0 \\ 0 & g_2 \end{bmatrix}, g_1 \in R^{p \times p}, g_2 \in R^{(q+m) \times (q+m)}, \tag{4}$$

where g_1 and g_2 are all-one-element matrices. In order to obtain the optimal solution of Formula (3), we can solve the following expression:

$$\underset{D_{new},\gamma}{arg\ min}\|Y_{new} - D_{new}\gamma\|_2^2 + \lambda\|\gamma\|_1, \tag{5}$$

where $Y_{new} = \left(Y^T, \sqrt{\beta}G^T\right)^T$, $D_{new} = \left(D^T, \sqrt{\beta}A^T\right)^T$. Formula (5) can be solved using the K-SVD algorithm. The learning process of the dictionary D_{new} will generate a sparse coding value γ, and we can obtain the dictionary D.

When we have got the sparse dictionary, we assign weights to each base vector of the dictionary, according to the center distance from the samples to the target. We use the Gaussian function centered on the target as the weight function, and the weight of the dictionary's base vector is only related to the center distance $d(i)$. The weight of the base vector is defined as follows:

$$W(i) = exp(-d^2(i)/2\sigma^2), \tag{6}$$

where σ is the standard deviation of normal distribution. This weight reflects the similarity between the target and the samples. Finally, we can get a discriminative dictionary with a weight table, namely the weight dictionary, as shown in Fig. 2.

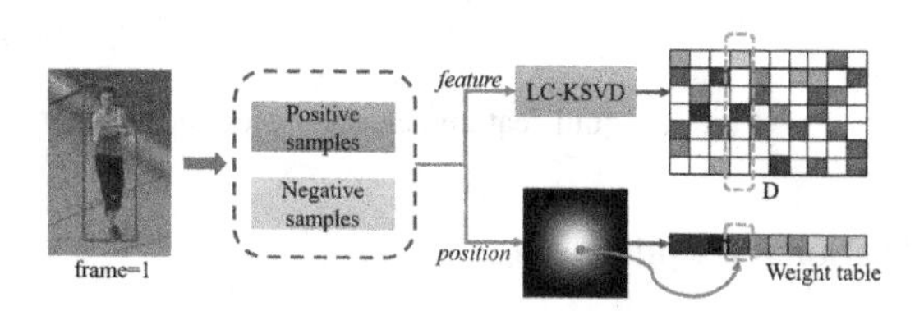

Fig. 2. Initial dictionary learning and weight assignment of the dictionary's base vectors

2.2 Multi-feature Selection Strategy

In the frame t, we perform Gaussian sampling centered on the target position of the previous frame to obtain samples S_i (i = 1, 2, …, n). Using two feature dictionaries D_k (k = 1, 2) to perform sparse decomposition on all samples, we can get sparse coefficients γ_k^i, where k is a feature tag (k = 1 denotes color histogram, k = 2 denotes Haar-like features [20]) and i is the sample index.

In the sparse coefficients γ_k^i, all coefficient values reflect the correlation strength between the sample feature and the dictionary's base vector. A base vector (sparse feature) corresponding to the maximum value has the strongest correlation with the sample. In the tracking process, we combine the weights of two features to get the synthetic weights W^i. Its definition is as follows:

$$W^i = \prod_k W_k^i, \tag{7}$$

where W_k^i represents the *k-feature* weight of sample s_i. The candidate samples CS_j are the samples with the largest feature synthetic weight among all samples.

Then we use the synthetic reconstruction error to select the best sample from candidate samples. The expression of the synthetic reconstruction error is as follows:

$$R^j = \prod_k R_k^j, \tag{8}$$

where R_k^j represents the reconstruction error of the sample s_j in *k-feature*, j is the label of the candidate samples. Finally, in the candidate samples, the sample label of the best tracking result can be expressed as follows:

$$\hat{j} = arg\, min_j R^j. \tag{9}$$

The multi-feature selection process is shown in Fig. 3.

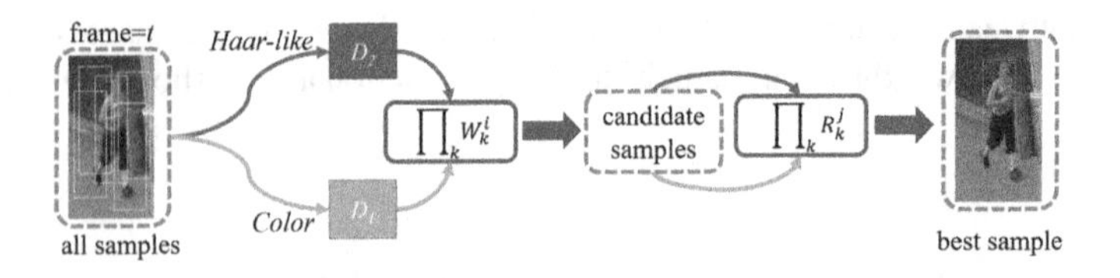

Fig. 3. Multi-feature selection process

2.3 Adaptive Dictionary Update

In the sparse coefficient γ_k^i, the maximum sparse coefficient represents most information of the sample and the noise factor e (see Eq. (2)) is much smaller than the maximum coefficient. Noise coefficient e can reflect the situation of target occlusion and tracking drift to some extent. We should not update the dictionary for these two situations. Our method analyzes the noise energy u (the sum of the noise coefficients e) to determine the time of the dictionary update.

In frame t, the average noise energy expression for all samples in the current frame is $\overline{u_k^T} = \sum_i u_k^i$, where u_k^i is the noise energy of sample s_i. The threshold x_k^α is the upper quantile of set U_k (all $\overline{u_k^T}$ from frame 1 to frame t). The threshold is defined as:

$$P\{U_k > x_k^\alpha\} = \alpha. \tag{10}$$

We only perform the weight dictionary update when the following three conditions are met. (1) The noise energy of the current best sample is less than the average noise energy of all samples; (2) The average noise energy change curve intersects the threshold curve at the last two frames; (3) The interval time between two updates must be more than tm. The update result is shown in Fig. 4.

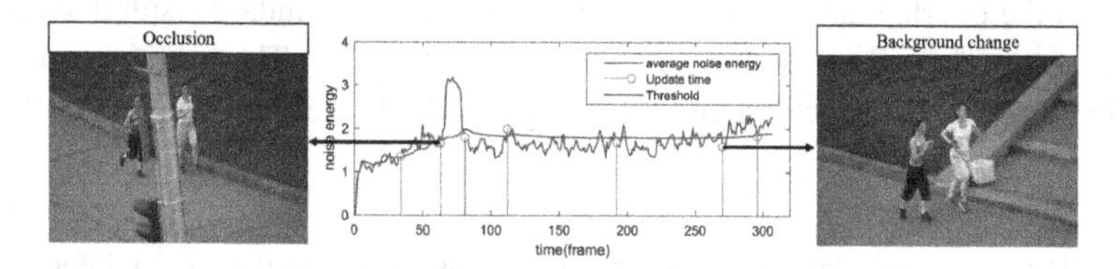

Fig. 4. Update time and corresponding scene

The learning process of the new dictionary is shown in Fig. 1. We sample the positive and negative samples in the current frame and form a new training dataset with the positive samples of the first frame. We use this new training dataset to learn a new dictionary based on LC-KSVD method [19] and replace the old one.

3 Experimental Results and Comparison

3.1 Experimental Settings

In this paper, 14 representative video sequences in the OTB100 datasets [21] are selected as the evaluation test set of the algorithm. These standard test videos are: basketball, Panda, Skater, Shaking, jumping, football, BlurFace, BlurOwl, couple, Man, jogging-1, david3, david2, carDark. These video clips cover a variety of challenging attributes, including target occlusion, target deformation, illumination changes, target rotation, background interference. In the comparative experiment, we not only selected 8 tracking models related to our method (ASLA [1], IVT [2], L1APG [3], CT [5], CXT [6], ORIA [8], OAB [7], TLD [9]), but also selected 9 excellent methods (DCF [10], KCF [10], DSST [11], SRDCF [12], LMCF [13], SiamFC [14], ACFN [15], SAMF [22], STAPLE [23]) in recent years including methods based on CF and deep-learning.

We use the open code and default parameters of these methods to experiment in the same computer environment. The computer environment used in the experiment is: Intel (R) Core (TM) i3-3.7 GHz, RAM-12 GB, matlabR2017a.

The method of this paper adopts uniform parameter settings. The number of Gaussian samples in the tracking process is 500 and the sampling radius is 25. The sampling parameter of the training sample is set to: $r_0 = 4$, $r_1 = 7$, $r_2 = 15$. The Haar-like [20] feature dimension is set to 150, and the bin of the color statistics histogram is set to 32. So the color-feature dimension of the single-channel image is 32, and the RGB image is 96. Update time interval is $tm = 6$ frames, and noise energy threshold parameter is $\alpha = 0.2$.

3.2 Experimental Results and Analysis

We use the average center error and the average overlap score [21] as evaluation criteria for comparative experiments. The center error is the Euclidean distance between the tracking result and the standard target position. The overlap rate is a measure of the overlap range of the tracking result and the standard result tracking box. The calculation formula is defined as: $score = \frac{intersection\,area}{union\,area}$. The average center error and overlap rate for our method and the related methods are shown in Tables 1 and 2.

Table 1. The average overlap rate of the related methods and our method on 14 different videos (bold indicates the best two methods). DSST and KCF were added as evaluation baseline.

Video	Ours	DSST	KCF	ASLA	IVT	OAB	TLD	L1APG	ORIA	CT	CXT
Basketball	**0.715**	0.606	**0.676**	0.277	0.123	0.026	0.310	0.202	0.065	0.212	0.019
Panda	0.512	0.142	0.159	**0.518**	0.138	0.152	**0.539**	0.285	0.109	0.489	0.182
Skater	**0.632**	**0.629**	0.611	0.548	0.551	0.532	0.542	0.567	0.597	0.597	0.426
Shaking	**0.668**	**0.706**	0.040	0.427	0.034	0.034	0.101	0.276	0.468	0.171	0.308
Jumping	**0.652**	0.070	0.275	0.086	0.122	0.059	0.646	0.105	0.082	0.031	**0.773**
Football	**0.628**	0.560	0.552	**0.590**	0.560	0.529	0.542	0.462	0.512	0.403	0.538
BlurFace	0.772	**0.841**	0.796	0.218	0.158	0.481	**0.864**	0.450	0.176	0.221	0.835
BlurOwl	**0.743**	0.190	0.195	0.194	0.055	**0.768**	0.610	0.253	0.069	0.067	0.312
Couple	**0.594**	0.092	0.201	0.100	0.074	0.420	0.188	**0.471**	0.047	0.297	0.467
Man	**0.878**	**0.883**	0.831	0.836	0.745	0.859	0.793	0.874	0.848	0.074	0.873
Jogging-1	0.701	0.187	0.186	0.186	0.177	0.612	**0.767**	0.184	0.223	0.160	**0.766**
David3	**0.657**	0.458	**0.772**	0.314	0.512	0.286	0.276	0.292	0.132	0.400	0.122
David2	0.698	0.830	0.828	**0.899**	0.702	0.754	0.782	0.839	0.468	0.003	**0.854**
carDark	0.587	0.845	0.615	**0.854**	0.663	0.767	0.446	**0.852**	0.419	0.007	0.540

In Tables 1 and 2, we can see that our method show favorably performance in comparison with the methods based on dense sampling or sparse representation.

Table 2. The average center error of the related methods and our method on 14 different videos (bold indicates the best two methods). DSST and KCF were added as evaluation baseline.

Video	Ours	DSST	KCF	ASLA	IVT	OAB	TLD	L1APG	ORIA	CT	CXT
Basketball	**6.9**	10.9	**7.9**	71.2	81.5	160.9	65.2	111.9	110.7	112.9	188.3
Panda	**6.8**	43.6	42.1	6.9	51.2	143.2	**5.9**	26.9	69.9	6.9	81.4
Skater	8.8	**8.4**	10.7	**7.5**	8.5	20.7	11.3	16.1	11.7	11.8	40.5
Shaking	**10.6**	**8.4**	112.5	27.0	87.2	155.3	68.5	37.9	24.4	65.0	122.1
Jumping	**6.2**	36.9	26.1	49.5	61.6	69.6	7.6	57.6	57.7	52.0	**3.5**
Football	**9.0**	15.8	14.6	15.0	13.9	15.8	14.3	41.3	**13.2**	19.3	14.3
BlurFace	10.9	**5.2**	8.4	117.2	148.9	53.6	**3.8**	62.8	75.6	109.9	6.5
BlurOwl	**8.9**	196.1	183.4	64.6	167.2	11.8	30.3	120.6	179.4	164.7	**6.9**
Couple	**8.9**	125.6	47.6	93.9	109.4	**26.5**	64.3	28.4	98.8	29.3	49.2
Man	1.8	1.6	2.3	**1.3**	3.4	2.3	3.1	**1.4**	1.9	45.8	2.1
Jogging-1	**6.9**	110.7	88.3	104.0	88.3	13.7	7.2	83.3	45.2	91.8	**5.6**
David3	**12.0**	88.2	**4.3**	104.6	53.0	91.1	135.7	86.0	182.6	68.5	221.8
David2	4.8	2.0	2.1	1.5	**1.2**	3.5	2.6	1.5	19.5	78.2	**1.3**
carDark	7.6	1.5	6.0	**1.4**	8.4	3.5	26.9	**1.2**	25.9	118.7	18.6

In order to objectively evaluate our approach, we also use the tracking precision and success rate [21] under different thresholds to compare our method with 17 different methods (ASLA [1], IVT [2], L1APG [3], CT [5], CXT [6], ORIA [8], OAB [7], TLD [9], DCF [10], KCF [10], DSST [11], SRDCF [12], LMCF [13], SiamFC [14], ACFN [15], SAMF [22], STAPLE [23]). The overall tracking accuracy and success rate for all test videos is shown in Fig. 5. In comparison with some advanced methods in recent years, our method also shows excellent tracking performance.

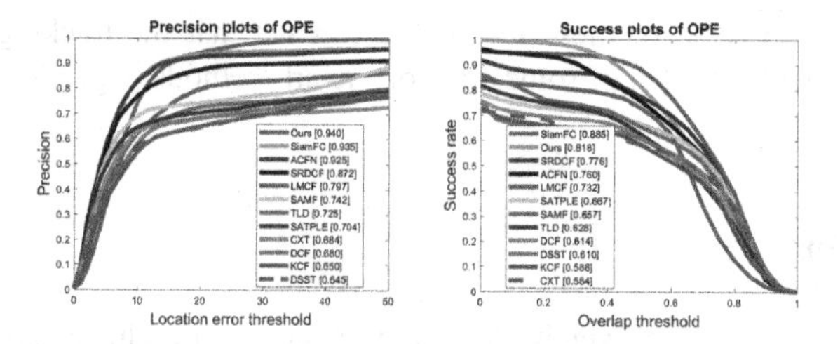

Fig. 5. Precision and success plots of overall performance comparison for 14 videos

The tracking performance evaluation of different video attributes is showed in Fig. 6. Our tracking performance is second (only below SiamFC) on attribute *deformation*, *rotation* and *scale variation*, and we achieve the best performance on attribute *background clutter* (see Fig. 6).

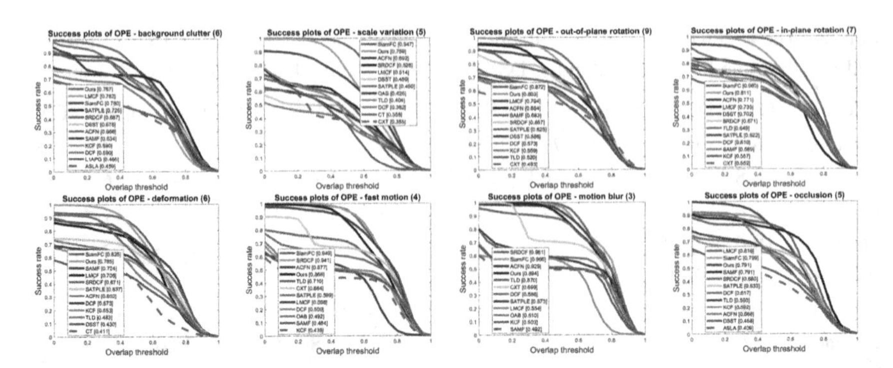

Fig. 6. Attribute based evaluation. Success plots compare our tracker with other 17 trackers on all test videos. Our tracker has favorably tracking effects in most attributes.

The color features have properties that are insensitive to the deformation of the target. The use of color feature dictionary greatly enhances the tracking effect of our tracking model when the target is blurred. In comparison with the related methods, our tracker has the best tracking effect on attribute *motion blur* and *fast motion* (see Fig. 6). The tracking results in videos *BlurOwl*, *jumping* and *couple* are shown in Fig. 7.

Fig. 7. Tracking results of 6 related methods and our method in videos BlurOwl, jumping and couple

From the comparison of these results we can see that the tracking effect of our method has reached the level of some state-of-the-art methods (e.g. LMCF, ACFN and SRDCF).

4 Conclusion

This paper proposes a novel weight dictionary model with multi-feature selection and adaptive dictionary learning to represent the appearance of the target, and noise energy analysis and sample similarity weights are introduced to improve the performance of sparse feature selection. Using different features can complement the feature representation capabilities of the target and reduce background noise interference to increase tracking accuracy. The sample similarity weight is used to narrow the search range of the optimal sample to select candidate samples, which can effectively reduce the interference of abnormal samples. A new updating algorithm has been proposed via noise energy analysis which compares the noise energy with the dynamic threshold.

Experimental results on the OTB100 dataset show the effectiveness of the proposed method. In the future, we will further solve the issue of scale change, improve our algorithm by investigating more sophisticated sparse representation-based methods [24], and extend our method to multi-camera target tracking application scenarios [25].

Acknowledgment. This research is supported by National Natural Science Foundation of China (61772144, 61672008), Innovation Research Project of Education Department of Guangdong Province (Natural Science) (2016KTSCX077), Foreign Science and Technology Cooperation Plan Project of Guangzhou Science Technology and Innovation Commission (201807010059), Guangdong Provincial Application-oriented Technical Research and Development Special Fund Project (2016B010127006), the Natural Science Foundation of Guangdong Province (2016A030311013), and the Scientific and Technological Projects of Guangdong Province (2017A050501039). The corresponding authors are Jin Zhan and Huimin Zhao.

References

1. Lu, H., Jia, X., Yang, M.H.: Visual tracking via adaptive structural local sparse appearance model. In: Proceedings of Computer Vision and Pattern Recognition (CVPR), pp. 1822–1829. IEEE (2012)
2. Ross, D.A., Lim, J., Lin, R.S., et al.: Incremental learning for robust visual tracking. Int. J. Comput. Vis. (IJCV) **77**(1–3), 125–141 (2008)
3. Bao, C., Wu, Y., Ling, H., Ji, H.: Real time robust l1 tracker using accelerated proximal gradient approach. In: Proceedings of Computer Vision and Pattern Recognition (CVPR), pp. 1830–1837 (2012)
4. Liu, Q.: Decontaminate feature for tracking: adaptive tracking via evolutionary feature subset. J. Electron. Imaging **26**(6), 1 (2017)
5. Zhang, K., Zhang, L., Yang, M.H.: Real-time compressive tracking. In: Computer Vision (ECCV), pp. 864–877 (2012)
6. Dinh, T.B., Vo, N., Medioni, G.: Context tracker: Exploring supporters and distracters in unconstrained environments. In: Proceedings of Computer Vision and Pattern Recognition (CVPR), pp. 1177–1184. IEEE (2011)
7. Grabner, H., Bischof, H.: On-line boosting and vision. In: Proceedings of Computer Vision and Pattern Recognition (CVPR), pp. 260–267 (2006)
8. Ling, H.: Online robust image alignment via iterative convex optimization. In: Proceedings of Computer Vision and Pattern Recognition (CVPR), pp. 1808–1814. IEEE (2012)
9. Kalal, Z., Mikolajczyk, K., Matas, J.: Tracking-learning-detection. IEEE Trans. Pattern Anal. Mach. Intell. **34**(7), 1409–1422 (2012)
10. Henriques, J.F., Rui, C., Martins, P., et al.: High-speed tracking with kernelized correlation filters. IEEE Trans. Pattern Anal. Mach. Intell. **37**(3), 583–596 (2014)
11. Danelljan, M., Häger, G., Khan, F.S., et al.: Accurate scale estimation for robust visual tracking. In: British Machine Vision Conference, pp. 65.1–65.11 (2014)
12. Danelljan, M., Hager, G., Khan, F.S., et al.: Learning spatially regularized correlation filters for visual tracking. In: Proceedings of International Conference on Computer Vision (ICCV), et al, pp. 4310–4318. IEEE Computer Society (2015)
13. Wang, M., Liu, Y., Huang, Z.: Large margin object tracking with circulant feature maps. In: Proceedings of Computer Vision and Pattern Recognition (CVPR), pp. 4800–4808. Honolulu, Hawaii (2017)

14. Bertinetto, L., Valmadre, J., Henriques, J.F., et al.: Fully-convolutional siamese networks for object tracking. In: Proceedings of European Conference on Computer Vision (ECCV), pp. 850–865. Springer, Cham (2016)
15. Choi, J., Chang, H.J., Yun, S., et al.: Attentional correlation filter network for adaptive visual tracking. In: Proceedings of Computer Vision and Pattern Recognition (CVPR), pp. 4828–4837. IEEE (2017)
16. Wang, N., Li, S., Gupta, A., et al.: Transferring rich feature hierarchies for robust visual tracking. Comput. Sci. (2015)
17. Nam, H., Han, B.: Learning multi-domain convolutional neural networks for visual tracking. In: Proceedings of Computer Vision and Pattern Recognition (CVPR), pp. 4293–4302, IEEE (2016)
18. Jiang, Z., Lin, Z., Davis, L.S.: Label consistent K-SVD: learning a discriminative dictionary for recognition. IEEE Trans. Pattern Anal. Mach. Intell. **35**(11), 2651–2664 (2013)
19. Jin, Z., Su, Z., Wu, H., et al.: Robust tracking via discriminative sparse feature selection. Vis. Comput. **31**(5), 575–588 (2015)
20. Lienhart, R., Maydt, J.: An extended set of Haar-like features for rapid object detection. In: International Conference on Image Processing, vol. 1, pp. I-900–I-903. IEEE (2002)
21. Wu, Y., Lim, J., Yang, M.H.: Object Tracking Benchmark. IEEE Trans. Pattern Anal. Mach. Intell. **37**(9), 1834–1848 (2015)
22. Li, Y., Zhu, J.: A scale adaptive kernel correlation filter tracker with feature integration. In: Agapito, L., Bronstein, M.M., Rother, C. (eds.) ECCV 2014. LNCS, vol. 8926, pp. 254–265. Springer, Cham (2015). https://doi.org/10.1007/978-3-319-16181-5_18
23. Bertinetto, L., Valmadre, J., Golodetz, S., et al.: Staple: complementary learners for real-time tracking. In: Proceedings of Computer Vision and Pattern Recognition (CVPR), pp. 1401–1409. IEEE (2016)
24. Qiao, T., Yang, Z., Ren, J., et al.: Joint bilateral filtering and spectral similarity-based sparse representation: a generic framework for effective feature extraction and data classification in hyperspectral imaging. Pattern Recognit. (2017)
25. Ren, J., Orwell, J., Jones, G.A., et al.: Tracking the soccer ball using multiple fixed cameras. Comput. Vis. Image Underst. **113**(5), 633–642 (2009)

Saliency Detection via Bidirectional Absorbing Markov Chain

Fengling Jiang[1,2,3](✉), Bin Kong[1,4], Ahsan Adeel[5], Yun Xiao[6], and Amir Hussain[5]

[1] Institute of Intelligent Machines, Chinese Academy of Sciences, Hefei 230031, China
bkong@iim.ac.cn
[2] University of Science and Technology of China, Hefei 230026, China
fljiang@mail.ustc.edu.cn
[3] Hefei Normal University, Hefei 230061, China
[4] Anhui Engineering Laboratory for Intelligent Driving Technology and Application, Hefei 230088, China
[5] University of Stirling, Stirling FK9 4LA, UK
{aad,ahu}@cs.stir.ac.uk
[6] Anhui University, Hefei 230601, China
xiaoyun@ahu.edu.cn

Abstract. Traditional saliency detection via Markov chain only consider boundaries nodes. However, in addition to boundaries cues, background prior and foreground prior cues play a complementary role to enhance saliency detection. In this paper, we propose an absorbing Markov chain based saliency detection method considering both boundary information and foreground prior cues. The proposed approach combines both boundaries and foreground prior cues through bidirectional Markov chain. Specifically, the image is first segmented into superpixels and four boundaries nodes (duplicated as virtual nodes) are selected. Subsequently, the absorption time upon transition node's random walk to the absorbing state is calculated to obtain foreground possibility. Simultaneously, foreground prior as the virtual absorbing nodes is used to calculate the absorption time and obtain the background possibility. Finally, two obtained results are fused to obtain the combined saliency map using cost function for further optimization at multi-scale. Experimental results demonstrate the outperformance of our proposed model on 4 benchmark datasets as compared to 17 state-of-the-art methods.

Keywords: Saliency detection · Markov chain
Bidirectional absorbing

1 Introduction

Saliency detection aims to effectively highlight the most important pixels in an image. It helps to reduce computing costs and has widely been used in

J. Ren et al. (Eds.): BICS 2018, LNAI 10989, pp. 495–505, 2018.
https://doi.org/10.1007/978-3-030-00563-4_48

various computer vision applications, such as image segmentation [6], image retrieval [36], object detection [8], object recognition [21], image adaptation [23], and video segmentation [26]. Saliency detection could be summarized in three methods: bottom-up methods [22,33,37], top-down methods [10,15,35] and mixed methods [7,27,31]. The top-down methods are driven by tasks and could be used in object detection tasks. The authors in [34] proposed a top-down method that jointly learns a conditional random field and a discriminative dictionary. Top-down methods could be applied to address complex and special tasks but they lack versatility. The bottom-up methods are driven by data, such as color, light, texture and other basic features. Itti et al. [13] proposed a saliency method by using these basic features. It could be effectively used for real-time systems. The mixed methods are considered both bottom-up and top-down methods.

In this paper, we focus on the bottom-up methods, the proposed method is based on the properties of Markov model, there are many works based on Markov model, such as [3,4]. Traditional saliency detection via Markov chain [14] is based on Marov model as well, but it only consider boundaries nodes. However, in addition to boundaries cues, background prior and foreground prior cues play a complementary role to enhance saliency detection. We consider four boundaries information and the foreground prior saliency object, using absorbing Markov chain, namely, both boundary absorbing and foreground prior are considered to get background and foreground possibility. In addition, we further optimize our model by fusing these two possibilities, and exploite multi-scale processing. Figure 1 demonstrates and compares the results of our proposed method with the traditional saliency detection absorbing Markov chain (MC) method [14], where the outperformance of our method is evident.

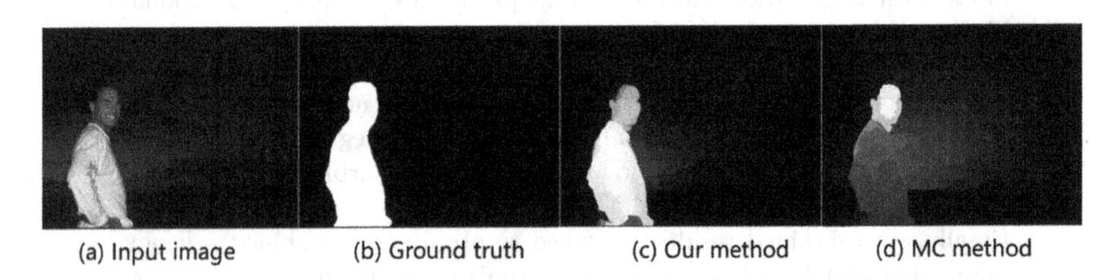

Fig. 1. Comparison of the proposed method with the ground truth and MC method.

2 Principle of Absorbing Markov Chain

In absorbing Markov chain, the transition matrix P is primitive [9], by definition, state i is absorbing when $P(i,i) = 1$, and $P(i,j) = 0$ for all $i \neq j$. If the Markov chain satisfies the following two conditions, it means there is at least one or more absorbing states in the Markov chain. In every state, it is possible to go to an absorbing state in a finite number of steps (not necessarily in one step), then we call it absorbing Markov chain. In an absorbing Markov chain, if a state is not a absorbing state, it is called transient state.

An absorbing chain has m absorbing states and n transient states, the transfer matrix P can be written as:

$$P \rightarrow \begin{pmatrix} Q & R \\ 0 & I \end{pmatrix}, \tag{1}$$

where Q is a n-by-n matrix, giving transient probabilities between any transient states, R is a nonzero n-by-m matrix giving these probabilities from transient state to any absorbing state, 0 is a m-by-n zero matrix and I is the m-by-m identity matrix.

For an absorbing chain P, all the transient states can achieve absorbing states in one or more steps, we can write the expected number of times $N(i,j)$ (which means the transient state moves from i state to the j state), its standard form is written as:

$$N = (I - Q)^{-1}, \tag{2}$$

namely, the matrix N with invertible matrix, where n_{ij} denotes the average transfer times between transient state i to transient state j. Supposing $c = [1, 1, \cdots, 1]_{1\times n}^{N}$, the absorbed time for each transient state can be expressed as:

$$z = N \times c. \tag{3}$$

3 Bidirectional Absorbing Markov Chain Model

To obtain more robust and accurate saliency maps, we propose a method via bidirectional absorbing Markov chain. This section explains the procedure to find the saliency area in an image in two orientations. Simple linear iterative clustering (SLIC) algorithm [2] has been used to get the superpixels. The pipeline is explained below (Fig. 2):

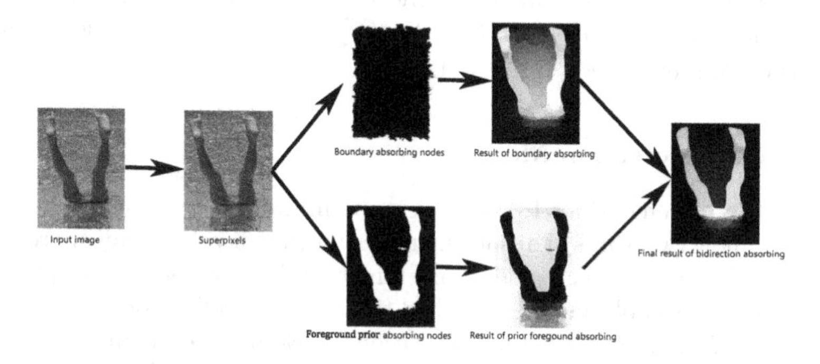

Fig. 2. The processing of our proposed method

3.1 Graph Construction

The SLIC algorithm is used to split the image into different pitches of superpixels. Afterwards, two kinds of graphs $G^1(V^1, E^1)$ and $G^2(V^2, E^2)$ are constructed, where G^1 represents the graph of boundary absorbing process and G^2 represents the graph of foreground prior absorbing process. In each of the graphs, V^1, V^2 represent the graph nodes and E^1, E^2 represent the edges between any nodes in the graphs. For the process of boundary absorbing, superpixels around the four boundaries as the virtual nodes are duplicated. For the process of foreground prior absorbing, superpixels from the regions (calculated by the foreground prior) are duplicated. There are two kinds of nodes in both graphs, transient nodes (superpixels) and absorbing nodes (duplicated nodes). The nodes in these two graphs constitute following three properties: (1) The nodes (including transient or absorbing) are associated with each other when superpixels in the image are adjacent nodes or have the same neighbors. And also boundary nodes (superpixels on the boundary of image) are fully connected with each other to reduce the geodesic distance between similar superpixels. (2) Any pair of absorbing nodes (which are duplicated from the boundaries or foreground nodes) are not connected (3) The nodes, which are duplicated from the four boundaries or foreground prior nodes, are also connected with original duplicated nodes. In this paper, the weight w_{ij} of the edges is defined as

$$w_{ij} = e^{-\frac{\|x_i - x_j\|}{\sigma^2}}, i, j \in V^1 \text{ or } i, j \in V^2 \tag{4}$$

where σ is the constant parameter to adjust the strength of the weights in CIELAB color space. Then we can get the affinity matrix A

$$a_{ij} = \begin{cases} w_{ij}, & \text{if } j \in M(i) \quad 1 \leq i \leq j \\ 1, & \text{if } i = j \\ 0, & \text{otherwise,} \end{cases} \tag{5}$$

where $M(i)$ is a nodes set, in which the nodes are all connected to nodes i. The diagonal matrix is given as: $D = diag(\sum_j a_{ij})$, and the obtained transient matrix is calculated as: $P = D^{-1} \times A$.

3.2 Saliency Detection Model

Following the aforementioned procedures, the initial image is transformed into superpixels, now two kinds of absorbing nodes for saliency detection are required. Firstly, we choose boundary nodes and foreground prior nodes to duplicate as absorbing nodes and obtain the absorbed times of transient nodes as foreground possibility and background possibility. Secondly, we use a cost function to optimize two possibility results together and obtain saliency results of all transient nodes.

Absorb Markov Chain via Boundary Nodes. In normal conditions, four boundaries of an image rarely have salient objects. Therefore, boundary nodes are assumed as background, and four boundaries nodes set H^1 are duplicated as absorbing nodes set D^1, $H^1, D^1 \subset V^1$. The graph G^1 is constructed and absorbed time z is calculated via Eq. 3. Finally, foreground possibility of transient nodes $z^f = \bar{z}(i) \quad i = 1, 2, \cdots, n$, is obtained, and $\bar{z}$ denotes the normalizing the absorbed time vector.

Absorb Markov Chain via Foreground Prior Nodes. We use boundary connectivity to get the foreground prior $\mathbf{f}_i$ without using the down-top method [38].

$$f_i = \sum_{j=1}^{N}(1 - \exp(-\frac{BC_j^2}{2\sigma_b^2}))d_a(i,j)\exp(-\frac{d_s^2(i,j)}{2\sigma_s^2}) \tag{6}$$

where $d_a(i,j)$ and $d_s(i,j)$ denote the CIELAB color feature distance and spatial distance respectively between superpixel i and j, the boundary connectivity (BC) of superpixel i is defined as $BC_i = \frac{\sum_{j\in\mathcal{H}} w_{ij}}{\sqrt{\sum_{j=1}^{N} w_{ij}}}$ in Fig. 3, $\sigma_b = 1$, $\sigma_s = 0.25$. $\mathcal{H}$ denotes the boundary area of image and w_{ij} is the similarity between nodes i and j. N is the number of superpixels. Afterwards, nodes $(\{i|f_i > avg(f)\})$ with high level values are selected to get a set H^2, which are duplicated as absorbing nodes set D^2, $H^2, D^2 \subset V^2$. The graph G^2 is constructed and absorbed time z is calculated using Eq. 3. Finally, the background possibility of transient nodes $z^b = \bar{z}(i) \quad i = 1, 2, \cdots, n$, is obtained, where $\bar{z}$ denotes the absorbed time vector normalization.

Fig. 3. An illustrative example of boundary connectivity. (a) input image (b) the superpixels of input image (c) the superpixels of similarity in each pitches (d) an illustrative example of boundary connectivity.

3.3 Saliency Optimization

In order to combine different cues, this paper has used the optimization model presented in [38], which fused background possibility and foreground possibility for final saliency map. It is defined as

$$\sum_{i=1}^{N} z_i^b s_i^2 + \sum_{i=1}^{N} z_i^f (s_i - 1)^2 + \sum_{i,j} w_{ij}(s_i - s_j)^2 \tag{7}$$

where the first term defines superpixel i with large background probability z^b to obtain a small value s_i (close to 0). The second term encourages a superpixel i with large foreground probability z^f to obtain a large value s_i (close to 1). The third term defines the smoothness to acquire continuous saliency values.

In this work, the used super-pixel numbers N are 200, 250, 300 in the superpixel element, and the final saliency map is given as: $\mathbf{S} = \sum_h S^h$ at each scale, where $h = 1, 2, 3$.

4 Simulation Results

The proposed method is evaluated on four benchmark datasets ASD [1], CSSD [30], ECSSD [30] and SED [5]. ASD dataset is a subset of the MSRA dataset, which contains 1000 images with accurate human-labeled ground truth. CSSD dataset, namely complex scene saliency detection contains 200 complex images. ECSSD dataset, an extension of CSSD dataset contains 1000 images and has accurate human-labeled ground truth. SED dataset has two parts, SED1 and SED2, images in SED1 contains one object, and images in SED2 contains two objects, in total they contain 200 images. We compare our model with 17 different state-of-the-art saliency detection algorithms: CA [12], FT [1], SEG [20], BM [28], SWD [11], SF [19], GCHC [32], LMLC [29], HS [30], PCA [18], DSR [17], MC [14], MR [33], MS [24], RBD [38], RR [16], MST [25]. The tuning parameters in the proposed algorithm is the edge weight $\sigma^2 = 0.1$ that controls the strength of weight between a pair of nodes.

The precision-recall curves and F-measure are used as performance metrics. The precision is defined as the ratio of salient pixels correctly assigned to all the pixels of extracted regions. The recall is defined as the ratio of detected salient pixels to the ground-truth number. A PR curve is obtained by the threshold sliding from 0 to 255 to get the difference between the saliency map (which is calculated) and ground truth (which is labeled manually). F-measure is calculated by the weighted average between the precision values and recall values, which can be regarded as overall performance measurement, given as:

$$F_\beta = \frac{(1+\beta^2)Precision \times Recall}{\beta^2 Precision + Recall}, \tag{8}$$

we set $\beta^2 = 0.3$ to stress precision more than recall. PR-curves and the F-measure curves are shown in Figs. 4–7, where the outperformance of our proposed method as compared to 17 state-of-the-art methods is evident. Figure 8 presets visual comparisons selected from four datasets. It can be seen that the proposed method achieved best saliency results as compared to the state-of-the-art methods.

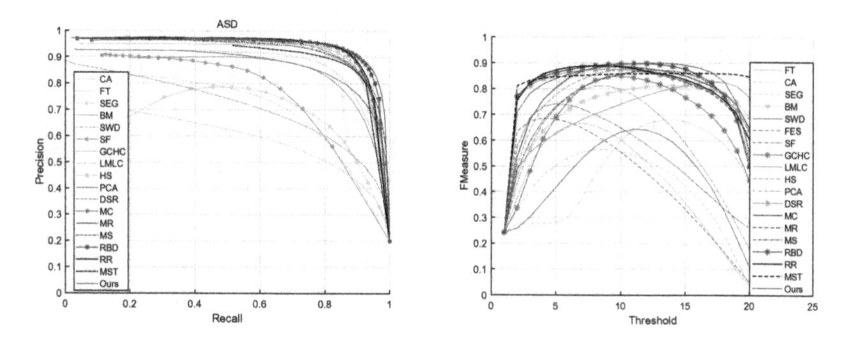

Fig. 4. PR-curves and F-measure curves comparing with different methods on ASD dataset.

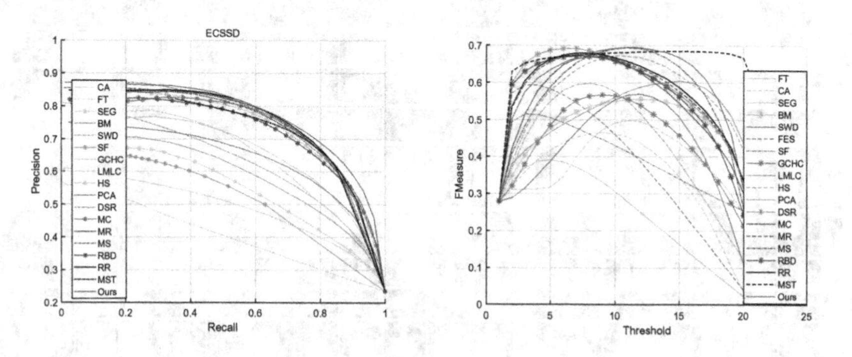

Fig. 5. PR-curves and F-value curves comparing with different methods on ECSSD dataset.

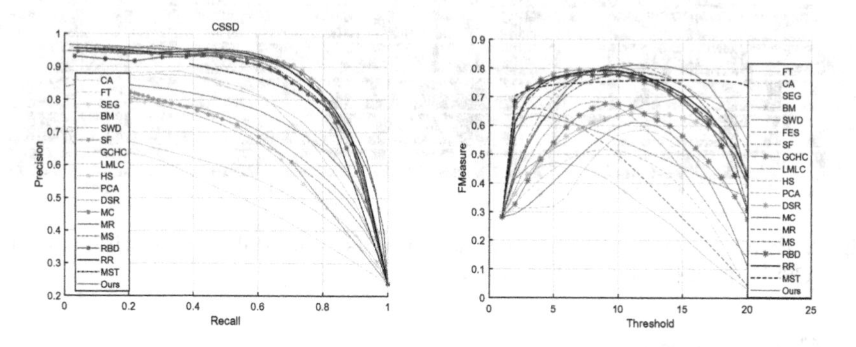

Fig. 6. PR-curves and F-measure curves comparing with different methods on CSSD dataset.

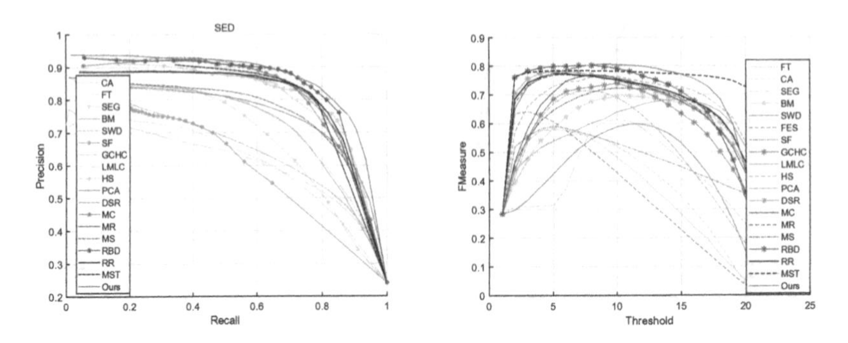

Fig. 7. PR-curves and F-measure curves comparing with different methods on SED dataset.

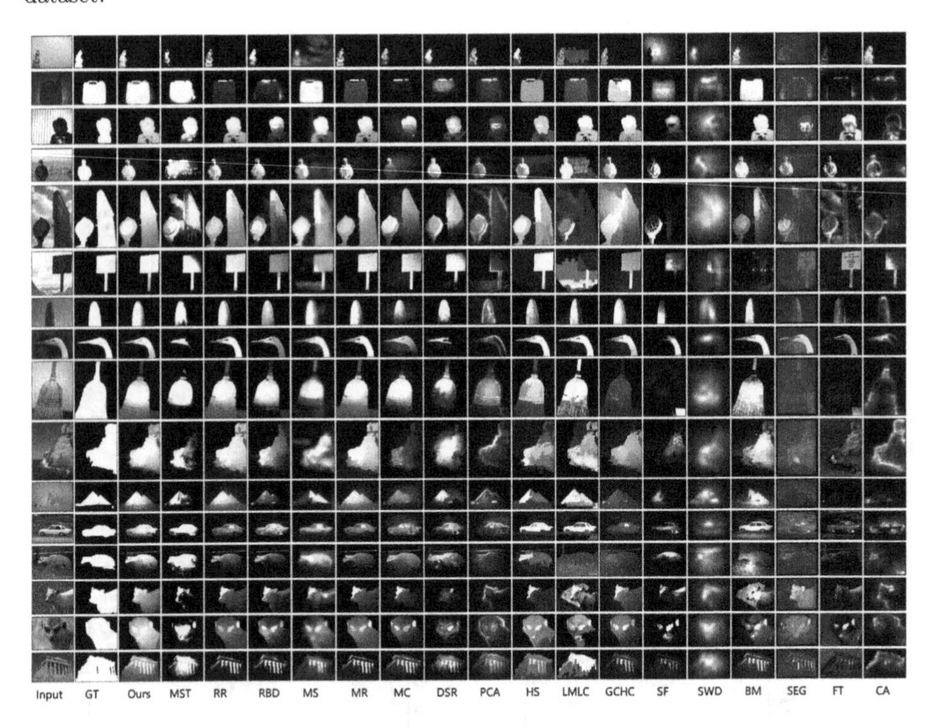

Fig. 8. Examples of output saliency maps results using different algorithms on the ASD, CSSD, ECSSD and SED datasets

5 Conclusion

In this paper, a bidirectional absorbing Markov chain based saliency detection method is proposed considering both boundary information and foreground prior cues. A novel optimization model is developed to combine both background and foreground possibilities, acquired through bidirectional absorbing Markov chain. The proposed approach outperformed 17 different state-of-the-art methods over four benchmark datasets, which demonstrate the superiority of our proposed approach. In future, we intend to apply our proposed saliency detection algorithm to problems such as multi-pose lipreading and audio-visual speech recognition.

Acknowledgement. This work was supported by China Scholarship Council, the National Natural Science Foundation of China (No. 913203002), the Pilot Project of Chinese Academy of Sciences (No. XDA08040109). Prof. Amir Hussain and Dr. Ahsan Adeel were supported by the UK Engineering and Physical Sciences Research Council (EPSRC) grant No. EP/M026981/1.

References

1. Achanta, R., Hemami, S., Estrada, F., Susstrunk, S.: Frequency-tuned salient region detection. In: Proceedings of IEEE Conference on Computer Vision and Pattern Recognition (CVPR), pp. 1597–1604. IEEE (2009)
2. Achanta, R., Shaji, A., Smith, K., Lucchi, A., Fua, P., Süsstrunk, S.: SLIC superpixels compared to state-of-the-art superpixel methods. IEEE Trans. Pattern Anal. Mach. Intell. (TPAMI) **34**(11), 2274–2282 (2012)
3. AlKhateeb, J.H., Pauplin, O., Ren, J., Jiang, J.: Performance of hidden Markov model and dynamic Bayesian network classifiers on handwritten Arabic word recognition. Knowl.-Based Syst. **24**(5), 680–688 (2011)
4. AlKhateeb, J.H., Ren, J., Jiang, J., Al-Muhtaseb, H.: Offline handwritten Arabic cursive text recognition using hidden Markov models and re-ranking. Pattern Recogn. Lett. **32**(8), 1081–1088 (2011)
5. Alpert, S., Galun, M., Brandt, A., Basri, R.: Image segmentation by probabilistic bottom-up aggregation and cue integration. IEEE Trans. Pattern Anal. Mach. Intell. (TPAMI) **34**(2), 315–327 (2012)
6. Arbelaez, P., Maire, M., Fowlkes, C., Malik, J.: Contour detection and hierarchical image segmentation. IEEE Trans. Pattern Anal. Mach. Intell. (TPAMI) **33**(5), 898–916 (2011)
7. Borji, A., Sihite, D.N., Itti, L.: Probabilistic learning of task-specific visual attention. In: Proceedings of IEEE Conference on Computer Vision and Pattern Recognition (CVPR), pp. 470–477. IEEE (2012)
8. Chang, K.Y., Liu, T.L., Chen, H.T., Lai, S.H.: Fusing generic objectness and visual saliency for salient object detection. In: Proceedings of IEEE International Conference on Computer Vision (ICCV), pp. 914–921. IEEE (2011)
9. Charles, M., Grinstead, J., Snell, L.: Introduction to Probability. American Mathematical Society, Providence (1997)
10. Cholakkal, H., Johnson, J., Rajan, D.: Backtracking SCSPM image classifier for weakly supervised top-down saliency. In: Proceedings of IEEE Conference on Computer Vision and Pattern Recognition (CVPR), pp. 5278–5287. IEEE (2016)
11. Duan, L., Wu, C., Miao, J., Qing, L., Fu, Y.: Visual saliency detection by spatially weighted dissimilarity. In: Proceedings of IEEE Conference on Computer Vision and Pattern Recognition (CVPR), pp. 473–480. IEEE (2011)
12. Goferman, S., Zelnik-Manor, L., Tal, A.: Context-aware saliency detection. IEEE Trans. Pattern Anal. Mach. Intell. (TPAMI) **34**(10), 1915–1926 (2012)
13. Itti, L., Koch, C., Niebur, E.: A model of saliency-based visual attention for rapid scene analysis. IEEE Trans. Pattern Anal. Mach. Intell. (TPAMI) **20**(11), 1254–1259 (1998)

14. Jiang, B., Zhang, L., Lu, H., Yang, C., Yang, M.H.: Saliency detection via absorbing Markov chain. In: Proceedings of IEEE International Conference on Computer Vision (ICCV), pp. 1665–1672. IEEE (2013)
15. Kocak, A., Cizmeciler, K., Erdem, A., Erdem, E.: Top down saliency estimation via superpixel-based discriminative dictionaries. BMVA Press (2014). https://doi.org/10.5244/C.28.73
16. Li, C., Yuan, Y., Cai, W., Xia, Y., Feng, D.D., et al.: Robust saliency detection via regularized random walks ranking. In: Proceedings of IEEE Conference on Computer Vision and Pattern Recognition (CVPR), pp. 2710–2717. IEEE (2015)
17. Li, X., Lu, H., Zhang, L., Ruan, X., Yang, M.H.: Saliency detection via dense and sparse reconstruction. In: Proceedings of IEEE International Conference on Computer Vision (ICCV), pp. 2976–2983. IEEE (2013)
18. Margolin, R., Tal, A., Zelnik-Manor, L.: What makes a patch distinct? In: Proceedings of IEEE Conference on Computer Vision and Pattern Recognition (CVPR), pp. 1139–1146. IEEE (2013)
19. Perazzi, F., Krähenbühl, P., Pritch, Y., Hornung, A.: Saliency filters: contrast based filtering for salient region detection. In: Proceedings of IEEE Conference on Computer Vision and Pattern Recognition (CVPR), pp. 733–740. IEEE (2012)
20. Rahtu, E., Kannala, J., Salo, M., Heikkilä, J.: Segmenting salient objects from images and videos. In: Daniilidis, K., Maragos, P., Paragios, N. (eds.) ECCV 2010. LNCS, vol. 6315, pp. 366–379. Springer, Heidelberg (2010). https://doi.org/10.1007/978-3-642-15555-0_27
21. Ren, Z., Gao, S., Chia, L.T., Tsang, I.W.H.: Region-based saliency detection and its application in object recognition. IEEE Trans. Circuits Syst. Video Technol. **24**(5), 769–779 (2014)
22. Riche, N., Mancas, M., Gosselin, B., Dutoit, T.: Rare: a new bottom-up saliency model. In: Proceedings of the 19th IEEE International Conference on Image Processing (ICIP), pp. 641–644. IEEE (2012)
23. Sun, J., Xie, J., Liu, J., Sikora, T.: Image adaptation and dynamic browsing based on two-layer saliency combination. IEEE Trans. Broadcast. **59**(4), 602–613 (2013)
24. Tong, N., Lu, H., Zhang, L., Ruan, X.: Saliency detection with multi-scale superpixels. IEEE Signal Process. Lett. **21**(9), 1035–1039 (2014)
25. Tu, W.C., He, S., Yang, Q., Chien, S.Y.: Real-time salient object detection with a minimum spanning tree. In: Proceedings of IEEE Conference on Computer Vision and Pattern Recognition (CVPR), pp. 2334–2342. IEEE (2016)
26. Wang, W., Shen, J., Yang, R., Porikli, F.: Saliency-aware video object segmentation. IEEE Trans. Pattern Anal. Mach. Intell. (TPAMI) **40**(1), 20–33 (2018)
27. Wang, Z., Ren, J., Zhang, D., Sun, M., Jiang, J.: A deep-learning based feature hybrid framework for spatiotemporal saliency detection inside videos. Neurocomputing **287**, 68–83 (2018)
28. Xie, Y., Lu, H.: Visual saliency detection based on Bayesian model. In: Proceedings of the 18th IEEE International Conference on Image Processing (ICIP), pp. 645–648. IEEE (2011)
29. Xie, Y., Lu, H., Yang, M.H.: Bayesian saliency via low and mid level cues. IEEE Trans. Image Process. **22**(5), 1689–1698 (2013)
30. Yan, Q., Xu, L., Shi, J., Jia, J.: Hierarchical saliency detection. In: Proceedings of IEEE Conference on Computer Vision and Pattern Recognition (CVPR), pp. 1155–1162. IEEE (2013)
31. Yan, Y., et al.: Unsupervised image saliency detection with Gestalt-laws guided optimization and visual attention based refinement. Pattern Recogn. **79**, 65–78 (2018)

32. Yang, C., Zhang, L., Lu, H.: Graph-regularized saliency detection with convex-hull-based center prior. IEEE Signal Process. Lett. **20**(7), 637–640 (2013)
33. Yang, C., Zhang, L., Lu, H., Ruan, X., Yang, M.H.: Saliency detection via graph-based manifold ranking. In: Proceedings of IEEE Conference on Computer Vision and Pattern Recognition (CVPR), pp. 3166–3173. IEEE (2013)
34. Yang, J., Yang, M.H.: Top-down visual saliency via joint CRF and dictionary learning. In: Proceedings of IEEE Conference on Computer Vision and Pattern Recognition (CVPR), pp. 2296–2303. IEEE (2012)
35. Yang, J., Yang, M.H.: Top-down visual saliency via joint CRF and dictionary learning. IEEE Trans. Pattern Anal. Mach. Intell. (TPAMI) **39**(3), 576–588 (2017)
36. Yang, X., Qian, X., Xue, Y.: Scalable mobile image retrieval by exploring contextual saliency. IEEE Trans. Image Process. **24**(6), 1709–1721 (2015)
37. Zhao, R., Ouyang, W., Li, H., Wang, X.: Saliency detection by multi-context deep learning. In: Proceedings of IEEE Conference on Computer Vision and Pattern Recognition (CVPR), pp. 1265–1274. IEEE (2015)
38. Zhu, W., Liang, S., Wei, Y., Sun, J.: Saliency optimization from robust background detection. In: Proceedings of IEEE Conference on Computer Vision and Pattern Recognition (CVPR), pp. 2814–2821. IEEE (2014)

Pedestrian Detection Based on Visual Saliency and Supervised Learning

Wanhan Zhang(✉), Jie Ren, and Meihua Gu

College of Electronics and Information, Xi'an Polytechnic University, Xi'an 710048, Shanxi, People's Republic of China
1612149374@qq.com

Abstract. Pedestrian detection is a key issue in computer vision, which received extensive attentions. Supervised learning methods with feature extraction and classification are widely used in the pedestrian detection. This paper proposed a pedestrian detection method based on visual saliency and supervised learning. The LC algorithm is used to calculate the saliency value of each training image, followed by the LBP feature extraction. The saliency LBP features and HOG features are combined together as the input of SVM classifier to detect pedestrians. Experimental results show that this method is more accurate and efficient compared with the traditional HOG and LBP feature fusion based method.

Keywords: Pedestrian detection · HOG · LBP · SVM · Visual significance

1 Introduction

Pedestrian detection is an important research topic in computer vision and pattern recognition. It is widely used in many fields such as intelligent assisted driving, intelligent monitoring and augmented reality. Pedestrian detection uses computer vision techniques to determine whether there are pedestrians in an image or a video sequence, followed by the pedestrian extraction and localization. It is a basic task of people identification, trajectory tracking, and crowd detection. Due to the differences in the appearance and movement of pedestrians and the influence of the environment, it is very difficult to identify pedestrians in the complex situation and the realistic environment.

However, human vision systems have a natural ability to locate interest regions in complex scenes. Several researches have shown that the incorporation of the visual saliency mechanism into the pedestrian detection can improve the accuracy of detection. Visual significance detection is a process to predict which information in an image or video is more noticeable. This research has received extensive attention in recent years. The processing and analyzing of the image are more focuses on the regions with more information.

Pedestrian detection methods using machine learning can be divided into two categories: extracting features manually or using neural networks to extract features. In the first class, features and the classifier are selected manually. The common used features to describe pedestrians are color, texture, edge, and gradient histogram. Dala

J. Ren et al. (Eds.): BICS 2018, LNAI 10989, pp. 506–513, 2018.
https://doi.org/10.1007/978-3-030-00563-4_49

et al. proposed a Histograms of Oriented Gradients (HOG) feature to describe the appearance and shape of targets [1]. Ojala et al. used the Local Binary Patterns (LBP) to classify texture information, which is widely used in face recognition [2]. According to the characteristics of the pedestrian, Mu et al. proposed two improved algorithms: Semantic-LBP (S-LBP) and Fourier LBP (F-LBP) [3]. Census transform histogram, which is similar to LBP features, can describe the global information of the scene and is used in the scene classification [4]. Wu uses Centrist in the pedestrian detection, in which the integral graph technology is applied for a faster feature extraction and a cascade classifier is combined to detect pedestrians in real time [5]. Viola et al. proposed a face detection method based on Haar feature and AdaBoost classifier. As a week classifier, AdaBoost can select features with strong discriminability from a large number of Haar features. This method is then successfully applied in the pedestrian detection [6]. The fusion of multiple underlying features can improve the accuracy of detection. However, the computation time of feature estimation increases with the increase of features dimension, which means that the pedestrian detection unable to work in real time. Wang et al. simply combined the LBP histogram feature of each local image block as a feature descriptor of the pedestrian. This method shows a similar performance to that of S-LBP [7]. Walk et al. used other datasets to evaluate the detection results based on the combination of HOG and LBP features. However, the performance of the detection is not improved because LBP cannot describe texture features effectively when the image is blurred or the light is suddenly changed [8]. Tuzel et al. used the covariance matrix of various features to describe the local feature of each pedestrian, and then classified pedestrians in Riemann geometric space [9]. Watanable et al. proposed the Co-occurrence Histograms of Oriented Gradients (CoHOG) feature which is similar to gray-level co-occurrence matrix [10]. Zheng et al. improved HOG and LBP method, which uses K-singular value decomposition (K-SVD) to extract sparse representation features from the combination of HOG and LBP features. These features are further used in the fast pedestrian detection for still images [11].

The second category uses neural networks to learn the features from the original image directly. These learned features are more distinguish in the classification. Du et al. proposed a deep neural network with a fused architecture for a faster and powerful pedestrian detection [12]. Ouyang et al. developed a joint deep learning network, which includes the feature extraction, deformation treatment, occlusion treatment and classification, for the pedestrian detection [13].

2 Proposed Method

Although the neural network based methods show a high performance in pedestrian detection, the classification result is closely depended on the hardware with high quality and the training sample with representative features. This paper still uses the method with manual feature extraction and classification. Since LBP features cannot effectively represent the texture of images when the image is relatively blurred and the light is stronger.

Therefore, the visual significance is applied as a new feature and combined to HOG-LBP features in the pedestrian detection [14]. In the saliency calculation step, LC algorithm is selected because of its fast processing speed. There are two parts of the proposed method: training and testing. Its flowchart is shown in Fig. 1. In the training process, the LC algorithm is used to calculate the saliency value of each training image, followed by the LBP feature extraction step. The saliency LBP feature and HOG feature are combined together as the input of SVM to build a training model. In the test process, saliency LBP features and HOG features are extracted for each test image. Then fused features are input into the trained SVM classifier to decide whether there is a pedestrian or not.

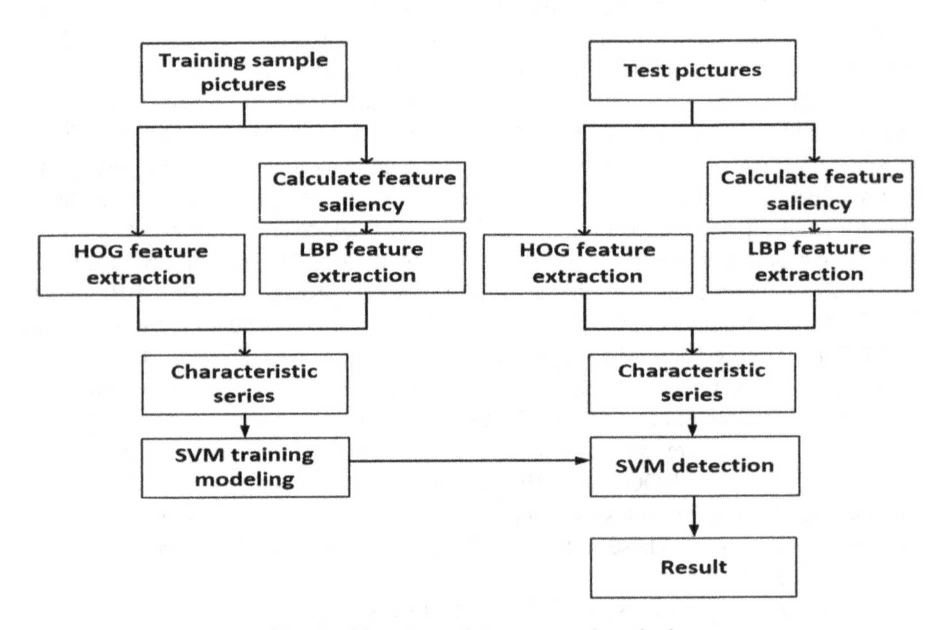

Fig. 1. Flowchart of the proposed method.

3 HOG Feature Extraction

HOG, a local feature descriptor with the gradient statistical histogram of the local region, can effectively express the appearance and shape information of objects and are used to detect these objects [1]. Firstly, the image is divided into several small regions called cells. Then the gradient of each pixel in a cell is calculated to generate a direction histogram of that cell. Finally, the histograms are combined to form a feature descriptor. The main steps are:

Step 1: Let $I_0(x, y)$ be a grey value of the pixel at (x, y) in the input image. Its Gamma standardized grey value is:

$$I(x, y) = I_0(x, y)^g \tag{1}$$

where g usually uses 0.5.
Step 2: Calculate the gradient amplitude $G(x, y)$ and gradient direction $\alpha(x, y)$ of pixel (x, y).

$$G_x(x, y) = I(x+1, y) - I(x-1, y) \tag{2}$$

$$G_y(x, y) = I(x, y+1) - I(x, y-1) \tag{3}$$

$$G(x, y) = \sqrt{G_x(x, y)^2 + G_y(x, y)^2} \tag{4}$$

$$\alpha(x, y) = \tan^{-1}(G_y(x, y)/G_x(x, y)) \tag{5}$$

where $G_x(x, y)$ and $G_y(x, y)$ are gradients in horizontal direction and vertical direction respectively.
Step 3: Generate the statistical histogram of gradient directions. The image is evenly divided into several non-overlapped cells. The histogram of gradient direction is calculated in each cell. If all gradient directions are divided into 9 intervals, each cell generates a 9 dimensional vector.
Step 4: After merging several cells into a block, the histogram vector of the block, which is a combination of the histogram of all cells in that block, is used as the final descriptor. In fact, there is an overlap between adjacent blocks, which means the histogram of each cell is used to calculate the final descriptor many times. The calculation redundancy can significantly improve the final classification performance.

A schematic diagram of HOG is shown in Fig. 2.

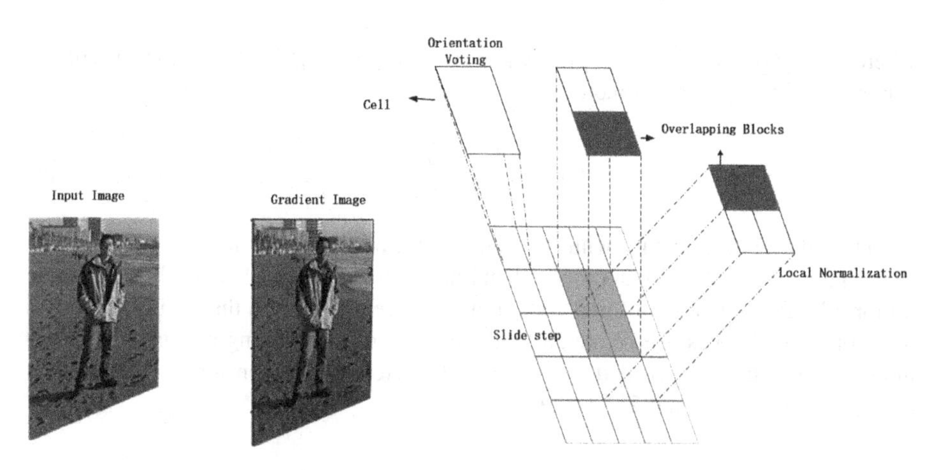

Fig. 2. Schematic diagram of HOG feature detection

4 S-LBP Feature Extraction

4.1 LC Algorithm

It is widely believed that the brain responds more easily to high contrast regions [15]. Based on the psychological studies, human perception system is sensitive to the contrast of visual signals, such as color, intensity and texture [16]. Under this assumption, Zhai and Shah proposed LC algorithm to compute the spatial saliency map based on the color contrast between image pixels [17]. The saliency of a pixel (x, y) in the image I is the sum of the color distance between that pixel and each of other pixels.

$$\mathrm{S}(x, y) = \sum\nolimits_{\forall \mathrm{I}(x_0, y_0) \in I} \|\mathrm{I}(x, y) - \mathrm{I}(x_0, y_0)\| \tag{6}$$

where the value of $\mathrm{I}(x, y)$ is in the range of [0, 255], $\| * \|$ represents the color distance metric, and $\mathrm{I}(x_0, y_0)$ represents other pixels in the image.

Then, the histogram method is used to reduce the computational complexity. Finally, the spatial saliency map is normalized.

4.2 The LBP Feature Extraction

LBP operator is used to describe the local texture features of an image [3]. Firstly, the gray value $\mathrm{I}(x, y)$ is selected as the threshold, in which pixel (x, y) is the center of a 3 * 3 region. Then, the gray values of the other 8 pixels in that region are compared with the threshold. The pixel with a value larger than the threshold is marked as 1. On the contrary, if its value is less than the threshold, that pixel is labeled as 0. After comparing these 8 pixels, an 8 bit binary is generated. The decimal of that binary $\mathrm{L}(x, y)$ is the LBP value of the pixel, which represents the texture information of the region.

$$\mathrm{L}(x, y) = \sum\nolimits_{m=0}^{m-1} 2^m \mathrm{c}(\mathrm{I}(x, y) - \mathrm{I}(x_m, y_m)) \tag{7}$$

where $\mathrm{I}(x_m, y_m)$ represents the gray value of pixel (x_m, y_m) in the region except the center. $\mathrm{c}(x)$ is a symbolic function.

$$\mathrm{c}(x) = \begin{cases} 1, & \textit{if } x \geq 0 \\ 0, & \textit{else} \end{cases} \tag{8}$$

To adapt the texture feature with different scales, and keep the invariant of the gray scale and rotation, Ojala et al. proposed an improved uniform LBP algorithm [2]. In the uniform LBP, the number of transformations between 0 and 1 in the coding process is not more than 2 times. There are 58 kinds of uniform LBP coding results. Other non-uniformed results are classified as one class. Therefore, the dimension of the feature is reduced from the original 256 to 59.

5 SVM Classifier

In this paper, the support vector machine (SVM) is selected as the classifier in the pedestrian detection. Firstly, the training dataset is mapped to the Hilbert space. The non-linear and non-separable data is transformed into the Hilbert space and becomes linear separable. The optimal separation hyper-plane with maximum isolation distance is established in the feature space, which generates an optimal nonlinear decision boundary in the input space. In the feature space, the hyper-plane of support vector machine is the optimal one. The support vector is the smallest number of sample vectors that determine the optimal separation hyper-plane.

6 Pedestrian Detection

The pedestrian detection can be classified into 5 steps:

Step 1: The LC algorithm is used to calculate the salient map of the input image.
Step 2: The input image with a dimension of 128 * 64 is divided into 16 * 16 dimensional sub-images. The number of sub-images is 8 * 4 = 32. Then the LBP feature of each pixel is used to obtain LBP feature histogram of individual sub-image. Using the uniform method, the feature of each sub-image is a vector with 59 dimensions. Then, the histograms of the whole image are normalized. The feature vector has 1888 dimensions.
Step 3: In HOG feature detection, the size of each cell is 8 * 8, and the size of each block is 16 * 16. Then input image contains 105 blocks and each block contains a 36 dimensional vector. Therefore, the feature vector of HOG for the whole image has 105 * 36 = 3780 dimensions.
Step 4: The HOG and S-LBP features are connected in series. The final feature has 5668 dimensions.
Step 5: The feature data is the input of SVM to learn a classifier of the pedestrian detection. The classifier can be used to detect pedestrians using the sliding window method.

7 Experimental Results

In order to evaluate the effectiveness and reliability, the proposed method is compared with HOG and HOG-LBP based methods. To compare the time consuming, this paper uses a computer with FX (TM) 8300 CPU. The software includes python3.5 and opencv3.

INRIA Dataset is a widely used static pedestrian detection dataset. It provides original images and corresponding annotation files. The training set has 614 positive samples (including 2416 pedestrians) and 1218 negative samples; the test set has 288 positive samples (including 1126 pedestrians) and 453 negative samples.

In this paper, images in the training set are preprocessed according to the tagging files. There are 1613 images with pedestrians, which have a size of 64 * 128 pixels.

1218 images with a size of 64 * 128 contain no pedestrians. The 1613 pictures are randomly divided into two categories: 1024 training images and 598 test images. For the classifier, the V-SVC is applied in this paper. The kernel function type is LINEAR, and the maximum iteration number of the algorithm termination condition is set to 1000. Using the cross validation method, the average recognition rates of three methods are shown in Table 1.

Table 1. Comparison of the average recognition rate of three methods.

Test method	Feature dimensions (dimension)	Training time (s)	Testing time (s/image)	Recognition rate (%)
HOG + SVM	3780	270.68	0.0214	79.31
HOG + LBP + SVM	5668	270.04	0.0389	89.04
HOG + LC + LBP + SVM	5668	157.02	0. 0289	92.25

8 Conclusion

In this paper, a visual saliency and HOG + LBP based pedestrian feature extraction method is proposed. The LBP feature and HOG feature guided by LC algorithm are fused, and SVM is used for pedestrian detection. Experimental result shows that this method is more faster and accuracy compared with the traditional HOG and LBP method. In the future work, it is necessary to improve the visual saliency algorithm, and also add neural network to further improve the speed and detection rate.

Acknowledgment. This work is supported by the Shaanxi natural science basic research project under Grant 2017JQ6058.

References

1. Dalal, N., Triggs, B.: Histograms of oriented gradients for human detection. In: Dalal, N., Triggs, B. (eds.) Proceedings 2005 IEEE Computer Society Conference on Computer Vision and Pattern Recognition, CVPR 2005, pp. 886–893. IEEE Computer Society, San Diego (2005)
2. Ojala, T., Pietikäinen, M., Mäenpää, T.: Multiresolution gray-scale and rotation invariant texture classification with local binary patterns. IEEE Trans. Pattern Anal. Mach. Intell. **24** (7), 971–987 (2002)
3. Mu, Y., Yan, S., Liu, Y., et al.: Discriminative local binary patterns for human detection in personal album. In: Mu, Y., Yan, S., Liu, Y., et al. (eds.) 26th IEEE Conference on Computer Vision and Pattern Recognition, CVPR, pp. 1–8. IEEE Computer Society, Anchorage (2008)
4. Wu, J., Rehg, M.: A visual descriptor for scene categorization. IEEE Trans. Pattern Anal. Mach. Intell. **33**(8), 1489–1501 (2011)

5. Wu, J., Geyer, C., Rehg, M.: Real-time human detection using contour cues. In: 2011 IEEE International Conference on Robotics and Automation, ICRA 2011, pp. 860–867. Institute of Electrical and Electronics Engineers Inc., Shanghai (2011)
6. Viola, P., Jones, M., Snow, D.: Detecting pedestrians using patterns of motion and appearance. Int. J. Comput. Vis. **63**(2), 153–161 (2003)
7. Wang, X.: An HOG-LBP human detector with partial occlusion handling. In: Computer Vision, Kyoto Japan, vol. 30, pp. 32–39 (2009)
8. Walk, S., Majer, N., Schindler, K., et al.: New features and insights for pedestrian detection. In: 2010 IEEE Computer Society Conference on Computer Vision and Pattern Recognition, CVPR 2010, pp. 1030–1037. IEEE Computer Society, San Francisco (2010)
9. Tuzel, O., Porikli, F., Meer, P.: Pedestrian detection via classification on Riemannian manifolds. IEEE Trans. Pattern Anal. Mach. Intell. **30**(10), 1713–1727 (2008)
10. Wantanbe, T., Ito, S., Yokoi K.: Co-occurrence histograms of oriented gradients for pedestrian detection. In: Advances in Image and Video Technology - Third Pacific Rim Symposium, PSIVT 2009, Proceedings, pp. 37–47. Springer, Tokyo (2009)
11. Zheng, C.H., Pei, W.J., Yan, Q., Chong, Y.W.: Pedestrian detection based on gradient and texture feature integration. Neurocomputing **228**, 71–78 (2017)
12. Du, X., El-Khamy, M., Lee, J., Davis, L.: Fused DNN: a deep neural network fusion approach to fast and robust pedestrian detection. In: Proceedings 2017 IEEE Winter Conference on Applications of Computer Vision, WACV 2017, pp. 953–961. Institute of Electrical and Electronics Engineers Inc, Santa Rosa (2017)
13. Ouyang, W., Zhou, H., Li, H., Li, Q., Yan, J., Wang, X.: Jointly learning deep features, deformable parts, occlusion and classification for pedestrian detection. IEEE Trans. Pattern Anal. Mach. Intell. **40**(8), 1874–1887 (2017)
14. Zheng, J., Yanan, L., Jinchang, R., Tingge, Z., Yijun, Y.: Fusion of block and keypoints based approaches for effective copy-move image forgery detection. Multidimens. Syst. Signal Process. **27**(4), 989–1005 (2016)
15. Yan, Y., et al.: Unsupervised image saliency detection with Gestalt-laws guided optimization and visual attention based refinement. Pattern Recognit. **79**, 65–78 (2018)
16. Ren, J., Jiang, J., Wang, D., Ipson, S.S.: Fusion of intensity and inter-component chromatic difference for effective and robust colour edge detection. IET Image Process. **4**(4), 294–301 (2010)
17. Zhai, Y., Shah, M.: Visual attention detection in video sequences using spatiotemporal cues. In: Proceedings of the 14th Annual ACM International Conference on Multimedia, MM 2006, pp. 815–824. Association for Computing Machinery, Santa Barbara (2006)

Data Analysis and Natural Language Processing

Hadoop Massive Small File Merging Technology Based on Visiting Hot-Spot and Associated File Optimization

Jian-feng Peng[1], Wen-guo Wei[1(✉)], Hui-min Zhao[1], Qing-yun Dai[1], Gui-yuan Xie[1], Jun Cai[1], and Ke-jing He[2]

[1] College of Electronics and Information, Guangdong Polytechnic Normal University, Guangzhou 510665, China
447402586@qq.com
[2] School of Computer Science and Engineering, South China University of Technology, Guangzhou 510641, China

Abstract. Hadoop Distributed File System (HDFS) is designed to reliably storage and manage large-scale files. All the files in HDFS are managed by a single server, the NameNode. The NameNode stores metadata, in its main memory, for each file stored into HDFS. HDFS suffers the penalty of performance with increased number of small files. It imposes a heavy burden to the NameNode to store and manage a mass of small files. The number of files that can be stored into HDFS is constrained by the size of NameNode's main memory. In order to improve the efficiency of storing and accessing the small files on HDFS, we propose Small Hadoop Distributed File System (SHDFS), which bases on original HDFS. Compared to original HDFS, we add two novel modules in the proposed SHDFS: merging module and caching module. In merging module, the correlated files model is proposed, which is used to find out the correlated files by user-based collaborative filtering and then merge correlated files into a single large file to reduce the total number of files. In caching module, we use Log - linear model to dig out some hot-spot data that user frequently access to, and then design a special memory subsystem to cache these hot-spot data. Caching mechanism speeds up access to hot-spot data.

The experimental results indicate that SHDFS is able to reduce the metadata footprint on NameNode's main memory and also improve the efficiency of storing and accessing large number of small files.

Keywords: HDFS · Small files problem · SHDFS · Merge · Cache

1 Introduction

HDFS [1, 2] is the flagship file system component of Hadoop. Inspired by the design of proprietary Google File System (GFS) [3]. HDFS follows the pattern of write-once and read-many-times. HDFS has a master-slave architecture, with a single master called the NameNode and multiple slaves called DataNode. NameNode manages the metadata and the file system configuration data within the HDFS. The metadata is maintained in the main memory of the NameNode to ensure fast access to the client, on read/write

J. Ren et al. (Eds.): BICS 2018, LNAI 10989, pp. 517–524, 2018.
https://doi.org/10.1007/978-3-030-00563-4_50

requests. DataNode store and service read/write requests on files in HDFS, as directed by the NameNode. The files stored into HDFS are replicated into any number of DataNode as per configuration, to ensure reliability and data availability.

But storing large-scale files into HDFS becomes an overhead in terms of memory usage by metadata stored in NameNode. In such scenarios, a single NameNode becomes a bottleneck for handling metadata requests, when an application accesses a larger set of these small files. For example, in [4], a novel framework for Content-based image retrieval (CBIR) was proposing to improved retrieval performance offered. The framework is applied to retrieve images from HDFS which are similar to each other in terms of their visual contents. If we can not solve the small files problem, it will affect retrieval performance.

We design a SHDFS to reduce the metadata footprint in NameNode's main memory. This needs an efficient way of storing small files into HDFS. The basic approach is to combine correlated small files, as identified by the client, into a single large file. This helps in reducing the file count. An caching mechanism has been built to access the frequently visited data from the combined file. It will help decrease the load due to metadata requests on NameNode.

The paper is organized as follows: Sect. 2 discusses the background on HDFS, small files problem and the existing work that addresses this problem; Sect. 3 describes the proposed system architecture and the modules that provide changes to the system; Sect. 4 discusses the experimental results and evaluations; Sect. 5 concludes and provides possible future directions.

2 Background

2.1 HDFS

HDFS provides distributed storage in the cluster [5]. HDFS consists of two services namely, the NameNode and DataNode. The NameNode is a centralized server, responsible for maintaining the metadata for files inside HDFS. It also maintains the configuration data such as, the count of replicas for each block of a file called replication factor, size of a block and other such parameters for HDFS. NameNode maintains the directory tree structure for the files in the file system. The DataNode store the files in the form of blocks on behalf of the client. Every block is stored as a separate file in node's local file system. As DataNode abstract away the details of underlying file system, all nodes need not be identical in their features. DataNode is responsible for storing, retrieving and deleting blocks on the request of NameNode. Files in HDFS are divided into blocks, with a default block size of 128 MB, and each block is replicated and stored in multiple DataNode.

NameNode maintains the metadata for each file stored into HDFS, in its main memory. This includes a mapping between stored file names, the corresponding blocks of each file and the DataNode that host these blocks. Using the metadata stored, NameNode has to direct every request from client to the appropriate set of DataNode. The client then communicates with the DataNode to perform file operations. NameNode, storing metadata in its main memory, becomes a bottleneck when it has to handle massive number of small files. A small file is any file whose size is significantly lesser than the block size of HDFS. This small files problem [6], prevents many potential applications from using the benefits of Hadoop framework.

Small Files Problem. NameNode stores the entire metadata in the main memory for faster and efficient servicing of client requests. When a file whose size is larger than the block size is stored, the amount of metadata stored is justified by the file size. Whereas, when a large number of small files, each less than the block size are Stored, each file forms a block and hence, the corresponding metadata stored is considerably high. For example, assume that, metadata in memory for each block of a file takes up about 150 bytes. Thus, a large number of small files takes less space on ile system but a significant amount of NameNode's main memory. This results in unfair use of the cluster space available. Further, accessing a large number of these files results in a bottleneck in NameNode.

3 Design

3.1 File Merging

The file merging technique reduces both the file metadata and the block metadata maintained by the NameNode for small files. It capitalizes on the fact that most of the file metadata remains the same for all the files whenever a user groups them together and uploads them to HDFS. File merging ensures that the NameNode maintains metadata only for the combined file and not for all the small files present in it. The names of the constituent files and their block information are maintained as part of a special data structure in the NameNode.

In the merge module, if we consider the correlation between several small files which are combined into a large file, we can only not just improve the efficiency of storing but improve the efficiency of accessing large number of small files. So, we design the correlated files model which bases on user-based collaborative filtering to find out the correlated files. Then a set of correlated files is combined, as identified by the client, into a single large file to reduce huge number of files.

Here is an example of applying the user-based collaborative filtering to find the associated file. Table 1 lists the users' access records.

Table 1. The users' access records

	42_avatar_middle.jpg	51_avatar_middle.jpg	9_avatar_middle.jpg
John	3	0	2
User A	0	0	3
User B	1	2	0

User-based collaborative filtering idea [7] is that firstly analyze a data set and the currently active user's ID to find out other users who have similar access preferences to the current user. The potential assumption of this approach is that if users have similar access preferences in the past, they will also have similar access preferences in the future.

$U = \{U_1, \ldots U_n\}$ represents user set, $P = \{P_1, \ldots P_m\}$ represents file sets accessed on behalf of users. Once a user has visited a file, the score is 1, If the user have visited the file again, the score is 2, and if the user have not visited it, the score will be 0. represents use's scoring matrix, $i \in 1 \ldots n$, $j \in 1 \ldots m$. represents user's average score. Pearson correlation coefficients: $sim(a, b)$ represents correlation between users access behavior.

$$sim(a,b) = \frac{\sum_{p \in P}(r_{a,p} - \bar{r}_a)(r_{b,p} - \bar{r}_b)}{\sqrt{\sum_{p \in P}(r_{a,p} - \bar{r}_a)^2}\sqrt{\sum_{p \in P}(r_{b,p} - \bar{r}_b)^2}} \quad (1)$$

So, we user user-based collaborative filtering to find out correlated files. The data, the history of user access to the file, were assessed by the Pearson correlation coefficients. By calculation, get the similarity between users. Pearson correlation coefficients is shown in Formula 1.

We introduce Pearson correlation coefficient to calculate nearest neighbors' rating. The Pearson correlation coefficient ranges from -1 (strong negative correlation) to +1 (strong positive correlation). When the value greater than zero, the files they have accessed must have some degree of relevance. The files which they have accessed have some degree of relevance.

3.2 File Caching

When a file is being read from HDFS, a request is sent to the NameNode initially to obtain the metadata associated with the file. This metadata provides information about the list of blocks containing the file and the DataNode that hold these blocks. This is essential for reading the contents of the file. Communication with the NameNode happens via Remote Procedure Calls (RPC). Therefore, for every file that is being opened, an RPC request has to be initiated to obtain the metadata. This poses a problem at the NameNode, when a large number of small files are accessed. The number of requests and the frequency with which they are generated, while reading small files making NameNode a bottleneck in the system.

The proposed SHDFS overcomes this bottleneck by providing a special memory subsystem Caching mechanism speeds up access to already visited folders. Caching mechanism speeds up access to already visited folders. Whenever the file is present in the cache, the client need not initiate an RPC request to the NameNode. This ensures that the number of requests sent to the NameNode is reduced considerably, thereby improving the performance of read operation. We use Log - linear model to dig out hot-spot data which user frequently access to.

The Log - linear model was put forward in reference [8]. By means of logarithmic transformation of variables, the linear relationship between the files visits in the past and the file visits in the future was found. The formula of the Log – linear model is shown in Formula 2.

$$ln N_i = k(t) ln N_i(t) + b(t) \quad (2)$$

N_i represents the number of access to file in the future, $N_i(t)$ the number of access to file in the past, t represents observation time length. $k(t)$ and $b(t)$ are related parameters of linear relation, the optimal value can be obtained by using linear regression method.

By Formula 2, we can calculate N_i. We use N_i to definite hot-spot data. we use Hbase database to cache these hot-spot data.

4 Evaluation and Result

The performance of the HDFS cluster with respect to the main memory usage and the time taken to complete read operations was initially benchmarked with the original default HDFS and then compared with results obtained using SHDFS. This process is described in the following sections.

4.1 Experimental Environment and Workload Overview

The test platform is built on a cluster with 5 PC servers. One node acts as NameNode, which has Inter(R) Core CPU (i7-4790, 3.4 GHz), 4 GB memory, and 1 TB disk. The other four nodes act as DataNode. Each of them has Inter(R) Core CPU (i7-4790, 3.4 GHz), 4 GB memory, and 1 TB disk. In each machine, Ubuntu 12.04.1 LTS with the kernel of version 2.6.32.70 is installed. Hadoop version is 2.6.3 and Java version is 1.8.0_73. The number of replicas is set to 3 and the default block size is 128 MB.

The workload for the main memory usage measurement contains a total of 50,000 picture files and a total of 50,000 txt files. The size of picture files range from 4 KB to 100 KB. The cumulative size of picture files is approximately 1.975 GB. The size of txt files range from 1 MB to 2 MB. The size of txt files is approximately 6.83 GB.

Memory Usage Analysis. For original HDFS, and the used memories of NameNode is evaluated when the system stores 10000, 20000, 30000, 40000, 50000 picture files and txt files respectively. The memory usage results are shown in Figs. 1 and 2.

Figures 1 and 2 show the memory usage comparison among HDFS and SHDFS. As expected, SHDFS achieves much better efficiency of storing picture files than original HDFS, increasing by an average of 15%. And storing txt files, SHDFS also achieves much better efficiency of storing picture files than original HDFS, increasing by an average of 25%.

Generally speaking, there is a linear increase in memory usage as the number of files increases when system store small files. SHDFS maintains additional data structures in the NameNode for efficient file access. The memory used by the SHDFS is lesser than the memory used by HDFS to store the same number of files. The SHDFS only maintains the file metadata for each small file and not the block metadata. The block metadata is maintained by the Name Node for the single combined file alone and not for every single small file. From these figures, we can see that, SHDFS spend much less memory space than original HDFS.

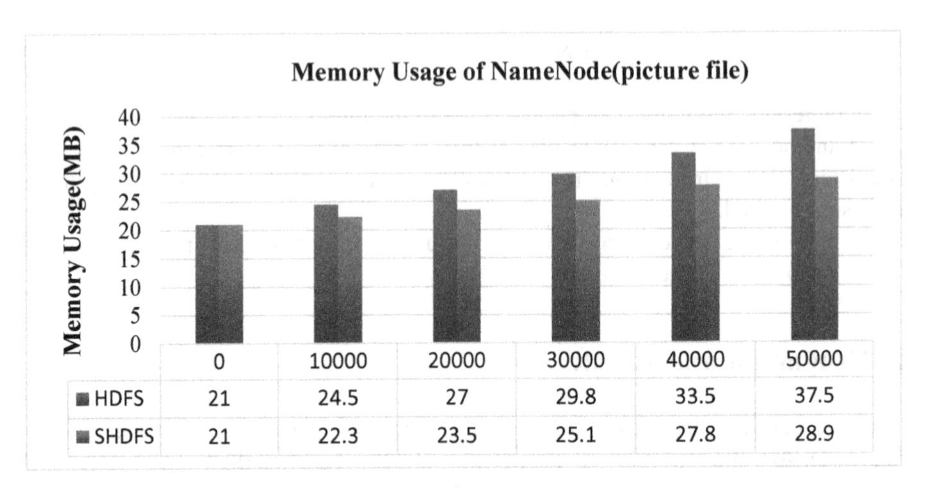

Fig. 1. Memory usages of HDFS and SHDFS (picture file)

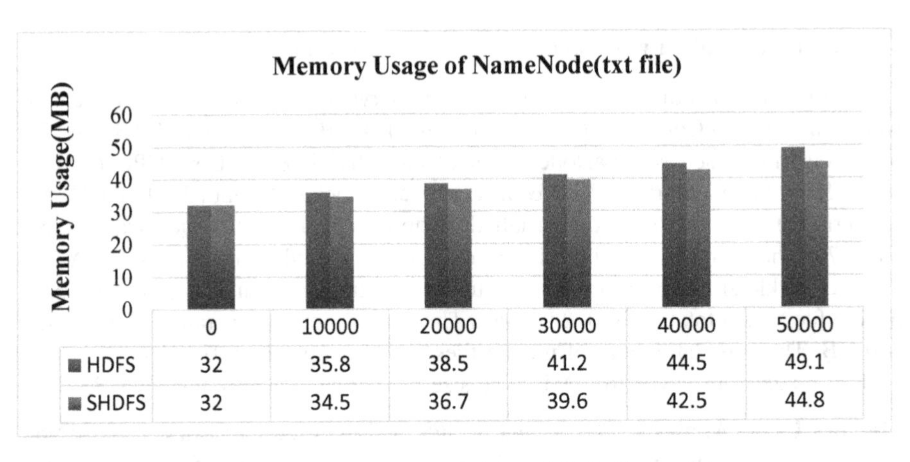

Fig. 2. Memory usages of HDFS and SHDFS (txt file)

Time Taken for File Access. In this experiment, the time taken to complete read operations was measured for both the original HDFS and the SHDFS. A set of 10000 files were placing into HDFS and SHDFS, which includes some hot-spot data. This was then repeated five times, the time taken for read operation in HDFS and SHDFS is depicted in the graph shown in Figs. 3 and 4.

The graph in Fig. 3 shows that when the average time taken to read a files from original HDFS is 0.16 s, and the average time taken to read a files from SHDFS is 0.03 s. Figure 4 shows that when the average time taken to read a files from original HDFS is 0.73 s, and the average time taken to read a files from SHDFS is 0. 37 s. The data obtained clearly indicates that the SHDFS is faster than the default original HDFS for read operation.

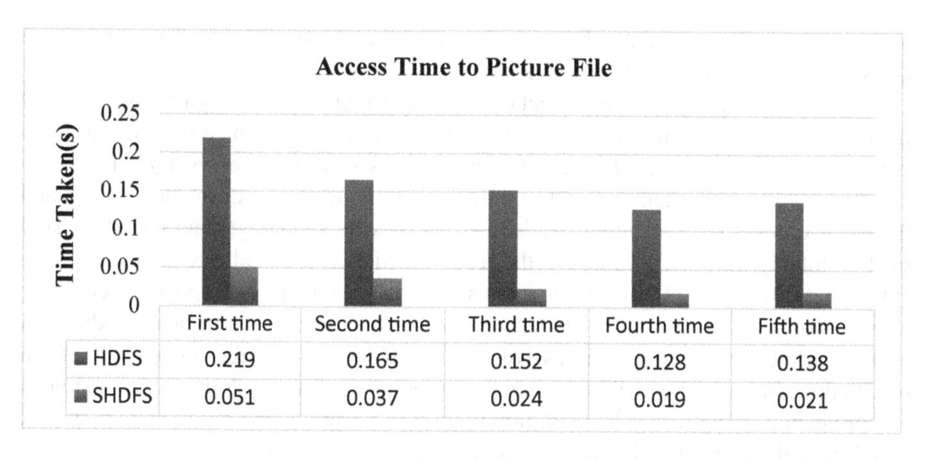

Fig. 3. Access time to picture file

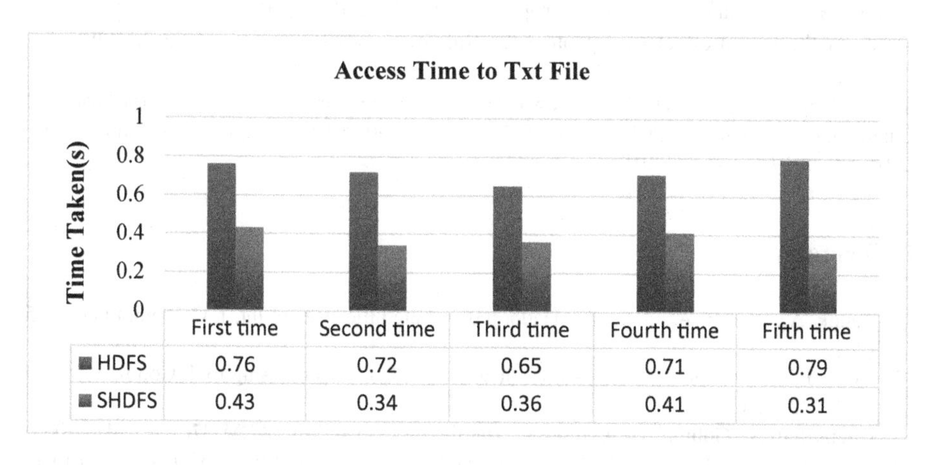

Fig. 4. Access time to txt file

This is evident from the fact that as SHDFS has a special memory subsystem. Some hot-spot data are stored in a client side cache. If the file is being opened is already present in the cache, no request is sent to the NameNode. This considerably improves the response time for read operations. It also reduces the number of requests that are being sent to the NameNode, thus reducing the load on the NameNode while improving the speed of consecutive read operations.

5 Conclusions and Future Directions

We have propose a SHDFS, which bases on original HDFS. Compared to original HDFS. SHDFS adds new two module: merging module and caching module. In merging module, a set of correlated files is combined, as identified by the client, into a single large file to reduce the file count. In caching module, we use Log - linear model to dig out some hot-spot data, then design a special memory subsystem in which some hot-spot data are duplicated for quick access.

For future work, in order to protect data which stored in SHDFS, some conventional image steganalysis method can be deployed in SHDFS. Efficient image steganalysis method can be applied including an efficient recovery method of secret signal for image steganalysis [9] and saliency detection [10]. In addition, video information hiding and transmission over noisy channels leads to errors on video and degradation of the visual quality notably. In order to improve the reconstruction video quality without requiring significant extra channel resource, a video signal fusion scheme is proposed to combine sensed host signal and the hidden signal with quantization index modulation (QIM) technology in the compressive sensing (CS) and discrete cosine transform (DCT) domain [11]. This will be extremely important for low-resolution video analytics and protection in big data era. As an important tool for protecting multimedia contents, which stored in SHDFS, in [12], based on the neural perception mechanism of our human brains in dealing with multidimensional data, a novel cognitive computation-based CS-watermark approach is proposed for information hiding inside videos. The above methods can effectively protect the transmission of data security in SHDFS.

Acknowledgements. This work was supported in part by the Science and Technology Project of Guangdong Province (2015B010131017, 2017B030306016) and Guangzhou City (201802020019, 201806040010).

References

1. Taunk, A., Parmar, A., et al.: The Hadoop distributed file system. Int. J. Comput. **8**(1), 8–15 (2013)
2. Dean, J., Ghemawat, S., et al.: MapReduce:a flexible data processing tool. Commun. ACM **53**(1), 72–77 (2010)
3. Ghemawat, S., Gobioff, H., Leung, S.: The Google file system. ACM **37**(5), 29–43 (2003)
4. Zhou, Y., Zeng, F., Zhao, H., et al.: Hierarchical visual perception and two-dimensional compressive sensing for effective content-based color image retrieval. Cognit. Comput. **8**(5), 877–889 (2016)
5. White, T.: Hadoop: The Definitive Guide. O'Reilly Media, Inc., Newton
6. Cloudera Engineer Blog: http://www.cloudera.com. Accessed 21 Mar 2018
7. Herlocker, J., Konstan, J., Riedl, J.: An empirical analysis of design choices in neighborhood-based collaborative filtering algorithms. Inf. Retrieval **5**(4), 287–310 (2002)
8. Szabo, G., Huberman, B.A.: Predicting the popularity of online content. Commun. ACM **53**(8), 80–88 (2010)
9. Zhao, H., Ren J., Zhan, J., et al.: Compressive sensing based secret signals recovery for effective image Steganalysis in secure communications. Multimed. Tools Appl. 1–14 (2018)
10. Yan, Y., Ren, J., Sun, G., et al.: Unsupervised image saliency detection with Gestalt-laws guided optimization and visual attention based refinement. Pattern Recogn. **79**(7), 65–78 (2018)
11. Zhao, H., Dai, Q., Ren, J.C., et al.: Robust information hiding in low-resolution videos with quantization index modulation in DCT-CS domain. Multimed. Tools Appl. **1**, 1–21 (2017)
12. Zhao, H., Ren, J.: Cognitive computation of compressed sensing for watermark signal measurement. Cognit. Comput. **8**(2), 246–260 (2016)

A Reversible Data Hiding Scheme Using Compressive Sensing and Random Embedding

Guo-Liang Xie[1,2], Hui-Min Zhao[1,2(✉)], Ju-Jian Lv[1,2], and Can-Yao Li[1,2]

[1] School of Computer Science, Guangdong Polytechnic Normal University, Guangzhou, China
zhaohuimin@gpnu.edu.cn

[2] Guangzhou Key Laboratory of Digital Content Processing and Security Technology, Guangzhou, China

Abstract. Steganography is a kind of technique which hides data under the cover file so as not to arouse any suspicion. In this paper, a new image steganography algorithm combining compressive sensing (CS) and random embedding is proposed. There are two security parts in this algorithm. The first part is the random projection inherited from CS, and the second is the random embedding process. CS serves to create the encrypted data, and acts as a tool to reduce the dimensionality of the secret data. Random-embedding algorithm is proposed to choose the position of cover image randomly for hiding the secret image. This algorithm uses symmetric key method, which means the sender and the receiver use the same key. Numerical experiments show that this steganography algorithm provides high embedding capacity and high Peak Signal Noise Ratio (PSNR).

Keywords: Data hiding · Steganography · Subsampling
Compressive sensing

1 Introduction

In steganography, secret images are hidden into other multimedia carriers such as digital audio, video and images [6]. Basically, the sender and the receiver agree on a steganographic system and a shared key that decides how a message is encoded in the cover medium [12]. In general, there are two different ways to hide the data into the cover medium. The first is in spatial domain, and the second is in frequency domain. In spatial domain, intensity values of the cover image are used to hide the secret data [15].

Different methods of spatial domain steganography techniques have been proposed using Watermarking [20], Least significant bit (LSB) substitution [1], Modulus function [5], Pixel Value Differencing method [10], LSB matching [15] and optimal pixel adjustment process [3]. Among these, LSB substitution is the one that manipulates the least significant bit planes by directly replacing the LSBs of the cover image with the message bits. LSB methods typically achieve high capacity.

J. Ren et al. (Eds.): BICS 2018, LNAI 10989, pp. 525–534, 2018.
https://doi.org/10.1007/978-3-030-00563-4_51

Embedding directly may cause some issues. For instance, the amount of secret data is more than the amount of embedding positions. Therefore, compressive sensing (CS) is used to compress the secret data owing to its excellent coding efficiency. Besides, CS can encrypt the secret data simultaneously [4, 7, 19].

Moreover, the theorem makes the compression and encryption synchronously. Since the reconstruction process of the original data is nonlinear, this merit can be utilized to encrypt the secret data. Besides, if the measurement matrix is not correct in the decoding side, the reconstruction of the original data is not possible. The measurement matrix, in another way, can be regarded as a secret key.

Direct-embedding can also cause another problem. In LSB based embedding technique, the set of the LSB pixels in cover image is substituted by the bits of secret image. This process can be done either in sequential or in random manner. But embedding directly is not safe enough. Therefore, chosen pixels randomly for hiding provides better security than a sequential manner. The randomly choose scheme is described as random embedding in this paper. Usually, a key is used to control the randomness in the embedding process.

In this paper, a reversible data hiding scheme by simple LSB substitution with CS and random embedding technique (CSRE) is proposed. The results show the validity and the reliability of the proposed algorithm. The remaining section of the paper is structured as follows. Brief descriptions of LSB substitution, CS and random embedding in Sect. 2. Proposed data hiding scheme is illustrated in Sect. 3. Experimental results and their analysis are discussed in Sect. 4. Conclusion is drawn in Sect. 5.

2 Related Work

2.1 Least Significant Bit Substitution

Let C be the original 8-bit grayscale cover-image of $M_C \times N_C$ pixels represented as

$$C = \{p_{ij} \mid 0 \le i < M_C, 0 \le j < N_C, p_{ij} \in \{0, 1, \ldots, 255\}\} \tag{1}$$

Q be the n-bit secret message represented as below.

$$Q = \{q_i \mid 0 \le i < n, q_i \in \{0, 1\}\} \tag{2}$$

Suppose that the n-bit secret message Q is to be embedded into the k-rightmost LSBs of the cover image C. Firstly, the secret message Q is rearranged to form a conceptually k-bit virtual image Q' represented as:

$$Q' = \{q'_i \mid 0 \le i < n', q'_i \in \{0, 1, \ldots, 2^k - 1\}\} \tag{3}$$

where $n' < M_C \times N_C$. The mapping between the n-bit secret message $Q' = \{q'\}$ can be defined as follows:

$$q'_i = \sum_{j=0}^{k-1} q_{i\times k+j} \times 2^{k-1-j} \tag{4}$$

Secondly, a subset of n' pixels $\{p_{l_1}, p_{l_2}, \ldots, p_{l_{n'}}\}$ is chosen from the cover image C in a predefined sequence. The embedding process is completed by replacing the k LSBs of p_{l_i} by q'_i. Mathematically, the pixel value p_{l_i} of the chosen pixel for storing the k-bit message q'_i is modified to form the stego pixel p'_{l_i} as follows:

$$p'_{l_i} = p_{l_i} - p_{l_i} \bmod 2^k + q'_i \tag{5}$$

where $\mathrm{mod}(\cdot,\cdot)$ is the remainder of the integer division.

2.2 Compressive Sensing Basics

Compressive sensing theory mainly includes sparse representation of signals, linear measurement and reconstruction method [7].

Sparse Representation of Signal. Suppose x is an original signal of length H. According to the signal theory, x can be represented by a set of basis $\Psi^T = \{\psi_1, \psi_2, \ldots, \psi_H\}$, so x is

$$x = \sum_{t=1}^{H} \psi_t \alpha_t = \Psi\alpha \tag{6}$$

where $\alpha_t = <x, \psi_t>$, $\Psi \in R^{H\times H}$ is an orthogonal transform matrix, x and α are both H dimensional vectors. When signal x is composed of only w non-zero coefficient α_w under a certain set Ψ, then Ψ is known as a sparse basis.

Linear Measurement. Given an original signal x, we can obtain measurements y through compressive sensing

$$y = \Phi x = \Phi\Psi\alpha = A\alpha \tag{7}$$

where $\Phi \in R^{G\times H}$ is known as sensing matrix or measurement matrix, A is a $G \times H$ matrix $(G << H)$.

Sparse Reconstruction. When matrix A satisfies RIP [4] principle, CS theory can firstly solve the sparse coefficients' problem by solving inverse problem of (2), then substitute the result into equation $y = \Phi x = \Phi\Psi\alpha = A\alpha$ to get the solution for x. We can accurately reconstruct signal x from H dimensional measurements y. The most direct method of sparse reconstruction problem is to solve equation by l_0 norm

$$\min_{\alpha} \|\alpha\|_{l_0} \ \text{s.t.}\ y = \Phi\Psi\alpha \tag{8}$$

In this paper, OMP (Orthogonal Matching Pursuit) [13] algorithm is adopted to recover the stego-image for its fast implementation capability.

2.3 Random Embedding Algorithm

Consider the cover image $C = [p_{i,j}]$ for $i = 1, 2, \ldots, M_C$ and $j = 1, 2, \ldots, N_C$, where $p_{i,j}$ are the pixel values. K1 and K2 are predefined numbers, L is the length of secret message in binary format.

Algorithm 0: Random embedding

```
    Input: CoverImg, SecretImg, K1, K2, L, SecretMessage
    Output: SecretImg
1   Compute a pseudo-random sequence r = [r_1, r_2, ..., r_L] with uniform distribution in
    the interval [0,1]
2   for row=1: M
3       for c=1: N
          if r_i >0.5: then c+K1
          else c+K2
          S(row(i) col(i)) = C(row(i),col(i)) - mod(C(row(i),col(i)),2) + Q(i,1)
          if c>=N: row+1,c=1
4   end
```

In this way, a stego image $S = [p'_{i,j}]$ is obtained.

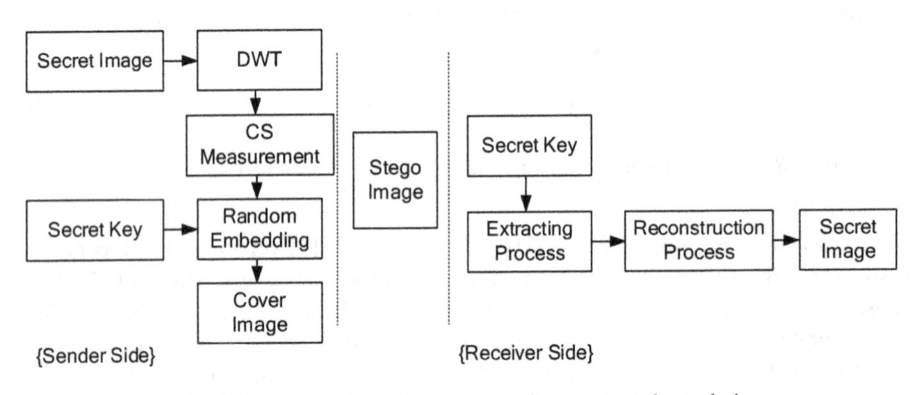

Fig. 1. The overall view of the proposed steganography technique.

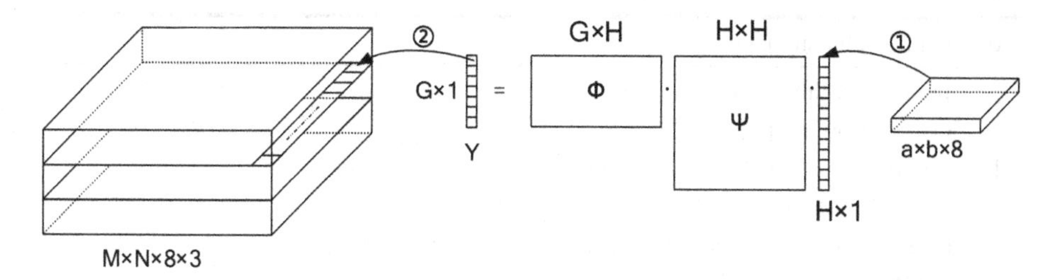

Fig. 2. The embedding method of the proposed paper. Where ① is the vectorization of the secret image, ② is the embedding of the measurement vector.

3 Compressive Sensing and Random Embedding Scheme

In this section, a novel symmetric key steganography (CSRE) is proposed. The overall view of the proposed steganography technique is shown in Fig. 1. The embedding method of the proposed paper is shown in Fig. 2. To establish a secure communication channel between the sender and the receiver, three algorithms need to be defined in our scheme, which include: Sending, Randompixel, and Receiving. They are shown below.

3.1 Sender Side

Step by step procedure of the proposed steganography technique is illustrated below.

Algorithm 1: Sending		
	Input: CoverImg, SecretImg, Key_1, S_RATE	
	Output: StegoImg, Key_2, Key_3	
1	X1←DWT(SecretImg), P←0.5	
2	M←S_RATE*(SecretImg.height)	//Generating the measurement matrix
4	A←rand(M,SecretImg.width)	
5	A←A<P, Y←A*X1	//Acquire measurement
6	Key_2←A, Key_3←L	
7	Y_1←transform Y to binary form	//Embedding(CoverImg,Y,Key_1)
8	L←length of vector Y_1	
9	[row,col]←Randompixel(CoverImg,L,Key_1)	
10	for i =1 : L	
11	embedding using formula (4)	
12	end	

```
Algorithm 2: Randompixel
     Input: CoverImg, L, Key_1
     Output: [row, col]
 1   N← (CoverImg.width)*(CoverImg.height)
 2   K1←floor(N/L), K2←K1-2, rand('seed',Key_1)
 5   a←rand(1,L), row←zeros(1,L), col←zeros(1,L) , r←1,c←1
 6   row(1,1)←r, col(1,1)←c
 7   for i←2:L
 8       if a(i)>0.5, c←c+K1;
 9       else, c←c+ K2;
10   end
11      if c> CoverImg.height, r←r+1;
12       if r> CoverImg.width, error("CoverImg is too small")
13      end
14   c←mod(c, CoverImg.height);
15     if c==0, c←1;
16   end
```

3.2 Receiver Side

```
Algorithm 3: Receiving
     Input: StegoImg, Key_1, Key_2, Key_3
     Output: SecretImg
 1   Y'←GetSecret(StegoImg, Key_3, Key_1)
 2   [row,col]←Randompixel(StegoImg, Key_3,K')
 3   S←zeros(1, Key_3)
 4   for i=1: Key_3
 5       S(1:i)←mod(StegoImg (row(i),col(i),2))
 6   end
 7   SC←zeros(1, Key_3)                          // Transform to ASCII code
 8   SA← (Key_3)/8
 9   for i=1:SA
10       for j=1:8
11       SC(1,i)←SC(1,i)+S(1,(i-1)*8+j)*power(2,(j-1))
12      end
13   end
14   A'←Key_2
16   Reconstruct SecretImg using formula (7)
```

4 Experimental Result and Discussion

Four test images from the USC-SIPI image database are shown below in Fig. 3 [18]. Three groups of experiments are performed in this section: (1) to estimate the visual quality of the stego iamges;(2) to estimate the recovery capability; and (3) to estimate the histogram comparison.

In Wu-Tsai's steganographic method [8], the secret data is hidden into a cover image by pixel-value-differencing. Wu-Tsai's scheme hides more secret data into edge area than smooth area, and this act maintains the good quality of the stego-image. Wu's PVD [17] is an improved version of [8], they share the same basic idea of PVD.

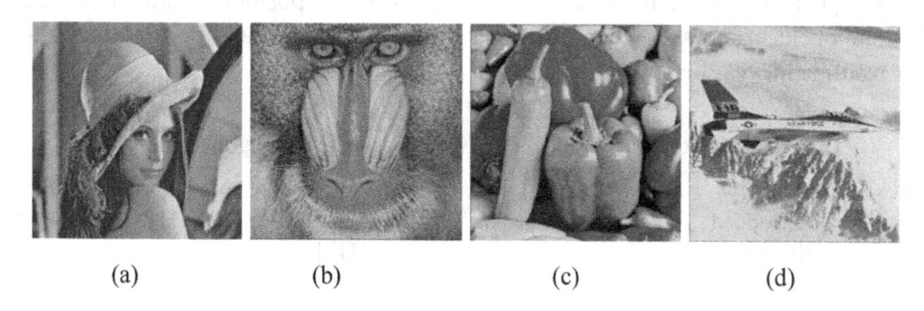

(a) (b) (c) (d)

Fig. 3. The four 512 × 512 cover images.

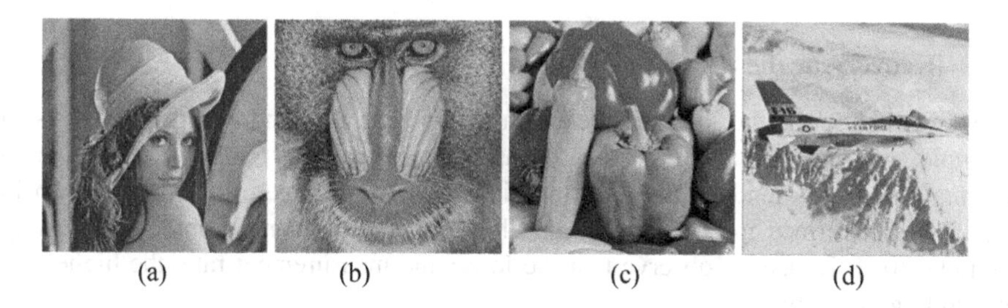

(a) (b) (c) (d)

Fig. 4. The four 512 × 512 stego images of Fig. 3.

4.1 Estimate the Visual Quality of the Stego Images

Figure 3 shows the four cover images. Figure 4 shows the corresponding stego images. Their hidden content is the same 15064 KB data. The objective quality of the stego images is measured by the peak-signal-to-noise ratio (PSNR), which is defined as

$$PSNR = 10\log_{10}(\frac{255^2}{MSE})dB \tag{9}$$

where MSE is the mean square error between the cover image and the stego image.

$$MSE = \frac{1}{M \times N} \sum_{i=1}^{N} \sum_{j=1}^{M} (C_{i,j} - S_{i,j})^2 \tag{10}$$

C represents the original cover image, and S represents the stego image.

Table 1 shows the PSNR of the stego images. The data are collected from the corresponding references. As the table shows, CSRE scheme achieves the best result in 5 algorithms. Wu's PVD [17] achieves a much better result than Wu Tsai's [8] PVD after improving their algorithm. But their algorithms mainly focus on the edge area, so they may achieve less good in images that are composed of a large number of smooth area. Ref [11] embeds the information within 2nd to 8th bit position of blue (B) or green (G) component of a pixel, which increases the MSE slightly, and perhaps that's why their result achieves the second best.

Table 1. PSNR value of different cover images after hiding the same data

Cover image	Data embedded (bytes)	Wu-Tsai's PVD [8]	Method in Ref [2]	Wu's PVD [17]	Method in Ref [11]	CSRE scheme
Lena	15064	34.58	53.77	57.03	66.36	71.75
Baboon	15064	34.33	53.76	49.67	67.98	71.66
Pepper	15064	36.91	53.80	52.60	69.29	71.46
Airplane	15064	33.72	53.78	54.30	67.87	71.49

4.2 Recovery of the Secret Image

The cover image and the secret image are shown in Figs. 3(a) and 5 respectively. As an example, we choose encoding basis Ψ as discrete wavelet transform (DWT) and sensing basis Φ as random Bernoulli matrix. A 64 × 64 fingerprint image shown in Fig. 5 is transformed in DWT basis, and then the measurement is obtained by using formula (6). It is easy to observe that the lower the measurement rate, the higher the embedding capacity.

Fig. 5. The secret image fingerprint

To ensure a good quality of the recovered secret image, we make full sampling here. The fingerprint image is recovered with average PSNR = 53.01 dB over 100 trials. The exact recovery of the secret image makes it suitable for applications where accuracy is in demand, such as fingerprint recognition.

Since there many details and arcs in the secret image, the reconstruction seems satisfactory only after the measurement rate is higher than 0.9 (22 dB). By using the more advanced reconstruction algorithm, less time will be needed to run the algorithm, and higher PSNR will be acquired, such as ROMP, CoSAMP, StOMP [13].

4.3 Histogram Analysis

Histogram shows the exact occurrence of each pixels in the image. High similarity between the cover image histogram and stego image histogram shows that a tiny distortion occurred after embedding the secret image into cover image [19]. Figure 6(a) shows the histogram of cover image Lena and Fig. 6(e) shows histogram after embedding the fingerprint image into Lena image. As a result, the proposed scheme fight against visual attack and statistical attack.

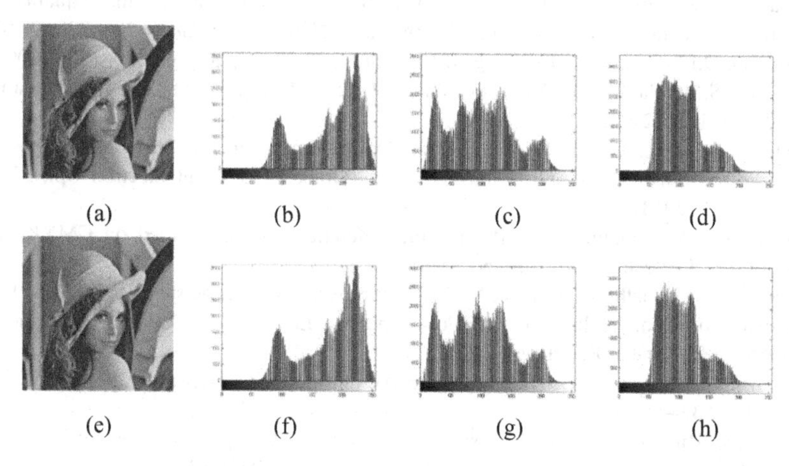

Fig. 6. Histogram analysis (a) Cover image (b) the Red plane of cover image (c) the Green plane of cover image (d) the Blue plane of cover image (e) Stego image (f) the Red plane of stego image (g) the Green plane of stego image (h) the Blue plane of stego image (Color figure online)

5 Conclusion

In this paper, we have presented a practical data hiding scheme in which the secret data is encoded via CS and random embedding scheme. Cover image pixel positions are chosen randomly to embed the secret image bits and this work will minimize the security risk. The hidden data can be extracted using the algorithm we designed. Lastly, the secret image will be reconstructed with the help of correct key and measurement. The experimental results show the validity and the reliability of the proposed algorithm.

Acknowledgements. This work was partly supported by the National Natural Science Foundation of China (61672008), Guangdong Provincial Application-oriented Technical Research and Development Special fund project (2016B010127006), the Natural Science Foundation of Guangdong Province (2016A030311013), and the Scientific and Technological Projects of Guangdong Province (2017A050501039).

References

1. Amirtharajan, R., Rajesh, V., Archana, P., Rayappan, J.B.B.: Pixel indicates, standard deviates: a way for random image steganography. Res. J. Inf. Technol. **5**(3), 383–392 (2013)
2. Bairagi, A.K., Mondal, S., Debnath, R.: A robust RGB channel based image steganography technique using a secret key. In: International Conference on Computer and Information Technology, Khulna, Bangladesh, pp. 81–87 (2014)
3. Banimelhem, O., Tawalbeh, L., Mowafi, M., Al-Batati, M.: A more secure image hiding scheme using pixel adjustment and genetic algorithm. Int. J. Inf. Secur. Priv. **7**(3), 1–15 (2013)
4. Cands, E.J.: The restricted isometry property and its implications for compressed sensing. C. R. Math. **346**(9), 589–592 (2008)
5. Chan, C.S., Chang, C.C., Hu, Y.C.: Image hiding scheme using modulus function and optimal substitution table. Pattern Recognit. Image Anal. **16**(2), 208–217 (2006)
6. Chang, C.C., Nguyen, T.S., Lin, C.C.: Reversible image hiding for high image quality based on histogram shifting and local complexity. Int. J. Netw. Secur. **16**(3), 208–220 (2014)
7. Donoho, D.L.: Compressed sensing. IEEE Trans. Inf. Theory **52**(4), 1289–1306 (2006)
8. Hossain, S.M., Haider, M.: A hybrid method of data hiding into digital images. Dhaka Univ. Stud. Part B **55**(2), 203–210 (2007)
9. Liu, X., Cao, Y., Lu, P., Lu, X., Li, Y.: Optical image encryption technique based on compressed sensing and Arnold transformation. Optik Int. J. Light Electron Opt. **124**(24), 6590–6593 (2013)
10. Manoharan, S., Rajkumar, D.: Pixel value differencing method based on CMYK colour model. Int. J. Electron. Inf. Eng. **5** (2016)
11. Mondal, S., Debnath, R., Mondal, B.K.: An improved color image steganography technique in spatial domain. In: International Conference on Electrical and Computer Engineering, pp. 582–585. Dhaka, Bangladesh (2017)
12. Provos, N., Honeyman, P.: Hide and seek: An introduction to steganography. IEEE Secur. Priv. **1**(3), 32–44 (2003)
13. Qaisar, S., Bilal, R.M., Iqbal, W., Naureen, M., Lee, S.: Compressive sensing: From theory to applications, a survey. J. Commun. Netw. **15**(5), 443–456 (2013)
14. Rachlin, Y., Baron, D.: The secrecy of compressed sensing measurements. In: 2008 Allerton Conference on Communication, Control, and Computing, pp. 813–817. Urbana-Champaign, IL, USA (2008)
15. Rajendran, S., Doraipandian, M.: Chaotic map based random image steganography using LSB technique. Int. J. Netw. Secur. **19** (2017)
16. Romberg, J., Tao, T.: Exact signal reconstruction from highly incomplete frequency information. IEEE Trans. Inf. Theory **52**(2), 489–509 (2006)
17. Singh, A., Singh, H.: An improved LSB based image Steganography technique for RGB images. In: IEEE International Conference on Electrical, Computer and Communication Technologies, pp. 1–4. Coimbatore, India (2015)
18. The USC-SIPI Image Database. http://sipi.usc.edu/database/. Accessed 28 April 2018
19. Wang, X., Zhao, J., Liu, H.: A new image encryption algorithm based on chaos. Opt. Commun. **285**(5), 562–566 (2012)
20. Zhao, H., Ren, J.: Cognitive computation of compressed sensing for watermark signal measurement. Cognit. Comput. **8**(2), 246–260 (2016)

An Abnormal Behavior Clustering Algorithm Based on K-means

Jianbiao Zhang[1,2], Fan Yang[1,2(✉)], Shanshan Tu[1,2], and Ai Zhang[3]

[1] Faculty of Information, Beijing University of Technology, Beijing, China
supperdoof@sina.com
[2] Beijing Key Laboratory of Trusted Computing, Beijing, China
[3] Beijing-Dublin International College, Beijing University of Technology, Beijing, China

Abstract. With the development of abnormal behavior analysis technology, measuring the similarity of abnormal behavior has become a core part of abnormal behavior detection. However, there are general problems of central selection distortion and slow iterative convergence with existing clustering-based analysis algorithms. Therefore, this paper proposes an improved clustering-based abnormal behavior analysis algorithm by using K-means. Firstly, an abnormal behavior set is constructed for each user from his or her behavioral data. A weight calculation method for abnormal behaviors and an eigenvalue extraction method for abnormal behavior sets are proposed by using all the behavior sets. Secondly, an improved algorithm is developed, in which we calculate the tightness of all data points and select the initial cluster centers from the data points with high density and low density to improve the clustering effect based on the K-means clustering algorithm. Finally, clustering result of the abnormal behavior is got with the input of the eigenvalues of the abnormal behavior set. The results show that, the proposed algorithm is superior to the traditional clustering algorithm in clustering performance, and can effectively enhance the clustering effect of abnormal behavior.

Keywords: Abnormal behavior analysis · K-means algorithm
Similarity · Clustering algorithm

1 Introduction

With the explosive growth of data in the past few years, data has been accumulated at a speed never seen before. In the area of information security, the behavior data generated by abnormal users has shown a distinct diversity and complexity. Constructing abnormal behavior clustering for each user and differentiating the similarities among different abnormal behavior clustering is valuable for analyzing similar behavior clustering, which results in the improvement in analytical efficiency of abnormal behavior [1, 2]. Thus, studying clustering algorithm for abnormal behavior has become a new method to distinguish the similarities of abnormal behavior.

K-means algorithm is a typical unsupervised learning algorithm which is mainly used to group similar datasets to the same class [3, 4]. However, as the initial clustering

J. Ren et al. (Eds.): BICS 2018, LNAI 10989, pp. 535–544, 2018.
https://doi.org/10.1007/978-3-030-00563-4_52

center for this algorithm is selected randomly, the final clustering result is a local optimal solution in a certain area rather than a global optimal solution [5, 6]. To address the selection issue of initial clustering center, MinMax k-Means clustering algorithm is developed by Grigorios [7]. One data point is chosen as the first initial center randomly, then the data point farthest from the first initial center is chosen as the second one; and the other initial centers should meet the following requirements: initial center K has the maximum value among the points within shortest distance from initial center $K - 1$. This method can separate each initial clustering center from one another, but cannot ensure that the separated clustering center is the optimal one. The concept of tightness based on the nature of optimal initial clustering center is proposed by Zuo [8]. The outlier area is removed and k initial clustering centers are selected in the dense area evenly. Though this method makes the initial clustering center seem more reasonable, it also increases time complexity of the algorithm. Considering the sparse data sets, identifying initial clustering center is discussed by Song [9], which is based on the concept of density parameter and distance theory. This method removes all the outlier points successfully, but still could not ensure that the initial clustering centers are distributed uniformly. A clustering method based on the distance assumption is proposed by Liu [10]. Assuming there is a clustering radius, the first data point is the first clustering center, so the distance between the second data point and the first clustering center can be figured out. In the case that the distance is smaller than or equal to the clustering radius, the second data point is classified into the first cluster and the clustering center is recalculated, otherwise, the second data point turns to be the new clustering center when the distance is larger than the clustering radius. This method can separate the data points based on the clustering radius and help to achieve uniform distribution. The limit of this method is the uncertainty for selecting clustering radius, so that the clustering effect cannot be guaranteed.

In this paper, the distribution of the actual cluster centers is studied, and the initial clustering center of data points is selected from the high-density or low-density area by calculating the degree of tightness of the data. The clustering algorithm based on abnormal behavior is proposed according to this method. Experiment results show that this algorithm can effectively improve the clustering effects of the abnormal data and perform better in both of iteration speed and iteration convergence.

2 Related Work

K-means algorithm divides the data set into several similar classes based on a certain metric (similarity or dissimilarity) and ensures that the samples in the same class have the highest similarity.

K-means algorithm divides N samples to K clusters: $D = \{D_1, D_2, \ldots, D_K\}$. The similarity of the samples is as high as possible in the same class and as low as possible in different classes. It is assumed that $c = \{c_1, c_2, \ldots, c_K\}$ is K classes with corresponding cluster centers, in which c_k is the mean clustering center of D_k cluster. In the k-means algorithm, the sample is segmented according to the minimum squared error function as follows:

$$J = \sum_{k=1}^{K} \sum_{x_i \in D_k} \|x_i - c_k\|^2 \tag{1}$$

If the sample is the closest one to the center c_k of k cluster, which means that the sample belongs to cluster D_k, it can be defined by formula (2) and (3).

$$D_k = \left\{ x_i \in X \middle| k = \underset{j \in \{1,2,\ldots,k\}}{\arg\min} \|x_i - c_j\|^2 \right\} \tag{2}$$

$$c_k = \frac{\sum_{x_i \in D_k} x_i}{|D_k|} \tag{3}$$

The k-means algorithm is simple and efficient, but it also has some disadvantages. As the initial cluster center is selected randomly, there is some uncertainty in the clustering result. If the initial clustering center can be chosen to be very similar to the actual cluster center, it will greatly improve the clustering effect.

3 Method

3.1 Model Overview

Abnormal behavior clustering algorithm consists of weight calculation module, eigenvalue extraction module and clustering analysis module. The flow chart of the algorithm is shown in Fig. 1. The details of each module are given below:

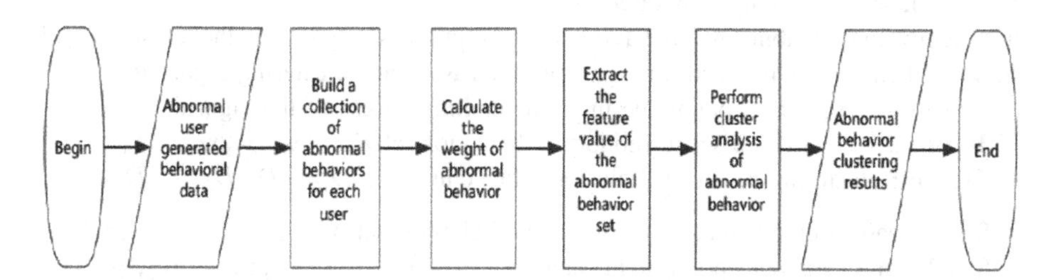

Fig. 1. Abnormal behavior clustering algorithm flow chart

Weight calculation module: this module works to calculate the frequency of each abnormal behavior based on the abnormal behavior data and get the corresponding weight according to this frequency.

Eigenvalue extraction module: as the abnormal behavior is usually presented in the form of behavioral set, the weighted average of abnormal behavior set is extracted as the eigenvalue based on the weight of each abnormal behavior.

Clustering analysis model: it is used to read in eigenvalue of abnormal behavior set, improve selection method about initial clustering center based on K-means clustering algorithm, make algorithm more pertinent to the special feature of abnormal behavior, optimize execution efficiency of the algorithm, and improve the clustering effect and the final clustering result.

3.2 Module Introduction

3.2.1 Weight Calculation Module

First of all, the module calculates the frequency N_{A_i} of each abnormal behavior $A_i (i = 1, 2, \ldots, n)$ based on abnormal behavior data, and then gives the corresponding weight according to the frequency. The weight calculation is defined as formula (4).

$$W_{A_i} = \frac{N_{A_i}}{\sum_{j=1}^{n} N_{A_j}} \quad (4)$$

3.2.2 Eigenvalue Extraction Module

This model takes into account that abnormal behavior comes up in the form of behavior set, $S_i = (A_1, A_2, \ldots, A_n)\ i = 1, 2, \ldots, n$. Based on the weight W_{A_i} of each abnormal behavior, we can extract the weighted average of abnormal behavior set as the eigenvalue x_i. The formula of eigenvalue extraction is shown as follows:

$$x_i = \frac{\sum_{i=1}^{n} W_{A_i}}{n} \quad (5)$$

3.2.3 Clustering Analysis Model

The eigenvalue of abnormal behavior set is input first, and then the clustering of abnormal behavior is realized through improved K-means clustering algorithm.

The following part explains the implementation process of the algorithm.
Input: the eigenvalue set for abnormal behavior set $X = \{x_1, \ldots, x_i, \ldots, x_n\}$;
Output: clustering result of k clusters after clustering $D = \{D_1, D_2, \ldots, D_k\}$;

- Step1: read in eigenvalue set of abnormal behavior set $X = \{x_1, \ldots, x_i, \ldots, x_n\}$;
- Step2: for every data point x_i in data set $X = \{x_1, \ldots, x_i, \ldots, x_j, \ldots, x_n\}$, we calculate the tightness level of x_i with the formula $T(x_i) = \frac{\sum_{j=1, x_j \in X}^{n} D(x_i, x_j)}{n}$, where $D(x_i, x_j)$ is the Euclidean distance function between x_i and x_j;
- Step3: choose the point x_i with the maximum $T(x_i)$ as the first clustering center;
- Step4: choose the point x_j with minimum $T(x_j)$ as the second initial clustering center;
- Step5: remove the data points in the tight area, whose level of tightness meets $T > \frac{\sum_{x \in X} T(x)}{n}$ and get the new set of data points in the sparse area X;

- Step6: if $K \geq 3$, in the data points set X' in sparse area, the *k-th* $(3 \leq k \leq K)$ initial clustering center c_k should meet the following conditions. $x_i \in X'$ meet $\min(D(x_i, c_1))$ and $c_k = x_i$. If x_i is chosen as the initial clustering center, remove data point x_i from X' and repeat step5 until k initial clustering centers are chosen;
- Step7: calculate the euclidean distance between every single data points in X and cluster center $D(x_i, c_j)$ where $i = 1, 2, \ldots, n$ and $j = 1, 2, \ldots, K$. When the data point x_m meets the requirement $D(x_m, c_j) = \min(D(x_m, c_j))$ and $j = 1, 2, \ldots, K$, x_m, it will be represented by c_j and classified into Cluster D_j;
- Step8: when all the data points are classified into the corresponding cluster, update the cluster center $c = \{c_1, c_2, \ldots, c_k\}$ and calculate the clustering criteria function $J = \sum_{i=1}^{K} \sum_{d_j \in D_i} D(d_j, c_i)$;
- Step9: repeat step7 and step8 until J no longer changes, and then export the clustering result of K clusters, namely, $D = \{D_1, D_2, \ldots, D_k\}$.

4 Experiments

In this experiment, the clustering effect of abnormal behaviors was tested by comparing main evaluation indicator such as clustering criteria functions, number of iterations and convergence time. The lab configuration consists of Ubuntu 16.04, IDEA, CPU 2.6 GHz and 8.0 GB memory. The data set used is Yeast data set from UCI machine learning database [11].

4.1 Clustering Criterion Functions

To validate the reasonableness of selection about the initial clustering center in this algorithm, the paper adopts the first clustering criterion function J_1 following the selection about initial clustering center to make judgment. The smaller the J_1 is, the more reasonable initial clustering center selected is and the closer it is to the real clustering center. The result of this experiment is shown in Fig. 2.

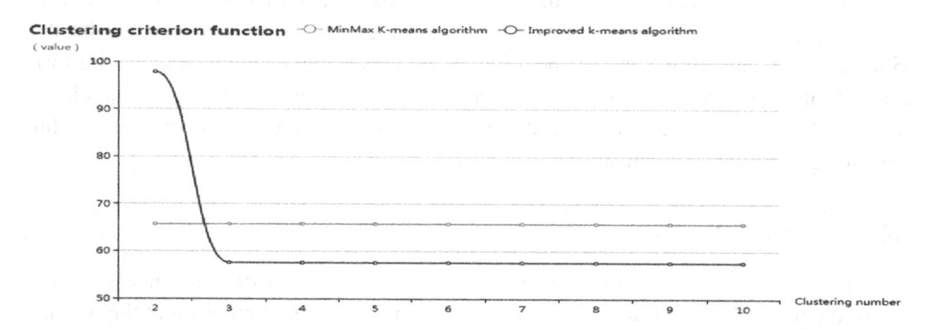

Fig. 2. Clustering criterion function value of MinMax K means and our proposed algorithm

As shown in the figure, when k = 2, the improved algorithm chooses the data point with minimum density as the second initial clustering center. As the number of clustering is small, the second initial clustering center chosen is far away from the real clustering center, which results in the increased value of clustering criterion function. The improved algorithm takes the distribution of real clustering center into account and focuses even more on distribution, so the data points uniformly distributed can represent the distribution of optimized clustering centers better when the clustering number increases. It greatly reduces the clustering criterion function value of improved algorithm, which leads to the improvement in clustering quality. The values of the clustering criterion function are shown in Table 1.

Table 1. Clustering criterion function value of MinMax K means and our proposed algorithm

Clustering number (k)	MinMax K means algorithm (value)	Improved algorithm (value)	Difference (value)
2	65.7199	97.8214	−32.1015
3	65.7197	57.5323	8.1874
4	65.7200	57.5275	8.1925
5	65.7200	57.5268	8.1932
6	65.7200	57.5265	8.1935
7	65.7200	57.5247	8.1953
8	65.7201	57.5237	8.1964
9	65.7200	57.5204	8.1996
10	65.7201	57.5198	8.2003

As is shown in Table 1, the difference of clustering criterion function value increases steadily with the increase of clustering number K. This is because the improved algorithm proposed in this paper selects the maximum and minimum points first, thus ensuring that two initial clustering centers belong to different clustering. What's more, the data points from the first initial cluster center are selected as the initial clustering centers in the sparse data region, and the selected data points can be distributed more uniformly. When the number of clustering K increases, the uniform distribution of data points is more consistent with the distribution of the optimal cluster center, which makes the clustering criterion function value decrease obviously, thus improving the quality of clustering.

4.2 Number of Iterations

To validate the clustering quality of the algorithm, the number of iterations is used as one of the metrics. If the number of iterations is small enough, it means that the initially selected clustering center is close to the real clustering center and the selection result is reasonable. The experiment result is shown in Fig. 3.

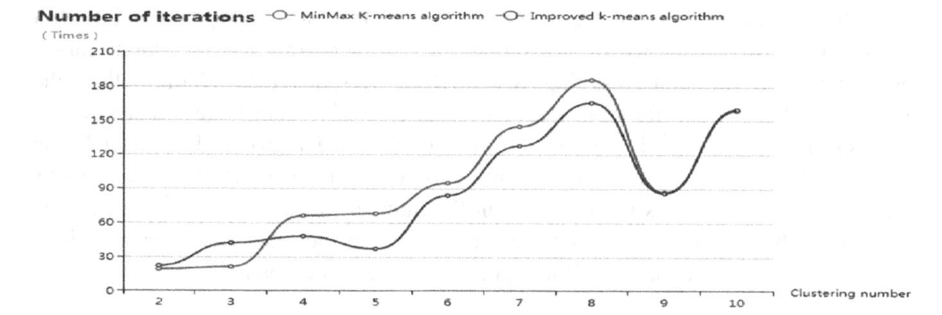

Fig. 3. Number of iterations of MinMax K means and our proposed algorithm

As is shown in Fig. 3, when K $\geq$ 4, the number of iteration of MinMax K means algorithm increases dramatically, because MinMax K means algorithm doesn't consider the distribution of real clustering center while the improved algorithm takes this into consideration. The data points have significant impacts on the level of density which leads to the increase of number of iterations. When the clustering number K increases, the data points with low density are much closer to the clustering center of the new cluster, which can reduce the number of iterations of the improved algorithm effectively. When K is large enough, the random selection about the first initial clustering center with the MinMax K means algorithm affects the clustering quality less, and the selection rules of the initial clustering center of the two algorithms become approximate to each other, which leads the numbers of iteration to overlap. The number of iteration is shown in Table 2.

Table 2. Number of iterations of MinMax K means and our proposed algorithm

Clustering number (k)	MinMax K means algorithm (number)	Improved algorithm (number)	Decrease (number)
2	19	22	−3
3	21	42	−21
4	66	48	18
5	68	37	31
6	95	84	11
7	145	128	17
8	186	166	20
9	87	86	1
10	159	160	−1

As is shown in Table 2, when K reaches 3, the number of the iterations drops by −21, which is the lowest value. With the increase of the cluster number K, the drop of iteration number increases steadily. When k = 5, the drop of the number of iteration reaches the highest one, 31. The number of iterations drops by 8.6% on average, which results from that the improved algorithm proposed in this paper selects the points with the highest density and lowest density first, thus ensuring that the two initial cluster centers belong to different clustering. Secondly, in the sparse data region, both of the data points close to and far from the first initial clustering center are selected as the initial cluster center, which ensures the obvious distance between the selected data points. In this way we can ensure that the clustering which the choosed data points belong to is as different as possible. When the number of clustering K increases, the selection of the initial cluster center becomes closer to the real cluster center, which makes the number of iteration of the algorithm decrease obviously.

4.3 Convergence Time

In order to validate the execution efficiency of the algorithm, the experiment uses convergence time for judgment, too. The shorter convergence time we use, the faster and the more efficient the algorithm execution is. The experiment results are shown in Fig. 4.

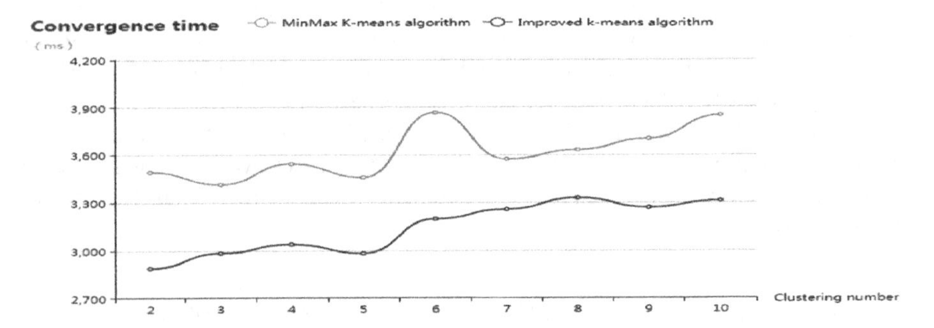

Fig. 4. Convergence time of MinMax K means and our proposed algorithm

As is shown in Fig. 4, with the increase of clustering number K, convergence time of MinMax K means algorithm and that of the improved algorithm is gradually getting closer. The MinMax K means algorithm selects the initial clustering center evenly, which results in a large number of distance operations in the selection process and affects the efficiency of the algorithm seriously. However, the improved algorithm takes the distribution of the real clustering center into consideration and selects the initial cluster center from the data points with low density, which greatly reduces the amount of data in the distance operation and ensures the clustering efficiency, and improves the efficiency of algorithm at the same time. The time of convergence is as shown in Table 3.

As is shown in Table 3, as the clustering number K increases, the speed-up ration decreases gradually. The convergence time declines by 13.1% on average, which results from that the improved algorithm proposed in the paper selects data points from sparse data area. This selection method greatly reduces the computation burden in the process of selecting initial clustering centers and drastically improves execution speed

Table 3. Convergence time of MinMax K means and our proposed algorithm

Clustering number (k)	MinMax K means algorithm (ms)	Improved algorithm (ms)	Speed-up ratio (%)
2	3493	2889	17.3
3	3415	2984	12.6
4	3543	3039	14.2
5	3458	2982	13.8
6	3867	3198	17.3
7	3574	3257	8.9
8	3633	3329	8.4
9	3703	3268	11.7
10	3849	3311	14.0

of algorithm. Besides, the data points selected from sparse data area can ensure obvious distances among them. In this way, we can make sure that the data points selected are most possible to belong to different clusters without reducing the execution efficiency of the algorithm. So the execution efficiency can be improved and relatively good initial clustering centers can be got. The convergence time of the algorithm declines sharply with convergence being accelerated and execution efficiency of the algorithm being improved.

5 Conclusions

This paper proposes a weight calculation method for abnormal behavior and an eigenvalue extraction method for abnormal behavior set by distinguishing the risk level of abnormal behavior and similarity level of abnormal behavior set. Through dividing the data points based on the level of density, the author optimizes the selection process of initial clustering center so as to get more reasonable initial clustering centers before the execution of K-means algorithm. The author has developed the clustering algorithm especially for abnormal behavior based on this. The experiment results show that the algorithm can effectively improve the clustering effects for abnormal behavior and perform better in both number of iteration and convergence time. With the abnormal behavior becoming more diversified, the future research will focus on higher dimensions, so larger-scale deep learning algorithm is the future direction for this paper.

Acknowledgements. This work was partly financially supported through grants from the Beijing Science and Technology Plan Project (No. Z171100004717001), Beijing Municipal Natural Science Fund Project (No. L172049), National Natural Science Foundation Project (No. 61671030), Beijing University of Technology Graduate Science and Technology Fund (No. YKJ-2017-00850).

References

1. Choi, S., Choi, Y., et al.: Network abnormal behavior analysis system. In: ICACT, 19–12 February 2017 (2017)
2. Hu, Y.J., Pang, L.J., Pei, Q.Q., Wang, X.A.: Instruction clustering analysis for network protocol's abnormal behavior. In: 2015 10th International Conference on P2P, Parallel, Grid, Cloud and Internet Computing, pp. 791–793 (2015)
3. Liu, H.F., Li, X.: Greedy optimization for K-means-based consensus clustering. Tsinghua Sci. Technol. **23**(2), 184–194 (2018)
4. Rahim, M.S., Ahmed, T.: An initial centroid selection method based on radial and angular coordinates for K-means algorithm. In: 2017 20th International Conference of Computer and Information Technology (ICCIT), 22–24 December 2017 (2017)
5. Celeb, M., Kingravi, H., Vela, P.: A comparative study of efficient initialization methods for the K-methods for the K-means clustering algorithm. Expert Syst. Appl. **40**(1), 200–210 (2013)
6. Ganesh, S.H., Premkumar, M.S.: A median based external initial centroid selection method for K-means clustering. In: World Congress on Computing and Communication Technologies (WCCCT). IEEE (2017)
7. Tzortzis, G., Likas, A.: The MinMax K-means clustering algorithm. Pattern Recognit. **44**(4), 866–876 (2011)
8. Chen, Z.M., Zuo, J.: Abnormal test algorithm based on improved K means algorithm. Comput. Sci. **08**, 258–261 (2016)
9. Gao, Z.H., Liu, L., Song, X.Q.: The research into the network abnormity test method based on data digging. Electron Technol. **45**(11), 30–32 (2016)
10. Hou, X.N., Liu, H.C., Yang, Z.: Algorithm-based and related intrusion test system research and design. Comput. Sci. Dev. **07**, 133–137 (2015)
11. Asuncion, A., Newman, D.: UCI Machine Learning Respository [EB/OL]. http://archive.ics.uci.edu/ml/datasets.html. 1 June 2015
12. Feng, W., et al.: Class imbalance ensemble learning based on the margin theory. Appl. Sci. **8** (5), 815 (2018)
13. Yan, Y., et al.: Unsupervised image saliency detection with Gestalt-laws guided optimization and visual attention based refinement. Pattern Recognit. **79**, 65–78 (2018)
14. Yan, Y., et al.: Cognitive fusion of thermal and visible imagery for effective detection and tracking of pedestrians in videos. Cognit. Comput. **10**(1), 94–104 (2018)
15. Sun, G., et al.: A stability constrained adaptive alpha for gravitational search algorithm. Knowl.-Based Syst. **139**, 200–213 (2018)
16. Zhang, A., et al.: A dynamic neighborhood learning-based gravitational search algorithm. IEEE Trans. Cybernet. **48**(1), 436–447 (2018)
17. Han, J., et al.: Background prior-based salient object detection via deep reconstruction residual. IEEE Trans. Circ. Syst. Video Technol. **25**(8), 1309–1321 (2015)
18. Han, J., et al.: Object detection in optical remote sensing images based on weakly supervised learning and high-level feature learning. IEEE Trans. Geosci. Remote Sens. **53**(6), 3325–3337 (2015)

Manifold-Regularized Adaptive Lasso

Si-Bao Chen(✉), Yu-Mei Zhang, and Bin Luo

Key Lab of Intelligent Computing and Signal Processing of Ministry of Education, School of Computer Science and Technology, Anhui University, Hefei 230601, China
sbchen@ahu.edu.cn

Abstract. Adaptive Lasso preserves oracle properties comparing to classical Lasso. It performs as well as if the true underlying model is provided in advance. In order to let feature subset selected by Adaptive Lasso preserve more local information, which is discriminative and benefit for classification, Manifold-regularized Adaptive Lasso (MrALasso) is proposed for feature selection. Reconstructing response by linear sum of features is considered in manifold embedded in high-dimensional space. A similarity graph of data points is built. Connected points are restricted to stay together as close as possible so that the intrinsic geometry of the data and the local structure are preserved. An effective iterative algorithm, with detailed proof of convergence, is proposed to solve the optimization problem. Experimental results of feature selection on several classical gene datasets show the effectiveness and superiority of the proposed method.

Keywords: Lasso · Manifold-regularization · Sparse minimization
Feature selection

1 Introduction

In many applications of pattern recognition and machine learning, feature dimension is very high which may hide the relationship between response and the most related features. A common way to resolve this problem is feature selection, which is to select a subset of the most representative or discriminative features from the input feature set.

In classical feature selection methods, filter-type feature selection methods are independent of classifiers, such as: t-test, ReliefF [13], F-statistic [5], information gain [15] and mRMR [14]. Wrapper-type feature selection methods take classifier as a black box to evaluate subsets of features [12]. Embedded-type feature selection methods train model to get the weight coefficient of each feature, such as: l_1-norm penalized Lasso (Least Absolute Shrinkage and Selection Operator) [19] and Elastic Net [23].

B. Luo—This work was supported in part by National Natural Science Foundation of China under Grant 61472002, 61572030 and 61671018, and Collegiate Natural Science Fund of Anhui Province under Grant KJ2017A014.

J. Ren et al. (Eds.): BICS 2018, LNAI 10989, pp. 545–556, 2018.
https://doi.org/10.1007/978-3-030-00563-4_53

Lasso [19] receives increasing research attention due to its good performance in feature selection [8]. However, the solution of Lasso is inconsistent in some cases [24]. Recently, Adaptive Lasso [24] was proposed, where adaptive weights [17] were designed to penalize different coefficients in the l_1-norm penalty. Zou [24] showed that Adaptive Lasso preserves oracle properties of identifying the correct subset model and having the optimal estimation accuracy comparing to classical Lasso. It performs as well as if the true underlying model is provided in advance. However, the feature subset selected by Adaptive Lasso does not contain adequate local and discriminative information for classification.

On the other hand, manifold learning can discover the intrinsic low-dimensional structure in high-dimensional data. Typical manifold learning methods include Isomap [18], Locally Linear Embedding (LLE) [16] and Laplacian Eigenmaps [3]. Linear projection method Locality Preserving Projections (LPP) [11] is a linear extension of Laplacian Eigenmaps. It constructs nearest neighbor graph of data points and utilizes graph Laplacians to preserve local structure among the original data. Experiments show graph Laplacians can discover local structure of original data very well. Recently, graph Laplacians was further applied to feature selection to help selecting those features containing local information, such as: Sparse Induced Graph Regularized Group Lasso [4].

In order to let feature subset selected by Adaptive Lasso preserve more local information, which contains more discriminative information and is benefit for classification, we propose Manifold-regularized Adaptive Lasso (MrALasso) for feature selection. Reconstructing response by linear sum of features is considered in manifold embedded in high-dimensional space. A similarity nearest neighbor graph of data points is built. Connected points are restricted to stay together as close as possible so that the intrinsic geometry of the data and the local structure are preserved [21].

2 Manifold-Regularized Adaptive Lasso

To select more informative and discriminative feature subset, we consider to add locality preserving restriction into Adaptive Lasso, which should contain more discriminative information. We investigate response reconstruction by linear sum of features in manifold embedded in high-dimensional space.

2.1 Formulation

Suppose there is a training data matrix with n samples of p features $\mathbf{X} = [\mathbf{x}_1, \mathbf{x}_2, \cdots, \mathbf{x}_p] = [\mathbf{x}^{(1)}, \mathbf{x}^{(2)}, \cdots, \mathbf{x}^{(n)}]^\top \in \mathbb{R}^{n\times p}$. Each column of $\mathbf{X}$ corresponds to a feature with the i-th feature (the i-th column of $\mathbf{X}$) being $\mathbf{x}_i = (x_{1i}, x_{2i}, \cdots, x_{ni})^\top \in \mathbb{R}^n$ $(i = 1, 2, \cdots, p)$. Each row of $\mathbf{X}$ corresponds to a training sample with the j-th training sample (the j-th row vector of $\mathbf{X}$) being $\mathbf{x}^{(j)} = (x_{j1}, x_{j2}, \cdots, x_{jp})^\top \in \mathbb{R}^p$ $(j = 1, 2, \cdots, n)$. The corresponding response vector $\mathbf{y} = (y_1, y_2, \cdots, y_n)^\top \in \{0, 1\}^n$. Suppose all p features and response are reprocessed through normalization of zero mean and unit variance.

Denote diagonal adaptive weights matrix $\mathbf{W} = diag(w_{11}, w_{22}, \cdots, w_{pp}) \in \mathbb{R}^{p\times p}$ with the i-th diagonal element

$$w_{ii} = 1/(|\beta_i^{(0)}| + \epsilon), \tag{1}$$

where $\beta_i^{(0)}$ means the i-th element of initial regression coefficient vector $\beta^{(\mathbf{0})}$, which could be the solution of classical Lasso or just least squares. $\epsilon > 0$ is a small positive constant which is added for avoiding dividing 0. The weight in the proposed method is fixed at the beginning, which has several advantages: oracle properties, not needing to update and compressing to 0 quickly.

Reconstructing response by linear sum of features with a sparsity constraint is actually a kind of linear dimensionality reduction. Based on the idea of linear projection-based dimensionality reduction method LPP [11], we restrict "close" data points should stay as close as possible in reduced subspace, which can preserve the intrinsic geometry of data and manifold local structure is preserved. A locality preserving constraint with a Laplacian matrix of the nearest neighbor graph is considered.

Suppose k-nearest neighbor graph (NN-graph) [22] among n training sample points is initially constructed. Then data similarity matrix $\mathbf{S} = (s_{ij}) \in \mathbb{R}^{n\times n}$ is computed with the (i,j)-th element s_{ij} being the heat kernel similarity between the i-th data point $\mathbf{x}^{(i)}$ and the j-th data point $\mathbf{x}^{(j)}$, which is defined as,

$$s_{ij} = \begin{cases} exp\{\frac{-||\mathbf{x}^{(i)} - \mathbf{x}^{(j)}||^2}{t}\}, & \mathbf{x}^{(i)} \text{ and } \mathbf{x}^{(j)} \text{ are neighbors;} \\ 0, & \text{otherwise,} \end{cases} \tag{2}$$

where t is an empirical parameter which is usually set as $t = \sigma \max\{||\mathbf{x}^{(i)} - \mathbf{x}^{(j)}||^2\}$. σ is a tuning parameter. It is worth noting that $s_{ij} = s_{ji}$ and similarity matrix $\mathbf{S}$ is symmetric.

Based on NN-graph of data points, we minimize the following locality preserving constraint of response estimation,

$$\min \frac{1}{2} \sum_{i,j=1}^{n} (\hat{y}_i - \hat{y}_j)^2 s_{ij}, \tag{3}$$

where $\hat{y}_i = \mathbf{x}^{(i)\top}\beta$ is the response estimation (low-dimensional representation) of the i-th sample $\mathbf{x}^{(i)}$. "Local" data have higher similarity s_{ij}, which enforces higher weight on the square difference of their response estimation. Minimizing the locality constraint (3) can enforce that "local" data stay close in the reduced subspace.

Substituting $\hat{y}_i = \mathbf{x}^{(i)\top}\beta$ or $\hat{\mathbf{y}} = \mathbf{X}\beta$ into Eq. (3), the locality preserving constraint can be rewritten as,

$$\begin{aligned} \frac{1}{2} \sum_{i,j=1}^{n} s_{ij}(\hat{y}_i - \hat{y}_j)^2 &= \sum_{i=1}^{n} D_{ii}\hat{y}_i^2 - \sum_{i=1}^{n}\sum_{j=1}^{n} s_{ij}\hat{y}_i\hat{y}_j \\ &= \hat{\mathbf{y}}^\top(\mathbf{D} - \mathbf{S})\hat{\mathbf{y}} = \beta^\top \mathbf{X}^\top \mathbf{L}\mathbf{X}\beta, \end{aligned} \tag{4}$$

where $\mathbf{D}$ is a diagonal matrix, $D_{ii} = \sum_{j=1}^{n} s_{ij}$, $\mathbf{L} = \mathbf{D} - \mathbf{S}$ is Laplacian matrix. The matrix $\mathbf{D}$ can measure how important the data is. In other words, the larger D_{ii} is, the important the corresponding response $\hat{y}_i$ is.

Therefore, we incorporate the above locality preserving constraint (4) into Adaptive Lasso [24], which is named Manifold-regularized Adaptive Lasso (MrALasso). The formal objective function of the proposed MrALasso is formulated as

$$\min_{\beta \in \mathbb{R}^p} ||\mathbf{y} - \mathbf{X}\beta||_2^2 + \lambda_1 \beta^\top \mathbf{X}^\top \mathbf{L} \mathbf{X} \beta + \lambda_2 ||\beta^\top \mathbf{W}||_1, \tag{5}$$

where λ_1 and λ_2 are tuning parameters which can balance between locality preserving constraint and sparsity constraint.

Since all three items of Eq. (5) are convex, the objective function is a convex optimization problem as a whole, which implies that it has a unique global optimal solution.

2.2 Optimization Algorithm

In this section, we present an iterative algorithm to solve the objective function (5), which is summarized in Algorithm 1.

Algorithm 1. Optimization Procedure of MrALasso

1: **Input:** Feature matrix $\mathbf{X} \in \mathbb{R}^{n \times p}$ with n samples and p-dimensional features (normalized by zero-mean and unit-variance), corresponding response vector $\mathbf{y} \in \{0, 1\}^n$, initial regression coefficient $\beta^{(0)} \in \mathbb{R}^p$, tuning parameter $\lambda_1, \lambda_2 \geq 0$, maximum number of iteration t_{max}, residual bound $\varepsilon > 0$;

2: Compute diagonal weight matrix $\mathbf{W}$ with the ith element $w_{ii} = 1/(|\beta_i^{(0)}| + \epsilon)$, set $t = 0$;

3: Update the following diagonal matrix $\mathbf{H}^{(t)}$,

$$\mathbf{H}^{(t)} = diag(\sqrt{\beta_1^{(t)}}, \sqrt{\beta_2^{(t)}}, \cdots, \sqrt{\beta_p^{(t)}}), \tag{6}$$

4: Use the following equation to update $\beta^{(t+1)}$,

$$\beta^{(t+1)} = \mathbf{H}^{(t)}[\mathbf{H}^{(t)}(\mathbf{X}^\top \mathbf{X} + \lambda_1 \mathbf{X}^\top \mathbf{L} \mathbf{X})\mathbf{H}^{(t)} + \frac{\lambda_2}{2}\mathbf{W}]^{-1}\mathbf{H}^{(t)}\mathbf{X}^\top \mathbf{y}. \tag{7}$$

5: If $t > t_{max}$ or $||\beta^{(t+1)} - \beta^{(t)}|| < \varepsilon$, go to Step 6; otherwise, let $t = t + 1$ and go to Step 3;

6: **Output:** The optimal regression coefficient $\beta^* = \beta^{(t+1)}$.

In each iteration, diagonal matrix $\mathbf{H}$ is calculated with the current β as in Eq. (6) and β is updated via the just obtained $\mathbf{H}$ as in Eq. (7). The alternate iteration between $\mathbf{H}$ (Step 3) and β (Step 4) are repeated until the algorithm converges.

2.3 Justification

In this section, we will give the detailed convergence proof of Algorithm 1. Let $J(\beta)$ represent the objective function (5). Note that $J(\beta)$ is a convex optimization problem with respect to regression coefficient β. We will prove that the objective function Eq. (5) is non-increasing with the iteration Algorithm 1, which is stated in Theorem 1.

Theorem 1. *The objective function value $J(\beta)$ in (5) is non-increasing during the whole iterative procedure of Algorithm 1. In other words, $J(\beta^{(t+1)}) \leq J(\beta^{(t)})$ holds along with each iteration of Eqs. (6) and (7) in Algorithm 1.*

To prove the Theorem 1, we need the help of the following two Lemmas.

Lemma 1. *An auxiliary function is defined as:*

$$Q(\beta, \beta^{(t)}) = ||\mathbf{y} - \mathbf{X}\beta||_2^2 + \lambda_1 \beta^\top \mathbf{X}^\top \mathbf{L} \mathbf{X} \beta + \lambda_2 \sum_{i \in C^{(t)}} w_{ii} \frac{{\beta_i}^2}{2|{\beta_i}^{(t)}|}, \tag{8}$$

where $C_{(t)} = \{i \mid |\beta_i^{(t)}| \neq 0, i = 1, 2, \cdots, p\}$. With the iteration of Algorithm 1, the following inequality holds:

$$Q(\beta^{(t+1)}, \beta^{(t)}) \leq Q(\beta^{(t)}, \beta^{(t)}). \tag{9}$$

Proof. This auxiliary function $Q(\beta, \beta^{(t)})$ is a convex quadratic function with respect to the regression coefficient β. Therefore, we can obtain the unique global optimal solution by taking the derivatives and set them equal to 0.

Let diagonal matrix $\mathbf{E}^{(t)} = diag(\sqrt{\frac{w_{11}}{2|{\beta_1}^{(t)}|}}, \sqrt{\frac{w_{22}}{2|{\beta_2}^{(t)}|}}, \cdots, \sqrt{\frac{w_{pp}}{2|{\beta_p}^{(t)}|}}) \in \mathbb{R}^{p \times p}$, and substitute $\mathbf{E}^{(t)}$ into Eq. (8), then Eq. (8) can be rewritten as

$$Q(\beta, \beta^{(t)}) = ||\mathbf{y} - \mathbf{X}\beta||_2^2 + \lambda_1 \beta^\top \mathbf{X}^\top \mathbf{L} \mathbf{X} \beta + \lambda_2 ||\mathbf{E}^{(t)} \beta||_2^2. \tag{10}$$

Take the derivative of Eq. (10) with respect to β, we obtain

$$\frac{\partial Q(\beta, \beta^{(t)})}{\partial \beta} = 2\mathbf{X}^\top \mathbf{X}\beta - 2\mathbf{X}^\top \mathbf{y} + 2\lambda_1 \mathbf{X}^\top \mathbf{L} \mathbf{X} \beta + 2\lambda_2 \mathbf{E}^{(t)\top} \mathbf{E}^{(t)} \beta. \tag{11}$$

Substitute $\mathbf{H}^{(t)}$ in Eq. (6) into the above Eq. (11). Equation(11) can be rewritten as

$$\frac{\partial Q(\beta, \beta^{(t)})}{\partial \beta} = 2\mathbf{X}^\top \mathbf{X}\beta - 2\mathbf{X}^\top \mathbf{y} + 2\lambda_1 \mathbf{X}^\top \mathbf{L} \mathbf{X} \beta + \lambda_2 \mathbf{W} (\mathbf{H}^{(t)})^{-2} \beta. \tag{12}$$

By setting $\frac{\partial Q(\beta, \beta^{(t)})}{\partial \beta} = 0$, we can get the following equation

$$\beta^* = [\mathbf{X}^\top \mathbf{X} + \lambda_1 \mathbf{X}^\top \mathbf{L} \mathbf{X} + \frac{\lambda_2}{2} \mathbf{W} (\mathbf{H}^{(t)})^{-2}]^{-1} \mathbf{X}^\top \mathbf{y}, \tag{13}$$

$$= \mathbf{H}^{(t)} [\mathbf{H}^{(t)} (\mathbf{X}^\top \mathbf{X} + \lambda_1 \mathbf{X}^\top \mathbf{L} \mathbf{X}) \mathbf{H}^{(t)} + \frac{\lambda_2}{2} \mathbf{W}]^{-1} \mathbf{H}^{(t)} \mathbf{X}^\top \mathbf{y}. \tag{14}$$

From this, we obtain the optimal solution of β. That is to say, the inequality $Q(\beta^*, \beta^{(t)}) \le Q(\beta, \beta^{(t)})$ is true with respect to arbitrary β. That is $Q(\beta^*, \beta^{(t)}) \le Q(\beta^{(t)}, \beta^{(t)})$. Comparing Eq. (7) with Eq. (14), we know that both of $\beta^* = \beta^{(t+1)}$ and $Q(\beta^{(t+1)}, \beta^{(t)}) \le Q(\beta^{(t)}, \beta^{(t)})$ are right in our model. This completes the proof of Lemma 1.

We explain why we are replacing the simpler Eq. (13) with the seemingly more complicated Eq. (14). Due to the nature of l_1-penalty, many elements of regression coefficient β are shrunk to exact or near 0. This phenomenon cannot realize the inverse operator of matrix $\mathbf{H}^{(t)}$ due to matrix singularity. Consequently, in order to avoid this case, we make use of Eq. (14) rather than Eq. (13) in Algorithm 1.

Besides of the above Lemma 1, we further need Lemma 2 to prove Theorem 1.

Lemma 2. *With each iteration of Algorithm 1, the regression coefficient β has the following property*

$$J(\beta^{(t+1)}) - J(\beta^{(t)}) \le Q(\beta^{(t+1)}, \beta^{(t)}) - Q(\beta^{(t)}, \beta^{(t)}). \tag{15}$$

Proof. Let $\triangle = (J(\beta^{(t+1)}) - J(\beta^{(t)})) - (Q(\beta^{(t+1)}, \beta^{(t)}) - Q(\beta^{(t)}, \beta^{(t)}))$, we only need to prove $\triangle \le 0$ holds. Substitute Eqs. (5) and (8) into $\triangle$, we arrive at

$$\begin{aligned}
\triangle &= \lambda_2 ||\mathbf{W}\beta^{(t+1)}||_1 - \lambda_2 ||\mathbf{W}\beta^{(t)}||_1 - \lambda_2 \sum_{i \in \mathcal{C}^{(t)}} w_{ii} \frac{({\beta_i}^{(t+1)})^2}{2|{\beta_i}^{(t)}|} + \lambda_2 \sum_{i \in \mathcal{C}^{(t)}} w_{ii} \frac{({\beta_i}^{(t)})^2}{2|{\beta_i}^{(t)}|} \\
&= \lambda_2 \sum_{i \in \mathcal{C}^{(t)}} \frac{w_{ii}}{2|{\beta_i}^{(t)}|} (2|{\beta_i}^{(t+1)}||\beta_i(t)| - ({\beta_i}^{(t)})^2 - ({\beta_i}^{(t+1)})^2) \\
&= -\lambda_2 \sum_{i \in \mathcal{C}^{(t)}} \frac{w_{ii}}{2|{\beta_i}^{(t)}|} ({\beta_i}^{(t+1)} - {\beta_i}^{(t)})^2 \le 0.
\end{aligned} \tag{16}$$

Here, $\mathcal{C}_{(t)} = \{i \mid |\beta_i^{(t)}| \ne 0, i = 1, 2, \cdots, p\}$. Then Eq. (15) is obtained and the proof of Lemma 2 is completed.

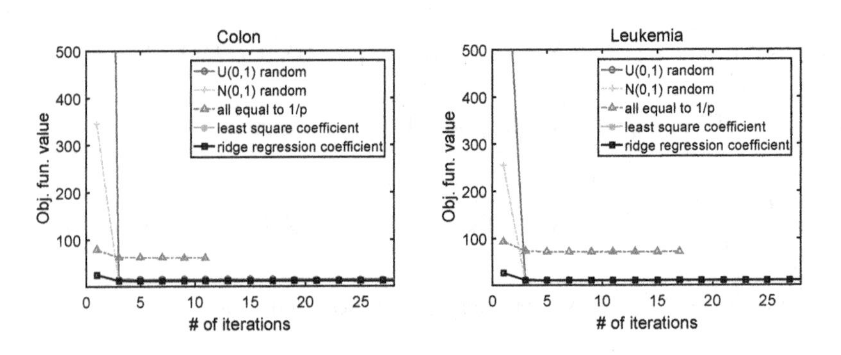

Fig. 1. Effect of different initial regression coefficients on Colon cancer and Leukemia datasets.

Based on Lemmas 1 and 2, the proof of Theorem 1 is easy. We can get $Q(\beta^{(t+1)}, \beta^{(t)}) - Q(\beta^{(t)}, \beta^{(t)}) \leq 0$ from Lemma 1. Combining with Lemma 2, we have $J(\beta^{(t+1)}) - J(\beta^{(t)}) \leq 0$, which is to say

$$J(\beta^{(t+1)}) \leq J(\beta^{(t)}). \tag{17}$$

This is the exact result of Theorem 1. The entire proof of Theorem 1 is accomplished.

3 Experiments

In this section, we evaluate the performance of the proposed MrALasso feature selection method. The effects of regression coefficient initialization and tuning parameters in the algorithm are initially evaluated. Then classification experiments of the proposed MrALasso feature selection method is compared with several closely related popular feature selection methods.

We choose two well-known gene datasets for experiments, which are Colon cancer dataset [7] and Leukemia dataset [1]. Although there are small number of samples, the number of features (data dimensionality) are quite large, which is benefit for feature selection. Colon cancer dataset [7] contains 62 samples in total. Each sample contains 2,000 features [20]. The number of two categories of samples 22 and 40 respectively. Leukemia dataset [1] is composed of 72 samples and each sample has 7,129 genes. The number of two categories of sample is 47 and 25 respectively.

3.1 Effect of Coefficient Initialization

The iteration of Algorithm 1 requires the initial regression coefficient $\beta^{(0)}$ starts with a non-zero vector. The convergence speed of the algorithm may be affected by different initial regression coefficients. In this subsection, we test different types of coefficient initialization $\beta^{(0)}$ to evaluate their effects on the convergence speed of Algorithm 1.

Five types of initial regression coefficients $\beta^{(0)}$ are given as follows: First, all elements of $\beta^{(0)}$ are uniform random number between 0 and 1, which is denoted as "U(0, 1) random"; Second, all elements of $\beta^{(0)}$ are Gaussian random number of zero-mean and unit-variance, which is denoted as "N(0, 1) random"; Third, all elements of $\beta^{(0)}$ are equal to $1/p$; Fourth, least square coefficients $\beta^{(0)} = (\mathbf{X}^\top \mathbf{X})^{-1} \mathbf{X}^\top \mathbf{y}$; Last, ridge regression coefficients $\beta^{(0)} = (\mathbf{X}^\top \mathbf{X} + \frac{1}{2}\lambda_1 \mathbf{I}_p + \lambda_2 \mathbf{I}_p)^{-1} \mathbf{X}^\top \mathbf{y}$.

To evaluate the effect of these five initial coefficients on the convergence speed of Algorithm 1, we test the iteration of the proposed MrALasso method on Colon cancer and Leukemia datasets. Figure 1 shows the variation of objective function values along with each iteration using five different initial regression coefficients on Colon cancer and Leukemia datasets. For the first and second initial regression coefficients, the initial objective function values are larger. But They drop rapidly

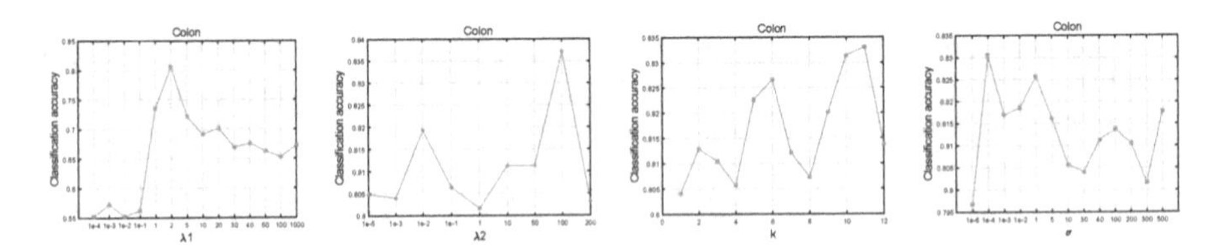

Fig. 2. Effects of λ_1, λ_2, k and σ on Colon cancer dataset.

and converge along with the increasing of iterations. Comparing with the first and second initial regression coefficients, the remaining three types of regression coefficients make the initial objective function values smaller, more closer to their convergent values.

From both the sub-figures of Fig. 1, we can see that no matter what the initial coefficient is. Algorithm 1 can converge quickly. To simplify the experiments, we just choose the simplest and efficient initialization, the third type of initialization (all elements being $1/p$), in all the following experiments.

3.2 Effects of Tuning Parameters

The proposed method has four tuning parameters: model regularization parameters λ_1 and λ_2, nearest neighbor parameter k and heat kernel parameter σ in constructing NN-graph. To test the effects of these tuning parameters on final recognition performance, we conduct classification experiments on Colon cancer dataset after feature selection by the proposed MrALasso method. The default values of these tuning parameters are set to be $\lambda_1 = 1$, $\lambda_2 = 1$, $k = 5$ and $\sigma = 1$. To simplify the experiments, when one parameter is examined, all the other parameters are set to be their default values.

Figure 2 shows the effects of λ_1, λ_2, k and σ of the proposed MrALasso method on classification performance on Colon cancer dataset. From the four sub-figures we can see that the classification recognition accuracies are stable around the default values of these four tuning parameters. Note that when $\lambda_1 \to 0$, the proposed MrAlasso method turns to classical Adaptive Lasso. From

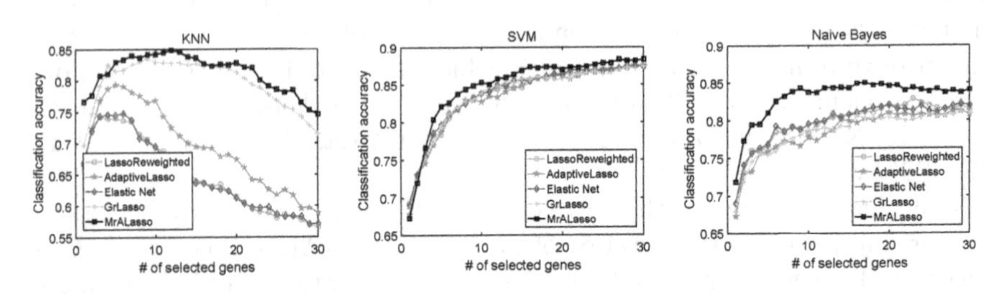

Fig. 3. Variation of classification accuracy along with different number of genes selected by different feature selection methods on Colon cancer dataset with KNN (left), SVM (middle) and Naive Bayes (right) classifiers.

the first sub-figure of Fig. 2, we can see that the classification accuracy is higher when λ_1 is equal to default value 1 than that when $\lambda_1 \to 0$, which shows the effectiveness of locality preserving constraint in the proposed MrALasso method. To simplify the subsequent experiments, we only set these four tuning parameters to be their default values.

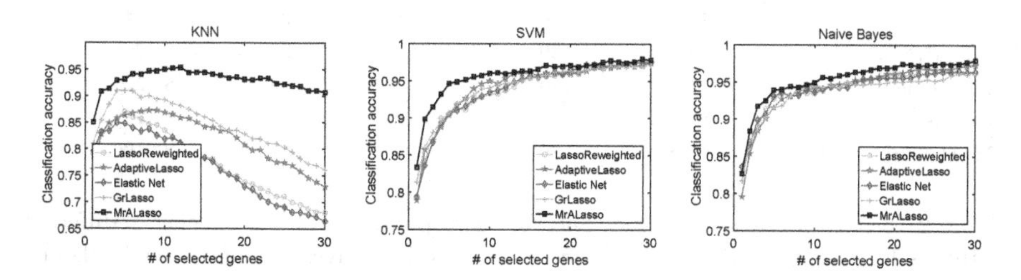

Fig. 4. Variation of classification accuracy along with different number of genes selected by different feature selection methods on Leukemia dataset with KNN (left), SVM (middle) and Naive Bayes (right) classifiers.

3.3 Classification Results

In this subsection, we evaluate the classification performance of our proposed MrALasso method on Colon cancer dataset and Leukemia dataset, comparing with other closely related feature selection methods. Before the experiments, each feature is normalized to zero-mean and unit-variance. We adopt 10-fold cross validation to all experiments and further twenty runs are conducted to let the average experimental results more reliable. Three classifiers, which are KNN, SVM [6] and Naive Bayes classifiers, are adopted to calculate classification accuracy.

Figures 3 and 4 show variation of classification performance along with different number of genes selected by MrALasso feature selection method on Colon cancer dataset and Leukemia dataset respectively, comparing with closely related feature selection methods: Lasso [19], Adaptive Lasso [24], Elastic net [23] and GrLasso [4].

From all of the sub-figures of Figs. 3 and 4, we can see that the classification accuracy of all feature selection methods increase at first and then gradually decrease (as KNN) or saturate (as SVM and Naive Bayes) along with more selected genes. This is because when the number of selected genes is small, the discriminative information provided by the selected genes is insufficient. More genes are needed to obtain more discriminative information for better classification performance. However, when the number of genes is greater than a certain amount, that is more genes are selected, some redundant or noisy genes will be involved, which can cause perturbations to the discriminative ability and decrease the final classification performance. Comparing with SVM and Naive Bayes, KNN shows sensitive to noises.

Table 1. Top classification accuracy and the corresponding number of genes of different feature selection methods via KNN, SVM and Naive Bayes classifiers on Colon cancer dataset.

Method	KNN classifier		SVM classifier		Naive Bayes classifier	
	# of genes	Accuracy (%)	# of genes	Accuracy (%)	# of genes	Accuracy (%)
MAVE-LD	50	83.87	-	-	-	-
Lasso	3	74.27	30	87.80	23	82.94
Adaptive Lasso	5	79.43	30	87.44	28	81.29
Elastic net	6	74.84	30	87.39	29	82.22
GrLasso	9	83.54	30	87.46	29	81.21
MrALasso	12	**84.84**	30	**88.37**	17	**85.03**

Table 2. Top classification accuracy and the corresponding number of genes of different feature selection methods via KNN, SVM and Naive Bayes classifiers on Leukemia dataset.

Method	KNN classifier		SVM classifier		Naive Bayes classifier	
	# of genes	Accuracy (%)	# of genes	Accuracy (%)	# of genes	Accuracy (%)
WVM	50	85.29	-	-	-	-
Lasso	5	87.01	29	97.73	27	96.31
Adaptive Lasso	8	87.29	30	97.44	30	97.28
Elastic Net	4	84.93	29	97.52	28	96.51
GrLasso	5	90.97	30	97.16	28	96.16
MrALasso	12	**95.35**	29	**97.99**	30	**97.89**

We can see from all of the sub-figures of Figs. 3 and 4 that the proposed MrALasso method has significant improvements comparing with other feature selection methods, which indicates that our proposed method can effectively select the most representative and discriminative features. The experimental results show that our method can significantly outperform state-of-the-art methods with different classifiers.

To further evaluate the effectiveness of our proposed method, the top classification accuracy and the corresponding number of genes of the proposed MrALasso on Colon cancer dataset and Leukemia dataset are listed in Table 1 [9,10] and Table 2 respectively, comparing with its closely related feature selection methods: MAVE-LD [2], weighted voting machine (WVM) [7], Lasso [19], Adaptive Lasso [24], Elastic net [23] and GrLasso [4]. From the tables we can see that the proposed MrALasso method achieves the best classification results consistent with KNN, SVM and Naive Bayes classifiers.

4 Conclusion

Motivated by the oracle properties of Adaptive Lasso and locality-preserving property of manifold Laplacians, we proposed Manifold-regularized Adaptive Lasso (MrALasso) for feature selection. Reconstructing response by linear sum of features is considered in manifold. A similarity graph of data points is built. Connected points are restricted to stay together as close as possible so that the intrinsic geometry of the data and the local structure are preserved. An effective iteration algorithm, with proof of convergence, is presented to solve the optimization problem of MrALasso. The experiments on two gene datasets demonstrate that the proposed MrALasso outperforms other feature selection methods.

References

1. Alon, U., Barkai, N.: Broad patterns of gene expression revealed by clustering analysis of tumor and normal colon tissues probed by oligonucleotide arrays. Proc. Natl. Acad. Sci. USA **96**(12), 6745–6750 (1999)
2. Antoniadis, A., Lambertlacroix, S., Leblanc, F.: Effective dimension reduction methods for tumor classification using gene expression data. Bioinformatics **19**(5), 563–570 (2003)
3. Belkin, M., Niyogi, P.: Laplacian eigenmaps for dimensionality reduction and data representation. Neural Comput. **15**(6), 1373–1396 (2003)
4. Chen, X., Xu, Y.: Discriminative feature selection for multiple ocular diseases classification by sparse induced graph regularized group Lasso. In: Navab, N., Hornegger, J., Wells, W.M., Frangi, A.F. (eds.) MICCAI 2015. LNCS, vol. 9350, pp. 11–19. Springer, Cham (2015). https://doi.org/10.1007/978-3-319-24571-3_2
5. Ding, C.H.Q., Peng, H.: Minimum redundancy feature selection from microarray gene expression data. J. Bioinform. Comput. Biol. **3**(2), 185–206 (2005)
6. Feng, W., Huang, W., Ren, J.: Class imbalance ensemble learning based on the margin theory. Appl. Sci. **8**(5), 815 (2018)
7. Golub, T.R., Slonim, D.K., et al.: Molecular classification of cancer: class discovery and class prediction by gene expression monitoring. Science **286**(5439), 531–537 (1999)
8. Gui, J., Sun, Z., Ji, S., Tao, D., Tan, T.: Feature selection based on structured sparsity: a comprehensive study. IEEE T-NNLS **28**(7), 1490–1507 (2017)
9. Han, J., Zhang, D., et al.: Object detection in optical remote sensing images based on weakly supervised learning and high-level feature learning. IEEE TGRS **53**(6), 3325–3337 (2015)
10. Han, J., Zhang, D., Hu, X., Guo, L., Ren, J., Wu, F.: Background prior-based salient object detection via deep reconstruction residual. IEEE T-CSVT **25**(8), 1309–1321 (2015)
11. He, X., Yan, S., Hu, Y., Niyogi, P., Zhang, H.: Face recognition using laplacianfaces. IEEE Trans. Pattern Anal. Mach. Intell. **27**(3), 328–340 (2005)
12. Kohavi, R., John, G.H.: Wrappers for feature subset selection. Artif. Intell. **97**(1–2), 273–324 (1997)
13. Kononenko, I.: Estimating attributes: analysis and extensions of RELIEF. In: Bergadano, F., De Raedt, L. (eds.) ECML 1994. LNCS, vol. 784, pp. 171–182. Springer, Heidelberg (1994). https://doi.org/10.1007/3-540-57868-4_57
14. Peng, H., Long, F., Ding, C.: Feature selection based on mutual information: criteria of max-dependency, max-relevance, and min-redundancy. IEEE TPAMI **27**(8), 1226–1238 (2005)
15. Raileanu, L.E., Stoffel, K.: Theoretical comparison between the gini index and information gain criteria. Ann. Math. Artif. Intell. **41**(1), 77–93 (2004)

16. Roweis, S., Saul, L.K.: Nonlinear dimensionality reduction by locally linear embedding. Science **290**(5500), 2323–2326 (2000)
17. Sun, G., Ma, P., Ren, J., Zhang, A., Jia, X.: A stability constrained adaptive alpha for gravitational search algorithm. Knowl.-Based Syst. **139**, 200–213 (2018)
18. Tenenbaum, J.B., De Silva, V., Langford, J.: A global geometric framework for nonlinear dimensionality reduction. Science **290**(5500), 2319–2323 (2000)
19. Tibshirani, R.: Regression shrinkage and selection via the Lasso. J. R. Stat. Soc. Ser. B (Methodol.) **58**(1), 267–288 (1996)
20. Wang, Z., Ren, J., et al.: A deep-learning based feature hybrid framework for spatiotemporal saliency detection inside videos. Neurocomputing **287**, 68–83 (2018)
21. Yan, Y., Ren, J., et al.: Unsupervised image saliency detection with gestalt-laws guided optimization and visual attention based refinement. Pattern Recogn. **79**, 65–78 (2018)
22. Zhang, A., Sun, G., Ren, J., Li, X., Wang, Z., Jia, X.: A dynamic neighborhood learning-based gravitational search algorithm. IEEE Trans. Cybern. **48**(1), 436–447 (2018)
23. Zou, H., Hastie, T.: Regularization and variable selection via the elastic net. J. R. Stat. Soc.: Ser. B (Stat. Methodol.) **67**(2), 301–320 (2005)
24. Zou, H.: The adaptive Lasso and its oracle properties. J. Am. Stat. Assoc. **101**(476), 1418–1429 (2006)

SentiALG: Automated Corpus Annotation for Algerian Sentiment Analysis

Imane Guellil[1,2](✉), Ahsan Adeel[3], Faical Azouaou[2], and Amir Hussain[3]

[1] Ecole Superieure des Sciences Appliquées d'Alger ESSA-alger, Alger, Algeria
i.guellil@essa-alger.dz

[2] Laboratoire des Méthodes de Conception des Systèmes (LMCS), Ecole Nationale Supérieure d'Informatique, BP 68M, 16309 Oued-Smar, Alger, Algérie
{i_guellil,f_azouaou}@esi.dz

[3] Institute of Computing Science and Mathematics, School of Natural Sciences University of Stirling, Stirling, UK
ahsan.adeel@stir.ac.uk, ahu@cs.stir.ac.uk

Abstract. Data annotation is an important but time-consuming and costly procedure. To sort a text into two classes, the very first thing we need is a good annotation guideline, establishing what is required to qualify for each class. In the literature, the difficulties associated with an appropriate data annotation has been underestimated. In this paper, we present a novel approach to automatically construct an annotated sentiment corpus for Algerian dialect (A Maghrebi Arabic dialect). The construction of this corpus is based on an Algerian sentiment lexicon that is also constructed automatically. The presented work deals with the two widely used scripts on Arabic social media: Arabic and Arabizi. The proposed approach automatically constructs a sentiment corpus containing 8000 messages (where 4000 are dedicated to Arabic and 4000 to Arabizi). The achieved F1-score is up to 72% and 78% for an Arabic and Arabizi test sets, respectively. Ongoing work is aimed at integrating transliteration process for Arabizi messages to further improve the obtained results.

Keywords: Arabic sentiment analysis · Algerian dialect
Sentiment lexicon · Sentiment corpus · Sentiment classification

1 Introduction

Sentiment analysis is defined as an interdisciplinary domain among the natural language processing (NLP), artificial intelligence (AI), and text mining [17]. To determine whether a document or a sentence expresses a positive or negative sentiment, three main approaches are commonly used: the lexicon based approach [26], machine learning (ML) based approach [20] and a hybrid approach [18].

J. Ren et al. (Eds.): BICS 2018, LNAI 10989, pp. 557–567, 2018.
https://doi.org/10.1007/978-3-030-00563-4_54

English has the greatest number of sentiment analysis studies , while research is more limited for other languages including Arabic and its dialects [5].

ML based sentiment analysis requires an annotated data. The lexicon based approach needs an annotated sentiment lexicon (containing the valence and/or intensity of its terms and/or expressions). One of the majors problems related to the treatment of Arabic and its dialect is the lack of resources. Other dominant problems include the standard romanization (called Arabizi) that Arabic speakers often use in social media. Arabizi uses Latin alphabet, numbers, punctuation for writing an Arabic word (For example the word "mli7", combining between Latin letters and numbers, is the romanized form of the Arabic word "مليح" meaning "good"). To the best of our knowledge, limited work has been conducted on sentiment analysis of Arabizi and it is dedicated to Arabic and not to its dialect [11]. However, not much work has been conducted on sentiment analysis of Algerian Arabizi.

To bridge the gap, this paper proposes an approach that automatically construct a sentiment lexicon for a Magheribi dialect (i.e. Algerian dialect). Based on the constructed lexicon, we automatically annotate a sentiment corpus into positive and negative. To validate the build corpus, we applied a set of classifiers and tested our corpus on two different test sets: internal (which is a part of the constructed corpus) and external (which represent a set of messages that we manually annotated). However, the general experimental results have shown better performance with Arabic test sets which is attributed to the complexity of Arabizi.

This paper is organized as following: Sect. 2 presents the related work on sentiment analysis by focusing on the work done on Arabic and its dialects. Section 3 presents our approach and the different parts that composed it. Section 4 presents the different results that we collected in this study. Section 5 presents conclusion containing some opening for our futures works.

2 Arabic Sentiment Analysis

2.1 Lexicon-Based Approaches

A lexicon of 120,000 Arabic terms is build in [3], following infinitives collection, transliteration to English, and exploitation of English lexicon to determine the valence and intensity of each word. Another large lexicon has been constructed in [10]. It contains 157 969 synonymous and 28 760 lemmas. To build this big dataset, the authors combined several Arabic resources including English WordNet, Arabic WordNet, English SentiWordNet, Standard Arabic Morphological Analyzer (SAMA). In [24], the authors develop a lexicon of sentiment containing 14 182 English unigram classified into positive or negative using the "Mechanical Turk of Amazon"[1]. This lexicon is then translated into 40 languages including MSA. The authors in [2] studied three lexical construction techniques including

[1] https://www.mturk.com/.

one manual and two automatics. In addition, a SA tool was developed within this work. Experiments showed that the use of a lexicon containing 16 800 words (created by integrating three techniques, so one manual and the two others automatic) gives the best results. In [21], the authors manually construct a lexicon of sentiment starting with an existing Arabic and Egyptian lexicon. They analyzed messages containing MSA as well as DALG. To answer to the morphological characteristics of this language and dialect, the authors used the lemmatization tool "khoja" (developed for MSA).

Most of the proposed lexicon construction methods are based on three: (1) manual; (2) automatic translation and (3) annotated corpus. In this paper, we exploited the second technique to construct our Algerian sentiment lexicon.

2.2 Machine Learning Based Approaches

Supervised approaches essentially depends on the existence of annotated data. Among the corpora presented in the literature, we cite: OCA [25], AWATIF [1],LABR [9], TSAC [22], AraSenTi-Tweet [4]. OCA contains 500 Arabic comments (250 positive and 250 negative), manually preprocessed, then segmented, and root extracted with a tool dedicated to Arabic. AWATIF is a multi-genre corpus containing 10 723 sentences in Arabic manually annotated in objective and subjective sentences. Then annotation of the subjective sentences in positive, negative or neutral. LABR contains 63 257 Arabic comments annotated with stars ranging from 1 to 5 by users. The authors considered positive comments containing 4 or 5 stars, negative ones containing 1 or 2 stars and neutral ones containing 3 stars. TSAC contains 17 060 comments (including 8215 positive and 8845 negative) in Tunisian dialect annotated manually. AraSenTi-Tweet contains 17 573 Saudi tweets, manually annotated into four classes (positive, negative, neutral and mixed).

Almost all works are based on the constructed corpus to classify sentiment (by using classification algorithm). The most used classification Algorithm are: Support Vector Machine (SVM) and Naive Bays(NB). However, most of the aforementioned works suffer from: manual annotation, almost all resources are not publicly available and constructed corpora are not dedicated to DALG. To the best of our knowledge, one work only has been done on Arabizi sentiment analysis [11]. However, it is not focus on Algerian Arabizi. Emergent works have been done on Algerian Arabizi treatment [12–16] but no one concentrate on sentiment analysis.

3 Contribution

In this paper, we present an approach for sentiment analysis of DALG messages. This approach is based on an annotated corpus that we constructed automatically. The construction of this corpus is based on a sentiment lexicon (that we also constructed automatically) and on a sentiment algorithm (handling DALG characteristics). Figure 1 presents the proposed sentiment analysis approach. The proposed approach constitutes three general steps: (1) Automatic construction of DALG sentiment lexicon. (2) Polarity calculation of DALG messages and (3) Sentiment classification of DALG messages. The three steps are comprehensively explained in subsequent sections.

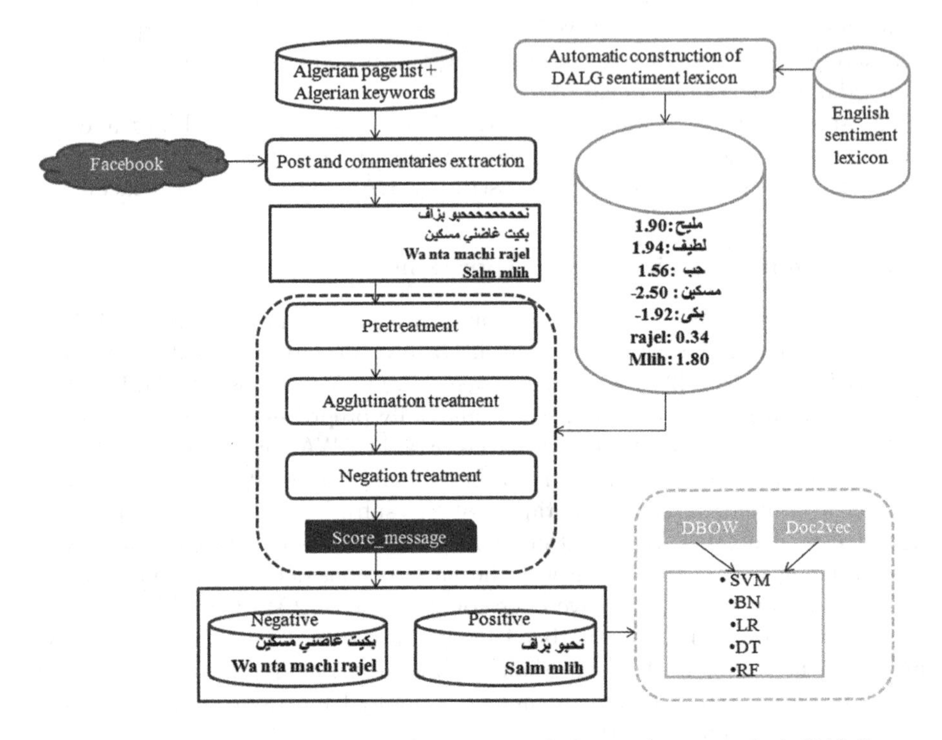

Fig. 1. A general architecture of our approach for sentiment analysis DALG

3.1 Automatic Construction of DALG Sentiment Lexicon

Our approach receives a lexicon of sentiments in English as input. Each word in this lexicon is translated using a translation API ([2]). The specificity of this API is that the translation is performed by ordinary users native of the DALG. The same score is assigned to all collected words. For example, the English word 'excellent' (with a score of +5) gives different DALG words such as: 'بَاهي' baAhiy, 'لطيف' lTiyf, 'مليح', mliyH, etc. All these words receive a score of +5, similarly to the word 'excellent'. However, a word in DALG is associated with several words in English and can therefore have several scores. For example the word مليح mliyH, 'good' is associated with several English words such as: excellent, generous, delicious, etc. The word 'excellent' has a score equal to (+5); the

[2] https://glosbe.com/en/arq/excellent.

word 'generous' has the score (+2) and the others words have different scores. Therefore we extract, within this part, all the words in DALG and calculating their scores. Concerning the calculation of the score, we take the average of the scores of all the English words to which our word in DALG is associated.

3.2 Polarity Calculation of DALG Messages

The goal of this step is to automatically annotate a set of Facebook messages (extracted from Algerian pages) as positive and negative. For example, the sentence: 'نحبو بزاف' translated into 'I love him a lot' should recognized as positive and the sentence 'wa nta machi rajel' translated into 'and you are not man' should recognized as negative. To correctly annotate this sentences and others, we need to proceed to a set of treatments: (1) Pretreatment of the messages. (2) Agglutination treatment. (3) Negation treatment.

3.2.1 Pretreatment of the Messages

- Deleting of the repeated messages in the corpus to keep only one occurrence of each message.
- Deleting of exaggerations, for example the word نحّحّحب is transformed into: نحب and nhhhhhab is transformed into nhab. The different repetitions of the different letter 'ح' and 'h' are removed to keep a single occurrence.
- Deleting of the '#' character and spaces of the different punctuations '.,!,?' of the related word .
- Deleting of consecutive whites spaces as well as Tatweel ('–') within Arabic characters.

3.2.2 Agglutination Treatment

We first form all the possible n-gram in the messages. For example, the second message ('بكيت غاظني مسكين') gives us 3 uni-gram ('بكيت، غاظني' and 'مسكين'), 2 bi-gram ('بكيت غاظني، غاظني مسكين') and one tri-gram ('بكيت غاظني مسكين'). Then, we look for each n-gram in the lexicon and add the score of the finding ones into the global score (if they are not proceeded by a negation). If no n-gram is found, we extract stem from each word and look for it in the lexicon. To extract the DALG stems, we define a set of prefixes and suffixes (Personnel pronouns, complement pronouns, feminine pronouns, plural pronouns, etc.) of DALG. For example: The stem of the word 'نحبو' is 'حب' because the two letters 'ن' and 'و' are respectively represent a prefix and a suffix in DALG and the stem 'حب' is recognized in our lexicon. However, some words which are conjugated into the past like 'بكيت' to be transformed before being recognized. So, the stem of 'بكيت' is 'بكى'. To recognize it, we have to extract the part without affixes (so 'بك' and add the letter 'ى' at the end).

3.2.3 Negation Treatment

Negation analysis is an important research challenge for all languages. Nevertheless this challenge is accentuated in the case of Arabic and its dialects where the negation is usually attached to the word as well as the different pronouns. Users can use negation in different ways, for example the word مَانحبكمش can be written in the following way: مَا نحبكمش or مَانحبكم ش or مَا نحبكم ش. Therefore, we notice that negation can be attached to or separated from terms. We have found, however, that in most cases negation does not only affect the preceding word but also some other words in the sentence. Once a prefix or negation suffix is detected, we reverse the score of the words succeeding this negation (multiplying the score by (-1)).

After calculating the score of each messages, we annotate it as positive (if its score is bigger than 0), and negative in the other case (so if its score is smaller that 0). Finally, we are able to automatically annotate the extracted corpus.

3.3 Sentiment Classification of DALG Messages

In this paper, we propose to compare different shallow classification models. We used two vectorization techniques: Bag of Words (BOW) and document embedding where we rely on the Doc2vec algorithm presented within [19]. For Doc2vec, we apply the two methods presented in [19]: (1) Distributed Memory Version Of Paragraph Vector (PV-DM) et (2) Distributed Bag of Words Version of Paragraph Vector (PV-DBOW). We also use the implementation merging these two methods. In the method (PV-DM), the paragraph vector (document or sentence) is concatenated to the word vectors in order to predict the next word within a text window. Unlike this method, (PV-BOW) ignores the context of the words within the inputs and this to force the prediction of these words randomly focusing on the paragraph vector. For the classification part, we use different classifiers: (1) Support Vector Machine (SVM). (2) Naive Bayes (NB). (3) Logistic regression (LR). (4) Decision Tree (DT) and (5) Random Forest (RF).

4 Experimentations and Results

4.1 Constructed Resources

In this work we constructed three kind of resources: (1) An Algerian sentiment lexicon (containing words in both Arabic and Arabizi). (2) A monolingual Algerian dialect corpus. (3) An annotated Algerian sentiment corpus.

For the construction of lexicons, we used SOCAL (an English sentiment lexicon) presented in [26]. SOCAL contains 6769 terms whose sentiment is labeled between $(-1, -5)$ for negative terms and between $(+1, +5)$ for positive terms. However only 3968 terms in English have been recognized and translated by the Glosbe API. After the extraction of Algerian dialect terms we obtain a lexicon containing 4873 words annotated from (−5 to +5), where 2390 are in Arabic and 2483 are in Arabizi.

We use Socialbekers website[3] to collect the name of the 226 most famous Algerian Facebook pages including Ooredoo, HamoudBoualem, Algeria Telecom, Ruiba, etc. We also extracted some strong dialectal Algerian keywords from PADIC corpus [23] (for example, يفرح which means "he is happy", الكدّاب which means "a lier"). Then, we use RestFB[4] API implemented with JAVA to extract all post and commentaries present in the target pages and present in others pages but containing Algerian keywords. At the end, we were able to collect **15,407,910** messages where **7,926,504** are in Arabic and **3,976,700** are in Arabizi.

Based on the constructed lexicon, on the extracted corpus and on the sentiment analysis algorithm that we developed, we are able to automatically annotate a sentiment corpus. Then we randomly form a training corpus containing 8000 messages (where 4000 messages are in Arabic and 4000 messages are in Arabizi with 2000 positives messages and 2000 negative. After, this corpus is divided into three part (train, dev and test) for internal experiment and (train, dev) for external experiment. The dev set is used only for deep classification. For shallow classification, we use the entire annotated corpus as training.

4.2 Experimental Results

The constructed automatically annotated sentiment corpus has been critically analyzed by applying shallow algorithms. Difficulties to deal with a non-resourced dialect (such as Algerian dialect which uses two different alphabets) have also been highlighted. Table 1 presents the performance of difference classification algorithms in terms of Accuracy (Acc)) and F1-score (F1) for each vectorization method (BOW, Doc2vec).

Based on simulations and analysis, our three major observations are: (1) The results with Arabic sets are better than Arabizi sets in most of the cases. (2) The results on internal data sets are better than external ones. (3) Bow vectorization gives better results than Doc2vec. These results are principally related to five facts and could substantially be improved by handling these lack:

- Arabizi is very complex and one term could have different writing manner (sometimes more than 100 manners). Handling it with one lexicon is almost impossible. To address this issues, we could enrich the used lexicon by all variation of Arabizi word. We also propose to integrate a transliteration module to transform Arabizi into Arabic before analyzing the sentiment of Arabizi messages.
- Our lexicon contains lots of noise. For example the different words: (1) "ب، و، مع", etc. (with) have a negative polarity when these words are neural. (2) The word ("رب" meaning "god" has a positive polarity in Arabic

[3] https://www.socialbakers.com/statistics/facebook/pages/total/algeria/.
[4] http://restfb.com/.

Table 1. DALG sentiment analysis results

Vectorization		Classification	Arabic				Arabizi			
			Internal		External		Internal		External	
			F1	Acc	F1	Acc	F1	Acc	F1	Acc
BOW		SVM	0.51	0.54	0.40	0.47	0.57	0.61	0.42	0.45
		NB	0.56	0.57	0.51	0.55	0.56	0.58	0.55	0.57
		LR	**0.72**	**0.72**	**0.68**	**0.68**	**0.78**	**0.78**	0.51	0.52
		DT	0.67	0.67	0.58	0.59	0.75	0.75	0.49	0.49
		RF	0.67	0.67	0.59	0.61	0.73	0.73	0.49	0.49
Doc2vec	PV-DBOW	SVM	0.27	0.58	0.63	0.63	0.51	0.54	0.61	0.61
		NB	0.52	0.52	**0.67**	**0.67**	0.52	0.52	0.59	0.60
		LR	**0.59**	**0.59**	0.63	0.64	0.54	0.54	0.53	0.55
		DT	0.55	0.56	0.58	0.58	0.54	0.54	0.53	0.53
		RF	0.58	0.59	0.61	0.61	0.55	0.56	0.55	0.56
	PV-DM	SVM	0.48	0.52	0.51	0.54	0.50	0.52	0.61	0.62
		NB	0.41	0.48	0.45	0.53	0.52	0.52	0.65	0.65
		LR	0.53	0.53	0.57	0.58	0.52	0.52	0.63	0.63
		DT	0.54	0.54	0.56	0.56	0.51	0.51	0.49	0.49
		RF	0.52	0.53	0.53	0.54	0.52	0.53	0.51	0.51
	PV-DBOW/PV-DM	SVM	0.44	0.49	0.51	0.53	0.51	0.54	0.61	0.63
		NB	0.41	0.48	0.48	0.55	0.51	0.51	**0.66**	**0.66**
		LR	0.51	0.51	0.55	0.56	0.54	0.54	**0.66**	**0.66**
		DT	0.53	0.53	0.45	0.45	0.49	0.49	0.55	0.55
		RF	0.46	0.47	0.53	0.54	0.49	0.50	0.55	0.56

when the word "lah" representing a part of "alah" in Arabizi (meaning god too) has a negative polarity. To address this problem, a manual review of lexicons could be used to increase the precision of annotation.

- Other parameters than score involved in the annotation process such as: number of positives and negatives words, length of the sentence, the comparison of score to other threshold than 0, etc. The integration of these parameters to our algorithm and testing and the influence of each one on the annotation process could considerably improve the results.
- Some irregular plurals such as ملاح in arabic and "mlah" in Arabizi are not recognize by our algorithm which is only based on soft stemming. The proposition of a stemmer tool dedicated to DALG could improve the annotation process.
- The vectorization used techniques are complementary. Hence, some messages are recognized by using DBOW and are not recognized by using Doc2vec and vice versa. The combination between the different vectorization technique will considerably improve the results.

5 Conclusion and Perspectives

In this paper, we present a novel approach to automatically construct an annotated sentiment corpus for Algerian dialect (A Maghrebi Arabic dialect). The construction of this corpus is based on an Algerian sentiment lexicon that is also constructed automatically. The presented work deals with the two widely used scripts on Arabic social media: Arabic and Arabizi. The proposed approach automatically constructs a sentiment corpus containing 8000 messages (where 4000 are dedicated to Arabic and 4000 to Arabizi). The achieved F1-score is up to 72% and 78% for an Arabic and Arabizi internal test sets, and up to 68% and 66% for an Arabic and Arabizi internal test sets respectively.

This study represents the baseline for our future work where we plan to augmenting the lexicon size based on embedding algorithm such as word2vec. Additionally, enlarging the dataset with focusing on more annotated words will provide much better results. One thing more, one arabizi word could have many different writing manners. This phenomena leads to misinterpretation and consequently a wrong polarity classification. Hence, proceeding to transliterate arabizi messages absolutely improve the results.

We also plan to extend our work for handling handwriting Arabic based on the work proposed in [6–8].

Acknowledgment. Amir Hussain and Ahsan Adeel were supported by the UK Engineering and Physical Sciences Research Council (EPSRC) grant No.EP/M026981/1.

References

1. Abdul-Mageed, M., Diab, M.T.: AWATIF: A multi-genre corpus for modern standard Arabic subjectivity and sentiment analysis. In: LREC, pp. 3907–3914. Citeseer (2012)
2. Abdulla, N., Mohammed, S., Al-Ayyoub, M., Al-Kabi, M., et al.: Automatic lexicon construction for Arabic sentiment analysis. In: Future Internet of Things and Cloud (FiCloud), International Conference on 2014, pp. 547–552. IEEE (2014)
3. Al-Ayyoub, M., Essa, S.B., Alsmadi, I.: Lexicon-based sentiment analysis of Arabic tweets. Int. J. Soc. Netw. Min. **2**(2), 101–114 (2015)
4. Al-Twairesh, N., Al-Khalifa, H., Al-Salman, A., Al-Ohali, Y.: Arasenti-tweet: a corpus for Arabic sentiment analysis of Saudi tweets. Procedia Comput. Sci. **117**, 63–72 (2017)
5. Alayba, A.M., Palade, V., England, M., Iqbal, R.: Arabic language sentiment analysis on health services. In: Arabic Script Analysis and Recognition (ASAR), 1st International Workshop on 2017, pp. 114–118. IEEE (2017)
6. AlKhateeb, J.H., Jiang, J., Ren, J., Ipson, S.: Component-based segmentation of words from handwritten Arabic text. Int. J. Comput. Syst. Sci. Eng. **5**(1), 54–58 (2009)
7. AlKhateeb, J.H., Pauplin, O., Ren, J., Jiang, J.: Performance of hidden markov model and dynamic bayesian network classifiers on handwritten Arabic word recognition. knowl.-Based Syst. **24**(5), 680–688 (2011)

8. AlKhateeb, J.H., Ren, J., Jiang, J., Al-Muhtaseb, H.: Offline handwritten Arabic cursive text recognition using hidden Markov models and re-ranking. Pattern Recogn. Lett. **32**(8), 1081–1088 (2011)
9. Aly, M., Atiya, A.: Labr: A large scale Arabic book reviews dataset. In: Proceedings of the 51st Annual Meeting of the Association for Computational Linguistics, vol. 2, pp. 494–498 (2013). (Volume 2: Short Papers)
10. Badaro, G., Baly, R., Hajj, H., Habash, N., El-Hajj, W.: A large scale arabic sentiment lexicon for Arabic opinion mining. In: Proceedings of the EMNLP 2014 Workshop on Arabic Natural Language Processing (ANLP), pp. 165–173 (2014)
11. Duwairi, R.M., Alfaqeh, M., Wardat, M., Alrabadi, A.: Sentiment analysis for arabizi text. In: Information and Communication Systems (ICICS), 7th International Conference on 2016, pp. 127–132. IEEE (2016)
12. Guellil, I., Azouaou, F.: Bilingual lexicon for algerian arabic dialect treatment in social media (2017)
13. Guellil, I., Azouaou, F., Abbas, M.: Comparison between neural and statistical translation after transliteration of algerian arabic dialect. In: WiNLP: Women and Underrepresented Minorities in Natural Language Processing (co-located withACL 2017), pp. 1–5 (2017)
14. Guellil, I., Azouaou, F., Abbas, M., Fatiha, S.: Arabizi transliteration of algerian Arabic dialect into modern standard Arabic. In: Social MT First workshop on Social Media and User Generated Content Machine Translation, pp. 1–8 2017
15. Guellil, I., Azouaou, F.: Asda: Analyseur syntaxique du dialecte alg {\'e} rien dans un but d'analyse s {\'e} mantique
16. Guellil, I., Azouaou, F.: Arabic dialect identification with an unsupervised learning (based on a lexicon) application case: algerian dialect. In: Computational Science and Engineering (CSE) and IEEE International Conference on 2016 Embedded and Ubiquitous Computing (EUC) and 15th Intl Symposium on Distributed Computing and Applications for Business Engineering (DCABES), pp. 724–731. IEEE (2016)
17. Guellil, I., Boukhalfa, K.: Social big data mining: A survey focused on opinion mining and sentiments analysis. In: Programming and Systems (ISPS), 12th International Symposium on 2015, pp. 1–10. IEEE (2015)
18. Khan, A.Z., Atique, M., Thakare, V.: Combining lexicon-based and learning-based methods for twitter sentiment analysis. Int. J. Electron. Commun. Soft Comput. Sci. Eng. (IJECSCSE) **89**, 89 (2015)
19. Le, Q., Mikolov, T.: Distributed representations of sentences and documents. In: International Conference on Machine Learning, pp. 1188–1196 (2014)
20. Maas, A.L., Daly, R.E., Pham, P.T., Huang, D., Ng, A.Y., Potts, C.: Learning word vectors for sentiment analysis. In: Proceedings of the 49th Annual Meeting of the Association for Computational Linguistics: Human language technologies, vol. 1, pp. 142–150. Association for Computational Linguistics (2011)
21. Mataoui, M., Zelmati, O., Boumechache, M.: A proposed lexicon-based sentiment analysis approach for the vernacular algerian Arabic. Res. Comput. Sci. **110**, 55–70 (2016)
22. Medhaffar, S., Bougares, F., Esteve, Y., Hadrich-Belguith, L.: Sentiment analysis of Tunisian dialects: Linguistic ressources and experiments. In: Proceedings of the Third Arabic Natural Language Processing Workshop, pp. 55–61 (2017)
23. Meftouh, K., Harrat, S., Jamoussi, S., Abbas, M., Smaili, K.: Machine translation experiments on PADIC: a parallel Arabic dialect corpus. In: The 29th Pacific Asia Conference on Language, Information and Computation, pp. 1–9 (2015)

24. Mohammad, S.M., Turney, P.D.: Crowdsourcing a word-emotion association lexicon. Comput. Intell. **29**(3), 436–465 (2013)
25. Rushdi-Saleh, M., Martín-Valdivia, M.T., Ureña-López, L.A., Perea-Ortega, J.M.: OCA: opinion corpus for Arabic. J. Assoc. Inf. Sci. Technol. **62**(10), 2045–2054 (2011)
26. Taboada, M., Brooke, J., Tofiloski, M., Voll, K., Stede, M.: Lexicon-based methods for sentiment analysis. Comput. Linguist. **37**(2), 267–307 (2011)

Self-validated Story Segmentation of Chinese Broadcast News

Wei Feng[1], Lei Xie[2(✉)], Jin Zhang[2], Yujun Zhang[1], and Yanning Zhang[2]

[1] School of Computer Science and Technology, Tianjin University, Tianjin 300350, China
{wfeng,yujunzhang}@tju.edu.cn

[2] School of Computer Science, Northwestern Polytechnical University, Xi'an 710129, China
{lxie,jzhang,ynzhang}@nwpu.edu.cn

Abstract. Automatic story segmentation is an important prerequisite for semantic-level applications. The normalized cuts (NCuts) method has recently shown great promise for segmenting English spoken lectures. However, the availability assumption of the exact story number per file significantly limits its capability to handle a large number of transcripts. Besides, how to apply such method to Chinese language in the presence of speech recognition errors is unclear yet. Addressesing these two problems, we propose a self-validated NCuts (SNCuts) algorithm for segmenting Chinese broadcast news via inaccurate lexical cues, generated by the Chinese large vocabulary continuous speech recognizer (LVCSR). Due to the specialty of Chinese language, we present a subword-level graph embedding for the erroneous LVCSR transcripts. We regularize the NCuts criterion by a general exponential prior of story numbers, respecting the principle of Occam's razor. Given the maximum story number as a general parameter, we can automatically obtain reasonable segmentations for a large number of news transcripts, with the story numbers automatically determined for each file, and with comparable complexity to alternative non-self-validated methods. Extensive experiments on benchmark corpus show that: (i) the proposed SNCuts algorithm can efficiently produce comparable or even better segmentation quality, as compared to other state-of-the-art methods with true story number as an input parameter; and (ii) the subword-level embedding always helps to recovering lexical cohesion in Chinese erroneous transcripts, thus improving both segmentation accuracy and robustness to LVCSR errors.

Keywords: Story segmentation · Self-validation · Topic detection Chinese broadcast news · Subwords · Normalized cuts

L. Xie—This work is supported by NSFC 61671325, 61572354.

J. Ren et al. (Eds.): BICS 2018, LNAI 10989, pp. 568–578, 2018.
https://doi.org/10.1007/978-3-030-00563-4_55

1 Introduction

As the explosive growth of multimedia content, there is an urgent demand for automatic organization of the massive multimedia data to facilitate efficient topic-based retrieval and analysis [7,10,15]. Hence, a well-segmented multimedia document is clearly an important *prerequisite* for various tasks of high-level semantic browsing [10]. Story segmentation aims to partition a text, audio and/or video stream into a sequence of topically coherent segments, namely stories.

Previous efforts on story segmentation have focused on topic modeling and the selection of topical boundary cues. Such as lexical chaining [17], C99 [3], latent semantic analysis (LSA) [4], etc., detect word-level semantic variations in a document via various cohesive measures, and produce local similarity minima as story boundaries. Recently, graph-theoretic approaches have shown promising potentials in segmenting natural data, such as images [6,16] and real-world discourses [12]. It has been shown that the graph embedding of linguistic units and the normalized cuts (NCuts) criterion [16] lead to effective story segmentations of English spoken lectures [12]. Our preliminary results [13,23] also showed that the NCuts approach can obtain superior performance than previous lexical-based methods [4,22] in handling subtle and ambiguous topical boundaries of Chinese broadcast news. Indeed, we prefer an automatic story segmentation approach that meets the following four requirements. *Self-validation*: it should be able to automatically determine the number of stories in a document. *Efficiency*: it should be fast enough to be able to segment a large number of documents. *Accuracy*: the segmentation result should be reasonable and as accurate as possible. *Robustness*: since the segmentation may be based on erroneous transcripts generated by LVCSR [12], it should be robust to various recognition errors.

In this paper, we study how to segment inaccurate news transcripts, transcribed from audio via LVCSR [9]. Firstly, the inevitable Chinese LVCSR errors, resulted from adverse acoustic conditions, multiple speakers and out-of-vocabulary (OOV) words, pose significant difficulties in word-level lexical story segmentation [11,23]. Secondly, the specialty of Chinese language makes previous successful methods for English story segmentation [12], not directly applicable. We propose a simple yet effective approach, namely self-validate normalized cuts (SNCuts) using subword-level graph embedding. We demonstrate the effectiveness of the proposed approach to both error-free manual transcripts and erroneous LVCSR transcripts at different error rates using two benchmark corpora.

2 Self-validated Story Segmentation

In this section, we show how to realize self-validated story segmentation for erroneous LVCSR transcripts of Chinese broadcast news. The core of our approach is: (i) a subword-level graph embedding, and (ii) a new self-validated SNCuts graph partitioning criterion.

2.1 Subword-Level Graph Embedding

The LVCSR transcript $\mathcal{T}$ of a Chinese broadcast news stream is constituted by a sequence of recognized words $\{w_1 w_2 \dots w_M\}$. Due to the inevitable LVCSR errors, we use subwords (i.e., characters/syllables subsequences), rather than the raw recognized words, to build the graph $\mathcal{G} = (\mathcal{V}, \mathcal{E})$.

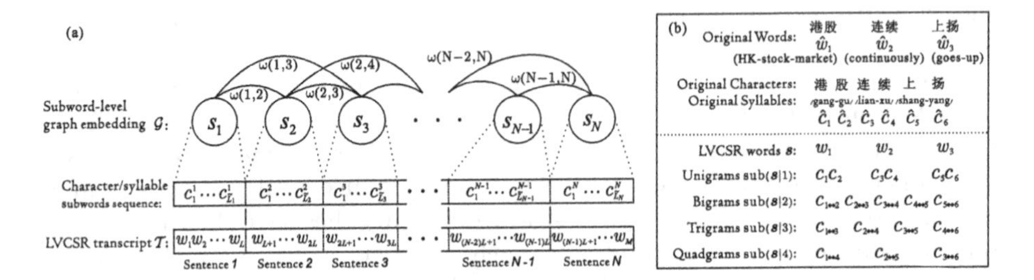

Fig. 1. Subword-level graph embedding: (a) is the subword-level graph embedding of an LVCSR transcript with cutoff distance $\tau = 2$; (b) shows an example of a Chinese sentence and the corresponding LVCSR recognized word sequence $\mathbf{s} = \{w_1 w_2 w_3\}$ and the subword-level n-gram representations $\text{sub}(\mathbf{s}|n)$ with $1 \le n \le 4$.

Node Extraction. Instead of relying on automatic Chinese sentence segmentation, we extract sentences from an LVCSR transcript as fixed number of consecutive word sequences. As shown in Fig. 1(a), we split the input LVCSR transcript $\mathcal{T} = \{w_1 w_2 \dots w_M\}$ into $N = \lceil \frac{M}{L} \rceil$ sentences $\{s_1 \dots s_N\}$ with the same number of words L. In our experiments, the sentence length L was empirically tuned based on training datasets.

For sentence $\mathbf{s}_i = \{w_1^i \dots w_L^i\}$, let $\text{comp}(\mathbf{s}_i) = \{c_1^i \dots c_{\tilde{L}_i}^i\}$ be its component characters/syllables sequence. We define the subword-level representation $\text{sub}(\mathbf{s}_i|n)$ of sentence $\mathbf{s}_i$ as the overlapping n-gram subsequence of characters/syllables:

$$\text{sub}(\mathbf{s}_i|n) = \{c_{p \leftrightarrow p+n-1}^i\}_{p=1}^{\tilde{L}_i - n+1} = \{c_{1 \leftrightarrow n}^i, c_{2 \leftrightarrow n+1}^i, c_{3 \leftrightarrow n+2}^i, \dots\}, \tag{1}$$

where $\tilde{L}_i$ is the number of subwords in sentence $\mathbf{s}_i$. $c_{p \leftrightarrow p+n-1}^i$ denotes the subwords subsequence in $\text{comp}(\mathbf{s}_i)$ starting from the pth to the $p+n-1$th subwords, can be viewed as a *subword* representation, where n refers to the number of local components used to compose a subword. The purpose of overlapping is to reduce the possibility of missing useful information and to provide more chances for partial matching. In order to maintain the finer granularity of the representation, n should not be very large. As shown in Fig. 1(b), we restricted $n \le 4$.

Edge Cutoff. To construct the weighted edge set $\mathcal{E}$, we need to choose a proper edge link range. The same topic, e.g., a breaking news, may be intermittently reported from different angles for several times in a program. In story segmentation, these discontinuous reoccurrences of the same topic should be labeled as different stories, otherwise those inbetween stories would be falsely missed. Therefore, an appropriate edge *cutoff*, properly balancing lone-term correlation and short-term discrimination, is more applicable to news story segmentation. In practice, we set up an edge cutoff value τ and simply discard those nodes-links whose distances exceed the threshold, See Fig. 1(a) for an example of the graph embedding with cutoff value $\tau = 2$.

Subwords Similarity. For two connected sentences $\mathbf{s}_i$ and $\mathbf{s}_j$ in the graph embedding, we assign the edge weight $\omega(i, j)$ as the exponential cosine similarity at subword level:

$$\omega(i,j) = \exp\big(\cos(\mathbf{f}_i, \mathbf{f}_j)\big) = \exp\Big(\frac{\mathbf{f}_i \cdot \mathbf{f}_j}{\|\mathbf{f}_i\|\|\mathbf{f}_j\|}\Big). \tag{2}$$

Note that, the n-gram representation of subwords may exponentially increase the subword vocabulary size. To make the similarity computation tractable, in practice, the subwords frequency vectors $\mathbf{f}_i$ and $\mathbf{f}_j$ are derived based on the local vocabulary $\mathcal{D}_{ij}$ instead of the global one, where the local vocabulary $\mathcal{D}_{ij}$ is composed of all the subwords occurred in $\mathrm{sub}(\mathbf{s}_i|n)$ and $\mathrm{sub}(\mathbf{s}_j|n)$.

Sentence similarities are inclined to be high within the same story and low at story boundaries. To alleviate this, in Eq. (2), we use *temporally smoothed* frequency vectors instead of the original ones to compute the sentence similarity $\tilde{\mathbf{f}}_i = \frac{1}{Z}\sum_{p=i-\frac{T}{2}}^{i+\frac{T}{2}} \exp\Big(-\frac{|p-i|}{\sigma}\Big)\mathbf{f}_p$, where σ controls the degree of smoothing, T is the size of sliding window, and Z is the constant normalization factor.

2.2 Self-validated Normalized Cuts

Dealing with multi-class tasks with different misclassification costs of classes is harder than dealing with two-class ones [5]. For a particular story number K, the dynamic programming normalized cuts(DP-NCuts) solution can efficiently produce a globally optimal K-partitioning to the input news transcript. In the next, we show how to enable the DP-NCuts method to self-validated story segmentation using the general principle of Occam's razor with reasonable complexity.

A Probabilistic Formulation. In order to seek the best segment number $\hat{K}$ and an optimal linear $\hat{K}$-labeling $\hat{X} = \{\hat{x}_1, \ldots, \hat{x}_N\}$ to each node of $\mathcal{G}$ with $\hat{x}_i \in \{1, \ldots, \hat{K}\}$, by maximizing the following posterior probability:

$$(\hat{K}, \hat{X}) = \arg\max_{K,X} \Pr(X, K \,|\, \mathcal{G}) = \arg\max_{K,X} \Pr(X \,|\, \mathcal{G}, K)\Pr(K), \tag{3}$$

where $\Pr(X, K \,|\, \mathcal{G})$ is the joint posterior likelihood of labeling X and segment number K given the observation; $\Pr(X \,|\, \mathcal{G}, K)$ measures the segmentation goodness; $\Pr(K)$ is the prior preference of story numbers. From Eq. (3), the self-validated story segmentation converts to a joint optimization problem. Due to the efficiency and efficacy of the non self-validated DP-NCuts algorithm, we simplify the formulation of self-validated labeling as:

$$(\hat{K}, \hat{X}) = \arg\max_{K} \Pr(K)\big[\arg\max_{X} \Pr(X \,|\, \mathcal{G}, K)\big] \tag{4}$$

$$= \arg\max_{K,X} \Pr(\hat{X}(K) \,|\, \mathcal{G}, K)\Pr(K), \tag{5}$$

where $\hat{X}(K) = \arg\max_X \Pr(X \mid \mathcal{G}, K)$ is the optimal K-labeling of $\mathcal{G}$, and $\Pr(\hat{X}(K) \mid \mathcal{G}, K)$ is the corresponding maximum K-labeling likelihood. Note that the joint optimization of K and X in Eq. (3) is decoupled in Eqs. (4)–(5).

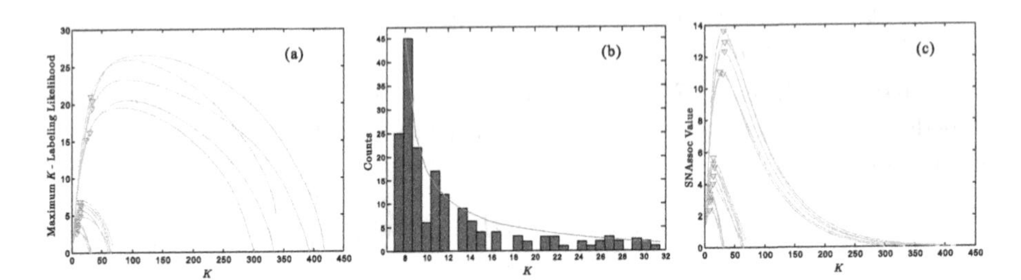

Fig. 2. Exemplar curves of K-labeling likelihood, prior of story numbers and the SNCuts score: (a) the maximum K-labeling likelihood $\Pr(\hat{X}(K) \mid \mathcal{G}, K)$ curves of TDT2 dataset; (b) the empirical histogram of TDT2 corpus and the fitted exponential distribution (red curve); (c) the SNAssoc curves of the transcripts shown in (a). The red triangles in (a) and (c) indicate the real story number for each transcript. (Color figure online)

Maximum K-Labeling Likelihood. $\Pr(\hat{X}(K) \mid \mathcal{G}, K)$ In Eq. (5), $\Pr(\hat{X}(K) \mid \mathcal{G}, K)$ indeed measures the goodness of the optimal K-segmentation of $\mathcal{G}$. We can naturally define $\Pr(\hat{X}(K) \mid \mathcal{G}, K)$ as the sum of normalized intra-sentence associations, so smaller NCuts value corresponds to better K-labeling to the $\mathcal{G}$. Thus,

$$\Pr(\hat{X}(K) \mid \mathcal{G}, K) \propto \sum_{k=1}^{K} \frac{\mathrm{assoc}(\hat{\mathbf{s}}_k)}{\mathrm{vol}(\hat{\mathbf{s}}_k)} = K - \mathrm{NCuts}\big(\hat{X}(K)\big), \tag{6}$$

where $\mathrm{assoc}(\hat{\mathbf{s}}_k)$, $\mathrm{vol}(\hat{\mathbf{s}}_k)$ indicate the association and volume of the optimal sentence $\hat{\mathbf{s}}_k$. In Eq. (6), $\mathrm{NCuts}(\hat{X}(K)) = \sum_{k=1}^{K} \mathrm{NCuts}(\hat{\mathbf{s}}_k)$ denotes the minimum NCuts value of K-segmentations of $\mathcal{G}$. There are two important properties of $\Pr(\hat{X}(K) \mid \mathcal{G}, K)$. First, a better K-labeling X to graph $\mathcal{G}$ has larger likelihood value $\Pr(X \mid \mathcal{G}, K)$. Second, as shown in Fig. 2(a), the value of $\Pr(\hat{X}(K) \mid \mathcal{G}, K)$ is quickly increases first as K becomes larger, then slowly goes down after some critical point to penalize fragmental segments in the labeling $\hat{X}(K)$.

General Exponential Prior. $\Pr(K)$ The prior probability of story number K should reflect the empirical distribution of story numbers in real data, and respect the general principle of Occam's razor [6]. As shown in Fig. 2(b), in real-world transcripts with unfixed lengths, the story number in a transcript approximately follows an exponential distribution:

$$\Pr(K) \propto \alpha^K, \quad \text{with } 0 < \alpha < 1, \tag{7}$$

where α is the scaling parameter that controls the suppression strength to the possibility of choosing larger K. We believe that such exponential prior reflects the similar fact that described by the well-known power-law distribution. The exponential prior defined in Eq. (7) has similar property of the power-law, and is empirically more suitable to the task of news story segmentation. On the other hand, the rationale of the exponential prior of K can also be explained as a natural respect to the general principle of Occam's razor, since it clearly favors smaller K and suppresses larger ones.

SNCuts Score. From Eqs. (3)–(7), we can define a new graph partitioning criterion, namely self-validated NCuts, which takes accounts of both the segmentation goodness and the labeling cost. We use the posterior energy to measure the segmentation quality. Accordingly, we define the SNCuts score of labeling X as $\mathrm{SNCuts}(X \mid \mathcal{G}) = -\log(\Pr(X, K(X) \mid \mathcal{G}))$, thus yielding

$$\begin{aligned} \mathrm{SNCuts}(X \mid \mathcal{G}) &= -\log\left(\mathrm{SNAssoc}(X \mid \mathcal{G})\right) \\ &= -\log\left(\left[K(X) - \mathrm{NCuts}(X)\right] \alpha^{K(X)}\right), \end{aligned} \tag{8}$$

where $\mathrm{SNAssoc}(X \mid \mathcal{G}) = \Pr(X \mid \mathcal{G}, K(X)) \Pr(K(X))$ indicates the posterior likelihood of labeling X. Clearly, the optimal labeling $\hat{X}$ to graph $\mathcal{G}$ corresponds to the minimum SNCuts and maximum SNAssoc value. Note that, α balances the relative importance of segmentation goodness and the log labeling cost in the energy function of Eq. (8). Figure 2(c) shows that with an appropriate scaling parameter α, the real story numbers $\hat{K}$ approximately coincide with the points of maximum SNAssoc and minimum SNCuts values.

3 Experiments

3.1 Corpus and Experimental Setup

We carry out the experiments on two benchmark Mandarin broadcast news corpora, TDT2 [19] and CCTV [1]. The TDT2 Mandarin corpus [19] contains about 53 h of VOA Chinese broadcast news audio (177 recordings in total) from Feb to June, 1998. We separate the corpus into two non-overlapping subsets: a training set of 90 recordings (1321 boundaries) for parameter tuning, and a test set of 87 recordings (1262 boundaries) for evaluation. The CCTV corpus records 71 news episodes of 27 h of CCTV (i.e., China Central Television) Mandarin broadcast news from July to Dec, 2007. Due to the particular news production rules of CCTV, we further label CCTV news stories as either detailed ('-f') or brief ('-s') ones. Similar to TDT2, we separate the CCTV corpus into a training set with 40 audio files (1209 story boundaries) and a test set with 31 audio files (892 story boundaries). Accord with the TDT2 convention [14], we consider a detected story boundary on CCTV corpus as being correct if it lies in a K-word-length tolerance window on each side of the exact boundary position ($K = 10$ for brief stories, and $K = 30$ for detailed stories).

In all our experiments, we assess story segmentation accuracy using the F1-measure, i.e., $\frac{2 \cdot \mathrm{Recall} \cdot \mathrm{Precision}}{\mathrm{Recall} + \mathrm{Precision}}$. For a particular word or subword level, we use two forms to represent a news transcript $\mathcal{T}$: (1) the sequence of Chinese characters (denoted by char for short) and (2) the sequence of base-syllables (denoted by syll).

3.2 Comparison to State-of-the-Art Methods

We use TDT2 corpus to compare the proposed SNCuts approach with nine state-of-the-art story segmentation methods: (1) TextTiling (TT) [8]; (2) latent semantic analysis (LSA) [4]; (3) LSA-TextTiling (LSA-TT) [22]; (4) lexical chains (LC) [2]; (5) conditional random field (CRF) [20]; (6) maximum lexical cohesion (MLC) [11]; (7) LE-TextTiling (LE-TT) [21]; (8) spectral clustering (SC) [21]; (9) LE-DP [21]. To maintain the fairness of comparison, for all competing methods, we compare the best segmentation results reported by their authors. On CCTV corpus, besides comparing the best segmentation accuracy, we further investigate the behavior and sensitivity of different methods for erroneous transcripts with increasing ASR error rates.

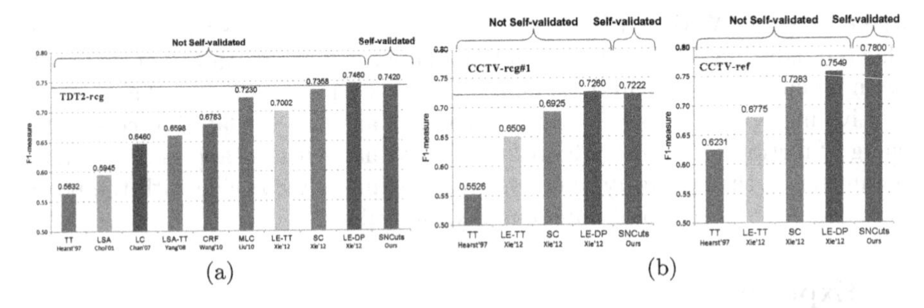

Fig. 3. Comparative best performance of the proposed SNCuts approach and state-of-the-art story segmentation methods on (a) TDT2-rcg dataset, (b) CCTV-rcg#1 dataset (left) and CCTV-ref dataset (right).

Figure 3(a) shows that almost all existing story segmentation methods are not self-validated, which is a major drawback. Besides self-validation, the proposed SNCuts approach has achieved the second highest accuracy and is only 0.004 less than the highest one on TDT2-rcg dataset. As shown in Fig. 3(b), on CCTV-rcg#1, SNCuts has also obtained the second highest accuracy with 0.0038 disparity to the best one; and on CCTV-ref, SNCuts has achieved the highest F1-measure 0.78 that is 0.0251 higher than the second best one.

In Table 1, we compare the relative degradation ratio of different methods (with valid reported performance) for transcripts with increasing ASR errors. We can see that for all methods, increasing ASR errors may degrade their segmentation accuracy. On CCTV-rcg#1, both SNCuts and NCuts exhibit more robustness to ASR errors than TextTiling (TT) [8]. LE-DP [21] has the lowest degradation ratio on CCTV-rcg#1. But due to the lack of results on CCTV-rcg#2 and CCTV-rcg#3 [21], we cannot further check its robustness for higher ASR error rates. SNCuts has obtained comparable degradation ratio to NCuts.

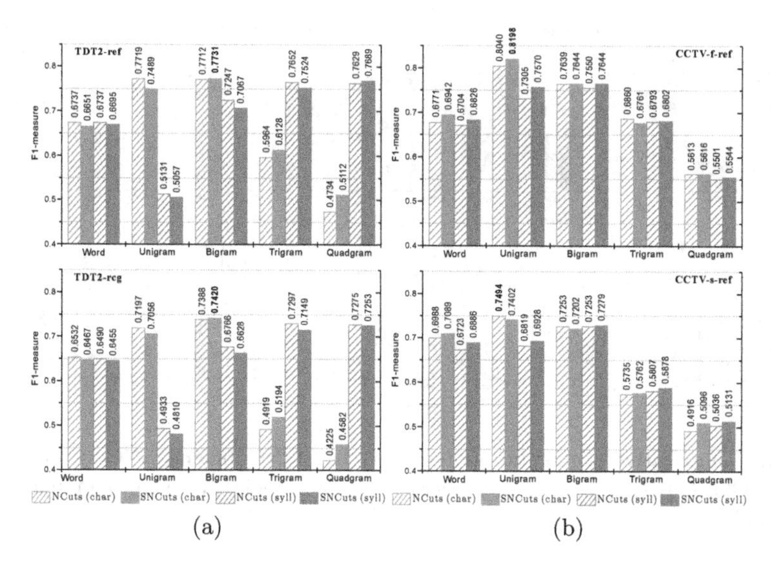

Fig. 4. Comparative segmentation performance of NCuts and SNCuts on (a) TDT2 corpus, (b) CCTV-ref. Best accuracies are shown in red. (Color figure online)

3.3 SNCuts Vs. NCuts

Since our SNCuts is a self-validated extension to the NCuts criterion, we specifically interest in comparing their *best* capabilities in story segmentation on different datasets. For this purpose, we first use TDT2 and CCTV training sets to individually seek the best parameters with the highest average F1-measure, and then compare their accuracies on test sets. For comparison fairness, we conduct automatic parameter-tuning using the Differential Evolution (DE) algorithm [18] with the same (reasonably large enough) number of generations and the same proper parameters ranges.

Accuracy. We first evaluate the segmentation accuracy. As shown in Fig. 4(a), for both TDT2-ref and TDT2-rcg, the best accuracies are achieved by SNCuts using Bigram (char) representation. In some cases (e.g., for n-gram subwords with $n \geq 2$), the NCuts algorithm [12,23] fed by the true story number K may result in worse segmentation than SNCuts does. This is mainly due to an inherent limitation of NCuts criterion that tends to generate false-positive segmentation boundaries and miss correct ones [6]. As validated by our experiments, besides self-validation, SNCuts also helps to amend the inherent limitation of NCuts criterion.

Figures 4(b) and 5 respectively show the detailed best segmentation results of SNCuts and NCuts at every word/subword-level via either 'char' or 'syll' representations on CCTV-rcg datasets with increasing ASR error rates. Similarly, at some particular levels, SNCuts can even outperform NCuts with the correct story number K as an input parameter. And, in most cases, SNCuts can achieve comparable accuracy with NCuts.

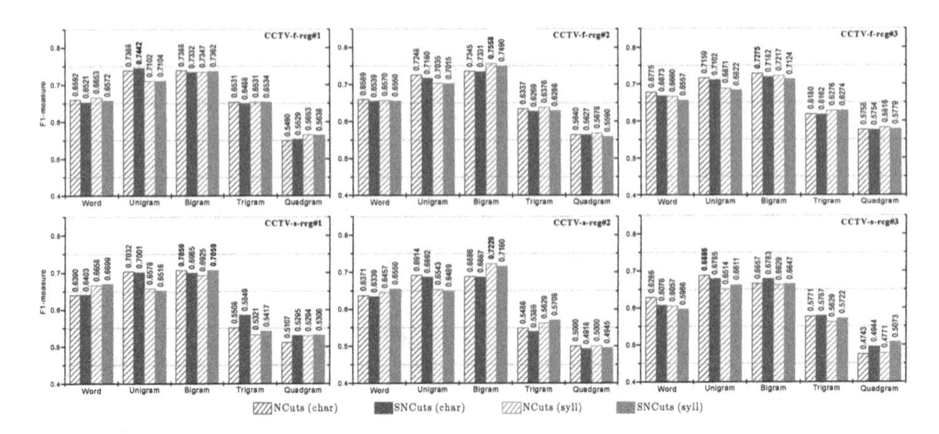

Fig. 5. Comparative segmentation performance of NCuts and SNCuts on CCTV-rcg#1, CCTV-rcg#2, and CCTV-rcg#3. Best accuracies are shown in red. (Color figure online)

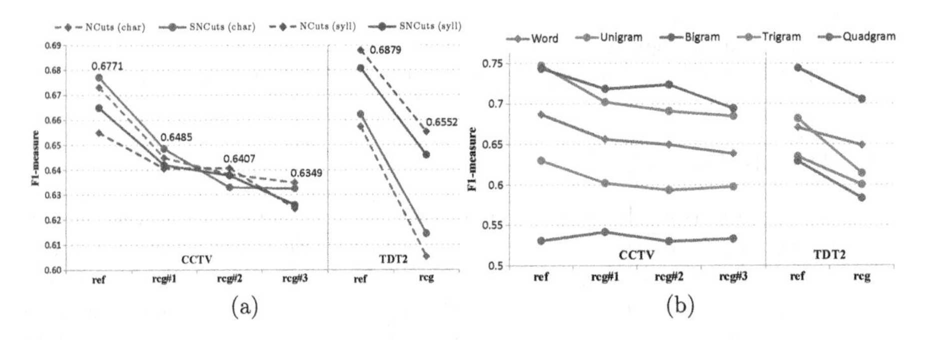

Fig. 6. Influence of ASR errors on story segmentation performance. (a) Mean segmentation accuracy of NCuts and SNCuts on CCTV and TDT2 corpora. (b) Average story segmentation accuracy for different word/subword-levels on CCTV and TDT2 corpora.

Influence of ASR Errors. Figure 6(a) compares the average segmentation accuracy of NCuts and SNCuts for benchmark datasets with increasing ASR error rates. Averagely speaking, both mean segmentation accuracies and the degradation ratios of NCuts and SNCuts are comparable. Specifically, on CCTV corpus, SNCuts (char) obtained the best accuracy for low ASR errors, and SNCuts (syll) performed the best for higher ASR errors. On TDT2 corpus, NCuts (syll) achieved the highest mean accuracy; and for 'char' representation, SNCuts performed better than NCuts. We then evaluate the robustness of word/subword-levels to ASR errors in Fig. 6(b). The degradation effect of ASR error is also evident. Among all word/subword-levels, bigram and unigram performed the best for CCTV corpus; while for TDT2 corpus, bigram evidently outmatched the other levels. On both corpora, we can clearly see the robustness of subword representations to ASR errors.

Table 1. Comparison of best segmentation accuracy (Acc.) and relative degradation (Degrad.) ratio of different methods on CCTV corpus. For each dataset, the best accuracy is in red font.

Approach	CCTV-ref	CCTV-rcg#1		CCTV-rcg#2		CCTV-rcg#3	
	Acc.	Acc.	Degrad. ratio	Acc.	Degrad. ratio	Acc.	Degrad. ratio
TT [8]	0.6231	0.5526	11.31%	-	-	-	-
LE-TT [21]	0.6775	0.6509	3.93%	-	-	-	-
SC [21]	0.7283	0.6925	4.92%	-	-	-	-
LE-DP [21]	0.7549	0.7260	3.83%	-	-	-	-
NCuts	0.7767	0.7224	6.99%	0.7393	4.82%	0.7023	9.85%
SNCuts	0.7800	0.7222	7.41%	0.7325	6.09%	0.6983	10.47%

4 Conclusions

In this paper, we have proposed a simple yet effective approach, namely n-gram subword SNCuts, to accurately segmenting Chinese broadcast news via inaccurate lexical cues. Our approach can automatically determine the story number, and can properly take care of inter- and intra-story similarity. Extensive experiments have validated that our approach can achieve comparable or better accuracy to state-of-the-art non-self-validated methods on benchmark corpora.

Besides accuracy and efficiency, self-validation is also an important requirement in segmentation, especially in the era of Big Data, to automatically handle huge number of media data. At last, we believe properly encoding soft similarity measurements in the classical cosine similarity may further improve the segmentation performance.

References

1. CCTV Corpus: Story segmentation and topic detection of CCTV Mandarin broadcast news (2010)
2. Chan, S.K., Xie, L., Meng, H.M.L.: Modeling the statistical behavior of lexical chains to capture word cohesiveness for automatic story segmentation. In: INTERSPEECH, pp. 2408–2411 (2007)
3. Choi, F.: Advances in domain independent linear text segmentation. In: NAACL, pp. 26–33 (2000)
4. Choi, F., Wiemer-Hastings, P., Moore, J.: Latent semantic analysis for story segmentation. In: EMNLP (2001)
5. Feng, W., Huang, W., Ren, J.: Class imbalance ensemble learning based on the margin theory. Appl. Sci. **8**(5), 815 (2018)
6. Feng, W., Jia, J., Liu, Z.Q.: Self-validated labeling of Markov random fields for image segmentation. IEEE Trans. Pattern Anal. Mach. Intell. **32**(10), 1871–1887 (2010)
7. Guo, Q., Sun, S., Ren, X., Dong, F., Gao, B.Z., Feng, W.: Freqeuncy-tuned active contour model. Neurocomputing **275**(31), 2307–2316 (2018)

8. Hearst, M.: TextTiling: segmentation text into multi-paragraph subtopic passages. Comput. Linguist. **23**(1), 33–64 (1997)
9. Kyoto University: Multipurpose large vocabulary continuous speech recognition engine - Julius (rev 3.2) (2001)
10. Lee, L.S., Chen, B.: Spoken document understanding and organization. IEEE Signal Process. Mag. **22**(5), 42–60 (2005)
11. Liu, Z., Xie, L., Feng, W.: Maximum lexical cohesion for fine-grained news story segmentation. In: INTERSPEECH (2010)
12. Malioutov, I., Barzilay, R.: Minimum cut model for spoken lecture segmentation. In: ACL, pp. 25–32 (2006)
13. Nie, X., Feng, W., Wan, L., Xie, L.: Measuring similarity by contextual word connections in Chinese news story segmentation. In: ICASSP (2013)
14. NIST: The topic detection and tracking phase 2 (TDT2) evaluation plan, version 35 (1998)
15. Ren, J., Jiang, J.: Hierarchical modeling and adaptive clustering for real-time summarization of rush videos. IEEE Trans. Multimed. **11**(5), 906–917 (2009)
16. Shi, J., Malik, J.: Normalized cuts and image segmentation. IEEE Trans. Pattern Anal. Mach. Intell. **22**(8), 888–905 (2000)
17. Stokes, N., Carthy, J., Smeaton, A.: SeLeCT: a lexical cohesion based news story segmentation system. J. AI Commun. **17**(1), 3–12 (2004)
18. Storn, R., Price, K.: Differential evolution - a simple and efficient heuristic for global optimization over continuous spaces. J. Glob. Optim. **11**, 341–359 (1997)
19. TDT2 Corpus: Topic detection and tracking phase 2, July 2000. http://projects.ldc.upenn.edu/TDT2/
20. Wang, X., Xie, L., Ma, B., Chng, E.S., Li, H.: Modeling broadcast news prosody using conditional random fields for story segmentation. In: APSIPA ASC (2010)
21. Xie, L., Zheng, L., Liu, Z., Zhang, Y.: Laplacian Eigenmaps for automatic story segmentation of broadcast news. IEEE Trans Audio Speech Lang. Process. **20**(1), 264–277 (2012)
22. Yang, Y., Xie, L.: Subword latent semantic analysis for texttiling-based automatic story segmentation of Chinese broadcast news. In: ISCSLP, pp. 358–361 (2008)
23. Zhang, J., Xie, L., Feng, W., Zhang, Y.: A subword normalized cut approach to automatic story segmentation of Chinese broadcast news. In: Lee, G.G., Song, D., Lin, C.-Y., Aizawa, A., Kuriyama, K., Yoshioka, M., Sakai, T. (eds.) AIRS 2009. LNCS, vol. 5839, pp. 136–148. Springer, Heidelberg (2009). https://doi.org/10.1007/978-3-642-04769-5_12

Improved Big Data Analytics Solution Using Deep Learning Model and Real-Time Sentiment Data Analysis Approach

Chun-I Philip Chen[1](✉) and Jiangbin Zheng[2]

[1] College of Engineering and Computer Science, California State University, Fullerton, USA
chuchen@fullerton.edu

[2] School of Software and Microelectronics, Northwestern Polytechnical University, Xi'an, China
zhengjb@nwpu.edu.cn

Abstract. Deep Learning has been considered as an effective tool for Big Data Analytics due to its capabilities of dealing with massive amounts of complex structured and unstructured data. Deep Learning has recently come to play a significant role in solutions for Big Data Analytics. The Sentiment Analysis is also considered the most effective tool for performing the real-time analytics to know "what is really happening now" queries.

This paper studies the method that integrated the Deep Learning Model with a Real-Time Sentiment Analysis technique to perform predictive analytics that could improve the outcomes of the Big Data Analytics solution for an informed decision-making process. A proof of concept project on Stock Market Prediction System was developed to demonstrate the real value of our approach for an improved Big Data Analytics solution.

Keywords: Big data analytics · Machine learning · Deep learning
Neural network model · Sentiment analysis

1 Introduction

Big Data Analytics has been a 'hot topic' for industry and academic during the past few years. Big data analytics examines large amounts of data to uncover previously hidden patterns, correlations and make highly accurate predictions from structured and unstructured information using machine learning algorithms. Organizations will use real-time analysis of current activity to anticipate what will be likely to happen and identify the drivers of various business outcomes, so they can make the strategic decision wisely.

This paper studies the method that integrated the Deep Learning Model with a Real-Time Sentiment Analysis technique to perform predictive analytics that could improve the outcomes of Big Data Analytics solution for an informed decision-making process. A proof of concept project on Stock Market Prediction System was developed to demonstrate the real value of our approach for an improved Big Data Analytics solution.

J. Ren et al. (Eds.): BICS 2018, LNAI 10989, pp. 579–588, 2018.
https://doi.org/10.1007/978-3-030-00563-4_56

2 Literature Review

2.1 Big Data and Big Data Analytics

Big Data is defined as large and complex data sets that are generated from internal and external sources of the organization, including systems, users, applications and sensor. Big Data consists of four characteristics (4 Vs); (1) Volume: the size of data generated is very large, and it goes from terabytes to petabytes; (2) Velocity: Data grows continuously at an exponential rate; (3) Variety: data are generated in different forms; structured, semi-structured, and unstructured data, which require new techniques that can handle data heterogeneously and (4) Value: the challenge in Big Data is to identify what is valuable so as to be able to capture, transform, and extract data for analysis.

De Mauro et al. [1] proposed a new definition of "Big Data" which reads as "Big Data is the Information asset characterized by such a High Volume, Velocity and Variety to require specific Technology and Analytical Methods for its transformation into Value". Thus, Big Data requires a new generation of technologies and architectures designed to extract value economically from very large volumes of a wide variety of data by enabling high-velocity capture, discovery and analysis. Data has many hidden "value". Big Data use ranges of data mining and machine learning algorithm techniques to derive "value" from data for decision making and competitive advantages.

What is Big Data Analytics? Big Data Analytics is the process of analyzing Big Data to provide past, current, and future statistics and useful insights that can be used to make better business decisions [2]. Big Data Analytics stands for the processing of large sets of data to derive some meaningful and actionable knowledge. This knowledge can be in the form of patterns, correlations or useful insights which can help an organization understand the current market trends, customer preferences, and new opportunities. The process of examining large amounts of structured and unstructured data to uncover hidden patterns, unknown corrections and other useful and actionable information.

There are four types of Big Data Analytics. See Fig. 1.

Descriptive Analytics: Descriptive Analytics which use data aggregation and data mining to provide insight into the past and answer: "What has happened?"

Diagnostic Analytics: Diagnostic Analytics are used for discovery or to determine "why did it happen?". It can be useful for identifying and validating a causal relationship between two events as part of diagnostics analytics.

Predictive Analytics: The Predictive Analytics uses statistical models and forecasts techniques to understand the future and answer: "what is likely to happen?"

Prescriptive Analytics: Prescriptive Analytics, which use optimization and simulation algorithms to advise on possible outcomes and answer: "What should we do?"

Machine Learning and Deep Learning. "Machine learning is the training of a model from data that generalizes a decision against a performance measure." – Jason Brownlee [4]. A "concept" is a set of objects, symbols, or events grouped together

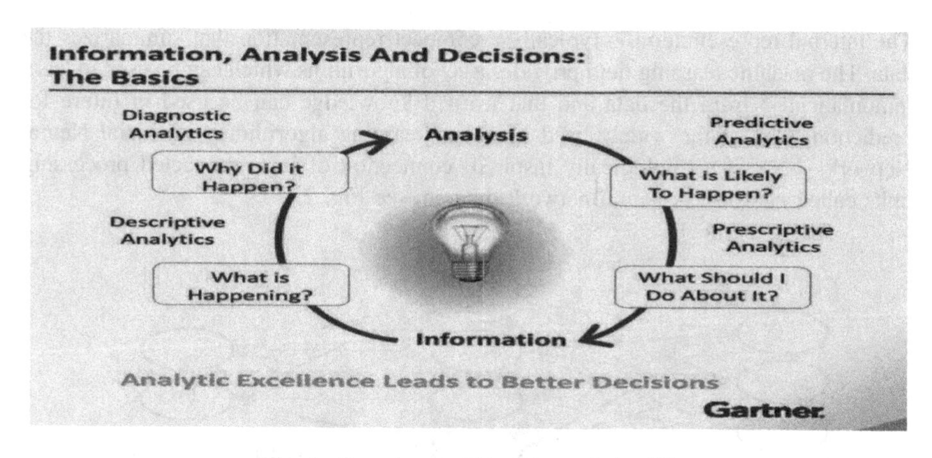

Fig. 1. Four types of big data analytics [3]

because they share certain characteristics, Such as "Pattern". Computers are good at learning "concepts" or "pattern". The concepts are the output of a data mining session. Thus, we could train the computer to learn a model from labeled training data that allows us to make predictions about unknown data. There are two kinds of common used Machine Learnings; Supervised and Unsupervised.

Supervised Learning. Supervised learning deals with training algorithms with labeled data, inputs for which the outcome or target variables are known, and then predicting the outcome (target) with the trained model for unseen future data [5]. For example, historical e-mail data will have individual e-mails marked as ham (not-spam) or spam; this data is then used for training a model that can predict future e-mails as ham or spam. Supervised learning problems can be broadly divided into two major areas, classification and regression.

Unsupervised Learning. Unsupervised learning is about analyzing the data and discovering hidden structures in unlabeled data [11]. Unsupervised learning refers to techniques with finding relationships and patterns in the data without any labeled training data set. For example, Amazon uses a machine learning technique called collaborative filtering, to determine which products users will like based on their history and similarity to other users. The "clustering" and "Associations" algorithms are typical examples of unsupervised learning.

Deep Learning = Deep + Learning

Deep learning is a class of methods and techniques that employ artificial neural networks with multiple layers of increasingly richer functionality. Major classes of deep neural networks include feed-forward networks with convolution and pooling layers. They have no notion of sequence and inputs and outputs are assumed independent. In contrast, in recurrent and recursive neural networks outputs are dependent on the previous states of the computation.

Learning - The process of Learning is to take prior knowledge and data and to create an internal representation (knowledge base) that can be used by the agent to act.

The internal representation is typically a compact representation that summarizes the data. The machine learning field provides a set of algorithms which can be used to learn (automatically) from the data and that learned knowledge can be used in future for prediction. One of the widely used Machine Learning algorithm is Artificial Neural Network, ANN is a (biologically inspired) connection of inter-connected processing units called neurons. A neural network diagram see Fig. 2.

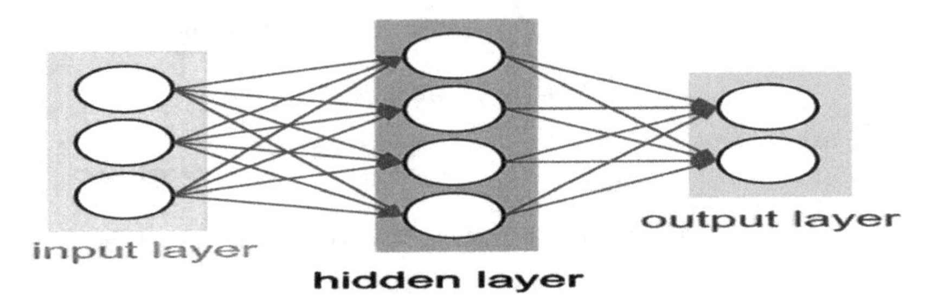

Fig. 2. A neural network diagram [6].

2.2 Deep Learning for Big Data Analytics Solutions

In this digitalized world, we are dealing with enormous data from multiple sources known as big data. The biggest challenges in Big Data Analytics is to extract complex patterns from the massive volume of data. Deal with these big data can be supported by Deep Learning capabilities, especially its ability of dealing with both the labeled and unlabeled data often collected abundantly in Big Data [7]. The key benefit of Deep Learning is the analysis and learning of massive amounts of unsupervised data, making it a valuable tool for big data analytics solutions [8].

2.3 Real-Time Sentiment Analysis for Big Data Analytics

It's software for automatically extracting opinions, emotions and sentiments in text. It allows us to track attitudes and feelings on the web. People write blog posts, comments, reviews and tweets about all sorts of different topics. We can track products, brands and people for example and determine whether they are viewed positively or negatively on the web.

This opinion or "sentiment" data, generated through social channels in the form of reviews, chats, shares, like tweets, etc., often includes comments that can be invaluable for businesses looking to improve products and services, make more informed decisions, and better promote their brands.

The key to Big Data Analytics for business success with sentiment data lies in the ability to mine vast stores of unstructured social data for actionable insights.

3 Designing a Stock Market Prediction System Uses Deep Learning Model and Sentiment Analysis

To demonstrate our approach for an improved big data analytics solution, we design a stock prediction system which integrated a Deep Learning Model with a social sentiment analysis dashboard.

3.1 Project Introduction

Predictive modeling is the process by which a model is created or chosen to try to best predict the probability of an outcome. Being considered as one of the most common data mining tasks, it involves the process of taking historical data, identifying patterns in the data that are seen though some methodology and then using the model to make predictions about what will happen in the future [12]. There has been a lot of research done on the predictive power of neural networks in carrying out prediction tasks. In our project we use a multilayer perceptron (MLP) neural network model for predicting stock markets.

Companies need to be aware of what is said about them in the public sphere as it may impact them either positively or negatively and have a direct influence on their values in the stock market thus impacting on either gaining returns or losing their investment's value. Use of sentiment analysis models on social media news as a predictive factor for prices in stock exchange companies would also be essential in knowing the mood and sentiment factor of companies and thus inform investors/traders on the company sentiment portrayal by the public as a considerable factor in forming decisions on which company to invest in.

The purpose of this project is to demonstrate and prove our approach using predictive analysis and integrating with real-time sentiment analysis that could improve a decision-making process significantly based on the outcomes of the big data analytics.

3.2 Project Design Methodology

For our project we use Python, which contains the main business logic. We also use Python libraries like Tweepy, Numpy, Pandas, TextBlob and TkInter.

On the implementation side, we have used twitter API for fetching tweets and analyzing sentiment i.e. positive, negative or neutral. For stock prediction, we have used Multilayer perceptron model which is a deep learning model.

Data Analysis and Model Used

Though deep neural networks have been proven to be very powerful, creating an optimum network is an arduous task. The performance of the network is markedly dependent upon its width (number of neurons per layer), depth (number of hidden layers), and activation function, training algorithm, feature set and input data. This section will shed some light on our proposed model to predict stock using MLP. Multilayer Perceptron (MLP) Neural Network MLP consists of a network of densely connected neurons between adjoining layers (See Fig. 3). One of the peculiarities of Feed Forward Neural Networks is that the output of one layer is never fed back to the previous layers. The input which goes to every neuron is the weighted sum of all the outputs from the previous layer of the neural network. The conversion of this input into the output is performed by a continuous and differentiable activation function. The output of one pass is produced after the signals propagate from the input to the output layer. The error for the pass is calculated, for regression it is usually root mean squared error or mean squared error [9]. The learning algorithm, generally a kind of gradient descent algorithm, adjusts the weights of the neurons necessary to reduce the error. The data is passed to the model several times to adjust the weights to reduce the errors until the preset number of epochs is reached.

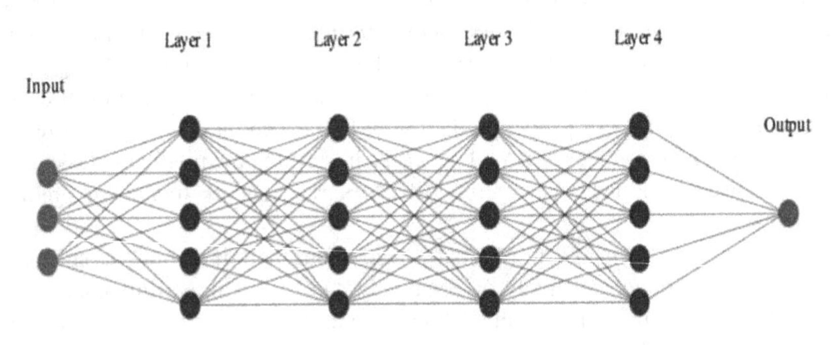

Fig. 3. MLP architecture [10].

Training and Test Data Preparation
The dataset we have is in the form of .csv file imported through the Google Finance API. We have used Google finance sample data from April 2017 to August 2017 for fortune 500 companies. (Total Number of records, 41266 rows). The dataset has been divided into training data, (80%), April, 2017 to July, 2017, 33013 rows, and test data, (20%), August, 2017, Total size of test data: 8253 rows. Indexes and stocks are arranged in wide format in a .csv file.

Placeholders. We create an abstract representation of the model using placeholders and variables. In order to fit our model we needed two placeholders: X contains the network's inputs (the stock prices of all S&P 500 constituents at time T = t) and Y the network's outputs (the index value of the S&P 500 at time T = t + 1). The inputs are a 2-dimensional matrix and the output is a 1-dimensional vector.

Variables. Apart from placeholders, variables are also important in the TensorFlow universe. Placeholders store input and target data in the graph, while variables are flexible containers that are allowed to change during graph execution. Our model consists of four hidden layers (See Fig. 3). The first layer consists 1024 neurons which is slightly more than double the size of inputs. Subsequent layers are half the size of the previous layer i.e. it contains 512, 256 and 128 neurons respectively. Number of neurons is reduced so that the information that the network identifies is compressed.

The Multilayer Perceptron model that we used here, each layer passes its output as an input to the next layer.

Network Architecture Design

In this the placeholders (data) and the variables (weights and biases) need to be combined into a system of sequential matrix multiplications. Furthermore, hidden layers are transformed by activation functions which introduce non-linearity to the system. We have used ReLU (Rectified Linear Unit) as an activation function for this model.

The model consists of three major building blocks. The input layer, the hidden layers and the output layer. This architecture is called a feedforward network. Feedforward indicates that the batch of data solely flows from left to right.

Cost Function

The cost function of the network is used to calculate the deviation of the network's predictions from the actual observed value. Mean Squared error computes the average squared deviation between predictions and targets.

Model Fitting

The model training is done in mini batches. In this random data sample of n = batch size are drawn from the training data and is fed into the network. The training dataset, then gets divided into n/batch size batches that are fed into the network sequentially. The placeholders X and Y store the input and target data and present them to the network as inputs and targets.

A sampled data batch of X flows through the network until it reaches the output layer. There, TensorFlow compares the model predictions against the actual observed targets Y in the current batch. Afterwards, TensorFlow conducts an optimization step and updates the network parameters, corresponding to the selected learning scheme. After having updated the weights and biases, the next batch is sampled and the process is repeated. The procedure continues until all batches have been presented to the network. One full sweep over all batches is called an epoch.

We evaluated network's predictions on the test data which is not learned, but is set aside for every 5th batch and visualize it.

4 Project Results and Discussion

4.1 Sentiment Analysis Result

Here we enter the company symbol to get social sentiment. A Browser window opens with Kibana dashboard loaded and running. The dashboard updates itself every 5 s with the new Sentiment Analyzed data sent by the Python code.

On touching the components of the dashboard, we can get additional information. The values keep getting updated and with updated values we get to observe changes in the Visualizations.

The Sentiment Dashboard Visualization has two sections:

A section displays a list of positive and negative tweets on the word (company name) which make these classifications Circle has the separation based on a broader range of Positive, Negative and Neutral.

A section show bar Chart which displays a list of positive and negative tweets on the words which make these classifications hashtags. When we hover the mouse over the sections we get information in percentage of a particular range e.g. Positive 60%.

Apart from the Total positive, negative and Natural percentages shown on the Pie chart, we have other components which cover Trend line for Positive, Negative and Neutral Sentiments based on the time and a majority components of both categories hashtags (See Fig. 4).

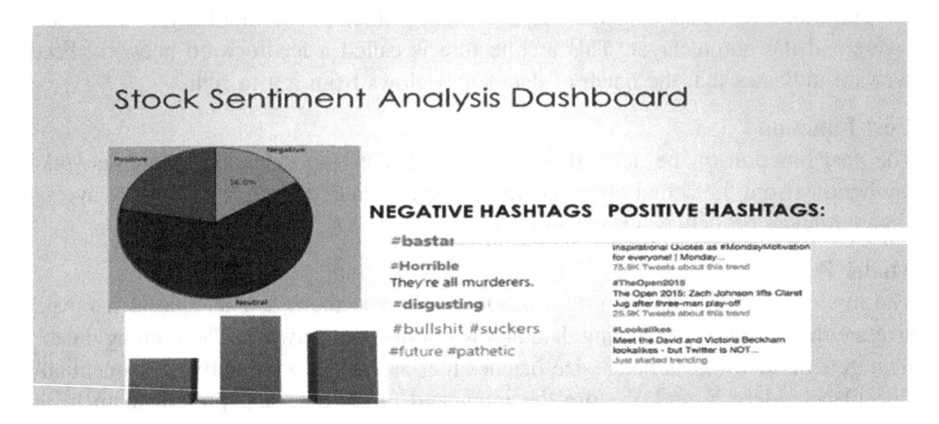

Fig. 4. Stock sentiment analysis dashboard.

4.2 Stock Prediction Result

In this study we observe the relation between the number of epochs and the graph. Our model learns the shape and location of the time series in the test data and is able to produce a somewhat accurate prediction after 19 epochs (See Fig. 5). The blue line denotes the actual value and the green denotes the predicted value of the stocks.

The final test MSE equals 0.00078 (it is very low, because the target is scaled). The mean absolute percentage error of the forecast on the test set is equal to 5.31% which is pretty good. Below are the screenshots of the visualizations:

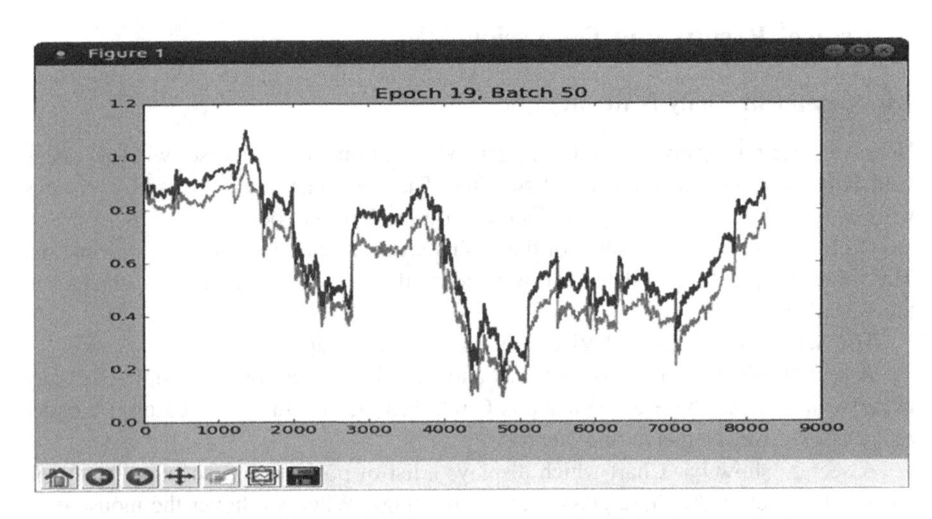

Fig. 5. Actual vs. predicted value at epoch 19. (Color figure online)

5 Conclusion and Future Work

The predictive analysis using Deep Learning model could dramatically improve the accuracy of the prediction. However, Machine Learning or deep learning model can learn on their own, but only by recognizing patterns in large datasets and making decisions based on similar situations. Machine Learning is dependent on large amounts of data to be able to predict outcomes. If there are few or no structured inputs to extract patterns, Machine Learning systems can't solve a new problem or situation that has no apparent relation to its prior knowledge. The new problem or situation such as stock price could be influenced by new, unexpected economic policy, product defects, legal disputes or bad news media coverages about the company that might not be detected as a new pattern until it has collected enough instances from a large amount of data. Since there's a strong correlation exists between the rise and falls in stock prices with the public sentiments in tweets [13], Integrating the predictive analytics and real-time sentiment analysis, could eventually help to make a better decision strategically and effectively on buying or selling stocks upon reviewing the results from the sentiment analysis for a selected company in addition to the predictive analytics.

In this project, we calculated the sentiment score of tweets using the sentiment analyzer for a given company and developed a deep neural network model called Multilayer Perceptron model to predict the future stock price. Our project provided descriptive and predictive analytics simultaneously whereby investors can use this prediction model to predict future stock market trend based on historic data while at the same time get live insights about the current stock trends for a better informed decision on purchasing or selling stocks influenced by a real-time sentiment data analysis.

As a result of building a stock market prediction system using Deep Learning model and integrated with a real-time social sentiment analysis dashboard could thus make more informed decisions for an improved Big Data Prediction Analytics solution.

This study was based on numeric data input to the Deep Learning Model with text contents extractions on the real-time sentiment analysis for an improved decision solution of the big data analytics application. Future research may consider extending to non-structured data, such as videos and images which extracts and integrated hybrid features from videos using Deep Learning Model [14, 15] and sensing images [16] on broader data extractions from the real world big data, structured and non-structured, using Deep Learning Models for an ultimate goal of providing more effective Big Data Analytics solutions.

References

1. De Mauro, A., Greco, M., Grimaldi, M.: A formal definition of big data based on its essential features. Libr. Rev. **65**(3), 122–135 (2016)
2. Ankam, V.: Big Data Analytics. Packt Publishing, Birmingham (2016)
3. Corcoran, M.: The Five Types of Analytics. http://www.informationbuilders.es/sites/www.informationbuilders.com/files/intl/co.uk/presentations/four_types_of_analytics.pdf?redir=true. Accessed 1 May 2018
4. Gollapudi, S.: Practical Machine Learning. Packt Publishing, Birmingham (2016)

5. Tiwary, C.: Learning Apache Mahout. Packt Publishing, Birmingham (2015)
6. Kashyap, A.: Neural Networks for Decision Boundary in Python! https://medium.com/ml-algorithms/neural-networks-for-decision-boundary-in-python-b243440fb7d1. Accessed 5 Nov 2018
7. Elaraby, N.M., Elmogy, M., Barakat, S.: Deep learning: effective tool for big data analytics. Int. J. Comput. Sci. Eng. (IJCSE) **5**, 254–262 (2016)
8. Najafabadi, M.M., Villanustre, F., Khoshgoftaar, T.M., et al.: Deep learning applications and challenges in big data analytics. J. Big Data **2**, 1–21 (2015)
9. Khare, K., Darekar, O., et al.: Short term stock price prediction using deep learning. In: Recent Trends in Electronics, Information and Communication Technology, pp. 482–486 (2017)
10. Vargas, M.R., de Lima, B.S.L.P., Evsukoff, A.G.: Deep learning for stock market prediction from financial news articles. In: Computational Intelligence and Virtual Environments for Measurement Systems and Applications (CIVEMSA), pp. 60–65 (2017)
11. Kaluža, B.: Machine Learning in Java. Packt Publishing, Birmingham (2016)
12. Ondieki, A.R., Okeyo, G.O., Kibe, A.: Stock price prediction using neural network models based on tweets sentiment scores. J. Comput. Sci. Appl. **5**, 64–75 (2017)
13. Liu, V., Banea, C., et al.: Grounded emotions. In: 7th International Conference on Affective Computing and Intelligent Interaction, pp. 477–483 (2017)
14. Wang, Z., et al.: A deep-learning based feature hybrid framework for spatiotemporal saliency detection inside videos. Neurocomputing **287**, 68–83 (2018)
15. Ren, J., Jiang, J.: Hierarchical modeling and adaptive clustering for real-time summarization of rush videos. IEEE Trans. Multimed. **11**(5), 906–917 (2009)
16. Han, J., et al.: Object detection in optical remote sensing images based on weakly supervised learning and high-level feature learning. IEEE Trans. Geosci. Remote Sens. **53**(6), 3325–3337 (2015)

A Semi-supervised Corpus Annotation for Saudi Sentiment Analysis Using Twitter

Abdulrahman Alqarafi[1,2], Ahsan Adeel[1(✉)], Ahmed Hawalah[2], Kevin Swingler[1], and Amir Hussain[1]

[1] CogBID Lab, Department of Computing Science and Mathematics, University of Stirling, Stirling FK9 4LA, UK
ahsan.adeel@gcu.ac.uk
[2] University of Taibah, Medina, Saudi Arabia

Abstract. In the literature, limited work has been conducted to develop sentiment resources for Saudi dialect. The lack of resources such as dialectical lexicons and corpora are some of the major bottlenecks to the successful development of Arabic sentiment analysis models. In this paper, a semi-supervised approach is presented to construct an annotated sentiment corpus for Saudi dialect using Twitter. The presented approach is primarily based on a list of lexicons built by using word embedding techniques such as word2vec. A huge corpus extracted from twitter is annotated and manually reviewed to exclude incorrect annotated tweets which is publicly available. For corpus validation, state-of-the-art classification algorithms (such as Logistic Regression, Support Vector Machine, and Naive Bayes) are applied and evaluated. Simulation results demonstrate that the Naive Bayes algorithm outperformed all other approaches and achieved accuracy up to 91%.

Keywords: Sentiment analysis · Saudi dialect · Word embedding

1 Introduction

Sentiment analysis has gained a lot more research attention due to the emergence of social media. The principal goal of sentiment analysis is to classify text as positive, negative or neutral [10]. Sentiment analysis for Arabic language possesses different challenges compared to other languages such as dealing with Modern Standard Language (MSA) and Dialects that significantly varies from one region to another [5,18]. Sentiment analysis is based on three main approaches: (1) Supervised approach. (2) Unsupervised approach and (3) Hybrid approach [13]. The supervised approach is based on a set of annotated messages (that is usually constructed manually [3,15]). The unsupervised approach is based on sentiment lexicon (which is often built automatically by exploiting English dictionaries such as Wordnet or Sentimentwordnet, etc) [6,8]. The hybrid approach is a combination of these two [14,19]. However, most of the existing related

J. Ren et al. (Eds.): BICS 2018, LNAI 10989, pp. 589–596, 2018.
https://doi.org/10.1007/978-3-030-00563-4_57

research works have concentrated more on dialects such as Egyptian, Levantine, Jordanian etc. In addition, the constructed resources are not publicly available. In this work a publicly available lexicons are developed based on word embedding for Saudi dialect (Dialect which suffers from a subsequent lack of works and studies). In addition, the developed lexicons are evaluated on a semi-supervised constructed corpus. The developed corpus is collected from Twitter, automatically annotated, and reviewed by a native Saudi dialect speaker. The resulted corpus contains 4000 messages (2000 positive and 2000 negative sentiments)[1].

The paper is organized as follows: Sect. 2 presents the developed novel corpus. Simulation results are presented in Sect. 4. Finally, Sect. 5 concludes this work with some future directions.

2 Related Works

In this paper, two kind of resources are considered: (1)sentiment lexicons and (2) An annotated sentiment corpus. This section is divided into two parts, the first part presents related work on sentiment lexicon construction, whereas the second part presents the works on building and annotating corpus.

2.1 Sentiment Lexicon Construction

Approaches for building lexicons include, manual approach, dictionary-based approach, and corpus-based approach. Building lexicons manually is time consuming and requires more time and resource. In the dictionary-based approach, number of seeds words are collected manually and then utilized the synonym and antonym of the list using common dictionary such as WordNet. In the corpus-based approach, a seed list is used to extract the similar words from the corpus. To build lexicons for Arabic language, a number of techniques have been utilized in the literature. However, most of them have focused on Modern Standard Arabic (MSA) and other dialects such as Egyptian and Levantine, while only few researches studied building lexicons for Saudi dialect. El-Beltagy and Ali [11] proposed a lexicon-based method that learns the weights of the lexicon words from a large corpus of tweets. They reported the achieved accuracy up to 70%. However, it was based on Egyptian dialect. Abdul-Majeed etl [1] built a large scale multi-genre multi dialect Arabic sentiment lexicon and contains only two dialects Egyptian and Levantine. Furthermore, a large-scale Arabic Sentiment Lexicon (ArSenL) was proposed by Badaro et al. [9]. The authors constructed ArSenLis using a combination of English SentiWordnet (ESWN), Arabic WordNet, and the Arabic Morphological Analyzer (AraMorph). However, it only covers MSA. Eskander elt in [12] followed the same approach in ArSenLis and built a Sentiment Lexicon for Standard Arabic SLSA. In the proposed approach, the authors linked an Arabic morphological analyzer Aramorph lexicon with SentiWordNet and included MSA only. For Saudi dialect, there are some proposed

[1] Please contact aaq@cs.stir.ac.uk or ahu@stir.ac.uk to access the dataset.

lexicons such as Adayel and Azmi [4] for Saudi dialect lexicon. This lexicon contains only around 1500 terms. AraSenTi [3] developed an Arabic sentiment lexicons based on tweets called AraSenTi-Trans and AraSenTi-PMI. Assiri [7] built a large lexicon that contains 14,000 sentiment terms based on a pre-created lexicon developed by Badaro et al. [9] and encoded using the Buckwalter translation. It is to be noted that most of the aforementioned approaches focused on other dialects and ignored Saudi dialect. In addition, lexicons were built without using word-embedding.

2.2 Annotated Corpus Construction

The supervised approach depends essentially on the existence of annotated data. Most of the existing approaches adopt manual annotation; hence, develop a restricted corpus which lacks good generalization. Foe example, OCA corpus contains 500 Arabic comments (250 positive and 250 negative), manually preprocessed, then segmented, and root extracted with a tool dedicated to Arabic [17]. AWATIF is a multi-genre corpus containing 10 723 sentences in Arabic manually annotated in objective and subjective polarity and then annotated the subjective sentences in positive, negative or neutral [2]. ASTD used 10,000 Arab Tweets, annotated in objective and subjective polarities and mixed with annotators of Amazon Mechanical Turk [15]. AraSenTi-Tweet used 17 573 Saudi tweets, manually annotated into four classes (positive, negative, neutral and mixed) [3]. In contrast to aforementioned work, in this work word embedding has been used to extend a lexicon (composed from a set of seeds that we constructed manually). The sentiment corpus is constructed in a semi-supervised manner depending on the constructed lexicon. The validation of this corpus is performed using three different classifiers. The corpus is available online.

3 Data Collection

3.1 Building Lexicon

We manually built the sentiment lexicon based on deep learning word embedding technique for Arabic language developed by [20]. It contains approximately 3000 words (1500 positive and 1500 negative). A group of seeds words were collected manually and annotated by an expert in the language. We searched for the similar words in the dictionary. Each word in the lexicon is assigned a similarity value from the word embedding. Any value below 60% similarity is excluded. To make this enrichment, we utilized AraVec which is a pre-trained Arabic word embedding model. It is trained using word2vec and includes data from Tweets, World Wide Web pages and Wikipedia articles. The total number of utlized tokens are approximately around 3 billion. The lexicon contains some words which were written incorrectly but they are very common. In dialect, people sometimes do not follow the writing standards or rules and use slang. This is more clear in negations. MSA contains some negations which could change the meaning from positive to negative and vice versa. However, users sometimes link the negation with the words. The existing Arabic stemmers find it difficult to deal with dialects. For example (مو حلو) they combine them into (موحلو) which could be considered as different words (Table 1).

Table 1. Example of negations

words	Translation	Negations	Translation
أحب	I love	لا أحب	I hate
حلو	Beautiful	مو حلو	Ugly
يعجبني	I like	ما يعجبني	Don't like
مزبوط	Good	مش مزبوط	Not good

3.2 Building Corpus

Saudi people are one of the largest Twitter users. In Twitter, people express their opinions in few words and short sentences due to the restrictions in number of letters. Consequently, people try to create new ways to overcome this challenge. For example, they combine some phrase together such as "ما يعجبني" contains negation "ما" and word "يعجبني" which means like to become "مايعجبني" without space. This is challenging because most of the available Arabic NLP tools fail in stemming the dialects. In order to build the corpus, the approach presented in [16] is followed. In this case we collected approximately 15000 tweets and classified them into positive and negative polarities. The adopted approach first separated the tweets into two classes: positive and negative based on a list of strong emoticons such as heart, devil, etc. Figure 1 illustrates the different steps of building the corpus.

The preprocessing steps include (1) Normalization: Where we removed any punctuations in the corpus that includes 'Tashkeel'. (2) Remove mentions such as names, retweets etc. Based on the constructed lexicon, we extracted tweets containing sentiments words. (3) Remove longation, in order to delete repeated letters. However, the suppression begin with more than two repeated letters (because we could find words with two repeated letters like "ممتتع" and "ممتاز"). Finally, the collected data were annotated manually into two different classes positive and negative. For annotation, the annotators followed some guidelines for annotating the tweets such as,

- it should hold an opinion (حقيقة قرار مزبوط) "A really great decision"
- the speaker expresses emotion (انا مغرم باجهزة ابل) "I am in love with Apple devices"

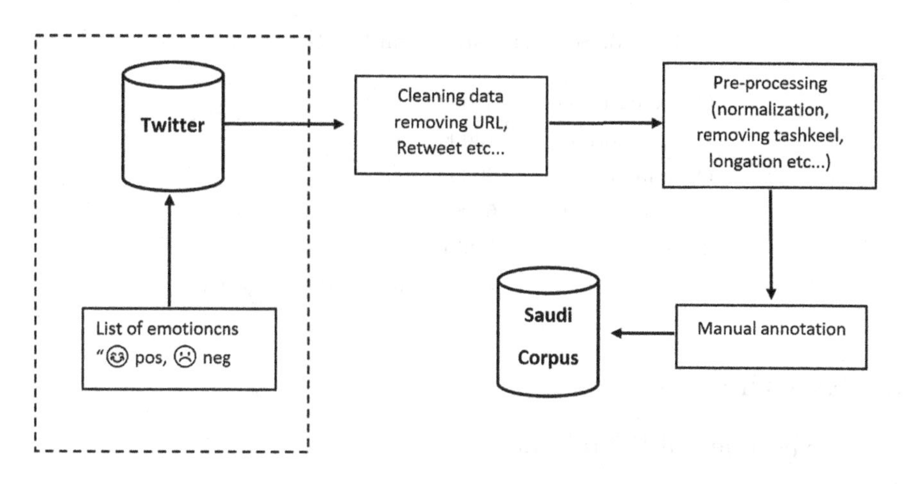

Fig. 1. Constructing Twitter corpus framework

- does not include news (وقد أفاد المصدر عن وقوع حادث شنيع في في طريق العقبة) "According to the reporter, a terrible accident took place in Alaqaba road" etc.

The resulted dataset contains 4000 tweets classified as 2000 positive and 2000 negative. Table 2. presents few examples from our dataset. In addition, Table 3 shows some statistics regarding the corpus.

Table 2. Positive and negative tweets examples

Tweets	Annotation
انا عن نفسي اشوف تركيا من افضل الاماكن للسياحة "I would say Turkey is one of the best places to travel"	Positive
دعاية خرافية عن الايفون بعد ٣٠ سنة "A beautiful advertisement about iPhone after 30 years"	Positive
عشاء مطنوخ من أبو ريان الليلة "A delicious dinner from Abu Rayan tonight"	Positive
الفندق خايس وكله صراصير ولا خدمة ولا شي "The hotel is disgusting and there is no service as well"	Negative
مع نفسك يا رجال هذا متغطرس ومهايطي ولا يشوف احد "This man is arrogant and hypocritical"	Negative
فاشلين هم وبرنامجهم اللي مايشتغل ابد كرهوني اطلب هالزلابة "These are failures and their program is not working"	Negative

Table 3. Some statistics regarding the corpus

Collected tweets	35000 tweets	
Using emotions list	15000	
Cleaning data	8000	
annotating data	6000	
Total	**4000**	
	2000 Positive	2000 Negative

4 Experiments

4.1 Experimental Environment

For the experiment part, we divided our corpus into training and testing using 5 cross validation and Stratified K-Folds cross-validator. In addition, Term frequency-Inverse document frequency (TF-IDF) is used for feature extraction. For lexicon, only words having more that 60% similarity with initial our seed words are used.

4.2 Classification

Four different classifiers (Logistic-Regression, Support Vector Machine (SVM), Stochastic Gradient Descent Classifier (SGD), and Naive Bayes) were applied to the annotated corpus. For evaluation, f1 Score, precision and recall performance are used. The tf-idf for the annotated corpus are calculated and classified. Table 4 shows the achieved result of the first experiment. In the second experiment, constructed lexicon are considered and improved results are presented in Table 5.

Table 4. The accuracy result before adding the lexicon features

Classifier	F1 score	Precision	Recall
Logistic-regression	0.88	0.83	**0.89**
SGD	0.87	0.86	0.88
SVM	0.74	0.61	0.87
Naïve Bayes	**0.89**	**0.90**	0.88

It can be seen that Naive Bayes classifier achieved the best accuracy in both f1 score and precision 89% and 90% respectively, where Logistics Regression achieved the highest score in recall with 89%.

Adding lexicon features in the second experiment showed a slight improve in the accuracy. Naive Bayes achieved the best accuracy with an increase of 1% in f1-score and precision respectively where Logistic Regression had around 1 % increase in recall and achieving 90% .

Table 5. The overall accuracy

Classifier	F1 score	Precision	Recall
Logistic-regression	0.89	0.87	**0.90**
SGD	0.88	0.89	0.87
SVM	0.83	0.78	0.89
Naïve Bayes	**0.90**	**0.91**	0.89

5 Conclusion

In this paper, a semi-supervised approach is presented to construct an annotated sentiment corpus from Saudi tweets. In addition, word embedding techniques such as word2vec are exploited to build a lexicon and annotate the corpus. A set of experiments based on different classification algorithms are conducted. Simulation results demonstrate that the Naive Bayes classifier achieved the best precision of 91%, revealing the benefits of using word embedding technique for building the lexicon. There are still few challenges to be addressed such as processing for different dialects and limited resources (e.g. PoS tagging, stemming etc.). In addition, there are some linguistic features which require more investigation such as negations. Hence, the future work includes the investigation of linguistic features and development of algorithms to better deal with these features.

References

1. Abdul-Mageed, M., Diab, M.: Sana: a large scale multi-genre, multi-dialect lexicon for arabic subjectivity and sentiment analysis. In: Proceedings of the Ninth International Conference on Language Resources and Evaluation (LREC-2014), European Language Resources Association (ELRA) (2014). http://www.aclweb.org/anthology/L14-1702
2. Abdul-Mageed, M., Diab, M.T.: Awatif: A multi-genre corpus for modern standard Arabic subjectivity and sentiment analysis. In: LREC, pp. 3907–3914. Citeseer (2012)
3. Al-Twairesh, N., Al-Khalifa, H.S., Al-Salman, A.S.: Arasenti: Large-scale twitter-specific Arabic sentiment lexicons. In: ACL (2016)
4. Aldayel, H.K., Azmi, A.M.: Arabic tweets sentiment analysis - a hybrid scheme. J. Inf. Sci. **42**(6), 782–797 (2016)
5. Alqarafi, A.S., Adeel, A., Gogate, M., Dashitpour, K., Hussain, A., Durrani, T.: Toward's arabic multi-modal sentiment analysis. In: Liang, Q., Mu, J., Jia, M., Wang, W., Feng, X., Zhang, B. (eds.) Communications, Signal Processing, and Systems, pp. 2378–2386. Springer, Singapore (2019). https://doi.org/10.1007/978-981-10-6571-2_290
6. Altrabsheh, N., El-Masri, M., Mansour, H.: Combining sentiment lexicons of Arabic terms (2017)

7. Assiri, A., Emam, A., Al-Dossari, H.: Towards enhancement of a lexicon-based approach for Saudi dialect sentiment analysis. J. Inf. Sci. **44**(2), 184–202 (2018). https://doi.org/10.1177/0165551516688143
8. Badaro, G., Baly, R., Hajj, H., Habash, N., El-Hajj, W.: A large scale Arabic sentiment lexicon for Arabic opinion mining. In: Proceedings of the EMNLP 2014 Workshop on Arabic Natural Language Processing (ANLP), pp. 165–173 (2014)
9. Badaro, G., Baly, R., Hajj, H.M., Habash, N., El-Hajj, W.: A large scale Arabic sentiment lexicon for Arabic opinion mining. In: ANLP@EMNLP (2014)
10. Dashtipour, K., et al.: Multilingual sentiment analysis: state of the art and independent comparison of techniques. Cogn. Comput. **8**(4), 757–771 (2016). https://doi.org/10.1007/s12559-016-9415-7
11. El-Beltagy, S.R., Ali, A.: Open issues in the sentiment analysis of Arabic social media: a case study. In: 2013 9th International Conference on Innovations in Information Technology (IIT), pp. 215–220 (2013)
12. Eskander, R., Rambow, O.: Slsa: A sentiment lexicon for standard Arabic. In: EMNLP (2015)
13. Guellil, I., Boukhalfa, K.: Social big data mining: A survey focused on opinion mining and sentiments analysis. In: Programming and Systems (ISPS), 12th International Symposium on 2015, pp. 1–10. IEEE (2015)
14. Khalifa, K., Omar, N.: A hybrid method using lexicon-based approach and naive bayes classifier for arabic opinion question answering. J. Comput. Sci. **10**(10), 1961 (2014)
15. Nabil, M., Aly, M., Atiya, A.: ASTD: Arabic sentiment tweets dataset. In: Proceedings of the 2015 Conference on Empirical Methods in Natural Language Processing, pp. 2515–2519 (2015)
16. Pak, A., Paroubek, P.: Twitter as a corpus for sentiment analysis and opinion mining. In: Calzolari, N., et al. (eds.) Proceedings of the Seventh International Conference on Language Resources and Evaluation (LREC 2010), European Language Resources Association (ELRA), Valletta, Malta (may 2010)
17. Rushdi-Saleh, M., Martín-Valdivia, M.T., Ureña-López, L.A., Perea-Ortega, J.M.: OCA: opinion corpus for Arabic. J. Assoc. Inf. Sci. Technol. **62**(10), 2045–2054 (2011)
18. Sadat, F., Kazemi, F., Farzindar, A.: Automatic identification of Arabic dialects in social media. In: Proceedings of the First International Workshop on Social Media Retrieval and Analysis, pp. 35–40. ACM (2014)
19. Shoukry, A., Rafea, A.: A hybrid approach for sentiment classification of Egyptian dialect tweets. In: Arabic Computational Linguistics (ACLing), First International Conference on 2015, pp. 78–85. IEEE (2015)
20. Soliman, A.B., Eissa, K., El-Beltagy, S.R.: Aravec: a set of Arabic word embedding models for use in Arabic NLP. Proced. Comput. Sci. **117**, 256–265 (2017)

Exploiting Deep Learning for Persian Sentiment Analysis

Kia Dashtipour[1(✉)], Mandar Gogate[1], Ahsan Adeel[1], Cosimo Ieracitano[2], Hadi Larijani[3], and Amir Hussain[1]

[1] Department of Computing Science and Mathematics, Faculty of Natural Sciences, University of Stirling, Stirling FK9 4LA, UK
kd28@cs.stir.ac.uk

[2] DICEAM Department, University Mediterranea of Reggio Calabria, 89124 Reggio Calabria, Italy

[3] Department of Communication, Network and Electronic Engineering, Glasgow Caledonian University, Glasgow G4 0BA, UK

Abstract. The rise of social media is enabling people to freely express their opinions about products and services. The aim of sentiment analysis is to automatically determine subject's sentiment (e.g., positive, negative, or neutral) towards a particular aspect such as topic, product, movie, news etc. Deep learning has recently emerged as a powerful machine learning technique to tackle a growing demand of accurate sentiment analysis. However, limited work has been conducted to apply deep learning algorithms to languages other than English, such as Persian. In this work, two deep learning models (deep autoencoders and deep convolutional neural networks (CNNs)) are developed and applied to a novel Persian movie reviews dataset. The proposed deep learning models are analyzed and compared with the state-of-the-art shallow multilayer perceptron (MLP) based machine learning model. Simulation results demonstrate the enhanced performance of deep learning over state-of-the-art MLP.

Keywords: Persian sentiment analysis · Persian movie reviews Deep learning

1 Introduction

In recent years, social media, forums, blogs and other forms of online communication tools have radically affected everyday life, especially how people express their opinions and comments. The extraction of useful information (such as people's opinion about companies brand) from the huge amount of unstructured data is vital for most companies and organizations [5]. The product reviews are important for business owners as they can take business decision accordingly to automatically classify user's opinions towards products and services. The application of sentiment analysis is not limited to product or movie reviews but can

J. Ren et al. (Eds.): BICS 2018, LNAI 10989, pp. 597–604, 2018.
https://doi.org/10.1007/978-3-030-00563-4_58

be applied to different fields such as news, politics, sport etc. For example, in online political debates, the sentiment analysis can be used to identify people's opinions on a certain election candidate or political parties [19,20,27]. In this context, sentiment analysis has been widely used in different languages by using traditional and advanced machine learning techniques. However, limited research has been conducted to develop models for the Persian language.

The sentiment analysis is a method to automatically process large amounts of data and classify text into positive or negative sentiments) [2,8]. Sentiment analysis can be performed at two levels: at the document level or at the sentence level. At document level it is used to classify the sentiment expressed in the document (positive or negative), whereas, at sentence level is used to identify the sentiments expressed only in the sentence under analysis [6,7].

In the literature, deep learning based automated feature extraction has been shown to outperform state-of-the-art manual feature engineering based classifiers such as Support Vector Machine (SVM), Naive Bayes (NB) or Multilayer Perceptron (MLP) etc. One of the important techniques in deep learning is the autoencoder that generally involves reducing the number of feature dimensions under consideration. The aim of dimensionality reduction is to obtain a set of principal variables to improve the performance of the approach. Similarly, CNNs have been proven to be very effective in sentiment analysis. However, little work has been carried out to exploit deep learning based feature representation for Persian sentiment analysis [10,16]. In this paper, we present two deep learning models (deep autoencoders and CNNs) for Persian sentiment analysis. The obtained deep learning results are compared with MLP.

The rest of the paper is organized as follows: Sect. 2 presents related work. Section 3 presents methodology and experimental results. Finally, Sect. 4 concludes this paper.

2 Related Works

In the literature, extensive research has been carried out to model novel sentiment analysis models using both shallow and deep learning algorithms. For example, the authors in [3] proposed a novel deep learning approach for polarity detection in product reviews. The authors addressed two major limitations of stacked denoising of autoencoders, high computational cost and the lack of scalability of high dimensional features. Their experimental results showed the effectiveness of proposed autoencoders in achieving accuracy upto 87%. Zhai et al. [28] proposed a five layers autoencoder for learning the specific representation of textual data. The autoencoders are generalised using loss function and derived discriminative loss function from label information. The experimental results showed that the model outperformed bag of words, denoising autoencoders and other traditional methods, achieving accuracy rate up to 85%. Sun et al. [26] proposed a novel method to extract contextual information from text using a convolutional autoencoder architecture. The experimental results showed that the proposed model outperformed traditional SVM and Nave Bayes models, reporting accuracy of 83.1 %, 63.9% and 67.8% respectively.

Su et al. [24] proposed an approach for a neural generative autoencoder for learning bilingual word embedding. The experimental results showed the effectiveness of their approach on English-Chinese, English-German, English-French and English-Spanish (75.36% accuracy). Kim et al. [14] proposed a method to capture the non-linear structure of data using CNN classifier. The experimental results showed the effectiveness of the method on the multi-domain dataset (movie reviews and product reviews). However, the disadvantage is only SVM and Naive Bayes classifiers are used to evaluate the performance of the method and deep learning classifiers are not exploited. Zhang et al. [29] proposed an approach using deep learning classifiers to detect polarity in Japanese movie reviews. The approach used denoising autoencoder and adapted to other domains such as product reviews. The advantage of the approach is not depended on any language and could be used for various languages by applying different datasets. AP et al. [1] proposed a CNN based model for cross-language learning of vectorial word representations that is coherent between two languages. The method is evaluated using English and German movie reviews dataset. The experimental results showed CNN (83.45% accuracy) outperformed as compared to SVM (65.25% accuracy).

Zhou et al. [30] proposed an autoencoder architecture constituting an LSTM-encoder and decoder in order to capture features in the text and reduce dimensionality of data. The LSTM encoder used the interactive scheme to go through the sequence of sentences and LSTM decoder reconstructed the vector of sentences. The model is evaluated using different datasets such as book reviews, DVD reviews, and music reviews, acquiring accuracy up to 81.05%, 81.06%, and 79.40% respectively. Mesnil et al. [17] proposed an approach using ensemble classification to detect polarity in the movie reviews. The authors combined several machine learning algorithms such as SVM, Naive Bayes and RNN to achieve better results, where autoencoders were used to reduce the dimensionality of features. The experimental results showed the combination of unigram, bigram and trigram features (91.87% accuracy) outperformed unigram (91.56% accuracy) and bigram (88.61% accuracy).

Scheible et al. [22] trained an approach using semi-supervised recursive autoencoder to detect polarity in movie reviews dataset, consisted of 5000 positive and 5000 negative sentiments. The experimental results demonstrated that the proposed approach successfully detected polarity in movie reviews dataset (83.13% accuracy) and outperformed standard SVM (68.36% accuracy) model. Dai et al. [4] developed an autoencoder to detect polarity in the text using deep learning classifier. The LSTM was trained on IMDB movie reviews dataset. The experimental results showed the outperformance of their proposed approach over SVM. In Table 1 some of the autoencoder approaches are depicted.

3 Methodology and Experimental Results

The novel dataset used in this work was collected manually and includes Persian movie reviews from 2014 to 2016. A subset of dataset was used to train the neural network (60% training dataset) and rest of the data (40%) was used to test and validate the performance of the trained neural network (testing set (30%), validation set (10%)). There are two types of labels in the dataset: positive or negative. The reviews were manually annotated by three native Persian speakers aged between 30 and 50 years old.

After data collection, the corpus was pre-processed using tokenisation, normalisation and stemming techniques. The process of converting sentences into single word or token is called tokenisation. For example, "The movie is great" is changed to "The", "movie", "is", "great" [25]. There are some words which contain numbers. For example, "great" is written as "gr8" or "gooood" as written as "good". The normalisation is used to convert these words into normal forms [21]. The process of converting words into their root is called stemming. For example, going was changed to go [15]. Words were converted into vectors. The fasttext was used to convert each word into 300-dimensions vectors. Fasttext is a library for text classification and representation [10,13,18].

For classification, MLP, autoencoders and CNNs have been used. Figure 1 depicts the modelled MLP architectures. MLP classifer was trained for 100 iterations [9]. Figure 2 depicts the modelled autoencoder architecture. Autoencoder is a feed-forward deep neural network with unsupervised learning and it is used for dimensionality reduction. The autoencoder consists of input, output and hidden layers. Autoencoder is used to compress the input into a latent-space and then the output is reconstructed [11,12,23]. The exploited autoencoder model is depcited in Fig. 1. The autoencoder consists of one input layer three hidden layers (1500, 512, 1500) and an output layer. Convolutional Neural Networks contains three layers (input, hidden and output layer). The hidden layer consists of convolutional layers, pooling layers, fully connected layers and normalisation layer. The h_j is denotes the hidden neurons of j, with bias of b_j , is a weight sum over continuous visible nodes v which is given by:

$$h_j = b_j + \sum v_i w_{ij} \quad (1)$$

The modelled CNN architecture is depicted in Fig. 3 [11,12]. For CNN modelling, each utterance was represented as a concatenation vector of constituent words. The network has total 11 layers: 4 convolution layers, 4 max pooling and 3 fully connected layers. Convolution layers have filters of size 2 and with 15 feature maps. Each convolution layer is followed by a max polling layer with window size 2. The last max pooling layer is followed by fully connected layers of size 5000, 500 and 4. For final layer, softmax activation is used.

To evaluate the performance of the proposed approach, precision (1), recall (2), f-Measure (3), and prediction accuracy (4) have been used as a performance matrices. The experimental results are shown in Table 1, where it can be seen that autoencoders outperformed MLP and CNN outperformed autoencoders with the highest achieved accuracy of 82.6%.

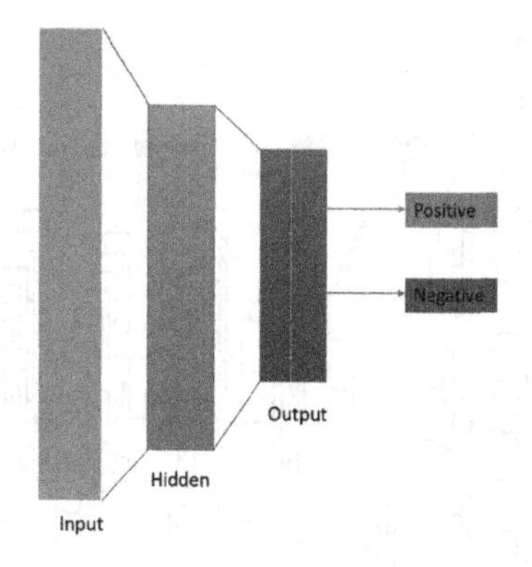

Fig. 1. Multilayer perceptron

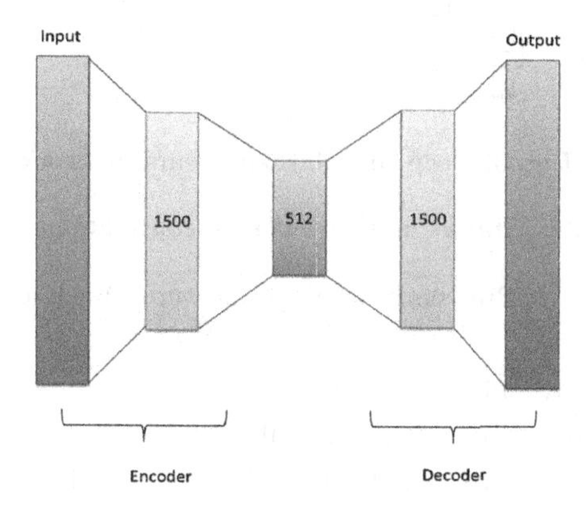

Fig. 2. Autoencoder

$$Precision = \frac{TP}{TP + FP} \tag{2}$$

$$Recall = \frac{TP}{TP + FN} \tag{3}$$

$$F\_measure = 2 * \frac{Precision * Recall}{Precision + Recall} \tag{4}$$

$$Accuracy = \frac{TP + TN}{TP + TN + FP + FN} \tag{5}$$

where TP is denotes true positive, TN is true negative, FP is false positive, and FN is false negative.

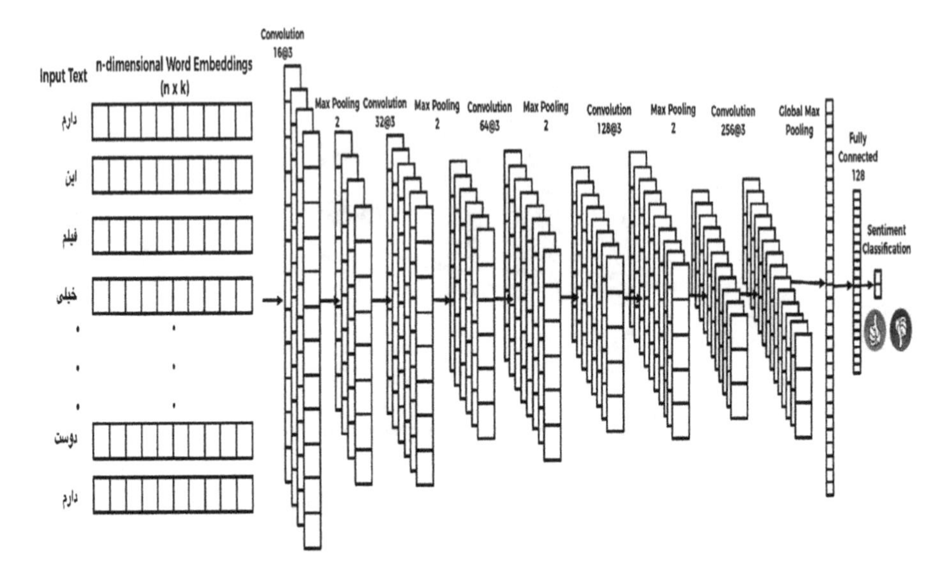

Fig. 3. Deep convolutional neural network

Table 1. Results: MLP vs. autoencoder vs. convolutional neural network

	Precision	Recall	F-measure	Accuracy (%)
MLP				
Negative	0.78	0.76	0.77	
Positive	0.79	0.81	0.8	
AVG	0.78	0.78	0.78	78.49
MLP-autoencoder				
Negative	0.78	0.81	0.79	
Positive	0.82	0.8	0.81	
AVG	0.8	0.8	0.8	80.08
1D-CNN				
Negative	0.90	0.78	0.83	
Positive	0.77	0.89	0.82	
AVG	0.84	0.83	0.83	82.86

4 Conclusion

Sentiment analysis has been used extensively for a wide of range of real-world applications, ranging from product reviews, surveys feedback, to business intelligence, and operational improvements. However, the majority of research efforts are devoted to English-language only, where information of great importance is also available in other languages. In this work, we focus on developing sentiment analysis models for Persian language, specifically for Persian movie reviews. Two deep learning models (deep autoencoders and deep CNNs) are developed and compared with the state-of-the-art shallow MLP based machine learning model. Simulations results revealed the outperformance of our proposed CNN model over autoencoders and MLP. In future, we intend to exploit more advanced deep learning models such as Long Short-Term Memory (LSTM) and LSTM-CNNs to further evaluate the performance of our developed novel Persian dataset.

Acknowledgment. Amir Hussain and Ahsan Adeel were supported by the UK Engineering and Physical Sciences Research Council (EPSRC) grant No. EP/M026981/1.

References

1. AP, S.C., et al.: An autoencoder approach to learning bilingual word representations. In: Advances in Neural Information Processing Systems, pp. 1853–1861 (2014)
2. Cambria, E., Poria, S., Hazarika, D., Kwok, K.: SenticNet 5: discovering conceptual primitives for sentiment analysis by means of context embeddings. In: AAAI (2018)
3. Chen, M., Xu, Z., Weinberger, K., Sha, F.: Marginalized denoising autoencoders for domain adaptation. arXiv preprint arXiv:1206.4683 (2012)
4. Dai, A.M., Le, Q.V.: Semi-supervised sequence learning. In: Advances in Neural Information Processing Systems, pp. 3079–3087 (2015)
5. Dashtipour, K., Gogate, M., Adeel, A., Hussain, A., Alqarafi, A., Durrani, T.: A comparative study of persian sentiment analysis based on different feature combinations. In: Liang, Q., Mu, J., Jia, M., Wang, W., Feng, X., Zhang, B. (eds.) CSPS 2017. LNEE, vol. 463, pp. 2288–2294. Springer, Singapore (2019). https://doi.org/10.1007/978-981-10-6571-2_279
6. Dashtipour, K., Gogate, M., Adeel, A., Algarafi, A., Howard, N., Hussain, A.: Persian named entity recognition. In: 2017 IEEE 16th International Conference on Cognitive Informatics and Cognitive Computing (ICCI* CC), pp. 79–83. IEEE (2017)
7. Dashtipour, K., Hussain, A., Zhou, Q., Gelbukh, A., Hawalah, A.Y.A., Cambria, E.: PerSent: a freely available persian sentiment lexicon. In: Liu, C.-L., Hussain, A., Luo, B., Tan, K.C., Zeng, Y., Zhang, Z. (eds.) BICS 2016. LNCS (LNAI), vol. 10023, pp. 310–320. Springer, Cham (2016). https://doi.org/10.1007/978-3-319-49685-6_28
8. Dashtipour, K., et al.: Multilingual sentiment analysis: state of the art and independent comparison of techniques. Cogn. Comput. **8**(4), 757–771 (2016)
9. Gardner, M.W., Dorling, S.: Artificial neural networks (the multilayer perceptron) a review of applications in the atmospheric sciences. Atmos. Environ. **32**(14–15), 2627–2636 (1998)
10. Gasparini, S.: Information theoretic-based interpretation of a deep neural network approach in diagnosing psychogenic non-epileptic seizures. Entropy **20**(2), 43 (2018)
11. Gogate, M., Adeel, A., Hussain, A.: Deep learning driven multimodal fusion for automated deception detection. In: 2017 IEEE Symposium Series on Computational Intelligence (SSCI), pp. 1–6. IEEE (2017)
12. Gogate, M., Adeel, A., Hussain, A.: A novel brain-inspired compression-based optimised multimodal fusion for emotion recognition. In: 2017 IEEE Symposium Series on Computational Intelligence (SSCI), pp. 1–7. IEEE (2017)

13. Joulin, A., Grave, E., Bojanowski, P., Douze, M., Jégou, H., Mikolov, T.: Fast-text.zip: Compressing text classification models. arXiv preprint arXiv:1612.03651 (2016)
14. Kim, Y.: Convolutional neural networks for sentence classification. arXiv preprint arXiv:1408.5882 (2014)
15. Korenius, T., Laurikkala, J., Järvelin, K., Juhola, M.: Stemming and lemmatization in the clustering of finnish text documents. In: Proceedings of the thirteenth ACM international conference on Information and knowledge management, pp. 625–633. ACM (2004)
16. LeCun, Y., Bengio, Y., Hinton, G.: Deep learning. Nature **521**(7553), 436 (2015)
17. Mesnil, G., Mikolov, T., Ranzato, M., Bengio, Y.: Ensemble of generative and discriminative techniques for sentiment analysis of movie reviews. arXiv preprint arXiv:1412.5335 (2014)
18. Morabito, F.C., et al.: Deep convolutional neural networks for classification of mild cognitive impaired and alzheimer's disease patients from scalp eeg recordings. In: 2016 IEEE 2nd International Forum on Research and Technologies for Society and Industry Leveraging a Better Tomorrow (RTSI), pp. 1–6. IEEE (2016)
19. Ren, J., Jiang, J.: Hierarchical modeling and adaptive clustering for real-time summarization of rush videos. IEEE Trans. Multimed. **11**(5), 906–917 (2009)
20. Ren, J., Jiang, J., Feng, Y.: Activity-driven content adaptation for effective video summarization. J. Vis. Commun. Image Represent. **21**(8), 930–938 (2010)
21. Reynolds, D.A.: Comparison of background normalization methods for text-independent speaker verification. In: Fifth European Conference on Speech Communication and Technology (1997)
22. Scheible, C., Schütze, H.: Cutting recursive autoencoder trees. arXiv preprint arXiv:1301.2811 (2013)
23. Semeniuta, S., Severyn, A., Barth, E.: A hybrid convolutional variational autoencoder for text generation. arXiv preprint arXiv:1702.02390 (2017)
24. Su, J., Wu, S., Zhang, B., Wu, C., Qin, Y., Xiong, D.: A neural generative autoencoder for bilingual word embeddings. Inf. Sci. **424**, 287–300 (2018)
25. Sumathy, K., Chidambaram, M.: Text mining: concepts, applications, tools and issues-an overview. Int. J. Comput. Appl. **80**(4) (2013)
26. Sun, X., Li, C., Ren, F.: Sentiment analysis for chinese microblog based on deep neural networks with convolutional extension features. Neurocomputing **210**, 227–236 (2016)
27. Tan, S.-S., Na, J.-C.: Mining semantic patterns for sentiment analysis of product reviews. In: Kamps, J., Tsakonas, G., Manolopoulos, Y., Iliadis, L., Karydis, I. (eds.) TPDL 2017. LNCS, vol. 10450, pp. 382–393. Springer, Cham (2017). https://doi.org/10.1007/978-3-319-67008-9_30
28. Zhai, S., Zhang, Z.M.: Semisupervised autoencoder for sentiment analysis. In: AAAI, pp. 1394–1400 (2016)
29. Zhang, P., Komachi, M.: Japanese sentiment classification with stacked denoising auto-encoder using distributed word representation. In: Proceedings of the 29th Pacific Asia Conference on Language, Information and Computation, pp. 150–159 (2015)
30. Zhou, H., Chen, L., Shi, F., Huang, D.: Learning bilingual sentiment word embeddings for cross-language sentiment classification. In: Proceedings of the 53rd Annual Meeting of the Association for Computational Linguistics and the 7th International Joint Conference on Natural Language Processing (Volume 1: Long Papers), vol. 1, pp. 430–440 (2015)

Big Data Analytics and Mining for Crime Data Analysis, Visualization and Prediction

Mingchen Feng[1,2], Jiangbin Zheng[1(✉)], Yukang Han[2], Jinchang Ren[2], and Qiaoyuan Liu[2,3]

[1] School of Computer Science, Northwestern Polytechnical University, Xi'an, China
mingchen.feng@strath.ac.uk, zhengjb@nwpu.edu.cn
[2] Department of Electronic and Electrical Engineering, University of Strathclyde, Glasgow, UK
{yukang.han, jinchang.ren, qiaoyuan.liu}@strath.ac.uk
[3] Department of Information Science and Technology, Northeast Normal University, Changchun, China

Abstract. Crime analysis and prediction is a systematic approach for analyzing and identifying different patterns, relations and trends in crime. In this paper we conduct exploratory data analysis to analyze criminal data in San Francisco, Chicago and Philadelphia. We first explored time series of the data, and forecast crime trends in the following years. Then predicted crime category given time and location, to overcome the problem of imbalance, we merged multiple classes into larger classes and did feature selection to improve accuracy. We have applied several state-of-the-art data mining techniques that are specifically used for crime prediction. The experimental results show that the Tree classification models performed better on our classification task over k-NN and Naive Bayesian approaches. Holt-Winters with multiplicative seasonality gives best results when predicting crime trends. The promising outcomes will be beneficial for police department and law enforcement to speed up the process of solving crimes and provide insights that enable them track criminal activities, predict the likelihood of incidents, effectively deploy resources and make faster decisions.

Keywords: Crime data analysis · Big data analytics · Data mining Visualization

1 Introduction

The increasing number of crime incidents is a challenge issue to both police department and law enforcement. It not only concerned with personal safety but also affected culture and economic growth. Therefore it is an important task for safety analysts to carry out comprehensive study of crime incidents to identify factors that cause a crime to happen. Analysis of crime data lets officers effectively keep track of crime activity, find similarity of different incidents, deploy resources and make faster decisions. With the fast development of computer network and storage technology, a large number of

J. Ren et al. (Eds.): BICS 2018, LNAI 10989, pp. 605–614, 2018.
https://doi.org/10.1007/978-3-030-00563-4_59

crime data was collected and made public, such big data can provide new insights for understanding crime patterns.

Data mining [1] is an innovative, interdisciplinary, and a growing area of research and analysis to build paradigms and techniques across various fields for deducing useful information and hidden patterns from data. It can help us not only in knowledge discovery, that is, the identification of new phenomena, but also it is useful in enhancing our understanding of known phenomena. Using data mining techniques, we can easily discover the pattern of crime which take place in a particular area and how they are related with time. The implications of machine learning and mathematical techniques on crime data or specifically time series data will enable us to know the pattern and trends of crimes in a country and further assist society to be able to plan for the prevention and curtailment of crime.

In this paper, we explored crime data from three different cities. We first did feature normalization and implemented feature selection to get the most important features in order to get better classification results, then we explored time series of the data, and forecast crime trends in the following four years. Finally we predicted crime category given time and location, to overcome the problem of imbalance, we merged multiple classes into larger classes and used oversampling strategy to improve classification accuracy. We tried different widely adapted data mining techniques that are specifically used for multi-class crime prediction.

2 Related Work

In the criminology literature researchers have devoted attention to study the relationship between crime and various factors. Examples are historical crime records [2], unemployment rate [3], and spatial similarity [4]. Using data mining and statistical techniques, new algorithms and systems have been developed and new types data are used in the study. For instance, there are studies using classification and statistical models to mining crime pattern and predict crime [5, 6], and studies employing transfer learning to exploit spatio-temporal patterns in New York city [7]. Wu et al. [8] developed a system that automatically collects crime-logged data and mining crime pattern to help devise more effective crime prevention practices within and around a university campus. Vineeth et al. [9], obtained correlation between the crime types and then used random forest to classify the state based on their crime intensity point. There are also methods which applied unsupervised learning to find crime patterns and crime hotpot, Rodríguez et al. [10] used memetic differential fuzzy cluster to produce a forecast of criminal patterns, while in [11] fuzzy C-means algorithm was applied to cluster criminal events in space. Noor et al. [12] accomplished association rule mining to find relationship between different crimes. With deep learning and neural networks become hot topics, researchers also applied deep learning and neueral network models to predict crime occurrence, which can be found in [13].

In our proposed approach, we share certain similarities with some of the work described above, which include visualization, classification and prediction of crime trends in three cities, i.e. Chicago, San Francisco and Philadelphia. Statistical visualization is used to show relationships of crime data using time series model to estimate crime trends in the following years. We also tackle the problem of imbalanced classification by merging similar categories along with the oversampling strategy.

3 Data Analysis

Our data is publicly available datasets that consist of crime activities from 3 different countries, San-Francisco, Chicago, and Philadelphia. The San-Francisco crime data contains 2,142,685 crime incidents from 01/01/2003 to 11/08/2017. Data from Chicago contains a total of 5,541,398 records, dating back to 2003, while relevant data in Philadelphia include data captured from 01/01/2006 to 12/31/2017, the total size is 2,371,416 crime incidents.

3.1 Features

Every entry in our data set is about a particular crime, and each data record has the following features:

- Dates - Date and timestamp of the crime incident.
- Category - Type of the crime. This is the target/label that we need to predict in the classification stage.
- Descript - A brief note describing any pertinent details of the crime.
- DayOfWeek - Day of the week that crime occurred.
- PdDistrict - Police Department District where the crime is assigned.
- Resolution - How the crime incident was resolved (with the perpetrator being, say, arrest or booked).
- Address - The approximate street address of the crime incident.
- X - Longitude of the location of a crime.
- Y - Latitude of the location of a crime.
- Dome - whether crime id domestic or not
- Arrest - Arrested or not

3.2 Preprocessing

Before implementing any algorithms on our datasets, a series of preprocessing steps are performed in order to get better classification results. These include:

- Time is discretized into a couple of columns to allow for time series forecasting for the overall trend in the data.
- To make data perform better on classification tasks, we normalized features like DayofWeek, PdDistrict, and Category into numbers.
- The timestamp indicates the date and time of occurrence of each crime, we deduced these attributes into five features: Year (2003–2017), Month (1–12), Day (1–31), Hour (0–23), and Minute (0–59).
- We also omit some features that unneeded like incidentNum, coordinate.

3.3 Collapsing Crime Categories

When we summarize crime category in each city, shown in Fig. 1, we found that the number of classification label in original data is too high for accurate prediction. The data is heavily skewed. The categories are too fine-grained, and we realized that several crime incidents are similar to one another, and could therefore be collapsed into smaller classes for better classification.

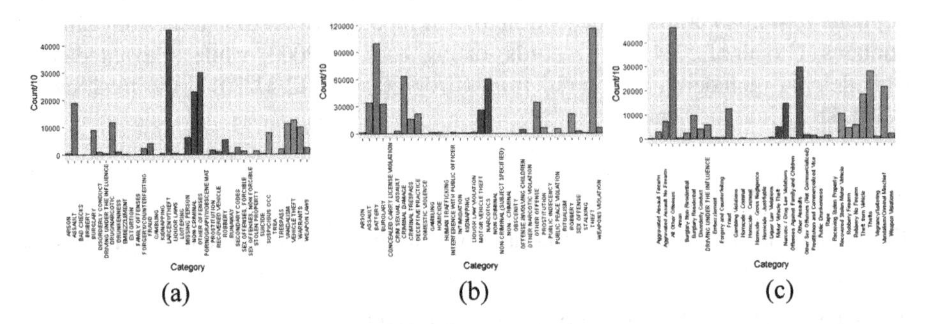

Fig. 1. Occurrence of each category of crime in (a) San Francisco, (b) Chicago and (c) Philadelphia. Theft is the most common crime in all cities. In San Francisco other offenses is the second highest crime, while in Chicago and Philadelphia is assault.

We can also find that there are many non-criminal records in the datasets which do no harm to society, we eliminate these rows in order to focus on criminal incidents. Finally the new categories and their distribution are shown in Fig. 2.

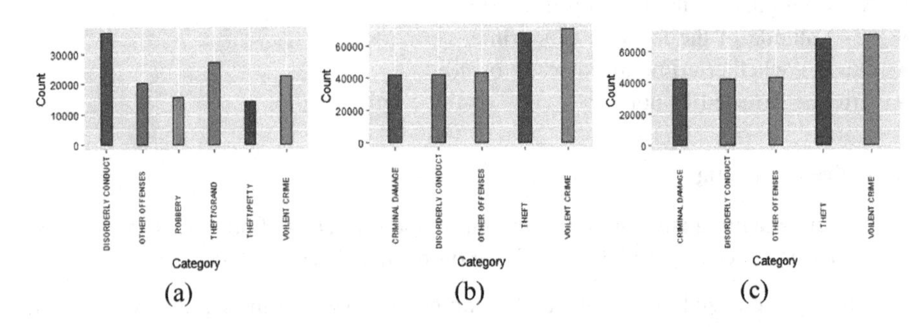

Fig. 2. After collapsing and merging similar categories, we got new categories and the distribution of categories in (a) San Francisco, (b) Chicago and (c) Philadelphia looks more balanced.

3.4 Feature Selection

Before doing classification model, we explored which of the features actually help predict crime category. We plot the correlation coefficient between each feature to analyse the importance of features in our model. As shown in Fig. 3, for San Francisco we chose Latitude, PdDistrict, Minute, Hour, Day and DayofWeek as our features, and for Chicago we used Hour, Minute, Longitude, Latitude, Dome, Arrest, for Philadelphia we used Month, Longitude, PSA, UCR and Hour.

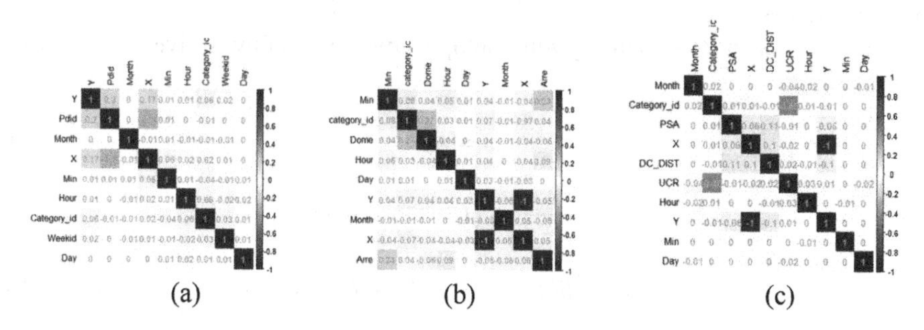

Fig. 3. The correlation coefficient diagram of each feature. (a) in San Francisco Latitude, Hour and DayofWeek are the most important features. (b) in Chicago Minute, Latitude, Longitude are top-3 important features. (c) in Philadelphia UCR and Month are the most important features.

4 Methods

4.1 Time Series

In order to tackle crime trends forecasting problem we explored time series model. A time series is a series of data points indexed (or listed or graphed) in time order. Usually, time series takes successive equally spaced points in time. Thus it is a discrete-time data. Figure 4 demonstrates how the amount of crime incidents changed over time. It can conclude that there exists some trend and seasonality in the data. So we applied Triple Exponential Smoothing (Holt-Winters) on our data. Holt-Winters applies exponential smoothing three times, which is commonly used when there are three high frequency signals to be removed from a time series under study.

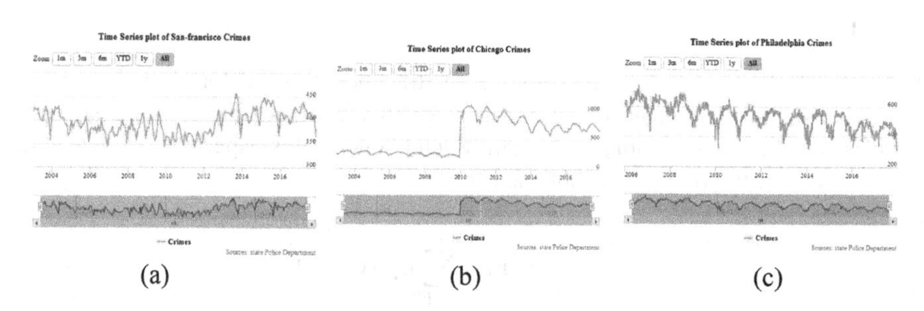

Fig. 4. Time series plot of crime in each city (a) San Francisco, (b) Chicago and (c) Philadelphia.

Holt-Winters exponential smoothing estimates the level, slope and seasonal component at the current time point. Smoothing is controlled by three parameters: alpha, beta, and gamma, for the estimates of the level, slope b of the trend component, and the seasonal component, respectively, at the current time point. The parameters alpha, beta and gamma all have values between 0 and 1, and values that are close to 0 mean that relatively little weight is placed on the most recent observations when making forecasts of future values.

Triple exponential smoothing with multiplicative seasonality is given by following formulas.

$$\mathrm{s}_0 = \mathrm{x}_0 \tag{1}$$

$$s_t = \alpha \frac{x_t}{c_t - L} + (1 - \alpha)(s_{t-1} + b_{t-1}) \tag{2}$$

$$b_t = \beta(s_t - s_{t-1}) + (1 - \beta)b_{t-1} \tag{3}$$

$$c_t = \gamma \frac{x_t}{s_t} + (1 - \gamma)c_{t-L} \tag{4}$$

$$F_{t+m} = (s_t + mb_t)c_{t-L+1+(m-1)} \bmod L \tag{5}$$

4.2 Naive Bayes

Naive Bayes classifiers are a family of simple “probabilistic classifiers” based on applying Bayes’ theorem with strong independence assumptions between the features. In this paper we implemented a Naive Bayes based on multi-label classification model with Laplace smoothing. Given a dataset $\{a_1, a_2, \ldots, a_j\}$ with labels $\{v_1, v_2, \ldots, v_j\}$ the results are estimated using the following equation:

$$v_{NB} = \arg\max_{v_j \in V} P(v_j) \prod\nolimits_i P(a_i|v_j) \tag{6}$$

4.3 KNN

K-Nearest-Neighbors (k-NN) is a non-parametric method used for classification. An object is classified by a majority vote of its neighbors, with the object being assigned to the class most common among its k nearest neighbors. In this paper we use a weighted KNN classifier, the output y is obtained by:

$$f(x_q) \leftarrow \arg\max_{v \in V} \sum_{i=1}^{k} w_i \delta(v, f(x_i)) \tag{7}$$

$$w_i \equiv \frac{1}{d(x_q, x_i)^2} \tag{8}$$

4.4 Random Forest

Random Forest is one of the important methods of ensemble learning, which builds a number of classifiers on the training set and compares all their results to make their best performance on the testing set. Given a series of classifiers $h(x|\theta_j)$, the output is obtained by aggregating the results thus:

$$y = \arg \max_{p \in \{h(x_1)...h(x_k)\}} \{\sum_{j=1}^{k} (I(h(x|\theta_j) = p))\} \tag{9}$$

where *I* denotes the indicator function.

4.5 Gradient Boosted Decision Trees

Gradient Tree Boosting is another popular ensemble method used for regression and classification. Given a training sample (x, y), the goal is to find a function $F^*(x)$ that maps x to y such that the expected value of some loss function $\Psi(y, F(x))$ is minimized. Boosting approximates $F^*(x)$ by the following equation:

$$F(x) = \sum_{m=0}^{M} \beta_m h(x; a_m) \tag{10}$$

where functions $h(x;a_m)$ are function x with parameter a. β_m and a_m are in function $F_m(x)$ and $F_m(x)$ is updated as:

$$F_m(x) = F_{m-1}(x) + \beta_m h(x; a_m) \tag{11}$$

5 Experimental Results

5.1 Time Series for Crime Trend Prediction

We adopt MSE (mean square error) to evaluate our time series model, we divided the data into two parts: data before year 2014 as training data, and the rest as testing data. Before conduct any model, we first decomposed time series data to estimate trend component, seasonal component and irregular component shown in Fig. 5. When applied Holt-Winters with multiplicative seasonality we got the lowest MSE (Fig. 6).

5.2 Classification Performance

In this section we compared the results of classification models in previous section on both original data and our collapsed categories data.

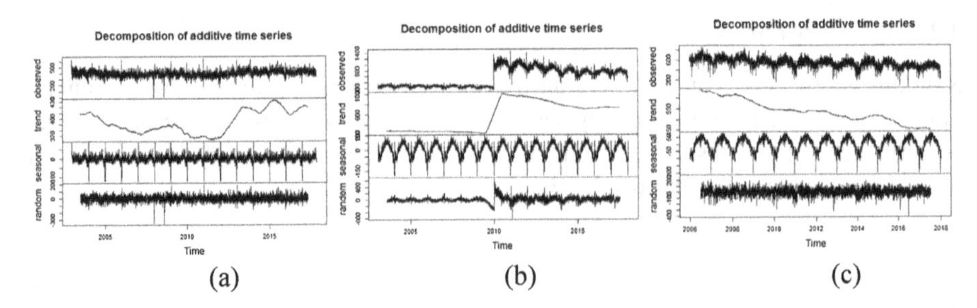

Fig. 5. Decompose of time series in each city (a) San Francisco, (b) Chicago and (c) Philadelphia. The plots show the original time series, the estimated trend component, the estimated seasonal component, and the estimated irregular component. We can see how crime evolved over time.

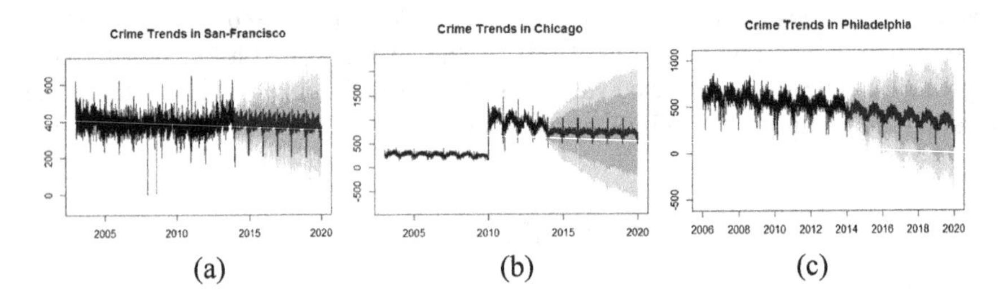

Fig. 6. Crime trends in each city (a) San Francisco, (b) Chicago and (c) Philadelphia, we used Holt-Winters with multiplicative seasonality to forecast the mount of crime everyday

Naive Bayes Classifier
The Naive Bayes model was tested using cross validation, we used 60% of the data as training data and the rest for validation. The prediction accuracy is summarized in Fig. 7, we can see that Naive Bayes is not good enough to do our classification task.

K-Nearest-Neighbors
We ran KNN classifier using rectangular kernel and k = 150 to train our data, we found that larger k does not guarantee smaller error, larger k may lead to under-fitting. The results of KNN is better than Naive Bayes.

Random Forest
For Random Forest we tried different combinations of parameters. Finally we choose the maximum accuracy when we set number of trees = 150 and depth = 15.

Gradient Tree Boosting
The Gradient boosted trees performs well when set proper parameters (i.e.the number of trees and the maximum depth of each tree). We tested the algorithm on the data for permutation of the parameters. Finally we set estimators = 170 and maximum depth = 12.

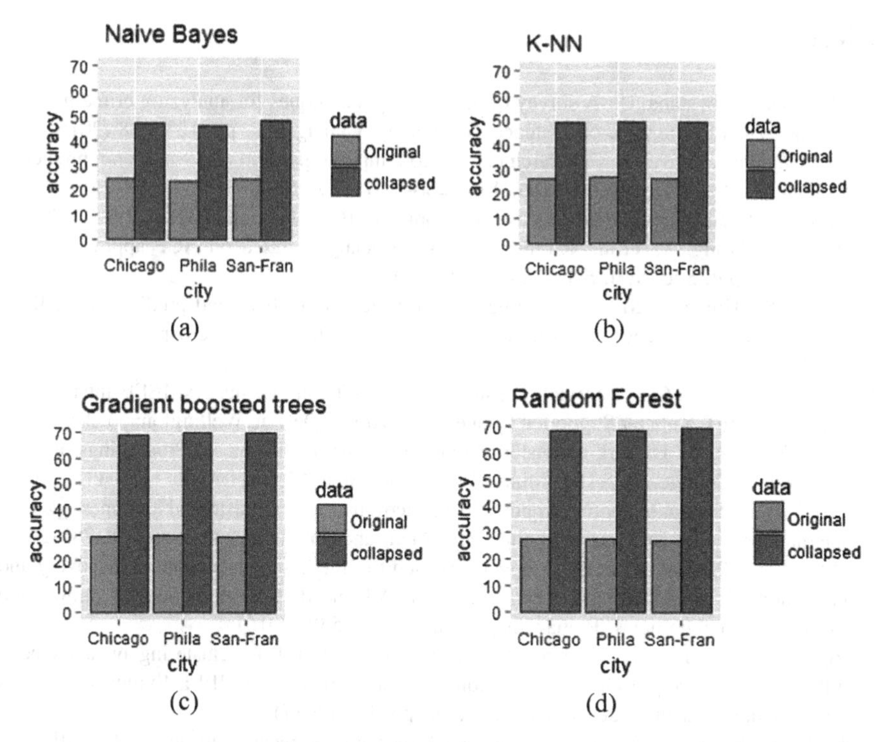

Fig. 7. The classification accuracy using different classifiers and data, we can see the Tree models (a) Naive Bayes, (b) KNN (c) Gradient boosted trees outperform (d) Random Forest, and after collapsing the accuracy of classification improves a lot.

6 Conclusion and Future Work

In this paper we analyzed crime data from 3 cities with two purpose:visualization and prediction. The initial problem of crime prediction is a multi-label classification task where the data is skewed, in order to improve accuracy we collapsed the categories to make the data balanced and chose the most important features to train data. We found that tree classification models performed better for our dataset. We also explored crime trend using time series model. In the future, we plan to add more features that related to crime incidents and using more state-of-the-art algorithms to get higher accuracy for multi-class classification problem. Besides, as Deep Learning [14–16] and Artificial Intelligence [17, 18] has achieved big success in computer vision, we also want to perform more deep learning models and other learning algorithms [19, 20] on our datasets.

Acknowledgements. This work has been supported by HJSW and Research & Development plan of Shaanxi Province (Program No. 2017ZDXM-GY-094, 2015KTZDGY04-01).

References

1. Thongsatapornwatana, U.: A survey of data mining techniques for analyzing crime patterns. In: 2nd Asian Conference on Defence Technology, Chiang Mai, pp. 123–128 (2016)
2. Yu, C., Ding, W., et al.: Hierarchical spatio-temporal pattern discovery and predictive modeling. IEEE Trans. Knowl. Data Eng. **28**(4), 979–993 (2016)
3. Musa, S.: Smart cities-a road map for development. IEEE Potentials **37**(2), 19–23 (2018)
4. Wang, S., Wang, X., et al.: Parallel crime scene analysis based on ACP approach. IEEE Trans. Comput. Soc. Syst. **5**(1), 244–255 (2018)
5. Yadav, S., Timbadia, M., et al: Crime pattern detection, analysis and prediction. In: IEEE International Conference on Electronics, Communication and Aerospace Technology, pp. 225–230 (2017)
6. Baloian, N., et al.: Crime prediction using patterns and context. In: 21st IEEE International Conference on Computer Supported Cooperative Work in Design, Wellington, pp. 2–9 (2017)
7. Zhao, X., Tang, J.: Exploring transfer learning for crime prediction. In: Proceedings of IEEE International Conference on Data Mining Workshops, New Orleans, LA, pp. 1158–1159 (2017)
8. Wu, S. et al.: Spatial-temporal campus crime pattern mining from historical alert messages. In: International Conference on Computing, Networking and Communications, pp. 778–782 (2017)
9. Vineeth, K., Pandey, A., et al.: A novel approach for intelligent crime pattern discovery and prediction. In: International Conference on Advanced Communication Control and Computing Technologies, Ramanathapuram, pp. 531–538 (2016)
10. Rodríguez, C., Gomez, D., et al.: Forecasting time series from clustering by a memetic differential fuzzy approach: an application to crime prediction. In: IEEE Symposium Series on Computational Intelligence, Honolulu, HI, pp. 1–8 (2017)
11. Joshi, A., Sabitha, A.S., et al.: Crime analysis using K-means clustering. In: 2017 3rd International Conference on Computational Intelligence and Networks, Odisha, pp. 33–39 (2017)
12. Noor, N., Ghazali, A., et al.: Supporting decision making in situational crime prevention using fuzzy association rule. In: International Conference on Computer, Control, Informatics and Its Applications (IC3INA), Jakarta, pp. 225–229 (2013)
13. Wang, M., Zhang, F., et al.: Hybrid neural network mixed with random forests and perlin noise. In: 2nd IEEE International Conference on Computer and Communications (ICCC), Chengdu, pp. 1937–1941 (2016)
14. Wang, Z., Ren, J., et al.: A deep-learning based feature hybrid framework for spatiotemporal saliency detection inside videos. Neurocomputing **287**, 68–83 (2018)
15. Ren, J., Jiang, J.: Hierarchical modeling and adaptive clustering for real-time summarization of rush videos. IEEE Trans. Multimed. **11**(5), 906–917 (2009)
16. Han, J., Zhang, D., et al.: Object detection in optical remote sensing images based on weakly supervised learning and high-level feature learning. IEEE Trans. Geosci. Remote Sens. **53** (6), 3325–3337 (2015)
17. Chen, J., Ren, J.: Modelling of content-aware indicators for effective determination of shot boundaries in compressed MPEG videos. Multimed. Tools Appl. **54**(2), 219–239 (2011)
18. Ren, J., Vlachos, T.: Immersive and perceptual human-computer interaction using computer vision techniques. In: 2010 IEEE Computer Society Conference on Computer Vision and Pattern Recognition Workshops. IEEE, pp. 66–72 (2010)
19. Yan, Y., Ren, J., et al.: Cognitive fusion of thermal and visible imagery for effective detection and tracking of pedestrians in videos. Cognit. Comput. 1–11 (2017)
20. Yan, Y., Ren, J., et al.: Unsupervised image saliency detection with Gestalt-laws guided optimization and visual attention based refinement. Pattern Recognit. **79**, 65–78 (2018)

Comparison of Sentiment Analysis Approaches Using Modern Arabic and Sudanese Dialect

Intisar O. Hussien[1], Kia Dashtipour[2](✉), and Amir Hussain[2]

[1] Faculty of Computer Science, Arab Open University, Kuwait City, Kuwait
[2] Department of Computing Science and Mathematics, University of Stirling, Stirling, UK
Kd28@cs.stir.ac.uk

Abstract. Sentiment analysis mainly focused on the automatic recognition of opinions' polarity, as positive or negative. Nowadays, sentiment analysis is replacing the web-based and traditional survey methods commonly conducted by companies for finding the public opinion about their products and services to improve their marketing strategy and product advertisement and help to improve customer service. The online availability of large text makes it important to be analyzed. The automatic analysis of this information involves a deep understanding of natural languages. Sentiments and emotions play a pivotal role in our daily lives. They assist decision-making, learning, communication, and situation awareness in human environments. The importance of processing and understanding dialect text is increasing due to the growth of socially generated dialectal content in social media. In addition to existing materials such as local proverbs, advice and folklore that are found spread on the web. This paper focused on text sentiment analysis as dialect text, as quick review to identify relevant contributions that address languages aspect for a specific dialect.

Keywords: Sentiment analysis · Affecting analysis · Arabic text Dialect

1 Introduction

Nowadays, sentiment analysis is replacing the web-based and traditional survey methods that are usually implied by companies for finding public opinion about their products and services. The surveys helped the business providers to improve their marketing strategy, customer service and product advertisement. This paper focused on text sentiment analysis as dialect text, since most users on social networks use dialectal Arabic, by giving a complete image and related dataset available and providing brief details for each type. In addition to that present the recent trend of researches in the Arabic dialect sentiment analysis, the Modern Arabic sentiment analysis and its related fields will be explored.

In the last two decades, many studies have been conducted to investigate sentiment analysis, and opinion, with a focused on English language. However, with the growth of Internet around the world, users write their comments and opinion in different languages such as Arabic. Sentiment analysis in only single languages increase the risk

J. Ren et al. (Eds.): BICS 2018, LNAI 10989, pp. 615–624, 2018.
https://doi.org/10.1007/978-3-030-00563-4_60

of missing information in text for other languages. In order to analyse data in different language, we review current approaches in Arabic sentiment analysis. In addition, we compared general Arabic dialects sentiment analysis and Sudanese dialects Arabic sentiment analysis approaches.

There are large number of dialect text is available online every day, which contain opinion features that infer what opinion behind it. The automatic analysis of text opinion involves a deep understanding of natural languages, text processing, whereas researchers are continuing to improve them. Languages depending on different factors in its morphology, syntax or lexical combinations, according to that, Arabic language is classified into three different categories: (1) MSA - Modern Standard Arabic, (2) CA - Classical Arabic and (3) DA - Dialectal Arabic. On social networks, most users typically use the latter, i.e. Dialectal Arabic. Arabic sentiment analysis faces many challenges, especially dialect sentiment analysis. One of the most problems is language itself and significant lack of its related resource, since there are no resources available, at the beginning most researchers address their work, by transformation, and get knowledge from rich language to poor recourse.

This paper is organized as follows: Sect. 2 is related work on Arabic language and the domain of dialect sentiment analysis, presents the reviewed literature on sentiment analysis, Sect. 3 comparison of modern Arabic and dialects, Sect. 4 is conclusion, concludes the paper with future research directions.

2 Related Work

In this section, we review current approaches in Arabic sentiment analysis and dialects sentiment analysis.

2.1 Linguistic Features

Sentimental analysis gained from textual aims at the extraction of appraising meaning which starts by automatic detection of the state's subjective. Here, an overview is provided about the sentiment analysis approaches in NLP (Natural Language Processing), including supervised and unsupervised methods, and future directions and limitations in the field Dialect. In natural language processing, Sentiment Analysis refers to find whether sentiment of a text which is written in natural language is positive, neural or negative, [24] this can be achieved using *supervised* "Corpus-based" sentiment analysis approach, which relies on manually labeled samples, *unsupervised.*

"Knowledge or Lexicon-based" sentiment analysis approach, or *hybrid* (both lexiconbased and corpus-based) approach.

Supervised sentiment analysis aims at building predictive models for sentiment based by exploiting machine learning classifier that is trained on a labeled data, which in turn, tests data based on it. This approach builds a feature vector of each text entry in which certain aspects or word frequencies are quantified, and then, training the standard machine learning tools and validating them against reference annotated texts. However, most of supervised approaches related to sentiment analysis are trained on specific domain and require a huge annotated corpus that manually labeled, this process is expensive and time consuming. Unsupervised sentiment analysis approaches allow an estimation that is based on expert knowledge without the need to annotated data. The expert knowledge, which is used for the estimation, is often encoded in a lexicon, in which words or phrases are annotated with their sentimental meanings. These lexica can be manually annotated by means of raters who can interpret the meaning of words. Hybrid sentiment analysis is a combination of both feature-level and decision-level methods. It aims to obtain the advantages of both feature and decision level fusion approaches and overcomes the disadvantages of both. Sentiment analysis can be grouped into three different levels based on the target of study: document level, the entire document is classified either positive or negative using machine learning approach or lexicon based approach. Sentences level, evaluation of opinion is done sentence by sentence in order to decide whether it is positive, neutral or negative. But the drawback of both levels, they provide high level of classification, the researches illustrate the previous described levels are [6, 27, 28, 30, 36, 37, 49, 50].

2.2 Modern Arabic Sentiment Analysis

Analysis using sentiment analysis requires a corpus or dataset to train a classifier and to evaluate it. This part covers Arabic Sentiment Analysis datasets, and reviews that used corpora, Table 1. Mostly used corpora were collected from social media, the content is easily and freely provided. Users can express, reach, and share opinions in public. Aly [20] proposed a corpus for Modern Standard Arabic sentiment analysis, 63,257 book reviews. The datasets contain positive reviews those with ratings 4 or 5, negative reviews those with ratings 1 or 2 and reviews with rating 3 are considered neutral. The performance of proposed corpus is evaluated using Multinomial Naive Bayes, Bernoulli Naive Bayes (BNB), and Support Vector Machines (SVM). The results showed SVM (90%) outperformed as compared to BNB. The disadvantage of the approach is the number of positive reviews is much larger than that of negative reviews, to avoid the bias of having more positive than negative reviews, they explored two set: a balanced and unbalanced, this leads to a small corpus, another disadvantage is lacks handling the neutral cases, reviews with rating 3 are considered neutral and not included in the polarity classification.

Rushdi [21] proposed corpus for Modern Standard Arabic sentiment analysis, 500 movie reviews. The dataset contains 250 positive and 250 negative reviews. The performance of proposed corpus is evaluated using Naive Bayes (NB), and Support Vector Machines (SVM). The results showed SVM (90%) outperformed as compared to NB (84.6%). The disadvantage of the approach is exploiting a small corpus and lacks handling the neutral cases, neutral cases are not included in the polarity classification. Abdul-Mageed [22] proposed a multi-genre corpus for Modern Standard Arabic sentiment analysis and also Abdul-Mageed [23] proposed a corpus for Modern Standard Arabic sentiment analysis. The datasets contain 1281 objects, 1574 subjects, 491 positive, 689 negative and 394 neutral. The performance of proposed corpus is evaluated using Support Vector Machines (SVM). The results showed SVM (90%–95%) outperformed as compared to under different parameters. The disadvantage of the approach is exploits a small corpus and. Al-Smadi [25, 26] proposed coups for Modern Standard Arabic sentiment analysis. The performance of proposed corpus is evaluated

Table 1. Modern Arabic sentiment analysis datasets.

References	Dataset	Dataset size	Techniques
Aly et al. 2013 [20]	LABR	63,257 book reviews	MNB, BNB, SVM
Rushdi et al. 2012 [21]	OCA	500 reviews(250 +ve & 250 −ve)	NB, SVM
Mageed et al. 2012 [22]	sub PATB	400 doc., 2855 sentences	SVM
Mageed et al. 2012 [23]	AWATIF	2855 sentences, 1508 web, 1019 threaded	J48, CRF
Al-Smadi et al. 2015 [25]	HAAD, sub LABR	2838 reviews	Lexicon based
Obaidat 2015 [24]	Sub HAAD	1,513 reviews	Lexicon based

using J48 and Conditional Random Filed (CRF). The results showed J48 (81%) outperformed as compared to NB (73%). The disadvantage of the approach is exploits a small corpus domain dependent. Obaidat [24] proposed a corpus lexicon-based for Modern Standard Arabic sentiment analysis, from HAAD datasets. This work focuses on the aspect based sentiment analysis for the Arabic language. Specifically, on aspect category determination and aspect category polarity determination, using lexicon-based approaches.

2.3 Arabic Dialects Sentiment Analysis

Arabic dialects and MSA share a considerable number of semantic, syntactic, morphological and lexical features, these features have many differences. However, most of the research done in these fields was focused on English texts with very limited research done for other languages such as Spanish [9, 18, 51], and Arabic [1–17], particularly the Sudanese dialect which is the language of interest for this research. There are rare study and research works on sentiment analysis for Arabic dialects sentiment analysis, majorly for the following reasons: (1) Morphological complexities (2) Dialectal varieties of the Arabic language which require advanced special lexicon building and preprocessing steps beyond what is applicable for the standard Arabic language domain, The Dialect sentiment analysis techniques and sentiment analysis corpus are summarized in Table 2.

Rizkallah [1] proposed a corpus for Saudi dialect. Compared between two sentiment strategies, sentiment analysis directly on the dialect; and sentiment after transforms from dialect to MSA. The performance of proposed corpus is evaluated using seven different classifiers such as Logistic Regression, Passive Aggressive, SVM, Perceptron, Multinomial Naive Bayes, SGD and KNN. The result showed that Logistic Regression (76.2%) outperformed as compared to other classifiers. The disadvantage of this corpus is only used for Saudi dialect. Shoukry [2] proposed a corpus for Egyptian dialect. The corpus contains 500 positive and 500 negative tweets. The performance of proposed corpus is evaluated using Naive Bayes classifier and Support Vector

Table 2. Arabic dialects sentiment analysis corpus and sentiment techniques.

References	Dialect languages	Dataset	Techniques	Accuracy
Rizkallah et al. 2018 [1]	Saudi	Saudi twitter data	SVM, NB, KNN	76.2%
Assiri et al. 2016 [16]	Saudi	4700 tweets	ML	80.2%
Abdulla, et al. 2013 [3]	MSA + DA, Jordanian	2000 tweets	Lexicon, SVM, NB, KNN, D-Tree	80%
Mageed 2014 [6]	MSA, DA, Egyptian	4 diff datasets	SVM	84–67%
Salamah et al. 2014 [5]	Kuwait	340,000 tweets	SVM, J48, AD-Tree & R-Tree	76%
Mahgouba et al. 2015	Egyptian + other	3015 tweets	Arab SentiNet Lexicon	-
Shoukry et al. 2012 [2]	Egyptian	1000 tweets	SVM and NB	72%
Sadat et al. 2014 [15]	18 differ Dialects	2000 words	NB Markov	98%
Zribi et al. 2017 [14]	Tunisian	42388 words	SVM, PART and PIPER	87.32%
Ibrahim et al. 2015 [30]	Egyptian, MSA	4000 tweets	-	
AL-Twairesh 2015 [38]	Saudi	17,573 tweets	Support Vector Machines with a linear kernel	62.27%

Machine. The result showed SVM (72%) outperformed as compared to SO approach (65%). The disadvantage of this approach is only used for Egyptian dialect, lacks handling the neutral cases and exploits a small corpus. Abdulla [3] proposed a corpus-based and lexicon-based for Jordanian dialect and MSA. The corpus contains 1000 positive and 1000 negative tweets. The performance of the proposed corpus is evaluated using SVM, NB, KNN, and Decision tree classifiers. The experimental results showed SVM & NB (80%) outperformed as compared to other classifiers. The disadvantage of the approach is lacks handling the neutral cases and exploits a small corpus and exploits a small Jordanian dialect tweets. Mageed [4] proposed a corpus for MSA and dialect. The corpus contains 3015, where 1549 different dialects and 1466 MSN. The polarity lexicon used was Arab SentiNet which contains 3982 adjectives extracted from the news domain. Salamah [5] proposed a corpus for Kuwaiti dialect. The corpus contains 340,000 tweets. The performance of proposed corpus is evaluated using SVM J48, AD Tree, Random Tree, and Random Tree classifier. The results showed SVM (76%) outperformed as compared to others. The disadvantage of the approach is only used for Kuwaiti dialect, unknown of number of negative and positive tweets. Mageed [6] proposed a corpus for MSN and dialect. The corpus contains four datasets. The performance of proposed corpus is evaluated using SVM classifier. The results showed SVM (84–67%) outperformed. The disadvantage of the approach is only used for Egyptian dialect. Alayba [7] proposed a corpus for health dialect. The corpus contains 2026 tweets, 628 positive and 1398 negative words. The performance of proposed corpus is evaluated using Naïve Bayes, Support Vector Machine and Logistic Regression classifier and Deep and Convolutional Neural Networks. The results showed SVM (91%) outperformed as compared to other rang to 80%. The disadvantage of the approach is domain dependent, number of positive large compare to negative. Al-Harbi [8] proposed a corpus for Saudi dialect. The corpus contains 5,500 tweets, 1,415 positive, 2,434 negative and 1,634 Neutral. The performance of proposed corpus is evaluated using NB, SVM and KNN classifiers. The results showed KNN (73%) outperformed as compared to SVM (57%). The disadvantage of the approach is only used for Egyptian dialect.

Sadat [15] proposed a multi dialect corpus for 18 different countries. The corpus contains 1000 positive and 1000 negative words. The performance of proposed corpus is evaluated using Naive Bayes classifier. The results showed Naive Bayes 98% outperformed as average. The disadvantage of the approach is the corpus is small to represent 8 countries, and used only one classifier, Naïve Bayes. Assiri [16] proposed a corpus for Saudi dialect. The corpus contains 1830 positive, 1991 negative and 904 neutral twitter. The performance of proposed corpus is evaluated using ML classifier. The results showed (80%). The disadvantage of the approach is only used for Saudi dialect, and only one classifier used. Al-Shargi [19] proposed two corpora for Moroccan (MOR) and Yemeni (YEMS). The MOR corpus contains 64K words, while the YEMS corpus has 32.5K words. The performance of proposed corpus is evaluated using Blogmeter's classifier. The results showed Blogmeter's technique (62.7%) outperformed. The disadvantage of the approach is only used for Italy and it is focusing only on detecting irony in the sentences. Al-Ayyoub [37] proposed lexicon based corpus for Modern Standard Arabic sentiment analysis, 900 tweets. The dataset contains 300 positive, 300 negative and 300 natural. The performance of proposed corpus is evaluated using SVM. The results showed SVM (86.89%) outperformed. Nabil [29] proposed a corpus for Egyptian dialect. The corpus contains 10,000 tweets. The performance of proposed corpus is evaluated using SVM, MNB, BNB, SVM, SGD KNN, Logistic Regression, Linear Perceptron, Passive Aggressive classifier. The results showed SVM and MNB outperformed better compared to others. The disadvantage of the approach is only used for Egyptian dialect. Medhaffar [39] proposed a corpus for Tunisian dialect. The corpus contains 17,000 tweets. The performance of proposed corpus is evaluated using SVM, NB and MLP classifiers. The results showed SVM and MLP outperformed similar results for all experimental setups as compared to others. The disadvantage of the approach is only used for Tunisian dialect, unknown of number of negative and positive tweets. Al-Twairesh [38] proposed a corpus for Saudi dialect. The corpus contains 17,573 tweets, 4957 Positive, 6155 Negative, 4639 Neutral and 1822 Mixed. The performance of proposed corpus is evaluated using Support Vector Machines with a linear kernel classifier with three different datasets. The results showed positive and negative method (62.27%) outperformed compared to others. The disadvantage of the approach is used only one classifier.

3 Dialect Distinction in Modern Standard Arabic

In this section, we compared Arabic dialects sentiment analysis and Sudanese dialects sentiment analysis.

3.1 Arabic Dialects Sentiment Analysis

The written form of the Native languages of Arabic speakers for each region (dialects) is different from Modern Standard Arabic language. The various spoken regional dialects of Arabic differ somewhat from each other. Since written form is almost in Modern Standard Arabic, and all Arabic datasets have mainly Modern Standard Arabic content. However, dialects have many challenges for NLP searches working on NLP, mainly spoken dialects, they lack standardization, are written in free-text and showed significant variation from MSA [31]. Habash breakdown of regional dialects into main six groups is as Egyptian, Levantine, Gulf, Iraqi, Maghrebi and others. There are large number of linguistic differences between the regional dialects and MSA [32].

- The level of short vowels, which do not appear in written form or omitted in Arabic text. another difference, In MSA addition to the singular and plural forms MSA has a dual form, one masculine and one feminine, whereas the dialects mostly lack the dual form and many dialects often make no such gendered uniqueness, also, dialects have a more complex open system than MSA, allowing for the combination of a prefix and a suffix that attach to a base, negation, pronouns to act as indirect objects.
- MSA has a complex grammatical case system, while Dialects is lack of that. Dialects lack diacritics, while in MSA most cases are expressed with diacritics that are rarely explicitly written, as it is expressed using a suffix as on adverbs and objects.
- Orthography standardization, there are lexical choice differences in the vocabulary itself, e.g. {Money, (نقود – مصاري – فلوس – قروش)} {Beautiful girl, (مزيونة - زينةجميلة – حلوة -} and {Now, (الان – هلا – الحين – دلوقت – هسه - هلحزة)}, these differences go beyond a lack of orthography standardization.
- Differences in verb conjugation, even when the root is kept e.g. conjugations of the root, (ل - ع - ب){He play, (يلعب – بيلعب - بلعب)}.
Negation, (بلا – لا –ما – ما في – عكس- مش كدة –غير -عديم).

3.2 Sudanese Dialects Sentiment Analysis

Modern Arabic is the superclass of Arabic dialects spoken in the North Africa region, principally Egypt, Sudan and Maghreb region. Sudanese Arabic dialects include principally Modern Standard Arabic in additional to it is dialects. At phonological level, Sudanese Arabic dialects share the most features of standard Arabic. In additional, 28 Arabic consonants phonemes, the used of (ذ as د)ث(as ت). At Lexical level, Sudanese dialects' vocabulary is mostly inspired from Modern Standard Arabic but it is phonologically altered, with significant Greek, Turkish and English. The morphology of Sudanese dialectal words shares a lot of features with MSA morphology. But dialect inflection method is more complicated in some aspect than MSA, an example, the affixation system method. To our knowledge specific research related to Sudanese sentiment analysis was not found, only three researchers include Sudanese dialect within their corpus as multi dialect corpus. Almeman and Lee [33] proposed a multi dialect corpus for Egyptian, Levantine Gulf North Africa dialect. Two morphological analyzers were used, the first, MSA morphological analyzer and in the second applies word segmentation and uses web data as a corpus to produce statistical information in the second one. The performance of proposed corpus is evaluated using linguistic rules. The results showed improved to (69%) outperformed as overall accuracy. Sadat [35] proposed a multi dialect corpus for six different regions, Egypt; Iraq, Iraq; Gulf (Bahrein, Emirates, Kuwait, Qatar, Oman and Saudi Arabia); Maghrebi (Algeria, Tunisia, Morocco, Libya, Mauritania); Levantine (Jordan, Lebanon, Palestine, Syria); Others: Sudan. The corpus contains 100 sentences for each country. The performance of proposed corpus is evaluated using Naïve Bayes and Support Vector Machine classifier. The results showed Naïve Bayes (98%) outperformed as compared to SVM (78%). Mubarak proposed Multi-dialectic corpus based on twitter data was built in [34] for seven different dialects, Sudan is one of them. The results accuracy for Saudi (93%).

4 Conclusion

Dialect gained high interest from the research community. Different techniques have been used for Arabic sentiment analysis of Arabic and direct Arabic too; supervised learning using machine learning methods, unsupervised learning using sentiment lexicons and a hybrid approach, which combines the two techniques, which have proven to gain high accuracy. In this paper, we tried to review all the literature that was found on Arabic sentiment analysis, include the proposed corpus and highlighting the results and accuracies reached by each research. The complexity of Arabic language has led to the rise of different challenges in SSA of Arabic. However, there are still many gaps in SSA of Arabic research, such as Opinion summarization, target extraction opinion and Aspect level techniques have not been addressed in detail as other languishes. Dialect Arabic is still a poor language resource, so most research works have been spent on building and annotating dialectical corpora. Morphology and syntactical, are frequently used to perform towards building language resources, however many paper researches addressed the morphology of dialectical Arabic, while most of them ignored the syntactical analysis. Future work; we will start a new process for Sudanese dialect sentiment analysis.

Acknowledgment. Amir Hussain was supported by the UK Engineering and Physical Sciences Research Council (EPSRC) grant No. EP/M026981/1.

References

1. Abdul-Mageed, M., Kübler, S., Diab, M.: SAMAR: subjectivity and sentiment analysis for Arabic social media. In: Proceedings of WASSA 2012, vol. 28, no. 1, pp. 19–28 (2012)
2. Salamah, J.B., Elkhlifi, A.: Microblogging opinion mining approach for Kuwaiti dialect. In: The International Conference on Computing Technology and Information Management (ICCTIM2014), pp. 388–396. The Society of Digital Information and Wireless Communication (2014)

3. Abdul-Mageed, M., Diab, M., Kübler, S.: SAMAR: subjectivity and sentiment analysis for Arabic social media. Comput. Speech Lang. **28**(1), 20–37 (2014)
4. Alayba, A.M., Palade, V., England, M., Iqbal, R.: Arabic language sentiment analysis on health services. In: 2017 1st International Workshop on Arabic Script Analysis and Recognition (ASAR), pp. 114–118. IEEE (2017)
5. Al-Harbi, W.A., Emam, A.: Effect of Saudi dialect preprocessing on Arabic sentiment analysis. Int. J. Adv. Comput. Technol. (IJACT) (2015)
6. Jarrar, M., Habash, N., Alrimawi, F., Akra, D., Zalmout, N.: Curras: an annotated corpus for the Palestinian Arabic dialect. Lang. Resour. Eval. **51**(3), 745–775 (2017)
7. Zaidan, O.F., Callison-Burch, C.: The Arabic online commentary dataset: an annotated dataset of informal Arabic with high dialectal content. In: Proceedings of the 49th Annual Meeting of the Association for Computational Linguistics: Human Language Technologies: Short Papers, vol. 2, pp. 37–41. Association for Computational Linguistics (2011)
8. Ieracitano, C., Duun-Henriksen, J., Mammone, N., La Foresta, F., Morabito, F.C.: Wavelet coherence-based clustering of EEG signals to estimate the brain connectivity in absence epileptic patients. In: 2017 International Joint Conference on Neural Networks (IJCNN), pp. 1297–1304. IEEE (2017)
9. Khalifa, S., Habash, N., Abdulrahim, D., Hassan, S.: A large-scale corpus of Gulf Arabic. arXiv preprint arXiv:1609.02960 (2016)
10. Diab, M., Habash, N., Rambow, O., Altantawy, M., Benajiba, Y.: COLABA: Arabic dialect annotation and processing. In: LREC Workshop on Semitic Language Processing, pp. 66–74 (2010)
11. Al- Sabbagh, R., Girju, R.: YADAC: yet another dialectal arabic corpus. In: LREC, pp. 2882–2889 (2012)
12. Zribi, I., Ellouze, M., Belguith, L.H., Blache, P.: Morphological disambiguation of Tunisian dialect. J. King Saud Univ. Comput. Inf. Sci. **29**(2), 147–155 (2017)
13. Sadat, F., Kazemi, F., Farzindar, A.: Automatic identification of Arabic dialects in social media. In: Proceedings of the First International Workshop on Social Media Retrieval and Analysis, pp. 35–40. ACM (2014)
14. Assiri, A., Emam, A., Al-Dossari, H.: Saudi twitter corpus for sentiment analysis. World Acad. Sci. Eng. Technol. Int. J. Comput. Electr. Autom. Control Inf. Eng. **10**(2), 272 (2016)
15. Bosco, C., Patti, V., Bolioli, A.: Developing corpora for sentiment analysis and opinion mining: a survey and the Senti-TUT case study. IEEE Intell. Syst. **28**(2), 55–63 (2013). [12] A. Weichselbraun, S. Gindl, A. Scharl, Ext
16. Rosas, V.P., Mihalcea, R., Morency, L.P.: Multimodal sentiment analysis of Spanish online videos. IEEE Intell. Syst. **28**(3), 38–45 (2013)
17. Al-Shargi, F., Kaplan, A., Eskander, R., Habash, N., Rambow, O.: Morphologically annotated corpora and morphological analyzers for Moroccan and Sanaani Yemeni Arabic. In: 10th Language Resources and Evaluation Conference (LREC 2016) (2016)
18. Aly, M., Atiya, A.: LABR: a large scale Arabic book reviews dataset. In: Proceedings of the 51st Annual Meeting of the Association for Computational Linguistics, Short Papers, vol. 2, pp. 494–498 (2013)
19. Rushdi Saleh, M., Martín Valdivia, M.T., Ureña López, L.A., Perea Ortega, J.M.: OCA: opinion corpus for Arabic. J. Assoc. Inf. Sci. Technol. **62**(10), 2045–2054 (2011)
20. Abdul-Mageed, M., Diab, M.T.: AWATIF: a multi-genre corpus for modern standard Arabic subjectivity and sentiment analysis. In: LREC, pp. 3907–3914 (2012)
21. Abdul-Mageed, M., Diab, M.T., Korayem, M.: Subjectivity and sentiment analysis of modern standard Arabic. In: Proceedings of the 49th Annual Meeting of the Association for Computational Linguistics: Human Language Technologies: Short Papers, vol. 2, pp. 587–591. Association for Computational Linguistics (2011)

22. Obaidat, I., Mohawesh, R., Al-Ayyoub, M., Mohammad, A.S., Jararweh, Y.: Enhancing the determination of aspect categories and their polarities in Arabic reviews using lexicon-based approaches. In: IEEE Jordan Conference on Applied Electrical Engineering and Computing Technologies (AEECT), pp. 1–6. IEEE (2015)
23. Al-Smadi, M., Qawasmeh, O., Talafha, B., Quwaider, M.: Human annotated Arabic dataset of book reviews for aspect based sentiment analysis. In: 2015 3rd International Conference on Future Internet of Things and Cloud (FiCloud), pp. 726–730 (2015)
24. Al-Smadi, M., et al.: Using aspect-based sentiment analysis to evaluate Arabic news affect on readers. In: 2015 IEEE/ACM 8th International Conference on Utility and Cloud Computing (UCC). IEEE (2015)
25. Duwairi, R.M., Marji, R., Sha'ban, N., Rushaidat, S.: Sentiment analysis in Arabic tweets. In: 2014 5th International Conference on Information and Communication Systems (ICICS), pp. 1–6. IEEE (2014)
26. Duwairi, R.M.: Sentiment analysis for dialectical Arabic. In: 2015 6th International Conference on Information and Communication Systems (ICICS), pp. 166–170. IEEE (2015)
27. Nabil, M., Aly, M., Atiya, A.F.: ASTD: Arabic sentiment tweets dataset. In: Proceedings of the 2015 Conference on Empirical Methods in Natural Language Processing, pp. 2515–2519 (2015)
28. Ibrahim, H.S., Abdou, S.M., Gheith, M.: MIKA: a tagged corpus for modern standard Arabic and colloquial sentiment analysis. In: 2015 IEEE 2nd International Conference on Recent Trends in Information Systems (ReTIS), vol. 2, pp. 353–358 (2015)
29. Zaidan, O.F., Callison-Burch, C.: Arabic dialect identification. Comput. Linguist. **40**(1), 171–202 (2014)
30. Mubarak, H., Darwish, K. (2014). Using Twitter to collect a multi-dialectal corpus of Arabic. In: ANLP 2014, pp. 1–7 (2014)
31. Sadat, F., Kazemi, F., Farzindar, A.: Automatic identification of Arabic language varieties and dialects in social media. In: SocialNLP 2014, pp. 22–27 (2014)
32. Dashtipour, K., et al.: Multilingual sentiment analysis: state of the art and independent comparison of techniques. Cognit. Comput. **8**(4), 757–771 (2016)
33. Al-Ayyoub, M., Essa, S.B., Alsmadi, I.: Lexicon-based sentiment analysis of Arabic tweets. Int. J. Soc. Netw. Min. **2**(2), 101–114 (2015)
34. Al-Twairesh, N., Al-Khalifa, H., Al-Salman, A., Al-Ohali, Y.: AraSenTi-Tweet: a corpus for arabic sentiment analysis of Saudi tweets. Procedia Comput. Sci. **117**, 63–72 (2017)
35. Medhaffar, S., Bougares, F., Esteve, Y., Hadrich-Belguith, L.: Sentiment analysis of Tunisian dialects: linguistic resources and experiments. In: Proceedings of the Third Arabic Natural Language Processing Workshop, pp. 55–61 (2017)
36. Pang, B., Lee, L.: Opinion mining and sentiment analysis. Foundations and Trends®. Inf. Retr. **2**(1–2), 1–135 (2008)
37. Chen, J., Ren, J., Jiang, J.: Modelling of content-aware indicators for effective determination of shot boundaries in compressed MPEG videos. Multimed. Tools Appl. **54**(2), 219–239 (2011)
38. Morabito, F.C., et al.: Deep convolutional neural networks for classification of mild cognitive impaired and Alzheimer's disease patients from scalp EEG recordings. In: 2016 IEEE 2nd International Forum on Research and Technologies for Society and Industry Leveraging a Better Tomorrow (RTSI), pp. 1–6. IEEE (2016)
39. Gasparini, S., et al.: Information theoretic-based interpretation of a deep neural network approach in diagnosing psychogenic non-epileptic seizures. Entropy **20**(2), 43 (2018)

An Intelligent Question Answering System for University Courses Based on BiLSTM and Keywords Similarity

Chunyan Ma, Baomin Li(✉), Tong Zhao, and Wei Wei

School of Software and Microelectronics, Northwestern Polytechical Universiy, Xi'an, China
machunyan@nwpu.edu.cn, libaomin_NWPU@163.com

Abstract. The application of intelligent question answering system in college assistant teaching is an effective way to reduce the workload of university teachers and improve students' learning efficiency. With the rapid development of related technologies, the intelligent question answering system has made great progress, but there is little related work in answering students' university course questions, and there are some problems such as poor accuracy and non universality. Because of this reason, it cannot fully meet the demands of universities. Therefore, this paper proposes an intelligent question answering system for professional questions. First, we select candidate question-and-answer pairs in the knowledge base through professional word matching, and then use the attention mechanism proposed in this paper and bi-directional long short term memory network (BiLSTM) to calculate the semantic similarity between query questions and candidate questions. Multiplying the semantic similarity by the keywords similarity of the two questions as the final similarity. Finally, we push the three most similar candidate questions and the corresponding answers to students. The experimental results show that the system improves the accuracy of answering students' university course questions, and is applicable to any university course.

Keywords: Intelligent question answering system · Semantic similarity Keywords similarity

1 Introduction

At present, college students rely mainly on the Internet or teacher to solve the problem. However, the former requires students to filter the required content in a large number of resources, and the latter will bring greater workload to university teachers whose research tasks are increasing year by year. Therefore, how to balance students' learning efficiency and teachers' work pressure becomes an urgent problem to be solved.

In order to solve the above problem, by using bidirectional long short term memory network (BiLSTM) and keywords similarity algorithms, this paper proposes an intelligent question answering system for college teaching assistants, which aims at the characteristics of college course professional questions. The system can provide direct

J. Ren et al. (Eds.): BICS 2018, LNAI 10989, pp. 625–632, 2018.
https://doi.org/10.1007/978-3-030-00563-4_61

and effective answers to students and can be a part of the Intelligent Computer Aided Instruction (ICAI) System [1].

2 Related Works

Intelligent question answering system as the next generation of search engines has attracted the attention of a large number of researchers. Previous researches mainly include semantic analysis and information retrieval methods [2]. Devi et al. [3] and Kahaduwa et al. [4] queried the answers through SPARQL. Yih et al. [5] proposed a semantic analysis framework for the knowledge base question answering system to simplify the semantic analysis into the query graph generation problem. Xu et al. [6] proposed a neural network based relation extraction method to retrieve candidate answers from FreeBase.

With the advent of related data resources such as WebQuestions [7] and SQuAD [8], the intelligent question answering system has been further developed. Researchers have now tended to use artificial neural networks to convert questions and answers into semantic vectors and select correct answers by calculating the distance between the question vector and the answer vector. Minaee et al. [9] used an insurance question and answer dataset to train an automated QA model based on deep learning, and select the most similar answers to user questions as the best answer. Lei et al. [10] used the NLPCC2016KBQA dataset to train bidirectional long short term memory network for calculating the similarity between the question and the candidate answer, and used the candidate answer with the highest similarity as the correct answer.

Through the efforts of a large number of researchers, the intelligent question answering system has made a fruitful achievement, but there are still many deficiencies in answering university course questions. Zhou [11] based on domain knowledge ontology and extended key terms set, built SPARQL query to find answers. However, this method takes a lot of time to construct domain ontology for each course, thus, its portability is poor. Chen [12] got the correct answer by keyword matching, Wang [13] proposed an intelligent question answering system for college course, combining TF-IDF, semantic dictionary and sentence structure. However, the above two methods lack the semantic analysis of the question context. In contrary, this paper constructs the FAQ knowledge base which is quite convenient for teachers; in addition, this paper using BiLSTM analyzes the context semantics of the question, and calculates the keywords similarity between the questions, and improves the accuracy of the intelligent question answering system by combining the sentence structure information and semantic information.

3 Overview

The current intelligent question answering system includes open domain question answering system and knowledge base (KB) question answering system. The open domain question answering system searches for relevant content on the Internet through search engines and processes related content to return the answer [14]. The information of professional questions is mainly from related community forums and cannot guarantee the accuracy of the answer. Therefore, this paper adopts the question answering system based on knowledge base.

The existing intelligent question answering system based on knowledge base is mainly used to calculate the semantic similarity between the query question and the answer in knowledge base, but there is still a certain sentence pattern difference between the question and the answer, which will cause a certain degree interference to semantic similarity calculation; therefore, this paper calculates the similarity between the query question and the question in knowledge base. The overview of the system is shown in Fig. 1. First, we generate candidate questions through professional vocabulary matching. Then the semantic similarity between the query question and each candidate question is calculated through the attention mechanism proposed in this paper and the bidirectional long short term memory network. At last, we calculate the keywords similarity between the query question and each candidate question, and use the product of the semantic similarity calculated by the neural network and the keywords similarity as the final similarity, and the three most similar candidate questions and the corresponding answers will be shown to students.

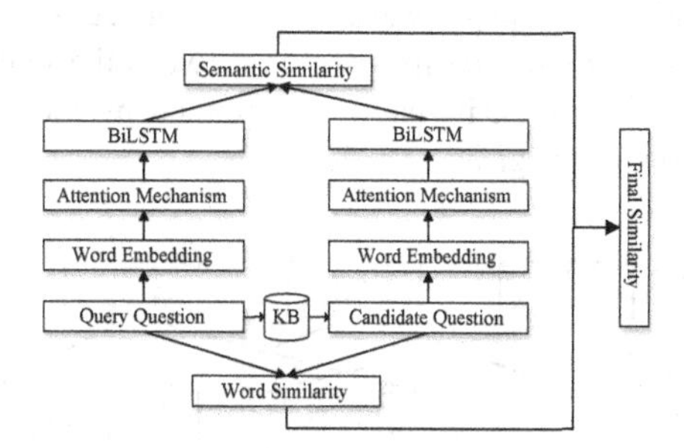

Fig. 1. The overview of the proposed KB-QA system.

4 Our Approach

4.1 Candidate Question Generation Using Professional Vocabulary Matching

In theory, calculating the similarity between the query question and each question in the knowledge base separately will produce the highest accuracy, but at the same time it will also bring huge time cost. Different from the description method of daily language, the description method of the question in the university course has a certain degree of professionalism, that is, the two questions with the same meaning must have the same professional vocabulary. Therefore, candidates can be selected in the knowledge base through professional vocabulary matching.

As we all know, professional vocabulary has the highest degree of importance in the corresponding course materials. Therefore, this paper adopts the TF-IDF algorithm [15] to process each chapter in the electronic textbook of the corresponding course, and obtain the importance of each vocabulary in each chapter of the textbook. In this paper, it is called "Chapter Vocabulary Importance Table". Then, we select the vocabulary of the first 10% (acquired by the crossover experiment) of the importance of each chapter as the professional vocabulary of the corresponding course. After that, we search the professional vocabulary in the query question through the professional vocabulary set, and select the question containing the same professional vocabulary in knowledge base as candidate questions.

4.2 Proposed Attention Mechanism

The attention mechanism [16] has been widely applied in many natural language processing tasks such as reading comprehension [17], semantic similarity calculation [18], and machine translation [19], which has greatly improved the effect of these tasks. At present, the value of attention is mainly calculated by means of vector dot product, cosine similarity, and neural network, but the above methods will additionally generate parameters that need training. Based on the previous work, this paper proposes a new attention mechanism for the above problems.

The distance between the sentence vectors represents the similarity between the sentences, and is determined by the respective subvectors, that is, the word embedding in the sentence. Therefore, this paper weakens the influence of the unimportant words on the sentence vectors. As a result, the distance between the sentence vectors, that is, the similarity between sentences, is mainly determined by the important words. The specific method is shown in Fig. 2.

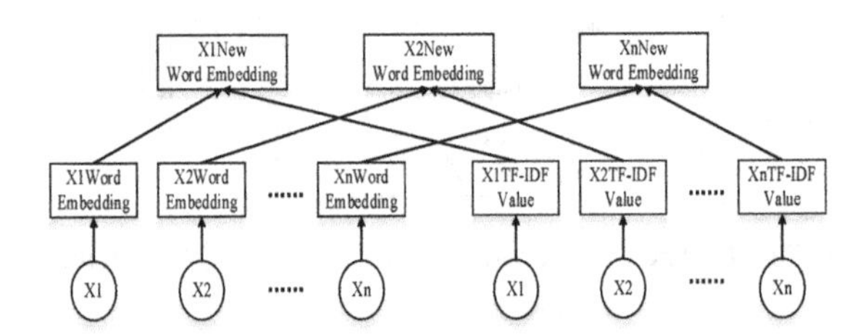

Fig. 2. The architecture of the proposed attention mechanism.

(1) Get the word embedding of each word in the question according to the pre-training word vector table;
(2) Find the importance degree of each word of the query question in the "Chapter Vocabulary Importance Table" where the query question belongs to;
(3) Multiply the word embedding of each word in the sentence by its important degree value to obtain a new word embedding. The sentence vector consisted of the new word embedding will be used as the input of the neural network.

4.3 Question-Question Semantic Similarity Based on BiLSTM

To better obtain the semantics of the question, this paper uses a bidirectional long short term memory network (BiLSTM) with contextual memory to deal with the question.

The neural network uses memory blocks instead of the traditional hidden nodes to reduce the gradient disappearance or the gradient explosion. LSTM enters the question forward one time, when dealing with a word, it only gets the above information of the word, but BiLSTM can input the question in the forward and reverse directions, not only obtaining the above information of the word but also capturing the following information of the word, which has a better result and has been proven to be effective in many natural language processing tasks [2].

In this paper, the question is taken as the input of the BiLSTM, and the vector representing the semantic of the question is obtained. The distance which represents the similarity of the two questions between the two vectors is calculated as follows [20].

$$dis = \exp(-\|h_1 - h_2\|_1) \tag{1}$$

h_1 and h_2 represent the output of the last hidden state of the two BiLSTMs respectively.

4.4 Final Predictions Combining Semantic Similarity and Keywords Similarity

As mentioned above, the question description method in the university curriculum has a certain degree of professionalism. No matter how the sentence pattern of a professional question changes, two professional questions must have the same professional vocabulary to achieve a similar effect. The degree of similarity between two questions can be further determined by the keywords similarity. The keywords similarity is calculated as follows.

$$keyWordSim = \frac{SameKeyWords(Q1, Q2) * 2}{Q1KeyWords + Q2KeyWords} \tag{2}$$

$SameKeyWords(Q1, Q2)$ represents the same number of keywords in question1 and question2, $Q1KeyWords$ represents the number of keywords in question1, $Q2KeyWords$ represents the number of keywords in question2. In particular, the synonyms of the keywords are also used as the same keywords. For example, "feature" is a keyword in question1, and "characteristics" is a keyword in question2; since "feature" and "characteristics" are synonyms, then "feature" and "characteristics" can be used as the same keywords. Multiplying the keywords similarity calculated in this section and the semantic similarity calculated by the neural network as the final similarity value, and using the answer corresponding to the three most similar candidate questions as the correct answer.

4.5 Training

This paper calculates the similarity between the query question and the candidate questions, and pushes the three most similar candidate questions and the corresponding answers to students. Therefore, the accuracy of similarity calculation represents the accuracy of the proposed intelligent question answering system in this paper. Quora-

Question-Pairs [21], an authoritative dataset provided by Quora, is now widely used in semantic similarity calculation tasks. There are over 400000 question-question pairs, and each pair includes two questions and a label which indicates whether the two questions are similar (label value is "1") or not (label value is "0"). This paper uses this dataset as training data to train the neural network. Finally, it uses the mean square error (MSE) loss function to calculate the error between the predicted value and the label value.

5 Experiments

To evaluate the proposed intelligent question answering system, we conducted experiments on the dataset collected in this paper.

5.1 Settings

This paper uses Stanford's pre-trained 300-dimensional word vector table to obtain the word vector. Adam function is used as the optimization function. The learning rate is set to 0.001. The hidden embedding of the bidirectional long short term memory network is set to 100, and the state of the hidden layer of the BiLSTM is initialized for Gaussian distribution. In order to avoid overfitting, we set the Dropout value to 0.5.

5.2 Results

This paper takes the course of "Object-oriented Analysis and Design" as an example. The frequently asked questions collected by university teachers who have been teaching for many years are taken as the question-answer pairs in knowledge base; in addition, 100 students query the relevant course questions through the system to verify the accuracy of the system. The result is shown in Table 1. In addition, Table 2 shows the effectiveness of each module in our method.

Table 1. Experiment results.

Methods	Accuracy
Zhou	74%
Wang	92.5%
Our approach	95%

Zhou [11] and Wang [13] proposed intelligent question answering system for college courses based on SPARQL and sentence structure respectively. As shown in Table 1, our approach outperforms the previous related research work.

As shown in Table 2, if we only use BiLSTM, the accuracy of the system is 78%; however, when we add keywords similarity and attention mechanism, the accuracy of the system gradually increases.

Table 2. The effectiveness of each module.

Methods	Accuracy
BiLSTM	78%
BiLSTM + keywordsSimilarity	86%
BiLSTM + keywordsSimilarity + AM	95%

6 Conclusion and Future Work

This paper proposes an intelligent question answering system which is suitable for college professional courses. First, according to the characteristics of the college course questions with certain specialties, the method of using professional vocabulary matching to generate candidate questions is proposed. Second, this paper uses the BiLSTM and the keywords similarity algorithm to calculate the similarity between query question and each candidate question. At last, this paper selects the three candidate questions with the highest degree of similarity to the query question, and uses the corresponding answer as the correct answer. Experiments show that this method is suitable for the question and answer task of college professional courses.

Recently, many state-of-the-art deep learning [22, 23] and feature selection [24–26] algorithms have made great progress in computer vision and image processing. In the future, we plan to employ these methods to our system to further improve the effectiveness.

Acknowledgements. The project is supported by HJSW and Research & Development plan of Shaanxi Province (Program No. 2017ZDXM-GY-094, 2015KTZDGY04-01).

References

1. Zhang, J., Ma, Y., et al.: A research on student model based on intelligent computer assisted instruction. In: International Conference on IC4E 2010, pp. 308–310. IEEE (2010)
2. Hao, Y., Zhang, Y., et al.: An end-to-end model for question answering over knowledge base with cross-attention combining global knowledge. In: Proceedings of the 55th Annual Meeting of the Association for Computational Linguistics, Long Papers, vol. 1, pp. 221–231 (2017)
3. Devi, M., Dua, M., et al.: An agriculture domain question answering system using ontologies. In: International Conference on Computing, Communication and Automation, pp. 122–127 (2017)
4. Kahaduwa, H., Pathirana, D., et al.: Question answering system for the travel domain. In: Engineering Research Conference, pp. 449–454. IEEE (2017)
5. Yih, S.W., Chang, M.W., et al.: Semantic parsing via staged query graph generation: question answering with knowledge base (2015)
6. Xu, K., Reddy, S., et al.: Question answering on freebase via relation extraction and textual evidence. arXiv preprint arXiv:1603.00957 (2016)
7. Berant, J., Chou, A., et al.: Semantic parsing on freebase from question–answer pairs. In: Proceedings of the 2013 Conference on Empirical Methods in Natural Language Processing, pp. 1533–1544 (2013)

8. Rajpurkar, P., Zhang, J., et al.: Squad: 100,000+ questions for machine comprehension of text. arXiv preprint arXiv:1606.05250 (2016)
9. Minaee, S., Liu, Z.: Automatic question–answering using a deep similarity neural network. arXiv preprint arXiv:1708.01713 (2017)
10. Lei, K., Deng, Y., et al.: Open domain question answering with character-level deep learning models. In: 10th International Symposium on, vol. 2, pp. 30–33. IEEE (2017)
11. Zhou, Y.: An Automatic Question Answering System Based on Ontology. Jiangsu University of Science and Technology, Zhenjiang (2011)
12. Chen, X.: Research and implementation of curriculum knowledge quiz system based on community Q & a technology (2017)
13. Wang, X.: Research on Intelligent Question Answering System Based on Chinese Word Segmentation and Knowledge Ontology Technology. Hunan University, Changsha (2015)
14. Chen, D., Fisch, A., et al.: Reading Wikipedia to answer open-domain questions. arXiv preprint arXiv:1704.00051 (2017)
15. Larson, R.R., et al.: Introduction to information retrieval. J. Am. Soc. Inf. Sci. Technol. **61** (4), 852–853 (2010)
16. Mnih, V., Heess, N., Graves, A.: Recurrent models of visual attention. In: Advances in Neural Information Processing Systems, pp. 2204–2212 (2014)
17. Wang, W., Yang, N., et al.: Gated self-matching networks for reading comprehension and question answering. In: Proceedings of the 55th Annual Meeting of the Association for Computational Linguistics, Long Papers, vol. 1, pp. 189–198 (2017)
18. Wang, Z., Hamza, W., et al.: Bilateral multi-perspective matching for natural language sentences (2017)
19. Bahdanau, D., Cho, K., et al.: Neural machine translation by jointly learning to align and translate. arXiv preprint arXiv:1409.0473 (2014)
20. Mueller, J., Thyagarajan, A.: Siamese recurrent architectures for learning sentence similarity. In: Thirtieth AAAI Conference on Artificial Intelligence, pp. 2786–2792. AAAI Press (2016)
21. Xiao, H., Meng, L.: Hungarian layer: logics empowered neural architecture (2017)
22. Wang, Z., Ren, J., et al.: A deep-learning based feature hybrid framework for spatiotemporal saliency detection inside videos. Neurocomputing **287**, 68–83 (2018)
23. Ren, J., Jiang, J.: Hierarchical modeling and adaptive clustering for real-time summarization of rush videos. IEEE Trans. Multimed. **11**(5), 906–917 (2009)
24. Han, J., et al.: Object detection in optical remote sensing images based on weakly supervised learning and high-level feature learning. IEEE Trans. Geosci. Remote Sens. **53**(6), 3325–3337 (2015)
25. Chen, J.: Modelling of content-aware indicators for effective determination of shot boundaries in compressed MPEG videos. Multimed. Tools Appl. **54**(2), 219–239 (2011)
26. Zaihidee, E.M.: A hybrid thermal-visible fusion for outdoor human detection. J. Telecommun. Electron. Comput. Eng. (JTEC) **10**, 79–83 (2018)

A Method for Calculating Patent Similarity Using Patent Model Tree Based on Neural Network

Chunyan Ma, Tong Zhao(✉), and Hao Li

School of Software and Microelectronics,
Northwestern Polytechnical University, Xi'an, China
machunyan@nwpu.edu.cn, zhaotong_94@163.com,
lihao_93@126.com

Abstract. To make full use of patent information and help companies find similar patent pairs by calculating the similarity of patents, help them deal with the issue of patent infringement detection, patent search, enterprise competition analysis, and patent layout, this paper proposes a method for calculation of patent similarity based on patent text using patent model tree. This method not only simplifies the process of understanding the patent text but also increases the accuracy of calculating the similarity among patents effectively. In this paper, the similarity between patents is calculated based on the patent model tree, and different similarity calculation methods are used according to different properties of tree nodes. Among them, in order to improve the accuracy of the claims node similarity measurement results, the Siamese LSTM network is applied. The experimental results show that the patent similarity calculation method based on text has an outstanding accuracy.

Keywords: Patent similarity · Patent text · Patent model tree

1 Introduction

As the core representative of intellectual property rights, patents are a concentrated expression of the competitiveness of a company, an industry or a country. Making full use of the patent information can help analyze the company's strategic layout, R&D progress, technology orientation, and future market outlook. Similar patents are the embodiment of technological similarity and competitiveness. They represent the distribution of the competitive situation of the company's technology level. The similarity of patents is of great significance to patent layout, identify new technologies, infringement detection and patent early warning. Therefore, improving the accuracy and validity of patent similarity measurement is significant to patent analysis.

There have been some studies on patent similarity calculation, mainly based on patent text and citation technologies. Both text mining and citation analysis can be used for patent similarity. However, patent texts are distinguished from general texts; they contain names, abstracts, citations, and much other information that cannot be obtained by a single method. Therefore, the comprehensive utilization of various information is of great significance to improve the measurement of patent similarity.

J. Ren et al. (Eds.): BICS 2018, LNAI 10989, pp. 633–643, 2018.
https://doi.org/10.1007/978-3-030-00563-4_62

This paper proposes a method for calculation of patent similarity using patent model tree based on Siamese LSTM. The concept of patent model tree was introduced to translate the patent text into a structured patent model tree. The paper builds a patent model tree based on the information features of patent text, defines the nodes of the patent model tree and adopts different methods according to the nature of different nodes. Among them, similarity calculation methods consist of neural network computing text node similarity, deep learning computing time node similarity, and etc. The benefits of this method is that it fully considers the unique features of patent texts.

The rest of this paper is organized as follows. The second part is related works. The third part describes the concept of the patent model tree and the different similarity calculate methods of the patent model tree node. The fourth part evaluates indicators and experimental results. Finally, conclusions are drawn in the last section.

2 Related Works

2.1 Similarity Calculation Based on Patent Text

Sam Arts used text mining tools to measure the technical similarity between patents. Kyoko Yanagihori [2] used "notice of reasons for refusal" of patent to calculate the similarity. Yi Zhang [3] constructed a hybrid similarity measuring method for the patent portfolio analysis that includes both IPCs and text elements. The limits of these approaches are the dependence of authors' word choice and writing style. To solve these problems, Ji [4] proposed the concept of patent model tree, using the patent model tree to calculate the similarity between patents, and used for patent collaborative filtering recommendation. However, the structure and content characteristics of the patent claims are not taken into consideration, and the text similarity cannot be accurately calculated based on the keyword.

2.2 Similarity Calculation Based on Patent Citation

Andrew R [6] used similarity measures for patents in a patent citation network. Hsiao Wu [8] adopted a method for assessing patent compound similarity that includes direct and indirect similarities. A multivariate approach for calculating the similarity of patents is used, including text mining, IPC classification and patent citation [7].

3 Patent Model Tree and Similarity Calculation

3.1 Patent Model Tree

Patent document is a form of semi-structured data, including structured data such as IPC codes, application dates, publication dates, inventor names, and applicant names, as well as text data such as claims, abstracts, and some non-structured data. Each element contains different information. According to the characteristics of the patent text, this paper constructs a patent model tree, which uses the nodes of the patent model tree to represent each feature element and its attributes in the patent text. A typical patent model tree structure is shown in Fig. 1.

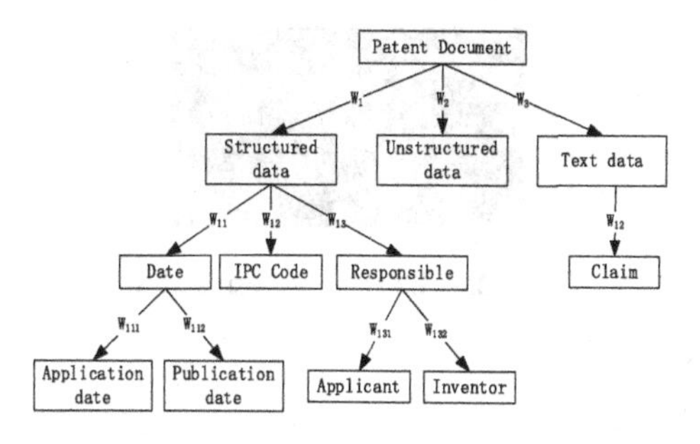

Fig. 1. The structure of the patent model tree

3.2 PMT Similarity Calculation Method

Due to the diversity of patent data, PMT nodes have multiple data forms, including structured data, unstructured data, and text data. The different data forms of nodes determine different similarity calculation formulas.

The similarity Calculation of Structured Data. The structured data in the PMT includes numerical data and text data. Take the following different similarity calculation formulas for different data:

Date Data. Date data include application date and publication date. The similarity between the date nodes of the patent tree can be obtained by calculating the distance between the dates. The similarity is calculated using the following formula:

$$Sim(P1, P2) = \frac{a}{a + D} \tag{1}$$

Sim(P1, P2) refers to the similarity between the patent model trees P1 and P2, D is the distance between T1 and T2 calculated by formula (2).

$$D = |T1 - T2| \tag{2}$$

T1 and T2 refer to the data nodes of different PMTs. A is an adjustable parameter obtained by training using linear regression analysis in depth learning. The training process is shown as follows:

- Formula (1) is changed by mathematical formula (3).

$$\frac{1}{Sim(P1, P2)} = 1 + \frac{1}{a} \times D \tag{3}$$

- Using java to achieve linear regression analysis of training parameters, the experimental results are shown as Fig. 2.

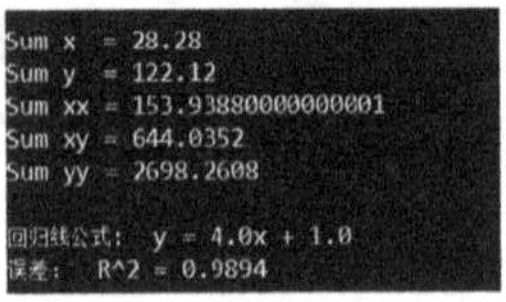

Sum x = 28.28
Sum y = 122.12
Sum xx = 153.93880000000001
Sum xy = 644.0352
Sum yy = 2698.2608
回归线公式: y = 4.0x + 1.0
误差: R^2 = 0.9894

Fig. 2. The training result of a

- Transform to get a.

$$a = \frac{1}{4.0} = 0.25 \tag{4}$$

IPC classified data. The distances between IPC nodes of different PMTs are calculated using the IPC code tree. The IPC code tree is shown in Fig. 3.

Tree root
department
A
B
C
D
E
F
G
H
Class symbol
00
05
SubClass
A
A
Group
1
1
SubGroup
00
00
A00A1/00
A05A1/00

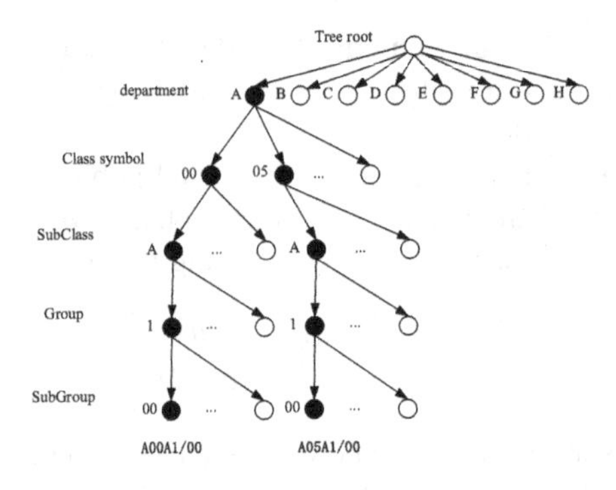

Fig. 3. The structure of IPC code tree

The IPC code is split into 5 parts: department, class symbol, subclass, group, and subgroup. The distances between the IPC nodes are calculated by finding the common parent nodes of the IPC codes. The similarity calculation process is as follows:

- Get the IPC nodes value of the PMTs to compare.
- Find the distance D between two IPC nodes in the IPC code tree.
- Calculate the similarity according to formula (1).

Personal data. The personal data include applicant and inventor information. Although these elements are in the form of characters, their contents have only two possibilities, same or different. Therefore, the values are:

$$SimP(Ai, Bi) = \begin{cases} 1, & |Ai = Bi| \\ 0, & |Ai \neq Bi| \end{cases} \tag{5}$$

Ai, Bi denote the corresponding elements in PMT A and B, and SimP(Ai, Bi) denotes the similarity of the corresponding elements in PMT A and B.

The Similarity Calculation of Unstructured Data. Unstructured data includes drawings, codes, tables, and etc. They are not considered due to the diversity of expressions and difficulty in judging similarities.

The Similarity Calculation of Patent Claims. Patent text includes abstract, full text, and claim. The patent claims are clear, complete, detailed descriptions and are submitted to the patent organization for reviewing and approving written materials. They explain the method adopted by the present invention to overcome these drawbacks and illustrate the advanced nature and novelty of the present invention. Therefore, the claims are used herein as textual experimental data.

The claim is different from ordinary texts. The former not only reflects the main technical content of the patent as a whole but also writes in accordance with a certain format and structure requirements. The use of words and words therein are relatively accurate and refined, and show strong regularity both in terms of content and structure. Therefore, the similarity of patent claims can illustrate the similarity of patents text best. Therefore, this paper uses the patent claims as the target document for patent similarity detection.
Analysis of characteristics of patent claims

- Content features of the patent claims

The patent claims focus on the technical features of the invention or utility model patent application, and clearly state the content and scope of the protection in the patent. Since patents should be novel in the application process, a large number of vocabulary words appear to be technical terms that have not yet been popularized.

- Structure features of the patent claims

The text format of the patent claims is usually divided into two parts. One is the preamble and the other is the characteristic part. The former is used to describe the technical field described in this patent, and the prior art is related to the technical features of the patent research subject. The latter deals with the technical characteristics of this patent and elaborates on it.

Through the analysis of the content and structure of the patent claims, it can be found that the patent claims have certain structural features in terms of structure, but they have unstructured features in content; therefore, in the process of text processing, attention shall be paid from two aspects.
Key sentence extraction of patent claims.

In order to obtain key sentences from the patent claims and as the input of the Siamese LSTM, the paper extracts key sentences from the claims firstly. First, through the elimination and merging of multiple mainstream stop word lists, a professional stop word list is obtained. A patent stop word is extracted from the patent text database using the TF-IDF algorithm. By combining the patent word list with the professional stop word list, our patent stop word list can be obtained. Second, use the patent stop word list for the improved TextRank algorithm, extracting the key sentences from the patent claims, and obtaining the key Sentence collection.

The paper uses TF-IDF algorithm to construct a patent stop word list firstly. In order to construct a stop word list devoted to patent texts, the paper first removes duplicate from the three market mainstream stop words (Harbin Institute of Technology, Sichuan University's Machine Learning Smart Lab and Baidu) and merges them, obtaining the patent stop word list. Then, by using the TF-IDF algorithm to extract all the corpus feature keywords from each patent claim from the acquired corpus database, the weights of the corpus feature words are constructed and sorted. The keywords with lower weights are selected in turn (weight less than 0.2), and the feature subsets that need to be deleted are obtained and added to the general stop word list obtained by the paper to obtain a special stop word list for patents. Finally, use the stop word list to process the patent claims.

Then, the paper improves the classic TextRank [10] algorithm and extracts key sentences from processed patent claims. The classic TextRank algorithm often considers the similarity between sentence nodes in the automatic abstract extraction of documents more, ignoring the textual structure of the documents and the context information of the sentences. Combined with the structural characteristics of the patent claims, this paper introduces information such as titles, paragraphs, special sentences, sentence positions and lengths into the structure of TextRank network graphs, improving the TextRank algorithm. The improved TextRank algorithm flow is shown in Fig. 4. The processed patent claims are processed using the improved TextRank algorithm to obtain a set of key sentences.

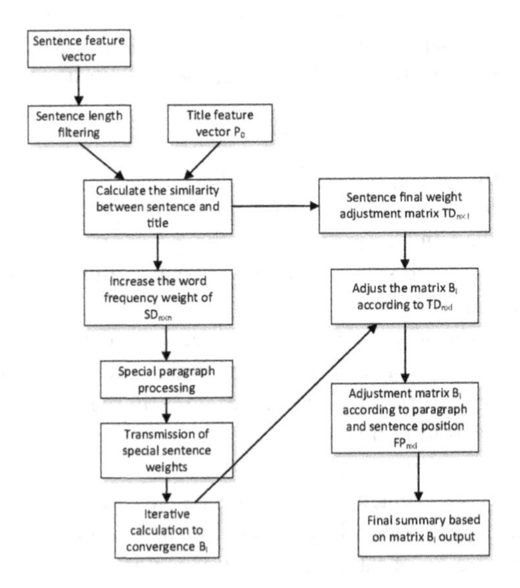

Fig. 4. The improved TextRank algorithm flow

Calculating similarity of claims nodes using the Siamese LSTM.

In order to calculate the similarity of the patent claims more accurately, this paper compares several popular text similarity calculation methods. The comparison results are shown in Table 1:

Table 1. Techniques for calculating similarity of text

Technical name	Advantage	Shortcomings
CNN	Context information retention is good	Poor retention of contextual information for long intervals
RNN	Use context-sensitive information	The range of context information that can be accessed is very limited, so that the impact of the input of the hidden layer on the network output is degraded with the continuous recursion of the network loop
LSTM	Contextual information that is closely spaced is preserved	The result represents the vector of each sentence, and the sentences are independent
Siamese LSTM	Constituted by two parallel bidirectional LSTMs, the resulting sentence vectors are related	When measuring the similarity between particularly long sentences, the last part of the sentence occupies a high proportion
CNN	Context information retention is good	Poor retention of contextual information for long intervals

The Siamese LSTM has obvious advantages and is by far the best method for calculating similarity of texts. The Siamese LSTM refers to an LSTM network with a Siamese structure. It consists of two parallel bidirectional LSTMs. The structure is shown in the following Fig. 5 [11, 12].

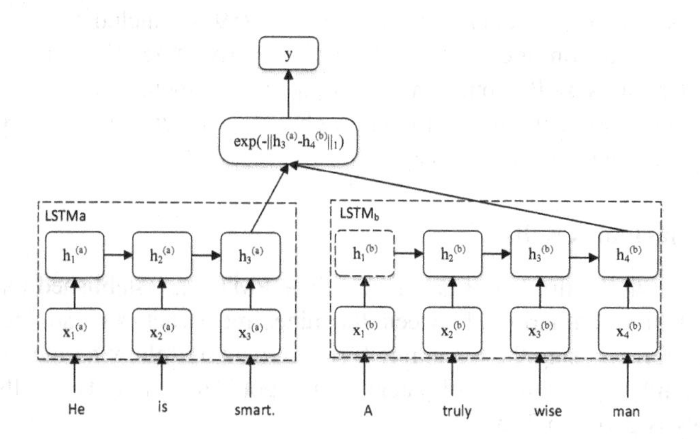

Fig. 5. The structure of Siamese LSTM

Quora-Question-Pairs, an authoritative dataset provided by Quora, is now widely used in semantic similarity calculation tasks. This paper uses this dataset as training data to train the Siamese LSTM, and the mean square error (error (MSE) loss function is to calculate the error between the predicted value and the label value. The hidden embedding of the bidirectional long short term memory network is set to 100, and the state of the hidden layer of the Siamese LSTM is initialized for Gaussian distribution.

After the Siamese LSTM was trained, we used the acquired key sentence sets as input to calculate the similarity of the patent claims. To complete the process, the multiple key sentence sets to be compared are all arranged and merged to get the set of sentence pairs, then the Siamese LSTM network is used to calculate the similarity between sentence pairs. Finally, the similarity between patent texts is obtained by weighted summation of the similarity of multiple sentence pairs.

After computing the nodes similarity, the PMT similarity can be defined as:

$$Sim(P1, P2) = \sum_{i=1}^{i=n} Wi \times Sim(Ai, Bi) \tag{6}$$

Sim(P1, P2) refers to the similarity between PMT P1 and P2, n refers to the number of leaf nodes of PMT, W_i refers to the weight of each leaf node, Sim(Ai, Bi) refers to the similarity of the corresponding leaf nodes.

4 Experiment

In this section, a set of experiments were done to confirm the effectiveness of the proposed method.

4.1 Dataset

The storage space of raw data is approximately 789 M, including all 2016 patent documents obtained from the State Intellectual Property Office (SIPO) of the People's Republic of China using Python. Ten sets of patent documents were selected from the original dataset as the experimental data. Each set of documents included one target patent and nine patents to be compared.

4.2 Experimental Results

First, dealing with the first set of patent data. The PMT was established for all patents, then calculate the similarities between the nine tree structures and the target tree structure; then, processing the remaining 9 sets of data by following the same method; finally, the similarity of ten sets of patent data is got. The similarity results of the first set of patents is given in Table 2:

It is shown that, patents with high similarity to target patents also have high similarities in terms of claims, and application dates. It shows that the comprehensive use of patent texts to calculate patent similarity is of great significance.

Table 2. The similarity result of the first patent set

PMT node	(1)	(2)	(3)	(4)	(5)	(6)	(7)	(8)	(9)
Applicant date	0.01	0.1	0.02	0.11	0	0	0.18	0.03	0.03
Publish date	0	0.01	0.11	0.01	0	0.02	0	0.18	0.03
Inventor	0	0	0	0	0	0	0	0	0
Applicant	0	0	0	0	0	0	0	0	0
Ipc	0	0	0	0	0	0	0.11	0	0
Claim	0.07	0.19	0.16	0.17	0.08	0.06	0.12	0.02	0.06
Result	0.09	0.39	0.37	0.35	0.08	0.08	0.52	0.28	0.14

4.3 Comparison of Experimental Results

To test the effectiveness of the proposed method, we found 10 students to manually compare the similarity of dataset and compared the results with the experimental results. Students manually compared the similarities of each set of data and ranked each set of patents based on similarity. We compared the experimental results with the students' results. Three of the comparison results are shown as Table 3(c represents the results calculated by the method proposed in this paper, m represents the results of the students' manual sorting. The following serial number indicates the group.):

Table 3. Experimental comparison results

PMT	(1)	(2)	(3)	(4)	(5)	(6)	(7)	(8)	(9)
c [1]	0.09	0.39	0.37	0.35	0.08	0.08	0.52	0.28	0.14
m [1]	7	2	3	4	9	8	1	5	6
c [2]	0.5	0.0	0.01	0.0	0.03	0.0	0.3	0.01	0.01
m [2]	1	3	3	3	3	3	2	3	3
c [3]	0.37	0.19	0.16	0.17	0.08	0.06	0.12	0.02	0.06
m [3]	1	2	4	3	6	6	5	6	7

The results show that the experimental results calculated using the proposed method are highly consistent with the students' manual comparisons. When two patents are basically unrelated, the similarity is as low as 0.0. When two patents are especially relevant, the similarity between patents is as high as 0.52. The result also indicates that we can accurately find the most similar patents using our proposed method when there are multiple patents to be compared.

5 Conclusion and Future Work

Patent text is an important source of knowledge. Its proper use has the potential to shorten the development cycle and save research funding, however, the complexity of the patent text structure and content makes it difficult. Thus, combined with the neural network, a new method based on patent text to calculate patent similarity is proposed. This method introduces the concept of PMT, adopts different similarity calculation methods through the nature of different nodes in PMT, and obtains the final similarity result through the method of weighted summation. Experiments show that this method has good performance in the measurement of similarity of patents, and it helps to improve the ability to use patents. Deep learning [13, 14] and advanced machine learning [15–17] algorithms have achieved many successes in areas such as computer vision. In the future, we hope to introduce the patent citation into the patent model tree, and use deep learning or machine learning methods to calculate the similarity between citations, which will make the calculation of patent similarity more accurate.

Acknowledgements. The project is supported by HJSW and Research & Development plan of Shaanxi Province (Program No. 2017ZDXM-GY-094, 2015KTZDGY04-01).

References

1. Arts, S., Cassiman, B., Gomez, J.C.: Text Matching to Measure Patent Similarity. Social Science Electronic Publishing, Rochester (2017)
2. Yanagihori, K, Tsuda, K.: Verification of patent document similarity of using dictionary data extracted from notification of reasons for refusal. In: IEEE, Computer Software and Applications Conference, pp. 349–354. IEEE Computer Society (2015)
3. Zhang, Y., Shang, L., Huang, L., et al.: A hybrid similarity measure method for patent portfolio analysis. J. Informetr. **10**, 1108–1130 (2016)
4. Ji, X, Gu, X, Dai, F, et al.: Patent collaborative filtering recommendation approach based on patent similarity. In: Eighth International Conference on Fuzzy Systems and Knowledge Discovery, pp. 1699–1703. IEEE (2011)
5. Chen, J.-X., Gu, X.-J., Chen, G.-H.: Method of discovering similar patents based on vector space model and characteristics of patent documents. J. Zhejiang Univ. Eng. Sci. **43**(10), 1848–1852 (2009)
6. Rodriguez, A., Kim, B., Turkoz, M., et al.: New multi-stage similarity measure for calculation of pairwise patent similarity in a patent citation network. Scientometrics **103**, 565–581 (2015)
7. Kasravi, K., Risov, M.: Multivariate patent similarity detection, pp. 1–8 (2009)
8. Wu, H.C., Chen, H.Y., Lee, K.Y., et al.: A method for assessing patent similarity using direct and indirect citation links. In: IEEE International Conference on Industrial Engineering and Engineering Management. IEEE (2010)
9. Yu. S., Su, J., Li, P.: Automatic abstract extraction method based on improved TextRank. In: Computer Science, pp. 240–247 (2016)
10. Mihalcea, R., Tarau, P.: TextRank: bringing order into texts. In: Emnlp, pp. 404–411 (2004)
11. Mueller, J., Thyagarajan, A.: Siamese recurrent architectures for learning sentence similarity. In: Thirtieth AAAI Conference on Artificial Intelligence, pp. 2786–2792. AAAI Press (2016)
12. Foland, W., Martin, J.H.: Abstract meaning representation parsing using LSTM recurrent neural networks. In: Meeting of the Association for Computational Linguistics, pp. 463–472 (2017)
13. Wang, Z., et al.: A deep-learning based feature hybrid framework for spatiotemporal saliency detection inside videos. Neurocomputing **287**, 68–83 (2018)

14. Ren, J., Jiang, J.: Hierarchical modeling and adaptive clustering for real-time summarization of rush videos. IEEE Trans. Multimed. **11**(5), 906–917 (2009)
15. Chen, Z.-Y., Gogoi, A., et al.: Coherent narrow-band light source for miniature endoscopes. IEEE J. Sel. Top. Quantum Electron. (2018), (In press)
16. Zhang A., Sun G., et al.: A dynamic neighborhood learning-based gravitational search algorithm. IEEE Trans. Cynernetics (2017). (In press)
17. Cao, F., Yang, Z., Ren, J., et al.: Extreme sparse multinomial logistic regression: a fast and robust framework for hyperspectral image classification. Remote Sens. **9**(12), 1255 (2017)

An Optimal Solution of Storing and Processing Small Image Files on Hadoop

Qiubin Su[1], Lu Lu[1,2(✉)], and QiuYan Feng[1]

[1] School of Computer Science and Engineering, South China University of Technology, Guangzhou, Guangdong, China
lul@scut.edu.cn
[2] Modern Industrial Technology Research Institute, South China University of Technology, Zhongshan, China

Abstract. The rapid development of the Internet, especially mobile Internet, makes it much easier for people to make social contacts online. Nowadays people tend to spend more and more time on social network service, and produce a lot of image files. This brings a challenge to traditional standalone framework on handing the continued increasing image files. Therefore, it is advisable to find a new way to settle the challenge. Hadoop is a notable, widely-used project for distributed storage and computations with high efficiency, data integrity, reliability and fault tolerance. Hadoop Distributed File System and MapReduce are two primary subprojects respectively for big data storage and computations. However, Hadoop does not provide any interface for image processing. Moreover, both Hadoop Distributed File System and MapReduce have trouble in processing largė amount of small files, which result in decreasing efficiency of files access and distributed computations. This prevents us from performing images processing actions on Hadoop. In view of this, this paper proposes a new method to optimize the storage of small image files on Hadoop and self-defines an input/output format to enable Hadoop to process image files.

Keywords: Hadoop Distributed File System (HDFS) · MapReduce
Small images files · Self-dined storage and IO format

1 Introduction

Nowadays, with the increasing growth of data, the researches on big data are becoming more and more important especially for image processing [1, 2]. Lots of novel methods for feature extractions and classification are proposed for big data applications [3–5]. Besides, Hadoop is also very important and widely used in the recent years when big data and distributed computing are attracting more and more attentions. As a famous project of Apache [6], Hadoop is an open-source java based software framework with the subprojects including Hadoop Common, Hadoop Distributed File System, Hadoop Map Reduce and Hadoop Yarn [7]. This framework shows its irreplaceable merits of high reliability, availability and data integrity while dealing with large data storage and processing massive distributed computations.

J. Ren et al. (Eds.): BICS 2018, LNAI 10989, pp. 644–653, 2018.
https://doi.org/10.1007/978-3-030-00563-4_63

At the meantime, the rapid development of mobile technology and the wide spread of the Internet give rise to the time people spend on social networking service every day [8]. They chat and share their life by pictures or videos with friends whenever they access to the net. It is common that if something amazing catches your eyes, you will capture it and immediately post to Facebook, for instance, and then all your friends get amazed too [9]. Take Weibo as an example. According to The Report of Weibo Users Development 2016, the number of monthly active users on Weibo has reached 297 million while daily active users have got to 132 million by September, 2016. The report also revealed that these users active on Weibo mainly write tweet in the form of images with some text description, which accounts for 60%. We can simply estimate that even if we take Weibo alone into consideration, about 70 million of images will be created, stored and uploaded every day. And clearly there are many other network services similar to Weibo, popular and producing large amount of data especially images data. Thus it is hard for traditional standalone framework to store and handle such a large number of image files. A solution to this problem is needed.

Considering that Hadoop is created to handle big data, turning to Hadoop for help can be a good choice [10]. However, since Hadoop is designed for text file, there is no interface offered to store and process image files. Besides, big data does not mean a great amount of data. Although Hadoop is useful in storing and processing big files, it has great weakness in the face of numerous small files, while image files are always not very big. On the one hand, Hadoop Distributed File System (HDFS) stores data on the node called DataNode in the cluster, and the only one NameNode will keep the metadata of every file on the DataNode. Therefore, when it comes to a lot of small files like images, NameNode will soon run out of its memory [11]. On the other hand, the more files there are, the more MapReduce tasks are needed, and thus more interactions and communications between nodes will be necessary too, which will add to the overhead and clearly decrease the efficiency of the cluster [12]. Hence this paper presents our solution to enable small image files storing and processing on Hadoop and optimize the performance so that it can help managing the large amount of image files flowing through the network.

2 Background

2.1 Hadoop Distributed File System

The Hadoop Distributed File System (HDFS) is a file system designed for big data storage to support distributed computations in Hadoop clusters. It is inspired by Google File System, implemented in Java, running on commodity machines.

A basic concept of HDFS is block, the default size of which is 64 MB. That is to say the files in HDFS will be split into blocks of 64 MB and stored in a series of nodes. A node can be a physical machine or a virtual one with HDFS installed. It should be noting that a file smaller than 64 MB will be similarly split as a block, though it does not exactly occupy 64 MB of space. With its master-slave structure [13], HDFS assigns one single node in the cluster as NameNode, and all other nodes are DataNodes. As the master in HDFS, NameNode is responsible for storing all the metadata of files as well as managing the namespace of the file system. The information of the data blocks constituting the files are all recorded in NameNode so that if a user wants to perform a read or write operation, he has to send request to NameNode first in order to get the response about the locations of the blocks. Then the user can read data from or write to the specific DataNode. DataNode, as mentioned above, keeps all the actual data.

HDFS is of high data integrity, reliability and fault tolerance. Each data block has its own replicas of 3 by default on different nodes. When one of them breaks down, HDFS will get information from NameNode and create a new replica from the other two. Besides, every DataNode will periodically send heartbeats to NameNode informing its availability and the block replicas it holds. In case that NameNode does not receive any report from a DataNode within a particular time, it will consider the DataNode broken and start to create new replicas on other healthy nodes [14]. It is easy for users to perform CRUD (Create, Read, Update and Delete) operations on HDFS as how they do on no-distributed file systems. The structure of the HDFS is shown in Fig. 1.

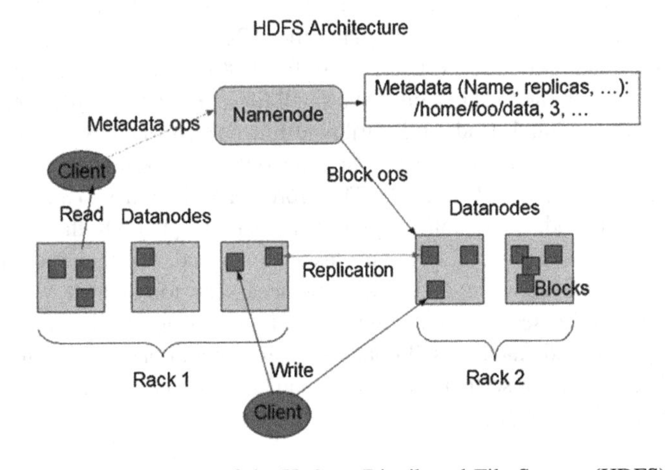

Fig. 1. The structure of the Hadoop Distributed File System (HDFS)

2.2 Small Files and Image-Processing Problems on Hadoop

A great number of image files are being produced at the time people surfing the Internet with their computers or smartphones. As netizens increase with great speed, we need to come up with new solutions to handle these image files. Hadoop is designed for big data so theoretically is a rational choice for us. But Hadoop have no interface for users to operate image files, designed to process big text file. Also, Hadoop do not work well in large amount of small files. Generally, a file smaller than 64 MB (the default size of a block) is thought to be a small file and will be split into an individual block in HDFS. NameNode will keep the metadata of each file storing in the DataNode. Therefore, if there are lots of small files in the DataNode, NameNode will have to take much storage space to hold a large amount of metadata. For example, assuming that we are going to store a 1 GB big file in HDFS, it will be split into 16 blocks. The size of metadata for one block is about 150 bytes. So the 1 GB file takes up 2.4 KB storage space in the NameNode. However, if there are 2048 small files of 512 KB, the size of their metadata will increase by 125 times, to 300 KB. In addition, with more blocks in the HDFS, the more time will be taken to search for a required file block. Besides, speaking of the impact on MapReduce, more blocks mean that more MapReduce tasks have to be established to finish the job. Since a MapReduce job only processes a block of data, it is a waste of the potential, sharply decreasing the performance. Therefore, to apply Hadoop to store and process so many small image files, it is imperative to self-define an image file format and do some improvement on HDFS and MapReduce.

2.3 Existing Solutions to Small Files Problem

Small files problems can be avoided by transforming small files into a part of a large file. The key is how to group the files together so as to maximize the performance of Hadoop. Here are some existing solutions for this problem.

2.3.1 SequenceFile

SequenceFile, provided by Hadoop, is a kind of flat file of binary key/value pairs. Acting like a container, SequenceFile merges the small files into a big file in some way. Key/value pairs make up the SequenceFile. Key here refers to the name of the small file, and value is the file content. Nevertheless, SequenceFile does not support adding a key/value pair to the end of the file. Additionally, since SequenceFile do not record the mapping relation between itself and the small files constituting it, it is time-consuming to search a certain file in it. We have to traverse the whole file, resulting in a bad file accessing efficiency.

2.3.2 MapFile

MapFile also provided by Hadoop can be treated as SequenceFile with an index. MapFile can be divided into two parts, index and data. Index stores the mapping relation of the MapFile and its small files. Data is made up of a series of key/value pairs, in which key is the file name and value is the content, similar to SequenceFile. Now that index marks down the offset of each key/value pair in the data, MapFile has a better performance in looking for a certain file than SequenceFile. But to pay for that MapFile costs more storage space. Similarly, adding new small files to an existing MapFile is not allowed.

2.3.3 Hadoop Archives (HAR Files)

Hadoop Archives is a special archive format with an extension of *.har. A Hadoop Archives contains an index file, a master index file and lots of data files, the name of which starts with part-*. The index file records the files and their locations in the data file [7]. And the master index file refers to the index file. Packing the small files in HDFS into a HAR file reduces the number of files on Hadoop, but users will not notice the existence of index and master index files. We don't have to expand a HAR file to access the files in it because this access is done in main memory [15]. The reading efficiency of HAR file is not satisfying because users have to search through two layers of index files before they read the actual data file. Besides, addition of new files is not allowed in HAR File, either.

3 The Proposed Solution

It has been shown that MapFile is better to store image files than SequenceFile, and HAR file, with better performance. But none of them allows users to modify the file, which leads to great inconvenience since in real life people might need to do some change based on the original file instead of generating a new one. So this paper puts forward a solution to optimize small image files storage in HDFS by self-defining an image storage file format, naming it ImageMergeFile. At the same time, to overcome the difficulty of lacking in APIs for image-processing on Hadoop, ImageInputFormat and ImageOutputFormat are defined to provide the I/O interface for MapReduce jobs.

3.1 The Storage of Small Image Files on HDFS

3.1.1 The Design of ImageMergeFile

MapFile is of high efficiency in storing and reading the file because of the index file. The design of ImageMergeFile learns from that advantage and meanwhile is open to being appended. An ImageMergeFile composes of an index file and a data file. Index file stores each image file's name and offset in the data file as a key/value pair. The offset part is a String containing the point where the small image's data begins and ends in the data file, which makes it possible and convenient to locate the image rapidly in the data file. The data file is simply all images' data jointing together in a certain order. What's more, it is available to append extra image at the end of the file.

3.1.2 Implementation

ImageMergeFile takes lots of image files as input. In its implementation, first read the configuration file written by the users to get the path of input files and the output directory. Actually users just need to fill in the blank in the configuration file with some important arguments like file path. Next is to start a loop collecting the images from input path together. In the loop, for each small image file, designate its name as key and its offset as value. This String key/value pair will be stored in an object of a kind of data structure named TreeMap. TreeMap, based on Red-Black Tree, is a sorted HashMap provided by Java. By default, the TreeMap sorts in lexicographical order of the key. Then save the TreeMap object into index file by serializing it. Serializing an object means encoding it into a byte stream. Java has offered object serialization mechanism to help with this. The actual image data is added to the data file. In this way the order of the keys matches the order of the image data added to the data file since files are read in lexicographical order by default from the file system. This helps a lot in speeding up searching a certain image in the ImageMergeFile. What is needed to extract an image is its file name. Take it as key and then we can get the value (offset) from the TreeMap object in the index file (by deserializing), and eventually locate it in the data file and read it.

In order to serve the goal of appending an image at the end of the ImageMergeFile, the output path has to be detected first. If the path is discovered to be already existed, it means that the ImageMergeFile has been created before. What it is supposed to do at this moment is to open it and add content to the end of the file instead of creating a new one. This is the optimal design of storing a bunch of image files in HDFS. It is just the first step to process lots of image files in Hadoop since when the way of storing the images is changed, we have to redefine the InputFormat and OutputFormat in MapReduce jobs to adapt to the change. We will discuss it in detail in the next part.

3.2 Image Processing with ImageMergeFile by MapReduce

As introduced in Sect. 2, MapReduce takes key/value pairs as input and generates key/value pairs as output. By consulting the source code, it is concluded that the InputFormat interface is in charge of controlling the input files, defining how to split the file and read the record. And OutputFormat is applied to define the format of output files.

The InputFormat interface is defined in org.apache.hadoop.mapreduce package, including two main functions: getSplits() and createRecordReader(). Inside the getSplits() function, file will be split into InputSplits in a particular way. One InputSplit will be assigned to one mapper (the TaskStracker conducting a map job). The createRecoedReader() function creates a RecordReader, which states the way to read a record from the InputSplit. In other words, RecordReader transforms the InputSplit into key/value pairs so that they become available for the mapper.

The OutputFormat interface specifies where to store the output data and how to write them into a file. getRecordWriter() function and checkOutputSpecs() function are two primary functions of the interface which need to be covered. getRecordWriter() creates a RecordWriter, inside which there is a write() function defining the form of the key/value pairs. Except write() function, a close() function is used to close the output stream. And additionally the checkOutputSpecs() function will check the availability of the output path before a MapReduce job takes action.

The proposed image processing framework is shown in Fig. 2 with self-defined ImageInputFormat and ImageOutputFormat. During the map phase, ImageInputFormat will first load the index file to get the offsets and determine the number of splits, after which InputSplits are created according to the split amount and image data from data file. Next its ImageRecordReader makes input splits available by separating them into key/value pairs in the forms of <Text, BytesWritable> . That is to say that ImageRecordReader will set the image's file name as Text type and convert the image into BytesWritable type. Text class and BytesWritable class are the data types in Hadoop implementing the Writable Interface, which is the core of Hadoop Serialization Mechanism. Transforming the image to BytesWritable benefits a lot in transferring them between nodes, making the best use of the bandwidth and reducing the consumption of transmission time. These pairs will be pushed to the mappers. After mappers and reducers finish processing each record (each image), they output it to the HDFS as what the ImageOutputFormat defines. Before outputting the image files, we can merge them as ImageMergeFile again to reduce the burden of the NameNode.

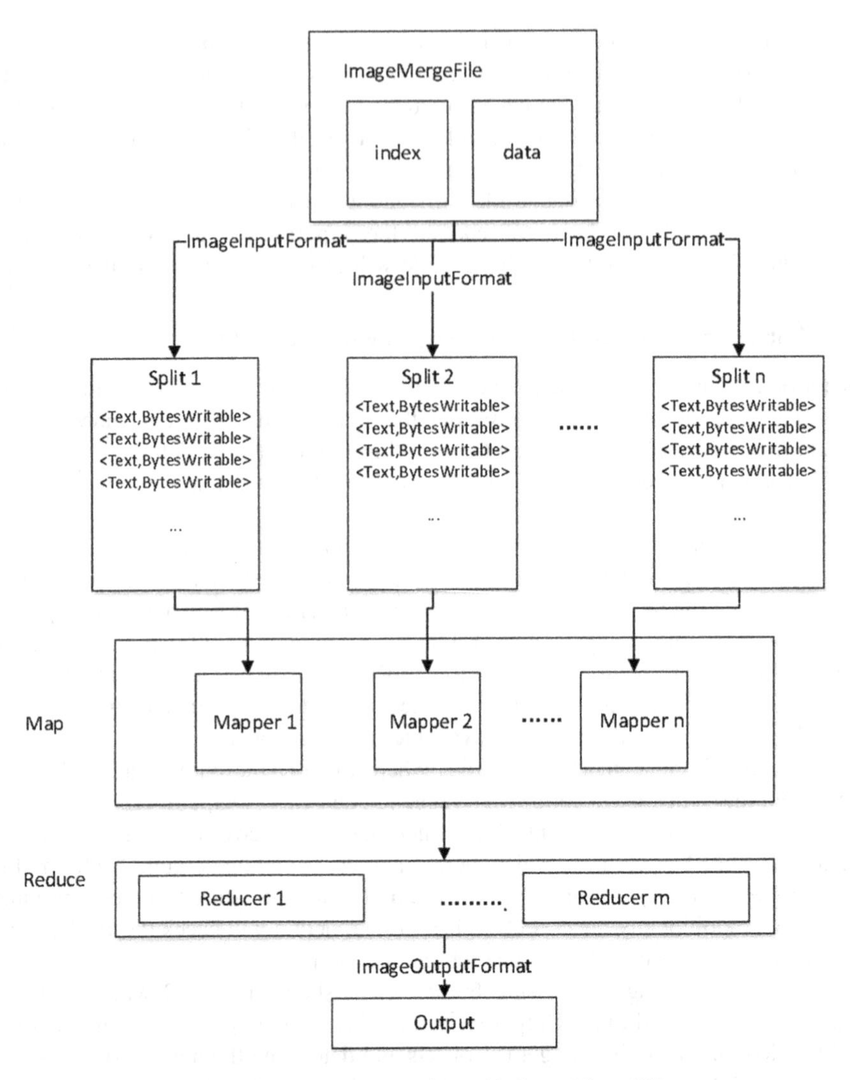

Fig. 2. The image processing with ImageMergeFile.

Then we can handle lots of small image files with better efficiency by mean of Hadoop overcoming its bottleneck. The whole process is shown in Fig. 3.

4 Results and Discussion

4.1 Set up Experimental Hadoop Cluster

This paper uses a Hadoop architecture of three nodes considering of the existing experimental condition. These three nodes are physical machines with 64-bit CentOS 7 installed, whose detail information is given in Table 1.

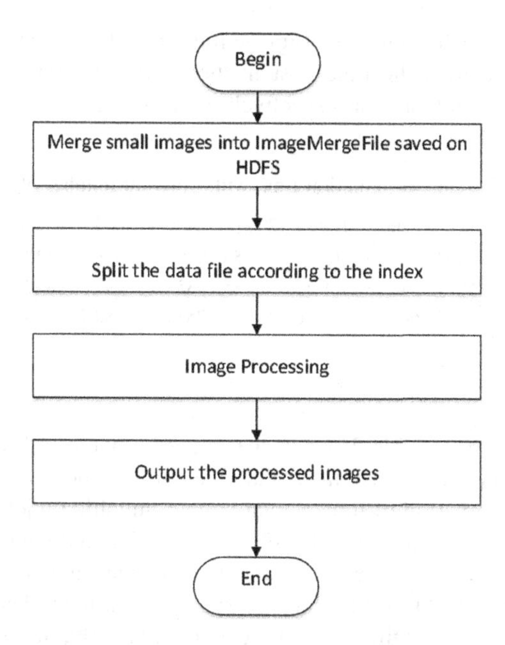

Fig. 3. The flow chart of image processing.

Table 1. The detail information of the three Hadoop nodes used here.

Hostname	Master	Slave1	Slave2
Role	Master	Slave	Slave
NameNode/DataNode	NameNode	DataNode	DateNode
JobTracker/TaskTracker	JobTracker	TaskTracker	TaskTracker
Operating system	CentOS 7	CentOS 7	CentOS 7
CPU	2 cores 2.5 GHz	2 cores 2.5 GHz	2 cores 2.5 GHz
Memory	8 GB	4 GB	4 GB
Java version	1.7	1.7	1.7
Hadoop version	2.6.0	2.6.0	2.6.0

4.2 Control Experiments

In this subsection, the experiments are conducted to test the availability of the proposed method and compare its performance (on time consumption while handling lots of image files) with the stand-alone machines performing the same process on the images. We prepared 4000 images of JPG type, whose size is less than 1 MB for the experiments. In order to make comparison of the consuming time between our Hadoop cluster and the single machines, we run an image binaryzation program respectively on Slave1 and Slave2, recording the consuming time after increasing the image files' amount by 400 each time. Then a MapReduce job was set for the same purpose of binarizing images but took the self-defined ImageMergeFile as input. Run the job on the Hadoop cluster and also change the numbers of image files constituting the ImageMergeFile by 400 every time. Recorded the time cost in the chart and drew into a line chart to visually present the result, shown respectively in Table 2.

Table 2. The consumption time with different number of images

Image number	400	800	1200	1600	2000	2400	2800	3200	3600	4000
Slave1 (s)	171.97	365.63	521.18	701.89	832.84	945.35	1058.12	1171.57	1280.17	1395.75
Slave2 (s)	186.59	384.31	548.13	739.15	876.85	985.76	1097.28	1208.79	1312.23	1443.61
Hadoop (s)	462.15	577.13	643.23	681.76	723.87	753.64	780.73	805.98	827.12	846.37

As can be seen from Table 2, when the images amount is lower than 1600, the single machines complete the task faster than the cluster. The reason is that the cluster has to spend a certain period of time activating and initialling a job. Besides, the time spending in extracting the files from HDFS cannot be ignored which may probably be longer than the time for the image processing when images' amount is small. When the amount is larger than 1600, our Hadoop cluster behaves much better than the single machines, costing much less time. When the amount is 4000, the computation time of the proposed Hadoop cluster is almost just a half of that of the single machine. It is worth noticing that with the increase of the images' amount, the processing time needed for Hadoop cluster roses slowly while the single machines have a sharper increasing trend. That is because the job initialization time of the cluster is hardly changed and the nodes share the burden of increasing image files, resulting in the gentle rise of the Hadoop.

Therefore, we come to a conclusion that our design of ImageMergeFile and its relative self-dined input format and output format work in processing small image files. When there is a substantial amount of small images files, it is of better performance than traditional standalone machines.

5 Conclusion

This paper presents a complete process of handling small image files on Hadoop overcoming its shortcomings of lacking interface for image processing as well as low efficiency in dealing with the storage and management of small files. In the respect of storage, a method is put forward to group all the small image files into a big file named ImageMergeFile before uploading them to HDFS. ImageMergeFile is divided into two parts, index and data, supporting addition of new file at the end of it. Then to make it possible for MapReduce to do with the ImageMergeFile, the redefinition of input format and output format was presented. Experiments show that the proposed method works and helps to improve the performance of Hadoop when handling large number of image files.

Acknowledgements. This paper is supported by the National Nature Science Foundation of China (No. 61370103), Guangdong Province Application Major Fund (2015B010131013) and Zhongshan Produce & Research Fund (2017A1014).

References

1. Ren, J., Zabalza, J., Marshall, S., Zheng, J.: Effective feature extraction and data reduction in remote sensing using hyperspectral imaging. IEEE Signal Process. Mag. **31**(4), 149–154 (2014)
2. Qiao, T., Yang, Z., Ren, J., et al.: Joint bilateral filtering and spectral similarity-based sparse representation: a generic framework for effective feature extraction and data classification in hyperspectral imaging. Pattern Recogn. **77**, 316–328 (2017)
3. Zabalza, J., et al.: Novel two dimensional singular spectrum analysis for effective feature extraction and data classification in hyperspectral imaging. IEEE Trans. Geosci. Remote Sens. **53**, 4418–4433 (2015)
4. Qiao, T., Ren, J., et al.: Effective denoising and classification of hyperspectral images using curve let transform and singular spectrum analysis. IEEE Trans. Geosci. Remote Sens. **55**, 119–133 (2017)
5. Cao, F., Yang, Z., Ren, J., Ling, W.K., Zhao, H., Marshall, S.: Extreme sparse multinomial logistic regression: a fast and robust framework for hyperspectral image classification. Remote Sens. **9**(12), 1255 (2017)
6. Mohandas, N., Thampi, S.M.: Improving Hadoop performance in handling small files. In: Abraham, A., Mauri, J.L., Buford, J.F., Suzuki, J., Thampi, S.M. (eds.) ACC 2011. CCIS, vol. 193, pp. 187–194. Springer, Heidelberg (2011). https://doi.org/10.1007/978-3-642-22726-4_20
7. Bende, S., Shedge, R.: Dealing with small files problem in Hadoop distributed file system. Proced. Comput. Sci. **79**, 1001–1012 (2016)
8. Ghazi, M.R., Gangodkar, D.: Hadoop, MapReduce and HDFS: a developers perspective. Proced. Comput. Sci. **48**, 45–50 (2015)
9. Dean, J., Ghemawat, S.: MapReduce: simplified data processing on large clusters. Commun. ACM **51**, 107–113 (2008)
10. He, H., Du, Z., Zhang, W., Chen, A.: Optimization strategy of Hadoop small file storage for big data in healthcare. J. Supercomput. **72**, 3696–3707 (2015)
11. Mackey, G., Sehrish, S., Wang, J.: Improving metadata management for small files in HDFS. In: IEEE International Conference on Cluster Computing, pp. 1–4 (2009)
12. Cao, Z., Lin, J., Wan, C., Song, Y., Taylor, G., Li, M.: Hadoop-based framework for big data analysis of synchronised harmonics in active distribution network. IET Gener. Transm. Distrib. **11**, 3930–3937 (2017)
13. Zhao, S., Medhi, D.: Application-aware network design for Hadoop MapReduce optimization using software-defined networking. IEEE Trans. Netw. Serv. Manage. **14**, 804–816 (2017)
14. George, J., Chen, C.-A., Stoleru, R., Xie, G.G.: Hadoop MapReduce for mobile clouds. IEEE Trans. Cloud Comput. **3**(1), 1–14 (2014)
15. Won, H., Nguyen, M., Gil, M., Moon, Y.: Advanced resource management with access control for multitenant Hadoop. J. Commun. Netw. **17**, 592–601 (2015)

A Big Data Analytics Platform for Information Sharing in the Connection Between Administrative Law and Criminal Justice

Na Li[1], Jiangbin Zheng[2(✉)], and Mingchen Feng[2]

[1] School of Humanities, Economics and Law, Northwestern Polytechnical University, Xi'an, China
lina8460@sina.com

[2] School of Computer Science, Northwestern Polytechnical University, Xi'an, China
zhengjb@nwpu.edu.cn

Abstract. Big data analysis and application is an efficient approach for analyzing and identifying different patterns, relations and trends in daily life. In this paper we proposed an intelligent big data platform for information sharing in connection to administrative law and criminal justice. We first explored the structure of the data and utilized Apache Pig and Hadoop to handle structured, semi-structured and unstructured data. We extracted and transformed useful features from data and delivered and stored them in database using Cassandra and Zookeeper. After obtaining required features we applied machine learning and neural network algorithms in the data sets, to classify or mine potential knowledge. Finally we stored the results in MongoDB in which all staff from law enforce departments can have access to them through Web APP. We have applied several state-of-the-art data mining techniques and big data analytic tools that are specifically used for data processing and feature extraction. The experimental results show that our system is efficient in improving the filing rate, and also time-saving in processing large number of data. The promising outcomes will be beneficial for administrative enforcement and law enforcement to speed up the process of solving law cases and provide insights that enable them track case activities, predict the likelihood of warnings, effectively deploy resources and make faster decisions.

Keywords: Big data analytics · Information sharing · Linkage of two laws
Data mining

1 Introduction

With the advancement of the "linkage between administrative enforcement and criminal justice" working mechanism, an information sharing platform has become the hub for administrative law enforcement and criminal justice department to exchange information thus to realize case inquiry, clue transfer, case statistics, monitoring analysis, risk warning, etc. However, there still exists some problem in that it can't play its role in fully supervising the whole law systems, guaranteeing justice and regulating

J. Ren et al. (Eds.): BICS 2018, LNAI 10989, pp. 654–662, 2018.
https://doi.org/10.1007/978-3-030-00563-4_64

market due to insufficient funds and ineffective data processing tools. As shown in Fig. 1, we calculated the filing rate in five cities in china who using the current system, and were surprised to found that nearly half of the cases were left unsolved. With the fast development of computer network and storage technology, a large number of legal cases was collected and made public to all law enforcement departments. These big data can provide new insights for understanding patterns and share information through big data platform.

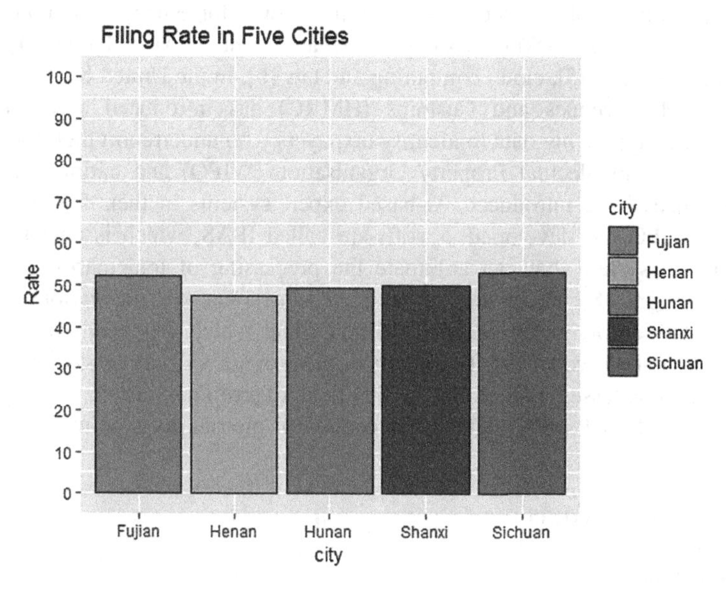

Fig. 1. Using current system the filing rate in five China cities, we can conclude that nearly half of the cases is left unsolved.

Big data and its analysis are at the center of modern science and business [1]. These data are generated from online transactions, emails, videos, audios, images, click streams, logs, posts, search queries, health records, social networking interactions, science data, sensors and mobile phones and their applications [2, 3]. They are stored in databases grow massively and become difficult to capture, form, store, manage, share, analyze and visualize via typical database software tools. Big Data is driving a trend towards behavioral optimization and "personalized law" in which legal decisions and rules are optimized for best outcomes and where law is tailored to individual consumers based on analysis of past data.

In this paper we proposed an effective big data analytics platform, first we utilize the existing government network, facilities and data to achieve a communication platform for law enforcement resource sharing among administrative law enforcement agencies, public security organs and judicial organs. Then by using big data processing tools and data mining algorithms, we realized real-time information analysis and decision making. We tried different state-of-the-art tools and algorithms, our platform greatly promote the effectiveness and usage of law resources, and ensure the stable and development of the society and economy.

2 Related Work

In the recent studies leading AI and Law researchers have devoted attention to apply novel and effective tools and technologies to help law enforcement work more effective and to assist decision making. Examples are argument in AI and Law [4], Natural Intelligence and Law [5], cloud computing and law [6]. In the United Kingdom, the tax authority HM Revenues and Customs (HMRC) has introduced a system called "Connect" which uses big data to identify taxpayers who underreport their total income [7]. The World Intellectual Property Organisation (WIPO) and national intellectual property offices have introduced AI-based expert systems in their law enforcement processes. WIPO has developed as software called IPAS, which is an integrated IP administration system that can automate the processing of trademarks, patents and industrial designs [8]. Poole and others have conceptualized the various tasks that automated law enforcement systems (ALES) entail which can exert surveillance of "large areas at little cost" [9]. Blomberg et al. provide an overview of the use and evolution of risk assessment tools in the field of criminal justice, with particular attention given to risk assessment in the context of pretrial decision-making [10].

3 Theory and Tools

3.1 Law Theory

Connection between administrative law and criminal justice is a new concept which refers to procuratorial organs, together with the public security organs and relevant administrative law enforcement agencies, who divided the cases beyond the scope of administrative law enforcement and suspected crimes from the general administrative law enforcement, and then let judicial organs be responsible for the criminal investigation. It deepens the reform of the justice system to vest real power of supervision to the pro-curatorial organs, and establish the supervisory system connection of the People's Congress and the procuratorial organs, and the People's Congress should obey the Constitution to take the responsibility to supervise the procuratorial power of procuratorial organs.

3.2 Hadoop and MapReduce

Hadoop and MapReduce provide a common and integrated base on which you can add a great diversity of tools that will provide a wide variety of functionalities. MapReduce is a programming model based on two functions: Map and Reduce, it allows to process large amounts of data without the need for immense systems architectures. The Hadoop Distributed File System (HDFS) is designed to store very large data sets reliably, and to stream those data sets at high bandwidth to user applications. In a large cluster, thousands of servers both host directly attached storage and execute user application tasks. By distributing storage and computation across many servers, the resource can grow with demand while remaining economical at every size. Figure 2 demonstrates the work flow of Hadoop.

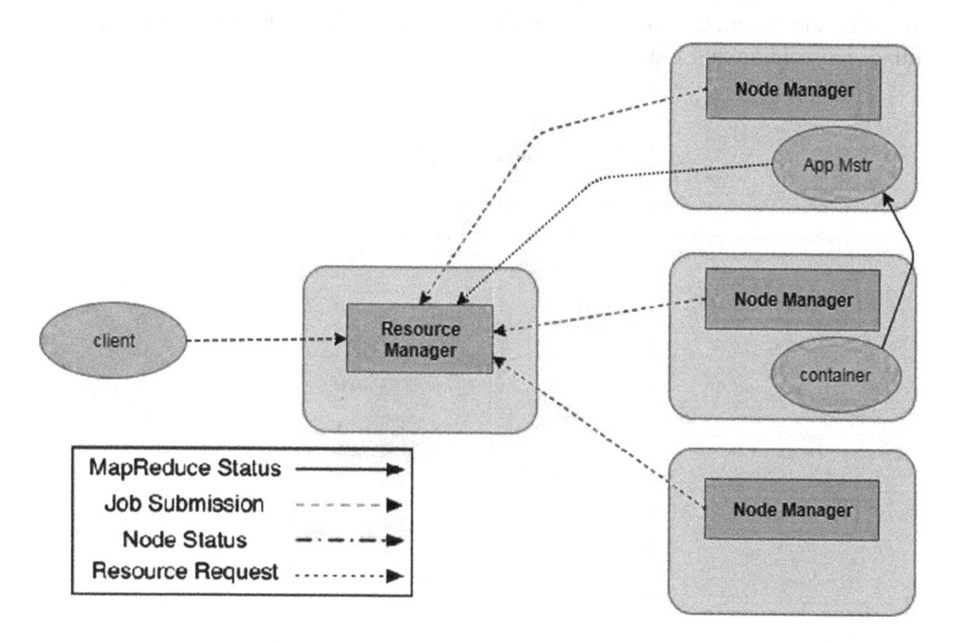

Fig. 2. Work flow of Hadoop2 - Yarn.

3.3 MongoDB

MongoDB is an open-source document database and leading NoSQL database. It is also a cross-platform, document oriented database that provides, high performance, high availability, and easy scalability. MongoDB works on concept of collection and document. MongoDB has the following advantages:

(1) MongoDB is a document database in which one collection holds different documents. Number of fields, content and size of the document can differ from one document to another.
(2) Structure of a single object is clear.
(3) No complex joins.
(4) Deep query-ability. MongoDB supports dynamic queries on documents using a document-based query language that's nearly as powerful as SQL.
(5) Ease of scale-out – MongoDB is easy to scale.
(6) Conversion/mapping of application objects to database objects not needed.
(7) Uses internal memory for storing the (windowed) working set, enabling faster access of data.

4 System Overview

As the existing information sharing system can store large amount of data, as shown in Fig. 3. But it cannot handle large datasets efficiently. Motivated by this, we designed a big data intelligent analysis platform allowing users to explore and analyse data and information shared in the databases. Based on data shared by relevant administrative agencies, the system can supervise the whole process of case uploading, case screening, filing, prosecution and trial.

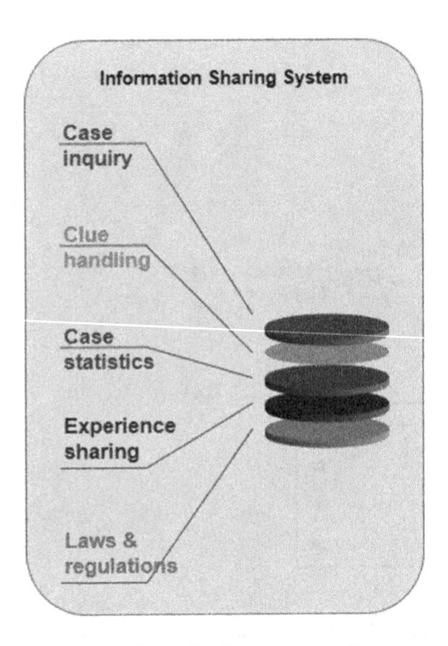

Fig. 3. The model of existing information sharing system, it can store large mount of data and do some basic work, i.e. case inquiry, clue handling etc.

The framework of our system is shown in Fig. 4. Our system can handle structured, semi-structured, unstructured data. We used Apache Pig and Hadoop to analyze large data sets, extract and transform useful information. Then used zookeeper for maintaining configuration information, naming, providing distributed synchronization, and providing group services. Then applied data mining techniques to the data sets, finally the results were stored in MongoDB. Staff from all department of law enforcement can have access to the system through web app.

The data flow of our system is shown in Fig. 5. First, each administrative agency uploads the administrative cases it handles to the platform. The public security organ decides whether to solve the case according to the pre-judgment of the platform. The procuratorial organ supervises whether the public security organ has settled the case through the warning message. The court combines the evidence uploaded to the platform to conduct the case according to law. Our system can automatically classify cases into administrative personnel crimes and cases involving serious criminal offences. As data between departments is not connected to each other, each

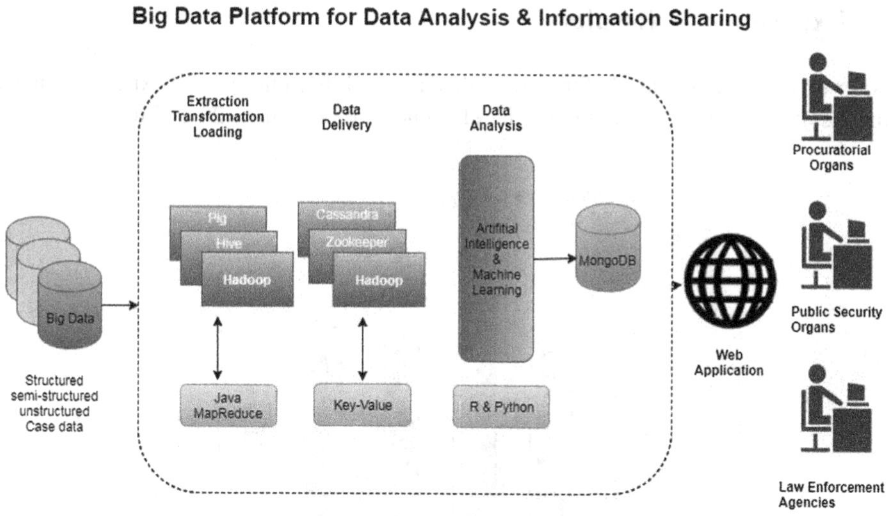

Big Data Platform for Data Analysis & Information Sharing
Extraction Transformation Loading
Data Delivery
Data Analysis
Pig
Hive
Hadoop
Cassandra
Zookeeper
Hadoop
Artifitial Intelligence & Machine Learning
MongoDB
Big Data
Structured semi-structured unstructured Case data
Java MapReduce
Key-Value
R & Python
Web Application
Procuratorial Organs
Public Security Organs
Law Enforcement Agencies

Fig. 4. Framework of our system.

administrative agency needs to upload its own case data to the platform. Then the public security organ obtains case data uploaded by each administrative agency, and the procuratorial organ also obtain data from various other administrative departments and public security organs, and the law court obtains data from all the above units, finally the supervisory committee can obtain data for the entire process.

Supervision Committee
Public Safety Agency
Procuratorate Department
Law Court
Administrative case of Environmental Protection Department
Administrative case of Food and Drug Supervision Department
Administrative case of Industry and Commerce Department
Other Data
Other Data
Evidence data
Other Data

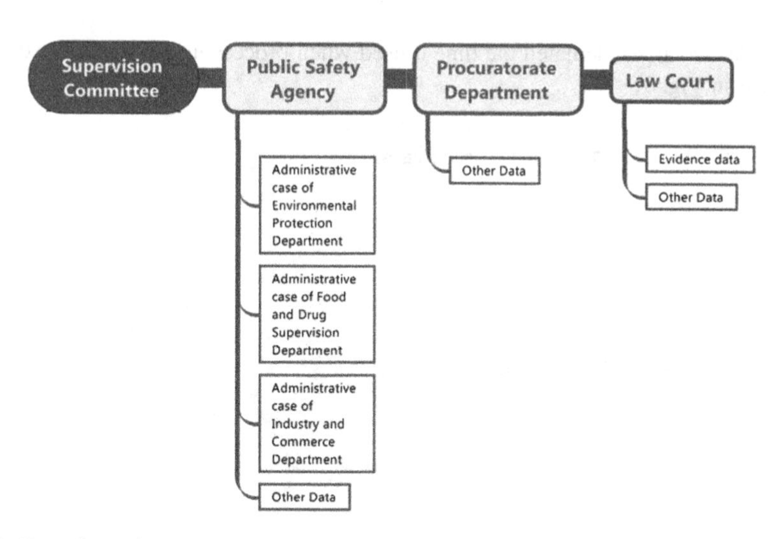

Fig. 5. Data flow of our system. Monitoring Committee supervises the whole system and the activities of entire departments.

5 Experimental Results

After using our big data platform, we calculate the filing rate in the next two months, the results show that we improved the efficiency by more than 20% (Fig. 6).

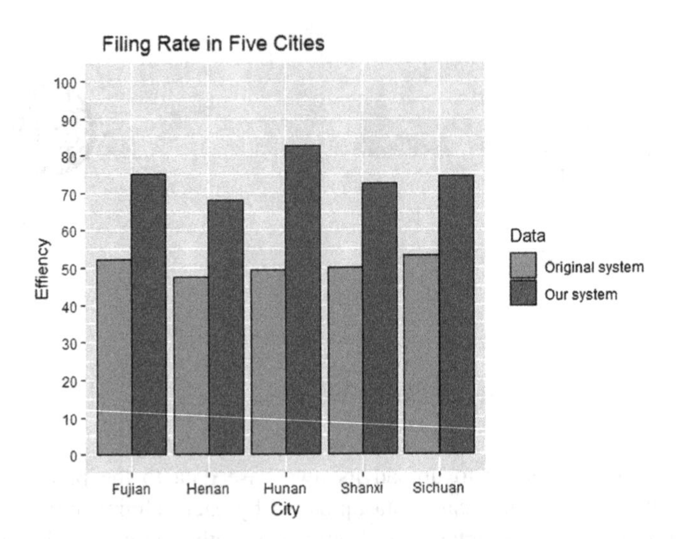

Fig. 6. The filing rate of law cases handled by police department, the results show that we improved Hunan Province by nearly 30% which is the highest, while the number in Sichuan is 20.9% which is the lowest.

Besides we also calculated the time it used when processing large number of cases, as shown in Fig. 7.

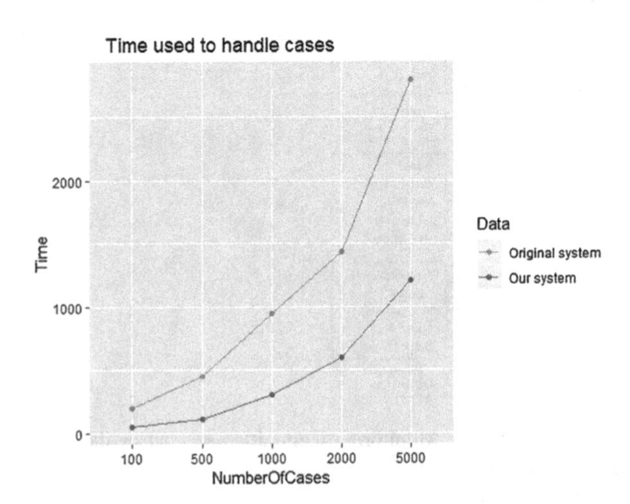

Fig. 7. Time used for processing large number of cases, the promising results show that our system is faster and time saving.

6 Conclusion and Future Work

In the era of big data and artificial intelligence, it is an inevitable choice to create a big data platform for efficient information sharing in the connection between administrative law and criminal justice. Efficient and accurate data storage, statistics, analysis, and early warning mechanisms are important factors to strengthen the relationship. In this paper we propose a big data analysis platform which will not only enable administrative law enforcement and criminal justice to be more closely integrated, but also promote the procuratorial organs to achieve their supervisory functions, guarantee administrative agencies to effectively use the law and more importantly, help combat infringement and counterfeiting, thus promote the steady and healthy development of society and economic development. In the future we will deploy more big data tools such as spark and more machine learning and natural language processing algorithms to our system. Besides, as Deep Learning [11–13] and Artificial Intelligence [14, 15] has achieved big success in computer vision, we also want to perform more deep learning models and other learning algorithms [16, 17] on our platform.

Acknowledgements. This work has been supported by HJSW and Research & Development plan of Shaanxi Province (Program No. 2017ZDXM-GY-094,2015KTZDGY04-01) and Central Fund of High Education, The Legal Issue of Silk Road (Program No. 3102017JC19003).

References

1. Sagiroglu, S., Sinanc, D.: Big data: a review. In: 2013 International Conference on Collaboration Technologies and Systems (CTS), pp. 42–47 (2013)
2. Yacchirema, D., Sarabia-Jácome, D., et al.: A smart system for sleep monitoring by integrating IoT with big data analytics. IEEE Access **6**, 35988–36001 (2018)
3. Zakir, J., Seymour, T.: Big data analytics. Issues Inf. Syst. **16**(2) (2015)
4. Bench-Capon, T.: Argument in artificial intelligence and law. Artif. Intell. Law **5**(4), 249–261 (1997)
5. Hoeschl, H.C., Barcellos, V.: Artificial intelligence and law. In: Bramer, M., Devedzic, V. (eds.) AIAI 2004. IIFIP, vol. 154, pp. 25–34. Springer, Boston (2004). https://doi.org/10.1007/1-4020-8151-0_3
6. Reingold, B., Mrazik, R.: Cloud computing: whose law governs the cloud? (Part III). LegalWorks (2010)
7. HMRC homepage: https://www.gov.uk/government/organisations/hm-revenue-customs
8. IPAS Homepage. http://www.wipo.int/tad/en/activitysearchresult.jsp?vcntry=JO
9. Poole, B., Johnson, S.: An overview of automated enforcement systems and their potential for improving pedestrian and bicyclist safety (2017)
10. Blomberg, T., Bales, W., et al.: Validation of the COMPAS risk assessment classification instrument. College of Criminology and Criminal Justice, Florida State University (2010)
11. Wang, Z., Ren, J., et al.: A deep-learning based feature hybrid framework for spatiotemporal saliency detection inside videos. Neurocomputing **287**, 68–83 (2018)
12. Ren, J., Jiang, J.: Hierarchical modeling and adaptive clustering for real-time summarization of rush videos. IEEE Trans. Multimed. **11**(5), 906–917 (2009)

13. Han, J., Zhang, D., et al.: Object detection in optical remote sensing images based on weakly supervised learning and high-level feature learning. IEEE Trans. Geosci. Remote Sens. **53** (6), 3325–3337 (2015)
14. Chen, J., Ren, J.: Modelling of content-aware indicators for effective determination of shot boundaries in compressed MPEG videos. Multimed. Tools Appl. **54**(2), 219–239 (2011)
15. Ren, J., Vlachos, T.: Immersive and perceptual human–computer interaction using computer vision techniques. In: 2010 IEEE Computer Society Conference on Computer Vision and Pattern Recognition Workshops, pp. 66–72. IEEE (2010)
16. Yan, Y., Ren, J., et al.: Cognitive fusion of thermal and visible imagery for effective detection and tracking of pedestrians in videos. Cognit. Comput. **10**, 1–11 (2017)
17. Yan, Y., Ren, J., et al.: Unsupervised image saliency detection with Gestalt-laws guided optimization and visual attention based refinement. Pattern Recognit. **79**, 65–78 (2018)

Applications

RST Invariant Watermarking Scheme Using Genetic Algorithm and DWT-SVD

Yan Chao(✉), Hao Wang, Shuying Liu, and Huaming Liu

School of Computer and Information, Fuyang Normal College, Fuyang, Anhui, China
910984320@qq.com

Abstract. In recent research, geometric attack is one of the most challenging problems in digital watermark. Such attacks are very simple to defeat most of the existing digital watermark algorithms without destroying watermark itself. In this paper, a point matching measure is adopted for estimating the geometric transformation parameters. First, the affine invariant points of the original and probe image are computed. Then, the best embedded coefficients are found via GA in which the fitness function is defined as the minimal change of the significant region after the watermarking embedding. Finally, the watermark embedding and extraction were implemented in digital wavelet transform (DWT) domain. The propose scheme actualizes blind extraction since not requiring the original image information. The watermark is embedded adaptively according to image texture. This method has been proved its robustness to various attacks through experiments, and it can recover the watermarking image when the watermarking is aggressed.

Keywords: DWT · Affine invariant interest point · Genetic algorithm

1 Introduction

In recent years, research and application of robust image watermarking technology have made some progress, in which the choice of watermark embedding coefficient and watermark embedding strength is still a hot research topic because of it will directly affect the basic performance of digital watermarking: Robustness and invisibility [1]. After comparing the similar algorithms in recent years [2–6], it is found that most of the watermarking algorithms based on the frequency domain are used to randomly select the embedding coefficient and embedding strength of watermark. It's not only has a lot of subjectivity, but it needs a lot of experiments to come to the conclusion that the efficiency is very poor.

So, a robust watermark scheme that can embed watermark adaptively and achieve self-synchronizing is proposed in this paper, which combines the genetic algorithm [2] and the singular value decomposition [3]. The eigenvalues of the singular value decomposition of matrices have characteristics that are not easily altered by geometric attacks, so, the watermark image is decomposed by singular value to generate the watermark sequence to improve the robustness and anti-interference ability of the watermark; Genetic algorithm is an optimization algorithm that simulates natural selection and genetic mechanism [14], it can select the best solution from many

J. Ren et al. (Eds.): BICS 2018, LNAI 10989, pp. 665–675, 2018.
https://doi.org/10.1007/978-3-030-00563-4_65

possible solutions. This feature can solve the uncertain problem when selecting watermark embedding coefficient [4].

Therefore, genetic algorithm is used to select the optimal embedding coefficient, and in the process of embedding, the watermark embedding strength coefficient is adaptively obtained according to the texture characteristics of the carrier image. To the self-synchronizing, we used the affine invariant interest points [10] to extract the feature points of the carrier image before and after embedding the watermark, and the fitness function in genetic algorithm is constructed to optimize the robustness and invisibility of the watermark [12]. In the watermark extraction, the carrier image and the original watermark information are not needed, and blind extraction is realized. Experimental results show that the watermark can still be successfully extracted after being subjected to common geometric attacks and general signal processing.

2 Affine Invariant Interest Point Detector

Affine invariant features in object recognition and image registration applications have recently been studied [13]. These features are highly distinctive and matched with high probability against large image distortions. For robust watermarking, we adopt affine invariant interest points, which were proposed by Mikolajczyk and Schmid [5]. The points have been proved to be invariant to image rotation, scaling, translation, viewpoint changing and affine transformation.

Supposing the point set detected from original image is called reference point set and detected from the probe image is called probe point set. These two point sets denoted by $P = \{(x_i, y_i)^T | i = 1, 2, \ldots, m\}$ and $Q = \{(u_j, v_j)^T | j = 1, 2, \ldots, n\}$ respectively. The estimated geometry parameters are scaling factor ρ, rotting factor θ, horizontal translation factor e and vertical translation factor f. Transformation point set $P' = \{(u_i', v_i')^T | i = 1, 2, \ldots, m.\}$ is obtained from reference point set by following transformation:

$$\begin{pmatrix} u' \\ v' \end{pmatrix} = \rho \begin{pmatrix} \cos\theta & \sin\theta \\ -\sin\theta & \cos\theta \end{pmatrix} \begin{pmatrix} x \\ y \end{pmatrix} + \begin{pmatrix} e \\ f \end{pmatrix} \tag{1}$$

We can consider that points in P' are similar to the points in Q except unmatched points.

3 Watermark Embedding and Extraction

In this section, the watermark scheme is departed into three parts.

3.1 Watermark Generation and Recovery

For security and robustness, the original watermark image is not directly embedded into the original image. Firstly, Arnold transformation [6] is carried out on the watermark image W, the scrambled image W' is obtained after key_1 transformation. Then, performing SVD decomposition [7] on the scrambled watermark image to obtain a watermark sequence $W = w_1, w_2,\ldots,w_N$. Watermark values are divided into two categories [11]: the first element value is the first category δ_1. Other element values are of the second class $\eta = \{\delta_2, \delta_3 \ldots \delta_N\}$. Finally, the embedded watermark sequences are generated. The watermark recovery process is an inverse procedure of generation.

3.2 Watermark Embedding

In this paper, DWT method [7] is employed and the approximate component is considered as operation target. This method obtains great robustness. Since that multiresolution analysis of wavelet is consistent with human visual characteristics [9].

Step 1: After two levels DWT, the original image can be decomposed into seven partials denoted by approximate component LL_2, horizontal components HL_2 and HL_1, vertical components LH_2 and LH_1 and diagonal components HH_2 and HH_1 respectively. Notice that the affine invariant feature point set of carrier image should be processed before DWT for determining the fitness function in genetic algorithm.

Step 2: For one thing, the watermark embedded in the approximate component is limited, so watermark belonging to the first category will be embedded into approximate component of the second level by the following rule:

$$I'_{LL\,2}(p,q) = I_{LL\,2}(p,q) + \alpha_i \cdot \delta_1 \tag{2}$$

For another thing, The more watermarks can be embedded in the detail components, therefore, the genetic algorithm is used to obtain the optimal embedding coefficient point (i, j), and then the second kind of watermark value is embedded into the detail component of the first level with formula such as:

$$I'^{\theta}_{sub1}(i,j) = I^{\theta}_{sub1}(i,j) + \alpha_i \cdot \eta(k) \tag{3}$$

Where $p, q = \{1, 2\ldots N/2\}$, $i, j = \{1, 2\ldots N\}$, $k = \{2, 3\ldots N\}$, $\theta \in \{HL_1, LH_1, HH_1\}$ is the detail component of the first level in wavelet domain, $I_{LL2}(p, q)$ is the approximate component of the second level in wavelet domain, $I'_{LL2}(p,q)$ is the approximate component of watermarked images at level 2; I^{θ}_{sub1} is the detail component of the first level, I'^{θ}_{sub1} is the detail component of watermarked images at first level; α_i is the embedding strength coefficients which self-adapt according to texture masking characteristics.

Step 3: embedding strength coefficient also should be confirmed successfully before embedding algorithm executed. The embedding strength coefficients which self-adapt according to texture masking characteristics can be obtained by:

$$\alpha_i = \alpha_{base} + \left(\frac{f_i - f_{\min}}{f_{\max} - f_{\min}}\right) \times \alpha_{base} \quad (i = 1, 2, \ldots, N) \tag{4}$$

Where N is the length of the watermark sequence. And α_i can be regulated into a certain range by changing α_{base}. Parameter f_i reflects image texture. The lager f_i, the more complex the texture is. That is we can amend more to enhance robustness. Parameter $f_{\min}$ is the minimum of f_i and $f_{\max}$ is the maximum of f_i.

Variance value reflects the complexity of the texture. So f_i is constructed by the variance of details components.

$$f_i = weight_{i,1} \times (\sigma_{i,LH_1} + \sigma_{i,HL_1} + \gamma\sigma_{i,HH_1}) + weight_{i,2} \times (\sigma_{i,LH_2} + \sigma_{i,HL_2} + \gamma\sigma_{i,HH_2}) \quad (i = 1, 2, \ldots, N)$$
$$\begin{cases} weight_{i,1} = \frac{\sigma_{i,LH_1} + \sigma_{i,HL_1} + \sigma_{i,HH_1}}{\sigma_{i,LH_1} + \sigma_{i,HL_1} + \sigma_{i,HH_1} + \sigma_{i,LH_2} + \sigma_{i,HL_2} + \sigma_{i,HH_2}} \\ weight_{i,2} = \frac{\sigma_{i,LH_2} + \sigma_{i,HL_2} + \sigma_{i,HH_2}}{\sigma_{i,LH_1} + \sigma_{i,HL_1} + \sigma_{i,HH_1} + \sigma_{i,LH_2} + \sigma_{i,HL_2} + \sigma_{i,HH_2}} \end{cases} \quad (5)$$

Where σ_{i,HL_j} is the variance of ith embedding position in details components HL_j $(j = 1,\ 2)$ and $\gamma(\gamma > 1)$ responses impact of diagonal components, because human eye is not sensitive to diagonal direction.

Then the watermarked image is obtained by inverse discrete wavelet transform (IDWT).

3.3 Watermark Extraction

To extract watermark in a probe image, firstly, Two-layer wavelet decomposition is carry out on that original image and the watermarked image respectively. Because executed without the information of original image and original watermark, the extraction algorithm is blind. The extraction rule is:

$$\tilde{\delta}_1^* = \frac{sum\left\{\left\{I'_{LL_1}(p,q) - I_{LL_1}(p,q)\right\}/a_i\right\}}{((N/2) * (N/2))} \quad (6)$$

$$\tilde{\eta} * (j) = \left\{ \begin{array}{l} (I'_{sub1}{}^0(i,j) - I_{sub1}{}^0(i,j))/a_i + (I'_{sub1}{}^1(i,j) - I_{sub1}{}^1(i,j))/a_i \\ + (I'_{sub1}{}^2(i,j) - I_{sub1}{}^2(i,j))/a_i \end{array} \right\} /3 \quad (7)$$

The extracted singular value sequence is $\tilde{\delta}_1^*, \tilde{\eta}^*(2), \tilde{\eta}^*(3)\ldots\tilde{\eta}^*(N)$, that is, the extracted watermark sequence. Therefore, the extract watermark signal is $W' = UW^*V^T$, where $W^* = diag(\tilde{\delta}_1^*, \tilde{\eta}^*(2), \tilde{\eta}^*(3)\ldots\tilde{\eta}^*(N))$.

In order to make the extracted watermark still be a binary image, a detection threshold T_t is introduced. If the pixel point value of the extracted watermark image is larger than the threshold T_t, the watermark value is 1; if the value of the pixel point is less than the threshold T_t, the watermark value is 0.

$$W'(m,n) = \begin{cases} 1, & if\ W'(m,n) > T_t(m,n = 1,2\ldots N) \\ 0, & else \end{cases} \quad (8)$$

4 Optimization of Embedding Coefficient Using GA

We can adjust the probe image to achieve the synchronization by matching reference point set P with probe point set Q and the fitness function is constructed according to the principle of minimizing the significant region change of the image feature points after embedding watermark, and the best embedding point is found by genetic algorithm. Fitness function constructed by the summation of distance square [8], which is used for measuring the matched degree between P and Q.

Suppose that points order in Q has been resorted according to points order in P. For the sake of calculation simply, confirming that $a = \rho\cos\theta$ and $b = \rho\sin\theta$ in Eq. (1). So the summation of distance square definition is:

$$\begin{aligned}\varepsilon^2 &= \sum_{i=1}^{m}\left(\left(u_i - u_i'\right)^2 + \left(v_i - v_i'\right)^2\right) \\ &= \sum_{i=1}^{m}\left((u_i - ax_i - by_i - e)^2 + (v_i + bx_i - ay_i - f)^2\right)\end{aligned} \tag{9}$$

We can improve this equation by introducing the penalty of not completely matching. The improved ε^2 is:

$$\hat{\varepsilon} = \begin{cases}\varepsilon^2\left(1 + \left(\frac{m-2}{k-2}\right)\log\left(\frac{m-2}{k-2}\right)\right) & k \geq 3 \\ \infty & k = 0, 1, 2\end{cases} \tag{10}$$

Where k is the matched points number on two point set P and Q. Equation (10) is considered as object function in GA, which is a part of fitness function.

4.1 Initial Population Generation and Chromosome Encoding

The initial population is generated randomly. We suppose that there are m points in reference point set P and n points in probe point set Q. So the chromosome should consist of m genes and each gene value is in the range of $[0,\ n]$. If the value of ith gene is j except zero, the representation is that j^{th} point in Q is matched with i^{th} point in P. When the value of ith gene is zero, the representation is that no point in Q is matched with i^{th} point in P. The resulting population can not only ensure the diversity of the population, but cannot generate new individual gene conflict due to cross operation.

The coding method chosen in this paper is real number coding, that is to count the position of watermark embedding point, and directly use it as genotype of decision variable for genetic operation. The problem of the same individual in the same chromosome caused by crossover and mutation can be avoided by using real coding [15].

4.2 Fitness Function

The optimization goal of this algorithm is to minimize the significant region change of the feature points before and after embedding the watermark in the image, and obtain the final embedding position of the watermark according to the corresponding solution of the best fitness of the last generation.

Considering the summation of distance square between point sets P and Q. The smaller the object function value is, the larger the match degree between P and Q has. Consequently, the fitness function should be inversed to the object function:

$$fitness = \frac{1}{c + Object(P,\ Q)} \tag{11}$$

Where c is a positive constant to avoid the denominator is a zero. In experiment, c is selected as*1*.

4.3 Genetic Operators and Point Match Algorithm

As we all know, there are three main operators in GA. Selection processing is used for choosing chromosomes which fitness function value are greater and put them into offspring [11]. The greater the fitness function value of chromosome is, the more likely the chromosome can be choosing. In this paper, random selection with competing is adopted as selection operator.

The crossing processing and the mutation processing are used to produce new chromosome to increase the diversity of new population. There are performed according to a certain probability called crossing probability P_c and predefined probability P_m. In this paper, single point crossover operator and mutation operator are adopted here.

The input of GA is reference point set P and probe point set Q. And the output of GA is the best matched point set and best transformation parameters. The main steps of the proposed are summarized in Algorithm 1.

Algorithm 1: Point Match via Genetic Algorithm

Input: reference point set P and probe point set Q

1) Define population size N, crossing probability P_c, mutation probability P_m, maximum generation $G_{\max}$, generation counter G_{num}, selection operator, crossing operator, and mutation operator respectively.

2) Initialize $P(G_{num})$ randomly using chromosome encoding method.

3) Evaluate each chromosome fitness value in $P(G_{num})$ by fitness function.

4)While ($G_{num} \le G_{\max}$)

5) {If $Object(P, Q)$ >threshold

6){Change generation counter value $G_{num} = G_{num} + 1$;

7) Selecting process to $P(G_{num})$ from $P(G_{num} - 1)$;

8) Cross process to $P(G_{num})$;

9) Mutate process to $P(G_{num})$;

10) Evaluate $P(G_{num})$;}}

11) Compute the best embedding positions which are determined by the best chromosome in current population. And the best chromosome is the best matched two-point set.

Output: best matched point set and best transformation parameters

---

5 Optimization of Embedding Coefficient Using GA

In this section, proposed scheme has been tested under various attacks. The standard gray level image is "*Elain*" (512 × 512 pixels). The algorithm is manipulated under Matlab7.2. In the experiments, the algorithm parameters are set as, Diagonal components impact factor $\gamma = 2$, Arnold scrambling key_1 is 33. "dwt2" is used to compute the DWT, which wavelet name is "db1". "gatbx" toolbox is employed to implement the genetic algorithm, and parameters are population size $N = 30$, maximum generation $G_{\max} = 50$, crossing probability $P_c = 0.08$ and mutation probability $P_m = 0.03$. In the process of extracting watermark, the threshold $T_t = 0.5$ is used. After embedding the watermark, the Peak Signal to Noise Ratio (PSNR) of the image is 43.62.

Figure 1(a)–(d) is respectively the original image, the secret image, the original watermark and the extracted watermark.

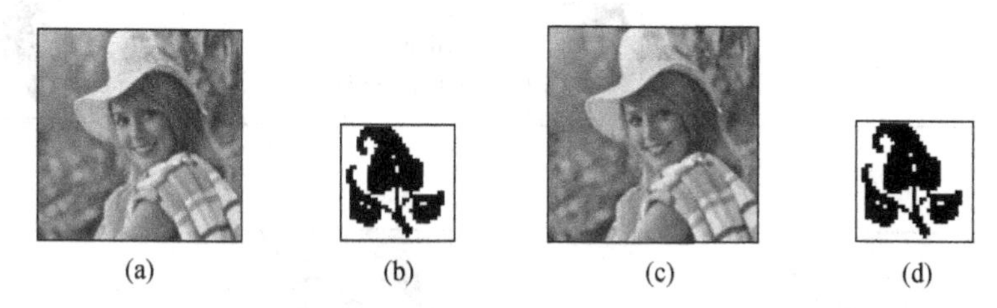

Fig. 1. Watermark embedding and extraction: (a) Original image, (b) Watermark image, (c) Watermarked image, (d) Extracted watermark image

5.1 Robustness of Watermark

(1) Robustness to conventional signal processing operations. Simulation results are shown in Table 1.
(2) Robustness to geometric attacks. Fig. 2 shows the experimental results after Gaussian blur with radius = 1.0 and USM sharpening attack with number = 300%, radius = 3, and threshold = 50. Fig. 3 is the experimental results of deforming different parts of the image. Figure 4 is the experimental results of tailoring attacks with different sizes to watermark images. It can be seen that the extracted watermark image is still relatively clear.

The experimental results show that the proposed algorithm has good watermark invisibility and good robustness against conventional signal processing operations and geometric attacks.

5.2 Comparison with Other Algorithm

In Table 2, proposed method is compared with Hai method [12]. Hai scheme is invariant to RST based on log-polar mapping (LPM) and phase correlation. The watermark is embed in the log-polar mappings of Fourier magnitude spectrum of

Table 1. NC and PSNR of image under different operation (JPEG compression, Gaussian noising, Salt& Pepper noising, Median filtering (3 × 3))

Signal processing operation	NC	PSNR	extracted watermark image	Signal processing operation	NC	PSNR	extracted watermark image
JPEG compression 90%	1.0000	34.0165		Gaussian noising 0.003	0.9269	19.0816	
JPEG compression 75%	0.9767	31.8043		Salt& Pepper noising 0.01	1.0000	24.0471	
JPEG compression 60%	0.9201	29.0634		Salt& Pepper noising 0.02	0.9819	21.0116	
Gaussian noising 0.001	0.9864	20.3648		Median filtering(3×3)	0.9423	16.7850	

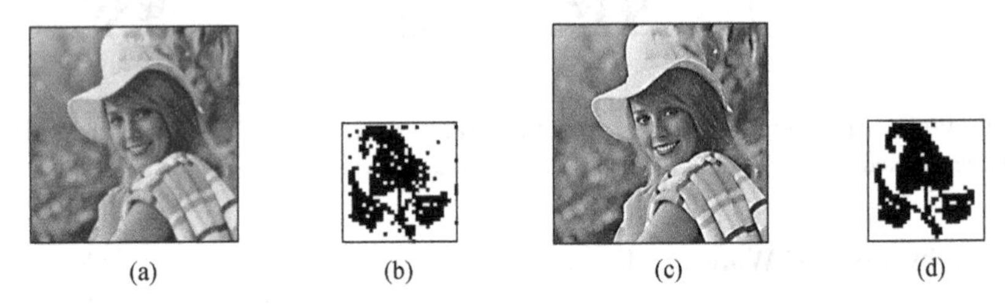

Fig. 2. Watermark image (a, c) and extracted watermark image (b, d) after Gaussian blur and USM sharpening attack

Fig. 3. Watermarked image (a, c, e) and extracted watermark image (b, d, f) after geometric deformation attack

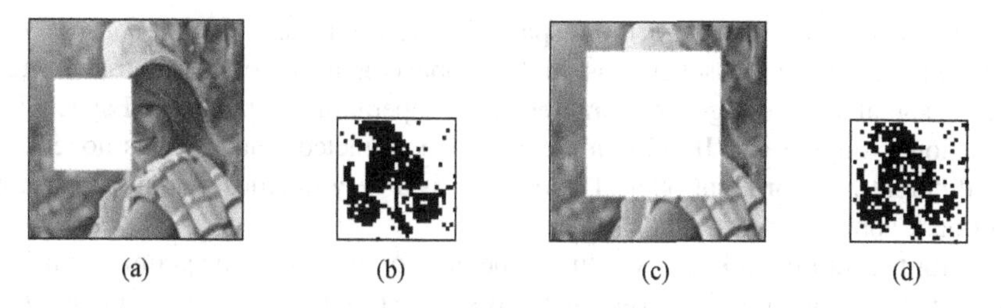

Fig. 4. Watermarked image (a, c) and extracted watermark image (b, d) after tailoring attacks with different sizes

original image, and use the phase correlation between the LPM of the original image and the LPM of the watermarked image to calculate the displacement of watermark positions in LPM domain. Experiment results show that proposed method is better than Hai [12] method in most attacks.

Table 2. The comparison of invisibility and robustness between proposed method and the algorithm [12] under different attack

Attacks	Proposed method		Hai method [12]	
	PSNR	NC	PSNR	NC
JPEG compression 90%	37.0387	1.0000	35.69	0.9979
JPEG compression 50%	33.1537	0.9995	31.14	0.7986
Gaussian noising 0.001	31.3259	0.9767	31.82	0.9120
Gaussian noising 0.003	29.4648	0.8719	29.37	0.7885
USM sharpening attack	28.2351	0.9553	26.72	0.8173
Cropping 25%	39.3012	0.8862	37.04	0.8312
Translation 15 left & 10 up	39.1843	0.9284	34.15	0.7987

We can see that this new scheme is highly robust against geometric attacks and signal processing operations separately. Moreover, the performance of geometric transformation is much better than signal processing. For comprehensive attacks, it can achieve the poor performance of geometric transformation or signal processing basically. The above simulations and analyses have all confirmed that the proposed scheme has high robustness against among geometric transformations, signal processing and comprehensive attacks.

6 Conclusions

In this paper, we have proposed a novel watermark algorithm. This scheme introduces the affine invariant point technique and point matching method by GA for standing against geometric attacks. At the same time, watermark embedding algorithm is self-adaptive to compromise between transparency and robustness. Simulations have substantiated that this new scheme is highly robust against geometric transformation attacks, signal processing and comprehensive operations separately. Especially for translation, cropping and JPEG compression, the extracted watermark is none or very little different from original ones. Therefore, it is a very practical technique for image watermark applications.

As for the future work, we will find a method for extracting the geometric invariant interest point, which provides low time and space complexity. Fitness function of GA will be improved from RST invariant to affine invariant [6]. And the watermark algorithm also can be betterment to better deal with noising and filtering. The algorithm is also the further research on the robustness of the algorithm to the general signal attack.

Acknowledgements. This work was supported by the Key Project of the Education Department of Anhui Province (Grant No. KJ2018A0345) and Natural Science Foundation of Fuyang Normal University (Grant No. 2018FSKJ04ZD).

References

1. Zhu, H., Liu, M., Li, Y.: The RST invariant digital image watermarking using Radon transforms and complex moments. Digit. Signal Process. **20**(6), 1612–1628 (2010)
2. Lee, D., Kim, T., Lee, S., Paik, J.: Genetic algorithm-based watermarking in discrete wavelet transform domain. Intell. Comput. **4113**, 709–716 (2006)
3. Liu, R., Tan, T.: An SVD-based watermarking scheme for protecting rightful ownership. IEEE Trans. Multimed. **4**(1), 121–128 (2002)
4. Bhatnagar, G., Raman, B.: A new robust reference watermarking scheme based on DWT-SVD. Comput. Stand. Interfaces **31**(5), 1002–1013 (2009)
5. Mikolajczyk, K., Schmid, C.: Scale & affine invariant interest point detectors. Int. J. Comput. Vis. **60**(1), 63–86 (2004)
6. Zhao, H., Ren, J.: Cognitive computation of compressed sensing for watermark signal measurement. Cogn. Comput. **8**(2), 246–260 (2016)
7. Lai, C.C.: An improved SVD-based watermark-ing scheme using human visual characteristics. Opt. Commun. **284**(4), 938–944 (2011)
8. Ali, M., Chang, W.A., Siarry, P.: Differential evolution algorithm for the selection of optimal scaling factors in image watermarking. Eng. Appl. Artif. Intell. **31**(31), 15–26 (2014)
9. Chen, C.H., Tang, Y.L., Wang, C.P.: A robust watermarking algorithm based on salient image features. Optik Int. J. Light. Electron Opt. **125**(3), 1134–1140 (2014)
10. Elshazly, E.H., Faragallah, O.S., Abbas, A.M.: Robust and secure fractional wavelet image watermarking. Signal Image Video Process. **9**(1), 89–98 (2015)
11. Lang, J., Zhang, Z.: Blind digital watermarking method in the fractional Fourier transform domain. Opt. Lasers Eng. **53**(2), 112–121 (2014)
12. Hai, L.S., Nan, W., Zi, H.W.: An RST invariant image watermarking scheme using DWT-SVD. In: International Symposium on Instrumentation & Measurement, Sensor Network and Automation (IMSNA), pp. 214–217. IEEE, Sanya (2012)

13. Li, L., Xu, H.H., Chang, C.C.: A novel image watermarking in redistributed invariant wavelet domain. J. Syst. Softw. **84**(6), 923–929 (2011)
14. Fan, M.Q., Wang, H.X., Li, S.K.: Restudy on SVD-based watermarking scheme. Appl. Math. Comput. **203**(2), 926–930 (2008)
15. Akay, B.: A study on particle swarm optimization and artificial bee colony algorithms for multilevel thresholding. Appl. Soft Comput. **13**(6), 3066–3091 (2013)

Application of VPN Based on L2TP and User's Access Rights in Campus Network

Shuying Liu[1(✉)], Tao Zeng[2], Yan Chao[1], and Hao Wang[1]

[1] School of Computer and Information, Fuyang Normal College, Fuyang, Anhui, China
654670459@qq.com
[2] Information Center, Fuyang Normal College, Fuyang, Anhui, China

Abstract. VPN is widely used in colleges and universities at present, having brought great convenience to teachers and students in their study and life. Due to the fact that the current VPN in colleges and universities has the same access rights to all users, as long as VPN users login successfully via VPN account, they can access the campus network. As a result, not only is the management of the VPN administrators troublesome, but also the security of the network environment in the school is not very good. In view of this problem, this paper proposes a method that people visit the campus network resources according to user's access authority in which the distribution of access rights can be distributed according to user's identity category or individual way, and gives the application in college campus network. Finally, the simulation results show that this system is feasible to guarantee the security of communication.

Keywords: VPN · L2TP · Access · Security

1 Introduction

With the continuous development of computer technology and digital campuses, all colleges and universities are advocating information construction. However, with the increasing application of information technology in colleges and universities, a series of problems have also emerged, among which the security issues are comparatively outstanding. Taking the campus network as an example, many resources in the school are protected, such as resources in the e-government system, educational administration system, financial system and library management system. Once the campus network is attacked by illegal users, it will cause the campus network to be inaccessible, and even leak confidential data on the campus network. From the perspective of security, the access to these resources must be implemented. Only users with legitimate IP addresses within the campus network are allowed to access these resources. As a result, the schoolteachers and system maintenance personnel cannot access these resources on the campus network. As a networking technology, VPN is a logical and virtual private network, which establishes a virtual private network over the Internet and performs encrypted communication. Off-campus personnel can access campus resources through VPN. For example, students at home can check the results of this semester and teachers can access the school's internal resources at home, such as viewing documents in

J. Ren et al. (Eds.): BICS 2018, LNAI 10989, pp. 676–686, 2018.
https://doi.org/10.1007/978-3-030-00563-4_66

e-government, logging in to the educational administration system to enter student grades and so on. Whether it is for students or teachers, VPN brings great flexibility and convenience to everyone's work and study [1, 2].

At the same time, with the expansion of colleges and universities, there are nearly 20,000 teachers and students in general undergraduate colleges and universities, even bigger, who are all users of campus VPN users. Such a large number of VPN users access the campus network through the VPN and accesses various types of school resources. The security of campus resources remains to be solved [3]. At present, in most colleges and universities, any person who has the VPN username and password of the university can access the campus. But at the same time there are the following problems. Firstly, the user name and password may be revealed, as a result that illegal users can enter the campus network through the VPN, and even easily access all the school resources, including some sensitive information. Therefore, it is difficult to guarantee the security of remote access to the campus network through VPN. Secondly, because every school's VPN users are in a library, VPN administrators are relatively cumbersome to manage VPN users of such a large scale. And it is time-consuming to search for her information when the VPN user has problems (for example, the password needs to be reset when it is forgotten).

To solve the above problems, the university urgently needs a system of VPN with strong adaptability, high security and efficient. At present, there are many kinds of VPN, such as SSL VPN, IPSec VPN, L2TP VPN and so on [2, 6]. Compared with other protocols such as IPSec VPN [3, 4], L2TP's greatest advantage is its simplicity. Currently, the VPN system used by universities is based on the L2TP protocol. This article presents a system that can assign access rights to resources within a school based on the user's identity and the L2TP protocol. This VPN system not only brings convenience to everyone's office, but also solves security problems when using a VPN system by restricting the access rights of VPN members and classifying VPN members.

2 Related Technologies—VPN and L2TP

2.1 The Concept of VPN

The full name of VPN is the Virtual Private Network, which uses encapsulation technology, encryption technology, switching technology, and PKI technology to establish a dedicated data communication network in the public Internet. It can establish a proprietary communication line through a special encrypted communication protocol which is located in different places connected to Internet, between external networks and campus networks, multiple intranets. The reason why it is called a virtual network is that the link between any two nodes of the entire VPN does not have the end-to-end physical links required by the traditional private network. It is a kind of logical networks built on the network platform (Internet, ATM, Frame, Relay and so on) provided by the public network service provider, and the user data is transmitted in the logical links.

2.2 VPN Features

The construction of Virtual Private Network is fast. It only needs to connect the network node to the private network in dedicated lines and configures the network accordingly.

The cost is low. VPN is a virtual private network established on the basis of public networks, thus avoiding the high investment in hardware and software required for the construction of traditional private networks. At the same time, users can greatly reduce link rental fees and network maintenance costs through VPN networking, thereby reducing the operating costs of campuses or enterprises.

The security is good. VPN mainly adopts the international standard network security technology, and establishes logical tunnels and network layer encryption on the public network to prevent network data from being modified and stolen, thus ensuring the security and integrity of user data [5, 11].

The network maintenance is simple. A lot of network management and maintenance work are done by public network service providers.

2.3 L2TP

L2TP is an industry-standard Internet tunneling protocol that enables the encryption of network data streams. L2TP operates at the data link layer and its packets are classified into data messages and control messages. The data messages are used to deliver a PPP frame [7], which serves as the data area of the L2TP packet. L2TP does not guarantee the reliable delivery of data messages. If a data message is lost, it will not be retransmitted, and the traffic control and congestion control of data messages are not supported. Control messages are used to establish, maintain, and terminate control connections and sessions. L2TP ensures reliable delivery and supports flow control and congestion control of control messages.

The L2TP protocol structure shown in Fig. 1 describes the relationship between PPP frames and control channels, data channels. PPP frames are transmitted on the unreliable L2TP data channels, and control messages are transmitted on a reliable L2TP control channel.

<table>
<tr><td>PPP Frame</td><td></td><td></td></tr>
<tr><td>L2TP date message</td><td></td><td>L2TP control message</td></tr>
<tr><td>L2TP date channel
(unreliable)</td><td></td><td>L2TP control channel
(reliable)</td></tr>
<tr><td colspan="3">Packet transmission network (e.g. UDP[13])</td></tr>
</table>

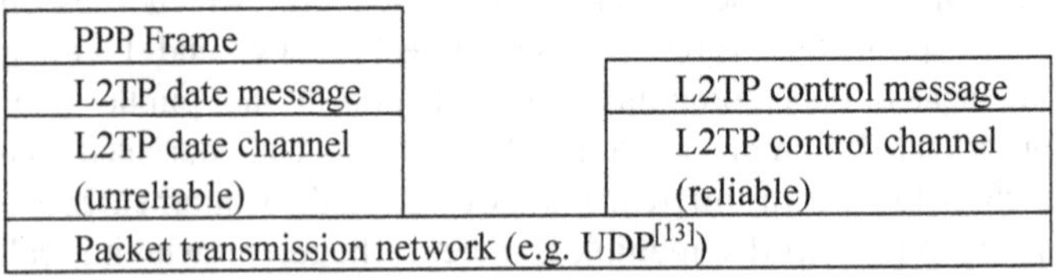

Fig. 1. L2TP protocol architecture [8]

Normally, L2TP data is sent as UDP packets. L2TP registers the UDPport1701, but this port is only used for the initial tunneling process. The L2TP tunnel initiator chooses a free port to send a message to the receiver's port1701, and after receiving the message, the receiver also selects a free port and sends the message back to the sender's specified port. At this point, the ports of both parties are selected and will not change during the time period when the tunnel remains connected [3].

3 Application of VPN Based on L2TP and User's Access Permission in Campus Network

3.1 General Idea of VPN Based on User's Access Permission

Currently, users of VPN in colleges and universities have a unique VPN account. Once the account is stolen by illegal users, illegal users can access all resources in the school and may attack the school website. In order to clarify the access process and security of VPN system based on user's access rights, the VPN remote access architecture is given, as shown in Fig. 2.

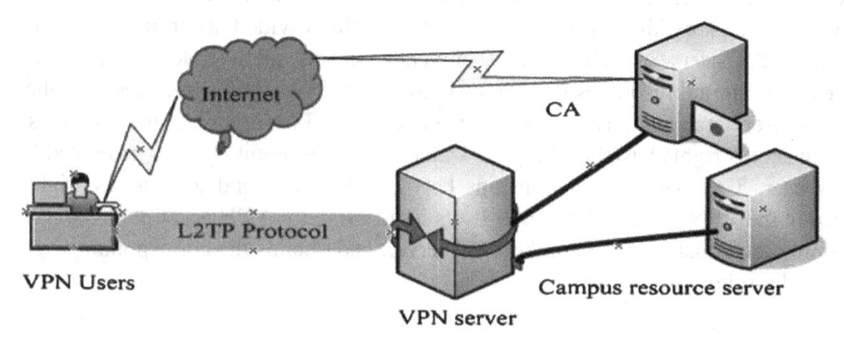

Fig. 2. Remote access block diagram of VPN based on L2TP and user's access rights

In the remote access architecture shown in Fig. 2, different remote users access the CA certification center via the Internet, and it is determined whether the user's identity is legal through the CA certification center. If it is legal, the account is assigned to the user, and his identity is saved to the VPN server. The VPN server divides users into different user groups. The mapping relationship between the VPN user and the school resources is saved in the VPN server. The L2TP protocol is used to establish a secure channel for user communication between VPN users and VPN servers. After the VPN user logs in successfully next time, the user can directly enter the campus network to obtain the corresponding permission resources. This not only reduces the workload of the VPN account manager, but also ensures the security of VPN usage. Due to the different access rights of each user, even though VPN access to the campus network, it is not possible to see resources beyond its jurisdiction, thus further ensuring the security of campus resources.

3.2 The Composition of the VPN

The composition of the VPN is roughly divided into four parts. Firstly, VPN users are users of VPN, which can be divided into teachers, students and maintenance personnel according to the specific situation of colleges and universities. Secondly, the administrator is responsible for the maintenance of the VPN system, such as the registration of VPN users, password recovery and information management. Thirdly, the server is divided into the management server and resource server, the management server provides an information storage device for administrators to manage VPN users. The resource server stores resources in the campus network, which can be divided into educational system, e-government, scientific research management system. Fourthly, CA that it is provided by a VPN server is a complete CA center. It is a Public Key Infrastructure (PKI) public key infrastructure technology that provides network identity authentication. Specifically, it is responsible for issuing digital certificates to users who have been authenticated to enter the campus network, and at the same time, they give credentials for VPN users.

The flow chart of each user in campus network accessing the VPN system is shown in Fig. 3. According to the classification of campus network resources, it can be divided into educational system, scientific research management system and e-government. Three kinds of strategies can be roughly divided according to the identity of the VPN users in colleges and universities, and each strategy determines the accessible internal resources of campus network. VPN user authenticates with the CA, and the user name and passwords are obtained. The VPN server assigns resources with certain access rights based on the user's identity and different policies generated by the VPN user. The mapping relationships between the users and their access rights are saved in the VPN server. The remote users login using the VPN account, comparing the mapping relationships saved in the VPN server, and obtains the corresponding rights to access the school resources.

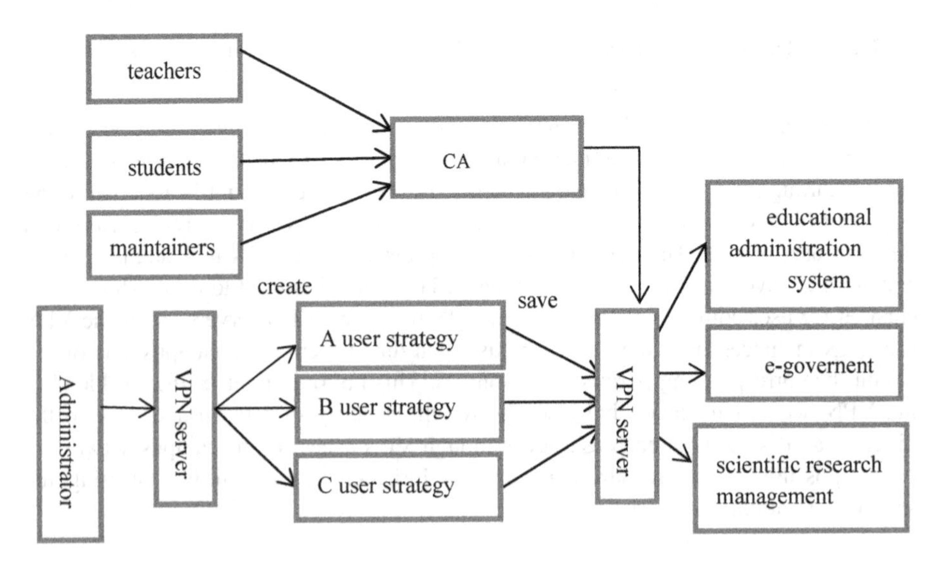

Fig. 3. VPN access flow chart

The Division of User Type. VPN users in campus network can be divided into students, teachers and administrators and administrators. Among them, the administrative staff is divided into the secretary, the President, the secretary, the administrative secretary and other users. The administrator is the maintenance personnel of each website in the campus network, and different website modules have different maintainers. Adding the different user groups to the user management bar under the user authentication of the original VPN system and adding different users to their respective user groups are needed in this VPN system [9].

Resource Classification in Campus Network. In general, campus network resources are stored in educational administration management system server, library server, financial management system server, scientific research management system server, the e-government affairs server and so on. VPN users can access different resources according to their access rights. The same resources in the original VPN server are placed in a resource group, and the mapping relationships are established between the user groups and the resource groups (Fig. 4).

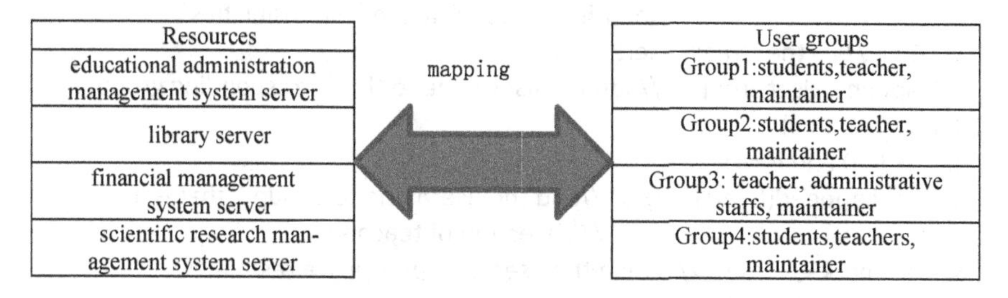

Fig. 4. The mapping relationship of resource groups and user groups

Allocation of Permissions. *Permissions resources allocated according to user type.*

Users will be divided into different user groups when they request VPN to access campus resources. According to the actual situation of university users applying for a VPN account, the users generally can be divided into students, teachers and maintenance personnel. These three kinds of users enter their corresponding user groups through their own VPN accounts. The user groups are mapped to the corresponding resource groups, that is, the set of resources that can be accessed within the scope of the user's authority, so as to control the access to campus resources through user types.

Permissions Resources Allocated According to Single Person. If for special reasons or management needs, it is also possible to allocate the authorized resources according to personal requirements when assigning the access rights to the university resources for users. Because the access rights may be different for different users who access the same campus resources, such as accessing to the educational system, the system administrator can view the system's operation and teachers can enter the score, however, students can only check the information inside. In this case users' access rights need be set by personal identity in order to achieve the purpose of limiting their access to campus resources [10].

3.3 The Implementation Process of VPN Based on User's Access Rights in University Campus Network

This chapter is divided into two parts: the algorithm description and the practical application steps. At present, most colleges and universities adopt L2TP protocol, which is not introduced in detail. This paper mainly introduces the division of user permissions and the mapping of use groups and resource groups. The main steps of the proposed are summarized in Algorithms 1 and 2.

Algorithm 1. Algorithm of user group allocation [11]

```
Input: user's number i that the server assigned to it
Output: UserGroup[] // It is a kind of users collection who have the same
                    //identity or the same job responsibilities
1. j←0 //j is the largest users' number
2. S.append(UserGroup[]) //add the username to the corresponding group
3. IF(i>0 and i<j)
4.    IF (i>0 and i<=n)
5.        i.append(UserGroup 1) //add the username to Group 1 that is a
                                // collection of teachers
6.        mark←true    // assign the user the appropriate resources
7.        Break
8.    ELSE IF(i>n and i<=m)
9.        i.append(UserGroup 2) //add the username to Group 2 that is a
                                //collection of students
10.       mark← true //assign the user the appropriate resources
11.       Break
12.     ELSE IF(i>m and i<j)
13.       i.append(UserGroup 3) // add the username to Group 3 that is a
                                //collection of  administrations
14.       mark← true // assign the user the appropriate resources
15.       Break
16.       ELSE  mark←FALSE  //return allocation failure
```

```
Algorithm 2. Algorithm of resource group allocation
Input: UserGroup Number i that the user is in //the number is determined by
                                              //Algorithm 1
Output: ResourceGroup[] // It is a collection of campus resources that the user
                          //can access
1.  S.append(ResourceGroup[]) // Map the UserGroup to the corresponding
                                //ResourceGrou.p.
2. IF(i=1)
3.  i.append(ResourceGroup 1) //Map UserGroup 1 to ResourceGroup 1 that
                                //teachers can access
4.  mark←true  // the users in UserGroup 1 can access the appropriate
                 //resources
5.  Break
6. ELSE IF(i=2)
7.   i.append(UserGroup 2) // Map UserGroup 2 to ResourceGroup 2 that
                             //students can access
8.   mark←true // the users in UserGroup 2 can access the appropriate
                 //resources
9.   Break
10.   ELSE IF(i=3)
11.          i.append(UserGroup 3) // Map UserGroup 3 to ResourceGroup 3
                                     //that administrations can access
11.         mark←true // the users in UserGroup 3 can access the appropri-
                         ate //resources
12.         Break
13. ELSE  mark ←FALSE //return mapping failure
```

The Concrete Implementation Steps of the VPN System. Step 1: Through the above introduction to the VPN system based on the users' access right, we adopt safe VPN equipment, terminal server structures and L2TP protocol to establish the platform system, and configure the related parameters as well as IP address. At last all kinds of resources server in the campus network also need to be configured.

Step 2: The L2TP protocol is configured on the firewall to provide related parameters such as the IP address range of campus users accessing the campus network, and an account is created for user who is divided into the corresponding UserGroup according to Algorithm 1. After the connection is successful, the user can only access the corresponding resources in the campus network according to Algorithm 2. Users can open the network and share center to view the VPN server and the IP address obtained by the user in the connection details. For example, it can be seen that the remote user connects to the VPN server using L2TP protocol, and use the MS CHAP V2 protocol for authentication. At the same time, the IP addresses of client and VPN server can also be seen [12].

Step 3: Configure user groups and resource groups on the VPN server and establish mappings between user groups and resource groups. After the user is registered successfully, the VPN server automatically opens the corresponding resource server for the VPN user.

Step 4: After users successfully log in through VPN, through the analysis of the network information in detail, as you can see client have two IP addresses. One is the IP address of the local public network, and the other is the IP address assigned by the campus network VPN server to the L2TP remote user requesting access to the campus network.

4 Experiment

Due to the development of a complete set of VPN system workload is very large, so we make some changes on the basis of the original system, such as adding the user's identity and classifying the original resources and so on. Then we use the IxChariot 6.70 soft to test the indexes, such as throughput, response, etc. The educational system and e-government server are set in the campus network, the computers out of campus visit the servers located in campus through the VPN system based on L2TP and user access rights. The results of testing at different time are shown in Table 1. The records in Table 1 are shown the various latency and throughput of off-campus access to the educational system and e-government [12].

Table 1. The indexes of that user visit the campus resources

Test times	Types of resource	Response time (s)			Throughput (Mbps)		
		Min	Max	Average	Min	Max	Average
1	Educational system	0.129	0.135	0.131	0.632	1.453	1.152
	E-government	0.126	0.212	0.189	2.478	4.369	3.951
2	Educational system	0.229	0.279	0.235	1.329	2.851	2.163
	E-government	0.151	0.213	0.196	2.970	3.476	3.252
3	Educational system	0.149	0.251	0.223	2.893	3.941	3.529
	E-government	0.133	0.230	0.198	1.431	2.790	2.282

Through the test of the simulation software, it is found that, first of all, remote users can access the internal resources of the campus network within permissions, not resources outside them through this VPN system. From the results of testing at different time, we can see that the maximum of throughput for the educational system can reach 3.941 Mbps. For e-government service, maximum of throughput is 4.369 Mbps.

For response time, the slowest of all test indexes is 0.279 s. In such response time, the existing of delay is very short, and it is perfectly acceptable to the users.

From the results of testing for aforementioned two types of indexes, we can see that the VPN system based on L2TP and user's access rights can entirety satisfy the demands for actual use.

5 Conclusions and Prospect

In the VPN system based on L2TP and user's access rights, the system administrator is responsible for assigning the rights for the VPN users in the entire campus network. To access campus resources, each user must pass through the VPN server to perform identity authentication and get certain rights. The VPN system based on L2TP and user's access rights not only solves the problems of off-campus teachers and students accessing the campus network remotely, but also can further protect the safety of campus network resources, preventing the illegal user's access.

This paper focuses on user access rights, and presents the processes the application in campus network. The experiment only gives that the VPN system can satisfy the demands for actual use. In the next work, we will do further study how to improve the access speed and the security of the system when it is used [14, 15]. Of course, the VPN system of the experiment and the completeness of the function need to be further improved.

Acknowledgements. This work was funded by the ministry of education has a collaborative education Project (Grant No. 201702109077), Natural Science Foundation of Fuyang Normal University (Grant No. 2016PPWL19), Anhui provincial university student innovation and entrepreneurship Project (Grant No. 201710371103), the Key Project of Fuyang Normal University (Grant No. hx2017007), Natural Science Foundation of Fuyang Normal University (Grant No. 2017PPJY04).

References

1. Liu, J., Li, Y., et al.: A real-time network simulation infrastructure based on OpenVPN. J. Syst. Softw. **82**(3), 473–485 (2008). https://doi.org/10.1016/j.jss.2008.08.015
2. Zhao, G.: Research on VPN network system using IPSec protocol. Energy Procedia **13**, 2367–2373 (2011). https://doi.org/10.1016/j.egypro.2011.11.339
3. Yang, F.F., Sun, Q., Wang, B.: Application of L2TP over IPSec technology in private desktop cloud. Comput. Technol. Dev. **25**(10), 160–165 (2015). https://doi.org/10.3969/j.issn.1673-629X.2015.10.035
4. Zhang, W., Wang, F.Y.: Research and implementation of GRE over IPsec VPN in combination with NAT. J. Shandong Univ. Technol. **31**(3), 6–10 (2017). https://doi.org/10.13367/j.cnki.sdgc.2017.03.002
5. Tatsuya, T., et al.: Evaluation of remote access VPN with dynamic port randomization function by mobile codes. J-STAGE **37**, 119–124 (2009). https://doi.org/10.11485/itetr.33.37.0_119
6. Sun, G.Y.: VPN simulation based on GRE and IPSec protocols. J. Shaanxi Univ. Technol. (Nat. Sci. Ed.) **34**(1), 49–55 (2018)
7. Jiang, Y.F.: VPN experiment design and implementation based on Windows Server 2012. Comput. Sci. Appl. **7**(8), 793–803 (2017). https://doi.org/10.12677/csa.2017.78091
8. Li, C.: The implementation and performance analysis of Campus network IPSec VPN system. J. Panzhihua Univ. **34**(2), 35–40 (2017)
9. Zhang, Z.: Application of SSL VPN in campus network. J. Puer Univ. **31**(3), 33–37 (2015)
10. Qing, H.: A new method of VPN based on LSP technology. In: 2nd Joint International Mechanical, Electronic and Information Technology Conference, Chongqing, China (2017)

11. Lu, B.: Research on user identification algorithm based on massive multi-site VPN log. In: 17th IEEE International Conference on Communication Technology, Chengdu, Sichuan, China (2017)
12. Chen, H.: Design and implementation of secure enterprise network based on DMVPN. In: International Conference on Business Management and Electronic Information, Guangzhou Guangdong, China (2011)
13. Gao, P., Ren, J.: Analysis and realization of Snort-based intrusion detection system. Comput. Appl. Softw. **23**(8), 134–135+138 (2006)
14. Zhao, H., Ren, J.: Cognitive computation of compressed sensing for watermark signal measurement. Cogn. Comput. **8**(2), 246–260 (2016)
15. Zhou, Y.: Hierarchical visual perception and two-dimensional compressive sensing for effective content-based color image retrieval. Cogn. Comput. **8**(5), 877–889 (2016)

Improved Reversible Data Hiding in JPEG Images Based on Interval Correlation

Zhigao Hong[1], Zhaoxia Yin[1,2(✉)], and Bin Luo[1]

[1] Key Laboratory of Intelligent Computing and Signal Processing, Ministry of Education, Anhui University, Hefei 230601, People's Republic of China
yinzhaoxia@ahu.edu.cn

[2] School of Communication and Information Engineering, Shanghai University, Shanghai 200072, People's Republic of China

Abstract. The redundancy of JPEG images is lower than that of non-compressed images, so any modification will greatly reduce the visual effect and produce file expansion. In this paper, a new RDH algorithm for JPEG images based on interval correlation is proposed. Through the quantization of DCT, the secret message is embedded into a continuous interval with large correlation and low distortion by using histogram shifting (HS). Experimental result shows that the proposed algorithm has better peak signal noise ratio (PSNR) and file expansion than the state-of-the-art HS algorithms for JPEG.

Keywords: Reversible information hiding · Histogram shifting
JPEG · Interval correlation

1 Introduction

With the rapid development of Internet, multimedia plays an important role in information communication. People transmit and acquire all kinds of multimedia information through the Internet. The image is an important transmission carrier, which provides not only convenience but also potential security problems. In the open and complex network environment, no individual or organization can guarantee the absolute non-acquisition of data, so data hiding for security is becoming more and more popular with researchers.

In 1997, Barton [1] first proposed the concept about reversible information hiding (RDH), and then various frameworks of RDH were proposed in a few short years, which can be divided into the following categories: lossless compression [2, 3], difference expansion (DE) [4, 5], and histogram shifting (HS) [6–8]. RDH algorithms in uncompressed images have been well established. Compared with uncompressed images, compressed images have less redundancy, thus are considerably more difficult for RDH. Joint Photographic Experts Group (JPEG) is the most popular format of compressed image. Therefore, RDH in JPEG image is important and useful for many applications, such as archive management and image authentication.

Recently, more and more RDH algorithms have been developed for JPEG images. Some works [9–11] embed messages by modifying Huffman table, which can well preserve the file size of JPEG image, yet their embedding capacities are rather limited.

J. Ren et al. (Eds.): BICS 2018, LNAI 10989, pp. 687–696, 2018.
https://doi.org/10.1007/978-3-030-00563-4_67

Currently the most popular schemes [12–17] for RDH in JPEG image are based on modifying quantified DCT coefficients. Huang et al. [16] propose a HS-based RDH scheme for JPEG image, by which zero coefficients remain unchanged and only coefficients with values "1" and "−1" are selected to carry messages. Moreover, a block selection strategy based on the number of zero coefficients in each 8×8 block is presented to adaptively choose DCT blocks for embedding to achieve high embedding capacity, good visual quality and low file expansion. However, a DCT block having more zero coefficients does not always means smaller distortion after embedding. So Wedaj et al. [17] proposed an improved HS algorithm by utilizing quantification table to compute embedding efficiency R of each position in DCT block, and then select AC coefficients in blocks with higher R for minimizing distortions. However, the above algorithms do not take into account the correlation among images. There is a large association between a general and the surroundings, which is called the smoothness of the pixels.

This paper proposes a new RHD algorithm of selectin intervals for HS to minimize distortions based on correlation among images. According to the required embedding capacity, we find some DCT coefficient intervals to embed, which balance the visual effect and the file expansion well.

The rest of the paper is organized as follows: In the Sect. 2, we will give a detail introduction of the proposed RDH method. Experimental results and comparison study are given in Sect. 3 to show the advantages of the proposed method, and finally we concluded in Sect. 4.

2 Proposed Scheme

2.1 HS Algorithm in JPEG

Joint Photographic Experts Group (JPEG) is an international image compression standard, which has been widely applied in daily life. JPEG image coding involves three key processes as shown in Fig. 1, which are discrete cosine transform (DCT), quantization step, and entropy encoding.

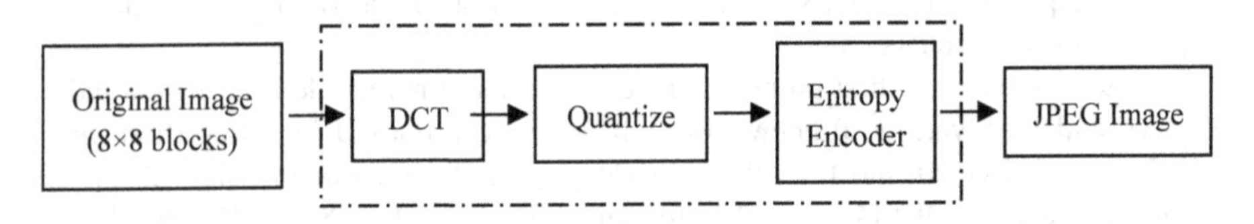

Fig. 1. JPEG compression processes

After decoding a JPEG image, we can get the quantized DCT coefficients. In an $8 * 8$ quantized coefficient block, without any loss of generality, the 63 nonzero AC coefficients are selected. According to Huang et al.'s analysis, the peak points of nonzero AC coefficient histogram are generally located at points "1" and "−1", so for each AC coefficient C, the following method is used:

$$C' = \begin{cases} C + sign(C) * b, & \text{if } |C| = 1 \\ C + sign(C) * 1, & \text{if } |C| \neq 1 \end{cases} \tag{1}$$

Where

$$sign(C) = \begin{cases} 1, & \text{if } C > 0 \\ 0, & \text{if } C = 0 \\ -1, & \text{if } C > 0 \end{cases} \tag{2}$$

In (1), $b \in \{0, 1\}$ denotes the message bit to be embedded and C' represents the corresponding AC coefficient in the marked image. As shown in (2), we can get:

- if C is ± 1, it can embed one-bit secret message, which is called Embeddable Coefficient;
- if C is greater than +1 or less than -1, it is shifted by 1, which is called Shiftable Coefficient;
- if C is 0, it is not modify, which is called Zero Coefficient.

2.2 Interval Correlation in JPEG

In one image, the rule object and the regular background (refers to the surface color distribution that is ordered and not chaotic) of the surface physical properties of the correlation, the correlation of the optical imaging structure in the digital image is represented as a digital correlation. Digital Association, that is, the over expression of numerical value is a continuous gradual process.

Taking the 512 * 512 Lena of QF = 70 as an example, in order to reflect the correlation between the adjacent 8 * 8 DCT sub blocks, we transform the original 4096 blocks into block vector $B = \{b_1, b_2, \ldots, b_{4096}\}$ by zigzag scanning. Then the 63 AC coefficients in each block are expanded into a column vector in turn. Therefore, the whole DCT coefficient matrix forms a 63 * 4096 table as shown in Fig. 2. Among them, $C(i,j)$ represents the AC value at the jth position of ith block.

4096 columns

63 rows

1	2	0	...	-3	-3	-12
-1	-1	0	...	3	3	-1
⋮	⋮	⋮	⋮	⋮	⋮	⋮
0	0	0	...	0	0	0
0	0	0	...	0	0	0

Fig. 2. Example of AC coefficient table

2.3 Embedded Priority and Distortion Efficiency

For the all 63 positions (rows) in the AC coefficient table, 4096 AC coefficients in one position is divided into some intervals, which contains T AC coefficients in one interval. For each interval, the embedding priority is calculated as following:

$$R = \sum_{j=1}^{N} \frac{1}{Q_i^2} \tag{3}$$

Where N is the number of Zero Coefficient in an certain interval, $0 \leq N \leq T$; Q_i is the quantization table entry corresponding to the position of the interval. The standard JPGE quantization table is shown in Fig. 3.

16	11	10	16	24	40	51	61
12	12	14	19	26	58	60	55
14	13	16	24	40	57	69	56
14	17	22	29	51	87	80	62
18	22	37	56	68	109	103	77
24	35	55	64	81	104	113	92
49	64	78	87	103	121	120	101
72	92	95	98	112	100	103	99

Fig. 3. Standard JPEG quantification table

Huang et al. found that blocks with many Zero Coefficients will likely contain many Embeddable Coefficients. Using this statistical feature, we can approximately predict the number of Embeddable Coefficient according to the number of Zero Coefficient in a certain area, to calculate the priority R embedded in the area.

The reason to squaring the quantization table entry is, to consider its effect on quantization phase. Although the number of embeddable coefficients are many and Shiftable Coefficient are small on a given position, if the quantization table entry is a large number, then image may be highly distorted after data embedding. To make clear the difference between positions with respect to the value of R, we squared the quantization table values. Figure 4 shows the squared quantization entries for each position for Lena with QF = 70. It can be observed that modifying AC coefficients in the position 47 will cause huge distortion, while the position 1 will cause little distortion.

For the unification of data, the range of T is $\{X \mid \text{MOD}(4096, X) = 0\}$. However, the value of T should not be too large or too small. If the length of the interval is too large in the general assembly, the algorithm tends to the simplicity algorithm, and the complexity of the algorithm will be increased if too small. $T \in \{4, 8, 32, 64\}$ is

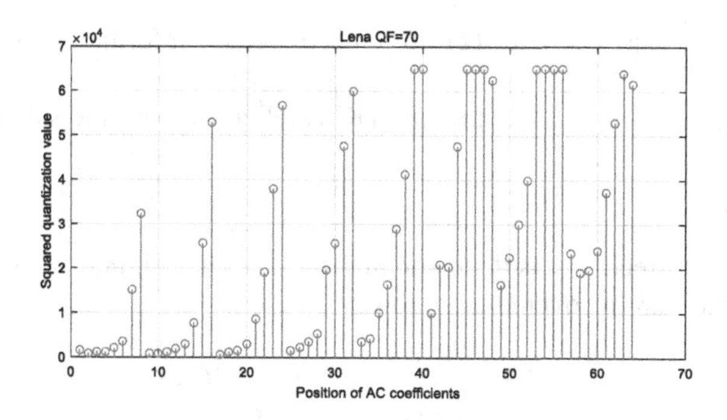

Fig. 4. Squared quantization entries for each position

generally chosen in practice, and the following experiments are conducted according to this range.

In order to find the most suitable value T for minimizing distortions, we give the following equations:

$$SUM1 = \sum_{j=1}^{T} abs(AC_j) = 1 \tag{4}$$

$$SUM2 = \sum_{j=1}^{T} abs(AC_j) \geq 2 \tag{5}$$

$$T = \underset{T \in \{4,8,32,64\}}{\arg\min} \{(\frac{SUM1}{2} + SUM2) \times Q_i^2\} \tag{6}$$

In the equations, we quantify the distortion of the image based on the number of Embeddable Coefficient and Shiftable Coefficient.

2.4 Encoder

To restore host image and embedded messages, we need to record T and payload length as side information, in which payload length is regarded as a part of the payloads to be embedded. Because of $T \in \{4, 8, 32, 64\}$, so T can be represented by 2 bits such as 00, 01, 10, 11. Therefore, T can be embedded in the first 2 LSBs of the DC values. In order to facilitate perfect recovery of the LSB of the original DC values, the original DC values are appended as part of the payload before embedding.

Now, the detailed processes of embedding are described as follows:

Step 1: Decode original JPEG image to get the quantified DCT coefficients, and then get AC coefficient table;

Step 2: Compute best distortion efficiency T for getting intervals, then compute embedded priority R for each interval and sort intervals according to the ascending order of Rs;

Step 3: Use Eqs. (1) and (2) to embed secret information (including side information);

Step 4: Replace the LSBs of the first DC coefficients with the side information.

2.5 Decoder

The extraction and recovery is done simultaneously. The original AC coefficients and secret information are recovered as follows:

$$C = \begin{cases} sign(C), & if\ 1 \leq |C'| \leq 2 \\ C' - sign(C'), & if\ |C'| > 2 \end{cases} \tag{7}$$

$$b = \begin{cases} 0, & if\ |C'| = 1 \\ 1, & if\ |C'| = 2 \end{cases} \tag{8}$$

Now, the detailed processes of embedding are described as follows:

Step 1: Decode marked JPEG image to get the quantified DCT coefficients, and then get marked AC coefficient table;

Step 2: Read the LSBs of the first 2 DC coefficients to extract T, then get intervals and compute embedded priority R for each interval and sort intervals according to the ascending order of Rs;

Step 3: Extract payload length and the original LSBs of the DC coefficients first;

Step 4: Extract secret information and recovery original AC coefficient table according to the payload length;

Step 5: Replace the LSBs of the DC coefficients with the original values.

3 Experimental Results and Discussion

In all experiments, the secret messages are randomly generated and 100 standard 512 * 512 JPEG images are experimental materials from CVG-UGR database [18] and the USC-SIPI database [19]. For each experiment, not only PSNR with dB but also file expansion with bits is adopted to evaluate the performance of an RDH algorithm in JPEG image.

Firstly, we compare the proposed algorithm with the two state-of-the-art RDH algorithms based on HS in JPEG image – Huang et al.'s and Wedaj et al.'s work on 6 typical test images as shown in Fig. 5. The comparative results are listed in Table 1. From Table 1, the proposed algorithm has a good experimental effect under QF = 60 compared with the other two algorithms. Simultaneously, it can be observed that, the affection of the proposed algorithm tends to gradually decrease with the increase of the payload and close to the other 2 algorithms.

To further verify the average advantages of the proposed method, we test the proposed method with Huang et al.'s and Wedaj et al.'s work on 100 images and the average results generated by such three algorithms are figured in Figs. 6 and 7. Note that, we will ignore some test images with some QFs that cannot provide enough capacities in experiments. Because the all the three algorithms are based on HS method,

Fig. 5. Six test images: (a) Baboon. (b) Boat. (c) House. (d) Barbara. (e) Lena.

Table 1. Comparison in terms of PSNR (dB) with different payload base on QF = 60

Images		Payload (bits)/PSNR (dB)				
		4000	6000	8000	10000	120000
Baboon	Huang et al.	41.6292	39.6411	38.3768	37.0705	36.3569
	Wedaj et al.	42.4274	40.7553	39.4249	37.7216	36.7317
	Proposed	43.4202	41.3573	39.8080	38.5896	37.4733
Boat	Huang et al.	44.1428	42.1220	40.4407	38.9576	37.7936
	Wedaj et al.	44.0611	41.4388	40.4950	39.0900	38.0499
	Proposed	44.2932	42.0677	40.4485	39.2217	38.2122
House	Huang et al.	44.3822	42.4522	41.2621	40.2653	39.4005
	Wedaj et al.	42.7945	42.6797	41.4402	40.1956	39.1621
	Proposed	44.9769	42.8880	41.4127	40.3581	39.3878
Barbara	Huang et al.	43.6504	41.8896	40.5739	38.9833	37.5838
	Wedaj et al.	43.4992	42.1739	40.5565	39.4102	38.6302
	Proposed	44.9008	42.7855	41.2021	39.9609	38.8448
Lena	Huang et al.	46.5117	44.6028	42.7461	41.1829	39.6356
	Wedaj et al.	45.0363	43.1874	41.6598	40.3515	39.3753
	Proposed	46.3358	44.0285	42.3115	40.8457	39.5046

thus the influence of ignoring the images with some QFs on experimental results will be the same.

Figure 6 shows the average PSNR between the marked and the host images. In Fig. 6(a)–(d), the horizontal axes represent the embedding payloads and the vertical axes represent the PSNR (dB). It is observed from Fig. 6 that the proposed method can preserve the PSNR and better than other two methods, especially in lower QF. According to our analysis in Sects. 2.2 and 2.3, under lower QF, the AC coefficients are almost 0 and ± 1, considering that Zero Coefficient does not affect the algorithm, so most of the AC are Embeddable Coefficient, and very few parts are Shiftable Coefficient. In the high QF, the proportion of the Shiftable Coefficient in the AC coefficient table increases and presents the characteristic of the discrete distribution, so the algorithm is not rather better.

Figure 7 shows the average increased file sizes between the marked and the original images. In Fig. 7(a)–(d), the horizontal axes represent the embedding payloads and the vertical axes represent the increased file sizes. The result shows the proposed method

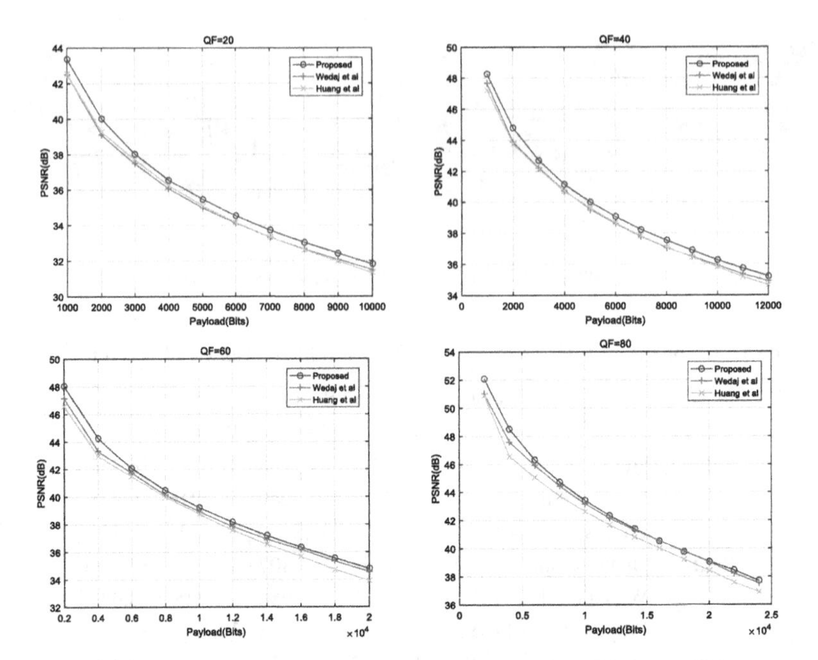

Fig. 6. Average PSNR values under different embedding payloads

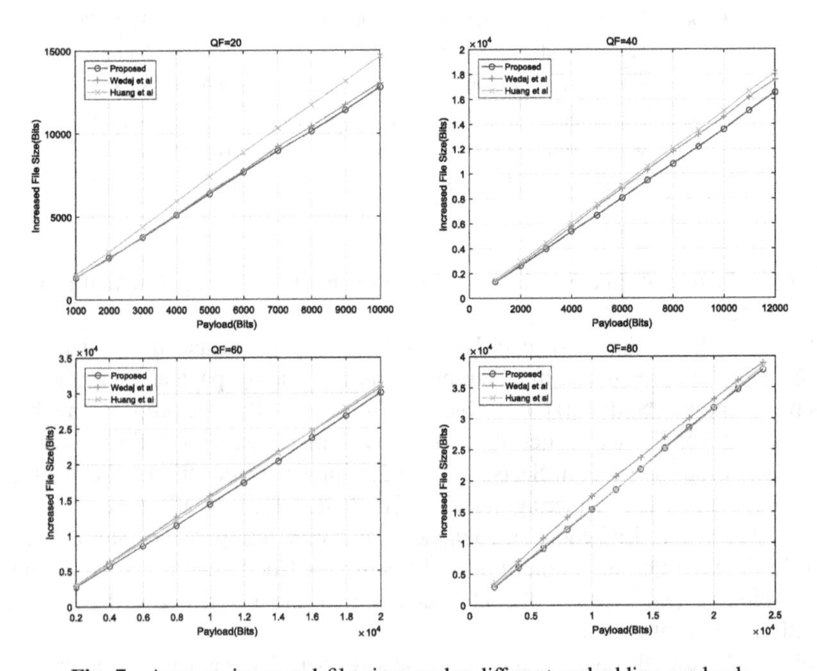

Fig. 7. Average increased file sizes under different embedding payloads

can has a low file increment at low QF. With the increase of QF, the file incremental curve is closer to the algorithm of Huang et al. The reason mainly is that all the selected coefficients belonging to Non-Zero Coefficients, which is encoded with the VLI code. If the coefficient value is increased to twice its value, the length of the VLI code may increase by two times. In higher QF, more Shiftable Coefficients dopes in the interval, and causes the proportion of Shiftable Coefficients becomes higher compared with lower QF. Thus, the file size may increase even if the messages of the same size bits are embedded in higher QF images

4 Conclusion

In this paper, we propose a new RDH algorithm for JPEG images based on interval correlation considering about embedded capacity, visual effect, and file expansion together. In the AC coefficient table after zigzag scanning, by calculating the embedding priority and distortion of the partition interval, the two factors – Embedded Priority and Distortion Efficiency are integrated to obtain the best intervals in balance.

Then HS is carried out in these intervals. Therefore, this algorithm can obtain a better PSNR and file expansion.

References

1. Barton, J.M.: Method and apparatus for embedding authentication information within digital data. U.S. Patent 5646997 (1997)
2. Fridrich, J., Goljan, M., Du, R.: Lossless data embedding for all image formats. In: Proceedings of SPIE, pp. 572–583 (2002)
3. Celik, M.U., Sharma, G., Tekalp, A.M., Saber, E.: Lossless generalized-LSB data embedding. IEEE Trans. Image Process. **14**(2), 253–266 (2005)
4. Alattar, A.M.: Reversible watermark using the difference expansion of a generalized integer transform. IEEE Trans. Image Process. **13**(8), 1147–1156 (2004)
5. Thodi, D.M., Rodriguez, J.J.: Expansion embedding techniques for reversible watermarking. IEEE Trans. Image Process. **16**(3), 721–730 (2007)
6. Lee, S.-K., Suh, Y.-H., Ho, Y.-S.: Reversible image authentication based on watermarking. In: Proceedings of the IEEE International Conference on Multimedia and Expo, pp. 1321–1324 (2006)
7. Hong, W., Chen, T.-S., Shiu, C.-W.: Reversible data hiding for high quality images using modification of prediction errors. J. Syst. Softw. **82**(11), 1833–1842 (2009)
8. Li, X., Li, B., Yang, B., Zeng, T.: General framework to histogram-shifting-based reversible data hiding. IEEE Trans. Image Process. **22**(6), 2181–2191 (2013)
9. Mobasseri, B.G., Berger, R.J., Marcinak, M.P., NaikRaikar, Y.J.: Data embedding in JPEG bitstream by code mapping. IEEE Trans. Image Process. **19**(4), 958–966 (2010)
10. Qian, Z., Zhang, X.: Lossless data hiding in JPEG bitstream. J. Syst. Softw. **85**(2), 309–313 (2012)
11. Hu, Y., Wang, K., Lu, Z.M.: An improved VLC-based lossless data hiding scheme for JPEG images. J. Syst. Softw. **86**(8), 2166–2173 (2013)
12. Chang, C.C., Lin, C.C., Tseng, C.S., Tai, W.L.: Reversible hiding in DCT-based compressed images. Inf. Sci. **177**(13), 2768–2786 (2007)

13. Sakai, H., Kuribayashi, M., Morii, M.: Adaptive reversible data hiding for JPEG images. In: Proceedings of the International Symposium on Information Theory and Its Applications, pp. 1–6 (2008)
14. Zhang, X., Wang, S., Qian, Z.: Reversible fragile watermarking for locating tampered blocks in JPEG images. Signal Process. **90**(12), 3026–3036 (2010)
15. Efimushkina, T., Egiazarian, K., Gabbouj, M.: Rate-distortion based reversible watermarking for JPEG images with quality factors selection. In: Proceedings of the 4th European Workshop on Visual Information Processing, pp. 94–99 (2013)
16. Huang, F., Qu, X., Kim, H.J., Huang, J.: Reversible data hiding in JPEG images. IEEE Trans. Circuits Syst. Video Technol. **26**(9), 1610–1621 (2016)
17. Wedaj, F.T., Kim, S., Kim, H.J., Huang, F.: Improved reversible data hiding in JPEG images based on new coefficient selection strategy. EURASIP J. Image Video Process. **2017**(1), 63 (2017)
18. CVG-UGR database. http://decsai.ugr.es/cvg/dbimagenes/g512.php. Accessed May 2018
19. USC-SIPI database. http://sipi.usc.edu/database/. Accessed May 2018

Representing RCPBAC (Role-Involved Conditional Purpose-Based Access Control) in Ontology and SWRL

Ronghan Li(✉), Zejun Jiang, and Lifang Wang

Computer Institute, Northwestern Polytechnical University, Xi'an, China
{claud,wanglf}@nwpu.edu.cn, lrh000@mail.nwpu.edu.cn

Abstract. Privacy preservation in a data-sharing computing environment is becoming a challenging problem. A purpose is defined as the intention of data accesses or usages and purpose-based access control (PBAC) has been proposed to extend traditional models for privacy-preserving. However, in existing research, the purpose is often to bind to data by using labeling schemes or building privacy metadata databases separately, which leads to redundancy of data tables and decreasing of query efficiency. Moreover, privacy policies involving purpose lack sufficient semantics. In this paper, we present a semantic model for the role-involved conditional purpose-based access control (RCPBAC) with ontology. Purpose, data, and role are represented by ontology and their relationships are described with object or data properties, which is based on *Web Ontology Language* (OWL). We use *Semantic Web Rule Language* (SWRL) to represent privacy policies for reasoning. This model can help data providers to define and share their own information more easily and securely.

Keywords: Access control · Personal privacy · Semantic Web

1 Introduction

Nowadays, enterprises are required to comply with existing privacy protection regulations on data collection, use, and disclosure. In the data sharing environment, more and more attention has been paid to privacy issues. Data providers, on the one hand, want to meet the needs of sharing their own data and, on the other hand, express their concerns about their potential privacy. In the business world, enterprises and companies gather data about transactions or their customers to analyze customer buying behavior and discover hidden business opportunities [8]. They share data on third-party platforms or partners, but for their own sake, they don't want to expose hide information or disclose customer privacy. In healthcare industry, people's electronic health records (EHR) includes basic information, summaries of major diseases and health issues, and records of major health services [15]. Electronic information can be more conveniently

J. Ren et al. (Eds.): BICS 2018, LNAI 10989, pp. 697–706, 2018.
https://doi.org/10.1007/978-3-030-00563-4_68

and quickly integrated into the daily diagnosis and treatment work of medical and health institutions. The standardization and digitization of various records realize the sharing of information among medical institutions, patients/ordinary people and health management departments. However, because these medical data contain a large number of personal privacy information, it will inevitably face huge security risks. Both malicious attacks outside the platform attacker, or internal managers intentionally or unintentionally operation, may lead to leakage of private information. Considering the privacy of patients, people with different roles should get the different content of EHR.

For these issues, access control is an effective solution. Traditional access control relies on permission tables or role assignments and does not consider privacy issues or data access granularity from a semantic perspective. This paper combines ontology and SWRL based on role-involved conditional purpose-based access control and proposes an access control method based on privacy ontology. By giving detailed ontology and SWRL rule definitions, we use the dual attributes of role and access purpose to represent the semantics that needs to be considered in the access control scenario. Finally, the effectiveness of this method is verified by experiments in an EHR scene, and the logical completeness is discussed.

2 Related Work

2.1 RCPBAC

Byun et al. [2] proposed a privacy-preserving access control model for relational databases. They bind purpose to data by using labeling schemes. Yang et al. [16] specified the entities of the purpose-based access control model formally and investigated their proof obligations. Ni et al. [11] introduced several privacy-aware role-based access control (P-RBAC) models. Privacy data permissions include data permissions, purposes, conditions, obligations. In their hierarchical P-RBAC, role hierarchy, data hierarchy, purpose hierarchy were specified. Masoumzadeh et al. [9] proposed purpose-aware role-based access control. They considered purpose as an intermediary entity between role and permission entities. The model assigned permissions to roles based on purpose related to privacy policies. In [14], the RBAC was extended to incorporate the notion of purpose. Relationships between purposes are defined. It is investigated that how different components in the RBAC model are related to purpose and how the purpose information can be used to determine whether a subject has access to a given object. Colombo et al. [3] argued that database management systems still do not provide the proper support for privacy policies. They proposed a systematic approach to the automatic development of a monitor that regulates the execution of SQL queries based on purpose based privacy policies. Farzad et al. [4] proposed a role-based access control requirements model with purpose extension. However, examples they illustrated lack of executable formal semantic expression.

However, these works did not consider to extract more information or specific implementation environment and tools. Kabir et al. [7] presents a role-involved conditional purpose-based access control model, which is the model we represent with ontology in this paper. RCPBAC allows users using some data for certain purpose with conditions. An algorithm is developed to achieve the compliance computation between access purposes (related to data access) and intended purposes (related to data objects) and is illustrated with role-based access control (RBAC) to support RCPBAC. Although intended purpose are extended to AIP, CIP, and PIP, purpose compliance computation is based on extra purpose table. Access decision algorithm relies on the calculation of data tables, which leads to redundancy of data tables and decreasing of query efficiency.

2.2 Ontology-Based Access Control

A lot of works [1,5,6,12,13] has proposed many valuable schemes for representing access control policies with ontology. There are developed policy languages for access control. These include XACML [10], Ponder, Rei, and KAos. Hsu [6] argued that conventional XACML lacks the computer interoperability needed to support knowledge representation and the OWL has no mechanism for defining arbitrary, multi-element antecedents. He proposed an intelligent XACML shell based on a Multi-layer Semantic XACML Framework (MSACF), which includes URI layer, XML (XACML) layer, ontology (OWL) layer, and rule (SWRL) layer. However, he did not elaborate on the specific access control model and consider purpose that has more semantic and practical scenes. Other works rely purely on ontology capabilities, which cannot represent complex rules.

Finin et al. [5] studied the relationship between the OWL and RBAC. They showed two different ways to support RBAC in OWL and discussed how the OWL constructions can be extended to model attribute-based RBAC model or more generally attribute-based access control (ABAC). Priebe [12] focused on the reasoning supplemental role of ontology in the XACML framework and the translation from OWL and SWRL to XACML. Sharma et al. [13] represented the basic user, subject, object, and permission in ABAC as classes and discussed the representation of attributes and rules in the MAC, DAC, and RBAC namespaces. Beimel [1] proposed a situation-based access control strategy in the healthcare system and introduced context into access decision rules. OWL is used to represent the objective things in the medical system, including patients, hospitals, doctors, etc. SWRL describes specific visit scenarios. Through the description logic (DL) inference engine, the access situation is classified into the established ontology, and the access decision result is obtained. However, none of them considered privacy issues or used the access purpose as a deciding factor.

3 Ontology Design for RCPBAC

We present a semantic model for role-involved conditional purpose-based access control (RCPBAC) with ontology. A user can be assigned to different roles that have different privileges including purposes data and actions. The system accepts a request if and only if the access purpose of the request is compliant to the intended purpose being bound to the requested data object according to the SWRL policies. In order to simplify the discussion, we assume that the third-party authority certifies the role assignment and no longer discuss the ontology definition of data and actions.

3.1 Concepts

In this section, we introduce concepts and object properties in detail. The ontology design for RCPBAC is shown in Fig. 1 where concepts are represented by box and properties among concepts are represented by one-way arrows that names, domain, and range of object properties. We discuss which of and how these components are associated with purpose.

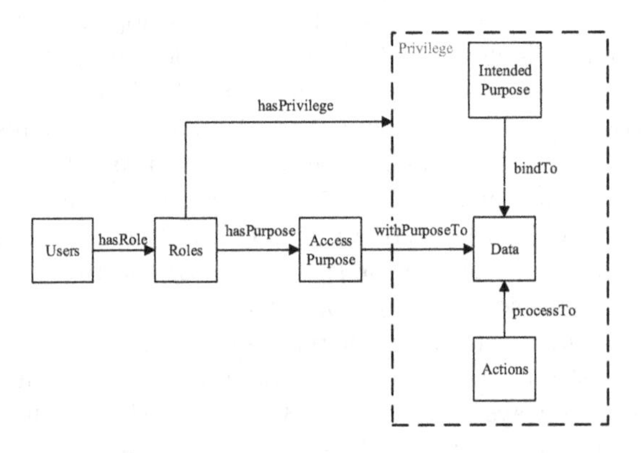

Fig. 1. The ontology design for RCPBAC

Users. In traditional RBAC, users request an access to data by issuing a query which includes the object accessed and the action or access mode. Considering privacy issues, we require users to state additional access purpose *ap* when initiating an access request. Of course, the user must choose the character set that describes the purpose from the consensus.

Roles and Purposes. Usually, in the typical situation, roles and purposes are organized in a hierarchical structure based on some principles. Purposes can be specified based on generalization/specialization semantics and role hierarchies are a natural means to reflect an organization's lines of authority and responsibility. Mathematically, role and purpose hierarchies are partial orders. We denote *Access Purpose* with a purpose tree. There is a close logical relationship between purpose and role hierarchy, which we will discuss in the next section. Compared to previous studies, we simplified the definition of the purpose set. Considering the purpose of the concept of data providers and requesters as a common agreement, the character set used to express the access purpose can be divided into different subclasses of *Access Purpose* by semantics. Strings in the same class (individuals in a class) can be treated as the same purpose. On the other hand, we refer to purposes associated with data and thus regulating data accesses as *Intended Purpose*, which has three subclasses AIP, CIP, and PIP. We refer to Kabir's definition, but we do not take the method of dividing the purpose tree into a binary operation. The strings expressing access purpose are also in AIP, CIP and PIP. Roles and data are linked by purpose, allowing the data provider to define access to their own data in a richer semantic context.

Privilege. This class is defined as an anonymous subclass of ontology constraints, and is used to express what the data can hold for what purpose. It is a constraint definition for the intended purpose, action, and data. The authority class expresses the semantics of the authority, which are divided into three subclasses: PermitPrivilege, DenyPrivilege, and ConditionalPrivilege according to the effect of the intended purpose binding.

3.2 Properties

Properties let us assert general facts about the members of classes and specific facts about individuals. The ontology contains a number of Object Properties in order to establish the relations between the instances of the classes in ontology. In Table 1 the main relationships are shown.

Table 1. ObjectProperties in ontology

Name	Domain	Range
hasRole	Users	Roles
hasPurpose	Roles	Access_Purpose
withPruposeTo	Access_Purpose	Data
hasAction	Privilege	Actions
bindTo	Intended_Purpose	Data
hasPrivilege	Roles	Privilege
processTo	Actions	Data
hasIntPurpose	Privilege	Intended_Purpose
hasProhibitedPermission	Users ∪ Roles	Data
hasCompletePermission	Users ∪ Roles	Data
hasConditionalPermission	Users ∪ Roles	Data

Brief descriptions about these properties are explained here:

- **seniorRoleof:** Specifies the partial ordering between roles. The inverse property is **juniorRoleof**.
- **seniorPurposeof:** Specifies the partial ordering between purposes. The inverse property is **juniorPurposeof**.

- **hasRole:** Specifies the roles that a user has.
- **hasAccPurpose:** Specifies the access purpose that the role has.
- **withPruposeTo:** Specifies that the data object can be requested with which access purpose.
- **hasAction:** Specifies the actions that the privilege has.
- **bindTo:** Specifies the intended purpose bound to data objects. Contains three sub-attributes, asAIPBindTo, asPIPBindTo, asCIPBindTo, respectively, as three kinds of intended purpose binded with the data.
- **processTo:** Specifies that the action can process which data object.
- **hasProhibitedPermission:** Specifies that a user is prohibited from accessing the requested data object.
- **hasCompletePermission:** Specifies that a user have complete permission to access the requested data object.
- **hasConditionalPermission:** If according to the purpose of matching rules to access the purpose of the CIP, it is clear that the user can access part of the data or the processed data.

In addition, the ontology also contains some Data Properties to establish values like name, codes, etc., but these properties are not important for the study of this article so no more mention will be done.

4 Privacy Policies in SWRL

The core of ontology establishment is the reasoning. OWL DL can well define the concepts and relationships among concepts, and realize the satisfiability reasoning based on ontology knowledge bases. However, it lacks the ability to express the universal causation that exists in the real world. The purpose of the *Semantic Web Rule Language* (SWRL) is to drive the Horn-like rules into combination with the OWL knowledge base and to implement the reasoning of applied logic that the ontology itself cannot describe.

In this section, we discuss some core reasoning rules in SWRL, including the semantic description of roles and purposes in inheritance relations and grant of access rights in common scenes.

Rule 1 defines the most basic inclusion relationship between roles (positions). Although the object property seniorRoleof in the ontology definition can be simply set to be transitive, we still explicitly define its formal rule, to provide the basis for the definition of semantic relationships between role and purpose. The following is the formal definition of role inclusion relationship in SWRL.

$$seniorRoleof(?r1, ?r2) \land seniorRoleof(?r2, ?r3) \rightarrow seniorRoleof(?r1, ?r3)$$

The inclusion relationship definition *seniorPurposeof* is the same as *seniorRoleof.*

Rule 2. Take the authority and responsibility assignment of enterprise or organization as an example, the top of the role tree is often the highest authority position. The closer to the leaf node, the more detailed the authority are distributed, and the smaller the corresponding authority is. So if a role r has a purpose p, its superior also has p semantically.

$$\begin{aligned}&Roles(?r1) \wedge hasAccPurpose(?r1,?p) \wedge seniorRoleof(?r2,?r1)\wedge \\ &Roles(?r2) \rightarrow hasAccPurpose(?r2,?p)\end{aligned} \tag{2-1}$$

Similarly, if a character has a purpose, the character has at least the general purpose of this purpose. The rule is as follows.

$$\begin{aligned}&Roles(?r) \wedge hasAccPurpose(?r,?p1) \wedge seniorPurposeof(?p2,?p1) \\ &\rightarrow hasAccPurpose(?r,?p2)\end{aligned} \tag{2-2}$$

Rule 3 is mainly for the intended purpose and the binding of the data, because the intended purpose of three, but the semantic relationship between the definition of the purpose and the data between the mapping is different. Rule 3-1 and Rule 3–4 indicate that if an object is bound to data for the purpose of allowing or condition permitting, then its sub-purpose will all be bound to data with permission or conditional permission, semantically speaking The purpose is allowed to refine the purpose are allowed; Rule 3-2 and Rule 3-3 shows that if a purpose is prohibited for access to a data, the purpose of the branch will be banned, which is same as the PBAC core idea from the semantic point of view.

$$\begin{aligned}&Intended\_Purpose(?p1) \wedge Data(?d) \wedge asAIPBindTo(?p1,?d)\wedge \\ &seniorPurposeof(?p1,?p2) \wedge Intended\_Purpose(?p2) \rightarrow asAIPBindTo(?p2,?d)\end{aligned} \tag{3-1}$$

$$\begin{aligned}&Intended\_Purpose(?p1) \wedge Data(?d) \wedge asPIPBindTo(?p1,?d)\wedge \\ &seniorPurposeof(?p1,?p2) \wedge Intended\_Purpose(?p2) \rightarrow asPIPBindTo(?p2,?d)\end{aligned} \tag{3-2}$$

$$\begin{aligned}&Intended\_Purpose(?p1) \wedge Data(?d) \wedge asPIPBindTo(?p1,?d)\wedge \\ &seniorPurposeof(?p2,?p1) \wedge Intended\_Purpose(?p2) \rightarrow asPIPBindTo(?p2,?d)\end{aligned} \tag{3-3}$$

$$\begin{aligned}&Intended\_Purpose(?p1) \wedge Data(?d) \wedge asCIPBindTo(?p1,?d)\wedge \\ &seniorPurposeof(?p1,?p2) \wedge Intended\_Purpose(?p2) \rightarrow asCIPBindTo(?p2,?d)\end{aligned} \tag{3-4}$$

Rule 4 explains the function of the role of access to three kinds of data access reasoning relationship. We define the privilege that the role has and decide what kind of permissions the role has based on the type of intended purpose in the privilege. If the access purpose provided by the role matches one kind of the intended purpose(AIP, CIP and PIP), return corresponding decision result. The rules for allowing access are as follows:

$$\begin{aligned}&Roles(?r) \wedge hasAccPurpose(?r,?p) \wedge hasPrivilege(?r,?pr) \wedge Privilege(?pr)\wedge \\ &hasIntPurpose(?pr,?p) \wedge asAIPBindTo(?p,?d) \wedge Data(?d) \\ &\rightarrow hasCompletepermission(?r,?d)\end{aligned}$$

The same form applies to conditional access and forbidden access rules.

Rule 5 describes the role - the inheritance of the permission, but in the opposite direction from the denial of access. If a role has permission, its parent role also owns the permission. If a role is denied, its child role will be rejected. Rule 5-1 and Rule 5-2 represent the above two meanings respectively. It is noteworthy that, Rule 5-3 provides that when a role has a conditional permission, its sub-role provisions of this document will not be able to obtain access to the data.

$$Roles(?r1) \wedge hasCompletePermission(?r1, ?d) \wedge seniorRoleOf(?r2, ?r1) \wedge \\ Roles(?r2) \wedge Data(?d) \rightarrow hasCompletepermission(?r2, ?d) \tag{5-1}$$

$$Roles(?r1) \wedge hasProhibitedPermission(?r1, ?d) \wedge seniorRoleOf(?r1, ?r2) \wedge \\ Roles(?r2) \wedge Data(?d) \rightarrow hasProhibitedpermission(?r2, ?d) \tag{5-2}$$

$$Roles(?r1) \wedge hasConditionalPermission(?r1, ?d) \wedge seniorRoleOf(?r1, ?r2) \wedge \\ Roles(?r2) \wedge Data(?d) \rightarrow hasProhibitedpermission(?r2, ?d) \tag{5-3}$$

Rule 6 means that when a user has a certain role and the user who has passed the previous rule has the authority of the role, the permission is granted to the actual user. The other two cases are also the same form definition:

$$Users(?u) \wedge hasRole(?u, ?r) \wedge hasCompletePermission(?r, ?d) \wedge \\ Data(?d) \rightarrow hasCompletePermission(?u, ?d)$$

Different rules can be combined as access policies, which can lead to policy conflicts and redundancy. At present, there are sophisticated access control policies, redundancy and conflict detection methods, which we will not discuss in this article.

5 Experiment and Discussion

Our experiments in [17] illustrate the effectiveness of the proposed method. We defined the classes and relationships mentioned in the above section in the ontology, and also defined the positions in the hospital and additional roles. SWRL was used to describe the core access control rules and business semantics in the healthcare system, for example, low-level doctors have only a small privilege to access a portion of the complete EHR table. The JESS inference engine was responsible for utilizing the knowledge of OWL and SWRL to reason and get new facts, which converted to XACML access control policies through XSLT. For example, Table 2 is the original data table, and Table 3 shows the actual returned query result.

In W3C's OWL Semantics and Abstract Syntax document, direct model-Theoretic semantics of OWL goes directly from ontologies in the OWL DL abstract syntax, which includes the OWL Lite abstract syntax, to a standard model theory. Interpretations of vocabularies, embedded constructs, axioms,

Table 2. Original EHR table

Name	Gender	Age	ID	Job	Status	Medical history
Zhangsan	Male	45	12345	Programmer	Heart disease	Hypertension

Table 3. Actual returned query result

Name	Gender	Age	ID	Job	Status	Medical history
—	Male	40–50	123XX	Programmer	Heart disease	——

facts and ontologies guarantee the decidability of logical reasoning. The model-theoretic semantics for SWRL is a straightforward extension of the semantics for the OWL. A rule is satisfied by an interpretation iff every binding that satisfies the antecedent also satisfies the consequent. The semantic conditions relating to axioms and ontologies are unchanged, e.g., an interpretation satisfies an ontology iff it satisfies every axiom (including rules) and facts in the ontology.

6 Conclusions

In this work, we design an ontology for role-involved conditional purpose-based access control (RCPBAC) and define privacy policies in SWRL. Compared to previous studies based on purpose-based access control, our proposal reserve the original methods of data storage, and enable data providers to define access to their own data in a richer semantic context. Finally, we give experiments to prove the effectiveness of the proposed method and discuss the decidability and completeness of logic. In the future, we will try simpler and more general access control methods in more areas [18–21].

References

1. Beimel, D., Peleg, M.: Editorial: using OWL and SWRL to represent and reason with situation-based access control policies. Data Knowl. Eng. **70**(6), 596–615 (2011)
2. Byun, J.W., Li, N.: Purpose based access control for privacy protection in relational database systems. VLDB J. Int. J. Very Large Data Bases **17**(4), 603–619 (2008)
3. Colombo, P., Ferrari, E.: Enforcement of purpose based access control within relational database management systems. IEEE Trans. Knowl. Data Eng. **26**(11), 2703–2716 (2014)
4. Farzad, F., Yu, E., Hung, P.C.K.: Role-based access control requirements model with purpose extension. In: Anais Do WER 2007 - Workshop Em Engenharia De Requisitos, Toronto, Canada, May 2007, pp. 207–216 (2007)
5. Finin, T., et al.: R OWL BAC: representing role based access control in OWL. In: ACM Symposium on Access Control Models and Technologies, pp. 73–82 (2008)
6. Hsu, I.C.: Extensible access control markup language integrated with semantic web technologies. Inf. Sci. **238**(7), 33–51 (2013)

7. Kabir, M.E., Wang, H., Bertino, E.: A role-involved conditional purpose-based access control model. Kluwer Academic Publishers (2012)
8. Li, Y., Gai, K., Ming, Z., Zhao, H., Qiu, M.: Intercrossed access controls for secure financial services on multimedia big data in cloud systems. ACM Trans. Multimed. Comput. Commun. Appl. 12(4) (2016)
9. Masoumzadeh, A., Joshi, J.B.D.: PuRBAC: purpose-aware role-based access control. In: Meersman, R., Tari, Z. (eds.) OTM 2008. LNCS, vol. 5332, pp. 1104–1121. Springer, Heidelberg (2008). https://doi.org/10.1007/978-3-540-88873-4_12
10. Moses, T.: Extensible access control markup language (xacml) version 3.0. oasis standard (2013)
11. Ni, Q., Bertino, E., Lobo, J., Calo, S.B.: Privacy-aware role-based access control. IEEE Secur. Priv. **13**(3), 1–31 (2010)
12. Priebe, T., Dobmeier, W., Kamprath, N.: Supporting attribute-based access control with ontologies. In: International Conference on Availability, Reliability and Security, p. 8 pp. (2006)
13. Sharma, N.K., Joshi, A.: Representing attribute based access control policies in OWL. In: IEEE Tenth International Conference on Semantic Computing, pp. 333–336 (2016)
14. Wang, Y., Zhou, Z., Li, J.: A purpose-involved role-based access control model. In: Wen, Z., Li, T. (eds.) Foundations of Intelligent Systems. AISC, vol. 277, pp. 1119–1131. Springer, Heidelberg (2014). https://doi.org/10.1007/978-3-642-54924-3_106
15. Yang, L., Sinnott, R.O.: Semantic-based privacy protection of electronic health records for collaborative research. In: Trustcom/BigDataSE/I SPA, pp. 519–526 (2017)
16. Yang, N., Barringer, H., Zhang, N.: A purpose-based access control model. In: International Symposium on Information Assurance and Security, pp. 143–148 (2007)
17. Ronghan, L.: Research on access control method based on privacy ontology reasoning. Master, Northwestern Polytechnical University (2017)
18. Zhao, H.: Robust information hiding in low-resolution videos with quantization index modulation in DCT-CS domain. Multimed. Tools Appl. **1**, 1–14 (2018)
19. Zhao, H., Dai, Q., Ren, J.C., Wei, W., Xiao, Y., Li, C.: Robust information hiding in low-resolution videos with quantization index modulation in DCT-CS domain. Multimed. Tools Appl. **1**, 1–21 (2017)
20. Zhao, H., Ren, J.: Cognitive computation of compressed sensing for watermark signal measurement. Cogn. Comput. **8**(2), 246–260 (2016)
21. Zhou, Y., Zeng, F.Z., Zhao, H.M., Murray, P., Ren, J.: Hierarchical visual perception and two-dimensional compressive sensing for effective content-based color image retrieval. Cogn. Comput. **8**(5), 877–889 (2016)

Real-Time Image Deformation Using Locally-Weighted Moving Least Squares

Li Zhao[1,2], Xi Chen[2(✉)], Chang Shu[2,3], Chong Yu[1,2], and Hua Han[2,4,5]

[1] Faculty of Mathematics and Statistics, Hubei University, Wuhan 430062, China
[2] Institute of Automation, Chinese Academy of Sciences, Beijing 100190, China
xi.chen@ia.ac.cn
[3] University of Chinese Academy of Sciences, Beijing, China
[4] CAS Center for Excellence in Brain Science and Intelligence Technology, Beijing, China
[5] School of Future Technology, University of Chinese Academy of Sciences, Beijing, China

Abstract. In this paper, we provide a real-time image deformation method based on *Locally-weighted Moving Least Squares* (LW-MLS). To achieve a detail-preserving and realistic deformation of images, a concise deformation formula is proposed as the deformation function. Compared with two state-of-the-art methods, Moving Least Squares (MLS) and Moving Regularized Least Squares (MRLS), the main improvement of our method is preprocessing the control points, which adopts sparse approximation to achieve a fast deformation. With the traditional methods of image deformation, each pixel is affected by all control points, which consume too much time to deform an image. So in our method, each pixel is mainly affected by surrounding control points, and every pixel is almost not affected by the control points which are far away from the deformed pixel. The novel method we proposed can be performed in real time and could supply promising performance for the deformation of large image.

Keywords: Control points · Image deformation · Real time
Reproducing kernel Hilbert space
Locally-weighted moving least squares

1 Introduction

A reconstruction effort on the scale of mammalian brains, however, would be enormously expensive and difficult to justify without assurances that this kind of information would be of value [4,7,11]; In order to reconstruct mammalian brains, it is necessary to do image deformation for smooth effect, which has long been an active research area in image processing and has a number of useful applications. Many specialists have done similar work [1,3,10,16,17]. Control points p are fixed, while the user creates these deformations by manipulating

J. Ren et al. (Eds.): BICS 2018, LNAI 10989, pp. 707–716, 2018.
https://doi.org/10.1007/978-3-030-00563-4_69

the corresponding points q [14]. In order to realize automatically real-time distortion of large images, we need to achieve an effect that the image could be distorted fleetly after selecting the corresponding points q. The question that real-time deformation of large images has not been solved. There are plenty of similar works with no complete solution to this problem, such as [8,14]. We naturally do such a work to make it realism: we derive a closed-form solution of the transformation and adopt the idea of sparse approximation to achieve a fast implementation, which largely reduces the computation complexity without performance sacrifice [15]. On the basis of MLS, the nonrigid transformation f viewed to map points in the raw image to the deformed image is specified in a reproducing kernel Hilbert space [8]. The transformation function f is applied to create the deformed image.

(a) original image (b) deformed image

Fig. 1. Schematic illustration of image deformation. (a): the original image (Burning Candle) with the control points marked by red points and corresponding target points marked by yellow points; (b): a deformed image with the deformed control points marked by red points. (Color figure online)

With our method, the real-time deformation of electron microscope images has a good deformation performance (as shown in Fig. 2), at the same time, we have pretty results for natural images (as shown in Fig. 1). To illustrate, we choose a set of control points firstly, as marked by the red points in the left flame, then the red control points located on the flame are adjusted to a new position marked by the yellow points. The image on the right is the result of the candle deformation. To fix the candle, red points and yellow points in the candle are almost complete overlap. Now consider an image with a set of handles p that the user moves to new positions q. For f to be useful for deformations it must satisfy the following properties [14]:

(1) Interpolation: The handles p should map directly to q under deformation. (i.e.; $f(p_i) = q_i$).
(2) Smoothness: f should produce smooth deformations.
(3) Identity: If the deformed handles q are the same as the p, then f should be the identity function. (i.e.; $q_i = p_i \Rightarrow f(v) = v$).

The rest of this paper is organized as follows: In Sect. 2, this study detailedly introduces the proposed method and several implementation details. Then, experimental results are reported in Sect. 3; Finally, this paper presents conclusions and points out our future works in Sect. 4.

2 Method

For high resolution electron microscope sequence slice image deformation, the structure of biological tissue is complex and diverse, so the structure of each slice image needs to be deformed variably. We naturally need to select a large number of control points before deforming an image. We know that the computational complexity of MRLS and MLS is too high to realize real-time distortion of high resolution electron microscope images. In this chapter, we use the locally-weighted moving least squares method to do the deformation, and find a closed-form solution for the deformation function. Then we compare the computational complexity of our method with MLS and MRLS.

2.1 Locally-Weighted Moving Least Squares

Let $P = \{p_i\}_{i=1}^{n}$ be a set of control points and $Q = \{q_i\}_{i=1}^{n}$ be their corresponding deformed positions, where p_i and q_i are column vectors. We add mesh to speed up the deformation efficiency, and bilinear interpolation is applied to the non grid points [2]. We deform an image with a uniform grid and select point set P as control points, and every grid v is almost controlled by the nearest k control points $P_v(k)$. In this section, our formula is based on MLS but different from MLS. For any point v in the image, the method of MLS deformation requires that all the control points affect the displacement of each pixel, which will cause real-time deformation of large images unrealistic. MLS solves for a rigid-body transformation f_v that minimizes weighted least squares error functional

$$\sum_{i=1}^{n} \omega_i \left\| f_v(p_i) - q_i \right\|^2, \tag{1}$$

where $\omega_i(v)$ is nonnegative weight matrix, and it is defined as

$$\omega_i(v) = \left\| v - p_i \right\|^{-2\alpha}. \tag{2}$$

α controls the weight norm and Euclidean distance of each control point. The global deformation function f belongs to affine transformation in linear space, and it is derivable. Here we introduce a regularized term and extend the deformation function to the case of nonlinear function, so that we can achieve better deformation effect. We need to preprocess the selected control points in advance. Note that remote control points does not influence on one pixel. Therefore, we restrict the set of control points used in the deformation at a pixel v to its k nearest neighbors according to the Euclidean distance. We denote the k nearest neighbor control points as $P_v(k)$, the corresponding points of which are denoted as $Q_v(k)$. And the weighted matric is denoted as $W_v(k)$. We solve for the optimal displacement function f_v that minimizes a weighted regularized least squares error function

$$\sum_{i=1}^{k} \omega_i \left\| f_v(p_i) - q_i \right\|^2 + \lambda \Psi(h_v), \tag{3}$$

where $\omega_i(v) = \|v - p_i\|^{-2\alpha} \in W_v(k)$, $P \in P_v(k)$, $Q \in Q_v(k)$, and $\Psi(h_v)$ is a regularization term with $\lambda > 0$, controlling the trade-off between the two terms. The regularization technique is used to impose smoothness. For each pixel, we need to get a different transformation function $h_v(\cdot)$, which is nonrigid and belongs to a special function space reproducing kernel Hilbert space. The function $h_v(\cdot)$ is a vector-valued function built on the set $\{p_i\}_{i=1}^{n}$, and for any correspondence (p_i, q_i), it has $q_i = p_i + h_v(p_i)$. We lie it in a specific functional space $\mathscr{H}$, namely a Reproducing Kernel Hilbert Space (RKHS) [8,9,13]. Thus the functional has the form:

$$\Psi(h_p) = \|h_p\|_{\mathscr{H}}^2, \tag{4}$$

where $\|\cdot\|_{\mathscr{H}}$ denotes the norm of $\mathscr{H}$. We will discuss the detailed forms of h_v and $\|\cdot\|_{\mathscr{H}}$ later. We define an RKHS $\mathscr{H}$ by a positive definite Gram matrix valued kernel:

$$\Gamma(p_i, p_j) = \kappa(p_i, p_j) \cdot I = e^{-\|p_i - p_j\|^2/\beta^2} \cdot I \in \Gamma_{2\times 2} \tag{5}$$

with β determining the width of the range of interaction between points, and I is an identity matrix. The transformation function takes the form:

$$h_v(\cdot) = \sum_{i=1}^{k} \Gamma(\cdot, p_i) C_i, \tag{6}$$

where the coefficient C_i is a 2×1 dimensional vector (to be determined). Hence, the minimization over the infinite dimensional Hilbert space reduces to finding a finite set of coefficients C_i. Note that the smooth regularization term now can be defined as

$$\|h_v\|_{\mathscr{H}}^2 = \sum_{i=1}^{k} \sum_{j=1}^{k} \langle \Gamma(p_i, p_j) C_i, C_j \rangle = tr(C^T T C). \tag{7}$$

Now we define our deformation function as the initial position plus the displacement function

$$f_v(x) = x + h_v(x). \tag{8}$$

This deformation function f is smooth, and as p approaches v, $\omega_i(v)$ approaches infinity and then the function f interpolates, i.e., $f(p_i) = q_i$. Moreover, if $\forall i, p_i = q_i$, then $h_v(p_i) \equiv 0$, therefore, f is the identity transformation, i.e., $h(p) = p$. Compared with MLS and MRLS, we select some control points around the pixel to approximate all the control points. This is consistent with the actual situation, because when the control point is far away from a pixel, it will hardly produce deformable effect on this pixel. At the same time, we can greatly reduce the amount of computation time. As a result, our novel method is denoted as locally-weighted deformation.

2.2 A Closed-Form Solution

To solve for the coefficients, the regularized least squares error can be conveniently expressed in the following matrix form:

$$E(C) = \left\| W_v(k)^{1/2}(P_v(k) + \Gamma C) - Q_v(k) \right\|_F^2 + \lambda \cdot tr(C^T \Gamma C), \tag{9}$$

where the weight matrix $W_v(k) = diag(\omega_v(i))_{i=1}^k$, P and Q are the control points and deformed control points respectively. Equation (9) is quadratic in C. Taking the derivative of it with respect to C and setting it to zero, we obtain a closed form solution

$$C = (\Gamma_v(k) + \lambda \cdot W_v(k)^{-1})^{-1}(Q_v(k) - P_v(k)). \tag{10}$$

With this closed-form solution for C, we can write a simple expression for the deformation function:

$$f(v) = v + (\Gamma_v(\Gamma + \lambda \cdot W_v(k)^{-1})^{-1}(Q_v(k) - P_v(k)), \tag{11}$$

where Γ_v is a $1 \times k$ row vector with the $i - th$ entry $e^{-\|v-p_i\|^2/\beta^2}$. To create a instant deformation, we approximate the image with a grid and apply the deformation function to each vertex, followed by a bilinear interpolation in each lattice.

The points p are fixed, while the user creates these deformations by manipulating the points q. Since the p are stationary during deformation, much of Eq. (11) can be precomputed yielding instant deformations. In particular, we can rewrite Eq. (11) in the form:

$$f(v) = M + (N \cdot Q_v(k))^T, \tag{12}$$

where $N = \Gamma_v(\Gamma + \lambda W_v(k)^{-1})^{-1}$, $M = v - (N \cdot P_v(k))^T$. M and N could be precomputed for they are irrelevant to Q. And the complexity of computing $f(v)$ is $1 \times k$. Therefore, our method LW-MLS with nonrigid model can perform more efficiently (see Tables 1, 2 and 3).

2.3 Computational Complexity

The algorithm proposed by MRLS involves the inversion of a matrix of size $n \times n$ at each grid point, which spends plenty of time on deforming large images with large number of control points to meet the needs of practical application (3D reconstruction) [6]. This leads to the algorithm consuming tens of hours of computation time, and it is not convenient for real-time deformation of medical images; The algorithm proposed by MLS, when a large number of control points are selected for high resolution images, will take several seconds after precomputing, and there is no way to make large images deformed in real time.

Our approach is to use the idea of sparse approximation to select the nearest k control points around pixels instead of using all control points, which greatly reduces the complexity of the operation from $O(l \cdot n^3)$ to $O(l \cdot k^3)$ $(k \ll n)$. So the time to do deformation with our method is almost unaffected by the number of control points. And it takes less than one second after precomputing. The complexity of computing (12) is $O(l \cdot k)$. Therefore, our method LW-MLS with nonrigid model can perform more efficiently (see Tables 1, 2 and 3).

3 Experiments

In this chapter, some details of the experiment are added, and we provide the effect and time comparison between three different methods.

Parameter Initialization: There are mainly five parameters in our deformation algorithm: $(\alpha, \beta, \lambda, k, ctrl - pt)$. Parameter α controls the weight of each control point. The parameters β and λ react to the smoothness of the constraint. Parameter β determines how wide the range of interaction between points. Parameter λ controls the trade-off between the closeness to the data and the smoothness of the solution [8]. Parameter $ctrl - pt$ represents the number of total control points and parameter k determines the number of control points affecting each grid point. In our evaluation, we found our method was very robust to parameter tuning, and we set $\alpha = 2, \beta = 10^3, \lambda = 10^{-5}, k = 10$, with different $ctrl - pt$ throughout our experiments (see Tables 1, 2 and 3).

Tables 1, 2 and 3 summarize the runtimes on an Intel Core 2 GHz PC with MATLAB code. We use three different size of rat brain images to make real-time deformation with the resolution of 1024×1024, 4096×4096 and 8192×8192 respectively, and the runtime of MLS, MRLS and LW-MLS are displayed in Tables 1, 2 and 3. We see that both algorithms MRLS and LW-MLS perform quite faster than algorithm MRS and can be performed in real-time. Due to the closed-form solution (12) only involves simple matrix operations such as addition and multiplication, the computing complexity of the operation is reduced from $O(l \cdot n^3)$ to $O(l \cdot k^3)$ $(k \ll n)$. And the time we spend is almost unaffected by the number of control points. For a rat brain image with the resolution of 4096×4096, when two hundred control points are selected, the total time of MLS is a few minutes, our method is dozens of minutes, but the MRLS spends several hours. All in all, according to the total time and precomputing time consumption with three different approaches, our method can be used to do real-time deformation of large images, while MLS and MRLS are not suitable. Then, let's look at their effect of the deformation.

Table 1. Runtime of MLS, MRLS and LW-MLS on an image with the resolution of 1024×1024.

methods / #ctrl-pt \ time(s)	MLS	MRLS	LW-MLS
121	0.0150	0.0003	0.0003
225	0.0276	0.0006	0.0004
324	0.0392	0.0010	0.0010
400	0.0470	0.0014	0.0005
529	0.0578	0.0012	0.0005
625	0.0656	0.0023	0.0004

Table 2. Runtime of MLS, MRLS and LW-MLS on an image with the resolution of 4096×4096.

methods / #ctrl-pt \ time(s)	MLS	MRLS	LW-MLS
100	0.4554	0.0029	0.0029
225	1.024	0.0064	0.0133
324	1.7134	0.0100	0.0110
400	2.4714	0.0243	0.0125
529	4.1404	0.0093	0.0114
625	4.9176	0.0091	0.0118

We present a few representative deformation results obtained with our technique in Fig. 2. For comparison, we also provide the results of MLS and MRLS, two state-of-the-arts algorithm which operates on the rigid transformation and non-rigid transformation respectively. In order to show the whole and local deformation effect, the red control points located on original image are adjusted to a new position marked by the lower right corner yellow points, at the same time, a green point in the blue rectangle is select to move to the blue point. And the local deformation result are placed in the green rectangle in the upper right corner seeing Fig. 2(b), (c) and (d). Comparing the deformation results of the three methods, for the result of MRLS shows that many pixels do not follow the control points to do corresponding movement, and many pixels in the green rectangle deformed messly. MLS and LW-MLS have better deformation effect than MRLS from the whole effect to the local effect. And combined with the problem of deformation efficiency, our method is more suitable for real-time deformation of large images.

Table 3. Runtime of MLS, MRLS and LW-MLS on an image with the resolution of 8192×8192.

#ctrl-pt \ methods / time(s)	MLS	MRLS	LW-MLS
121	1.8905	0.1026	0.0276
272	3.2160	0.0420	0.0442
380	4.1750	0.0424	0.0375
462	5.6863	0.0766	0.0356

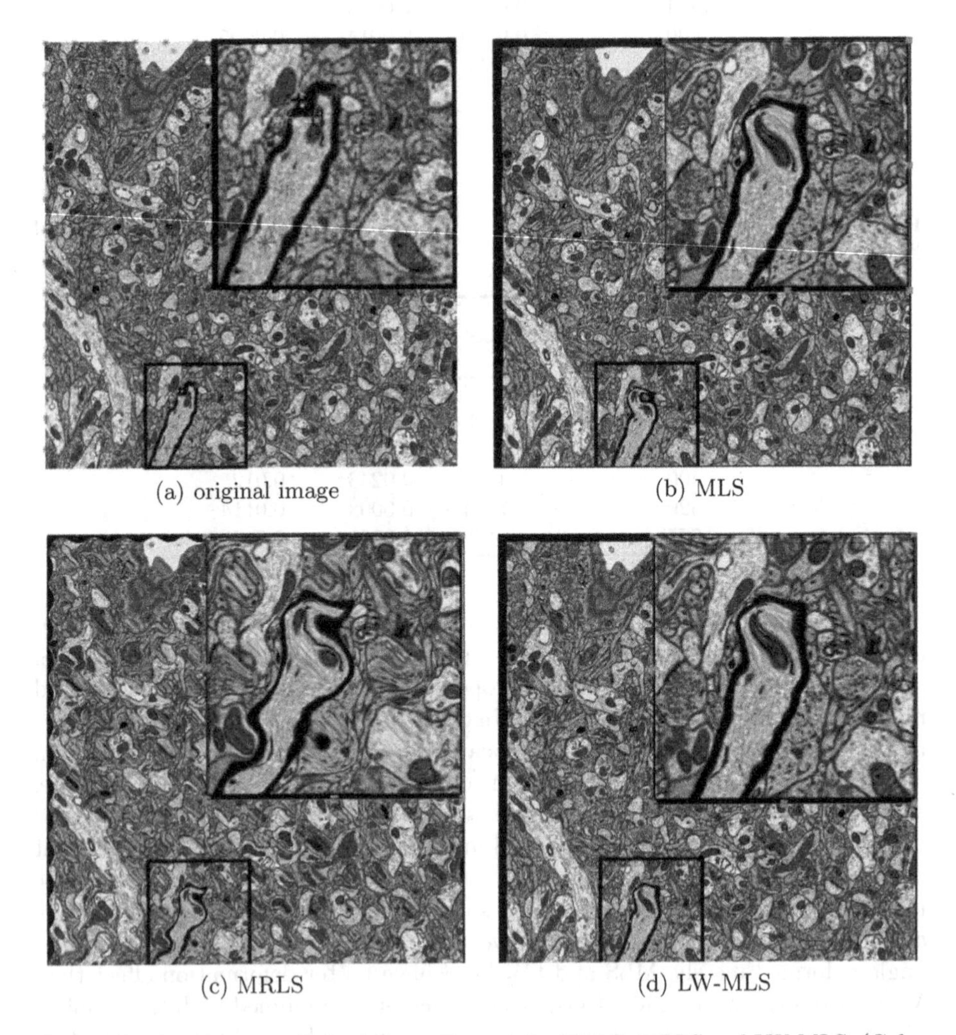

(a) original image (b) MLS (c) MRLS (d) LW-MLS

Fig. 2. Original image and the deformation result of MLS, MRLS and LW-MLS. (Color figure online)

4 Conclusions

This paper presents a new technique for real time image deformation using LW-MLS. The displacement function f is nonrigid, and the function space is modeled within a reproducing kernel Hilbert space. We adopt the idea of sparse approximation to refine the affected control points for locally-weighted deformation, and also write a closed-form solution of the deformation function. We can realize the real-time deformation of multiple control points on large image after the pre-computing. Considering time consumption and performance of the deformation, our method is better than two state-of-the-art methods MLS and MRLS.

Along the line of present research, several problems deserve further study. Firstly, we attempt to apply many other function spaces in [5,12]. Secondly, our real-time deformation technique has a broad application for real-time registration of electron microscope images. Thirdly, color and spatial features [18] of deformed images could be considered for achieving better performance. All these problems are under our research.

Acknowledgments. This paper is supported by National Science Foundation of China (No. 11771130, 61673381, 61201050, 61701497), Scientific Instrument Developing Project of Chinese Academy of Sciences (No. YZ201671), Bureau of International Cooperation, CAS (No. 153D31KYSB20170059), and Special Program of Beijing Municipal Science & Technology Commission (No. Z161100000216146).

References

1. Bookstein, F.L.: Principal warps: thin-plate splines and the decomposition of deformations. IEEE Trans. Pattern Anal. Mach. Intell. **11**(6), 567–585 (1989)
2. Chen, X., Xie, Q., Shen, L., Han, H.: Wrinkle image registration for serial microscopy sections. In: International Conference on Signal-Image Technology & Internet-Based Systems, pp. 23–26 (2016)
3. Ju, T., Warren, J., Eichele, G., Thaller, C., Chiu, W., Carson, J.: A geometric database for gene expression data. Symp. Geom. Process. **2003**, 166–176 (2003)
4. Kasthuri, N., et al.: Saturated reconstruction of a volume of neocortex. Cell **162**(3), 648–661 (2015)
5. Li, L., Li, W., Zou, B., Wang, Y., Tang, Y., Han, H.: Learning with coefficient-based regularized regression on Markov resampling. IEEE Trans. Neural Netw. Learn. Syst. (2017)
6. Li, W., Deng, H., Rao, Q., Xie, Q., Chen, X., Han, H.: An automated pipeline for mitochondrial segmentation on atum-sem stacks. J. Bioinform. Comput. Biol. **15**(3), 1750015 (2017)
7. Lichtman, J.W., Pfister, H., Shavit, N.: The big data challenges of connectomics. Nat. Neurosci. **17**(11), 1448–1454 (2014)
8. Ma, J., Zhao, J., Tian, J.: Nonrigid image deformation using moving regularized least squares. IEEE Signal Process. Lett. **20**(10), 988–991 (2013)
9. Ma, J., Zhao, J., Tian, J., Tu, Z., Yuille, A.L.: Robust estimation of nonrigid transformation for point set registration. In: IEEE Conference on Computer Vision and Pattern Recognition, pp. 2147–2154 (2013)

10. Maccracken, R., Joy, K.I.: Free-form deformations with lattices of arbitrary topology. In: Conference on Computer Graphics and Interactive Techniques, pp. 181–188 (1996)
11. Marblestone, A.H., et al.: Conneconomics: the economics of large-scale neural connectomics, pp. 337–349 (2013)
12. Qiao, T., et al.: Effective denoising and classification of hyperspectral images using curvelet transform and singular spectrum analysis. IEEE Trans. Geosci. Remote Sens. **55**(99), 1–15 (2017)
13. Saitoh, S.: Theory of reproducing kernels. Trans. Am. Math. Soc. **68**(3), 337–404 (2003)
14. Schaefer, S., Mcphail, T., Warren, J.: Image deformation using moving least squares. In: ACM SIGGRAPH, pp. 533–540 (2006)
15. Thompson, P., Toga, A.W.: A surface-based technique for warping three-dimensional images of the brain. IEEE Trans. Med. Imaging **15**(4), 402 (1996)
16. Tsai, Y.C., Lin, H.D., Hu, Y.C., Yu, C.L., Lin, K.P.: Thin-plate spline technique for medical image deformation. J. Med. Biol. Eng. **20**(4), 203–210 (2000)
17. Wittek, A., Miller, K., Kikinis, R., Warfield, S.K.: Patient-specific model of brain deformation: application to medical image registration. J. Biomech. **40**(4), 919–929 (2007)
18. Yan, Y., Ren, J., Li, Y., Windmill, J.F.C., Ijomah, W., Chao, K.M.: Adaptive fusion of color and spatial features for noise-robust retrieval of colored logo and trademark images. Multidimens. Syst. Signal Process. **27**(4), 1–24 (2016)

Machine-Learning-Based Malware Detection for Virtual Machine by Analyzing Opcode Sequence

Xiao Wang[1,2], Jianbiao Zhang[1,2](✉), and Ai Zhang[3]

[1] Faculty of Information, Beijing University of Technology, Beijing, China
zjb@bjut.edu.cn
[2] Beijing Key Laboratory of Trusted Computing, Beijing, China
[3] Beijing-Dublin International College, Beijing University of Technology, Beijing, China

Abstract. With the rapid development of cloud computing, cloud security is increasingly an important issue. Virtual machine (VM) is the main form to provide cloud service. To protect VMs against malware attack, a cloud needs to have the ability to react not only to known malware, but also to the new emerged ones. Virtual Machine Introspection (VMI) is a good solution for VM monitoring, which can obtain the raw memory state of the VM at Virtual Machine Monitor (VMM) level. Through analyzing the memory dumps, the significant features of malware can be obtained. In our research, we propose a novel static analysis method for unknown malware detection based on the feature of opcode n-gram of the executable files. Different feature sizes ranging from 2-gram to 4-gram are implemented with the feature length of 100, 200, 300 respectively. The feature selection criterion of Term Frequency (TF)-Inverse Document Frequency (IDF) and Information Gain (IG) are leveraged to extract the top features for classifier training. Different classifiers are trained with the preprocessed dataset. The experimental results show that the weighted integrated classifier with opcode 4-gram of 300 features has the optimal accuracy of 98.2%.

Keywords: Machine learning · Malware detection
Virtual machine introspection · Cloud security

1 Introduction

Nowadays, with the scalability and cost effectiveness of cloud computing, more and more individuals and enterprises are willing to accept cloud services. At the same time, security has become an urgent issue and will be more important in the future [1, 2]. Virtual Machine (VM) is the main form to provide cloud service for customers. The security vulnerability of cloud environment exposes VMs at risk. To protect VMs against malware-based attacks, malware detection technique is emerging as a highly crucial concern.

As the core technology used in cloud computing, virtualization technology has brought new solutions to malware detection. Virtual Machine Monitor (VMM), which is the key component of virtualization, works at a higher privilege level than VMs.

J. Ren et al. (Eds.): BICS 2018, LNAI 10989, pp. 717–726, 2018.
https://doi.org/10.1007/978-3-030-00563-4_70

From a security point of view, it is an ideal place to deploy security infrastructures. Virtual Machine Introspection (VMI) [3] has been a powerful monitoring technique out-of-VM. It can reconstruct the memory state of the VM at the VMM layer without the consent of the monitored VM. All executable files must be loaded into memory before execution. Therefore, there are unique advantages of analyzing the key features from memory snapshot, such as avoiding hidden issues of malicious processes like rootkits.

Traditional signature-based detection is no longer adequate to detect unknown malwares [4], while the heuristic approaches can construct models to detect unknown malwares by using machine learning techniques. It is a very new research topic to combine machine learning and data mining technology with VMI for VM memory analysis to detect malicious behaviors [5]. In this paper, our main goal is to filter out unknown malwares in the VM guest OS. The opcode n-gram includes program control flow information, which can be tracked back for further analysis in the executable [6]. Therefore we investigate the opcode n-gram as feature for classification.

The main contributions of this paper are as follows. Firstly, VMI technique was leveraged to capture the memory state of VM to extract the executable binary codes. The binary codes were disassembled into assembly pattern. Opcode n-gram were selected from the assembly program. It is the basis for determining whether the software is a malware. Secondly, the machine learning classifier was trained to detect malware symptoms. Different feature sizes ranging from 2-gram to 4-gram were implemented with the feature length of 100, 200, 300 respectively. Feature selection criterions TF-IDF and IG were used to extract the top features for classifier training. Weighted integrated classifier was introduced to improve the performance of classification. At last, the classifier was leveraged to detect malware symptoms in the VM memory dump.

2 Related Work

The works related to our research consists of virtual machine introspection and malware detection.

2.1 Virtual Machine Introspection

Virtual Machine Introspection (VMI) has emerged as a promising out-of-VM security solution. It gathers the information of the monitored VM at the VMM level for further deduction to determine the security state of the VMs. It is widely used in intrusion detection systems (IDS) [7], forensic analysis [8] and integrity checking etc.

VMI can introspect the volatile memory state of the introspected guest OS. Information in memory includes [9]: processes, threads, network objects, kernel modules, registry keys etc., which can be viewed and acquired by VMI from memory image. Memory forensic analysis (MFA) is an approach to analyze the memory snapshots or dumps to observe the running state of the physical or virtual machine, which is a branch of digital forensics [10]. Since every OS object is transferred to memory before the execution, RAM is a great place to look for malicious artifacts.

There are many advantages [11] by leveraging the MFA with the VMI at the VMM level to obtain the memory state of the guest OS, it is easy to monitor the low-level details of a running virtual machine by viewing its memory.

2.2 Malware Detection

The two main approaches commonly applied to malware detection are dynamic malware analysis and static malware analysis. Both the dynamic analysis and the static analysis have their advantages and disadvantages [12]. The dynamic malware analysis, which is also known as behavioral analysis, collects features such as API calls, system calls, network access and memory modifications [13] during the running of the executable files. For the dynamic malware analysis approach, the appropriate time to observe the malicious activity is not clear, and it is hard to capture all of the execution flows. In the static analysis, the features of the executable, such as byte n-gram, byte opcode, n-gram opcode sequence, are extracted from the binary/source code without running it, thereby providing rapid classification. In our research, we choose n-gram opcode sequence as the classifying feature. Static analysis does not need to run the malware and analyzes it from static characteristics, but it is incapable for detecting unseen malware [6]. In our work, the features are extracted from memory image to avoid malware hiding problem, which can remedy the drawback of static malware analysis. The features selected from different analysis approach are shown in Table 1.

Table 1. Features selected from different analysis approaches

Analysis approach	Features selected
Dynamic analysis	DNS requests, system call, API call
Static analysis	Byte n-gram, byte opcode, opcode n-gram

3 Method

3.1 The Process of Malware Detection for VM Memory

The procedure of malware detection for VM is as follows: The first stage is data generation, in which the VMI tools such as LibVMI [14] are used to capture the memory state of the monitored VM from outside the VM at the hypervisor level. The raw memory information is binary. For the purpose of extracting opcode features, it is necessary to disassemble the binary code into assembly pattern. Disassembly tools such as IDA-Pro, Windbdg and Ndisasm can be leveraged. In our research, we choose IDA-Pro for binary disassembling, which uses the method of gradient descent to emphasize the concept of control flow.

The second stage is data extraction. Opcode n-gram provides a more semantic representation of the program and is a feasible way to detect unknown malware. We choose n-gram opcode as the feature for malware detection. The disassembly file contains additional information, such as register name, register address, and function names. Only the normal assembly code are considered for n-gram opcode extraction.

The third stage is malware detection. According to the extracted feature, the trained classifiers determine whether the executable files are malware or not. The whole process of malware detection for VM memory is shown in Fig. 1.

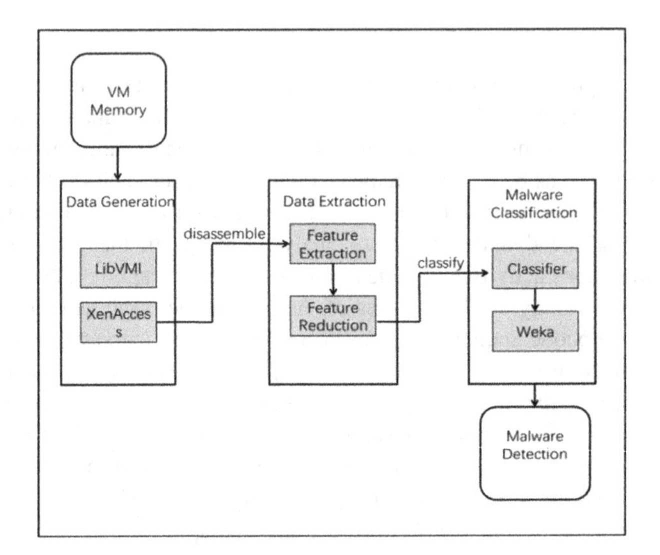

Fig. 1. The whole process for malware detection for VM memory

3.2 Using Machine Learning Method to Train Classifier

Dataset Creation

The learning process of classifier is divided into two phases: classifier training and classifier testing. The training dataset is composed of about 7342 malicious files acquired from the VX Heaven website [15], and about 2578 benign files collected from the freshly installed Windows 10 64-bit OS. The malicious samples can be identified by the antivirus software such as Kaspersky, or on-line detection. The common website for malicious code detection are Virus Total, Viruscan, Malwr etc. Through the detection, it can determine whether the data is a malicious sample, and get the malicious type, so as to complete the basic preparation. The training dataset can be divided into actual training dataset and validation dataset used to verify the training process. In our research, we use Kaspersky to identify the malicious files and verify that the benign files did not contain any malicious code.

Before disassembling the malicious and benign samples, we need to complete file type recognition and shell file shelling. File type recognition is mainly based on the extracted executable files from data samples. Many malwares confuse the original code by the shell, and it can not be directly disassembled. The shell generates inaccurate disassembly code, which affects the analysis. By using PEiD, most of the shell types and specific version information can be detected. According to the detected shell type, the corresponding shelling tools, such as Upxunpacker and Pecompact2 can be used to take off the shell. In the process of actual experiment, it is found that using python-magic to detect the file type can also identify the shell type for most of the files. With those preprocesses, the binary code of the executable files are get. They need to be disassembled for the subsequent feature selection.

Feature Extraction

In order to convert the binary executables into assembly program files, a disassembly tool called IDA-Pro was used. Then the opcode n-gram is extracted from the assembly files. An executable file is composed of a series of instructions, and an instruction contains an opcode and one or more operands. Since opcode is more representative of the behavior of the software, we discard the operands, and only consider the opcodes.

It may not be possible to use all the extracted features for training, because the total number (feature length) will be very large. Not only the requirement for memory may be huge, but also the speed of training will be very slow. On top of that, most of the features would be redundant, noisy, or irrelevant. Consequently, we use Term Frequency (TF)-Inverse Document Frequency (IDF) and Information Gain (IG) to extract a relevant useful subset of features.

TF-IDF is a statistical method to evaluate the importance of a n-gram opcode feature to classifying a sample. TF is defined as Eq. (1).

$$\mathrm{TF} = \frac{n_{i,j}}{\sum_k n_{k,j}} \tag{1}$$

$n_{i,j}$ is the appearance number of n-gram in j^{th} sample, $\sum_k n_{k,j}$ is the total appearance number of all the n-grams in j^{th} sample. The IDF is defined as Eq. (2).

$$\mathrm{IDF}_i = \log \frac{|D|}{|\{j : t_i \in d_i\}|} \tag{2}$$

$|D|$ is the total number of samples, and $|\{j{:}t_i \in d_i\}|$ is the number of samples containing an n-gram. TF-IDF is calculated by TF multiply $\mathrm{IDF}_{i,}$ which used to represent the weight of each n-gram.

IG is one of the best criterions for selecting appropriate features, which has the ability to measure an attribute A to distinguish a sample B. The greater the IG (B, A) is, the more important the attribute A is. So IG can be defined as a measure of effectiveness of the feature in classifier training. IG of an attribute A on a collection of instances B is given by Eqs. (3, 4, 5):

$$Entropy(A) = -\sum_{i=1}^{n} p_i \log p_i \tag{3}$$

$$Entropy(B|A) = -\sum_{i=1}^{n} p_i(B|A) \log p_i(B|A) \tag{4}$$

$$Gain(B, A) = Entrop(B) - Entropy(B|A) \tag{5}$$

Based on these two criteria, we selected the top 100, 200, 300 opcode sequence for 2-gram, 3-gram and 4-gram to find the optimal feature length and size for classification. The machine learning analysis tool WEKA were utilized for training the classifier.

4 Experiment and Evaluation

Through experiment, two questions need to be clarified: the first one is that which size is the best for n-gram and how many features should be extracted to achieve the best classification result. The second question is that which classifier is the optimal between NB, RF, DT and LR or the combination of them has a superior performance. To answer the above questions, 2-gram, 3-gram and 4-gram opcode sequences were extracted with the feature number of 100, 200, 300 respectively. The performance of the classifier is presented in Table 2.

Table 2. The performance of various classifiers with different feature size and length

Feature length		100			200			300		
Feature size	Classifier	TPR	FPR	Accuracy	TPR	FPR	Accuracy	TPR	FPR	Accuracy
2-gram	NB	0.795	0.203	0.831	0.801	0.193	0.842	0.813	0.187	0.853
	DT	0.883	0.115	0.845	0.894	0.095	0.867	0.903	0.089	0.878
	RF	0.871	0.131	0.859	0.882	0.113	0.869	0.905	0.107	0.882
	LR	0.752	0.342	0.796	0.776	0.336	0.812	0.807	0.307	0.836
3-gram	NB	0.798	0.198	0.846	0.812	0.189	0.847	0.818	0.179	0.859
	DT	0.890	0.102	0.858	0.899	0.091	0.871	0.906	0.083	0.898
	RF	0.881	0.123	0.879	0.887	0.101	0.879	0.914	0.096	0.903
	LR	0.781	0.332	0.814	0.783	0.317	0.817	0.812	0.296	0.847
4-gram	NB	0.817	0.184	0.878	0.823	0.180	0.885	0.836	0.152	0.905
	DT	0.921	0.092	0.889	0.936	0.087	0.926	0.955	0.063	0.963
	RF	0.894	0.103	0.881	0.897	0.095	0.893	0.923	0.087	0.946
	LR	0.796	0.302	0.845	0.807	0.286	0.852	0.835	0.271	0.876

The results of the experiment show that when the feature size is the same, the bigger the feature length is, the better the performance is. For example, it can be seen that when the feature size is 3-gram, the accuracy of Decision Trees is 0.858, 0.871, 0.898 corresponding with the feature lengths of 100, 200, and 300. Other classifiers follow the same rule. It can also be observed that when the feature length is the same, the feature size determines the performance of the classifier. When the feature length is 300, the accuracy of Decision Trees is 0.889, 0.896, 0.963 respectively corresponding to feature sizes of 2-gram, 3-gram, 4-gram. Consequently, the best performance generates in the condition of 4-gram and 300 features. The experiment results show that the highest accuracy is 0.963 generated by the Decision Tree classifier with 4-gram, 300 features. In our experiment, 300 features of 4-gram opcode is extracted to the greatest extent. Maybe there are different rules in other feature ranges. It will be verified in further experiments. The comparison of the TPR, FPR and Accuracy of each classifiers with different feature size and length is shown in Figs. 2, 3 and 4.

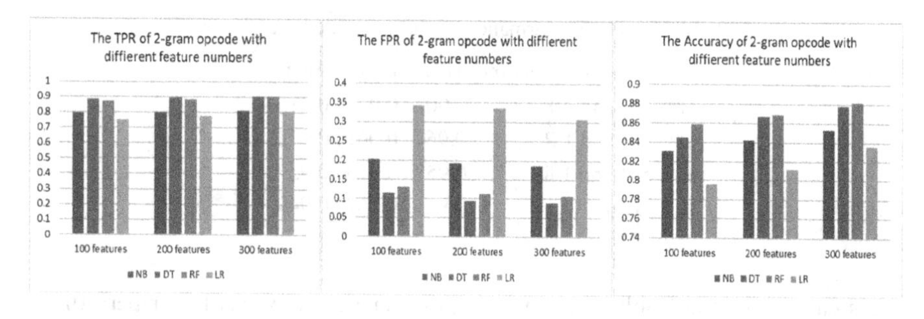

Fig. 2. The TPR, FPR and Accuracy of 2-gram opcode with feature number of 100, 200 and 300

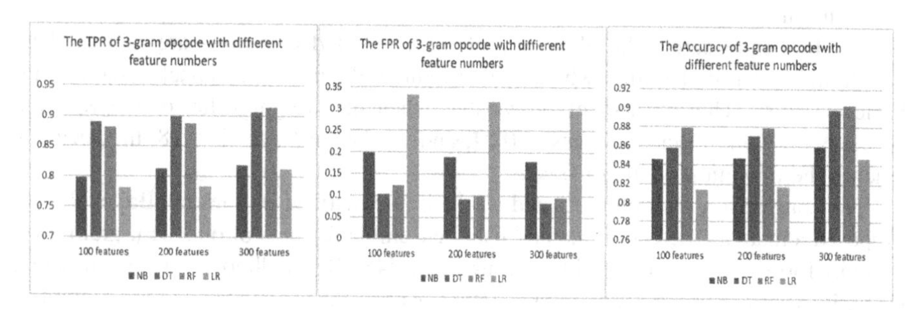

Fig. 3. The TPR, FPR and Accuracy of 3-gram opcode with feature number of 100, 200 and 300

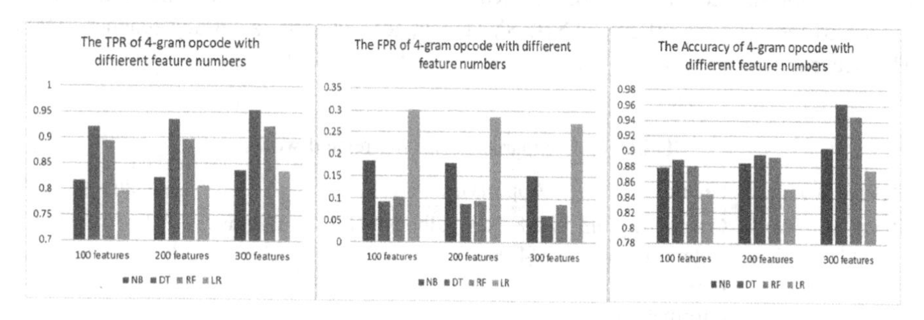

Fig. 4. The TPR, FPR and Accuracy of 4-gram opcode with feature number of 100, 200 and 300

The previous experiment is based on a single basic classifier. In order to verify whether the integrated classifier has better performance, further experiments on 4-gram of 300 features are carried out. Three classifiers of the four are selected for combination, in which each basic classifier makes the same contribution in classifying. The performance of the test is shown in Table 3.

Table 3. The performance of the integrated classifiers

Classifier combination	TPR	FPR	Accuracy
DT, RF and NB	0.903	0.072	0.915
DT, RF and LR	0.964	0.061	0.972
RF, NB and LR	0.957	0.053	0.957
DT, NB and LR	0.911	0.067	0.949

As can be seen in Table 3, integrated classifier generally has better performance than single basic classifier. This is because the average of probabilities rule mitigates the side effects of the inferior basic classifier and elevates the positive effects of the excellent ones.

For further research, the efficiency of the integrated classifiers are improved by weighting the basic classifier, which further reduces the negative impact of the inferior basic classifier. The experiment shows that when the weight value of the Random Forest is 0.78, the Decision Trees is 0.04, and the Naive Bayes is 0.18, the accuracy reaches the maximum value of 0.982.

The comparison with other related works is summarized in Table 4. Bai et al. [16] proposed a malware detection method using ensemble features of opcode n-gram, byte n-gram, format information with classifiers of J48, RF, AdboostM1(J48), Bagging (J48). Its accuracy achieved as high as 0.967. Kang et al. [17] used opcode n-gram as feature to train classifier of NB, SVM, PART, RF, reaching an accuracy of 0.96. The feature of Zak et al. [18] is also opcode n-gram, and the classifier includes SVM, NN, RF. The optimal accuracy is 0.925. Kumara et al. [19] leveraged the byte n-gram feature to feed the classifiers of NB, SVM, RF, RT, J48, the accuracy reached 0.995. The accuracy of our proposed work reached as high as 0.982.

Table 4. Comparison with the related works

Related work	Feature types	Approaches	Accuracy	FPR
Bai et al. [16]	Opcode n-gram Byte n-gram Format information	J48, RF, AdboostM1(J48), Bagging (J48)	0.967	0.2
Kang et al. [17]	Opcode n-gram	NB, SVM, PART, RF	0.980	□
Zak et al. [18]	Opcode n-gram Byte n-gram	SVM, NN, RF	0.925	□
Kumara et al. [19]	Byte n-gram	NB, SVM, RF, RT, J48	0.995	0.04
Proposed work	Opcode n-gram	DT, RF, NB, LR	0.981	0.02

Naïve Bayes (NB), support vector machine (SVM), partial decision tree (PART) and random forest (RF), Logistic Regression (LR), Decision Trees (DT), Nearest Neighbor (NN). □: Information not explicitly mentioned in the previous work.

5 Conclusion and Future Work

Aiming at the security problem of virtual machine in cloud computing environment, a method of detecting unknown malware based on machine learning is proposed. We leveraged VMI and memory forensic technology to capture the memory state of the virtual machine. Machine learning technology is used to analysis the malicious behavior of the executables. Machine learning classifier was trained to detect malware attacks in the VMs. The experimental results show that the efficiency of the weighted integrated classifier can meet our requirement and reached an accuracy of 0.982.

In our research, opcode n-gram feature is utilized for malware static analysis. Classifiers are DT, RF, NB and LR. In the future work, deep learning methods [20] such as S-SAE [21] will be using to extract features from malware samples. It can not only reduce complexity but also improve the efficacy of data abstraction and accuracy of data classification. What is more, other classifiers such as SVM-GRBF and CNNs [22] will be investigated to find the optimal classifying way for malware detection.

References

1. Ren, J., Shen, J., Wang, J., Han, J., Lee, S.: Mutual verifiable provable data auditing in public cloud storage. J. Internet Technol. **2**(16), 317–323 (2015)
2. Xia, Z., Wang, X., Sun, X., et al.: A secure and dynamic multi-keyword ranked search scheme over encrypted cloud data. IEEE Trans. Parallel Distrib. Syst. **27**, 340–352 (2015)
3. Garfinkel, T., Rosenblum, M.: A virtual machine introspection based architecture for intrusion detection. In: Proceedings of the Network and Distributed Systems Security Symposium, pp. 191–206 (2003)
4. Markel, Z., Bilzor, M.: Building a machine learning classifier for malware detection. In: 2014 Second Workshop on Anti-malware Testing Research (WATeR), pp. 1–4. IEEE (2014)
5. Ajay Kumara, M.A., Jaidhar, C.D.: Automated multi-level malware detection system based on reconstructed semantic view of executables using machine learning techniques at VMM. Future Gener. Comput. Syst. **1**(79), 431–446 (2018)
6. Shabtai, A., Moskovitch, R., Feher, C., et al.: Detecting unknown malicious code by applying classification techniques on opcode patterns. Secur. Inform. **1**(1), 1 (2012)
7. Srinivasan, D., Wang, Z., Jiang, X., Xu, D.: Process out-grafting: an efficient "out-of-VM" approach for fine-grained process execution monitoring. In: Proceedings of the ACM Conference on Computer and Communications Security, CCS 2011, Chicago, Illinois, USA, pp. 363–374 (2011)
8. Mosli, R., Li, R., Yuan, B.: Automated malware detection using artifacts in forensic memory images. In: 2016 IEEE Symposium on Technologies for Homeland Security (HST), pp. 1–6. IEEE (2016)
9. Dolan-Gavitt, B., Leek, T., Zhivich, M., Giffin, J., Lee, W.: Virtuoso: narrowing these mantic gap in virtual machine introspection. In: 2011 IEEE Symposium on Security and Privacy, pp. 297–312. IEEE (2011)
10. Jain, B., Baig, M.B., Zhang, D.: Introspections on trust and the semantic gap. In: 2014 IEEE Symposium on Security and Privacy, pp. 605–620. IEEE (2014)
11. Fu, Y., Lin, Z.: Bridging the semantic gap in virtual machine introspection via online kernel data redirection. ACM Trans. Inf. Syst. Secur. **16**(2), 1–29 (2013)

12. Saberi, A., Fu, Y., Lin, Z.: HYBRID-BRIDGE: efficiently bridging the semantic gap in virtual machine introspection via decoupled execution and training memorization. In: Proceedings of the 21st Annual Network and Distributed System Security Symposium, NDSS14 (2014)
13. Teller, T., Hayon, A.: Enhancing automated malware analysis machines with memory analysis. Black Hat USA (2014)
14. Libvmi Homepage. http://libvmi.com/. Accessed 8 June 2018
15. VX Heaven Homepage. http://83.133.184.251/virensimulation.org/. Accessed 8 June 2018
16. Bai, J., Wang, J.: Improving malware detection using multi-view ensemble learning. Secur. Commun. Netw. **9**(17), 4227–4241 (2016)
17. Kang, B., Yerima, S.Y., McLaughlin, K., Sezer, S.: N-opcode analysis for android malware classification and categorization. In: 2016 International Conference on Cyber Security and Protection of Digital Services (Cyber Security), pp. 1–7. IEEE (2016)
18. Zak, R., Raff, E., Nicholas, C.: What can N-grams learn for malware detection? In: 2017 12th International Conference on Malicious and Unwanted Software (MALWARE), pp. 109–118. IEEE (2017)
19. Kumara, M.A., Jaidhar, C.D.: Leveraging virtual machine introspection with memory forensics to detect and characterize unknown malware using machine learning techniques at hypervisor. Digit. Investig. **23**, 99–123 (2017)
20. Wang, Z., Ren, J., Zhang, D., et al.: A deep-learning based feature hybrid framework for spatiotemporal saliency detection inside videos. Neurocomputing **287**, 68–83 (2018)
21. Zabalza, J., Ren, J., Zheng, J., et al.: Novel segmented stacked autoencoder for effective dimensionality reduction and feature extraction in hyperspectral imaging. Neurocomputing **185**, 1–10 (2016)
22. Noor, S.S.M., Michael, K., Marshall, S., Ren, J.: Hyperspectral image enhancement and mixture deep-learning classification of corneal epithelium injuries. Sensors **17**(11), 2644 (2017)

A Trusted Connection Authentication Reinforced by Bayes Algorithm

WanShan Xu[1,2], JianBiao Zhang[1,2(✉)], and YaHao Zhang[1,2]

[1] Faculty of Information Technology, Beijing University of Technology, Beijing 100124, China
zjb@bjut.edu.cn
[2] Beijing Key Laboratory of Trusted Computing, Beijing 100124, China

Abstract. Trusted Connection Authentication (TCA) is a critical part of network security access solution. TCA is a kind of high level trusted network access techniques which can create trusted connections between client and remote networks through two-way user authentication and platform identification in TTP. However, there are general security problems after accessed to the network which are not much considered by existing TCA schemes. Therefore, this paper proposes a reinforced TCA architecture, TCA-BA, which extends a network behavior layer on the basis of TCA. Firstly, network behavior eigenvalue extraction is proposed by using time and host network flow characteristics. Secondly, a new method is illustrated in which we classify the behavior by Naïve Bayes Algorithm, measure the network abnormal behavior by minimum risk bayes rules, identify these behaviors which have accessed to the network. Finally, the experimental results present that our architecture can effectively identify the abnormal behavior in the network and protect the network security.

Keywords: TCA · Behavior analysis · Naive bayes · Network security

1 Introduction

TCA which is also called the Trusted Connect Authentication is a kind of Trusted Network Connection (TNC) but has TPCM (Trusted Platform Control Module) proposed by National Standard GB/T29828-2013 in the People's Republic of China, TCA was proposed to solve the problem in TNC security. TCA which was developed on Tri-element Entity Authentication technique is a kind of trusted network connection technique with high security level. Figure 1 shows the architecture of TCA.

TCA has realized bidirectional and platform integrity authentication for network access terminals and intermediate devices through a trusted third party (TTP). After passing the authentication, we allow the terminal to access the network, otherwise, the terminal is prevented from accessing the network. Compared with the existing network connection method based on the username and password mechanism, the TCA includes some mechanisms such as authentication on accessing terminal identification and integrity verification of the access platform which is intended to greatly improve the security [1]. Moreover, TCA can achieve trusted authentication on network middleware

J. Ren et al. (Eds.): BICS 2018, LNAI 10989, pp. 727–737, 2018.
https://doi.org/10.1007/978-3-030-00563-4_71

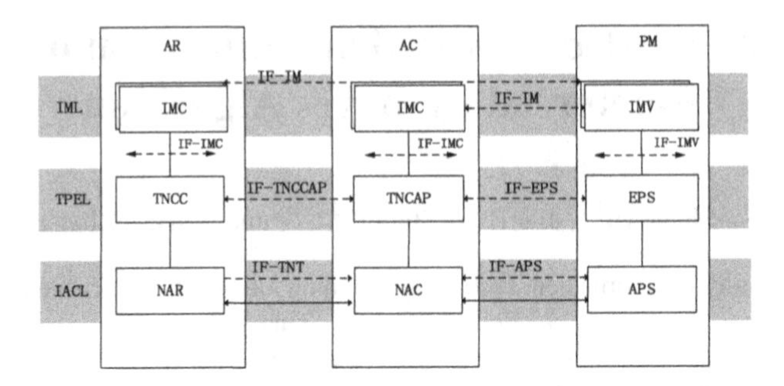

Fig. 1. Architecture of TCA

(such as routers, switches, etc.) with the help of TTP. Therefore, it can effectively resist against those network attacks such as Man-in-the-Middle attacks [2].

Although TCA has more security, it mainly deals with static online threats before the access to the network, and often lacks of effective detection tests for dynamic security risks during network connection, such as DDOS, SYN Flood. Through the development of the internet, more cyber attackers tend to use machine learning techniques to automate their attacks or bypass intrusion-detection. Cyber attacks present a clear trend of intelligence and clustering [3]. In this situation, network security should be performed based on machine learning techniques.

Thus, we propose a method of extending TCA by machine learning techniques. First, we use Naïve Bayes algorithm to construct a network behavior classifier and create a network behavior analysis layer with the help of existing data sets. Secondly, we combine the network behavior analysis layer with the original TCA architecture to generate four-tier architecture called TCA-BA. Finally, we use TCA-BA to collect the actual operation parameters in the network running, through the preset loss functions, we use the Bayes minimum risk rule to implement the trusted identification for network behavior. Since this method detects every network data transmission process and exists in the entire transmission life cycle, it can achieve dynamic defense on network security [4].

2 Related Work

Network behavior analysis is an important means to detect dynamic network security threats. It refers to the techniques of detecting network abnormal state through the analysis of network flow. This method obtains main network performance indicators through statistical analysis and calculation of collected data packets. Then it gets the current network security status and detect abnormal behavior by comparing the result of the performance indicators with the preset reference values. Network behavior analysis plays an important role in detecting abnormal network conditions. For example, the average packet length of normal flow is a relatively stable data, but those malicious scanning attack can cause bursts of traffic in a short period of time. So we have high sensitivity to scanning attacks through monitoring the average length of packets over time. Also, threats can be detected according to the key parameters of the network protocol. For example, attacks such as the DoS (Denial of Service), DDoS (Distributed Denial of Service) and SYN Flood, can be detected by calculating the percentage of "SYN" incorrect connections.

In view of the important role of network behavior analysis in detecting network security, many scholars combine the network behavior analysis technology with the existing trusted network connection technology to enhance the security of the network. Liu [5] and other scholars proposed a trusted network connection control scheme based on terminal behavior. However, this scheme is oriented towards the terminal and cannot handle abnormal behavior due to network changes. Zhang [6] proposed an improved trusted network connection research based on user behavior analysis by using a double sliding window. This method is mainly aimed at the research of user behavior, which is based on access control technology. It solves the problem of malicious operation and illegal access to the terminal users and does not solve the problem of network behavior.

3 Method

3.1 Framework of TCA-BA

We classify the network behavior by Bayes algorithm and create new architecture TCA-BA to reinforce the existing TCA. The framework of the TCA-BA is shown in Fig. 2 as follows.

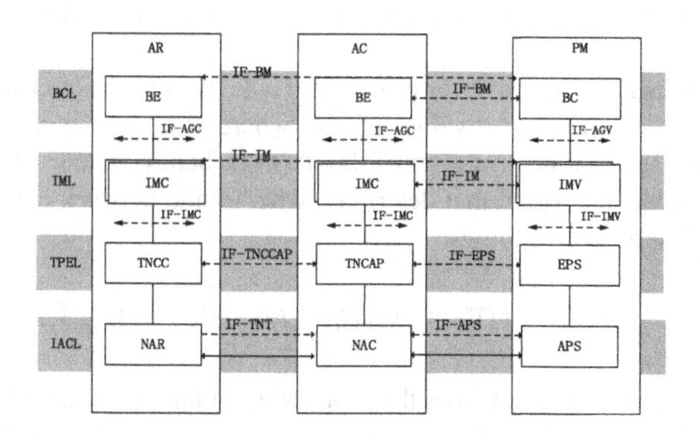

Fig. 2. Framework of TCA-BA

Compared the reinforced trusted connection framework TCA-BA in Fig. 2 with the existing trusted connection architecture shown in Fig. 1, we add a layer of behavior analysis (BCL). The BCL collects network behavior parameters and implements behavior classification through the Bayesian algorithm. Through the network behavior analysis layer, dynamic security detection after network access can be implemented.

3.2 Construction of Behavior Analysis Layer (BCL)

The behavior analysis layer mainly implements data acquisition, classification and discrimination of network behavior. Firstly, a classifier is built using Bayesian algorithm, and the classifier is trained by machine learning method to improve the classification accuracy. Then we get the value of network parameters through API in the TCA-BA architecture system and classify behaviors by Bayes algorithm classifiers. Finally, we use Minimum Risk Bayesian Rule and Loss Function to Realize the judgment of network behavior.

Network Behavior Classification Based on Bayesian Algorithm
The network behavior in the field of network security can be divided into two categories, normal and abnormal, and their classification can be achieved through the Bayes algorithm. The Bayesian algorithm uses the prior probability and the conditional probability to calculate the posterior probability. The prior probability and the conditional probability are obtained through the sample values. After the sample value is obtained, a set of feature vectors that can reflect the sample features needs to be selected, and the prior probability and the conditional probability are obtained by the operation of the feature vector. Since most network attacks have time and host characteristics, the following 10 variables based on time and host traffic are selected to construct eigenvectors.

Since the Bayesian algorithm handles discrete data, it is necessary to discretize the continuous variables in the eigenvalues. We can discretize the continuous variables by dividing the interval, because the sample eigenvalues have high clustering characteristics. In order to generate a discrete eigenvalue $U_i = (U_0, U_1)$, we illustrate U_0 as the interval with high frequency of occurrence and U_1 as the interval with low frequency of occurrence.

After the derivation of the eigenvalues in Table 1, we construct a set of vectors X = (x1, x2, x3,..., xn) by eigenvalues above, where xi is the eigenvalue in Table 1, and vector X is used to represent a set of the network behavior state. According to the Bayes algorithm, the algorithm that determine whether the network behavior is normal or not can be described as follows:

$$C_{NB} = \max\left(P(C_i)\,\Pi_{j=1}^{n} P\left(X_j \mid C_i\right)\right), i = 0, 1; j = 1, 2, 3, \ldots, 10 \tag{1}$$

In this case, the $P(x_j|C_i)$ indicates the probability of features x_j given class C_i, There are only two values in C_i, C_0 indicates the abnormal network behavior, C_1 indicates the normal network behavior. $P(C_i)$ is the prior probability of C_i.

Minimum Risk Bayes Rule for Network Behavior Determination
The Minimum Risk Bayes Decision is an optimal decision after considering different losses caused by various errors. In this paper, we set the decision table in Table 2.

Moreover, λ indicates the loss function, λ (d_1, c_2) represents a normal loss in a set of abnormal network behaviors, and $\lambda(d_2, c_1)$ represents the abnormal loss in a set of normal network behavior. Evidently though, $\lambda(d_1, c_1) = \lambda(d_2, c_2) = 0$.

We assume network behavior B has occurred, the conditional risk of taking decision D_i is described as follows:

Table 1. Eigenvalue set of network behavior

Eigenvalue	Definition
X1	The number of connections with the same destination address in the past two seconds
X2	The same number of connections for the connection service in the past two seconds
X3	The percentage of connections with "SYN" errors in the same destination address connection in the past two seconds
X4	The percentage of connections that have "SYN" errors in the same connection for the connection service in the past two seconds
X5	The percentage of connections that have the same destination address and the same connection service in the past two seconds
X6	Number of connections with the same destination address and connection service in the first 100 connections
X7	Percentage of connections in the first 100 connections that have the same destination address and connection service
X8	Percentage of connections with the same destination address and the same source port in the first 100 connections
X9	Percentage of connections that have SYN errors in connections with the same destination host for the top 100 connections
X10	Percentage of connections that have SYN errors connections with the same service as the current target host in the top 100 connections

Table 2. Risk decision table

Decision	Condition	
	C_1 normal behavior	C_2 abnormal behavior
D_1 normal decision	$\lambda(d_1, c_1)$	$\lambda(d_1, c_2)$
D_2 abnormal decision	$\lambda(d_2, c_1)$	$\lambda(d_2, c_2)$

$$R(D_i \mid B) = \sum_{j=1}^{c} \lambda(D_i, C_j) \mathrm{P}(C_j \mid D) \\ (i = 1, 2; j = 1, 2) \tag{2}$$

$R(D_i|B)$ shows the average loss value when the observation value B was judged as D_i. Obviously, the smaller the average value, the smaller the risk of decision-making and the more realistic it is. So we could find the minimum risk decision by calculating min $R(D_i|B)$. When i = 1, 2, we can get the following formula:

$$R(D_2 \mid B) = \lambda(D_2, C_1) \mathrm{P}(C_1 \mid D) \tag{3}$$

$$R(D_1 \mid B) = \lambda(D_1, C_2) \mathrm{P}(C_2 \mid D) \tag{4}$$

3.3 TCA-BA Connect Process

The connection process of TCA-BA is shown in Fig. 3.

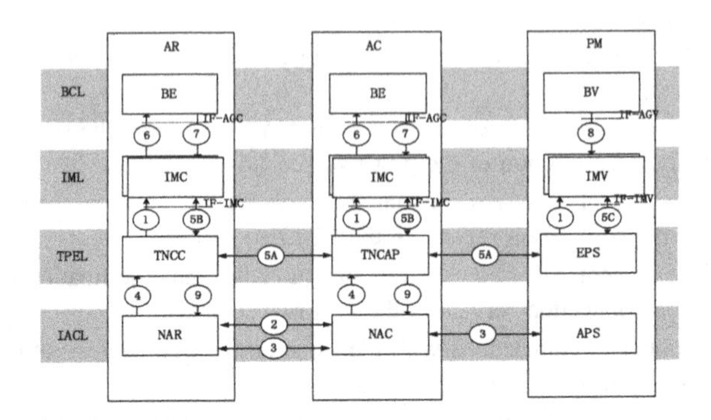

Fig. 3. TCA-BA connect process

(1) Connection preparation: before the connection starts, the TNCC (TNC Client) and the TNCAP (TNC Access Point) load the interface to collect relevant information according to the specific platform binding function.
(2) NAR (Network Access Requestor) initiates a network access request to NAC (Network Access Controller).
(3) NAR and NAC execute user authentication. After receiving the network access request sent by NAR, the NAC finishes the two-way user identification with NAR under the help of APS (Authentication Policy Server). APS acts as trusted third party if it participates in identity authentication.
(4) NAR and NAC send platform identification requests to the TNCC and TNCAP.
(5A) After receiving the platform authentication request, the TNCAP performs a round or multi- platform authentication protocol with TNCC and APS in order to implement the platform authentication between TNCC and ANCAP.
(5B) In the platform authentication process, the TNCC and TNCAP interacts with each IMC (Integrity Measure Collector) through the platform's IF-IMC, getting the integrity information M (hard disk information, memory information, operating system version, important patch, network information, related drive, etc.) of the platform.
(5C) EPS (Evaluation Policy Server) completes the integrity verification of the platform through the IF-IMV with IMV (Integrity Measure Verifier). The integrity evaluation results are generated and returned to the TNCC and TNCAP.
(6) When the network behavior needs to identify, the TNCC and TNCAP send behavior identification requests to the BCL.
(7) In the process of platform behavior identification, the TNCC and TNCAP interacts with each BE (Behavior Collector) to get the information of the platform network behavior, and extracts the related network characteristic parameters, which shown in Table 1.

(8) APS completes the validation to the credibility of the platform behavior with the help of IF-IMV and BV (Behavior Verifier). The result of the behavior credibility is generated and returned to the TNCC and TNCAP.
(9) After the network behavior authentication is completed, the TNCC and TNCAP generate access decision (permission/ prohibition/ isolation) by using the platform integrity and behavior credibility evaluation results, which is sent to NAR and NAC respectively.
(10) NAR and NAC implement access control based on generated access decisions.

4 Experiments

The test environment was constructed in Windows 7 x64 while our analyze program is written in C# language by Visual Studio 2010. Moreover, we choose KDD99 data set as our experimental test data set which consists of a full set of 5,000,000 records and a 10% training subset. We use the training subset to train the classification algorithm. The subset contains 494,020 records, each record contains 41 attributes and is marked as normal or exception, and the exception type is subdivided into 4 classes in a total of 39 different attack types.

After post-training analyzing to 494020 records in training subset, we get 97279 correct records and 396742 abnormal ones. Therefore, two priori probabilities P $(C_0) = 0.8$ and P $(C_1) = 0.2$ are obtained.

Since some of the eigenvalues in Table 1 are continuous, it is necessary to discretize these attributes. In this paper, we use the method of dividing the interval to discretize the data in order to cope with the large data interval in Fig. 4(a) and (b).

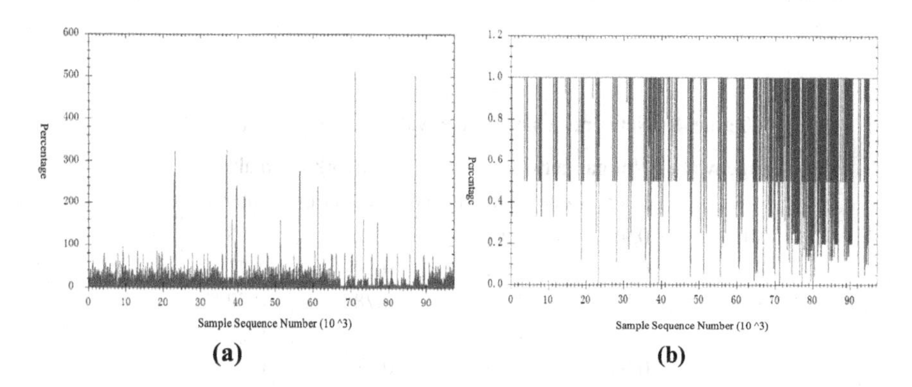

Fig. 4. The percentage of connections that have "SYN" errors in the same connection for the connection service in the past two seconds and the percentage of connections that have the same destination address and the same connection service in the past two seconds

From the sample data in Fig. 4(a), we can get the percentage of connections that have "SYN" errors in the same connection for the connection service in the past two seconds. By statistics, the number of sample connections of 98.2% is below 0.4.

Therefore, the eigenvalue X4 (percentage of connections that have "SYN" errors in the same connection for the connection service in the past two seconds) can be divided into interval [0, 0.4] and (0.4, 1].

Similarly, the eigenvalue X5 which indicates the percentage of connections that have the same destination address with the same connection service in the past two seconds in Fig. 4(b) is more than 99% on 0.5 point, so the eigenvalue X5 can be divided into interval [0.5, 1] and [0, 0.5).

The result of sorted interval in each eigenvalue is divided as follows (Table 3):

Table 3. Interval division of network behavior eigenvalues

Eigenvalue	Interval one	Interval two
X1	[0, 60]	(60, ∞]
X2	[0, 120]	(120, ∞]
X3	[0, 0.4]	(0.4, 1]
X4	[0, 0.4]	(0.4, 1]
X5	[0.5, 1]	[0, 0.5)
X6	[2, ∞]	[0, 2)
X7	[0.01, 1]	[0, 0.01)
X8	[0, 0.99]	(0.99, 1]
X9	[0, 0.01]	(0.1, 1]
X10	[0, 0.01]	(0.1, 1]

Based on the analysis of the sample data of the first 10% of the KDD99 dataset, the conditional probability of normal and abnormal network conditions is as follows (Table 4):

Table 4. Network behavior eigenvalue conditional probability

Eigenvalue	Normal network		Network anomaly	
	Interval one	Interval two	Interval one	Interval two
X1	0.98	0.02	0.02	0.98
X2	0.98	0.02	0.29	0.71
X3	0.99	0.01	0.78	0.22
X4	0.99	0.01	0.78	0.22
X5	0.99	0.01	0.73	0.27
X6	0.96	0.04	0.98	0.02
X7	0.96	0.04	0.98	0.02
X8	0.95	0.05	0.28	0.72
X9	0.98	0.02	0.77	0.23
X10	0.99	0.01	0.78	0.22

According to the prior probability $P(C_i)$ and conditional probability $P(x_j|C_i)$, the posterior probability $P(C_i|x_j)$ can be obtained by the Bayes formula, because there are several independent eigenvalues, so the posterior probability $P(C_i|x_j)$ calculation formula is as follows:

$$P(c_i \mid x_j) = \frac{P(c_i) * \Pi P(x_j \mid c_i)}{\Sigma P(c_i) * \Pi P(x_j \mid c_i)} \quad (i = 0, 1; j = 1, 2, 3, \ldots, 10) \tag{5}$$

In order to evaluate the performance of this method, we compare it with the Improved NB algorithm proposed in literatures [7] and the PCA-AKM proposed in literatures [8] which use the same data set. Accuracy and error rate was used as evaluation indicators, the results are shown in Figs. 5 and 6.

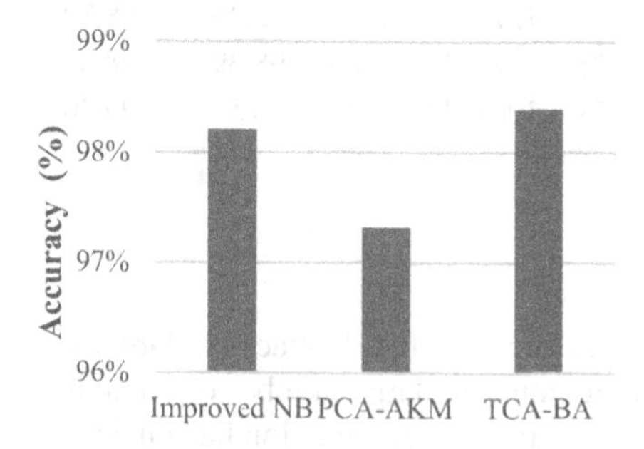

Fig. 5. Accuracy of the three methods

As in shown in Figs. 5 and 6, the accuracy of TCA-BA is 98.46%, higher than Improved NB (98.21%) and PCA-AKM (97.32%). Although the error rate sees a small rise between the PCA-AKM (1.03%) with the TCA-BA (1.62%), the error rate of our method drops significantly by around 4.6% compared with the Improved NB. Experimental results show that TCA-BA can identify abnormal network behaviors efficiently while remaining lower error rate.

According to the minimum risk Bayes decision rule and the loss function, formula 2 is used to calculate the conditional risk. Because the loss function is set up artificially, those difference between the loss function may lead to different experimental results. In our experiment, we set several different sets of loss function values and get the results that are shown in Table 5.

The experiment results of Table 5 show that the result is different when setting different loss functions. Therefore, the corresponding loss function can be set up according to the specific requirements of the environment in order to achieve the desired purpose in the actual environment.

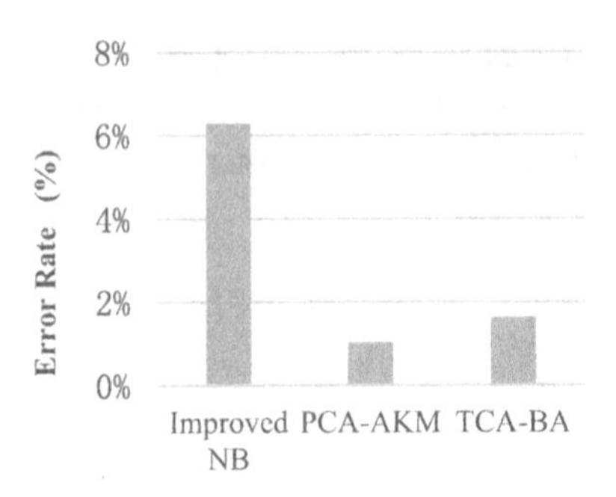

Fig. 6. Error rate of the three methods

Table 5. Comparison of experimental results of different risk functions (%)

Number	Loss function	Accuracy	Precision	Recall	FPR
I	λ(d1, c2) = 1, λ(d2, c1) = 1	98.46	98.89	99.09	3.59
II	λ(d1, c2) = 6, λ(d2, c1) = 1	98.39	98.89	98.98	3.59
III	λ(d1, c2) = 10, λ(d2, c1) = 1	96.58	99.20	96.32	2.60

5 Conclusion

At present, cyber attackers launch network attacks in larger scale and higher density by using machine learning to control a large number of computers. Thus, Researching on network security techniques in this new situation has vital practical significance. In this paper, a trusted connection architecture reinforced by Bayes algorithm (TCA-BA) is proposed by adding a network behavior analysis layer on the basis of TCA. Compared with the original TCA architecture, TCA-BA can not only guarantee the security when the terminal is accessed from the network, but also implement trusted identification on the network behavior through the naive Bayes algorithm and the minimum risk analysis rules. The authentication method solves the dynamic security problem after accessing to network and improves the security of TCA. The experiment results show that the accuracy rate can reach more than 98%, achieving network state discrimination well. Compared with existing trusted connection techniques, TCA-BA has stronger security and scalability, and can greatly guarantee the reliable connection of the network.

Future work can focus on increasing the accuracy of the proposed technique by using another well-trained model generated by more efficient training algorithms. Furthermore, more deep learning [9] algorithms such as LSTM and SAE [10] can also be utilized, as these have been proven to be highly efficient in features selection and classification.

References

1. Wang, Y., Yi, X., Li, K., et al.: Formal verification of trusted connection architecture. Comput. Sci. **39**(s3), 230–233 (2012)
2. Xiao, Y.L., Wang, Y.M., Pang, L.J.: Security analysis and improvement of TNC IF-T protocol binding to TLS. China Commun. (Engl. Ed.) **10**(7), 85–92 (2013)
3. Vidal, J.M., Orozco, A.L.S., Villalba, L.J.G.: Adaptive artificial immune networks for mitigating DoS flooding attacks. Swarm Evol. Comput. **38** (2017)
4. Luo, Y.B., Wang, B.S., Wang, X.F., et al.: RPAH: a moving target network defense mechanism naturally resists reconnaissances and attacks. IEICE Trans. Inf. Syst. **100**(3), 496–510 (2017)
5. Liu, W.W., Han, Z., Shen, C.X.: Trusted network connection control scheme based on terminal behavior. J. Commun. **30**(11), 127–134 (2009)
6. Zhang, J.L., Zhang, G.L., Zhang, X.F.: Real-time evaluation mechanism based on double evidence classification of user behavior. Int. J. Secur. Appl. 31–42 (2016)
7. Wang, H., Chen, Y.Y., Liu, S.F.: Intrusion detection system based on improved Naive Bayes algorithm. Comput. Sci. **41**(4), 111–115 (2014)
8. Niu, L., Sun, Z.L.: PCA-AKM algorithm and its application in intrusion detection. computer. Science **45**(2), 226–230 (2018)
9. Wang, Z., Ren, J., Zhang, D.: A deep-learning based feature hybrid framework for spatiotemporal saliency detection inside videos. Neurocomputing (2018)
10. Zhang, J.M., Ren, J.C., Zhao, H.M.: Novel segmented stacked autoencoder for effective dimensionality reduction and feature extraction in hyperspectral imaging. Neurocomputing **185**, 1–10 (2016)

A Proactive Caching Strategy Based on Deep Learning in EPC of 5G

FangYuan Lei[1], QinYun Dai[1], Jun Cai[1](✉), HuiMin Zhao[2], Xun Liu[1], and Yan Liu[1]

[1] School of Electronic and Information, Guangdong Polytechnic Normal University, Guangzhou 510640, China
gzhcaijun@126.com
[2] School of Computer, Guangdong Polytechnic Normal University, Guangzhou 510640, China

Abstract. In 5G mobile network, SDN/NFV as a key technology is widely used in EPC networks. In order to cope with the increasing data service in the EPC of 5G network, we propose a proactive cache strategy based on the deep learning network SSAEs for content popularity prediction based on the SDN/NFV architecture, SNDLPC. Firstly, NFV/SDN technique is used to build a virtual distributed deep learning network SSAEs. Then, the SSAEs network parameters are unsupervised trained by the historical users' data. Finally, the content popularity is predicted by SSAEs using the data of user request in whole network collected by SDN controller. The SDN controller generates the proactive caching strategy according to the prediction results and synchronizes it to each cache node through flowtable to implement the strategy. In the simulation, the SSAEs network structure parameters are compared and determined. Compared with other strategies, such as the typical Hash + LRU and Betw + LRU caching strategies, SVM prediction and the BPNN prediction algorithm, the proposed SNDLPC proactive cache strategy can significantly improve cache performance.

Keywords: Proactive caching strategy · Content popularity prediction · Deep learning · EPC · 5G

1 Introduction

According to the latest Cisco release of the Visual Network Index (VNI) forecast [4], global mobile data traffic in 2021 will be seven times than in 2016, of which mobile video traffic will be closer to 80% of mobile traffic. Therefore, this requires the deployment of a costly infrastructure and a considerable incensement of the backbone link capacity, special the capacity of EPC backbone. However, relying solely on network expansion cannot efficiently solve network capacity problems. In fact, most of the growth of mobile traffic comes from a large number of users repeatedly requesting the same popular content in a short period of

J. Ren et al. (Eds.): BICS 2018, LNAI 10989, pp. 738–747, 2018.
https://doi.org/10.1007/978-3-030-00563-4_72

time. Consequently, proactively caching popular contents in mobile networks can reduce the requirement of backbone network capacity and greatly improve user experience at the same time. Therefore, reducing the EPC traffic becomes an urgent problem to be solved.

In traditional mobile networks, the implementation of network functions is often tightly coupled with hardware devices. In EPC of 5G, SDN [11] decoupled the network element hardware and software and NFV [10] virtualized the decoupled hardware and software resources. In 5G, Which content is cached network should depend on the popularity of the content. Therefore, the content popularity is a key factor in improving cache performance and reducing network traffic. Obviously, the popularity of the content is determined by the level of user attention. By effectively reducing the duplicate content transmission in the network, the caching technology based on content popularity prediction has received extensive attention in wireless mobile networks [2,3,13,15].

Therefore, we propose an efficient cache mechanism SNDLPC (SDN/NFV based deep learning popularity prediction cache strategy) in EPC of 5G. First, NFV are used to virtual part of hardware resources in EPC. Then, a distributed deep learning network is constructed and trained. Next, the global cache SDN controller generates cache strategy based on content popularity prediction. Finally, the strategy is synchronized to the relevant network elements to implement content caching and replacement.

The contributions of this paper are as follows: (1) In the 5G core network, based on the SDN/NFV technology, a method of constructing a SSAEs plus Softmax distributed deep learning network is proposed; (2) the user history request information is used to predict the popularity of the network content; (3) In the cooperation of the SDN controller, proactive caching and replacement are implemented to make the cache content object more reasonable in the temporal and spatial distribution; (4) Simulation results show that compared with Betw [8], Hash [14] and Opportunistic [13], this strategy can better improve network cache performance including network traffic, cache hit rate.

The remainder of this article is organized as follows. In Sect. 2, related works is described. In Sect. 3, The SNDLPC approach is proposed. In Sect. 4, numerical simulation results are analyzed. Finally, we draw our conclusions in Sect. 5.

2 Related Works

Since the NFV concept was proposed, the cache technology was considered as one of the key application scenarios of the NFV architecture. Recently, the research on the introduction of the cache function into the EPC of 5G mobile communications has attracted extensive attention. Liu [9] studied the use of SDN/NFV technology to manage the core network cache content. Wang [16] proposed to incorporate CCN's caching technology into 5G EPC to further reduce network caching. Katsaros [7] proposed a cache sharing mechanism between multiple virtual operators of 5G networks basis on NFV/SDN. Ren [12] decomposed the EPC caching problem as content layout and request routing issue. Jia [6] proposed an efficient 5G network slice buffer resource allocation scheme. SDN based 5G packet core hierarchical architecture was proposed [1].

In terms of content popularity prediction, Suksomboon [14] proposed a caching decision policy PopCache based on content popularity. Trzcixski [15] proposed a regression method to predict the popularity of YouTube and Facebook online videos. Stokowiec [13] proposed a bi-directional long-term short-term memory (Bi-LSTM) neural network to predict online news texts and video. Cai [3] translated the content popularity prediction into a classification problem, and used an depth neural network to implement an end-to-end multi-mode prediction model. Bastug [2] proposed the prediction of user needs based on the relevance of the file popularity and user and file patterns, and proactively cached files during off-peak demand to reduce backhaul network traffic congestion.

3 System Model

3.1 Deep Learning Networks Construct on EPC

In EPC of 5G networks, the core network elements are SDN enable architecture. The NFV can be used to virtualize part of the hardware resources such as P-GW, MCC, CSC, and MME in EPC to construct virtual distributed deep learning network architecture. The calculation resource of the deep learning network is decentralized into the different virtual node and Softmax is used to obtain the prediction of the content popularity in the SDN controller.

In order to implement a global caching mechanism based on content popularity prediction, it is necessary to know the global requested content of all users in the network. Therefore, the virtual content request statistics server in the EPC is used to collect the content information of the locally received request message through the SDN controller. The statistics request server inputs historical content request information and real-time user content request information into a distributed deep learning network. The content popularity prediction is implemented on the SDN controller, and then the generalized, cache scheme is synchronized to a corresponding core network node to implement proactive caching. The system architecture of the network model is shown in Fig. 1.

3.2 SSAE Network

Sparse AutoEncoder (SAE) [18], which is one of the famous unsupervised feature learning methods, has been widely studied to realize deep learning [5,17] which can predict the content request distribution for all users, since it is highly effective for finding succinct and high-level representations of complex data. The SSAE (Stacked Sparse AutoEncoder) is a neural network consisting of multiple layers of basic SAE in which the outputs of each layer are wired to the inputs of the successive layer. Considering the limitation of resources, the SSAE deep learning network is utilized in our system.

The SSAE is composed by two layers sparse auto-encoders, where the hidden layer of the first sparse auto-encoder is treated as the input layer of the second

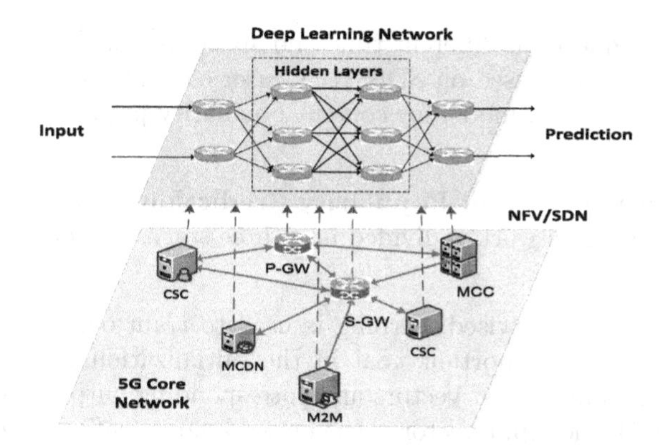

Fig. 1. Deep learning network structure in EPC of 5G.

sparse auto-encoder. A greedy layer-wise unsupervised algorithm is used to train each sparse auto-encoder independently. After the SSAE is trained to learn the features, the parameters of SSAE are used to initialize the Softmax classifier to get the features for classification.

3.3 Proactive Cache Scheme Based on Content Prediction SSAEs

SSAEs network parameters. On the structure of the SSAEs network, the dimension of the input layer, the number of the layers of the hidden layer, the number of neurons in each hidden layer, and the activation function of each layer should be considered in advance.

For each timeslot, there are p types measurement parameters should be collected for the EPC nodes. These measure parameters contain the spatial distribute information of different element node. Then for t timeslot, there are $p \times t$ categories parameters. Therefore, there are $p \times t$ virtual nodes are used to construct the input layer of the SSAEs network.

Specially, when $t > 1$ is used, the collected data contain spatial correlation of content popularity. The traffic data has relation with i timeslot and also with the past t time, that is, the $X^{i-1}, X^{i-2}, ..., X^{i-t}$ used to predict the content popularity. The input data of the SSAE contain time dependence of content popularity. The $p{\times}t$ parameters represent the traffic patterns of all nodes in EPC. Therefore, the input data of SSAE contains the temporal and spatial distribution of the content popularity. Then the SSAEs can predict the popularity more accurately according to the deep learning network.

In this article, the content popularity is discretized into q types, and the category of the Softmax classifier's output content popularity is also q types, which is output by one-hot coding in the prediction, and the corresponding category is the category of content popularity.

In EPC, the number of requests for content reflects the popularity of the content and can predict the popularity of the content in the future by analyzing the number of requests in different time and space. In the SSAE deep learning model are constructed based on SDN/NFV, user content request data collected by SDN is sent to SSAE model for content popularity prediction.

The Procedure of Content Popularity Prediction. The prediction process of the deep learning network is divided into three stages: initialization, training, and running.

InitializationStage. Supervised learning is used to train our SSAE predication model. Therefore, an important goal in the initialization phase is to obtain labeled data, including input vectors and corresponding output vectors. As previously described, the input vector is the network node traffic patterns based on our proposed model. The output vector is one-hot type which indicates the class of content popularity. The input vector can be collected through the virtualized EPC network node.

TrainingStage. The training stage contains two parts, pre-training and fine-tuning. In the pre-training, the Greedy Layer-Wise unsupervised learning algorithm is used to train SAE in down-top of the SSAEs. Then the BP with the gradient-based optimization technique is used to tune the model's parameters in a top-down direction.

RunningStage. After the training, we can obtain the optimal depth learning network model parameters, including the number of hidden layers, neurons in each layer and the weight values and the bias value of SSAEs. The connection between deep learning neurons is relative fixed. The SSAEs models deploy on the virtual node based on SDN/NFV of EPC network elements.

In the running stage, the m class measure parameters should be regularly recorded as traffic models. These traffic models are used as input vectors to predict category of content popularity in SSAES deep learning content popularity prediction model.

Proactive Caching Strategy with SNDLPC. In the implementation of the SNDLPC caching strategy, NFV provides the virtual function of the network element. As the upper control plane, SDN aware of the topology routing information of the EPC network element node and dynamically updates the cache node of the EPC network element cache node to maintain a detailed record of the cache of each EPC cache node. All caching strategies are generated by SDN controller, and EPC cache nodes are only responsible to implement. SDN fully considers the topology of the network and the caching of each node, thus making the cache of the entire EPC network efficient, avoiding the waste of caching resources and reducing the communication overhead between the cached nodes.

SDN controller is responsible for routine work, at the same time it is also responsible for the deployment and maintenance the SNDLPC. The controller also responsible to establish the routing forwarding table of EPC node. When the SNDLPC make prediction, the SDN controller creates a routing forwarding table for the content and actively inserts it into the normal switch routing table before the packet arrives. The content will be cached when the packet arrives, at the same time some packet which also decide by SDN controller be replaced if the cache space is full.

According to the results of the content popularity prediction, the SDN controller flow table is used to identify the content of the content of the future content, and to replace the content with low popularity. The flow table is synchronized to the control plane of the core network. The control plane of the core network element achieves the proactive cache and replacement of contents in storage devices after receiving the storage and replacement instructions.

4 Experiment and Evaluation

4.1 Experimental Environments

In the simulation environment, the Openflow table is used to construct the SDN model control plane and data plane. The SSAEs deep learning is based on the tensorflow framework. They run on Ubuntu 14.04 and a platform that possesses 4 GPU cards- NVIDIA GeForce TitanX 12G GDDR5 and 64G RAM memories.

The content in EPC is represented by the set $F = f_1, f_2, ..., f_R$,and the content server in the network is represented by the set $S = s_1, s_2, ..., s_p$ .It is assumed that one content packet randomly keeps in only one content server, and the content serve connects to one node. Assuming that the content units of each content server have the same size, each cache node has the same size of cache space, and a cache slot in the cache memory can only hold one content unit. Assume that the content request reaches obey Poisson process. Assuming the distribution of user data packet requests from a fixed virtual node accords with Zipf's law, which means user request frequency for content popularity $i(1 \leq i \leq M)$ as following:

$$P(X = i) = \left(i^{-a}\right)/C, C = \sum_{j=1}^{M} j^{-a} \tag{1}$$

where the M is the total category.

During the experiment, those measure parameters of user content request are collected at the virtual EPC nodes and are constructed as spatial-temporal joint distribution data. In order to input the parameters into SSAEs input layer, those data are normalized into [0,1].

When the content packet is requested, the content match is matched in the corresponding node. If the content is found, a cache hit is expressed; otherwise, the cache is not hit. In cache missed events, content requests traverse the entire content distribution path to content servers. When the requested packet is returned, the SNDLPC make a prediction for the timeslot, and predict the content popularity levels, and send them to the SDN controller. The cache nodes synchronizes the information of the packet through the Openflow flow table of the SDN controller and send the cache decision to the EPC cache node data plane by the flow table.

4.2 Evaluation Metrics

The research goal is to make full use of the cache resources in the network, reduce the redundancy in the EPC network cache, and improve the content difference rate. Therefore, for the system level, resource cost, cache hit rate, and caching routing hops reduction rate are selected as evaluation criteria, and the impact of the parameters of content popularity Zipf on these evaluation metrics is also considered.

To evaluate the performance of the prediction of SNDLPC model, we adopted three performance indexes: the root-mean-square error (RMSE), the mean absolute error (MAE), and the mean absolute percentage error (MAPE). These indexes are calculated as follows:

$$RMSE = \sqrt{\frac{1}{N}\sum_{i=1}^{n}(o_i - p_i)^2} \tag{2}$$

$$MAE = \frac{1}{N}\sum_{i=1}^{n}|o_i - p_i| \tag{3}$$

$$MAPE = \frac{1}{N}\sum_{i=1}^{n}\frac{|o_i - p_i|}{o_i} \tag{4}$$

where o_i denotes the observed number of content block being requested, p_i denotes the predicted number of content block being requested, and N denotes the number of evaluation samples.The optimal structure of our model was determined when the $MAPE$ was minimized.

4.3 SSAEs Architecture Structure

The SSAEs architecture structure parameter should be determined, including the dimension of the input layer, the number of hidden layers, and the number of hidden units in each hidden layer. For the input layer, we use the user request data collected from node in EPC in every k timeslot as the input; thus, the model could be built upon a monitoring network that considers temporal correlations. We compare the timeslot k from the set $2, 4, 6, 8, 10$; thus, the input dimensions vary from 400 to 2000. The optimal structure of our model was determined when the $MAPE$ was minimized.

The effect of timeslot is tested, as shown in Table 1. A large k would increase the dimension of the input layer from 400 to 2000 and provide a sufficient number of temporally correlated features, although it increases the training time. The prediction performance MAPE obviously decreased initially but failed to show improved performance after k = 6. The minim of MAPE is about 22.11%. If k is greater than 6, then additional latent unrelated inputs make it more difficult for the complicated architecture to learn a good representation. In the following experiments, the SNDLPC use the timeslot 6 with the hidden layers units [300 200 100] and input dimension of input layer set as 1200.

Table 1. Architecture structure for SSAEs.

Timeslot	Dimension of input layer	Hidden layers	Hidden layers units	MAPE (%)	MAE	RMSE
2	400	3	[300 200 100]	25.73	13.92	24.79
4	800	3	[300 200 100]	23.68	12.89	21.91
6	1200	3	[300 200 100]	22.11	13.95	20.24
8	1600	3	[300 200 100]	24.64	15.94	23.52
10	2000	4	[300 300 200 100]	26.32	16.28	25.73

4.4 Experimental Results

In this section, it is assumed that the EPC network is constructed by 100 virtual nodes and 1004 links. The other design parameters are as follows: the total number of users's request is set to 120000, the average content is 1MB, and the node cache unit is also a unit of 1MB. All the following results are averaged after 10 tests. The prediction and generalization capabilities of our SNDLPC are investigated. We compared it with some cache strategies without SDN supporting, such as Betw + LRU, Hash + LRU and Opportunistic. And also compared it with SDN support strategies, SDN + BPNN, SDN + SVM. The BPNN is the traditional neural network and attempts to learn features through hidden layers, and the SVM is a classic model for prediction. All models are trained and tested using the same data sets.

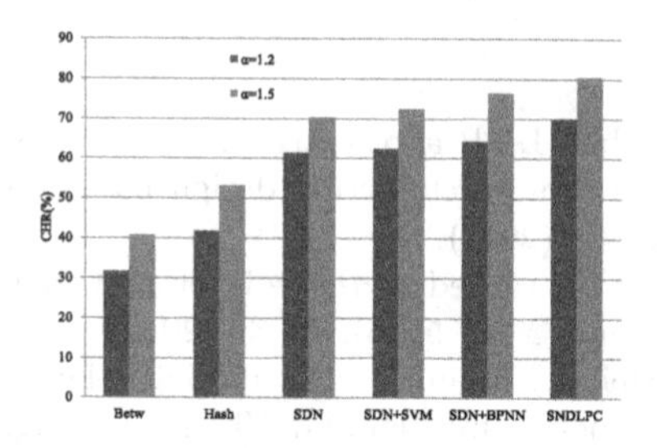

Fig. 2. Effect of content popularity.

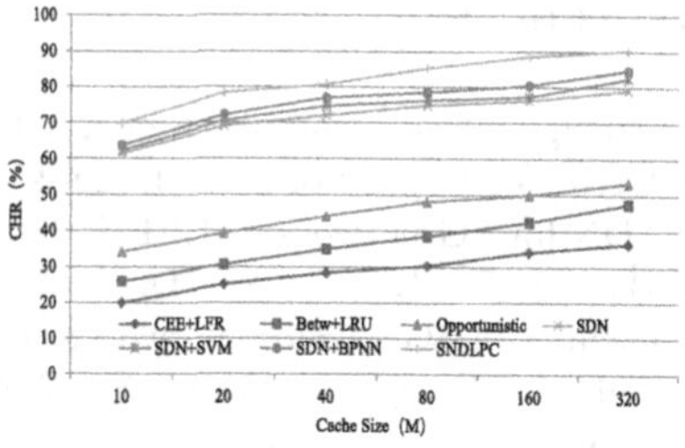

Fig. 3. Effect of cache size.

Figure 2 shows the effect of content popularity for CHR. With the increase of the value of alpha, the concentration and locality of the content request is strengthened, the probability and the hit rate of the popular caching resources are increasing, and the CHR of all the schemes has been improved accordingly. The SNDLPC achieves 80.56% and 69.83%, when alpha = 1.5 and alpha = 1.2 respectively, better than others.

Figure 3 shows the impact of cache space size on cache hit rate. With the cache size increasing, the cache hit rate also increases for all cache schemes. Because with the cache size increasing, there are more content packet can be cached, the following user requests have higher probability to send the cached content packet. As the cache space increased from 10M to 320M, the cache hit rate of SNDLPC is the best, increase from 69.8% to 90.2%.

5 Conclusions

In this paper, we have proposed a proactive caching strategy based on SSAE network in EPC of 5G. The distributed SSAE network is constructed, trained for prediction the content popularity. The SDN controller make the cache strategy based on the prediction. The experiments show that the SSAEs can be greatly improve the prediction accuracy, and then the proactive cache performance can be improved. In further, we will research the effect of sparse parameter of SSAE and the Zipf parameter for cache. Also we will research on proactive cache in heterogeneous network of 5G by deep learning.

Acknowledgment. This work was supported in part by the National Natural Science Foundation of China under Grant 61571141, Grant 61702120 and Grant 61672008, in part by Guangdong Science and technology development project under Grant 2017A090905023, in part by Guangdong Natural Science Foundation under Grant 2016A030311013, in part by the Excellent Young Teachers in Universities in Guangdong(Grant No. YQ2015105), in part by the Scientific and Technological Projects of Guangdong Province (2017A050501039), in part by Guangdong Provincial Application-oriented Technical Research and Development Special fund project (Grant 2016B010127006, Grant 2017B010125003).

References

1. Ameigeiras, P., Ramos-Munoz, J.J., Schumacher, L., Prados-Garzon, J., Navarro-Ortiz, J., Lopez-Soler, J.M.: Link-level access cloud architecture design based on SDN for 5G networks. IEEE Netw. **29**(2), 24–31 (2015)
2. Bastug, E., Bennis, M., Debbah, M.: Living on the edge: the role of proactive caching in 5G wireless networks. IEEE Commun. Mag. **52**(8), 82–89 (2014)
3. Cai, H., Zhang, Y., Wang, Y., Wang, X., Mei, J., Huang, Z.: Predicting relative popularity via an end-to-end multi-modality model. In: Zhai, G., Zhou, J., Yang, X. (eds.) IFTC 2017. CCIS, vol. 815, pp. 343–353. Springer, Singapore (2018). https://doi.org/10.1007/978-981-10-8108-8_32
4. Cisco visual: Cisco visual networking index: Forecast and methodology 2016–2021 (2017)
5. Han, J., Zhang, D., Hu, X., Guo, L., Ren, J., Wu, F.: Background prior-based salient object detection via deep reconstruction residual. IEEE Trans. Circ. Syst. Video Technol. **25**(8), 1309–1321 (2015)
6. Jia, Q., Xie, R., Huang, T., Liu, J., Liu, Y.: Efficient caching resource allocation for network slicing in 5G core network. IET Commun. **11**(18), 2792–2799 (2017)
7. Katsaros, K.V., Glykantzis, V., Petropoulos, G.: Cache peering in multi-tenant 5G networks. In: 2017 IFIP/IEEE Symposium on Integrated Network and Service Management (IM), pp. 1131–1134. IEEE (2017)

8. Liu, D., Chen, B., Yang, C., Molisch, A.F.: Caching at the wireless edge: design aspects, challenges, and future directions. IEEE Commun. Mag. **54**(9), 22–28 (2016)
9. Liu, Y., Point, J.C., Katsaros, K.V., Glykantzis, V., Siddiqui, M.S., Escalona, E.: SDN/NFV based caching solution for future mobile network (5G). In: 2017 European Conference on Networks and Communications (EuCNC), pp. 1–5. IEEE (2017)
10. Mijumbi, R., Serrat, J., Gorricho, J.L., Bouten, N., De Turck, F., Boutaba, R.: Network function virtualization: state-of-the-art and research challenges. IEEE Commun. Surv. Tutor. **18**(1), 236–262 (2016)
11. Nguyen, V.G., Brunstrom, A., Grinnemo, K.J., Taheri, J.: SDN/NFV-based mobile packet core network architectures: a survey. IEEE Commun. Surv. Tutor. **19**(3), 1567–1602 (2017)
12. Ren, S., et al.: Design and analysis of collaborative EPC and RAN caching for LTE mobile networks. Computer Networks **93**, 80–95 (2015)
13. Stokowiec, W., Trzciński, T., Wołk, K., Marasek, K., Rokita, P.: Shallow reading with deep learning: predicting popularity of online content using only its title. In: Kryszkiewicz, M., Appice, A., Ślęzak, D., Rybinski, H., Skowron, A., Raś, Z.W. (eds.) ISMIS 2017. LNCS (LNAI), vol. 10352, pp. 136–145. Springer, Cham (2017). https://doi.org/10.1007/978-3-319-60438-1_14
14. Suksomboon, K., et al.: PopCache: Cache more or less based on content popularity for information-centric networking. In: 2013 IEEE 38th Conference on Local Computer Networks (LCN), pp. 236–243. IEEE (2013)
15. Trzciński, T., Rokita, P.: Predicting popularity of online videos using support vector regression. IEEE Trans. Multimed. **19**(11), 2561–2570 (2017)
16. Wang, X., Chen, M., Taleb, T., Ksentini, A., Leung, V.: Cache in the air: exploiting content caching and delivery techniques for 5G systems. IEEE Commun. Mag. **52**(2), 131–139 (2014)
17. Wang, Z., Ren, J., Zhang, D., Sun, M., Jiang, J.: A deep-learning based feature hybrid framework for spatiotemporal saliency detection inside videos. Neurocomputing **287**, 68–83 (2018)
18. Zabalza, J., et al.: Novel segmented stacked autoencoder for effective dimensionality reduction and feature extraction in hyperspectral imaging. Neurocomputing **185**, 1–10 (2016)

Dynamic Hybrid Approaching for Robust Hand-Eye Calibration

Chen Meng[1,2], Wei Feng[1,2](✉), and Jinchang Ren[3]

[1] School of Computer Science and Technology, Tianjin University, Tianjin, China
{chmeng,wfeng}@tju.edu.cn
[2] Key Research Center for Surface Monitoring and Analysis of Cultural Relics, SACH, Beijing, China
[3] Department of Electronic and Electrical Engineering, University of Strathclyde, Glasgow, UK
jinchang.ren@strath.ac.uk

Abstract. The hand-eye calibration problem is to compute the relative pose between a robot platform (hand) and a camera (eye) mounted rigidly on the robot platform. To solve the problem, the motion pairs of the robot platform movement and the corresponding camera movement are collected and then use a linear algorithm or nonlinear minimization algorithm to find the optimal solution from the collected motion pairs. Because there are noises in the motion pairs, the previous method uses the motion pairs directly can't effectively reduce the impact of the noise. In this paper, we focus on how to ease the impact of the noises of the motion pairs. We use active vision approach to hybrid the robot platform movement and camera movement with different credibility and generate a series of special motion pairs, this can dynamically get a more accurate initial estimation of the relative pose between the robot platform and the camera. Then we use a recursive way to filter matching points and update the estimation of the relative pose, which can improve the robustness of our hand-eye calibration algorithm effectively. Both virtual and real experiments show the superiority of our approach over the previous methods.

Keywords: Hand-eye calibration · Active vision
Nonlinear minimization · Feature matching

1 Introduction

Hand-eye calibration plays an important role in computer vision and robotics applications such as: visual servo [9], 3D tracking and mapping [11], simultaneous localization and mapping (SLAM) [2]. It can also help to accelerate the convergence of camera relocalization [4,10,15] and improve the precision of fine-grained change detection task [5,18].

W. Feng—This work is supported by NSFC 61671325 and 61572354.

J. Ren et al. (Eds.): BICS 2018, LNAI 10989, pp. 748–758, 2018.
https://doi.org/10.1007/978-3-030-00563-4_73

A number of approaches have been proposed to solve the problem. Early works [16,17] calculate the rotation part $\mathbf{R}$ and translation part $\mathbf{t}$ of the relative pose $\mathbf{X}$ between robot platform (hand) and camera (eye) separately. The drawback of the separation method is that the estimation error of $\mathbf{R}$ will propagate to the estimation of $\mathbf{t}$. To eliminate the error propagation, simultaneously identify the $\mathbf{R}$ and $\mathbf{t}$ approaches are proposed, such as [1,7,8]. However, whether the separation approaches or the simultaneous approaches ignore the important fact that the magnitude of the estimation error of hand movements and eye movements are different. We should not treat them equally. Some approaches [6,14] use image measurements directly and do not need to care about the estimation error of the eye movements, but these method do not address the impact of the matching points error, which may cause these approaches to fail.

In this paper, we take the credibility of the movement estimation into consideration by instructing hand to perform a series of special movements. The rotation axis of the hand movements will approach to the rotation axis of the relative pose $\mathbf{X}$. This has two advantages: (1) The introduction of the credibility of the movement estimation helps to provide a more accurate initial estimation to $\mathbf{X}$ than previous method; (2) The dynamic process of approaching to the rotation axis of $\mathbf{X}$ will be more robust to outliers. After the initial estimation, the calculated $\mathbf{X}$ is used to filter the matching points based on the re-mapping error, and then minimize the objective function based on the re-mapping error will get a more accurate estimation of $\mathbf{X}$. This recursive way to filter matching points and update the estimation of $\mathbf{X}$ will effectively reduce the impact of the matching points error and improve the robustness of our hand-eye calibration algorithm.

2 Robust Hand-Eye Calibration

2.1 Problem Formulation

The rigid transformation can be denoted by a homogeneous matrix $\mathbf{T} = \begin{pmatrix} \mathbf{R} & \mathbf{t} \\ \mathbf{0}^{\mathrm{T}} & 1 \end{pmatrix}$, where the rotation part $\mathbf{R} \in \mathbf{SO}(3) \subseteq \mathbb{R}^{3\times3}$ and translation part $\mathbf{t} \in \mathbb{R}^{3\times3}$. The rotation part $\mathbf{R}$ can be expressed by axis-angle representation $\langle\theta, \mathbf{e}\rangle$, where unit vector $\mathbf{e}$ is the rotation axis and θ is the rotation magnitude about $\mathbf{e}$. We use $\mathbf{R} \cong \langle\theta, \mathbf{e}\rangle$ to indicate the equivalence of the two kinds of representations for the rotation part. Similarly, the rigid transformation can be denoted as $\mathbf{T} \cong \langle\mathbf{R}, \mathbf{t}\rangle$.

According to the notations above, we use $\mathbf{X} \cong \langle\mathbf{R}_{\mathrm{X}}, \mathbf{t}_{\mathrm{X}}\rangle$ denote the transformation of scene points from the hand coordinate system to the eye coordinate system. Let $\mathbf{B}^{(t)} \cong \langle\mathbf{R}_{\mathrm{B}}^{(t)}, \mathbf{t}_{\mathrm{B}}^{(t)}\rangle, t = 1, 2, ...n$ be the t-th hand relative movement from the position i to the position $(i+1)$. Suppose the camera is rigidly mounted on the robot platform, so the movements of hand will give rise to a series of eye relative movements denoted by $\mathbf{A}^{(t)} \cong \langle\mathbf{R}_{\mathrm{A}}^{(t)}, \mathbf{t}_{\mathrm{A}}^{(t)}\rangle$. From [17], we have the well-known equation

$$\mathbf{A}^{(t)}\mathbf{X} = \mathbf{X}\mathbf{B}^{(t)} \tag{1}$$

and the Eq. (1) can be decomposed to

$$\mathbf{R}_{\mathrm{A}}^{(t)}\mathbf{R}_{\mathrm{X}} = \mathbf{R}_{\mathrm{X}}\mathbf{R}_{\mathrm{B}}^{(t)} \tag{2}$$

$$\mathbf{R}_{\mathrm{A}}^{(t)}\mathbf{t}_{\mathrm{x}} + \mathbf{t}_{\mathrm{A}}^{(t)} = \mathbf{R}_{\mathrm{X}}\mathbf{t}_{\mathrm{B}}^{(t)} + \mathbf{t}_{\mathrm{X}} \tag{3}$$

Further, in the t-th movement of camera, we set the camera in position i as the t-th reference camera and the camera in position $(i+1)$ as the t-th current camera. $\mathbf{P}^j$ denotes the j-th matching point's between the reference image and current image, $j = 1, 2, ..., m$. We use $\mathbf{P}_{ref}^{tj}$ indicate the point $\mathbf{P}^j$ in the t-th reference camera coordinate system and $\mathbf{P}_{cur}^{tj}$ indicate the point $\mathbf{P}^j$ in the t-th current camera coordinate system. In the absence of noise and matching errors, we know that $\mathbf{A}^{(t)}\mathbf{P}_{cur}^{tj} - \mathbf{P}_{ref}^{tj} = 0$. By substituting $\mathbf{A}^{(t)} = \mathbf{X}\mathbf{B}^{(t)}\mathbf{X}^{-1}$, we get

$$\mathbf{X}\mathbf{B}^{(t)}\mathbf{X}^{-1}\mathbf{P}_{cur}^{tj} - \mathbf{P}_{ref}^{tj} = 0 \tag{4}$$

When noise present, we can convert the hand-eye calibration to an optimization problem:

$$\mathbf{X}^* = \arg\min_{\mathbf{X}} \sum_{t=1}^{n}\sum_{j=1}^{m} \|\mathbf{X}\mathbf{B}^{(t)}\mathbf{X}^{-1}\mathbf{P}_{cur}^{tj} - \mathbf{P}_{ref}^{tj}\|_2, \tag{5}$$

where $\mathbf{X}^*$ denotes the optimal solution of the hand-eye calibration. We will use a dynamic hybrid approaching to get an initial estimation of $\mathbf{X}$ based on Eqs. (2) and (3), then use a recursive method to filter the matching points and update the $\mathbf{X}$ based on the optimization problem depicted by Eq. (5).

2.2 Robust and Fast Estimation of $\mathbf{e}_{\mathrm{X}}$

Hybrid Approaching. From [17], we know that Eq. (2) is equivalent to Eq. (6). The equation $\mathbf{e}_{\mathrm{A}}^{(t)} = \mathbf{R}_{\mathrm{X}}\mathbf{e}_{\mathrm{B}}^{(t)}$ means that the $\mathbf{e}_{\mathrm{B}}$ rotates θ_{X} around $\mathbf{e}_{\mathrm{A}}$. Thus we can design a novel strategy by guiding the rotation axis of $\mathbf{R}_{\mathrm{B}}^{(t)}$ approaching to the rotation axis of $\mathbf{R}_{\mathrm{X}}$ via iteratively adjustments using Eq. (7). The λ in Eq. (7) indicates the credibility of the estimation of $\mathbf{A}^{(t)}$ and $\mathbf{A}^{(t)}$. From Fig. 1, we can see that if there exist noise in $\mathbf{A}^{(t)}$ and $\mathbf{B}^{(t)}$, to approach the $\mathbf{e}_{\mathrm{B}}^{(t)}$ to $\mathbf{e}_{\mathrm{X}}$, point $\mathbf{C}$ in Fig. 1(a) should be inside the circle, which implies that the more accurate the estimation of $\mathbf{B}^{(t)}$, the smaller the value of λ should be. Figure 1(b) shows the process of $\mathbf{e}_{\mathrm{B}}$ approaching to $\mathbf{e}_{\mathrm{X}}$. The following theorem theoretically guarantees the convergence of the dynamic hybrid approaching method.

$$\begin{cases} \theta_{\mathrm{A}} = \theta_{\mathrm{B}} \\ \mathbf{e}_{\mathrm{A}}^{(t)} = \mathbf{R}_{\mathrm{X}}\mathbf{e}_{\mathrm{B}}^{(t)} \end{cases} \tag{6}$$

$$\mathbf{e}_{\mathbf{X}}^{(t+1)} = \frac{\lambda(\mathbf{e}_{\mathrm{A}}^{(t)} - \mathbf{e}_{\mathrm{B}}^{(t)}) + \mathbf{e}_{\mathrm{B}}^{(t)}}{\|\lambda(\mathbf{e}_{\mathrm{A}}^{(t)} - \mathbf{e}_{\mathrm{B}}^{(t)}) + \mathbf{e}_{\mathrm{B}}^{(t)}\|}, \lambda \in (0,1) \tag{7}$$

Theorem 1. *By the rotation axis approaching strategy defined by Eq. (7),* $\lim_{t\to+\infty}\alpha^{(t)}=0$. $\alpha^{(t)}$ *is the angle between* $\mathbf{e}_{\mathrm{B}}^{(t)}$ *and* $\mathbf{e}_{\mathrm{X}}^{(t)}$ *and* $\alpha^{(t)}\in(0,\frac{\pi}{2})$.

Proof. From Eq. (6), According to the geometric relationship of $\mathbf{e}_{\mathrm{B}}^{(t)}$, θ_{X}, $\alpha^{(t)}$ and λ, we have

$$tan(\alpha^{(t+1)})=tan(\alpha^{(0)})(\sqrt{cos^2\frac{\theta_{\mathrm{X}}}{2}+((1-2\lambda)sin(\frac{\theta_{\mathrm{X}}}{2}))^2})^{(t+1)},\lambda\in(0,1). \quad (8)$$

Because the $\lambda\in(0,1)$ and $\alpha^{(t)}\in(0,\frac{\pi}{2})$, we have $cos^2\frac{\theta_{\mathrm{X}}}{2}+((1-2\lambda)sin(\frac{\theta_{\mathrm{X}}}{2}))^2<1$. We can get the conclusion that $\lim_{t\to+\infty}\alpha^{(t)}=0$.

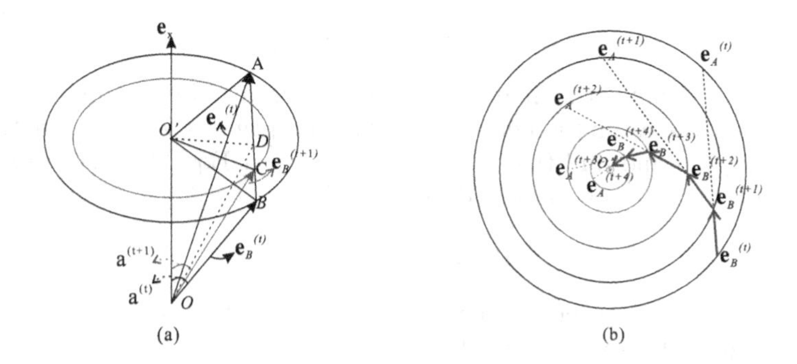

Fig. 1. (a) Indicate the process of $\mathbf{e}_{\mathrm{B}}^{(t)}$ approaching to $\mathbf{e}_{\mathrm{B}}^{(t+1)}$. (b) A schematic diagram of $\mathbf{e}_{\mathrm{B}}^{(t)}$ updating trajectory.

Acceleration by Relative Pose Amplification. To accelerate the approaching speed, we study the Eq. (8) and get the Theorem 2.

Theorem 2. *By the rotation axis approaching strategy defined by Eq. (7), the greater the value of* θ_{X}*, the faster the* $\mathbf{e}_{\mathrm{X}}^{(t)}$ *approach to* $\mathbf{e}_{\mathrm{X}}$.

Proof. From Eq. (8), we have the first derivative of $\tan(\alpha^{(t+1)})$:

$$\begin{aligned}&tan(\alpha^{(t+1)})=\tfrac{tan(\alpha^{(0)})(t+1)}{2}\Delta_{\theta_{\mathrm{X}}},\\&\Delta_{\theta_{\mathrm{X}}}=(\cos^2\tfrac{\theta_{\mathrm{X}}}{2}+((1-2\lambda)\sin(\tfrac{\theta_{\mathrm{X}}}{2}))^2)^{\frac{(t-1)}{2}}(4\lambda(\lambda-1)\sin\tfrac{\theta_{\mathrm{X}}}{2}),\\&\lambda\in(0,1).\end{aligned} \quad (9)$$

Because $\lambda-1<0$, $\theta_{\mathrm{X}}\in[0,\pi]$, $\sin\frac{\theta_{\mathrm{X}}}{2}$, we have $(tan(\alpha^{(t+1)}))'<0$ and the $\tan(\alpha^{(t+1)})$ is a decreasing function. Thus we can get the conclusion that the greater the value of θ_{X}, the faster the $\mathbf{e}_{\mathrm{X}}^{(t)}$ approach to $\mathbf{e}_{\mathrm{X}}$.

Therefore, we set a virtual hand, its relative motion is indicated by $\tilde{\mathbf{B}}$ and the relative pose between the relative hand and the eye is $\tilde{\mathbf{X}}$, i.e.,$\mathbf{A}^{(t)}\tilde{\mathbf{X}} = \tilde{\mathbf{X}}\tilde{\mathbf{B}}^{(t)}$, the $\tilde{\theta}_{\mathrm{X}}$ of $\tilde{\mathbf{X}}$ is much larger than θ_{X}. We use $\mathbf{X}_{\delta}$ denote the relative pose between the real hand and virtual hand, i.e., $\mathbf{B}^{(t)} = \mathbf{X}_{\delta}\tilde{\mathbf{B}}\mathbf{X}_{\delta}^{-1}$, by substituting the relative pose to Eq. (1), we have $\mathbf{A}^{(t)}\mathbf{X}\mathbf{X}_{\delta} = \mathbf{X}\mathbf{X}_{\delta}\tilde{\mathbf{B}}^{(t)}$ and $\tilde{\mathbf{X}} = \mathbf{X}\mathbf{X}_{\delta}$. From Theorem (2), we know that the relative pose amplification will help accelerate the approaching speed.

2.3 Estimation of θ_{X} and $\mathbf{t}_{\mathrm{X}}$

After we get the estimation of $\mathbf{e}_{\mathrm{X}}$, we will guide the hand to perform a special movement, that the rotation axis of the movement is perpendicular to the $\mathbf{e}_{\mathrm{X}}$, this gives rise to an eye movement. From Eq. (6) we know that θ_{X} is equal to the angle between $\mathbf{e}_{\mathrm{B}}$ and $\mathbf{e}_{\mathrm{A}}$. The Eq. (9) is the solution to the θ_{X}.

$$\theta_{\mathrm{X}} = \arccos\langle \mathbf{e}_{\mathrm{B}}, \mathbf{e}_{\mathrm{A}} \rangle, \tag{10}$$

where $\langle \mathbf{e}_{\mathrm{B}}, \mathbf{e}_{\mathrm{A}} \rangle$ denotes the inner product of the vector of $\mathbf{e}_{\mathrm{B}}$ and $\mathbf{e}_{\mathrm{A}}$.

To prevent the estimation error of rotation propagates to the estimation, we study the Eq. (2) and find that if $\mathbf{t}_{\mathrm{B}} = 0$, we can get Eq. (11), that implies the estimation error propagation will disappeared.

$$\mathbf{R}_{\mathrm{A}}^{(t)}\mathbf{t}_{\mathrm{x}} + \mathbf{t}_{\mathrm{A}}^{(t)} = \mathbf{t}_{\mathrm{X}}, \tag{11}$$

Therefore, we will instruct the hand to move without translation and use the same method in [17] to calculate the $\mathbf{t}_{\mathrm{X}}$.

2.4 Bundle Optimization

The dynamic hybrid approaching method will provide an initial value $\mathbf{X}^{(0)}$ that very close to the ground truth of $\mathbf{X}$. Thus we can use the $\mathbf{X}^{(0)}$ to filter the matching points by Eq. (12).

$$\|\mathbf{X}\mathbf{B}^{(t)}\mathbf{X}^{-1}\mathbf{P}_{\mathrm{cur}}^{tj} - \mathbf{P}_{\mathrm{ref}}^{tj}\|_2 < \varepsilon, \tag{12}$$

where the ε is a threshold of the re-mapping error. We only use the filtered matching points as the parameters of the objective function Eq. (5). We rewrite Eq. (5) here:

$$\mathbf{X}^* = \arg\min_{\mathbf{X}} \sum_{t=1}^{n}\sum_{j=1}^{m} \|\mathbf{X}\mathbf{B}^{(t)}\mathbf{X}^{-1}\mathbf{P}_{\mathrm{cur}}^{tj} - \mathbf{P}_{\mathrm{ref}}^{tj}\|_2. \tag{13}$$

This is a nonlinear minimization problem and we adopt Gauss-Newton method to solve it. Because $\mathbf{X} \in \mathbf{SE}(3), \mathbf{B} \in \mathbf{SE}(3)$, we calculate the Newton direction and update $\mathbf{X}^{(t)}$ in $\mathbf{se}(3)$. The optimal solution provides a more accurate estimation of $\mathbf{X}$ and we can use it to filter more accurate matching points. The recursive approach can improve the accuracy of the estimation of $\mathbf{X}$ and robustness of our algorithm.

2.5 The Algorithm and Discussion

This section will show the pseudocode of our algorithms and discuss the detail of the algorithm to make it more understandable.

To decrease the approaching steps, we will use the previous method such as [1,17] to provide the initial estimation of the relative pose and we denote the rotation part of the estimation by $\mathbf{R}_{\mathrm{X}}^{(0)} \cong \langle \mathbf{e}_{\mathrm{X}}^{(0)}, \theta_{\mathrm{X}}^{(0)} \rangle$. These methods should be fast and do not need many motion pairs. According to Theorem (2), we will set $\theta_\delta = \pi - \theta_{\mathrm{X}}^{(0)}$ and $\mathbf{e}_\delta = \mathbf{e}_{\mathrm{X}}^{(0)}$. The credibility of the estimation of $\mathbf{A}^{(t)}$ and $\mathbf{B}^{(t)}$ need not to be very accurate. We simply verify which one is more accurate and give a corresponding λ is enough. This make our algorithm very easy to use. The estimation of θ_{X} and $\mathbf{t}_{\mathrm{X}}$ is very simple and similar to [17], so we do not discuss it in detail here. Note that we will instruct the hand to do pure rotation action in Algorithm (1) to prevent the estimation error of rotation propagates to the estimation of translation.

Algorithm 1. Robust and fast estimation of $\mathbf{e}_{\mathrm{X}}$

Input: Stopping threshold ϵ_{min}, $\mathbf{R}_{\mathrm{X}}^{(0)}$, $\mathbf{R}_\delta$, λ
Output: $\mathbf{e}_{\mathrm{X}}^{(t)}$

1 Initialization: initialize platform to zero position, initial angle $\epsilon = 2\pi$, $t = 0$;
2 Set $\tilde{\mathbf{R}}_{\mathrm{X}}^{(0)} = \mathbf{R}_{\mathrm{X}}^{(0)} \mathbf{R}_\delta$, $\mathbf{X}_\delta \cong \langle \mathbf{R}_\delta, 0 \rangle$;
3 **while** $\epsilon > \epsilon_{min}$ **do**
4   Capture current image $\mathbf{I}_{\mathbf{ref}}^{(t)}$;
5   Set $\tilde{\mathbf{R}}_{\mathrm{B}}^{(t)} = \tilde{\mathbf{R}}_{\mathrm{X}}^{(t)}$, $\tilde{\mathbf{B}}^{(t)} \cong \langle \tilde{\mathbf{R}}_{\mathrm{B}}^{(t)}, 0 \rangle$, move robot platform by $\mathbf{B}^{(t)} = \mathbf{X}_\delta \tilde{\mathbf{B}}^{(t)} \mathbf{X}_\delta^{-1}$;
6   Capture current image $\mathbf{I}_{\mathbf{cur}}^{(t)}$ and calculate the relative pose of camera $\mathbf{R}_{\mathrm{A}}^{(t)} \cong \langle \mathbf{e}_{\mathrm{A}}^{(t)}, \theta_{\mathrm{A}}^{(t)} \rangle$;
7   Calculate $\tilde{\mathbf{e}}_{\mathrm{X}}^{(t+1)}$ by Eq. (7) ;
8   $\tilde{\mathbf{R}}_{\mathrm{X}}^{(t+1)} \cong \langle \tilde{\mathbf{e}}_{\mathrm{X}}^{(t+1)}, \tilde{\theta}_{\mathrm{X}}^{(0)} \rangle$, $\epsilon = \arccos \frac{\langle \mathbf{e}_{\mathrm{B}}^{(t)}, \mathbf{e}_{\mathrm{A}}^{(t)} \rangle}{\|\tilde{\mathbf{e}}_{\mathrm{B}}^{(t)}\| \|\tilde{\mathbf{e}}_{\mathrm{A}}^{(t)}\|}$;
9   Retrun to the zero position;
10   $t++$;
11 $\mathbf{R}_{\mathrm{X}}^{(t)} = \tilde{\mathbf{R}}_{\mathrm{X}}^{(t)} \mathbf{R}_\delta$, $\mathbf{R}_{\mathrm{X}}^{(t)} \cong \langle \mathbf{e}_{\mathrm{X}}^{(t)}, \theta_{\mathrm{X}}^{(0)} \rangle$;
12 return $\mathbf{e}_{\mathrm{X}}^{(t)}$.

3 Experimental Results

3.1 Setup

Baselines. We select the following methods as baselines: the Tsai-Lenz method (T89) [17], the dual-quaternion method (D99) [1] and the convex LMI relaxations method (Hec14) [7]. Our dynamic approaching method is represented by "DHA"

Algorithm 2. Bundle Optimization

Input: $\mathbf{X}^{(00)}$, the set of hand motions $\{\mathbf{B}^{(t)}\}$, matching points set $\{\mathbf{P}_{ref}^{(tj)}, \mathbf{P}_{cur}^{(tj)}\}$

Output: $\mathbf{X}^{(kn)}$

1 Initialization: $k = 0$, threshold for filter mathing points ε;
2 **while** $k < k_{max}$ **do**
3 Select mathing points by Eq. (12);
4 Calculate the number of matching points $\eta(k)$;
5 **if** $k > 2$ **then**
6 **if** $\eta(k) = \eta(k-1) = \eta(k-2)$ **then**
7 break;
8 $n = 0$;
9 **while** $n < n_{max}$ **do**
10 Map $\mathbf{X}^{(kn)}$ to $\xi^{(kn)} \in \mathbf{se}(3)$;
11 Calculate the Newton direction of Eq. (13) in $\mathbf{se}(3)$, which is indicated by $g^{(kn)}$;
12 $\xi^{(k(n+1))} = \xi^{(k(n))} - g^{(kn)}$;
13 Map $\xi^{(k(n+1))}$ to $\mathbf{X}^{(k(n+1))}$;
14 $n++$;
15 $k++$;
16 return $\mathbf{X}^{(kn)}$.

and the dynamic approaching method with bundle optimization is represented by "DHAbo". We compare these methods using both virtual and real-world environments. In the real-world experiments, we use a depth camera as the eye and the camera pose were recovered by EPnP algorithm. The approaches "T89", "D99" and "Hec14" use the same motion pair sets to solve the hand-eye calibration problem.

Criteria. To evaluate the accuracy and robustness of the above methods in multiple perspectives, we consider the fellowing criteria measures, namely, $\mathbf{F}_{\text{norm}}$ error, rotation angle error, rotation axis error, translation error and average feature-point displacement (AFD) [4].

The $\mathbf{F}_{\text{norm}}$ error corresponds to the agreement between the result of hand-eye calibration $\mathbf{X}$ and the ground truth of the transformation matrices,

$$\mathrm{F}_{\text{norm}} = \left\| \mathbf{X} - \mathbf{X}^{(t)} \right\|_2. \tag{14}$$

The rotation angle error is the absolute value of the difference between $\theta_{\mathrm{X}}^{(t)}$ and the ground truth θ_{X}. The rotation axis error is the Euclidean norm of the rotation axis for $\mathbf{R}_{\mathrm{X}}^{(t)}$ and $\mathbf{R}_{\mathrm{X}}$. The translation error is the relative errors in translation $\frac{\left\|\mathbf{t}_{\mathrm{X}}^{(t)} - \mathbf{t}_{\mathrm{X}}\right\|_2}{\|\mathbf{t}_{\mathrm{X}}\|_2}$.

In real-world environments, we can not get the ground truth of $\mathbf{X}$, so we use AFD to evaluate the accurate of hand-eye calibration. AFD measures the camera relocalization accuracy:

$$\text{AFD}(\mathbf{O}_{\text{ref}}, \mathbf{O}_{\text{cur}}) = \frac{1}{n}\sum_{i=1}^{n} \|\mathbf{O}_{\text{ref}} - \mathbf{O}_{\text{cur}}\|_2, \tag{15}$$

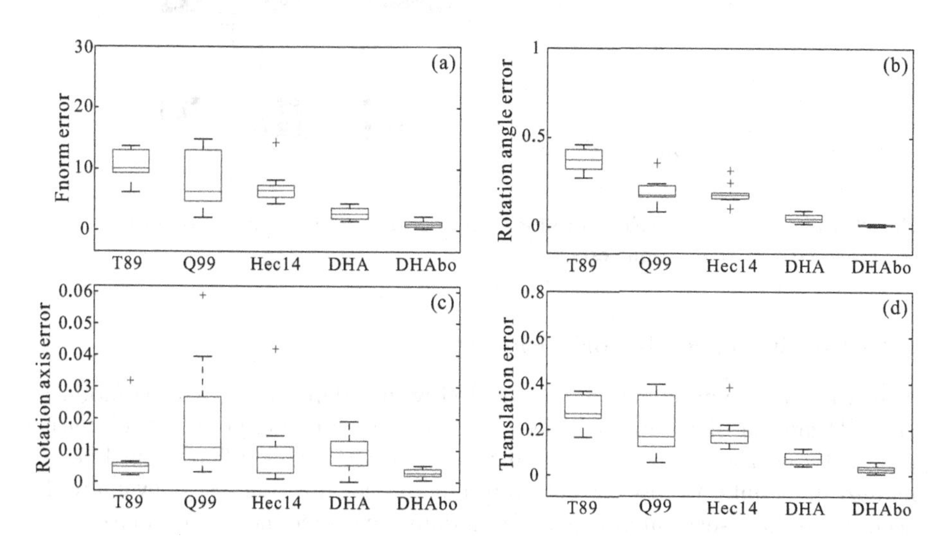

Fig. 2. Results in virtual environments. (a) The $\mathbf{F}_{\text{norm}}$ error. (b) The rotation angle error. (c) The rotation axis error. (d) The translation error. The central mark indicates the median, and the bottom and top edges of the box indicate the 25th and 75th percentiles, respectively. The outliers are plotted individually using the + symbol.

where n is the number of the matches and $\mathbf{O}_{\text{ref}}$ is the matched feature-point coordinates in reference image and $\mathbf{O}_{\text{cur}}$ is the matched feature-point coordinates in current image.

3.2 Results in Virtual Environment

A virtual environment based on Open MVG can provide motion pairs and corresponding images for the experiment that is very close to the real scene. 10 monitoring points, 3 random ground truth of $\mathbf{X}$ are set up for tests. We will provide 30 motion pairs for every monitoring point and every $\mathbf{X}$. This is the input of the approaches "T89", "D99" and "Hec14". Note that our algorithm is a dynamic approach, so we cannot use the same motion pairs sets, but we guarantee the monitoring points used are the same. The camera movements $\mathbf{A}^{(t)}$ are calculated by EPnP algorithm. In the virtual environment we do not add noise to the robot platform movements $\mathbf{B}^{(t)}$, so the value of λ is set 0.1. The average errors of results for the experiments are shown in Fig. 2, from which we can observe the superior performance of our algorithm.

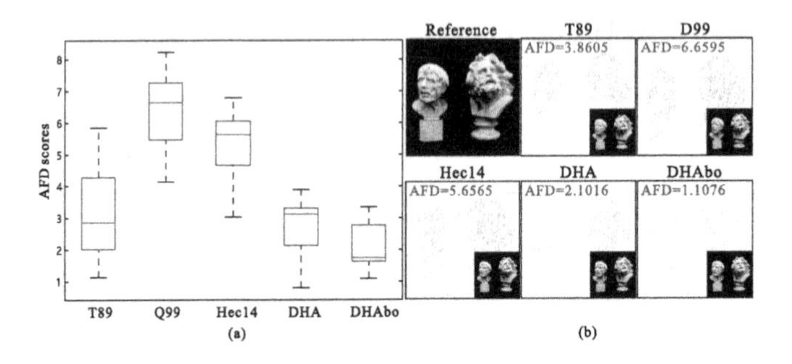

Fig. 3. (a) The average AFD score for each approach. (b) Visualization of the results of an one-step relocalization tests.

3.3 Results on Real-World Platform

The real-world experiments are conducted with a depth camera ZED mounted on a 6D motion platform. We select 3 different monitoring points. The relative pose between the camera and the 6D motion platform is different in different monitoring points. We use the one-step camera relocalization test to evaluate the accuracy of hand-eye calibration. We randomly instruct the motion platform to move 30 times and the platform movements $\mathbf{B}^{(t)}$ can be read from the motion system. The same to virtual experiments, camera motions $\mathbf{A}^{(t)}$ can be calculated by EPnP algorithm. Considering the noise level of $\mathbf{B}^{(t)}$ is lower than the noise level of $\mathbf{A}^{(t)}$, we set $\lambda = 0.3$.

After hand-eye calibration has been done by all the methods above, we test the accuracy of the estimation results of these methods by the one-step relocalization tests. The camera takes a reference image in position 1, and then we instruct the 6D motion platform to move to position 2 and grab another image. From the two image we can calculate the movements of the camera by EPnP algorithm and generate motion instruction by $\mathbf{B} = (\mathbf{X}^{-1}\mathbf{A}\mathbf{X})^{-1}$. The platform will drive the camera back to position 1 and we can get the current image. The test is repeated 10 times for every estimation result of the hand-eye calibration approaches. We take the average value of the 10 times one-step relocalization tests results as our criteria for assessing the effectiveness of the method. Note that the camera's pose in position 1 and position 2 is guaranteed same by camera relocalization strategy [4] in each one-step relocalization test. The average AFD score of all the one-step relocalization tests for each approach is shown in Fig. 3(a), which shows the effectiveness of our approaches. We use a sparse field of feature-point displacement vectors, which is called feature-point displacement flow (FDF) to visualize the results of an one-step relocalization test, which is shown in Fig. 3(b).

4 Conclusion

In this paper, we have proposed a dynamic hybrid approaching method for hand-eye calibration. The method uses a simple strategy to take the credibility of the movement estimation into consideration and the dynamic approaching process can be robust to the outliers. Furthermore, we use the estimation result of hand-eye calibration to filter matching points, which in return will help to improve the accuracy of hand-eye calibration. Virtual and real-world experiments both validate the accuracy and robustness of our approach. In the future we plan to unify the dynamic hybrid approaching algorithm and nonlinear minimization algorithm to get a faster, simpler and more robustness approach. Besides we want to utilize image information by some approaches such as [3,12,13] to provide more powerful restrictions to help improve the accuracy and robustness of hand-eye calibration.

References

1. Daniilidis, K.: Hand-eye calibration using dual quaternions. Int. J. Robot. Res. **18**(3), 286–298 (1999)
2. Davison, A.J.: Real-time simultaneous localisation and mapping with a single camera. In: ICCV, p. 1403 (2003)
3. Feng, W., Jia, J.Y., Liu, Z.Q.: Self-validated labeling of markov random fields for image segmentation. IEEE Trans. Pattern Anal. Mach. Intell. **32**(10), 1871–1887 (2010)
4. Feng, W., Tian, F.P., Zhang, Q., Zhang, N., Sun, J.: 6D dynamic camera relocalization from single reference image. In: CVPR (2016)
5. Feng, W., Tian, F.P., Zhang, Q., Zhang, N., Wan, L., Sun, J.Z.: Fine-grained change detection of misaligned scenes with varied illuminations. In: ICCV (2015)
6. Heller, J., Havlena, M., Pajdla, T.: A branch-and-bound algorithm for globally optimal hand-eye calibration. In: CVPR (2012)
7. Heller, J., Henrion, D., Pajdla, T.: Hand-eye and robot-world calibration by global polynomial optimization. In: ICRA (2014)
8. Horaud, R., Dornaika, F.: Hand-eye calibration. Int. J. Robot. Res. **14**(3), 195–210 (1995)
9. Hutchinson, S., Hager, G.D., Corke, P.I.: A tutorial on visual servo control. IEEE Trans. Robot. Autom. **12**(5), 651–670 (1996)
10. Miao, D., Tian, F.P., Feng, W.: Active camera relocalization with RGBD camera from a single 2D image. In: ICASSP (2018)
11. Newcombe, R.A., Lovegrove, S.J., Davison, A.J.: DTAM: dense tracking and mapping in real-time. In: ICCV (2011)
12. Ren, J.C., Jiang, J.M., Vlachos, T.: High-accuracy sub-pixel motion estimation from noisy images in fourier domain. IEEE Trans. Image Process. **19**(5), 1379–1384 (2010)
13. Ren, J.C., Vlachos, T., Zhang, Y., Zheng, J.B., Jiang, J.M.: Gradient-based subspace phase correlation for fast and effective image alignment. J. Vis. Commun. Image Represent. **25**(7), 1558–1565 (2014)
14. Seo, Y., Choi, Y.J., Lee, S.W.: A branch-and-bound algorithm for globally optimal calibration of a camera-and-rotation-sensor system. In: ICCV (2009)

15. Shi, Y.B., Tian, F.P., Miao, D., Feng, W.: Fast and reliable computational rephotography on mobile device. In: ICME (2018)
16. Shiu, Y.C., Ahmad, S.: Calibration of wrist-mounted robotic sensors by solving homogeneous transform equations of the form AX = XB. IEEE Trans. Robot. Autom. **5**(1), 16–29 (1989)
17. Tsai, R., Lenz, R.: A new technique for fully autonomous and efficient 3D robotics hand/eye calibration. IEEE Trans. Robot. Autom. **5**(3), 345–358 (1989)
18. Zhang, Q., Feng, W., Wan, L., Tian, F.P., Tan, P.: Active recurrence of lighting condition for fine-grained change detection. In: IJCAI (2018)

Statistical Analysis Driven Optimized Deep Learning System for Intrusion Detection

Cosimo Ieracitano[1(✉)], Ahsan Adeel[2], Mandar Gogate[2], Kia Dashtipour[2], Francesco Carlo Morabito[1], Hadi Larijani[3], Ali Raza[4], and Amir Hussain[2]

[1] DICEAM Department, University Mediterranea of Reggio Calabria, 89124 Reggio Calabria, Italy
cosimo.ieracitano@unirc.it
[2] Department of Computing Science and Mathematics, Faculty of Natural Sciences, University of Stirling, Stirling FK9 4LA, UK
[3] Department of Communication, Network and Electronic Engineering, Glasgow Caledonian University, Glasgow G4 0BA, UK
[4] Department of Networks and Security Rochester, Institute of Applied Technology, Dubai, United Arab Emirates

Abstract. Attackers have developed ever more sophisticated and intelligent ways to hack information and communication technology (ICT) systems. The extent of damage an individual hacker can carry out upon infiltrating a system is well understood. A potentially catastrophic scenario can be envisaged where a nation-state intercepting encrypted financial data gets hacked. Thus, intelligent cybersecurity systems have become inevitably important for improved protection against malicious threats. However, as malware attacks continue to dramatically increase in volume and complexity, it has become ever more challenging for traditional analytic tools to detect and mitigate threat. Furthermore, a huge amount of data produced by large networks have made the recognition task even more complicated and challenging. In this work, we propose an innovative statistical analysis driven optimized deep learning system for intrusion detection. The proposed intrusion detection system (IDS) extracts optimized and more correlated features using big data visualization and statistical analysis methods, followed by a deep autoencoder (AE) for potential threat detection. Specifically, a preprocessing module eliminates the outliers and converts categorical variables into one-hot-encoded vectors. The feature extraction module discards features with null values grater than 80% and selects the most significant features as input to the deep autoencoder model trained in a greedy-wise manner. The NSL-KDD dataset (an improved version of the original KDD dataset) from the Canadian Institute for Cybersecurity is used as a benchmark to evaluate the feasibility and effectiveness of the proposed architecture. Simulation results demonstrate the potential of our proposed IDS system for improving intrusion detection as compared to existing state-of-the-art methods.

J. Ren et al. (Eds.): BICS 2018, LNAI 10989, pp. 759–769, 2018.
https://doi.org/10.1007/978-3-030-00563-4_74

Keywords: Cybersecurity · Deep learning · Auroencoder
NSL-KDD dataset

1 Introduction

The heterogeneity of data in modern networks and variety of new protocols have made the intrusion detection ever more complex and challenging. In this context, there is a great deal of interest in developing intelligent, robust and efficient Intrusion Detection Systems (IDS) capable of identifying the potential or unforeseen threat and consequently denying access to the system. In the literature, traditional machine learning algorithms have been widely employed to develop IDS [19]. However, these techniques are based on handcrafted features by expert users and remain deficient to handle high-dimensional volume of training data. Deep learning (DL) is an advanced machine learning technique that addresses the limitations of shallow machine learning algorithms [11] by learning feature representation at varying level of granularity directly from raw input data through a deep hierarchical structure. Since DL has shown to achieve human-level performances in several real-world applications (i.e. health care [7,13], sentiment analysis [4,5], saliency detection [20,21]) recently, researchers have proposed several novel DL driven cybersecurity algorithms [14]. DL driven solutions are capable of efficiently analyzing big data and identifying temporal structures in long complex sequences in real-time.

In this paper, an innovative Statistical Analysis Driven Optimized DL System for Intrusion Detection is proposed. Specifically, a statistical-driven deep autoencoder (AE) is developed to detect normal and abnormal traffic patterns. The proposed framework has been evaluated using the recent NSL-KDD dataset (updated version of the previous KDD Cup 99 (KDD99) dataset [17]). The proposed framework constitutes three main modules as shown in Fig. 1: *data preprocessing*, *feature extraction*, and *classification*. *Data preprocessing* discards the outliers and converts categorical variables into one-hot-encoded vectors. *Feature extraction* selects the most correlated features and discards features with null values grater than 80%; For *classification*, a deep autoencoder and a shallow multilayer perceptron (MLP) classifier are used to classify different categories of the NSL-KDD dataset (Normal, DoS, R2L, Probe). The deep AE and shallow MLP classifiers are compared with four recent models which have been on NSL-KDD dataset. Experimental results (Table 5) showed that the deep AE classifier outperformed all other approaches and achieved accuracy up to 87%.

The remainder of this paper is organized as follows. Section 2, illustrates previous approaches, especially based on DL architectures trained with NSL-KDD dataset. Section 3 describes the proposed methodology, including NSL-KDD dataset description, data preprocessing, feature extraction and classification. Section 4 discusses the experimental results. Finally, Sect. 5 concludes the paper.

2 Related Work

The KDD99 and NSL-KDD datasets have been widely employed as benchmarks to assess the performance and effectiveness of different intrusion detection models. Alrawashdeh et al. [3] developed a deep belief network (DBN) based on Restricted Boltzmann Machine (RBM) modules, followed by a multi-class softmax layer. The model was tested on 10% of the KDD99 test dataset and achieved a detection accuracy up to 97.9% with a false alarm rate of 2.47%. Tang et al. [16] proposed a deep learning approach for flow-based anomaly detection in an Software Defined Networking (SDN) environment. The authors developed a Deep Neural Network (DNN) with 3 hidden layers, trained on the NSL-KDD dataset to perform only binary classification (normal, anomaly) using six basic features. However, the reported accuracy was 75.75%. Kim et al. [10] developed a different DNN architecture (with 4 hidden layers and 100 hidden units) and optimized trained using adam optimization algorithm. However, the performance was measured using the KDD99 dataset. Javaid et al. [9] proposed a self-taught learning (STL) approach based on sparse autoencoders for anomaly detection. The NSL-KDD dataset was employed as benchmark to quantify the performance. In [22] proposed a Recurrent Neural Network (RNN) for anomaly detection using the same benchmark, claiming accuracies of 83.28% and 81.29% in binary and multi-class classification, respectively. Shone et al. [15] proposed a non-symmetric deep auto-encoder (NDAE) model for intrusion detection tested on both KDD99 and NSL-KDD dataset, achieving 5-class accuracy rate up to 97.85% and 85.42%, respectively. Recently, Abeshu et al. [1] proposed a novel DL architecture based on autoencoders for attack detection in fog-to-things computing, using the NSL-KDD. However, the evaluation restricted to binary detection (normal, anomaly) only. In this paper, we propose an innovative statistical driven deep learning method for detecting network intrusion. The NSL-KDD dataset is used to estimate the reliability of the model for binary and multi-class classification and aforementioned limitations have been addressed.

3 Methodology

The flowchart of the proposed method is illustrated in Fig. 1. The KDD dataset is first filtered by eliminating the outliers, followed by the transformation of categorical features into *one-hot-encoded vectors*. Afterwards a statistical analysis has been carried out over 38 numeric features in order to extract more correlated features. Finally, a deep and shallow classifiers are employed to test the detection accuracy.

3.1 NSL-KDD Dataset

The used NSL-KDD dataset [18] is arranged into a training set of 125973 samples (KDDTrain+) and a testing set of 22544 samples (KDDTest+). The dataset has x_i (i=1, 2, ... 41) features with 38 numeric and 3 categorical features. Specifically, *protocol_type*, *service*, *flag* (x_2, x_3, x_4) represent 3 categorical variables. Table 1 summarizes attack types and 4 different categories: (1) DoS (Denial of Service attacks), (2) R2L (Root to Local attacks), (3) U2R (User to Root attack), (4) Probe (Probing attacks). The structure of the NSL-KDD dataset is shown in Table 2.

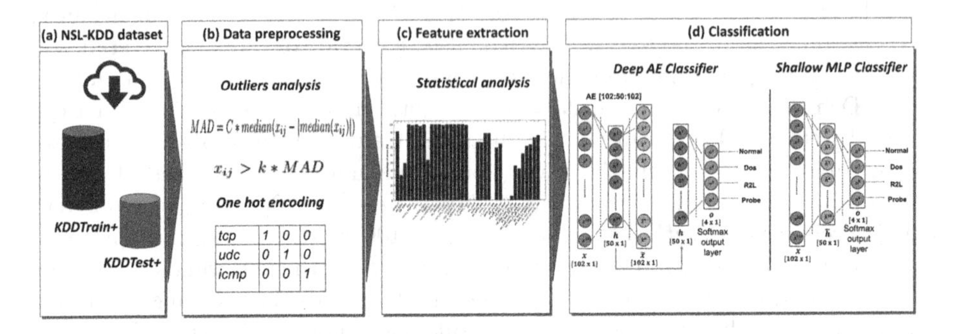

Fig. 1. Flowchart of the proposed method

Table 1. Attack types of DoS, R2L, U2R, Probe categories.

Attack class	Attack type
Dos	back, land, neptune, pod, smurf, teardrop
R2L	ftp_write, guess_passwd, imap, multihop, phf, spy, warezclient, warezmaster
U2R	buffer_overflow, loadmodule, perl, rootkit
Probe	ipsweep, nmap, portsweep, satan

Table 2. NSL-KDD dataset composition without additional test attacks types.

NSL-KDD	Total	Normal	Dos	Probe	R2L	U2R
KDDTrain+	125973	67343	45927	11656	995	52
KDDTest+	18793	9710	5741	1106	2199	37

3.2 Data Preprocessing

Outliers Analysis: Removing outliers from the dataset before performing the data normalization has proven to be an essential task. This operation removes inconsistent values that makes the learning difficult. In this study, the Median

Absolute Deviation (MAD) estimator is used for detecting the outliers. It is defined as follow:

$$MAD = C * median(x_{ij} - |median(x_{ij})|) \quad (1)$$

where $C = 1.4826$ is a multiplicative constant typically used under the assumption of data normality and x_{ij} is the instance belonged to the feature x_i.

Specifically, x_{ij} was considered an outlier when $x_{ij} > k * MAD$ (with k = 10). The original size of training and testing sets was reduced from 125973 to 85421 and from 22544 to 11925, respectively. Table 3 summarizes the dataset after removing outliers. It is to be noted that, the dataset is highly unbalanced with only 18 test samples in the U2R attack class. Therefore, the final dataset removed U2R class.

Table 3. NSL-KDD* dataset composition after removing outliers.

NSL-KDD*	Total	Normal	Dos	Probe	R2L	U2R
*KDDTrain+**	85421	51551	23272	9683	874	41
*KDDTest+**	11925	7341	1975	620	1971	18

One Hot Encoding: Since features x_2, x_3, x_4 (*protocol type*, *service* and *flag*) consist of categorical values, these features were converted into *one hot encoded vectors*. For example, the *protocol type* feature includes 3 attributes: *tcp*, *udp* and *icmp*, and were represented as (1, 0, 0), (0, 1, 0), (0, 0, 1), respectively. Similarly, *service* and *flag* features were represented by binary values. This procedure maps the 41-dimensional features into 122-dimensional features: 38 continuous and 84 with binary values associated to the 3 categorical features (*protocol*, *flag*, and *service*).

3.3 Feature Extraction

Several feature extraction techniques exist in literature (i.e. [12]). However, in this study, the proposed feature extraction module selects the most correlated features according to the following procedure. Firstly, the percentage of null values are quantified for 38 numeric features vectors. The histogram in Fig. 2 shows the distribution of zeros of each numeric feature in the training set. In this study, variables with number of zeros greater than 80% are not included in the analyses. It is to be noted that 20 features (depicted in red in Fig. 2) out of 38 consists of mostly zeros which are discarded. Therefore, the remaining 18 numeric features are combined with 84 one-hot-encoded features forming 102-dimensional input vector for deep AE and shallow MLP classifier.

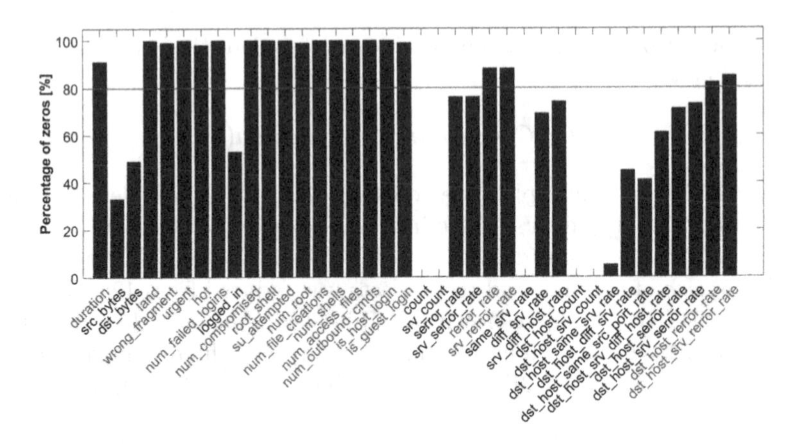

Fig. 2. Distribution of the number of zeros in each numeric features of the training set. Features with null values greater than 80% are depicted in red and are discarded from the analysis. (Color figure online)

3.4 Classification

In this section, two machine learning algorithms are presented to classify different categories of the NSL-KDD dataset (Normal, DoS, R2L and Probe). Specifically, a deep architecture based on Autoencoder and a shallow architecture based on standard Multi Layer Perceptron are implemented. Details of the proposed frameworks are described in the following subsections.

Deep AE Classifier: An autoencoder is a type of unsupervised learning algorithm, typically used for dimensionality reduction purposes. The AE standard configuration includes one input layer, one output layer and one hidden layer, as showed in Fig. 3(a). It compresses the input data x into a lower dimension h through the encoding process:

$$h = g(xw + b) \tag{2}$$

where x, w, b are the input vector, weight matrix, the bias vector, respectively and g is the activation function. Then, it attempts to reconstruct the same set of input (x) from the compressed representation (h) through the decoding process:

$$\tilde{x} = g(hw^T + b) \tag{3}$$

The architecture of the deep AE classifier is showed in Fig. 3(a). The extracted 102 features are the input of the single hidden layer AE that compressed the input space from 102 into 50 latent features ($AE_{[50]}$). At this stage, the AE is trained with unsupervised learning through the scaled conjugate gradient algorithm, for 100 iterations. The *saturating linear transfer function* ($g(z) = 0$ if $z \leq 0$, $g(z) = z$ if $0 < z < 1$, $g(z) = 0$ if $z \geq 1$) and the *linear transfer function* ($g(z) = z$) is used for encoding and decoding operations. The reconstruction of the input features (x) is measured through the mean squared error (MSE) coefficient. The proposed AE achieved the reconstruction error of 0.0083. Subsequently, the 50 compressed features are fed into a softmax output layer trained with supervised learning for performing the multi-class detection task. Finally, the whole network (AE+softmax) is trained with supervised learning (back-propagation algorithm) to improve the classification performance (fine-tuning method). The training is stopped when the cross-entropy loss function [6] saturates. In this study, the convergence is observed after 300 iterations.

Shallow MLP Classifier: The architecture of the shallow MLP classifier is showed in Fig. 3(b). It constitutes standard feed-forward neural network trained with supervising learning through scaled conjugate gradient algorithm. For fair comparative analysis, both shallow and deep AE models have adopted same architecture. The shallow MLP architecture has used a single hidden layer with 50 hidden neurons followed by a softmax output layer.

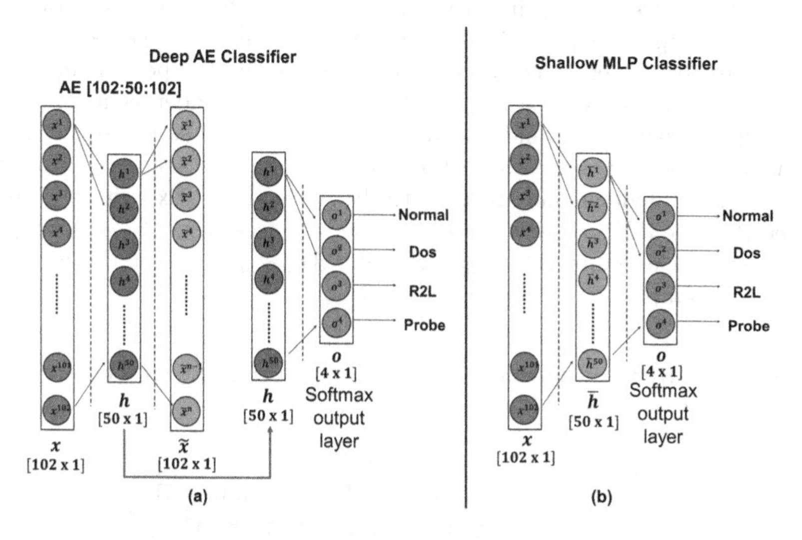

Fig. 3. (a) Proposed Deep AE Classifier: The AE [102:50:102] compresses the 102 features ($\boldsymbol{x}$) into 50 most significant variables ($\boldsymbol{h}$) used as input for a final softmax output layer ($\boldsymbol{o}$) to perform the multi-class detection. (b) Shallow MLP Classifier: standard single layer feed-forward neural network with 50 hidden neurons ($\tilde{h}$) followed by a softmax output layer ($\boldsymbol{o}$).

4 Experimental Results

The effectiveness of the proposed deep (AE) and shallow (MLP) classifier is evaluated using standard metrics: Precision (PR), recall (RC), F_measure (or F_score) and accuracy (ACC):

$$Precision = \frac{TP}{TP + FP} \tag{4}$$

$$Recall = \frac{TP}{TP + FN} \tag{5}$$

$$F\_measure = 2 * \frac{Precision * Recall}{Precision + Recall} \tag{6}$$

$$Accuracy = \frac{TP + TN}{TP + TN + FP + FN} \tag{7}$$

where true positives (TP) represent the number of anomalous samples correctly identified as anomaly; true negatives (TN) represent the number of normal samples correctly identified as normal; false positives (FP) are the number of normal samples missclassified as anomaly; false negatives (FN) are the number of anomaly samples missclassified as normal. Table 4 reports the outcome of the experiments. The shallow MLP classifier showed good performances in detecting Normal, Dos and Probe categories, reporting F_measure values of 87.10%, 97.08%, 77.13%, respectively. However remained deficient to classify the R2L attack class accurately (achieving F_measure of 11.74%). The deep AE classifier achieved better results in terms of F_measure rate in all categories, with performances up to 98%. To find out the most optimal AE architecture, different numbers of hidden layers were tested. Specifically, the performance of the proposed deep AE classifier (having one layer) with 50 hidden neurons ($AE_{[50]}$) was compared with a two hidden layers AE architecture (with 50 and 25 hidden neurons respectively, $AE_{[50,25]}$) and a three hidden layers AE architecture (with 50, 25, 12 hidden neurons respectively, $AE_{[50,25,12]}$). Experimental results showed that the $AE_{[50]}$ classifier achieved the best accuracy of 87% as compared to accuracies achieved by $AE_{[50,25]}$ (82%) and $AE_{[50,25,12]}$ (81%), this is possibly due to over compression in multilayered AE.

Table 4. NSL-KDD* performance (Precision, Recall, F_measure) for the deep AE classifier and the shallow MLP classifier.

Attack class	Precision		Recall		F_measure	
	MLP	AE	MLP	AE	MLP	AE
Normal	96.35	96.19	79.46	85.03	87.10	90.27
Dos	96.96	98.18	97.21	97.05	97.08	97.61
Probe	96.29	94.03	64.33	69.82	77.13	80.14
R2L	6.24	39.78	99.19	99.49	11.74	56.83

Table 5 reports the comparison of proposed deep AE and shallow MLP classifier with four recently proposed approaches in the literature. In order to compare our results, we referred to studies that focused on multi-classification tasks using the NSL-KDD dataset. It is to be noted that, the proposed AE based deep learning architecture, outperformed all other approaches, achieving accuracy up to 87%. However, the MLP classifier achieved maximum accuracy of 81.6%. In [8] the authors proposed a sequential learning algorithm achieving an accuracy of 76.04%. In [9] the authors developed a sparse autoencoder based classifier and reported 79.10% accuracy. In [22] the authors developed a RNN based system and reported multiclass accuracy of 81.29%. In [15], the authors proposed a stacked non-symmetric deep autoencoders and reported 5-class accuracy of 85.42%. Here, instead, we propose an alternative statistical analysis driven deep AE classifier able to achieve multiclass accuracy of 87%.

Table 5. Accuracy performance and comparison with state of the art models.

Model	Accuracy (%)
AE proposed	**87**
MLP proposed	81.43
Huang et al. [8]	76.04
Abeshu et al. [9]	79.10
Yin et al. [22]	81.29
Shone et al. [15]	85.42

5 Conclusion

The proposed approach leverages the complementary strengths of both automated feature engineering (provided by deep learning) and manual statistical driven optimized feature engineering (based on human-in-the-loop and big data visualization) that helps the learning model to better correlate the input-output relationship. Specifically, we introduced a statistical driven optimized DL system for intrusion detection. The NSL-KDD dataset was employed as benchmark to identify normal and abnormal network traffic patterns. The most correlated features were extracted using statistical methods and were the input of a deep AE classifier. The feasibility and effectiveness of the proposed model were evaluated using precision, recall, F_measure and accuracy metrics. The comparative evaluation of proposed deep autoencoder with a shallow MLP classifier and state-of-the-art models showed that the proposed deep AE classifier outperformed all other approaches and achieved upto 87% accuracy. Future works include a more robust system capable of handling real-time traffic similar to NSL-KDD dataset to contextually detect intrusions in real-time applications. In addition, to concurrently acquire long-term learning, fast decision making, and low computational complexity for real-time Big Data processing, we intend to integrate the work presented in [2] with the work presented in this paper.

Acknowledgment. Amir Hussain and Ahsan Adeel were supported by the UK Engineering and Physical Sciences Research Council (EPSRC) grant No. EP/M026981/1.

References

1. Abeshu, A., Chilamkurti, N.: Deep learning: the frontier for distributed attack detection in Fog-to-Things computing. IEEE Commun. Mag. **56**(2), 169–175 (2018)
2. Adeel, A., Larijani, H., Ahmadinia, A.: Random neural network based novel decision making framework for optimized and autonomous power control in lte uplink system. Phys. Commun. **19**, 106–117 (2016)
3. Alrawashdeh, K., Purdy, C.: Toward an online anomaly intrusion detection system based on deep learning. In: 2016 15th IEEE International Conference on Machine Learning and Applications (ICMLA), pp. 195–200. IEEE (2016)
4. Dashtipour, K., Gogate, M., Adeel, A., Algarafi, A., Howard, N., Hussain, A.: Persian named entity recognition. In: 2017 IEEE 16th International Conference on Cognitive Informatics and Cognitive Computing (ICCI* CC), pp. 79–83. IEEE (2017)
5. Dashtipour, K., Hussain, A., Zhou, Q., Gelbukh, A., Hawalah, A.Y.A., Cambria, E.: PerSent: a freely available persian sentiment lexicon. In: Liu, C.-L., Hussain, A., Luo, B., Tan, K.C., Zeng, Y., Zhang, Z. (eds.) BICS 2016. LNCS (LNAI), vol. 10023, pp. 310–320. Springer, Cham (2016). https://doi.org/10.1007/978-3-319-49685-6_28
6. De Boer, P.T., Kroese, D.P., Mannor, S., Rubinstein, R.Y.: A tutorial on the cross-entropy method. Ann. Oper. Res. **134**(1), 19–67 (2005)
7. Gasparini, S., et al.: Information theoretic-based interpretation of a deep neural network approach in diagnosing psychogenic non-epileptic seizures. Entropy **20**(2), 43 (2018)
8. Huang, H., Khalid, R.S., Liu, W., Yu, H.: Work-in-progress: a fast online sequential learning accelerator for IoT network intrusion detection. In: 2017 International Conference on Hardware/Software Codesign and System Synthesis (CODES+ ISSS), pp. 1–2. IEEE (2017)
9. Javaid, A., Niyaz, Q., Sun, W., Alam, M.: A deep learning approach for network intrusion detection system. In: Proceedings of the 9th EAI International Conference on Bio-Inspired Information and Communications Technologies (Formerly BIONETICS), pp. 21–26. ICST (Institute for Computer Sciences, Social-Informatics and Telecommunications Engineering) (2016)
10. Kim, J., Shin, N., Jo, S.Y., Kim, S.H.: Method of intrusion detection using deep neural network. In: 2017 IEEE International Conference on Big Data and Smart Computing (BigComp), pp. 313–316. IEEE (2017)
11. LeCun, Y., Bengio, Y., Hinton, G.: Deep learning. Nature **521**(7553), 436 (2015)
12. Morabito, C.F.: Independent component analysis and feature extraction techniques for NDT data. Mater. Eval. **58**(1), 85–92 (2000)
13. Morabito, F.C., et al.: Deep convolutional neural networks for classification of mild cognitive impaired and Alzheimer's disease patients from scalp EEG recordings. In: 2016 IEEE 2nd International Forum on Research and Technologies for Society and Industry Leveraging a Better Tomorrow (RTSI), pp. 1–6. IEEE (2016)
14. Najafabadi, M.M., Villanustre, F., Khoshgoftaar, T.M., Seliya, N., Wald, R., Muharemagic, E.: Deep learning applications and challenges in big data analytics. J. Big Data **2**(1), 1 (2015)
15. Shone, N., Ngoc, T.N., Phai, V.D., Shi, Q.: A deep learning approach to network intrusion detection. IEEE Trans. Emerg. Top. Comput. Intell. **2**(1), 41–50 (2018)

16. Tang, T.A., Mhamdi, L., McLernon, D., Zaidi, S.A.R., Ghogho, M.: Deep learning approach for network intrusion detection in software defined networking. In: 2016 International Conference on Wireless Networks and Mobile Communications (WINCOM), pp. 258–263. IEEE (2016)
17. Tavallaee, M., Bagheri, E., Lu, W., Ghorbani, A.A.: A detailed analysis of the KDD cup 99 data set. In: 2009 IEEE Symposium on Computational Intelligence for Security and Defense Applications, CISDA 2009, pp. 1–6. IEEE (2009)
18. Tavallaee, M., Bagheri, E., Lu, W., Ghorbani, A.A.: NSL-KDD dataset (2012). http://www.unb.ca/research/iscx/dataset/iscx-NSL-KDD-dataset.html). Accessed 28 Feb 2016
19. Tsai, C.F., Hsu, Y.F., Lin, C.Y., Lin, W.Y.: Intrusion detection by machine learning: a review. Expert. Syst. Appl. **36**(10), 11994–12000 (2009)
20. Wang, Z., Ren, J., Zhang, D., Sun, M., Jiang, J.: A deep-learning based feature hybrid framework for spatiotemporal saliency detection inside videos. Neurocomputing **287**, 68–83 (2018)
21. Yan, Y., et al.: Unsupervised image saliency detection with Gestalt-laws guided optimization and visual attention based refinement. Pattern Recogn. **79**, 65–78 (2018)
22. Yin, C., Zhu, Y., Fei, J., He, X.: A deep learning approach for intrusion detection using recurrent neural networks. IEEE Access **5**, 21954–21961 (2017)

Comparing Event Related Arousal-Valence and Focus Among Different Viewing Perspectives in VR Gaming

Diego Monteiro, Hai-Ning Liang(✉), Yuxuan Zhao, and Andrew Abel

Xi'an Jiaotong-Liverpool University, Suzhou, China
haining.liang@xjtlu.edu.cn

Abstract. Games are both a way to enjoy leisure time and to learn. Understanding how mental processes associated with gaming work at a deeper level is very important, especially with emerging technologies such as consumer VR head-mounted display systems. One approach to better understand games is through the analysis of how individual events and components of the game affect our autonomic responses. To this end, in this paper, we analyze how the component of viewing perspectives and display types affect the reaction to specific in-game events. We do this through the collection of EEG data using a consumer EEG headset. The collected values are used to calculate Arousal-Valence and Engagement indexes. Finally, these values are compared to events happening at the collection time, and the data is analyzed to identify patterns and draw conclusions from the data. This initial analysis of selected events does not identify any representative change in values amongst different displays and viewing perspectives. These results suggest that viewing perspective and display are of less importance than may be expected for our selected events, whereas other factors such as ranking play a greater role in emotional state changes.

Keywords: ERP · EEG metrics · Arousal-Valence · VR · Game Engagement

1 Introduction

Games are both a way to enjoy leisure time and to learn [1, 2], and it can be said that virtually everybody has played some form of game in their lifetime [3]. Videogames (hereafter games) have increased in popularity and thus attracted the interest of researchers [4], for example to investigate and understand the factors that make a game enjoyable for the players [5].

While games have existed for decades, games in consumer Virtual Reality (VR) are relatively new and have recently been attracting attention, especially VR that makes use of Head-Mounted Displays (HMD) [6]. What is not often studied in VR is the difference in viewing perspective—that is, the difference between 1PP and 3PP (1st and 3rd person-perspective respectively) [6]. Despite receiving little attention, it is an important research topic because it could potentially influence both the sense of presence and simulator sickness [6–8]. Presence is a feeling commonly described as the

J. Ren et al. (Eds.): BICS 2018, LNAI 10989, pp. 770–779, 2018.
https://doi.org/10.1007/978-3-030-00563-4_75

feeling of "being there" [9], and it has been argued that such a thing as presence might bring a greater level of engagement [8].

To investigate how these changes in viewing perspective and display affect gaming in more depth we considered psychophysiological metrics. These metrics aim to capture not only subjective feelings from players, but also their bodily responses to those stimuli [10]. Examples of techniques used for this include Electroencephalogram (EEG), Electrocardiogram (ECG), and Electromyogram (EMG). Amongst psychophysiological metrics, one that helps to provide a deeper understanding of what is happening during gameplay is the analysis of Event Related Potential (ERP), which analyzes brain waves as an event is happening. Since the metrics are derived from these potentials, we can use them to analyze specific events.

In this paper we utilize psychophysiological metrics and their use in ERP for analyzing user responses to computer game events. We analyze how those metrics are affected by changes in viewing perspective and display type. We also analyze the data for patterns to improve our understanding of how VR affects the game experience. This is an important research topic as there has been very little prior investigation focusing on the different psychophysiological effects of different viewing perspectives, and this paper contributes a new study.

2 Theoretical Background

2.1 Brainwaves Metrics for Emotions

Brainwaves are electromagnetic waves generated by the brain as the neurons fire, and they can be observed through electroencephalography (EEG) data. They are useful for metrics because they can be used to identify certain consistent patterns in the brain that can be interpreted [11].

Brainwaves are generally divided into frequency bands, commonly known as Alpha, Beta, Delta, Gamma and Theta. These bands are normally associated with specific mental states (see Table 1) for more detail. Even though the frequency range is not universally agreed upon by all researchers, there seems to be agreement regarding the main frequency components [4, 11–14].

Table 1. Types of brainwave signals

Wave type	Frequency	Mental state
Delta	1–4 Hz	Deep sleep, unconscious
Theta	4–8 Hz	Creativity, dream sleep, drifting thoughts
Alpha	8–13 Hz	Relaxation, abstract thinking, calmness
Beta	13–30 Hz	Tension, excitement, stress
Gamma	30–50 Hz	Anxiety, nervous, stress

These waves can be used for several types of research, including being biomarkers for mental illness like depression and Alzheimer's disease [13, 15, 16], or for better understanding of emotional states ranging from boredom to fear [14, 17]. To better understand emotional states using brainwaves, a number of metrics have been created.

These metrics generally do not use the whole spectrum of waves, but just the most pertinent ones. For example, one metric for measuring engagement (a.k.a. focus) uses only Beta and Theta waves [15]. Another metric that calculates engagement was proposed by [18], and makes use of not only Beta and Theta but also Alpha waves. One advantage of these metrics is that the waves they use are somewhat more artifact (noise) resistant than Delta and Gamma because the frequency in which they occur is not commonly associated with blinking, which happens at lower frequencies, or with muscle movements, which happens at higher frequencies.

With regard to measuring emotions, there is one metric that requires only Alpha and Beta [17, 19]. This metric is based on a process that divides emotions through a Cartesian system in which one axis is called Arousal and the other Valence, and the emotions fall into one of their quadrants. Arousal reveals how exciting an emotion is, whereas Valence represents how "positive" the emotion is (Fig. 1).

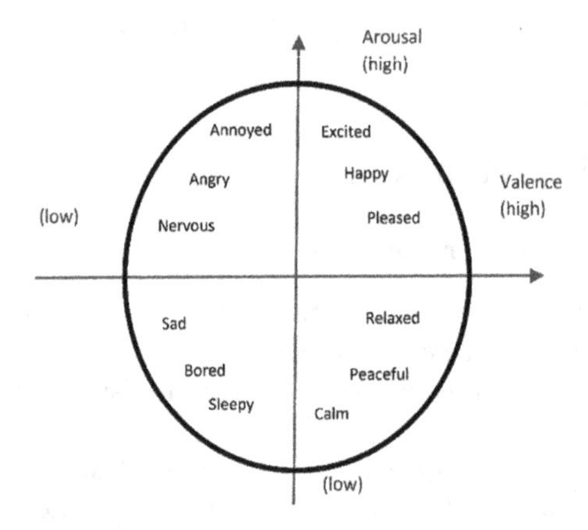

Fig. 1. Emotional states and their positions in the valence/arousal plane (image adapted from [20])

In order to be able to calculate any metrics, it is necessary to be able to record the brainwaves in the first place. One relatively straightforward way to do this is by using consumer EEG headsets such as MindWave Mobile [11, 21], MUSE EEG [22] and EMOTIV EPOC [17]. While these headsets are not necessarily as precise as medical ones, they are widely regarded as being precise enough for non-critical purposes [23], and therefore they have been used for different researches involving meditation [14] or lecture engagement [21].

For this work we decided to use the MUSE headset, which has been used and validated by previous research [23]. As discussed, the metrics chosen were Arousal-Valence [17, 19], which shows potential for this work, and the engagement metric presented by Shin et al. [15], which uses Alpha, Beta and Theta waves as parameters. As explained, these metrics should be artifact (noise) resistant.

2.2 Viewing Perspective in VE

When dealing with a virtual environment (VE), the viewing perspective may have great influence on user experience, as it influences presence [24] and enjoyment [6]. First-Person perspective (1PP) has been presented as bringing a greater sense of presence during a Role-Playing Game (RPG), when compared to playing the same game in Third-Person Perspective (3PP) [5]. One could infer that a similar effect would be carried over to a different VE.

Kalinen et al. [8] observed a analogous occurrence when performing a similar experiment. Their study also involved an RPG in 3PP and 1PP. However, unlike [5] they used physiological data in their analysis. In another study, volunteers, who were wearing a Head-Mounted Display, had the floor under their avatar's feet fall into a pit. The volunteers' fear response in 1PP was greater than their response in 3PP. To reach this conclusion, researchers collected galvanic skin response to measure the fear response [25]. However, even though 1PP may lead to a greater sense of presence, some research [6, 7] has suggested that 3PP induces lower levels of simulator sickness, while under delivering presence in a small manner. This tradeoff may be beneficial to some projects that require long term exposure.

2.3 EEG Analysis in Games and VR

One of the first studies to deal with games and EEG was [26]. This research used the game Super Monkey Ball 2 as a parameter. They defined events within the game and analyzed the Event Related Potential (ERP) of the brain when those events were performed. The results of this experiment showed an increase in Beta and decrease in Alpha on the frontal electrodes when participants faced challenges.

Later research [4] investigated how the use of different kinds of controllers affects the brain during gameplay. In this study participants played Resident Evil 4 using either a Nintendo Wiimote or a regular PS2 controller. Their results indicate that intuitive controllers like the Wiimote may cause a lower workload on the brain.

In a recent study that evaluated serious games [3], PSD (Power Spectrum Density) decreased in Theta, associated with relaxation, when the participants were gaming. The researchers expected Beta, which is associated with anxiety and focus, and was assumed to be needed for playing games, to raise during gaming, which did not happen. This is interesting because the metrics for engagement use both those waves.

Another recent work related to learning investigated possible differences in learning with a VR-HMD and with a regular display [27]. When students used a virtual lab to study advanced biology, they felt more present when using VR-HMD. However, in this condition, they scored lower in the acquired knowledge test and their brain workload was greater, according to the researchers' metrics.

Several different studies investigated Wall-VR systems compared to a regular monitor [28, 29]. Wall-VR are projections on a wall (often three-dimensional (3D)), that normally have 1:1 ratio models, which immerses the user in the environment. These studies found that VR generally provides a greater sense of presence and that Alpha and Theta waves change when using the different displays. This is important because the metrics in this paper are based on those waves.

3 Experiment

Based on the reviewed literature, in this paper, we want to test the ERP of specific events in a VR game and how they compare to a regular screen, and how changing perspective in VR affects the ERP.

We decided that Mario Kart Wii was a suitable game to use, because of its gender neutrality [30], how easily reproducible phases between players can be, its "spoiler" resistance, and because it is relatively easy to reproduce events [6]. To convert the game to VR we used the Dolphin VR emulator (version 5.0) [31], and the configuration follows what was reported in [6].

We then chose the events to be evaluated. The game has many possible events to be evaluated, and we decided to focus on three: One ubiquitous to every interaction of the game and two that the researchers observed on previous iterations to be frequent. Event 1 is Crossing the Finish Line; Event 2 is Collecting an Item; Event 3 is Falling off Map. We hypothesized that all events present greater indexes of Arousal-Valence and Focus/Engagement in VR when compared to a Common Display (CD), and also that indexes in 1PP-VR would be even greater than in 3PP-VR.

We recruited volunteers from a local university, regardless of their course of study. We had a total of 13 volunteers—(one female) with an average age of 23.69 ± 3.76, median of 23, mode of 22, and range between 19 and 32. All volunteers had normal or normal to corrected vision, and none declared any history of color blindness or mental illness. 84.6% of the participants had experience with the chosen game before but had never played it on a PC emulator nor in any kind of VR systems. 53.8% of them had already had experience playing other games in VR, 69.2% played "regular" games at least once a week, and of these, 44.4% played at least 3 times a week.

All the volunteers received an explanation about the experiment, particularly the collection of their psychophysiological data. After understanding the process and what psychophysiological data would be collected, there was verbal agreement to continue with the experiment.

We used an Oculus Rift CV1 as our HMD. Our PC had 16 GB RAM, an Intel Core i7-7700k CPU @ 4.20 GHz, and a GeForce GTX 1080Ti dedicated GPU. We used a Betop Pandora 2.4G Wireless Gamepad as the controller. We used it instead of the traditional Rift Touch Controller because the Betop could be used both with an HMD and without it.

The standard data collection procedure was to introduce the players to the game and controllers using the 3PP-CD. We had the players play the game once under this perspective, while the EEG device calibrated on the volunteers' head. This part of the process took approximately 11 min for each volunteer. The races were recorded so we could observe the events later.

The players played one of the three conditions, followed by answering questionnaires about their experience. The process was repeated for all three conditions and the order of conditions was determined by a Latin square design. Due to space limitations the questionnaires are not discussed in this paper.

4 Results and Discussion

We collected data from 13 participants. However, the data of 2 participants were discarded because they had stopped the experiment before it finished due to excessive simulator sickness.

During the analysis we evaluated Arousal-Valence and Focus. We calculated the scores as presented in the relevant literature. In order to evaluate those components for each of the predetermined events, we graphed the scores starting one second before and finishing one second after the event had happened. In total, we had over 360 graphs charactering the events.

The analysis first identified that one of the initially chosen conditions had to be ignored, due to it occurring less commonly than expected, namely condition 3 - “Fall”. Based on our previous experience, we expected participants to fall off the chosen map with a certain consistency. However, the results showed that was not the case. Even though people did fall, they did not do so consistently across versions, which means there was not a solid basis to make comparisons.

Events 1 and 2 happened constantly and thus were evaluated in this paper. Both of these events had relatively consistent graphs across versions, meaning that while each volunteer showed a different response to each of these events, the same volunteer presented similar responses across different versions to similar stimuli. This suggests that the impact of the events themselves have a higher impact on the players’ minds than the display or point of view the event is presented in.

The data was challenging to compare across volunteers, with most of them showing changes in different indexes and in very dissimilar ranges. However, for Event 2, general patterns within volunteers could be observed. However, this event presented another challenge: to isolate it from other forms of interaction.

Event 1 almost ubiquitously lead to a spike in valence, generally a few milliseconds before the actual crossing of the finish line. However, the peak either turned into a plunge if the ranking was not, we hypothesize, the desired position for the player, or flattened straight away. We could not find a specific pattern to determine what a desired position was, as this would require complex investigation. Thus, we are going to present a number of selected cases we felt were particularly interesting.

Subject A finished the first game (3PP-CD) in 1st place, and it seems his positive feelings peaked; however, on the next version when obtaining the same result, even though the level of positive feelings increased, it was closer to apathy. And finally, when obtaining a worse result than in the previous versions, subject A presented a plunge in positive feelings, which could have been caused by either the result or the experiment being over. This is shown in Fig. 2.

Subject B presented mixed feelings regarding his positions, we can see that in all his interactions there is an alternation between peaks and valleys. However, his data shows very clearly that patterns are closer within volunteers than across volunteers (Fig. 3).

With regards to Event 2, Fig. 4 represents the first time Player A gets an item in each version. On the first graph (which represents the Subject’s first race), Valence shows a very high peak when compared to the other two graphs. The range that the

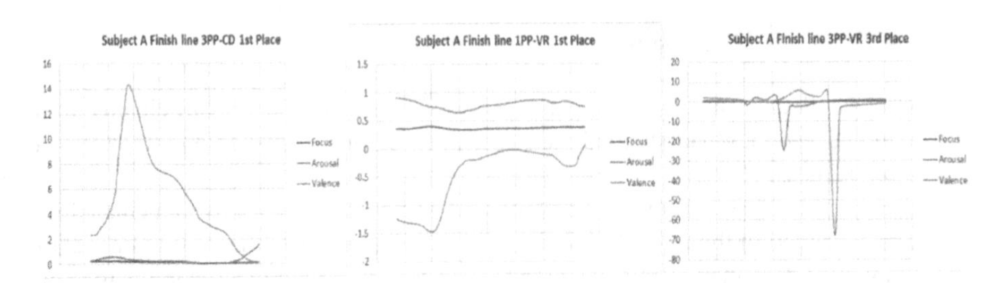

Fig. 2. Graphs of ERP of Subject A's Event 1 under different conditions.

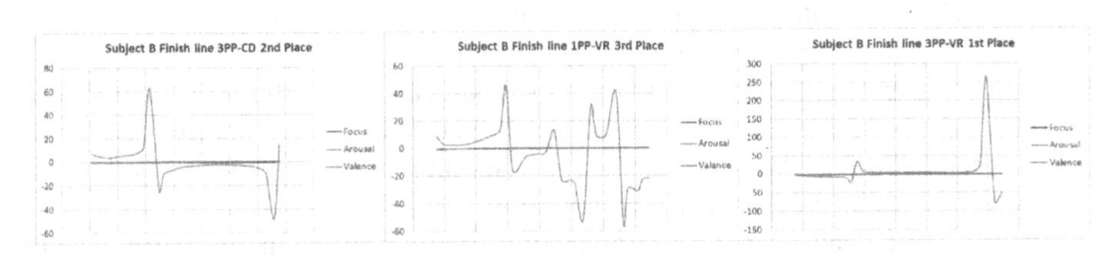

Fig. 3. Graphs of ERP of Subject B's Event 1 of under different conditions.

indexes varies in the later graphs is closer than the variation of the first. We speculate that this occurred because the rewards caused by getting an item were greater on the first iteration; and based on the law of diminishing returns the rewards in later iterations of getting an item probably became lower and lower (the player had acquired over 12 items by then). Another plausible explanation is that it was the beginning of the first race and expectations and the feelings of excitement may have been higher.

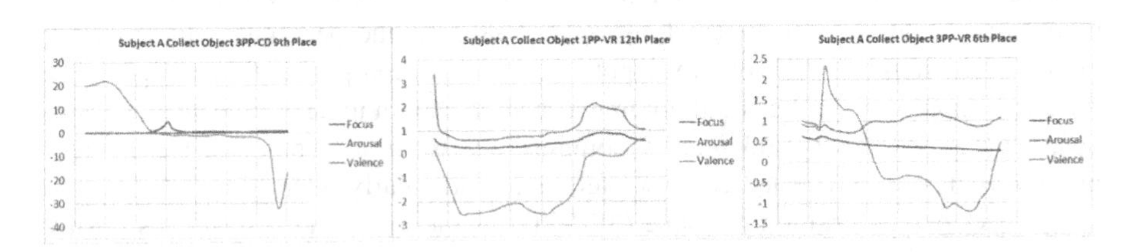

Fig. 4. Graphs of ERP of Subject A's Event 2 of under different conditions.

Our hypothesis that events 1 and 2 in VR would cause greater indexes of Valence and Arousal was not confirmed, nor was the hypothesis that 3PP would have lower indexes than 1PP. Our hypothesis that "Falls" would have a greater impact in VR was not verified due to challenges with data collection.

It is possible that events such as falling, being hit by an object, or hitting another driver might elicit stronger reactions, since the brain might interpret it as something likely to have actually hit the player; whereas a victory is regarded as a victory, regardless of medium. The polluted data of events 1 and 2 provided some supporting evidence of this, when these events happened simultaneously with hitting another player, causing different reactions.

One possible direction we could take for a future work is to try to summarize the patterns and identify interruptions using techniques similar to those used in activity-driven video summarization (see [32–34]).

5 Conclusions

Even though we did not confirm our initial hypothesis, these results are relevant. They suggest that certain feelings are not so connected to how the experience is being seen (i.e., 1PP or 3PP), but rather to what it means to the gamers. We can therefore extrapolate that this lack of difference may also be behind why people feel so involved with sports in which they are simply spectators.

Our sample data is not big, and this is by design because we wanted to examine the data for each subject in detail, and also because there is no analytical framework from prior research we could follow in our analysis, meaning that it was vital to perform this experiment with a small sample size. Data from subject A makes us believe that for a game to be enjoyable it should increase in challenge gradually, since after the first victory, the only strong feeling present is that of disappointment.

To the best of our knowledge this is the first work that investigates the differences between viewing perspective and display type in virtual reality gaming using ERP based metrics. We believe this work can provide some foundations for other studies of psychophysiological analysis of viewing perspectives in VR gaming. Further analyses of our data and future studies may help shed some light on the reasons why we could not identify specific patterns in the data.

Acknowledgements. We would like to thank the participants for their time. This research was partially funded by the XJTLU Key Program Special Fund (KSF-A-03) and the XJTLU Research Development Fund.

References

1. Martončik, M.: E-Sports: playing just for fun or playing to satisfy life goals? Comput. Hum. Behav. **48**, 208–211 (2015)
2. Horta, A.S., de Almeida, L.F., Monteiro, R.C.R.V., Monteiro, D.V.: A proposal of a game for education and environmental consciousness. In: Proceedings of the 24th International Association for Management of Technology Conference (2015)
3. Hosťovecký, M., Babušiak, B.: Brain activity: beta wave analysis of 2D and 3D serious games using EEG. JAMSI **13**, 39–53 (2017)
4. Nacke, L.E.: Wiimote vs. controller: electroencephalographic measurement of affective gameplay interaction. In: Proceedings of the International Academic Conference on the Future of Game Design and Technology, pp. 159–166 (2010)
5. Denisova, A., Cairns, P.: First person vs. third person perspective in digital games. In: Proceedings of the 33rd Annual ACM Conference on Human Factors in Computing Systems, CHI 2015, pp. 145–148 (2015)

6. Monteiro, D., Liang, H., Xu, W., Brucker, M., Yue, Y.: Evaluating enjoyment, presence, and emulator sickness in VR games based on first- and third-person viewing perspectives. Comput. Animat. Virtual Worlds **29**, e1830 (2018)
7. Medina, E., Fruland, R., Weghorst, S.: VIRTUSPHERE: walking in a human size VR "hamster ball". In: Proceedings of the Human Factors and Ergonomics Society 52nd Annual Meeting, New York, NY, USA, pp. 2102–2106 (2008)
8. Kallinen, K., Salminen, M., Ravaja, N., Kedzior, R., Sääksjärvi, M.: Presence and emotion in computer game players during 1st person vs. 3rd person playing view: evidence from self-report, eye-tracking, and facial muscle activity data. In: Proceedings of the Presence, pp. 187–190 (2007)
9. Cummings, J.J., Bailenson, J.N.: How immersive is enough? A meta-analysis of the effect of immersive technology on user presence. Media Psychol. **19**, 272–309 (2016)
10. Kivikangas, J.M., Ekman, I., Chanel, G., Järvelä, S., Cowley, B., Henttonen, P., Ravaja, N.: Review on psychophysiological methods in game research. In: Proceedings of the 1st Nordic DiGRA (2010)
11. Liu, N.H., Chiang, C.Y., Chu, H.C.: Recognizing the degree of human attention using EEG signals from mobile sensors. Sensors **13**, 10273–10286 (2013)
12. Balconi, M., Lucchiari, C.: Consciousness and arousal effects on emotional face processing as revealed by brain oscillations: a gamma band analysis. Int. J. Psychophysiol. **67**, 41–46 (2008)
13. Güntekin, B., Başar, E.: Review of evoked and event-related delta responses in the human brain. Int. J. Psychophysiol. **103**, 43–52 (2016)
14. Kosunen, I., Salminen, M., Järvelä, S., Ruonala, A., Ravaja, N., Jacucci, G.: RelaWorld: neuroadaptive and immersive virtual reality meditation system. In: IUI 2016, pp. 208–217 (2016)
15. Shin, D., Lee, G., Shin, D., Shin, D.: Mental state measurement system using EEG analysis. In: Park, J.J., Pan, Y., Kim, C.-S., Yang, Y. (eds.) Future Information Technology. LNEE, vol. 309, pp. 451–456. Springer, Heidelberg (2014). https://doi.org/10.1007/978-3-642-55038-6_70
16. Knyazev, G.G.: EEG delta oscillations as a correlate of basic homeostatic and motivational processes. Neurosci. Biobehav. Rev. **36**, 677–695 (2012)
17. McMahan, T., Parberry, I., Parsons, T.D.: Evaluating player task engagement and arousal using electroencephalography. Proc. Manuf. **3**, 2303–2310 (2015)
18. Pope, A.T., Bogart, E.H., Bartolome, D.S.: Biocybernetic system evaluates indices of operator engagement in automated task. Biol. Psychol. **40**, 187–195 (1995)
19. Petrantonakis, P.C., Hadjileontiadis, L.J.: Emotion recognition from brain signals using hybrid adaptive filtering and higher order crossings analysis. IEEE Trans. Affect. Comput. **1**, 81–97 (2010)
20. Thirunavukkarasu, G.S., Abdi, H., Mohajer, N.: A smart HMI for driving safety using emotion prediction of EEG signals. In: Proceedings of the IEEE International Conference on Systems, Man, and Cybernetics, pp. 004148–004153 (2016)
21. Hassib, M., Schneegass, S., Eiglsperger, P., Henze, N., Schmidt, A., Alt, F.: EngageMeter. In: Proceedings of the CHI Conference on Human Factors in Computing Systems, CHI 2017, pp. 5114–5119. ACM Press, New York (2017)
22. Krigolson, O.E., Williams, C.C., Norton, A., Hassall, C.D., Colino, F.L.: Choosing MUSE: validation of a low-cost, portable EEG system for ERP research. Front. Neurosci. **11**, 1–10 (2017)
23. Mondéjar, T., Hervás, R., Johnson, E., Gutierrez, C., Latorre, J.M.: Correlation between videogame mechanics and executive functions through EEG analysis. J. Biomed. Inform. **63**, 131–140 (2016)

24. Gorisse, G., Christmann, O., Amato, E.A., Richir, S.: First- and third-person perspectives in immersive virtual environments: presence and performance analysis of embodied users. Front. Robot. AI **4**, 1–12 (2017)
25. Debarba, H.G., Bovet, S., Salomon, R., Blanke, O., Herbelin, B., Boulic, R.: Characterizing first and third person viewpoints and their alternation for embodied interaction in virtual reality. PLoS ONE **12**, 1–19 (2017)
26. Salminen, M., Ravaja, N.: Oscillatory brain responses evoked by video game events: the case of Super Monkey Ball 2. CyberPsychol. Behav. **10**, 330–338 (2007)
27. Makransky, G., Terkildsen, T.S., Mayer, R.E.: Adding immersive virtual reality to a science lab simulation causes more presence but less learning. Learn. Instr. 0–1 (2017)
28. Kober, S.E., Kurzmann, J., Neuper, C.: Cortical correlate of spatial presence in 2D and 3D interactive virtual reality: an EEG study. Int. J. Psychophysiol. **83**, 365–374 (2012)
29. Clemente, M., Rodríguez, A., Rey, B., Alcañiz, M.: Assessment of the influence of navigation control and screen size on the sense of presence in virtual reality using EEG. Expert Syst. Appl. **41**, 1584–1592 (2014)
30. Iwata, S.: The 72nd annual general meeting of shareholders Q&A. https://www.nintendo.co.jp/ir/en/stock/meeting/120628qa/index.html
31. Dolphin VR: Dolphin VR – a gamecube and WII emulator with VR support. https://dolphinvr.wordpress.com/
32. Ren, J., Jiang, J., Feng, Y.: Activity-driven content adaptation for effective video summarization. J. Vis. Commun. Image Represent. **21**, 930–938 (2010)
33. Chen, J., Ren, J., Jiang, J.: Modelling of content-aware indicators for effective determination of shot boundaries in compressed MPEG videos. Multimed. Tools Appl. **54**, 219–239 (2011)
34. Ren, J., Jiang, J.: Hierarchical modeling and adaptive clustering for real-time summarization of rush videos. IEEE Trans. Multimed. **11**, 906–917 (2009)

A Novel Loop Subdivision for Continuity Surface

Lichun Gu[1,2](✉), Jinjin Zheng[1], Chuangyin Dang[2], Zhengtian Wu[3], and Baochuan Fu[3]

[1] Department of Precision Machinery and Precision Instrumentation, University of Science and Technology of China, Hefei 230027, Anhui, People's Republic of China
gulichun0299@163.com

[2] Department of Machinery Engineering and Engineering Management, City University of Hong Kong, Hong Kong, China

[3] School of Electronic and Information Engineering, Suzhou University of Science and Technology, Suzhou, China

Abstract. This paper introduces a novel Loop subdivision method, which produces a C^1 continuity surface including boundaries and creases. The new rules develop Loop subdivision surface by adding a parameter known as a knot interval. Sederberg et al. used knot intervals for sharp features in subdivision surface modeling for the first time. This paper extends the subdivision rule to triangular subdivision meshes. It can generate a pleasant result in Loop subdivision surfaces.

Keywords: Subdivision · Crease · Dart · Corner · Cone · Knot interval

1 Introduction

Subdivision can be tracked back in 1978 in Chaikin's [1] corner-cutting algorithm for free-form curves, which deforms from an initial control mesh into a dense one by recursive refinements. It is one approach to obtaining maximally smooth curves. Its mathematical translation results in a uniform quadratic B-spline curve.

Chaikin's scheme was extended by Catmull-Clark [2] and Doo-Sabin [3]. These two subdivision methods gave the advanced results over conventional modeling techniques, especially NURBS, with the use of an extension of uniform bi-cubic and bi-quadratic B-spline surfaces for control meshes of arbitrary topology. The Catmull-Clark subdivision surface has a high level of symmetry [4].

In 1987, Loop's subdivision method [5] was proposed. It is an approximation subdivision method using triangular mesh. This scheme obtains a C^1 continuity surface,

Supported by NSFC-CAS Joint Fund (No. U1332130, U1713206), 111 Projects (No. B07033), 973 Project (No. 2014CB931804), NSFC under Grant No. 61672371, Jiangsu Provincial Department of Housing and Urban-Rural Development under grants No. 2017ZD253 and China Scholarship Council.

J. Ren et al. (Eds.): BICS 2018, LNAI 10989, pp. 780–789, 2018.
https://doi.org/10.1007/978-3-030-00563-4_76

including the boundary and sharp features. In 1990, another important kind of subdivision method, the interpolation subdivision method, was proposed by Dyn, Gregory and Levin [6, 7]. This scheme refines an arbitrary triangular mesh by interpolatory subdivision. However, because of its topology rules, it only obtains C^1 continuity on regular meshes. In 1996, Zorin developed a modified Butterfly scheme which obtains a satisfactory result on a limit surface [8]. This modified scheme achieves C^1 continuity everywhere. Loop present an improved Catmull-Clark subdivision surface with bi-cubic patches in 2008 [9], it can get a smooth surface including extraordinary vertex.

Subdivision schemes have some applications in other research areas. In 2010 thin plate splines surfaces design using subdivision methods was proposed by Henrik [10]. Bornemann [11] presents a novel method to facilitate the implementation of b-splines and their interfacing with conventional finite element implementations in 2013. Wang [12] proposed the scheme of approximation Catmull-Clark subdivision surfaces on Graphics Processing Unit in 2010. Subdivision can also use in building materials modeling [13, 14], it builds a smooth surface for any kinds of materials control points.

Subdivision has an advantage to model smooth surface by arbitrary topological mesh, but it lost many features in the control mesh through subdivision refinement. In 1994 Hoppe et al. [15] proposed an algorithm based on Loop subdivision scheme. It tagged the sharp features such as crease, dart, corner, and developed special rules to these features. DeRose et al. [16] generalized the Hoppe algorithm into Catmull-Clark subdivision scheme in 1998. Jerome et al. [17] employ subdivision rules as a surface modeling tool to add other details to meshes. These algorithms did well in some subdivision surface, but they changed subdivision rules in their schemes and broke the uniform surfaces.

This paper proposes a new rule for the Loop subdivision scheme to preserve sharp features. The new rules develop Loop subdivision surface by adding a parameter known as a knot interval. It extends the subdivision rule to triangular subdivision meshes. This novel rules based on Loop subdivision scheme has proven efficient with the models we have simulated, and it could extend to the other subdivision scheme.

This paper organized as follows. In Sects. 2 and 3 we briefly introduce Loop subdivision scheme and knot intervals. A novel subdivision algorithm will discuss in Sect. 4 and we draw a conclusion in the end.

2 Loop Subdivision

Loop subdivision is probably the simplest scheme, but the results are very impressive. It is an approximation face split subdivision for triangular meshes and was proposed by Loop [5] in 1987. The limit subdivision surface achieves C^1 continuity everywhere, including the boundary and extraordinary areas, as been demonstrated [18, 19].

The limit surface is a three-directional box spline, and attains C^2 continuity in regular areas, namely everywhere except at the boundary and areas containing extraordinary vertices, where there is C^1 continuity. In 1994 Hoppe et al. [15] created an extension of the Loop subdivision algorithm which classified the edges and vertices into different types. Subsequently some new algorithms were proposed to model boundaries and concave corners. This subdivision method is an approximation scheme that renews all the vertices at every step of refinement.

The subdivision mask for Loop's scheme is depicted in Fig. 1. The geometric rules are as follows:

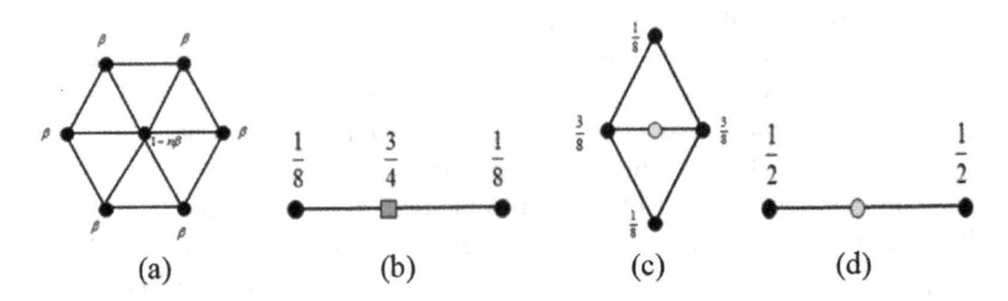

Fig. 1. The Loop subdivision mask (a) inner vertex point, (b) boundary or crease vertex point, (c) inner edge point, (d) boundary or crease edge point

New inner vertex points:

$$P^{k+1} = (1 - n\beta_n)P^k + \beta_n\left(P_0^k + P_1^k + \cdots + P_{n-1}^k\right) \tag{1}$$

New inner edge points:

$$P_i^{k+1} = \frac{3P^k + 3P_i^k + P_{i-1}^k + P_{i+1}^k}{8}, \quad i = 0, 1, \ldots, n-1 \tag{2}$$

Where the parameter $\beta_n = \frac{1}{64n}\left(40 - \left(3 + 2\cos\left(\frac{2\pi}{n}\right)\right)^2\right)$. To avoid the trigonometric function, Warren and Weimer [20] proposed $\beta_n = \frac{3}{n(n+2)}$.

An improved method was developed to help to ensure C^1 continuity [21, 22]. The authors created a modification to the rule of extraordinary areas, which depend on the valence of the vertex. For vertex valences of no more than 7, the Loop scheme is still used, while for the other, extraordinary vertices a new rule was created, as illustrated in the mask shown in Fig. 2. The limit surface can thus achieve C^1 continuity around the boundary.

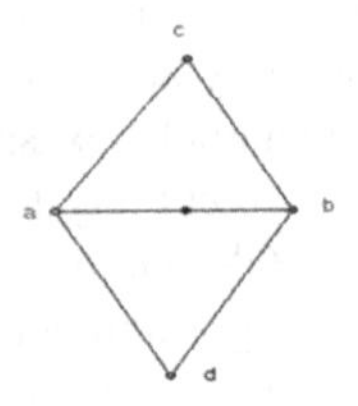

Fig. 2. The mask for extraordinary vertices (Color figure online)

In Fig. 2, the green dot represents the extraordinary vertex with the parameter $a = \frac{1}{4} + \frac{1}{4}\cos\frac{2\pi}{k-1}$, $b = \frac{1}{4} - \frac{1}{4}\cos\frac{2\pi}{k-1}$, $c = d = \frac{1}{8}$, where k is the valence of the extraordinary vertex.

The Loop subdivision method topology rule is presented in Fig. 3. The new face points on each original face are connected with each other, and the new face points are also connected with the new vertex points. Figure 3 demonstrates one step of the Loop subdivision algorithm.

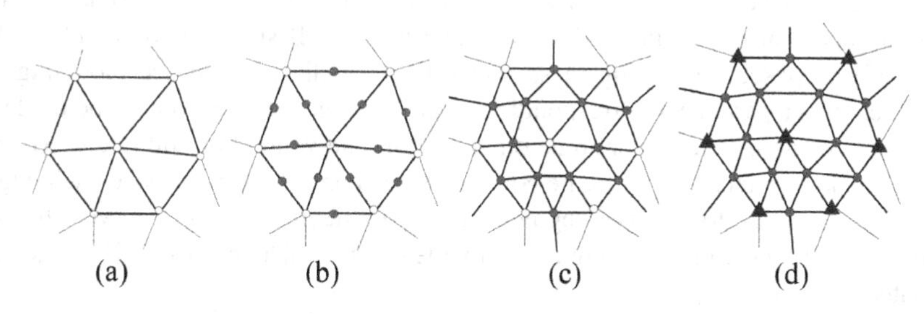

Fig. 3. The Loop scheme topology rule (a) control mesh, (b) new edge points, (c) connection of the edge points, (d) new vertex points in blue (Color figure online)

The Loop subdivision method is an approximation subdivision surface using triangular meshes. The simplicity of the rules has contributed to its popularity and wide use. As an example, a rabbit is modeled in Fig. 4, using the Loop subdivision method. The bottom right image has been refined 6 times: by this point, the surface achieves C^2 continuity almost everywhere. Satisfactory results can be obtained by using this system with most surface rendering applications.

Fig. 4. The Loop algorithm applied to modeling a rabbit (a) control mesh, (b) subdivide once, (c) subdivide 3 times, (d) subdivide 6 times

We can obtain the limit position for a fixed vertex in the initial mesh. For interior vertices, the formulation is similar to Eq. 3, with the parameter β' replaced by $\beta' = \frac{1}{3/8\beta + k}$.

The boundary vertices are expressed as:

$$p_k^{\infty} = \frac{1}{5}(p_{k-1} + p_{k+1}) + \frac{3}{5}p_k \tag{3}$$

3 Knot Intervals

A B-spline can be classified as a class of control points, a knot vector or a degree. Knot information can also be expressed as knot intervals on a B-spline curve, and Sederberg et al. [22] proposed employing these intervals in subdivision surface modeling. The knot interval is a parameter corresponding to the adjacent edge, and could be the length of a B-spline curve segment or some other appropriate value. For odd-degree B-spline curves, the knot interval is set to the corresponding control edge, because each edge of the curve is related to a curve segment. For even-degree B-spline curves, the knot interval is set to the corresponding control vertex, since each vertex of a B-spline curve is related to a curve segment.

Knot intervals have some attractive properties, so knot interval notation is often used to represent knot vectors. For example, knot interval notation has a closer relationship to the control mesh than knot vector notation. Knot intervals are better to represent periodic B-splines. Knot intervals also offer greater flexibility in geometric design, because a knot interval can easily be set to the desired value.

A knot interval can express a B-spline curve, just as a knot vector does, as it contains all the information of a knot vector, except at a knot origin. Opting to use knot interval notation will not alter any property of the vertices of a curve, since the representation of a B-spline curve is consistent under linear transformation of a knot vector. B-splines were first used in approximation theory with approximation functions. In 2D and 3D shape modeling, knot values are important for shape control.

As stated above, for odd-degree B-spline curves, the knot interval is set to the corresponding control edge, while for even-degree B-spline curves, the knot interval is set to the corresponding control vertex. Each control edge and control vertex has only one knot interval. For a B-spline that is not a periodic curve, $\frac{n-1}{2}$ end-condition knot intervals must be set through each of the two end control points.

Figure 5 presents a cubic B-spline curve. Left one shows the control points, which are labeled P with corresponding values, and right one shows the control edges, which are labeled d with special values. We enlarge the control mesh in the end knots with an additional knot interval.

Periodic B-spline curves are a little simpler than the curve in Fig. 5, because of the lack of end knots. Periodic B-spline curves are closed curves, so we do not need to add an additional knot interval.

Figure 6 shows the cubic periodic B-splines with the same control mesh and different knot intervals. In (b), we increase the knot interval values of d_1 and d_2 to 3 and 2 respectively. It will be noted that the shape of the curve has changed slightly. The length of the corresponding curve is enlarged. In (c) the knot interval is set at $d_0 = 0$: the corresponding curve has shrunk to 0 and disappeared from the figure. When we set $d_0 = d_1 = 0$ in (d), the finial curve only contains 3 curve segments.

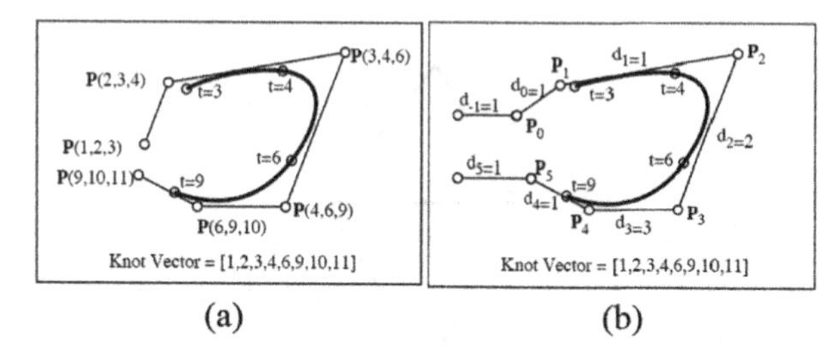

Fig. 5. Sample cubic B-spline (a) control points, (b) control edges

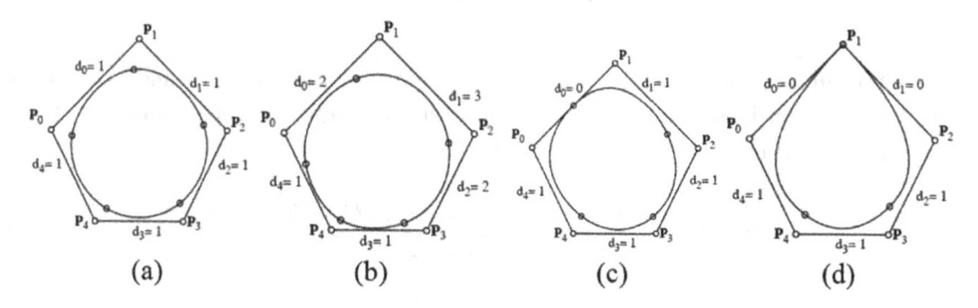

Fig. 6. Periodic B-spline curves (a)–(d) is for the same control mesh and different knot intervals

The polar labels corresponding to the control points are useful in some applications, such as knot insertion with knot intervals. Polar algebra is a powerful tool for the analysis of B-spline curves. The arguments of polar labels are sums of knot intervals. We are free to choose any parameter for the knot. In Fig. 7, we set the knot origin to coincide with control vertex P_0: the polar values are explained in (b).

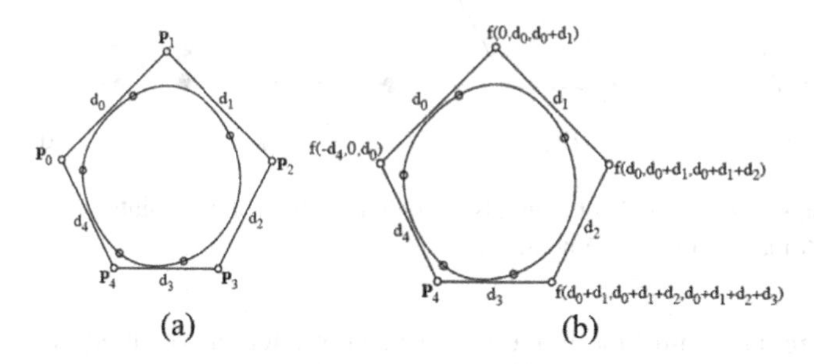

Fig. 7. Polar labels with knot intervals (a) and (b) control vertex and the polar values

4 A New Loop Subdivision

The subdivision mask presented in Fig. 8 and the geometric rules are much like those of the Loop subdivision method. The new rules add a knot interval parameter at each edge next to the corresponding control points.

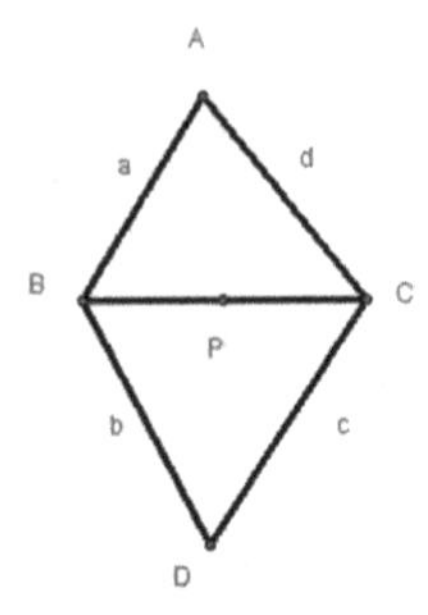

Fig. 8. Loop scheme using knot intervals which add to the edges

The formulation of the geometric rules is given in Eq. 4. A, B, C and D represent the positions of vertices, and a, b, c and d represent the knot intervals, which may be set to any desired value, allowing great flexibility in modeling.

$$P = \frac{(a+b)B + (a+d)A + (c+d)C + (b+c)D}{2(a+b+c+d)} \tag{4}$$

And we could also add a knot interval parameter at each control point, the rules are shown in Fig. 9. In figures (a) and (b), the A, B, C, D, E, F are the control points of the mesh, the knot interval is the a, b, c, d, e and f.

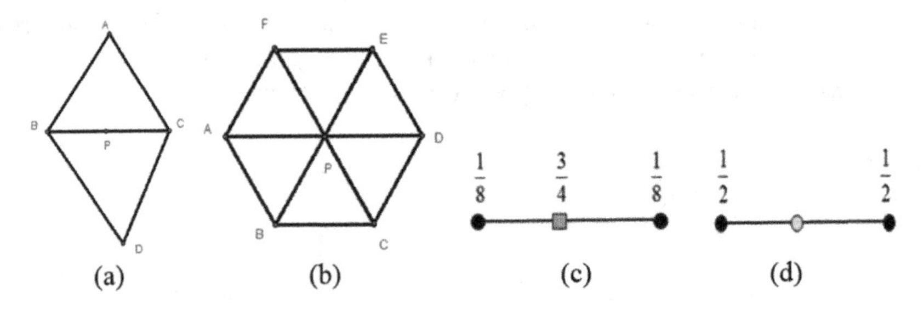

Fig. 9. Loop scheme using knot intervals which add to the control points (a) and (b) the vertex point rules, (c) and (d) the edge point rules

In the regular control mesh, the values of knot interval which add to the edges are $a = d = \frac{1}{8}$, $b = c = \frac{3}{8}$. And the values of knot interval which adds to the control points are $a = \frac{1}{64n}\left(40 - \left(3 + 2\cos\left(\frac{2\pi}{n}\right)\right)^2\right)$, $p = 1 - \frac{1}{64}\left(40 - \left(3 + 2\cos\left(\frac{2\pi}{n}\right)\right)^2\right)$.

For the infinite sharp features, the values of knot interval which add to the edges are $a = d = 0$, $b = c = \frac{1}{2}$. The values of knot interval add to the control points are $a = b = c = d = e = f = 0, p = 1$.

For the semi-sharp features, we can change the value of each parameter to control the sharpness of the surface.

Figure 10 provides some examples to illustrate the subdivision rules. The left image is the control mesh. It can be seen that by setting appropriate knot interval values, the features in the final model are well preserved.

Fig. 10. A human model (a) control mesh, (b) limit surface by our rules

Figure 11 gives a comparison between the Loop subdivision rules and our novel rules. The left one is the control mesh, the middle one subdivides 5 times by Loop rules, and the right one also subdivides 5 times our novel rules. We can easily find the right one preserves the sharp features from the control mesh.

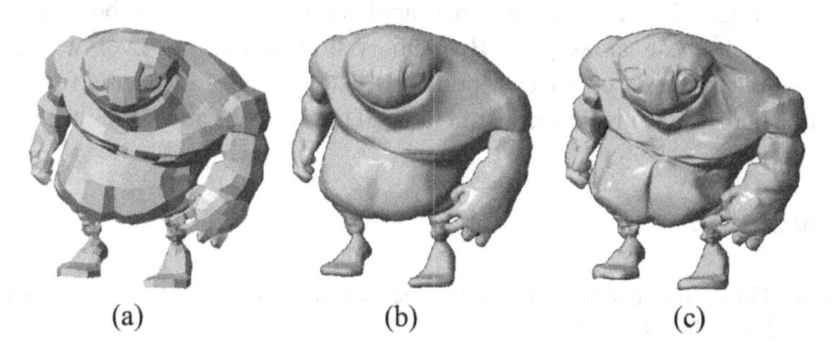

Fig. 11. A carton model (a) control mesh, (b) subdivide by loop rules, (c) subdivide by our rules

This rule describes a flexible method for adjusting the shape of the subdivision surface. By setting appropriate values of knot interval, a variety of sharp features from 'infinitely sharp' to 'semi sharp' can be modeled. Compared with other subdivision methods, this approach offers much greater freedom of surface expression. Figure 12 demonstrates the surface in the same control mesh with the different values of the knot interval. From the same control mesh we get a comparison limit surface models by different values of knot interval.

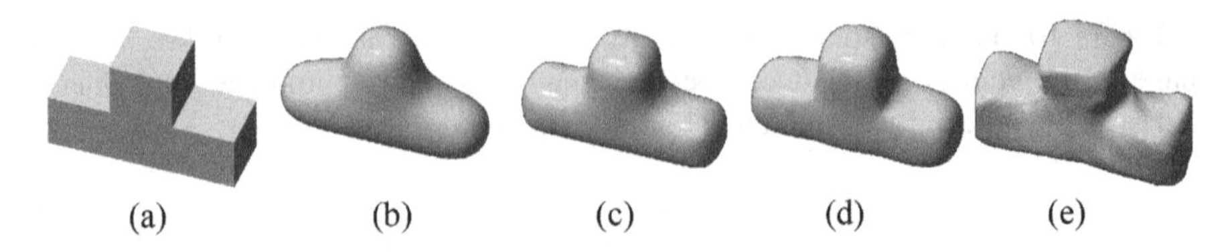

Fig. 12. Different knot interval model (a) control mesh, (b)–(e) limit surface by different values of knot interval

5 Conclusion and Future Work

Knot intervals were introduced into subdivision surfaces for triangular meshes. This method increases the flexibility of subdivision surface shape control. Since the topology of the control mesh is unaltered, one can easily decide to adopt the modification or not at any given refinement step. From the figures presented in this paper, it can be seen that sharp features can be preserved very well. The limit surface can attain the same continuity as achieved by butterfly surface modeling, with the exception of the areas around infinitely sharp features.

When using the knot interval method, appropriate values of knot intervals must be selected. Further research is needed to determine the optimum values of knot intervals to model different degrees of surface sharpness.

In computer vision we often have to model some animation characters, 3D reconstruction [23–25], and some other applications [26–29]. Subdivision surface could involve in these areas [16]. But subdivision models an everywhere smooth surface. Some features in characters, buildings, and etc. are lost. In the future we will discuss the subdivision in 3D reconstruction, 3D rendering, and computer animation.

References

1. Chaikin, G.M.: An algorithm for high-speed curve generation. Comput. Graph. Image Process. **3**(4), 346–349 (1974)
2. Catmull, E., Clark, J.: Recursively generated B-spline surfaces on arbitrary topological meshes. Comput. Aided Des. **10**(6), 350–355 (1978)
3. Doo, D., Sabin, M.: Behaviors of recursive division surfaces near extraordinary points. Comput. Aided Des. **10**(6), 356–360 (1978)
4. Kavan, L., Collins, S., O'Sullivan, C.: Automatic linearization of non-linear skinning. In: Proceedings of Symposium on interactive 3D Graphics and Games, Boston, 27 February–1 March (2009)
5. Loop, C.: Smooth subdivision surfaces based on triangles. Master's thesis, Department of Mathematics, University of Utah (1987)
6. Dyn, N.: A butterfly subdivision method for surface interpolation with tension control. ACM Trans. Graph. **9**(2), 160–169 (1990)
7. Dyn, N., Levin, D., Micchelli, C.A.: Using parameters to increase smoothness of curves and surfaces generated by subdivision. Comput. Aided Geom. Des. **7**(1), 129–140 (1990)
8. Zorin, D., Sweldens, W.: Interactive multiresolution mesh editing. In: Conference on Computer Graphics and Interactive Techniques, Los Angeles, 3–8 August (1997)

9. Loop, C., Schaefer, S.: Approximating Catmull-Clark subdivision surfaces with bi-cubic patches. ACM Trans. Graph. **27**(1), 1–11 (2008)
10. Henrik, W., Joe, W.: Subdivision schemes for thin plate splines. Comput. Graph. Forum **17** (3), 303–313 (2010)
11. Bornemann, P.B., Cirak, F.: A subdivision-based implementation of the hierarchical b-spline finite element method. Comput. Methods Appl. Mech. Eng. **253**(1), 584–598 (2013)
12. Wang, L.Z., Liu, W., Xu, L.: Approximating Catmull-Clark subdivision surfaces with bicubic Bezier patches on GPU. J. Comput. Appl. **30**(2), 37–39 (2010)
13. Wu, Z., Hu, F., Zhang, Y., Gao, Q., Chen, Z.: Mechanical analysis of double-layered circular graphene sheets as building material embedded in an elastic medium. J. Cent. South Univ. **24**, 2717–2724 (2017)
14. Wu, Z., Zhang, Y., Hu, F., Gao, Q., Xu, X., Zheng, R.: Vibration analysis of bilayered graphene sheets for building materials in thermal environments based on the element-free method. J. Nanomater. (2018). https://doi.org/10.1155/2018/6568061
15. Hoppe, H., DeRose, T., Duhamp, T., et al.: Piecewise smooth surface reconstruction. In: Proceedings of the 21st Annual Conference on Computer Graphics and Interactive Techniques, Orlando, 24–29 July (1994)
16. DeRose, T., Kass, M., Truong, T.: Subdivision surfaces in character animation. In: Proceedings of the 25th Annual Conference on Computer Graphics and Interactive Techniques, Orlando, 19–24 July (1998)
17. Jerome, M., Jos, S.: A unified subdivision scheme for polygonal modeling. Comput. Graph. Forum **20**(3), 471–479 (2010)
18. Schweitzer, J.E.: Analysis and application of subdivision surfaces. Ph.D thesis, University of Washington, Seattle (1996)
19. Zorin, D.: Subdivision and multiresolution surface representations. Ph.D thesis, Caltech, Pasaedna (1997)
20. Warren, J., Weimer, H.: Subdivision Methods for Geometric Design, pp. 276–285. Morgan Kaufmann Publishers, Boston (2002)
21. Biermann, H., Levin, A., Zorin, D.: Piecewise smooth subdivision surfaces with normal control. In: Proceedings of the 27th Annual Conference on Computer Graphics and Interactive Techniques, New Orleans, 23–28 July (2000)
22. Sederberg, T.W., Zheng, J., Sewell, D., Sabin, M.: Non-uniform recursive subdivision surfaces. In: Proceedings of the 25th Annual Conference on Computer Graphics and Interactive Techniques, Orlando, 19–24 July (1998)
23. Feng, Y.: Object-based 2D-to-3D video conversion for effective stereoscopic content generation in 3D-TV applications. IEEE Trans. Broadcast. **57**(2), 500–509 (2011)
24. Ren, J.: Multi-camera video surveillance for real-time analysis and reconstruction of soccer games. Mach. Vis. Appl. **21**(6), 855–863 (2010)
25. Ren, J.: Real-time modeling of 3-D soccer ball trajectories from multiple fixed cameras. IEEE Trans. Circuits Syst. Video Technol. **18**(3), 350–362 (2008)
26. Zheng, J., Zuo, X., Ren, J., et al.: Multiple depth maps integration for 3D reconstruction using geodesic graph cuts. Int. J. Software Eng. Knowl. Eng. **25**(03), 473–792 (2015)
27. Zhao, D., Zheng, J., Ren, J.: Effective removal of artifacts from views synthesized using depth image based rendering, Vancouver, Canada, 31 August–2 September (2015)
28. Wu, Z., Li, B., Dang, C., et al.: Solving long haul airline disruption problem caused by groundings using a distributed fixed-point computational approach to integer programming. Neurocomputing **269**, 232–255 (2017)
29. Wu, Z., Li, B., Dang, C.: Solving multiple fleet airline disruption problems using a distributed-computation approach to integer programming. IEEE Access **5**, 19116–19131 (2017)

Making Industrial Robots Smarter with Adaptive Reasoning and Autonomous Thinking for Real-Time Tasks in Dynamic Environments: A Case Study

Jaime Zabalza[1], Zixiang Fei[2], Cuebong Wong[2], Yijun Yan[1], Carmelo Mineo[1], Erfu Yang[2(✉)], Tony Rodden[3], Jorn Mehnen[2], Quang-Cuong Pham[4], and Jinchang Ren[1]

[1] Department of Electronic and Electrical Engineering, University of Strathclyde, Glasgow G1 1XJ, UK
[2] Department of Design, Manufacture and Engineering Management, University of Strathclyde, Glasgow G1 1XJ, UK
erfu.yang@strath.ac.uk
[3] Advanced Forming Research Centre, University of Strathclyde, Glasgow G1 1XJ, UK
[4] School of Mechanical and Aerospace Engineering, Nanyang Technological University, 50 Nanyang Avenue, Singapore 639798, Singapore

Abstract. In order to extend the abilities of current robots in industrial applications towards more autonomous and flexible manufacturing, this work presents an integrated system comprising real-time sensing, path-planning and control of industrial robots to provide them with adaptive reasoning, autonomous thinking and environment interaction under dynamic and challenging conditions. The developed system consists of an intelligent motion planner for a 6 degrees-of-freedom robotic manipulator, which performs pick-and-place tasks according to an optimized path computed in real-time while avoiding a moving obstacle in the workspace. This moving obstacle is tracked by a sensing strategy based on machine vision, working on the HSV space for color detection in order to deal with changing conditions including non-uniform background, lighting reflections and shadows projection. The proposed machine vision is implemented by an off-board scheme with two low-cost cameras, where the second camera is aimed at solving the problem of vision obstruction when the robot invades the field of view of the main sensor. Real-time performance of the overall system has been experimentally tested, using a KUKA KR90 R3100 robot.

Keywords: Machine vision · Path planning · Robot control Adaptive reasoning · Dynamic environment

1 Introduction

The integration of robotic systems in human life has become a reality thanks to the major advancements in the field of robotics [1]. Comprising of many applications [2, 3], smart robotic systems are not only able to perform faster and more accurately but are also to

J. Ren et al. (Eds.): BICS 2018, LNAI 10989, pp. 790–800, 2018.
https://doi.org/10.1007/978-3-030-00563-4_77

learn, adapt to the environment and make decisions in several degrees of intelligence [4], achieving collaborative systems able to interact with humans [5]. Most real-world systems are based on predefined series of tasks planned offline [6, 7], and have the advantage of being highly effective for traditional mass-production processes based on repetition. However, predefined planning lacks the capability for adapting to changes, which becomes a huge shortcoming in industrial systems. Hence, some barriers need to be removed before robots and humans can share the same workspace [8].

In order to provide robotic systems with autonomous adaptability and smart interaction with the environment [9], new capabilities linked to sensory attributes are required. Although there is a number of potential sensing approaches, including ultrasonic [8] or laser, machine vision [9] is widely used not only in robotics [10] but also in many other applications [11, 12], due to its satisfactory performance and/or affordable cost. Therefore, the use of cameras, in conjunction with effective image processing, is a feasible approach to dealing with non-uniform lighting conditions and shadows [13] and other problem requirements such as adaptability and robustness [14]. In the same terms, multiple cameras can be used to overcome problems such as vision obstruction [15–17].

In this work, a real-time approach for smart path planning [18] and control of robotic arms is developed. The integration of machine vision provides the whole system with sensory capabilities. Although it is possible to find some research literature evaluating real-time path planning or related adaptability in robot manipulators [7, 18, 19], such previous works possess a number of drawbacks including the use of expensive sensors, non-integrated implementations and lack of modularity. In this work, the KUKA QUANTEC KR90 R3100 [20] is selected as a platform for testing an intelligent system, able to adapt to a dynamically changing environment. This is achieved through a modular machine vision software platform, based on low-cost cameras running in parallel.

The robot performs pick-and-place tasks in a challenging scenario, where a moving obstacle can intercept any planned path between the start (pick) and goal (place) locations. Therefore, collision with the moving obstacle has to be avoided, adapting the robot path to the workspace conditions in real-time. With a biological inspired integration of vision, reasoned planning and motion control, including cognitive structures that can be identified as offline training and calibration, the main objective of this work is to achieve an adaptive intelligent system with environmental awareness. Whenever a potential collision is detected, the robot has to divert towards an alternative effective collision-free path, in a prompt fashion. The aim is to have a better reaction time than the average human reaction time, whose average is equal to 180 ms [18].

This manuscript is organized as follows. Section 2 gives a brief overview of the path planning and robot control implementation. Section 3 presents and develops the sensing strategy adopted to provide the whole system with sensory capabilities. The experimental setup for a physical demonstrator is detailed in Sect. 4, while Sect. 5 evaluates the achieved performance. Final remarks are drawn in Sect. 6.

2 Path Planning and Robot Control

2.1 Overview

Pick and place tasks are traditionally automated through offline programming, by defining predefined paths between the two points. While this approach is suitable for structured and static environments, this study addresses dynamic, changing environments, where an obstacle, moving within the workspace, can invalidate the currently active robot path at any point in time. Thus an additional requirement of the path planning module is to find a feasible (collision-free) path in real-time, such that the robot trajectory can be updated quickly enough, when an interfering obstacle is detected.

This real-time path planning problem is solved using the dynamic roadmaps method, which is a real-time variant of the configuration space (C-space) sampling-based probabilistic road maps technique [21]. The dynamic roadmap method has been proven effective for motion planning in changing environments due to its high-speed online computation. This speed is achieved through an offline pre-processing phase, which is required to be computed only once for any particular robot.

After the path planning procedure, the robot is controlled through a novel approach based on a KUKA software add-on, known as Robot-Sensor Interface (RSI). This allows sending command positional packets at a rate of 250 Hz. With this method, motion paths can be updated rapidly in response to changes in the environment, as determined by the machine vision module. The path planning stages are explained below.

2.2 Offline Stage

During offline pre-processing, mapping between a C-space roadmap and a discretized Cartesian (geometric) workspace is created such that an entirely feasible roadmap can be quickly obtained when the geometric information about the obstacles in the environment is known. The offline pre-processing stage comprises: (i) robot C-space sampling, (ii) workspace discretization and (iii) mapping between C-space and Cartesian space.

The C-space sampling involves randomly sampling the entire C-space to obtain nodes of the roadmap. This is performed assuming a completely obstacle-free space. Then, pairs of neighbouring nodes are connected to form the edges of the roadmap. Next, the workspace is discretized into uniform cells. The spatial resolution available is obviously dependent on this size, with a subsequent trade-off between finer resolution and faster computation. Increasing the number of cells increases the computation time of the third stage exponentially. Finally, the mapping between C-Space and workspace is obtained by iteratively checking every robot configuration associated with all sampled nodes and along each edge of the roadmap. All workspace cells that collide with the robot at these configurations are mapped to the associated nodes and edges. Hence during online execution, when the cells that are pre-occupied by an obstacle is known, the roadmap can be "trimmed" to leave only feasible segments.

2.3 Online Stage

In real-time operation, the algorithm combines the vision information about the position of a moving obstacle and the offline-computed mapping to create a graph representation of the collision-free regions of the C-space. The desired start and goal configuration (which may differ in each instance of path planning) is connected to the nearest node in the roadmap. Then, the A* search algorithm [22], which is an extension of the Dijkstra's algorithm, is used to search for the shortest route within the graph in order to find a path between start and goal that guarantees no collision with the moving obstacle. Afterwards, B-splines [23] are used to smooth the obtained path and provide continuous smooth motion from any start to goal configuration. A diagram is given in Fig. 1.

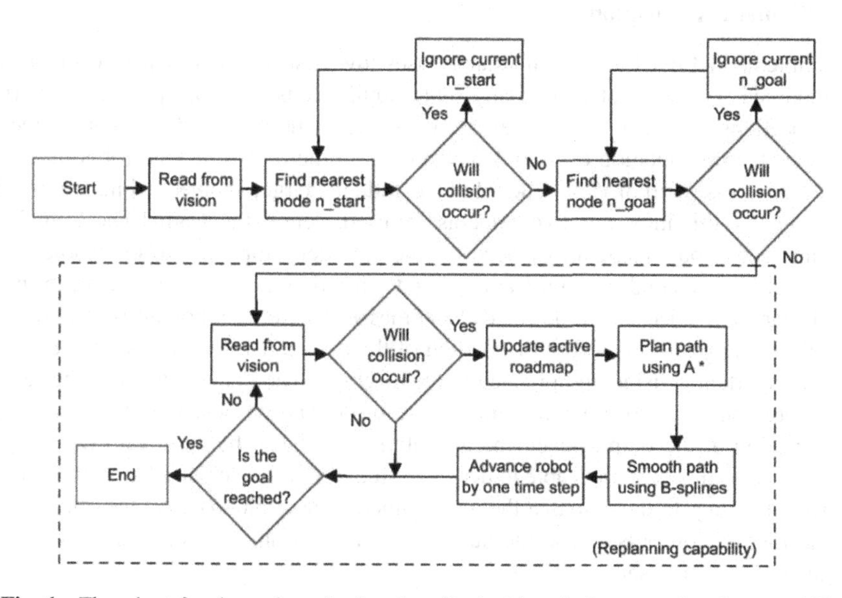

Fig. 1. Flowchart for dynamic path planning. Dashed box indicates replanning capability.

As the robot executes the initially planned path, the path planner continues to monitor the obstacles in the environment. When a change results in a collision with the previously planned path, a new updated path is planned using the same approach described above. This is made possible by the low computation time (<50 ms) achieved using the dynamic roadmaps approach.

3 Machine Vision

3.1 Overview

In order to provide the robotic system with vision capabilities, a sensing strategy based on machine vision was developed. It uses optical cameras and runs independently but simultaneously to the rest of the system, comprising path planning and robot control.

The machine vision code architecture is made up of three independent stages, which also run in parallel by the implementation of three threads: (i) frames acquisition, (ii) image processing and (iii) communication. First, the acquisition thread manages the use of cameras for video stream acquisition. Second, the obtained frames are treated by the image processing stage, which performs object detection based on color and additional filtering. Third, the communication thread stores the detection information in a package, to be sent directly to the path planner by TCP/IP communication sockets [24]. This enables the main control module and the machine vision module to communicate with each other in real-time. The computation time for acquisition, processing and communication do not cumulate.

3.2 Camera Acquisition

The implemented machine vision strategy uses low-cost webcams. These cameras are not mounted on the robot as in many other applications [25], but placed at external fixed locations. In order words, they are off-board cameras. Fixed off-board cameras facilitates the computation of spatial coordinates, at the cost of having robot intrusion into the cameras' field of view. The robot can hide the targeted object while moving. In order to solve this intrusion, two cameras are used, denoted as Cam-1 and Cam-2.

Cam-1, the main camera, is placed overhead to get a top view of the whole robot workspace. The second camera, Cam-2, is introduced as an auxiliary sensor, to make sure the targeted object can be detected at all times and solve the robot intrusion issue into the field of view of Cam-1. The disposition of the two cameras is discussed in Sect. 4.

An important consideration related to the machine vision is how to solve the sensor fusion problem, as two different cameras are used. The proposed strategy addresses sensor fusion at the output level: the algorithm prioritizes the main camera (Cam-1) and, as long as this camera is able to detect the moving obstacle, its information is used for path planning. In the case that the main camera is not able to detect the object, then the machine vision opts to use the auxiliary camera (Cam-2), using its information. A related diagram is shown in Fig. 2.

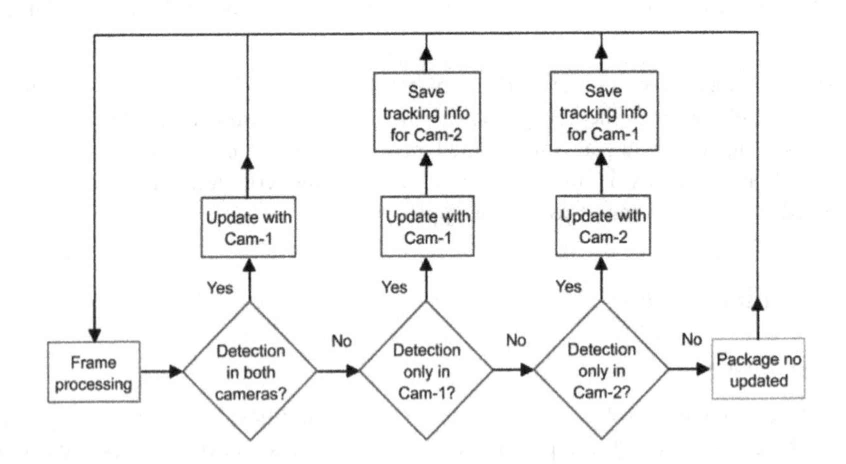

Fig. 2. Flowchart for sensor fusion in real-time.

3.3 Image Processing

Object detection is based on color discrimination, implemented in the hue-saturation-value (HSV) color space. This space, which differs from others such as the red-green-blue (RGB) [26, 27], comprises parameters related not only to the true color targeted (hue), but also the color depth (saturation) and color darkness (value). A good selection of allowed parameter ranges in the HSV color space can deal with reflections, shadows and other related issues, achieving satisfactory object detection performance.

In a similar way to the path planning implementation, there are two stages for the image processing: (i) offline calibration and (ii) online workflow.

Offline implementation involves some calibration procedures. First, a contour mask is defined for masking the frames. Second, some calibration points are measured in the workspace and translated into pixel coordinates in the images. These calibration points are used for training a projection algorithm, which will translate coordinate pixels to 2D real-world coordinates. Finally, the selection of range values to target in the HSV color space make up the last part of the calibration procedures.

The online workflow involves the following steps: (i) transformation from RGB image to HSV image, (ii) transformation from HSV image to binary image, by means of applying a selected HSV color range, and (iii) posterior treatment of the binary image, including size and tracking filtering, avoiding the detection of undesired objects.

3.4 Communication

While running in parallel, the machine vision can communicate in real-time with the main control software by means of TCP/IP sockets communication [24]. In the TCP/IP configuration, the machine vision software acts as a server (slave), while the main control software acts as a client (master). Therefore, the machine vision waits for any request and replies immediately with the latest information available. In order to do so, an information package is defined, which is made up of several bytes containing the coordinates (x, y) and approximated dimensions (bounding box) of the detected object.

4 Experimental Setup

4.1 Robotic Manipulator

The implementation of the integrated system is based on the KR90 R3100 from KUKA [20], a robotic arm usually found in many factories. This robot is a 6-axis jointed-arm manipulator, with volume of 66 m^3 and 50 kg weight. In order to control this robot, dynamic link libraries (DLLs) were developed in C++ language.

The KR90 R3100 has been selected for experiments because of its wide use in industry, however, the implemented approach is easily transferable to other robots and experimental conditions.

4.2 Workspace and Moving Obstacle

In the experiments, a table with dimensions 160 × 110 cm was selected as the robot workspace (Fig. 3). The table is covered by a recycled tablecloth containing different textile traces with the purpose of simulating a dirty, noisy environment.

The moving obstacle is implemented by a remote controlled car (20 × 10 cm) covered by cardboard that is yellow in colour (intending to reproduce a similar safety jacket tonality). Being remotely controlled, the car can be driven by an operator behind safety barriers, complying with all safety regulations.

Fig. 3. Workspace table (left) with pick-and-place box (top) and moving obstacle (bottom).

4.3 Cameras and Location

Two Advent HD Pro (AWCAMHD15) were selected as sensors to prove that an inexpensive machine vision implementation is possible. These are low-cost cameras able to capture images with an original resolution of 640 × 480 pixels and frame rate of 30 fps.

The main camera, Cam-1, was placed in an overhead location approximately 3 m high over the ground, capturing images of the workspace table in landscape mode. The auxiliary Cam-2 was placed at a much lower height of 1.5 m, and provided a side view of the workspace in relation to Cam-1. The selected disposition for Cam-2 covered all blind points in Cam-1 when the robotic arm intruded its field of view.

4.4 Host Computer and Related Software

A laptop was used to run all software modules in parallel. The path planning module was implemented in Matlab. Robot control and machine vision were implemented in C++ language and called from Matlab through DLLs and executable files.

The laptop was based on a quad-core Intel i7 CPU with 16 GB RAM, running the 64-bit Windows 10 operating system. Matlab R2016b and the OpenCV 3.1 library (for machine vision) were used. Two USB ports (one for each camera) and an Ethernet port for connecting to the robot were required.

5 Performance Evaluations

The performed experimental tests proved that the proposed machine vision works effectively and robustly, as it was able to continuously track the moving obstacle under changing conditions including reflections and shadows. Additionally, the intrusion of the robot into the field of view of Cam-1 was successfully solved by the introduction of the auxiliary Cam-2.

The precision (resolution) of the vision system has been measured to be approximately 0.3 cm per pixel, with an estimated positional accuracy of approximately ±3 cm for the obstacle, which are acceptable figures for the performed tasks.

Thanks to the machine vision, the path planning module was able to detect potential collisions in the predefined paths between start and goal locations, allowing the robotic manipulator to trace alternative trajectories to avoid the moving obstacle in real-time during pick-and-place tasks. Figure 4 shows a frame from a video acquired during demonstrations. In conclusion, the integrated system performed satisfactorily.

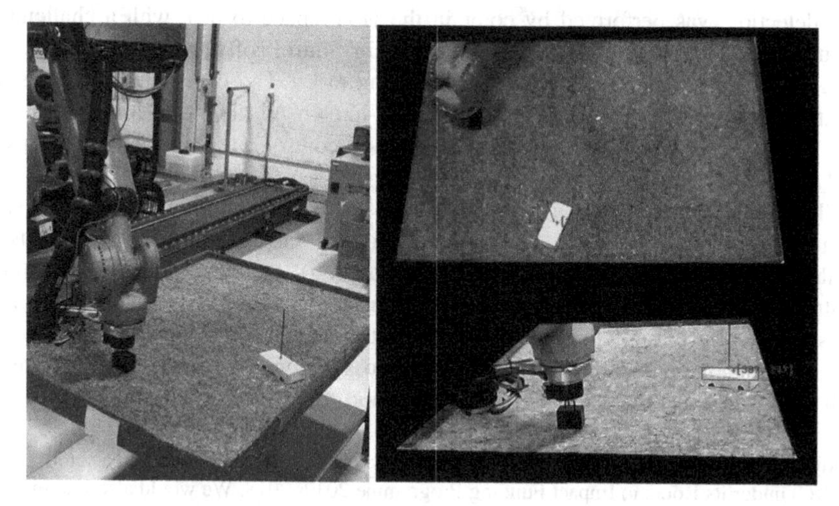

Fig. 4. A real video frame (left) with related captures by Cam-1 (top) and Cam-2 (bottom).

In relation to the computation time (Table 1), the main bottleneck lies in the image acquisition, due to the cameras' limited frame rate. However, the parallel execution of machine vision and path planning avoids accumulation of the computation times. Therefore, the overall time for the integrated system (around 60 ms) is faster than the one in [18] (around 90 ms) and much lower than that of the average human reaction time, estimated as 180 ms.

Table 1. Estimated computation time for machine vision, path planning and overall system.

Machine vision		Path planning		Overall time (ms)
Stage	Time (ms)	Stage	Time (ms)	
Camera acquisition	45	Read package	12	Proposed ~60
Image processing	14	Check collision	15	Reference [18] ~90
Communication	<1	Replanning	30	Human reaction ~180

6 Conclusions

In this work, a sensing strategy based on machine vision using low-cost optical cameras was developed for a robot manipulator system with real-time path planning and dynamic collision-avoidance capabilities. An integrated system was developed and tested with the KUKA KR90 R3100, a traditional industrial robot with 6 degrees of freedom.

The machine vision is based on two cameras placed off-board in fixed locations. The detection was performed by color in the HSV space to deal with a challenging environment. Computed in parallel with the main control software, they communicate in real-time for efficient pick-and-place planning tasks. The path planner was implemented using dynamic roadmaps, with the well-known A* algorithm for graph search and B-splines for smoothing, while robot motion control was achieved by means of DLLs.

The motivation of this work was to build a flexible and autonomous smart system with environmental awareness through a biological inspired integration of sensory attributes (machine vision), reasoning (path planning), coordinated movement (robot control) and cognitive learning (offline training and calibration). Performance in a physical demonstrator showed that intelligent behavior of robots for challenging environments in the manufacturing industry is possible, with a global system frequency well below 180 ms, the estimated human reaction time.

Acknowledgements. This research is supported by the Advanced Forming Research Centre (AFRC) under its Route to Impact Funding Programme 2017–2018. We would also like to thank Dr. Remi Christopher Zante, Dr. Wenjuan Wang (AFRC, University of Strathclyde), Prof. Stephen Gareth Pierce, Dr. Gordon Dobie, and Dr. Charles MacLeod (Centre for Ultrasonic Engineering, University of Strathclyde), and Dr. Francisco Suarez-Ruiz (Nanyang Technological University, Singapore) for their contribution and support towards the completion of this project.

References

1. Zeng, Y., Zhao, Y., Bai, J., Bo, X.: Toward robot self-consciousness (II): brain-inspired robot bodily self-model for self-recognition. Cogn. Comput. **10**(2), 307–320 (2018)
2. Liu, Y., Tian, Z., Liu, Y., Li, J., Fu, F., Bian, J.: Cognitive modeling for robotic assembly/maintenance task in space exploration. In: Baldwin, C. (ed.) AHFE 2017. AISC, vol. 586, pp. 143–153. Springer, Cham (2018). https://doi.org/10.1007/978-3-319-60642-2_13

3. Mineo, C., Pierce, S.G., Nicholson, P.I., Cooper, I.: Robotic path planning for non-destructive testing – a custom MATLAB toolbox approach. Robot. Comput. Integr. Manuf. **37**, 1–12 (2016)
4. Chella, A.: A robot architecture based on higher order perception loop. In: Hussain, A., Aleksander, I., Smith, L., Barros, A., Chrisley, R., Cutsuridis, V. (eds.) Brain Inspired Cognitive Systems, vol. 657, pp. 267–283. Springer, New York (2008). https://doi.org/10.1007/978-0-387-79100-5_15
5. Cherubini, A., Passama, R., Crosnier, A., Lasnier, A., Fraisse, P.: Collaborative manufacturing with physical human–robot interaction. Robot. Comput. Integr. Manuf. **40**, 1–13 (2016)
6. Ajwad, S.A., Ullah, M.I., Khelifa, B., Iqbal, J.: A comprehensive state-of-the-art on control of industrial articulated robots. J. Balkan Tribol. Assoc. **20**(4), 499–521 (2014)
7. Lopez-Juarez, I.: Skill acquisition for industrial robots: from stand-alone to distributed learning. In: The 2016 IEEE International Conference on Automatica, pp. 1–5 (2016)
8. Anand, G., Rahul, E.S., Bhavani, R.R.: A sensor framework for human–robot collaboration in industrial robot work-cell. In: International Conference on Intelligent Computing, Instrumentation and Control Technologies, Kerala State, Kannur, India, pp. 715–720 (2017)
9. Perez, L., Rodriguez, I., Rodriguez, N., Usamentiaga, R., Garcia, D.F.: Robot guidance using machine vision techniques in industrial environments: a comparative review. Sensors **16**(3), 335 (2016)
10. Feng, Y., Ren, J., Jiang, J., Halvey, M., Jose, J.M.: Effective venue image retrieval using robust feature extraction and model constrained matching for mobile robot localization. Mach. Vis. Appl. **23**, 1011–1027 (2012)
11. Wang, Z., Ren, J., Zhang, D., Sun, M., Jiang, J.: A deep-learning based feature hybrid framework for spatiotemporal saliency detection inside videos. Neurocomputing **287**, 68–83 (2018)
12. Han, J., Zhang, D., Cheng, G., Guo, L., Ren, J.: Object detection in optical remote sensing images based on weakly supervised learning and high-level feature learning. IEEE Trans. Geosci. Remote Sens. **53**(6), 3325–3337 (2015)
13. Yan, Y., et al.: Cognitive fusion of thermal and visible imagery for effective detection and tracking of pedestrians in videos. Cogn. Comput. **10**, 94–104 (2018)
14. Liu, Q., Wang, Y., Minghao, Y., Ren, J., Li, R.: Decontaminate feature for tracking: adaptive tracking via evolutionary feature subset. J. Electron. Imaging **26**(6), 063025 (2017)
15. Ren, J., Orwell, J., Jones, G.A., Xu, M.: Real-time modeling of 3-D soccer ball trajectories from multiple fixed cameras. IEEE Trans. Circ. Syst. Video Technol. **18**(3), 350–362 (2008)
16. Ren, J., Orwell, J., Jones, G.A., Xu, M.: Tracking the soccer ball using multiple fixed cameras. Comput. Vis. Image Underst. **113**(5), 633–642 (2009)
17. Ren, J., Xu, M., Orwell, J., Jones, G.A.: Multi-camera video surveillance for real-time analysis and reconstruction of soccer games. Mach. Vis. Appl. **21**, 855–863 (2010)
18. Kunz, T., Reiser, U., Stilman, M., Verl, A.: Real-time path planning for a robot arm in changing environments. In: The 2010 IEEE/RSJ International Conference on Intelligent Robots and Systems, Taipei, Taiwan (2010)
19. Galvao-Wall, D., Economou, J., Goyder, H., Knowles, K., Silson, P., Lawrance, M.: Mobile robot arm trajectory generation for operation in confined environments. J. Syst. Control Eng. **229**(3), 215–234 (2015)
20. KR QUANTEC extra HA Specifications (2013). https://www.kuka.com/en-de/products/robot-systems/industrial-robots/kr-quantec-extra. Accessed May 2018
21. Leven, P., Hutchinson, S.: A framework for real-time path planning in changing environments. Int. J. Robot. Res. **21**(12), 999–1030 (2002)

22. Cui, S.G., Wang, H., Yang, L.: A simulation study of A-star algorithm for robot path planning. In: 16th International Conference on Mechatronics Technology, pp. 506–510 (2012)
23. De Boor, C.: A Practical Guide to Splines. Applied Mathematical Sciences. Springer, New York (1978)
24. Donahoo, M.J., Calvert, K.L.: TCP/IP Sockets in C Practical Guide for Programmers. Morgan Kaufmann, Burlington (2009)
25. Mutlu, M., Melo, K., Vespignani, M., Bernardino, A., Ijspeert, A.J.: Where to place cameras on a snake robot: focus on camera trajectory and motion blur. In: 2015 IEEE International Symposium on Safety, Security, and Rescue Robotics (SSRR), pp. 1–8 (2015)
26. Abu, P.A., Fernandez, P.: Performance comparison of the Teknomo–Fernandez algorithm on the RGB and HSV color spaces. In: Humanoid, Nanotechnology, Information Technology, Communication and Control, Environment and Management, Palawan, pp. 1–6 (2014)
27. Zhou, Y., Zeng, F.Z., Zhao, H., Murray, P., Ren, J.: Hierarchical visual perception and two-dimensional compressive sensing for effective content-based color image retrieval. Cogn. Comput. **8**, 877–889 (2016)

Shading Structure-Guided Depth Image Restoration

Xiuxiu Li[1(✉)], Haiyan Jin[1], Yanjuan Liu[1], and Liwen Shi[2]

[1] Xi'an University of Technology, Xi'an 710048, China
{lixiuxiu, jinhaiyan}@xaut.edu.cn,
liuyanjuan@stu.xaut.edu.cn

[2] China Life Data Center, Shanghai 201201, China
shiliwen@e-chinalife.com

Abstract. Color-guided depth image restoration is an issue of great interest. However, the edge in color image is not always consistent with the depth image. There is a certain relationship between the shading component of RGB image and the depth, so a depth image restoration method is proposed with shading structure guidance. First, the RGB image is decomposed into the shading component and the reflectance component based on Retinex Theory; next, calculate the structure tensors of the shading component and the depth image respectively, and the corresponding eigenvalues and eigenvectors; then, design the diffusion tensor with the eigenvalues and eigenvectors of the depth structure tensor to make the diffusion be along the level lines isophotes, finally the shading structure is introduced to inhibit the diffusion in the direction perpendicular to the edge, and the depth image is restored by diffusion. Experiments show, visually and quantitatively, the better restoration results are achieved by the introduction of the shading structure.

Keywords: Depth image restoration · Image decomposition · Diffusion tensor

1 Introduction

With the increasing application of machine learning and computer vision, computer vision tasks are becoming more and more complex. This puts forward higher requirements for the quality of the images obtained. Because depth images can reflect the spatial information of the scene, it plays an important role in understanding and analyzing the scene. The development of multi vision and depth sensors makes it easier to get depth images. However, Due to the limitation of acquisition range and noise interference, etc., usually there are missing depth values in the depth images, especially at the edges. The missing depth values would affect the further usage of depth images, e.g. views synthesis [2], 3D Reconstruction [1] and so on.

Several techniques and methods for image restoration have been proposed and can be divided into two categories: methods based on PDE and methods based on texture copy or synthesis. Methods based on PDE mainly imitate the thermal diffusion mechanism to spread the known information with the structural continuity along the level lines isophotes to the missing area [1]. In [4], a non-linear diffusion tensor is

J. Ren et al. (Eds.): BICS 2018, LNAI 10989, pp. 801–807, 2018.
https://doi.org/10.1007/978-3-030-00563-4_78

designed to diffuse known information along the level lines isophotes. Based on [1], a Total Variation repair model is proposed, which produced ladder effect easily in the flat area, and its computational complexity is large. In [5, 6], a diffusion model based on curvature driven is proposed to restore larger damaged areas, but this model would produce blur. Methods based on PDE are effective on small scratches and cracks in images. Methods based on texture copy or syntheses are mainly used for restoring the large missing areas [7, 8]. However, these methods need to search most matching block in images, so their computation complexity is large. The above methods restore the depth image with information from the image itself.

Some interests is to restore the depth image with the guidance of aligned RGB image. In [12], the Joint Bilateral Upsampling based on the geodesic distance is used to get a high resolution depth image. In [9, 13], the optimization framework is used to get a high resolution or complete depth image. In [14], with the relevance between the high resolution intensity image and the low resolution depth image, a graph transduction is used to reconstruct the high resolution depth image.

Above methods restore depth images with either constraints of depth structural continuity or assumptions of consistency between the depth discontinuities and the aligned RGB edges. In fact, the depth discontinuities are not always consistency with the RGB edges. Most state-of-the-art methods solve it by designing the weight of the aligned RGB image constraints. In [9], a penalty function is used to be against the inconsistency.

In this paper, the shading structure is involved in the depth image restoration. It is well known that the shading depicts the amount of reflected light, which is related to the normal direction and relative depth of the scene surface. So the structure of the shading component of the RGB image is consistency with the structure of the depth image. Different from the representation of the spatial structure [19, 20], in which the spatial structure are mainly used to represent texture, the purpose of using shading structure is to determine the edge direction. In this paper, the shading structure is represented with the structure tenor, whose eigenvectors can reflect the direction of the edges. Furthermore, the introduction of the shading structure can inhibit the diffusion of the depth image to a certain extent, which is effective to preserve the structure of the missing regions in the depth image.

2 Image Decomposition Based on Retinex Theory

Retinex theory on the human visual perception is used to decompose the RGB image into the shading component and the reflection component. According to Retinex theory, at the pixel p of the RGB image I, the pixel value is a multiplication between the shading component $B(\mathrm{p})$ and the reflectance component $R(\mathrm{p})$:

$$I(\mathrm{p}) = B(\mathrm{p}) \cdot R(\mathrm{p}) \tag{1}$$

The reflectance component $R(p)$ depicts the intrinsic color of the material at p, which is invariant to illumination conditions, and the shading component $B(p)$ is what the proposed method needs in this paper.

In this paper, the retinex model is used to acquire the shading component [16]. This model obeys to the reflectance gradient sparsity prior and the reflectance gradient fidelity priors, and an optimal quasi-gradient are used to fit the gradient of the reflectance, furthermore, the shading component can be calculated with Eq. (1).

3 Depth Image Restoration with Shading Structure

To restore the depth image, an objective function is constructed as following:

$$E = \iint_{(x,y)} (D_0(x,y) - D(x,y))^2 dxdy + \alpha \cdot \iint_{(x,y)} \phi(|\nabla D|) dxdy \tag{2}$$

Where $\iint_{(x,y)} (D_0(x,y) - D(x,y))^2$ is a data fidelity term, which can guarantee the consistence between known data before and after the restoration. D_0 and D are the initial depth image and the restored image respectively; $\iint_{(x,y)} \phi(|\nabla D|) dxdy$ is a regularization term to transfer the ill-posed problem to well-posed problem, and ∇ is the gradient operator, α is the weight of the regularization term.

The objective function is solved with PDE, and a diffusion equation is get:

$$D(x,y,t) = D(x,y,t-1) + \alpha \cdot div(\phi(|\nabla D(x,y,t-1)|)) \tag{3}$$

Where $\nabla D = [D_x, D_y]^T$, D_x and D_y are the partial derivatives along the direction of x and y respectively. $div(\cdot)$ is the divergence function.

In the restoration, to preserve the structure of the missing region, the diffusion along edge should be greater, and in the direction perpendicular to the edge, the diffusion along edge should be tiny or 0. So in Eq. (3), the key is to design the function $\phi(\cdot)$. In this paper, the diffusion tensor and the gradient are used to represent the function $\phi(\cdot)$.

3.1 Diffusion Tensor

Structure tensor can be used to reflect the local gradient variation of the image. Structure tensor S of an image D has the following form:

$$S = \begin{bmatrix} s_{11} & s_{12} \\ s_{12} & s_{22} \end{bmatrix} = G_\rho * \left(\nabla D_\sigma \cdot \nabla D_\sigma^{\mathrm{T}}\right) = \begin{bmatrix} G_\rho * D_{\sigma,x}^2 & G_\rho * (D_{\sigma,x} D_{\sigma,y}) \\ G_\rho * (D_{\sigma,y} D_{\sigma,x}) & G_\rho * D_{\sigma,y}^2 \end{bmatrix} \tag{4}$$

Where D_σ is the smoothed depth image D with Gaussian kernel whose standard deviation is σ, and G_ρ is the Gaussian kernel with standard deviation. S is used to describe the local gradient feature of image precisely. In [17], some deductions show that eigenvalues of S reflect the local variation of pixel values in the image D, and eigenvectors reflect the local variation directions of pixel values.

Let λ_1, λ_2 $(\lambda_1 > \lambda_2)$ be eigenvalues of tensor structure S, and v_1, v_2 are the corresponding eigenvectors $(v_1 \perp v_2)$. The eigenvalues λ_1, λ_2 are given by:

$$\begin{cases} \lambda_1 = \frac{1}{2}\left(s_{11} + s_{22} + \sqrt{(s_{11} - s_{22})^2 + 4s_{12}^2}\right) \\ \lambda_2 = \frac{1}{2}\left(s_{11} + s_{22} - \sqrt{(s_{11} - s_{22})^2 + 4s_{12}^2}\right) \end{cases} \tag{5}$$

With eigenvalues of the tensor structure, some analysis are given: in flat regions, $\lambda_1 \approx \lambda_2 \approx 0$, the variation of pixel values is small in the directions of eigenvectors v_1, v_2; in the region with edge, $\lambda_1 \gg \lambda_2 \approx 0$, the variation of pixel values is bigger along the direction v_1 than the direction v_2; in region with cross point, $\lambda_1 \approx \lambda_2 \gg 0$, the variations of pixel values are bigger along the directions v_1 and v_2.

Based on the above analysis, the function $\phi(\cdot)$ can be designed to make the diffusion equation satisfy:

(1) In flat regions, the diffusion is implemented in the direction of v_1 or v_2.
(2) In the region with edge, the diffusion is implemented along the direction of the edge v_2.
(3) In the region with cross point, the diffusion is tiny along the direction of v_1 or v_2.

In this paper, let $\phi(|\nabla D(x, y, t-1)|)$ be represented by a diffusion tensor $d\_S(x, y)$ and gradient $\nabla D(x, y)$:

$$\phi(|\nabla D(x, y)|) = d\_S(x, y) \cdot \nabla D(x, y) \tag{6}$$

In Eq. (5), eigenvectors of the diffusion tensor $d\_S(x, y)$ are v_1 and v_2, and the corresponding eigenvalues are used to control the diffusion of different directions: promote the diffusion along edge, and inhibit the diffusion in the direction perpendicular to the edge. So the choice of eigenvalues is crucial.

3.2 Shading Structure-Guided Eigenvalues of Diffusion Tensor

In the traditional design, the diffusion tensor is designed with the structure continuity of the depth image only. In this paper, the design of the diffusion tensor not only involves the structure tensor of the depth image but also the guidance of the shading structure. The introduction of the shading structure can control the diffusion in different directions.

The RGB image I which is aligned with the depth image D is decomposed to get its shading component B. The shading structure tensor of B is calculated with the method in Sect. 3.1, and the corresponding eigenvalues and eigenvectors are $\lambda_{s,1}$, $\lambda_{s,2}$ and $v_{s,1}$, $v_{s,2}$. The eigenvalue of the diffusion tensor are designed as followings:

$$\begin{cases} u_1 = e^{-\lambda_{s,1}} \cdot c \\ u_2 = e^{-\lambda_{s,2}} \cdot \dfrac{1}{1 + \cdot \frac{\sqrt{\lambda_1 + \lambda_2}}{k}} \end{cases} \tag{7}$$

where c is a very small number, and k is a parameter to control the diffusion. $e^{-\lambda_{s,1}}$ and $e^{-\lambda_{s,2}}$ are the guidance from the shading structure.

In Eq. (7), if $\lambda_{s,1} \approx \lambda_{s,2} \approx 0$, the shading structure would not affect the diffusion of the depth image; if $\lambda_{s,1} \gg \lambda_{s,2} \approx 0$, the shading structure would inhibit the diffusion in the direction of v_1; if $\lambda_{s,1} \approx \lambda_{s,2} \gg 0$, the shading structure would inhibit the diffusion in the direction of v_1 and v_2 at the same time.

With the eigenvalues in Eq. (7) and the corresponding eigenvectors, the diffusion tensor can be obtained based on the Eigen decomposition theorem:

$$d\_S(x,y) = u_1 v_1 v_1^T + u_2 v_2 v_2^T \tag{8}$$

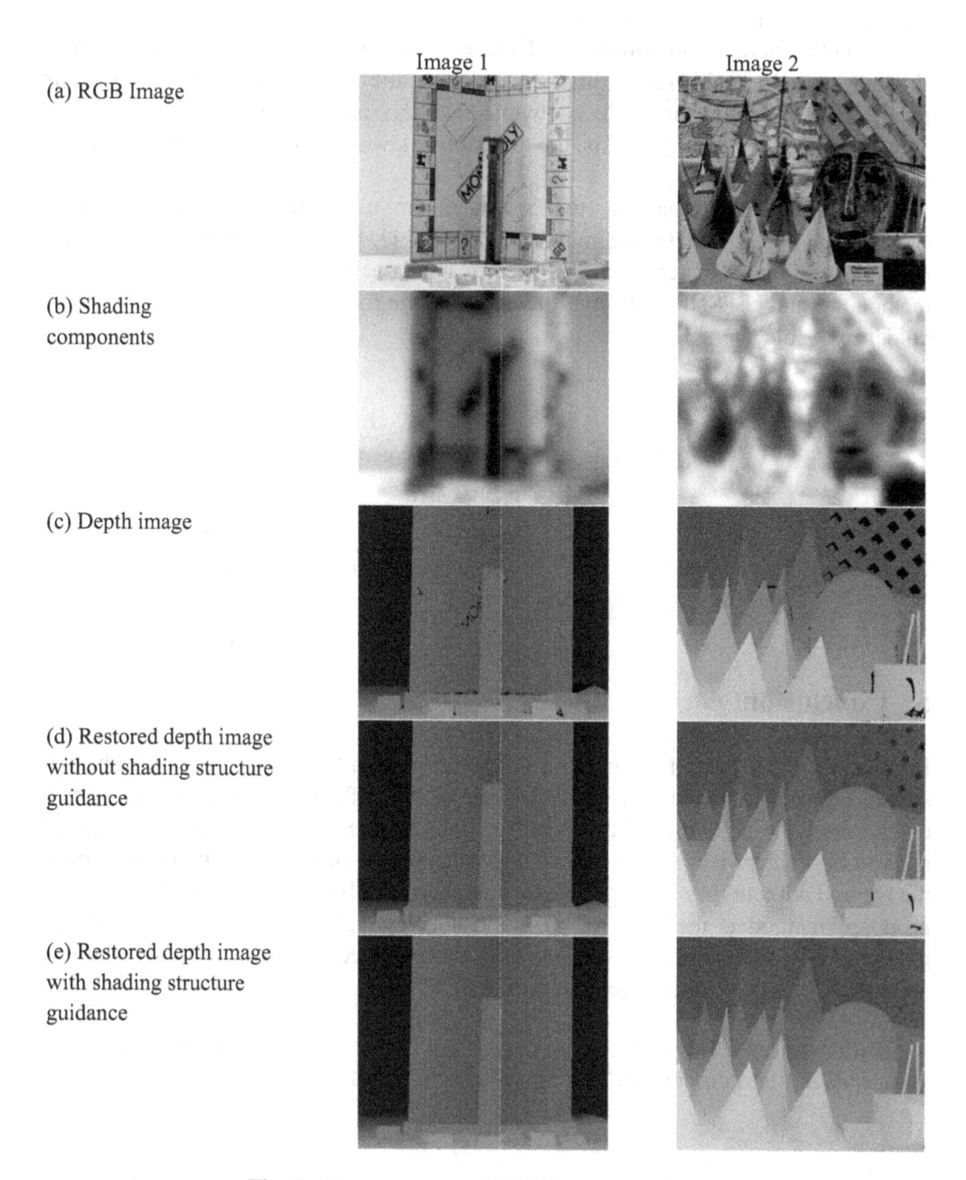

Fig. 1. Experiments on Middlebury stereo dataset

4 Experiments

In this section, the proposed method is implemented on the public dataset: the Middlebury stereo dataset [9]. In the experiments, the disparity images are used as depth images simply. In the dataset, the ground truth is not provided, so the enhancement result from [10] is used in experiments. To validate the proposed method, the visual comparison and quantitative comparison are taken.

In visual comparison, the restoration of depth images is carried out with and without shading structure guidance respectively (Fig. 1d and e). In experiments, the parameters are set in terms of [18].

Visually, there is no obvious difference between the results with and without shading structure guidance in Image 1, because the missing regions are small. In Image 2, the difference of results is obvious with the same iterations. In Fig. 1d, some holes still exist in Image 2, that is, the diffusion is lower due to the lack of the shading structure guidance.

In quantitative comparison, two measures are used: peak signal-to-noise ratio (PNSR) and Mean Structural Similarity (MSSIM) [11]. MSSISM takes values in the interval [0, 1], and increases as the quality increase. By comparison, the proposed method has higher PSNR and better MSSIM than the method without shading structure guidance (Table 1).

Table 1. The quantitative comparison

Mehod	PSNR (dB)		MSSIM	
	Image 1	Image 2	Image 1	Image 2
Method in [18]	37.2451	29.7910	0.9786	0.9546
Method in [18] with shading	38.9628	37.6141	0.9801	0.9708

5 Conclusion

In this paper, a method for the depth image restoration is proposed with the shading structure guidance. Due to the shading structure, the diffusion is inhibited to a certain extent, thus the structure of the depth is preserved. By comparison, the proposed method has better visual effect. On the quantitative, the proposed method outperforms the method without the shading structure guidance in PSNR and MSSIM. However, the proposed method is used for restoring the smaller regions only. In the future, the guidance of the shading structure would be extended to other methods and the restoration of larger missing regions would be studied.

Acknowledgements. This work has been partially supported by the National Natural Science Foundation of China under Grant Nos. 6150238 and 61501370.

References

1. Zheng, J., Zuo, X., Ren, J., Wang, S.: Multiple depth maps integration for 3D reconstruction using geodesic graph cuts. Int. J. Softw. Eng. Knowl. Eng. **25**(3), 473–492 (2015)
2. Zhao, D., Zheng, J., Ren, J.: Effective removal of artifacts from views synthesized using depth image based rendering, pp. 65–71 (2015)
3. Bertalmio, M., Sapiro, G., Caselles, V., Ballester, C.: Image inpainting. In: Proceedings of 27th Annual Conference on Computer Graphics, New Orleans, pp. 417–422 (2000)
4. Benzarti, F., Amiri, H: Image inpainting via isophotes propagation. In: 6th International Conference on Sciences of Electronics, Technologies of Information and Telecommunications, Sousse, pp. 359–364 (2012)
5. Shen, J.H., Kang, S.H., Chan, T.F.: Euler's elastica and curvature-based inpainting. SIAM J. Math. Anal. **63**(2), 564–592 (2002)
6. Shen, J.H., Chan, T.F.: Non-texure inpainting by curvature-driven diffusion. J. Vis. Commun. Image Represent. **12**(4), 436–449 (2001)
7. Wu, J.Y., Ruan, Q.Q.: A novel exemplar-based image completion model. J. Inf. Sci. Eng. **25** (2), 481–497 (2009)
8. Criminisi, A., Perez, P., Toyama, K.: Object removal by exemplar-based inpainting. In: IEEE Computer Society Conference on Computer Vision and Pattern Recognition, Madison, pp. 721–728 (2003)
9. Liu, W., Chen, X.G., Yang, J., Wu, Q.: Robust color guided depth map restoration. IEEE Trans. Image Process. **26**(1), 315–327 (2017)
10. Lu, S., Ren, X.F., Liu, F.: Depth enhancement via low-rank matrix completion. In: IEEE Conference on Computer Vision and Pattern Recognition, Columbus, pp. 4321–4328 (2014)
11. Wang, Z., Bovik, A.C., Sheikh, H.R., Simoncelli, E.P.: Image quality assessment: from error visibility to structural similarity. IEEE Trans. Image Process. **13**(4), 600–611 (2004)
12. Liu, M.Y., Tuzek, O., Taguohi, Y.: Joint geodesic upsampling of depth images. In: IEEE Conference on Computer Vision and Pattern Recognition, Portland, pp. 169–176 (2013)
13. Park, J., Kim, H., Tai, Y.W., Brown, M.S., Kweon, I.: High quality depth map upsampling for 3D-TOF cameras. In: IEEE International Conference on Computer Vision, Barcelona, pp. 1623–1630 (2011)
14. Wichkert, J.: Coherence-enhancing diffusion filtering. Int. J. Comput. Vis. **31**, 111–127 (1999)
15. Ham, B., Min, D., Sohn, K.: Depth supersolution by transduction. IEEE Trans. Image Process. **24**(5), 1524–1535 (2015)
16. Zosso, D., Tran, G., Osher, S.: A unifying Retinex model based on non-local differential operators. Proc. SPIE **8657**, 1–12 (2013)
17. Wichkert, J.: Anisotropic Diffusion in Image Processing. Teubner-Verlag, Leipzig (1998)
18. Benzarit, F., Amiri, H.: Repairing and inpainting damaged image using diffusion. Int. J. Comput. Sci. **9**(3), 1–7 (2012)
19. Zhou, Y., Zeng, F., Zhao, H., Murray, P., Ren, J.: Hierarchical visual perception and two-dimensional compressive sensing for effective content-based color image retrieval. Cogn. Comput. **8**(5), 877–889 (2016)
20. Yan, Y., Ren, J., Li, Y., Chao, K.: Adaptive fusion of color and spatial features for noise-robust retrieval of colored logo and trademark images. Multidimension. Syst. Signal Process. **27**(4), 945–968 (2016)

Machine Learning for Muon Imaging

Guangliang Yang(✉), David Ireland, Ralf Kaiser, and David Mahon

School of Physics and Astronomy, Glasgow University, Glasgow G12 8QQ, UK
Guangliang.yang@glasgow.ac.uk

Abstract. Muon imaging is a new imaging technique which can be used to image large bulky objects, especially objects with heavy shielding where other techniques like X-ray CT scanning will often fail. This is due to the fact that high energy cosmic rays have a very high penetrative power and can easily penetrate hundreds of meters of rock. Muon imaging is essentially an inverse problem. There are two popular forms of muon imaging techniques - absorption muon imaging based on the attenuation of muons in matter and multiple scattering muon imaging based on the multiple scattering effect of muons. Muon imaging can be used in many areas, ranging from volcanology and searching for secret cavities in pyramids over border monitoring for special nuclear materials to nuclear safeguards applications for monitoring the spent fuel casks. Due to the lack of man-made muon sources, both of the muon imaging techniques rely on cosmic ray muons. One important shortcoming of comic ray muons are the very low intensities. In order to get high image resolutions, very long exposure times are needed. In this paper, we will study how machine learning techniques can be used to improve the muon imaging techniques.

Keywords: Muon imaging · Machine learning · Inverse problem

1 Introduction

1.1 History

Muons are elementary particles, which are similar to electrons but more than 200 times heavier. They were discovered by Carl D. Anderson and Seth Neddermeyer at Caltech in 1936. The naturally occurring muons on earth are mostly coming from the upper atmosphere as the results of the interaction of primary cosmic rays with the atoms and molecules in the atmosphere.

Muon Absorption Imaging. Shortly after the discovery of muon, George used muons to measure the depth of the overburden of a tunnel in Australia in the 1950s [1], and Luis Alvarez used muons to search for hidden chambers in a pyramid in the 1960s [2]. Recently, muon imaging has been successfully used by geophysicists to measure the internal structure of volcanoes [3–6]. There are also studies to use the muon absorption imaging technique to investigate underground cavities in Italy [7]. A Canadian company CRM Geotomography Technologies, Inc. has used the muon absorption muon imaging technique for mining and oil industry applications [8]. There are also intensive studies to use the muon imaging technique to monitor CO_2 stored in geological

J. Ren et al. (Eds.): BICS 2018, LNAI 10989, pp. 808–817, 2018.
https://doi.org/10.1007/978-3-030-00563-4_79

reservoirs [9]. The most famous project was the recent discovery of a secret hidden chamber inside Egypt's Great Pyramid of Giza [10]. Muon absorption imaging has also been used to monitor some historical buildings [11].

Muon Multiple Scattering Imaging. Inspired by the proton imaging technique developed by the Los Alamos Laboratory, scientists from this lab developed a new kind of muon multiple scattering imaging technique in the early 2000s [12, 13]. This new technique was developed to tackle the problems of the smuggling of nuclear devices and special nuclear materials across the borders of countries to deter terrorists from harming the United States. This new technique soon gained popularity and stirred broad interest around world. Apart from the application for monitoring transport containers [14], there are also applications imaging shielded nuclear waste containers [15, 16], for verifying the contents of spent nuclear fuel casks [17, 18], and for looking into the debris of the nuclear reactor core in Fukushima [19, 20]. It can also be used in civil engineering to study the corrosion of reinforced steel bars inside concrete and to monitor large steel pipes for industries [21].

1.2 Theories of Muon Imaging

Muon imaging techniques are essentially inverse problems. We need to understand what data we can get and know what parameters we want to investigate, and most importantly, we need good models to link the data and the parameters together.

Muon Absorption Imaging. Due to the lack of man-made muon sources, cosmic ray muons have to be used for the muon imaging techniques. The muon absorption imaging technique is based on the attenuation of the cosmic ray muon flux by matter. At the surface of the earth, cosmic ray muons span quite a large energy range up to TeV. Roughly speaking, the energy spectrum for cosmic ray muons below 1 GeV is almost flat, and at higher energy ranges, it reflects the primary cosmic ray energy spectrum [22].

Muons lose energy when passing through matter due to electromagnetic processes. The rate of energy loss depends on the muon's energy and also on the properties of the matter [22]. If the thickness of the matter is sufficient, some of the muons will lose all of their energy and be stopped inside the matter, and the remaining muon flux will be reduced. With increasing thickness of the matter, the muon flux decreases. If the original muon flux and the energy spectrum of the muons are known, the cutting-off-energy can be decided for that material and thickness by measuring the muon beam flux after it has passed through a certain thickness of matter. The cutting-off-energy is defined as the energy of a muon which is just sufficient to let the muon passing through the matter. Inversely, if the cutting-off-energy is known, the thickness of the matter can be estimated from it. For complicated objects, if a 2D or 3D image is desired, measurements should be taken by varying the angles and positions. The image reconstruction algorithm is similar to imaging algorithms used in medical imaging.

Muon Multiple Scattering Imaging. When passing through matter, muons suffer from repeated elastic Coulomb scatterings from nuclei. The measurable effects of the multiple scattering are the scattering angle and the displacement. The scattering angle is the angle between the original muon track and the exiting muon track, and the displacement is the distance between the expected striking position by extending the original muon track and the actual striking position. The multiple scattering effect has been very well studied, and the Moliere theory [23] is the most commonly used theory to describe this effect. Despite the Moliere theory being one of the earliest theories in this area, it still remains one of the most accurate. It can give an exact solution to the multiple scattering effect, however it is rather difficult to implement. As a result, approximations to the Moliere theory were also developed for practical applications. The Rossi formula [24] is one of them, which describes the muon multiple scattering angle approximately as a Gaussian distribution. According to this theory, for a uniform matter, the standard deviation σ of the scattering angle can be described approximately by the following formula,

$$\sigma \cong \frac{15\ \mathrm{MeV}}{\beta c p}\sqrt{\frac{L}{X_0}} \tag{1}$$

here L is the length of the matter, βc is the particle velocity ($\beta = 1$), and p is the particle momentum in MeV/c, and X_0 is the radiation length of the matter, which can be described by the following equation.

$$X_0 = \frac{716.4\ \mathrm{g\ cm}^{-2} A}{\rho Z(Z+1)\ln\left(\frac{287}{\sqrt{Z}}\right)} \tag{2}$$

where A is the atomic mass, Z the atomic number and ρ the material density. By combining (1) and (2), it can be seen that the standard deviation of the scattering angle depends on the radiation length of the material which is dependent on the atomic number of the material, i.e. materials with higher atomic numbers will typically give larger scattering angles.

The Eq. (1) serves as the basis for muon multiple scattering tomography. However, it technically is only valid for uniform matter, while in practice, we are more interested in mixtures or more complicated structures. With a simple substitution of the radiation length we will be able to do that. The material's radiation length for compounds or mixtures can be described by using the following equations [25]:

$$\frac{1}{X_0} = \sum \frac{w_i}{X_i} \tag{3}$$

where the X_i is the radiation length for the ith component along the muon path, and w_i is the weight for the ith component.

Combining (1) to (3), we have:

$$\sigma^2 = \sum_i \left(\frac{15\ \mathrm{MeV}}{p_i c \beta_i}\right)^2 \frac{l_i}{X_i} \tag{4}$$

The Eq. (4) links the square of the variance of the muon scattering angle with the radiation length of the matter encountered along each muon's path. If we measure the muon multiple scattering at different positions and different angles, we will get a system of linear equations. By solving these linear equations, we will be able to get a map of the radiation length.

Because the variance of the muon scattering angle rather than the scattering angle itself is needed in the muon multiple scattering imaging, ideally, we have to use a beam of muons to determine the variance for each direction. But in reality, cosmic ray muons are generated at random positions and orientations, and at a random time. We therefore may have to group muons with similar positions and orientations together to form a quasi-beam.

Apart from solving a system of linear functions, another way to do the image reconstruction for the muon multiple scattering imaging is to use the maximum likelihood method. For details about the maximum likelihood method, please refer to reference [26]. The benefit of using the maximum likelihood method is that there is no need to explicitly find out the variance of the scattering angles for each muon track.

1.3 Problems with Muon Imaging

Although there are a number of benefits to use cosmic ray muons for muon imaging, e.g. the fact that they are ubiquitous, cost free and do not lead to any additional radiation dose, there is a fundamental shortcoming, which is the very low intensities of cosmic ray muons. At sea level, the cosmic ray muon flux is about 1 muon/min/cm^2. For some applications of muon imaging, there is a very strict time limit, for example, the scanning of shipping containers requires to finish the scan in less than 1 min. With such a short time, the resulting images are very noisy, which can cause false alarms or fail to find the target. For other applications, like the monitoring of the spent fuel casks, hours or even days are allowed for the imaging. However, there are still requirements to speed it up for economic reasons. Therefore, we propose to use machine learning method to further improve the performance of the muon imaging techniques. This can be achieved by using the artificial neural network to do the image reconstruction, and we proposed a new method to reduce the number of input needed for the ANN method. In the future we also plan to use other machine learning tool such as the SVM to do image segmentation and materials classification.

2 Machine Learning for Muon Imaging

Machine learning is not something new to tomographic imaging. In medical and industrial applications, machine learning is widely used. In the era of big data, machine learning can help to find features otherwise too time consuming or difficult for humans to find. Machine learning can also be used for image reconstruction, for example by using an artificial neural network. Although substantial work has already been carried out in the inverse imaging field, special attention still needs to be paid to muon imaging. This is due to the special imaging reconstruction algorithms used for muon imaging and also the very high noise level. In this paper, we will discuss how muon imaging will benefit from machine learning.

2.1 Image Reconstruction with an Artificial Neural Network

One possible application is to use an artificial neural network for the image reconstruction. Artificial neural networks are superior to the traditional imaging reconstruction methods because there is no need to know the exact forward modeling - the modeling can be learnt from training if enough data is provided. This is particularly useful for the muon multiple scattering imaging, where the forward modeling that we used is only a rough estimation of reality. Apart from that, the muon energy loss and the lack of knowledge of the muon's momentum for each individual muon make things even more complicated.

In addition, with an artificial neural network, the image reconstruction speed can be very fast. Although the training stage is very time consuming, once trained, the image reconstruction with an artificial neural network can be very quick. The image quality can be superior than other fast image reconstruction methods such as the filtered backprojection (FBP) method [27] for low dose imaging applications. Yang has shown that the acquired X-ray tomographic signal was increased at least by a factor of 10 in a low dose CT study by using a deep convolutional neural network [28]. If this dose reduction can also be applied to the muon imaging application, those applications with very tight time limits such as at the border control point will greatly benefit from this.

The very low flux rate of the cosmic ray muons will also affect the way of how to use the artificial neural network to carry out the image reconstruction. For muon multiple scattering imaging, the total number of the input values is not fixed, because the data is not taken a regular intervals in angles and position. Furthermore, each of the muons will take random positions and directions - and its scattering angle is also a random value; all of this information has to be taken into account for the image reconstruction. It therefore is not possible to design a neural network by simply taking each muon as the input. One way to overcome this difficulty is to preprocess the data to reduce the number of input. One effective approach to preprocess the data is to use the back projection method. The reader can refer to reference [29] for the application of the back projection method for muon imaging.

2.2 Classification with Machine Learning Tools

Often, there are needs for the muon imaging to discriminate different materials or to verify if a device is defective or not. Good practice for this is to combine the muon absorption and multiple scattering imaging results, and if available other prior information. In this way, it becomes a multi-dimensional classification problem, and suitable for using machine learning.

It is very possible that within one image there are several different kinds of material. Before material discrimination, we have to separate all these different materials, which means that clustering by using machine learning tools is a possibility. There are already studies using machine learning tools for clustering etc. for muon imaging [30].

3 Method and Preliminary Results

Using machine learning to study the muon imaging needs a large amount of data. This data can be collected by running the muon imaging experiments in the laboratory or in a commercial site. However, taking real data is very time consuming, and sometimes not even possible. One alternative way to generate data is to simulate the muon imaging process through Monte Carlo simulations. This can be done by using the software toolkit Geant4 [31], which is designed by the physicists from CERN for high energy particle and nuclear applications.

For muon imaging, one has to know the muon striking positions and directions. This can be realized by using position sensitive charged particle detectors. The position sensitive detectors can be simulated using Geant4 [31]. With the help of position sensitive detectors, muon striking positions on the detector can be measured. By using many sets of position sensitive detectors, we will be able to get an array of the muon positions, which can be used to infer muon trajectories.

The shape and material properties of the imaging target can be defined using the Geant4 libraries. All of the interactions of muons with matter, including the energy loss, multiple scattering and the generation of second particles, can be simulated with Geant4. Geant4 also allows the user to define the parameters for each muon. A dedicated muon generator is used to produce muon events. Muons are sampled according to the cosmic ray muon energy spectrum and angular distribution at sea level [32]. Figure 1 shows the muon energy spectrum used in the simulation.

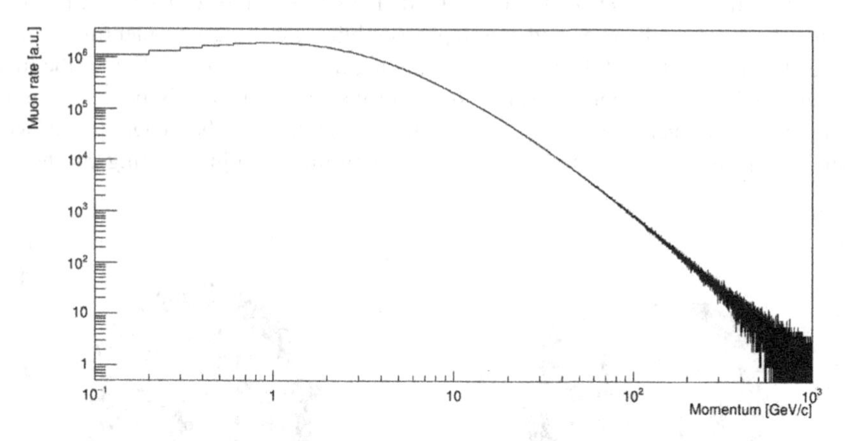

Fig. 1. Energy spectrum of the muons used in the Geant4 simulations.

As an example, a partially loaded Westinghouse MC-10 cask was simulated. In the simulation, the MC-10 has a 25 cm thick steel wall, and an aluminium basket to hold the fuel assemblies in the centre of the cask. 20 out of 24 of the aluminium basket holder slots were filled with pressurized water reactor fuel assemblies and left 4 of them empty. Each fuel assembly contains 204 fuel rods, 20 control rod guide tubes, and one instrument tube. The fuel rods are filled with UO_2 and surrounded by a zirconium alloy cladding. The control rods and instrument tube were simulated with empty cladding, and with no fuel present. The dimensions and geometry of the MC-10 cask and the water pressure fuel assembly used in the simulation was found in reference [33, 34]. The layout of the fuel bundles in this MC-10 cask is shown in Fig. 2.

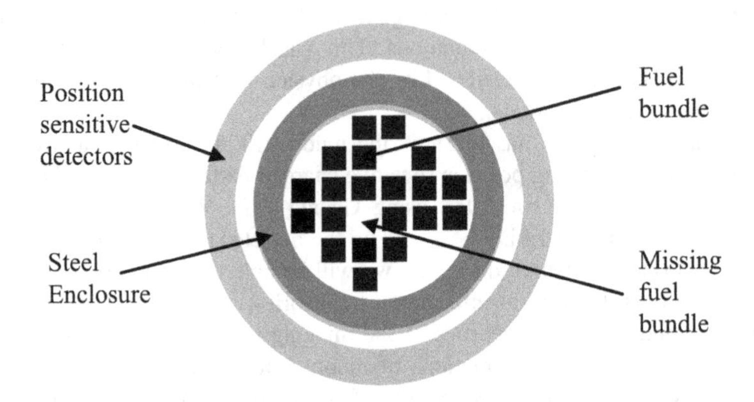

Fig. 2. Sketch of a MC10 spent fuel cask in the Geant4 simulation.

Both the multiple scattering signal and the absorption signal are used in the image reconstruction. In Fig. 3, images reconstructed with 4 million and 0.2 million muons are shown. It can be seen that each individual fuel assembly can be clearly distinguished between each other and missing assemblies can be easily identified for the image showing on the left. For the image showing on the right side of Fig. 3, the muon number used is significantly smaller, therefore the image quality is poorer. Figure 3 highlights the problem for muon imaging, that is how to keep the image quality while reducing the measurements time, this is something that machine learning can help.

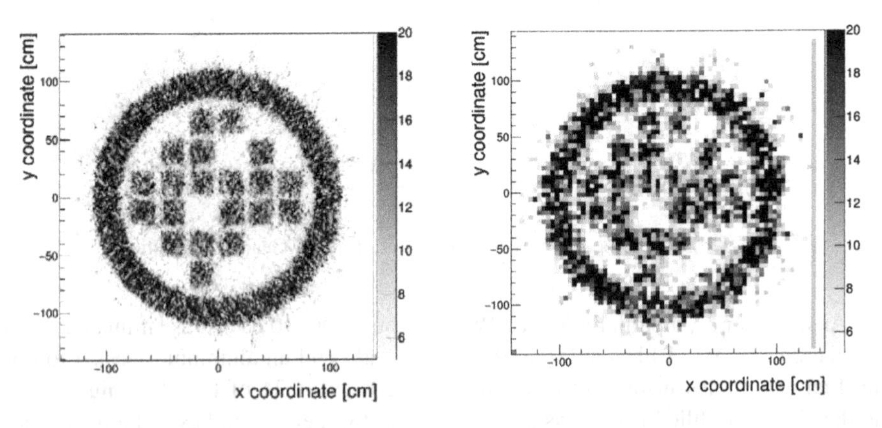

Fig. 3. Reconstructed images of the partially loaded MC 10 spent fuel cask (left) 4 million muons, (right) 0.2 million muons.

Although there wasn't much activity of using machine learning technique in the muon imaging field in the past, but there was a lot of work done in the medical imaging field. In reference [35], Jian et al. reviewed the applications of neural network in the medical imaging field. Since the image reconstruction techniques used for the muon imaging are quite similar to the techniques used in the medical imaging, it is natural to believe that the machine learning techniques developed for the medical applications can be transferred to the muon imaging without much difficulty. Inspired by the work done for the medical field, we plan to use an artificial neural network classifier to improve our capability in imaging the nuclear spent fuel casks. This is because, to some extent, this problem can be reduced into a two classes classification problem, i.e. to see if there is a nuclear spent fuel assembly, or there isn't a nuclear spent fuel assembly. This will be done by using a small artificial neural network classifier, with one input layer and one output layer and one hidden layer. Each input represents a feature of a pixel, and for each of the pixels there are 3 features that can be extracted, which are the density calculated with the absorption method, and radiation lengths reconstructed with the multiple scattering method by using the scattering angle or the displacement as input respectively. There are in total 27 inputs parameters from 9 pixels which form a square region with 3 pixels on each side. The size of this square region can be increased if necessary. The output of this ANN classifier will tell if there exists a nuclear fuel assembly or not in the center position of this square region. This process will be repeated for the whole imaging area. To further improve the performance of this small neural network classifier, an optimal decision making technique will be applied. For details about this optimal decision making for neural network, please refer to reference [36, 37]. This work is currently ongoing, and results will be reported in a later publication.

4 Conclusions

Muon imaging is a promising new technique that offers unique capabilities to image large objects that other techniques will often fail at. However, due to the low intensities of the cosmic ray muons, the images often are very noisy in the time limited applications. Iterative image reconstruction algorithms can offer better quality images, but they need very long computation times and a large amount of computing resources. On the other hand, machine learning can help to speed up the image reconstruction and improve the image quality. The possible procedure to use machine learning for the muon imaging is discussed in this paper.

Acknowledgement. This work was partially supported by the EPSRC and STFC Impact Accelerator Accounts at the University of Glasgow and by Lynkeos Technology Ltd.

References

1. George, E.P.: Cosmic rays measure overburden of tunnel. Commonwealth Eng. 455–457 (1955)
2. Alvarez, L.W., et al.: Search for hidden chambers in the pyramids using cosmic rays. Science **167**, 832–839 (1970)

3. Nagamine, K.: Geo-tomographic observation of inner structure of volcano with cosmic-ray muons. J. Geogr. **104**, 998–1007 (1995)
4. Tanaka, H., Nagamine, K., Kawamura, N., Nakamura, S.N., Ishida, K., Shimomura, K.: Development of the cosmic-ray muon detection system for probing internal-structure of a volcano. Hyperfine Interact. **138**, 521–526 (2001)
5. Tanaka, H., Nagamine, K., Nakamura, S.N., Ishida, K.: Radiographic measurements of the internal structure of Mt. West Iwate with near horizontal cosmic ray muons and future developments. Nucl. Instrum. Methods A **555**, 164–172 (2005)
6. Carbone, D., Gibert, D., Marteau, J., Diament, M., Zuccarello, L., Galichet, E.: An experiment of muon radiography at Mt. Etna (Italy). Geophys. J. Int. **196**, 633–643 (2014)
7. Saracino, G., et al.: Imaging of underground cavities with cosmic-ray muons from observations at Mt. Echia (Naples). Sci. Rep. **7**(1), 1181 (2017). https://doi.org/10.1038/s41598-017-01277-3
8. http://www.crmgtm.com/home/applications/. Accessed 24 May 2018
9. Klinger, J., et al.: Simulation of muon radiography for monitoring CO_2 stored in a geological reservoir. Int. J. Greenhouse Gas Control **42**, 644–654 (2015)
10. Morishima, K., et al.: Discovery of a big void in Khufu's Pyramid by observation of cosmic-ray muons. Nature **552**, 386–390 (2017)
11. Zenoni, A., et al.: Historical building stability monitoring by means of a cosmic ray tracking system. arXiv:1403.1709v1
12. Borozdin, K.N., et al.: Surveillance: radiographic imaging with cosmic-ray muons. Nature **422**, 277 (2003)
13. Schultz, L.: Cosmic ray muon radiography, Ph.D. dissertation, Portland State University, Portland, OR (2003)
14. Schultz, L., et al.: Image reconstruction and material Z discrimination via cosmic ray muon radiography. Nucl. Instrum. Methods A **519**, 687 (2004)
15. Clarkson, A., et al.: The design and performance of a scintillating-fibre tracker for the cosmic-ray muon tomography of legacy nuclear waste containers. Nucl. Instrum. Methods A **745**, 138 (2014)
16. Mahon, D.F., et al.: A prototype scintillating-fibre tracker for the cosmic-ray muon tomography of legacy nuclear waste containers. Nucl. Instrum. Methods A **732**, 408 (2013)
17. Jonkmans, G., et al.: Nuclear waste imaging and spent fuel verification by muon tomography. Ann. Nucl. Energy **53**, 267–273 (2013)
18. Durham, J.M., et al.: Verification of spent nuclear fuel in sealed dry storage casks via measurements of cosmic-ray muon scattering. Phys. Rev. Appl. **9**, 044013 (2018)
19. Miyadera, H., et al.: Imaging Fukushima Daiichi reactors with muons. AIP Adv. **3**, 052133 (2013)
20. Borozdin, K., et al.: Cosmic ray radiography of the damaged cores of the Fukushima reactors. Phys. Rev. Lett. **109**, 152501 (2012)
21. Durham, J.M., et al.: Tests of cosmic ray radiography for power industry applications. http://arxiv.org/abs/1503.07550
22. Nakamura, K., et al.: Particle data group. J. Phys. G **37**, 075021 (2010). (2011 partial update for the 2012 edition)
23. Molière, G.: Theorie der Streuung schneller geladenen Teilchen II Mehrfach- und Vielfachstreuung. Z. Naturforschg. **3A**, 78–97 (1948)
24. Rossi, B.: High Energy Particles. Prentice-Hall, Englewood Cliffs (1952)
25. Beringer, J., et al.: (PDG), PR D86, 010001 (2012) and 2013 update for the 2014 edition. http://pdg.lbl.gov
26. Schultz, L., et al.: Statistical reconstruction for cosmic ray muon tomography. IEEE Trans. Image Process. **16**, 1985 (2007)

27. Fessler, J.: Analytical tomographic image reconstruction methods, Chap. 3, 19 November 2009
28. Yang, X., et al.: Low-dose X-ray tomography through a deep convolutional neural network. Sci. Rep. **8**, 2575 (2018)
29. Morris, C.L., et al.: Tomographic imaging with cosmic ray muons. Sci. Glob. Secur. **16**, 37–53 (2008)
30. Stocki, T.J., et al.: Machine learning for the cosmic ray inspection and passive tomography project (CRIPT). In: 2012 IEEE Nuclear Science Symposium and Medical Imaging Conference Record (NSS/MIC), Anaheim, CA, pp. 91–94 (2012)
31. Agostinelli, S., et al.: GEANT4: a simulation toolkit. Nucl. Instrum. Methods A **506**, 250 (2003)
32. Chatzidakis, S., et al.: A Geant4 MATLAB muon generator for Monte-Carlo simulations. Internal Report (2015)
33. McKinnon, M.A., et al.: The MC-10 PWR spent-fuel storage cask: testing and analysis. Electric Power Research Institute Report NP-5268 (1987)
34. O'Donnell, G.M.: A New Comparative Analysis of LWR Fuel Designs, NUREG-1754. U.S. Nuclear Regulatory Commission, Rockville (2001)
35. Jiang, J.: Medical image analysis with artificial neural networks. Comput. Med. Imaging Graph. **34**(8), 617–631 (2010)
36. Ren, J.: ANN vs. SVM: which one performs better in classification of MCCs in mammogram imaging. Knowl.-Based Syst. **26**, 144–153 (2012)
37. Ren, J.: Effective recognition of MCCs in mammograms using an improved neural classifier. Eng. Appl. Artif. Intell. **24**(4), 638–645 (2011)

Night View Road Scene Enhancement Based on Mixed Multi-scale Retinex and Fractional Differentiation

Yuanfang Zhang, Jiangbin Zheng(✉), Xuejiao Kou, and Yefan Xie

Northwestern Polytechnical University, Xi'an, Shaanxi Province, People's Republic of China
robinzhang.zyf@gmail.com

Abstract. In recent years, image processing has been applied in various industries. In the part of the public road scene, the vehicle camera in night could not be used perfectly as it does in daytime, because it usually gains low visibility by the faint illumination. In order to enhance the visual clear visibility, in this paper, the mixed multi-Retinex algorithm is first introduced to deal with the night view scene, and then using fractional differentiation to make the edge information much clearer. Finally we combined the two methods with center surround function to make the effects better. In the experiment, processing speed is faster than the comparing methods and dark regions has boosted the brightness of the image.

Keywords: Multi-scale Retinex · Fractional differentiation · Night view image

1 Introduction

The traffic safety is regarded as the top goal in the daily life, and it can be a threat for drivers that vehicle cameras or monitor devices could not find the unnoticeable person or other things at night. The low visibility makes drivers' sight ability nearly blind and it also misleads the drivers when they couldn't figure out the road condition. Besides, the monitors could not adjust the low light at night, because its core component has little ambient illumination processing capacity, and image is not discernible due to the noise. All these can attributed to the dark vision.

Several scientists and researchers have developed the significant new methods of image enhancement in the dark vision successfully. Xiao et al. [1] make a fast image enhancement based on color space fusion and Zhu et al. [2] developed local contrast preserving method for cloud removing. Li et al. [3] developed a detection method as on-line detection based on single-scale Retinex method; Lee et al. [4] makes a new method to satisfy the multi-scale morphology; Nikonorov et al. [5] think out a method to correcting color and hyperspectral images; Al-Ameen et al. [6] developed a new method to use single-scale method to meet the needs of the image enhancement; And Chen et al. [7] developed a new method to be applied in tone reproduction; Guo [8] proposed a haziness analysis method to deal with the haze images; Hu et al. [9]

J. Ren et al. (Eds.): BICS 2018, LNAI 10989, pp. 818–826, 2018.
https://doi.org/10.1007/978-3-030-00563-4_80

designed a algorithm to deal with the degraded fog images; Sun et al. [10] created a method to speed up the process of image enhancement.

Retinex theory is proposed by R. Land in the 20th century and it is often applied in the image processing field. The main idea is that the original image is calculated as the input image, and researchers take several different image estimation methods to develop various Retinex algorithm. The counterpart Retinex methods in the night image research are single–scale Retinex (SSR) and multi-scale Retinex (MSR) and multi-scale Retinex with color restoration (MSRCR). Meanwhile, Retinex algorithm has the ability of dynamic range adjustment and lightness constancy to fulfill the need during the processing procedure of night road view scene. However, traditional Retinex theory can not make a correspondence between R, G, B value in the RGB color space with the color attribution. It could easily makes color distortion with the difference of every color channel enhancement and makes the edge information loss, especially when the image has abundant scene depth.

This paper proposed a mixed multi-Retinex combined with fractional differentiation method. It can adjust the ambient illumination processing capacity in the dynamic range under the low light conditions at night and it could enhance the night view image and also depress the noise.

2 Mixed Multi-scale Retinex

The basic idea of Retinex theory is that people can perceive color and brightness of a point which does not only depend on the absolute value. This conclusion is based on a series of experiments. Generic Retinex algorithm makes the low visibility image become much clear, and it can also deal with the night view road scene [11, 12]. However, applying the method could not satisfy the need of dynamic range in the image which has abundant image depth.

The algorithm is designed for this kind of image, for the Retinex theory think that the object's color is determined by the attribution of the surface and has no relationship with the light source irradiation condition. The reflecting component represents the object reflection attribution and incident component reflects the incident component. Retinex theory mathematical expression could be defined as Eq. (1):

$$S(x,y) = L(x,y)R(x,y) \tag{1}$$

wherein, $S(x, y)$ is the original image; $L(x, y)$ is the incident component; $R(x, y)$ is the reflection component.

The main idea of multi-Retinex is to choose different Gauss surround scale to calculate based on the SSR algorithm [13, 14], and then makes the output results weighted sum. MSR could be described as Eq. (2):

$$logR_i(x,y) = \sum_{k=1}^{k} w_k\{\log S_i(x,y) - \log[F_k(x,y) * S_i(x,y)]\} \tag{2}$$

wherein, (x, y) is the coordinates of the pixel, and i is the color channel, $i \in \{R, G, B\}$, $S(x, y)$ is the original image and $R(x, y)$ is the reflection component. $F_k(x, y)$ is the Gauss surround function, k is the number of scales. W is the weighted value of the Gauss surround function and * means convolution calculation. A large number of experimental tests show that the value of K has a set standard, according to the results that the actual application need to choose scales from small, middle to large range. The large range is regulated at least 200, and the small one is designed no more than 20. And Eq. (3) shows:

$$\sum_{k=1}^{K} w_k = 1 \tag{3}$$

For most images after the relevant experiments:

The mixed multi-scale Retinex (MMSR) adopts several technique to deal with noise and dark shadows.

This paper introduced the change form of $F(x, y)$, which is the flexible part that can change its form. C means the circle's circumference. This paper defined $F(x, y)$ like Eqs. (4) and (5):

$$F(x, y) = \mu \exp\left(\frac{-(x^2 + y^2)^2}{c^2}\right) \tag{4}$$

$$\int\int F(x, y)dxdy = 1 \tag{5}$$

3 Fractional Differentiation

With the use of fractional differentiation, the edge information of the night view image can be more specific and clear. This part use the definition of Grumwald–Letnikov in this theory, like Eq. (6) shows:

$$_a^G D_t^V = lim \frac{1}{h^v} \sum_{m=0}^{\left[\frac{t-a}{h}\right]} (-1)^m \frac{!\Gamma(v+1)}{m!\Gamma(v-m+1)} f(t-mh)(h \to 0) \tag{6}$$

Wherein, $\Gamma(n)$ is Gamma function, for a single signal, Follow the steps of 1 to divide, let

$$m = [(t-a)/h]^{(h=1)} = [t-a] \tag{7}$$

thus, this gives a differential expression Eq. (8):

$$d^{v}f(t)/dt^{v} = f(t) + (-v)f(t-1) + \frac{(-v)(-v+1)}{2} f(t-2) + \cdots + \frac{(-v+1)}{n!\Gamma(-v+n+1)} f(t-n) \quad (8)$$

The fractional differential operator has different processing performance at different orders [15]. It can be learnt from the amplitude spectrum diagram that the fractional differential operator preserves the low frequency components of the signal in a non-linearity way and enhances the high frequency signal component at the same time. As the frequency increases, the signal is nonlinearly attenuated.

For the different order of the fractional differential operator, the result is not same. High-frequency signal processing will have a certain growth [16], and after several different signal processing, low-frequency signal will have a certain degree of weakening. For the differential processing effect, specifically, the best effect is between the first-order differential effect and the second-order differential effect. Not only can make the UHF key information have a outstanding performance, but also depress the noise in a degree.

In order to achieve the anti-rotation of the algorithm, we set the differential coefficients of 8 symmetrical directions in the matrix, which are positive and negative directions of the X axis, and the Y-axis Positive and negative direction, diagonal 4 directions.

In practical applications, in order to achieve the goal that the filter does not have much error, we use 5 × 5 template for filtering and choose the classic fractional differential operator named tiansi template (Fig. 1).

$\frac{v^2-v}{2}$	0	$\frac{v^2-v}{2}$	0	$\frac{v^2-v}{2}$
0	-v	-v	-v	0
$\frac{v^2-v}{2}$	-v	$\frac{(-v)(-v+1)}{2}$	-v	$\frac{v^2-v}{2}$
0	-v	0	-v	0
$\frac{v^2-v}{2}$	0	$\frac{v^2-v}{2}$	0	$\frac{v^2-v}{2}$

Fig. 1. The tiansi template

People's eyes are very difficult to directly determine the small differences in image processing. With the fractional order's increase, the effect is not always enhanced. And after a great number of experiments indicates that, the best order of the night road scene is 0.45.

After operating all these above, we have finished the step about using the way of fractional differentiation to enhance the edge information in the dark image.

4 Algorithm Design

For the traditional Retinex algorithm, the goal can be achieved on the small scale. However, when it get closer to the target and achieve a large scale, the advantages of such a mixed mode is to enhance some of the details, but also to reduce the presence of halo.

So this paper give the improved algorithm like flow chart to solve this problem:

From Fig. 2, first input image should be set the differential coefficients of 8 symmetrical directions in the matrix, and then choosing a proper order for the calculation. Thus, through fractional differentiation calculation, with using MMSR to enhance the image effect.

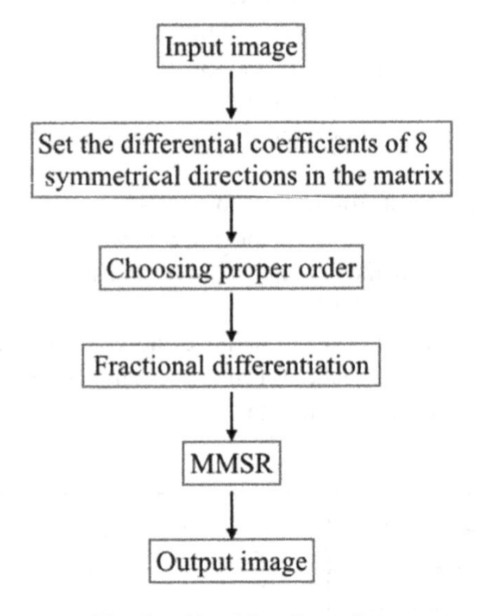

Fig. 2. Algorithm flow chart

5 Experiment

In order to highlight the effect of the algorithm, we chose the common-used method, contrasting with enhancement method (DCE, Combined with contrast enhancement and histogram equalization). The results is shown in Figs. 3 and 4. This paper selects the scene as a sample for comparison. This paper employs desktop PC which has Intel Core2Duo CPU, 4 GB Ram memory, and we use matlab 2014b platform to conduct the experiment.

All the first pictures in Figs. 2 and 3 are the original image, through SSR (scales 100), MSR (scales 200). The results are in weak conditions, the overall effect is more like gloomy picture. Image detail is good, and the halo phenomenon is not obvious.

Lowering the time-consuming is the final aim of the improved MSR, it was led to different results according to different programming languages, different platforms and

Fig. 3. The result of image separately using the methods of DCE (b), SSR (c), MSR (d), improved SSR (e) and Improved MSR (f)

different optimization ways. Therefore, in this algorithm result analysis, the experiments use consuming time as the basis of statistics. As is shown in Table 1, our final aim is to compare the time-consuming of these different algorithms under the same platform.

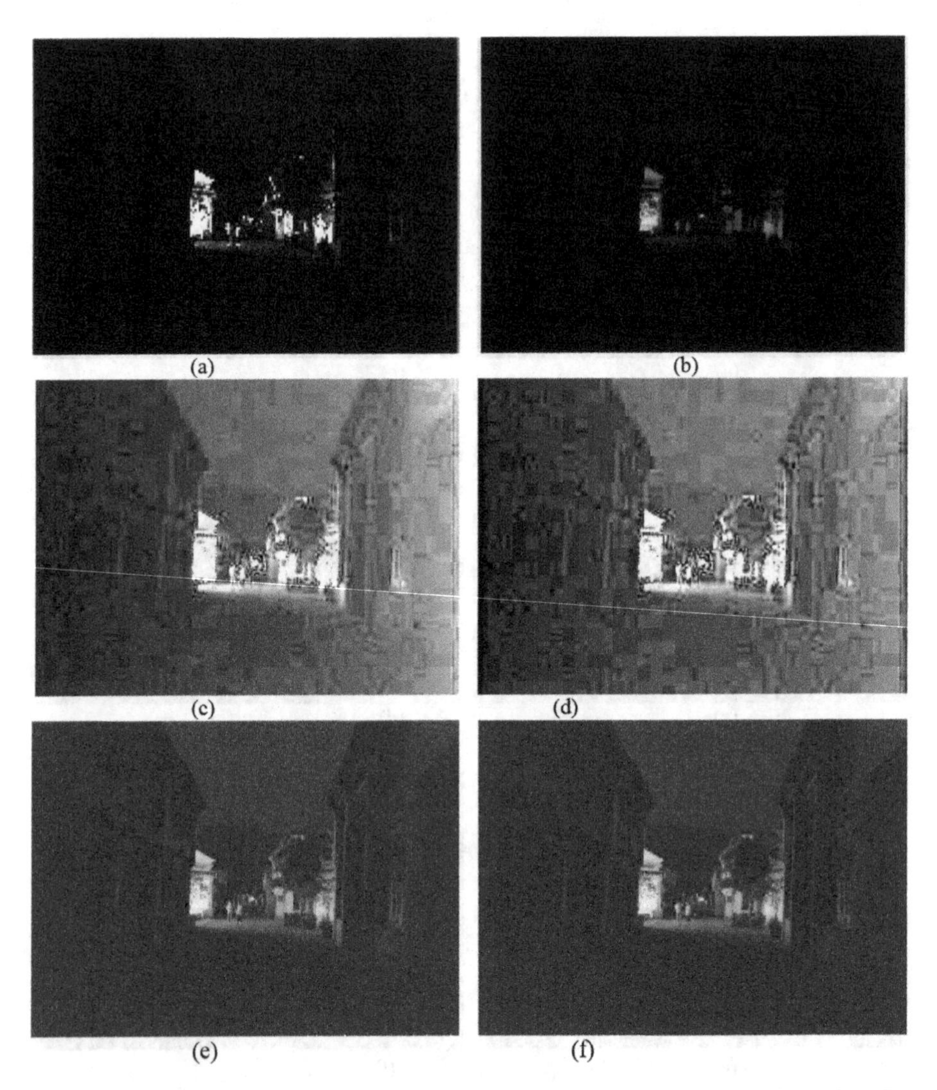

Fig. 4. The result of image separately using the methods of (b) DCE, (c) SSR, (d) MSR, (e) improved SSR and (f) improved MSR

Table 1. Results comparison in time consume and PSNR

Image	Method	Time consume/s	PSNR/dB
Figure 3(a)	DCE	4.805	14.7
	SSR	11.454	20.6
	MSR	17.712	29.1
	Improved SSR	6.756	32.7
	Improved MSR	8.322	36.1
Figure 4(a)	DCE	20.377	19.2
	SSR	22.379	19.8
	MSR	24.656	21.7
	Improved SSR	19.212	34.8
	Improved MSR	18.45	38.6

6 Conclusion

From Figs. 3 and 4, we know that the recovering effect from darkness to the brightness is distinct. the method in this text show more abundant details in the whole comparison, meanwhile, it still give a unsmooth feeling. The DCE method only sharpen and brighten the lighting areas but ignore the darkness place without enhance them. In summary, the method in this paper can enhance the picture through little details in order to get a enhanced image. We take two representative phenomenon separately in narrow streets, broad street, covering 80% roads classification in the modern urban traffic designation. In the end, we compare the time consume in these methods, and we draw a conclusion that DCE consume a lot and make less PSNR in Table 1.

Also, this method could be adapt to using in text [17, 18] which have the same night occasion.

Acknowledgements. This work has been supported by HGJ, HJSW and Research & Development plan of Shaanxi Province (Program No. 2017ZDXM-GY-094, 2015KTZDGY04-01).

References

1. Xiao, J., Peng, H., Zhang, Y., Chaoping, T., Li, Q.: Fast image enhancement based on color space fusion. Color Res. Appl. **41**(1), 22–31 (2016)
2. Zhu, H., Wan, G.: Local contrast preserving technique for the removal of thin cloud in aerial image. Optik Int. J. Light Electron Opt. **127**(2), 742–747 (2016)
3. Li, J., Miao, C.: The conveyor belt longitudinal tear on-line detection based on improved SSR algorithm. Optik Int. J. Light Electron Opt. **127**(19), 8002–8010 (2016)
4. Lee, S., Lee, C.: Multiscale morphology based illumination normalization with enhanced local textures for face recognition. Expert Syst. Appl. **62**, 347–357 (2016)
5. Nikonorov, A., Bibikov, S., Myasnikov, V., Yuzifovich, Y., Fursov, V.: Correcting color and hyperspectral images with identification of distortion model. Pattern Recogn. Lett. **83**, 178–187 (2016)
6. Al-Ameen, Z., Sulong, G.: A new algorithm for improving the low contrast of computed tomography images using tuned brightness controlled single-scale Retinex. Scanning **37**(2), 116–125 (2015)
7. Chen, Z.-S., Tai, S.-C.: Corrected center-surround Retinex: application to tone reproduction for high dynamic range images. Int. J. Comput. Appl. **37**(1), 37–51 (2015)
8. Guo, F., Tang, J., Cai, Z.-X.: Image dehazing based on haziness analysis. Int. J. Autom. Comput. **11**(1), 78–86 (2014)
9. Hu, X., Gao, X., Wang, H.: A novel Retinex algorithm and its application to fog-degraded image enhancement. Sens. Transducers **175**(7), 138–143 (2014)
10. Sun, W., Han, L., Guo, B., Jia, W., Sun, M.: A fast color image enhancement algorithm based on max intensity channel. J. Mod. Opt. **61**(6), 466–477 (2014)
11. Tang, J., Peli, E., Acton, S.: Image enhancement using a contrast measure in the compressed domain. IEEE Signal Process. Lett. **10**(10), 289–292 (2003)
12. Xueming, L., et al.: Night image enhancement algorithm based on Retinex theory. Appl. Res. Comput. **3**(10), 235–237 (2005)
13. Wang, W., et.al.: A fast multi-scale retinex algorithm for color image enhancement, vol. 1, pp. 80–85. IEEE (2008)

14. Tao, L., Asari, V.: Modified luminance based MSR for fast and efficient image enhancement. IEEE Appl. Imag. Pattern Recogn. **1**, 174–179 (2003)
15. Huang, G., Lib, X.U., Yi-Fei, P.U.: Summary of research on image processing using fractional calculus. Appl. Res. Comput. **2**, 1 (2012)
16. Yuan, Y.H., Sun, Q.S., Ge, H.W.: Fractional-order embedding canonical correlation analysis and its applications to multi-view dimensionality reduction and recognition. Pattern Recogn. **47**(3), 1411–1424 (2014)
17. Yan, Y., et al.: Cognitive fusion of thermal and visible imagery for effective detection and tracking of pedestrians in videos. Cogn. Comput. **10**(1), 94–104 (2018)
18. Wang, Z., et al.: A deep-learning based feature hybrid framework for spatiotemporal saliency detection inside videos. Neurocomputing **287**, 68–83 (2018)

Traffic Image Defogging Based on Bit-Plane Decomposition

Yuanfang Zhang, Jiangbin Zheng(✉), Xuejiao Kou, and Yefan Xie

Northwestern Polytechnical University,
Xi'an, Shaanxi, People's Republic of China
robinzhang.zyf@gmail.com

Abstract. The image of Highway Traffic defogging has become an important part in the traffic security monitoring system. The studies in the image field on this topic are mainly based on the optical image transform theory and mathematical physics, with a number of fruitful results have been achieved, this paper proposes a method combining the mathematical morphology and the bit plane decomposition coding for traffic image defogging, compared with the traditional image defogging methods, the new method makes the effect increased displayed on PSNR values.

Keywords: Mathematical morphology · Bit-planes · Image defogging

1 Introduction

The haze and fog removal which is caused by the particles in the air, is a typical research topic. Haze is composed of aerosol particles suspended in gas. It occurs when the dust and smoke particles accumulate in dry air, which gives people a cloudy impression. Under a foggy scene, many reactions of smoke particles like scattering, refraction and absorption will occur very often. The presence of this haze leads to considerable distortion of the scene. Thus we can reduce its visibility drastically at times. Defogging and dehazing images are highly required for receiving high quality of images, especially in the road traffic area.

Srinvasa and Narasimhan [1] proposed a method which thought to be the same image scene depth point launch has no relation with weather; Zhai [2] etc. presented a method which put forward a genetic algorithm with an adaptive function, in the meantime, it put the image gradient as the contrast evaluation index to acquire ideal image defogging results. He [3] suggested a method based on the dark channel prior, which is based on the soft computing and dark channel image to make image enhancement.

Nowadays, the methods toward the clearance of the fog-degraded images have two directions: the first one is to manipulate image recovery based on physical models, which build a mathematical analyzed prototype to realize scene recovery; the another way is to enhance the contrast of images, so as to increase object visibility.

Knowing image depth is the principle of a recovery method; Oakley et al. built a multiple parameter degradation model which can successfully recover the gray level scenes. Tan et al. improved the model as the recovery of the color pictures under an

J. Ren et al. (Eds.): BICS 2018, LNAI 10989, pp. 827–837, 2018.
https://doi.org/10.1007/978-3-030-00563-4_81

unusual weather. However, it costs a lot for the hardware and memory so that it is difficult to be applied in society. Narasimhan et al. dealt with at least two series of degraded images in order to get the structure and depth information of scenes so it can make the color and contrast recovered.

Narasimhan et al. put forward an interactive image depth estimation method to realize the scene recovery. But it needs to assemble the disappearing points and to make instructions around the maximum and minimum image depths. Some Chinese scholars let their main items on the image processing field accomplish tasks. The two ways are the general enhancement and local enhancement respectively. While executing the entropy of information, the image contrast is enhanced for a single image. The depth of the scene changing has proved that it can not reflect the changes in such an image. Hence, the local enhancement method can make the results perfectly and match what we want.

2 Basic Theory

2.1 Atmospheric Delusion Model

In the foggy weather, the reflected light rays could scatter because small particles make the image equipment do not detect complete launch light rays. That is why the light may be reduced in a transmission way. The particles existed in the air generates the light scattering procedure more complicated [4]. In order to explain the procedure which has many influences on the light transmission way, there is a formula has been put forward as:

$$I(x) = J(x)t(x) + A(1 - t(x)) \tag{1}$$

Where, $I(x)$ represents an adopting image; A as the atmospheric light intensity; $J(x)$ is for the true image; $t(x)$ for the transmissity. The defog procedure means using known $I(x)$ to solve $J(x)$. Because this formula contains multi unknown factors, so we need some prior knowledge at first.

Concentration and visibility from the fog have a close relationship, based on the level of visibility from fog can be divided into the following categories:

(1) The horizontal visibility distance between 1–10 km is called mist.
(2) The horizontal visibility is less than 1 km is called fog.
(3) The level of visibility in fog distance between 200–500 m is called fog.
(4) The horizontal visibility distance in foggy weather between 50–200 m is called fog.
(5) The level of less than 50 m visibility fog is called strong fog.

2.2 Top-Hat and Bottom-Hat

Image edges contain a wealth of information and abundant data, so the edge detection technology plays an important role in image segmentation. Edges are essentially dramatic changes within the local point range of pixel gray scales. The traditional edge detection method using edge neighborhood detection for noise sensitive detection. For this reason researchers put forward many new algorithms, mathematical theories and tools which have been applied to the image edge detection, such as neural network, wavelet transform, the blur detection method, mathematical morphology method [4]. Wherein, the edge detection based on mathematical morphology has the better performance.

Mathematical morphology is based on a set of theory, integral geometry and algebra on the grid discipline, the basic idea is to have some form of structural elements to measure and extract the image corresponding shape in order to achieve the purpose of image analysis and recognition [5]. Image processing method has a simplified mathematical morphology image data which can maintain the basic characteristics of the image. In order to facilitate parallel processing advantages of easy hardware implementation, therefore, the mathematical morphology in image processing is widely used.

Top hat transformation and low hat transformation are important forms for mathematical morphology algorithms. Hat transform has the characteristics of high-pass filter, and the low hat transform can detect valley points. With the low cat could better transform image enhancement, and the top-hat transformation can do better for low cap edge detection [6].

This text put forward a defogging method based on Top-Hat and Bottom-Hat transform, which is suits for such image processing. The principle dealt with the brighter background to explore some dark pixel particles or adversely get the bright pixel in the darker background. These transform can detect the image signals which are smaller than structure elements including grayscale wave top and wave bottom.

Here is the Top-Hat and Bottom-Hat transform formulas, c means, g means:

$$Top - Hat(f) = f - (f^{c}g) \tag{2}$$

$$Bottom - hat(f) = (f^{c}g) - f \tag{3}$$

3 Math Morphology Basic Principle

Math morphology basic principle is using a set of scientific transform to describe basic pattern of images or its structure. Erosion and dilation are the main character in the theory and other concrete transform is defined by their combinations.

3.1 Morphological Opening and Closing Operation

Mathematical Morphology basic operations include erosion, dilation, opening operation and closing operation. Generally, corrosion shrink images get bigger picture. Let A as input image, B as structure element, so we define B does opening operation on A as following:

$$A \circ B = (A \otimes B) \oplus B \tag{4}$$

Opening operation has the advantages of removing smaller scatter and burr, cutting the bridge between them and make image smooth, making low-pass filter. But opening operation can only make company with the shape as same as the structure element of the image.

Closing operation means the dual computations of the opening. It is defined as dilation and then erosion conception. When we put the image B does closing operation on image A, we define it like following:

$$A \cdot B = (A \oplus B) \otimes B \tag{5}$$

Closing operation could fill the gap and hole in an image smaller than structure elements, paternering with short cut so it could lead to connection. It also does wave filter to polish up the convex interior angle in an image.

3.2 Freeman Chain Code Method

Freeman Chain code with the starting point of the curve point coordinates and the direction of the border or boundary curve code to describe a method often used to denote the area boundary curves and image processing, computer graphics, pattern recognition and other fields. It is a coded representation of the border, with the direction of the border as the basis for coding, to simplify the description of the boundary, a general description of the boundary point set [5].

Conventional chain code in accordance with the number of different center pixel is adjacent to the direction of the communication. Chain code is divided into 4 and 8 communication chain code. 4-connected neighbors chain code has four, respectively, in the center of the upper, lower, left and right. 8 communication chain code chain code communication adds four oblique directions, because any one of the eight surrounding pixels are neighbors, and 8 communication chain code just in case of actual pixels, it is possible to accurately describe the center pixel and its information of the adjacent points. Therefore, the 8 communication chain code relatively high [6].

Usually a pixel (usually already refined image) as the reference point, respectively, adjacent pixels in eight different locations, they give direction to a value of 0 to 7 (Fig. 1) [7], referred to 0 bit to 7 direction chain code value. Figure 2 gives a bitmap of 9×9, wherein a line segment, S is the starting point, E is the end point, as do this line segment is expressed as L = 43322100000066.

Selecting the disc-shaped element 3×3 structure morphology operation. Determining the shape of the structural elements, the structural elements of the size is critical. Structural elements denoised is weak in small size, but it can detect a good edge detail; denoised strong structural elements of large size, but the coarse edge has been detected. Large structural elements can be small-sized structural element which can be obtained by multiple expansion, dilation structuring element's shape has been shown in Fig. 3.

3	2	1
4	P	0
5	6	7

Fig. 1. Freeman chain code sample

		1	1	1	1	1	1	1
	1							1
	1							E
	1							
		1						
			1	S	1			
				1				
				1				

Fig. 2. Freeman chain code running sample

$$b = \begin{bmatrix} 0 & 1 & 0 \\ 1 & 1 & 1 \\ 0 & 1 & 0 \end{bmatrix} \quad b_n = \underbrace{b \oplus b \oplus b \oplus \cdots \oplus b}_{n}$$

Fig. 3. Structure element sample

3.3 Bit-Planes Decomposition

Bit-plane decomposition is presented by Schwarz and its basic idea is to decompose an image into a collection of binary images. Thus, any grey-scaled image can be split into a series of binary layers. For bit-plane decomposition, the gray levels of the gray-scaled image are represented in binary. Therefore, for possible distinct gray levels L, the each pixel of the image is represented by a k ($k = \lceil \log 2L \rceil$) bit binary code. Reducing in value of L can result in the significant loss of information and this often adversely affects the performance of the classifier. If L is too large, it will be time-consuming. So the suitable size is necessary for value of L. The image is decomposed into k layers where layer 'i' is composed of the i-th bits of the gray level values. Thus, layer '1' is formed by collecting all the least significant bits (LSB) and layer '8' is formed by collecting the Most Significant Bits (MSB) of the binary coded gray-scale image [5].

Several bits can describe a grayscale value as a whole photo, every bit could also regard as a one binary plane, also, it can be called a bit plane [8, 9] in Fig. 4.

Let a photo divided into several bit planes, which described its data in a binary system. Then we encode these planes, which is called bit-plane decomposition method.

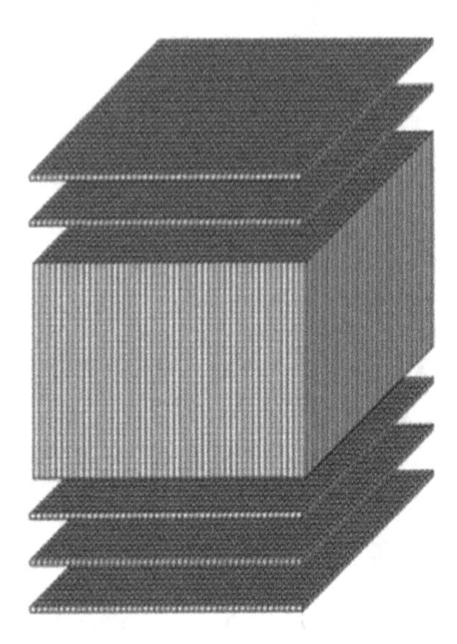

Fig. 4. Bit-plane decomposition method sample image

An image is decomposed into a series of binary image and then use binary compression method to conduct a compression in a degree, and this is called bit-plane encode technology. Bit-plane decomposition means a photo with m bits grayscales can be divided into m layers, which can be expressed in a formula description:

$$I(x, y) = a_{m-1}2^{m-1} + a_{m-2}2^{m-2} + \cdots + a_1 2^1 + a_0 2^0 \tag{6}$$

In formula 6, a_i is a coefficient related to standard binary value. m number M * N dimensional binary vectors are composed of m layers Bit-plane and their points, the right side of the formula, we draw its value 0 or 1. According to this, we recognize we divided m coefficient into m 1-bit bit-planes, thus we can get a series of binary value images.

4 Algorithm Design and Experiment

From the above research, we design an algorithm procedure to come up with results as following:

(1) Load the image first, and then use top-hat or bottom-hat transform to display the image gray peaks and valleys of the original image, then make the top-hat value subtract the bottom-hat value in order to get the enhance effect;
(2) Use the bit-plane decomposition method to deal with the input picture, and then use the freeman chain code to strengthen the object boundary from both horizon and vertical directions;
(3) Make histogram analysis for each bit image and according the histogram result, selecting the most flat picture as the final result.

Fig. 5. Experiment results under different scenes using various methods

Fig. 5. *(continued)*

We were on the highways and urban roads, high-rise city view photos, residential scene is processed by our method, and obtains a histogram of the image after the picture and defogging them. Highways usually comes across the vehicle accident and trouble because of fog; urban roads crowded condition has become worse and worse under foggy circumstances. Especially in traffic lights visibility. And high-rise city views assisted the police and security to handle the city condition, especially the low airspace security when some unknown flying objects occurred in a very important meeting; residential scene are needed for the property to monitor the real-time condition in residential district.

We can see that, because of fog quality, with scattering its subject, contrast severely reduced, the histogram is compressed within a small range, contrast histogram defogging later [10], we can clearly see the gray value image is stretched to the entire gray degree-level space, and maintains the brightness of the image midfield landscape distribution. It does not lead to recovery after a serious distortion of the image, but this histogram equalization algorithm will lead to block and color distortion, and its occurrence different mechanisms, we can see that our algorithm is better (Fig. 5).

Table 1. Comparison about different scenes using various methods

Method	PSNR value of image (a)	PSNR value of image (b)
Dark channel prior (DCP)	37.4	39.6
Adaptive color contrast methods (ACC)	31.5	34.2
Adaptive histogram equalization (AHE)	31.2	32.3
Retinex (MCR)	35.5	37.8
Bit-plane decomposition	33.5	32.9

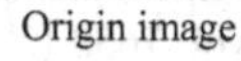

Origin image

Bit-decomposition method result

Fig. 6. Crowded road under foggy days view using bit-decomposition method

5 Analysis and Conclusion

In order to illustrate our method have a relative obvious performance after defogging image, we make a comparison with other methods (Table 1).

And we can adopt this method to deal with the road view scene certainly, especially in some crowded area, it can lead the supervisor to monitor the real-time situation. Like Fig. 6 :

Through the fog image using the Top-Hat and Bottom-Hat transformation, and then bit-plane decomposition, in order to get the fog image in each plane coded by Freeman chain code [11, 12, 18, 19], by comparison with the description of the histogram equalization, contrast enhancement methods which these restoration effect method is thought to be ideal. Besides all these above, our method has the advantage in other field, such as video processing [20], CT technology [12], 3D image sensing [17], ultrasound image [15] et al. Some researchers attempt to develop the method and apply it to different kinds of fields [13, 14].

Acknowledgements. This work has been supported by HGJ, HJSW and Research & Development plan of Shaanxi Province (Program No. 2017ZDXM-GY-094, 2015KTZDGY04-01).

References

1. Narasimhan, S.G., Shree, K.N., et al.: Chromatic framework for vision in bad weather. In: IEEE Conference on Computer vision and Pattern Recognition, pp. 598–605 (2000)
2. Zhai, Y., Zhang, Y.: Contrast restoration for fog degraded images. In: International Conference on Computational Intelligence and Security, pp. 619–623 (2009)
3. He, K., et al.: Single image haze removal using dark channel prior. In: IEEE Conference on Computer Vision and Pattern Recognition (2009)
4. Chavez, P.: An improved dark-object substraction technique for atmospheric scattering correction of multispectral data. Remote Sens. Environ. **24**, 450–479 (1988)
5. Hough, P.V.: Methods and means for recognizing complex patterns. 2069654, USA (1962)
6. Kabir, S., Azad, T., Alam, A.A.S.M.: Freeman chain code with digits of unequal cost. In: 2014 8th International Conference on Software Knowledge Information Management and Application, SKIMA (2014)
7. Lee, D., Park, C., Jang, M., Kim, J.: Human internal state recognition using modified chain-code method. In: 2015 12th International Conference on Ubiquitous Robots and Ambient Intelligence, URAI (2015)
8. Dutta, A., Mandal, A., Chatterji, B.N., Kar, A: Bit-plane extension to a class of intensity-based corner detection algorithms. In: 2007 15th European Signal Processing Conference (2007)
9. Noruma, T.: Optical encryption using a joint transform correlator architecture. Opt. Eng. **39** (8), 2031–2035 (2000)
10. Jia, G., Xiaotong, W., Chengpeng, H., Changqing, Y.: Simple defogging method for outdoor images based on physical model. In: Proceedings of SPIE 5th International Symposium on Advanced Optical Manufacturing and Testing Technologies, vol. 7658 (2010)
11. Chen, T.-S., Wu, H.-C., Tsai, H.-F., Hsieh, M., Chiou, S.-F.: Progressive transmission of two-dimensional gel electrophoresis image based on context features and bit-plane method. In: 2004 IEEE International Conference on Networking, Sensing and Control (2004)
12. Sammouda, R., Mathkour, H.B., Touir, A.: A modified bit-plane based method for lung region extraction from 3D chest CT images. In: 2013 Japan–Egypt International Conference on Electronics, Communications and Computers, JEC-ECC (2013)

13. Karthika, M., James, A.: A proposed method for document image binarization based on bit plane slicing. In: 2014 International Conference on Advances in Engineering and Technology Research, ICAETR (2014)
14. Shakoor, M.H., Moattari, M.: A fuzzy method based on bit-plane images for stabilizing digital images. In: 2010 20th International Conference on Electronics, Communications and Computer, CONIELECOMP (2010)
15. Rahman, M.M., Kumar, P.K.M., Arefin, M.G., Uddin, M.S.: Speckle noise reduction from ultrasound images using principal component analysis with bit plane slicing and nonlinear diffusion method. In: 2012 15th International Conference on Computer and Information Technology, ICCIT (2012)
16. Yoon, I., Jeon, J., Lee, J., Paik, J.: Weighted image defogging method using statistical RGB channel feature extraction. In: 2010 International SoC Design Conference, ISOCC (2010)
17. Loganathan, D., Mehata, K.M.: 3D image sensing for bit plane method of progressive transmission. In: Proceedings of the 2nd International Symposium on 3D Data Processing, Visualization and Transmission, 3DPVT 2004 (2004)
18. Zheng, Y., Chen, C., Sarem, M.: An improved gray image representation method based on binary-bit plane decomposition. In: 2008 4th International Conference on Natural Computation (2008)
19. Gibson, K.B., Nguyen, T.Q.: Fast single image fog removal using the adaptive Wiener filter. In: 2013 IEEE International Conference on Image Processing (2013)
20. Venugopala, P.S., Sarojadevi, H., Chiplunkar, N.N., Bhat, V.: Video watermarking by adjusting the pixel values and using scene change detection. In: 2014 5th International Conference on Signal and Image Processing, ICSIP (2014)

The Simulation of Non-Gaussian Scattering on Rough Sea Surface

Lei Fan[1] and Guoxing Gao[2(✉)]

[1] School of Marine Science and Technology, Northwestern Polytechnical University, Xi'an, China
[2] Navy Submarine of Academy, Qingdao, China
gaogx999@163.com

Abstract. The simulation of a non-Gaussian scattering on rough surface based on local curvature approximation (NG-LCA) model is presented. The comparison between the NRCS result of LCA and the QuikSCAT scatterometer data shows that NG-LCA model can well explain the scattering way of the Upwind/downwind asymmetry.

Keywords: Local curvature approximation (LCA) · Non-Gaussian sea surface Normalized Radar Cross Section (NRCS)

1 Introduction

It's much critical to research and develop the electromagnetic scattering model on the non-Gaussian rough surface because of its important roles in many fields such as the oceanic environmental parameters retrieval and oceanic supervision using remote sensing. In the last two decades, several scattering models such as small slope approximation model (SSA) and integral equation model (IEM), have been reported and developed for the scattering from stochastic rough surface under various condition [1, 2]. Concerning on the estimation of the electromagnetic scattering from the sea surface, the correlation components of the sea surface vertical displacement, statistically, often required to be calculated on the large/short-scale waves such as Short Gravity Waves and Capillarity Gravity Waves. Generally, due to the complexity of the processing, the Gaussian stochastic process is firstly assumed, thus a complex question will became simply and its reduction will be done. However, the ocean surface often exhibits non-Gaussian features such as non-normal distribution of wave height and slope of the sea surface, moreover the function of the surface vertical displacement is anisotropy and shows strongly dependence on the relative wind direction.

Non-Gaussian characteristics on sea surface can be described by the vertical displacement's or slope distribution of third or fourth-order statistical description. Chen [4, 5] shown an ad-hoc empirical bispectrum function and selected several forms of the skewness function in order to present the sea surface slope, while Quilfen [6] suggested that a physical basis has not been given to support this formulation. Guan et al. [7] also studied the forth-order probability density function of the wave-height distribution. Bourier [11] also researches the non-Gaussian characteristics of the sea surface

J. Ren et al. (Eds.): BICS 2018, LNAI 10989, pp. 838–846, 2018.
https://doi.org/10.1007/978-3-030-00563-4_82

electromagnetic scattering. Actually, an earlier derivation of surface slope distribution model is shown by Cox and Munk in 1954 [12], and the higher order statistic moments and behaviors of the corresponding correlation functions are also presented. It is noted that the corresponding formulation of correlation functions is seemed as the composited model which a parameter should be indicted. Besides, as computer vision has achieved great success on many fields [20, 21], there are also studies focusing on sea surface and sea ice image processing [22–25].

In this paper, we present a modified non-Gaussian mode based on Local Curvature Approximation (LCA) model [13] in which Bourier's third and fourth-order statistical moment is adopted. The model calculation result is compared with the measured Normalized Radar Cross Section (NRCS) by QuikSCAT's SeaWinds scatterometer.

2 Non-Gaussian Scattering Model Based on LCA

2.1 Coordinates System and Definitions

To expose the general scattering problem, we adopt the same vectorial conventions as the Elfouhaily's [3]. According to these conventions, we consider that incident downward propagating electromagnetic plane wave interactive with the stochastic rough sea surface and produces the up-going scattering wave. The wave-height or displacement of the sea surface function is expressed as $\eta(\mathbf{r})$, where $\mathbf{r}$ is horizontal component of the three-dimensional position wave vector. The incident and scattering wave number vector is presented as $(\mathbf{k}_0, -q_0)$ and $(\mathbf{k}, q_k)$ respectively. The horizontal wave number vector, $\mathbf{k}$, is corresponding to the scattering wave, and $\mathbf{k}_0$ is the horizontal component of the incident wave. Equation (1) shows their relations.

$$\begin{aligned} \mathbf{k}_0 &= (K\cos\phi_i \sin\theta_i,\ K\sin\phi_i \sin\theta_i) \\ \mathbf{k} &= (K\cos\phi_s \sin\theta_s,\ K\sin\phi_s \sin\theta_s) \end{aligned} \tag{1}$$

where K is the electromagnetic wave number, θ_{i} and $\boldsymbol{\phi}_i$ are incident and azimuth viewing angle of incident wave whereas θ_{s} and $\boldsymbol{\phi}_s$ are the scattering waves' and the variables q_0 and q_{k} are the horizontal projection component of the incident and scattering wave respectively. And we have

$$q_0 = \sqrt{\frac{\omega^2}{c^2} - k_0^2},\ q_k = \sqrt{\frac{\omega^2}{c^2} - k^2},\ \text{Im}q_0,\ q_k > 0 \tag{2}$$

where ω is circle frequency, c is velocity of light in the medium, and k0 = |k0|, k = |k|. In order to convenience, two variables are introduced following as QH = k − k0 and Qz = qk + q0.

To show the polarization characteristics, We also introduce an 2 × 2 matrix named as scattering amplitude into the radar scattering cross section. The scattering amplitude [2, 13] is expressed as (3)

$$S = \frac{1}{Q_z} \int_A \mathbf{H}(\mathbf{k}, \mathbf{k}_0; \eta(\mathbf{r})) \exp\{-j[\mathbf{Q}_H \cdot \mathbf{r} + Q_z \eta(\mathbf{r})]\} d\mathbf{r} \tag{3}$$

where **S** is S-matrix with four different polarization configuration such as HH, VV, VH and HV. S^{pq} is scattering amplitude (SA) for the given polarization, pq, configuration.

$$S^{pq} = \frac{1}{Q_z} \int_A \mathbf{H}^{pq}(\mathbf{k}, \mathbf{k}_0; \eta(\mathbf{r})) \exp\{-j[\mathbf{Q}_H \cdot \mathbf{r} + Q_z \eta(\mathbf{r})]\} d\mathbf{r} \tag{4}$$

where $\mathbf{H}^{pq}(\cdot)$ is kernel function. If we obtain the special expression of the SA, the incoherent bi-static scattering cross section is proportional to the second-order centered statistical moment of the SA.

$$\sigma^{pq}(\mathbf{k}, \mathbf{k}_0) \propto \left\langle |S^{qp}(\mathbf{k}, \mathbf{k}_0)|^2 \right\rangle - |\langle S^{qp}(\mathbf{k}, \mathbf{k}_0) \rangle|^2 \tag{5}$$

2.2 The General Formulation of the LCA-2

The Local curvature approximation (LCA) model is proposed by Elfouhaily and it is one of the "unified" scattering models since it is satisfied the low and high frequent limits simultaneously. For model of LCA-2 [15], the kernel function [13] can be expressed as (6),

$$\mathbf{H}^{pq}(\mathbf{k}, \mathbf{k}_0; \eta(\mathbf{r})) = N_1^{pq}(\mathbf{k}, \mathbf{k}_0) + N_2^{pq}(\mathbf{k}, \mathbf{k}_0; \eta(\mathbf{r})) \tag{6}$$

Where

$$\begin{aligned} N_1^{pq}(\cdot) &= \mathbf{K}(\mathbf{k}, \mathbf{k}_0) \\ N_2^{pq}(\cdot) &= \int_\xi \mathrm{B}(\mathbf{k}, \mathbf{k}_0; \xi) \hat{\eta}(\xi) e^{j\xi \cdot r} d\xi \\ &\quad - \int_\xi \mathbf{K}(\mathbf{k}, \mathbf{k}_0) \hat{\eta}(\xi) e^{j\xi \cdot r} d\xi \end{aligned}$$

The expression form, K(k, k0), B(k, k0; ξ), can be found in [3]. In (6), $\hat{\eta}(\xi)$ is presents the Fourier translation of the sea surface vertical displacement function.

Following the description above, we can see that the LCA can be degraded into small slope approximate (SSA) model if the second kernel function is omitted. For a Gaussian sea surface, although the model can interpret the radar scattering cross section variation with the wind velocity changes, it can not show the upwind/downwind difference. However, the fact, for the real sea surface, that the scattering measurements such as scatterometer or synthetic aperture radar (SAR) are dependent on the wind direction and show the asymmetry of upwind and downwind direction [16]. The dependence of measured data on wind direction have been the basis of the sea surface wind field retrieval yet, however the asymmetry of upwind and downwind can not introduce the operational model [6], owning to the asymmetry of upwind and downwind is a small component of sigma 0 measurement and subsequent, leaving a 180° ambiguity. Consequently, it is important to develop for the scattering approximation model in which the upwind/downwind asymmetry should be considered.

2.3 Non-Gaussian LCA Model

Considering the non-Gaussian characteristics of the sea surface, we should renew to derive the statistics of the SA in the (5). Here we adopt the phase perturbation technique, subsequently, obtain the formulation of bi-static radar cross section based on LCA-2,

$$\sigma^{pq}(\mathbf{k},\mathbf{k}_0) = \frac{1}{\pi Q_z^2}\int_{\mathbf{r}} \exp(-jQ_H\cdot\mathbf{r})\psi(\mathbf{r})P(\mathbf{r})d\mathbf{r} \tag{7}$$

Where

$$\begin{aligned}
P(\mathbf{r}) &= \left[|N_1^{pq}|^2 + N_1^{pq}\chi_1^{pq}(-\mathbf{r})^* + N_1^{pq*}\chi_1^{pq}(\mathbf{r})\right] \\
&\quad - e^{-Q_z^2 C_\eta(0)}\left[|N_1^{pq}|^2 + 2\mathrm{Re}\{N_1^{pq*}Q_z W_m^{pq}(0)\}\right] \\
\chi_1^{pq}(\mathbf{r}) &= jQ_z[W_m^{pq}(r) - W_m^{pq}(0)] \\
W_m^{pq}(\mathbf{r}) &= \int_\xi \hat{N}_2^{pq}(\xi)S(\xi)e^{j\xi\cdot\mathbf{r}}d\xi
\end{aligned}$$

It is noted in (7) that $\psi(\mathbf{r})$ is including non-Gaussian characteristic function of the surface vertical displacement and it can be expressed as different-order statistics. If we retained the forth-order statistics, the expression of $\psi(\mathbf{r})$ can be obtained as (8)

$$\psi(\mathbf{r}) = \exp[-Q^2(C_\eta(0) - C_2(\mathbf{r})) + jQ^3C_3(\mathbf{r}) + \frac{Q^4}{2}C_4(\mathbf{r})] \tag{8}$$

where $C_3(\mathbf{r})$ and $C_4(\mathbf{r})$ are the third and fourth order moment, respectively. We will discuss in next section.

In (7), $\hat{N}_2^{pq}(\xi)$ is the Fourier translation of the $N_2^{pq}(\mathbf{k},\mathbf{k}_0;\xi)$. Given the suggestion proposed by Bourier [14], the second moment can be shown as following,

$$C_\eta(\mathbf{r}) = C_2(\mathbf{r}) = C_{20}(r) - \cos(2\phi)C_{22}(r) \tag{9}$$

where $C_{20}(r) = \int_0^\infty dkS(k)J_0(kr)$, $C_{22}(r) = \int_0^\infty dkS(k)J_2(kr)\Delta(k)$.

In (10), C_{20} (r) and $C_{22}(r)$ are functions of surface vertical displacement of isotropic and anisotropic part, respectively. The J_n, $n = 0, 2$, is the first kind of Bessel function of n-order.

Accounting for the frequency of electromagnetic wave in microwave band and given the incident angle in the moderate scale, the expression $P(\mathbf{r})$ can be reduced to (10),

$$P(\mathbf{r}) \approx \left[|N_1^{pq}|^2 + N_1^{pq} \chi_1^{pq}(-\mathbf{r})^* + N_1^{pq*} \chi_1^{pq}(\mathbf{r}) \right] \tag{10}$$

From the derivation of the bi-static radar cross section, we can see that the problem is relatively easier if we only consider up to second statistics; while the derivation is appear to be more intricate for higher order. Bourier [11] has obtained the higher order correlation function for the third and fourth statistics. We will give the higher order statistics which are shown the non-Gaussian feature of the wind droved sea surface in next section.

2.4 The Higher Order Statistics

To date, the ocean surface slope probability density function given by Cox and Munk [12] and subsequently analyzed by Wu [17] is yet critical for the research and application of oceanography. The slope probability density function is expressed as (11),

$$p_s(\gamma_x, \gamma_y) = \frac{1}{2\pi\sigma_{sx}\sigma_{sy}} \exp\left(-\frac{\gamma_x^2}{2\sigma_{sx}^2} - \frac{\gamma_y^2}{2\sigma_{sy}^2} \right) G(\gamma_x, \gamma_y) \tag{11}$$

Where

$$\begin{aligned} G(\gamma_x, \gamma_y) &= 1 - c_{21}(\Gamma_y^2 - 1)\Gamma_x/2 - c_{03}(\Gamma_x^2 - 1)\Gamma_x/6 \\ &\quad + c_{22}(\Gamma_x^2 - 1)(\Gamma_y^2 - 1)/4 + c_{40}(\Gamma_y^4 - 6\Gamma_y^2 + 3)/24 \\ &\quad + c_{04}(\Gamma_x^4 - 6\Gamma_x^2 + 3)/24, \\ \Gamma_x &= \gamma_x/\sigma_{sx}, \ \Gamma_y = \gamma_y/\sigma_{sy} \end{aligned}$$

In (2–11), γ_x and γ_y are normalized slopes in the windward and crosswind directions, respectively, and the coefficients σ_{sx}^2 and σ_{sy}^2 are slopes variance. Other coefficients in (11) are shown in [12].

From the slope probability density function proposed by Cox and Munk, the higher order statistics is presented in (12) by Bourier [14, 18] who combined the slope density function with the symmetry properties of correlation function.

$$\begin{aligned} C_3(r, \phi) &= -\frac{1}{6} c_{03}\sigma_{sx}^3 r^3 \exp\left[0.3029 \frac{c_{03}^{2/3} \sigma_{sx}^2 r^2}{\sigma_{zS}^2} \right] \cos\phi \\ C_4(r) &= \frac{c_{22}\sigma_{sx}^2\sigma_{sy}^2 r^4}{4} \exp\left(-\frac{c_{22}\sigma_{sx}^2\sigma_{sy}^2 r^4}{\sigma_{zL}^4} \right) \end{aligned} \tag{12}$$

In (12), σ_{zL}^2 and σ_{zS}^2 are the variance of large- and small-scale wave, respectively, and these two parameters can be determined by the following equation.

$$\sigma_z^2 = \sigma_{zL}^2 + \sigma_{zS}^2 = \int_0^{K_c} S_{20}(k)dk + \int_{K_c}^{\infty} S_{20}(k)dk \tag{13}$$

From (13), we can see that a parameter, K_c, will be indicated in prior. Bourier suggested that the parameter would be associated with the wind speed and it is an intrinsic parameter of the sea. A simply relation between wind speed and this parameter can be given by (14).

$$\sigma_{zL}^2 = \int_0^{Kc} S(k)k^2 dk \approx (1.62u_{12} + 8) \times 10^{-3} \tag{14}$$

Here, *S(k)* is a form of wave number spectrum one can be referred from Elfouhaily [19]. Here, we fit it by least squares approach and then obtain four coefficients for it. The fitting expression is

$$K_c(u) = \beta_0 + \beta_1 u_{10} + \beta_2 u_{10}^2 + \beta_3 u_{10}^3 \tag{15}$$

where the coefficients β_0, β_1, β_2 and β_3, are set values −416.98, 182.62, −26.36 and 1.30, respectively. So the parameter, K_c, can be easier to be determined by wind velocity measured at 10 m above the sea. Next section will present the calculation results from NG-LCA model and compare with the radar scattering cross section measured by QuikSCAT SeaWinds scatterometer.

3 Simulation and Comparison

3.1 QuikSCAT Data

To explain the reasonableness of the analyzed model, the SeaWinds scatterometer on QuikSCAT data is applied for comparison with the calculation results of the scattering model. The Ku band (frequency is 13.402 GHz) scatterometer, operated by NASA, a dual pencil-beam instrument with two viewing angles (40° and 46°) and two polarizations configuration (VV for outer wave beam and HH for inner).

3.2 Results of the Model Calculation and Comparison with Measured Data

From the NG-LCA model, calculation is be done as different configuration. Figure 1 shows the result for SSA model which not considering non-Gaussian characteristics. The degree, 0 and 90°, indicate upwind and downwind direction, respectively. Whatever low or high wind speed, the dependence of the NRCS on wind direction is clear but the difference between upwind and downwind direction is not shown. Figure 2 presents the NRCS calculation with the NG-LCA and the upwind/downwind astrometry is shown since the higher statistic moment of surface vertical displacement is taken account for. The difference of upwind and downwind is smaller at the lower than higher for wind speed.

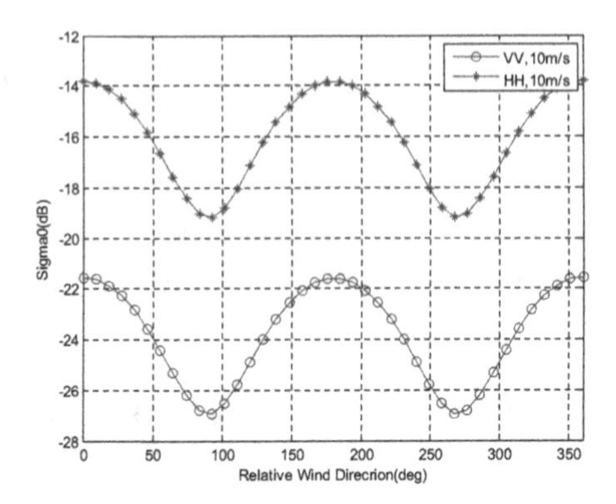

Fig. 1. SSA's NRCS versus wind direction of Gaussian feature of sea surface.

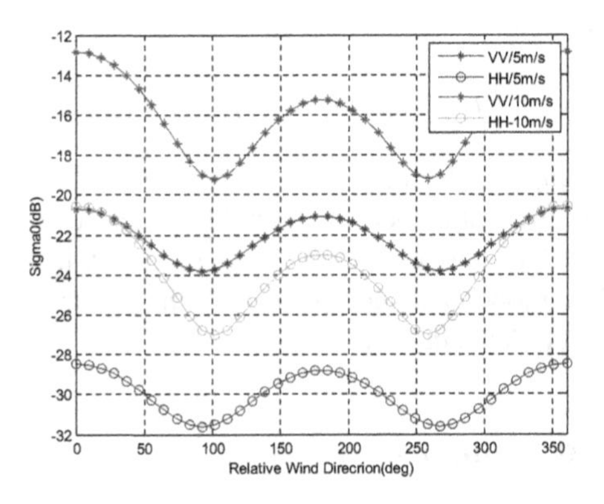

Fig. 2. NRCS of NG-LCA Model versus wind direction (i = 46°)

Figure 3(a) and (b) show the results for the model and the NRCS measured by QuikSCAT scatterometer on 2003 with different wind velocity and relative direction between wind direction and the azimuth angles. Note that the direction and velocity of

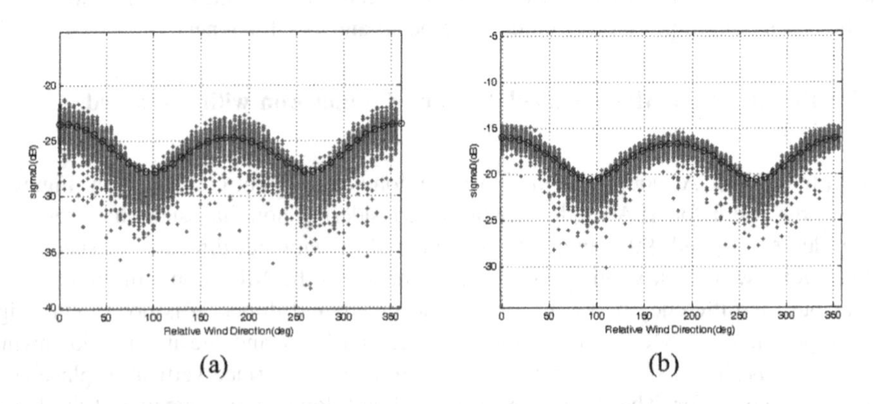

Fig. 3. Comparison the model result with the measured NRCS by QuikSCAT (a) Wind speed is 5 m/s; (b) Wind speed is 10 m/s

the wind fields come from L2B Data whereas the NRCS value obtained from L2A Data.

4 Conclusion and Future Work

A Non-Gaussian scattering model based on LCA and higher-order statistic moments is presented. The model's NRCS which is configured as the QuikSCAT scatterometer of is simulated and the results are compared with data measured by QuikSCAT scatterometer. It shows that the LCA model have a sensibility to changes in wind direction especially for the up-down wind direction, which is consistent with the previous work [6] and show the model is reasonable to describe the rough surface scattering characteristic. In the future, we plan to employ machine learning [26], deep learning [27] and computer vision techniques [28] to train our model and get more valuable results.

References

1. Voronovich, A.G.: Wave Scattering from Rough Surfaces, vol. 17. Springer, Heidelberg (2013). no. 1
2. Elfouhaily, T.M., Guérin, C.A.: A critical survey of approximate scattering wave theories from random rough surfaces. Waves Random Med. **14**(4), R1–R40 (2004)
3. Guoxing, G., Zhenzhan, W., et al.: Study of non-Gaussian scattering characteristic based on FDTD algorithm for rough sea surface, In: 4th IEEE Conference on Industrial Electronics and Applications, pp. 1477–1482. IEEE (2009)
4. Chen, K.S., Fung, A.K., et al.: A backscattering model for ocean surface. IEEE Trans. Geosci. Remote Sens. **30**(4), 811–817 (1992)
5. Fung, A.K., Chen, K.S., et al.: Microwave Scattering and Emission Models for User. Artech House, Norwood (2010)
6. Quilfen, Y., Chapron, B., et al.: Global ERS 1 and 2 and NSCAT observations: upwind/crosswind and upwind/downwind measurements. J. Geophys. Res. Oceans **104**(C5), 11459–11469 (1999)
7. Guan, C.L., Sun, F.: Fourth order statistic distribution of the non-linearity height wave. Sci. China (D Compile) **27**(4), 501–508 (1997)
8. McDaniel, S.T.: Microwave backscatter from non-Gaussian seas. IEEE Trans. Geosci. Remote Sens. **41**(1), 52–58 (2003)
9. Liu, Y., Yan, X.H., et al.: The probability density function of ocean surface slopes and its effects on radar backscatter. J. Phys. Oceanogr. **27**(5), 782–797 (1997)
10. Xu, D.L.: Theory on Statistic Ocean Wave. High Education Press, Beijing (2001)
11. Bourlier, C.: Azimuthal harmonic coefficients of the microwave backscattering from a non-Gaussian ocean surface with the first-order SSA model. IEEE Trans. Geosci. Remote Sens. **42**(11), 2600–2611 (2004)
12. Cox, C., Munk, W.: Statistics of the seasurface derived from sun glitter. J. Mar. Res. **17**(2), 198–227 (1954)
13. Thompson, D.R.: Local and non-local curvature approximation: a new asymptotic theory for wave scattering. Waves Random Med. **13**(4), 321–337 (2003)
14. Bourlier, C., Pinel, N.: Numerical implementation of local unified models for backscattering from random rough sea surfaces. Waves Random Complex Med. **19**(3), 455–479 (2009)

15. Mouche, A., Chapron, B., et al.: Importance of the sea surface curvature to interpret the normalized radar cross section. J. Geophys. Res. Oceans **112**(C10), 12 (2007)
16. Stoffelen, A., Anderson, D.: Scatterometer data interpretation: measurement space and inversion. J. Atmos. Ocean. Technol. **14**(6), 1298–1313 (1997)
17. Wu, J.: Mean square slopes of the wind-disturbed water surface, their magnitude, directionality, and composition. Radio Sci. **25**(1), 37–48 (1990)
18. Bourlier, C., Saillard, J., et al.: Intrinsic infrared radiation of the sea surface. J. Electromagn. Waves Appl. **14**(4), 551–561 (2000)
19. Elfouhaily, T., Chapron, B., et al.: A unified directional spectrum for long and short wind-driven waves. J. Geophys. Res. Oceans **102**(C7), 15781–15796 (1997)
20. Hwang, B., Wilkinson, J., et al.: Winter-to-summer transition of Arctic sea ice breakup and floe size distribution in the Beaufort Sea. Elem. Sci. Anth. **5**, 40 (2017)
21. Ren, J., Hwang, B., et al.: Effective SAR sea ice image segmentation and touch floe separation using a combined multi-stage approach. In: 2015 IEEE International Geoscience and Remote Sensing Symposium, IGARSS, pp. 1040–1043. IEEE (2015)
22. Yan, Y., Ren, J., et al.: Unsupervised image saliency detection with Gestalt-laws guided optimization and visual attention based refinement. Pattern Recogn. **49**, 65–78 (2018)
23. Hwang, B., Ren, J., et al.: A practical algorithm for the retrieval of floe size distribution of Arctic sea ice from high-resolution satellite synthetic aperture radar imagery. Elem. Sci. Anth. **5**, 38 (2017)
24. Polak, A., Ren, J., et al.: Remote oil spill detection and monitoring beneath sea ICE. In: The 2016 European Space Agency Living Planet Symposium (2016)
25. Ijitona, T.B., Ren, J., et al.: SAR sea ice image segmentation using watershed with intensity-based region merging, In: 2014 IEEE International Conference on Computer and Information Technology, CIT, pp. 168–172. IEEE (2014)
26. Cao, F., Yang, Z., Ren, J., et al.: Sparse representation-based augmented multinomial logistic extreme learning machine with weighted composite features for spectral-spatial classification of hyperspectral images. IEEE Trans. Geosci. Remote Sens. **1**, 1–17 (2018)
27. Wang, Z., Ren, J., Zhang, D., et al.: A deep-learning based feature hybrid framework for spatiotemporal saliency detection inside videos. Neurocomputing **1**, 68–83 (2018)
28. Qiao, T., Ren, J., Wang, Z., et al.: Effective denoising and classification of hyperspectral images using curvelet transform and singular spectrum analysis. IEEE Trans. Geosci. Remote Sens. **55**(1), 119–133 (2017)

Distributed Multi-node of Fuzzy Control Considering Adjacent Node Effect for Temperature Control

Jianyu Wei(✉) and Yameng Jiao

School of Electronic Information, Xi'an Polytechnic University, Xi'an, China
wssb2dtd@126.com, jiaoyameng@mail.nwpu.edu.cn

Abstract. This paper presents a fuzzy logic control for a distributed multi-node temperature control. The fuzzy logic controller is also introduced to the system for keeping temperature index to be constant. Because real-time induction temperature has many differences with correlation in industry. So the temperature control of induction is more important to control temperature of each node. The result of main fuzzy controller and five node fuzzy controllers of temperature will be conducted in this paper. It is observed that the effect of adjacent node fuzzy controller on performance of distributed multi-node temperature. The node of adjacent fuzzy controller can avoid strong sway phenomenon, and industrial temperature control system introduced in paper can get good regulation quality.

Keywords: Temperature control · Fuzzy control · The adjacent node Multi-node

1 Introduction

An efficient induction temperature of distributed multi-node regulation is fundamental in terms of reduction of power demands and industrial production process sector accounts for about 40% of total final energy consumption. In recent years, many studies were performed in order to optimize energy efficiency of induction systems, but these traditional controllers most commonly used still PID and thermostats [1]. Thus, the challenge for distributed multi-node temperature control is to find a compromise between the control precision and the energy consumption. The Model Predictive Control relies on the physically mathematical model of induction system [2], not always so simply to obtain. In this respect, one principal approach is proposed in paper: fuzzy logic control.

The fuzzy logic control does not require a mathematical the process model, it could be applied to many systems where conventional control theory could not be used due to a lack of mathematical models. The fuzzy systems are multi-input-single-output mappings from a real-valued vector to a real-valued scalar, a multi-output mapping can be decomposed into a collection of single-output mappings [3], and precise mathematical formulas of these mappings can be obtained; the fuzzy systems are knowledge-based systems constructed from human knowledge in the form of fuzzy IF-THEN rules.

J. Ren et al. (Eds.): BICS 2018, LNAI 10989, pp. 847–855, 2018.
https://doi.org/10.1007/978-3-030-00563-4_83

An important contribution of fuzzy systems is that it provides systematic procedure for transforming a knowledge base into a nonlinear mapping. Because this transformation, So peoples are able to use knowledge-based systems (fuzzy systems) in complex industrial applications in the same manner as the Model Predictive Control use mathematical models and sensory measurements.

2 Theory

A fuzzy system consists of four components: fuzzy rule base, fuzzy inference engine, fuzzifier and defuzzifier, as shown in Fig. 1.

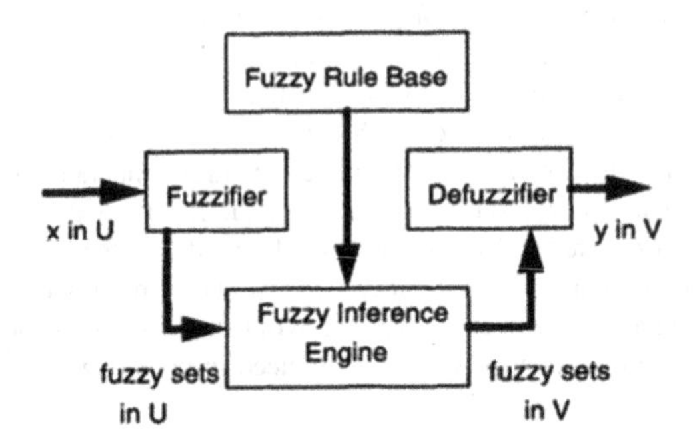

Fig. 1. Basic fuzzy systems with fuzzifier and defuzzifier

A fuzzy rule base consists of a set of fuzzy IF-THEN rules. It is the core of the fuzzy system in the sense that all other components are used to implement these rules in a reasonable and efficient manner. Specifically, the fuzzy rule base comprises the following fuzzy IF-THEN rules:

$$Ru^{(l)} : \text{IF } x_1 \text{is } A_1^l \text{and } \ldots \text{and } x_n \text{ is } A_n^l, \text{THEN y is } B^l \tag{1}$$

where A_i^l and B^l are fuzzy sets in $U_i \subset R$ and V $\subset R$, respectively, and x = $(x_1, x_2, \ldots, x_n)^T \in$ U and y $\in$ V are the input and output variables of the fuzzy system, respectively. Let M be the number of rules in the fuzzy rule base; that is, l = 1, 2, …, M in (1).

Product Inference Engine: individual-rule based inference with union combination, Mamdani's product implication, and algebraic product for all the t-norm operators and max for all the s-norm operators. The product inference engine as

$$\mu_{B'}(y) = \max_{l=1}[\sup_{X \in U}(\mu A'(x) \prod_{i=1}^{n} \mu_{A_i'(x_i)} \mu_{B^l}(y))] \tag{2}$$

Gaussian fuzzifier: The Gaussian fuzzifier maps x* $\in$ U into fuzzy set A' in U, which has the following Gaussian membership function:

$$\mu_{A'}(X) = e^{-(\frac{x_1 - x_1^*}{a_1})^2} \star \ldots \star e^{-\left(\frac{x_n - x_n^*}{a_n}\right)^2} \quad (3)$$

where a_i are positive parameters and the t-norm $\star$ is usually chosen as algebraic product or min.

Triangular fuzzifier: The triangular fuzzifier maps x* ∊ U into fuzzy set A' in U, which has the following triangular membership function

$$\mu_{A'}(X) = \begin{cases} \left(1 - \frac{|x_1 - x_1^*|}{b_1}\right) \star \ldots \star \left(1 - \frac{|x_n - x_n^*|}{b_n}\right) if |x_1 - x_1^*| \leq b_i, i = 1,2,\ldots,n \\ 0 \ otherwise \end{cases} \quad (4)$$

where b_i are positive parameters and the t-norm $\star$ is usually chosen as algebraic product or min.

Center Average defuzzifier: $\bar{y}^l$ be the center of the l'th fuzzy set and ω_l be its height, with the weights equal the heights of the corresponding fuzzy sets the center average defuzzifier determines y* as

$$y^* = \frac{\sum_{l=1}^{M} \bar{y}^l \omega_l}{\sum_{l=1}^{M} \omega_l} \quad (5)$$

The fuzzy systems with fuzzy rule base, product inference engine, Gaussian fuzzifier with $\star$ = product, center average defuzzifier, and Gaussian membership functions are following form:

$$f(x) = \frac{\sum_{l=1}^{M} \bar{y}^l \left[\prod_{i=1}^{n} \exp\left(-\frac{(x_i - \bar{x}_i^l)^2}{a_i^2 + \left(\sigma_i^l\right)^2}\right)\right]}{\sum_{l=1}^{M} \left[\prod_{i=1}^{n} \exp\left(-\frac{(x_i - \bar{x}_i^l)^2}{a_i^2 + \left(\sigma_i^l\right)^2}\right)\right]} \quad (6)$$

3 Design

MATLAB Fuzzy logic Toolbox is used to design fuzzy logic controller. The Fuzzy Logic controller consists of four basic components: fuzzification, a knowledge base, inference engine, and a defuzzification each component affects the effectiveness of fuzzy controller and the behavior of controlled system [4]. In the fuzzification interface, a measurement of inputs and a transformation, which converts input data into suitable linguistic variables, are performed which mimic human decision making. The results obtained by fuzzy logic depend on fuzzy inference rules and fuzzy implication operators. The knowledge base provides necessary information for linguistic control rules and information for fuzzification and defuzzification [5]. In the defuzzification interface, an actual control action is obtained from results of fuzzy inference engine.

Figure 2 shows the flow chart of the methodology for fuzzy logic controller part.

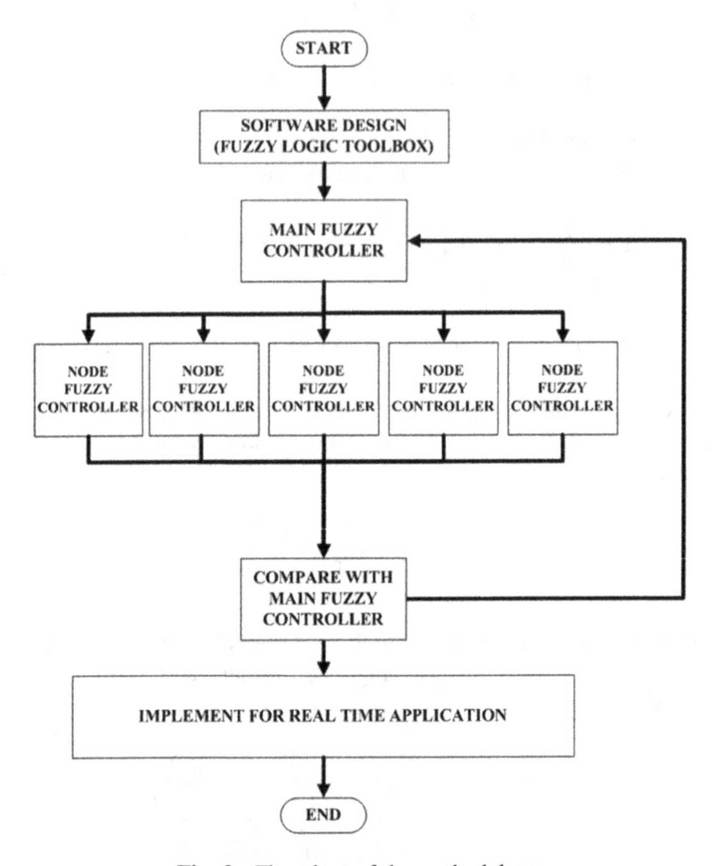

Fig. 2. Flowchart of the methodology

In this project, main fuzzy controller is the first stage of fuzzy logic controller process. This process converts information of temperature parameters into controller that the node fuzzy controller can easily use to active and apply rules of differences with correlation in the industries temperature.

The Mamdani techniques will be used in main fuzzy controller of three control inputs and five control outputs as shown in Fig. 3.

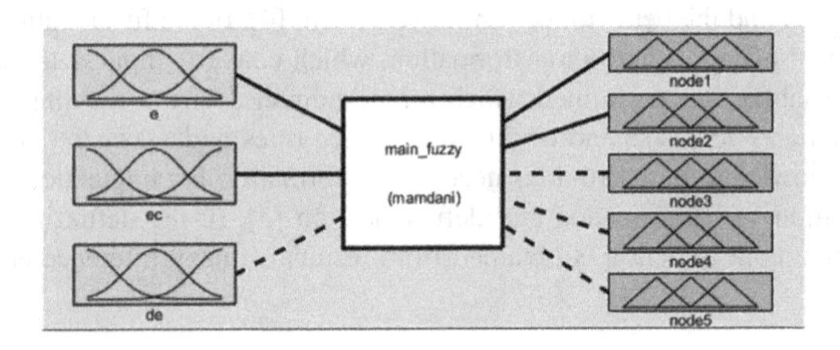

Fig. 3. The main fuzzy controller

To adapt the temperature change of each node error, the variety rate of the error and comparisons values of difference node temperature will be considered in terms of node temperature changing as shown in Fig. 4. The node fuzzy controller contains that cover for the 2 inputs of the main fuzzy controller output and variety rate of the error as shown in Fig. 5.

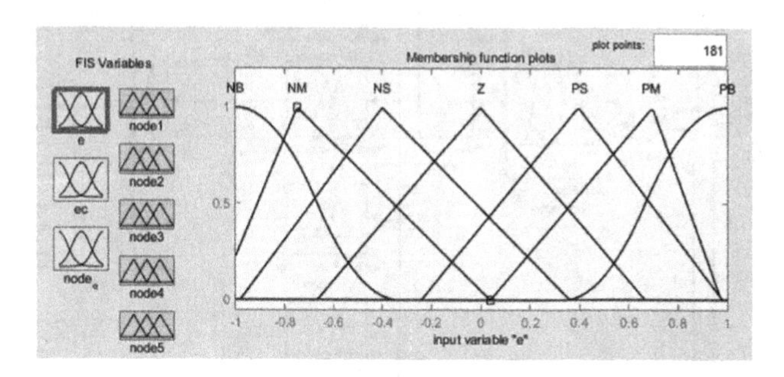

Fig. 4. Input values of the main fuzzy controller

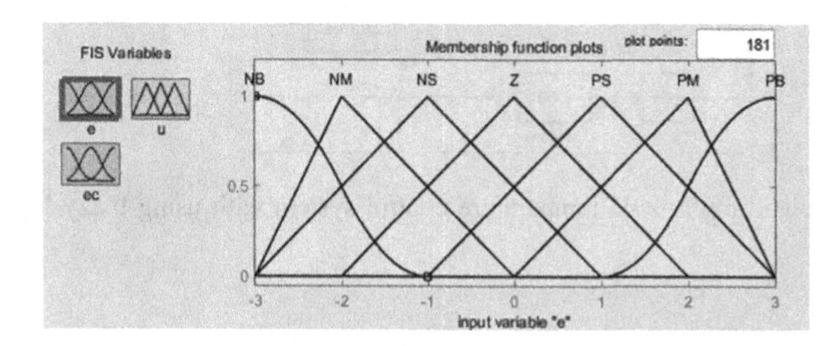

Fig. 5. Input values of the node fuzzy controller

The node fuzzy controller contains 30 rules that cover for the 2 inputs and one output, and main fuzzy controller contains 89 rules that cover 3 inputs and 5 outputs membership functions as shown in Fig. 6.

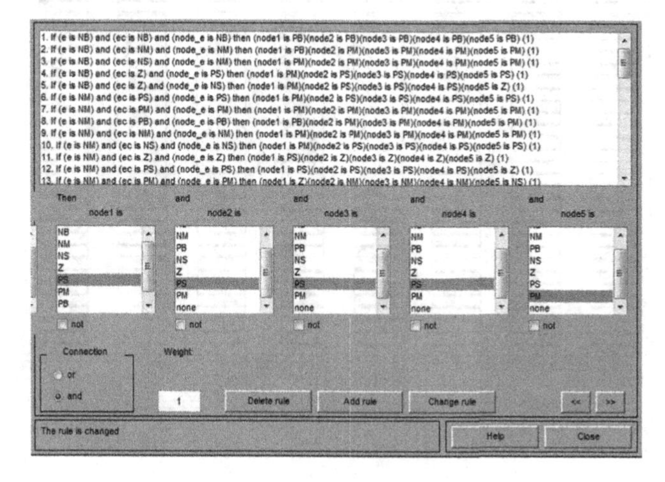

Fig. 6. Rule editor in MATLAB

The block diagram, as shown in Fig. 7, is representing fuzzy logic controller by using MATLAB of simulink. It consists of main fuzzy controller, node fuzzy controller, a difference interface module and etc.

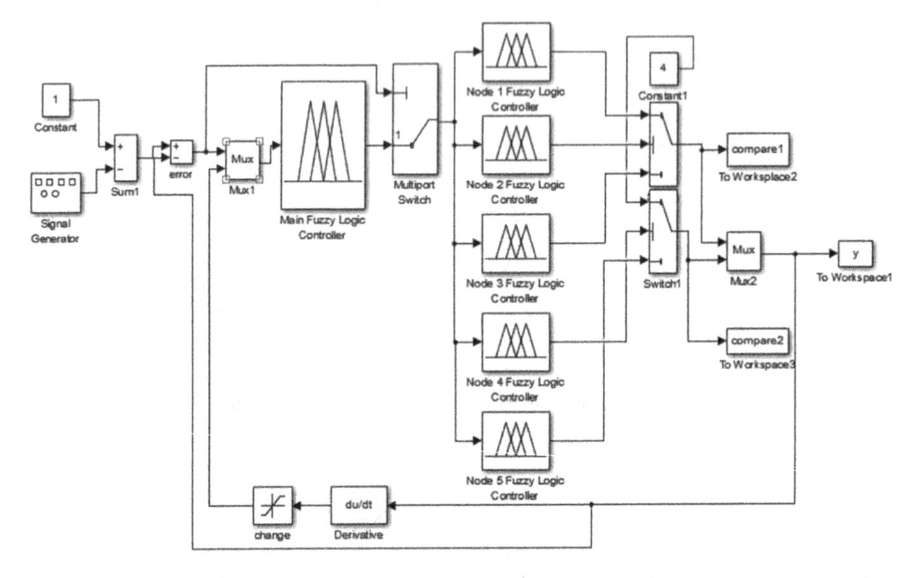

Fig. 7. Distributed multi-node temperature control system with using fuzzy logic controller

4 Result

After adding rules to system, as shown in Fig. 8, the result of main fuzzy controller can be obtained from 'Rule Viewer' in MATLAB of FIS tools. The result of the main fuzzy controller can be obtained as shown in Fig. 9.

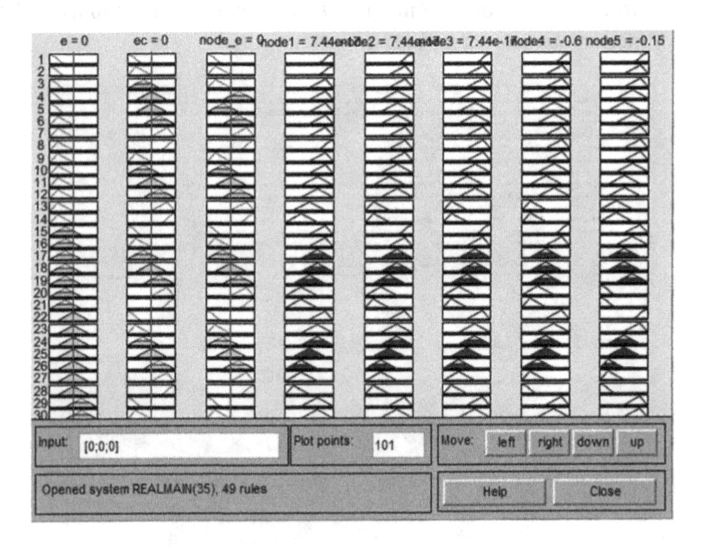

Fig. 8. The main fuzzy logic control rule

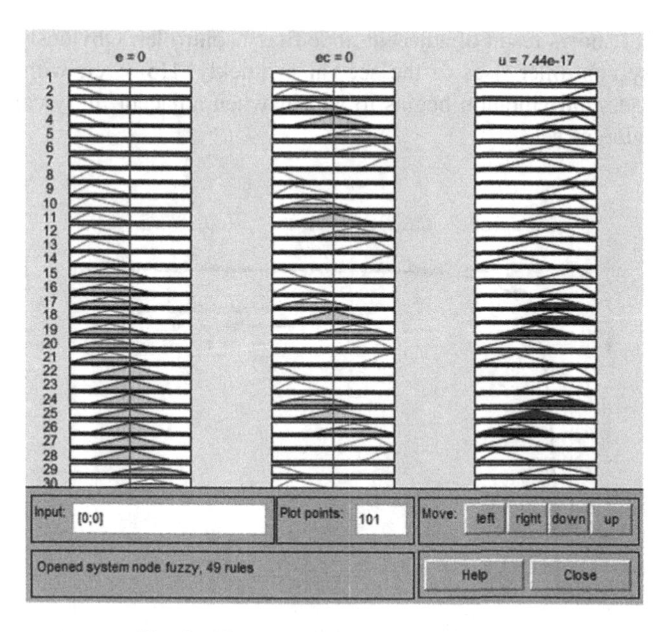

Fig. 9. The node fuzzy logic control rule

Figure 10 shows, when inputting unit step signal, the response consist of the ordinary PID controller and the node fuzzy controller, the contrast of two curves, the overshoot of the node fuzzy is less than the ordinary PID controller.

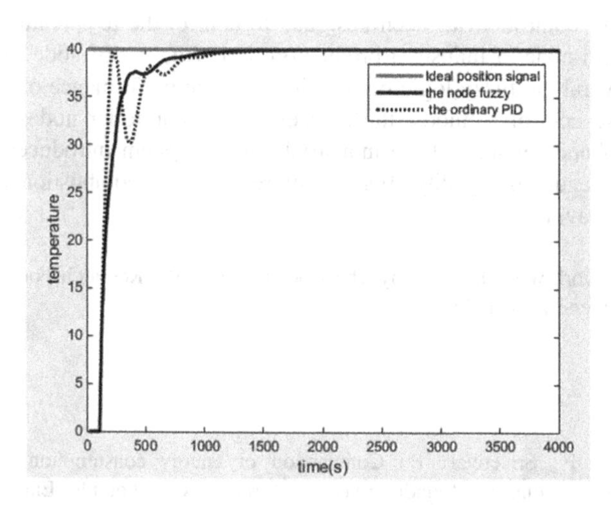

Fig. 10. The result of the main fuzzy controller and the ordinary PID controller

The Fig. 11 shows result of adjacent node fuzzy controller. Obviously, the node of adjacent fuzzy controller rises to the set value quickly. However, with influence of adjacent of node, the vibration begins to appear when adjacent fuzzy controller node reaches the value of set.

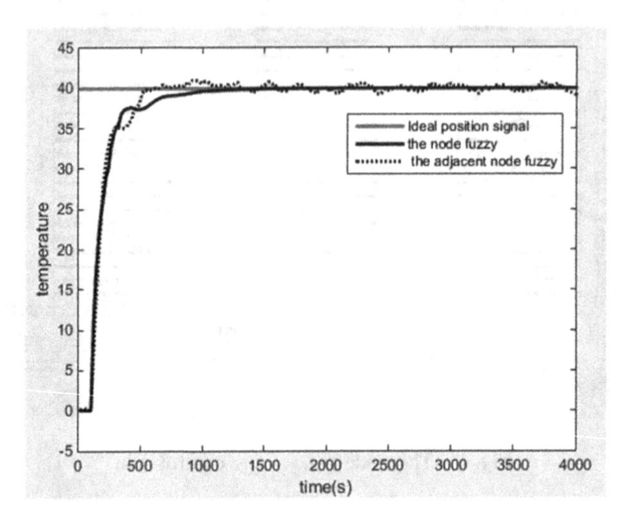

Fig. 11. The result of the node of adjacent fuzzy controller

5 Conclusion

The main fuzzy controller has been designed to control the temperature according to distributed multi-node of industrial production. Every output of node fuzzy controller consists of several the fuzzy logic rules to increase the performance of the system. So based on these control methods, the adjacent fuzzy controller nodes can avoid the strong sway phenomenon, and the industrial control system introduced in this paper can get good regulation quality. For the more, enhance combustion efficiency and realize energy-saving.

Funding. This work was supported by The Doctoral Scientific Research Foundation of Xi'an Polytechnic University (BS1413).

References

1. Ziółkowskia, E., Śmierciak, P.: Comparison of energy consumption in the classical (PID) and fuzzy control of foundry resistance furnace. Arch. Foundry Eng. **12**(3), 349–350 (2012)
2. Dambrosio, L.: Data-based fuzzy logic control tenchnique appied to a wind system. Energy Proc. **126**, 690–697 (2017)

3. Shahid, H., et al.: Design of a fuzzy logic based controller for fluid level application. World J. Eng. Technol. **04**(3), 469–476 (2016)
4. Ugaji, N.: Fuzzy logic toolbox for MATLAB. J. Jpn. Soc. Fuzzy Theory Syst. **7**(2), 797 (1995)
5. Ramya, T., Kannan, A.C., Balasenthil, R.S., Bagirathi, B.A.: Fuzzy logic modeling for decision making processes using MATLAB. Adv. Mater. Res. **3269**, 984 (2014)
6. Debnath, M.K., Mallick, R.K., Sahu, B.K.: Application of hybrid differential evolution–grey wolf optimization algorithm for automatic generation control of a multi-source interconnected power system using optimal fuzzy–PID controller. Electr. Power Compon. Syst. **45**, 19 (2017)
7. Cheng, C.-H.: Design of output filter for inverters using fuzzy logic. Expert Syst. Appl. **38** (7), 8639–8647 (2011)
8. Martínez, L.G., Licea, G., Rodríguez, A., Castro, J.R., Castillo, O.: Using MatLab's fuzzy logic toolbox to create an application for RAMSET in software engineering courses. Comput. Appl. Eng. Educ. **21**(4), 1753–1766 (2013)
9. Yameng, J., Jianguo, H., Jing, W.: An information criterion for source number detection with the peak-to-average power ratio modified by Gerschgorin radii. In: IEEE International Conference on Signal Processing, Communications and Computing (ICSPCC), Xi'an, China, pp. 1048–1052 (2011)
10. Cao, F., Yang, Z., Ren, J., Ling, W.K., et al.: Sparse representation based augmented multinomial logistic extreme learning machine with weighted composite features for spectral-spatial classification of hyperspectral images. IEEE Trans. Geosci. Remote Sens. **185**, 1–10 (2018)
11. Gomaa Haroun, A.H., Li, Y.: A novel optimized hybrid fuzzy logic intelligent PID controller for an interconnected multi-area power system with physical constraints and boiler dynamics. ISA Trans. **71**, 364–379 (2017)
12. Zhang, A., Sun, G., Ren, J., et al.: A dynamic neighborhood learning-based gravitational search algorithm. IEEE Trans. Cynern. **12**, 644–654 (2017)
13. Wang, C.-L., Ren, J., et al.: Spectral-spatial classification of hyperspectral data using spectral-domain local binary patterns. Multimed. Tools Appl. **13**, 2019 (2018)
14. Wang, Z., Ren, J., Zhang, D., Sun, M., Jiang, J.: A deep-learning based feature hybrid framework for spatiotemporal saliency detection inside videos. Neurocomputing **229**, 279–292 (2018)
15. Ramesh, T., Panda, A.K., Kumar, S.S.: Type-1 and type-2 fuzzy logic and sliding-mode based speed control of direct torque and flux control induction motor drives – a comparative study. Int. J. Emerg. Electr. Power Syst. **14**(5), 385 (2013)

An Improved Tentative Q Learning Algorithm for Robot Learning

Lixiang Zhang(✉), Yi'an Zhu, and Junhua Duan

School of Computer Science, Northwestern Polytechnical University, NWPU, Xi'an, China
297125741@qq.com

Abstract. Aiming at the problem of the slow speed of reinforcement learning, a tentative Q learning algorithm is proposed. By improving the number of exploration in each learning iteration and the updating method of Q table, tentative Q learning algorithm accelerates the learning speed and ensures the balance between exploration and exploitation. Finally, the feasibility and effectiveness of the algorithm are proved by the experiment of robot path planning.

Keywords: Q-learning · Exploration · Exploitation · Path-planning

1 Introduction

Reinforcement learning (RL) has emerged as a strong approach in the field of Artificial intelligence, specifically, in the field of machine learning, robotic navigation, etc. [1, 2]. RL can increase the adaptability of robotics systems, and the use of RL for robot control is gaining popularity over the last few years. Reinforcement learning improves the performance of robot by rewarding and punishing signals from the environment [6]. In the learning process, robot performs an action on the environment and receives a point scored reward, as in the game of soccer, and a negative score punishment. Robot usually adapts its parameter based on the current and cumulative rewards, and it learns by experiencing in the environment – what is a good action and what is not. The controller's aim is to maximise its expected future rewards for state-action pairs, represented by the action values [7].

Slow convergence is a difficult problem to overcome in reinforcement learning [8]. In order to obtain the optimal learning result of reinforcement learning, we must first guarantee the full detection of the state space. The convergence rate of reinforcement learning is slow. When the state space of the learning task is very large, the convergence rate is slower. How to make the robot fully detect the state space and learn the optimal solution in the least number of learning times is a key problem to be solved for robot learning.

This paper puts forward tentative Q learning algorithm (Tentative Q learning, TQL). TQL utilizes the Q value update characteristics in each state and takes full exploration of the successor states. TQL algorithm speeds up the learning convergence speed based on the balance of exploration and exploitation.

J. Ren et al. (Eds.): BICS 2018, LNAI 10989, pp. 856–865, 2018.
https://doi.org/10.1007/978-3-030-00563-4_84

2 Tentative Q Learning Algorithm

The reinforcement learning process in a static environment is generally assumed to be the Markov Decision Process [9] (MDP), which is an important prerequisite for the reinforcement learning algorithm. An MDP process is usually defined as $M = <S, A, T, R>$, where S is a discrete state set, A is a discrete action set, T is a state transition function, and $T:S \times A \rightarrow S$, R is a reward function.

There are many Reinforcement learning algorithm which have their own characteristics and can adapt to different environments. Q learning due to its needless to establish environmental model and ensure convergence under certain conditions, becomes one of the most widely used reinforcement learning methods [10]. The Q-learning formula is:

$$Q_t(s_t, a_t) = \begin{cases} (1 - \alpha_t)Q_{t-1}(s_t, a_t) + \alpha_t[r_t + \gamma \max_{a \in A}\{Q_{t-1}(s_{t+1}, a)\}], & s = s_t, a = a_t \\ Q_{t-1}(s_t, a_t), & otherwise \end{cases} \tag{1}$$

In the formula, s_t is the current state, a_t is the selected action among all possible actions, s_{t+1} is the next state, r_t is the received immediate reward after a_t is executed, α_t is learning rate, and γ is discount factor.

One of the key issues in Q learning is how to balance the relationship of exploration and exploitation [6]. The process of "exploration" is to search the optional behavior based on a certain rule, which is often random or blind, and is beneficial to the discovery of unknown areas. The process of "exploitation" is to select a learning behavior, which generally have the highest cumulative discount reward value (Q value) of the behavior. However the Q values are often unreliable because of the incomplete information of learning in the early learning stage. And the unreliable Q values will mislead future learning process. If the proportion of exploration behavior is too large and the choice of individual behavior will be blind, and the speed of convergence is too slow. If the exploitation of behavior is too large, it is difficult for individuals to find the potential optimization results and easily fall into the local optimal. So it is necessary to compromise between acquiring knowledge and obtaining high returns, that is, to balance exploration and exploitation.

The classical method to balance exploration and exploitation is Greedy, ε-*greedy* [11] and Boltzmann [12] exploration mechanism. ε-*greedy* strategy follows the greedy strategy with probability ε, and acts randomly with probability $(1-\varepsilon)$. If ε is too large, there will be more actions to take greedy strategy; and if ε is too small, random actions will be increased. Boltzmann strategy chooses different selection pressure according to different stages of learning, so it do not fall into the "local trap", but it causes slow convergence speed.

In addition, for traditional Q learning, all candidate states will be investigated in each learning step. Then one state will be selected as the next state according certain principles, and its Q value will be updated. However, the Q value of other states will not be changed, and the investigation process is wasted.

Assuming that the robot is in a state of s_t at time t, it needs to select a new action, and enter the following state s_{t+1}, and then perform the corresponding action a_{to}.

Definition 1. Tentative action a_{ti} $(1 \leq i \leq n)$ is used to perform a trial action before the action a_t is implemented. Tentative action is used to explore all the subsequent states of the current state, and the number n is the total number of subsequent states.

Definition 2. Tentative state s_{ti} $(1 \leq i \leq n, i \in z)$ is the successor state that the system will enter after the selection of the tentative action a_{ti}.

Definition 3. Tentative reward value r_{ti} $(1 \leq i \leq n, i \in z)$ is the reward value after selecting the tentative action a_{ti} and enters the tentative state s_{ti}.

The Q table update formula of the tentative results is as follows:

$$Q_t(s_t, a_{ti}) = \begin{cases} (1-\alpha_t)Q_{t-1}(s_t, a_{ti}) + \alpha_t[r_{ti} + \gamma Q_{t-1}(s_t, a_{ti})] & s = s_t; a = a_{ti} \\ Q_{t-1}(s_t, a_t), & otherwise \end{cases} \quad (2)$$

Where, α_t is learning rate to control the speed of learning. γ is the factor of discount.

After all the successor states are explored and updated, the successor state with maximum Q value is selected as the next state, and the corresponding Q value is updated again. The formulas are as follows:

$$select = \arg \max_{1<i<4}(\{Q(s_t, a_{ti})\}) \quad (3)$$

$$Q_t(s_t, a_{select}) = \begin{cases} (1-\alpha_t)Q_{t-1}(s_t, a_{select}) + \alpha_t[r_{select} + \gamma V(s_{select})] & s = s_t; a = a_t \\ Q_{t-1}(s_t, a_t), & otherwise \end{cases} \quad (4)$$

$$V(s_{select}) = \max_{\alpha \in A}\{Q_{t-1}(s_{select}, a)\} \quad (5)$$

The difference between the TQL learning algorithm and the traditional Q learning is the Q table update process. The TQL algorithm explores all successor states and updates the corresponding Q values, and then update Q value of the selected successor state for the second time. Yet traditional Q learning explores all or part successor states, and only updates the selected successor state Q values, the rest of other explore results are not recorded. Traditional Q learning wastes a lot of exploration.

A basic learning process of Q learning is a search process from initial state to target state, and it is called a round. Q learning is the process of multiple rounds of iterative execution. Assuming that traditional Q learning needs to explore the H step in a round, a total of H nodes are explored, and the Q value is updated H times. However TQL algorithm will explore four successor nodes in each step of state exploration, and the Q table will be updated for 5 times. So in TQL algorithm, it will explore 4th nodes, and the Q value will be updated for 5th times. So the number of exploration in TQL algorithm in single round is far more than the traditional Q learning. The exploration is more sufficient, so the speed of convergence is faster.

The pseudo code of the TQL learning algorithm is as follows:

TQL learning algorithm

Input : $Q(s,a)=0(\forall s\in S, a\in A)$, S0, Final_State

Output : Q

```
 // Initialize
1 Set initial state : s =S0 ;
2 Set next state as initial state : s'= S0 ;
3 Set initial action : a = null ;
4 Set initial rewards as initial state rewards : r = r0 ;
5 Set iteration number : t=0 ;
6 for t=1: Max_EPISODES
7   While(s!=Final_State)
//Perform tentative Q-learning :
8       for i = 1 to 4
9         Receive next action as the ith tentative action : a_ti = i;
10        Receive rewards as the ith tentative state rewards : r_ti = r(s_ti);
11        Update Q_t(s_t, a_ti) :
```

$Q_t(s_t,a_{ti})=(1-\alpha_t)Q_{t-1}(s_t,a_{ti})+\alpha_t\left[r_{ti}+\gamma Q_{t-1}(s_t,a_{ti})\right]$;

```
12      end_for
//Select the best action as performing action
```

13 $k=\arg\max(\{Q(s_t,a_{ti})\})$;

14 $a_t=a_{tk}$;

15 $s'=s_{tk}$;

16 $r_t=r_{tk}$;

17 $Q_t(s_t,a_t)=(1-\alpha_t)Q_{t-1}(s_t,a_t)+\alpha_t\left[r_t+\gamma\max_{\alpha\in A}\{Q_{t-1}(s',a)\}\right]$;

```
18   end_while
19 end_for
```

The TQL algorithm requires the robot to observe all subsequent states and receive all the corresponding environmental reward values under the current state st. If the robot can not get all the successor states and corresponding rewards, then the TQL algorithm will become the traditional Q learning algorithm.

3 Avoidance of Local Traps by TQL

TQL algorithm is able to converge at a faster speed. In the whole process of learning, TQL algorithm adopts a complete greedy selection strategy, that is, to choose the next step with the biggest Q value. Therefore, in the same state space, the TQL learning process is a deterministic exploration process. However, the TQL learning process generally does not trap into a "local trap" state.

In the traditional Q learning algorithm, the greedy strategy is used to select the action with maximum Q value, which is called the greedy Q learning algorithm [13]. When robot uses greedy Q learning algorithm, it is easy for robot to produce a dead cycle between two points when learning is not enough (i.e., walking between two adjacent points). Taking the case map shown in Fig. 1 as an example, the white grid shows the feasible grid, and the dark grid represents the obstacle. The reward value of the successor state for point A and point B is shown in Fig. 1. At some step in the initial period of learning, robot takes action based on the formula (1), and the Q value of the subsequent state of each point is shown as Table 1 when the greedy strategy is adopted.

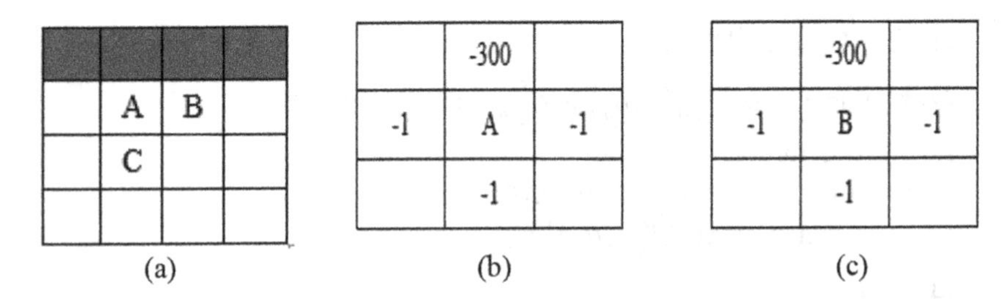

Fig. 1. (a) Case map, (b) the successor status rewards value of point A, (c) the successor status.

The direction of robot actions is shown in Table 1. Robot will select right state as next state when it is on point A, and will select left state as next state when it is on point B. At each step, robot will update the corresponding Q value. The Q values are showed in Table 3. It can be found that the Q value of right direction state of point A and the Q value of left direction state of point B become more and more bigger with the increase of learning step (Because of the length of the text, this article only intercepts some of the data). Robot will fall into the dead cycle. So it can be find that the traditional Q learning will produce a dead cycle in the case of inadequate learning.

Under the same initial conditions as Fig. 1(a), reward value (Fig. 1(b) and (c)), and initial Q value (Table 3), the Q value of TQL learning algorithm is shown in Table 4. The robot moving direction is shown in Table 2. The TQL algorithm first updates the four directions' Q value when robot is in point A, and then selects the direction with maximum Q value (i.e. point B) as moving direction and updates corresponding Q value. After that, the TQL algorithm also updates the 4 directions' Q value when robot is in point B, and then selects the direction with maximum Q value (i.e. point A) as moving direction and updates corresponding Q value. But when robot returns to the point A, it updates the Q value of four directions, and the maximum value of Q value is the down direction (i.e. point C), and it becomes the new moving direction. The robot does not fall into the dead cycle (i.e. the local trap).

TQL algorithm updates all Q values of all subsequent nodes in each learning step, and updates the selected successor state nodes for second times, so Q tables are fully accessed. Nodes that are not selected also updates their Q values continuously according to their own successor nodes. So the Q table has higher rate to be changed, and the transfer speed of the Q value of excellent solutions is faster, which has greatly reduced the probability of falling into the dead cycle.

Table 1. Robot moving direction under the greedy exploration.

Step	Moving direction
1st step	Point A → Point B
2nd step	Point B → Point A
3rd step	Point A → Point B
4th step	Point B → Point A

Table 2. Robot moving direction under TQL algorithm.

Step	Moving direction
1st step	Point A → Point B
2nd step	Point B → Point A
3rd step	Point A → Point C

Table 3. Robot moving direction under TQL algorithm.

Step	Point	Q-value (up)	Q-value (down)	Q-value (left)	Q-value (right)
Initial	A	0	−3.6202	−4.9082	−2.6134
	B	0	−4.9204	−4.9017	−4.9419
1st step	A	0	−3.6202	−4.9082	**−1.8067**
	B	0	−4.9204	−4.9017	−4.9419
2nd step	A	0	−3.6202	−4.9082	−1.8067
	B	0	−4.9204	**−2.9509**	−4.9419
3rd step	A	0	−3.6202	−4.9082	**−1.4034**
	B	0	−4.9204	−2.9509	−4.9419
4th step	A	0	−3.6202	−4.9082	−1.4034
	B	0	−4.9204	**−1.9755**	−4.9419

Table 4. The Q value of the TQL algorithm.

Step	Point	Q-value (up)	Q-value (down)	Q-value (left)	Q-value (right)
Initial	A	0	−3.6202	−4.9082	**−2.6134**
	B	0	−4.9204	**−4.9017**	−4.9419
1st step	A	−150.0	−3.7582	−4.9174	**−2.8521**
	B	0	−4.9204	−4.9017	−4.9419
	A	−150.0	**−3.7582**	−4.9174	−3.8860
	B	0	−4.9204	−4.9017	−4.9419
2nd step	A	−150.0	−3.7582	−4.9174	−3.8860
	B	−150.0	−4.9284	**−4.9115**	−4.9471
	A	−150.0	−3.7582	−4.9174	−3.8860
	B	−150.0	−4.9284	**−4.4590**	−4.9471
3rd step	A	−285.0	**−3.8823**	−4.9257	−3.9974
	B	−150.0	−4.9284	−4.4590	−4.9471

4 Simulation Experiment and Analysis

The simulation experiment is carried out under Visual C++ 2010, and the environment of simulation experiment is as shown in Fig. 2. S represents the starting point of the robot, and D represents the target point. The robot can only move up, down, left, and right, and each time moves one grid. Each experiment starts when the robot is at the starting point and ends when the robot reaches the target point. At the beginning, robot has no experiences in an unfamiliar environment, so the initial value in Q are all 0. The reward of obstacles in environment is −300. The reward of edge of the map is −300. The reward of target point is 100, others are −1. In experiment, α is 0.5 and γ is 0.8. Under the same circumstances with same starting and end points, robot respectively use Q-learning based Boltzmann selection strategy and ε - greedy selection strategy (the value of ε is set in stages) and TQL algorithm to conduct experiment 400 times. Path length of each experiment is recorded. The experimental results are shown in Figs. 3, 4 and 5. In the charts, the ordinate represents length of path robot takes to get the target point. The horizontal axis represents the number of iterations.

When robot uses segmented *ε-greedy* selection strategy, in early times, robot learns with smaller value of ϵ and has little probability to select the action with the maximum Q value. In the late times, robot learns with bigger value of ϵ. The experimental results are shown in Fig. 5. This method is faster than Boltzmann selection strategy, but it sometimes falls into "local trap".

When the robot using TQL strategy, it can quickly converge to an optimal path. Robot has been updated Q value of all directions and selected the direction corresponding to maximum Q value before it actually moved. TQL improves the efficiency of robot learning. The results is shown in Fig. 5.

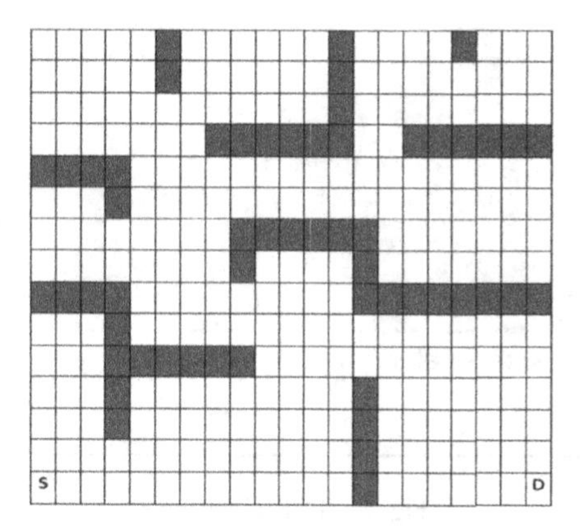

Fig. 2. Simulation experiments map.

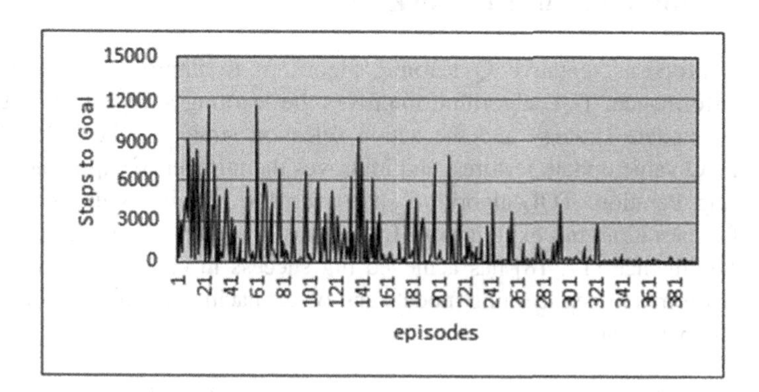

Fig. 3. Boltzmann selection strategy.

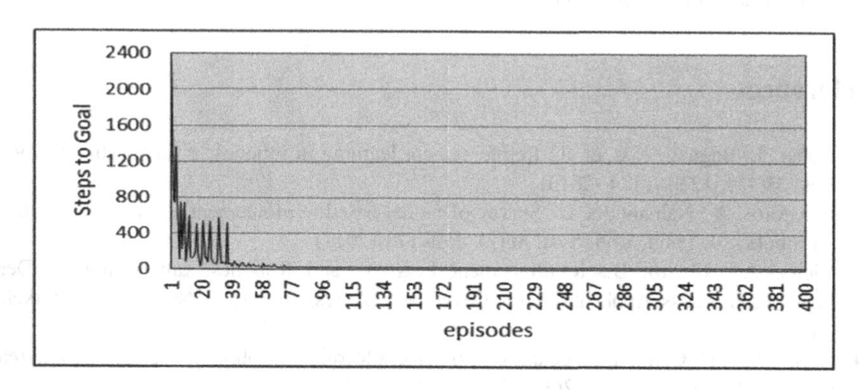

Fig. 4. Segmented ε-greedy strategy.

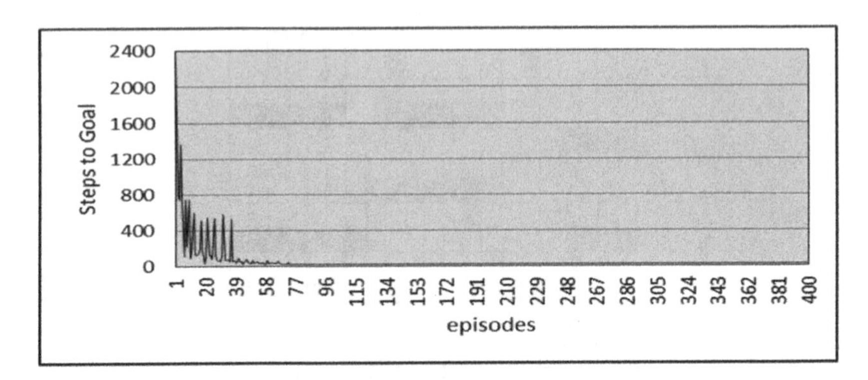

Fig. 5. TQL algorithm.

5 Conclusion and Future Work

This paper proposes tentative Q learning algorithm to improve the traditional Q learning performance. TQL algorithm improves the learning speed of the robot from the Q value update strategy and the action selection strategy. The TQL algorithm analyses the Q value update features, and improves the number of exploration times in each learning iteration. TQL algorithm speeds up the learning speed based on the balance of exploration and exploitation. In the future, as Deep Learning [14–16] and Artificial Intelligence [17, 18] has achieved big success in computer vision, we also want to deploy more deep learning models and other machine learning algorithms [19, 20] on our experiments.

Acknowledgements. This research project was supported by two Shaanxi Province Founds (Program No. 2017ZDXM-GY-008 and 2016MSZD-G-8-1), and supported by two National Funds (Program No. 2017KF100037 and MJ-2015-D-66).

References

1. Kober, J., Bagnell, J.A., et al.: Reinforcement learning in robotics: a survey. Int. J. Robot. Res. **32**(11), 1238–1274 (2013)
2. Polydoros, A., Nalpantidis, L.: Survey of model-based reinforcement learning: applications on robotics. J. Intell. Rob. Syst. **86**(2), 153–173 (2017)
3. Vieira, A., Ribeiro, B.: Reinforcement Learning and Robotics, Introduction to Deep Learning Business Applications for Developers. Apress, pp. 137–168. A Press, Berkeley (2018)
4. Kormushev, P., Calinon, S., et al.: Reinforcement learning in robotics: applications and real-world challenges. Robotics **2**(3), 122–148 (2013)
5. Wawrzynski, P.: Control policy with autocorrelated noise in reinforcement learning for robotics. Int. J. Mach. Learn. Comput. **5**(2), 91 (2015)
6. Sutton, R.S., Barto, A.G.: Reinforcement learning: an introduction (2011)
7. Ravishankar, R., Vijayakumar, V.: Reinforcement learning algorithms: survey and classification. Indian J. Sci. Technol. **10**(1), 1–8 (2017)

8. Koga, M.L., Silva, V.F., et al.: Speeding-up reinforcement learning through abstraction and transfer learning. In: Proc. of Int. Cof. on Autonomous Agents and Multi-agent Systems. International Foundation for Autonomous Agents and Multiagent Systems, pp. 119–126 (2013)
9. Azar, G., Munos, R., Ghavamzadeh, M., et al.: Speedy Q-learning: a computationally efficient reinforcement learning algorithm with a near optimal rate of convergence (2013)
10. Matignon, L., Laurent, G., et al.: Improving reinforcement learning speed for robot control. In: IEEE/RSJ Int. Conf. on Intelligent Robots and Systems, pp. 3172–3177 (2008)
11. Tokic, M.: Adaptive ε-greedy exploration in reinforcement learning based on value differences. In: Annual Conference on Artificial Intelligence, pp. 203–210 (2010)
12. Achbany, Y., Fouss, F., et al.: Tuning continual exploration in reinforcement learning: An optimality property of the Boltzmann strategy. Neurocomputing **71**(13–15), 2507–2520 (2008)
13. Viet, H.H., Kyaw, P.H., et al.: Simulation-based evaluations of reinforcement learning algorithms for autonomous mobile robot path planning. In: Park, J., Arabnia, H., Chang, H. B., Shon, T. (eds.) IT Convergence and Services, pp. 467–476. Springer, Dordrecht (2011)
14. Wang, Z., Ren, J., et al.: A deep-learning based feature hybrid framework for spatiotemporal saliency detection inside videos. Neurocomputing **287**, 68–83 (2018)
15. Ren, J., Jiang, J.: Hierarchical modeling and adaptive clustering for real-time summarization of rush videos. IEEE Trans. Multimed. **11**(5), 906–917 (2009)
16. Han, J., Zhang, D., et al.: Object detection in optical remote sensing images based on weakly supervised learning and high-level feature learning. IEEE Trans. Geosci. Remote Sens. **53** (6), 3325–3337 (2015)
17. Chen, J., Ren, J.: Modelling of content-aware indicators for effective determination of shot boundaries in compressed MPEG videos. Multimed. Tools Appl. **54**(2), 219–239 (2011)
18. Ren, J., Vlachos, T.: Immersive and perceptual human–computer interaction using computer vision techniques. In: 2010 IEEE Computer Society Conference on Computer Vision and Pattern Recognition Workshops, pp. 66–72. IEEE (2010)
19. Yan, Y., Ren, J., et al.: Cognitive fusion of thermal and visible imagery for effective detection and tracking of pedestrians in videos. Cogn. Comput. **61**, 1–11 (2017)
20. Yan, Y., Ren, J., et al.: Unsupervised image saliency detection with Gestalt-laws guided optimization and visual attention based refinement. Pattern Recogn. **79**, 65–78 (2018)

Author Index

Printed in the United States
By Bookmasters